Information Systems Today
Managing in the Digital World

SIXTH EDITION

Information Systems Today
Managing in the Digital World

Joe Valacich
University of Arizona

Christoph Schneider
City University of Hong Kong

International Edition contributions by
Ramesh Behl
IMI Bhubaneswar

PEARSON

Boston   Columbus   Indianapolis   New York   San Francisco   Upper Saddle River
Amsterdam   Cape Town   Dubai   London   Madrid   Milan   Munich   Paris   Montréal   Toronto
Delhi   Mexico City   São Paulo   Sydney   Hong Kong   Seoul   Singapore   Taipei   Tokyo

Editor in Chief: Stephanie Wall
Executive Editor: Bob Horan
Editorial Project Manager: Kelly Loftus
Editorial Assistant: Ashlee Bradbury
Director of Marketing: Maggie Moylan
Executive Marketing Manager: Anne Fahlgren
Marketing Assistant: Gianna Sandri
Senior Managing Editor: Judy Leale
Production Project Manager: Jane Bonnell
Publisher, International Edition: Angshuman
  Chakraborty
**Publishing Administrator and Business Analyst,
  International Edition:** Shokhi Shah Khandelwal
Senior Print and Media Editor, International Edition:
  Ashwitha Jayakumar
Acquisitions Editor, International Edition:
  Sandhya Ghoshal

Publishing Administrator, International Edition:
  Hema Mehta
Project Editor, International Edition:
  Daniel Luiz
**Senior Manufacturing Controller, Production,
  International Edition:** Trudy Kimber
Operations Specialist: Maura Zaldivar-Garcia
Creative Director: Blair Brown
Senior Art Director: Janet Slowik
Cover Designer: Jodi Notowitz
Interior Designer: ElectraGraphics, Inc.
Media Project Manager, Editorial: Alana Coles
Media Project Manager, Production: Lisa Rinaldi
Full-Service Project Management: PreMediaGlobal
Cover Printer: Courier/Kendallville

Pearson Education Limited
Edinburgh Gate
Harlow
Essex CM20 2JE
England

and Associated Companies throughout the world

Visit us on the World Wide Web at: www.pearsoninternationaleditions.com

© Pearson Education Limited 2014

The rights of Joe Valacich and Christoph Schneider to be identified as authors of this work have been asserted by them in accordance with the Copyright, Designs and Patents Act 1988.

Authorized adaptation from the United States edition, entitled Information Systems Today: Managing in the Digital World, 6th edition, ISBN 978-0-13-297121-8, by Joe Valacich and Christoph Schneider, published by Pearson Education, Inc., © 2014.

ISBN 10: 1-292-00000-7
ISBN 13: 978-1-292-00000-8

British Library Cataloguing-in-Publication Data
A catalogue record for this book is available from the British Library

10 9 8 7 6 5 4 3 2
14 13

Typeset in 10/12 TimesLTStd-Roman by PreMediaGlobal
Printed and bound by Courier Kendallville in The United States of America

The publisher's policy is to use paper manufactured from sustainable forests.

Dedication

To Jackie, Jordan, and James for your sacrifices, love, and support.
—Joe

To Birgit for your love and support.
—Christoph

About the Authors

Joe Valacich is an Eller Professor at The University of Arizona, Eller College of Management. He was previously on the faculty at Indiana University, Bloomington, and Washington State University, Pullman. He has had visiting faculty appointments at City University of Hong Kong, Buskerud College (Norway), the Helsinki School of Economics and Business, and the Norwegian University of Life Sciences. He currently teaches in a program for Riga Technical University (Latvia). He received a PhD degree from The University of Arizona (MIS) and MBA and BS (Computer Science) degrees from the University of Montana. Prior to his academic career, Dr. Valacich worked in the software industry in Seattle in both large and start-up organizations.

Dr. Valacich has served on various national task forces designing model curricula for the information systems discipline, including *IS '97, IS 2002,* and *IS 2010: The Model Curriculum and Guidelines for Undergraduate Degree Programs in Information Systems,* where he was co-chairperson. He also served on the task force that designed *MSIS 2000* and *2006: The Master of Science in Information Systems Model Curriculum.* He served on the executive committee, funded by the National Science Foundation, to define the *IS Program Accreditation Standards* and served on the board of directors for CSAB (formally, the Computing Sciences Accreditation Board) representing the Association for Information Systems (AIS). He was the general conference co-chair for the 2003 International Conference on Information Systems (ICIS) and the 2012 Americas Conference on Information Systems (AMCIS); both were held in Seattle.

Dr. Valacich has conducted numerous corporate training and executive development programs for organizations, including AT&T, Boeing, Dow Chemical, EDS, Exxon, FedEx, General Motors, Microsoft, and Xerox. He is currently a senior editor at *MIS Quarterly.* His primary research interests include human–computer interaction, technology-mediated collaboration, mobile and emerging technologies, e-business, and distance education. He has published more than 90 scholarly articles in numerous prestigious journals, including *MIS Quarterly, Information Systems Research, Management Science, Academy of Management Journal, Journal of MIS, Decision Sciences, Journal of the AIS, Communications of the ACM, Organizational Behavior and Human Decision Processes,* and *Journal of Applied Psychology.* He is a coauthor of the leading textbooks *Modern Systems Analysis and Design* (7th ed.) and *Essentials of Systems Analysis and Design* (5th ed.); both published by Prentice Hall.

Dr. Valacich was awarded the 2012 Distinguished Alumnus Award from the University of Montana Alumni Association and the 2009 Outstanding Alumnus Award from the University of Montana's School of Business Administration. Dr. Valacich is also ranked as one of most prolific scholars in the history of *MIS Quarterly* over the life of the journal (1977–2012) (see www.misq.org). In 2009, he was named a Fellow of the Association for Information Systems. Throughout his career, he has won numerous teaching, service, and research awards.

Christoph Schneider is an assistant professor in the Department of Information Systems at City University of Hong Kong and previously held a visiting faculty appointment at Boise State University. He earned a Swiss Higher Diploma in Hotel Management at the University Centre César Ritz in Brig, Switzerland, and a BA in Hotel and Restaurant Administration at Washington State University. Following extensive experience in the international hospitality industry, he studied information systems at the Martin Luther University in Halle, Germany, before joining the information systems department at Washington State University to earn his PhD degree. His teaching interests include the management of information systems, business intelligence, and enterprise-wide information systems.

Dr. Schneider is an active researcher. His primary research interests include human–computer interaction, electronic commerce, and computer-mediated collaboration. His research has appeared in peer-reviewed journals, such as *Information Systems Research, Management Information Systems Quarterly, Management Science,* and *IEEE Transactions on Professional Communication*; further, he has presented his research at various national and international conferences, such as the International Conference on Information Systems, the European Conference on Information Systems, and the Hawaii International Conference on System Sciences. He is a member of the International Steering Committee of the International Conference on Information Systems Development (ISD) and associate editor at *Information Systems Journal.*

Brief Contents

Contents

Preface

APPROACH

Information systems have become *pervasive. Mobile devices, social media,* and *cloud computing* have transformed organizations and society. Organizations see the impacts of *consumerization of IT,* in that many innovative technologies such as tablets and smartphones are first introduced in the consumer marketplace before being harnessed by organizations. People argue that we're living in the *post-PC era.* Businesses face unprecedented opportunities, but also challenges, through the ability to utilize *Big Data.* What does all this mean? What are the catalysts of these concepts and of all this change? More important, how can organizations thrive in this dynamic and highly competitive marketplace? The answer to these and many similar questions is that information systems and related information technologies are driving globalization, new business models, and hypercompetition. It is little wonder that teaching an introductory course on information systems has never been more crucial—or more challenging.

One of the greatest challenges that we face in teaching information systems courses is how to keep pace in the class with what is happening out in the real world. Being relevant to students while at the same time providing the necessary foundation for understanding the breadth, depth, and complexity of information systems has never been more difficult. We wrote *Information Systems Today,* Sixth Edition, with this overarching goal in mind, to be both rigorous *and* relevant. To accomplish this, we want students not only to learn about information systems, but also to clearly understand the importance of information systems for individuals, organizations, and society. Additionally, we do not want to simply spoon-feed students with technical terms and the history of information systems. Instead, students must understand exactly what innovative organizations are doing with contemporary information systems and, more important, where things are heading. Finally, we want to empower students with the essential knowledge needed to be successful in the use and understanding of information technology in their careers.

To this end, we wrote *Information Systems Today,* Sixth Edition, so that it is contemporary, fun to read, and useful, focusing on what business students need to know about information systems to survive and thrive in the digital world.

AUDIENCE

Information Systems Today, Sixth Edition, is primarily for the undergraduate introductory information systems course required of all business students. The introductory information systems course typically has a diverse audience of students majoring in many different areas, such as accounting, economics, finance, marketing, general management, human resource management, production and operations, international business, entrepreneurship, and information systems. This book was also written for students studying topics outside of business, especially in the growing and broad area of information sciences. Given the range of students taking this type of course, we have written this book so that it is a valuable guide to all students, providing them with the essential information they need to know. Therefore, this book has been written to appeal to a diverse audience.

Information Systems Today, Sixth Edition, can also be used for the introductory course offered at the graduate level—for example, in the first year of an MBA program. Such usage would be especially appropriate if the course heavily focused on the diverse set of cases provided in each chapter.

WHAT'S NEW TO THE SIXTH EDITION

Our primary goal for *Information Systems Today,* Sixth Edition, was to emphasize the importance of information systems to all business students as the role of information technology and systems continues to expand within organizations and society. Most notably, we extensively examine how five big megatrends—mobile, social, cloud computing, Big Data, and consumerization of IT—are transforming how individuals and organizations use information systems. Given this clear focus, we are better able to identify those topics most critical to students and future business professionals. Consequently, we have made substantial revisions to the basic content of the chapters and pedagogical elements that we believe achieve this goal. New or expanded chapter topics include the following:

- An extensively revised chapter—Chapter 1, "Managing in the Digital World"—focusing on defining not only what an information system consists of but also discussing the role of the five big megatrends as catalysts for tremendous change, as evidenced by the rise of globalization and emerging ethical issues.
- A revised chapter—Chapter 2, "Gaining Competitive Advantage Through Information Systems"—providing new content describing how information systems play a key part in most organization's business and revenue models.
- A revised chapter—Chapter 3, "Managing the Information Systems Infrastructure and Services"—providing a stronger focus on the need for a reliable, adaptable, and scalable infrastructure to support the needs of today's organizations. Chapter 3 also covers essential infrastructure concepts related to hardware, software, storage, networking and the Internet, and data centers, and an extended discussion on cloud computing and related concepts and their role in supporting an organization's information systems infrastructure.
- An extensively revised chapter—Chapter 4, "Enabling Business-to-Consumer Electronic Commerce"—that now focuses primarily on topics related to e-commerce involving the end consumer, with expanded coverage of mobile commerce and payment and related issues.
- An extensively revised chapter—Chapter 5, "Enhancing Organizational Communication and Collaboration Using Social Media" —that is centered around various topics related to the need for organizational communication, and discusses how organizations use both traditional communication and collaboration tools and social media for communication, collaboration, cooperation, and connection.
- A revised chapter—Chapter 6, "Enhancing Business Intelligence Using Information Systems" —providing extended coverage on databases to include Big Data and organizations' use of non-relational databases for handling and analyzing the ever-increasing amount of data.
- An extensively revised chapter—Chapter 8, "Strengthening Business-to-Business Relationships Via Supply Chain and Customer Relationship Management"—that greatly expands the coverage of supply chain management by including foundational topics of business-to-business electronic commerce. This chapter further provides extended coverage of customer relationship management by including evolving topics such as social CRM.
- A revised chapter—Chapter 10, "Securing Information Systems"—providing extended coverage on pertinent topics such as IS risk management.
- An updated and streamlined Technology Briefing covers foundational concepts related to various information technologies. The Technology Briefing provides the foundations for a deeper understanding of the topics introduced in Chapter 3 and is intended for use in more technically oriented courses. Each section of this briefing was designed to be stand-alone—it can be read with or without the other sections.

http://goo.gl/FeHGg

In addition to the changes within the main chapter content, we have also added two new features to each chapter—"Key Players" and "Who's Going Mobile." "Key Players" briefly introduces major companies in the information systems industry, as well as their products or services, and highlights why every business student needs to know about these companies. "Who's Going Mobile" discusses various issues related to the growing importance of mobile devices in organizations and society. We also provide QR codes throughout the book at the beginning of each major chapter section. These codes can be scanned with your smartphone and you will be directed to our blog, where we provide links to interesting videos and other content related to the current topic.

Beyond the chapter content and features, we have also made substantial changes and refinements to the end of each chapter. First, we carefully revised the end-of-chapter problems and exercises to reflect content changes and new material. Second, we have carefully updated the end-of-chapter cases about contemporary organizations and issues to illustrate the complexities of the digital world. Each case mirrors the primary content of its chapter to better emphasize its relevancy within the context of a real organization. Third, we have further introduced all new Team Work Exercises based on interesting, important trends related to Internet usage within a variety of contexts; this exercise encourages students to keep up to date on these topics, discuss the significance of changes brought about by the Internet, and to visualize and present the most pertinent findings. All these elements are discussed more thoroughly next.

Our goal has always been to provide only the information that is relevant to all business students, nothing more and nothing less. We believe that we have again achieved this goal with *Information Systems Today,* Sixth Edition. We hope you agree.

KEY FEATURES

As authors, teachers, developers, and managers of information systems, we understand that in order for students to best learn about information systems with this book, they must be motivated to learn. To this end, we have included a number of unique features to help students quickly and easily assess the true value of information systems and their impact on everyday life. We show how today's professionals are using information systems to help modern organizations become more efficient and competitive. Our focus is on the application of technology to real-world, contemporary situations. Next, we describe each of the features that contribute to that focus.

A Multi-tiered Approach

Each chapter utilizes cases in a variety of ways to emphasize and highlight how contemporary organizations are utilizing information systems to gain competitive advantage, streamline organizational processes, or improve customer relationships.

OPENING CASE—MANAGING IN THE DIGITAL WORLD. All chapters begin with an opening case describing a real-world company, technology, and/or issue to spark students' interest in the chapter topic. We have chosen engaging cases that relate to students' interests and concerns by highlighting why information systems have become central for managing in the digital world. Each opening case includes a series of associated questions the students will be able to answer after reading the chapter contents. The organizations, technologies, or issues highlighted in these cases include the following:

- Apple's rise, fall, and reemergence as a global technology giant
- How Groupon achieved a first mover advantage by reinventing the business model of group buying
- Google's meteoric rise and the challenges associated with maintaining its success
- How Chinese e-commerce company Taobao became a leader in the world of e-commerce
- How Facebook has emerged as one of the most successful and powerful social media sites
- Intelligence agencies' use of social media to gather intelligence about changes in worldwide public sentiment
- Amazon.com's use of its sophisticated infrastructure to automate the supply chain for both large and small customers
- How natural disasters disrupt the global supply chains of countless organizations throughout the world
- How Microsoft's Xbox rose to the top with the help of an ecosystem of devices and apps
- How the hacking group "Anonymous" uses various tactics to further its ideological goals

BRIEF CASE. Each chapter also includes a brief case that discusses important issues related to companies, technologies, or society. These are embedded in the text of the chapter and highlight concepts from the surrounding chapter material. Discussion questions are provided to seed critical thinking assignments or class discussions. The organizations, trends, and products highlighted in these cases include the following:

- How Starbuck's new CIO is turning the organizational IS-ship around by introducing various internal and external IS-based innovations
- How domainers—those who buy and sell lucrative domain names on the Internet—have grown into a multi-billion-dollar industry

- How data centers in Japan survived a devastating earthquake and tsunami
- How organizations such as Catchafire are helping to bring together non-profit organizations and volunteers
- How Iceland used crowdsourcing to obtain input and buy-in into its new constitution
- How companies such as eLoyalty use business intelligence to identify hotline callers' personality types
- How Amazon Studios crowdsources movie ideas and scripts, allowing aspiring screenwriters to bypass Hollywood production companies
- How Demand Media creates a supply chain for content published on sites such as eHow, Livestrong.com, Trails.com, or GolfLink.com
- How hardware and software companies are fighting a global patent war
- How law enforcement uses 3D technology to recreate crime scenes

END-OF-CHAPTER CASE. To test and reinforce chapter content, we present two current real-world cases at the end of each chapter. Sources for these cases include *InformationWeek, BusinessWeek, CIO* magazine, and various Web sites. Like the Brief Cases within the chapter, these are taken from the news and are contemporary. However, these are longer and more substantive than the Brief Cases. They too are followed by discussion questions that help the student apply and master the chapter content. The organizations and products highlighted in these cases include the following:

- How the One Laptop per Child program is attempting to bridge the digital divide
- How PayPal created a global currency to enable worldwide collaboration and commerce
- How Netflix is transforming the movie industry
- How LinkedIn, a social networking site for professionals, can help people find jobs, useful business contacts, and business opportunities
- How broadband Internet access in airplanes has overcome its teething problems and will soon become common
- How Facebook's infrastructure has evolved to support social games like FarmVille and Mafia Wars
- How the picture exchange site Flickr has gone through ups and downs over its lifetime
- How YouTube has grown into a mainstream Web marvel
- How Wikipedia has become both a useful and a sometimes controversial Web resource
- How Digg.com's stellar ascent has abruptly ended
- How Netflix is utilizing crowdsourcing to improve its ability to make movie recommendations to customers
- How online mapping services like Google maps are enabling many innovative products and services
- How enterprise resource planning systems transform business processes but often do not satisfy the needs of the users and the organization
- How Software as a Service has enabled small and medium-sized organizations to utilize enterprise resource planning systems
- How customer relationship management is evolving to include social media capabilities
- How the automobile industry is expanding their supply chains as cars become more reliant on information systems for information services, navigation, and communication
- How the rise of open source software systems, such as the Linux operating system, Apache Web server, and Firefox Web browser, is transforming the software industry
- How the FBI and DHS joined forces in developing a comprehensive database of biometric information to better track and apprehend criminals
- How and why cybercriminals target eBay, PayPal, and other popular Web sites and resources
- How China limits information exchange within its society through its "great firewall"

COMMON CHAPTER FEATURES

Throughout every chapter, a variety of short pedagogical elements are presented to highlight key information systems issues and concepts in a variety of contexts. These elements help to show students the broader organizational and societal implications of various topics.

Industry Analysis

Every industry is being transformed by the Internet and the increasing use of information systems by individuals and organizations. To give you a feel for just how pervasive and profound these changes are, each chapter presents an analysis of a specific industry to highlight the new rules for operating in the digital world. Given that no industry or profession is immune from these changes, each Industry Analysis highlights the importance of understanding information systems for *every* business student, not only for information systems majors. Discussion questions help students better understand the rapidly changing opportunities and risks of operating in the digital world. Chapter 1 examines how the digital world is transforming the opportunities for virtually all business professions. Subsequent chapters examine how globalization and the digital world have forever transformed various industries, including banking, movie, retail, travel, health care, automobile, manufacturing, broadcasting, and law enforcement. Clearly, we are in a time of tremendous change, and understanding this evolution will better equip students to not only survive but also thrive in the digital world.

Coming Attractions

We worked to ensure that this book is contemporary. We cover literally hundreds of different current and emerging technologies throughout the book. This feature, however, focuses on innovations that are likely to soon have an impact on organizations or society. Topics include the following:

- The future of cloud-based communications
- Google's augmented reality glasses
- Optical WLAN
- Very smart phones and services of the future
- Bio-storing files in bacteria
- The Internet of Things
- Swarm intelligence learned from ants, bees, termites, and wasps
- Saving lives through 3D bioprinting
- Microsoft's PixelSense user interface
- Speeding security screening using the AVATAR kiosk

When Things Go Wrong

Textbooks don't usually describe what not to do, but this can be very helpful to students. This feature enables students to learn about a real-world situation in which information systems did not work or were not built or used well. Topics include the following:

- Apple's numerous product and strategy failures
- Groupon and the dangers of miscalculating coupons
- Dirty data centers and the environmental impact of cloud computing
- How companies who try to rig search results often pay a big price
- Nestlé's social media fiasco after blocking a YouTube video posted by Greenpeace
- How the Internet can quickly disseminate false information with unforeseen consequences
- How New York City's "City Time" project failed due to fraud and corruption
- How faulty DRM code stalled iOS apps
- How an Internet security startup couldn't fight fire with fire
- How whistleblower sites such as WikiLeaks can cause security concerns

Who's Going Mobile

Mobile technologies have become pervasive throughout society. New opportunities and issues have emerged with the growing importance of mobile devices, such as smartphones and tablets, which are in people's immediate reach 24/7. Related to each chapter's content, this feature examines topics related to the growth in mobile device usage throughout the world. Topics include the following:

- The evolution of post-PC devices
- The battle of mobile phone operating systems
- How the cloud phone revolutionizes connectivity in sub-Saharan Africa

- The rise of mobile payments
- Mobile social media
- Mobile mapping services
- Managing businesses on the road using mobile ERP
- The power of mobile CRM
- How to succeed in mobile app development
- Mobile security threats

Ethical Dilemma

Ethical business practices are now a predominant part of contemporary management education and practice. This feature examines contemporary dilemmas related to the chapter content and highlights the implications of these dilemmas for managers, organizations, and society. Topics include the following:

- The human cost of the newest gadgets
- An underground gaming industry selling virtual goods for "real" money
- The ethics of publishing street photography on the Web
- The ethics of reputation management
- Social networks and people's diminishing sense of self
- Tracking shoppers using mobile phone signals
- Privacy of radio-frequency identification
- Using customer relationship management systems to target or discriminate
- Genetic testing and discrimination
- Industrial espionage

Key Players

A variety of key companies have shaped the information technology industry. While there are countless companies that have contributed to today's digital world, this feature presents some of the more prominent organizations that have significantly advanced technologies or are the leaders in their respective markets. These key players include the following:

- Wipro and Infosys, the global outsourcing leaders
- Samsung et al.: The global technology elite
- Dell, IBM, Rackspace, and other giants of the infrastructure
- Amazon, GoDaddy, Shopify, and other players behind online storefronts
- You: The content creator
- SAS, MicroStrategy, and other business intelligence leaders
- SAP, Oracle, and Microsoft: The titans of ERP
- Salesforce.com, an SaaS pioneer
- Activision Blizzard, Electronics Arts, and other players in game development
- TrendMicro, McAfee, and other white knights of the Internet Age

End-of-Chapter Material

Our end-of-chapter material is designed to accommodate various teaching and learning styles. It promotes learning beyond the book and the classroom. Elements include the following:

- *Key Terms*—Highlight key concepts within the chapter.
- *Review Questions*—Test students' understanding of basic content.
- *Self-Study Questions*—Enable students to assess whether they are ready for a test.
- *Matching Questions*—Check quickly to see if students understand basic terms.
- *Problems and Exercises*—Push students deeper into the material and encourage them to synthesize and apply it.
- *Application Exercises*—Challenge students to solve two real-world management problems using spreadsheet and database applications from a running case centered on a university travel agency. Student data files referenced within the exercises are available on the book's Web site: www.pearsoninternationaleditions.com/valacich.
- *Team Work Exercise* (**NEW**)—Encourage students to keep up with, discuss, visualize, and present interesting, important trends and forecasts related to Internet usage within a variety of contexts.

We have extensively updated these elements to reflect new chapter content and the natural evolution of the material.

Pedagogy

In addition to the features described above, we provide a list of learning objectives to lay the foundation for each chapter. At the end of the chapter, the Key Points Review repeats these learning objectives and describes how each objective was achieved. A list of references is located at the end of the text, organized by chapter.

Organization

The content and organization of this book are based on our own teaching as well as on feedback from reviewers and colleagues throughout the field. Each chapter builds on the others to reinforce key concepts and allow for a seamless learning experience. Essentially, the book has been structured to answer three fundamental questions:

1. What are contemporary information systems, and how are they being used in innovative ways?
2. Why are information systems so important and interesting?
3. How best can we build, acquire, manage, and safeguard information systems?

The ordering and content of our chapters was also significantly influenced by the "IS 2010 Curriculum Guidelines for Undergraduate Degree Programs in Information Systems," with a particular focus on "What Every Business Student Needs to Know About Information Systems."[1] These articles, written by prominent information systems scholars, define the information systems core body of knowledge for all business students. By design, the content of *Information Systems Today,* Sixth Edition, carefully follows the guidance of these articles. We are, therefore, very confident that our book provides a solid and widely agreed-on foundation for any introductory information systems course.

The chapters are organized as follows:

- *Chapter 1: Managing in the Digital World*—This chapter helps the student understand what information systems are, how the big five megatrends mobile, social, cloud computing, big data, and consumerization of IT influence organizations and society, and how information systems have become a vital part of modern organizations. We walk the student through the technology, people, and organizational components of an information system, and lay out types of jobs and career opportunities in information systems and in related fields. We also focus on how technology is driving globalization and creating countless ethical concerns. We use a number of cases and examples, such as that of Apple, to show the student the types of systems being used and to point out common "best practices" in information systems use and management.
- *Chapter 2: Gaining Competitive Advantage Through Information Systems*—Here, we discuss how companies such as Groupon can use information systems for automation, organizational learning, and strategic advantage by creating new and innovative business models. Given the rapid advancement of new technologies, we explain why and how companies are continually looking for innovative ways to use information systems for competitive advantage, and how information systems support organizations' international business strategies.
- *Chapter 3: Managing the Information Systems Infrastructure and Services*—In this extensively updated chapter, we provide an overview of the essential information systems

---

[1]Topi, H., Valacich, J., Wright, R.T., Kaiser, K., Nunamaker Jr., J.F., Sipior, J.C., and de Vreede, G.J. (2010). IS 2010: Curriculum guidelines for undergraduate degree programs in information systems. *Communications of the Association for Information Systems,* 26(18); Ives, B., Valacich, J., Watson, R., Zmud, R. (2002). What every business student needs to know about information systems. *Communications of the Association for Information Systems,* 9(30). Other contributing scholars to this article include Maryam Alavi, Richard Baskerville, Jack J. Baroudi, Cynthia Beath, Thomas Clark, Eric K. Clemons, Gordon B. Davis, Fred Davis, Alan R. Dennis, Omar A. El Sawy, Jane Fedorowicz, Robert D. Galliers, Joey George, Michael Ginzberg, Paul Gray, Rudy Hirschheim, Sirkka Jarvenpaa, Len Jessup, Chris F. Kemerer, John L. King, Benn Konsynski, Ken Kraemer, Jerry N. Luftman, Salvatore T. March, M. Lynne Markus, Richard O. Mason, F. Warren McFarlan, Ephraim R. McLean, Lorne Olfman, Margrethe H. Olson, John Rockart, V. Sambamurthy, Peter Todd, Michael Vitale, Ron Weber, and Andrew B. Whinston.

infrastructure components and describe why they are necessary for satisfying an organization's informational needs. With the ever-increasing complexity of maintaining a solid information systems infrastructure, it becomes increasingly important for organizations such as Google to design a reliable, robust, and secure infrastructure. We also examine the rapid evolution toward the delivery of infrastructure capabilities through a variety of technology services.

- *Chapter 4: Enabling Business-to-Consumer Electronic Commerce*—Perhaps nothing has changed the landscape of business more than the use of the Internet for electronic commerce. In this extensively updated chapter, we describe how a number of firms, such as US Airways, Timbuk2, or Taobao, use the Internet to conduct commerce in cyberspace. Further, we describe the stages of business-to-consumer electronic commerce and discuss Internet marketing and mobile commerce, as well as consumer-to-consumer and consumer-to-business e-commerce. Finally, we discuss payment and legal issues in e-commerce and explain different forms of e-government.

- *Chapter 5: Enhancing Organizational Communication and Collaboration Using Social Media*—Social media have forever changed how people interact. In addition to enabling various business opportunities, social media have also enabled companies to better harness the power and creativity of their workforce. In this extensively updated chapter, we provide an overview of traditional communication and collaboration tools, and examine how different social media can enhance communication, collaboration, cooperation, and connection within organizations but also between organizations and their customers. Further, we discuss the importance of carefully managing an Enterprise 2.0 strategy. Finally, using examples such as Twitter and Facebook, we describe how companies can deal with potential pitfalls associated with social media.

- *Chapter 6: Enhancing Business Intelligence Using Information Systems*—Given how many different types of information systems organizations use to run their business and gain business intelligence, in this chapter we use examples from Williams Sonoma and other firms to describe the various types of systems. In this chapter, we describe key business intelligence concepts and explain how databases serve as a foundation for gaining business intelligence. Further, we discuss three components of business intelligence: information and knowledge discovery, business analytics, and information visualization.

- *Chapter 7: Enhancing Business Processes Using Enterprise Information Systems*—In this chapter, we focus on enterprise systems, which are a popular type of information system used to integrate information and span organizations' boundaries to better connect a firm with customers, suppliers, and other partners. We walk students through various core business processes and then examine how enterprise resource planning systems can be applied to improve these processes and organizational performance.

- *Chapter 8: Strengthening Business-to-Business Relationships via Supply Chain and Customer Relationship Management*—In this extensively updated chapter, we continue our focus on enterprise systems by examining the complexities of supply networks and the rise of business-to-business electronic commerce, before examining how supply chain management systems can support the effective management of supply networks. Additionally, we examine customer relationship management systems and their role in the attraction and retention of customers, and, using examples from companies such as Dell, discuss how organizations can integrate social media in their CRM efforts.

- *Chapter 9: Developing and Acquiring Information Systems*—In this chapter, we begin by describing how to formulate and present the business case to build or acquire a new information system. We then walk the student through the traditional systems development approach and explain how numerous other approaches, such as prototyping, rapid application development, and object-oriented analysis and design, can be utilized depending on the situation. Finally, we examine the steps followed when acquiring an information system from an outside vendor.

- *Chapter 10: Securing Information Systems*—With the pervasive use of information systems, new dangers have arisen for organizations, and the interplay between threats, vulnerabilities, and potential impacts has become a paramount issue within the context of global information management. In this chapter, we define computer crime and contrast several types of computer crime, and discuss the growing significance of cyberwar and cyberterrorism. We then highlight the primary threats to information systems security and explain how systems can be compromised and safeguarded. We conclude this chapter with a discussion of the role of auditing, information systems controls, and the Sarbanes–Oxley Act. Note that some instructors may choose to introduce this chapter prior to the discussion of the information systems infrastructure in Chapter 3.

■ *Technology Briefing*—In addition to these ten chapters, we include a Technology Briefing that focuses on foundational concepts regarding hardware, software, networking and the Internet, and databases. While Chapter 3, "Managing the Information Systems Infrastructure and Services," provides a more managerial focus to these enabling technologies, this foundational material is intended to provide a more in-depth examination of these topics. By delivering this material as a Technology Briefing, we provide instructors the greatest flexibility in how and when they can apply it.

SUPPLEMENT SUPPORT

Online Instructor's Resource Center

The convenient Online Instructor's Resource Center is accessible from the Web site www .pearsoninternationaleditions.com/valacich by choosing the "Instructor Resources" link from the catalog page. The online center includes the following supplements: Instructor's Manual, Test Item File, PowerPoint presentations, and Image Library (text art).

The Instructor's Manual includes answers to all review and discussion questions, exercises, and case questions. The Test Item File (Test Bank) includes multiple-choice, true-or-false, and essay questions for each chapter. The Test Bank is delivered in Microsoft Word as well as in the form of TestGen. The PowerPoint presentations highlight text learning objectives and key topics. Finally, the Image Library is a collection of the figures and tables from the text for instructor use in PowerPoint slides and class lectures.

CourseSmart eTextbooks Online

CourseSmart eTextbooks were developed for students looking to save on required or recommended textbooks. Students simply select their eText by title or author and purchase immediate access to the content for the duration of the course using any major credit card. With a CourseSmart eText, students can search for specific keywords or page numbers, take notes online, print out reading assignments that incorporate lecture notes, and bookmark important passages for later review. For more information or to purchase a CourseSmart eTextbook, visit www.coursesmart.co.uk

MyMISLab

MyMISLab is now available to bring a greater software applications emphasis to your class. Included is MyITLab, a Microsoft Office simulation currently used by thousands of students allowing them to gain practical skills in the use of spreadsheet and database software. End-of Chapter applications are tied to this unique tutorial.

Please visit www.pearsoninternationaleditions.com/mymislab and contact your local rep for more details.

REVIEWERS

We wish to thank the following faculty who participated in reviews for this and previous editions:

Lawrence L. Andrew, *Western Illinois University*

Karin A. Bast, *University of Wisconsin–La Crosse*

David Bradbard, *Winthrop University*

Rochelle Brooks, *Viterbo University*

Brian Carpani, *Southwestern College*

Amita Chin, *Virginia Commonwealth University*

Jon D. Clark, *Colorado State University*

Paul Clay, *Washington State University*

Khaled Deeb, *Barry University*

Thomas Engler, *Florida Institute of Technology*

Badie Farah, *Eastern Michigan University*

Roy H. Farmer, *California Lutheran University*

Mauricio Featherman, *Washington State University*

David Firth, *University of Montana*

Frederick Fisher, *Florida State University*

James Frost, *Idaho State University*

Frederick Gallegos, *California State Polytechnic University–Pomona*

Dale Gust, *Central Michigan University*

Peter Haried, *University of Wisconsin- La Crosse*

Albert Harris, *Appalachian State University*
Michelle Hepner, *University of Central Oklahoma*
Traci Hess, *University of Massachusetts*
Bruce Hunt, *California State University–Fullerton*
Carol Jensen, *Southwestern College*
Bhushan Kapoor, *California State University–Fullerton*
Elizabeth Kemm, *Central Michigan University*
Beth Kiggins, *University of Indianapolis*
Chang E. Koh, *University of North Texas*
Brian R. Kovar, *Kansas State University*
Kapil Ladha, *Drexel University*
Linda K. Lau, *Longwood University*
Cameron Lawrence, *University of Montana*
Martha Leva, *Penn State University–Abington*
Weiqi Li, *University of Michigan–Flint*
Clayton Looney, *University of Montana*
Dana L. McCann, *Central Michigan University*
Richard McCarthy, *Quinnipiac University*
Patricia McQuaid, *California State Polytechnic University, San Louis Obispo*
Michael Newby, *California State University–Fullerton*
Kathleen Noce, *Penn State University–Erie*
W. J. Patterson, *Sullivan University*

Timothy Peterson, *University of Minnesota–Duluth*
Lara Preiser-Houy, *California State Polytechnic University, Pomona*
Sridhar Ramachandran, *Indiana University Southeast*
Eugene Rathswohl, *University of San Diego*
Rene F. Reitsma, *Oregon State University*
Jose Rodriguez, *Barry University*
Bonnie Rohde, *Albright College*
Kenneth Rowe, *Purdue University*
Dana Schwieger, *Southeast Missouri State University*
G. Shankaranarayanan, *Boston University*
James Sneeringer, *St. Edward's University*
Cheri Speier, *Michigan State University*
Bill Turnquist, *Central Washington University*
Craig K. Tyran, *Western Washington University*
William Wagner, *Villanova University*
Minhua Wang, *State University of New York–Canton*
John Wells, *University of Massachusetts*
Nilmini Wickramasinghe, *Cleveland State University*
Yue Zhang, *California State University–Northridge*

ACKNOWLEDGMENTS

Although only our two names are listed as the authors for this book, this was truly a team effort that went well beyond the two of us. Pearson Prentice Hall has been an outstanding publishing company to work with. They are innovative, have high standards, and are as competitive as we are.

Among the many amazingly helpful people at Pearson Prentice Hall, there are a handful of people we wish to thank specifically. First, Kelly Loftus, our editorial project manager, helped to whip us and this book into shape and get it finished on time. Additionally, Jane Bonnell, our production project manager, and Haylee Schwenk of PreMediaGlobal helped in getting approval for photos, figures, Web sites, and other graphics, as well as coordinating refinements as the book moved through the stages of production. Finally, our executive editor, Bob Horan, guided the book and us from its inception, and he dared us to dream of and to write the best introductory information systems textbook ever.

In addition to our colleagues at Pearson Prentice Hall, several individuals have been particularly instrumental in making the sixth edition the best ever. First, Jackie Valacich did an outstanding job on editing and revising several of our case elements; Tracy Hess from the University of Massachusetts and Mauricio Featherman from Washington State University provided valuable inputs into our revision of Chapters 7 and 8. Likewise, Ryan Wright from the University of Massachusetts provided many ideas that shaped the current edition. Also, Kannis Tam, Felix Chiu, Hugo Cheung, and Leo Chu from City University of Hong Kong have provided many new and exciting ideas for the revised chapter elements. Finally, a special thanks goes out to Catherine Chan from Hong Kong Baptist University, who has been instrumental in drafting chapter elements. Thanks team! We could not have done it without you.

Most important, we thank our families for their patience and assistance in helping us to complete this book. Joe's wife Jackie, daughter Jordan, and son James were a constant inspiration, as was Christoph's wife Birgit. This one is for all of you.

The publishers would like to thank Susmi Routray of IMT Ghaziabad for reviewing the content of the International Edition.

Information Systems Today
Managing in the Digital World

Managing in the Digital World

Preview

Today, organizations from Apple to Zales Jewelers use computer-based information systems to better manage their organizations in the digital world. These organizations use information systems to provide high-quality goods and services as well as to gain or sustain competitive advantage over rivals. In addition to helping organizations to be competitive, information systems have contributed to tremendous societal changes. Our objective for this chapter is to help you understand the role of information systems as we move into the digital world, and how they have helped fuel globalization. We then highlight what information systems are, how they have evolved to become a vital part of modern organizations, and why this understanding is necessary for you to become an effective manager in the digital world. We conclude by discussing ethical issues associated with the use of information systems.

Managing in the Digital World:
Apple

On October 5, 2011, a legend died. Steve Jobs lost his battle to pancreatic cancer, and the world mourned. Outside Jobs' Palo Alto home, flowers and scrawled chalk messages were found in front of the gates; apple-shaped pizza was made in Naples as a tribute to the tech guru. In Tokyo, people left iPads and iPhones displaying candle graphics at a store in the Ginza district, and in Hong Kong, newspaper headlines were dominated by the death of the Apple founder. Everywhere, people cried; "iSad" became a trending topic on Twitter. Bill Gates recalled the profound impact Jobs made, Facebook founder Mark Zuckerberg thanked him for changing the world, and Barack Obama credited Steve Jobs for transforming the world and redefining industries. It is undeniable how esteemed Jobs had become—a technological innovator turned "visionary" and "hero"—and how information systems have come to play a crucial part in today's global community. Think how waiting in line at the grocery store or waiting for the next train is more productive, or at least no longer tedious, when you get to check your inbox or play a round of Angry Birds (see Figure 1.1). Now remember how insecure you felt the last time you left your smartphone sitting on your living room sofa. Whichever way you look at it, the Apple craze is certainly here to stay. People camp out for days to get their hands on the latest Apple gadgets; when the iPhone 4S was launched in China, mayhem broke out, forcing Apple to close their stores in Beijing and Shanghai due to the overwhelming crowds.

FIGURE 1.1

Smartphones have taken the dreadfulness out of waiting.
Source: diego cervo/Fotolia

Looking at the company today, it is hard to imagine how everything started; two college drop-outs, a bedroom, and a garage. The Apple I, selling for US$666.66, debuted shortly after Steve "Woz" Wozniak and Steve Paul Jobs formed the Apple Computer Company in 1976. Soon after, the Apple II, an attractive and functional addition to one's living space, sold 50,000 units, dominating the market until 1993. Despite a series of lows (the Lisa and the Apple III were disastrous), the company took off; after a power struggle, Jobs left Apple in 1985, followed by Wozniak, who left two years later. After Jobs' return to Apple in 1996, successful additions to the company's product line included the iMac, a PowerBook featuring a 14-inch display, and a new operating system known as the Mac OS X. Late 2001 saw the iPod kickoff, with the MP3 music player going mainstream in 2003. During this time, Apple came up with iTunes, a virtual store where users could download digital music for 99 cents per track.

In 2007, the iPhone was introduced, selling 1.4 million units in the first 90 days. Also introduced at that time was the "App Store," extending iTunes to apps for the popular smartphone. Then came the iPod touch—which was simply an iPhone minus the phone, for those who chose to separate listening to music or playing games from answering the phone. The era of iPhones continued as the iPhone 3G sold over 1 million units on its first weekend. In 2010 the iPhone 4 was released, and not long after Jobs' death people lined up in endless queues for a first-hand experience of the newly released iPhone 4S. Adding to the series of innovations were 2008's MacBook Air and, of course, the revolutionary iPad (2010), touted by Jobs as a "third-category" device between smartphones and laptops. From the newest music players and computers, to a series of smartphones and tablets, you name it, Apple has it. The distribution and use of the products have become so immense that as of November 2011, one in every ten American mobile phone subscribers owned an iPhone, while 5 percent of UK kids under the age of 10 owned an iPad. Clearly, innovations fueled by Apple have changed the lives of many people all over the world.

Numerous cases have shown that corporations, schools, and other social institutions are using the iPad to improve both internal operations and external communications. For example, Mercedes-Benz deployed iPads in all 355 of their car dealerships in the United States. This innovation allows sales people instant access to Mercedes-Benz's point of sale system, information on car models, and other related marketing programs. In addition, an iPad app was created to enable customers to electronically sign documents, expediting the sales process. Doctors have also found iPads and related apps such as "DrChrono" extremely useful in scheduling patient appointments, writing prescriptions and sending them to pharmacies, setting reminders, taking clinical notes, inputting electronic health records, accessing lab results, and more. The iPad is also bringing innovations to education: the iBooks 2 app makes learning more fun with full-screen books, interactive 3D objects, exciting videos, informative diagrams, and gorgeous photos. Adding creativity and inventing new concepts with each new product, Apple has indeed transformed our world with one swipe of a finger.

Thanks to the innovative designs, clever marketing tactics, and significant practicality, Apple has managed to become not only a hardware vendor, but also a keeper of people's (often private) information. As it is being stored in the cloud, personal information can easily be (ab)used to predict future behavior, potential trends, music tastes, and more. Connected as we may be to the rest of the world, salient concerns are warranted regarding issues of privacy and information property; who has access to what and how private information is being used. Certainly, there are potential risks associated with being an active participant in the digital world, so the next time you purchase an app, think about how much you reveal about yourself with the swipe of your finger.

After reading this chapter, you will be able to answer the following:

1. Given the pace at which technology is converging (e.g., phones, music players, cameras, and so on), what do you think is next in the post-PC era?

2. How have Apple's products influenced the way we work and socialize?

3. How can a company like Apple balance the ethical aspects of relying on global manufacturers for their products?

Based on:

Anonymous. (2012, January 19). Apple Reinvents Textbooks with iBooks 2 for iPad. *apple.com*. Retrieved March 19, 2012, from http://www.apple.com/pr/library/2012/01/19Apple-Reinvents-Textbooks-with-iBooks-2-for-iPad.html.

Anonymous. (n.d.). Apple-history.com: Recent changes. Retrieved March 19, 2012, from http://www.apple-history.com.

comScore. (2011, November 4). comScore Reports September 2011 U.S. Mobile Subscriber Market Share. *comscore*. Retrieved March 20, 2012, from http://www.comscore.com/Press_Events/Press_Releases/2011/11/comScore_Reports_September_2011_U.S._Mobile_Subscriber_Market_Share.

Cutter, C. (2011, October 14). New iPhone launch turns into remembrance for Jobs. *Yahoo! News*. Retrieved March 19, 2012, from http://news.yahoo.com/iphone-launch-turns-remembrance-jobs-203012050.html.

Martin, S. (2011, March 1). More companies put iPads to work. *USA Today*. Retrieved March 20, 2012, from http://www.usatoday.com/tech/products/2011-02-28-ipad-enterprise_N.htm.

Parker, R. (2011, October 7). Steve Jobs dead: Tributes as Apple's legions of fans mark death of hero. *Mail Online*. Retrieved March 19, 2012, from http://www.dailymail.co.uk/news/article-2045903/Steve-Jobs-dead-Tributes-Apples-legions-fans-mark-death-hero.html.

http://goo.gl/iqGeV

INFORMATION SYSTEMS TODAY

Today, computers—the core components of information systems (IS)— are ubiquitous: be it e-book readers, laptop computers, digital cameras, smartphones, etc., you name it; computers are all around us, whether you see them or not. Companies such as FedEx or UPS use information systems to route trucks and track packages. Retailers such as Walgreens and Walmart use information systems for everything from optimizing supply chains to recording purchases and analyzing customer tastes and preferences. Cities use information systems for adaptive traffic control systems or variable speed limits. Cars use small computers for everything from ignition control to airbags to distance control and park assist systems; in fact, U.S. automaker Ford now considers itself a technology company, pioneering, for example, applications that allow accessing smartphone apps from an in-dash touch screen. Alternatively, just look around your school or place of work. At your school, you register for classes online, use e-mail, Twitter, or Facebook to communicate with fellow students and your instructors, access e-books from your library, and complete or submit assignments on online learning platforms such as BlackBoard, Moodle, or Sakai. At work, you may use a PC for e-mail and many other tasks. Your paychecks are probably generated by computer and automatically deposited in your banking account via high-speed networks. Even in your spare time, information technology is ubiquitous: you use social networking sites like Facebook to stay connected with your friends and family, you watch videos on YouTube, you upload pictures taken with your cell phone or digital camera to picture sharing sites like Flickr, and you use your smartphone for playing games, sending e-mails, or even reading books. Chances are that each year you see more information technology than you did the year before, and this technology is a more fundamental and important part of your social, learning, and work life than ever before.

Over the past decades, the advent of powerful, relatively inexpensive, easy-to-use computers has had a major impact on business. When you stop and think about it, it is easy to see why information technology is important. Increasing global competitiveness has forced companies to find ways to be better and to do things less expensively. The answer for many firms continues to be to use information systems to do things better, faster, and cheaper. Using global telecommunications networks, companies can more easily integrate their operations to access new markets for their products and services as well as access a large pool of talented labor in countries with lower wages.

Clearly, we are living in a digital world. Given the proliferation of new form factors, such as tablets or smartphones, some even argue that we are living in the **post-PC era**, where wireless, mobile devices allow for novel ways of interacting with information systems. In fact, already in 2011, the majority of Apple's revenues came from "post-PC devices," and in the last quarter of 2011, Apple sold more iPads than HP (traditionally one of the world's leading PC makers) sold PCs. With Apple's introduction of the latest iPad in early 2012, this trend is likely to continue; analysts forecast that Apple will sell 55 million iPads in 2012 worldwide. Forrester research predicts that by 2016, one in every three U.S. adults will own a tablet, be it Apple's iPad, a tablet manufactured by electronics manufacturers such as Samsung, ASUS, or Motorola, or a tablet designed by the online bookseller Amazon.com (Kindle) or Barnes & Noble (Nook). Initially created as consumer devices, tablets have already made their way into various business settings, including warehouses, showrooms, airplane cockpits, and hospitals (see Figure 1.2).

Yet, desktop personal computers (PCs) and laptops are unlikely to go away. Rather, devices with newer form factors will work in tandem with older form factors to provide truly ubiquitous experiences, and the changes we've seen so far will give rise to future developments, including wearable computers, augmented reality devices, or surface computers (Epps, 2011).

Changes in technology have enabled new ways of working and socializing; whereas traditionally, people were bound to a stationary PC to do essential tasks, they can now perform such tasks from almost anywhere where they have a cell phone signal. At the same time, work days traditionally had a clear beginning and a clear end—from when you power your computer on to when you turn it off at night. Today, many tasks (especially more casual tasks such as reading or sending e-mails) can be done at any time, often in small chunks in between other tasks, such as when waiting in line at the supermarket cashier.

FIGURE 1.2

Post-PC devices are increasingly being used in various business settings.

Source: Minerva Studio/Fotolia

Computing has changed from an activity primarily focused on automating work to encompass various social and casual activities. Devices such as smartphones or tablets, paired with mobile broadband networks, allow for instant-on computing experiences, whenever and wherever; advances in *cloud computing* (think Gmail, Evernote, or DropBox) allow for accessing e-mails, files, notes, and the like from different devices, further enhancing portability and mobility.

In effect, we are in a virtuous cycle (or in a vicious cycle, considering the creep of work life into people's leisure time, and the increasing fixation on being permanently "on call"), where changes in technology enable social changes, and social changes shape technological changes. For example, communication, social networking, or online investing almost necessitate mobility and connectivity, as people have grown accustomed to checking e-mails, posting status updates, or checking on real-time stock quotes while on the go. In addition, the boundaries between work and leisure time are blurring, so that employees increasingly demand devices that can support both, often bringing their own devices into the workplace. In fact, a study conducted by research firm Forrester in 2011 found that 54 percent of online consumers in the U.S. and 70 percent of iPad owners believe that technology helps them to optimize both work and personal life.

In 1959, Peter Drucker predicted that information and information technology (IT) would become increasingly important, and at that point, over four decades ago, he coined the term **knowledge worker**. Knowledge workers are typically professionals who are relatively well educated and who create, modify, and/or synthesize knowledge as a fundamental part of their jobs.

Drucker's predictions about knowledge workers were very accurate. As he predicted, they are generally paid better than their prior agricultural and industrial counterparts; they rely on and are empowered by formal education, yet they often also possess valuable real-world skills; they are continually learning how to do their jobs better; they have much better career opportunities and far more bargaining power than workers ever had before; they make up about a quarter of the workforce in the United States and in other developed nations; and their numbers are rising quickly.

Drucker also predicted that, with the growth in the number of knowledge workers and with their rise in importance and leadership, a **knowledge society** would emerge. He reasoned that, given the importance of education and learning to knowledge workers and the firms that need them, education would become the cornerstone of the knowledge society. Possessing knowledge, he argued, would be as important as possessing land, labor, or capital (if not more so) (see Figure 1.3). Indeed, research shows that people equipped to prosper in the knowledge society, such as those with a college education, earn far more on average than people without a college education, and that gap is increasing. In fact, the most recent data from the U.S. Census Bureau (2011 data) reinforce the value of a college education: workers 18 and over with a bachelor's degree earn an average of US$57,026 a year, while those with a high school diploma earn

FIGURE 1.3

In the knowledge society, information has become as important as—and many feel more important than—land, labor, and capital resources.

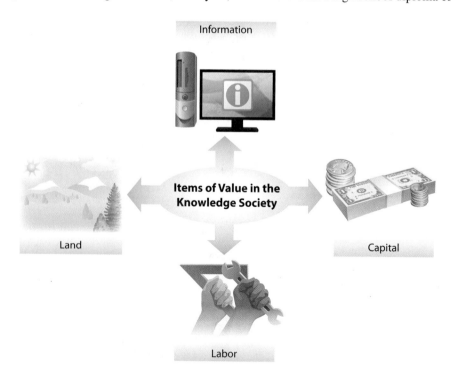

US$34,197. Workers with a master's degree make an average of US$69,958, and those without a high school diploma average US$23,227. The Census Bureau data suggest that a bachelor's degree is worth about US$1 million in additional lifetime earnings compared to a worker with only a high school diploma. Additionally, getting a college degree will qualify you for many jobs that would not be available to you otherwise and will distinguish you from other job candidates. Finally, a college degree is often a requirement to qualify for career advancement and promotion opportunities once you do get that job.

People generally agree that Drucker was accurate about knowledge workers and the evolution of society. While people have settled on Drucker's term "knowledge worker," there are many alternatives to the term "knowledge society." Others have referred to this phenomenon as the knowledge economy, new economy, the digital society, the network era, the Internet era, and other names. We simply refer to this as the *digital world*. All these ideas have in common the premise that information and related technologies and systems have become very important to us and that knowledge workers are vital.

Similarly, many "traditional" occupations now increasingly use information technologies—from the UPS package delivery person using global positioning system (GPS) technology to plan the best route to deliver parcels, to the farmer in Iowa who uses precision agriculture to plan the use of fertilizers to increase crop yield. The lines between "knowledge workers" and "manual workers" are blurring, to the point that some argue that "every worker is a knowledge worker" (Rosen, 2011). The people at the front lines typically have a very good understanding of how certain business processes work, and can provide valuable input for improving or optimizing those processes; further, knowing how their work contributes to business results can foster commitment, leading to higher job performance.

Some have argued, however, that there is a downside to being a knowledge worker and to living in the digital world. For example, some have argued that knowledge workers will be the first to be replaced by automation with information technology. Others have argued that in the new economy there is a *digital divide,* where those with access to information technology have great advantages over those without access to information technology (discussed later in this chapter).

To be sure, there is a downside to overreliance on information technology, but one thing is for certain: Knowledge workers and information technologies are now critical to the success of modern organizations, economies, and societies. How did information systems become so pervasive throughout our lives and society? This is examined next.

The Rise of the Information Age

In his book *The Third Wave,* futurist Alvin Toffler describes three distinct phases, or "waves of change," that have taken place in the past or are presently taking place within the world's civilizations (see Figure 1.4). The first wave—a civilization based on agriculture and handwork—was a comparatively primitive stage that replaced hunter-gatherer cultures and lasted for thousands of years. The second wave of change—the industrial revolution—overlapped with the first wave. The industrial revolution began in Great Britain toward the end of the eighteenth century and continued over the next 150 years, moving society from a predominantly agrarian culture to the urbanized machine age. Where once families supported themselves by working the land or handcrafting items for sale or trade, now mothers, fathers, and children left home to work in factories. Steel mills, textile factories, and eventually automobile assembly lines replaced farming and handwork as the principal source of family income.

FIGURE 1.4

The Information Age is the biggest wave of change.

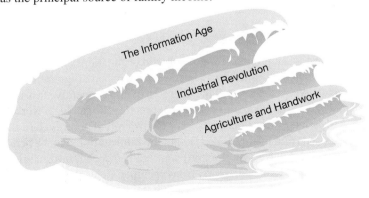

The Information Age

Industrial Revolution

Agriculture and Handwork

BRIEF CASE   Technology at Starbucks

When hearing the name "Starbucks," people immediately think about the global chain of coffeehouses. Since its founding in Seattle in the early 1970's, Starbucks has managed to attract a loyal crowd of customers, not only by offering a variety of coffees and related drinks, but also by providing a comfortable place to meet friends and colleagues, study, work, or just hang out. Having introduced Italian-style espresso bars to the United States in the mid-1980's, Starbucks quickly expanded its business, with (as of spring 2012) almost 20,000 stores in 58 countries (McDonald's, founded decades earlier, thus far operates over 33,000 stores). Yet, this fast pace of growth came at a cost: around 2008, same-store sales slowed. During Starbucks' growth phase (during certain periods, they opened on average one store per day) the role of the IS department was to support the sustained growth, with little focus on systems that would facilitate the management of stores or enhance the customer experience. In 2008, Starbucks hired Steve Gillett (named "CIO of the Year" by *InformationWeek* in 2011) to turn the IS-ship around. Blending marketing with technology, Gillett started a number of initiatives, both with a focus on the customers and Starbucks' employees. Here are just a few examples of how technology is being used at Starbucks:

1. Connecting with Customers—A key component of Starbucks' coffeehouse atmosphere is connectivity. At stores throughout the United States, customers can enjoy free Wi-Fi access, paired with free access to music, as well as content from the *Wall Street Journal*, *The Economist*, and other sources through Starbucks' newly created portal. Another way to connect with customers is "My Starbucks Idea." On this online platform, customers can post ideas and suggestions, as well as vote on or discuss others' ideas. As of March 2012, over 200 customer-generated ideas have been launched, with many more being on the way. The company's Facebook page, which has almost 30 million "likes," serves as another avenue for customers to stay close to the coffee chain.

2. Mobile Payment—Since Stephen Gillett took the helm at Starbucks' IS department, the company has quickly become a retail leader in mobile payments. A smartphone app tied to the customer's loyalty and payment cards generates a 2D bar code that can be read by an in-store payment terminal. This enables making transactions, but

also generates a wealth of information about Starbucks' loyal customers. In the year 2011 alone, Starbucks saw a record of 20 million transactions on the app.

3. Virtual Talent—A new addition to Starbucks' headquarters is the "Tech Cafe," a new IS help desk for employees. Resembling Apple's "Genius Bars," the Tech Cafe was created not only to help employees with IS-related problems, but also to allow employees to choose the technologies they need for their own workplace (not unlike in a retail store, where you can "play around" with different devices before making a choice), and to discuss their needs and suggestions. Having recognized the increasing IS-related knowledge of its employees, Starbucks hopes to obtain valuable new ideas and suggestions from each employee.

4. Contextual Retailing—The next frontier for Starbucks is to offer an individualized experience for every customer. For example, using mobile technologies, the baristas at Starbucks can be alerted if a regular customer enters the store, know the customer's preferred drinks, or suggest new alternatives based on the customer's history. Even further, the music played within a store could be based on the collective preferences of the customers sitting in the store.

These are but some examples that show that in today's highly competitive world, brewing successful coffee is not as simple as it looks.

Questions:

1. What are other ways in which Starbucks could use technology to connect with its customers?

2. To what extent do such innovations influence your choice of coffee shops? What would make you switch to another store? Why?

Based on:

Murphy, C. (2011, December 12). How Starbucks blends marketing and tech. *InformationWeek*. Retrieved May 10, 2012, from http://www.informationweek.com/news/mobility/business/232200561.

Murphy, C. (2011, December 12). Starbucks' help desk secret: model an Apple store. *InformationWeek*. Retrieved May 10, 2012, from http://www.informationweek.com/news/232200550.

Murphy, C. (2011, December 12). Starbucks' Stephen Gillett: InformationWeek's IT Chief of The Year. *InformationWeek*. Retrieved May 10, 2012, from http://www.informationweek.com/news/global-cio/interviews/232200549.

As the industrial revolution progressed, not only did occupations change to accommodate the mechanized society, but so did educational, business, social, and religious institutions. On an individual level, punctuality, obedience, and the ability to perform repetitive tasks became qualities to be instilled and valued in children in public schools and, ultimately, in workers.

In a much shorter period of time than it took for civilization to progress past the first wave, societies worldwide moved from the machine age into the **information age**—a period of change Toffler has dubbed the "third wave." As the third wave gained speed, information became the currency of the realm. For thousands of years, from primitive times through the Middle Ages, information, or the body of knowledge known to that point, was limited. It was transmitted

FIGURE 1.5

The printing press gave birth to the Information Age.
Source: ChipPix/Shutterstock

verbally within families, clans, and villages, from person to person and generation to generation. Then came Johannes Gutenberg's invention of the printing press with movable type in the middle of the fifteenth century, and a tremendous acceleration occurred in the amount and kinds of information available to populations (see Figure 1.5). Now knowledge could be imparted in written form and sometimes came from distant locations. Information could be saved, absorbed, debated, and written about in publications, thus adding to the exploding data pool.

Five IT Megatrends in the Information Age

Today, in most developed societies, information technologies have become pervasive—information technologies are in fact used throughout society. The development of sophisticated Web technologies has brought about a fundamental shift in types of information technologies that are being used, and we're seeing five (intertwined) "megatrends" that shape organizations and society (Hinchcliffe, 2011; see Figure 1.6). Knowing about the influence of these megatrends will be increasingly important for both your work life and your personal life.

- *Mobile.* As indicated in the opening section of this chapter, many believe that we're living in a post-PC era, and one of the biggest trends we're seeing today is the move toward mobile devices. In most developed countries, the vast majority of adults has a mobile phone, and typically, people have their mobile phones within their reach 24/7. Compare that with the access to your laptop or PC. In the developing world, mobile devices are frequently seen leapfrogging traditional PCs, often owing to the lack of stable, reliable power or lacking landline telephone infrastructures, making mobile devices the primary means of accessing the Internet. For organizations, this increase in mobility has a wide range of implications, from increased collaboration to the ability to manage a business in

FIGURE 1.6

Five IT Megatrends.

FIGURE 1.7

Mobile devices allow running business in real-time—anytime, from anywhere.

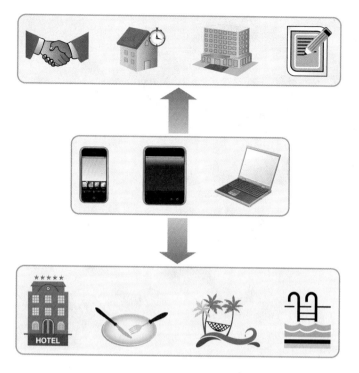

real-time—anytime, from anywhere—to changes in the way new (or existing) customers can be reached (see Figure 1.7). In fact, Wendy Clark, Coca-Cola's senior vice president for integrated marketing, is quoted as saying when advising about the development of marketing campaigns that "if your plans don't include mobile, then your plans aren't finished." Throughout the text, we will introduce issues and new developments associated with increases in mobility.

- *Social media.* A second megatrend, as you have undoubtedly noticed, is social media. You may be one of the over 900 million (and growing) Facebook users who share status updates or pictures with friends and family, or you may use a social network such as Google+ to stay informed about the activities of your social "circles." University professors use social networks to provide students with updates about course-related topics, and organizations use social media to encourage employee collaboration or to connect with their customers (see Figure 1.8). In addition, companies can harness the power of the crowd, by using social media to get people to participate in innovation and other activities. Another example of the power of social media is Wikipedia, the online encyclopedia that everyone can contribute to. As you can imagine, social media are here to stay; while we will touch on social media–related aspects throughout the book, we will devote Chapter 5, "Enhancing Organizational Communication and Collaboration Using Social Media," to social media and related topics.

- *Big Data.* Together, the transformation of our social and work interactions enabled by 24/7 connectivity has given rise to a third trend, *Big Data*. Following the old adage that information is power, organizations are continuously seeking to get the right information to make the best business decisions. Yet, organizations are generating and collecting ever

FIGURE 1.8

Social media are used in various personal and business settings.

more data from internal and external sources. The rise of social media has further increased the amount of unstructured data available to organizations; for example, people frequently voice their thoughts about products or companies on social media sites. In addition, increasingly, devices and sensors are connected to the Internet, measuring, among other things, location, temperature, humidity, or movement, further contributing to the growth of data available to organizations and individuals. A study by research firm IDC estimated that in 2011, 1.8 zettabytes of data were generated and consumed. How much is 1.8 zettabytes? 1.8 zettabytes equals 1.8 trillion gigabytes, or the equivalent of 57 billion 32GB iPads (Voorhout, 2012). The number is forecast to be 50 times more by the end of the decade. For many organizations in the information age, value is created from data: for example, whereas the largest/most valuable organizations in the "old economy" (such as GE, Dow, or Ford) have 100,000–200,000 employees and the largest organizations in the "new economy" (such as Microsoft, HP, or Oracle) have 50,000–100,000 employees, companies in the "information age economy" (such as Facebook, Twitter, or Groupon) have risen to the top with a mere 5,000–20,000 employees by creating value from data (Hofmann, 2011) (see Figure 1.9). However, analyzing tremendous amounts of (often unstructured) data (i.e., Big Data) poses tremendous challenges for organizations. In Chapter 6, "Enhancing Business Intelligence Using Information Systems," we will discuss how organizations can harness Big Data to gain business intelligence and make better business decisions.

■ **Cloud computing.** Another megatrend is **cloud computing**. Whereas traditionally each user would install applications for various tasks—from creating documents to listening to music—as well as store documents, pictures, and other data on his or her computer, Web technologies enable using the Internet as the platform for applications and data. Now, much of the functionality previously offered by applications installed on each individual computer is offered by applications "in the cloud," accessed via your Web browser (see Figure 1.10). In fact, many regard cloud computing as the beginning of the "fourth wave" of change, where not only the applications but also the data reside in the cloud, to be accessed anytime from anywhere. A good example of cloud computing are various services offered by Google, such as Gmail (e-mail), Google docs (word processing), or Google Calendar, all of which are accessed via a Web browser, freeing users from the task of installing or updating traditional desktop applications or worrying about storing or backing up data. If you have your data stored in the cloud, you don't have to worry if your laptop dies on your way to an important meeting; all you have to do is purchase a new laptop at the next store, and you immediately have access to all your important data. Cloud computing has made inroads in a variety of organizational applications, and many organizations rely on an information systems infrastructure in the cloud. We will extensively discuss cloud computing in Chapter 3, "Managing the Information Systems Infrastructure and Services."

■ **Consumerization of IT.** The most significant trend affecting organizational IS personnel in the next decade—according to research firm Gartner—is **consumerization of IT**. Fueled by societal changes, many technological innovations are first introduced in the consumer marketplace, before being used by organizations. In addition, fueled by advances

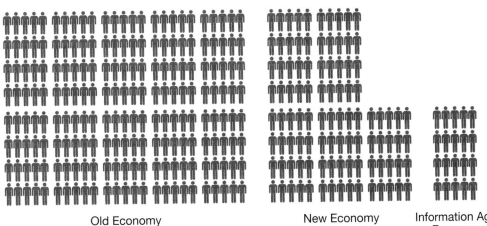

Old Economy   New Economy   Information Age Economy

FIGURE 1.9

Companies in the information age economy are creating value not from people, but from data.

FIGURE 1.10

Applications and data stored in the cloud can be accessed from different devices.

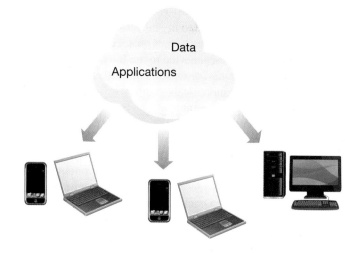

in consumer oriented mobile devices (such as smartphones and tablets) and the ability to access data and applications "in the cloud," today's employees are increasingly using their own devices for work-related purposes, or are using software they are used to (such as social networks for communicating) in the workplace (see Figure 1.11). While initially, workers tended to use their own devices primarily for checking e-mails or visiting social networking sites, they now use their own devices for various other important tasks, including customer relationship management or enterprise resource planning (Savitz, 2012). For organizations, this trend can be worrying (due to concerns related to security or compliance, or increasing need to support the workers' own devices), but it can also provide a host of opportunities, such as increased productivity, higher retention rates of talented employees, or higher customer satisfaction (TrendMicro, 2011). Managing this trend of "bring your own device" (**BYOD**) is clearly a major concern of business and IT managers alike.

What do these megatrends mean for today's workforce? On a most basic level, it implies that being able to use information systems, to assess the impacts of new technologies on one's work or private life, and to learn new technologies as they come along will be increasingly important skills.

Most modern-day high school and university students have grown up in a computerized world. If by some chance they do not know how to operate a computer by the time they graduate from high school, they soon acquire computer skills, because in today's work world, knowing how to use a computer—called **computer literacy** (or information literacy)—can mean the difference between being employed and being unemployed. Knowing how to use a computer can also open up myriad sources of information to those who have learned how to use the computer as a device to gather, store, organize, and otherwise process information. In fact, some fear that the

FIGURE 1.11

People increasingly bring their own mobile devices into the workplace.

information age will not provide the same advantages to "information haves"—those computer-literate individuals who have unlimited access to information—and "information have-nots"—those with limited or no computer access or skills.

Computer-related occupations have evolved as computers have become more sophisticated and more widely used. Where once we thought of computer workers as primarily programmers, data entry clerks, systems analysts, or computer repairpersons, today many more job categories in virtually all industries, from accounting to the medical field, involve the use of computers. In fact, today there are few occupations where computers are not somehow in use. Computers manage air traffic, perform medical tests, monitor investment portfolios, control construction machinery, and more. Since they are especially adept at processing large amounts of data, they are used extensively by universities and public schools, in businesses of all sizes, and in all levels and departments of government. Engineers, architects, interior designers, and artists use special purpose computer-aided design programs. Musicians play computerized instruments, and they write and record songs with the help of computers. Not only do we use computers at work, we also use them in our personal lives. We teach our children on them, manage our finances, do our taxes, compose letters and term papers, create greeting cards, send and receive electronic mail, surf the Internet, purchase products, and play games on them. With the increasing use of computers in all areas of society, many argue that being computer literate—knowing how to use a computer and use certain applications—is not sufficient in today's world; rather, **computer fluency**—the ability to independently learn new technologies as they emerge and assess their impact on your work and life—is what will set you apart in the future.

WHO'S GOING MOBILE

The Evolution of Post-PC Devices

Smartphones have come a long way from the first emergence of mobile devices. In 1989, the first tablet-like computer, the GRiDPad, was launched, sporting a black-and-white screen and a stylus. In 1992, one of the pioneers of the GRiDPad, Jeff Hawkins, founded Palm Computing; this set off the beginning of PDAs (personal digital assistants) in the history of mobile technology. The company launched a series of PDAs in the 1990s, allowing people to update and edit calendars, contacts, edit documents, or even check e-mail while on the go.

In 1993, PDAs went mainstream with the Newton MessagePad, which was developed, not surprisingly, by Apple. The Newton OS came to be Apple's first tablet operating system, carrying two familiar features often offered in today's smartphones and tablets—voice and handwriting recognition. A wave of PDAs came to the market afterwards, primarily based on the Newton OS, Windows Mobile, or Palm OS. However, the high price and lack of processing power of PDAs soon led to a decline in popularity as few found the technology useful aside from its note-taking and voice recognition capabilities; further, although many later PDAs featured Wi-Fi connectivity, the lack of Internet or phone connectivity limited the usefulness of the PDAs. Apple's Newton was discontinued in 1998, and Palm was acquired by HP in 2010. In the early 2000's, Microsoft released one of the first tablet PCs. Yet, the market did not seem to be ready for tablets, so this device, too, failed due to its high price and usability problems.

In the decade that followed, BlackBerry took the lead by enabling push-based e-mail on a mobile device. In 2007,

Apple's iPhone was launched, quickly followed by Google's Android mobile phone operating system in 2008, both of which marked the breakthrough for smartphones, bringing mobile devices to new heights by providing connectivity for instant Web browsing and e-mail, complemented by multimedia capabilities and various interesting and useful applications. At this time, advances in mobile and touchscreen technologies, paired with an ecosystem of apps, created an opportunity for a new (or not so new?) device form factor—the tablet, with Apple's iPad (launched in 2010) being the first player in this market. The success of the iPad has spurred much competition, with companies from Amazon.com to Samsung now offering a variety of "post-PC" tablets.

Looking back at the evolution of mobile devices, there has been much discussion over whether smartphones and tablets have officially taken over the PDA. Some reckon that the Palm PDA was a progress from pocket computers and the smartphone another step forward from the PDA. What do you think?

Based on:

Po, A. (2012, February 28). Palm PDAs: Better than a smartphone? *Squidoo*. Retrieved March 19, 2012, from http://www.squidoo.com/palm-pda-tx-t5-t3-e2-z22-vs-palm-pre.

Vogel, S. (2011, November 11). Tablets: a history. *PC Advisor*. Retrieved March 19, 2012, from http://www.pcadvisor.co.uk/features/tablets/3317718/tablets-history.

In addition to changing the way people work and interact, information technology has also enabled *globalization,* the integration of economies throughout the world, fundamentally changing how not only people but also organizations and countries interact. In the next section, we examine the evolution of globalization and the effects on our daily lives.

http://goo.gl/v3PSX

EVOLUTION OF GLOBALIZATION

You can see the effects of globalization in many ways, such as the greater international movement of commodities, money, information, and labor, as well as the development of technologies, standards, and processes to facilitate this movement (see Figure 1.12). Specifically, a more global and competitive world spurs visible economic, cultural, and technological changes, including the following:

- **Economic Changes.** Increases in international trade, in the development of global financial systems and currency, and in the outsourcing of labor.
- **Cultural Changes.** Increases in the availability of multiculturalism through television and movies; the frequency of international travel, tourism, and immigration; the availability of ethnic foods and restaurants; and the frequency of worldwide fads and phenomena such as Facebook, Groupon, Twitter, and YouTube.
- **Technological Changes.** The development of low-cost computing platforms and communication technologies; the availability of low-cost communication systems such as e-mail, Skype, and instant messaging; the ubiquitous nature of a low-cost global telecommunications infrastructure like the Internet; and the enforcement of global patent and copyright laws to spur further innovation.

Through economic and cultural changes, fueled by a rapidly evolving global technology infrastructure, the world has forever changed.

Over the past centuries, **globalization**—the integration of economies throughout the world, enabled by innovation and technological progress (International Monetary Fund, 2002)—has come a long way, from separate nation-states on different continents to what we see today, a world where people and companies can enjoy worldwide communication and collaboration, with fewer and fewer barriers. What are some of the drivers of globalization? In his book *The World Is Flat, New York Times* foreign affairs columnist Thomas L. Friedman discussed some of the factors spurring globalization. In the next section, we will discuss some of the most pertinent ones.

Key Factors Enabling Globalization

THE FALL OF THE BERLIN WALL. The fall of the Berlin Wall marked the end of the Cold War between communist and capitalist countries and the breakup of the Eastern bloc, freeing millions of people. At once, people in many former communist countries could enjoy greater freedoms. For many companies, this meant a tremendous increase in potential customers as well as access to a huge, talented labor pool in the former Eastern bloc countries. Similarly, the opening up of China in the late 1970's spurred profound changes, by lowering the costs of production of goods, providing access to talented labor, and by opening up a potentially huge market for goods and services.

FIGURE 1.12

Globalization can be seen in visible economic, cultural, and technological changes.

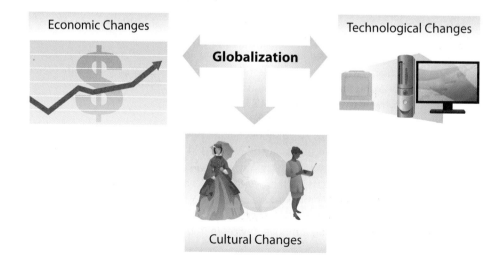

THE WINDOWS OPERATING SYSTEM. In 1990, Microsoft released the first version of the Windows operating system, which over time became the *de facto* world standard in PC operating systems, enabling people from all over the world to use a common computing platform. Now, Windows (in various versions), Mac OS X, and Linux (in various versions) are the most popular operating systems for personal computers, and these systems can communicate fairly effortlessly.

THE INTERNET — RELEASE OF THE NETSCAPE WEB BROWSER. Another factor contributing greatly to the globalized society we see today was the Internet browser—the "killer app" that enabled anyone who had a computer and a modem to view Web pages (see Figure 1.13). A company called Netscape released the first mainstream Web browser in 1994. In addition to opening up the possibilities of the Internet for the general public, Netscape helped set a standard for the transport and display of data that other companies and individuals could build on, making the Internet even easier to use and more powerful than ever.

FALLING TELECOMMUNICATIONS COSTS. In the final years of the last millennium, companies supplying the network infrastructure saw the need to provide more and faster connections, leading to a tremendous *overinvestment* in telecommunications infrastructure, such as fiber-optic cable, which is used to transmit very large amounts of data at the speed of light. With the bursting of the dot-com bubble, the plummeting demand for telecommunications infrastructure (that had been installed just a few years before) led to an oversupply, causing infrastructure providers to fail; and much of the infrastructure had to be sold for a fraction of the cost. The most notable long-term consequence was falling telecommunications costs, enabling the collaboration of individuals and small groups that we see today.

OUTSOURCING. **Outsourcing** is the moving of business processes or tasks (such as accounting or security) to another company (outsourcing is discussed in detail shortly). The tremendous decrease in communication costs has added another dimension to outsourcing, as now companies can outsource business processes on a global scale. For example, companies commonly outsource customer service functions (such as call centers) or accounting to companies specializing in these services. Often, companies located in countries such as India can provide these services much cheaper because of lower labor costs. Sometimes, companies also perform certain functions in a different country to reduce costs or harness skilled labor. For example, aircraft manufacturer Boeing offshored design work (such as computational fluid dynamics) for its new 787 Dreamliner aircraft to Russia, making use of the availability of highly skilled aeronautical engineers.

When China officially joined the World Trade Organization in 2001, it agreed to follow certain accepted standards of trade and fair business practices. Now, companies can set up entire

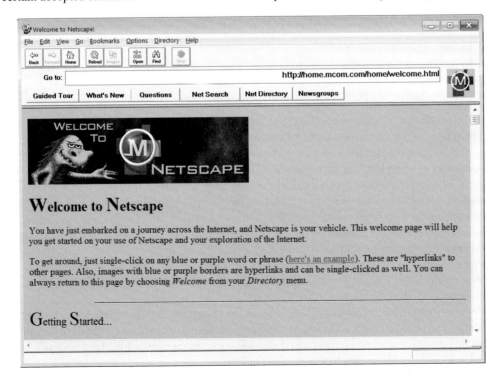

FIGURE 1.13

The Netscape browser was a cornerstone in giving individuals easy access to the Internet.
Source: © 2010 Netscape Communications Corporation. Used with permissions.

FIGURE 1.14

Companies are offshoring production to overseas countries (such as China) to utilize talented workers or reduce costs.
Source: lianxun zhang/Fotolia

factories in emerging countries in order to mass-produce goods at a fraction of the price it would cost to produce these goods in the United States, Canada, or even in Mexico (see Figure 1.14).

The Rise of Information Systems Outsourcing

Many organizations that are **downsizing**, or rightsizing as some call it, are looking for ways to streamline business functions and, in some cases, to slash costs and replace people. Often, these organizations try to use the IS function and technology as the lever for simultaneously shrinking the organization by reducing personnel head count and making the organization more productive (i.e., doing more with less). Although this approach may not be fair for the people who lose their jobs, many firms are forced to do this to remain competitive and, in some cases, to continue to exist.

Similarly, as discussed previously, one phenomenon that has seen a huge increase because of the decrease in telecommunication costs is outsourcing, both onshore (domestically) and offshore. Traditionally, organizations (domestically) outsourced many of the more routine jobs or entire business functions, such as accounting, to other companies. In 2011, the global market for IT outsourcing alone was US$315 billion, with a projected compound annual growth rate of 4.4 percent through 2015 (Gartner, 2011). Companies are choosing to outsource business activities for a variety of reasons; the most important reasons include the following (King, 2003):

- To reduce or control costs
- To free up internal resources
- To gain access to world-class capabilities
- To increase revenue potential of the organization
- To reduce time to market
- To increase process efficiencies
- To be able to focus on core activities
- To compensate for a lack of specific capabilities or skills

Early examples of offshore outsourcing in the United States included the manufacturing of goods in countries such as Mexico to take advantage of lower wages and less stringent regulations. Then, companies started to introduce offshore outsourcing of *services,* starting with the development of computer software and the staffing of customer support and telemarketing call centers. Today, a wide variety of services—ranging from telephone support to tax returns—are candidates for offshore outsourcing to different countries, be it Ireland, China, or India. Even highly specialized services, such as reading X-rays by skilled radiologists, are outsourced by U.S. hospitals to doctors around the globe, often while doctors in the United States are sleeping. However, companies operating in the digital world have to carefully choose offshore outsourcing locations, considering factors such as English proficiency, salaries, or geopolitical risk. While countries such as India remain popular for offshore outsourcing, other formerly popular countries (such as Singapore, Canada, or Ireland) are declining because of rising salaries. With these shifts, outsourcers are constantly looking at nascent and emerging countries such as Bulgaria, Egypt, Ghana, Bangladesh, or Vietnam. Obviously, organizations have to weigh the potential benefits (e.g., cost savings) and drawbacks (e.g., higher geopolitical risk or less experienced workers) of outsourcing to a particular country.

As you can see, outsourcing is now a fact of life, and no matter which industry you're in, you will likely feel the effects of outsourcing (see Table 1.1). Today, individuals will have to ask themselves how they can seize the global opportunities and how they will be able to compete with individuals from all over the world who might be able to do their job at the same quality but at a lower cost.

However, offshore outsourcing does not always prove to be the best approach for an organization. For example, only about a decade ago, German companies manufacturing highly specialized products such as large crankshafts, ship cranes, or road-paving equipment offshored parts of their operations to Eastern European countries in order to cut costs. However, the cost savings have turned out to be negligible because of added overhead, such as customs, shipping, or training, and quality problems ran rampant, leading to a reversal of this trend. Today, many companies are moving production back to Germany in order to better control production quality and costs. Similarly, *InformationWeek,* a leading publication targeting business IT users, found that 20 percent of the 500 most innovative companies in terms of using IT took back previously offshored projects. Similarly, the noted technology author Nicholas Carr recently suggested that cloud computing may contribute to a decline in outsourcing; because much of an IT outsourcer's business is built around managing complex internal systems, a shift to a simpler cloud-based IT infrastructure (see Chapter 3) should reduce the need for outsourcing.

The next sections will outline some opportunities made possible by increasing globalization.

Opportunities of Operating in the Digital World

Clearly, globalization has opened up many opportunities, brought about by falling transportation and telecommunication costs. Today, shipping a bottle of wine from Australia to Europe merely costs a few cents, and using the Internet, people can make PC-to-PC phone calls around the globe for free. To a large extent fueled by television and other forms of media, the increasing globalization has moved cultures closer together—to the point where people now talk about a "global village." Customers in all corners of the world can receive television programming from other countries or watch movies produced in Hollywood, Munich, or Mumbai (sometimes called "Bollywood"), helping to create a shared understanding about forms of behavior or interaction, desirable goods or services, or even forms of government. Over the past decades, the world has seen a democratization of many nations, enabling millions of people to enjoy freedoms they had never experienced before. All this makes operating and living in the digital world much easier than ever before.

TABLE 1.1   Examples of Outsourcing

Industry	Examples
Airlines	British Airways moves customer relations and passenger revenue accounting to India.
	Delta outsources reservation functions to India.
Airplane design	Parts of Airbus and Boeing airplanes are designed and engineered in Moscow, Russia.
Consulting	McKinsey moves global research division to India.
	Ernst & Young moves part of its tax preparation to India.
Insurance	British firm Prudential PLC moves call center operations to India.
Investment banking	J.P. Morgan moves investment research to India.
Retail banking	Worldwide banking group HSBC moves back-office operations to China and India.
Credit card operations	American Express moves a variety of services to India.
Government	The Greater London Authority outsources the development of a road toll system to India.
Telecommunications	T-Mobile outsources part of its content development and portal configuration to India.

Source: Based on http://www.ebstrategy.com (2006).

OPPORTUNITIES FOR REACHING NEW MARKETS.   After the fall of communism, new markets opened up for countless companies. The fall of communism in Eastern bloc countries, as well as the rise of a new middle class in China, enabled the sales of products to literally millions of new customers.

OPPORTUNITIES OF A GLOBAL WORKFORCE.   With the decrease in communication costs, companies can now draw on a large pool of skilled professionals from all over the globe. Many countries, such as Russia, China, and India, offer high-quality education, leading to an ample supply of well-trained people at low cost. While enrollment in the sciences or engineering is dropping in the United States, other countries are producing engineering graduates at an unprecedented pace (Mallaby, 2006). Annually, about 200,000 young engineers graduate from Indian universities, while the United States produce only about a third as many; likewise, Europe produces only about half the number of India (although critics of such statistics point out that countries such as India or China have different, often more inclusive definitions of the field "engineering"). Some countries are actively building entire industries around certain competencies, such as software development or tax preparation in India and call centers in Ireland. For companies operating in the digital world, this can be a huge opportunity, as they can "shop" for qualified, low-cost labor all over the world. On the other hand, studies have shown that 75 pecent of graduates in technical fields are unsuitable for employment in India's global industries, such as call centers or IT outsourcing, mainly because of slow progress in educational reforms and poor language skills (Anand, 2011).

These factors translate into a number of direct opportunities for companies, including greater and larger markets to sell products and larger pools of qualified labor. Nevertheless, while globalization has brought tremendous opportunities to companies, they also face a number of daunting challenges when operating in the global marketplace. These will be discussed next.

Challenges of Operating in the Digital World

Traditionally, companies acquired resources and produced and sold goods or services all within the same country. Such domestic businesses did not have to deal with any challenges posed by globalization but also could not leverage the host of opportunities. The challenges faced can be broadly classified into governmental, geoeconomic, and cultural challenges. See Table 1.2 for a summary of the challenges of operating in the digital world.

TABLE 1.2   Challenges of Operating in the Digital World

Broad Challenges	Specific Challenges	Examples
Governmental	Political system	Market versus planned economy; political instability
	Regulatory	Taxes and tariffs; embargoes; import and export regulations
	Data sharing	European Union Data Protection Directive
	Standards	Differences in measurement units, bar code standards, address conventions, academic degrees, and so on
	Internet access and individual freedom	Internet censorship in various countries
Geoeconomic	Time zone differences	Videoconferences across different time zones
	Infrastructure-related reliability	Differences in network infrastructures throughout the world
	Differences in welfare	Migration and political instability caused by welfare differences between rich and poor countries
	Demographic	Aging population in the United States and Western Europe; younger workforce in other countries
	Expertise	Availability of labor force and salary differences
Cultural	Working with different cultures	Differences in power distance, uncertainty avoidance, individualism/collectivism, masculinity/femininity, concept of time, and life focus; differences in languages, perceptions of aesthetics, beliefs, attitudes, religion, or social organizations
	Challenges of offering products or services in different cultures	Naming and advertising for products; intellectual property

KEY PLAYERS

Wipro and Infosys—The Global Outsourcing Leaders

For students majoring in any business discipline, it is important to be aware of the key players in the information systems area. Infosys and Wipro are two global giants to remember; both companies work to improve business efficiency by providing consulting and IT services, bringing offshore outsourcing to another level with their fast-expanding networks and growing patronage.

Infosys Limited, founded in Pune, India, in 1981 with only seven people and US$250, was one of the pioneers of offshore outsourcing. Rather than companies trying to hire the best talents, and trying to get these talents to relocate to where the work should be done, Infosys helped introduce the "global delivery model," taking the work to where the talent is, where it is most economical, and where the potential risk involved is minimized. Now headquartered in Bangalore, India, Infosys uses this approach to provide services from business and technology consulting to product engineering, IT infrastructure services, testing and validation services, and others to Global 2000 companies. Based on the rationale of making the most out of location and talent at the lowest risk, Infosys has thus far expanded to 64 offices and 68 development centers in more than a dozen countries, and employs well over 145,000 people from 85 nationalities.

One of its closest competitors, Wipro, also found success in providing IS development and technical support to businesses. Initially incorporated in 1945 as a producer of vegetable oil,

Wipro has emerged as one of the biggest players in the IT outsourcing business, with now over 120,000 employees. Headquartered in Bangalore, India, Wipro has produced many innovations in the IT area, including large-scale projects such as India's most powerful supercomputer. Due to the growing influence of technology in enabling and improving business processes, Wipro has grown from its humble beginnings in pre-independent India to become a service provider for 150 global Fortune 500 clients in fields like financial services, manufacturing, telecommunications, and media.

In today's digital world, information systems are crucial in developing successful business models. Yet, for many companies, hiring the best employees to get the job done is close to impossible; global outsourcing giants such as Infosys and Wipro help to take the jobs to where the talent needed to get the job done is located. No matter which discipline you are in, chances are that someday, you will find yourself working together with someone who introduces herself as coming from Infosys, Wipro, or some other company focusing on providing outsourcing services.

Based on:

Infosys (n.d.). What we do. *Infosys.com.* Retrieved March 19, 2012, from http://www.infosys.com/about/what-we-do/pages/index.aspx.

Wipro (n.d.). About Wipro. *Wipro.com.* Retrieved March 19, 2012, from http://www.wipro.com/about-wipro.

INFORMATION SYSTEMS DEFINED

http://goo.gl/BRT3M

Information systems are combinations of **hardware**, **software**, and **telecommunications networks** that *people* build and use to collect, create, and distribute useful *data*, typically in organizational settings. Hardware refers to physical computer equipment, such as the computer monitor, central processing unit, or keyboard. Software refers to a program or set of programs that tell the computer to perform certain tasks. Telecommunications networks refer to a group of two or more computer systems linked together with communications equipment. Although we discuss the design, implementation, use, and implications of hardware, software, and telecommunications throughout the text, the specifics on hardware, software, and telecommunications are discussed in Chapter 3 and the Technology Briefing. Often, you will hear the term **information technology** used to refer to the hardware, software, and networking components of an information system; when looking at degree programs or job opportunities, you will find that IT programs or jobs are a bit more technical in nature, whereas IS programs have a stronger managerial focus. However, the difference is shrinking, with many using the terms IS and IT synonymously. In Figure 1.15, we show the relationships among these IS components.

People in organizations use information systems to process sales transactions, manage loan applications, or help financial analysts decide where, when, and how to invest. Product managers also use them to help decide where, when, and how to market their products and related services, and production managers use them to help decide when and how to manufacture products. Information systems also enable us to get cash from ATMs, communicate by live video with people in other parts of the world, or buy concert or airline tickets. (Note that the term

FIGURE 1.15

An information system is a combination of five key elements: people, hardware, software, data, and telecommunications networks.

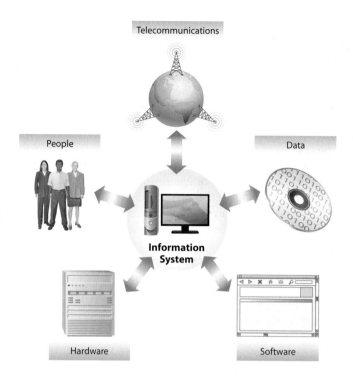

"information systems" is also used to describe the field comprising people who develop, use, manage, and study information systems in organizations.)

It is important to note that people use various terms to describe the field of information systems, such as management information systems, business information systems, computer information systems, and simply "systems." Next, we more thoroughly examine each of the key components of the IS definition.

Data: The Root and Purpose of Information Systems

Earlier, we defined information systems as combinations of hardware, software, and telecommunications networks that people build and use to collect, create, and distribute useful data, typically in organizational settings. We begin by talking about data, the most basic element of any information system.

DATA.   Before you can understand how information systems work, it is important to distinguish between raw, unformatted data and information. Unformatted data, or simply **data**, are raw symbols, such as words and numbers. Data have no meaning in and of themselves, and are of little value until processed (Ackoff, 1989). For example, if we asked you what 465889727 meant or stood for, you could not tell us (see Figure 1.16). However, if we presented the same data as 465-88-9727 and told you it was located in a certain database, in John Doe's record, in a field labeled "SSN," you might rightly surmise that the number was actually the Social Security number of someone named John Doe.

INFORMATION.   Data can be formatted, organized, or processed to be *useful*; it is transformed into **information**, which can be defined as a representation of reality, and can help to answer questions about who, what, where, and when (Ackoff, 1989). In the previous example, 465-88-9727 was used to represent and identify an individual person, John Doe (see Figure 1.16). Contextual cues, such as a label, are needed to turn data into information that is familiar and useful to the reader. Think about your experience with ATMs. A list of all the transactions at a bank's ATMs over the course of a month would be fairly useless data. However, a table that divided ATM users into two categories, bank customers and non–bank customers, and compared the two groups' use of the machine—their purpose for using the ATMs and the times and days on which they use them—would be incredibly useful information. A bank manager could use this information to create marketing mailings to attract new customers. Without information systems, it would be difficult to transform raw data into useful information.

Data	Information	Knowledge
465889727	465-88-9727	465-88-9727 → John Doe
Raw Symbols	Formatted Data	Data Relationships
Meaning:	Meaning:	Meaning:
???	SSN	SSN → Unique Person

FIGURE 1.16

Data, information, and knowledge.

KNOWLEDGE.   In order to actually use information, knowledge is needed. **Knowledge** is the ability to understand information, form opinions, and make decisions or predictions based on the information. For example, you must have knowledge to be aware that only one Social Security number can uniquely identify each individual (see Figure 1.16). Knowledge is a body of governing procedures, such as guidelines or rules, which are used to organize or manipulate data to make it suitable for a given task.

Understanding the distinctions between data, information, and knowledge is important because all are used in the study, development, and use of information systems.

Hardware, Software, and Telecommunications Networks: The Components of Information Systems

When we use the term "information system," we are talking about **computer-based information systems**. Remember that we defined an information system as a combination of hardware, software, and telecommunications networks that people build and use to collect, create, and distribute data. Ever since the dawn of mankind, there was a need to transform data into useful information for people, and people have invented various calculating devices, such as the abacus or the slide rule. Before the introduction of the first computers (which worked on a mechanical basis using punch cards), almost all business and government information systems consisted of file folders, filing cabinets, and document repositories. Computer hardware has replaced these physical artifacts, providing the technologies to input and process data and output useful information; software enables organizations to utilize the hardware to execute their business processes and competitive strategy by providing the computer hardware with instructions on what processing functions to perform. Finally, the telecommunications networks allow computers to share information and services, enabling the global collaboration, communication, and commerce we see today.

People: The Builders, Managers, and Users of Information Systems

The IS field includes a vast collection of people who develop, maintain, manage, and study information systems. Yet, an information system does not exist in a vacuum, and is of little use if it weren't for you—the user. We will begin by discussing the IS profession, and then talk about why knowing about fundamental concepts of information systems is of crucial importance in your personal and professional life.

If you are choosing a career in the IS field, you will find countless opportunities. The career opportunities for a person with IS training continue to be strong, and they are expected to continue to improve over the next 10 years. For example, the 2012–13 Edition of the Occupational Outlook Handbook published by the U.S. Bureau of Labor Statistics predicted that employment for computer and IS managers will grow 18 percent through 2020, faster than the average for all occupations (http://www.bls.gov/oco/ocos258.htm). This boost in employment will occur in nearly every industry, not just computer hardware and software companies, as more and more organizations rely more heavily on IS professionals. Likewise, *Money* magazine (http://money.cnn.com/magazines/moneymag/bestjobs) ranked software developers, IT consultants, and database administrators as three of its top 10 best jobs in America (see Table 1.3); also, *U.S. News* magazine (http://money.usnews.com/money/careers/articles/2012/02/27/the-best-jobs-of-2012) rated computer programmers, computer systems analysts, Web developers, database administrators, and software developers as being among the top 10 jobs, stressing that the industry is looking for people who can balance business and technology.

TABLE 1.3   Best Jobs in America

Rank	Career	Job Growth (10-year forecast)	Median Pay (in US$)
1	Software developer	32%	82,400
2	Physical therapist	30%	75,900
3	Financial adviser	30%	93,900
4	Civil engineer	24%	74,700
5	Marketing specialist	28%	52,200
6	Management consultant	24%	111,000
7	IT consultant	20%	96,500
8	Database administrator	20%	86,600
9	Financial analyst	20%	62,600
10	Environmental engineer	31%	81,200

Source: Based on http://money.cnn.com/magazines/moneymag/best-jobs.

In addition to an ample supply of jobs, earnings for IS professionals will remain strong. According to the U.S. Bureau of Labor Statistics, median annual earnings of these managers in May 2011 were US$118,010. The middle 50 percent earned between US$92,470 and US$148,500. Also, according to Salary.com, the median salary in 2012 for IT managers was US$106,935. According to a 2011 survey by the National Association of Colleges and Employers, starting salary offers for IS majors, with one year or less of experience, averaged US$56,868, making it one of the 10 top-paid bachelor's degrees. Finally, computer and IS managers, especially those at higher levels, often receive more employment-related benefits—such as expense accounts, stock option plans, and bonuses—than do non-managerial workers in their organizations (a study by Payscale.com found that IS majors were—post-graduation—among the most satisfied with their careers).

As you can see, even with some lower-level, highly technical jobs (such as systems programmers) being outsourced to organizations in other countries, there continues to be a very strong need for people with IS knowledge, skills, and abilities—in particular, people with advanced IS skills, as we describe here. In fact, IS careers are regularly selected as not only one of the fastest growing but also a career with far-above-average opportunities for greater personal growth, stability, and advancement. Although technology continues to become easier to use, there is still and is likely to continue to be an acute need for people within the organization that have the responsibility of planning for, designing, developing, maintaining, and managing technologies. Much of this will happen within the business units and will be done by those with primarily business duties and tasks as opposed to systems duties and tasks. However, we are a long way from the day when technology is so easy to deploy that a need no longer exists for people with advanced IS knowledge and skills. In fact, many people believe that this day may never come. Although increasing numbers of people will incorporate systems responsibilities within their nonsystems jobs, there will continue to be a need for people with primarily systems responsibilities. In short, IS staffs and departments will likely continue to exist and play an important role in the foreseeable future.

Given that information systems continue to be a critical tool for business success, it is not likely that IS departments will go away or even shrink significantly. Indeed, all projections are for long-term growth of information systems in both scale and scope. Also, as is the case in any area of business, those people who are continually learning, continuing to grow, and continuing to find new ways to add value and who have advanced and/or unique skills will always be sought after, whether in information systems or in any area of the firm.

The future opportunities in the IS field are likely to be found in a variety of areas, which is good news for everyone. Diversity in the technology area can embrace us all. It really does not matter much which area of information systems you choose to pursue—there will likely be a promising future there for you. Even if your career interests are outside information systems, being a well-informed and capable user of information technologies will greatly enhance your career prospects.

CAREERS IN INFORMATION SYSTEMS.   The field of information systems includes those people in organizations who design and build systems, those who use these systems, and those responsible for managing these systems. The people who help develop and manage systems in organizations include systems analysts, systems programmers, systems operators, network administrators, database administrators, systems designers, systems managers, and chief information officers. In Table 1.5 we describe some of these careers. This list is not exhaustive; rather, it is intended to provide a sampling of IS management positions. Furthermore, many firms will use the same job title, but each is likely to define it in a different way, or companies will have different titles for the same basic function. As you can see from Table 1.4, the range of career opportunities for IS managers is very broad, and salary expectations are very high.

WHAT MAKES IS PERSONNEL SO VALUABLE?   In addition to the growing importance of people in the IS field, there have been changes in the nature of this type of work. No longer are IS departments in organizations filled only with nerdy men with pocket protectors. Many more women are in IS positions now. Also, it is now more common for an IS professional to be a polished, professional systems analyst who can speak fluently about both business and technology. IS personnel are now well-trained, highly skilled, valuable professionals who garner high wages and prestige and who play a pivotal role in helping firms be successful.

Many studies have been aimed at helping us understand what knowledge and skills are necessary for a person in the IS area to be successful (see, e.g., Todd, McKeen, & Gallupe, 1995). Interestingly, these studies also point out just what it is about IS personnel that makes them so valuable to their organizations. In a nutshell, good IS personnel possess valuable, integrated knowledge and skills in three areas—technical, business, and systems—as outlined in Table 1.5 (see also Figure 1.17).

Technical Competency   The technical competency area includes knowledge and skills in hardware, software, networking, and security. In a sense, this is the "nuts and bolts" of information

TABLE 1.4   Some IS Management Job Titles and Brief Job Descriptions

IS Activities	Job Title	Job Description	Salary Ranges, in US$, in Percentiles (25%–75%)
Develop	Systems analyst	Responsible for analyzing business requirements and selecting information systems that meet those needs	54,000–87,000
	Programmer	Responsible for coding, testing, debugging, and installing programs	50,000–80,000
	Systems consultant	Provide IS knowledge to external clients	80,000–120,000
Maintain	IS auditor	Responsible for auditing information systems and operating procedures for compliance with internal and external standards	45,000–75,000
	Database administrator	Responsible for managing database and database management software use	75,000–100,000
	Webmaster	Responsible for managing the firm's Web site	50,000–83,000
Manage	IS manager	Responsible for the management of an existing information system	60,000–90,000
	IS security manager	Responsible for managing security measures and disaster recovery	55,000–85,000
	Chief information officer	Highest-ranking IS manager; responsible for strategic planning and IS use throughout the firm	150,000–180,000
Study	University professor	Teach undergraduate and graduate students; study the use of information systems in organizations and society	70,000–180,000
	Government scientist	Research and development of information systems for homeland security, intelligence, and other related applications	60,000–200,000

Source: Based on http://www.salary.com; http://cnnmoney.com and http://www.payscale.com.

TABLE 1.5 IS Professional Core Competencies

Domain	Description
Technical Knowledge and Skills	
Hardware	Hardware platforms, infrastructure, cloud computing, virtualization, peripherals
Software	Operating systems, application software, drivers
Networking	Network operating systems, cabling and network interface cards, local area networks, wide area networks, wireless, Internet, security
Business Knowledge and Skills	
Business integration, industry	Business processes, functional areas of business and their integration, industry characteristics
Managing people and projects	Planning, organizing, leading, controlling, managing people and projects
Social	Interpersonal, group dynamics, political
Communication	Verbal, written, and technological communication and presentation
Systems Knowledge and Skills	
Systems integration	Connectivity, compatibility, integrating subsystems and systems
Development methodologies	Steps in systems analysis and design, systems development life cycle, alternative development methodologies
Critical thinking	Challenging one's and others' assumptions and ideas
Problem solving	Information gathering and synthesis, problem identification, solution formulation, comparison, choice

systems. This is not to say that the IS professional must be a technical expert in these areas. On the contrary, the IS professional must know just enough about these areas to understand how they work, what they can do for an organization, and how they can and should be applied. Typically, the IS professional manages or directs those who have deeper, more detailed technical knowledge.

The technical area of competency is, perhaps, the most difficult to maintain because of the rapid pace of technological innovation in the digital world. With the economy rebounding, organizations are starting new projects or are reviving projects put on hold during the economic downturn; hence, while it once appeared as if most programming jobs or support jobs would be outsourced to third-party providers abroad (Collett, 2006), there is an increased demand in many

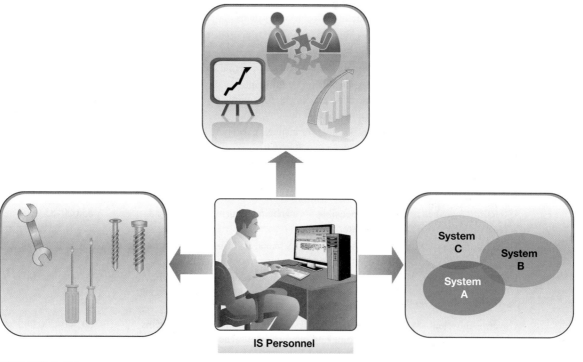

IS Personnel

FIGURE 1.17

Good IS personnel possess valuable, integrated knowledge and skills in three areas—technical, business, and systems.

companies for people with application development skills, especially in combination with sound business analysis and project management skills (Brandel, 2009). In fact, many of the hot skills listed in Table 1.6 are focused on the business domain, which is discussed next.

Business Competency The business competency area is one that sets the IS professional apart from others who have only technical knowledge and skills, and in an era of increased outsourcing, it may well save a person's job. For example, even though some low-level technology jobs may be outsourced, the Bureau of Labor Statistics recently reported that there is an increased need for IS managers as organizations embrace mobility and cloud computing (http://www.bls.gov/oco/ocos258.htm). As a result, it is absolutely vital for IS professionals to understand the technical areas *and* the nature of the business as well. IS professionals must also be able to understand and manage people and projects, not just the technology. These business skills propel IS professionals into project management and, ultimately, high-paying middle- and upper-level management positions.

Systems Competency Systems competency is another area that sets the IS professional apart from others with only technical knowledge and skills. Those who understand how to build and integrate systems and how to solve problems will ultimately manage large, complex systems projects as well as manage those in the firm who have only technical knowledge and skills.

TABLE 1.6   Hot Skills For the Next Decade

Domain	Hot Skills
Business	▪ Business–IT alignment ▪ Business analysis ▪ Enterprise solutions ▪ Project management ▪ Business process modeling ▪ Project planning, budgeting, and scheduling ▪ Third-party provider management ▪ Enterprise 2.0 and social media
Technology infrastructure and services	▪ Virtualization ▪ Cloud computing/Infrastructure as a service ▪ Systems analysis ▪ Systems design ▪ Network design ▪ Systems auditing ▪ Wireless ▪ Telecommunications/VoIP (Voice over Internet Protocol) ▪ Data center
Security	▪ IT security planning and management ▪ BYOD ▪ Governance ▪ Compliance
Applications	▪ Customer-facing application development ▪ Web development, open source, portal technologies ▪ Cloud computing ▪ Legacy systems integration
Internet	▪ Social media ▪ Customer-facing Web application systems ▪ Mobile apps ▪ Search engine optimization ▪ Artificial intelligence ▪ Web mining
Business intelligence	▪ Business intelligence ▪ Data warehousing ▪ Data mining ▪ Big Data

Source: Based on Brandel (2009), Leung (2009), and Veritude (2009).

Perhaps now you can see why IS professionals are so valuable to their organizations. These individuals have a solid, integrated foundation in technical, business, and systems knowledge and skills. Perhaps most important, they also have the social skills to understand how to work well with and motivate others. It is these core competencies that continue to make IS professionals valuable employees.

Given how important technology is, what does this mean for your career? Technology is being used to radically change how business is conducted—from the way products and services are produced, distributed, and accounted for to the ways they are marketed and sold. Whether you are majoring in information systems, finance, accounting, operations management, human resource management, business law, or marketing, knowledge of technology is critical to a successful career in business.

FINDING QUALIFIED PERSONNEL.   Unfortunately, given the increased sophistication of modern information systems, organizations can often have a difficult time finding qualified personnel, and attracting the right people with the right skills is not possible in some areas. Consequently, many technology-focused organizations tend to cluster in areas where talented workers are available. Such areas are often characterized by a high quality of life for the people living there, and it is no surprise that many companies in the IT sector within the United States are headquartered in Silicon Valley, California; Boston, Massachusetts; Austin, Texas; or Seattle, Washington. With increasing globalization, other regions throughout the world are boasting about their highly skilled personnel. One such example is the Indian city of Bangalore, where, over a century ago, Maharajas started to lure talented technology-oriented people to the region, building a world-class human resource infrastructure that attracted companies from around the world. In other areas, organizations may have to find creative ways to attract and retain people, such as by offering favorable benefits packages that include educational grants or expense-matching programs to encourage employees to improve their education and skills. Other human resource policies, such as telecommuting, flextime, and creative benefit packages, can also help to attract and retain the best employees.

YOU—THE USER.   Clearly, the field of information systems offers a wide variety of interesting career choices, and you will likely find a career that offers a host of opportunities for lifelong learning and advancement. Yet, an information system does not exist in a vacuum, and understanding fundamental concepts related to information systems will be critical in almost any career, as well as in your private life. In almost any business-related field, you will be extensively using information systems, and you will likely be involved in various information systems–related decisions within your organization. Understanding what information systems are capable of doing (as well as what they cannot do), being able to communicate with the "techies," and being able to make educated IS-related decisions is likely to set you apart from your competition. Especially in smaller organizations (that may not have dedicated IS departments), you are likely to be involved in IS-related investment decisions, and lacking a basic understanding of fundamental issues associated with topics such as IS infrastructure, systems analysis and design, or information systems security will put you at the mercy of outside consultants or (worse yet) vendors who are likely to act out of their own interests, often trying to sell you their "technology of the week/month/year."

In addition, as you have undoubtedly noticed, you are facing a number of IS-related decisions in your private life. Examples of such decisions abound; for example, you may face the question of what mobile phone to purchase next; an iPhone, a phone using some version of the Android operating system, or a phone sporting Microsoft's new Windows Phone operating system. Such decisions are likely to include your own preferences or influence by your peers, but there are a number of critical differences in terms of privacy, security, applications, and the like. Likewise, you may face the problem of how to best secure your wireless network at home, or may wonder how to best keep your various files in sync across different computers or mobile devices. Throughout this text, we will touch on those issues, and hope that you will gain valuable knowledge to understand the trade-offs involved when selecting new information systems.

Organizations: The Context of Information Systems

We have talked about data versus information, the technology side of information systems, and the people side of information systems. The last part of our IS definition is the term "organization." Organizations use information systems to become more productive and profitable, to gain competitive advantage, to reach more customers, or to improve customer service. This holds true

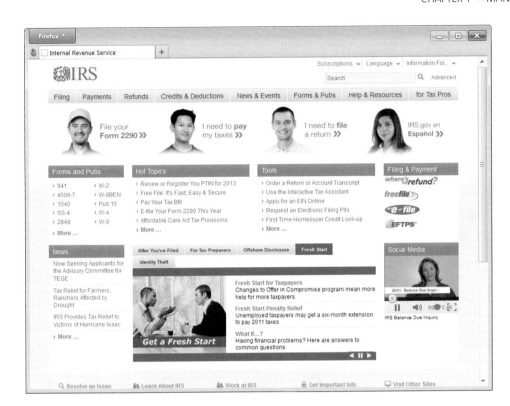

FIGURE 1.18

Web site of the U.S. Department of the Treasury, Internal Revenue Service, http://www.irs.gov.
Source: Courtesy of the United States Department of the Treasury.

for all types of organizations—professional, social, religious, educational, and governmental. In fact, the U.S. Internal Revenue Service launched its own Web site for the reasons just described (see Figure 1.18). The Web site was so popular that approximately 220,000 users visited it during the first 24 hours and more than a million visited it in its first week—even before the Web address for the site was officially announced. Today, popular Web sites like Facebook.com and WSJ.com receive millions of visitors every day.

TYPES OF INFORMATION SYSTEMS.   Throughout this text, we explore various types of information systems commonly used in organizations. It makes sense, however, for us to describe briefly here the various types of systems used so that you will better understand what we mean by the term "information system" as we use it throughout the rest of the book. Table 1.7 provides a list of the major types of information systems used in organizations.

Topping the list in the table are some of the more traditional, major categories that are used to describe information systems. For example, **transaction processing systems (TPS)** are used by a broad range of organizations to not only more efficiently process customer transactions, but also generate a tremendous amount of data that can be used by the organization to learn about customers or ever-changing product trends. Your local grocery store uses a TPS at the checkout that scans bar codes on products; as this occurs, many stores will print discount coupons on the backs of receipts for products related to current purchases. Every hour, online retailer Amazon.com's Web site processes thousands of transactions from around the world. This massive amount of data is fed into large data warehouses and is then analyzed to provide purchase recommendations to future customers. In addition, TPS data are sorted and organized to support a broad range of managerial decision making using a variety of systems; the most common of these is generally referred to as a **management information system**. TPS data also provide input into a variety of information systems within organizations, including *decision support systems, intelligent systems, data mining and visualization systems, knowledge management systems, social software, geographic information systems,* and *functional area information systems.* Five to 10 years ago, it would have been typical to see systems that fell cleanly into one of these categories. Today, with **internetworking**—connecting host computers and their networks together to form even larger networks like the Internet—and **systems integration**—connecting separate information systems and data to improve business processes and decision making—it is difficult to say that any given information system fits into only one of these categories (e.g., that a system is a management information system only and nothing else). Modern-day information systems tend to span several of these categories of information systems, helping not only to collect data from

TABLE 1.7 Types of Information Systems Used in Organizations

Type of System	Purpose	Sample Application
Transaction processing system	Process day-to-day business event data at the operational level of the organization	Grocery store checkout cash register with connection to network
Management information system	Produce detailed information to help manage a firm or a part of the firm	Inventory management and planning system
Decision support system	Provide analysis tools and access to databases in order to support quantitative decision making	Product demand forecasting system
Intelligent system	Emulate or enhance human capabilities	Automated system for analyzing bank loan applications
Data mining and visualization system	Methods and systems for analyzing data warehouses to better understand various aspects of a business	Online Analytical Processing (OLAP) system
Office automation system (personal productivity software)	Support a wide range of predefined day-to-day work activities of individuals and small groups	Word processor
Collaboration system	Enable people to communicate, collaborate, and coordinate with each other	Electronic mail system with automated, shared calendar
Knowledge management system	Collection of technology-based tools to enable the generation, storage, sharing, and management of knowledge assets	Knowledge portal
Social software	Facilitates collaboration and knowledge sharing	Social network
Geographic information system	Create, store, analyze, and manage spatial data	Site selection for new shopping mall
Functional area information system	Support the activities within a specific functional area of the firm	System for planning for personnel training and work assignments
Customer relationship management system	Support interaction between the firm and its customers	Sales force automation
Enterprise resource planning system	Support and integrate all facets of the business, including planning, manufacturing, sales, marketing, and so on	Financial, operations, and human resource management
Supply chain management system	Support the coordination of suppliers, product or service production, and distribution	Procurement planning
Electronic commerce system	Enable customers to buy goods and services from a firm's Web site	Amazon.com

throughout the firm and from customers but also to integrate data from diverse sources and present it to busy decision makers, along with tools to manipulate and analyze those data. *Customer relationship management, supply chain management,* and *enterprise resource planning* systems are good examples of these types of systems that encompass many features and types of data and cannot easily be categorized.

Office automation systems such as Microsoft Office and the OpenOffice.org Productivity Suite provide word processing, spreadsheet, and other personal productivity tools, enabling knowledge workers to accomplish their tasks; *collaboration systems,* such as Microsoft's Exchange/Outlook, Lotus Notes, or Google Apps, provide people with e-mail, automated calendaring, and online, threaded discussions, enabling close collaboration with others, regardless of their location.

Systems for electronic commerce, such as corporate Web sites, are also very popular and important. These systems are typically Internet-based and enable (1) consumers to find information about and to purchase goods and services from each other and from business firms and (2) business firms to electronically exchange products, services, and information. In Chapter 4, "Enabling Business-to-Consumer Electronic Commerce," we talk about different forms of electronic commerce involving the end consumer; in Chapter 8, "Strengthening Business-to-Business Relationships Via Supply Chain and Customer Relationship Management," we discuss how organizations use the Internet to enable or facilitate business-to-business transactions.

While many modern-day information systems span several of these IS categories, it is still useful to understand these categories. Doing so enables you to better understand the myriad approaches, goals, features, and functions of modern information systems.

We have talked about each of the parts of our definition of information systems, and we have talked about different types of information systems. In the next section, we focus on how information systems can be managed within organizations.

ORGANIZING THE IS FUNCTION.   Old-school IS personnel believed that they owned and controlled the computing resources, that they knew better than users did, and that they should tell users what they could and could not do with the computing resources; in addition, early IS departments typically had huge project backlogs, and IS personnel would often deliver systems that were over budget, were completed much too late, were difficult to use, and did not always work well. The increasing pervasiveness of technology in businesses and societies has led to a shifting mindset about information systems within organizations. Increasingly fast-paced competition is forcing businesses to regard IS as an enabler, so as to streamline business processes, provide better customer service, and better connect and collaborate with various stakeholders inside and outside the organization. Many organizations, for example, have realized that some of the best ideas for solving business problems come from the employees using the system; as a result, personnel within many IS units have taken on more of a consulting relationship with their users, helping the users solve problems, implement ideas, and be more productive. As shown in the example of Starbucks' Tech Cafe (see the Brief Case earlier in this chapter), IS personnel are increasingly reaching out to their internal customers and proactively seek their input and needs rather than waiting for customers to come in with systems complaints. They modify the systems at a moment's notice just to meet customer needs quickly and effectively. They celebrate the customer's new systems ideas rather than putting up roadblocks and giving reasons that the new ideas cannot or will not work. They fundamentally believe that the customers own the technology and the information and that the technology and information are there for the customers, not for the systems personnel. They create help desks, hotlines, information centers, and training centers to support customers. These service-oriented IS units structure the IS function so that it can better serve the customer.

The implications of this new service mentality for the IS function are staggering. It is simply amazing how unproductive a company can be when the IS personnel and other people within the firm are at odds with one another. On the other hand, it is even more amazing how productive and enjoyable work can be when people in the IS function work hand in hand with people throughout the organization. Technology is, potentially, the great lever, but it works best when people work together, not against each other, to use it.

THE SPREAD OF TECHNOLOGY IN ORGANIZATIONS.   Another phenomenon that shows how integral and vital information systems and their proper management have become to organizations is the extent to which the technology is firmly integrated and entrenched within the various business units (such as accounting, sales, and marketing).

In many organizations today, you will find that the builders and managers of a particular information system or subsystem spend most of their time out in the business unit, along with the users of that particular system. Many times, these systems personnel are permanently placed—with an office, desk, phone, and PC—in the business unit along with the users.

In addition, it is not uncommon for systems personnel to have formal education, training, and work experience in information systems as well as in the functional area that the system supports, such as finance. It is becoming increasingly more difficult to separate the technology from the business or the systems staff from the other people in the organization. For this reason, how information systems are managed is important to you, no matter what career option you pursue.

As information systems are used more broadly throughout organizations, IS personnel often have dual-reporting relationships—reporting both to the central IS group and to the business function they serve. Therefore, at least some need for centralized IS planning, deployment, and management continues—particularly with respect to achieving economies of scale in systems acquisition and development and in optimizing systems integration, enterprise networking, and the like. Even in organizations that are decentralizing technology and related decisions, a need to coordinate technology and related decisions across the firm still persists. This coordination is likely to continue to happen through some form of a centralized (or, at least, centrally coordinated) IS staff. Organizations are likely to continue to want to reap the benefits of IS decentralization (flexibility, adaptability, and systems responsiveness), but it is equally likely that they will not want to—and will not be able to—forgo the benefits of IS centralization (coordination, economies of scale, compatibility, and connectivity).

Given the trend toward pushing people from the IS staff out into the various business units of the firm and given the need for people within each of the functional areas of the business to have technology skills, there is clearly a need for people who know the technology side *and* the business side of the business. This is becoming increasingly important due to ever faster IT cycles: where traditionally, IS departments thought in time frames of about five years, nowadays, new devices (such as new versions of Apple's iPad) come out every 6–18 months, and organizations wanting to harness the opportunities brought about by new devices have to adjust to this change in pace.

http://goo.gl/2RNbR

THE DUAL NATURE OF INFORMATION SYSTEMS

Given how important and expensive information systems have become, information technology is like a sword—you can use it effectively as a competitive weapon, but, as the old saying goes, those who live by the sword sometimes die by the sword. The two following cases illustrate this dual nature of information systems.

Case in Point: An Information System Gone Awry: Leap Year Glitch Stops Government Cloud Computing Services (or Doesn't?)

All over the world, not only business organizations, but also governments and public sector organizations are facing tightening budgets. For many businesses, cloud computing offers the promise for significant cost savings—the business only pays for the services used. As businesses, the public sector has started to realize the benefits of cloud computing. Similar to many business organizations, many public sector organizations have similar needs for certain applications or services. For example, each city needs systems for controlling traffic lights or for managing emergency dispatch centers. In addition to having similar needs, each city would also go through a lengthy approval process for new software. Having realized the massive duplication of efforts by municipal governments, the government of the United Kingdom recently launched the "G-Cloud" initiative, where public sector organizations can access cloud-based services via a so-called "CloudStore," hosted on Microsoft's Windows Azure cloud servers (see Figure 1.19). The aim of this initiative was to reduce the costs associated with procuring and maintaining information systems, with an estimated cost saving of US$312 million by 2014. Instead of having to develop or purchase own systems, public sector organizations can now choose from over 1,700 services offered by over 250 providers, and pay for these services on an as-needed basis. Each service is accredited centrally, so that municipalities do not have to go through separate accreditation processes, further speeding up the procurement process and reducing costs. In addition, the CloudStore encourages participation by small and medium enterprises, in addition to large IT service providers; the CloudStore boasts 50 percent services offered by SMEs.

What happens when such information systems do not function as planned? In early 2012, there was a problem with Microsoft's Windows Azure cloud computing service. Specifically, due to a programming error, there was a mistake in the date calculation. As it happened, 2012 was a leap year, and the 29th of February brought down important parts of the system, making the services hosted in the CloudStore inaccessible for several hours.

This story has a happy ending; as the CloudStore project was just started, and was not intended for maximum reliability (so as to benefit from maximum cost savings), the CloudStore was not used for mission critical systems, and no data were lost.

FIGURE 1.19

The "CloudStore" offers various systems to public sector organizations in the United Kingdom.

Case in Point: An Information System That Works: FedEx

Just as there are examples of information systems gone wrong, there are many examples of information systems gone right. FedEx, a US$40 billion family of companies (2012 data), is the world's largest express transportation company and delivers millions of packages and millions of pounds of freight to 220 countries and territories each business day. FedEx uses extensive, interconnected information systems to coordinate more than 290,000 employees, hundreds of aircraft, and tens of thousands of ground vehicles worldwide. To improve its services and sustain a competitive advantage, FedEx continuously updates and fine tunes its systems. For example, FedEx.com has more than 15 million unique visitors per month and over 3 million tracking requests per day, and FedEx strives to provide the most accurate tracking information to each visitor. Similarly, in FedEx's ground hubs, automation is another enabler of competitive advantage. En route to its destination, each package typically travels through at least one sorting facility, where it is routed to its intermediate and final destinations (see Figure 1.20). Traveling through an extensive network of conveyor belts, each package is scanned multiple times, and can be rerouted as needed. Once a package passes an overhead scanner, there is between 1 and 2 seconds time to divert a package, so decisions have to be made in a few hundred milliseconds (King, 2011). On average, FedEx reengineers and improves the performance twice a year, and now manages to deliver a quarter of all daily packages handled within one business day. These and other information systems have positioned FedEx as the global leader in express transportation.

Information Systems for Competitive Advantage

The United Kingdom's G-Cloud initiative and FedEx's systems are typical of systems that are pervasive in today's life or used in large, complex organizations. These systems are so large in scale and scope that they are difficult to build. It is important to handle the development of such systems the right way the first time around. These examples also show that as we rely more and more on information systems, the capabilities of these systems are paramount to business success.

Not only were these systems large and complicated, but they were—and continue to be—critical to the success of the organizations that built them. The choices made in developing the systems in the UK government and at FedEx were **strategic** in their intent. The UK government developed the CloudStore to achieve economies of scale across the government, enhance flexibility, and reduce costs; the systems developed by FedEx are developed and continuously updated to help gain or sustain some **competitive advantage** (Porter, 1985; Porter & Millar, 1985) over its rivals. Let us not let this notion slip by us—while the use of technology can enable efficiency and while information systems must provide a return on investment, technology use can also be strategic and a powerful enabler of competitive advantage.

Although we described the use of information systems at two very large organizations, firms of all types and sizes can use information systems to gain or sustain a competitive advantage over their rivals. Whether it is a small mom-and-pop boutique or a large government agency, every organization can find a way to use information technology to beat its rivals.

FIGURE 1.20

Packages travel through an extensive network of conveyor belts, where they are routed to their intermediate and final destinations.
Source: Stephen Mahar/Shutterstock

WHEN THINGS GO WRONG

Failure: The Path to Success?

Management consultant Tom Peters, author and coauthor of 10 international best-sellers, including *In Search of Excellence, Thriving on Chaos, The Pursuit of Wow!*, and his latest, *Re-Imagine! Business Excellence in a Disruptive Age*, often tells business managers that a company's survival may depend upon those employees who fail over and over again as they try new ideas. There's little that is more important to tomorrow's managers than failure, Peters maintains.

Apparently Apple Computers lives by Peters' philosophy. In January 2008, to help celebrate 24 years of the Mac, first introduced to consumers in 1984, *Wired* magazine recalled some of Apple's more infamous failures.

One of Apple's most visible flops was the Newton, actually the name of a newly conceived operating system that stuck to the product as a whole. The Newton, which Apple promised would "reinvent personal computing," fell far short of its hype when it was introduced in 1993 as a not-so-revolutionary PDA. The Newton was on the market for six years—a relatively long time for an unsuccessful product—but one of Steve Jobs' first acts when he returned to Apple's helm in 1997 was to cut the Newton Systems Group.

Other Apple product failures include:

- The Pippin, introduced in 1993, an inexpensive game player/network computer that couldn't compete with Nintendo's 64 or the Sony PlayStation.
- The TAM (Twentieth Anniversary Macintosh), which debuted in 1997 and lasted only a year. The sleek design was contemporary and attractive, but the machine was panned as overpriced and underpowered.
- The Macintosh television, of which only 10,000 units were produced, from 1993 to 1994. It tanked because it was incapable of showing television feeds in a desktop window.
- The PowerMac G4 Cube, an 8" × 8" × 8" designer machine that needed a separate monitor (as opposed to the popular iMac series). Often regarded as overpriced, it was never popular with consumers.

- The Apple IIc (the "c" is for compact), which was meant to be the world's first portable computer (coming complete with carrying case). It lacked internal expansion slots and direct access to the motherboard, however, and thus was less popular than other Apple II models that allowed users to upgrade.
- The puck mouse that came with the iMac G3. Apple made the mouse popular, but miscued when it expected consumers to adapt to this too-small, awkward-to-control device that users often mistakenly used upside down. The puck was soon replaced with the Mighty Mouse—a consumer favorite.
- The Lisa, introduced in 1983, primarily intended for business use. Its whopping US$9,995 price tag (more than US$20,000 in current dollars) made it too expensive for most businesses, which preferred to buy PCs at much lower prices. The Lisa was retired in 1986, after the Mac had captured consumers' attention.

In recent years, Apple has introduced a large variety of new products, all with remarkable success. Innovative products that consumers stand in line to get include the Macbook Air, a line of iPods, iPhones, and iPads. Time will tell if Apple's current success streak continues, or if, at some point, Apple will yet again introduce a product that is "too innovative" for the consumers. Although Apple's failures are often cited by its competitors, the company has proved Peters right time and time again: Any company without an interesting list of failures probably isn't trying hard enough.

Based on:

Claburn, T. (2010, April 8). Can 300,000 iPads equal failure? *InformationWeek*. Retrieved May 9, 2012, from http://www.informationweek.com/news/security/management/showArticle.jhtml?articleID=224202035.

Gardiner, B. (2008, January 24). Learning from failure: Apple's most notorious flops. *Wired*. Retrieved May 9, 2012, from http://www.wired.com/gadgets/mac/multimedia/2008/01/gallery_apple_flops.

Why Information Systems Matter

In 2003, Nicholas Carr (then editor-at-large at *Harvard Business Review*) published an article titled "IT Doesn't Matter," arguing that as information technology becomes more pervasive, it will become more standardized and ubiquitous, more of a commodity that is absolutely necessary for every company. He reasoned, then, that companies should focus information technology strictly on cost reduction and risk mitigation and that investing in information technology for differentiation or for competitive advantage is futile. With advances in information systems (e.g., cloud computing), you may think that indeed, information technology has become commoditized. Indeed, there is no real *strategic* advantage of having one's systems run in-house as compared to on some cloud computing provider's systems, or vice-versa. Yet, as others rightly pointed out, and as evidenced by the advances in smartphones, emergence of social networks, or changes in various creative industries, IT is changing rapidly, and many companies have gained competitive advantage by innovatively using the potential of new technologies. Specifically, companies from Amazon.com to Zynga created competitive advantage by combining certain commoditized technologies with proprietary systems and business processes. As argued by noted technology author Don Tapscott, companies with bad business models tend to fail regardless of whether they use information technology or not, but companies that have good business models and use information technology successfully to carry out those business models tend to be very successful. For companies such as Google or Facebook, data generated by the customers create value, and how data are being gathered, processed, and used can be a source of sustained competitive advantage (Vellante, 2011); companies such as Amazon.com use their IT expertise to sell cloud computing services to other businesses, directly generating revenue from their IT investments.

In sum, we believe that information systems are a necessary part of doing business and that they can be used to create efficiencies, but that they can also be used as an enabler of competitive advantage. We do agree with Carr, however, that the competitive advantage from the use of information systems can be fleeting, as competitors can eventually do the same thing.

IS ETHICS

A broad range of ethical issues have emerged through the use and proliferation of computers. Especially with the rise of companies such as Google, which generate tremendous profits by collecting, analyzing, and using their customers' data, and the emergence of social networks such as Facebook, many people fear negative impacts such as social decay, increased consumerism, or loss of privacy. **Computer ethics** is used to describe moral issues and standards of conduct as they pertain to the use of information systems. In 1986, Richard O. Mason wrote a classic and very insightful article on the issues central to this debate—information privacy, accuracy, property, and accessibility (aka, "PAPA"). These issues focus on what information an individual should have to reveal to others in the workplace or through other transactions, such as online

http://goo.gl/pFZdf

COMING ATTRACTIONS

The Future of Cloud-Based Communications

In the coming decades, it is predicted that our lives will increasingly be linked with the cloud. According to AT&T's chief technology officer John Donovan, we may no longer need mobile phones and tablets by 2020—by then, many different kinds of communications-related information will be stored in the cloud. Being detached from modern-day smartphones and tablets means that it could be possible to share mobile devices with each other: phone calls could be made and messages be sent from a friend's place by logging into the friend's wireless device or even television using a password or a fingerprint scan. Using information stored in the cloud, the user could easily access all kinds of information about the person she wants to call, including e-mail address, or even the names of the person's children.

Even better, saved data could be analyzed by algorithms and computing systems to yield useful reminders of names, addresses, and hidden facts. In short, this is information that, important or not-so-important, will prove valuable in organizing and innovating our lifestyle. AT&T is researching ways to bring Donovan's claims to life, using data as basic as calling patterns to determine which nights of the week people call

home most and from where, making communication and access to information more convenient as the cloud is aware of when and where phone calls should be routed. For example, if a person spent weekdays in the office and weekends at home, the cloud would know better than to ring the home phone on a Wednesday afternoon. Similarly, cloud-based calling data could be analyzed to find interesting patterns such as who a user's best friends are.

Yet for many, this may sound spooky, with the cloud knowing more about one's life and behavior than oneself. On the other hand, these forms of cloud-based communications can make life easier for many, freeing us from having to carry our own devices or having to memorize the best number to call our friend at a certain time of the day.

Based on:

Hamblen, M. (2011, February 15). What to expect in cloud-based communications in 2020. *Computerworld*. Retrieved March 19, 2012, from http://www.computerworld.com/s/article/9209579/What_to_expect_in_cloud_based_communications_in_2020.

shopping, ensuring the authenticity and fidelity of information, who owns information about individuals and how that information can be sold and exchanged, and what information a person or organization has the right to obtain about others and how this information can be accessed and used.

With the societal changes brought about by information systems, the issues surrounding privacy have moved to the forefront of public concern; in addition the ease of digitally duplicating and sharing information has not only raised privacy concerns, but also issues related to intellectual property. Next, we examine these issues.

Information Privacy

If you use the Internet regularly, sending e-mail messages, posting status updates on Facebook, or just visiting Web sites, you may have felt that your personal privacy is at risk. Several e-commerce Web sites where you like to shop greet you by name and seem to know which products you are most likely to buy (see Figure 1.21); other Web sites provide you with advertising that appears to be targeted extremely accurately at you. As a result, you may feel as though eyes are on you every time you go online. **Information privacy** is concerned with what information an individual should have to reveal to others in the workplace or through other transactions, such as online shopping.

While the information age has brought widespread access to information, the downside is that others may now have access to personal information that you would prefer to keep private. Personal information, such as Social Security numbers, credit card numbers, medical histories, and even family histories, is now available on the Internet. Using search engines, your friends, coworkers, current or future employers, or even your spouse can find out almost anything that has been posted by or about you on the Internet. For example, it is very easy to locate your personal blog, your most recent party pictures posted on Facebook, or even sensitive questions you asked in a public discussion forum about drug use or mental health. Moreover, many of these pages are stored in the search engines' long-term cache, so they remain accessible for a long time even after they have been taken off the Web.

It happens to all of us. Nearly every day in our physical or virtual mailboxes, we receive unwanted solicitations from credit card companies, department stores, magazines, or charitable organizations. Many of these items are never opened. We ask the same question over and over again: "How did I get on another mailing list?" Our names, addresses, and other personal information were most likely sold from one company to another for use in mass mailings.

INFORMATION PROPERTY ON THE WEB.   Who owns the computerized information about people—the information that is stored in thousands of databases by retailers, credit card companies, and marketing research companies? The answer is that the company that maintains

FIGURE 1.21

Just as the owners of your neighborhood bookstore, online merchants such as Amazon.com greet you by name and personalize their Web sites to individual customers.
Source: Jurgita Genyte/Shutterstock

the database of customers or subscribers legally owns the information and is free to sell it. Your name, address, and other information are all legally kept in a company database to be used for the company's future mailings and solicitations, and the company can sell its customer list or parts of it to other companies who want to send similar mailings.

There are limits, however, to what a company can do with such data. For example, if a company stated at one time that its collection of marketing data was to be used strictly internally as a gauge of its own customer base and then sold that data to a second company years later, it would be unethically and illegally breaking its original promise. Companies collect data from credit card purchases (by using a credit card, you indirectly allow this) or from surveys and questionnaires you fill out when applying for a card. They also collect data when you fill in a survey at a bar, restaurant, supermarket, or the mall about the quality of the service or product preferences. By providing this information, you implicitly agree that the data can be used as the company wishes (within legal limits, of course).

What is even more problematic is the combination of survey data with transaction data from your credit card purchases. As information systems are becoming more powerful it becomes easier to collect and analyze various types of information about people. For example, using demographic data (Who am I, and where do I live?) and psychographic data (What do I like, what are my tastes and preferences?), companies can piece together bits of information about people, creating highly accurate profiles of their customers or users, with each additional bit helping to create a more accurate picture. Such pictures, sometimes referred to as "the Database of Intentions" (Battelle, 2010), can contain information about what people want, purchase, like, are interested in, are doing, where they are, who they are, and whom they know (see Figure 1.22).

Needless to say, just because people provide data at different points does not mean that they agree for the data to be combined to create a holistic picture. Companies are often walking a fine line, as information about customers is becoming increasingly valuable; Facebook founder Mark Zuckerberg, for example, is known for stretching people's privacy expectations. Throughout its existence, Facebook has pushed the boundaries of people's privacy expectations, maintaining that privacy would no longer be a social norm, and unilaterally changing default privacy settings; this has gone so far that in 2011 the U.S. Federal Trade Commission (FTC) ordered Facebook to perform regular independent privacy audits for the following two years. In early 2012, Google similarly pushed the privacy boundary by combining the data gathered at Google's different services (be it Google, Gmail, or YouTube) into one database, enabling the company to create an even more complete picture of any user of Google's services.

How do you know who is accessing these databases? This is an issue that each company must address at both a strategic/ethical level (Is this something that we should be doing?) and a tactical level (If we do this, what can we do to ensure the security and integrity of the

FIGURE 1.22

The database of intentions.
Source: Based on Batelle (2010).

data?). The company needs to ensure proper hiring, training, and supervision of employees who have access to the data and implement the necessary software and hardware security safeguards.

In today's interconnected world, there are even more dangers to information privacy. Although more and more people are concerned about their privacy settings on social networks such as Facebook, there are things that you may not be able to control. For example, if one of your friends (or even a stranger) posts a photo of you on Facebook, it will be there for many others to view, whether you like it or not. By the time you realize it, most of your friends, coworkers, and family members may have already seen it. At other times, you may divulge sensitive information (such as your address or date of birth) when signing up for yet another social network; as newer, more exciting applications come up, you abandon your profile, but your information stays out there. Sometimes, you may forget who's following your activities at the various social networking sites, and you may tell people things you never wanted them to know. As these examples show, there are many more threats to your privacy than you may have thought.

E-MAIL PRIVACY.   The use of e-mail raises further privacy issues, as nowadays, almost everyone sends and receives electronic mail, whether or not they have a PC. All that is needed to participate is access to the Internet, whether through a home PC, a school's computer lab, a smartphone, or any other device that provides Internet access. Although it is slowly being supplanted by social networking services and text messages, e-mail is still one of the most popular software applications of all time, having contributed greatly to a steady decline of physical mail. However, recent court cases have not supported computer privacy for employee e-mail transmissions and Internet usage. For example, although most companies provide employees with access to the Internet and other outside e-mail systems, many periodically monitor the e-mail messages that employees send and receive. Monitoring employee behavior is nothing new, and for many businesses it was a natural extension to monitor employee e-mail messages.

Surprisingly, there is little legal recourse for those who support e-mail privacy. In 1986, Congress passed the Electronic Communications Privacy Act (ECPA), but it offered far stronger support for voice mail than it did for e-mail communications. This act made it much more difficult for anyone (including the government) to eavesdrop on phone conversations. E-mail privacy is, therefore, much harder to protect. In addition, no other laws at the federal or state levels protect e-mail privacy. However, some states, most notably California, have passed laws that define how companies should inform their employees of this situation and in which situations monitoring is legal. Even so, this law is more of a guideline for ethical practice than a protection of privacy (Sipior & Ward, 1995).

Fortunately, the ECPA and the court case judgments thus far on e-mail monitoring suggest that companies must be prudent and open about their monitoring of e-mail messages and Internet usage. Companies should use good judgment in monitoring e-mail and should make public their policy about monitoring messages. One primary reason that employees perceive their e-mail to be private is the fact that they are never told otherwise (Weisband & Reinig, 1995). In addition, employees should use e-mail only as appropriate, based on their company's policy and their own ethical standards. Given recent actions and rulings on the capture and usage of e-mail messages over the Internet, it appears that online privacy is in jeopardy both in and out of business organizations. As a general rule, we all need to realize that what we type and send via e-mail in and out of the workplace is likely to be read by others for whom the messages were not intended. It is wise to write only those e-mail messages that would not embarrass us if they were made public.

HOW TO MAINTAIN YOUR PRIVACY ONLINE.   In general, companies operating in the online world are not required by law to respect your privacy. In other words, a vendor can track what pages you look at, what products you examine in detail, which products you choose to buy, what method of payment you choose to use, and where you have the product delivered. After collecting all that information, unscrupulous vendors can sell it to others, resulting in more direct-mail advertising, electronic spam in your e-mail in-box, or calls from telemarketers.

When surveyed about concerns related to Internet use, most consumers list issues of information privacy as a top concern. As a result, governments have pressured businesses to post their privacy policies on their Web sites. As outlined in the U.S. Federal Trade Commission's "Fair Information Practice Principles" (http://www.ftc.gov/reports/privacy3/fairinfo.shtm, see also Figure 1.23), widely accepted fair information practices include:

FIGURE 1.23

Fair Information Practice Principles.

Source: Courtesy of the Federal Trade Commission, http://www.ftc.gov/reports/privacy3/fairinfo.shtm.

- **Notice/Awareness.** Providing information about what data are gathered, what the data are used for, who will have access to the data, whether provision of the data is required or voluntary, and how confidentiality will be ensured. Such information is typically contained in **data privacy statements** on a Web site.
- **Choice/Consent.** Providing options about what will be done with the data (e.g., subscription to mailing lists after a purchase). Typically, consumers are given a choice to **opt-in** (i.e., signal agreement to the collection/further use of the data, e.g., by checking a box) or **opt-out** (i.e., signal that data cannot be collected/used in other ways).
- **Access/Participation.** Providing customers with means to access data collected about them, check for accuracy, and request correction of inaccuracies.
- **Integrity/Security.** Ensuring integrity of the data (e.g., by using only reputable sources of data), as well as implementing safeguards against unauthorized access, disclosure, or destruction of data (we will discuss these safeguards in Chapter 10, "Securing Information Systems").
- **Enforcement/Redress.** Providing means to enforce these practices, and/or for customers to receive remedies, for example, through self-regulation or appropriate laws and regulations.

Unfortunately, while data privacy statements provide information about, for example, how data will be used, they often do not *protect* the privacy of consumers. To protect yourself, you should always review the privacy policy of all companies you do business with and refuse to do business with those that do not have a clear policy or do not respect your privacy. To make sure your shopping experience is a good one, you can take a few additional steps to maintain your privacy:

- *Choose Web Sites That Are Monitored by Independent Organizations.* Several independent organizations monitor the privacy and business practices of Web sites (e.g., www.truste.com).
- *Avoid Having "Cookies" Left on Your Machine.* Many commercial Web sites leave cookies on your machine so that the owner of the site can monitor where you go and what you do on the site. To enhance your privacy, you should carefully manage your browser's cookie settings or get special "cookie management" software (see Chapter 10 for more on cookies).
- *Visit Sites Anonymously.* There are ways to visit Web sites anonymously. Using services provided by companies such as Anonymizer (www.anonymizer.com), you have a high degree of privacy from marketers, identity thieves, or even coworkers when surfing the Web.
- *Use Caution When Requesting Confirmation E-Mail.* When you buy products online, many companies will send you a confirming e-mail message to let you know that the order was received correctly. A good strategy is to have a separate e-mail account, such

as one that is available for viewing via a Web browser, that you use when making online purchases.

- **_Beware What You Post or Say Online._** As an old adage goes, "the Internet never forgets"; anything from status updates to Twitter messages to blog posts can be stored forever, and most information remains somewhere on the Web, even after the original page has long been taken down. It is safe to say that probably almost everybody engages in some regrettable activities at some point in time. Yet, having such activities appear on the Web can be devastating for one's career, so use common sense before you post that drunken party pic on Facebook, or tweet that you are so bored on your job.

Of course, there are no guarantees that all your online experiences will be problem free, but if you follow the advice provided here, you are much more likely to maintain your privacy.

Intellectual Property

Another set of ethical issues centers around **intellectual property** (i.e., creations of the mind that have commercial value), and the ability to easily download, copy (and potentially modify), and share or distribute digital information. For example, back in the days of analog music, it was all but impossible to create a copy of a song without sacrificing quality. Nowadays, you can almost effortlessly copy your friend's entire digital music library without any quality loss (see Figure 1.24); with just a little more effort, you can share it with your friends, or even strangers using peer-to-peer networks. Alternatively, you may come across a great photograph or article on the Web, and share it on Facebook or Google+, without asking for permission from the creator.

Similarly, your school may have licensing agreements with certain vendors, allowing you to install and use certain software while you are a student; yet, you never uninstall the software after graduating, or you may lend the software to some friend or family member for personal use. In other cases, you may not be able to afford certain programs, and download a pirated version from the Web.

Obviously, there are legal issues associated with each of these scenarios. However, there are also ethical issues associated with such behaviors. You may argue that there was no real loss involved for the creator of the files or software, as otherwise, you would have gone for a free alternative or chosen not to purchase the product at all, or you may argue that students do not have the funds to purchase expensive software. These issues become even more complex when viewed from a global perspective. In many non-Western societies, using someone else's work is considered praise for the creator, and it is perfectly alright to use a famous song as background music in a YouTube video, or to include another person's writing in one's personal blog (or term paper).

In either case, you are using someone else's intellectual property without permission (and often without attribution), and without compensating the creator.

FIGURE 1.24

Digital media allows for lossless duplication.

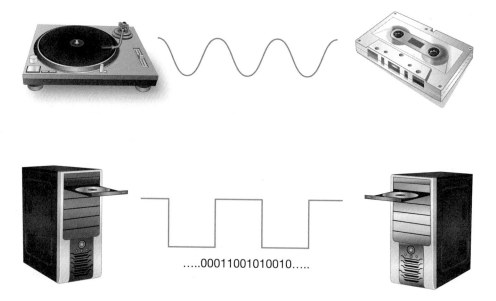

.....00011001010010.....

The Human Cost of the Newest Gadgets

Throughout our lives, we all face ethical dilemmas. Such situations, sometimes called moral dilemmas, occur when one has to choose between two different options, each of which involves breaking a moral imperative. Throughout this book, we will present situations that involve ethical dilemmas for the players involved. For most (if not all) of these situations, there are no definite solutions. In trying to resolve ethical dilemmas, decision makers should take into consideration both the consequences of and the actions involved in each approach: first, consider the *consequences* of each potential course of action, in terms of benefits and harms (in terms of degree, but also in consideration of long-term versus short-term), so as to identify the option that maximizes benefits while minimizing harms. The second step is to consider the *actions* involved (irrespective of the consequences), and evaluating which actions are least problematic from a moral standpoint (e.g., in terms of honesty, fairness, respect, etc.). While you may not arrive at a perfect solution, taking these two factors into account should give you some guidance on how to arrive at a decision.

There are various ethical dilemmas surrounding the production, use, and disposal of electronic devices, and Apple is no exception. For example, tiny silver letters printed on the back of an iPhone say: "Designed by Apple in California—Assembled in China." Globalization has enabled Apple to focus on designing electronics consumers crave, while outsourcing the manufacturing of components and assembling of the devices to contract manufacturers on a global scale. However, while Apple is keeping tight control over the designs of its devices, and prefers to keep mum about who is supplying or building which components, Apple does not always have complete control over *how* the suppliers build the components.

As a case in point, when taking over as Apple's CEO following the death of Steve Jobs, Tim Cook inherited the issues surrounding the working conditions at the Chinese factories of Foxconn, one of Apple's primary manufacturers. Foxconn, manufacturing products such as Apple's iPhones and iPads, but also electronic devices for a host of other companies ranging from Dell to Sony, employs more than 1.2 million people; there are few to no other suppliers who are able to meet the production volumes, quality, and costs demanded by Apple (and its customers) for its product line-up.

In 2010, a series of suicides occurred in Foxconn's 250,000-employee plant in Shenzhen, China: a total of 18 workers threw themselves off the company rooftops, resulting in 14 deaths. An additional 20 employees were stopped just in time; others were saved by newly installed safety nets surrounding the building. In 2011, an explosion killed 3 and injured 15 at a Foxconn plant manufacturing the iPad 2 in the Chinese city of Chengdu. In January 2012, around 150 workers at Foxconn's Wuhan, China, plant protested against their working conditions and threatened to commit mass suicide.

Reports have blamed these and other incidents on the less-than-desirable working conditions at Foxconn, where poor management is said to have prevented workers from talking to each other for fear of a bad mark on their record, severe scolding, or an unreasonable fine. The pressures of growing orders resulted in pushing workers to their limit, causing twitching hands, uncontrollable mimicking of the motion after work, and a rapid burn-out rate causing the resignation of 50,000 workers each month. The employees were worked 70 hours per week, 120 hours of overtime per month and paid a basic monthly wage of 900 yuan (about US$150). In light of the suicides, the company has gradually attempted to improve the working conditions by reducing overtime or offering counseling services. In addition, Apple has asked the non-profit Fair Labor Association to conduct an independent audit at various factories; this audit, among other things, confirmed that laborers worked excessive overtime and faced health and safety issues. Apple has agreed to address these issues, but they remind us that increasing consumerism and a focus on having the latest technologies carries a human cost.

Tim Cook faces a number of dilemmas. For its shareholders, Apple pursues a goal of profit maximization. In pursuing this goal, Apple introduces gadgets consumers crave at an ever-increasing pace, creating a hype around each new device, which, in turn, creates huge demand. There are few suppliers worldwide who can, on relatively short notice, produce the numbers needed to meet the demand for Apple's products, so shifting suppliers is not easy for Apple. At the same time, reducing working hours, raising salaries, or offering other fringe benefits negatively impacts Apple's profit margin. Further, for many young Chinese, working at Foxconn for a few months is better than the alternative of tilling the fields on their families' small farming operations, or not working at all, as evidenced by the thousands of workers lining up for Foxconn's recruiting sessions every week. If you were in Tim Cook's shoes, what would you do? As a consumer, what are your ethical dilemmas associated with the ever-increasing desire for new gadgets?

Based on:

Anonymous. (2012, March 29). Apple addresses China Foxconn factory report. *BBC News.* Retrieved May 11, 2012, from http://www.bbc.com/news/technology-17557630.

Duhigg, C., and Barboza, D. (2012, January 25). In China, human costs are built into an iPad. *The New York Times.* Retrieved May 11, 2012, from http://www.nytimes.com/2012/01/26/business/ieconomy-apples-ipad-and-the-human-costs-for-workers-in-china.html.

Moore, M. (2012, January 11). "Mass suicide" protest at Apple manufacturer Foxconn factory. *Telegraph.co.uk.* Retrieved March 19, 2012, from http://www.telegraph.co.uk/news/worldnews/asia/china/9006988/Mass-suicide-protest-at-Apple-manufacturer-Foxconn-factory.html.

Moore, M. (2010, May 27). Inside Foxconn's suicide factory. *Telegraph.co.uk.* Retrieved March 19, 2012, from http://www.telegraph.co.uk/finance/china-business/7773011/A-look-inside-the-Foxconn-suicide-factory.html.

Resolving an ethical dilemma. (n.d.). Retrieved May 11, 2012, from http://www.lmu.edu/Page27945.aspx.

The Need for a Code of Ethical Conduct

Not only has the Internet age found governments playing catch-up to pass legislation pertaining to computer crime, privacy, and security, it has also created an ethical conundrum. For instance, the technology exists to rearrange and otherwise change photographs, but is the practice ethical? If you can use a computer at your school or workplace for professional purposes but "steal" computer time to do personal business, is this ethical? Is it ethical for companies to compile information about your shopping habits, credit history, and other aspects of your life for the purpose of selling such data to others? Should guidelines be in place to dictate how businesses and others use information and computers? If so, what should the guidelines include, and who should write them? Should there be penalties imposed for those who violate established guidelines? If so, who should enforce such penalties?

Many businesses have devised guidelines for the ethical use of information technology and computer systems; similarly, most universities and many public school systems have written guidelines for students, faculty, and employees about the ethical use of computers. EduCom, a non-profit organization of colleges and universities, has developed a policy for ethics in information technology that many universities endorse. In part, the EduCom statement concerning software and intellectual rights says,

> Because electronic information is volatile and easily reproduced, respect for the work and personal expression of others is especially critical in computer environments. Violations of authorial integrity, including plagiarism, invasion of privacy, unauthorized access, and trade secret and copyright violations, may be grounds for sanctions against members of the academic community. (Courtesy of EduCom)

Most organization and school guidelines encourage all system users to act responsibly, ethically, and legally when using computers and to follow accepted rules of online etiquette as well as federal and state laws.

RESPONSIBLE COMPUTER USE.   The Computer Ethics Institute is a research, education, and policy study organization that studies how advances in information technology have impacted ethics and corporate and public policy. The institute has issued widely quoted guidelines for the ethical use of computers. The guidelines prohibit the following (Courtesy of Computer Ethics Institute):

- Using a computer to harm others
- Interfering with other people's computer work
- Snooping in other people's files
- Using a computer to steal
- Using a computer to bear false witness
- Copying or using proprietary software without paying for it
- Using other people's computer resources without authorization or compensation
- Appropriating other people's intellectual output

The guidelines recommend the following:

- Thinking about social consequences of programs you write and systems you design
- Using a computer in ways that show consideration and respect for others

Responsible computer use in the information age includes following the guidelines mentioned here. As a computer user, when in doubt, you should review the ethical guidelines published by your school, place of employment, and/or professional organization. Some users bent on illegal or unethical behavior are attracted by the anonymity they believe the Internet affords. But the fact is that we leave electronic tracks as we wander through the Web, and many perpetrators have been traced and successfully prosecuted when they thought they had hidden their trails. The fact is, too, that if you post objectionable material on the Internet and people complain about it, your Internet service provider can ask you to remove the material or remove yourself from the service.

The Digital Divide

Unfortunately, there are still many people in our society who are being left behind in the information age. The gap between those individuals in our society who are computer literate and have access to information resources like the Internet and those who do not is referred to as the **digital divide**. The digital divide is one of the major ethical challenges facing society today when you consider the strong linkage between computer literacy and a person's ability to compete in the information age. For example, access to raw materials and money fueled the industrial revolution, "but in the informational society, the fuel, the power, is knowledge," emphasized John Kenneth Galbraith, an American economist who specialized in emerging trends in the U.S. economy. "One has now come to see a new class structure divided by those who have information and those who must function out of ignorance. This new class has its power not from money, not from land, but from knowledge" (Galbraith, 1987).

The good news is that the digital divide in America is rapidly shrinking, but there are still major challenges to overcome. In particular, people in rural communities, the elderly, people with disabilities, and minorities lag behind national averages for Internet access and computer literacy. Outside the United States and other developed countries, the gap gets even wider, and the obstacles get much more difficult to overcome, particularly in the developing countries, where infrastructure and financial resources are lacking (see also Case 1 at the end of this chapter). For example, most developing countries are lacking modern informational resources such as affordable Internet access or efficient electronic payment methods like credit cards. Throughout this text, we will touch on various issues related to the digital divide.

INDUSTRY ANALYSIS

Business Career Outlook

Today, organizations are increasingly moving away from focusing exclusively on local markets. For example, PriceWaterhouseCoopers is focusing on forming overseas partnerships to increase its client base and to better serve the regions located away from its U.S. home. This means that it is not only more likely that you will need to travel overseas in your career or even take an overseas assignment, but it is also extremely likely that you will have to work with customers, suppliers, or colleagues from other parts of the world. Given this globalization trend, there is a shortage of business professionals with the necessary "global skills" for operating in the digital world. Three strategies for improving your skills include the following:

1. **Gain International Experience.** The first strategy is very straightforward. Simply put, by gaining international experiences, you will more likely possess the necessary cultural sensitivity to empathize with other cultures and, more important, you will be a valuable asset to any global organization.

2. **Learn More Than One Language.** A second strategy is to learn more than your native language. Language problems within global organizations are often hidden beneath the surface. Many people are embarrassed to admit when they don't completely understand a foreign colleague. Unfortunately, the miscommunication of important information can have disastrous effects on the business.

3. **Sensitize Yourself to Global Cultural and Political Issues.** A third strategy focuses on developing greater sensitivity to the various cultural and political differences within the world. Such sensitivity and awareness can be developed through coursework, seminars, and international travel. Understanding current events and the political climate of international colleagues will enhance communication, cohesiveness, and job performance.

In addition to these strategies, prior to making an international visit or taking an international assignment, there are many things you can do to improve your effectiveness as well as enhance your chances of having fun, including the following:

1. Read books, newspapers, magazines, and Web sites about the country.
2. Talk to people who already know the country and its culture.
3. Avoid literal translations of work materials, brochures, memos, and other important documents.
4. Watch locally produced television as well as follow the local news through international news stations and Web sites.
5. After arriving in the new country, take time to tour local parks, monuments, museums, entertainment locations, and other cultural venues.
6. Share meals and breaks with local workers and discuss more than just work-related issues, such as current local events and issues.
7. Learn several words and phrases in the local languages.

Regardless of what business profession you choose, globalization is a reality within the digital world. In addition to globalization, the proliferation of information systems is having specific ramifications for all business careers. This is discussed next.

For Accounting and Finance: In today's digital world, accounting and finance professionals rely heavily on information systems. Information systems are used to support various resource planning and control processes as well as to provide managers with up-to-date information. Accounting and finance professionals use a variety of information systems, networks, and databases to effectively perform their functions. In addition to changing the ways internal processes are managed and performed, information systems have also changed the ways organizations exchange financial information with suppliers, distributors, and customers. If you choose a career in accounting or finance, it is almost certain that you will be working with various types of information systems every day.

For Operations Management: Information systems have also greatly changed the operations management profession. In the past, orders for supplies had to be placed over the phone, production processes had to be optimized using tedious calculations, and forecasts were sometimes only educated guesses. Today, enterprise resource planning and supply chain management systems have eliminated much of the "busywork" associated with making production forecasts and placing orders. Additionally, with the use of corporate extranets, companies are connecting to their suppliers' and distributors' networks, helping to reduce costs in procurement and distribution processes. If you choose operations management as your profession, the use of information systems will likely be a big part of your workday.

For Human Resources Management: The human resources management profession has experienced widespread use of information systems for recruiting employees via Internet job sites, distributing information through corporate intranets, or analyzing employee data stored in databases. In addition to using information systems within your daily work activities, you will also have to deal with other issues related to information systems use and misuse within your organization. For example, what are the best methods for motivating employees to use a system they do not want to use? What policies should you use regarding monitoring employee productivity or Internet misuse? If you choose human resource management as a profession, information systems have become an invaluable addition to the recruitment and management of personnel.

For Marketing: Information systems have changed the way organizations promote and sell their products. For example, business-to-consumer electronic commerce, enabled by the Internet, allows companies to directly interact with their customers without the need for intermediaries; likewise, customer relationship management systems facilitate the targeting of narrow market segments with highly personalized promotional campaigns. Marketing professionals must therefore be proficient in the use of various types of information systems in order to attract and retain loyal customers.

For Information Systems: Information systems have become a ubiquitous part of organizational life, where systems are used by all organizational levels and functions. Because of this, there is a growing need for professionals to develop and support these systems. To most effectively utilize the investment in information systems, these professionals must be proficient in both business—management, marketing, finance, and accounting—and technology. In other words, information systems professionals must understand the business rationale for implementing a particular system as well as how organizations can use various systems to obtain a competitive advantage. Being able to bridge the business needs of the organization to information systems–based solutions will provide you with a competitive advantage in the job market.

Based on:

Treitel, R. (2000, October 9). Global Success. *Gantthead.com.* Retrieved April 23, 2012, from http://www.gantthead.com/articles/articlesPrint.cfm?ID=12706.

Key Points Review

1. *Describe the characteristics of the digital world and the advent of the information age.* Today, we live in a knowledge society, and information systems have become pervasive throughout our organizational and personal lives. Technological advances have enabled a move into the post-PC era, where mobility, social media, cloud computing, Big Data, and consumerization of IT have shaped the way we work and interact. The information age refers to a time in the history of civilization when information became the currency of the realm. Being successful in many careers today requires that people be computer literate, because the ability to access and effectively operate computing technology is a key part of many careers.

2. *Define globalization, describe how it evolved over time, and describe the key drivers of globalization.* A more global and competitive world includes visible economic, cultural, and technological changes. Globalization is the integration of economies throughout the world, fueled by technological progress and innovation, and has, among other changes, led to a rise in outsourcing and has helped to shape the world as we know it today. Companies operating in the digital world see a number of opportunities, such

as access to new markets and access to a talented labor pool in countries with lower wages. In addition to the opportunities, operating in the digital world also poses a number of challenges to companies. These challenges are of a governmental, geoeconomic, and cultural nature.

3. *Explain what an information system is, contrasting its data, technology, people, and organizational components.* Information systems are combinations of hardware, software, and telecommunications networks that people build and use to collect, create, and distribute useful data, typically in organizational settings. When data are organized in a way that is useful to people, these data are defined as information. The term "information systems" is also used to represent the field in which people develop, use, manage, and study computer-based information systems in organizations. The field of information systems is huge, diverse, and growing, and encompasses many different people, purposes, systems, and technologies. The technology part of information systems is the hardware, software, and telecommunications networks. The people who build, manage, use, and study information systems make up the people component. They include systems analysts, systems programmers, IS professors, and many others. Finally, information systems typically reside and are used within organizations, so they are said to have an organizational component. Together, these four aspects form an information system.

4. *Describe the dual nature of information systems in the success and failure of modern organizations.* If information systems are conceived, designed, used, and managed effectively and strategically, then together with a sound business model they can enable organizations to be more effective, to be more productive, to expand their reach, and to gain or sustain competitive advantage over rivals. If information systems are not conceived, designed, used, or managed well, they can have negative effects on organizations such as loss of money, loss of time, loss of customers' goodwill, and, ultimately, loss of customers. Modern organizations that embrace and manage information systems effectively and strategically and combine that with sound business models tend to be the organizations that are successful and competitive.

5. *Describe how computer ethics impact the use of information systems and discuss the ethical concerns associated with information privacy and intellectual property.* Information privacy is concerned with what information an individual should have to reveal to others through the course of employment or through other transactions, such as online shopping. While the information age has brought widespread access to information, the downside is that others may now have access to personal information that you would prefer to keep private. This becomes especially problematic as organizations are increasingly able to piece together information about you, forming an ever more complete picture. With the ease of duplicating, manipulating, and sharing digital information, intellectual property becomes an increasingly important issue, not only for companies, but also for individuals. Finally, the digital divide between people who are computer literate and have access to information resources and those who do not is one of the major ethical challenges facing society today. While the digital divide is shrinking in the United States, it continues to be a major challenge elsewhere, especially in developing countries.

Key Terms

BYOD 40
cloud computing 39
competitive advantage 59
computer ethics 61
computer fluency 41
computer literacy 40
computer-based information
   system 49
consumerization of IT 39
data 48
data privacy statement 65
digital divide 69
downsizing 44

globalization 42
hardware 47
information 48
information age 36
information privacy 62
information system 47
information technology 47
intellectual property 66
internetworking 55
knowledge 49
knowledge society 34
knowledge worker 34
management information system 55

office automation system 56
opt-in 65
opt-out 65
outsourcing 43
post-PC era 33
software 47
strategic 59
systems integration 55
telecommunications network 47
transaction processing
   systems (TPS) 55

Review Questions

1. List the three distinct phases of change within the world's civilizations.
2. List three examples of technology usage at Starbucks.
3. What are cloud-based systems? Give examples.
4. Describe and contrast the economic, cultural, and technological changes occurring in the digital world.
5. What is information technology and how is it different from information systems?
6. List and describe several reasons why companies are choosing to outsource business activities.
7. List and contrast several challenges of operating in the digital world.
8. Define the term "information systems" and explain its data, technology, people, and organizational components.
9. Define and contrast data, information, and knowledge.
10. Explain how decision support systems are different from knowledge management systems.
11. List and define three technical knowledge and/or skills core competencies.
12. Define the term "knowledge economy."
13. List and define four of the systems knowledge and/or skills core competencies.
14. List the effects of globalization on business.
15. Describe the evolution of the information systems function within organizations.
16. Discuss the issues surrounding information privacy, and how you can protect yourself.
17. How are the digital divide and computer literacy related?

Self-Study Questions

1. Information systems today are _____.
   A. slower than in the past
   B. ubiquitous
   C. utilized by only a few select individuals
   D. stable and should not change
2. Whereas data are raw unformatted symbols or lists of words or numbers, information is _____.
   A. data that have been organized in a form that is useful
   B. accumulated knowledge
   C. what you put in your computer
   D. what your computer prints out for you
3. Computer-based information systems were described in this chapter as _____.
   A. any complicated technology that requires expert use
   B. a combination of hardware, software, and telecommunications networks that people build and use to collect, create, and distribute data
   C. any technology (mechanical or electronic) used to supplement, extend, or replace human, manual labor
   D. any technology used to leverage human capital
4. Other terms that can be used to represent the knowledge society include _____.
   A. the new economy
   B. the network society
   C. the digital world
   D. all of the above
5. Which of the following was *not* discussed as a common type, or category, of information system used in organizations?
   A. transaction processing
   B. decision support
   C. enterprise resource planning
   D. Web graphics

6. What is meant by BYOD?
   A. the increased focus of hardware companies on the mass market
   B. the phenomenon that devices are becoming increasingly playful
   C. the use of personal devices and applications for work-related purposes
   D. the increase of technology in people's households
7. The release of the Netscape Web browser had the following effects on the flattening of the world *except* _____.
   A. helping setting standards for the display of Web data
   B. providing easy access to the Internet
   C. providing integrated e-mail
   D. helping setting standards for the transport of Web data
8. A Web site asking you for permission to send you a weekly newsletter is an example of _____.
   A. opt-in
   B. permissions
   C. opt-out
   D. data privacy
9. Which of the following is *not* considered an intellectual property violation?
   A. giving software licensed to your school or workplace to friends or family members
   B. downloading pirated movies or music
   C. making copies of music for your friends
   D. all of the above are considered intellectual property violations
10. Being _____, or knowing how to use the computer as a device to gather, store, organize, and process information, can open up myriad sources of information.
    A. technology literate
    B. digitally divided
    C. computer literate
    D. computer illiterate
    Answers are on page 75.

Problems and Exercises

1. Match the following terms with the appropriate definitions:
   i. Information
   ii. Downsizing
   iii. Information systems
   iv. Information privacy
   v. Computer fluency
   vi. Globalization
   vii. Outsourcing
   viii. Digital divide
   ix. Intellectual property
   x. Computer ethics

   a. The issues and standards of conduct as they pertain to the use of information systems
   b. Data that have been formatted in a way that is useful
   c. The integration of economies around the world, enabled by innovation and technological progress
   d. The ability to independently learn new technologies as they emerge and assess their impact on one's work and life
   e. The practice of slashing costs and streamlining operations by laying off employees
   f. Combinations of hardware, software, and telecommunications networks that people build and use to collect, create, and distribute useful data, typically in organizational settings
   g. The moving of routine jobs and/or tasks to people in another firm to reduce costs
   h. An area concerned with what information an individual should have to reveal to others through the course of employment or through other transactions, such as online shopping
   i. The gap between those individuals in our society who are computer literate and have access to information resources, such as the Internet, and those who do not
   j. Creations of the mind that have commercial value

2. Peter Drucker has defined the knowledge worker and knowledge society. What are his definitions? Do you agree with them? What examples can you give to support or disprove these concepts?

3. Of the several information systems listed in the chapter, how many do you have experience with? What systems would you like to work with? What types of systems do you encounter at the university you are attending? The Web is also a good source for additional information.

4. Identify someone who works within the field of information systems as an IS instructor, professor, or practitioner (e.g., as a systems analyst or systems manager). Find out why this individual got into this field and what this person likes and dislikes about working within the field of information systems. What advice can this person offer to someone entering the field?

5. As a small group, conduct a search on the Web for job placement services. Pick at least four of these services and find as many IS job titles as you can. You may want to try monster.com or careerbuilder.com. How many did you find? Were any of them different from those presented in this chapter? Could you determine the responsibilities of these positions based on the information given to you?

6. Visit Walmart China (www.wal-martchina.com/english/index.htm). Compare and contrast www.walmart.com with Walmart China's site. What is the focus of Walmart China's Web site? Discuss how the focus differs from www.walmart.com. What are possible reasons for the differences?

7. Select and study one process from your college or university. What type of information system would this process need?

8. What is the impact of mobility and social networks on your personal life? On the Web, find statistics about these topics. How does your own behavior compare to the statistics you found?

9. Should the U.S. government allow companies to use offshore outsourcing if qualified U.S. citizens are willing and able to do a job? Should the government regulate the amount that can be outsourced by any company? Why or why not?

10. Choose an organization and study the information systems solution it uses. Identify the types of information systems solutions that have been developed in the organization.

11. Compare and contrast the data privacy statements of three different e-commerce Web sites. What are the similarities and differences? Which business would you be least/most willing to do business with? Why?

12. Why do most organizations have only TPS and MIS as part of their information systems?

13. Global outsourcing appears to be here to stay. Use the Web to identify a company that is providing low-cost labor from some less developed part of the world. Provide a short report that explains who the company is, where it is located, who its customers are, what services and capabilities it provides, how long it has been in business, and any other interesting information you can find in your research.

14. The Electronic Frontier Foundation (www.eff.org) has a mission of protecting rights and promoting freedom in the "electronic frontier." The organization provides additional advice on how to protect your online privacy. Review its suggestions and provide a summary of what you can do to protect yourself.

15. Do you consider yourself computer literate? Do you know of any friends or relatives who are not computer literate? What can you do to improve your computer literacy? Is computer literacy necessary in today's job market? Why or why not?

16. Search the Web and identify what kind of business opportunities exist in the areas of accounting and finance, operations management and human capital management with respect to information systems.

17. Find your school's guidelines for ethical computer use on the Internet and answer the following questions: Are there limitations as to the type of Web sites and material that can be viewed (e.g., pornography)? Are students allowed to change the programs on the hard drives of the lab computers or download software for their own use? Are there rules governing personal use of computers and e-mail?

18. Do you believe that there is a need for a unified information systems code of ethics? Visit www.albion.com/netiquette/corerules.html. What do you think of this code? Should it be expanded, or is it too general? Search the Internet for additional codes for programmers or Web developers. What did you find?

Application Exercises

Note: The existing data files referenced in these exercises are available on the book's Web site: www.pearsonhighered.com/valacich.

Spreadsheet Application: Ticket Sales at Campus Travel

The local travel center, Campus Travel, has been losing sales. The presence of online ticketing Web sites, such as Travelocity.com and Expedia.com, has lured many students away. However, given the complexity of making international travel arrangements, Campus Travel could have a thriving and profitable business if it concentrated its efforts in this area. You have been asked by the director of sales and marketing to help with analyzing prior sales data in order to design better marketing strategies. Looking at these data, you realize that it is nearly impossible to perform a detailed analysis of ticket sales given that it is not summarized or organized in a useful way to inform business decision making. The spreadsheet TicketSales.csv contains the ticket sales data for spring 2012. Your director has asked you for the following information regarding ticket sales. Modify the TicketSales.csv spreadsheet to provide the following information for your director:

1. The total number of tickets sold.
   a. Select the data from the "tickets sold" column.
   b. Then select the "autosum" function.
2. The largest amount of tickets sold by a certain salesperson to any one location.
   a. Select the appropriate cell.
   b. Use the "MAX" function to calculate each salesperson's highest ticket total in one transaction.
3. The least amount of tickets sold by a certain salesperson to any one location.
   a. Select the appropriate cells.
   b. Use the "MIN" function to calculate the "least tickets sold."
4. The average number of tickets sold.
   a. Select the cells.

b. Use the "AVERAGE" function to calculate the "average number of tickets sold" using the same data you had selected in the previous steps.

Database Application: Tracking Frequent-Flier Miles at the Campus Travel Agency

The director of sales and marketing at the travel agency would like to increase the efficiency of handling those who have frequent-flier accounts. Often, frequent fliers have regular travel routes and a preferred seating area or meal category. In previous years, the data have been manually entered into a three-ring binder. In order to handle the frequent fliers' requests more efficiently, your director has asked you to build an Access database containing the following information:

- Name (first and last name)
- Address
- Phone number
- Frequent-flier number
- Frequent-flier airline
- Meal category
- Preferred seating area

To do this, you will need to do the following:

1. Create an empty database named "Frequent Flier."
2. Import the data contained in the file FrequentFliers.txt. Use "Text File" under "Import" in the "External Data" tab. Hint: Use tab delimiters when importing the data; note that the first row contains field names.

After importing the data, create a report displaying the names and addresses of all frequent fliers by doing the following:

1. Select "Report Wizard" under "Report" in the "Create" tab.
2. Include the fields "first name," "last name," and "address" in the report.
3. Save the report as "Frequent Fliers."

Team Work Exercise

Net Stats: Worldwide Internet Usage

In January 2012, 12 percent of the world's active Internet users were located in North America. As the rest of the world is getting online, this is about half of North America's nearly 30 percent share of 2004. Overall, it was estimated that there were over 2.3 billion active Internet users worldwide in early 2012: over 1 billion users in Asia, 500 million in Europe, and 273 million in North America (about 245 million active users in the United States alone) (see Table 1.8). The Internet is most heavily used in North America, with 78.6 percent of the total population going online; Africa has the lowest penetration (percentage of a region's population using the Internet) with 13.5 percent. China has the most users with 513 million, followed by the United States.

Based on:

Anonymous. (n.d.). World Internet usage statistics. Retrieved March 2, 2012, from http://www.internetworldstats.com/stats.htm.

TABLE 1.8 World Internet Usage Estimates

World Regions	Population (2011 estimates)	Internet Usage, Estimate	% Population (penetration)	Usage (% of world)
Africa/Middle East	1.2 billion	217 million	17.3%	9.6%
Asia	3.9 billion	1 billion	26.2%	44.8%
Europe	816 million	501 million	61.3%	22.1%
North America	347 million	273 million	78.6%	12%
Latin America/ Caribbean	597 million	236 million	39.5%	10.4%
Oceania/Australia	35 million	24 million	67.5%	1.1%
World total	6.9 billion	2.3 billion	32.7%	100.0%

Note: Internet usage and world population statistics were updated for December 31, 2011.

Source: Based on http://www.internetworldstats.com/stats.htm.

Questions and Exercises

1. Search the Web for the most up-to-date statistics.
2. As a team, interpret these numbers. What is striking/ important about these statistics?
3. As a team, discuss how these numbers will look like in 5 years and 10 years. What will the changes mean for globalization? What issues/opportunities do you see arising?
4. Using your spreadsheet software of choice, create a graph/ figure most effectively visualizing the statistics/changes you consider most important.

Answers to the Self-Study Questions

1. B, p. 32	**2.** A, p. 48	**3.** B, p. 49	**4.** D, p. 34	**5.** D, p. 55
6. C, p. 40	**7.** C, p. 43	**8.** A, p. 65	**9.** D, p. 66	**10.** C, p. 40

CASE 1 | Bridging the Digital Divide

An important ethical issue related to computer use is the *digital divide,* which refers to the unequal access to computer technology within various populations. The divide occurs on several levels: socioeconomic (rich/poor), racial (majority/minority), and geographical (urban/rural and developed/undeveloped countries). Studies have shown that as the information age progresses, those individuals who have access to computer technology and to opportunities for learning computer skills generally have an educational edge.

To bridge the divide, Nicholas Negroponte, an architect and computer scientist who founded the Massachusetts Institute of Technology's Media Lab, announced the creation of One Laptop per Child (OLPC), a non-profit organization, in 2005 at the World Economic Forum in Davos, Switzerland. As part of the project, the XO-1, a US$100 computer, was designed expressly for child use. With US$2 million start-up contributions, OLPC intended to distribute the computers to children around the world, including locations within the United States. The computers were to be given to children at an early age, were designed for child ownership and use, had built-in Internet access, were intended to accompany children from school to homes, and were designed for free and open programming access.

The project's goal was to close the digital divide and transform education by providing access to computers to children who would otherwise not have the opportunity to fully participate in the information age. Yet, the project was off to a slow start, as OLPC was not able to produce the laptop at the price initially envisioned; the XO-1 shipped for US$200, double the envisioned price.

In 2007, the project received a boost when the "Give 1 Get 1" program was launched. For US$399, a shopper could buy the XO laptop for themselves, and an additional XO laptop was given to the project. In six weeks, over 80,000 laptops were given to children through this initiative. Owing to this success, the program was relaunched in 2008, this time with online retail giant Amazon.com. After the end of the program on December 31, 2008, Amazon.com offered the XO-1 laptop for US$199, this time to be donated to a child in a developing country. In October 2009, every child in the country of Uruguay received a laptop (through Uruguay's official "Plan Ceibal" project), making Uruguay the first country to fulfill the mission of the OLPC program. The program has since delivered 110,000 laptops to Rwanda and, as of May 2012, even delivered 5,000 XOs to war-torn Afghanistan. Countries on the list that have received laptops include Uganda, Mongolia, Nicaragua, and Peru. Yet, the initiative is used not only for children in the developing world. In early 2012, the Australian federal budget included funds for 50,000 laptops to be purchased from OLPC. In total, OLPC has distributed over 2.4 million of the US$200 laptops to children all over the world.

Since the development of the first model, OLPC has continued evolving the design of the XO-1 series, with a focus on significantly reducing power consumption, while improving processing power. At the 2012 Consumer Electronics Show (CES) in Las Vegas, Nevada, OLPC presented the XO-3 model. Initially announced in late 2009, the XO-3 was designed as a tablet, and was expected to finally break the magic US$100 mark, depending on the configuration.

Critics of the program, however, claimed that Negroponte's policy of dealing only with heads of state and of requiring countries to purchase machines in lots of 1 million seemed in direct opposition to stated goals. (These requirements have since been modified.) In 2007, when Intel mounted competitive campaigns to sell the Classmate PC, a low-cost computer also designed for individuals previously underserved in the computer market, Negroponte complained about the competition, calling Intel's efforts "shameless." The competition, however, is proving beneficial to those who would otherwise not have had access to low-cost, educationally focused, top-of-the-line computer technology.

A recent study by the Inter-American Development Bank, however, revealed that the educational benefits from handing out laptops to children are far from given: in Peru, which spent US$225 million for 850,000 laptops (the largest number for any single country), there were no significant differences in math skills or literacy between children who received a laptop and those who did not. This is partially attributed to lack of training of teachers, who often do not know how to harness the potential of using these laptops in the classrooms. In addition, one of the main goals of the program in Peru was to give children a feeling of inclusion and self-esteem, rather than just improving learning.

Despite criticisms, the OLPC campaign continues to provide laptops to children around the world. Still, access to the Internet and digital information remains elusive for much of the human population, especially on the African continent. In light of this, the OLPC program continues to innovate and find ways to bring technology to children around the world. With every laptop delivered, the digital divide is lessened.

Questions:

1. Why does the digital divide matter to children and their families?
2. What will the rise in mobile devices in the developing world mean for the OLPC project?
3. Identify and discuss what you feel is the major challenge for making the OLPC a success. How can this challenge be overcome?

Based on:

Hernandez, C. (2010, February 8). Computers in Haiti and Afghanistan: One Laptop per Child expands its reach. *Smartplanet.com.* Retrieved May 10, 2012, from http://www.smartplanet.com/people/blog/pure-genius/computers-in-haiti-and-afghanistan-one-laptop-per-child-expands-its-reach/1813.

Negroponte, N. (n.d.). Retrieved May 10, 2012, from http://web.media.mit.edu/~nicholas.

Nysted, D. (2008, November 17). OLPC 'Give 1 Get 1' laptop program now available on Amazon. *PCWorld.* Retrieved May 10, 2012, from http://www.pcworld.com/article/153985/olpc_give_1_get_1_laptop_program_now_available_on_amazon.html.

Oppenheimer, A. (2012, April 21). Region's one laptop per child plan has a future. *The Miami Herald.* Retrieved May 10, 2012, from http://www.miamiherald.com/2012/04/21/2759975/regions-one-laptop-per-child-plan.html.

Osborne, C. (2012, April 9). One Laptop per Child: Disappointing results? *ZDNet.* Retrieved May 10, 2012, from http://www.zdnet.com/blog/igeneration/one-laptop-per-child-disappointing-results/15920.

Pearce, R. (2012, May 9). One Laptop Per Child Australia scores $11.7m in federal budget. *Techworld.com.au.* Retrieved May 10, 2012, from http://www.techworld.com.au/article/424025/one_laptop_per_child_australia_scores_11_7m_federal_budget.

Shah, A. (2012, January 7). OLPC's XO-3 tablet to debut at CES. *PCWorld.* Retrieved May 10, 2012, from http://www.pcworld.com/article/247448/olpcs_xo3_tablet_to_debut_at_ces.html.

Vota, W. (2007, May 21). OLPC XO vs. Intel Classmate PC, a beneficial competition. *OLPC News.* Retrieved May 10, 2012, from http://www.olpcnews.com/sales_talk/countries/olpc_xo_intel_classmates.html.

CASE 2   Enabling Global Payments at PayPal

If you have used eBay (and who hasn't?), you know how easy it is to pay for items you buy and to receive payment for items you have sold. Checks, credit card charges, and money orders are unnecessary. Instead of these traditional methods of payment, digital money is easily and effortlessly zapped to and from accounts at PayPal, the most frequently used digital money transfer service online.

Peter Thiel, a hedge fund manager, and Max Levchin, an online security specialist, founded what was to become PayPal—it was first named Field Link and then Confinity and finally, in 2001, PayPal. The company went online rather naively in 1999. The founders' vision was to create a digital currency exchange service free of government controls; however, hackers, con artists, and organized crime groups quickly realized the potential of using the site for scams and money laundering. After implementing tighter security measures to stop criminal activity and assuage customer complaints, the next hurdle to overcome was government regulators. Attorneys general in several states investigated PayPal's business practices, and New York and California levied fines for violations. Louisiana banned the company from operating in that state (the ban has since been lifted).

When PayPal began, payment for Web products could only be made through credit card charges at the purchase site and via checks and money orders sent through the U.S. Postal Service. Other companies, such as Beenz.com and Flooz.com, had tried to establish electronic payment systems based on a special digital currency, but merchants, banks, and customers were hesitant to accept "money" that wasn't based on real dollars. Thiel and Levchin saw the need for an electronic payment system that relied on real currency, especially when eBay became popular, and PayPal filled that niche.

After PayPal solved its security and customer support problems, customers liked the convenience and ease of using the service, and its client base grew. Buyers like not having to reveal their credit card numbers to every online merchant, and merchants appreciate having PayPal handle payment collection. New PayPal clients establish an account with a user name and password and fund the account by giving PayPal a credit card number or bank account transaction information. Although PayPal prefers the latter (because bank account transactions are cheaper than credit card transactions), half of PayPal's accounts are funded via credit cards.

eBay bought PayPal in 2002 for US$1.5 billion and since then has also been a major source of income for the money transfer site. At the same time, PayPal has expanded its client base both in the United States and abroad and is generating much of its revenue by charging fees for payment processing for a wide variety of online vendors, auction sites, and corporations. Services to buyers are free, but sellers are charged a fee, which is generally lower than fees charged by major credit card companies. PayPal now offers special merchant accounts for transferring larger amounts of money and also offers a donation box feature for blogs and other Web sites where visitors can make donations.

PayPal spawned many rivals after its initial launch, but most have since died, including Citigroup's C2it and Bank One's E-mail Money. As of 2012, the company operates in 190 worldwide markets, has localized Web sites in 21 countries, and manages over 110 million active accounts. It also allows customers to send, receive, and hold funds in 25 currencies worldwide, having handled over US$118 billion in transactions during the year 2011 alone.

PayPal has recently expanded its services into the realm of social media by partnering with Facebook. Facebook Credits, the social site's virtual online currency, can now be bought using PayPal. Facebook Credits allow Facebook users to buy virtual goods in their online gift shop and are used in social games and various other applications. Users who don't have access to a credit or debit account, but do have access to a PayPal account, will be able to purchase the virtual credits. This is an important move for many since the Credit Card Accountability, Responsibility and Disclosure Act of 2009 made it illegal for anyone under the age of 21 to be issued a credit card without a parent, guardian, or spouse's cosignature (or showing that they have the income to cover the credit obligation). The law hits at one of Facebook's key demographics: college students between the ages of 18 and 21. Since social gaming in the U.S. alone is forecast to grow to US$5.5 billion by 2015, PayPal sees virtual credits and, more importantly, a presence on Facebook as a revenue-generating opportunity. Additionally, the collaboration allows advertisers to buy self-serve ads on Facebook's pages using PayPal.

Another key element of PayPal's business is mobile payments. In 2011, PayPal's mobile transactions topped US$5 billion, nearly a five-fold increase from their 2010 mobile transaction figures. According to many analysts, the increasing number of smartphone applications is responsible for the increase. More and more mobile users are conducting business on eBay using their smartphones. With PayPal's mobile apps, sending money on the winning bid is easy and can be handled from nearly anywhere. PayPal's app for the iPhone and Android phones allows users to "bump" their phones together to transfer money between one another. The app also allows a user to request money from a group of people for things like a going-away gift at the office, a fund-raiser, or any other event where money needs to be pooled. Additionally, the app gives users the ability to "split the ticket" at a restaurant and send their portion of the check total to whoever paid the bill—including tax and tip!

While the company has had its share of problems with fraud and phishers (scamsters who send fraudulent e-mail messages and duplicate legitimate Web sites), PayPal continues to innovate and be the number one method of payment for the world's buyers and sellers.

Questions:

1. Why do you think PayPal has been so successful throughout the world?
2. What other opportunities will megatrends such as mobility and social networking provide for PayPal?
3. Do you use PayPal? Why or why not?

Based on:

Anonymous. (n.d.). PayPal—About us. Retrieved May 10, 2012, from https://www.paypal-media.com/mediacenter.cfm.

Anonymous. (n.d.). PayPal company history. Retrieved May 10, 2012, from http://www.fundinguniverse.com/company-histories/PayPal-Inc-Company-History.html.

Arellano, N. E. (2010, March 17). Bump, split and collect with PayPal's mobile payment iPhone app. *itbusiness.ca*. Retrieved May 10, 2012, from http://www.itbusiness.ca/it/client/en/home/News.asp?id=56825.

Gobry, P.-E. (2012, February 21). Social gaming market will grow to $5 billion+ by 2015. *Business Insider*. Retrieved May 10, 2012, from http://articles.businessinsider.com/2012-02-21/research/31081794_1_social-games-zynga-virtual-goods.

Grabianowski, E. (n.d.). How PayPal works. Retrieved May 10, 2012, from http://computer.howstuffworks.com/paypal3.htm.

PayPal. (2012, May 5). In *Wikipedia, the free encyclopedia*. Retrieved May 10, 2012, from http://en.wikipedia.org/w/index.php?title=PayPal&oldid=490814111.

Walker, L. (2005, May 19). PayPal looks to evolve beyond its auction roots. *Washingtonpost.com*. Retrieved May 10, 2012, from http://www.washingtonpost.com/wp-dyn/content/article/2005/05/18/AR2005051802187.html.

Walsh, M. (2010, February 18). Facebook and PayPal become payment pals. *Online Media Daily*. Retrieved May 10, 2012, from http://www.mediapost.com/publications/?fa=Articles.showArticle&art_aid=122775.

2

Gaining Competitive Advantage Through Information Systems

After reading this chapter, you will be able to do the following:

1. Discuss how information systems can be used for automation, organizational learning, and strategic advantage.

2. Describe international business and IS strategies used by companies operating in the digital world.

3. Explain why and how companies are continually looking for innovative ways to use information systems for competitive advantage.

4. Describe freeconomics and how organizations can leverage digital technologies to provide free goods and services to customers as a business strategy for gaining a competitive advantage.

Preview

This chapter examines how organizations can use information systems (IS) strategically, enabling them to gain or sustain competitive advantage over their rivals. As described in Chapter 1, "Managing in the Digital World," a firm has competitive advantage over rival firms when it can do something better, faster, more economically, or uniquely. In this chapter, we begin by examining the role of information systems at different levels of the organization. We then examine international business strategies that shape how information systems can be designed to support how data and controls flow across national borders. Finally, we talk about the continual need to find innovative ways to succeed with and through information systems.

Managing in the Digital World:
The Business of Merging "Groups" and "Coupons"

When formulating a business model, we typically strive to create a self-sustaining business which, of course, is done by generating sufficient revenue, followed by at least some profit. For example, a humble coffee shop owner provides feel-at-home service and good coffee to customers. In turn, customers pay for this service, and if they feel cozy enough to come back, revenue exceeds the cost of operation, resulting in a profit. Now, push the warm smell of coffee aside and imagine how information systems have applied, changed, and reinvented the idea of business models in today's world.

It comes as no surprise that the Internet has not only helped advance traditional business models, but also enabled entirely new kinds of business models, innovative, diverse, and no longer confined to traditional notions of business models. Some examples include virtual merchants like Amazon.com or so-called click and mortar merchants that maintain both virtual and traditional physical stores, such as Barnes & Noble. There is also the manufacturer-direct model that has been effectively deployed by Dell. And, of course, there is the auction broker model which immediately pin-points eBay. The Web appears more flexible than real-life society in so many ways, changing how we communicate with friends and family, changing how we work, and clearly changing the way we shop for products and services through the emergence of new business models. This flexibility is a catalyst to the creation of a seemingly endless array of new types of businesses or the reinvention of tried-and-true models of the past.

You may have heard of the concept called "network effect," which refers to the concept that the value of a network is proportional to its size (see Figure 2.1). For example, as more people use and share information on a social network such as Facebook, the network becomes more valuable. A similar concept, "economies of scale"—the idea that the average cost per unit falls as the scale of output increases—is applied by businesses in an attempt to drive down costs and increase profits through higher volume operations.

Consider combining both concepts in a new business model enabled through the power of the Internet. A highly popular Web site, Groupon, prompts consumers to get together with their friends and family, to shop in groups, and buy in volume, in order to benefit from higher discounts

from national and local businesses. Groupon's business model is to partner with established merchants looking to clear out seasonal stocks or excessive supply, or to work with newer businesses looking to build a customer base. Each day, for example, Groupon sends out an e-mail full of great deals about a variety of products and services to its growing list of subscribers (you can also visit the Groupon Web site when looking for a deal on a particular item, restaurant, or service). Groupon's business model helps partners ramp up their sales volume. Simply, as the sales volume increases, the cost per unit decreases, at least up to some point, for many types of merchants. This is where the "group" in Groupon comes in: a deal only goes through when a certain, predetermined number of Groupon subscribers sign up for it; once this number is reached, everyone who signed up for the deal enjoys the lower price. In essence, as sales volume per transaction increases, larger discounts can be provided by the seller. Groupon took the old-fashioned business model of using coupons to attract customers, marrying the network effects and economies of scale capabilities of the Internet to create a new and highly successful business model. How does Groupon make money? Acting as a deal broker, Groupon's sales team (Groupon's largest expense) negotiates deals with the merchants, and for every deal, Groupon takes a 40 percent share. Unfortunately, this business model can be easily copied.

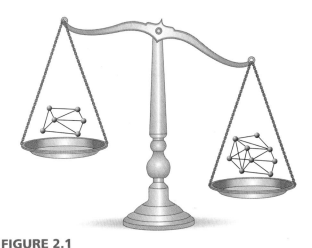

FIGURE 2.1

The Network Effect is central to many innovative business models.

If on a given day you find yourself craving a relaxation massage, you may be lucky and find a coupon at Groupon for US$40 (a 50 percent discount from the original price). The Groupon has already sold out? Don't worry, there are plenty of other sites potentially offering similar deals. Being an early player in the group buying market, and rapidly gaining market share, Groupon enjoyed a first-mover advantage, but due to its success, Groupon has been cloned and ripped off by numerous other "impersonators" around the globe. In 2010, the company decided to buy up its "clones" to reclaim its identity and, most importantly, fast-track its expansion into foreign markets in Europe and Asia. Thanks to the expansion facilitated by buying its "wannabe" clones, Groupon was quickly estimated to operate in 230 markets and 29 countries, having accumulated around 13 million subscribers.

However, the fast rising number of clones suggests that setting up another coupon site utilizing the same business model as Groupon is not that difficult, leaving Groupon rather vulnerable. Even though the company has attempted to buy up numerous potential clones, it has not been able keep up pace with the impostors. As of 2011, there were more than 500 similar sites worldwide with over 100 in the United States (e.g., check out LivingSocial.com); in the city of Hong Kong alone, there were already more than 20 group-buying sites available for browsing; in fact, daily deal aggregators have emerged as yet another business model, compiling deals from various group-buying sites. For merchants, the presence of other companies provides alternatives; like many consumers who shop on the Web, they too can choose whether Groupon or one of its competitors will provide the best deal. Groupon has never claimed or proved to carry the best deals, but is arguably the best known in this market space. So, while Groupon may have more customer traffic due to its better-known brand, other sites may bring in "enough" customers due to deeper discounts.

Unfortunately, Groupon's lack of uniqueness and inability to distinguish itself from others has so far resulted in a deficit of US$676.6 million by the end of 2011 (much of these losses were due to the cost of acquiring competitors). While it is certain that high-volume group couponing will continue to exist on the Internet, it is clear that the current instantiation of Groupon's business model does not provide a sustainable competitive advantage. Time will tell whether Groupon will be able to fine-tune its business model in order to have a lasting presence on the Web, or be another infamous Internet failure like Pets.com, Webvan.com, MVP.com, Kozmo.com, eToys.com, and countless others.

After reading this chapter, you will be able to answer the following:

1. How do information systems help organizations learn, automate, and improve their organizational strategies?

2. What are the sources of a competitive advantage?

3. What is a business model and its key components?

Based on:

Abdallah, M. (2011, December 5). Groupon's business model doomed to fail. *Seeking Alpha*. Retrieved June 11, 2012, from http://seekingalpha .com/article/311857-groupon-s-business-model-doomed-to-fail.

Anonymous. (n.d.). Top 10 Internet startup failures. *Marketing Mincfield*. Retrieved June 12, 2012, from http://www.marketingminefield.co.uk/ top-10-internet-startup-failures.

Mourdoukoutas, P. (2011, October 22). Is Groupon's business model sustainable? *Forbes*. Retrieved June 11, 2012, from http://www.forbes.com/sites/ panosmourdoukoutas/2011/10/22/is-groupons-business-model-sustainable.

Munarriz, R.A. (2012, February 9). Why Groupon will never be great again. *DailyFinance*. Retrieved June 14, 2012, from http://www.dailyfinance .com/2012/02/09/why-groupon-will-never-be-great-again.

Pan, J. (2012, February 17). Groupon Announces $30-per-year VIP program. *Mashable*. Retrieved June 11, 2012, from http://mashable .com/2012/02/17/groupon-vip-program.

Rappa, M. (2010, January 17). Business models on the Web. *Digitalenterprise.org*. Retrieved June 11, 2012, from http://digitalenterprise.org/ models/models.pdf.

Salmon, F. (2011, May 4). Grouponomics. *Reuters*. Retrieved June 11, 2012, from http://blogs.reuters.com/felix-salmon/2011/05/04/grouponomics.

http://goo.gl/9gnpG

ENABLING ORGANIZATIONAL STRATEGY THROUGH INFORMATION SYSTEMS

In Chapter 1, we introduced the notion that information systems can have strategic value to an organization. Because organizations are composed of different levels and functions, a broad range of information is needed to support an organization's business processes. **Business processes** are the activities organizations perform in order to reach their business goals, including core activities that transform inputs and produce outputs, and supporting activities that enable the core activities to take place. As a review, we briefly describe how organizations are generally structured as well as the common functional areas of most modern organizations. Understanding how organizations are structured helps to illustrate how different types of information systems can support various business processes and provide different levels of value to the organization.

FIGURE 2.2

Organizations are composed of different decision-making levels.

Organizational Decision-Making Levels

Every organization is composed of decision-making levels, as illustrated in Figure 2.2. Each level of an organization has different responsibilities and, therefore, different informational needs.

OPERATIONAL LEVEL. At the **operational level** of a firm, the routine, day-to-day business processes and interactions with customers occur. Information systems at this level are designed to automate repetitive activities, such as sales transaction processing, and to improve the efficiency of business processes at the customer interface. A **transaction** refers to anything that occurs as part of your daily business of which you must keep a record. Operational planning typically has a time frame of a few hours or days, and the managers at the operational level, such as foremen or supervisors, make day-to-day decisions that are highly structured and recurring. **Structured decisions** are those in which the procedures to follow for a given situation can be specified in advance. Because structured decisions are relatively straightforward, they can be programmed directly into operational information systems so that they can be made with little or no human intervention. For example, an inventory management system for a shoe store in the mall could keep track of inventory and issue an order for additional inventory when levels drop below a specified level. Operational managers within the store would simply need to confirm with the inventory management system that the order for additional shoes was needed. At the operational level, information systems are typically used to optimize processes and to better understand the underlying causes of any performance problems. Using information systems to optimize processes at the operational level can offer quick returns on the IS investment, as activities at this level are clearly delineated and well focused. Figure 2.3 summarizes the general characteristics of the operational level.

Who: Foremen and Supervisors

What: Automate Routine and Repetitive Activities and Events

Why: Improve Organizational Efficiency

FIGURE 2.3

Information systems at the operational level of an organization help to improve efficiency by automating routine and repetitive activities.

FIGURE 2.4

Information systems at
the managerial level of an
organization help to improve
effectiveness by automating the
monitoring and controlling of
operational activities.

MANAGERIAL/TACTICAL LEVEL. At the **managerial level** (or tactical level) of the organization, functional managers (e.g., marketing managers, finance managers, manufacturing managers, human resource managers, and so on) focus on monitoring and controlling operational-level activities and providing information to higher levels of the organization (see Figure 2.4). Managers at this level, referred to as midlevel managers, focus on effectively utilizing and deploying organizational resources to achieve the strategic objectives of the organization. Midlevel managers typically focus on problems within a specific business function, such as marketing or finance. Here, the scope of the decision usually is contained within the business function, is moderately complex, and has a time horizon of a few days to a few months (also referred to as tactical planning). For example, a marketing manager at Nike may decide how to allocate the advertising budget for the next business quarter or some other fixed time period.

Managerial-level decision making is not nearly as structured or routine as operational-level decision making. Managerial-level decision making is referred to as semistructured decision making because solutions and problems are not clear-cut and often require judgment and expertise. For **semistructured decisions**, some procedures to follow for a given situation can be specified in advance, but not to the extent where a specific recommendation can be made. For example, an information system could provide a production manager at Nike with performance analytics and forecasts about sales for multiple product lines, inventory levels, and overall production capacity. The metrics deemed most critical to assessing progress toward a certain goal (referred to as **key performance indicators [KPIs]**) are displayed on performance *dashboards* (described later in Chapter 6, "Enhancing Business Intelligence Using Information Systems"). The manager could use this information to create multiple hypothetical production schedules. With these schedules, the manager could then perform predictive analyses to examine inventory levels and potential sales profitability, depending on the order in which manufacturing resources were used to produce each type of product.

EXECUTIVE/STRATEGIC LEVEL. At the **executive level** (or strategic level) of the organization, managers focus on long-term strategic questions facing the organization, such as which products to produce, which countries to compete in, and what organizational strategy to follow (see Figure 2.5). Below we will examine various strategic decisions that executives need to address. Managers at this level include the president and chief executive officer, vice presidents, and possibly the board of directors; they are referred to as "executives." Executive-level decisions deal with complex problems with broad and long-term ramifications for the organization. Executive-level decisions are referred to as unstructured decisions because the problems are relatively complex and non-routine. In addition, executives must consider the ramifications of their decisions in terms of the overall organization. For **unstructured decisions**, few or no procedures to follow for a given situation can be specified in advance. For example, top managers may decide to develop a new product or discontinue an existing one. Such a decision may have vast, long-term effects on the organization's levels of employment and profitability. To assist

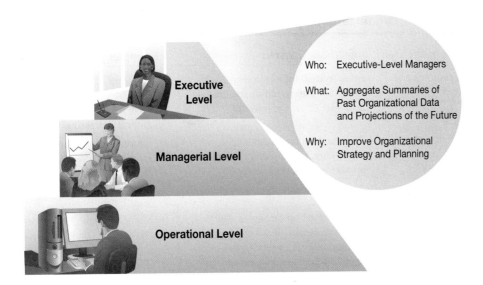

FIGURE 2.5

Information systems at the executive level of an organization help to improve strategy and planning by providing summaries of past data and projections of the future.

executive-level decision making, information systems are used to obtain aggregate summaries of trends and projections of the future. At the executive level, information systems provide KPIs that are focused on balancing performance across the organization, such that, for example, product launches are staggered to smooth out the effects of spikes in demand on the supply chain. Other KPIs are used to benchmark the organization's performance against its competitors.

In summary, most organizations have three general decision-making levels: operational, managerial, and executive. Each level has unique activities and business processes, each requiring different types of information. In other words, it is common that each decision-making level is supported by different types of information systems.

Organizational Functional Areas

In addition to different decision-making levels within an organization, there are also different functional areas. A functional area represents a discrete area of an organization that focuses on a specific set of activities. For example, people in the marketing function focus on the activities that promote the organization and its products in a way that attracts and retains customers; people in the accounting and finance functions focus on managing and controlling capital assets and financial resources of the organization. Table 2.1 lists various organizational functions and lists examples of the types of information systems that are commonly used. These **functional area information systems** are designed to support the unique business processes of specific functional areas (see Figure 2.6).

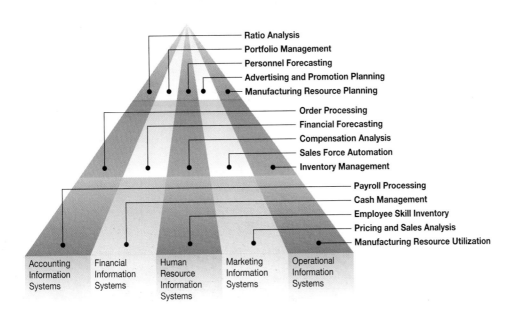

FIGURE 2.6

Business processes supported by various functional area information systems.

TABLE 2.1 Organizational Functions and Representative Information Systems

Functional Area	Information System	Examples of Typical Systems
Accounting and finance	Systems used for managing, controlling, and auditing the financial resources of the organization	• Accounts payable • Expense accounts • Cash management • Payroll processing
Human resources	Systems used for managing, controlling, and auditing the human resources of the organization	• Recruiting and hiring • Education and training • Benefits management • Employee termination • Workforce planning
Marketing	Systems used for managing new product development, distribution, pricing, promotional effectiveness, and sales forecasting of the products and services offered by the organization	• Market research and analysis • New product development • Promotion and advertising • Pricing and sales analysis • Product location analysis
Production and operations	Systems used for managing, controlling, and auditing the production and operations resources of the organization	• Inventory management • Cost and quality tracking • Materials and resource planning • Customer service tracking • Customer problem tracking • Job costing • Resource utilization

When deploying information systems across organizational levels and functions, there are three general ways the information system can provide value: to automate, to learn, and to execute organizational strategy (see Figure 2.7). These three ways are not necessarily mutually exclusive, but we believe that each is progressively more useful to the firm and thus adds more value to the business. This is examined next.

Information Systems for Automating: Doing Things Faster

Someone with an **automating** perspective thinks of technology as a way to help complete a task within an organization faster, more cheaply, and perhaps with greater accuracy and/or consistency. Let us look at a typical example. A person with an automating mentality would take a loan application screening process and automate it by inputting the loan applications into a computer database so that those involved in decision making for the loans could process the applications faster, more easily, and with fewer errors. Such a system might also enable customers to complete the loan application online. A transition from a manual to an automated loan application process might enable the organization to deploy employees more efficiently, leading to even more cost savings (see Table 2.2). Information systems at the operational level of an organization often help in automating repetitive activities, but they can also help to gather valuable information for higher decision-making levels within the organization.

FIGURE 2.7

The business value added from automating, learning, and strategizing with information systems.

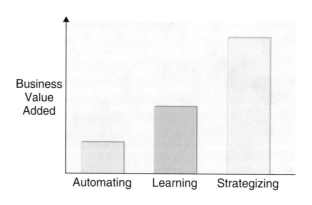

TABLE 2.2   Activities Involved Under Three Different Loan Application Processes and the Average Time for Each Activity

Primary Activities of Loan Processing	Manual Loan Process (Time)	Technology-Supported Process (Time)	Fully Automated Process (Time)
1. Complete and submit loan application	Customer takes the application home, completes it, and returns it (1.5 days)	Customer takes the application home, completes it, and returns it (1.5 days)	Customer fills out application from home via the Web (15 minutes)
2. Check application for errors	Employee does this in batches (2.5 days)	Employee does this in batches (2.5 days)	Computer does this as it is being completed (3.5 seconds)
3. Input data from application into the information system	Applications are kept in paper form, although there is handling time involved (1 hour)	Employee does this in batches (2.5 days)	Done as part of the online application process (no extra time needed)
4. Assess loan applications under $250,000 to determine whether to fund them	Employee does this completely by hand (15 days)	Employee does this with the help of the computer (1 hour)	Computer does this automatically (1 second)
5. Committee decides on any loan over $250,000	(15 days)	(15 days)	(15 days)
6. Applicant notified	Employee generates letters manually in batches (1 week)	Employee generates letters with the help of a computer (1 day)	System notifies applicant via e-mail (3.5 seconds)
Total time	Anywhere from 25 to 40 days, depending on size of loan	Anywhere from 5 to 20 days, depending on size of loan	Anywhere from 15 minutes to 15 days, depending on size of loan

Many online loan application services can now give you instant "tentative" approval pending verification of data you report in your online application. Also, only some of the activities within the manual and technology-supported processes can occur in parallel.

Information Systems for Organizational Learning: Doing Things Better

We can also use information systems to learn and improve. By analyzing information created when automating a process, improved understanding about the underlying work processes can be developed. The learning mentality builds on the automating mentality because it recognizes that information systems can be used as a vehicle for **organizational learning**—the ability of an organization to use past behavior and information to improve its business processes—and for change as well as for automation.

To illustrate a learning mentality, let us think again about our loan processing example. Figure 2.8 shows how a computer-based loan processing system tracks types of loan applications by date, month, and season. The manager easily sees the trends and can plan for the timely staffing and training of personnel in the loan department. The manager can also more efficiently manage the funds used to fulfill loans. This computer-based loan processing system, focusing on learning, is an example of an information system used at the managerial level of an organization.

A learning approach allows managers to track and learn about the types of applications filed by certain types of people at certain times of the year (e.g., more auto loan applications in the

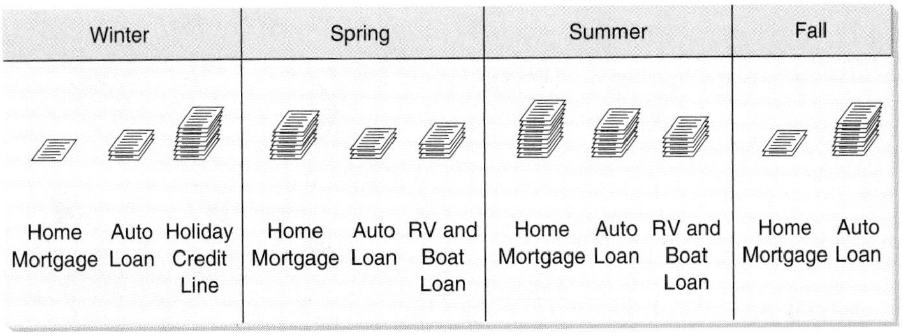

Winter	Spring	Summer	Fall
Home Mortgage Auto Loan Holiday Credit Line	Home Mortgage Auto Loan RV and Boat Loan	Home Mortgage Auto Loan RV and Boat Loan	Home Mortgage Auto Loan

FIGURE 2.8

A computer-based loan processing system enables the bank manager to identify trends in loan applications.

fall, mostly from men in their twenties and thirties), the patterns of the loan decisions made, or the subsequent performance of those loans. This new system creates data about the underlying business process that can be used to better monitor, control, and change that process. In other words, you *learn* from this information system about loan applications and approvals; as a result, you can do a better job at evaluating loan applications.

A combined automating and learning approach, in the long run, is more effective than an automating approach alone. If the underlying business process supported by technology is inherently flawed, a learning use of the technology might help you detect problems with the process and change it. For instance, in our loan processing example, a learning use of technology may help us uncover a pattern among the accepted loans that enables us to distinguish between low- and high-performing loans over their lives and subsequently to change the criteria for loan acceptance.

If, however, the underlying business process is bad and you are using technology only for automating (i.e., you would not uncover the data that would tell you this process is bad), you are more likely to continue with a flawed or less-than-optimal business process. In fact, such an automating use of technology may mask the process problems.

With a bad underlying set of loan acceptance criteria (e.g., rules that would allow you to approve a loan for someone who had a high level of debt as long as they had not been late on any payments recently), a person might manually review four applications in a day and, because of the problematic criteria used, inadvertently accept on average two "bad" applications per week. If you automated the same faulty process, with no learning aspects built in, the system might help a person review 12 applications per day, with six "bad" applications accepted per week on average. The technology would serve only to magnify the existing business problems (see Figure 2.9). Without learning, it is more difficult to uncover bad business processes underlying the information system.

Information Systems for Supporting Strategy: Doing Things Smarter

Using information systems to automate or improve processes has advantages, as described previously. In most cases, however, the best way to use an information system is to support the organization's strategy in a way that enables the firm to gain or sustain competitive advantage over rivals. To understand why, think about **organizational strategy**—a firm's plan to accomplish its mission and goals as well as to gain or sustain competitive advantage over rivals—and how it relates to information systems. When senior managers—at the executive level of the organization—conduct **strategic planning**, they form a vision of where the organization needs to head, convert that vision into measurable objectives and performance targets, and craft a strategy to achieve the desired results. In Figure 2.10, we show some common organizational strategies. An organization might decide to pursue a **low-cost leadership strategy**, as does Walmart, by which it offers the best prices in its industry on its goods and/or services. Alternatively, an organization might decide to pursue a **differentiation strategy**, as do Porsche, Nordstrom, and IBM, by which it tries to provide better products or services than its competitors. A company might aim that differentiation broadly at many different types of consumers, or it might focus on a particular segment of consumers, as Apple did for many years with its focus on high-quality computers for home and educational markets. Still other organizations might pursue a middle-of-the-road strategy, following a **best-cost provider strategy**, offering products or services of reasonably good quality at competitive prices, as does Dell.

FIGURE 2.9

Automating a loan processing system requires sound underlying business processes or errors will rapidly increase.

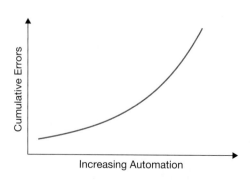

Cumulative Errors

Increasing Automation

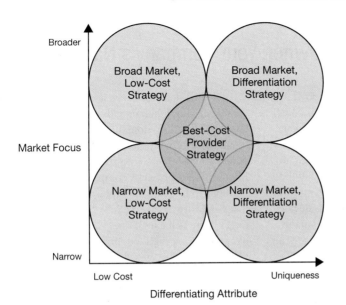

FIGURE 2.10

Five general types of organizational strategy: broad differentiation, focused differentiation, focused low-cost leadership, overall low-cost leadership, and best-cost provider.

A person with a strategic mentality toward information systems goes beyond mere automating and learning and instead tries to find ways to use information systems to achieve the organization's chosen strategy. This individual wants the benefits of automating and learning but also looks for some strategic, competitive advantage from the system. In fact, in today's business environment, if a proposed information system isn't going to clearly deliver some strategic value (i.e., help to improve the business so that it can compete better) while also helping people to work smarter and save money in the process, then it isn't likely to be funded.

Sources of Competitive Advantage

How do business firms typically get a competitive advantage? An organization has competitive advantage whenever it has an edge over rivals in attracting customers and defending against competitive forces (Porter, 1985, 2001). In order to be successful, a business must have a clear vision, one that focuses investments in resources such as information systems and technologies to help achieve a competitive advantage. Some sources of competitive advantage include the following (see Figure 2.11):

- Being the first to enter a market (i.e., having a **first mover advantage**)
- Having the best-made product on the market
- Delivering superior customer service
- Achieving lower costs than rivals
- Having a proprietary manufacturing technology, formula, or algorithm
- Having shorter lead times in developing and testing new products
- Having a well-known brand name and reputation
- Giving customers more value for their money

FIGURE 2.11

Sources of competitive advantage.

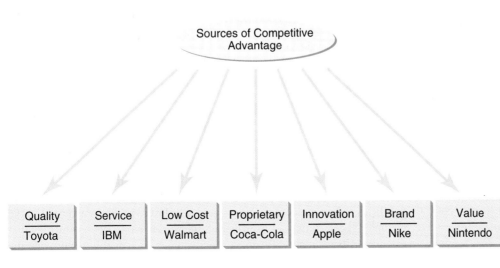

BRIEF CASE — For Sale By Owner: Your Company's Name.com

They don't sell houses or land, but they do deal in Internet real estate, and most turn a handsome profit. "They" are called domainers, and the real estate they buy and sell consists of domain names on the Web (such as www.candy.com). Although they keep a low profile and usually don't flaunt their success, domainers participated in a virtual land grab worth US$23 billion in 2009, with no end in sight. In January 2012, there were over 220 million registered domain names. Recently, it was decided to allow various other so-called "generic top level domains," such as .cola, .google, .auto, and so on, giving domainers an even larger market (see Chapter 3 for more on domain names).

As you know, every Web site has a domain name, also called a Uniform Resource Locator (URL), or Web address. For large companies such as Amazon.com, the domain name is an extremely valuable asset, as it clearly identifies the owner of the Web site. In 2012, for example, "PrivateJet.com" sold for US$30 million!

Domainers trade on the fact that many businesses, organizations, and celebrities want domain names for their Web sites that clearly identify the site's owner and are, therefore, easy for Web surfers to find. A domainer might buy the domain name "fordmotorcompany.com," for instance, and then try to sell it to the Ford Motor Company; that is exactly how the domain-buying business operated in the 1990s: buy a name, hold it, and wait for a buyer who wanted it to make an offer. But when pay-per-click advertising was developed, the game changed. Currently, domainers can profit most by renting advertising space on the domain names they hold to marketers. Here is how the domainer makes his or her profit from renting ad space:

1. Buy and hold a general domain name, such as "candy .com" or "cellphones.com." Alternatively, domainers buy domain names that represent common misspellings of popular domains (such as amazo.com), hoping to benefit from Web surfers' typos.
2. Direct Web traffic to a middleman, called an aggregator, who designs a Web site and then taps into Yahoo!, Google, or Microsoft's advertising networks and lists the best-paying clients. When a searcher enters the domain name, such as "cellphone.com," the "cellphone.com" Web page comes up with a list of cell phone Web site URLs.
3. Each time a searcher clicks on one of the URLs listed on the domain name's page, the search engine owner (Yahoo!, Google, or Microsoft) or advertiser pays the domainer a fee.

Renting domain names is a secondary market for domainers that can bring in hundreds of dollars per day. So, rather than buying and selling domain names, many domainers purchase hundreds of domain names. Then, they market these catchy names to customers who pay a monthly or annual fee, much like renting a physical company storefront in a commercial building. While domain rental is a fairly established business, many industry experts believe this to be a bad deal for the customer. Here is the big issue. When you rent, you don't own the name. Imagine that you are renting a domain name and your business is rapidly growing. At some point, the domain owner decides to either increase your rent, or worse yet, take back the domain name to sell or develop another business on the site you have developed. Given that buying a domain name outright isn't very expensive, most experts suggest the best and safest deal is to buy your own domain name rather than rent.

In March 2008, the U.S. Congress proposed the Anti-Phishing Consumer Protection Act, but this bill has stalled. In addition to fighting phishing, the bill was intended to levy heavy fines on domainers that violated company trademarks. While formal legislation has stalled, some actions have been taken to curb domainers. For instance, a number of large international corporations including Dell, DIRECTV, Hilton, Nike, and Wells Fargo joined together and formed the Coalition Against Domain Name Abuse, Inc. (CADNA), which aims to build awareness and stop this practice.

Questions:
1. How do you feel about domainers? Is it an ethical business?
2. Discuss the pros and cons of having Google, Yahoo!, Bing, and others "cut out" domainers as middlemen in the Web search process.

Based on:

Anonymous. (2012). CADNA—The Coalition Against Domain Name Abuse. Retrieved June 10, 2012, from http://www.cadna.org.

Anonymous. (2012). Internet 2011 in numbers. *Pingdom.com*. Retrieved June 10, 2012, from http://royal.pingdom.com/2012/01/17/internet-2011-in-numbers.

Shontell, A. (2011, May 3). The 20 most expensive domain names of all time. *Business Insider.com*. Retrieved June 10, 2012, from http://www.businessinsider .com/the-20-most-expensive-domain-names-urls-2011-4.

Sloan, P. (2005, December 1). Masters of their domains. *CNN Money.com*. Retrieved June 10, 2012, from http://money.cnn.com/magazines/business2/ business2_archive/2005/12/01/8364591/index.htm.

To develop and sustain a competitive advantage, organizations must have resources and/or capabilities that are superior to their competitors. **Resources** reflect the organization's specific assets that are utilized to create cost or product differentiation from their competitors. Examples of resources might include proprietary technology, brand equity, or a loyal and established customer base. **Capabilities** reflect the organization's ability to leverage these resources in the marketplace. For example, speed to market or efficient operations could be capabilities that help a firm effectively utilize its resources. Together, the resources and capabilities provide the

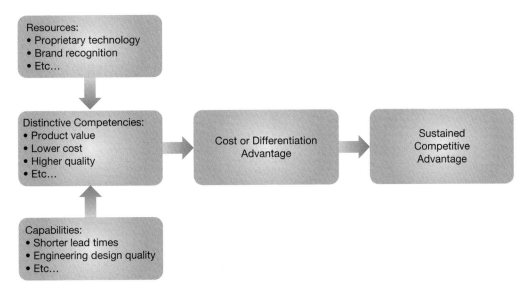

FIGURE 2.12

Distinctive competencies lead to value creation and a sustained competitive advantage.

Source: Based on http://www .quickmba.com/strategy/competitive-advantage.

organization with **distinctive competencies**—such as innovation, agility, quality, or low cost—in the marketplace. These competencies help to pursue the organizational strategy (i.e., low-cost leadership, differentiation, etc.) and make your product valuable to your customers relative to your competitors; superior **value creation** occurs when an organization can provide products at a lower cost or with superior (differentiated) benefits to the customer (see Figure 2.12). This is how organizations gain a competitive advantage.

Companies can gain or sustain each of these sources of competitive advantage by effectively using information systems. Returning to our loan example, a person with a strategic view of information systems would choose a computer-based loan application process because it can help achieve the organization's strategic plan to process loan applications faster and better than rivals and to improve the selection criteria for loans. This process and the supporting information system add value to the organization and match the organization's strategy. It is, therefore, essential to the long-term survival of the organization. If, on the other hand, managers determine that the organization's strategy is to grow and generate new products and services, the computer-based loan application process and the underlying system might not be an efficient, effective use of resources, even though the system could provide automating and learning benefits.

Identifying *Where* to Compete: Analyzing Competitive Forces

Organizations struggle with identifying the best uses of their resources to execute their strategy. Given that every industry is different, organizations can better understand where to focus their resources by analyzing the competitive forces within their industry. One framework often used to analyze the competition within an industry is Porter's (1979) notion of the five primary competitive forces: (1) the rivalry among competing sellers in your industry, (2) the threat of potential new entrants into your industry, (3) the bargaining power that customers have within your industry, (4) the bargaining power that suppliers have within your industry, and (5) the potential for substitute products from other industries (see Figure 2.13). Table 2.3 provides examples of how information systems can have an impact on the various competitive forces in an industry. Porter's five-forces model of competition can help you determine which specific technologies will be more or less useful, depending on the nature of your industry. You can then use this knowledge as the basis for identifying particular investments.

Identifying *How* to Compete: Analyzing the Value Chain

Managers use value chain analysis to identify opportunities where information systems can be used to develop a competitive advantage (Porter, 1985, 2001; Shank & Govindarajan, 1993). Think of an organization as a big input/output process. At one end, supplies are purchased and brought into the organization (see Figure 2.14). The organization integrates those supplies to create products and services that it markets, sells, and then distributes to customers. The organization provides customer service after the sale of these products and services. Throughout this process, opportunities arise for employees to add value to the product or service by acquiring

FIGURE 2.13

Five forces influence the level of
competitiveness in an industry.

FIGURE 2.14

A sample generic organizational
value chain.

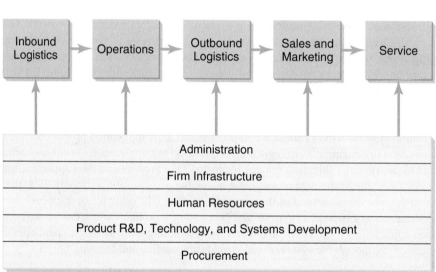

TABLE 2.3   Use of IS to Combat Competitive Forces

Competitive Force	Implication for Firm	Potential Use of Information Systems to Combat Competitive Force
Traditional rivals within your industry	Competition in price, product distribution, and service	Implement enterprise resource planning system to reduce costs and be able to act and react more quickly; implement Web site to offer better service to customers.
Threat of new entrants into your market	Increased capacity in the industry, reduced prices, and decreased market share	Improve Web site to reach customers and differentiate product; use inventory control system to lower costs and better manage excess capacity.
Customers' bargaining power	Reduced prices, need for increased quality, and demand for more services	Implement customer relationship management system to serve customers better; implement computer-aided design and/or computer-aided manufacturing system to improve product quality.
Suppliers' bargaining power	Increased costs and reduced quality	Use Internet to establish closer electronic ties with suppliers and to create relationships with new suppliers located far away.
Threat of substitute products from other industries	Potential returns on products, decreased market share, and losing customers for life	Use decision support system and customer purchase database to better assess trends and customer needs; use computer-aided design systems to redesign products.

Source: Based on Applegate, Austin, & Soule (2009).

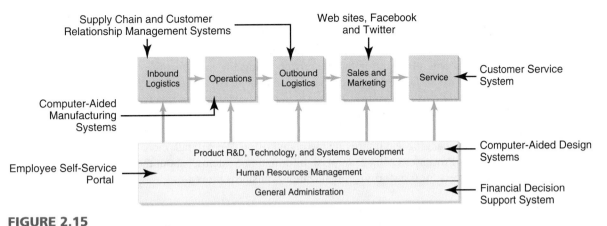

FIGURE 2.15

Information systems can improve an organization's value chain.

supplies in a more effective manner, improving products, and selling more products. This set of activities that add value throughout the organization is known as the **value chain** within an organization.

Value chain analysis is the process of analyzing an organization's activities to determine where value is added to products and/or services and what costs are incurred for doing so. Because information systems can automate many activities along the value chain, value chain analysis has become a popular tool for applying information systems for competitive advantage. In value chain analysis, you first draw the value chain for your organization by fleshing out each of the activities, functions, and processes where value is or should be added. Next, you determine the costs—and the factors that drive costs or cause them to fluctuate—within each of the areas in your value chain diagram. You then benchmark (compare) your value chain and associated costs with those of your competitors. You can then make changes and improvements in your value chain to either gain or sustain competitive advantage.

The Role of Information Systems in Value Chain Analysis

The use of information systems has become one of the primary ways that organizations improve their value chains. In Figure 2.15, we show a sample value chain and some ways that information systems can improve productivity within it. For example, many organizations use the Internet to connect businesses with one another electronically so that they can exchange orders, invoices, and receipts online in real-time. Using the Internet has become a popular method for improving the front end of the organizational value chain. In fact, many firms now use the Internet for such business-to-business interactions; these systems are described in greater detail in Chapter 8, "Strengthening Business-to-Business Relationships Via Supply Chain and Customer Relationship Management."

The Technology/Strategy Fit

You might be asking, if any information system helps do things faster and better and helps save money, who cares whether it matches the company's strategy? Good question. If money grew on trees, you probably would build and use just about every information system you could imagine. Organizations could build or acquire many different valuable systems, but they are constrained by time and money to build or acquire only those that add the most value: those that help automate and learn as well as have strategic value. In other words, organizations are trying to maximize **business/IT alignment**, and in most cases, you do not want systems that do not match the strategy, even if they offer automating and learning benefits. Further, while spending on information systems is rising, most companies are willing to spend money on projects only when they can see clear, significant value. Often, however, organizations have no choice in making some types of investments that may or may not coincide with their overall strategy. Such investments are called a **strategic necessity**—something the organization must do in order to survive.

Given this focus on the value that the system will add, you probably do not want a system that helps differentiate your products based on high quality when the organizational strategy is to be the overall industry low-cost leader. In other words, if a firm were pursuing a strategy for low-cost leadership, investments to help drive costs down would be valued over those that didn't. In Chapter 3, "Managing the Information Systems Infrastructure and Services," we introduce various technologies, infrastructures, and services that can help to support an organization's competitive strategy.

We should also caution that merely choosing and implementing an emerging information system is not sufficient to gain or sustain competitive advantage. In any significant IS implementation, there must be commensurate, significant organizational change. This typically comes in the form of *business process management* and other similar methods of improving the functioning of the organization, as opposed to merely dropping in an information system with no attempts at changing and improving the organization. We will talk more in Chapter 7, "Enhancing Business Processes Using Enterprise Information Systems," about the role of business process management for transforming organizational business processes.

Assessing Value for the IS Infrastructure

As you will read in Chapter 3, the IS infrastructure is a complex collection of technologies and capabilities that helps an organization execute its competitive strategy. While the infrastructure is critical and expensive to acquire and maintain, assessing its value, or some specific aspects of it, can be quite challenging. Depending on how an organization chooses to compete in its industry, different methods of assessing value may be warranted. Four possible approaches for assessing this value are discussed next (see Chapter 9, "Developing and Acquiring Information Systems", for more on assessing the value of IS investments).

ECONOMIC VALUE. First, economic value is the contribution an investment makes toward improving the infrastructure's ability to enhance the profitability of the business. To calculate such enhancements, you need to choose important business metrics in order to gauge the economic value of a given investment. An airline, for example, might use a metric such as revenue per passenger mile to determine effectiveness. To assess an investment, the airline could then calculate the IS infrastructure cost per passenger mile and observe how investments in the infrastructure over time have an impact on profitability.

ARCHITECTURAL VALUE. Second, architectural value can be derived from an investment's ability to extend the infrastructure's capabilities to meet business needs today and in the future. To measure architectural value, "before-and-after" assessments of infrastructure characteristics such as interoperability, portability, scalability, recoverability, and compatibility can be taken. Such assessments can be taken for each area of the business, where various infrastructure characteristics are rated on a scale of 1–10 as to how well various investments influence the infrastructure's ability to meet those needs.

OPERATIONAL VALUE. Third, operational value is derived from assessing an investment's impact on enabling the infrastructure to better meet business processing requirements. To assess this, you could measure the impact of not investing in a particular project. For example, what would be the cost of not investing in a new customer relationship management system in terms of lost staff productivity, lost business revenue, or even lost customers?

REGULATORY AND COMPLIANCE VALUE. Fourth, regulatory and compliance value is derived from assessing the extent to which an investment helps to meet requirements for control, security, and integrity as required by a governing body or a key customer. For example, what is the impact of, say, noncompliance with government reporting requirements necessitated by the Sarbanes-Oxley Act?

Finally, where possible, all evaluation measures should be compared with external benchmarks such as industry averages or your key competitors. In any event, these provide a useful framework for more broadly evaluating a particular investment.

Putting It All Together: Developing a Successful Business Model

We have examined how organizations can leverage technology investments faster, smarter, and more strategically. We also examined how to focus technology investments toward activities that provide competitive advantage and improve the performance of their value chain. Taken together, organizations need to align their technology investments with their business model. A **business model** is a summary of a business's strategic direction that outlines how the objectives will be achieved; a business model specifies how a company will create, deliver, and capture value (Osterwalder and Pigneur, 2010) and identifies its customer segments, value propositions, channels, customer relationships, revenue streams, key resources, key activities, key partners, and cost structure. In other words, a business model reflects the following:

1. What does a company do?
2. How does a company uniquely do it?
3. In what way (or ways) does the company get paid for doing it?
4. What are the key resources and activities needed?
5. What are the costs involved?

How a company answers these questions dictates how and where information systems investments can be utilized to execute a competitive strategy and sustain an advantage over competitors. There are several components of a proper business model (see Table 2.4). Each component plays a critical role in shaping all aspects of the business, including such factors as the expenses, revenues, operating strategies, corporate structure, and sales and marketing procedures. Generally speaking, anything that has to do with the day-to-day functioning of the organization is part of its business model. Perhaps the most important ingredient for any organization is determining how to generate revenue. A **revenue model** describes how the firm will earn revenue, generate profits, and produce a superior return on invested capital (even non-profit organizations need a revenue model). Information systems can be utilized to support and execute many aspects of your business model.

Changing Mind-Sets About Information Systems

One of the most significant changes in the IS field has been a change in mind-sets about technology. The old way for managers to think about information systems was that information systems were a necessary service, a necessary evil, and a necessary, distasteful expense that was to be minimized. Managers cannot afford to think this way anymore. Successful managers now think of information systems as a competitive asset to be nurtured and invested in. This does not mean

TABLE 2.4   Components of a Business Model

Component	Description	Questions to Ask
Customer segments	The customers targeted with the product/service offering	Who will be our target customers? Who are the most important customers?
Value proposition	The utility that the product/service has to offer to customers	Why do customers need our product/service? What problems will our product/service solve? Why would customers choose our product/service over our competitor's product/service?
Channels	The ways in which the product/service offerings reach the target customers	How will our customers be reached? Which channels are best in terms of cost and convenience for the customers?
Customer relationships	The relationships formed with the target customers	What types of relationships do we build with our customers? How do we maintain these relationships?
Revenue streams	The way a firm generates income	How do we generate income? What are we selling? What are customers willing to pay for?
Key resources	The most important assets needed to make the business model work	What key resources are needed to enable our value proposition, channels, customer relationships, and revenue streams?
Key activities	The most important activities needed to make the business model work	What key activities are needed to enable our value proposition, channels, customer relationships, and revenue streams?
Key partners	The network of partners and suppliers needed to make the business model work	Who are our key partners and suppliers? What resources do they offer, and what activities do they perform?
Cost structure	The costs incurred when operating the business model	What are the costs incurred when operating the business model? Which resources and activities are most expensive?

Source: Based on Osterwalder & Pigneur (2010).

that managers should not require a sound business case for every IS investment. Nor does this mean that managers need not base the business case for a system on solid facts (see Chapter 9). It does mean, however, that managers must stop thinking about systems as an expense and start thinking about systems as an asset to invest in wisely. Managers have to become strategic about information systems and have to think of them as an enabler of opportunities and mechanism for supporting or executing their business model.

http://goo.gl/vLRNb

INTERNATIONAL BUSINESS STRATEGIES IN THE DIGITAL WORLD

Before the era of globalization, most companies were solely operating in the domestic arena, conducting their activities exclusively in one country, starting from the acquisition of raw materials to the selling of final products. Although such businesses are likely to benefit from the enablers that also spurred globalization (see Chapter 1), many **domestic companies** also feel some negative effects brought about by globalization.

In today's digital world, the number of exclusively domestic companies is continually shrinking, with most domestic companies being relatively small (often local) businesses, such as local service providers, restaurants, farms, or independent grocery stores (and even those have international customers, suppliers, or products). Most of today's large companies, no matter if they are in car manufacturing (such as GM, Toyota, or Daimler), insurance (Allianz or Munich Re), or consumer goods (Nestlé or Procter & Gamble), have some **international business strategy** for competing in different global markets.

Such companies pursue either a home replication, multidomestic, global, or transnational strategy, depending on the degree of supply chain integration and necessary local customer responsiveness (Hitt, Ireland, & Hoskisson, 2013; Prahalad & Doz, 1987). On the one hand, businesses strive for global integration to realize economies of scale; on the other hand, a company's local subunits may benefit strongly from being able to quickly respond to changing conditions in local markets. Different international business strategies are suited better for different situations (see Figure 2.16 and Table 2.5).

Organizations use a variety of business strategies to manage international operations most effectively. For example, Nestlé, one of the world's largest food producers, with over 500 factories and operations in more than 70 countries, uses a transnational business strategy, supported by multiple distributed systems and Internet-enabled applications. For most organizations, the decision on which international business strategy to pursue is to a large extent determined by their **administrative heritage**, that is, the corporate culture that has evolved in the environment of the firm's home country. In the following sections, we describe each of these various business strategies, along with the appropriate IS strategies.

Home-Replication Strategy

The **home-replication strategy** (sometimes called export strategy or just international strategy) is the most basic form of going global. Companies using this strategy view international operations as secondary to their home operations. Thus, companies pursuing a home-replication

FIGURE 2.16

International business strategies.

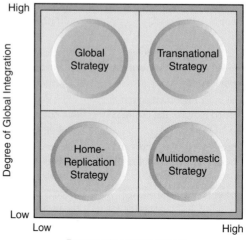

TABLE 2.5   When to Use International Business Strategies

Strategy	Description	Strengths	Weaknesses	When to Use
Home replication	International business seen as extension of home business	Focus on core competencies in home market	Inability to react to local market conditions	Homogeneous markets
Global	Centralized organization with standardized offerings across markets	Standardized product offerings allow achieving economies of scale	Inability to react to local market conditions	Homogeneous markets
Multidomestic	Federation of associated business units; decentralized	Ability to quickly react to local conditions	Differing product offerings limit economies of scale, and limited interunit communication limits knowledge sharing	Very heterogeneous markets
Transnational	Some aspects centralized, others decentralized; integrated network	Can achieve benefits of multidomestic and global strategies	Difficult to manage; very complex	Integrated global markets

WHEN THINGS GO WRONG

The Pains of Miscalculating Groupon

For customers and businesses alike, the Groupon coupon service is certainly a hot attraction. Imagine a perfect outcome where business owners boost profits and satisfy a vast number of new customers. A recent study, however, revealed that this doesn't always happen. Out of the 150 small-to-midsize businesses surveyed by Rice University in 2010, 32 percent found using Groupon unprofitable and 40 percent swore to never again use the service. So, what is the problem?

The buying frenzy that may result from coupon purchases is a tricky matter that should not be underestimated. For instance, judging from the experience of an Oregon-based coffee shop called Posies Café, the owner eventually lost more than US$8,000, thanks to unexpected increases in customer volume and the stress of hiring additional manpower, from a Groupon-enabled tidal-wave of customers. Most small businesses are not capable of coping with a sudden flood of 10s, or even 100s, of new customers. Think of the logistics of juggling overwhelming customer traffic and associated service quality issues. In addition, if a deal offers a 50 percent discount, Groupon takes about a 40 percent share of the deal's price (the numbers depend on factors such as size of the deal), leaving the merchant with 30 percent of the original price. Many businesses forget (or are not advised) to cap the number of deals, so that they end up having more business than they can handle, and may not be able to limit the losses incurred. Thus, businesses that miscalculate the impact of a Groupon campaign usually end up either suffering huge losses or garnering a crushed reputation as service quality goes down the drain.

Aside from miscalculating the capacity of one's business to handle a rush of new clients, businesses often overestimate the long-term impact of a deal on the business. Many customers are looking for a one-time deal, and never visit the business afterwards (how often would you repeat that helicopter trip if you had to pay full price, or how often do you need Lasik eye surgery?). Thus, businesses are advised to make the most out of the publicity brought about by Groupon's coupon campaign. Instead of relying solely on the one-time increase of buyers, which does not always generate profits, business owners should use the opportunity to sell additional products to customers. Likewise, service-oriented businesses should consider offering incentives for customers to come back by signing up for additional appointments. E-mail addresses and other personal information should be collected for future promotional needs. If Groupon is perceived more as an advertising strategy that requires careful management, business owners may, after all, achieve the ends of boosting their reputation and generating enhanced revenue.

Based on:

Hall, J. (2011, November 22). Groupon demand almost finishes cupcake-maker. *The Telegraph*. Retrieved June 12, 2012, from http://www.telegraph.co.uk/finance/newsbysector/retailandconsumer/8904653/Groupon-demand-almost-finishes-cupcake-maker.html.

Purewal, S.J. (2010, December 5). Groupon nightmares (and how to avoid them). *PCWorld*. Retrieved June 12, 2012, from http://www.pcworld.com/businesscenter/article/212328/groupon_nightmares_and_how_to_avoid_them.html.

TABLE 2.6 International IS Strategies

Business Strategy	Systems	Communications	Data Resources
Home replication	Domestic systems (if any)	Limited (if any)	Local databases (if any)
Global	Centralized systems	Multiple networks between home office and subsidiaries	Data sharing between central home office and subsidiaries
Multidomestic	Decentralized systems	Direct communication between home office and subsidiaries	Local databases
Transnational	Distributed/shared systems; Internet-enabled applications	Enterprise-wide linkages	Common global data resources

Source: Based on Alavi & Young (1992), Karimi & Konsynski (1991), and Ramarapu & Lado (1995).

strategy focus on their domestic customers' needs and wants and merely export their products to generate additional sales. This allows companies to focus on their core competencies in their respective domestic markets. In some cases, selling products internationally is used as a way to extend the life of products nearing the end of their life cycles domestically (e.g., last year's tennis shoes may still be considered "hip" in some countries). As the company places only secondary emphasis on international operations, there is no expectation of obtaining additional knowledge from foreign operations. For example, it can be argued that German automaker Porsche pursues a home-replication strategy. Specifically, Porsche designs very high performance automobiles geared toward driving on German Autobahns (many of which have no speed limits); although this style of driving is almost impossible in most countries, Porsche sells their cars with the promise of high performance, making only minor modifications for local markets. With a home-replication strategy, the organization provides a relatively low level of local responsiveness and requires a relatively low level of global integration. As such, information systems play a minor role in facilitating this strategy (see Table 2.6).

Global Business Strategy

Companies pursuing a **global business strategy** attempt to achieve economies of scale by producing identical products in large quantities for a variety of different markets. In contrast to the home-replication strategy, where a product is developed for the home country and then exported (with little or no modifications), companies pursuing a global strategy (such as Sony) develop products for the global market.

A global business strategy works much more in a centralized fashion. As the decisions are made at the headquarters, the organization can be characterized as a centralized hub (Bartlett & Ghoshal, 1998). The headquarters gives the overall strategic direction and thus has tight control of the entire company as well as the knowledge that is generated within the company. However, the need to achieve economies of scale prohibits implementation of local strategies, and thus a global company cannot quickly react to local challenges and opportunities. Here, data flow extensively from the subsidiaries to the home location, and the home location exerts strong control on the subsidiaries (see Figure 2.17). As the home office coordinates most of the strategic decisions of the local subsidiaries, companies pursuing a global business strategy utilize multiple networks between the home office and the subsidiaries to facilitate both communication and data sharing. As the data do not stay at the local subsidiaries, the potential for duplication is reduced, but organizations have to consider issues related to transborder data flows (primarily in EU countries) (see Table 2.6).

Multidomestic Business Strategy

The **multidomestic business strategy** is particularly suited for operations in markets differing widely. The multidomestic business strategy uses a loose federation of associated business units, each of which is rather independent in their strategic decisions. In other words, the degree of integration is very low, and the individual subunits can respond quickly to their respective market

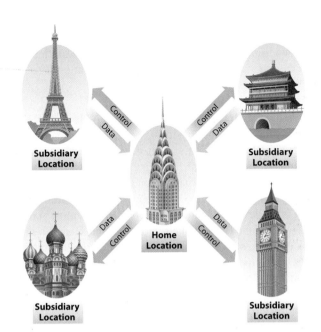

FIGURE 2.17
Global business strategy.

demands (Ghoshal, 1987). Multidomestic companies can thus be extremely flexible and responsive to the needs and demands of local markets, and any opportunities arising in local markets can be quickly seized. An example of a multidomestic company is the international arm of General Motors, the national subsidiaries of which produce cars that are customized to the specific local markets (e.g., Opel in Germany and Vauxhall in Great Britain). However, working in a decentralized fashion, much of the knowledge generated is retained at the local subsidiaries, and knowledge transfer between the individual subsidiaries is often limited, leading to inefficiencies and mistakes that potentially can be repeated across subsidiaries (Bartlett & Ghoshal, 1998). In sum, for companies following a multidomestic business strategy, very little data and control information flow between the home and subsidiary locations (see Figure 2.18).

In order to support the loose confederacy of various different local subsidiaries and the decentralized nature of the decision making within companies utilizing a multidomestic business strategy, each organizational subsidiary has its own decentralized information systems. Although the systems within the different business units may be integrated, there is no centralized IS infrastructure. The communications take place primarily between the different subsidiaries and the home office; thus, there is no focus on the communication between the different subsidiaries

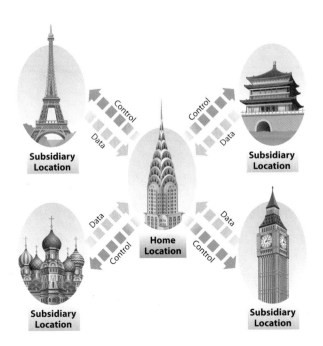

FIGURE 2.18
Multidomestic business strategy.

(this is why there is only limited knowledge transfer among the subsidiaries). As the different subsidiaries are very independent, they retain the decentralized local data processing centers that are responsive to local needs and regulations and at the same time use information technology to integrate them loosely into the framework of the parent organization (see Table 2.6).

Transnational Business Strategy

An emerging strategy is the **transnational business strategy**. Having realized the benefits and drawbacks of multidomestic and global business strategies, companies using a transnational business strategy selectively decide which aspects of the organization should be under central control and which should be decentralized. This business strategy allows companies to leverage the flexibility offered by a decentralized organization (to be more responsive to local conditions) while at the same time reaping economies of scale enjoyed by centralization. An example of a transnational company is Unilever, which decides when to centralize and when to decentralize, depending on the products and the local markets. However, this business strategy is also the most difficult, as the company has to strike a balance between centralization and decentralization. In contrast to global organizations, where most of the resources are centralized in a company's home country, different resources in a transnational company can be centralized in different countries, depending on where the company can achieve the greatest returns or cost savings. Further, different decentralized resources are interdependent; this is in contrast to the other organizational forms, where there is usually one direction of the flow of resources. In a transnational company, for example, semiconductors for computer chips might be produced in a state-of-the-art factory in Dresden, Germany, shipped to a Southeast Asian country to be assembled into a final product, and then shipped back to Western Europe to be sold to an individual customer. Bartlett and Ghoshal (1998) characterize transnational companies as integrated networks requiring a great deal of effort in terms of managing the different interdependencies, tasks, and communication among the different units. In sum, both data and control can flow in any direction, depending on the specific business process (see Figure 2.19).

Companies utilizing a transnational business strategy need to create integrated networks between the home office and the multiple local subsidiaries. Because of this requirement, there is much communication among the different subunits as well as between the home office and the subunits. Many systems are distributed and/or shared; in this way, a subsidiary can access the systems and resources of other subsidiaries. Similarly, key data are shared throughout the company to enable a seamless integration of processes. Much of the communication, data, and application sharing is enabled by intranet, extranet, and Web-based applications (see Table 2.6).

FIGURE 2.19

Transnational business strategy.

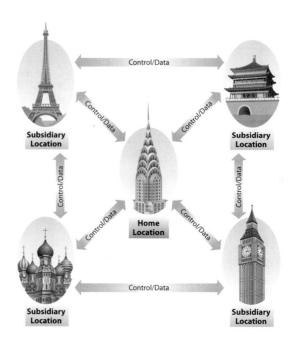

WHO'S GOING MOBILE

Mobile Operating Systems

Today, more and more people are enjoying the power and convenience of smartphones like Apple's iPhone or Motorola Droid. These mobile devices are having a significant impact on our lives, and are in fact redefining the way we access information and communicate with others. To make these gadgets "smart" they must have great hardware, useful apps, and a powerful operating system, all working together seamlessly.

Depending on the type of computer you own, it runs a particular type of operating system. If you have a Dell computer, you probably run some version of Windows (e.g., XP, Vista, 7, or 8). If you have an Apple, you run some version of the Mac OS X (e.g., Snow Leopard, Lion, or Mountain Lion). In a similar way, smartphones run a specific operating system they were designed for (in some exceptional cases, however, they might even be able to run operating systems they weren't made for): in general, an Android mobile device will only work with some version of Android and an iPhone will only run some version of iOS.

While Google's Android and Apple's iOS were the dominant mobile operating systems in 2012, others still had significant market share. Given the rapid growth in this market, there is likely to be a lot more change over the next several years. For instance, in late 2012, Microsoft released its widely anticipated Windows Phone 8 operating system; time will tell whether it will be able to battle the current market leaders. Figure 2.20 shows worldwide smartphone sales by operating system from 2007–2011. Notice the rapid growth of Android!

Google's strategy of having it run on a wide variety of phones from different manufacturers, and on a variety of networks, appears to be working. Apple's iOS has also done very well, especially considering it only runs on the iPhone and has had limited distribution to specific networks in some countries. While RIM's BlackBerry seems to be on the decline, Nokia's Symbian operating system keeps going strong, partly due to its heavy focus on low-cost phones for the developing world, with billions of potential customers. It used to be that people chose their phone only by their carrier and what brands they offered. Today, many choose their phone based on the manufacturer, its operating system's features, and the ecosystem of apps developed for the operating system.

Based on:

Anonymous. (n.d.). The evolution of mobile operating systems. *[x] cubelabs.* Retrieved June 3, 2012, from http://www.xcubelabs.com/evolution-of-mobile-operating-systems.php.

Mobile operating system. (2012, June 2). In *Wikipedia, The Free Encyclopedia.* Retrieved June 3, 2012, from http://en.wikipedia.org/w/index.php?title=Mobile_operating_system&oldid=495579867.

Raja, H.Q. (2011, May 14). An introduction to modern mobile operating systems. *addictivetips.com.* Retrieved June 3, 2012, from http://www.addictivetips.com/mobile/an-introduction-to-modern-mobile-operating-systems.

Siciliano, R. (2011, April 19). Five mobile operating system options. *fineextra.com.* Retrieved June 3, 2012, from http://www.finextra.com/community/fullblog.aspx?blogid=5230.

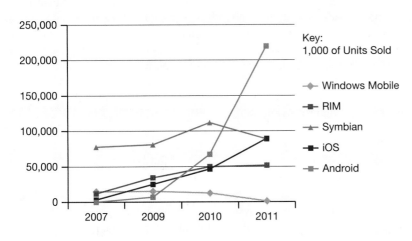

FIGURE 2.20

Worldwide smartphone sales by operating system.

VALUING INNOVATIONS

To differentiate itself, an organization often must deploy new, state-of-the-art technologies to do things even better, faster, and more cheaply than rivals that are using older technologies. Although firms can choose to continually upgrade older systems rather than investing in new systems, these improvements can at best give only a short-lived competitive edge. To gain and sustain significant competitive advantage, firms must often deploy the latest technologies or redeploy and reinvest in existing technologies in clever, new ways.

http://goo.gl/ZqMVM

FIGURE 2.21

Some enabling technologies on the horizon.

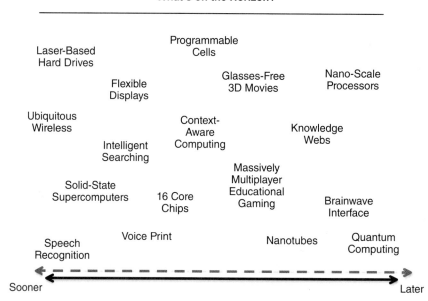

What's on the Horizon?

But with the plethora of new information technologies and systems available, how can you possibly choose winners? Indeed, how can you even keep track of all the new breakthroughs, new products, new versions, and new ways of using technologies? For example, in Figure 2.21 we present a small subset of some new information technologies and systems, ranging from some that are here now and currently being used to some that are easily a decade away from being a reality. Which one is important for you? Which one will make or break your business? Does this list even include the one that you need to be concerned about?

The Need for Constant IS Innovation

Sir John Maddox, a physicist and the editor of the influential scientific journal *Nature* for 22 years, was quoted in *Scientific American* in 1999 as saying "The most important discoveries of the next 50 years are likely to be ones of which we cannot now even conceive" (John Maddox. Reprinted from *Scientific American*, 1999). Think about that for a moment. Most of the important discoveries of the next 50 years are likely to be things that, at present, we have no clue about. To illustrate that point, think back to what the state of the Internet was back in 1999. Then, the Internet was not on the radar screens of many business organizations. Those that had Web sites were mostly providing an electronic brochure to customers and weren't exploiting the technology to streamline business processes as is the norm today. Look now at how the Internet has transformed modern business. How could something so transformational not have been easier for businesses to imagine or predict a decade earlier? It is difficult to see these things coming. Next, we examine how you can improve your ability to spot and exploit new innovations.

Successful Innovation Is Difficult

As we hinted at previously, there are limits to using emerging information systems to gain or sustain a competitive advantage. Information systems are often bought from or built by someone else. They are often either purchased from a vendor or developed by a consultant or outsourcing partner. In these situations, the information systems are usually not proprietary technologies owned by the organization. For example, although a soft-drink company can patent the formula of a cola or a pharmaceutical company can patent a new drug, an organization typically cannot patent its use of an information system, particularly if someone else developed it. The data in the system may be proprietary, but the information system typically is not. One classic counterexample, however, is Amazon.com's patented "one-click" ordering process that has been successfully defended in the courts.

INNOVATION IS OFTEN FLEETING. Given the pace of change in the digital world, advantages gained by innovations often have a limited life span. For example, even in situations where an organization has developed an innovative information system in-house, they usually do so with hardware, software, and networking components that others can purchase. In short, rivals can copy emerging information systems, so this form of competitive advantage can be short-lived. Indeed, if use of the new system causes one organization to gain a significant advantage over others, smart rivals are quick to duplicate or improve on that use of the system.

INNOVATION IS OFTEN RISKY. Developing innovative information systems always entails risk. The classic example from consumer electronics is the choice of a videocassette recorder (VCR) in the early days of that technology and the competing Betamax (developed by Sony) and VHS (developed by JVC) designs. Most experts agreed that the Betamax had superior recording and playback quality, but VHS ultimately won the battle in the marketplace. People who made the "smart" choice at the time probably would have chosen a VCR with the Betamax design. Ultimately, however, that turned out to be an unfortunate choice. Recently, consumers again had to choose between two competing formats, namely, for high-definition (HD) DVD players, where the Blu-ray and HD DVD format competed to become the industry standard. In this battle, Microsoft, Toshiba, and many others backed the HD DVD format, while Sony led the fight for Blu-ray (and even incorporated it into its PlayStation 3 gaming console). This time around, Sony (and the Blu-ray format) won the "format war," with the dissolution of the HD DVD Promotion Group in early 2008, effectively making Blu-ray the dominant format for HD video discs (see Figure 2.22).

INNOVATION CHOICES ARE OFTEN DIFFICULT. Choosing among innovative IS-related investments is just as difficult as choosing consumer electronics. In fact, for organizations, choosing among the plethora of available innovative technologies is far more difficult, given the size and often mission-critical nature of the investment. Choosing a suboptimal DVD player, although disappointing, is usually not devastating.

Choosing new technologies in the IS area is like trying to hit one of several equally attractive fast-moving targets. You can find examples of the difficulty of forecasting emerging technologies in the experiences that many organizations have had in forecasting the growth, use, and importance of the Internet. The 1994 Technology Forecast prepared by the major consulting firm Price Waterhouse (now PriceWaterhouseCoopers) mentioned the word "Internet" on only five pages of the 750-page document. The next year, more than 75 pages addressed the Internet. Only three years later, in the 1997 briefing, the Internet was a pervasive topic throughout. Back in 1994, it would have been difficult, perhaps even foolish, to forecast such pervasive, rapidly growing business use of the Internet today. Table 2.7 illustrates how many people and organizations have had difficulty making technology-related predictions.

Given the pace of research and development in the IS and components area, staying current has been nearly impossible. Probably one of the most famous metrics of computer evolution has been "Moore's Law." Intel founder Gordon Moore predicted that the number of transistors that could be squeezed onto a silicon chip would double every 24 months (this number is now often

FIGURE 2.22

Blu-ray has become the industry standard for high-definition DVD players.
Source: Matthew Jacques/Shutterstock

TABLE 2.7   Some Predictions About Technology That Were Not Quite Correct

Year	Source	Quote
1876	Western Union, internal memo	"This 'telephone' has too many shortcomings to be seriously considered as a means of communication. The device is inherently of no value to us."
1895	Lord Kelvin, president, British Royal Society	"Radio has no future. Heavier-than-air flying machines are impossible. X-rays will prove to be a hoax."
1899	C. H. Duell, commissioner, U.S. Office of Patents	"Everything that can be invented has been invented."
1927	H. M. Warner, Warner Brothers	"Who the hell wants to hear actors talk?"
1943	Thomas Watson, chairman, IBM	"I think there is a world market for maybe five computers."
1949	*Popular Mechanics*	"Where a calculator on the ENIAC is equipped with 18,000 vacuum tubes and weighs 30 tons, computers in the future may have only 1,000 vacuum tubes and weigh only 1.5 tons."
1957	Editor, business books, Prentice Hall	"I have traveled the length and breadth of this country and talked with the best people, and I can assure you that data processing is a fad that won't last out the year."
1968	*BusinessWeek*	"With over 50 foreign cars already on sale here, the Japanese auto industry isn't likely to carve out a big slice of the U.S. market."
1977	Ken Olsen, president, Digital Equipment Corporation	"There is no reason anyone would want a computer in their home."
1989	Bill Gates, Microsoft	"We will never make a 32-bit operating system."
2004	Bill Gates, Microsoft	"Spam will be a thing of the past in two years' time."
2005	Sir Alan Sugar	"Next Christmas the iPod will be dead, finished, gone, kaput."

reduced to 18 months), and this prediction has proven itself over the past 40 years (see Chapter 3). In fact, some computer hardware and software firms roll out new versions of their products every three months. Keeping up with this pace of change can be difficult for any organization.

Organizational Requirements for Innovation

Certain types of competitive environments require that organizations remain at the cutting edge in their use of information systems. For example, consider an organization that operates within an environment with strong competitive forces (Porter, 1979). The organization has competitive pressures coming from existing rival firms or from the threat of entry of new rivals. It is critical for these organizations to do things better, faster, and more cheaply than rivals. These organizations are driven to deploy innovative information systems.

These environmental characteristics alone, however, are not enough to determine whether an organization should deploy a particular information system. Before an organization can deploy any new system well, its processes, resources, and risk tolerance must be capable of adapting to and sustaining the development and implementation processes.

PROCESS REQUIREMENTS. To deploy innovative information systems well, people in the organization must be willing to do whatever they can to bypass and eliminate internal bureaucracy, set aside political squabbles, and pull together for the common good. Can you imagine, for example, a firm trying to deploy a Web-based order entry system that enables customers to access inventory information directly, when people in that firm do not even share such information with each other?

RESOURCE REQUIREMENTS. Organizations deploying innovative information systems must also have the human capital necessary to deploy the new systems. The organization must have enough employees available with the proper systems knowledge, skills, time, and other resources to deploy these systems. Alternatively, the organization must have resources and able systems partners available to outsource the development of such systems if necessary.

RISK TOLERANCE REQUIREMENTS. The last characteristic of an organization ready for the deployment of innovative information systems is that its members must have the appropriate

COMING ATTRACTIONS

Google's Project Glass: A Pair of Glasses

It's an early Monday morning, you're running late. Your friend from 5,000 miles away initiates a video-call so you can have a quick chat, but you simultaneously need to check the weather and find your way to where the meeting will be held in less than half an hour. There is no doubt that your smartphone usefully pops out to help, but Google has come up with an even more convenient answer—Project Glass.

Inside the secretive Google X Lab, researchers are constantly developing new innovations. At first glance, Project Glass looks like an ultramodern pair of glasses, but a closer look reveals a lot of innovation that seems closer to science fiction than science fact. These glasses augment reality by providing an embedded microphone and a partly transparent (and very tiny) screen slightly above the user's right eye. This screen enables displaying information about the wearer's surroundings, communicating with other people, browsing the Web, listening to music, and taking photos. In sum, these shades squeeze the various functions of a smartphone and a computer into a pair of glasses, including GPS location tracking capabilities. These are certainly not just another pair of geeky glasses!

As if living in a real-life sci-fi movie, users immediately see 14 different services displayed on the video screen once the glasses are put on, gliding between information about the weather, one's location, or your appointment schedule. For instance, when you look out the window on a cloudy day, Project Glass reminds you that there is an 80 percent chance of rain. When you stare at a blank wall, the screen displays that it is bowling night. When a friend sends a text message, an alert pops up to which a reply could be sent through voice command, courtesy of the built-in microphone.

Continuing your day, the sleek-looking glasses guide you to the nearest subway station while you're still happily chatting away, pausing in between to take a photo of a cute little dog that just walked past and, of course, easily sharing it with your friends right on the spot. After your busy day at work, the glasses allow you to stream news and current events to your ears or eyes, or if you choose, to listen to double doses of your favorite track from your favorite artist. The system can be controlled by a simple tilt of your head.

It is unclear if Project Glass will ever be commercially available, but many of the capabilities demonstrated in this project will surely arrive in the not too distant future. Such innovative capabilities will augment our day, reducing inefficiency and enriching our lives. While you may not like how you look in glasses, these glasses will surely be a fashion "must have" accessory.

Based on:

Anonymous. (2012, April 4). Google unveils Project Glass augmented reality eyeware. *BBC News*. Retrieved June 11, 2012, from http://www.bbc.com/news/technology-17618495.

Anonymous. (2012, May 16). Google patents augmented reality Project Glass design. *BBC News*. Retrieved June 11, 2012, from http://www.bbc.com/news/technology-18091697.

Julie. (2012, May 16). Google's Project Glass—Welcome to the future. Retrieved June 11, 2012, from http://www.coolest-gadgets.com/20120516/googles-project-glass-future.

Project Glass. (2012, June 9). In *Wikipedia, The Free Encyclopedia*. Retrieved June 11, 2012, from http://en.wikipedia.org/w/index.php?title=Project_Glass&oldid=496727230.

tolerance for risk and uncertainty as well as the willingness to deploy and use new systems that may not be as proven and pervasive as more traditional technologies. If people within the organization desire low risk in their use of information systems, then gambling on cutting-edge systems will probably not be desirable or tolerable for them.

Predicting the Next New Thing

As you can see, using information systems as a strategic innovation will be difficult to identify, implement, and sustain. As Bakos and Treacy (1986) and others have argued, if you are using information systems to gain a competitive advantage in the area of operating efficiencies, it is likely that your rivals can just as easily adopt the same types of information systems and achieve the same gains. For example, in the early days of online shopping, some progressive online retailers set up Web sites that enabled customers to check on the status of their order without requiring help from a customer service representative, which helped the retailers to cut costs and increase customer satisfaction. Rivals, however, quickly copied this approach, matching cost reductions and service improvements. Thus, the competitive advantage achieved with clever use of information systems did not last long, and the systems turned into strategic necessity for anyone in this industry.

There are certainly ways to use information systems to gain a longer lasting, sustainable competitive advantage; Bakos and Treacy argued that if you can use information systems to make your products or services unique or to cause your customers to invest so heavily in you that their switching costs are high (i.e., if switching to a competitor's product involves significant investment in terms of time and/or money for the customer), then you are better able to develop a competitive advantage that is sustainable over the long haul. For example, you might combine heavy investments in computer-aided design systems with very bright engineers in order to perfect your product and make it unique and something relatively difficult to copy. Alternatively, you might use a customer relationship management system to build an extensive database containing the entire history of your interaction with each of your customers, and then use that system to provide very high quality, intimate, rapid, and customized service that would convince customers that if they switched to a rival, it would take them years to build up that kind of relationship with the other firm.

The Innovator's Dilemma

Deciding which innovations to adopt and pursue has never been easy. In fact, there are many classic examples where so-called industry leaders failed to see the changing opportunities introduced by new innovations (see Table 2.8). In his influential book *Diffusion of Innovations*, Everett Rogers (2003) theorized that the adoption of innovations usually follows an S-shaped curve (see Figure 2.23). When an innovation is brought to market, initially only a small group of "innovators" will adopt that innovation. After some time, sales pick up as the innovators are followed by the "early adopters" and the "early majority," and the increase in sales is strongest. Then sales slowly level off when the "late majority" starts adopting the innovation. Finally, sales stay level as only the "laggards" are left to adopt the innovation.

However, some innovations are more disruptive, turning entire industries upside down. Clayton Christensen's (1997) *The Innovator's Dilemma* outlines how *disruptive innovations* undermine effective management practices, often leading to the demise of an organization or an industry. **Disruptive innovations** are new technologies, products, or services that eventually surpass the existing dominant technology or product in a market (see Table 2.8). For example, retail giant Sears nearly failed in the early 1990s when it did not recognize the transformational power of the disruptive innovation discount retailing; today, discounters like Walmart and segment-specific stores like Home Depot dominate retailing.

TABLE 2.8   Examples of Disruptive Innovations and Their Associated Displaced or Marginalized Technology

Disruptive Innovation	Displaced or Marginalized Technology
Digital photography	Chemical photography
Desktop publishing	Traditional publishing
Online stock brokerage	Full-service stock brokerages
Online retailing	Brick-and-mortar retailing
Free, downloadable greeting cards	Printed greeting cards
Distance education	Classroom education
Unmanned aircraft	Manned aircraft
Nurse practitioners	Medical doctors
Semiconductors	Vacuum tubes
Automobiles	Horses
Airplanes	Trains
Compact discs	Cassettes and records
MP3 players and music downloading	Compact discs and music stores
Smartphones	MP3 players, dedicated GPS navigation
Mobile telephony	Wire-line telephony
Tablets	Notebook computers
Xbox, PlayStation	Desktop computers

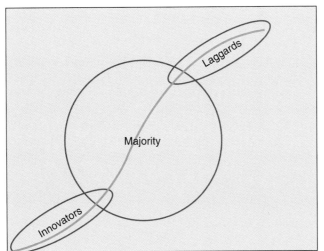

FIGURE 2.23

Diffusion of innovations.
Source: Based on Rogers (2003).

Within every market, there are customers who have relatively high, moderate, or low performance requirements from the existing product offerings. For example, within the mobile phone industry today, some low-performance customers demand very basic phones and services (e.g., no camera, touchscreen, or data services), whereas high-performance customers use devices and services that rival the capabilities of some personal computers with high-speed Internet connections. Over time, as disruptive innovations and incremental improvements are introduced into an industry, the capabilities of the products in all segments (i.e., low to high performance) improve; as product capabilities improve at the high-performance end of the market, the number of potential customers for these products gets relatively smaller. At the same time, as the low-end products also improve, they are increasingly able to capture more and more of the mainstream marketplace.

To illustrate this progression, Christensen provides compelling examples within several industries. In particular, the collapse of 1970's midrange computer giant Digital Equipment Company (DEC) (and the entire midrange industry for that matter) clearly illustrates the innovator's dilemma. DEC was ultimately surpassed in the marketplace by microprocessor-based computers, with the microprocessor being the disruptive innovation.

In the 1970's, when microcomputers were first introduced, DEC (and its customers) deemed them to be toys and ignored their potential. It is important to note that DEC was a well-run company and was touted as having one of the finest executive teams in the world. Additionally, DEC used leading management techniques, such as conducting extensive market research with its existing customers and industry (i.e., they put "marketing" ahead of technology; for a divergent view, see the discussion of the e-business innovation cycle later in this chapter). When surveyed, none of DEC's customers indicated a need for microcomputers, and thus DEC concluded that developing improved capabilities within its *existing* midrange computer product line is where they should focus. At this time, DEC's goal was to serve the needs of "high-" and "mid"-performance users, which made up the largest part of the total market for computers (see Figure 2.24). The increasing performance of DEC's products started meeting the needs of customers who would traditionally purchase mainframe computers, so DEC could try to "up sell" to mainframe customers of IBM, Burroughs, and Honeywell, where the margins were even greater than in the midrange computer industry.

Initially, there were virtually no competitive product offerings serving the needs of the low-performance users; in other words, current product offerings by established computer manufacturers, such as DEC, were either too powerful or too expensive (or both) for these low-end customers. In the 1980's, the microcomputer industry was launched by Apple, and the (disruptive) microprocessor, developed in the 1970's, was now being turned into a product that had the capabilities and price for users in the low-performance category of the marketplace. DEC was not alone in ignoring the introduction of microcomputers; virtually all established players in the computing industry continued to focus on their existing customers and existing product lines, incrementally improving their products over time. Meanwhile, in just a few years, the

FIGURE 2.24

Innovator's dilemma view of the evolution of the computing industry.

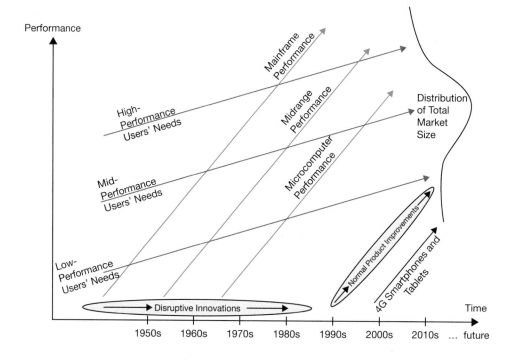

microcomputer industry grew and matured, going from toy to office automation device (e.g., a replacement for the typewriter or adding machine) to a multipurpose business computer for many small and medium-sized businesses that could never before afford a computer. As the low end of the market took shape in the 1980's, DEC continued to focus on its existing customers and business model (e.g., direct selling, personal service, and so on). Rapidly, the capabilities of the "disruptive" microcomputers improved, meeting the needs of not only the low end but also the mid-performance range of the marketplace, which was traditionally served by DEC's mid-range computers. Being far more inexpensive than DEC's products, the microcomputers took over the bulk of the market. Sadly, DEC continued to ignore the microcomputer industry until it was too late, and DEC could do nothing but watch the loss of its biggest traditional market segment. By January 26, 1998, what was left of DEC was sold to Compaq Computers; in 2002, Compaq was acquired by Hewlett-Packard.

Today, microprocessor-based computers from Dell, HP, Apple, and others meet or exceed the needs of much of the *entire* marketplace; additionally, only a handful of high-end computer manufacturers remain. So what is next for this industry? Many believe that the next disruptive innovations are 4G smartphones and tablets from companies like Apple and Samsung (see the Technology Briefing, "Foundations of Information Systems Infrastructure"). So, the **innovator's dilemma** refers to how disruptive innovations, typically ignored by established market leaders, cause these established firms or industries to lose market dominance, often leading to failure. What DEC experienced, so too have countless other companies in numerous industries. Table 2.9 summarizes the typical progression and effects of a disruptive innovation on an industry.

ORGANIZING TO MAKE INNOVATION CHOICES. Given the evolution of industries outlined in the innovator's dilemma, how do organizations make decisions on which innovations to embrace and which to ignore? In the follow-up book, *The Innovator's Solution,* Christensen & Raynor (2003) outline a process called the *disruptive growth engine,* which all organizations can follow to more effectively respond to disruptive innovations in their industry. This process has the following steps:

1. *Start Early.* To gain the greatest opportunities, become a leader in identifying, tracking, and adopting disruptive innovations by making these processes a formal part of the organization (i.e., budgets, personnel, and so on).
2. *Display Executive Leadership.* To gain credibility as well as to bridge sustaining and disruptive product development, visible and credible leadership is required.
3. *Build a Team of Expert Innovators.* To most effectively identify and evaluate potential disruptive innovations, build a competent team of expert innovators.

TABLE 2.9   Typical Progression and Effects of Disruptive Innovations on an Industry

1. The first mover introduces a new technology. It is expensive, focusing on a small number of high-performance, high-margin customers.

2. Over time, the first mover focuses on improving product capabilities to meet the needs of higher-performance customers in order to continue to reap the highest margins.

3. Later entrants, using a disruptive innovation, have an inferior market position, focusing on lower-performance, lower-margin customers.

4. Over time, later entrants focus on incremental product improvements to serve the needs of more lower-performance customers, also focusing on cost efficiencies to offset the lack of margins with economies of scale.

5. As the market matures, all products improve, competition increases, and margins diminish; the first mover rarely learns the efficiencies of the later entrants and is entrenched in high-margin business practices; the first mover's market share rapidly erodes as that of the later entrants rapidly grows.

6. Ultimately, the later entrants' products meet or exceed the requirements for the vast majority of the marketplace; they "win" with efficient, low-cost business processes demanded by the majority of the marketplace.

4. ***Educate the Organization.*** To see opportunities, those closest to customers and competitors (e.g., marketing, customer support, and engineering) need to understand how to identify disruptive innovations.

In addition to formalizing the identification of innovations within the organization, shifts in business processes and fundamental thinking about disruptive innovations are needed. Next, we examine how to implement the innovation identification process.

IMPLEMENTING THE INNOVATION PROCESS. Executives today who are serious about using information technology in innovative ways have made it a point to have their people be continually on the lookout for new disruptive innovations that will have a significant impact on their business. Wheeler (2002) has summarized this process nicely as the **e-business innovation cycle** (see Figure 2.25). Like the term "e-commerce," "e-business" refers to the use of information

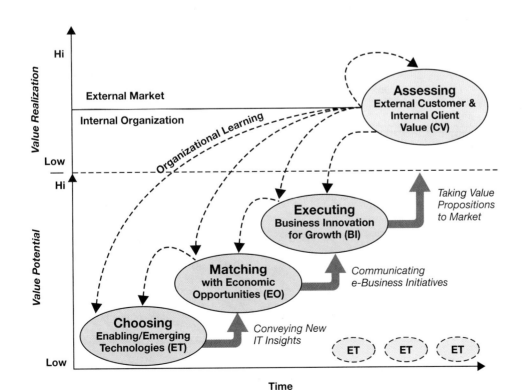

FIGURE 2.25

The e-business innovation cycle.
Source: Based on Wheeler (2002).

KEY PLAYERS

The Global Elite

Throughout the world, there are technology giants that provide us with gadgets and innovations that touch every aspect of our lives. For the U.S.-based companies, you probably can recognize their names, and maybe their primary markets. Companies like Hewlett-Packard, AT&T, Apple, IBM, Verizon, Microsoft, and Dell are just some of the global giants based in the U.S. What about the non-U.S.-based giants? Who are they, where are they from, and what are their primary markets? Table 2.10 provides a summary of the top 10, non-U.S.-based global technology giants. While you may not know all of their names, locations, or products, they are indeed key players in the global tech industry.

Based on:

China Mobile. (2012, May 28). In *Wikipedia, The Free Encyclopedia*. Retrieved June 14, 2012, from http://en.wikipedia.org/w/index.php?title=China_Mobile&oldid=494753470.

Deutsche Telekom. (2012, June 7). In *Wikipedia, The Free Encyclopedia*. Retrieved June 14, 2012, from http://en.wikipedia.org/w/index.php?title=Deutsche_Telekom&oldid=496437388.

Hitachi. (2012, June 10). In *Wikipedia, The Free Encyclopedia*. Retrieved June 14, 2012, from http://en.wikipedia.org/w/index.php?title=Hitachi&oldid=496964127.

Nippon Telegraph and Telephone. (2012, June 10). In *Wikipedia, The Free Encyclopedia*. Retrieved June 14, 2012, from http://en.wikipedia.org/w/index.php?title=Nippon_Telegraph_and_Telephone&oldid=496964312.

List of the largest technology companies. (2012, May 18). In *Wikipedia, The Free Encyclopedia*. Retrieved June 14, 2012, from http://en.wikipedia.org/w/index.php?title=List_of_the_largest_technology_companies&oldid=493196381.

Panasonic. (2012, June 14). In *Wikipedia, The Free Encyclopedia*. Retrieved June 14, 2012, from http://en.wikipedia.org/w/index.php?title=Panasonic&oldid=497621038.

Samsung Electronics. (2012, June 14). In *Wikipedia, The Free Encyclopedia*. Retrieved June 14, 2012, from http://en.wikipedia.org/w/index.php?title=Samsung_Electronics&oldid=497523414.

Siemens. (2012, June 12). In *Wikipedia, The Free Encyclopedia*. Retrieved June 14, 2012, from http://en.wikipedia.org/w/index.php?title=Siemens&oldid=497219180.

Sony. (2012, June 14). In *Wikipedia, The Free Encyclopedia*. Retrieved June 14, 2012, from http://en.wikipedia.org/w/index.php?title=Sony&oldid=497582729.

Telefónica. (2012, June 9). In *Wikipedia, The Free Encyclopedia*. Retrieved June 14, 2012, from http://en.wikipedia.org/w/index.php?title=Telef%C3%B3nica&oldid=496786288.

Toshiba. (2012, June 13). In *Wikipedia, The Free Encyclopedia*. Retrieved June 14, 2012, from http://en.wikipedia.org/w/index.php?title=Toshiba&oldid=497333303.

TABLE 2.10 Top 10 Largest Non-U.S.-Based Technology Companies (2011)

Rank	World Rank	Company	2011 Sales (in US$ million)	Headquarters	Founded	Employees (thousands)	Primary Markets
1	1	Samsung Electronics	133,780	South Korea	1969	164.6	Electronics, Information Technology
2	3	NTT	124,330	Japan	1985	219.3	Telecommunications
3	5	Hitachi	112,400	Japan	1910	400.2	Information technology, telecommunications, electrical systems, automotive systems, components, financial services
4	9	Panasonic	104,880	Japan	1918	384.6 (2010)	Electronics
5	10	Siemens	96,590	Germany	1847	360.0	Electronics, engineering
6	11	Sony	86,640	Japan	1946	180.5	Electronics, consumer products
7	12	Deutsche Telekom	82,650	Germany	1996	246.8	Telecommunications
8	13	Telefónica	80,830 (2010)	Spain	1924	269.0	Telecommunications
9	14	Toshiba	76,667 (2010)	Japan	1939	212.0	Electronics, Information Technology
10	15	China Mobile	73,366 (2010)	China	1997	207.4	Telecommunications

technologies and systems to support the business. Whereas "e-commerce" generally means the use of the Internet and related technologies to support commerce, **e-business** has a broader meaning: the use of nearly any information technologies or systems to support every part of the business. The model essentially holds that the key to success for modern organizations is the extent to which they use information technologies and systems in timely, innovative ways. The vertical dimension of the e-business innovation cycle shows the extent to which an organization derives value from a particular information technology, and the horizontal dimension shows time. Next, we examine the cycle.

Choosing Enabling/Emerging Technologies   The first bubble left of the graph shows that successful organizations first create jobs, groups, and processes that are all devoted to scanning the environment for new emerging and **enabling technologies** (i.e., information technologies that enable a firm to accomplish a task or goal or to gain or sustain competitive advantage in some way; also called disruptive innovations) that appear to be relevant for the organization. For example, an organization might designate a small group within the IS department as the "Emerging Technologies" unit and charge them with looking for new technologies that will have an impact on the business. As part of their job, this group will pore over current technology magazines, participate in Internet discussion forums on technology topics, go to technology conferences and conventions, and have strong, active relationships with technology researchers at universities and technology companies.

Matching Technologies to Opportunities   Next, in the second bubble, the organization matches the most promising new technologies with current **economic opportunities**. For example, the Emerging Technologies group might have identified advances in database management systems (and a dramatic drop in data storage costs) as a key enabling technology that now makes a massive data warehouse feasible. In addition, managers within the marketing function of the firm have recognized that competitors have really dropped the ball in terms of customer service and that there is an opportunity to gain customers and market share by serving customers better.

Executing Business Innovation for Growth   The third bubble represents the process of selecting—among myriad opportunities to take advantage of—the database and data storage advances and then addressing the current opportunity to grab customers and market share. The organization decides to implement an enterprise-wide data warehouse that enables them to have at their fingertips integrated corporate-wide data and an unparalleled capability to understand, react to, and better serve customers.

Assessing Value   The fourth bubble represents the process of assessing the value of that use of technology, not only to customers but also to internal clients (i.e., sales representatives, marketing managers, the chief operating officer, and so on).

THINKING ABOUT INVESTMENTS IN DISRUPTIVE INNOVATIONS.   The e-business innovation cycle suggests three new ways to think about investments in disruptive innovations:

1. *Put Technology Ahead of Strategy.* This approach says that technology is so important to strategy and to success that you have to begin with technology. Notice that the first bubble involves understanding, identifying, and choosing technologies that are important. The first bubble does not begin with strategy, as a traditional approach to running a business organization would suggest. In fact, many would argue that given how important technology is today and how fast it changes, if you start with a strategy and then try to retrofit technology into your aging strategy, you are doomed. This approach argues that you begin by understanding technology and develop a strategy from there. This approach is admittedly very uncomfortable for people who think in traditional ways and/or who are not comfortable with technology. We believe, however, that for many modern organizations, thinking about technology in this way is key.

2. *Put Technology Ahead of Marketing.* The second way that this approach turns conventional wisdom on its head is that, like strategy, marketing also takes a backseat to the technology. Think about it carefully, and you will see that marketing does not come into play

until later in this model. A very traditional marketing-oriented approach would be to go first to your customers and find out from them what their needs are and what you ought to be doing with technology (as did DEC). The trouble with this approach is that, given the rapid evolution of technology, your customers are not likely to know about new technologies and their capabilities. In some sense, they are the last place you ought to be looking for ideas about new technologies and their impact on your business. Indeed, if they know about the new technology, then chances are your competitors already do too, meaning that this technology is not the one to rest your competitive advantage on. As Steve Jobs of Apple put it, "You can't just ask people what they want and then try to give that to them. By the time you get it built, they'll want something new."

3. **Innovation Is Continuous.** The third way that this approach is interesting—and potentially troubling—is that the process has to be ongoing. As shown along the time dimension along the bottom of the graph, the first bubble repeats over and over again as the Emerging Technologies group is constantly on the lookout for the "next new thing" that will revolutionize the business. The rate of information technology evolution is not likely to slow down, and innovative organizations truly cannot—and do not—ever rest.

Today, dealing with rapid change caused by disruptive innovations is a reality for most industries. If you are a leader in an industry, you must continually learn to embrace and exploit disruptive innovations, potentially *destroying* your existing core business while at the same time building a new business around the disruptive innovation. If you fail to do this, your competition may do it for you.

http://goo.gl/jeQVA

FREECONOMICS: WHY FREE PRODUCTS ARE THE FUTURE OF THE DIGITAL WORLD

Chris Anderson (2009), editor in chief of *Wired Magazine,* has put forth a provocative idea that charging customers nothing for products and services may be the future of business in the digital world. In fact, he argues that this strategy is a viable approach for making a fortune in virtually any industry. Of course, obvious examples not likely to be easily replicated include Google making billions from its free search engine or Yahoo! making millions from its free Web e-mail service. Anderson convincingly argues, however, that such moneymaking principles are not limited to Google and Yahoo!, but can be applied to countless industries. Here we examine how **freeconomics**—the leveraging of digital technologies to provide *free* goods and services to customers as a business strategy for gaining a competitive advantage—can be utilized by organizations from virtually any industry in the highly competitive digital world.

How Freeconomics Works

According to basic economics within a competitive marketplace, the price of something is set by its marginal cost—the cost of producing an additional unit of output. Given the push toward globalization, the world has never been more competitive (see Chapter 1). Likewise, given the exponential increases in processing power (see Moore's Law in Chapter 3), along with even greater increases in storage and networking capacity, the prices of computer processing, storage, and bandwidth are in a free fall. For example, now that Yahoo! has built its Web e-mail environment, the cost to provide this service for each additional person is nearly zero. Consequently, the marginal cost for Web e-mail services is essentially zero. At the same time, huge profits are made giving away this service to more and more customers. For every additional customer, Yahoo! receives payments from companies placing banner advertisements on pages within the Web e-mail service (see Figure 2.26).

It is important to note that *any* industry that utilizes digital technologies (not just those like Google or Yahoo!) is on a path toward increasingly lower costs, ultimately toward a price of free—or at least "free" for consumers. As digital technologies increase in capabilities and at the same time decrease in cost, the industry as a whole will see rapid cost reductions. As costs are reduced, prices for consumers will drop. Moreover, as that industry relies more and more on

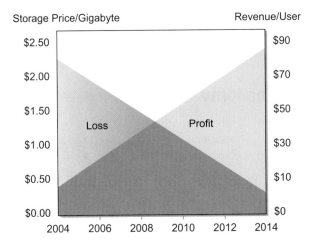

FIGURE 2.26

How Yahoo! makes millions of dollars from its *free* web-based e-mail service—as the cost of storage has dropped, revenue per user has increased.

digital technologies to further reduce costs and to further increase efficiencies, the competitiveness of the industry will further increase, pushing the price closer and closer toward its marginal cost. In other words, as an industry relies more and more on digital technologies, free becomes the inevitable price.

The Freeconomics Value Proposition

Within freeconomics, just because products are free to consumers doesn't mean that someone, somewhere, isn't paying for it and, most important, that someone else isn't also making a lot of money. For example, Google gets paid ad revenue from companies when someone using a Google search clicks on a sponsored link. Here the **value proposition**—what a business provides to a customer and what that customer is willing to pay for that product or service—is larger than simply buyers and sellers. For Google, the value proposition includes a broad ecosystem of many participants, only some of whom exchange payments (see Figure 2.27). This value proposition is very similar to that of the radio and television broadcast industries, where consumers receive free content, while advertisers make payments to stations to broadcast commercials. Freeconomics is therefore an extension of this basic advertising model and can be applied to virtually any industry. Additionally, this basic model can be applied in a variety of creative ways beyond advertising.

FIGURE 2.27

Google uses a value proposition similar to that of television and radio broadcasting advertising.
Source: Based on www.Google.com.

Underground Gaming Economy

The economy in real life is still not in good shape. The unemployment rate is still high, and the real estate market has been in dire straits, forcing many home owners (and speculators) into bankruptcy. Although health care reform has been approved in the United States, health care costs continue to spiral out of control. It's the real world, and those of us who live and work in it develop skills to cope.

Things in Entropia Universe, a virtual world with a real cash economy, aren't much better. Colonists on Calypso must still fight off dangerous enemies, the PED (Project Entropia Dollar) is still worth only 10 cents against the U.S. dollar, and the price of ore-rich property is rising.

Entropia Universe is one of many massively multiplayer online role-playing games (MMORPGs). Other online role-playing games include but are not limited to Sony's Everquest, EA's Star Wars: The Old Republic, and Blizzard's World of Warcraft. Players pay monthly subscription fees and assume virtual identities called avatars. Statistics show that the total virtual goods market in the United States was approximately US$2.9 billion in 2012, up from US$500 million in 2008.

In most MMORPGs, gamers slay enemies, build houses and businesses, choose professions, pick up mystical attributes, and fill their virtual bank accounts with gold and cash. Each player's avatar "lives" in the game's virtual community. A recent trend, however, is for serious players to play to collect virtual tools, gold, or cash and then sell the booty for real cash. The dollar amounts involved are usually relatively small, say, US$70 for 10 million gold sets in Ultima Online, but there have been notable exceptions. In April 2012, for example, an investor spent US$2.5 million on a plot of virtual real estate on Entropia's Planet Calypso. Land owners in the game share in the gross revenue generated on their planet from user-to-user transactions, which apparently totals around US$400 million a year on Calypso; reports estimate a 27 percent return on investment on these virtual land investments!

With the potential of such high returns, the practice of buying and selling assets from MMORPGs has become widespread. These virtual moguls of the MMORPG world often employ "gold farmers" to build their empires. Farming has become especially popular in China, where companies employ rows of gamers who play for up to 12 hours at a time, collecting virtual assets and ascending to the highest levels of a game—all of which the companies will sell. Items for sale range from characters that have advanced to higher levels of a game to weapons, gold, and other items captured in a game. Today, it is estimated that more than 400,000 people worldwide are employed as gold farmers, with nearly 90 percent from China. Like real farmers, these gold farmers work long hours, from 10- to 12-hour shifts, earning around US$250 per month, including room and board. In addition, many Chinese prisons are suspected of including gold farming as a form of hard labor. Rather than building furniture or mining coal, prisoners are given daily quotas to fill or face beatings and other punishment. Gold farming revenue is then converted into real-world cash.

As you might expect, gold farming is highly controversial. In addition to the human rights issues, critics of this new virtual economy say that buying gold on the virtual market penalizes gamers who play strictly for fun but allows those with cash to spend to advance through levels of a game they have not mastered. Others say there is nothing wrong with players buying advantages that let them play at higher levels without putting in large amounts of time.

Some game companies have banned farmers from the playing field. For example, Blizzard Entertainment, the makers of World of Warcraft, a game that boasted more than 10 million subscribers in 2012, has permanently banned thousands of users following its investigation into cheaters and farmers. Similarly, *PC Gamer*, America's largest gaming magazine, stopped taking advertisements from companies that trade in virtual goods and characters from MMORPGs; and in early 2007, eBay banned the sale of virtual goods such as currency or avatars. Nevertheless, countless sites remain that explain how the underground markets operate for the buying and selling of virtual goods. The companies cite ethical reasons for penalizing farmers, but they also realize that farmers can eventually impact revenues, as gamers who refuse to buy and sell attributes may refuse to play with those who do.

Based on:

Entropia Universe. (2012, May 10). In *Wikipedia, The Free Encyclopedia*. Retrieved June 12, 2012, from http://en.wikipedia.org/w/index.php?title=Entropia_Universe&oldid=491707837.

Gold farming. (2012, June 12). In *Wikipedia, The Free Encyclopedia*. Retrieved June 12, 2012, from http://en.wikipedia.org/w/index.php?title=Gold_farming&oldid=497157945.

Holisky, A. (2012, February 9). World of Warcraft subscriber numbers dip 100,000 to 10.2 million. *WOW Insider*. Retrieved June 12, 2012, from http://wow.joystiq.com/2012/02/09/world-of-warcraft-subscriber-numbers.

Lyons, D. (2010, March 29). Money for nothing. *Newsweek*. Retrieved June 12, 2012, from http://www.newsweek.com/id/235170.

Millard, E. (2006, January 4). Inside the underground economy of computer gaming. *Newsfactor*. Retrieved June 12, 2012, from http://www.newsfactor.com/story.xhtml?story_id=40592.

Reahard, J. (2012, April 4). Entropia Universe player drops $2.5 million on virtual land deeds. *Joystiq.com*. Retrieved June 12, 2012, from http://massively.joystiq.com/2012/04/04/entropia-universe-player-drops-2-5-million-on-virtual-land-deed.

Spohn, D. (2006, April 12). Thousands banned from World of Warcraft. *About.com*. Retrieved June 12, 2012, from http://internetgames.about.com/b/2006/04/12/thousands-banned-from-world-of-warcraft.htm.

Applying Freeconomics in the Digital World

To demonstrate how freeconomics can be applied to a variety of industries beyond Web e-mail or online searches, Anderson explains how cable TV giant Comcast gave a free DVR to millions of its customers, leading to huge profits for the company. The DVR cost Comcast around US$250 each, so giving them away needed to stimulate some other type of revenue. Specifically, once consumers had the DVR, they were charged a monthly subscription fee to utilize its capabilities. Comcast was also able to create a stronger relationship with its customers, leading to other revenue streams, including high-speed Internet access, digital telephony services, and pay-per-view movies. In the end, this free DVR generated tremendous revenue and profits for Comcast.

In another example, the music icon Prince gave away 2.8 million copies of his 2007 CD *Planet Earth*, retail value US$19, inside the Sunday edition of London's *Daily Mail*. Although Prince lost money on the giveaway—he received 36 cents per disc from the newspaper while the cost to produce each disc was around US$2—he more than made up for this loss through the sale of concert tickets. After the giveaway, he sold out a record-breaking 21 shows in the O_2 Arena in London, netting the entertainer nearly US$19 million in revenue after expenses. Indeed, there are many approaches for making money by giving things away.

Table 2.11 outlines six general approaches for applying the concepts of freeconomics to a broad range of industries. For example, the online photo sharing application Flickr (owned by Yahoo!) allows users to store, share, organize, and tag a limited number of pictures for free; applying the *freemium* approach, users can upgrade to a paid "pro account," providing additional features, such as unlimited storage and advertisement-free browsing, or can use other paid services, such as printing through Hewlett-Packard's print services, creating photo gifts, or creating books using blurb.com. Understanding how to leverage the value of IS investments is fundamental to thriving in the digital world.

TABLE 2.11 General Approaches for Applying Freeconomics to Various Industries

Approach	What It Means	Examples
Advertising	Free services are provided to customers and paid for by a third party.	▪ Yahoo!'s banner ads ▪ Google's pay-per-click ▪ Amazon's pay-per-transaction "affiliate ads"
Freemium	Basic services are offered for free, but a premium is charged for special features.	▪ Flickr ▪ Skype ▪ Dropbox.com ▪ Trillian
Cross subsidies	Sale price of one item is reduced in order to sell something else of value.	▪ Comcast DVR ▪ Free theater ticket for those willing to buy a large popcorn and beverage ▪ Free Wii to those willing to buy five new games ▪ Free cell phone with two-year contract
Zero marginal cost	Products are distributed to customers without an appreciable cost to anyone.	▪ Online music distribution at iTunes ▪ Software distribution ▪ Video content on YouTube
Labor exchange	Services are provided to customers; the act of using the services creates value for the company.	▪ Yahoo! Answers ▪ Answers.com
Gift economy	Environments are created that allow people to participate and collaborate to create something of value for everyone.	▪ Open source software development ▪ Wikipedia ▪ Freecycle—free secondhand goods to anyone willing to haul them away

Source: Based on Anderson (2009).

INDUSTRY ANALYSIS

Banking Industry

Like many other industries moving into the Internet age, the banking business is changing. Since the nineteenth century, banks in the United States have been heavily regulated. Federal and state laws passed in the 1800's and the 1930's have limited banks to certain geographic locations and have determined the services they could offer. For example, in many states each bank could maintain locations for accepting deposits in only that one state, and in some states they were allowed to maintain offices in just one county. Banks could offer traditional banking services, including deposits and loans, but little more. Insurance services were banned, and securities underwriting was limited. The many banking laws and regulations were intended to limit the number of bank failures after the Great Depression and to make banks safer, but they also limited services that banks could provide to customers, preventing them from competing with stockbrokers and insurance companies.

Nearly all these banking restrictions were eased or eliminated from the 1970's to the present, when banking deregulation took place. Deregulation resulted in increased acquisitions and consolidations, integration across state lines, and a larger market share for better-run banks as they gained ground over their less efficient rivals. As a result, banks could offer more customer services at lower prices, benefiting the country's overall economy.

Today, the Internet provides banks with another way to serve customers and another venue for competition. Banks can now offer customers the convenience and security of online banking services—from account management to loan applications and certificate-of-deposit purchases. No longer do customers judge banks simply according to hours open, ATM locations, fees charged, or travel distance to a brick-and-mortar site. Now banks offering online services can also expect potential customers to judge them according to the following:

1. The degree to which the online banking experience can be personalized
2. Ease of use
3. Responsiveness of the site

Online banking has become the norm, with millions of people logging onto their bank's Web site to pay bills, transfer money, or review transactions. Given the advent of 4G mobile networks, phones, and devices, the next wave of technology innovation within the banking industry is mobile banking. Mobile banking provides customers the convenience of conducting any banking service from virtually anywhere while at the same time providing increased security through the application of various encryption and authentications capabilities within the advanced 4G communication networks. For example, several large banks such as USAA, Chase, and Citibank now offer applications for the iPhone and Android-based smartphones that allow their customers to deposit a check by simply taking a photo of the endorsed check; the deposit will be instantly credited to the user's bank account.

Although mobile banking seems promising, it still has a ways to go. For instance, today, most banks provide only a limited set of mobile services, such as viewing balances or receiving text alerts about payments or overdrafts. Many mobile devices are not 4G compatible, and advanced 4G networks are only slowly extending outside major cities and population areas. Of course, banks are beginning to provide more advanced services, but there is still a substantial gap between what has been promised and what is reality. Nevertheless, it is clear that this industry is in a state of transition to provide enhanced services to customers that will lower costs and improve convenience, ultimately making the process of paying a bill as easy as sending a text message to a friend.

Questions:

1. What are your biggest security concerns related to online banking? How does/should your bank address these concerns?
2. Deregulation of the banking industry allowed banks to more freely operate across state lines; should international banks be allowed to operate in domestic markets? Why or why not?

Based on:

Anonymous. (2005, November 15). Delivering on the promise to change the banking experience. Retrieved June 12, 2012, from http://www.microsoft.com/presspass/features/2005/nov05/11-15Banking.mspx.

Gardner, N. (2009, September 28). The evolution of banking—From the Web to phones. *News.com.au.* Retrieved June 12, 2012, from http://www.news.com.au/money/banking/internet-banking-moves-onto-your-phone/story-e6frfmcr-1225780500924.

Strahan, P. E. (2003, July). The real effects of banking deregulation. Retrieved June 12, 2012, from http://research.stlouisfed.org/publications/review/03/07/Strahan.pdf.

Whitney, L. (2009, August 11). USAA app lets iPhone users deposit checks. *CNET News.com.* Retrieved June 12, 2012, from http://news.cnet.com/8301-13579_3-10307182-37.html.

Key Points Review

1. *Discuss how information systems can be used for automation, organizational learning, and strategic advantage.* Automating business activities occurs when information systems are used to do a business activity faster or more cheaply. Information systems can be used to help automate and can also be used to improve aspects of an operation in order to gain dramatic improvements in the operation as a whole. When this occurs, technology is said to help us learn because it provides information about its operation and the underlying work process that it supports. Using information systems to automate and learn about business processes is a good start. However, information systems can add even more value to an organization if they are conceived, designed, used, and managed with a strategic approach. To apply information systems strategically, you must understand the organization's value chain and be able to identify opportunities in which you can use information systems to make changes or improvements in the value chain to gain or sustain a competitive advantage. All of these factors influence how an organization utilizes information systems investments as a central component for executing its business model. This requires a change in mind-set from thinking about information systems as an expense to be minimized to thinking of information systems as an asset to be invested in.

2. *Describe international business and IS strategies used by companies operating in the digital world.* Companies operating in the digital world can use different business strategies. Some companies pursue a home-replication strategy, which entails selling products developed for the home market internationally. In contrast, other companies develop products for the global market. This strategy, known as global business strategy, includes having a centralized organization to offer standardized products in different markets. This helps to achieve economies of scale and is best suited for homogeneous markets. Information systems used by organizations pursuing this strategy are very centralized, and large quantities of data flow from the subsidiaries to the headquarters. The multidomestic business strategy is best suited for heterogeneous markets, as it allows companies to quickly respond to changing local conditions; this strategy includes having a decentralized federation of loosely associated business units in different countries. Companies pursuing this strategy employ decentralized systems, and data sharing is very limited. The transnational business strategy is very well suited for operating in the digital world, as it combines the benefits of the multidomestic and the global business strategies by enabling economies

of scale while being responsive to local market conditions. In a transnational business strategy, some aspects of the company are centralized, while others are decentralized. The information systems used are distributed, allowing for increased communication between the headquarters and the subsidiaries as well as between the subsidiaries and allowing for common access to critical data. Transnational information systems are enabled primarily by intranets, extranets, and the Internet.

3. *Explain why and how companies are continually looking for innovative ways to use information systems for competitive advantage.* Organizations are finding innovative ways to use new technologies to help them do things faster, better, and more efficiently than rivals. Being at the technological cutting edge has its disadvantages and is typically quite difficult to execute. Given that new technologies are not as stable as traditional ones, relying on innovative information systems and technologies can be problematic. Because constantly upgrading to newer and better systems is expensive, relying on emerging systems can hurt a firm financially. In addition, using innovative information systems for competitive advantage can provide short-lived advantages; competitors can quickly jump on the technological bandwagon and easily mimic the same system. Not every organization should deploy innovative information systems. Those organizations that find themselves in highly competitive environments probably most need to deploy new technologies to stay ahead of rivals. To best deploy these new technologies, organizations must be ready for the business process changes that will ensue, have the resources necessary to deploy new technologies successfully, and be tolerant of the risk and problems involved in being at the cutting edge. Deploying emerging information systems is essentially a risk/return gamble: The risks are relatively high, but the potential rewards are great. Organizations successfully utilizing innovative systems and technologies today have people (and in some cases, special units) who scan the environment, looking out for emerging and enabling (and potentially disruptive) technologies that can help their firm. They then narrow down the list to technologies that match with the challenges the firm faces or that create economic opportunities. Next, they choose a particular technology or a set of technologies and implement them in a way that enables them to gain or sustain a competitive advantage. Finally, they assess these technology projects in terms of their value, not only to internal people and groups but also to external clients and partners. This process is ongoing, as information technologies and systems continually evolve.

4. Describe freeconomics and how organizations can leverage digital technologies to provide free goods and services to customers as a business strategy for gaining a competitive advantage. Freeconomics refers to the leveraging of digital technologies to provide *free* goods and services to customers as a business strategy for gaining a competitive advantage. Virtually *any* industry that utilizes digital technologies (not just those like Google or Yahoo!) is on a path toward increasingly lower costs, ultimately toward a price of free—or at least "free" for consumers. Industries can apply freeconomics in a variety of ways to gain a competitive advantage, including using advertising (e.g., Yahoo! banner ads), using a freemium approach (e.g., Flickr providing limited storage for free to gain customers and then charging a fee to those customers who need additional storage and features), having one product cross subsidize another (e.g., Comcast giving away DVRs to charge for programming), having zero marginal costs for additional product offerings (e.g., constant expansion of content on iTunes), gaining labor exchanges for services (e.g., Yahoo!'s answer service), or facilitating a gift economy where people freely collaborate to create something of value to everyone (e.g., open source software development).

Key Terms

administrative heritage   94
automating   84
best-cost provider strategy   86
business/IT alignment   91
business model   92
business process   80
capabilities   88
differentiation strategy   86
disruptive innovation   104
distinctive competency   89
domestic company   94
e-business   109
e-business innovation cycle   107
economic opportunities   109
enabling technology   109

executive level   82
first-mover advantage   87
freeconomics   110
functional area information system   83
global business strategy   96
home-replication strategy   94
innovator's dilemma   106
international business strategy   94
key performance indicator (KPI)   82
low-cost leadership strategy   86
managerial level   82
multidomestic business strategy   96
operational level   81
organizational learning   85
organizational strategy   86

resources   88
revenue model   93
semistructured decision   82
strategic necessity   91
strategic planning   86
structured decision   81
transaction   81
transnational business strategy   98
unstructured decision   86
value chain   91
value chain analysis   91
value creation   91
value proposition   111

Review Questions

1. List the management levels and their corresponding information systems solutions.
2. Compare and contrast automating and learning.
3. List five general types of organizational strategy.
4. What are the sources of a competitive advantage?
5. How can information systems add value to a business organization?
6. What is a business model and what are its primary components?
7. Describe the multidomestic business strategy and how it affects the flow and control of information.
8. Why is successful application of innovative technologies and systems often difficult?
9. List the key requirements for implementing innovative projects.
10. Using past examples, explain what is meant by a disruptive innovation.
11. Describe the competitive forces model.
12. What is freeconomics, and what are several approaches for applying its concepts to various industries?

Self-Study Questions

1. _____ is using technology as a way to help complete a task within an organization faster and, perhaps, more cheaply.
   A. automating
   B. learning
   C. strategizing
   D. processing

2. What are new technologies, products, or services that eventually surpass the existing dominant technology or product in a market called?
   A. surpassing event
   B. disruptive innovation
   C. innovative technology
   D. technology change

3. Which of the following is *not* improving the value chain?
   A. improving procurement processes
   B. increasing operating costs
   C. minimizing marketing expenditures
   D. streamlining production processes

4. A company is said to have _____ when it has gained an edge over its rivals.
   A. monopoly
   B. profitability
   C. competitive advantage
   D. computer advantage

5. Each of the following was described in this chapter as a source of competitive advantage except for _____.
   A. delivering superior customer service
   B. achieving lower cost than rivals
   C. being the subject of a hostile takeover
   D. having shorter lead times in developing and testing new products

6. _____ refers to the emergence of disruptive innovations that undermine effective management practices, often leading to the demise of an organization or an industry.
   A. Moore's law
   B. Technological obsolescence
   C. Life cycle analysis
   D. Innovator's dilemma

7. What is the process of choosing, matching, executing, and assessing innovative technologies called?
   A. environmental scanning
   B. e-business innovation cycle
   C. strategic planning
   D. none of the above

8. What international business strategy is employed by companies that carefully decide which aspect should be under central control and which should be decentralized?
   A. global business strategy
   B. transnational business strategy
   C. multidomestic business strategy
   D. operational business strategy

9. At the _____ level of the organization, functional managers (e.g., marketing managers, finance managers, manufacturing managers, and human resource managers) focus on monitoring and controlling operational-level activities and providing information to higher levels of the organization.
   A. operational
   B. managerial
   C. organizational
   D. executive

10. A supervisor's having to decide when to reorder supplies or how best to allocate personnel for the completion of a project is an example of a(n) _____ decision.
    A. structured
    B. unstructured
    C. automated
    D. delegated

Answers are on page 120.

Problems and Exercises

1. Match the following terms with the appropriate definitions:
   i. value chain analysis
   ii. freeconomics
   iii. managerial level
   iv. value chain
   v. e-business innovation cycle
   vi. disruptive innovations
   vii. innovator's dilemma
   viii. transnational business strategy
   ix. multidomestic business strategy
   x. operational level

   a. The notion that disruptive innovations can cause established firms or industries to lose market dominance, often leading to failure
   b. The process of analyzing an organization's activities to determine where value is added to products and/or services and the costs that are incurred for doing so
   c. New technologies, products, or services that eventually surpass the existing dominant technology or product in a market
   d. The middle level of the organization, where functional managers focus on monitoring and controlling operational-level activities and providing information to higher levels of the organization
   e. A model suggesting that the extent to which modern organizations use information technologies and systems in timely, innovative ways is the key to success
   f. The leveraging of digital technologies to provide free goods and services to customers as a business strategy for gaining competitive advantage
   g. The set of primary and support activities in an organization where value is added to a product or service
   h. An international business strategy employed to be flexible and responsive to the needs and demands of heterogeneous local markets
   i. An international business strategy that allows companies to leverage the flexibility offered by a decentralized organization (to be more responsive to local conditions) while at the same time reaping economies of scale enjoyed by centralization
   j. The bottom level of an organization, where the routine day-to-day interaction with customers occurs

2. Using a business or organization that you are familiar with, contrast the operational, managerial, and executive levels by contrasting each level's typical activities, types of decisions, and information needs.

3. Using your own life, contrast several structured versus unstructured decisions that you regularly have to make.

4. Identify a company utilizing the distinct competitive strategies shown in Figure 2.10; provide evidence to support your selections.

5. Of the five industry forces presented in the chapter (Porter's model), which is the most significant for an organization in terms of making IS investment decisions? Why? Which is the least significant? Why?

6. Using a company or organization that you are familiar with, map their various business processes into a value chain.

7. Find an international organization not discussed in this chapter that is operating in multiple countries using a home-replication business strategy. Provide evidence and examples that help to support your selection.

8. Find an international organization not discussed in this chapter that is operating in multiple countries using a multidomestic business strategy. Provide evidence and examples that help to support your selection.

9. The travel industry has adopted Internet-based technology in a big way across the world. A number of travel Web sites now exist. In groups, select one travel site and find the success and failure parameters.

10. Several companies use internet, intranet, and extranet technologies to add value into their value chain. Illustrate with examples how some of these companies have integrated these technologies into their business processes to gain competitiveness.

11. A retail store in your neighborhood hires you as their IS consultant and ask you to develop a strategic information system for them. What key information would you gather?

12. Identify examples not discussed in the chapter of disruptive innovations that successfully displaced or marginalized an industry or technology.

13. Apply the progression and effects of disruptive innovation on an industry (see Table 2.9), describing the evolution of a disruptive technology to a product or industry.

14. Find and describe an example not discussed in the book that demonstrates the freeconomics concept of freemium.

15. Find and describe an example not discussed in the book that demonstrates the freeconomics concept of cross subsidy.

16. Find and describe an example not discussed in the book that demonstrates the freeconomics concept of zero marginal cost.

17. Create a value chain model for an insurance company. How has this company used the power of technology to gain a competitive advantage?

Application Exercises

Note: The existing data files referenced in these exercises are available on the book's Web site: www.pearsonhighered.com/valacich.

 **Spreadsheet Application:
Valuing Information Systems**

The cost of maintaining information systems is high for Campus Travel. You have been assigned to evaluate the total cost of ownership (TCO) of a few systems that are currently in use by Campus Travel employees. Take a look at the TCO.csv file to obtain the list of systems that are in use and the costs associated with maintaining the software, hardware, and the associated personnel for each type of system. Calculate the following for your operations manager:

1. The costs for server hardware by adding a new row to include Web servers. This includes US$4,500 for the main campus and US$2,200 for the other campuses.
2. The TCO for the entire information system in Campus Travel. Hint: Sum all the values for all the systems together.
3. The TCO for servers and network components of the information system.

4. Make sure that you format the table, including using the currency format, in a professional manner.

 **Database Application:
Building a System Usage Database**

To understand the assets in Campus Travel, the IS manager has asked you to design a database that would be able to store all the assets. Your manager asks you to do the following:

1. Create a new blank database called asset.mdb.
2. Create a new table called "assets" in the asset database with the following fields:
   a. Item ID (Text field)
   b. Item Name (Text field)
   c. Description (Memo field)
   d. Category (hardware, software, other)
   e. Condition (new, good, fair, poor)
   f. Acquisition Date (Date field)
   g. Purchase Price (Currency field)
   h. Current Value (Currency field)

Team Work Exercise

 **Net Stats:
Online Searching**

The Google search engine has become so popular with Internet users that the word "Google" is often used as a verb ("I 'Googled' the restaurant to see its reviews"), but there are other well-known search engines, such as Yahoo! and Microsoft's Bing. Table 2.12 shows the percentage of Internet surfers who used each search engine (i.e., the search engines' market share) in April 2012 as compared to April 2010.

TABLE 2.12 Top Search Engines by Market Share, April 2012 Compared with April 2010

Search Engine	April 2012 Market Share (%)	April 2010 Market Share (%)	Change (percentage points)
Google	79.7	86.3	−6.6
Yahoo!	6.5	5.3	1.2
Bing	4.5	3.1	1.4
Other	9.3	5.3	4.0

Source: Based on http://marketshare.hitslink.com/search-engine-market-share.aspx?qprid=5.

Questions and Exercises

1. Search the Web for the most up-to-date statistics about the search engine market.
2. As a team, interpret these numbers. What is striking/important about these statistics? How do the numbers compare to your own search behavior?
3. How have the numbers changed? Will there be other important players in the search engine market?
4. Using your spreadsheet software of choice, create a graph/figure most effectively visualizing the statistics/changes you consider most important.

Answers to the Self-Study Questions

1. A, p. 84	**2.** B, p. 104	**3.** B, p. 91	**4.** C, p. 87	**5.** C, p. 87
6. D, p. 104	**7.** B, p. 107	**8.** B, p. 98	**9.** B, p. 82	**10.** A, p. 81

CASE 1   LinkedIn

YouTube is for video entertainment; iTunes services is for music lovers; Facebook is primarily for socializing; Flickr is for photo exchange; World of Warcraft is for participating in virtual communities; Gamezone is for gamesters; and so on and so on. It would seem that the Web has anticipated all of our needs and responded. But wait, what's out there for those of us who want to further our professional lives—to visit with others in our field of expertise, to look at jobs that are available in other parts of the world, to find out what's happening in the business world outside our own familiar circle, and to garner introductions to those who might help us succeed? LinkedIn is an online service that fills this niche. LinkedIn advertises itself as "an interconnected network of experienced professionals from around the world, representing 150 industries and 200 countries. You can find, be introduced to, and collaborate with qualified professionals that you need to work with to accomplish your goals." As of 2012, LinkedIn had over 161 million members, with 61 percent from countries outside the United States, and has executives from all Fortune 500 companies in its ranks. LinkedIn is growing rapidly, with about two new members joining approximately every second. In addition to access via a Web browser, LinkedIn is also available on various smartphones and tablets using customized applications.

Reid Hoffman, a former executive vice president of PayPal, founded LinkedIn in 2002; the service was launched in May 2003. Hoffman remains chairman of the board at LinkedIn, which is based in Mountain View, California, but also has offices in Omaha, New York, and London. His LinkedIn profile is available at http://www.linkedin.com/in/reidhoffman.

LinkedIn uses a freemium approach, where joining is free, with the option of upgrading to a paid account with additional functionalities. Newcomers to LinkedIn create a profile, listing professional accomplishments. Each newcomer then links trusted colleagues, contacts, and clients—called *connections*—by inviting them to join and linking to him or her. In this way, LinkedIn participants create their own professional networks, where contacts may number in the thousands. Connections can be used in many ways:

- Users list trusted contacts, who then list their contacts, called second-degree connections. Second-degree connections list their trusted contacts, called third-degree connections. In this way, the original LinkedIn user brings together thousands of professionals, gaining many valuable contacts.
- Users can then find jobs, people, and business opportunities recommended by someone in the network.
- Employers using the network can list jobs and search for available candidates to fill job openings.
- Job seekers can search the connections of potential employers and find mutual connections who might introduce them.

A free feature called "LinkedIn Answers" lets users ask business-related questions for the community to answer. LinkedIn Groups is another free feature that allows users to make additional contacts by joining alumni, professional, or other job-related groups.

There are ways to enhance one's use of professional profile sites such as LinkedIn, writes Kevin Donlin for the *Minneapolis–St. Paul Star Tribune*. First, enhance your profile. One way to do this is to jazz up your profile with a few pertinent details and statements from colleagues. For example, staff members at LinkedIn advised Guy Kawasaki, managing director of Garage Technology Ventures in San Francisco, California, to add the following statement from a former colleague at Apple, where Guy said he was "chief evangelist." "Spirited and exceptionally bright with a highly developed sense of humor, Guy continues to be one of the most gifted marketing executives I know."

Enhance your profile, Donlin advises, but "keep your dirt to yourself. According to NBC News, 77 percent of employers will search the Internet to check your background, and 35 percent of employers have eliminated a candidate for consideration after finding 'digital dirt' about them online." So don't post that video of yourself imbibing too much at a party on Facebook, and remember that potential employers may not appreciate the video of the tasteless practical joke you played on a friend, so keep it off YouTube.

Like some other social media sites, LinkedIn has come under recent criticism for its threats to business and corporate security. According to a recent Security Threat Report by Sophos, an information security firm, LinkedIn is increasingly being used as a conduit for hackers and other malicious entities to develop "road maps" attacks. According to the report, LinkedIn is providing what amounts to a corporate directory of who works at a firm and what their responsibilities are as well as corporate e-mail addresses. In June 2012, 6.5 million LinkedIn passwords were posted on a hacker site. Armed with this type of information, hackers can easily set up a fake LinkedIn account or devise a social engineering attack—the act of manipulating people into divulging confidential information—and target who and what they want to attack to effectively meet their sinister goals. Security concerns aside, LinkedIn is clearly a valuable technological tool for Internet users and entrepreneurs alike who are looking for better ways to network.

Questions:

1. Do you think it is ethical for employers to search the Internet for information on potential employees?
2. Do you believe that you can gain a competitive advantage by joining a network such as LinkedIn? Why or why not?
3. Have you joined or do you plan to join LinkedIn (or a similar type of site)? Why or why not?

Based on:

Donlin, K. (2008, April 9). Three ways to get found and hired. *Star Tribune*. Retrieved June 12, 2012, from http://www.startribune.com/jobs/career/15116626.html.

Kawasaki, G. (2010, January 16). LinkedIn profile extreme makeover. Retrieved June 12, 2012, from http://blog.guykawasaki.com/2007/01/linkedin_profil.html.

LinkedIn. (2012, June 11). In *Wikipedia, The Free Encyclopedia*. Retrieved June 12, 2012, from http://en.wikipedia.org/w/index.php?title=LinkedIn&oldid=497074823.

Linkedin.com. (n.d.) Retrieved June 12, 2012, from http://press.linkedin.com/about.

Muncaster, P. (2010, February 15). LinkedIn hits 60 million global users. *CRN*. Retrieved June 12, 2012, from http://www.crn.com.au/News/167245,linkedin-hits-60-million-global-users.aspx.

Robertson, J. (2012, June 12). Stolen LinkedIn passwords can sell for as low as $1. *BusinessWeek*. Retrieved June 12, 2012, from http://www.businessweek.com/news/2012-06-12/stolen-linkedin-passwords-can-sell-for-as-low-as-1.

Sophos.com. (2010, February 1). Malware and spam rise 70% on social networks, security report reveals. Retrieved June 12, 2012, from http://www.sophos.com/pressoffice/news/articles/2010/02/security-report-2010.html.

CASE 2   Netflix

Remember the old brick-and-mortar movie rental services? You drove to the physical location, scanned shelves for your movie of choice (too frequently, it wasn't in), paid the clerk, and left. The flick was due back in 24 hours (or, at most, three to five days later), or you were billed a hefty late fee. In some cases, forgetful customers answered the door to find a police officer asking why they hadn't returned a rental movie.

Movie rental stores still exist, of course—Blockbuster may come to mind first, although many of its stores have closed—but now there are alternatives. Pay-per-view is an option for cable and satellite dish TV subscribers, but choices are limited to the services' picks and are available only after movies have been offered as rental DVDs and videos for 30 days. Since customers are not always satisfied with limits inherent in these options—late fees, unavailability of newer films, short turnaround times, and so on—it had to follow that someone would come up with the idea to offer a click-based online movie rental service.

Enter Netflix in 2002, the first and now the world's largest online movie rental service. As of March 2012, Netflix offered its nearly 30 million subscribers thousands of movie and television choices. The term "subscriber" is the key to Netflix's unique idea. Movie aficionados subscribe to the Netflix service by paying a monthly fee. Subscribers can have DVDs delivered, streamed over the Internet to computers and televisions, or both. Around 26.5 million customers selected the "streaming only" service, while 10.1 million subscribed to the movie delivery service (some subscribed to both, bringing the total to nearly 30 million). Although there are several subscription plans available, the most basic plan is US$7.99 per month for unlimited, and instant viewing, video streaming services. For customers subscribing to DVD delivery, you pay a bit more, and the turnaround time to receive the DVD is typically one business day after shipping. Movies are available in standard DVD format and many in Blu-ray, although at an additional charge. There are no late fees involved, you can keep the disc as long as you want, and postage is paid both ways. When one movie is returned, another is mailed back to the customer based on a tailored list of queued movies.

The "on-demand" type streaming service was added in 2007, allowing customers to view movies immediately on their PCs or Macs. In 2008, Netflix introduced a service that allowed subscribers to instantly watch streaming movies and TV shows on their television through Netflix-ready devices such as Internet-enabled Blu-ray players or Microsoft's Xbox 360. As of 2012, Netflix streaming has become its most popular subscription option, as more devices connect directly to the Netflix library of content and high-speed internet access is becoming ubiquitous. Additionally, the streaming content choices are ever growing, with over 60,000 items currently available in Netflix's "Watch Instantly" library (although, industry insiders say this number is somewhat inflated).

Soon after Netflix's inception in 2002, Blockbuster, the nation's largest movie rental chain, and Walmart, the largest business in the United States, began to offer in-store subscription services similar to Netflix's model. By 2006, however, Walmart had dropped its movie rental subscription service. As of 2012, Blockbuster's subscription service, Blockbuster By Mail, and their digital download service, Blockbuster On Demand, continue to provide competition to Netflix in some markets.

However, Netflix's extraordinary and, therefore, popular DVD rental service has outpaced competitive movie rental services, including pay-per-view, because it personalizes a customer's movie rental experience to a degree previously not possible. This personalized service asks the customer to rate up to 40 movies. From this information, software called Cinematch creates a profile of each customer and a list of recommended movies. If, for example, a customer liked 2012 blockbuster *Prometheus,* he or she may also like the 1979 sci-fi classic *Alien,* and that movie will be included in a list the customer accesses by clicking on "Suggestions." The customer can then opt to place any of the recommended movies in his or her queue. Customers manipulate the movies listed in the queue by adding new titles to the list, removing titles, and moving titles to the top or to other locations on the list. Netflix's Cinematch system allows customers to tap a wide database of movies, many of which they may not have been aware of at all since it will move to the next movie in a customer's queue if a more recent and popular listing is not immediately available.

Netflix is not without critics. It turns out that the service "rewards" customers with the fewest monthly rentals and "punishes" those with the most rentals in terms of popular movie availability and promptness of shipping. This policy is spelled out in the company's terms of service, published on the Netflix Web site:

In determining priority for shipping and inventory allocation, we may utilize many different factors, including the number and type of DVDs you rent through our service, the membership plan you select, as well as other uses of our service by you. For example, if all other factors are the same, we give priority to those members who receive the fewest DVDs through our service.

According to the Netflix site, when you add a popular movie that is currently unavailable, you are added to the internal list that rates customers according to profitability. There is an assumption by the customers that the service is linear, meaning that the first customer to request the movie would be the first customer to get the movie—or first in, first out. In reality, the priority service equation selects customers on the basis of their profitability. With shipping being the major cost for the online movie distributor, customers who cost the most in terms of shipping may not receive popular movies first.

What does this mean for the customers? If you are a customer who uses the service infrequently, then you are highly profitable for Netflix since your shipping costs are low. Therefore, your selections are prioritized. The customers who use the service frequently or what Netflix would deem "over-frequently" are seen as not as profitable and therefore do not receive priority.

In 2004, this policy caused a "frequent" Netflix customer to sue the company in a class-action lawsuit titled *Chavez v. Netflix, Inc.* The plaintiff in the case, Frank Chavez, claimed that Netflix's claims that a subscriber could rent "unlimited" DVDs each month and receive them in "a day's time" were false. (Chavez had attempted to rent hundreds of DVDs a month but sued when he found he could not.) Although Netflix denied any wrongdoing, they settled the suit in 2005. Chavez received US$2,000, and his lawyers got over US$2.5 million. Certain Netflix customers who joined the class-action suit were upgraded to a different rental plan for a short period, and Netflix instituted a limited try-the-plan-for-three-months-free offer. Although some customers have expressed dissatisfaction with the apparent "throttling" of their account, Netflix is working hard to understand this rapidly evolving market with various innovations in its product offerings and business model.

Consider how fast things are changing. Just a few years ago, a majority of Netflix's revenue came from DVD rentals. Today, a majority of Netflix customers exclusively utilize video streaming to their home. As streaming became popular, customers demanded better quality sound and video than is typical over the Internet (think of You-Tube). To address this, Netflix evolved its business model and associated infrastructure to support 1080p HD video with Dolby Digital 5.1 surround sound. Content delivered at this quality requires a lot of storage and bandwidth. Customers were happy and the streaming business is booming. However, industry insiders predict that streaming to mobile devices will be the next big thing, another megatrend that will continue to transform this industry. While allowing customers to enjoy content while on the go has the potential to greatly expand Netflix's customer base, most mobile devices have a limited data plan. Today, customers can stream content at various quality levels depending on their data plan. What's next for the online movie rental company? Clearly, their business model will need to continue to transform as technology and customer consumption patterns evolve.

Questions:

1. Can local video stores survive in the digital world? Contrast their evolution with that of local bookstores. What is similar? What is unique?
2. Forecast the future of Netflix in regard to the advent of on-demand video where any type of video content is available at any time on any device.
3. Discuss whether and how Netflix can maintain its competitive advantage.

Based on:

Elgan, M. (2006, January 30). How to hack Netflix. *Information Week*. Retrieved June 14, 2012, from http://www.informationweek.com/news/showArticle.jhtml?articleID=177105341.

Frauenfelder, M. (2005, November 2). Netflix settlement details. *Boing Boing*. Retrieved June 14, 2012, from http://www.boingboing.net/2005/11/02/netflix_lawsuit_sett.html.

Mullaney, T. J., & Hof, R. (2005, November 10). Netflix starring in merger story? *BusinessWeek*. Retrieved June 14, 2012, from http://www.businessweek.com/technology/content/nov2005/tc20051110_143721.htm.

Netflix. (n.d.). Retrieved June 14, 2012, from http://www.netflix.com.

Netflix. (2012, June 14). In Wikipedia, The Free Encyclopedia. Retrieved June 14, 2012, from http://en.wikipedia.org/w/index.php?title=Netflix&oldid=497566778.

O'Brien, J. M. (2002, December). The Netflix effect. *Wired*. Retrieved June 14, 2012, from http://www.wired.com/wired/archive/10.12/netflix.html.

Portnoy, S. (2010, February 8). Netflix will add 1080p, 5.1-channel surround sound streaming to its online video service later in 2010. *ZDNet*. Retrieved June 14, 2012, from http://blogs.zdnet.com/home-theater/?p=2641.

Managing the Information Systems Infrastructure and Services

Preview

Just as any city depends on a functioning infrastructure, companies operating in a digital world are relying on a comprehensive information systems (IS) infrastructure to support their business processes and competitive strategy. With ever-increasing speed, transactions are conducted; likewise, with ever-increasing amounts of data to be captured, analyzed, and stored, companies have to thoroughly plan and manage their infrastructure needs in order to gain the greatest returns on their IS investments. When planning and managing their IS architectures, organizations must answer many important and difficult questions. For example, how will we utilize information systems to enable our competitive strategy? What technologies and systems best support our core business processes? Which vendors should we partner with, which technologies do we adopt, and which do we avoid? What hardware, software, or services do we buy, build, or have managed by an outside service provider? How can we use cloud computing to increase our agility? How can we get the most out of the data captured from internal and external sources? Clearly, effectively managing an organization's IS infrastructure is a complex but necessary activity in today's digital world.

This chapter focuses on helping managers understand the key components of a comprehensive IS infrastructure and why its careful management is necessary. With the increasing complexity of an organization's information needs and the increasing complexity of the systems needed to satisfy these requirements, the topic of infrastructure management is fundamental for managing in the digital world.

Managing in the Digital World:
"I Googled You!"

"Supercalifragilisticexpialidocious." Not sure what that means? Google it. This search engine has become so associated with our daily lives that the Oxford English Dictionary officially incorporated Google as a verb in June 2006. More than any other American multinational Internet and software corporation, Google, best known for its search platform (see Figure 3.1), has thoroughly branched out to develop a number of Internet-based services and products. When searching for the nearest bookstore, Google Maps has the answer. Free for non-commercial use, the application offers street maps, a route planner, and high-resolution satellite images, and even "Street View" for urban areas. Another popular service is Gmail, a free e-mail service that provides users with (as of April 2012) over 10 GB of free storage, and allows sending and receiving attachments of up to 25 MB, larger than most other free e-mail services. Adding to its fast-growing empire, Google bought YouTube in November 2006 for US$1.65 billion. Since that time, the video sharing Web site, dubbed by Time magazine as the Walmart of video browsing, has operated as a subsidiary of Google. Google is, in fact, in every corner of the World Wide Web, and the different technologies it offers have been incorporated into our everyday lives.

Google's humble beginning started with Larry Page and Sergey Brin, two Stanford University graduate students in computer science. In January 1996, Page and Brin began collaborating on BackRub, a search engine whose name came from its unique ability to analyze the "back links" pointing to a given Web site. Afflicted by the perennial shortage of cash common to graduate students everywhere, the pair took to haunting the department's loading docks in hopes of tracking down newly arrived computers that they could borrow for their network. Page and Brin later changed the name of their project to "Google" which by definition describes the purpose of the Web site. Google is "a play on the word 'googol,' the mathematical term for a 1 followed by 100 zeros." Google's use of the term reflects the company's mission "to organize the world's information and make it universally accessible and useful" (Courtesy of Google, Inc.).

Flash-forward to 1998 and a picture of Page and Brin in a dorm room. The rest involves maxed out credit cards for a terabyte of memory and a series of adventures in search of investors to assist in the further development of their search engine technology. The good days were not far away as support came from two important figures. David Filo, a friend and one of the developers of Yahoo!, convinced the two to start up their own company. At the same time, Andy Bechtolsheim, a friend of a faculty member, offered "Google Inc." a check for US$100,000 after one brief meeting. With moral support and practical funding in place, Page and Brin scrambled to establish a corporation that would quickly see the companionship of other investors. In September 1998, Google Inc. began operations in a friend's garage in Menlo, California. From then on, Google's mission "to organize the world's information and make it universally accessible and useful" has gradually changed the technology of Web searching and more.

No longer garage-bound and innovating far beyond its 1996 beginning, it is worth noting that Google has stayed true to its initial mission. The company now offers a wide range of services ranging from communication and collaboration to entertainment. For example, Google offers e-mail, instant messaging, mobile text messaging services, and even phone numbers. In the entertainment field, Google's services include an automated news site, a site

FIGURE 3.1

Google search page inside Google's Chrome browser.
Source: Courtesy of Google, Inc.

hosting blogs (or Web logs, see Chapter 5, "Enhancing Organizational Communication and Collaboration Using Social Media"), free imaging software, and a site for programmers interested in creating new applications.

The biggest revenue generator for Google is its AdSense program, which allows any Web site to publish advertisements on its pages. The Web site publisher is paid every time someone clicks on an ad originating from that page; using AdSense, the Web site publisher can tailor the types of ads that are placed on a Web site, including the function of blocking competitor ads and the freedom to eliminate unwanted ads regarding death, war, or explicit materials. The advertisers, in turn, can specifically target their ads using various metrics provided by AdSense, including how many people look at the site, the cost per click, click through rates, and more.

The Google from 1998 is certainly no longer the Google we see today. The company has single-handedly expanded into a global empire. Simply google "Google" to see how many hits you come up with. Google News, Google Scholar, Google Finance, Google Translate, and Google Images, to name a handful. In addition, there is 2006's Google Docs; a suite of applications used for creating text documents, spreadsheets, and presentations (Google Docs has since been morphed into Google Drive, not only enabling the online editing of documents, but also providing users with 5 GB of space for storing any type of file in the cloud). OpenSocial, a set of application programming interfaces introduced in 2007, enables developers to create applications that work on all social networks. In 2008, Android was released as an open source operating system for mobile phones that directly and successfully competed against Apple's iPhone, Research in Motion's BlackBerry, and Microsoft's Windows Phone. That same year Google introduced Chrome, a Web browser lauded for its speed and unique features, thus attacking established companies such as Microsoft on yet another front. Rounding out the endless list are Google Voice (2009), which offers users the control over when and where a phone rings when their numbers are dialed, and Google's "Nexus" line of mobile phones and tablets, co-developed with manufacturers such as Samsung, and optimized for the Android operating system.

From e-mails to mobile devices, it may look as if Google's services have become so broad that it is impossible to find a common link, but this is not so. Many of these services are cloud-based, offering heavenly convenience and cloud-nine centralization. Do you remember the last time you had to download something to update your Gmail? Did you have to install an application to watch Madonna's Super Bowl half-time performance on YouTube? Of course not. In short, that is what Google is all about; no installation required. The magic begins and ends in Google's servers.

The success of Google cannot easily be summed up in a line or two. The company's search queries started at 10,000 back in 1998 and reached 500,000 by 1999, with a stunning 100 million by the end of the millennium. Google's stock sold for over US$600 per share in July 2012, compared with the initial US$85 in August 2004. The company reached US$37.91 billion in revenue and US$9.74 billion in net income in 2011. With the company growing at such astonishing pace, its infrastructure is of primary concern. While most of Google's systems and algorithms are self-developed and proprietary, and Google's services run on its own data centers, some have argued for incorporating open source solutions into the production environment to maintain portability, efficiency, and agility. Whatever the solution will be, the Google story is inspiring and still evolving. After all the fame and success, the company's initial dedication to its users and belief in the possibilities of the Internet remains grounded in the heart of Google.

After reading this chapter, you will be able to answer the following:

1. How does Google benefit from a well-functioning infrastructure?

2. How would you rank the various infrastructure components described in this chapter in their importance to Google's success? Explain your rationale.

3. How and why does Google's success rely on the cloud-computing model?

Based on:

Ager, M. (2010, May 4). Pedal to the Chrome metal: Our fastest beta to date for Windows, Mac and Linux. *Google Chrome Blog*. Retrieved May 24, 2012, from http://chrome.blogspot.com/2010/05/pedal-to-chrome-metal-our-fastest-beta.html.

Anonymous. (n.d.). Company overview. Retrieved May 24, 2012, from http://www.google.com/intl/en/company.

Anonymous. (n.d.). Google milestones. Retrieved May 24, 2012, from http://www.google.com/aoubt/company/history.

Baker, L. (2006, June 29). Google's a verb in the Oxford English Dictionary. Retrieved May 24, 2012, from http://www.searchenginejournal.com/googles-a-verb-in-the-oxford-english-dictionary/3590/.

Cauley, L. (2008, January 13). Introducing the first Android prototype. USA Today. Retrieved May 24, 2012, from http://www.usatoday.com/money/industries/technology/2008-01-13-android-google_N.htm.

U.S. Securities and Exchange Commission. (2012). Google 10-K Filing. Retrieved May 24, 2012, from http://www.sec.gov/Archives/edgar/data/1288776/000119312512025336/Financial_Report.xls.

THE IS INFRASTRUCTURE

Most people expect a variety of basic municipal services, such as sanitation, security, transportation, provision of energy and water, and so on, to be provided by the city they live in. Any area where people live or work needs a supporting **infrastructure**, which entails the technical structures enabling the provision of services (see Figure 3.2); many infrastructure components, such as power, telephone, water, and sewage lines, are "invisible" to the users, meaning that the users typically do not know (or even care) where, for example, their water comes from, as long as it flows when they open their faucets. Other, more visible, infrastructure components include streets, schools, retail stores, and law enforcement. Both the area's inhabitants and businesses depend on the services provided by that infrastructure, and cities with a good infrastructure are considered more livable than cities with poorer infrastructure and are much more likely to attract businesses and residents.

For organizations, many decisions are based on the provision of such services, such as when choosing a site for a new manufacturing plant or company headquarters. Indeed, many municipalities attempt to attract new businesses and industries by setting up new commercial zones with a well-planned infrastructure. In some cases, specific infrastructure components are of special importance. One such example is search engine giant Google, which needs data centers located all over the world to offer the best performance to its users. One of Google's newest data centers was built in an abandoned paper mill in Hamina, Finland. Why would a company such as Google choose such a rural location? First, the location offers connectivity, with a state-of-the-art fiber-optic network capable of providing high-speed data transfer to the Internet backbone. Second—and maybe more important—the location at the Baltic Sea allows the company to use sea water for its cooling needs (as a large number of computers generates a tremendous amount of heat), and the cool climate allows Google to reduce the need for air conditioning. As energy is one of the most important resources for Google, the company attempts to reduce consumption and use renewable sources whenever possible (see Figure 3.3). As you can see from this example, companies such as Google must consider far more than just the need for increased data storage space and processing power.

For organizations operating globally, local differences in infrastructure pose additional challenges, particularly when operating in developing nations. For example, in many parts of the world, organizations cannot count on an uninterrupted supply of water or electricity. Consequently, many of the large call centers in India that support customers around the world for companies like Dell Computers or Citibank have installed massive power generators to minimize the effects of frequent power outages, or have set up their own satellite links to be independent from the local, unreliable communications networks.

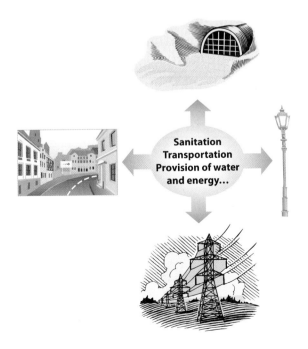

FIGURE 3.2

Infrastructure components of a city enable the provision of basic services.

FIGURE 3.3

Google uses solar energy to power its main campus in Mountain View, California.

Source: REUTERS/Kimberly White

Just as people and companies rely on basic municipal services to function, businesses rely on an **information systems infrastructure** (consisting of hardware, system software, storage, networking, and data centers) to support their decision making, business processes, and competitive strategy. Earlier, we defined business processes as the activities organizations perform in order to reach their business goals, including core activities that transform inputs and produce outputs, and supporting activities that enable the core activities to take place. To enable such processes, organizations rely on three basic capabilities supported by information systems: processing, storage, and transmission of data (see Figure 3.4). Hence, almost all of an organization's business processes depend on the underlying IS infrastructure, albeit to different degrees.

Organizations nowadays are facing continuously changing business environments. Traditionally, companies were operating in relatively stable markets, and could gain or sustain competitive advantage from relatively few innovations. Advances in information and communication

FIGURE 3.4

The information systems infrastructure enables processing, storing, and transmitting of data.

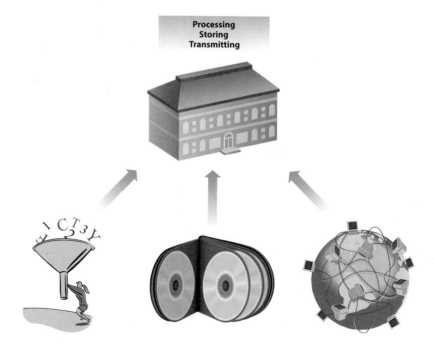

WHO'S GOING MOBILE

The Cloud Phone

In today's connected world, everybody seems to own a mobile phone, and many even go so far as to opt not to have a traditional landline phone anymore. In Sub-Saharan Africa, however, people often do not have the choice between fixed and mobile phones; lacking proper telecommunications infrastructure, mobile phones are for many the *only* means of providing not only connectivity, but also various other useful or even essential services to people. For example, as many people in Sub-Saharan Africa do not have bank accounts (and the nearest bank is often a few hours' or even days' walk away), a particularly successful application of mobile phones is the transfer of money through text messages. Yet, for people surviving on US$1–2 per day, owning a mobile phone is normally far out of reach.

Mobile phone manufacturers have long tried to manufacture affordable phones for developing countries; however, the three main components of a mobile phone (i.e., the display screen, the keyboard, and the radio frequency chip) cost US$5–6 each, and it is virtually impossible to build a phone for less than US$20–25, a price far too expensive for people in rural Africa. Therefore, people frequently share phones. Yet, traditionally, phone numbers are tied to so-called "subscriber identity modules" (integrated into SIM cards that can be inserted into a phone), meaning that typically only the owner of a phone and SIM card would have a phone number and could enjoy features such as text messaging or voice mail. To address this problem, and to provide access to mobile phones to more people, the British company Movirtu developed the "Cloud Phone," enabling individuals to access personal accounts and have their own phone numbers using shared mobile telephone handsets. Movirtu's phone works just like cloud-based e-mail. Rather than needing their own phone, people can just borrow another person's phone, log in with their own phone number and PIN code, and have instant access to placing phone calls, text messaging, voice mail, and so on. Setting up an account

with Movirtu costs a mere US$0.10–0.20, and following that, the user only incurs normal prepaid charges for making and/or receiving phone calls or messages. The owner of the phone receives additional airtime as incentive for sharing the phone.

Movirtu has successfully launched its cloud-based phone in Madagascar, Malawi, and Nigeria, enabling countless people to enjoy greater connectivity and access to mobile banking. However, another barrier has yet to be overcome: as the cloud-based phone allows sharing a phone amongst multiple users, the continuous usage quickly drains a phone's battery, rendering the phone useless (at least for a while). People in rural Africa sometimes need to walk two hours to have their phones charged and walk another two hours back home each week to keep their mobile phones up and going. If technology is to take another step in making lives easier, battery technology may just be the next problem to tackle.

Based on:

Byrne, C. (2011, May 31). Movirtu's "cloud phone" connects third world users. *The New York Times.* Retrieved May 23, 2012, from http://www.nytimes.com/external/venturebeat/2011/05/31/31venturebeat-movirtus-cloud-phone-connects-third-world-us-20932.html.

Lawson, S. (2011, August 5). Movirtu Cloud Phone brings mobile phone service to developing nations. *Computerworld UK.* Retrieved May 23, 2012, from http://www.computerworlduk.com/news/mobile-wireless/3295503/movirtu-cloud-phone-brings-mobile-phone-service-to-developing-nations.

Lopez, J. S., and Pfeifer, G. (2011, October 10). IFC, Movirtu, Airtel Madagascar announce innovative Cloud Phone to expand access to mobile network services in Madagascar. *Movirtu.com.* Retrieved May 23, 2012, from http://movirtu.com/internalnewsre-direct/item/297-ifc-movirtu-airtel-madagascar-announce-innovative-cloud-phone-to-expand-access-to-mobile-network-services-in-madagascar.

Sutter, J. D. (2010, October 21). Meet the 20-cent 'cloud phone'. *CNN.* Retrieved May 23, 2012, from http://edition.cnn.com/2010/TECH/innovation/10/21/cloud.phone/index.html.

technologies have leveled the playing field, allowing even small companies from all over the world to compete on a global scale. As new competitors can literally come out of nowhere, any competitive advantage will be increasingly short-lived, forcing organizations to keep innovating.

Facing this situation, organizations have to adapt, or will sooner or later go out of business. Quickly adapting to a constantly changing competitive environment necessitates that businesses are increasingly flexible and agile. In addition, any lack of availability, performance, or security (e.g., the news of an organization's Web site being attacked by hackers, or collapsing under unanticipated customer demand) is often immediately visible to customers or other stakeholders, potentially leading to loss of business, trust, and goodwill. Thus, organizations' business processes need to be supported by the right applications and the right data, which in turn rely on a solid underlying IS infrastructure (see Figure 3.5). In sum, organizations rely on a complex, interrelated IS infrastructure to effectively thrive in the ever-increasingly competitive digital world.

FIGURE 3.5

A solid IS infrastructure is needed to support an organization's business processes.

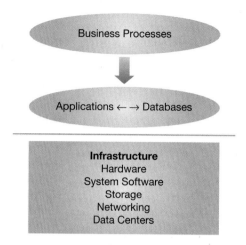

To get a better understanding of an IS infrastructure, we first provide a brief overview of how applications and databases support business processes, and then discuss how hardware, system software, storage, networking, and data centers interact to form an organization's IS infrastructure. Note that in this chapter, we will primarily focus on these components from a business perspective. For more technical details, please refer to the Technology Briefing.

Applications and Databases Supporting Business Processes

Data are probably among the most important assets an organization has, as data are essential for both executing business processes and gaining business intelligence. No matter what the business process is, data are used, processed, or generated along the way. For example, business processes associated with manufacturing products need data about inventory levels of raw materials, production capacities, and demand forecasts; likewise, back-office business processes associated with accounts receivable need data about customers, sales, receipts, and so on. In addition, increasing amounts of data are used for gaining business intelligence. Data once taken for granted or never collected at all are now used to make organizations more productive and competitive. Stock prices in the market, potential customers who meet a company's criteria for its products' target audiences, as well as the credit rating of wholesalers and customers are all types of data that organizations collect and analyze to turn into useful information. Yet, just having access to data is not sufficient; it is through applications that the data can be used effectively. Next, we briefly describe the role of application software in supporting an organization's business processes.

APPLICATION SOFTWARE. Organizations are continuously looking for ways to streamline and automate business processes, so as to generate more revenue or reduce costs, thus making the organization more profitable. **Application software** helps to automate business processes, and enables processes that would otherwise not even be possible. Accountants have for centuries used thick books for maintaining the accounting records of a business; automating the associated tasks using accounting software applications not only has helped to make the tasks less effortful and reduce error rates, but in addition allows quick analysis of accounting records, so as to examine sales trends, delinquencies, profit margins, and the like. Similarly, automating inventory management functions using specialized inventory management software not only helps keep a more accurate and up-to-date inventory, but can also generate a wealth of data that can be used to optimize inventory levels, taking into account the costs of keeping inventory and the potential costs of stockouts. E-commerce Web sites such as Amazon.com would not be possible without the applications needed for automatically processing transactions.

In addition to various types of application software for different business functions, other types of application software let users perform tasks such as writing business letters, managing stock portfolios, or manipulating forecasts to come up with the most efficient allocation of resources for a project. As discussed in Chapter 1, "Managing in the Digital World," application software also includes personal productivity software such as Microsoft Office; supply chain management systems to support the coordination of suppliers, product or service production, and distribution; or customer relationship management (CRM) systems to help companies win and retain customers, gain marketing and customer insight, and focus on customers.

ETHICAL DILEMMA

Putting People's Lives Online

Is that a man breaking into an apartment? There's obviously a house on fire. The lady in this picture looks exactly like my next-door-neighbor, and those are obviously my clothes drying in my backyard. Search a random location on Google Maps, and you may find—via the Street View feature—the most unexpected candid shots of your friends walking on the street, waiting for a bus, or even hanging out with people they don't want you to know about. Without doubt, Google Maps can be tremendously useful; combining traditional maps, information from the Web, and innovative technology, the application is a helpful assistant for planning trips, locating businesses, and so on. However, Google Maps has been under fire since the introduction of the Street View feature, with many questioning whether a strict line has been unnecessarily crossed in the invasion of public privacy.

The biggest argument behind the dilemma is the collective sense of intrusion that has stimulated concerns of losing one's safety—parents are worried pictures of their children could possibly make them targets of child predators, and people visiting adult shops simply do not find it essential for the entire world to know where they went last Saturday afternoon. Although Google has so far attempted to ease public concern by blurring the faces of people, license plate numbers, and house numbers, it still is rather awkward to find, say, a good shot of your underclothes hanging on the clothesline and be informed about it by another person. The way Street View operates indeed creates a sense of insecurity; many critics believe that Street View resembles having a gigantic security camera capturing their every move without their consent or further, even without their being aware of it (in fact, Google only periodically takes still photographs of streets, and these are quickly outdated).

The bottom line is: If taking random pictures is never a problem in a democratic society, is Google Maps engaging in illegal activity with its Street View feature? Attempts to come up with a definite answer make the issue even more controversial, as the concepts of free speech, open information, and the idea of privacy tend to have complex interrelationships. This creates a complex paradox that makes it almost impossible to determine whether Google is doing something good or bad. Nonetheless, Google Street View is not necessarily illegal; after all, it is not against the law to take pictures of public spaces and post them online for open viewing.

The Street View controversy took another turn when it became known that Google not only took pictures, but also intercepted and recorded Wi-Fi data when collecting imagery for the service. Initially, Google claimed that only the location of Wi-Fi access points should have been recorded, and that the cars had "inadvertently" recorded actual traffic (including e-mail messages, Internet traffic, and even passwords), blaming a programming error in the software used for data collection. Although an investigation by the U.S. Federal Communications Commission (FCC) revealed that Google did not break the law, it remains unclear whether Google was actually aware of the extent of the data collection. Clearly, this raises a number of important ethical issues.

The issues surrounding Google's Street View highlight an even broader issue: with ever more (often very personal) information being stored, shared, and exchanged in the cloud, companies such as Google, Facebook, and Apple effectively become the custodians of data that have the potential to ruin millions of people's lives. Having access to vast amounts of data provides the potential of monetizing the data in some way. Where can a company draw the line between the responsibility that comes with having access to the data and the responsibility toward the company's shareholders to maximize profits?

Based on:

Barnett, E. (2010, March 12). Google Street View: Survey raises privacy concerns. *Telegraph.co.uk*. Retrieved May 28, 2012, from http://www.telegraph.co.uk/technology/google/7430245/Google-Street-View-survey-raises-privacy-concerns.html.

Guynn, J. and Sarno, D. (2012, May 1). Google Street View privacy scandal broadens. *Los Angeles Times*. Retrieved May 28, 2012, from http://articles.latimes.com/2012/may/01/business/la-fi-google-street-view-20120502.

Snyder, S. J. (2007, June 12) Google Maps: An invasion of privacy? *Time.com*. Retrieved May 28, 2012, from http://www.time.com/time/business/article/0,8599,1631957,00.html.

Streitfeld, D. (2012, May 22). Google privacy inquiries get little cooperation. *The New York Times*. Retrieved May 28, 2012, from http://www.nytimes.com/2012/05/23/technology/google-privacy-inquiries-get-little-cooperation.html.

Many types of application software supporting business processes interact with databases, so as to efficiently retrieve and store the data needed for executing business processes and gaining business intelligence. Databases are discussed next.

DATABASES. **Databases**, which are collections of related data organized in a way that facilitates data searches, are vital to an organization's operations and often are vital to competitive advantage and success. In organizations, databases are performing various important functions. On the most fundamental level, databases are used to store data and to make the data accessible where and when needed. More specifically, the use of databases to store organizational data ranging from inventory to demand forecasts to customer data enables applications from across an organization to access the data needed. Typically, various business processes throughout an organization make use of the same data, and providing the associated applications with quick and easy access to the data can help streamline and optimize these processes. For example, if a salesperson has access to inventory levels, she can quickly give precise estimates of delivery times, which may help close the sale. Similarly, if business processes associated with inbound logistics or operations have access to order forecasts, this can help to streamline procurement and production processes, helping to avoid stockouts and minimize money tied up in excess inventory. Well-managed databases can help to provide organization-wide access to the data needed for different business processes.

Additionally, database technology fuels electronic commerce, from helping to track available products for sale to providing customer service. For example, any product information you see on e-commerce sites such as Amazon.com is dynamically retrieved from a database; any changes to product information, pricing, or shipping estimates do not require changes to the product's Web page itself, but can be accomplished by simply changing the associated entry in the database. In order to harness the power of the data contained in the databases, organizations use **database management systems**, which are a type of software that allows organizations to more easily store, retrieve, and analyze data.

Finally, databases support storing and analyzing Big Data from a variety of sources. Gaining insights from internal and external sources (such as social media) can provide valuable business intelligence for organizations.

How these data are collected, stored, and manipulated is a significant factor influencing the success of modern organizations. As databases have become a critical component for most organizations, they rely on a solid underlying IS infrastructure (note that sometimes, databases are considered part of the infrastructure; given their importance and role in an organization's business processes, we do not consider them infrastructure). In Chapter 6, we talk more about the benefits of effectively and efficiently collecting, storing, and manipulating data stored in databases.

IS INFRASTRUCTURE COMPONENTS

http://goo.gl/ZADx9

Computing, storage, and networking technologies can create value by enabling efficiency, effectiveness, and agility. In recent times, fueled by globalization, e-commerce, and advances in technology, a well-functioning IS infrastructure has become increasingly important for organizations, leading to the need for making informed infrastructure decisions. In this section, we will introduce hardware, system software, storage, networking, and data centers, and discuss how making the right choices about the IS infrastructure can contribute to business success.

Hardware

A fundamental component of the IS infrastructure is the hardware, that is, the computers that run the applications and databases necessary for processing transactions or analyzing business data. As organizations need to carry out hundreds or thousands of different activities belonging to various business processes, they need different types of computers to support these processes. The five general classes of computers are supercomputer, mainframe, server, workstation, and personal computer (see Table 3.1). A **supercomputer** is the most expensive and most powerful kind of computer; typically not used by business organizations, it is used primarily to assist in solving massive scientific problems. In contrast, **mainframe** computers, while being very large, are used primarily as the main, central computing system for major corporations; optimized for high availability, resource utilization, and security, mainframes are typically used for mission-critical applications, such as transaction processing. A **server** is any computer on a network that makes access to files, printing, communications, and other services available to users of the network. Servers are used to provide services to users within large organizations or to Web users. Servers are optimized for access by many concurrent users and therefore have more advanced microprocessors, more memory, a larger cache, and more disk storage than single-user computers; servers also boast high reliability and fast network connectivity. To support different business processes, organizations often have many different servers in different configurations. For example, whereas some Web servers display the same static Web pages for every visitor (as is the case with many informational Web sites), others are designed to dynamically create Web

TABLE 3.1   Characteristics of Computers Currently Being Used in Organizations

Type of Computer	Number of Simultaneous Users	Physical Size	Typical Use	Memory	Typical Cost Range (in US$)
Supercomputer	One to many	Like an automobile to as large as multiple rooms	Scientific research	5,000+ GB	Low: $1 million; high: more than $20 million
Mainframe	1,000+	Like a refrigerator	Transaction processing, enterprise-wide applications	Up to 3,000+ GB	Low: $500,000; high: $10 million
Server	10,000+	Like a DVD player and mounted in a rack to fitting on a desktop	Providing Web sites or access to databases, applications, or files	Up to 512 GB	Low: $300; high: $50,000
Workstation	Typically one	Fitting on a desktop to the size of a file cabinet	Engineering, medical, graphic design	Up to 512 GB	Low: $750; high: $100,000
Personal computer	One	Fitting on a desktop	Personal productivity	512 MB to 16 GB	Low: $200; high: $5,000

pages based on user requests (e.g., Facebook displays content based on each individual user's network of friends); such servers have different requirements (e.g., in terms of processing power, network connectivity, or software) than e-mail servers, print servers, or other types of servers.

In contrast to mainframes and servers, which are designed for multiple concurrent users, workstations and personal computers are typically used by one user at a time. **Workstations**, designed for medical, engineering, architectural, or animation and graphics design uses, are optimized for visualization and rendering of three-dimensional models, and typically have fast processors, large memory, and advanced video cards. **Personal Computers (PCs)** are used for personal computing and small business computing. In addition, portable computers—notebook computers, netbooks, tablets, and smartphones—have increasingly become part of an organization's information systems infrastructure.

The application software used for various business processes cannot directly interact with these various types of hardware. Rather, the application software interacts with the system software, which, in turn, interacts with the computer hardware.

System Software

System software is the collection of programs that control the basic operations of computer hardware. The most prominent type of system software, the **operating system** (e.g., Windows 8, OS X, Ubuntu Linux), coordinates the interaction between hardware components (e.g., the CPU and the monitor), peripherals (e.g., printers), application software (e.g., office programs), and users, as shown in Figure 3.6. Operating systems are often written in assembly language, a very low-level computer programming language that allows the computer to operate quickly and efficiently. The operating system is designed to insulate you from this low-level language and make computer operations unobtrusive. Further, the operating system provides a common layer for different underlying devices, so that applications only have to be developed for different operating systems, rather than for each different computer model (see Figure 3.7). The operating system performs all of the day-to-day operations that we often take for granted when using a computer, such as updating the system clock, printing documents, or saving data to a disk. Just as our brain and nervous system control our body's breathing, heartbeat, and senses without our conscious realization, the system software transparently controls the computer's basic operations.

COMMON OPERATING SYSTEM FUNCTIONS. Many tasks are common to almost all computers. These include getting input from a keyboard or mouse, reading from and/or writing to a storage device (such as a hard disk drive), and presenting information to you via a monitor. Each of these tasks is performed by the operating system. For example, if you want to copy a word processing file from a flash drive onto your computer, the operating system makes this very easy for you, as

FIGURE 3.6

Operating systems coordinate the interaction between users, application software, hardware, and peripherals.

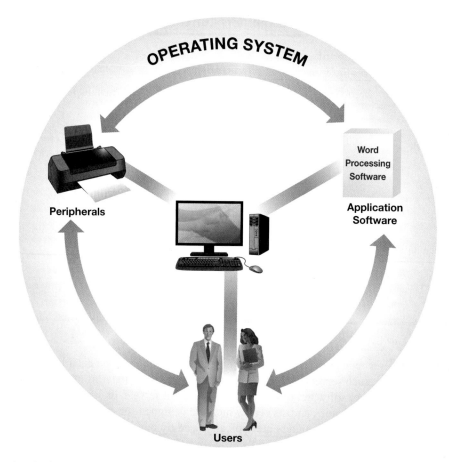

all it takes is simply using the mouse to point at a graphic icon of the word processing file on the flash drive, then clicking and dragging it onto an icon of your hard disk. The operating system makes this process appear easy. However, underlying the icons and simple dragging operations is a complex set of coded instructions that tell the electronic components of the computer that you are transferring a set of bits and bytes located on the flash drive to a location on your internal hard disk. Imagine if you had to program those sets of instructions every time you wanted to copy a file from one place to another. The operating system manages and executes these types of system operations so that you can spend your time on more important tasks.

MIDDLEWARE. Just as an operating system shields programmers from having to program applications for different devices, **middleware** is designed to shield programmers from having to build applications for different underlying operating systems, particularly in heterogeneous, distributed environments.

FIGURE 3.7

The operating system provides a common layer for different underlying devices, so that applications only have to be developed for different operating systems, rather than for each different computer model.

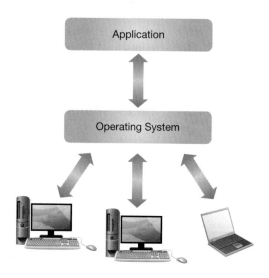

COMING ATTRACTIONS

Optical WLAN

Networking is facing a revolution faster than Silver Surfer. Scientists at the Fraunhofer Institute for Telecommunications at the Heinrich Hertz Institute (HHI) in Berlin have recently developed a new wireless transfer technology for data that is capable of streaming high definition media at the speed of 100 megabits per second. In other words, such bandwidth allows for simultaneously transferring four different videos in HD quality to four laptops. The secret behind this new technology is located right in your ceiling—integrated into LED lights.

You read it right: the optical WLAN uses white LEDs that flicker faster than the human eye can see to transmit data. A photo diode on one's laptop catches the light; the impulses are then decoded and translated into the zeros and ones a computer can understand. This form of data transmission is especially well suited for places where radio frequency devices are not allowed (e.g., due to potential for interference with sensitive devices); for instance, if in a surgical room lights can be used as a transfer medium, wireless surgical robots or faster transmission of x-ray images can be made possible. In addition the incredible bandwidth makes this data-transfer method a good option for transferring movies from one computer to another.

What about the down sides? Admittedly, the signal of optical WLAN can be easily blocked should the photo diode be covered or shaded. For the moment, this technology is unlikely to replace regular networking, but instead, it is assumed to work best as a companion to existing Wi-Fi or 3G technologies. In the near future, scientists are looking forward to further boosting transmission speed, targeting an ambitious eightfold increase in data rate through the use of red-blue-green-white light LEDs. If we look back at how fast the need for bandwidth has increased in the last decade, it definitely isn't hard to imagine that it will be easy to fill up that bandwidth as well.

Based on:

Davies, C. (2011, August 1). Optical WLAN uses LED light for up to 800 Mbit/s networking. *Slashgear.com*. Retrieved May 28, 2012, from http://www.slashgear.com/optical-wlan-uses-led-light-for-up-to-800-mbits-networking-01168674.

Paraskevopoulos, A. (2011). Optical WLAN-Internet from ceiling light. *Fraunhofer Heinrich Hertz Insititute*. Retrieved May 28, 2012, from http://www.hhi.fraunhofer.de/en/project-of-the-month/pdm-ov/archive/archive-2011/visible-light-communication.

Storage

In addition to processing and analyzing vast amounts of data, efficiently storing and retrieving data is key for organizational success. Further, governmental regulations such as the Sarbanes–Oxley Act mandate archiving business documents and relevant internal communication, including e-mail and instant messages. Hence, organizations are faced with the need to reliably process and store tremendous amounts of data, and this storage requirement is growing at an increasing rate. Earlier in this chapter, we discussed the role of databases in supporting organization-wide business processes. To enable efficient storage and retrieval of the content of such databases (as well as digital content not stored in databases), organizations need to have a solid storage infrastructure. Typically, organizations store data for three distinct purposes, each with distinct requirements in terms of timeliness, access speed, and life span (see Figure 3.8):

- Operational—for example, for processing transactions or for data analysis
- Backup—short-term copies of organizational data, used to recover from system-related disaster. Backup data are frequently overwritten with newer backups
- Archival—long-term copies of organizational data, often used for compliance and reporting purposes

These different uses of organizational data call for different physical storage technologies. For example, operational data are typically stored in databases (e.g., data from transaction processing systems or customer data) or files (e.g., business documents, images, or company brochures) using disk-based storage media such as hard drives. Hard drives offer high access speeds and are thus preferred for data that are frequently accessed or where response time is of the essence (as in an e-commerce Web site); in addition, flash-based storage is increasingly used for situations where access speed is of crucial importance. To ensure continuous business operations in case disaster strikes, organizations periodically back up their data to a secure location; often, companies have completely redundant systems so as to be able to seamlessly continue business

FIGURE 3.8

Operational, backup, and archival data have different requirements.

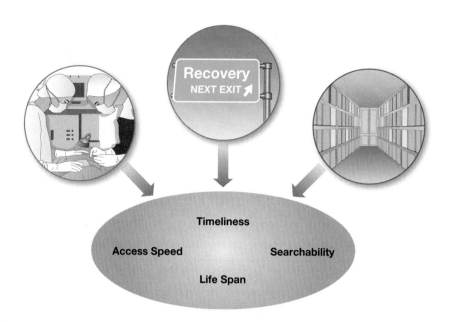

if the primary systems fail (see Chapter 10, "Securing Information Systems"). Storing backup data on hard drives enables quick recovery without slowing the company's operations. Data that are no longer used for operational purposes (such as old internal e-mails) are archived for long-term storage, typically on magnetic tapes. As data are stored sequentially on magnetic tapes, access speed can be very slow; however, magnetic tape has a shelf life of up to 30 years, is very low cost as compared to other storage media, and is removable, meaning that it is highly expandable and tapes can be easily stored in a secure, remote location (see the Technology Briefing for more on different storage technologies).

Networking

As you have seen, organizations depend on a variety of different applications, hardware, and storage technologies to support their business processes: organizations have servers, mainframes, personal computers, storage devices, mobile devices, environmental control systems, and various other devices. Yet, taken alone, each individual piece of technology has little value; it is through connecting the different pieces that business value can be realized: for example, the best performing database would be useless if it could not be accessed by those people or applications throughout the organization that depend on the data. Further, one of the reasons why information systems have become so powerful and important is the ability to interconnect, allowing internal and external constituents to communicate and collaborate with each other. The infrastructure supporting this consists of a variety of components, such as the networking hardware and software that facilitate the interconnection of different computers, enabling collaboration within organizations, across organizations, and literally around the world.

HUMAN COMMUNICATION AND COMPUTER NETWORKING. Human communication involves the sharing of information and messages between senders and receivers. The sender of a message formulates the message in his brain and codes the message into a form that can be communicated to the receiver—through voice, for example. The message is then transmitted along a communication pathway to the receiver. The receiver, using her ears and brain, then attempts to decode the message, as shown in Figure 3.9. This basic model of human communication helps us to understand telecommunications or computer networking. **Computer networking** is the sharing of data or services. The information source produces a message, which is encoded so that it can be transmitted via a communication channel; a receiver then decodes the message so that it can be understood by the destination. Thus, analogous to human communication, computer networks require three things:

- A sender (source) and a receiver (destination) that have something to share (a message)
- A pathway or transmission medium, such as a cable, to send the message
- Rules or protocols dictating communication between senders and receivers

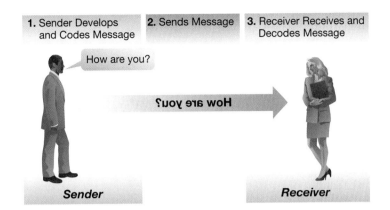

FIGURE 3.9

Communication requires senders, a message to share, and receivers.

The easiest way to understand computer networking is through the human communication model. Suppose you are applying for a job in France after graduation. You need information about different employers. The first requirement for a network—information to share—has now been met. After contacting a few potential employers, a company sends you information about their hiring process (the encoded message) via e-mail. This is the second requirement: a means of transmitting the coded message. The Internet is the pathway or transmission medium used to contact the receiver. **Transmission media** refers to the physical pathway—cable(s) and wireless—used to carry network information. At this point, you may run into some difficulties. If the potential employer has sent you information in French, you may not understand what they have written—that is, decode their message—because you don't speak French; if the message is not understood by the receiver, there is no communication. Although you have contacted the receiver, you and the receiver of your message must meet the third requirement for successful communication: you must establish a language of communication—the rules or protocols governing your communication. **Protocols** define the procedures that different computers follow when they transmit and receive data. You both might decide that one communication protocol will be that you communicate in English. This communication session is illustrated in Figure 3.10.

COMPUTER NETWORKS. A fundamental difference between human and computer communication is that human communication consists of words, whereas computer communication consists of bits, the fundamental information units of computers. Virtually all types of information can be transmitted on a computer network—documents, art, music, or film—although each type of information has vastly different requirements for effective transmission. For example, a single screen of text is approximately 14 KB of data, whereas a publication-quality photograph could be larger than 200 MB of data. Similarly, to support different business processes, vast amounts of data have to be transmitted. For example, a customer viewing a product on Amazon.com receives a Web page that is assembled by a Web server using data coming from different databases (e.g., containing data about products, inventory, pricing, or customer reviews), a content server (e.g., for product images), and other sources (see Figure 3.11); the actual transaction then involves product data, inventory data, customer data, payment data, confirmation e-mails, and so on. To

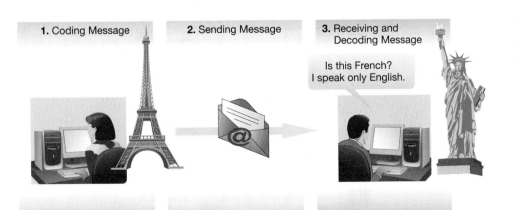

FIGURE 3.10

Coding, sending, and decoding a message.

FIGURE 3.11

Dynamic Web pages are assembled using data from various data sources.

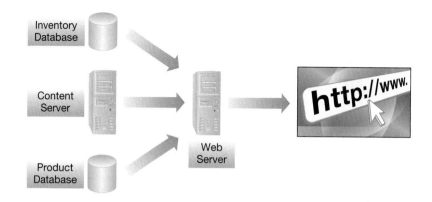

transmit such vast amounts of data in a timely manner from one location to another, adequate bandwidth is needed. **Bandwidth** is the transmission capacity of a computer or communications channel, measured in bits per second (bps) or multiples thereof, and represents how much binary data can be reliably transmitted over the medium in one second. To appreciate the importance of bandwidth for speed, consider how long it would take to transmit a document the length of this book (about 2 million characters, or 16 million bits). It would take about 1.6 seconds at 10 megabits per second (Mbps) and .16 seconds at 100 Mbps. In contrast, using an old-fashioned PC modem that transmits data at a rate of 56 kilobits per second (Kbps), it would take nearly five minutes to transmit the same document. Hence, different types of information have different communication bandwidth requirements (see www.numion.com/Calculators/Time.html for a tool that helps you calculate download times). Typical local area networks have a bandwidth of 10 Mbps to 1 Gbps.

Telecommunications advances have enabled individual computer networks—constructed with different hardware and software—to connect together in what appears to be a single network. Networks are increasingly being used to dynamically exchange relevant, value-adding information and knowledge throughout global organizations and institutions. The following sections take a closer look at the fundamental building blocks of these complex networks and the services they provide.

Servers, Clients, and Peers Computers in a **network** typically have one of three distinct roles—servers, clients, and peers—as depicted in Figure 3.12. A server is any computer on the network that makes access to files, printing, communications, and other services available to users of the network. Servers only provide services. A **client** is any computer, such as a user's PC or laptop, on the network, or any software application, such as Microsoft's Outlook e-mail client, that uses the services provided by the server. Clients only request services. A client usually has only one user, whereas many different users share the server. A **peer** is any computer that may both request and provide services. The trend in business is to use **client-server networks**,

FIGURE 3.12

A server is a computer on the network that enables multiple computers (or "clients") to access data. A peer is a computer that may both request and provide services.

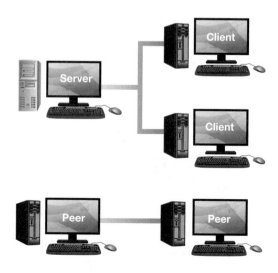

TABLE 3.2   Types of Networks

Type	Usage	Size
Private branch ex-change (PBX)	Telephone system serving a particular location	Within a business
Personal area network (PAN)	Wireless communication between devices, using technologies such as Bluetooth	Under 10 meters
Local area network (LAN)	Sharing of data, software applications, or other resources between several users	Typically within a building
Campus area network (CAN)	Connect multiple LANs, used by single organization	Spanning multiple buildings, such as a university or business campus
Metropolitan area network (MAN)	Connect multiple LANs, used by single organization	Larger than LAN or CAN, such as covering the area of a city
Wide area network (WAN)	Connect multiple LANs, distributed ownership and management	Large physical distance, up to worldwide (Internet)

in which servers and clients have defined roles. With ubiquitous access to company local area networks (LANs) and the Internet, almost everyone works in a client/server environment today. In contrast, **peer-to-peer networks** (often abbreviated as P2P) enable any computer or device on the network to provide and request services; these networks can be found in small offices and homes. In P2P networks, all peers have equivalent capabilities and responsibilities; this is the network architecture behind the Internet telephony service Skype and popular file sharing applications such as BitTorrent, where peers are able to connect directly to the hard drives of other peers on the Internet that are utilizing the software.

Types of Networks   Computing networks are commonly classified by size, distance covered, and structure. The most commonly used classifications are a **personal area network**, **local area network**, **campus area network**, **metropolitan area network**, and **wide area network** (see Table 3.2). These networks are typically used to connect devices within an organization, or across organizational subunits. To enable the connection of mobile devices, or to install a network where running cables is infeasible, organizations install **wireless local area networks (WLANs)** using high-frequency radio-wave technology; WLANs are also referred to as **Wi-Fi networks (wireless fidelity)**. The ease of installation has made WLANs popular for business and home use, and public WLANs can be found in many coffee shops, airports, or university campuses. In addition, organizations often install a dedicated telephone system called **private branch exchange** to route external phone calls or connect internal telephone extensions. For more on the different types of networks, see the Technology Briefing.

THE INTERNET.   One global network that has enabled organizations and individuals to interconnect in a variety of ways is the **Internet**, which is a large worldwide collection of networks that use a common protocol to communicate with each other. The name "Internet" is derived from the concept of internetworking, which means connecting host computers and their networks together to form even larger networks.

WORLD WIDE WEB.   One of the most powerful uses of the Internet is something that you probably use almost every day—the World Wide Web. The **World Wide Web** is a system of interlinked documents on the Internet, or a graphical user interface to the Internet that provides users with a simple, consistent interface to access a wide variety of information. A **Web browser** is a software application that can be used to locate and display Web pages, including text, graphics, and multimedia content.

A key feature of the Web is **hypertext**. A hypertext document, otherwise known as a **Web page**, contains not only information but also **hyperlinks**, which are references or links to other documents. The standard method of specifying the format of Web pages is called

FIGURE 3.13

Dissecting a URL.

Hypertext Markup Language (HTML). Specific content within each Web page is enclosed within codes, or markup tags, that stipulate how the content should appear to the user. These Web pages are stored on **Web servers**, which process user requests for pages using the **Hypertext Transfer Protocol (HTTP)**. Web servers typically host a collection of interlinked Web pages (called a **Web site**) that are owned by the same organization or by an individual. Web sites and specific Web pages within those sites have a unique Internet address. A user who wants to access a Web page enters the address, and the Web server hosting the Web site retrieves the desired page from its hard drive and delivers it to the user.

Web Domain Names and Addresses A **Uniform Resource Locator (URL)** is used to identify and locate a particular Web page. For example, www.google.com is the URL used to find the main Google Web server. The URL has three distinct parts: the domain, the top-level domain, and the host name (see Figure 3.13).

The **domain name** is a term that helps people recognize the company or person that the domain name represents. For example, Google's domain name is google.com. The prefix *google* lets you know that it is very likely that this domain name will lead you to the Web site of Google. Domain names also have a suffix that indicates which **top-level domain** they belong to. For example, the ".com" suffix is reserved for commercial organizations. Some other popular suffixes are listed here:

- .edu—educational institutions
- .org—organizations (non-profit)
- .gov—U.S. government entity
- .net—network organizations
- .de—Germany (there are over 240 two-letter "country code top-level domains")

Domain names can be registered through many different companies (known as registrars) that compete with one another. Given the proliferation of domain names, more generic top-level domains (gTLDs) have been added, such as .aero for the air transport industry, .name for individuals, .coop for business industry cooperatives, and .museum for museums. Recently, the ICANN (Internet Corporation for Assigned Names and Numbers—the organization that coordinates the domain name system) relaxed the strict rules for gTLDs, so that regions, businesses, or other entities can apply for their own gTLD. Applicants for such gTLDs, starting to be launched in 2013, include Canon (.canon) and Google, (e.g., .google, .youtube, and .docs), as well as many others applying for gTLDs such as .law, .bank, .hotel, .cashbackbonus, and .music.

The host name is the particular Web server or group of Web servers (if it is a larger Web site) that will respond to the request. In most cases, the "www" host name refers to the default Web site or the home page of the particular domain. Other host names can be used. For example, drive.google.com will take you to the group of Web servers that are responsible for serving up Google's cloud-based storage for documents. Larger companies have several host names for their different functions. Some examples used by Google are the following:

- mail.google.com (Google's free e-mail service)
- picasa.google.com (Google's application for organizing and editing photos)
- maps.google.com (Google's mapping application)

All the domain names and the host names are associated with one or more Internet protocol (IP) addresses. For example, the domain name google.com represents about a dozen underlying **IP addresses**. IP addresses serve to identify all the computers or devices on the Internet. The IP address serves as the destination address of that computer or device and enables the network to route messages to the proper destination. The format of an IP address is a 32-bit numeric address written as four numbers separated by periods. Each of the four numbers can be any number between 0 and 255. For example, 128.196.134.37 is an underlying IP address of www.arizona.edu, the University of Arizona's main Web page.

IP addresses can also be used instead of URLs to navigate to particular Web addresses. This practice is not done regularly, as IP addresses are far more difficult to remember than domain names, and an organization may assign their domain name to a server with a different IP address; for example, whereas the IP address behind google.com may change, the domain name stays the same.

World Wide Web Architecture The Web consists of a large number of interconnected Web servers, which host the sites users access with their Web browsers. The Internet uses the **Transmission Control Protocol/Internet Protocol (TCP/IP)** to facilitate the transmission of Web pages and other information. Users can access Web pages by entering the URL of the Web page into their Web browser. Once the user enters the URL into the address bar of the Web browser, TCP/IP breaks the request into packets and routes them over the Internet to the Web server where the requested Web page is stored. When the packets reach their destination, TCP/IP reassembles them and passes the request to the Web server. The Web server understands that the user is requesting a Web page (indicated by the http:// prefix in the URL) and retrieves the Web page, which is packetized by TCP/IP and transmitted over the Internet back to the user's computer. TCP/IP reassembles the packets at the destination and delivers the Web page to the Web browser. In turn, the Web browser translates the HTML code contained in the Web page, formats its physical appearance, and displays the results. If the Web page contains a hyperlink, the user can click on it and the process repeats.

INTRANETS AND EXTRANETS. As organizations have realized the advantage of using the Internet and Web to communicate public information outside corporate boundaries, they can also leverage Web-based technologies to support proprietary, internal communications through the implementation of an **intranet**. An intranet looks and acts just like a publicly accessible Web site and uses the same software, hardware, and networking technologies to communicate information. All intranet pages are behind the company's *firewall*, which secures proprietary information stored within the corporate local area network and/or wide area network so that the information can be viewed only by authorized users.

In the simplest form of an intranet, communications take place only within the confines of organizational boundaries and do not travel across the Internet. Organizations can use intranets for disseminating corporate information, employee training, project management, collaboration, or enabling employee self-service for administering benefits, managing retirement plans, or other human resources–based applications through *employee portals*.

Increases in employees' mobility necessitate that an intranet be accessible from anywhere. Thus, most companies allow their employees to use *virtual private networks (VPNs)* to connect to the company's intranet while on the road or working from home (i.e., telecommuting). Figure 3.14 depicts a typical intranet system architecture (see Chapter 10 for more on firewalls and VPNs).

Similar to an intranet, an **extranet**, which can be regarded as a private part of the Internet that is cordoned off from ordinary users, enables two or more firms to use the Internet to do business together. Although the content is "on the Web," only authorized users can access it after logging on to the company's extranet Web site. As an extranet uses the public (and normally insecure) Internet infrastructure to connect two or more business partners, it often uses VPNs to ensure the secured transmission of proprietary information between business partners (see Figure 3.15). To access information on an extranet, authorized business partners access their business partner's main extranet Web page using their Web browsers. Table 3.3 summarizes the similarities and differences between intranets, extranets, and the Internet.

Extranets benefit corporations in a number of ways. For example, extranets can dramatically improve the timeliness and accuracy of communications, reducing the number of

FIGURE 3.14

Typical intranet system architecture.

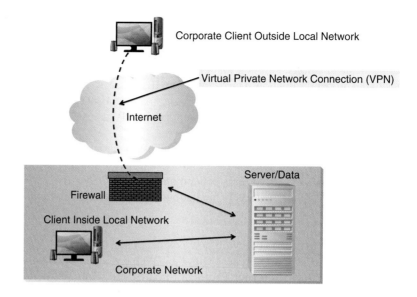

misunderstandings within the organization as well as with business partners and customers. In the business world, very little information is static; therefore, information must be continually updated and disseminated as it changes. Extranets facilitate this process by providing a cost-effective, global medium over which proprietary information can be distributed. Furthermore, they allow central management of documents, thus reducing the number of versions and the amount of out-of-date information that may be stored throughout the organization. While security is still considered to be better on proprietary networks, the Internet can be used as a relatively secure medium for business. Further, a company can use extranets to automate business transactions, reducing processing costs and achieving shortened cycle times. Extranets can also reduce errors by providing a single point of data entry from which the information can be updated on disparate corporate computing platforms without having to reenter the data. Management can then obtain real-time information to track and analyze business activities.

Data Centers

To satisfy the increasing requirements for processing and storing the ever-growing volume of data, large organizations need hundreds or even thousands of servers. Organizations such as UPS need tremendous amounts of computing power to route and track packages, online stores such as Zappos need to provide product information and track customer orders, and social networking game developers such as Zynga need to track each and every action users take on the popular game FarmVille (see Case 1 at the end of this chapter). As you can imagine, an organization's

FIGURE 3.15

Typical extranet system architecture.

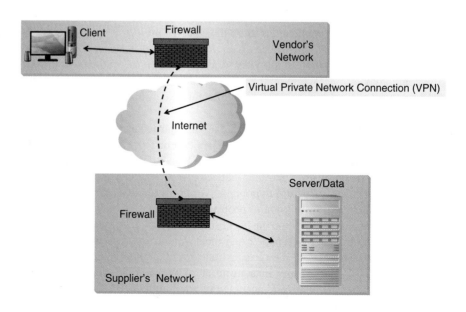

BRIEF CASE   Earthquake-Proofing a Data Center

Data centers play a crucial role in the information systems infrastructure, and a great deal of attention is given to their virtual safety and physical soundness. With the threat of natural disasters always looming, infrastructures have to be built to withstand almost any catastrophic event. In 2011, most of the data centers in Japan survived (with little damage) the 8.9 magnitude earthquake and tsunami that created unimaginable damage and triggered the Fukushima nuclear disaster. Despite the blackouts, shortages of generator fuel, and a complete power supply cut-off, the data centers remained unharmed.

There are a handful of measures that can be taken to avoid the failure of data centers. IDC Frontier, the data center operator which operates Yahoo!'s data centers in Japan, has imposed numerous measures in an attempt to avoid potential data center failure. Giant "shock absorbers," made from metal and rubber, allowed buildings to "float" while the ground shook from the shocks of the earthquake. In addition, uninterruptible power supplies and diesel-powered generators protected against power cut-off. Seventy percent of Japan's data centers are located in the Tokyo region, and the fact that data centers in the country are seldom built on the eastern seashore, where they would be more susceptible to a tsunami, also helps to keep Japan's data centers operational during natural disasters.

As a result, only five of IDC's server racks were reported to have encountered critical damage during the earthquake. Disaster recovery plans were executed smoothly and the information systems infrastructure successfully remained intact after the catastrophe.

Questions:
1. How do you secure your data?
2. When storing data in the cloud, how concerned are you about the security of your providers' data centers?
3. How do different cloud computing providers differ in terms of security and data recovery?

Based on:

Kern, J. (2011, March 11). Japan earthquake damages tech infrastructure. *Information Management.* Retrieved May 28, 2012, from http://www.information-management.com/news/Japan_earthquake_tsunami_data_center_cloud-10019922-1.html.

Miller, R. (2011, March 11). How Japan's data centers manage earthquakes. *Data-Center Knowledge.* Retrieved May 28, 2012, from http://www.datacenterknowledge.com/archives/2011/03/11/how-japans-data-centers-manage-earthquakes.

Nicolai, J. (2011, June 30). How Japan's data centers survived the earthquake. *Computerworld.* Retrieved May 28, 2012, from http://www.computerworld.com/s/article/9218091/How_Japan_s_data_centers_survived_the_earthquake.

hardware and storage infrastructure can quickly grow quite large, and companies typically set aside dedicated space for their infrastructure components (such data centers can range in size from a single dedicated server room to buildings the size of a large warehouse). Keeping this infrastructure in one location helps to manage, repair, upgrade, and secure the equipment.

Given that data are the lifeblood of organizations ranging from e-commerce companies to logistics companies to government agencies, these organizations are striving for the highest level of availability of their hardware, storage, and networking components, often reaching for "five-nines" (i.e., 99.999 percent availability, which translates into just over 5 minutes of downtime per year). To ensure this availability, there are not only specific demands for the individual components (e.g., being able to quickly swap hard drives or other parts in case of failure), but also for the data center overall (e.g., in terms of connectivity, floor space, provision of energy and cooling, and security). In addition, data centers need to be modular, so as to be easily expandable in case of changing needs. The facilities for UPS in Atlanta, Georgia and Mahwah, New Jersey are prime examples for such high-availability facilities. To ensure uninterrupted service, the data

TABLE 3.3   Characteristics of the Internet, Intranet, and Extranet

	Focus	Type of Information	Users	Access
Internet	External communications	General, public, and "advertorial" information	Any user with an Internet connection	Public and not restricted
Intranet	Internal communications	Specific, corporate, and proprietary information	Authorized employees	Private and restricted
Extranet	External communications	Communications between business partners	Authorized business partners	Private and restricted

Source: Based on Szuprowicz (1998) and Turban, King, Lee, Liang, and Turban (2012).

centers are self-sufficient, and each can operate for up to two days on self-generated power. The power is needed not only for the computers but also for air-conditioning, as each facility needs air-conditioning capacity equaling that of or more than 2,000 homes. In case power fails, the cooling is provided using more than 600,000 gallons of chilled water, and the UPS facilities even have backup wells in case the municipal water supply should fail. Other protective measures include raised floors (to protect from floods) and buildings designed to withstand winds of 200 miles per hour. Alternatively, organizations can rent space for their servers in collocation facilities, which are data centers managed by a third party that rents out space to multiple organizational customers (see Chapter 10 for more on securing data centers and collocation facilities).

http://goo.gl/Ut9pY

ISSUES ASSOCIATED WITH MANAGING THE IS INFRASTRUCTURE

Needless to say, for organizations, obtaining, operating, maintaining, and upgrading the information systems infrastructure can be a tremendous challenge, especially when this is not part of their core business.

As you have undoubtedly noticed, computing technology has evolved rapidly and will most likely continue to evolve rapidly in the future. In general, because of the increasing pace of change with modern technologies, most organizations face accelerating obsolescence of their hardware and software investments as well as increasing storage and space constraints, demand fluctuations, and increasing energy costs (see Figure 3.16). In the following section, we discuss how the interplay between the different infrastructure components both encourages and necessitates continuous upgrading of the infrastructure.

Rapid Obsolescence and Shorter IT Cycles

Over the past 75 years, information systems have gone through many radical changes. Rapid advances in both hardware and software capabilities have enabled or facilitated many business

FIGURE 3.16

Information systems infrastructure challenges for modern organizations.

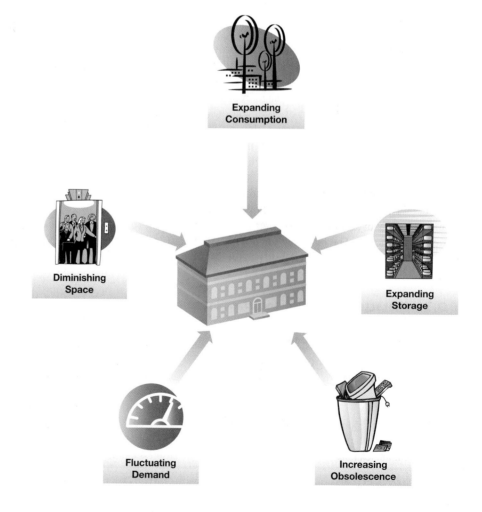

TABLE 3.4 Five Generations of Computing

Generation	Time Line	Major Event	Characteristics
1	1946–1958	Vacuum tubes	▪ Mainframe era begins ▪ ENIAC and UNIVAC were developed
2	1958–1964	Transistors	▪ Mainframe era expands ▪ UNIVAC is updated with transistors
3	1964–1990s	Integrated circuits	▪ Mainframe era ends ▪ Personal computer era begins ▪ IBM 360 with general purpose operating system ▪ Microprocessor revolution: Intel, Microsoft, Apple, IBM PC, MS-DOS
4	1990s–2000	Multimedia and low-cost PCs	▪ Personal computer era ends ▪ Interpersonal computing era begins ▪ High-speed microprocessor and networks ▪ High-capacity storage ▪ Low-cost, high-performance integrated video, audio, and data
5	2000–present	Widespread Internet accessibility	▪ Interpersonal computing era ends ▪ Internetworking era begins ▪ Ubiquitous access to Internet with a broad variety of devices ▪ Prices continue to drop; performance continues to expand ▪ Advent of powerful mobile devices ▪ Ubiquitous mobile connectivity

processes, and organizations are continuously faced with the need to upgrade the IS infrastructure so as to gain or maintain competitive advantage. In this section, we discuss the history of computing, as well as the effects of rapid advances in technology.

BRIEF HISTORY OF COMPUTING. When the Zuse Z1 Computer (a mechanical computer using program punch cards) was introduced in 1936, almost all business and government information systems consisted of file folders, filing cabinets, and document repositories. Huge rooms were dedicated to the storage of these records. Information was often difficult to find, and corporate knowledge and history were difficult to maintain. Only certain employees knew specific information. When these employees left the firm, so did all their knowledge about the organization. The computer provided the solution to the information storage and retrieval problems facing organizations up to the 1940's. Shifts in computing eras were facilitated by fundamental changes in the way computing technologies worked. Each of these fundamental changes is referred to as a distinct generation of computing. Table 3.4 highlights the technology that defined the five generations of computing.

MOORE'S LAW. In 1965, Intel cofounder Dr. Gordon Moore hypothesized that the number of transistors on a chip would double about every two years. When Moore made this bold prediction, he did not limit it to any specified period of time. This prediction became known as **Moore's Law**. Interestingly, whereas the first CPU had 2,200 transistors, the newest models have broken the 2-billion-transistor mark, so Dr. Moore's prediction has been fairly accurate so far (see www.intel.com/technology/mooreslaw). The number of transistors that can be packed into a modern CPU and the speed at which processing and other activities occur are remarkable. For example, the Intel Core i7 Extreme CPU can complete hundreds of millions of operations every second.

FASTER IT CYCLES AND CONSUMERIZATION. For organizations, this increase in capabilities is both a blessing and a curse. On the one hand, increases in processing power enable various applications; on the other hand, managers have to continuously think about when to upgrade the hardware components of the IS infrastructure. Beyond Moore's law, there are two other factors exacerbating this problem. First, IT cycles are becoming increasingly faster, with manufacturers releasing new devices at an ever-increasing pace. Whereas traditionally, IS managers would think in terms of 5 years, nowadays new versions of devices are released every 6–12 months. Further, with the increasing trends toward consumerization of IT, managers have to consider how to integrate their users' various mobile devices into the organization's IS infrastructure.

FIGURE 3.17

New hardware enables more powerful software; more powerful software often requires new hardware.

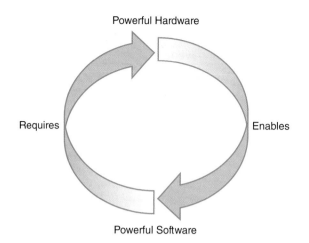

SOFTWARE OBSOLESCENCE. In addition to constant increases in hardware capabilities, companies such as Microsoft are continuously developing new and improved software that uses this power to help people be more productive. New operating systems such as Windows 7 and Windows 8 can use new processor architectures and offer a richer set of features than older operating systems such as Windows XP. However, these new operating systems often require new hardware, and older-generation application software may not be compatible with the new operating system (see Figure 3.17). Further, new generations of application software promise better performance and more (or improved) features, enabling higher productivity. One example is Microsoft Office 2007 (and its most recent successor Office 2013); when developing Office 2007, Microsoft conducted many usability studies to improve the human–computer interface (see Chapter 9, "Developing and Acquiring Information Systems") so as to facilitate the execution of common tasks and, as a result, introduced the so-called "Ribbon" interface. Although people used to the "old" interface were initially reluctant to switch—because of the associated learning curve—many have now realized the benefits this new feature brings. Manufacturers of hardware and software often apply the concept of **planned obsolescence**, meaning that the product is designed to last only for a certain life span. For hardware, this can mean that certain components are not built to be serviceable, and the device has to be replaced once one of these components breaks down; similarly, older versions of software may not be able to open newer file formats, or a company may cease support for a product (mainstream support for the Windows XP operating system ended in 2009, and paid support as well as critical security updates will be offered only until 2014), effectively forcing users to switch to newer versions. Hence, organizations are constantly faced with the decision of when and how to upgrade their current hardware and software infrastructure. Although such upgrades may increase productivity, often they do not but are still a large cost factor, both in terms of costs for hardware and software, and in terms of the time and resources needed for upgrading tens, hundreds, or thousands of computers. Further, the rapid obsolescence of computer hardware carries a high price tag for the environment in terms of resources needed both to manufacture the new systems and to dispose of the old ones (see Figure 3.18).

Big Data and Rapidly Increasing Storage Needs

Another issue organizations face is the amount of data available and the amount of data needed to stay ahead of the competition. Today, organizations can collect and analyze vast amounts of data for *business intelligence* (see Chapter 6) and other purposes (such as compliance). For example, organizations can analyze each visitor's actions on the company Web site in order to improve the site's performance. Similarly, organizations are increasingly trying to make use of "Big Data," that is, trying to analyze structured and unstructured data from media reports, social media, customer support calls, and other sources. Obviously, capturing more data requires ever more storage space and ever more powerful computing hardware and database management systems for managing and analyzing the data. Further, Internet bandwidth grew tremendously during the dot-com bubble, allowing organizations to provide their customers with richer (and more bandwidth-hungry) information. At the same time, services such as YouTube and videos streamed by Netflix create a need for even more bandwidth. Hence, this is another example of

FIGURE 3.18

The rapid obsolescence of computer hardware carries a high price tag for the environment.

Source: Tonis Valing/Shutterstock

a "vicious circle" where enhanced capabilities enable new applications, which in turn require a certain level of capabilities in terms of both data and communications infrastructure.

Demand Fluctuations

An additional challenge for many organizations is that the demands for computing resources are often fluctuating, leading to either having too few resources at some times or having too many idle resources most of the time (according to estimates, up to 70 percent of organizations' IS infrastructure is utilized at only 20 percent of its capacity). Companies engaged in (or supporting) business-to-consumer electronic commerce (such as Amazon.com or FedEx; see Chapter 4, "Enabling Business-to-Consumer Electronic Commerce"), for instance, face large spikes in demand during the pre-holiday season in December; consequently, increased capacity is needed to handle this demand. While it is relatively easy to hire temporary staff to handle an increase in orders, it is typically not that easy to make quick changes to the IS infrastructure based on changing needs. Just a few years ago, launching a start-up involved purchasing lots of hardware and installing Web servers in one's basement, with no real idea of how much demand would need to be met; fluctuation in demand for computing resources is especially difficult to cope with for new entrants who are not able to forecast demand and may not have the resources to quickly expand their IS infrastructure to meet increases in demand for their products or services.

For organizations with an increasing customer (or user) base, the facilities infrastructure has to grow along with any increase in computing needs (as Google grew, they eventually had to move their equipment out of their friend's garage; now Google is said to have more than 30 major data centers). This can be especially problematic for fast-growing companies, as renting (let alone building) additional facilities is expensive and significant time is needed for locating the right facilities, contract negotiations, and setup; further, long-term contracts limit the companies' flexibility to scale the infrastructure down in times of lower demand.

Increasing Energy Needs

Finally, the worldwide increase in demand for energy has become another concern for organizations. As computers process data, they consume electricity; further, various components (such as the CPU and the power supply) generate heat, and most computers have multiple fans to control the temperature. More powerful hardware needs more energy to enable the increase in computing power; at the same time, having more powerful hardware requires more energy for cooling.

WHEN THINGS GO WRONG

Dirty Data Centers

A 2011 report conducted by Greenpeace allowed a sneak peek into the environmental impact of data storage and transmission. The report, entitled "How Dirty Is Your Data?" measured the energy consumption of data centers owned by top technology companies to assess the environmental impacts of actions as simple as sending and receiving e-mail messages or posting status updates.

According to the study, Apple's data centers turned out to be the dirtiest of all companies, followed closely by HP, IBM, and Oracle. It was Apple's use of "dirtier" energy sources like coal and nuclear power as opposed to solar or wind power, that had the company landing in the top spot. Apple's 500,000 square-foot facility in Maiden, North Carolina (used to power Apple's iCloud) was estimated to consume energy that could provide for 80,000 homes in the United States—only 5 percent of this was considered clean energy.

Although Facebook came in fifth on the list of dirty data centers, the giant has since put much effort into going green with its data center located in Oregon's high desert—Prineville. Sitting on a plateau of about 2,800 feet above sea level gives Facebook's data center the advantage of using outside air to cool its servers; heating is done by using hot air that is produced by the servers themselves. Inside the data center, found water is used to run toilets, and the lighting system is controlled via Ethernet. Facebook put even more effort into designing highly efficient servers. For example, Facebook's servers have custom power supplies that reduce power loss by eliminating the need to transform power; similarly, the servers' fans spin slower, reducing energy consumption.

With environmental awareness fast on the rise, Google also claims to run its data center without chillers and is investing in wind and solar power. Similarly, Yahoo! has already located most of its data centers near sources of renewable energy. It is speculated that more technology companies will duly follow suit. As an encouraging step to clean up its dirty data center, Apple has confirmed plans to build a data center in Prineville; sources have further disclosed that the giant company is looking to take after Facebook's energy-conscious design to improve its record and make an effort to go environmental-friendly.

Based on:

Gross, D. (2012, April 22). Greenpeace: Apple has the dirtiest data. *CNN.com* Retrieved May 28, 2012, from http://edition.cnn.com/2011/TECH/web/04/22/greenpeace.apple.dirtiest.

McDonnell, T. and West, J. (2012, April 17). Apple, Google, Facebook: Whose data centers are the dirtiest? *MotherJones.* Retrieved May 28, 2012, from http://motherjones.com/environment/2012/04/apple-dirty-data-coal-google-amazon.

Metz, C. (2012, February 22). Apple mimics Facebook with high desert data center. *Wired.com.* Retrieved May 28, 2012, from http://www.wired.com/wiredenterprise/2012/02/apple-facebook-data-center.

Metz, C. (2011, December 1). Welcome to Prineville, Oregon: Population, 800 million. *Wired.com.* Retrieved May 28, 2012, from http://www.wired.com/wiredenterprise/2011/12/facebook-data-center/all/1.

West, C. (2012, April 17). Apple's North Carolina iCloud data center is dirty. *intomobile.* Retrieved May 28, 2012, from http://www.intomobile.com/2012/04/17/apples-north-carolina-icloud-data-center-dirty.

A typical desktop uses between 40 and 170 watts when idling and can use up to 300 watts or more under full load. A typical server rack (holding multiple servers) in a data center can easily consume 15–17 kilowatts, the equivalent of power needed for more than 10 homes. Although you may not feel the impact of your personal computer usage on your home energy bill, for organizations having hundreds or thousands of computers, rising energy costs are becoming a major issue. This is increasingly becoming an issue, as hardware manufacturers pack more and more processing power into servers, without providing much improvement in energy consumption, so that power consumption and heat emissions continue to rise. Thus, power and cooling can be a significant cost factor for companies. Google has invested many resources into developing more efficient data centers. Google now uses modular data centers that use specially equipped shipping containers for housing servers so as to be able to maximize efficiency by optimizing airflow, cooling, and power transformation (we will talk more about another trend, "green computing," later in the chapter).

Given these issues, organizations have been looking for ways to better manage their IS infrastructure so as to enhance flexibility and agility while reducing costs. In the following section, we will discuss cloud computing, and how it can address some of these infrastructure-related challenges.

CLOUD COMPUTING

Managing the IS infrastructure can be a challenge for many organizations, due to the evolution of hardware and software, the demand for more storage and networking bandwidth, and the rising costs of energy. Further, organizations need dedicated staff to support their infrastructure, which incurs further costs; often, managing the IS infrastructure is not among the organization's core competencies, so others may be better at managing the infrastructure for them.

As a result. over the past decades, there has been a shift away from thinking about the IS infrastructure toward thinking about what *services* the infrastructure should deliver. For example, people and organizations want to use e-mail rather than having to think about purchasing an e-mail server and dealing with associated issues such as administration, maintenance, storage, energy consumption, and so on. In addition, organizations increasingly buy or rent, rather than build, applications (except for highly specialized systems that help gain or sustain competitive advantage, as is the case with Amazon.com or Dell) to support their business processes; in other words, organizations leave the building of applications to other parties, and assume that these applications will work. Given this trend, a solid infrastructure is important, as the infrastructure determines how quickly new systems can be implemented, and how well they will function. This becomes even more important as any lack of robustness or integration of an organization's infrastructure will be immediately noticed by customers or other stakeholders, potentially leading to loss of business, trust, or goodwill.

What Is Cloud Computing?

Technological advances such as increasing Internet bandwidth and advances in virtualization have given rise to cloud computing (the "cloud" is a metaphor for the Internet; see Figure 3.19). As defined by the National Institute of Standards and Technology (NIST), "Cloud computing is a model for enabling ubiquitous, convenient, on-demand network access to a shared pool of configurable computing resources (e.g., networks, servers, storage, applications, and services) that can be rapidly provisioned and released with minimal management effort or service provider interaction" (Courtesy of the National Institute of Standards). Using a **utility computing** model (i.e., organizations "renting" resources such as processing, data storage, or networking from an external provider on an as-needed basis, and pay only for what is actually used), cloud computing thus helps to transform IT infrastructure costs from a capital expenditure to an operational expenditure (see Figure 3.20). One prime example of a cloud computing provider is Amazon Web Services; having built an immense infrastructure (in terms of both information technology and logistics) for supporting its online store, Amazon.com has decided to use these resources to generate additional revenue streams. For example, individuals and organizations

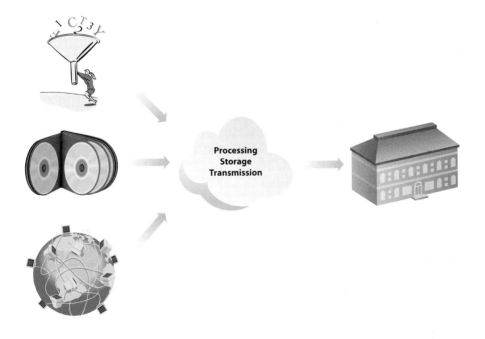

FIGURE 3.19

Processing, storage, and transmission of data taking place in the cloud.

FIGURE 3.20

Cloud computing uses a utility computing model, allowing companies to pay for computing resources on an as-needed basis.

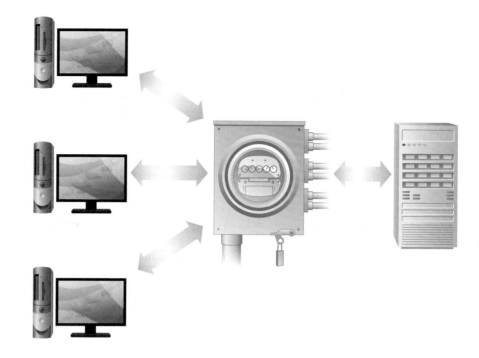

can rent storage space on Amazon's Simple Storage Service (S3) or computing time on Amazon's Elastic Compute Cloud (EC2), all on an as-needed basis. The ability to create an entire infrastructure by combining Amazon's various services has facilitated many successful start-up companies, such as Zynga, the makers of the Facebook application FarmVille, or Animoto, which offers a Web application that lets users create orchestrated videos from their own pictures and music. As Animoto became popular (it was featured on *CNN* and *BBC,* in the *New York Times,* and so on), it increased the number of EC2 server instances used from 50 to 3,500 within just three days; this would have been close to impossible were Animoto using their own data center because of both the time and the money needed to acquire this number of servers; and, at the time, who knew whether Animoto's business would actually take off? With a traditional in-house infrastructure, Animoto would have had to add capacity in "chunks," leading to either having too many unused resources or not being able to satisfy its users' demand; using a cloud infrastructure, Animoto can elastically scale the resources to be just above what is needed to keep the users satisfied (see Figure 3.21).

CLOUD CHARACTERISTICS. The cloud computing model has several unique and essential characteristics that distinguish cloud computing from an in-house infrastructure and provide various benefits to users (NIST, 2012). These characteristics are discussed next.

On-Demand Self-Service To allow for most flexibility, users can access cloud resources in a buffet-style fashion on an as-needed basis without the need for lengthy negotiations with the service provider; in many cases, resources in the cloud are accessible by the customer with no need for human interaction with the provider. In the case of Amazon Web Services, a customer needs only a credit card (for billing purposes) and can set up server instances or expand storage space via a Web-based control panel. For businesses, whose needs may rapidly change, this allows for unprecedented flexibility, as it greatly facilitates scaling the infrastructure up or down as needed.

Rapid Elasticity Typically, servers and other elements of an IS infrastructure take several weeks to be delivered and days or weeks to be configured (as a company's IS personnel has to install and configure system software, databases, and application software, depending on the organization's needs); in contrast, in a cloud environment, computing resources can be scaled up or down almost instantaneously and often automatically, based on user needs. Hence, there is no need to purchase expensive equipment to prepare for an anticipated surge in demand (which ultimately may not materialize) during the holiday season. If, however, the surge in demand does materialize, businesses can access the required resources instantaneously at almost any quantity.

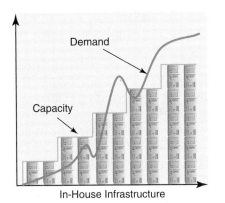

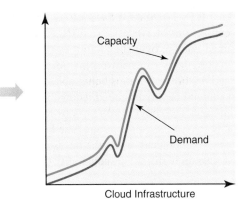

FIGURE 3.21

It is difficult to match demand using an in-house infrastructure; with a cloud infrastructure, resources can be added incrementally, on an as-needed basis.

Broad Network Access As cloud services are accessed via the Internet, they are accessible from almost anywhere and from almost any Web-enabled device. For organizations, this enables real-time management of business processes, as applications hosted in the cloud can be accessed whenever needed, from any location, be it from one's desktop or laptop, or using an iPhone, iPad, or Android smartphone application. Thus, knowledge workers can swiftly respond to anything that may require their immediate attention, without having to be physically in their office.

Resource Pooling Rather than renting out space or time to each customer on one specific, physical machine, cloud providers manage multiple distributed resources that are dynamically assigned to multiple customers based on their needs. Hence, the customer only rents a resource, with no knowledge or control over how it is provided or where it is located. In some cases, however, service providers allow for specifying particular geographic areas of the resources; for example, a California company may want to rent resources located in California (close to its customers) so as to reduce response latency, or a European company may need to rent storage space on servers located in Europe so as to comply with data protection directives (see Chapter 1).

Measured Service Service is typically provided using a utility computing model, where customers pay only for what they use, and the metering depends on type of resource. For example, customers are charged on an hourly basis for the use of server instances (the price typically depends on the instance's computing power, memory, and operating system) based on volume of data stored and/or on data transferred into or out of the cloud. For customers, the fixed costs associated with the IS infrastructure are thus transformed into variable costs, which are very easy to track and monitor.

SERVICE MODELS. As can be seen from the previously mentioned examples, various services are provided in the cloud. Whereas some users require access only to certain software, others want to have more control, being able to run the software of their choice on a server in the cloud (see Figure 3.22). Different cloud computing service models (NIST, 2012) are discussed next.

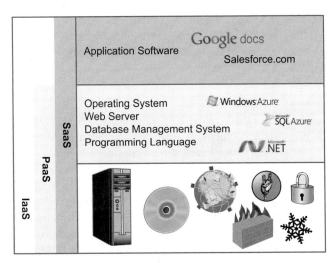

FIGURE 3.22

Services Provided by SaaS, PaaS, and IaaS Providers.

Infrastructure as a Service In the **infrastructure as a service (IaaS)** model, only the basic capabilities of processing, storage, and networking are provided. Hence, the customer has the most control over the resources. For example, using Amazon Web Services, customers can choose computing power, memory, operating system, and storage based on individual needs and requirements, thus being able to build (almost) their entire infrastructure in the cloud. For example, Netflix migrated its own IT infrastructure to Amazon Web Services using EC2 and S3 to transcode movies into various formats, powering its customer-focused Web site, and other mission-critical applications. The IaaS model provides the customer with the greatest flexibility; on the other hand, while the infrastructure is provided, managing licenses for operating systems and so on is still the responsibility of the customer, and setup costs are considerably higher.

Platform as a Service In the **platform as a service (PaaS)** model, the customer can run his or her own applications that are typically designed using tools provided by the service provider. In this model, the user has control over the applications but has limited or no control over the underlying infrastructure. One example is Microsoft's Windows Azure, which acts as a cloud services operating system that customers can use to deploy custom applications. For example, Outback Steakhouse launched a viral marketing campaign when it first introduced its Facebook Fan Page. To support the spikes in demand, Outback developed and deployed an e-mail marketing campaign using Windows Azure. As the underlying computing platform is provided, the customer does not have to worry about purchasing software licenses, for example, for the Web servers' operating systems or for database management systems, and the service provider manages the functioning and updating of the platform provided.

Software as a Service In the **software as a service (SaaS)** model, the customer uses only applications provided via a cloud infrastructure. Typically, such applications include Web-based e-mail services (e.g., Google's Gmail) and Web-based productivity suites (such as Zoho or Google Docs), but also advanced applications such as CRM systems, as provided by salesforce.com (see Chapter 8, "Strengthening Business-to-Business Relationships Via Supply Chain and Customer Relationship Management"). Typically, the customer cares only about the application, with no knowledge or control over the underlying infrastructure, and typically has only limited ability to control or configure application-specific settings; further, the customer does not have to worry about maintaining or updating the software, the underlying platform, or the hardware infrastructure. Thus, applications under the SaaS model are typically easiest to deploy.

TYPES OF CLOUDS. Cloud service providers such as Amazon.com offer what is referred to as a **public cloud**. Services in a public cloud can be used by any interested party on a pay-per-use basis; hence, they are often used for applications that need rapid **scalability** (i.e., the ability to adapt to increases or decreases in demand for processing or data storage), or in cases where there is insufficient capital or other resources to build or expand an IT infrastructure. In contrast, a **private cloud** (or internal cloud) is internal to an organization and can help the organization to balance demand and supply of computing resources within the organization; similar to a public cloud, a private cloud provides self-service access to resources, allowing business users to provision resources on-demand using a utility computing model. A private cloud does not free an organization from the issues associated with managing the cloud infrastructure, but it does give the organization a high degree of customizability, flexibility, and control over their data and applications (see Figure 3.23).

Managing the Cloud

Because of its various benefits, cloud computing has gained much popularity, especially among executives who try to harness the potential of scalability and increase the business' agility. However, there are also various issues management should consider when moving their infrastructure to the public cloud. The first consideration is which applications, services, or data to move to the cloud. Typically, there is no single cloud computing provider that can meet all needs of an organization. Rather, organizations often have to partner with different service providers, selecting IaaS, PaaS, and SaaS models based on the business' needs, often combining public and private clouds; hence, organizations have to weigh the benefits and downsides of cloud computing in a differentiated way, as there is not one solution that fits all. Organizations must also carefully

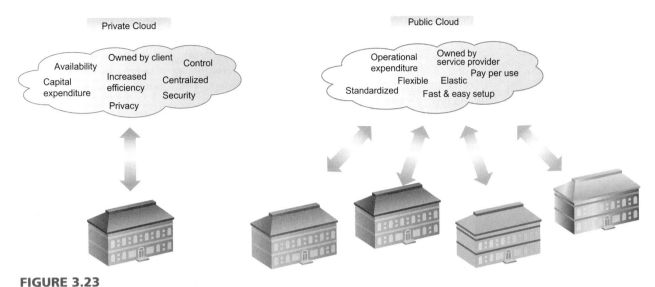

FIGURE 3.23

Public clouds versus private clouds.

consider which cloud services provider to choose. Some of the long-term, strategic issues that management should consider when evaluating different public cloud service providers include availability, reliability, scalability, viability, security, privacy, compliance, diversity of offerings, openness, and, not least, cost (see Figure 3.24). These are discussed next (see also Hofmann and Woods, 2010).

AVAILABILITY/RELIABILITY. Of primary concern for most organizations is the availability of the service. As shown by examples from Google, Amazon, or Microsoft, not even the largest public cloud computing providers are immune from failures, be it hardware failures, programming errors, or some network outage. Organizations thus have to evaluate which applications to move to the cloud, and how to ensure the availability of cloud-based applications. In addition to examining what the promised uptime of the application/system is, what backups are made to the servers and storage, or whether sufficient bandwidth will be provided to access large amounts of data, organizations have to provide their own precautionary measures. As it is often too costly (e.g., in terms of lost business or goodwill) to be affected by negative events, organizations should plan ahead and replicate their cloud-based infrastructure in different locations. Related to this, an important criterion to consider is the provider's support policies. In case something does not work as promised, how will issues be resolved? One of the beauties of cloud computing is self-service, allowing clients to provision resources as needed. At the same time, this can be a potential downside, as there is not always the guarantee of having help available, if needed. Thus, organizations must ensure that acceptable support capabilities and personnel are available, especially for mission-critical applications, to rapidly solve technical issues when they arise.

SCALABILITY. One of the biggest promises of cloud computing is scalability, such that organizations can scale up or down their infrastructure as needed. Yet, not every provider will be able to meet every organization's demands. Thus, organizations have to carefully evaluate to what extent the provider will be able to meet current and future business needs in terms of data storage, transaction volumes, and so on.

FIGURE 3.24

Organizations have to consider various issues when managing their cloud infrastructure.

VIABILITY. Another important issue is associated with the viability and stability of the provider in the long run. As an organization moves to a public cloud infrastructure, it puts much data and processing capabilities into the hands of an outside entity. If this outside entity happens to go out of business, this can have many repercussions for the organization, such as costs and efforts involved in setting up a new infrastructure, migrating applications, or transferring the data from the old provider to the new infrastructure.

SECURITY, PRIVACY, AND COMPLIANCE. In addition to concerns related to availability, reliability, scalability, and viability of the vendor, security, privacy, and compliance are critical aspects to consider when deciding which aspects to move to the cloud, and which provider to select. Especially when sensitive data are concerned, organizations have to question how secure the data will be from outside intruders, how the privacy of customer data will be protected, and whether the data storage complies with regulations such as the Sarbanes–Oxley Act, the Health Insurance Portability and Accountability Act (HIPAA), or standards such as the Payment Card Industry Data Security Standard. By definition, a public cloud infrastructure is shared among different companies, with different applications running on the same hardware; as a result, it is impossible for organizations to know where exactly (physically) the data are located, and thus auditing who has access to the data is extremely difficult, if not impossible. Whereas in an in-house infrastructure, a company has complete control over their own data, this control is lost in a cloud infrastructure, and organizations have less legal rights if their data is stored in the cloud. Similarly, cloud computing providers may be asked to hand over sensitive data stored on their servers to law enforcement, leaving the organization with little control. Especially for industries heavily concerned with privacy and data protection, such as firms in the medical or legal fields, these issues are of critical importance. On the other hand, public cloud computing providers are certainly aware of these issues, and organizations have to weigh which applications or data to move to the cloud, and which to keep in-house.

Issues such as availability, reliability, and security are normally covered in **service-level agreements**, which are contracts specifying the level of service provided in terms of performance (e.g., as measured by uptime), warranties, disaster recovery, and so on. A big caveat is that such service-level agreements do not *guarantee* the availability of resources; rather, they only promise certain service levels and provide for refunds or discounts if these promises are not met, and can thus be regarded mostly as a vehicle for resolving conflicts in case of problems. In effect, rather than guaranteeing the service, the service provider may just offer the service at a discount, without being able to keep his promises.

For businesses, this poses a serious dilemma, as such refunds and discounts only cover the costs paid for the service, but can never offset the opportunity costs arising from lost business. On the other hand, when evaluating the benefits and drawbacks of moving the infrastructure to the public cloud, organizations also have to critically evaluate how they would be able to maintain certain uptime using an in-house infrastructure, and at what costs; often, organizations realize that even though certain SLAs may not be met by the provider, the provider can still offer better uptime than a poorly managed in-house infrastructure. In evaluating their options, organizations often choose a hybrid approach, having certain mission-critical applications in-house, while moving other, less demanding applications (in terms of uptime, etc.) to the public cloud.

DIVERSITY OF OFFERINGS. As discussed earlier, there are various providers of cloud computing services, ranging from IaaS to SaaS. As an increasing number and diversity of providers is more difficult to manage, many organizations prefer to deal with fewer providers that can meet all needs. Thus, an important question to ask is which provider can offer the services needed both presently and in the future.

OPENNESS. A related question organizations face is the issue of interoperability. Most cloud providers use different infrastructures, different ways to store data, and so on. This, however, makes migrating data between providers extremely difficult, and can lead a company to be locked in by a certain provider. In addition to different infrastructures and storage models, existing network bandwidth (and data transmission costs) poses an additional limitation to interoperability, as moving terabytes of data from one provider to another, even using very high-speed networks, can prove extremely time consuming and expensive (as cloud computing providers often charge for transferring data into or out of their infrastructure).

COSTS. A final issue to consider when moving to a public cloud infrastructure is costs. The utility computing model used by cloud computing providers gives organizations control over the resources used and paid for—the organization only pays for the resources used, and can scale the resources up or down when needed. Thus, this provides the organization with much transparency over the cost of the resources. Yet, there is considerable disagreement over whether moving to the public cloud is cheaper than maintaining an in-house infrastructure. For example, the online game developer Zynga recently moved from a public cloud infrastructure to an in-house private cloud, and decided to own, rather than rent, its infrastructure. Comparing the costs of owning versus renting is not an easy feat. Whereas it is easy to calculate the costs per month of a server in Amazon's EC2 cloud, many organizations do not know how much exactly it costs to run a comparable server in an in-house infrastructure, including the costs of the server itself, the fees for software licenses, the electricity, the data center, the staff, and so on. Thus, organizations have to carefully balance the benefits and costs of the flexibility and scalability the cloud offers, such as by using a cloud infrastructure only for periods of peak demand; needless to say, this adds another layer of complexity to the IT operations.

In sum, there are various issues to consider when moving to a cloud infrastructure, and each organization has to make various informed choices about how to harness the opportunities the cloud offers while minimizing potential drawbacks. In the next section, we will provide a brief discussion of various other applications enabled by the cloud.

Advanced Cloud Applications

Clearly, the cloud offers many ways for businesses to solve their IT infrastructure–related issues. In addition to the different cloud services models, the cloud has enabled other trends, such as *grid computing* to help solve large-scale computing problems, *edge computing* for increasing Web application performance, and *IP convergence* for transmitting voice and video communication over the Internet. These applications are discussed next.

GRID COMPUTING. Businesses and public organizations heavily involved in research and development face an ever-increasing need for computing performance. For example, auto manufacturers, such as the GM German subsidiary Opel or Japanese Toyota, use large supercomputers to simulate automobile crashes and to evaluate design changes for vibrations and wind noise. Research facilities such as the U.S. National Center for Computational Science use supercomputers for simulating explosions of stars (see Figure 3.25), while others simulate earthquakes using supercomputers; such research sites have a tremendously complex hardware infrastructure.

Although today's supercomputers have tremendous computing power, some tasks are even beyond the capacity of a supercomputer. Indeed, some complex simulations can take a year or longer to calculate even on a supercomputer. Sometimes an organization or a research facility would have the need for a supercomputer but may not be able to afford one because of the extremely high cost. For example, the fastest supercomputers can cost more than US$200 million, and this does not represent the "total cost of ownership," which also includes all the other related

FIGURE 3.25

Jaguar, one of the world's fastest supercomputers, is used to simulate explosions of stars.
Source: National Center for Computational Sciences

KEY PLAYERS

Giants of the Infrastructure

In the world of information systems, there are a few crucial names that claim the center stage in infrastructure. In the game of hardware, three particular companies tend to stand out from the crowd:

1. Dell—an American multinational technology corporation that occupies the 41st spot in the Fortune 500 list. Being the third-largest PC maker in the world, Dell has become known for its innovative supply chain and its built-to-order model, building customized computers for each individual customer's needs. Founded in 1984 by Michael Dell, Dell has experienced rapid growth on a global scale. Facing intense competition from various other hardware manufacturers, Dell now focuses on higher margin business, offering servers, storage, and networking infrastructure components to enterprises, along with services ranging from cloud computing to IT consulting.

2. IBM—carrying a long history that dates back to 1911, IBM now operates both as a multinational technology corporation and a consulting firm, covering hardware, software, and services. Nicknamed "Big Blue," IBM also holds the most patents amongst all U.S.-based technology companies, including patents for transformative technologies such as the ATM, the floppy disk, and the hard disk drive. IBM is one of the market leaders in the area of servers and mainframe computers.

3. HP—founded, like many famous technology companies, in a garage, HP, formerly known as the Hewlett-Packard Company, has become one of the most important players in the IS infrastructure market. Among the first of its inventions was the HP Model 200A, a precision audio oscillator that was bought by Walt Disney Company. Aside from its well-known printers, HP is known for its personal computing devices, networking products, and servers that are sold to a broad range of clients from small households

to enterprises through online distribution, retailers, software partners, and major technology vendors.

In the now indispensable field of networking infrastructure, Cisco stands at the top. Having started out as a simple networking company, Cisco Systems, Inc. slowly worked its way to the top as a dominant force in routers and switches; until 1997, there was basically no other company that could successfully compete with Cisco. Since then, Cisco has branched out to different markets, ranging from networking hardware and software to various services, including WebEx collaboration solutions, as well as security services, data center services, and others.

In the area of cloud hosting, Rackspace is the big name. Having started out small in 1996, the Texas-based company now has data centers in various locations in the United States, the United Kingdom, and Hong Kong. In providing IT hosting services, Rackspace offers public and private cloud hosting to over 110,000 customers, ranging from Carlsberg and Wendy's to Skechers, the blogging site Posterous, and the University of British Columbia.

Without doubt, Dell, IBM, HP, Cisco, and Rackspace are some of the biggest players in the area of providing IS infrastructure solutions. With cross-partnership growing and multiple acquisitions going around, it is hard to tell who will come out as the long-standing survivor. Either way, the battle has just started and the fight will be on for years to come.

Based on:

Cisco. (n.d.). Retrieved May 30, 2012, from http://www.cisco.com.

Dell. (n.d.). Retrieved May 30, 2012, from http://www.dell.com.

HP. (n.d.). Retrieved May 30, 2012, from http://www.hp.com.

IBM. (n.d.). Retrieved May 30, 2012, from http://www.ibm.com.

Rackspace Hosting. (n.d.). Retrieved May 30, 2012, from http://www.rackspace.com.

costs for making the system operational (e.g., personnel, facilities, storage, software, and so on; see Chapter 9). Additionally, the organization may not be able to justify the costs because the supercomputer may be needed only occasionally to solve a few complex problems. In these situations, organizations either have had to rent time on a supercomputer or decided simply not to solve the problem.

One way for overcoming cost or use limitations is to utilize **grid computing**. Grid computing refers to combining the computing power of a large number of smaller, independent, networked computers (often regular desktop PCs) into a cohesive system in order to solve problems that only supercomputers were previously capable of solving. Similar to cloud computing, grid computing makes use of distributed resources; however, in contrast to cloud computing, the resources in a grid are typically applied to a single large problem (in fact, Amazon.com recently created the 42nd fastest supercomputer in the world using its cloud infrastructure). To make grid computing work, large computing tasks are broken into small chunks, each of which can then be completed by individual computers (see Figure 3.26). However, as the individual computers

FIGURE 3.26

Grid computing: Computers located around the world work on parts of a large, complex problem.

are also in regular use, the individual calculations are performed during the computers' idle time so as to maximize the use of existing resources. For example, when writing this book, we used only minimal resources on our computers (i.e., we typically used only a word processor, the Internet, and e-mail); if our computers were part of a grid, the unused resources could be utilized to solve large-scale computing problems. This is especially useful for companies operating on a global scale. In each country, many of the resources are idle during the night hours, often more than 12 hours per day. Because of time zone differences, grid computing helps utilize those resources constructively. One way to put these resources into use would be to join the Berkeley Open Infrastructure for Network Computing (http://boinc.berkeley.edu/), which lets individuals "donate" computing time for various research projects, such as searching for extraterrestrial intelligence (SETI@home) or running climate change simulations.

However, as you can imagine, grid computing poses a number of demands in terms of the underlying network infrastructure or the software managing the distribution of the tasks. Further, the slowest computer often creates a bottleneck, thus slowing down the entire grid. A **dedicated grid**, consisting of a large number of homogeneous computers (and not relying on underutilized resources), can help overcome these problems. A dedicated grid is easier to set up and manage and, for many companies, much more cost effective than purchasing a supercomputer.

EDGE COMPUTING. Another recent trend in IS hardware infrastructure management is **edge computing**, that is, moving processing and data storage away from a centralized location to the "edges" of a network. Many businesses use edge computing to improve performance of their online commerce sites. In such cases, customers interact with the servers of an edge computing service provider (such as Akamai). These edge servers, in turn, communicate with the business's computers (see Figure 3.27). This form of edge computing helps to reduce wait times for the consumers, as the sites (or media content, such as images or videos) are replicated on the provider's servers, while at the same time reducing the number of requests to the company's own infrastructure. This process not only saves valuable resources such as bandwidth but also offers superior performance that would otherwise be too expensive for organizations to offer. Akamai's services are utilized by organizations such as NBC, Fox Sports, BMW, and Victoria's Secret.

CONVERGENCE OF COMPUTING AND TELECOMMUNICATIONS. Today, much of an organization's communication and collaboration needs are supported by Internet technologies; for example, e-mail has become the communications medium of choice for many people. However, for some topics, other forms of communication are more suited, so managers turn to the telephone, instant messaging, meetings, or videoconferences. One recent trend to satisfy such diverse communication and collaboration needs is the growing convergence of computing and telecommunications. The computing industry is experiencing an ever-increasing convergence of functionality of various devices. Whereas just a few years ago a cell phone was just capable of making phone calls and people used personal digital assistants to support mobile computing needs, such devices are now converging such that the boundaries between devices are becoming increasingly blurred. Today, smartphones, such as the iPhone, BlackBerry, or Samsung's Galaxy S III, offer a variety of different functionalities—formerly often available only on separate

FIGURE 3.27

Edge computing brings computing resources closer to the end user.

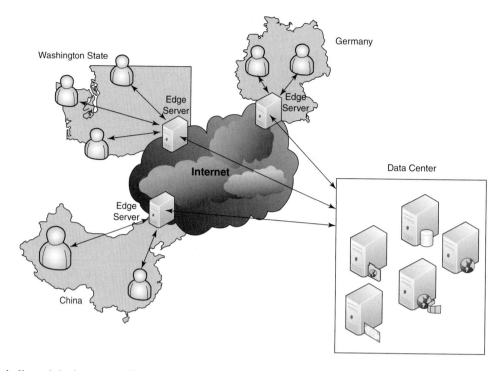

dedicated devices—to address differing needs of knowledge workers and consumers alike (e.g., phone, e-mail, Web browser, navigation system, camera, music player, and so on).

In addition to a convergence of capabilities of devices, there is also increasing convergence within the underlying infrastructures. For example, in the past, the backbone networks for the telephone and Internet were distinct. Today, increasingly, most voice and data traffic share a common network infrastructure. To facilitate this convergence, also termed **IP convergence**, the use of the *Internet protocol (IP)* for transporting voice, video, fax, and data traffic has allowed enterprises to make use of new forms of communication and collaboration (e.g., instant messaging and online whiteboard collaboration) as well as traditional forms of communication (such as phone and fax) at much lower costs (see Figure 3.28). In the following sections, we discuss two uses of IP for communication: voice over IP and videoconferencing over IP.

FIGURE 3.28

IP convergence allows various devices to communicate using IP technologies.

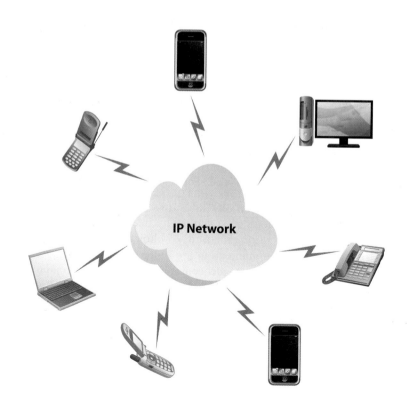

FIGURE 3.29

VoIP technology enables organizations and individuals to reduce their telecommunications costs.

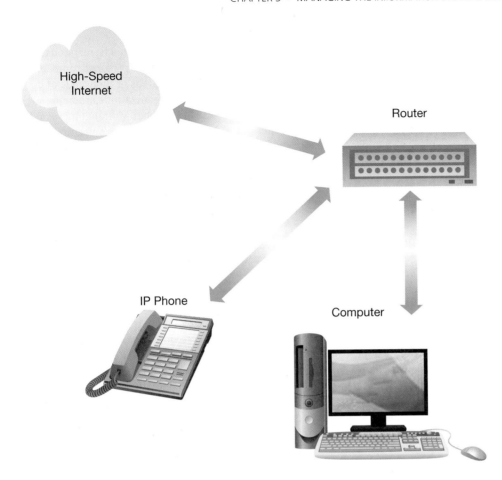

Voice Over IP Voice over IP (VoIP) (or IP telephony) refers to the use of Internet technologies for placing telephone calls (see Figure 3.29). Whereas just a few years ago the quality of VoIP calls was substandard, recent technological advances now allow the quality of calls to equal or even surpass the quality of traditional calls over (wired) telephone lines. In addition to the quality, VoIP offers a number of other benefits; for example, users can receive calls from almost anywhere they connect to the Internet. In other words, knowledge workers are not bound to their desk to receive VoIP calls; instead, using IP routing, their telephone number "follows" them to wherever they connect to the Internet. For example, Christoph, who lives in Hong Kong, has VoIP telephone numbers in the United States and Germany so that friends and family members living in these countries can call him at local rates. Organizations can also benefit from tremendous cost savings, as often there is little cost incurred over and above the costs for a broadband Internet connection (e.g., VoIP software such as Skype allows users to make frcc PC-to-PC calls).

Videoconferencing Over IP In addition to voice communications, IP can also be used to transmit video data. Traditionally, videoconferences were held either via traditional phone lines, which were not made to handle the transfer of data needed for high-quality videoconferencing, or via dedicated digital lines, which was a very costly option. Similar to VoIP, the Internet also helped to significantly reduce costs and enhance the versatility of videoconferences by enabling **videoconferencing over IP**.

For some videoconferences, desktop videoconferencing equipment (consisting of a webcam, a microphone, speakers, and software such as Microsoft Office Live Meeting or Skype) may be sufficient; for others, higher-end equipment may be needed. Such infrastructure can include specific videoconferencing hardware, or it can even be a US$400,000 Hewlett-Packard (HP) HALO meeting room featuring life-sized images allowing people from across the globe to meet as if they were sitting in the same room. In contrast to other applications, with the HALO room, HP provides a videoconferencing service to its customers, offering features such as access to a dedicated network infrastructure and support services for a fixed monthly fee. We discuss videoconferencing in more detail in Chapter 5, "Enhancing Organizational Communication and Collaboration Using Social Media."

Green Computing

Fueled by the rapid advances of developing nations, the world has seen a tremendous increase in demand for and cost of energy. You may not feel the impact of your personal computer usage on your home energy bill; however, for organizations having hundreds or thousands of computers, rising energy costs are becoming a major issue. Further, organizations are being increasingly scrutinized for their contribution to societal issues such as global warming; more and more organizations are trying to portray a "greener" image when it comes to the use of energy and natural resources, as company executives have realized that they cannot afford the consequences of inaction on the company's reputation. As "green" efforts can save money on energy and water use, waste disposal, and carbon taxes, and can be subsidized by grants, rebates, or free technical advice, they can also have positive impacts on a company's bottom line. Further, green efforts can improve the company's image and help to attract better employees and increase staff loyalty (Tebutt, 2010).

Green computing can contribute to these efforts by helping to use computers more efficiently, doing the same (or more) with less. For example, organizations can save large amounts of money for power and cooling by using virtualization to replace hundreds of individual servers with just a few powerful mainframe computers. As studies have shown, computing resources in organizations are often very much underutilized, and using virtualization can help lower an organization's energy bill and carbon footprint. Similarly, cloud computing has been argued to contribute to reduced energy consumption, as the service provider's infrastructure is shared by many users. Installing sophisticated power management software on individual desktops can save much energy that is wasted by leaving computers idling or on standby overnight; for instance, General Electric saved US$6.5 million in electricity annually by simply changing the power saving settings for its computers (Wheeland, 2007). Further, discouraging employees from printing out e-mails or business documents can help to reduce the waste of paper—an average office worker prints more than a tree's worth of paper each year.

A related issue is the retiring of obsolete hardware. Today, companies cannot just send retired equipment to a landfill. Rather, companies as well as individuals have to evaluate how to best dispose of unwanted computers, monitors, and parts. Whereas the first step is to make the decision *when* to retire equipment, the next steps are equally important. Needless to say, it has to be ensured that old computers are wiped of all user data. Many third-party outsourcers ("IT asset disposition" vendors) offer services including wiping all computer hard drives, and either refurbishing and selling usable equipment, or dismantling the components to recycle valuable raw materials and properly dispose of hazardous waste.

INDUSTRY ANALYSIS

Movie Industry

Do you remember the original *Star Wars* movies or movies such as *King Kong* (1976) or *Godzilla*? Compare these to recent box office hits such as the *Lord of the Rings Trilogy* (2001–2003), *2012* (2009), *Avatar* (2009), *Cowboys & Aliens* (2011), and *The Hobbit* (2012), or animated movies such as *Ice Age* (2002–2012), the *Shrek* series (2001–2010), *The Adventures of Tintin* (2011), or *Madagascar 3* (2012). The tremendous increase in computing power has enabled film studios such as Dreamworks and Universal Studios or special effects studios such as Weta Digital and Pixar to create animations and special effects of hitherto unimaginable quality using specialized powerful software and hardware for computer-generated imagery (CGI, also known as computer graphics).

As for major studios, rapidly evolving digital technology (specifically, recording hardware and sophisticated yet easy-to-use digital editing software) has opened vast opportunities for independent filmmakers who are producing studio-quality films without having to rely on expensive lighting, film development, and postproduction facilities. Thus, people who could never afford all the necessary equipment can now produce movies digitally. Further, digital cameras and projectors and advances in software have made the transition from celluloid to digital more attainable for filmmakers who until recently used traditional technology. In fact, over 30 percent of the submissions to the Sundance Film Festival (the primary film festival for independent movies, comparable to festivals in Cannes or Berlin for mainstream movies) are now in digital format.

However, the impact of technology on the movie industry does not stop with movie production. Many movie theaters across the world have shifted to digital projection technologies, reducing the need for duplicating and shipping large reels of film, reducing distribution costs by up to 90 percent, while speeding up the time from the studio to the theater. Rather than shipping reels of film (that are susceptible to out-of-focus projection, scratches, or "pops"), the movies are stored on central servers, from which they are accessed and downloaded via the Internet by individual theaters. Theater owners can much more swiftly react to fluctuating demand and easily show movies on more than one screen in case of high demand.

In addition, the extreme success of *Avatar* in 2010 accelerated the speed of the movie industry moving toward the 3D era. In fact, 3D movies have a pretty long history. The first commercially released 3D film can be traced back to 1922's *The Power of Love*. However, technology was a major limitation for early 3D films. As 3D projectors required two reels to be displayed in perfect synchronization, even very small errors in synchronization could result in eye strain and headache among viewers. Recently, the advances of information technology led to a resurrection of 3D films. James Cameron's *Avatar*, which broke several box office records during its release, was created using custom-built 3D cameras as well as specialized software, enabling the combined use of live action, miniature models, and computer-generated imagery; *Avatar* was nominated for nine Academy Awards and won three, including Best Cinematography, Best Visual Effects, and Best Art Direction. According to reports, there were around 22,300 3D screens in 2011 worldwide, an increase of 450 percent since mid-2009. Following *Avatar's* success, many other films were launched in 3D versions, including *Men in Black 3, Madagascar 3,* and *The Hobbit.*

Despite recent advances in technology, 3D remains an imperfect and relatively expensive technology. For instance, 3D versions of films aren't as sharp or rich in color as their 2D counterparts. Polarized glasses also reduce peripheral vision and leave viewers focused on the center of the screen. It is hoped that newer 3D technologies will fix these flaws. In addition, 3D manufacturers are working to break through the next significant barrier in 3D display. A number of autostereoscopic displays are currently being designed. Like stereoscopic screens, autostereoscopic screens display two images that are merged into one to simulate a 3D effect, thereby eliminating the need for glasses entirely. Using lenticular screens, autostereoscopic displays produce a variable image depending on the angle at which a person views the screen. Movement of the head produces a distinct image in each eye—the familiar stereoscopic effect.

With the advances in information technology, it shouldn't be too long for viewers to be able to sit down in a theater and enjoy a true 3D experience without the need for glasses. Clearly, the use of information systems has tremendously changed the movie industry.

Questions:

1. Can digital technologies help movie theaters compete with the increasing trend toward more sophisticated home theaters? How?
2. What are the ethical issues associated with special effects becoming more and more realistic with the help of digital technologies?
3. From the perspective of movie studios and theaters, list the pros and cons of using digital distribution technologies.

Based on:

Avatar (2009 film). (2012, May 30). In *Wikipedia, the free encyclopedia.* Retrieved May 30, 2012, from http://en.wikipedia.org/w/index.php?title=Avatar_(2009_film)&oldid=495051898.

Cieply, M. (2010, January 12). For all its success, will "Avatar" change the industry? *The New York Times.* Retrieved May 30, 2012, from http://www.nytimes.com/2010/01/13/movies/13avatar.html.

Hartvig, N. (2009, July 23). 3D projects new vision for the movie industry. *CNN.com.* Retrieved May 30, 2012, from http://www.cnn.com/2009/TECH/07/23/3D.cinema.business.

Jardin, X. (2005, July 28). Hollywood plots end of film reels. *Wired.* Retrieved May 30, 2012, from http://www.wired.com/entertainment/music/news/2005/07/68332.

Meyers, M. (2006, January 18). Tech plays supporting role at Sundance festival. *CNET News.com.* Retrieved May 30, 2012, from http://news.cnet.com/Tech-plays-supporting-role-at-Sundance-festival/2100-1025_3-6028354.html.

PRWeb. (2011, January 19). New report: 450% increase in 3D cinema screens in 18 months. *PRWeb.com.* Retrieved May 30, 2012, from http://www.prweb.com/releases/2011/01/prweb4979074.htm.

Schedeen, J. (2010, April 23). The history of 3D movie tech. *IGN.* Retrieved May 30, 2012, from http://gear.ign.com/articles/108/1085907p1.html.

Key Points Review

1. **Describe how changes in business' competitive landscape influence changing IS infrastructure needs.** Modern organizations use various applications and databases to support their business processes; these applications and databases rely on a solid underlying IS infrastructure.

2. **Describe the essential components of an organization's IS infrastructure.** The primary IS infrastructure components include hardware, system software, storage, networking, and data centers. Organizations use various types of IS hardware to meet their diverse computing needs. As applications and

databases cannot interact directly with the hardware, system software is used to control the basic operations of the computer hardware. The most prominent type of system software, the operating system, coordinates the interaction between hardware devices, peripherals, application software, and users. Thus, system software shields application developers from having to develop applications for individual devices. Further, organizations need to store massive amounts of data for operational, backup, and archival purposes. As each use has different requirements, managers have to consider various different storage technologies. Networking is one of the reasons why information systems have become so powerful and important to modern organizations. A computer network needs senders, receivers, transmission media, and protocols. The most widely used network is the Internet. The World Wide Web provides a graphical user interface to the Internet by using HTML documents called Web pages containing hyperlinks to other pages. Finally, organizations use data centers to house the different infrastructure components, so as to ensure security and availability.

3. *Discuss managerial issues associated with managing an organization's IS infrastructure.* Radical advances in information technology have opened many opportunities for organizations but have also brought about challenges. Advances in hardware have enabled advances in software. Hardware and software obsolescence, faster IT cycles, and consumerization present issues such as when and how to upgrade the current infrastructure. Further, organizations' storage needs are growing at an ever-increasing pace, and organizations also have to deal with fluctuations in demand for computing power while often being unable to quickly scale the IS infrastructure accordingly. The increasing need for both computing power and storage fuels an increasing demand for energy, which can affect a company's image as well as its bottom line.

4. *Describe cloud computing and other current trends that can help an organization address IS infrastructure–related challenges.* To cope with the ever-increasing complexity of managing the IS infrastructure, organizations can draw on various new technologies and services. Major IT service providers have introduced utility computing as a business model to address fluctuating computing needs by "renting" resources on an as-needed basis. Cloud computing uses a utility computing business model, where customers can draw on a variety of computing resources that can be accessed on demand, with minimal human interaction. Characteristics of cloud computing include on-demand self-service, rapid elasticity, broad network access, resource pooling, and measured service. Typical cloud computing service models are software as a service, platform as a service, and infrastructure as a service. When considering the move to a public cloud-based infrastructure, organizations have to weigh issues such as availability, reliability, scalability, viability, security, privacy, compliance, openness, diversity of offerings, and, not least, cost. Other applications in the cloud include grid computing for solving large-scale problems and edge computing for providing a more decentralized use of resources. The convergence of computing and telecommunications has helped organizations address their diverse communication needs, such as by enabling voice over IP or videoconferencing over IP. Finally, a recent trend is green computing, as companies realize potential cost savings and a positive effect on the company's image by implementing ways to reduce energy consumption and waste.

Key Terms

Review Questions

1. How do applications support organizational business processes?
2. What is middleware?
3. Describe the different types of computers and their key distinguishing characteristics.
4. Describe the key functions of system software.
5. List the five generations of computing.
4. What are the distinguishing characteristics of different storage media?
7. How does computer networking work?
8. What is a database?
9. What is the World Wide Web, and what is its relationship to the Internet?
10. What are URLs, and why are they important to the World Wide Web?
11. Define the terms "transmission media," "protocol," and "bandwidth."
12. Describe the characteristics of the cloud computing model.
13. What is Moore's law and how is it relevant to information technology?
14. Define grid computing and describe its advantages and disadvantages.
15. Give a few examples of advanced cloud applications.
16. Describe why green computing has become so important to modern organizations.

Self-Study Questions

1. All of the following are examples of infrastructure components except
   A. hardware
   B. system software
   C. data centers
   D. applications
2. Which of the following is *not* a consequence of lack of availability, performance, or security?
   A. loss of managerial oversight
   B. loss of business
   C. loss of trust
   D. loss of goodwill
3. Engineering drawings are typically prepared using _____.
   A. mainframes
   B. servers
   C. personal computers
   D. workstations
4. Tape drives are typically used for _____.
   A. storing operational data
   B. backing up critical data
   C. maintaining customer records
   D. archiving data
5. Which of the following is the protocol of the Internet?
   A. URL
   B. HTML
   C. TCP/IP
   D. ARPA
6. All of the following are correct domain suffixes except
   A. edu—educational institutions
   B. gov—U.S. government
   C. neo—network organizations
   D. com—commercial businesses
7. The ability to adapt to increases or decreases in demand for processing or storage is referred to as _____.
   A. adaptability
   B. flexibility
   C. scalability
   D. agility
8. In cloud computing, services are typically offered using _____.
   A. private clouds
   B. heterogeneous grids
   C. a utility computing model
   D. edge computing
9. For the most flexibility in the use of computing resources, companies choose a _____ provider.
   A. utility computing
   B. software as a service
   C. platform as a service
   D. infrastructure as a service
10. Large-scale computing problems can be solved using _____ computing.
   A. grid
   B. utility
   C. cloud
   D. edge

Answers are on page 165.

Problems and Exercises

1. Match the following terms with the appropriate definitions:
   i. Utility computing
   ii. Service-level agreement
   iii. System software
   iv. Software as a service
   v. Voice over IP
   vi. Cloud computing
   vii. Bandwidth
   viii. Server
   ix. Planned obsolescence
   x. Scalability

   a. The incorporation of a life span into the design of a product
   b. The use of Internet technology for placing telephone calls
   c. A cloud computing model in which the customer uses an application provided via a cloud infrastructure
   d. A model for enabling convenient, on-demand network access to a shared pool of configurable computing resources
   e. Any computer on a network that makes access to files, printing, communications, and other services available to users of the network
   f. The transmission capacity of a computer or communications channel
   g. A business model where computing resources are rented on an as-needed basis
   h. Contracts specifying the level of service provided in terms of performance, warranties, disaster recovery, and so on
   i. The collection of programs that control the basic operations of computer hardware
   j. The ability to adapt to increases or decreases in demand for processing or data storage

2. Take a look at the Web site of an online retailer. Which pieces of information are likely coming from information stored in databases?

3. How does a change in a business's competitive landscape influence changes in IS infrastructure needs?

4. How do software programs affect your life? Give examples of software from areas other than desktop computers. Are the uses for software increasing over time?

5. Interview an IS professional and ask him or her about IS infrastructure. Which infrastructure components does he or she regard as most important? Why?

6. Describe cloud computing and other current trends that can help an organization address IS infrastructure–related challenges.

7. Scan the popular press and/or the Web for clues concerning emerging technologies for computer networking. This may include new uses for current technologies or new technologies altogether. Discuss as a group the "hot" issues. Do you feel they will become a reality in the near future? Why or why not? Prepare a 10-minute presentation of your findings to be given to the class.

8. Do you have your own Web site with a specific domain name? How did you decide on the domain name? If you don't have your own domain, research the possibilities of obtaining one. Would your preferred name be available? Why might your preferred name not be available?

9. With the advent of GUI interface–based operating systems like Windows, is it necessary for the end user to study system software? Research the Web to support your answer.

10. A convergence of computing and telecommunication systems is taking place worldwide. How are companies using the power of convergence to their advantage?

11. Research the Web to identify the major trends in the hardware and software industry. How these trends are going to affect the existing computing infrastructure in your organization?

12. Are you using any services offered in the cloud? If so, what service model is offered by your provider? If not, what are your primary reasons for not using services offered in the cloud?

13. Interview an IS professional and ask him or her about cloud computing. Does he or she have a preference for public versus private clouds? Additionally, find out what data he or she would most likely entrust to a public cloud.

14. Research the Web for service-level agreements of two different providers of cloud services and compare these based on availability, security, and privacy. How do the agreements differ? Are the agreements reasonable? Which provider would you select for your cloud infrastructure if you were to start a company?

15. Internet, intranet, and extranet are three technological innovations of the decade. Research the Web and identify three organizations from different industries that are using these three to benefit their business. Provide illustrations.

Application Exercises

Note: The existing data files referenced in these exercises are available on the book's Web site: www.pearsonhighered.com/valacich.

Spreadsheet Application: Tracking Frequent-Flier Mileage

You have recently landed a part-time job as a business analyst for Campus Travel. In your first meeting, the operations manager learned that you are taking an introductory MIS class. As the manager is not very proficient in using office software tools, he is doing all frequent-flier mileage in two separate Excel workbooks. One is the customer's contact information, and the second is the miles flown. Being familiar with the possibilities of spreadsheet applications, you suggest setting up one workbook to handle both functions. To complete this, you must do the following:

1. Open the spreadsheet frequentflier2.csv. You will see a tab for customers and a tab labeled "miles flown."
2. Use the vlookup function to enter the miles flown column by looking up the frequent-flier number (Hint: If done correctly with absolute references, you should be able to enter the vlookup formula in the first cell in the "miles flown" column and copy it down for all the cells.)
3. Use conditional formatting to highlight all frequent fliers who have less than 4,000 total miles.
4. Finally, sort the frequent fliers by total miles in descending order and print out the spreadsheet.

Database Application: Building a Knowledge Database

Campus Travel seems to be growing quite rapidly. Now they have franchises in three different states, totaling 16 locations. As the company has grown tremendously over the past few years, it has become increasingly difficult to keep track of the areas of expertise of each travel consultant; often, consultants waste valuable time trying to find out who in the company possesses the knowledge about a particular region. Impressed with your skills, the general manager of Campus Travel has asked you to add, modify, and delete the following records from its employee database:

1. Open employeedata.mdb.
2. Select the "employee" tab.
3. Add the following records:
   a. Eric Tang, Spokane Office, Expert in Southwest, Phone (509)555-2311
   b. Janna Connell, Spokane Office, Expert in Delta, Phone (509)555-1144
4. Delete the following record:
   a. Carl Looney from the Pullman office
5. Modify the following:
   a. Change Frank Herman from the Pullman office to the Spokane office
   b. Change Ramon Sanchez's home number to (208)549-2544

Team Work Exercise

Net Stats: Broadband Access Increases

Reports show that broadband penetration in the United States is growing steadily. In early 2012, 66 percent of the U.S. population had access to broadband connections at home, and the gap between different population segments is shrinking. Still, a higher percentage of people with higher household income and higher educational attainment tend to have access to broadband Internet. Further, in terms of average connection speed, the United States is back in 13th place, not only behind South Korea and Hong Kong, but also behind countries like Latvia and Romania.

Questions and Exercises

1. Search the Web for the most up-to-date statistics.
2. As a team, interpret these numbers. What is striking/important about these statistics?

3. As a team, discuss how these numbers will look like in 5 years and 10 years. What changes have to be made to the global networking infrastructure? What issues/opportunities do you see arising?
4. Using your spreadsheet software of choice, create a graph/figure most effectively visualizing the statistics/changes you consider most important.

Based on:

Belson, D. (2012). The state of the Internet, 4th quarter, 2011. *Akamai.com*. Retrieved May 30, 2012, from http://www.akamai.com/dl/whitepapers/akamai_soti_q411.pdf.

Brenner, J., and Rainie, L. (2012, May 24). Pew Internet: Broadband. *Pew Internet*. Retrieved June 4, 2012, from http://pewinternet.org/Commentary/2012/May/Pew-Internet-Broadband.aspx.

Answers to the Self-Study Questions

1. D, p. 128	2. A, p. 129	3. D, p. 133	4. D, p. 136	5. C, p. 141
6. C, p. 140	7. C, p. 152	8. C, p. 149	9. D, p. 152	10. A, p. 155

CASE 1   FarmVille, CastleVille, Etc.: The Infrastructure Behind Social Games

Since its initial launch in 2004, Facebook has become the world's largest social network, helping people to communicate with friends, family members, and coworkers. In addition to communication capabilities (such as features that allow posting "status updates," a chat system, or photo albums), users can access a variety of third-party applications developed using Facebook's own development platform. Interestingly, a category of applications that has become hugely popular is social network games, such as FarmVille, CastleVille, or Restaurant City. Social network games are typically asynchronous, multiplayer games, where users tend a farm, build up a mafia clan, or own and manage a virtual restaurant, all while interacting with their online social network.

San Francisco–based game developer Zynga has become one of the most important players in this market, having developed games such as Mafia Wars, FarmVille, Bubble Safari, and Hidden Chronicles; in fact, six out of the seven most popular social games were developed by Zynga. Although joining the games is free, social network games are big business. Game developers make revenue through advertising or through the sale of relatively cheap game tokens (such as a special menu item for one's restaurant, sold for a few dollars or less) to large numbers of players. With over 290 million monthly active users, as of May 2012, the company was worth about US$5.2 billion.

Zynga's flagship game, FarmVille, grew from 1 million daily users after four days to 10 million daily users after just 60 days; nine months after launch, 75 million people logged in to FarmVille each month. On FarmVille, users can grow crops and trees, raise animals, build barns and fences, and so on. Fields need to be plowed and crops sowed and harvested before they wither, forcing the user to log in to the game frequently. Successful farmers advance and

receive "ribbons" that are announced in their Facebook news feed. Periodically, players receive game tokens (such as a mailbox, a flagpole, or a stray animal) that they can give away to their friends who also have a virtual farm; users can also buy game tokens if they want to add nicer features to their farms without having to wait for free tokens. In 2010, there were 30 million virtual farms with 38 million horse stables (and many more horses) on FarmVille, compared with 2 million farms and 9 million horses in the entire United States. At times, Zynga sells limited edition game tokens for a good cause, and has raised a total of more than US$10 million for various good causes, such as for victims of the 2010 Haiti earthquake.

Comparable to other Web applications, response time is critical for social network games, as time lags in the game's response can quickly kill a player's gaming experience. Further, the introduction of new features (such as new game tokens being offered) often cause spikes in user activity. Hence, supporting a successful social network game requires an IS infrastructure that is solid, responsive, and highly scalable. In addition, social network games place further demands on an IS infrastructure; most Web sites primarily serve content to the user and are thus very "read intensive." In contrast, social network games are "write intensive"; that is, large amounts of data are written to the games' underlying databases. Whenever a player plants a new crop, builds a windmill, moves a fence, or milks a cow, an object changes its state or a new object is created; all these actions have to be properly stored so as to avoid objects colliding or other "illegal" maneuvers. Overall, FarmVille's read-to-write ratio is three to one, which is considered incredibly high.

To support this demand, Zynga early on started using a cloud computing architecture. Using Amazon EC2, Zynga deployed more than a thousand servers for FarmVille alone.

To flexibly deal with changes in demand, Zynga uses a cloud management platform that automatically adds or removes servers based on predetermined parameters, such as when to start scaling or how fast to add or remove resources.

For Facebook, popular social games create synergies: These games entice people to log in to Facebook several times during the day, thus helping to drive advertising revenue; in addition, Facebook receives a share of the game developers' revenues from advertising or the sale of game tokens. However, this relationship is not always happy. Initially, social games could easily post notifications to a player's Facebook news feed, enticing the player to come back and advertising its presence to the player's friends. However, with an increasing number of games and players, many Facebook users have become increasingly annoyed with feeds about someone's lost duck or someone receiving yet another FarmVille ribbon. In 2010, Facebook modified the way news feeds are presented, allowing users to easily block notices from unwanted applications. Whereas this was seen as a blessing for many users, this hampered an important marketing channel for social network game developers. As the relationship between Facebook and Zynga has deteriorated, Zynga launched Zynga.com as its own online platform for social games, and has started offering its games on iPads, iPhones, and Android devices, as well as on other social networks such as Google+. Further realizing that the company was paying huge amounts of money to rent Amazon's infrastructure, Zynga decided to launch its own private cloud. This move allowed Zynga to fine-tune their infrastructure for gaming purposes, which was not possible using Amazon's all-purpose servers. Yet, Zynga maintains a hybrid cloud model, using Amazon's public cloud infrastructure as a fallback for times of unexpected spikes in demand.

Questions:

1. What infrastructure components are most critical for Zynga?
2. To what extent will Zynga be able to rely on its own cloud?
3. What are the benefits and drawbacks for Zynga in maintaining a hybrid cloud infrastructure?

Based on:

Anonymous. (n.d.). Zynga press room: Numbers. Retrieved May 30, 2012, from http://www.zynga.com/about/numbers.php.

Anonymous. (2012). Zynga.org. Retrieved May 30, 2012, from http://www.zynga.org.

Babcock, C. (2012, May 8). Zynga CTO: How to win hybrid cloud game. *InformationWeek.com*. Retrieved May 30, 2012, from http://www.informationweek.com/news/cloud-computing/platform/232901673.

Gannes, L. (2010, May 7). Facebook vs. Zynga: The turf war. *Gigaom*. Retrieved May 30, 2012, from http://gigaom.com/2010/05/07/facebook-vs-zynga-the-turf-war.

Hoff, T. (2010, February 8). How FarmVille scales to harvest 75 million players a month. *Highscalability.com*. Retrieved May 30, 2012, from http://highscalability.com/blog/2010/2/8/how-farmville-scales-to-harvest-75-million-players-a-month.html.

CASE 2   Broadband Service on Airplanes: Wi-Fi in the Sky

Broadband connectivity is fast becoming a competitive area in the airline industry. Since many passengers on long flights don't want to be deprived of their Wi-Fi-enabled digital devices, the industry is rushing to comply.

Although many airlines just recently started advertising such services, the concept isn't new. Already between 2004 and 2006, Boeing tried offering broadband service to passengers through its service called Connexion by Boeing. However, following the terrorist attacks of September 11, 2001, many U.S. domestic carriers faced severe financial difficulties and could not justify the costs associated with installing Connexion's systems. Thus, Connexion was launched internationally, and the first airline to use the service in 2004 was Lufthansa German Airlines. Soon after, several other international carriers installed the Connexion system.

Yet, despite indications supported by Boeing's market research, Boeing's broadband service was not as popular with passengers as anticipated, and Connexion was discontinued in 2006.

In 2008, broadband service was again positioned to take off, and various airlines announced that they would launch broadband access to flight passengers within a few months. Airlines such as Southwest Airlines, Norwegian Air Shuttle, and Russia's Transaero used satellite-based services via California-based Row 44. American and Virgin America Airlines used a cell phone tower system from Illinois-based Aircell (now rebranded as "GoGo").

As of 2012, Wi-Fi in the sky has become common among domestic carriers in the United States and is one of the key battlegrounds for attracting new passengers and keeping them loyal. Air Tran, Delta, Jet-Blue, US Airways, and Virgin America, as well as Southwest, Alaska, American, and United Airlines, all offer some form of wireless connectivity during flight. Some of the carriers provide Wi-Fi on all their planes, while others are in various stages of installation. Pricing for use of the service depends on the length of the flight, the type of device you are using (whether it is a laptop or a mobile device), and the carrier's Wi-Fi provider.

Aircell's cellular ground-based "GoGo" service has been installed on over 700 aircraft and is being used by most domestic airlines. It costs an airline company around US$100,000 per plane to install the system. Customers using GoGo pay for the service in increments by flight hour (e.g. US$9.95 for flights of 1.5 to 3 hours). Customers can also buy a single-airline 24-hour pass or a monthly pass. The costs also vary by device type being used. Users with mobile and handheld devices will pay slightly less than those using laptops. Row 44's satellite service is currently being installed in Southwest's entire fleet of aircraft, using a similar pricing model to that of GoGo.

Questions remain about if and how airlines will manage Internet content while in flight. Many airlines have chosen to block pornographic or other offensive sites, while other carriers have decided to leave the filtering to the user. One airline has gone as far to say that passengers are responsible for their surfing habits just as they are responsible for what books, magazines, and movies they bring on board.

Hoping to start using the plane's Wi-Fi connection to Skype with your friends and get around that pesky "no cell phone use" while in the air? Not so fast—the Federal Communications Commission (FCC) has already banned the use of VoIP for in-flight communications. In the meantime, the European Commission has lifted the cell phone ban aboard aircraft in European airspace. Other areas of the world have followed suit. As of 2010, four continents allowed cell phone use in flight. Ryanair, Qantas, Malaysia Airlines, Emirates, and Royal Jordanian Airlines all allow cell phone use on board. Other carriers, like Qatar Airways, Hong Kong Airlines, Virgin Atlantic, and British Airways, offer cell service on select routes. Although it has been determined that cell phone signals don't interfere with a plane's instrumentation, their use is prohibited in the United States while planes are in flight because of possible annoyance of other passengers. The last time the FCC brought up the subject of allowing cell phone use on planes, they were met with fierce resistance from frequent fliers and the largest flight attendants' union. In fact, there is legislation working its way through Congress called the Halting Airplane Noise to Give Us Peace Act. The "Hang Up" Act would ban all voice communications on wireless devices during commercial flights.

After a few stumbles, it appears that Wi-Fi in the sky is here to stay. Airline Wi-Fi services will undoubtedly continue to improve as Wi-Fi devices become more ubiquitous. Whether voice services for airline passengers will come to North America remains to be seen.

Questions:

1. What infrastructure components are most important for providing inflight Internet connectivity? How do the requirements differ between GoGo and Row 44?

2. How do you feel about cell phone use during the flight? Would you switch to or abandon carriers if cell phone use were allowed on one but not the other? Why?

3. Do you think that using the Internet or cell phones creates any security problems on a flight? Why or why not?

Based on:

Anonymous. (n.d.). Lessons from the failure of Connexion-by-Boeing. Retrieved May 30, 2012, from http://www.tmfassociates.com/LessonsfromConnexion.pdf.

Anonymous. (2010, January 22). Gogo gets $176 million for in-flight Wi-Fi. *The New York Times*. Retrieved May 30, 2012, from http://dealbook.blogs.nytimes.com/2010/01/22/gogo-lands-176-million-as-in-flight-wi-fi-takes-off.

Gardner, W. D. (2010, February 1). Southwest Airlines to offer Wi-Fi. *InformationWeek*. Retrieved May 30, 2012, from http://www.informationweek.com/news/telecom/business/showArticle.jhtml?articleID=222600648.

Gray, K. (2012, May 15). Virgin Atlantic rolls out in-flight cellphone service. *Reuters*. Retrieved May 30, 2012, from http://www.reuters.com/article/2012/05/16/net-us-virgin-cellphones-idUSBRE84F04720120516.

Lawson, S. (2010, February 25). Alaska Airlines switches to Aircell for Wi-Fi. *PCWorld*. Retrieved May 30, 2012, from http://www.pcworld.com/businesscenter/article/190256/alaska_airlines_switches_to_aircell_for_wifi.html.

Mayerowitz, S. (2009, November 23). Airlines add Internet access: The definitive guide to navigating airplane Wi-Fi. *ABC News*. May 30, 2012, from http://abcnews.go.com/Travel/BusinessTraveler/thanksgiving-travel-airline-wireless-Internet-access-guide/story?id=8936104.

Sharkey, J. (2009, September 28). Foreign airlines ahead of U.S. on cellphone use. *The New York Times*. Retrieved May 30, 2012, from http://www.nytimes.com/2009/09/29/technology/29phones.html.

4

Enabling Business-to-Consumer Electronic Commerce

After reading this chapter, you will be able to do the following:

1. Describe electronic commerce, how it has evolved, and the strategies that companies are adopting to compete in cyberspace.

2. Describe the stages of business-to-consumer electronic commerce, understand the keys to successful electronic commerce applications, and explain the different forms of Internet marketing.

3. Describe mobile commerce, consumer-to-consumer electronic commerce, and consumer-to-business electronic commerce.

4. Describe how to conduct financial transactions and navigate the legal issues of electronic commerce.

5. Explain different forms of electronic government.

Preview

This chapter focuses on electronic commerce (e-commerce, or EC), explaining how companies conduct business with customers over the Internet. The Internet and World Wide Web are extremely well suited for conducting business electronically on a global basis. Web-based e-commerce has introduced unprecedented opportunities for the marketing of products and services, accompanied by features, functionality, and innovative methods to serve and support consumers. With e-commerce representing a growing proportion of overall retail sales, an understanding of e-commerce can be a powerful tool in your arsenal. People with e-commerce skills are in high demand in the marketplace; therefore, the more you know about e-commerce, the more valuable you will become.

Managing in the Digital World:
Taobao and the World of e-Commerce

Most people in this world have heard of eBay and Amazon .com. Founded in 1995, eBay is the global online marketplace where trading is the name of the game. Anyone can trade practically anything, from baseball cards to rare vinyl records to private jets. Today, nearly 89 million people from 39 countries have active eBay accounts, trading over US$1,400 worth of goods every second of every day. If you are looking for an online shopping mall, then Amazon.com is the place for you. The company began in 1994 under Jeff Bezos, and has since grown from a garage-based online book seller to one of the world's largest retailers for everything from music, DVDs, videos, and wireless products to kitchen utensils and house wares. In 2011, sales topped US$48 billion, making Amazon.com the top online retailer in the United States. No matter what you want to buy or sell, you can do it all on the computer. Want to get rid of that Chinese scroll painting in your living room? Put it on eBay. Do you need a cool rug for your bedroom? Amazon.com has about 12,000 to choose from. Searching for that vintage Caddy to surprise your dad? You will most likely find one on eBay. Finally, do not forget to check out Amazon.com for this week's groceries.

The online shopping fever has spread to China in the form of Taobao and 360buy.com. Taobao, owned by Alibaba, was founded in 2003 and only eight years later had 370 million registered users, more than the entire population of the United States. If you have tried any of Taobao's services, you know that it has various branches. There's Taobao Marketplace, China's eBay, which dominates the country's online consumer-to-consumer (C2C) e-commerce business with its 90 percent market share. Then there's Taobao Mall, a separate site where renowned brands sell directly to consumers in a business-to-consumer (B2C) manner. In fact, Taobao has fostered such a holistic shopping experience that international names like Gap, Adidas, and Levi's, just to name a few, decided to launch their own official online retail storefronts in the virtual mall. By 2011, Taobao had become the third-most visited site in China, and the 15th most visited site in the entire world, holding a gross merchandise volume of an estimated US$60 billion. Compare that to

eBay, where the numbers during the same period stood at US$53 billion and 22nd in the list of most visited sites.

However, shoppers should beware. Taobao might be the talk of the town, but it is also known as a notorious market for piracy and counterfeit goods. According to the Office of the U.S. Trade Representative, there is a problem with the authenticity of the merchandise sold on the site and questions regarding whether or not Taobao is profiting from assisting with the illegal sale of these goods (an issue that has been disputed by China's Ministry of Commerce). You may want to try out 360buy .com instead, which as of late, has not made it to the list of notorious markets. The company is expanding fast, with an e-book platform that launched in February 2012 and a massive, ambitious plan of solving logistics and delivery troubles (long-running problems that continue to plague the geographically huge Chinese e-commerce market, see Figure 4.1).

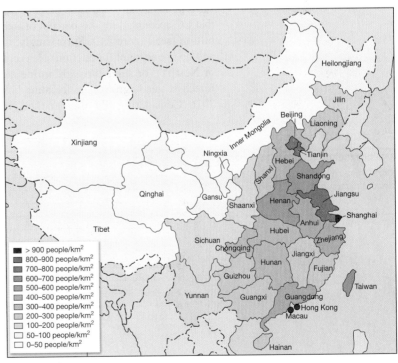

FIGURE 4.1

Companies serving the Chinese market face huge logistics problems.

360buy.com hopes to build a trucking fleet of close to 300 trucks and enter the logistics and distribution market, specifically to get rid of long-distance transport headaches. This comes on the heels of the many difficulties that discourage doing business in China. For example, offering one-day shipping to most locations is virtually impossible in a country the size of China. In terms of making payments, credit cards are not as widely used in China as they are in the United States. This has resulted in the launch of Alipay, a third-party online payment platform affiliated with Alibaba, which partners with more than 65 financial institutions, including Visa and MasterCard, and supports transactions in 12 major foreign currencies. The greatest barrier to online shopping in China remains trust; within China, people fear being defrauded or receiving substandard products. Outside China, potential customers often face language barriers when attempting to communicate with the suppliers. While low-priced offers directly from Chinese suppliers may seem tempting, these factors can easily convince overseas consumers to turn to the more familiar Amazon.com or eBay.

Based on:

Anonymous. (2011, March 29). Gap opens online store on Taobao Mall. *Alibaba.com.* Retrieved June 7, 2012, from http://news.alibaba.com/article/detail/alibaba/100461066-1-gap-opens-online-store-taobao.html.

Anonymous. (2012, February 20). 360buy.com opens e-book service today in China. *China Tech News.* Retrieved June 7, 2012, from http://www.chinatechnews.com/2012/02/20/16077-360buy-com-opens-e-book-service-today-in-china.

Bergman, J. (2011, November 2). The eBay of the east: Inside Taobao, China's online marketplace. *Time.com.* Retrieved June 7, 2012, from http://www.time.com/time/world/article/0,8599,2098451,00.html.

Drajem, M., and Lee, M. (2011, March 1). Baidu, Taobao identified as 'Notorious Markets' by U.S. for helping piracy. *Bloomberg.* Retrieved June 7, 2012, from http://www.bloomberg.com/news/2011-02-28/u-s-says-baidu-a-notorious-market-for-pirated-materials-1-.html.

Hille, K. (2011, December 8). China's 360buy to buy 300 trucks "out of frustration". *FT.com.* Retrieved June 7, 2012, from http://blogs.ft.com/beyond-brics/2011/12/08/chinas-360buy-to-buy-300-trucks-out-of-frustration.

Kan, M. (2012, January 18). China: US lacks evidence to put Taobao on "notorious markets" list. *PCWorld.* Retrieved June 7, 2012, from http://www.pcworld.com/businesscenter/article/248323/china_us_lacks_evidence_to_put_taobao_on_notorious_markets_list.html.

Mackie, N. (2011, August 29). Online shopping is growing rapidly in China. *BBC News.* Retrieved June 7, 2012, from http://www.bbc.co.uk/news/business-14679595.

http://goo.gl/nqEwf

ELECTRONIC COMMERCE DEFINED

The Internet provides a set of interconnected networks for individuals and businesses to complete transactions electronically. We define **electronic commerce (EC)** very broadly as the exchange of goods, services, and money[1] among firms, between firms and their customers, and between customers, supported by communication technologies and, in particular, the Internet. The Census Bureau of the Department of Commerce reported that while total U.S. annual retail sales in 2011 increased by 8 percent from 2010, online retail sales were up by 15 percent and that EC accounted for 4.6 percent of total retail sales, resulting in sales of more than US$193.7 billion (see Figure 4.2). Surprisingly, these figures include only traditional online retail sales and do not account for auction sales (e.g., eBay), movie and music content rentals (e.g., iTunes or Netflix), or sales through online classifieds (e.g., Craigslist). Research firm eMarketer forecasts steady growth, anticipating U.S. retail e-commerce sales to exceed US$360 billion by 2016. Considering all online markets, it is clear that online transactions have become a major

FIGURE 4.2

Online retailing continues to grow rapidly.

Source: Courtesy of the U.S. Census Bureau.

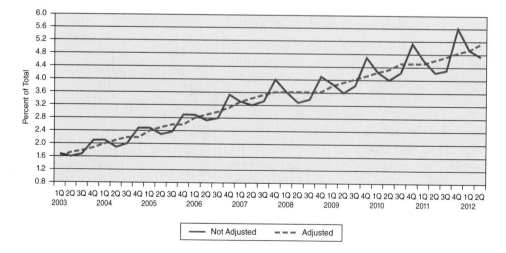

[1]EC can also include the distribution of digital products, such as software, music, movies, and digital images.

segment of the global economy. With this much money at stake, it is little wonder that no other information systems (IS) issue has captured as much attention as has EC. Already during the Berlin airlift in 1948, the foundations for EC transactions between businesses were laid, as the Military Air Transport Service of the U.S. Air Force in Europe realized that not only the airlifted cargo was important, but that *information* about the cargo was equally important, and devised standard universal codes for transmitting these data via teletype (Seidemann, 1996). The emergence of the Internet and Web further facilitated EC and, in addition, paved the way for marketing and selling products and services to individual consumers. This has led to the creation of an electronic marketplace where a virtually limitless array of services, features, and functionality can be offered. As a result, a presence on the Web has become a strategic necessity for most companies.

Contrary to popular belief, EC goes beyond consumers merely buying and selling products online. EC can involve the events leading up to the purchase of a product as well as customer service after the sale. Furthermore, EC is not limited to transactions between businesses and consumers, which is known as **business-to-consumer (B2C)** EC. EC is also used to conduct business with business partners such as suppliers and intermediaries. This form of EC, not involving the end consumer, is commonly referred to as **business-to-business (B2B)** EC. According to the U.S. Census Bureau, B2B EC is by far the largest form of EC in terms of revenues, and many firms concentrate solely on B2B EC. Further, almost all companies focusing on the B2C arena, such as the clothing and home furnishing retailer Eddie Bauer, also engage in B2B EC. In the process of producing goods and services, a business typically sources its raw materials from a variety of specialized suppliers (in B2B transactions); after the production, the business sells each finished product to a distributor or wholesaler (in a B2B transaction) or directly to the end consumer (in a B2C transaction). We will discuss B2B EC in Chapter 8, "Strengthening Business-to-Business Relationships Via Supply Chain and Customer Relationship Management."

Some forms of EC do not even involve business firms, as would be the case with an online auction site such as eBay; these forms of EC are referred to as **consumer-to-consumer (C2C)**. An emerging EC model that is referred to as **consumer-to-business (C2B)** is a complete reversal of the traditional B2C, where consumers offer products, labor, and services to companies. Finally, there are forms of EC that involve a country's government and its citizens (*government-to-citizen [G2C]*), businesses (*government-to-business [G2B]*), and other governments (*government-to-government [G2G]*). These basic types of EC are summarized in Table 4.1. The tremendous increase in the use of mobile devices such as smartphones and tablets has given rise to **m-commerce (mobile commerce)**, that is, any electronic transaction or information

TABLE 4.1   Types of EC

Types of EC	Description	Example
Business-to-consumer (B2C)	Transactions between businesses and their customers	A person buys a book from Amazon.com.
Business-to-business (B2B)	Transactions among businesses	A manufacturer conducts business over the Web with its suppliers.
Consumer-to-business (C2B)	Transactions between customers and businesses	A person offers his photography at shutterstock.com.
Consumer-to-consumer (C2C)	Transactions between people not necessarily working together	A person purchases some memorabilia from another person via eBay.com.
Government-to-citizen (G2C)	Transactions between a government and its citizens	A person files his or her income taxes online.
Government-to-business (G2B)	Transactions between a government and businesses	A government purchases supplies using an Internet-enabled procurement system.
Government-to-government (G2G)	Transactions among governments	A state agency reports birth and death information to the U.S. Social Security Administration using the Internet.

interaction conducted using a wireless, mobile device and mobile networks (wireless or switched public network) that leads to the transfer of real or perceived value in exchange for information, services, or goods (MobileInfo, 2008). In the following section, we examine the reasons that Web-based EC is revolutionizing the way business is being done.

Technological forces are driving business, and the Internet and Web have emerged as strong agents of change, lowering barriers to entry and leveling the playing field, allowing small businesses from around the globe to sell products to a global customer base (Looney & Chatterjee, 2002). For small companies, this opens up vast opportunities. Unlike in large sports tournaments such as the Ironman World Championship, where athletes have to compete locally to qualify for the big event, online businesses can "participate in the world championships" (i.e., compete on a global scale) right from the start. Companies are exploiting the capabilities of the Web to reach a wider customer base, offer a broader range of products, and develop closer relationships with customers by striving to meet their unique needs (Valacich, Parboteeah, & Wells, 2007). These wide-ranging capabilities include global information dissemination, integration, mass customization, interactive communication, collaboration, transactional support, and disintermediation (Chatterjee & Sambamurthy, 1999; Looney & Chatterjee, 2002; see Table 4.2).

Internet and World Wide Web Capabilities

INFORMATION DISSEMINATION. The powerful combination of Internet and Web technologies has given rise to a global platform where firms from across the world can effectively compete for customers and gain access to new markets. EC has wide geographical potential given that many countries have at least some type of Internet access. The worldwide connectivity of the Internet enables **global information dissemination**, a relatively economical medium for firms to market their products and services over vast distances. This increased geographical reach has been facilitated by virtual storefronts that can be accessed from every Web-enabled computer or mobile device in the world.

INTEGRATION. Web technologies also allow for **integration** of information via Web sites that can be linked to corporate databases to provide real-time access to personalized information. No longer must customers rely on old information from printed catalogs or account statements that arrive in the mail once a month. For example, like nearly every other major airline, US Airways (www.usairways.com) dynamically adjusts fares based on availability, booking time, current

TABLE 4.2 Capabilities of the Web

Web Capability	Description	Example
Global information dissemination	Products and services can be marketed over vast distances.	A global audience has access to the trailer for Universal Pictures' *Fast and Furious 6*.
Integration	Web sites can be linked to corporate databases to provide real-time access to personalized information.	Customers can view real-time fares on www.usairways.com.
Mass customization	Firms can tailor their products and services to meet a customer's particular needs.	Customers can build their own messenger bag on www.timbuk2.com.
Interactive communication	Companies can communicate with customers, improving their image of responsiveness.	Customers can receive live help through text or video chat on www.landsend.com.
Transactional support	Clients and businesses can conduct business online without human support.	Customers can purchase everything from books to kitchen ware on www.amazon.com.
Disintermediation	Cutting out the "middleman" and reaching customers more directly and efficiently	US Airways can sell tickets directly to customers, without the need for travel agents.

FIGURE 4.3

US Airways website.

Source: © NetPhotos/Alamy

and historical demand, forecast demand, and other factors to maximize revenues (a practice referred to as yield management); the most current fares are disseminated in real-time on the company's Web site (see Figure 4.3). This is particularly important for companies operating in highly competitive environments such as the air transport industry. Furthermore, US Airways offers their valued customers the ability to check the balances of their frequent-flier accounts, linking customers to information stored on the firm's corporate database. Customers do not have to wait for monthly statements to see if they are eligible for travel benefits and awards.

MASS CUSTOMIZATION. Web technologies are also helping firms realize their goal of mass customization. **Mass customization** helps firms tailor their products and services to meet a customer's particular needs on a large scale. For instance, Dell Computer Corporation allows customers to customize their computers based on their specific performance needs (see Figure 4.4). Dell began selling computers on the Web in mid-1996, and by early 1998, Dell was already experiencing around US$2 million in online sales per day. Dell derives about 90 percent of its overall revenues from sales to medium-sized and large businesses, yet more than half of its Web-based sales have been from individuals and small businesses

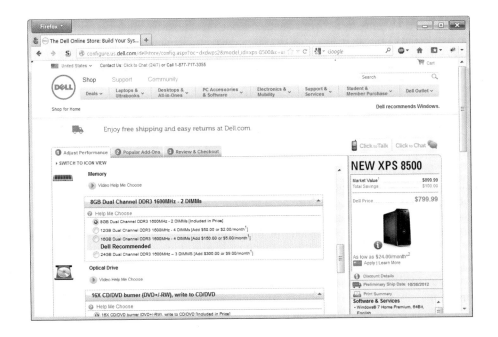

FIGURE 4.4

Customers can build their own computers at www.dell.com.

Source: © 2012 Dell Inc. All Rights Reserved.

that typically buy one computer at a time. Linking an online product configuration system with just-in-time production allows Dell to build each individual computer based on the customers' specifications.

INTERACTIVE COMMUNICATION. **Interactive communication** via the Web enables firms to build customer loyalty by providing immediate communication and feedback to and from customers, and this can dramatically improve the firm's image through demonstrated responsiveness. Many firms have augmented telephone-based ordering and customer support with Web-based applications and electronic mail. In many cases, online chat applications are provided to allow customers to communicate with a customer service representative in real-time through the corporate Web site.

Clothing retailer Lands' End, for example, offers online customer support through various channels. Whereas traditionally, customers would have to phone or even mail the retailer in case of order problems, Lands' End offers text chat and even one-way video chat (so that customers see they're actually communicating with a "real" person) for customers with problems, questions, or suggestions. This customer-driven approach far outdistances traditional, non-electronic means in terms of tailoring and timeliness.

TRANSACTION SUPPORT. By providing ways for clients and firms to conduct business online without human assistance, the Internet and Web have greatly reduced transaction costs while enhancing operational efficiency. Any company selling products or services online uses automated **transaction support** capabilities. For example, once a customer places an order, the customer's address and payment information is stored in the company's customer database, the customer's credit card is automatically charged, the inventory is checked, and the order is routed to the fulfillment center, where the shipping label is automatically generated. Asides from picking and packing the actual product, most of the transaction requires little to no human interaction. For the business, this tremendously reduces the costs associated with the transactions by reducing the demand for phone representatives taking the order or back-office staff handling the orders.

DISINTERMEDIATION. The Web has enabled manunfacturers of products (such as Dell computers) to sell their products directly to the end customers, without the need for distributors or retailers. This phenomenon of cutting out the "middleman" and reaching customers more directly and efficiently is known as **disintermediation**. Disintermediation creates both opportunities and challenges. While disintermediation allows producers or service providers to offer products at lower prices (or reap greater profits), they also have to take on those activities previously performed by the middleman. For example, when airlines started selling tickets online and dealing directly with customers, they disintermediated travel agents (and thus directly had to deal with upset travelers in case of delays or cancellations). To make up for this lost revenue, travel agents now charge booking fees when arranging a person's travel. In contrast, **reintermediation** refers to the design of business models that reintroduce middlemen in order to reduce the chaos brought on by disintermediation. For example, without middlemen like Travelocity.com, Orbitz .com, and other travel Web sites, a consumer would have to check all airline Web sites in order to find the flight with the best connection or lowest price.

EC Business Strategies

Given the vast capabilities of the Internet, the Web has moved traditional business operations into a hypercompetitive electronic marketplace. While it is beneficial for many small companies to access a global marketplace, this also means that every company participating in a market faces increased competition. Thus, companies must strategically position themselves to compete in the new EC environment. At one extreme, companies following a **brick-and-mortar business strategy** choose to operate solely in the traditional physical markets. These companies approach business activities in a traditional manner by operating physical locations such as retail stores, and not offering their products or services online. In contrast, companies following a **click-only business strategy** (i.e., **virtual companies**) conduct business electronically in cyberspace. These firms have no physical store locations, allowing them to focus purely on EC. An example of a click-only company is the online retailer Amazon.com, which does not have a physical storefront in the classic sense. In e-business terminology, click-only companies are sometimes called

BRIEF CASE Catchafire—Fueling "Volunteer-to-Charity" e-Commerce

Ever thought of giving a little for a good cause but confused where and how to start? Online charitable giving has been on the rise, reaching a whopping US$22 billion in 2010. Yet, many people do not want to donate money, but want to donate time or expertise for a cause, and finding the right organization to volunteer time or expertise is often difficult. Recognizing this problem, organizations such as Catchafire.org, MediaCause.org, or sparked.com, offer the answer to matching you with the right job and the exact non-profit enterprise you can offer your heart to.

The New York–based organization Catchafire is an online platform that bridges the gap between non-profits, social enterprises, and skilled individuals looking out to join charitable projects. That is, through an annual membership fee, enterprises are promised commitment to their agendas and allowed access to other Catchafire projects; volunteering professionals, on the other hand, are warmly welcomed free-of-charge. Catchafire then matches up professionals and organizations based on the organizations' needs and the individuals' skills, interests, and time availability; for the non-profits, this cuts the costs and time for identifying the best professionals and coming up with coordinated timeslots for the project to run smoothly. For example, design professionals can engage in the design of Web sites, infographics, or merchandise for various charitable organizations; communications specialists can develop press kits or public relations plans; fundraising specialists can assist in creating fundraising plans; and information systems professionals can create and update donor databases or create Web sites for charitable organizations. No matter what your skills are, the opportunities to help out are virtually limitless. As charitable organizations are increasingly looking for volunteers possessing some specific skills, such marketplaces open up new ways to find the people needed for their projects. For volunteers, volunteering their skills means not only "giving back"; volunteering is becoming an increasing part of people's résumés, provides the opportunity to gain important experience, and, last but not least, helps to build one's career network. When you're looking for an opportunity to volunteer your skills, be it just a few hours per week, you can "shop" on these online platforms to find the project that best fits your skills and availability.

Questions:

1. In what other ways can charitable organizations use the Internet for their purposes?
2. Do you feel that charities are becoming too commercialized? Justify your answer.

Based on:

ABC News (2012, February 23). Catchafire: skills-based volunteer matching. *ABC News* Retrieved June 13, 2012, from *http://abcnews.go.com/GMA/video/catchafire-skills-based-volunteer-matching-at-work-non-profit-companies-business-15780145.*

Catchafire.org (2012). Give what you're good at. Retrieved June 13, 2012, from *http://www.catchafire.org.*

Farrell, M. (2011, December 22). Charitable giving goes high tech. *Boston Globe.* Retrieved June 13, 2012, from *http://www.bostonglobe.com/business/2011/12/22/charitable-giving-goes-high-tech-with-start-ups-helping-nonprofits-raise-money/Qv9QAKsgDJivcQY54tNl4O/story.html.*

Leland, J. (2011, November 1). Volunteering rises on the résumé. *The New York Times.* Retrieved June 13, 2012, from *http://www.nytimes.com/2011/11/02/giving/volunteer-work-gains-stature-on-a-resume.html?pagewanted=all.*

"pure play companies," focusing on one very distinct way of doing business; other firms, such as the bookseller Barnes & Noble, choose to straddle the two environments, operating in both physical and virtual arenas. These firms employ a **click-and-mortar business strategy** approach (also referred to as the **bricks-and-clicks business strategy**). The three general approaches are depicted in Figure 4.5 (Looney & Chatterjee, 2002).

THE CLICK-AND-MORTAR STRATEGY. The greatest impact of the Web-based EC revolution has occurred in companies adopting the click-and-mortar approach. Click-and-mortars continue to operate their physical locations and have added the EC component to their business activities.

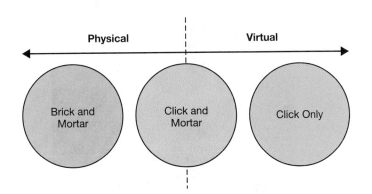

FIGURE 4.5

General approaches to EC.

With transactions occurring in both physical and virtual environments, it is imperative that click-and-mortars learn how to fully maximize commercial opportunities in both domains. Conducting physical and virtual operations presents special challenges for these firms, as business activities must be tailored to each of these different environments in order for the firms to compete effectively (e.g., differential pricing or shipping and inventory management can suddenly become huge concerns for companies selling physical products).

Another challenge for click-and-mortars involves increasing IS complexity. Design and development of complex computing systems are required to support each aspect of the click-and-mortar approach. Furthermore, different skills are necessary to support Web-based computing, requiring substantial resource investments. Companies must design, develop, and deploy systems and applications to accommodate an open computing architecture that must be globally and persistently available. For instance, with total client assets of over US$1 trillion, hundreds of thousands of daily trades by customers, a variety of ways that global customers use its Web site, and a dynamic, fast-changing set of online products and services, the click-and-mortar brokerage firm Charles Schwab has a large, diverse IS staff and a set of interrelated information systems (see Figure 4.6).

THE CLICK-ONLY STRATEGY. Click-only companies can often compete more effectively on price since they do not need to support the physical aspects of the click-and-mortar approach. Thus, these companies can reduce prices to rock-bottom levels (although a relatively small click-only firm may not sell enough products and/or may not order enough from suppliers to be able to realize economies of scale and thus reduce prices). Click-only firms, such as Amazon.com or eBay.com, also tend to be highly adept with technology and can innovate very rapidly as new technologies become available. This can enable them to stay one step ahead of their competition. However, conducting business in cyberspace has some problematic aspects. For example, it is more difficult for a customer to return a product to a purely online company than simply to return it to a local department store. In addition, some consumers may not be comfortable making purchases online. Individuals may be leery about the security of giving credit card numbers to a virtual company. We will discuss these potential drawbacks later in this chapter.

EC REVENUE MODELS. As discussed in Chapter 2, "Gaining Competitive Advantage Through Information Systems," any business that wants to succeed needs to have a sound underlying business model. Perhaps the most important ingredient for EC is determining how the firm will generate revenue streams. In addition to sales, transaction fees, and advertising-based business

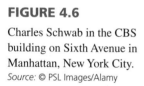

FIGURE 4.6

Charles Schwab in the CBS building on Sixth Avenue in Manhattan, New York City.
Source: © PSL Images/Alamy

TABLE 4.3   Typical Revenue Models for EC Businesses

Revenue Type	Description	Who Is Doing This?
Affiliate marketing	Paying businesses that bring or refer customers to another business. Revenue sharing is typically used.	Amazon.com's Associates program
Subscription	Users pay a monthly or yearly recurring fee for the use of the product/service.	Netflix.com, World of Warcraft
Licensing	Users pay a fee for using protected intellectual property (e.g., software)	Symantec, Norton
Transaction fees/Brokerage	A commission is paid to the business for aiding in the transaction.	PayPal.com, eBay.com, Groupon.com
Traditional sales	A consumer buys a product/service from the Web site.	Nordstrom.com, iTunes.com
Web advertising	A free service/product is supported by advertising displayed on the Web site.	Facebook.com, Answers.com

models common in the offline world, the Internet has enabled or enhanced other revenue models, such as affiliate marketing (see Table 4.3). Many companies selling products or services (such as Amazon.com) use the Web as an economic medium to reach a large customer base; large numbers of customers allow these companies to turn over their inventory quickly, thus enabling the company to offer low prices while still making a profit. Other companies (such as Netflix .com) generate revenue using a subscription model where customers pay a monthly or annual fee for using the product or service. In addition, the Internet has provided large and small companies alike with the ability to generate revenues in various other ways. Traditionally, revenue models based on advertising, referrals, or transaction fees were difficult to sustain. For example, free newspapers have to set their rates for advertising space sufficiently high so as to offset the paper's production costs; in contrast, advertising on the Web is typically rather inexpensive, and the advertiser is charged on a pay-per-click basis (see our discussion of Web advertising later in this chapter). The Web site on which the ad is placed generates it revenue by serving cheap ads to large numbers of visitors. Using such revenue models, Web sites like Google or Facebook, as well as companies such as Zynga (the maker of games such as FarmVille), make millions of dollars in revenue.

As you can see, firms can conduct EC in a variety of ways. In the next section, we describe in greater detail how firms have evolved toward using the Internet and Web to market to end consumers.

BUSINESS-TO-CONSUMER E-COMMERCE AND INTERNET MARKETING

http://goo.gl/mSXS5

The Internet and Web have evolved with mind-boggling speed, achieving mass acceptance faster than any other technology in modern history. The widespread availability and adoption of the Internet and Web, which are based on an economical, open, ubiquitous computing platform, has made the emergence of B2C EC economically feasible.

Stages of B2C EC

B2C-oriented Web sites typically range from passive to active. At one extreme are the relatively simple, passive Web sites that provide only product information, as well as company address and phone number, much like a traditional brochure would do. At the other extreme are the highly sophisticated, interactive Web sites that enable customers to view products, services, and related real-time information and to actually make purchases online. As shown in some early, pioneering research on EC (Kalakota, Olivia, & Donath, 1999; Quelch & Klein, 1996), companies usually start out with an electronic brochure and pass through a series of stages as depicted

The Ethics of Reputation Management

If you're trying to decide on which book to purchase, which movie to watch at the theater, which hotel to stay at, or which restaurant to go to for dinner, you are likely to use the power of the crowd—that is, you probably consult Web sites such as Amazon.com (books), Rottentomatoes.com (movies), Tripadvisor.com or Booking.com (hotels), or Yelp .com (restaurants) to read reviews from others. For consumers, online reviews can be a valuable decision aid. On the other hand, online reviews can make or break a business. For example, a restaurant receiving just a few negative reviews on Yelp.com during the pre-opening phase will be much less likely to attract diners in the future, and the restaurant may fail before it even started. For the restaurant owner, who has invested her life's savings, this would mean that she would have to declare bankruptcy; further, she may have to lay off the chef, the wait staff, and the dish washer, all of whom have families to feed. The owner is tempted to boost the reputation of the restaurant, and thinks about composing a few reviews herself, and publishing those under different pseudonyms. Alternatively, she is considering giving out free drinks or desserts to diners, as an incentive for posting positive reviews.

Needless to say, Web sites that publish customer reviews want to provide unbiased reviews, and often have (proprietary) mechanisms in place to minimize (or at least reduce) the potential of biased reviews. In addition, under rules of the U.S. Federal Trade Commission, paying someone to post reviews may actually be illegal. Yet, you may have noticed extensive, raving reviews about a 500-page book posted just a day after a book was released, or reviews that sound suspiciously like marketing copy.

The restaurant owner thus faces a dilemma. On the one hand, she may just ignore the negative reviews and hope that diners would keep coming in spite of these reviews; however, this may result in having to lay off all her staff and close the restaurant if customers are kept away by the reviews. On the other hand, she may engage in "reputation management" and try to provide a more "balanced" picture of her restaurant on the review site. What would you do? How about not providing any incentives, but merely asking all satisfied customers to write reviews? What would happen if the public found out about your reputation management? Imagine the owner knew that the initial negative reviews were posted by a competitor trying to drive her out of business, would this change your assessment? How?

Based on:

Mihalik, L. and Miles, K. (2011, August 25). The Yelp wars: false reviews, slander and anti-SLAPP – what's ethical in online reviewing? *SCPR.org*. Retrieved June 13, 2012, from http:// www.scpr.org/programs/patt-morrison/2011/08/25/20426/ yelpamazonfakereviewcitysearchtripadvisorantislapp.

Tijerina, A. (2011, February 11). The ethics of online reviews. *Drivingsales.com*. Retrieved June 13, 2012, from http://www.drivingsales .com/blogs/arnoldtijerina/2011/02/11/the-ethics-of-online-reviews.

Roggio, A. (2012, January 31). Fake reviews, a despicable practice? *Practical eCommerce*. Retrieved June 13, 2012, from http://www .practicalecommerce.com/articles/3330-Fake-Reviews-a-Despicable-Practice-.

Streitfeld, D. (2012, January 26). For $2 a star, an online retailer gets 5-star product reviews. *The New York Times*. Retrieved June 13, 2012, from http://www.nytimes.com/2012/01/27/technology/for-2-a-star-a-retailer-gets-5-star-reviews.html.

in Figure 4.7, adding additional capabilities as they become more comfortable with EC. These stages can be classified as **e-information** (i.e., providing electronic brochures and other types of information for customers), **e-integration** (i.e., providing customers with the ability to obtain personalized information by querying corporate databases and other information sources), and **e-transaction** (i.e., allowing customers to place orders and make payments).

FIGURE 4.7

Stages of B2C EC.

e-Information	e-Integration	e-Transaction
• Dissemination of promotional and marketing material	• Customers can access dynamic, customized information (such as bank statements)	• Customers get real-time access to information about products and services
• Global customers can access timely information, 24/7/365	• However, no transactional capabilities	• Customers can make purchases and payments and conduct banking or investment transactions
• Reduces cost and time needed to disseminate printed materials		
• However, no transactional capabilities		

Just a few years ago, integrating transactional capabilities into a company's Web site was very difficult, especially for smaller companies on a tight budget. Now, companies such as Yahoo! and Amazon.com offer small businesses the possibility to sell their goods and services online without having to invest large sums in an e-transaction infrastructure. Two major categories of e-transactions are the online sales of goods and services (or *e-tailing*, discussed next) and financial transactions (such as *online banking*, discussed later in the chapter).

e-Tailing: Selling Goods and Services in the Digital World

The online sales of goods and services, or **e-tailing**, can take many forms. For example, using the Internet, bricks-and-clicks retailers such as Walmart.com or click-only companies such as Amazon.com sell products or services in ways similar to traditional retail channels. In contrast, virtual companies such as Priceline.com have developed other innovative ways of generating revenue, such as offering consumers discounts on airline tickets, hotel rooms, rental cars, new cars, home financing, and long-distance telephone service. The revolutionary aspect of the Priceline.com Web site lies in its **reverse pricing** model called *Name Your Own Price*. Customers specify the product they are looking for and how much they are willing to pay for it and Priceline.com matches the customers' bids with offers from companies (who often use Priceline.com to get rid of excess inventory). This pricing scheme transcends traditional **menu-driven pricing**, in which companies set the prices that consumers pay for products. After a user searches for a service and submits a bid on priceline.com, the system routes the information to appropriate brand-name companies, such as United Airlines and Avis Rent-a-Car, which either accept or reject the consumer's offer (see Figure 4.8). In the first quarter of 2012, Priceline.com sold more than 45 million hotel room nights, 1.6 million airline tickets, and nearly 6.9 million rental car days, generating gross bookings of over US$6.7 billion (Priceline, 2012).

Another innovative B2C model enabled by the Internet is **group buying**. Companies such as Groupon or Livingsocial negotiate special volume discounts with local businesses and offer them to their members in the form of "daily deals"; if enough people agree to purchase the product or service, the customers typically get significant discounts over the original purchase price. The business offering the product or service uses these deals to either reduce unsold inventory, or to get new customers "into the door"; yet, local businesses face the danger of making significant losses on these deals, as the group purchasing site typically takes a hefty share of the deal's price (often around 50 percent), or they may not be able to cope with the sudden increase in demand (see Chapter 2 for more on Groupon's business model). Thus, e-tailing has both benefits and drawbacks, which are examined next.

FIGURE 4.8

Priceline.com lets consumers name their own price for travel-related services.

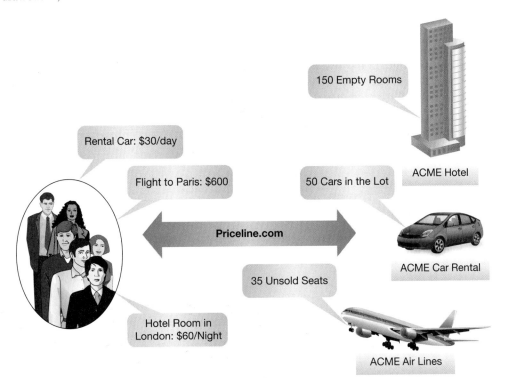

BENEFITS OF E-TAILING. e-Tailing can provide many benefits over traditional brick-and-mortar retailing in terms of the marketing concepts of product, place, and price. These are discussed next.

Product Benefits Web sites can offer a virtually unlimited number and variety of products because e-tailing is not limited by physical store and shelf space restrictions. For instance, e-tailer Amazon.com offers millions of book titles on the Web, compared to a local brick-and-mortar–only book retailer, which can offer "only" a few thousand titles in a store because of the restricted physical space.

For online customers, comparison shopping is much easier on the Web. In particular, a number of comparison shopping services that focus on aggregating content are available to consumers. Some companies fulfilling this niche are Google Shopping (focusing on a wide range of products), AllBookstores.com (books), or Booking.com (hotel rooms). These comparison shopping sites can literally force sellers to focus on relatively low prices in order to be successful. If sellers do not have the lowest price, they must be able to offer better quality, better service, or some other advantage. These comparison shopping sites generate revenue by charging a small commission on transactions, by charging usage fees to sellers, and/or through advertising on their site.

Place Benefits As company storefronts can (virtually) exist on every computer that is connected to the Web, e-tailers can compete more effectively for customers, giving e-tailers an advantage. Whereas traditional retailing can be accessed only at physical store locations during open hours, e-tailers can conduct business anywhere at anytime.

The ubiquity of the Internet has enabled companies to sell goods and services on a global scale. Consumers looking for a particular product are not limited to merchants from their own city or country; rather, they can search for the product where they are most likely to get it or where they may get the best quality. For example, if you're looking for fine wines from France, you can order directly from the French site Chateau Online (www.chateauonline.fr).

Price Benefits e-Tailers can also compete on price effectively since they can turn their inventory more often because of the sheer volume of products and customers who purchase them. Companies can sell more products, reducing prices for consumers while at the same time enhancing profits for the company. Further, virtual companies have no need to rent expensive retail space or employ sales clerks, allowing them to further reduce prices.

THE LONG TAIL. Together, these benefits of e-tailing have enabled a form of business model centered on the "Long Tails." Coined by Chris Anderson (2004, 2006), the concept of the **Long Tail** refers to catering to niche markets in addition to (or instead of) purely selling mainstream products. The distribution of consumers' needs and wants can be compared to a statistical normal distribution: the center of the distribution reflects the "mass market," characterized by relatively similar "mainstream" needs and wants shared by many people; the tails are the niche markets, catering to very diverse needs and wants (but very few of these people share the same needs and

FIGURE 4.9

The Long Tails.

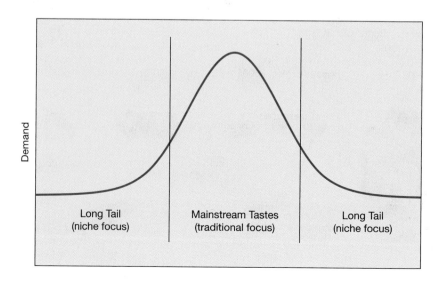

Long Tail (niche focus)   Mainstream Tastes (traditional focus)   Long Tail (niche focus)

wants) (see Figure 4.9). Because of high storage and distribution costs, most traditional brick-and-mortar retailers and service providers are forced to limit their product offerings to serving the needs and wants of the mainstream customers in the center of the distribution. For example, most independent movie productions are not shown at local cinemas, as they are unlikely to draw a large enough audience to cover the movie theater's costs to show the movie; in contrast, large mainstream productions typically draw a huge audience. Similarly, record stores carry only CDs of which a certain number of copies will be sold each year to cover the costs for shelf space, sales personnel, and so on. Given the limited local reach of brick-and-mortar stores, this ultimately limits the stores' product selection.

In contrast, enabled by their extended reach, many e-tailers can focus on the Long Tails, that is, on products outside the mainstream tastes. Whereas a local Blockbuster video rental store is unlikely to have a large selection of documentaries (because of a lack of local demand), Netflix can afford to have a very large selection of rather unpopular movies and still make a profit with it. Rather than renting a few "blockbusters" to many people, many (often outside the mainstream) titles are rented to a large number of people spread out on the Long Tails. Similarly, online bookseller Amazon.com can carry a tremendous selection of (often obscure) titles, as the costs for storage are far lower than those of their offline competitors. In fact, more than half of Amazon.com's book sales are titles that are *not* carried by the average physical bookstore, not even by megastores such as Barnes & Noble. In other words, focusing on those titles that are on the Long Tails of the distribution of consumers' wants can lead to a very successful business model in the digital world. A similar strategy is the mass-customization strategy pursued by Dell, which offers customized computers based on people's diverse needs and wants.

DRAWBACKS OF E-TAILING. Despite all the recent hype associated with e-tailing, there are some downsides to this approach, in particular, issues associated with product delivery and the customer's inability to adequately experience the capabilities and characteristics of a product prior to purchase.

Product Delivery Drawbacks Excepting products that you can download directly, such as music, games, or electronic magazines, e-tailing requires additional time for products to be delivered. If you have run out of ink for your printer and your research paper is due this afternoon, chances are that you will visit your local office supply store to purchase a new ink cartridge rather than ordering it online. The ink cartridge purchased electronically needs to be packaged and shipped, delaying use of the product until it is delivered. Other issues can also arise. The credit card information that you provided online may not be approved, or the shipper may try to deliver the package when you are not home.

Direct Product Experience Drawbacks Another problem associated with e-tailing relates to a lack of sensory information, such as taste, smell, and feel. When shopping for clothes at Lands' End, how can you be sure that you will like the feel of the material? Or what if you discover that the pair of size 9 EE hockey skates you just purchased online fits you like an 8 D? Products such as fragrances and foods can also be difficult for consumers to assess via the Web. Does the strawberry cheesecake offered online actually taste as good as it looks? How do you know if you will really like the smell of a perfume without actually sampling it? Finally, e-tailing eliminates the social aspects of the purchase. Although growing in popularity, e-tailers won't soon replace the local shopping mall, because going to the mall with some friends or interacting with a knowledgeable salesperson cannot be replicated online. On the other hand, online shopping provides certain anonymity, allowing people to shop for products they may not feel comfortable buying in an offline retail store.

EC Web Sites: Attracting and Retaining Online Customers

The basic rules of commerce are to offer valuable products and services at fair prices; a sound underlying business model is key for a successful business. This applies to EC as well as to any other business endeavor. However, having a good product at a fair price may not be enough to compete in the EC arena. Companies that were traditionally successful in the old markets will not necessarily dominate the new electronic markets, and e-tailers should keep in mind a few recommendations:

RECOMMENDATION 1—THE WEB SITE SHOULD OFFER SOMETHING UNIQUE. Providing visitors with information or products that they can find nowhere else leads to EC profitability. Many small firms have found success on the Web by offering hard-to-find goods to a global audience at reasonable prices. Such niche markets can be in almost any category, be it elk meat, art supplies, or hard-to-find auto parts.

RECOMMENDATION 2—THE WEB SITE MUST MOTIVATE PEOPLE TO VISIT, TO STAY, AND TO RETURN. Given the pervasiveness of e-tailing, online consumers can choose from a vast variety of vendors for any (mainstream) product they are looking for and are thus less likely to be loyal to a particular e-tailer. Rather, people go to the Web sites that offer the lowest prices, or they visit Web sites with which they have built a relationship, such as one that provides useful information, product ratings, and customer reviews, or offers free goods and services that they value. These sites help to establish an online community where members can build relationships, help each other, and feel at home. Likewise, e-tailers such as Amazon.com try to "learn" about their customers' interests in order to provide customized recommendations and strengthen virtual relationships.

RECOMMENDATION 3—YOU MUST ADVERTISE YOUR PRESENCE ON THE WEB. Like any other business, a Web site cannot be successful without customers. Companies must attract visitors to their site and away from the thousands of other sites they could be visiting. One method of attracting visitors involves advertising the Web site. The first way to advertise your firm's presence on the Web is to include the Web site address on all company materials, from business cards and letterheads to advertising copy. It is now common to see a company's URL listed at the end of its television commercials, and more and more companies integrate **QR codes** into their offline ads. QR codes are two-dimensional barcodes with a high storage capacity. In a consumer context, such bar codes are typically used to point the consumer to a particular Web page when he or she scans the barcode with a mobile device's camera (see Figure 4.10). Alternatively, QR codes can initiate certain actions, such as make a phone call to a sales representative, or send a text message to a pre-specified number.

RECOMMENDATION 4—YOU SHOULD LEARN FROM YOUR WEB SITE. Smart companies learn from their Web sites. A firm can track the path that visitors take through the many pages of its Web site and record the length of the visits, page views, common entry and exit pages, and even

FIGURE 4.10

Scanning a QR code can initiate certain actions, such as launching a Web site.
Source: Oleksiy Mark/Shutterstock

the user's region or Internet service provider, among other statistics. The company can then use this information to improve its Web site. If 75 percent of the visitors leave the company's site after visiting a certain page, the company can try to find out why this occurs and redesign the page to entice the users to stay. Similarly, pages that go unused can be eliminated from the site, reducing maintenance and upkeep. This process of analyzing Web surfers' behavior in order to improve Web site performance (and, ultimately, maximize sales) is known as **Web analytics** (for more on this topic, see Chapter 6, "Enhancing Business Intelligence Using Information Systems").

DESIGNING WEB SITES TO MEET ONLINE CONSUMERS' NEEDS. In addition to these recommendations, successful companies design their Web sites to enhance their online customers' experience when interacting with the Web site. Valacich, Parboteeah, and Wells (2007) found that online consumers' needs can be categorized in terms of the site's **structural firmness** (characteristics that influence the Web site's security and performance), **functional convenience** (characteristics that make the interaction with the Web site easier or more convenient), and **representational delight** (characteristics that stimulate a consumer's senses). These are discussed next.

Structural Firmness For Web sites to be successful, structural firmness is a must. Online consumers are unlikely to revisit a Web site (let alone make a transaction) if the Web site does not function well (at least reasonably well). For example, the Web site should not have (or at least minimize) bad links, it should provide understandable error messages should something go wrong, and it should ensure privacy and security of the consumer's data. Further, the Web site should be fast; if online consumers have to wait for screens to download, they are not apt to stay at the site long or to return. In fact, studies suggest that the average length of time that a Web surfer will wait for a Web page to download on his or her screen is only a couple of seconds.

Functional Convenience The Web site must be easy to use. As with nearly all software, Web sites that are easy to use are more popular. If Web surfers have trouble finding things at the site or navigating through the site's links, they are unlikely to make a transaction or return to the site. Thus, Web sites should provide easy navigation for users to find their way (and back), should provide feedback about where the users are on the site, and offer help features. Further, features such as one-click ordering, offering a variety of payment methods, or order tracking can increase the perceived functional convenience of a Web site.

Representational Delight Finally, the Web site must be aesthetically pleasing. Successful firms on the Web have sites that are nice to look at. People are more likely to visit, stay at, and return to a Web site that looks good, as the design of a Web site can signal other characteristics of an online business, such as professionalism (Wells, Valacich, and Hess, 2011). Creating a unique look and feel can separate a Web site from its competition. Aesthetics can include the use of color schemes, backgrounds, and high-quality images. Furthermore, Web sites should have a clear, concise, and consistent layout, taking care to avoid unnecessary clutter. Nowadays, online businesses can choose from various (often freely available) e-commerce solutions that offer numerous well-designed store templates.

THE ONLINE CONSUMERS' HIERARCHY OF NEEDS. In a perfect world, an organization would strive to maximize all three sets of characteristics. In reality, businesses constantly have to make trade-offs between complexity, resource limitations, and other factors; thus, it is important to understand online consumers' *relative* needs. Valacich et al's (2007) "online consumer's hierarchy of needs" suggests that overall, a site's structural firmness is most critical; once consumers' needs for structural firmness have been met, functional convenience is the next most important set of characteristics, followed by representational delight. In other words, if a Web site is only nice to look at, but difficult to navigate or appears not secure, consumers are likely to stay away.

Needless to say, a basic level of structural firmness, functional convenience, and representational delight should be provided by any Web site (in other words, online consumers have a "zone of intolerance"). Beyond this basic level, the importance of the different sets of characteristics depends

FIGURE 4.11

Different Web sites (pages) must focus on different design features.
Source: Based on Valacich et al. (2007).

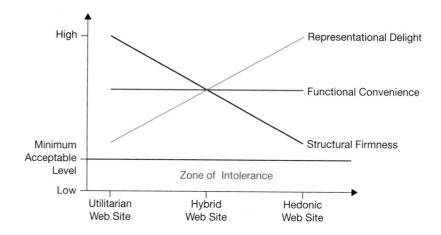

on the nature of the Web site and/or business (see Figure 4.11). For example, for a very utilitarian Web site, such as an online banking Web site, structural firmness will be most important (though both functional convenience and representational delight should not be neglected). In contrast, for a relatively more hedonic Web site, such as a music or movie site, representational delight will be the most important factor (again, not neglecting the other factors). Hybrid sites, offering both hedonic and utilitarian value, such as online shopping sites, should balance the different factors.

Internet Marketing

One fundamental mistake companies can make when taking a current business online or creating an online business is assuming that if you build it, they will come. As with an offline business, marketing is a critical activity in any online endeavor.

Traditionally, companies' advertising budgets were mostly spent on non-interactive advertising campaigns, such as billboards, newspaper, radio, or television ads. The interactivity of the Web has brought about unprecedented opportunities for marketers, resulting in a reduction of ad spending on traditional media; for example, a recent survey of 252 interactive marketing executives showed that 70 percent of the respondents believed that the effectiveness of television advertising will decrease or, at best, stay the same (VanBoskirk, 2011). In contrast, 55 percent of the respondents believed that the effectiveness of social media marketing will increase. In 2011, organizations spent 19 percent of their advertising budget on Internet marketing; research firm Forrester estimates that by 2016, companies will spend 35 percent of their advertising budget on Internet marketing, including search marketing, display ads, e-mail marketing, social media, and mobile marketing (VanBoskirk, 2011). All of these are discussed next.

SEARCH MARKETING. Whereas people would traditionally obtain information about products or companies from offline sources, many Web surfers now just enter the name of a product into a search engine such as Google or Bing and then visit the resulting pages. Given this trend, it is not surprising that search marketing is now big business. Research firm Forrester reports that by 2016, companies in the United States will spend US$33.3 billion on search marketing (see Figure 4.12).

FIGURE 4.12

Search marketing is forecasted to have the largest share of interactive marketing by 2016.
Source: Based on VanBoskirk (2011).

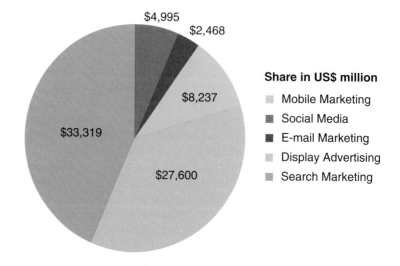

KEY PLAYERS

Behind the Online Storefront: How e-Commerce Giants Help Small Businesses Flourish

As numerous examples show, the Web allows almost anyone to set up an online store and start selling goods online. The first step in starting your B2C e-commerce business is to set up an online storefront that is easy to use, fast, reliable, and aesthetically pleasing. Luckily, you don't have to start from scratch, and there are numerous options to choose from, depending on your needs. If you want to benefit from being associated with large, successful e-businesses, and want to minimize your effort in setting up a storefront, you can simply turn to the e-commerce giants eBay or Amazon, which let you sell products on their sites on a large scale. Alternatively, you can set up your own storefront, complete with your own domain name, giving you the most flexibility in how to present your store and your products to your customers.

As a fledgling online merchant, you can choose from literally hundreds of providers offering their services. Typically, such providers offer various templates for your storefront, an integrated shopping cart, and so on. For example, you could download free open source e-commerce solutions from osCommerce or PrestaShop. Alternatively, many providers also host the online store for you. Having your online store in the cloud frees you from having to worry about infrastructure related issues. Among the biggest players offering hosted services are GoDaddy (known for a variety of Web hosting and cloud services), Intuit (known for its payroll services and QuickBooks accounting software), Shopify (primarily focusing on e-commerce solutions), and Yahoo! (known for its Web portal, search engine, and various other Internet services). Setting up your own storefront requires various decisions about the features you need; in addition to basic features such as product images, reviews, or search functionality, you may desire additional features such as reward programs, membership, coupons, and so on. Further, the online stores differ in features such as checkout/payment options, shipping calculation, or tracking integration; needless to say, different options come at different price points, and you will not only have to decide what your current needs are, but also how your business will grow and what your future needs will be.

Considering the range of different options, setting up an online storefront (complete with professional quality product photos and descriptions) may be time consuming up front, but once you have set up everything, you can sit back, relax, and wait for the orders to come in; as you do not have a physical store, you are likely to spend relatively little time interacting with your customers (though you may need to update products and/or prices periodically, or reply to customers' e-mails). However, handling the fulfillment of the orders can prove to be a challenging endeavor; if your online business starts to become successful, you will suddenly find yourself needing lots of time (and room) for keeping and managing your inventory and fulfilling your customers' orders. If your online shop is successful, your inventory will likely soon outgrow your living room, your garage, and your entire apartment. Further, while the customers complete the transactions without your help, you will still have to pick, pack, and ship the orders, all of which consume considerable time. What happens if your daily orders do not fit on the back of your pickup truck any more? At this point in time, you will likely not be able to run your online shop as a part-time business, and you may consider outsourcing your order fulfillment. Many companies offer e-commerce order fulfillment services; all you have to do is ship your products (in bulk) to their warehouses, where the products will be stored until an order is received. Employees from the fulfillment service then pick, pack, and ship the order for you, so you can concentrate on managing your online business. Crucial decisions include storage and handling costs, but also the number and location of warehouses, so as to reduce both time in transit and costs of shipping the packages. Not surprisingly, one of the biggest players offering such services is Amazon.com. Having built a state-of-the-art warehouse and information systems infrastructure, Fulfillment by Amazon "rents out" these services to anyone wanting to run a successful online business. With the help of these big players, you should be able quickly get up and running with your new online business.

Based on:

Amazon.com (2012). Fulfillment by Amazon. *Amazon.com.* Retrieved June 13, 2012, from http://www.amazonservices.com/content/fulfillment-by-amazon.htm.

GoDaddy.com (2012) Quick shopping cart. *GoDaddy.* Retrieved June 13, 2012, from http://www.godaddy.com/ecommerce/shopping-cart.aspx.

Intuit.com (2012). Sell online – the easy way. *Intuit.* Retrieved June 13, 2012, from http://www.intuit.com/ecommerce/create-your-online-store.

osCommerce.com (2012). Welcome to osCommerce! *osCommerce.* Retrieved June 13, 2012, from http://www.oscommerce.com.

Prestashop.com (2012). Build your online store. *Prestashop.* Retrieved June 13, 2012, from http://www.prestashop.com.

Shopify.com (2012). Create your ecommerce store today with Shopify. *Shopify.* Retrieved June 13, 2012, from http://www.shopify.com.

Yahoo.com (2012). We make ecommerce easier than ever. *Yahoo!.* Retrieved June 13, 2012, from http://smallbusiness.yahoo.com/ecommerce.

FIGURE 4.13

Companies pay per click for being included in the sponsored listings.
Source: Courtesy of Google, Inc.

Included in search marketing are paid search and search engine optimization, both of which are discussed next.

Paid Search The results presented by search engines such as Google or Bing are typically separated into organic results (i.e., based on the site's content) and sponsored results. A way to ensure that your company's site is on the first page users see when searching for a specific term is using **search advertising** (or **sponsored search**). For example, using Google's "AdWords," a company can bid for being listed in the sponsored search results for the term "LCD Monitor" (see Figure 4.13). In order to present the most relevant ads to its users, Google then determines the relevance of the ad's content to the search term, and, depending on the amount of the bid, the company's Web site is listed in the sponsored results; Google is paid on a pay-per-click basis (see the following discussion of pricing models). As you can imagine, this can quickly become very expensive for advertisers, especially when the sponsored link is associated with a popular search term, and the advertiser has to bid against many others. On the other hand, a system such as Google's AdWords ensures high-quality leads, as the ads are presented only to users actually searching for a specific key word (in contrast to traditional ads, which are presented to anyone). As programs such as AdWords can be tweaked in myriad ways (such as by key words, negative key words, region, time of day, and so on), many companies turn to professional consultants who help to optimize sponsored search campaigns. Alternatively, some search engines offer to elevate a company's position in the organic results after paying a fee (**paid inclusion**). Many search engines that pride themselves on offering unbiased results (such as Google), however, do not offer paid inclusion. Overall, Forrester Research estimates that spending on paid search will increase from US$16.5 billion to US$29 billion between 2011 and 2016.

Search Engine Optimization Internet search engines such as Google, Yahoo!, and Bing order the organic results of a user's search according to complex, proprietary formulas, and the ranking (position of the link to a company's Web site) on a search results page is largely outside the control of the Web site's owner (see Figure 4.14). Given the incredible numbers of results that are returned for common searches such as "apparel," "sportswear," or "digital camera," most surfers visit only the first few links that are presented and rarely go beyond the first page of the search results; thus, companies use **search engine optimization (SEO)** in an attempt to move up their Web sites in the organic search engine results. Although the exact formulas for a Web site's location in the organic results of a search engine are kept as trade secrets, the major search engines give tips on how to optimize a site's ranking, including having other pages link to one's site, keeping the content updated, and including key words for which a user might query. In other words, if a Web site is frequently updated, has content relevant to the search term, and is popular (as indicated by other pages linking to it), chances are that it will be positioned higher in the search results.

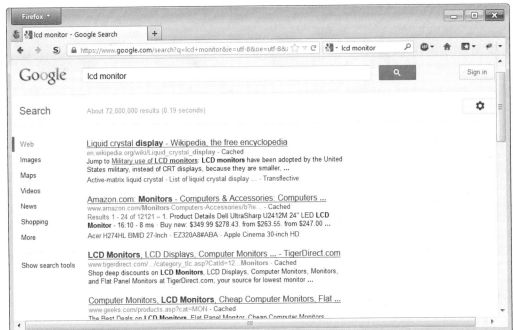

FIGURE 4.14

It is hard to influence the ranking of your company's page in the organic search results.
Source: Courtesy of Google, Inc.

There are a multitude of companies promising to improve a page's ranking, but because search engines' algorithms are usually proprietary and are frequently changed, and there can be literally hundreds of factors influencing a site's rank, the success of using such services is often limited. Further, search engines such as Google try to figure out whether a site is using unethical "tricks" (such as "hidden" key words) to improve its ranking and ban such sites from the listing altogether. Nevertheless, even slight modifications to a company's Web site can have a large impact on the site's ranking in search results, and investments in SEO are often worthwhile, especially in times of tight marketing budgets.

DISPLAY ADS. In the early days of the Web, display advertising was the prevalent form of online advertising. Similar to traditional newspaper ads, companies would advertise their presence on other popular Web sites, such as that of the *New York Times* (www.nytimes.com), using static banner ads, video ads, or interactive banner ads, where users can interact with the advertisement. A recent trend in display advertising has been contextual advertising, where the ads placed on a page are in some way related to the content of that page. If, for example, you are reading tournament results from a PGA golf event at a popular sports Web site such as espn.com, you will also likely see an advertisement to buy new golf equipment or to visit a golf resort. A variety of interactive features, rich media ads, the ability to place ads in online videos, as well as the ability to accurately measure an ad's impact, contribute to display advertising's increasing popularity.

E-MAIL MARKETING. E-mail marketing has been, and continues to be, very popular among advertisers, with over 95 percent of marketers using e-mail marketing in their overall interactive marketing mix (VanBoskirk, 2011). Given the low cost of less than US$0.01 per e-mail, advertisers are increasingly trying to move away from direct-mail advertising and replace it with e-mail advertising. In addition to low cost, the effectiveness of e-mail advertising campaigns can be measured directly (such as by including special links or images in the e-mail that allow tracking which e-mails the customers have read or reacted to). Further, e-mail marketing saves tremendous amounts of paper over direct marketing, allowing a company to build a positive green image.

SOCIAL MEDIA MARKETING. One relatively recent trend in Internet marketing is harnessing the power of social media, such as the social networking site Facebook. More and more people rely

WHEN THINGS GO WRONG

Rigging Search Results

Whenever you perform a Web search on Google, you normally expect that the most relevant search results will quickly show up. Yet, at times, people will try to fool Google, in an attempt to enhance their position in Google's search results. In its attempt to "organize the world's information and make it universally accessible and useful," the company faces a constant battle against "black hat" search engine optimization—the technique of raising a Web site's profile through methods that Google considers cheating, such as including "hidden" text to increase the site's relevance to the search engine. For example, in 2006, BMW's German Web site was caught red-handed and given a temporary removal. In late 2011, U.S. retailer J.C. Penney topped Google search results for keywords ranging from "dresses" to "area rugs"; surprisingly, a search for "Samsonite carry-on luggage" would return J.C. Penney's page ahead of Samsonite's official page. For months, J.C. Penney stayed on top of search results in dozens of product categories through the help of paid links scattered all over the Web on sites advertising cameras, travel, online games, fishing, even dentists, all carrying one similar feature; they led directly to JCPenney.com. Having always drawn a thick line between "white hat" and "black hat" approaches to search engine optimization, Google reacted by demoting J.C. Penney from the top spot to number 68 for "living room furniture" in a matter of two hours.

In the face of growing competition and innovative challenges, Google hopes to stick to its fundamental pledge of delivering the most relevant information at the highest convenience to its users. To tackle the problem of companies rigging search results, Google has made changes to its search algorithm, with the intention of punishing sites that practice "keyword stuffing" and "link schemes," and rewarding sites with high-quality content and less refined search engine optimization. Ideally, the company will be able to work its way to prevent future "black hat" strategies and come to deliver efficient, relevant search results where users can finally "google" at ease.

Based on:

Scott, C. (2012, April 24). Google begins penalizing search 'over-optimization'. *Computerworld.* Retrieved June 11, 2012, from http://www.computerworld.com/s/article/9226542/Google_begins_penalizing_search_39_over_optimization_39_.

Segal, D. (2011, February 11). The dirty little secrets of search. *The New York Times.* Retrieved June 11, 2012, from http://www.nytimes.com/2011/02/13/business/13search.html?_r=2&pagewanted=all.

Yin, S. (2011, February 14). JC Penney fires back at Google and New York Times over SEO controversy . *PCMag.* Retrieved June 11, 2012, from http://www.pcmag.com/article2/0,2817,2380306,00.asp.

on social media to stay in contact with their friends or business associates, so including such sites in the interactive marketing mix is a natural move for companies. In addition to placing display ads on such sites, companies increasingly use social networking sites for interactive communication with their customers. For example, the Coca-Cola Company has created a page on Facebook, allowing it to interact with its over 45 million "fans" (i.e., Facebook users who "like" the page) in various ways; Coke's fans can download free virtual goodies, can upload pictures related to everything Coke, or can use interactive applications. By creating this page (which is free for Coke, except for the time needed to set it up and maintain it), Coke can build strong relationships with a large group of its target customers. Similarly, people can follow Coke on Twitter or visit Coke's channel on the video sharing site YouTube. A recent trend for companies is establishing "social media listening centers" to feel the pulse of public opinion across a variety of social media. We discuss social media in more detail in Chapter 5, "Enhancing Organizational Communication and Collaboration Using Social Media."

MOBILE MARKETING. Finally, mobile marketing is forecast to skyrocket between 2011 and 2016 (VanBoskirk, 2011). Increasing use of smartphones and tablets has provided marketers with yet another channel for highly targeted advertising (such as based on a user's location). This is true especially for tablets (with their relatively large screens), which allow for various innovative interactive ad formats. Further, starting in early 2010, Apple allowed placing ads into iPhone applications, which allowed application developers to offer applications for lower prices (or free, under the freeconomics model; see Chapter 2) and gave marketers another opportunity to reach their target audience through their favorite channels. Finally, the growth in mobile commerce further contributes to the growth of mobile marketing, as companies are trying to reach their customers wherever, whenever.

PRICING MODELS. One common pricing model for online advertising is impression based, that is, based on the number of times the page containing an ad is viewed, typically expressed in cost per thousand impressions (i.e., cost per mille, or CPM). For example, for low-volume advertisers, the rates on the online edition of the *New York Times* are US$8 to US$10 per thousand impressions; on sites such as MSN or Yahoo!, the CPM is around US$20 and can be as high as US$40 per thousand impressions on the online video site Hulu.com. Although large advertisers negotiate special rates with such sites, these online ads can quickly become quite expensive. Given the fact that many Web surfers do not even look at the online ads (and Web browsers such as Firefox offer the option to block certain ads), the trend in Web advertising is moving toward performance-based pricing models whose return on investment is more direct, such as **pay-per-click** models. Under this type of pricing model, the firm running the advertisement pays only when a Web surfer actually clicks on the advertisement; the cost per click is typically between US$0.01 and US$0.50 per click, depending on the site, its viewers, and so on. The performance of this form of advertising can be assessed by metrics such as **click-through rate**, reflecting the ratio of surfers who click on an ad (i.e., clicks) divided by the number of times it was displayed (i.e., impressions), or **conversion rate**, reflecting the percentage of visitors who actually perform the marketer's desired action (such as making a purchase). These pricing models are also commonly used for affiliate marketing, that is, individual Web site owners' practice of allowing companies to post ads on their pages; the Web site owner can earn money from referrals or ensuing sales. Today, sophisticated tools help to match advertisers and content providers, allowing for targeting a well-defined audience with relative ease and helping to increase the ad campaign's return on investment. For the content provider, having high-quality ads is beneficial, as it increases the site's perceived quality; in turn, the site can charge higher fees for the placement of ads.

Click Fraud. One drawback, however, of pay-per-click models is the possibility of abuse by repeatedly clicking on a link to inflate revenue to the host or increase the costs for the advertiser; this is known as **click fraud**. The first form of click fraud is called **network click fraud**, where a site hosting an advertisement creates fake clicks in order to get money from the advertiser. In other cases, an entity—competitor, disgruntled employee, and so on—inflates an organization's online advertising costs by repeatedly clicking on an advertiser's link; this is called **competitive click fraud**.

MOBILE COMMERCE, CONSUMER-TO-CONSUMER EC, AND CONSUMER-TO-BUSINESS EC

http://goo.gl/4tTzW

One exciting new form of EC is mobile electronic commerce, or m-commerce. As defined earlier in the chapter, m-commerce is any electronic transaction or information interaction conducted using a wireless, mobile device and mobile networks (wireless or switched public network) that leads to the transfer of real or perceived value in exchange for information, services, or goods (MobileInfo, 2008).

The most notable driver of m-commerce is the phenomenal rise in the availability of powerful smartphones like Apple's iPhone or Samsung's Galaxy, supporting high-speed data transfer and "always-on" connectivity over high-speed cellular networks (see the Technology Briefing for a detailed description of these and other handheld devices). These powerful devices provide a wide variety of services and capabilities in addition to voice communication, such as multimedia data transfer, video streaming, video telephony, a sheer unlimited number of useful apps, and full Internet access, allowing consumers to access information or make transactions on the go. Indeed, Forrester Research forecasts the m-commerce market in the U.S. to grow from US$6 billion to US$31 billion from 2011 to 2016 (Rao, 2011).

In addition, the increasing use of tablets offers a host of new opportunities for marketers. Although providing for mobility, tablets are often used in people's living rooms as "couch computers"; thus, tablets allow people to shop from the comfort of their homes, without being tied to a desk and a computer screen (see Figure 4.15). In addition, tablets provide larger screen sizes, allowing for better product presentation. An analysis of 16.2 billion transactions from 150 online retailers showed that tablet users tend to spend significantly more per order than shoppers using smartphones or personal computers (Adobe, 2012); given that tablet users tend to have above average incomes, tablets may be an Internet marketer's dream. For companies operating in the

FIGURE 4.15

Tablets are often used as "couch computers."

Source: Diego Cervo/Shutterstock

digital world, this means that in order to harness the opportunities of mobile commerce, they have to ensure to provide their content in formats suited for the different devices' form factors.

LOCATION-BASED M-COMMERCE. A key driver for m-commerce is **location-based services**, which are highly personalized mobile services based on a user's location. Location-based services are implemented via the cellular network, Wi-Fi networks, and Global Positioning System (GPS) functionality, now built into most modern cell phones. Location-based services allow the service provider to offer information or services tailored to the consumers' needs, depending on their location. For example, search engines can provide specific information about attractions or restaurants located in the user's vicinity, retail stores can enhance store locators with navigation instructions, or users can receive real-time traffic or public transport information (see Table 4.4).

INFORMATION ON THE GO. Over the past decades, people have become increasingly used to having tremendous amounts of information available. Mobile devices have taken this to the next level, in that people now have the information available whenever, wherever. In the past, when people were sitting in a restaurant and would start arguing about certain facts and figures (such as a football player's statistics), they would typically leave in disagreement (and maybe start betting), and would only be able to validate the numbers after someone found a reputable information source to "prove" that he or she was right. Today, inevitably someone will pull out a smartphone and immediately resolve the argument (see Figure 4.16). When deciding on whether or not to enter a particular restaurant, people can get further information or customer reviews from sites such as yelp.com using their mobile devices; similarly, when standing in a retail store, customers can easily retrieve a host of information and reviews about particular products. For customers, this can help tremendously in the decision making. For companies operating in the offline world, this has turned into a mixed blessing. On the one hand, they can augment the offline shopping experience by being able to provide much more information than they would typically be able to. On the other hand, the rise in smartphone use has led to "showrooming," that is, shoppers coming into a store to evaluate the look and feel of a product, just to then purchase it online or at a competitor's store. Obviously, click-only companies benefit from

TABLE 4.4   GPS-Enabled Location-Based Services

Service	Example
Location	Determining the basic geographic position of the cell phone
Mapping	Capturing specific locations to be viewed on the phone
Navigation	The ability to give route directions from one point to another
Tracking	The ability to see another person's location

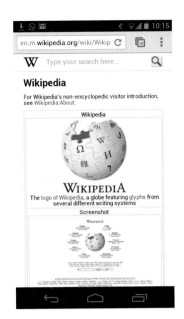

FIGURE 4.16

Using mobile devices, information is always at your fingertips.
Source: Courtesy of Wikimedia Foundation.

this practice; online retailer Amazon.com even offers an app that lets the user scan a product's barcode with the smartphone's camera, and then displays the product information and price offered by Amazon.com.

In addition to providing information on the go, service providers have started to offer mobile tickets or even mobile boarding passes; typically a QR barcode is sent to the smartphone of the user, who then just has to present the code to a barcode reader to verify the ticket or boarding pass. This adds convenience for the user, who does not have to keep track of paper tickets, physical boarding passes, and the like. In addition, the service provider can offer additional information and services, such as automatic notifications of delays or gate changes for passengers.

PRODUCT AND CONTENT SALES. Mobile users increasingly use their mobile devices to make purchases of products or content on the go. In an attempt to harness this trend, many online retailers designed mobile versions of their Web sites, so as to facilitate the shopping process on mobile devices. With the increasing popularity of mobile commerce, companies have to strategically decide whether to go beyond mobile versions of their Web sites and to compete in the ever growing market for mobile apps. While mobile apps can offer many interactive features, they are typically costly to develop, as they have to be tailored to different platforms (e.g., Apple's iOS vs. Android) and device form factors (such as different screen sizes of smartphones and tablets, see Figure 4.17). Recently, Home plus, the Korean subsidiary of the British grocery giant Tesco, built a "virtual supermarket" in a subway station. Using billboard-sized posters, Home

FIGURE 4.17

Businesses have to decide whether to build apps for different platforms and form factors.
Source: Scanrail/Fotolia

COMING ATTRACTIONS

Smartphones of the Future

What can we expect from the smartphone of the future? We cannot predict exactly what it will be, but we may get some clues from what the industry leaders are doing. The big smartphone manufacturers are typically mum about new features or capabilities. Apple, maker of the hugely successful iPhone and the iPad, is famous for its secrecy, to the point that the design department even has a separate kitchen to prevent the leakage of the company's best-kept secrets during lunch time. Aside from the occasional iPhone prototype left in a bar, it is mainly Apple's suppliers who are the source of leakage, and what some of these suppliers demonstrate may signal what will be part of the next generation of smartphones.

In addition to ever more powerful processors, one of the biggest areas of innovation has been the phones' touch screens. Whereas augmented reality apps are becoming more common and manufacturers such as LG have launched phones with 3D displays, there are even more exciting innovations on the horizon. Corning, the maker of the virtually indestructible "Gorilla Glass," recently unveiled "Willow Glass," a super-thin, flexible glass that can even be rolled up, and seems promising for a variety of innovative smartphone designs. Another innovation is related to the phones' keyboards. Some smartphones, such as RIM's BlackBerry, are lauded for their ergonomic keyboard; yet, physical keyboards need room, and many smartphone manufacturers have abandoned physical keyboards for virtual keyboards, which appear on the phone's touchscreen when needed. However, while being elegant, such virtual keyboards do not provide the tactile experience many users seek when typing. California-based Tactus Technology recently presented a prototype of the so-called Tactile Layer, a thin layer placed on top of the touch screen that can make shapes rise, thus enabling to virtually create a physical keyboard, or different other user interfaces. Using the Tactile Layer would enable mobile phone users to type blindly, and people could finally focus on their environment again while texting. Another innovative way to interact with your phone is through near field communication (NFC) technology. Samsung recently introduced NFC-enabled stickers to the market; these stickers can be attached to one's night stand, a business card, or any other place, and triggers an action (such as the setting of the alarm clock, a phone call, or some other action) once a user taps the sticker with her phone. The applications of such technologies are only limited by people's imagination. Clearly, there are many exciting developments on the horizon.

Based on:

Anonymous. (2012, June 5). Willow Glass: ultra-thin glass can 'wrap' around devices. *BBC News*. Retrieved June 13, 2012, from http://www.bbc.com/news/technology-18329974.

Ayala, D. (2010, February 4). Will your next smartphone shape-shift? One researcher presents his ideas. *PC World*. Retrieved June 13, 2012, from http://www.pcworld.com/article/188543/will_your_next_smartphone_shapeshift_one_researcher_presents_his_ideas.html.

Ayala, D. (2010, February 19). Dreaming up the smartphone of the future. *PC World*. Retrieved June 13, 2011, from http://www.pcworld.com/article/189732/dreaming_up_the_smartphone_of_the_future.html.

Brandon, J. (2010, February 16). The future of smartphones: 2010–2015 and beyond. *Digitaltrends.com*. Retrieved June 13, 2012, from http://www.digitaltrends.com/features/the-future-of-smartphones-2010–2015-and-beyond.

Gross, D. (2012, June 6). A touchscreen with keys that rise and disappear. *CNN.com*. Retrieved June 13, 2012, from http://whatsnext.blogs.cnn.com/2012/06/06/a-touchscreen-with-keys-that-rise-and-disappear.

Kassner, M. (2009, February 4). Smartphone patents foretell the future. *Tech Republic*. Retrieved March 20, 2010, from http://blogs.techrepublic.com.com/networking/?p=904.

Svensson, P. (2012, June 16). Phones gain ability to learn by touching. *USA Today*. Retrieved July 26, 2012, from http://www.usatoday.com/tech/news/story/2012–06–16/tapping-phones-nfc/55644082/1.

Waugh, R. (2011, March 20). How did a British polytechnic graduate become the design genius behind £200billion Apple? *MailOnline*. Retrieved June 13, 2012, from http://www.dailymail.co.uk/home/moslive/article-1367481/Apples-Jonathan-Ive-How-did-British-polytechnic-graduate-design-genius.html.

plus displayed pictures of all products that could be ordered; customers just had to scan the QR code beneath a product to make a purchase, which would then be delivered to the customer's home or office.

Especially among commuters, accessing content from mobile devices is extremely popular. Content providers ranging from newspapers to TV stations are now offering various ways to access their content from mobile devices. The increasing field of mobile content is obviously an important part of many companies' mobile marketing mix, as it allows reaching people in more places, and provides for extremely targeted marketing efforts (such as based on a user's location).

Mobile Social Networking is another trend fueled by the increasing penetration and increasing capabilities of mobile devices. With the success of social networking sites such as Facebook, many innovators are looking to social networks and mobile technologies. Social networks such as Facebook are offering various features supporting mobile social networking, such as allowing people to "check in" at places like restaurants or attractions using their mobile devices, letting their

TABLE 4.5   Opportunities and Threats of C2C EC

Opportunities	Threats
Consumers can buy and sell to broader markets	No quality control
Eliminates the middleman that increases the final price of products and services	Higher possibility of fraud
Always available for consumers, 24/7/365	Harder to use traditional methods to pay (checks, cash, ATM cards)
Market demand is an efficient mechanism for setting prices in the electronic environment	
Increases the numbers of buyers and sellers who can find each other	

friends know about their location or activities, and uploading pictures directly from the mobile phone. We will discuss more about (mobile) social networking in Chapter 5.

C2C EC

C2C commerce has been with us since the start of commerce itself. Whether it was bartering, auctions, or tendering, commerce has always included C2C economics. According to the American Life Project, 17 percent of online American adults, or 25 million people, have used the Internet to sell things. Electronically facilitated interactions create unique opportunities (such as a large pool of potential buyers) and unique problems (such as the potential of being defrauded; see Table 4.5). This section discusses *e-auctions* and *online classifieds,* two of the most popular mechanisms consumers use to buy, sell, and trade with other consumers.

E-AUCTIONS. As seen throughout this text, the Internet has provided the possibility to disseminate information and services that were previously unavailable in many locations. This dissemination can be seen clearly in the emergence of electronic auctions, or **e-auctions**. e-Auctions provide a place where sellers can post goods and services for sale and buyers can bid on these items or vice versa. e-Auctions can be categorized based on the number of sellers (one or many) and the number of buyers (one or many) involved, giving four distinct categories of e-auctions (see Figure 4.18). The most common form of e-auction is called **forward auction**, where the highest bid wins. A **reverse auction** is where buyers post a *request for quote*, which is similar to a request for proposal (for more on requests for proposal, see Chapter 9, "Developing and Acquiring Information Systems") in that the sellers respond with bids (and the seller with the lowest bid wins) rather than posting items or services for auction. Bartering typically takes place on a one-on-one basis, but Web sites such as swap.com bring together many people listing items to swap. Exchanges are typically taking place on a B2B level. Auctions are typically characterized as dynamic and competitive environments where market forces set the prices.

The largest e-auction site you probably know is eBay (www.ebay.com). eBay's revenue model is based on small fees that are associated with posting items, but these small fees quickly add up, so that in 2011 eBay's net revenues exceeded US$11.6 billion. Whereas eBay is hugely popular,

FIGURE 4.18

Types of e-auctions.
Source: Based on Turban et al. (2012).

FIGURE 4.19

Amateur and professional photographers can sell their creations through microstock photo sites such as shutterstock .com.

there continue to be cases of fraud. According to the Internet Crime Complaint Center, e-auctions are marred with fraud (ic3.gov, 2012), with e-auction fraud being among the top five most common crime types filed with the center. There are several different types of e-auction fraud:

- **Bid Luring.** Luring bidders to leave a legitimate auction to buy the same item at a lower price outside the auction space, where return policies and buyer protection do not apply.
- **Counterfeit items.** Selling something that is said to be an original, but it turns out to be a counterfeit item.
- **Bid Shielding.** Sometimes called "shill bidding." Using two different accounts to place a low followed by a very high bid on a desired item, leading other bidders to drop out of the auction. The high bid is then retracted, and the item is won at the low bid.
- **Shipping Fraud.** Charging excessive shipping and handling fees, far above actual cost.
- **Payment Failure.** Buyers not paying for item after auction conclusion.
- **Non-shipment.** Sellers failing to ship item after payment has been received.

e-Auction providers such as eBay use sophisticated business intelligence applications (see Chapter 6) to detect and minimize e-auction fraud, attempting to make C2C EC a safer shopping experience.

ONLINE CLASSIFIEDS. Another type of C2C e-commerce is online classifieds. Although online classifieds sites such as craigslist.com are enabled by Web capabilities, no transactions take place online. Yet, online classifieds have flourished in recent years, enabling people to sell anything from flowers to furniture. A related concept that has gained popularity is "freecycling," that is, giving away goods for free to anyone who is willing to pick them up.

C2B EC

Just as the Web has enabled small businesses to participate in global EC, it has also enabled consumers to sell goods or services to businesses, reversing the more typical B2C model. As a relatively new phenomenon, consumer-to-business (C2B) EC has seen a few implementations. One prime example is microstock photo sites such as www.shutterstock.com, which sells pictures, videos, or artwork to publishers, newspapers, Web designers, or advertising agencies; however, in contrast to traditional stock photo agencies, such as Getty Images, Shutterstock sources much of its content not from professionals but from amateur photographers (see Figure 4.19). Similarly, companies use crowdsourcing (see Chapter 5) in order to have small, well-defined tasks (such as tagging pictures or describing products) performed by a scalable ad hoc workforce of everyday people. However, it can be argued that consumers who regularly engage in C2B transactions and make parts of their living with such transactions can be considered businesses; hence, the line between C2B and B2B transactions is somewhat blurry.

http://goo.gl/PfqoA

MANAGING FINANCES AND NAVIGATING LEGAL ISSUES IN EC

Although EC is only a little over a decade old, radical developments in technology and systems have brought EC from a fringe economic activity to one of the most prevalent in today's global economy. This innovation has not slowed down and has opened some promising new areas within EC. This section outlines Web-based financial transactions and legal issues related to EC transactions.

WHO'S GOING MOBILE

Mobile Payments

How full is that jar on your kitchen counter used for keeping small change? Many people are annoyed by having to fumble for cash in a wallet filled up with small change whenever they make a purchase, or by having to wait in the checkout line for someone slowly writing a check. Both cash and checks have a number of drawbacks: for individuals and business alike, carrying large amounts of cash puts them at the risk of being robbed; for business organizations, handling checks can pose a tremendous burden; for countries, printing and distributing physical money is a large cost factor. The advent of the credit card and electronic funds transfer (EFT) mechanisms have paved the way for gradually making cash and checks obsolete, enabling societies to transform into cashless societies. Indeed, in the U.S., only 7 percent of all transactions are made in cash, and in Sweden, the number is only 3 percent.

Yet, even though the number of cash transactions seems to be on the decline, there are still various scenarios in which using EFT or credit cards is cumbersome or downright impossible. For example, many offline retailers resist accepting credit cards for small purchases, mainly due to the high costs involved, and many small amounts (such as paying at the parking meter) cannot be paid using credit cards. Similarly, the friend who lent you money for dinner is unlikely to accept credit cards, and paying for online purchases on your mobile phone (e.g., for movie tickets) is very cumbersome.

With increasing mobility in the digital world, the smartphone appears to be a natural payment companion: just like a wallet, most people carry their phone with them at all times. To harness this opportunity, companies have devised various ways to use a smartphone as a payment device. For example, near-field communication (NFC) allows for simply waving an NFC-enabled phone in front of a reading device; the payment amount is typically billed to a linked credit card. Similarly, the American coffee giant Starbucks developed an app that lets users pay for their coffee by having the barista scan a barcode generated by the app, and PayPal developed an app that allows for sending money to friends, or for ordering products by simply scanning a QR code.

In places like rural Africa where access to banks has remained, to date, rather limited, using mobile phones to transfer money by sending text messages has become increasingly popular. In Kenya, mobile phone giant Vodafone and Kenya's local operator Safaricom have formed a joint venture to launch a system called M-PESA (the word pesa means money in Swahili); to use M-PESA, the user has to register for the service, load money onto the phone, and can then transfer money or pay for goods or services simply by sending a text message. The recipient then shows the text message to the nearest M-PESA outlet (usually a gas station, shop, or pharmacy) and receives the cash. Going through life without having to carry cash is undoubtedly a convenience for many—traveling to the bank is no longer a headache, and the risk of being mugged is lessened to almost none. For stores, POS terminals are not needed, therefore even small and medium-sized enterprises have turned to mobile money transfer to make payments and deal with customer transactions. Today, M-PESA has more than 15 million subscribers, clearly showing how mobile technology has made people's lives easier.

As you can see, mobile payment appears to be here to stay. However, it is not without problems. For example, critics cite the lack of accessibility for older generations, as well as costs involved for the merchants, and, last but not least, privacy concerns: unlike cash, mobile transactions are always stored somewhere, and may put people's privacy at risk when making purchases or even donations. On the other hand, mobile payments offer a host of opportunities for retailers, enabling them to build ever closer relationships with their customers.

Based on:

Baker, N. (2012, April 9). Bump pay app helps transfer money. *Montreal Gazette*. Retrieved April 12, 2012, from http://www.montrealgazette.com/technology/Bump+helps+transfer+money/6430140/story.html.

Cave, A. (2012, April 10). Is mobile the way we'll all be paying? *Telegraph.co.uk*. Retrieved April 12, 2012, from http://www.telegraph.co.uk/finance/festival-of-business/9195540/Is-mobile-the-way-well-all-be-paying.html.

Gahran, A. (2011, November 22). Why mobile payments haven't gone mainstream. *CNN*. Retrieved April 12, 2012, from http://www.cnn.com/2011/11/22/tech/mobile/google-wallet-payment/index.html.

Graham, F. (2010, November 22). Kenya's mobile wallet revolution. *BBC News*. Retrieved April 12, 2012, from http://www.bbc.co.uk/news/business-11793290.

Hamblen, M. (2011, June 14). Starbucks extends smartphone payment app to Android devices. *Computerworld*. Retrieved April 12, 2012, from http://www.computerworld.com/s/article/9217626/Starbucks_extends_smartphone_payment_app_to_Android_devices.

e-Banking

One special form of services frequently offered online is managing financial transactions. Whereas traditionally consumers had to visit their bank to conduct financial transactions, they can now manage credit card, checking, or savings accounts online using **online banking** or pay their bills using **electronic bill pay** services. However, concerns about the security of online transactions have worried many online users, with 41 percent of the respondents to a survey by research firm Entersekt worrying about their account being compromised (Li, 2012).

In addition to online banking, **online investing** has seen steady growth over the past several years. The Internet has changed the investment landscape considerably; now, people use the Internet to get information about stock quotes or to manage their portfolios. For example, many consumers turn to sites such as MSN Money, Yahoo! Finance, or CNN Money to get the latest information about stock prices, firm performance, or mortgage rates. Then they can use online brokerage firms to buy or sell stocks. Increasingly, financial service providers offer ways for their customers to use their mobile devices for conducting banking transactions. For example, many banks created apps for checking account balances, or initiating transactions. Similarly, most large online brokerage services offer trading apps for various smartphone platforms. Large banks like Chase, Citibank, USAA, ING direct, or Charles Schwab offer mobile check deposit apps, allowing customers to deposit a check by simply taking a picture of the check with a smartphone's camera.

Securing Payments in the Digital World

One of the biggest impediments to B2C EC, C2C EC, and m-commerce is how to ensure that consumers can make secure transactions on the Web site. Although the transfer of money is a critical factor in online shopping, online banking, and online investing, security researchers and software companies are lamenting that people are often reluctant to change their habits when surfing the Web and carelessly reveal sensitive information to unknown or fraudulent sites. In fact, more than 11.6 million consumers in the U.S. (or 4.9 percent of U.S. adults) became victims of *identity theft* in 2011 (see Chapter 10, "Securing Information Systems"). Security concerns and other factors (such as impatience, lengthy checkout procedures, or comparison shopping) lead shoppers to frequently abandon their shopping carts and to not follow through with a purchase—reports show that more than half of the online shopping carts are abandoned. Traditionally, paying for goods and services was limited to using credit and debit cards, but now different companies offer payment services for buying and selling goods or services online. These different forms of online payment are discussed next.

CREDIT AND DEBIT CARDS. Credit and debit cards are still among the most accepted forms of payment in B2C EC. For customers, paying online using a credit card is easy; all the customer needs to do is to enter his or her name, billing address, credit card number, and expiration date to authorize a transaction. In many cases, the customer is also asked to provide the so-called **Card Verification Value (CVV2)**, a three-digit code located on the back of the card. This is one way to combat fraud in online purchases, as the code is used for authorization by the card-issuing bank. As the CVV2 is not included in the magnetic strip information, a person using a credit card for online transactions has to physically possess the actual credit card (see Table 4.6 for other guidelines on how to conduct safe transactions on the Internet).

For each transaction, an online customer has to transmit much personal information to a (sometimes unknown) merchant, and many Internet users (sometimes rightfully) fear being defrauded by an untrustworthy seller or falling victim to some other form of computer crime (see Chapter 10). For online merchants, the risk of people using fraudulent credit card data may be equally high. This is discussed next.

MANAGING RISK IN B2C TRANSACTIONS. As in offline transactions, online consumers at times dispute transactions for various reasons. In such cases, the merchant is financially responsible for the transactions, and credit card issuers typically charge back transactions that are disputed by cardholders. For the merchants, such chargebacks normally result in the loss of the transaction amount, loss of the merchandise, processing costs, and chargeback fees; in addition, the merchant's bank may charge higher fees or even close the merchant account if the chargeback rate is excessively high. Thus, minimizing chargebacks is of prime concern for online merchants. Some of the reasons for chargebacks, such as unclear store policies, product descriptions, shipping terms, or transaction currencies can be minimized through good Web store design; other reasons, such as stolen credit cards, require different safeguards (Visa, 2008).

Any credit card transactions must be authorized by the issuer of the credit card. However, this authorization merely assures that the credit card was not reported as lost or stolen, but does not assure that the person making the transaction is the actual cardholder. In e-commerce

TABLE 4.6   Ways to Protect Yourself When Shopping Online

Tip	Example
Use a secure browser	Make sure that your browser has the latest encryption capabilities; also, always look for the padlock icon in your browser's status bar before transmitting sensitive information
Check the site's privacy policy	Make sure that the company you're about to do business with does not share any information you would prefer not to be shared
Read and understand the refund and shipping policies	Make sure that you can return unwanted/defective products for a refund
Keep your personal information private	Make sure that you don't give out information, such as your Social Security Number, unless you know what the other entity is going to do with it
Give payment information only to businesses you know and trust	Make sure that you don't provide your payment information to fly-by-night operations
Keep records of your online transactions and check your e-mail	Make sure that you don't miss important information about your purchases
Review your monthly credit card and bank statements	Make sure to check for any erroneous or unauthorized transactions

Source: Based on Federal Trade Commission (2010).

transactions, there is no imprint of the physical card and no cardholder signature, so online merchants have to be especially careful when deciding whether or not to make a transaction. While online customers demand a quick checkout process, leaving the merchant with little time to authenticate whether the customer is indeed the cardholder, the transaction date is the date the merchandise is shipped; thus, online merchants typically have one or several days to verify the identity of the cardholder. To minimize risk, online merchants often use automated fraud screening services that provide the merchants with a risk score based on a number of variables such as match between shipping address, billing address, and phone number, the time of the order and the customer's time zone, transaction volume, and the customer's IP address and its geographic location. Based on the risk score, merchants can then decide whether or not to let the transaction go through. For such screening services to be most effective, the merchant should collect as much data as possible during the checkout process, which may lead some customers to abandon their shopping carts. In addition, online merchants can assess orders based on various fraud indicators (see Figure 4.20); Visa recommends looking for fraud indicators such as:

- **E-mail addresses.** Legitimate e-mail addresses often contain some parts of the customer's names; in contrast, fraudsters often set up e-mail addresses consisting of meaningless character combinations. Further, fraudsters typically use free e-mail addresses. However, rejecting transactions merely because of these reasons may reduce transaction volumes and alienate potential customers.
- **Shipping and billing addresses.** Fraudsters often have the merchandise shipped to foreign, high-risk countries. Thus, merchants may require billing and shipping addresses to be the same. In addition, as many fraudsters come from foreign countries, misspellings of common words or street names may serve as a potential fraud indicator.
- **Transaction patterns.** Fraudulent transactions often show very distinct patterns. For example, the orders may be larger than normal, may consist of multiple items of same type, or may consist largely of big ticket items. Similarly, fraudulent transactions often consist of multiple orders using the same credit card in a short period, or multiple orders using different cards shipped to the same address. Further, fraudsters often use overnight shipping, so as to reduce the merchant's time for verification checks, and to be able to quickly resell the merchandise.

Being alert for such fraud indicators can help an online merchant to reduce the risk of fraudulent transactions. Often, it is prudent to either call the customer for verification of the order (though this may be problematic for privacy reasons), or outright reject the transaction.

FIGURE 4.20

Various indicators can signal
potential e-commerce fraud.

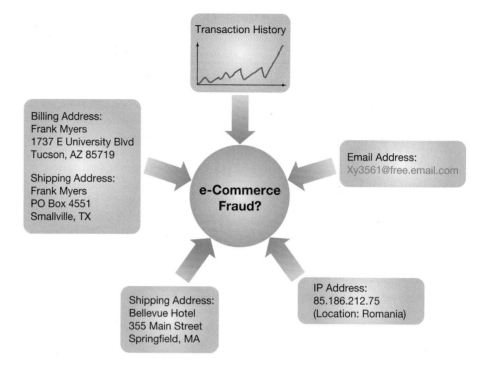

In contrast to merchants, ordinary people can only *make* payments by using credit cards—to receive payments, one has to open up a merchant account to accept credit card payments. For people who sell things online only once in a while (such as on the online auction site eBay), this is not a good option. To combat these problems, online shoppers (and sellers) are increasingly using third-party payment services. These are discussed next.

PAYMENT SERVICES. Concerns for security have led to the inception of independent payment services such as PayPal (owned by eBay) or Google Checkout. These services allow online customers to purchase goods online without having to give much private information to the actual sellers. Rather than paying a seller by providing credit card information, an online shopper can simply pay by using his or her account with the payment service. Thus, the customer has to provide the (sensitive) payment information only to the payment service, which keeps this information secure (along with other information such as e-mail address or purchase history) and does not share it with the online merchant. Google linked its payment service to the search results so that Internet users looking for a specific product can immediately see whether a merchant offers this payment option; this is intended to ease the online shopping experience for consumers, thus reducing the number of people abandoning their shopping carts. Another payment service, PayPal, goes a step further by allowing anyone with an e-mail address to send and receive money. In other words, using this service, you can send money to your friends or family members, or you can receive money for anything you're selling. This easy way to transfer money has been instrumental in the success of eBay, where anyone can sell or buy goods from other eBay users.

Legal Issues in EC

Although EC is now a viable and well-established business practice, there are issues that have changed the landscape for businesses and consumers and continue to do so. Two of the most important issues for EC businesses is taxation of online purchases and the protection of intellectual property, especially as it pertains to digital products, both of which are outlined next.

TAXATION. Although this issue is a relatively old one, it remains controversial within the American legal system. With EC global transactions increasing at an exponential rate, many governments are concerned that sales made via electronic sales channels have to be taxed in order to make up for the lost revenue in traditional sales methods. As people shop less in local

TABLE 4.7   Arguments For and Against Taxation of EC Transactions

For	Against
Increases tax income of local, state, and federal governments	Slows EC growth and opportunity
	Creates additional compliance burden for e-tailers
Removes unfair advantage for e-tailers over brick-and-mortar stores	e-Tailers located in one state would subsidize other states or jurisdictions
Increases accountability for e-tailers	Drives EC businesses to other countries

retail stores, cities, states, and even countries are now seeing a decrease in their sales tax income because of EC. Table 4.7 highlights issues associated with taxation of EC transactions.

The Internet Tax Freedom Act Starting in 1998, the **Internet Tax Freedom Act**, passed by the U.S. Senate, created a moratorium on EC taxation in the hopes of creating incentives for EC. The most recent version, called the Internet Tax Nondiscrimination Act, was signed into law in late 2004 by President George W. Bush. According to these tax laws (in addition to other provisions, such as a ban on Internet access or e-mail taxes), sales on the Internet were to be treated the same way as mail-order sales. As with mail-order sales, a company was required to collect sales tax only from customers residing in a state where the business had substantial presence. In other words, if an EC business had office facilities or a shipping warehouse in a certain state (say, California), it would have to collect sales tax only on sales to customers from that state (in that case, California). Many EC businesses thus strategically selected their home bases to offer "tax-free shopping" to most customers. For example, Jeff Bezos, the founder of Amazon.com, closely examined several states before choosing the state of Washington for Amazon.com's head office. This way, initially only the 6 million Washington State residents had to pay tax on Amazon.com purchases. As Amazon.com expanded, it continued to be very selective in where it located shipping facilities and warehouses. For example, Amazon.com selected Reno, Nevada, to serve the Californian market in order to allow its 36 million potential customers to avoid paying sales tax on purchases. Currently, Amazon.com collects sales tax only on purchases from customers located in Kansas, Kentucky, North Dakota, and Washington State. Walmart.com, on the other hand, charges taxes on all of their U.S. EC transactions, as they are physically present in every U.S. state.

However, the situation is not as easy as it seems. Even if the EC business does not *collect* sales tax on goods or services purchased outside your home state, you are still liable for *paying* "use tax" (usually equal to your state's sales tax) on those goods and services. For example, if an out-of-state e-tailer does not collect sales tax from its California customers, these customers are required to report that purchase and mail a check for the tax amount to the state. Other states have started adding a line for the use tax on their state income tax returns, and people have to report the taxes they owe on out-of-state purchases or else face stiff penalties for misrepresenting their tax liabilities.

On an international level, taxation is even more difficult. A customer ordering from a U.S. seller would not have to pay U.S. sales tax, but may be liable for paying tax in his or her home country on the shipment's arrival. For digital products (such as software or music downloads), the movement of the product is difficult to track, and the tax revenue is easily lost. Obviously, e-businesses actively doing business in other countries have to comply with the various different tax laws in different countries.

DIGITAL RIGHTS MANAGEMENT. With consumers increasingly using EC as viable alternatives for traditional commerce, the entertainment industry has no choice but to embrace the Internet as a distribution medium. At the same time, digital media are easily copied and shared by many people, as the entertainment industry has painfully learned after the introduction of the compact disc. Hence, the entertainment industry has turned to **digital rights management (DRM)**, which is a technological solution that allows publishers to control their digital media (music, movies, and so on) to discourage, limit, or prevent illegal copying and distribution. DRM restrictions include which devices will play the media, how many devices the media will play on, and even

FIGURE 4.21

Digital watermarks are used to trace illegal copies of digital media to the original purchaser.
Source: Courtesy of Microsoft, Inc.

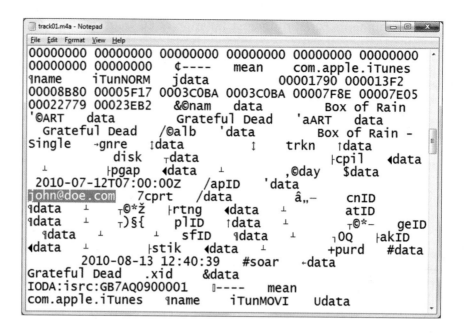

how many times the media can be played. The entertainment industry argues that DRM allows copyright holders to minimize sales losses by preventing unauthorized duplication.

Before 2009, songs or videos purchased from Apple's iTunes could only be played on a limited number of devices, but Apple and other online music retailers, such as Amazon.com, are now offering DRM-free downloads. Many users want the ability to freely move their media, typically music or videos, from one device to another with ease. To prevent illegal sharing of DRM-free content, it is often watermarked so that any illegal copy can be traced to the original purchaser (e.g., content purchased on iTunes contains the e-mail address used for the purchase, see Figure 4.21). A digital **watermark** is an electronic version of physical watermarks placed on paper currency to prevent counterfeiting. Likewise, to prevent counterfeiting of currency, most color laser printers print nearly invisible yellow dots uniquely identifying the originating printer on each page; privacy advocates argue that this could potentially be used to identify or persecute dissidents (EFF, 2010).

Critics refer to DRM as "digital restriction management," stating that publishers are arbitrary on how they enforce DRM. Further, critics argue that DRM enables publishers to infringe on existing consumer rights and to stifle innovation; for example, restrictions and limitations such as limiting the number of times a game can be activated, or limiting on which devices media can be accessed cause much inconvenience to users (such as when purchasing a new computer), and can thus breed piracy. Finally, critics argue that examples such as Amazon.com or Apple's iTunes show that businesses can be very successful with DRM-free content (CNet, 2012).

http://goo.gl/PWZoG

E-GOVERNMENT

e-Government is the use of information systems to provide citizens, organizations, and other governmental agencies with information about public services and to allow for interaction with the government. e-Government has become more widespread in the United States since the 1998 Government Paperwork Elimination Act. Similar to the EC business models, e-government involves three distinct relationships (see Figure 4.22).

GOVERNMENT-TO-CITIZENS The first form of e-government is known as **government-to-citizen (G2C)** EC. This category allows for interactions between federal, state, and local governments and their constituents. The Internal Revenue Service's Internet tax filing, or *e-filing,* is one of the more recognizable G2C tools, saving resources in terms of time and paper. Another e-government tool in wide use today is grants.gov. Of the over 2,200 funding opportunities

FIGURE 4.22

e-Government initiatives include interaction with citizens, corporations, and other governments.

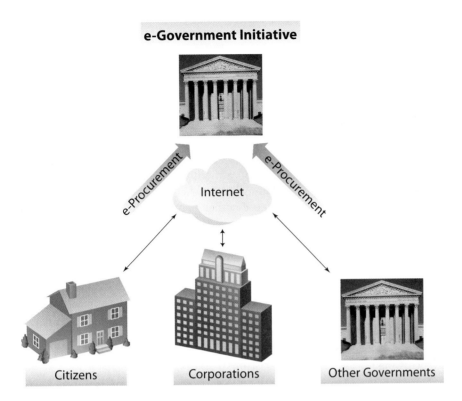

e-Government Initiative

for federal discretion, 54 percent were available for online submission (www.whitehouse .gov). Some states have begun working on e-voting initiatives, allowing citizens to vote online. However, concerns over security and protection from manipulation have thus far slowed the adoption of e-voting. Whereas e-voting initiatives are still hotly debated in many countries, several countries have started to introduce "smart" ID cards; for example, in 2003, Hong Kong introduced smart ID cards that allow its residents to use automated channels for immigration clearance for arrival and departure. Moreover, the smart ID card can be used as a library card in Hong Kong's public libraries or can be used as an electronic certificate to conduct secure transactions over the Internet.

GOVERNMENT-TO-BUSINESS. **Government-to-business (G2B)** is similar to G2C, but this form of EC involves businesses' relationships with all levels of government. This includes e-procurement, in which the government streamlines its supply chain by purchasing materials directly from suppliers using its proprietary Internet-enabled procurement system. Also included in G2B initiatives are forward auctions that allow businesses to buy seized and surplus government equipment. Similar to eBay.com, the U.S. government launched GovSales.gov to provide a marketplace for real-time auctions for surplus and seized goods. Other G2B services include online applications for export licenses, verification of employees' Social Security numbers, and online tax filing.

GOVERNMENT-TO-GOVERNMENT. Finally, **government-to-government (G2G)** EC is used for electronic interactions that take place between countries or between different levels of government within a country. Since 2002, the U.S. government has provided comprehensive e-government tools that allow foreign entities to find government-wide information related to business topics. This includes Regulations.gov and Export.gov; both allow information to be accessed regarding laws and regulations relevant to federal requirements. In addition, e-government has aligned its electronic capabilities with world issues. For example, the Consolidated Health Informatics Initiative has adopted electronic standards to allow worldwide health organizations to share information securely with government agencies. Other G2G transactions relate to the intergovernmental collaboration at the local, state, federal, and tribal levels.

INDUSTRY ANALYSIS

Retailing

You may make most of your large purchases online in order to benefit from greater convenience or lower prices, but most likely you will be setting your feet into a brick-and-mortar retail store at least once in a while, and you may have noticed some changes brought by technology. A few decades ago, large retail chains started introducing computerized point-of-sale inventory systems consisting of checkout computers and an inventory control system. A simple bar code scan captures a sale, and the item is automatically deducted from the store's inventory, allowing real-time tracking of purchases so that the retailer knows when to reorder merchandise or restock shelves. In addition to a speedier checkout process, such systems help to reduce stockouts, increasing customer satisfaction. In many grocery stores, this system has been taken a step further, allowing the customers to conduct the checkout process themselves, saving time and labor costs.

In the near future, many items will be equipped with radio frequency identification (RFID) tags, (see Chapter 8) eliminating the need to scan every individual item, so that the total price for a cart full of merchandise can be calculated within a second, saving even more time and adding convenience for the customer. Imagine the time you'll save when all you have to do is pass with your cart through an RFID reader and swipe your credit card. Similarly, a store's shelves will be equipped with RFID technology, tracking when an item is removed from the shelf or enabling the use of electronic shelf labels that can present much more than a product's price. With the capability to monitor stock levels and the best-before dates on all the items, RFID technology makes it possible to plan the in-house production of fresh vegetable and meat products extremely precisely, thereby optimizing the quality assurance processes. "Smart" dressing rooms, equipped with RFID technology, can help the customer find more information about a product, such as the availability of an item in additional sizes or different colors, or even suggest other matching items. Thus, the customer does not have to wait for a sales associate to go and look for items. A similar technology currently in use is handheld computers with bar code scanners. Linked to the store's inventory control system using wireless technologies, these handheld computers allow the sales associates to inquire about stock levels at the same store or even inquire about the availability at other stores of the same chain. In addition, a new "Pay by Fingerprint" system allows customers to complete a purchase by placing their finger onto a fingerprint scanner, without the need to sign a sales slip or enter a PIN; this makes the checkout process extremely convenient and secure. Another innovative way to pay for a purchase is via mobile phone. Using a technology called Near Field Communication (NFC; similar to Bluetooth), the customer's mobile phone communicates with the retailer's payment terminal, and the payment amount is automatically debited from the customer's bank account. NFC-based payment systems have already begun to be implemented; major smartphone manufacturers such as Samsung actively support this new technology by integrating it into new handsets, and third-party manufacturers offer solutions that allow using NFC by inserting a special micro-SD card into a cell phone.

As you can see, information systems have had a huge impact on retailing, and many more changes are yet to hit the shelves.

Questions:

1. How can technology help brick-and-mortar retailers compete against e-tailers?
2. Privacy advocates criticize the use of RFID, as it allows better tracking of purchasing habits. How can brick-and-mortar retailers alleviate these concerns?
3. As you have read, some of the "human element" in retailing is being replaced by technology. How can brick-and-mortar stores avoid becoming too "sterile" when using information systems to compete against e-tailers?

Based on:

Anonymous. (n.d.). *METRO Group Future Store Initiative*. Retrieved June 12, 2012, from http://www.future-store.org/fsi-internet/html/en/375/index.html.

Eler, A. (2011, December 2). Top 7 mobile commerce trends in 2011. *ReadWriteWeb*. Retrieved June 12, 2012, from http://www.readwriteweb.com/archives/top_7_mobile_commerce_trends_in_2011.php.

Voerste, A., & von Truchsess, A. (2008, May 28). METRO Group and Real open the store of the future. *METRO Group Future Store Initiative*. Retrieved June 12, 2012, from http://www.future-store.org/fsi-internet/html/en/16668/index.html.

Key Points Review

1. **Describe EC, how it has evolved, and the strategies that companies are adopting to compete in cyberspace.** EC is the online exchange of goods, services, and money between firms and between firms and their customers. Although EC was being used as far back as 1948 during the Berlin Airlift, the emergence of the Internet and World Wide Web has fueled a revolution in the manner in which products and services are marketed and sold. Their far-reaching effects have led to the creation of a global electronic marketplace that offers a virtually limitless array of new services, features, and functionality. Unlike the situation with traditional storefronts, time limitations are not a factor, allowing firms to sell and service products seven days a week, 24 hours a day, 365 days a year to anyone, anywhere. Companies are exploiting one or more of the capabilities of the Web to reach a wider customer base, offer a broader range of product offerings, and develop closer relationships with customers by striving to meet their unique needs. These wide-ranging capabilities include global information dissemination, integration, mass customization, interactive communication, transactional support, and disintermediation. The Web has moved traditional business operations into a hypercompetitive electronic marketplace. Companies must strategically position themselves to compete in the new EC environment. At one extreme, companies known as brick-and-mortars choose to operate solely in the traditional, physical markets. In contrast, click-only (or virtual) companies conduct business electronically in cyberspace. These firms have no physical locations, allowing them to focus purely on EC. Click-and-mortar (or bricks-and-clicks) companies straddle the two environments, operating in both physical and virtual arenas. Companies must also have a sound business model and define how they will generate revenue. Common EC revenue models include affiliate marketing, subscriptions, licensing, transactions fees, sales, and Web advertising revenue.

2. **Describe the stages of business-to-consumer electronic commerce, understand the keys to successful electronic commerce applications, and explain the different forms of Internet marketing.** B2C EC focuses on retail transactions between a company and end consumers. Business Web sites can be relatively simple or very sophisticated and can be classified as e-information, e-integration, or e-transaction sites. e-Information sites simply provide electronic brochures and other types of information for customers. e-Integration sites provide customers with the ability to gain personalized information by querying corporate databases and other information sources. e-Transaction sites allow customers to place orders and make payments. e-Tailers can benefit from being able to offer a wider variety of goods to more people at lower prices. On the other hand, drawbacks include delays introduced through shipping and customers' inability to directly evaluate the products. For successful B2C EC applications, companies should follow several rules. The basic rules of commerce are to offer valuable products and services at fair prices. These rules apply to EC as well as to any business endeavor. In addition to having a sound business model and plan for generating revenue, successful companies are found to follow a basic set of principles, or rules, related to Web-based EC. These rules include having a Web site that offers something unique, is aesthetically pleasing, is easy to use, and is fast, and that motivates people to visit, to stay, and to return. A company should also advertise its presence on the Web (e.g., using search engine marketing) and should try to learn from its Web site (using Web analytics). As with offline businesses, EC businesses have to market their product and services. Popular ways to advertise products or services on the Web are search marketing, display ads, e-mail marketing, social media, and mobile marketing. Advertisers pay for these types of Internet marketing on the basis of either the number of impressions or pay-per-click.

3. **Describe mobile commerce, consumer-to-consumer electronic commerce, and consumer-to-business electronic commerce.** Mobile EC, or m-commerce, enables people to take full advantage of the Internet on portable, wireless devices, such as smartphones or tablets. M-commerce is rapidly expanding with the continuing expansion of worldwide Internet adoption as well as the continued evolution of faster cellular networks, more powerful handheld devices, and more sophisticated applications. Location-based services, based on GPS technology, are a key driver enabling even more innovative m-commerce applications. As mobile consumers not only use their devices to obtain timely information on the go, but also increasingly purchase products or content in mobile settings, businesses have to consider the specific settings and devices of their target customers. Further, the Internet has fueled the development of a variety of ways people can trade goods, socialize, or voice their thoughts and opinions. Specifically, e-auctions allow private people to sell goods to large markets. Typical forms of e-auctions are forward auctions and reverse auctions. However, while e-auctions give people the availability to sell things to large markets, the potential of fraud is still considered a big problem. One emerging topic in EC is C2B EC, where individuals offer products or services to businesses.

4. Describe how to conduct financial transactions and navigate legal issues of electronic commerce. The Internet has enabled obtaining real-time financial information as well as making transactions online. Yet, securing payments in the digital world is still of concern, both for customers and for merchants, who have to minimize their risk arising from potentially fraudulent credit card transactions; as a result, many (especially smaller) retailers use online payment services. Finally, taxation of EC transactions and protecting intellectual property continue to be major issues and impediments to EC.

5. Explain different forms of e-government. e-Government is a government's use of IS to provide a variety of services to citizens, businesses, and other governmental agencies. Depending on the services, e-government initiatives can be targeted at citizens (government-to-citizens), businesses (government-to-business), or other governmental agencies (either within a country or between countries; government-to-government).

Key Terms

affiliate marketing   177
brick-and-mortar business strategy   174
bricks-and-clicks business strategy   175
business-to-business (B2B)   171
business-to-consumer (B2C)   171
Card Verification Value (CVV2)   196
click fraud   189
click-and-mortar business strategy   174
click-only business strategy   174
click-through rate   189
competitive click fraud   189
consumer-to-business (C2B)   171
consumer-to-consumer (C2C)   171
conversion rate   189
digital rights management (DRM)   199
disintermediation   174
e-auction   193
e-government   200
e-information   178

e-integration   178
electronic bill pay   195
electronic commerce (EC)   170
e-tailing   179
e-transaction   178
forward auction   193
functional convenience   183
global information dissemination   172
government-to-business (G2B)   201
government-to-citizen (G2C)   201
government-to-government (G2G)   201
group buying   179
integration   172
interactive communication   174
Internet Tax Freedom Act   199
location-based services   190
Long Tail   180
mass customization   173
menu-driven pricing   179

m-commerce (mobile commerce)   171
network click fraud   189
online banking   195
online investing   196
paid inclusion   186
pay-per-click   189
QR code   182
reintermediation   174
representational delight   183
reverse auction   193
reverse pricing   179
search advertising   186
search engine optimization (SEO)   186
sponsored search   186
structural firmness   183
transaction support   174
virtual company   174
watermark   200
Web analytics   183

Review Questions

1. What is EC, and how has it evolved?
2. List the various categories (forms) of e-commerce that are being used by organizations worldwide.
3. Compare and contrast two EC business strategies.
4. Describe the differences between affiliate marketing and Web advertising.
5. List the components of a business model.
6. What is a portal? How are organizations using this concept in their businesses?
7. Describe the differences between SEO, search marketing, and sponsored search.
8. Describe m-commerce and explain how it is different from regular EC.
9. Describe the various revenue streams that most of the e-commerce companies are following.
10. Explain the different forms of online auctions.
11. How can online retailers minimize risk associated with credit card transactions?
12. What is mass customization? Give one example.
13. Define the concepts of disintermediation and reintermediations, and explain how organizations are using them to their benefit.

Self-Study Questions

1. EC is the online exchange of _____ among firms, between firms and their customers, and between customers, supported by communication technologies and, in particular, the Internet.
   A. goods   B. services
   C. money   D. all of the above

2. _____ are those companies that operate in the traditional, physical markets and do not conduct business electronically in cyberspace.
   A. Brick-and-mortars
   B. Click-onlys
   C. both A and B
   D. Dot-coms

3. The revenue model involving referring customers to another business is called _____ .
   A. referral marketing
   B. internet marketing
   C. affiliate marketing
   D. ad marketing
4. According to the text, the three stages of B2C Web sites include all of the following except _____ .
   A. e-tailing
   B. e-integration
   C. e-transaction
   D. e-information
5. The revolutionary aspect of the Priceline.com Web site lies in its _____ model called Name Your Own Price. Customers specify the product they are looking for and how much they are willing to pay for it.
   A. immediate pricing
   B. menu-driven pricing
   C. forward pricing
   D. reverse pricing
6. _____ is a type of e-auction fraud where bidders are lured to leave a legitimate auction in order to buy the same item at a lower price.
   A. Bid luring
   B. Product luring
   C. Customer luring
   D. Low-price luring

7. A Web site should _____ .
   A. be easy to use and fast
   B. offer something unique and be aesthetically pleasing
   C. motivate people to visit, to stay, and to return
   D. all of the above
8. Trying to "outsmart" a search engine to improve a page's ranking is known as _____.
   A. rank enhancement
   B. SEO
   C. search engine hacking
   D. Google fooling
9. C2C EC can be categorized according to _____ .
   A. the number of goods sold
   B. the number of buyers and sellers
   C. the payment methods accepted
   D. all of the above
10. According to the Internet Tax Freedom Act, e-tailers

    _____ .

    A. have to collect sales tax from all customers, regardless of their location
    B. have to collect sales tax based on the place of the customer's residence
    C. have to collect sales tax based on the prevalent tax rate at the e-tailer's headquarters
    D. have to collect sales tax only from customers residing in a state where the business has substantial presence

Answers are on page 207.

Problems and Exercises

1. Match the following terms with the appropriate definitions:
   i. Search marketing
   ii. Reintermediation
   iii. Web analytics
   iv. Paid inclusion
   v. e-Transaction
   vi. Long Tails
   vii. Competitive click fraud
   viii. Search engine optimization
   ix. e-Government
   x. e-Integration

   a. The practice of trying to increase a company's visibility in search engine results
   b. The design of business models that reintroduce middlemen in order to reduce the chaos brought on by disintermediation
   c. The large parts of consumer demand that are outside the relatively small number of mainstream tastes
   d. A stage that takes the e-integration stage one step further by adding the ability for customers to enter orders and make payments online
   e. A stage in which Web pages are created on the fly to produce tailored information that addresses the particular needs of a consumer
   f. The use of information systems to provide citizens and organizations with handy information about public services

   g. Methods used to improve a site's ranking
   h. The analysis of Web surfers' behavior in order to improve a site's performance
   i. The practice of paying a fee to be included in a search engine's listing
   j. A competitor's attempt to inflate an organization's online advertising costs by repeatedly clicking on an advertiser's link
2. Visit Alaska Airlines' Web site (www.alaskaair.com) for real-time pricing and test the custom messenger bag builder at www.timbuk2.com. How have Internet technologies improved over the years?
3. Search the Web for a company that is purely web-based. Next, find the Web site of a company that is a hybrid (i.e., they have a traditional brick-and-mortar business plus a presence on the Web). What are the pros and cons of dealing with each type of company?
4. Have you purchased anything over the Internet? If so, how was it delivered? As compared to traditional shopping, how sustainable do you think EC is from an environmental perspective?
5. Do you receive advertisements through e-mail? Are they directed toward any specific audience or product category? Which ads seem to be most prevalent? Do you pay much attention or just delete them? How much work is it to get off an advertising list? Why would or wouldn't you try to get off the list?

6. What is it about a company's Web site that draws you to it, keeps you there on the site longer, and keeps you coming back for more? If you could summarize these answers into a set of criteria for Web sites, what would those criteria be?

7. Visit the following services for comparison shopping: Best-BookBuys (www.bestwebbuys.com/books), Bizrate (www.bizrate.com), and mySimon (www.mysimon.com). These companies focus on aggregating content for consumers. What are the advantages of these Web sites? What does the existence of such sites mean for the online merchants?

8. Compare three different search engines. What tips do they provide to improve a page's rankings? How much does it cost to advertise a page on their results pages? If you were a company, could you think of any situation where you would pay almost any amount to have the first listing on the first results page?

9. Your organization has recently developed an e-commerce model. Management wants you to develop the advertising strategy using both traditional and online media. Suggest a complete plan.

10. Study the security system followed by an online retailer like Amazon.com. Prepare a complete report and suggest how it can be improved.

11. Have you ever used a mobile, wireless device such as a smartphone for online shopping? If so, what do you like or dislike about it? In what ways could your shopping experience be made better? If you have not used a mobile device for shopping, what prevented you from doing so? What would have to happen before you would begin using a mobile device for shopping?

12. When you shop online, is sales tax a criterion for you? Do you try to purchase goods where you do not have to pay sales tax? If you would have to pay sales tax for everything you buy online, would that change your online shopping behavior?

13. Identify two service providers that organize reverse auctions. Study these organizations to understand how a reverse auction is conducted.

Application Exercises

Note: The existing data files referenced in these exercises are available on the book's Web site: www.pearsonhighered.com/valacich

 Spreadsheet Application: Analyzing Server Traffic

Campus Travel has recently found that its Internet connections between offices are becoming slow, especially during certain periods of the day. Since all the online traffic is maintained by another company, an increase in capacity requires a formal approval from the general manager. The IS manager has proposed to increase the capacity of the company's network; in a few days, he has to present the business case for this proposal at the weekly meeting of the department heads. You are asked to prepare graphs for the presentation to support the IS manager's business case. In the file ServerLogs.csv, you will find information about the network traffic for a one-week period. Prepare the following graphs:

1. Total bandwidth used for each day (line graph)
2. Bandwidth used per day, by time period (line graph)
3. Average bandwidth used in each two-hour period (line graph)

Format the graphs in a professional manner and print out each graph on a separate page (Hint: If you are using Microsoft Excel's Chart Wizard, select "Place chart: As New Sheet").

 Database Application: Tracking Network Hardware

As Campus Travel is new to EC, the management suggests following a stepwise approach for using the Internet to conduct business. Before using the Internet for conducting transactions, the managers recommend setting up a site that provides information to customers. Part of this informational site is an agency locator that shows the services each agency has. You have been asked to create a new database. This includes creating relationships between entities. To create this new database, do the following:

1. Create a database called "agency."
2. Create a table called "agencies" and include fields for agency ID, street address, city, state, ZIP code, phone number, number of service agents, and working hours.
3. Create a table called "services" that includes service ID, name (i.e., type of service), and description.
4. Create a third table called "agencyservices" that includes the agency ID field from the agencies table and the service ID field from the services table.
5. Once these tables are created, go to the relationship view and connect the agencies (one side) and agencyservices (many side) tables and the services (one side) and agencyservices (many side) tables using two one-to-many relationships (i.e., each agency can offer many services; each service can be offered by many agencies).

Team Work Exercise

 Net Stats:
Who Is Subsidizing Web Content?

When you subscribe to cable television, you typically have to decide between different packages, each offering various channels focusing on sports, movies, cartoons, and so on. In addition, you have the option of subscribing to other channels that interest you. Hence, the charges on your monthly cable bill are for your subscribed services. In contrast, the charges on your Internet bill are for connecting to the Internet rather than for the content on the Web. Hence, content providers on the Internet are dependent on other ways to generate revenue. Companies such as CNN, the Washington Post, Google, or Yahoo!, which provide content for free, subsidize their expenses by advertising revenue. One of the most common forms of advertising on the Web is display ads, which have moved from simple static images to rich, interactive advertisements. Although the CPM may be only between US$5 and US$20, display ads are big business.

Who are the biggest advertisers on the Web? Research firm comScore regularly provides rankings of the Web's top advertisers, based on the number of impressions. The top five advertisers in the year 2011 were the following:

1. AT&T: 105.8 billion impressions
2. Experian Interactive: 67.6 billion impressions
3. Verizon: 49.5 billion impressions
4. Scottrade Stock Brokerage: 44 billion impressions
5. Google: 40.5 billion impressions

Questions and Exercises

1. Search the Web for the most up-to-date statistics.
2. As a team, interpret these numbers. What is striking/important about these statistics?
3. How have the numbers changed? Which industries seem to be most interested in online advertising? Why?
4. Using your spreadsheet software of choice, create a graph/figure most effectively visualizing the statistics/changes you consider most important.

Based on:

ComScore (2012, February). U.S. digital future in focus 2012. *comScore*. Retrieved June 11, 2012, from http://www.comscore.com/Press_Events/Presentations_Whitepapers/2012/2012_US_Digital_Future_in_Focus.

Paparo, A. (2010, April 12). New frontiers in display advertising planning and measurement. *Google Blog*. Retrieved June 11, 2012, from http://googleblog.blogspot.com/2010/04/new-frontiers-in-display-advertising.html.

Wojcicki, S. (2010, March 15). The future of display advertising. *Google Blog*. Retrieved June 11, 2012, from http://googleblog.blogspot.com/2010/03/future-of-display-advertising.html.

Answers to the Self-Study Questions

1. D, p. 170	2. A, p. 174	3. C, p. 177	4. A, p. 178	5. D, p. 179
6. A, p. 194	7. D, p. 182	8. B, p. 186	9. B, p. 193	10. D, p. 199

CASE 1 — Global Picture Sharing: Flickr

Has there been a wedding, birth, confirmation, graduation, one-hundredth birthday celebration, or other commemorative event in your family lately? Would you like to see the photos your sister, Uncle Walt, and Grandma Mary took at the event? For quickly sharing snapshots, people often use social networking sites such as Facebook, Instagram, or Google+. Yet, some of these sites compress the images, leading to a loss of quality. Thus, Flickr.com remains the photo sharing site of choice for many professional or semiprofessional photographers.

Flickr.com was developed by Ludicorp, a Vancouver, Canada–based company founded in 2002 and launched online in 2004. Yahoo! purchased Flickr in 2005. In just over a year after Flickr's launch, the site had over 350,000 members, who had collectively uploaded 31 million images.

Flickr didn't invent online photo sharing, but the tools members can use to navigate the photos on the site were unique. "Tags" let photo owners and viewers label photos to prescribe a category that makes them easier to find. For example, popular tags include summer, winter, cute, Europe, dog, cat, and so on. Flickr has taken the tag concept further with clustering, a better way to explore photos through tags. Key in "summer beach vacations," for instance, and you can view a page of clustered photos with just those tags. Clustering has resulted in such far-out photo categories as confusing street signs, dogs' noses, Halloween costumes, margaritas, and mannequins.

Flickr sees photo sharing and the use of tags as a social process users call "folksonomy." That is, by adding tags to pictures, a classification, or taxonomy, is collaboratively created. For a person who is browsing through a set of photos, these notes on the photos tell little stories, as if that person were sitting by the photographer, who is explaining the photo.

Flickr photo viewers can also comment on pictures, add them to their favorites, and so on. Based on these factors, as well as the number of tags, the number of times a picture is viewed, and various other factors, Flickr calculates an "interestingness" score for each picture. Each calendar day, a few photos ranked as highly "interesting" are posted to a common page for easier viewer exploration.

Flickr also allows for basic photo manipulation, such as rotation, ordering prints, sharing with others, adding to a blog or even a map, and so on. Photos can be open for everyone everywhere to view, or viewing can be restricted to specified people or groups of people. In late 2009, Flickr also added the ability to tag people in photos uploaded to the site. The feature allows users to draw a small box around the person they want to tag, allowing the viewer to add names or notes about people in a picture.

Users can get a free basic account that allows them to upload two videos and 300MB worth of photos each calendar month. For US$25 a year, users can get a pro account that allows them an unlimited number of photo and video uploads per month, ad-free browsing, and a number of other advantages.

Since Flickr's basic photo sharing service is free, revenue for the company is based on Yahoo!-placed ads on Flickr Web pages. Photographers who post images on the Flickr site, however, are free to sell their photos. The legal aspects of copyright are handled by a license called the "creative commons." This license has many different levels of copyright protection but is primarily for not-for-profit use of a user's photographs. Flickr offers a simple interface that allows photographers to choose a license for protecting copyright.

For programming enthusiasts, Flickr has released all application program interfaces for public use. For example, programmers have used the interfaces to develop uploading applications for the Mac, Windows, smartphones, and other devices.

Flickr continues to expand their services to users and grow in popularity. Pro members of the site can now upload high-definition video, viewable in a 16:9 HD player. Although the site is focused on still photos, users who have that great little video clip they caught with their camera can now upload and share. Another popular addition to the site came in 2010 when Facebook Connect was added. The connection to the popular social media site allows users to update their Facebook status from within the photo page.

Flickr has also integrated Yahoo! maps. With this feature, users can see alternative photos that Flickr users have geotagged and uploaded. This is a significant enhancement to the service, owing to the huge amount of geotagged photos in the Flickr library, which, as of 2012, stands at over 188 million photos. Some estimates put the number of geotagged photos uploaded to Flickr at over 2 million *a month*. This growing amount of data will give users a wealth of photographic data to utilize when planning a trip using online mapping services (especially when going to regions where no "Street Views" are provided by online mapping services such as Google or Bing). For example, when planning a vacation, users can look for clusters of user-generated pictures to identify interesting sites that may be worth visiting.

Flickr's popularity has also reached the highest level of the U.S. government. In a historical move, the White House opened an official Flickr photo stream in April 2009. In its inaugural upload, the White House posted 293 photos of life surrounding President Obama and his first 100 days in office. Since the photo stream's inception, the Flickr page has chronicled most major events that surround the White House. For presidential history buffs and casual Web surfers alike, the photo stream has given an unprecedented look into the daily life of the president through Flickr's convenient and easy interface.

In the days before Facebook and other social networks, Flickr, being a social network centered around photo sharing, was far ahead of its time. Critics say, however, that the takeover by Yahoo! stifled the site's innovativeness, to the point that even a dedicated Flickr iPhone app was severely delayed and very poorly critiqued by early users.

Questions:

1. Why do you think Flickr has been so popular throughout the world?
2. What lessons could a Web site for a local business learn from Flickr?
3. Where do you see the future of Flickr in the face of many competing photo sharing applications?

Based on:

Anonymous. (2005, August 1). The new new things. *Flickr Blog.* Retrieved June 13, 2012, from http://blog.flickr.net/en/2005/08/01/the-new-new-things.

Axline, K. (2009, April 29). Presidential first: White House floods Flickr. *Wired.* Retrieved June 13, 2012, from http://www.wired.com/rawfile/2009/04/presidential-first-white-house-floods-flickr.

Gilbertson, S. (2009, March 3). Flickr video goes HD and opens to everyone. *Wired.* Retrieved June 13, 2012, from http://www.wired.com/epicenter/2009/03/flickr-video-go.

Honan, M. (2012, May 15). How Yahoo killed Flickr and lost the Internet. *Gizmodo.com.* Retrieved June 13, 2012, from http://gizmodo.com/5910223/how-yahoo-killed-flickr-and-lost-the-internet.

Terdiman, D. (2005, November 16). Tagging gives web a human meaning. *News.com.* Retrieved June 13, 2012, from http://news.com.com/Tagging+gives+Web+a+human+meaning/2009-1025_3-5944502.html.

Trenholm, R. (2009, October 22). Flickr adds face tagging. *CNET.co.uk.* Retrieved June 13, 2012, from, http://crave.cnet.co.uk/software/0,39029471,49304018,00.htm.

CASE 2 YouTube

It's the Web site everyone visits at least once, and most surfers come back again and again. It's the ubiquitous YouTube. Where else can you watch a video of a cat swimming contentedly in a bathtub, a 12-year-old rendering a professional performance of the "The Star Spangled Banner" at a small-town basketball game, or a public political debate where candidates answer questions visitors to the site have submitted?

YouTube, a video sharing Web site, went online in 2005. Two former PayPal employees, Steve Chen and Chad Hurley, created the site, and it was practically an overnight success. The San Bruno, California–based service displays a wide variety of user-generated video content, including movie and TV clips, music videos, video blogs, and short original videos. In July 2006, YouTube reported that visitors to the site were viewing more than 100 million video clips a day—a fact that compelled Google Inc. to buy the site that year for US$1.76 billion in stock. As of 2012, YouTube continues to be a successful video site and a top destination for Web surfers who watch over 4 billion videos each day. According to the site, over 3 billion hours of videos are watched each month, and 60 hours of video are uploaded every minute.

YouTube is free and registration is not necessary for visitors to view videos. To upload videos, however, registration is required. Videos with pornographic content and those showing nudity or that defame or harass are prohibited, as is advertising and anything encouraging criminal conduct. All of that video requires YouTube to have access to a lot of bandwidth. In 2012, the monthly bandwidth expenses for the service were estimated at US$30 million. In 2011, the viewing of videos on YouTube consumed about 22 percent of global mobile bandwidth. In fact, in 2007 the British publication *The Telegraph* expressed fears that the Internet could "grind to a halt within two years" without massive upgrades to the Internet infrastructure. Fortunately for YouTube fans and Internet users in general, that didn't happen. Bandwidth issues aside, YouTube continues to try to draw in more viewers. To that end, the site's user interface got a major overhaul in the spring of 2010. The main page was streamlined and redesigned to be more social-media friendly. In addition, the update made it easier to locate and watch a continuous stream of related video content.

As YouTube has gained in popularity, police forces around the country have used the service to help catch criminals. In April 2010, for example, homicide investigators in Vancouver, British Columbia, posted a video about a victim in an unsolved but high-profile murder case. Although the case was being actively investigated, the investigative team had exhausted their list of leads. The posted video included photos of the woman who had been killed and a recap of what the investigators had pieced together up to that point. Their hope was that by using social media and getting the story in front of viewers, it might help jog a memory of someone who might have seen something pertinent to the case. Some police departments, however, such as St. George County in Virginia, said they would not use YouTube for catching criminals because posting police videos next to those with "crazy" content would be "bad publicity" for the police.

Regardless of the propensity for catching criminals or lack thereof, YouTube has had its share of legal issues as well. After several lawsuits were filed alleging copyright violations over copyrighted material posted on YouTube, the company agreed to remove copyrighted material on request. In addition, YouTube installed software intended to automatically detect and remove copyrighted clips. In order to function correctly, however, the software needed to compare clips of copyrighted material to YouTube content, which meant that music, movie, and television companies would have to send decades of clips of copyrighted material to YouTube so that comparisons could be made.

In March 2010, the entertainment corporation Viacom entered into a US$1 billion lawsuit against YouTube alleging that the video site knowingly made a financial gain from 62,637 Viacom video clips that were viewed over 507 million times. YouTube has countered by alleging that Viacom was covertly uploading clips of their content in an attempt to sabotage YouTube's efforts to remove copyrighted material. Later that year, a U.S. district court ruled in favor of YouTube, a decision that Viacom was unlikely to accept; in April 2012, a judge at a U.S. federal appeals court sent the case back to a district court, asking the lower court to determine to what extent YouTube was aware of the copyright infringements. Although it remains to be seen how the lawsuit will be finally resolved, it is a sticky situation for the video site. Whatever YouTube's future, it's not likely that Internet users will soon lose interest in video sharing.

Questions:

1. Do you use YouTube? If so, what is your favorite type of content? If not, why not? What other video sharing sites do you use? Why?
2. How can businesses use YouTube to promote a good brand image? Have you seen any "good" campaigns on YouTube? If so, what made them appealing?
3. What potential dangers for a business' reputation can arise from user-generated content posted on sites such as YouTube? How can a business react to such dangers?

Based on:

Anonymous. (2007, October 17). YouTube installs copyright-protection filters. *Fox News*. Retrieved June 13, 2012, from http://www.foxnews.com/story/0,2933,302376,00.html.

Bolan, K. (2010, April 1). Police enlist YouTube in hunt for a killer. *Vancouver Sun*. Retrieved June 13, 2012, from http://www.canada.com/vancouversun/news/westcoastnews/story.html?id=acf3b299-6086-4e24-b68f-ede6543e3ed1.

Carroll, J. (2008, January 16). The shrinking planet and YouTube. *ZDNet.com*. Retrieved June 13, 2012, from http://blogs.zdnet.com/carroll/?p=1789.

Chmielewski, D.C. (2012, April 6). Judge revives Viacom copyright suit against YouTube. *Los Angeles Times*. Retrieved June 13, 2012, from http://articles.latimes.com/2012/apr/06/business/la-fi-ct-viacom-youtube-20120406.

Lane, T. (2010, April 2). YouTube's redesign focuses on social features & ease-of-use. *Sparxoo*. Retrieved June 13, 2012, from http://sparxoo.com/2010/04/02/youtubes-redesign-focuses-on-social-features-ease-of-use.

Mukherjee, M. (2012, January 20). How does YouTube make money? *Buzzle.com*. Retrieved June 13, 2012, from http://www.buzzle.com/articles/how-does-youtube-make-money.html.

Reisinger, D. (2010, February 15). In just five years, YouTube became the go-to video site. *Los Angeles Times*. Retrieved June 13, 2012, from http://latimesblogs.latimes.com/technology/2010/02/youtube-fifth-birthday.html.

Srinivasan, A. (2010, February 15). Average number of views on YouTube videos. *Tech Crunchies*. Retrieved June 10, 2012, from http://techcrunchies.com/youtube-average-views.

Yin, S. (2011, July 26). YouTube hogs 22 percent of world's mobile bandwidth. *PCMag.com*. Retrieved June 13, 2012, from http://www.pcmag.com/article2/0,2817,2389194,00.asp.

5

Enhancing Organizational Communication and Collaboration Using Social Media

Preview

This chapter focuses on social media, and how social media can enhance organizational communication and collaboration. Most likely, you are actively using various social media applications such as Facebook or Wikipedia, and you may ask, "Why do we need to have a chapter on this?" Social media introduce unprecedented ways to connect to friends, share knowledge with your colleagues, or collaborate with a team of engineers 5,000 miles away, and many of today's companies cannot afford to miss this trend. Most young people entering the workforce have grown accustomed to using Facebook or Twitter for their communication needs (and some even regard e-mail as an outmoded communication medium); if a company doesn't allow the use of these tools, some employees may leave and work for another company. Even more, you may have noticed your parents' generation joining sites such as Facebook, and those tools are more and more taken for granted by many.

With social media providing a new set of capabilities for individuals and businesses, an understanding of how they can be applied can be very helpful. Being able to understand and apply these emerging capabilities and strategies that are associated with social media is a highly valued skill.

Managing in the Digital World:
Facebook.com

When managing in the digital world, the past was certainly not as complex as the present. Governments did not have to deal with radical terrorists, Coca-Cola used only pin-up girls to boost their sales, and girls did not have to put up with their boyfriends mingling with girls from around the world on social networks. The same is true for companies. Interaction with customers was limited to one-way communication using TV ads, billboards, posters, or radio broadcasts. In return, people showed affinity to a particular brand by displaying bumper stickers, wearing t-shirts, or refusing to sample alternative brands. Nothing more than physical expression was ever apparent to companies. Thus, marketers played their own game in promoting products and consumers spread the good word around their circle of friends whenever they found something they loved. By the end of the day, no real interaction could be recorded between customers and brands; the two parties led separate lives and acted their own respective parts. The only connection between them was the product itself.

Things have changed since then. Take Facebook for example (see Figure 5.1). Do you recall that time you found your long-lost Uncle residing in Canada using Facebook's recommendations of people you may know? What about Facebook's Timeline feature which offers to tell the story of your life since you started using the social networking platform? You got married last year and, beside the fact you sent your invitations out through a Facebook event,

you can still laugh at all the candid photos friends and family have posted on their pages. Remember that nice Spanish gentleman who took your picture during your stay in Cambodia? He is now on your friends list. Facebook has definitely helped you become more connected with people all over the world.

In early 2012, eight years after its launch and six years after it was opened to the public, Facebook was still reporting impressive statistics. The least of which were more than 1 billion active users (of which 80 percent are from outside the U.S. and Canada), 500 million users accessing accounts through their mobile devices, and more than 42 million pages "liked" by ten or more Facebook users. Almost 400 million users access Facebook at least six days of the week. On average, Facebook users upload over 300 million photos per day and generate over 3 billion "likes" and comments.

Statistics have shown shifting demographics in social media as of late. A 2011 study found that 65 percent of adult Internet users spend time on social networking sites. That is a 4 percent increase from 2010 and a huge leap considering that the number stood at 29 percent in 2008 and a lowly 5 percent in 2005. This reflects the fact that over 50 percent of the adult population is now in touch with Facebook and other social media. So, beware. The next time you make a post on Facebook, think twice before you push the submit button, your mom might be hiding in your endless friends list.

Many companies have also joined Facebook, creating pages to extend their reach and promote new products. In addition, celebrities, musicians, public figures, movies, and almost any other product or service you can think of now appears to have a Facebook page. Facebook has become another get-together space for people who have acquaintances, friends, or beliefs in common. Businesses use it to build and track customer loyalty, and connections are made even tighter with the help of "Like" buttons that seem to be on almost every site on the Web. Facebook has changed the scope of social interactions, as consumer preferences, collective tastes, and future demands are now more easily analyzed and predicted through the number of "likes" or the comments left by consumers responding to photos regarding the latest smartphone or that new movie premiering next Thursday. Through this social media platform, companies can interact with customers like never before.

FIGURE 5.1

Facebook is the most popular social network, with over 1 billion active users.
Source: Thomas Pajot/Fotolia

If you think that Facebook pages are trivial and insignificant, you might want to go back and read this piece again. In March 2010, German drug maker Merck KGaA threatened Facebook with legal action after discovering that its page had been taken over by its U.S. rival Merck & Co. Facebook later apologized for the confusion and decided to suspend the page www.facebook.com/merck as unavailable until both Mercks had agreed which company may use it. Nonetheless, the companies could request other URLs and were allowed to remain on Facebook. Merck KGaA argued that the loss of the page deprived it of a crucial marketing device and the gravity of the fight demonstrated just how important Facebook has become for companies looking to market and promote their products.

Yet, while Facebook's tremendous success appears to continue, Facebook received a setback when it decided to go public in May 2012. Initially priced at US$38 per share (valuing the company at US$104 billion), the share price plunged on the opening day, remaining well below US$35 during summer 2012, and falling below US$20 after the first lock-up period ended and early investors were eligible to sell their shares. While this development has disappointed many investors, Facebook remains the social networking behemoth, and has raised enough funds to launch various new features and services, and to buy up almost any potential competitor in the social networking space.

After reading this chapter, you will be able to answer the following:

1. How can a social networking site such as Facebook become a part of everyday life?

2. Besides pure social interaction, what are some other ways Facebook can be used?

3. What are the pros and cons of using a social networking site in a business setting?

Based on:

Anonymous. (2012). Key Facts. Retrieved July 6, 2012, from http://newsroom.fb.com/content/default.aspx?NewsAreaId=22.

Anonymous. (2011, November 25). Drugmaker Merck challenges Facebook after 'losing' page. *BBC News*. Retrieved July 7, 2012, from http://www.bbc.com/news/technology-15888843.

Madden, K., and Zickuhr, K. (2011, August 26). 65% of online adults use social networking sites. *Pew Internet*. Retrieved July 7, 2012, from http://pewinternet.org/Reports/2011/Social-Networking-Sites.aspx.

Sengupta, S. (2012, August 16). Facebook shares hit new low as lockup period ends. *The New York Times*. Retrieved August 17, 2012, from http://www.nytimes.com/2012/08/17/technology/facebook-shares-hit-new-low-as-a-lockup-period-ends.html.

Swart, J. and Krantz, M. (2012, June 18). A month later, fallout from Facebook IPO persists. *USA Today*. Retrieved July 6, 2012, from http://www.usatoday.com/tech/news/story/2012-06-16/facebook-ipo-chill/55654700/1.

http://goo.gl/zMN2b

THE NEED FOR COMMUNICATION AND COLLABORATION

Just as you communicate with your friends when planning a vacation or organizing a party, or collaborate with your teammates on a class project, organizations rely on effective communication and **collaboration** (i.e., two or more people working together to achieve a common goal), both within and outside organizational boundaries. Most organizational business processes require communication and collaboration between employees of different departments, as well as with outside business partners (such as suppliers), customers, and other external stakeholders. Many organizations operate on a national or global scale, and rely on effective and efficient communication between various locations or subsidiaries, and even small, local companies need to communicate with suppliers or promote their products or services to customers. Further, globalization has enabled companies to source raw materials, parts, or components on a global scale, or manufacture products wherever they can find the lowest cost, best quality, or most qualified workforce. In all of these scenarios, effective and efficient communication is essential to convey specifications, coordinate production or delivery schedules, and so on. Similarly, salespeople rely on efficient communication with the customers and with other departments within the organization. With increased global reach of organizations, the needs for *internal* communication have also changed tremendously.

Virtual Teams

To be competitive, organizations constantly need to bring together the right combinations of people who have the appropriate set of knowledge, skills, information, and authority to solve problems quickly and easily. Traditionally, organizations have used task forces, which are temporary work groups with a finite task and life cycle, to solve problems that cannot be solved well by existing work groups. Unfortunately, traditional task forces, like traditional organizational structures, cannot always solve problems quickly. Structure and logistical problems often get in the way of people trying to get things done quickly. Thus, organizations routinely need flexible teams that can be assembled quickly and can solve problems effectively

FIGURE 5.2

Members of highly specialized virtual teams are often not collocated.

Source: Toria/Shutterstock

and efficiently. Time is of the essence, and organizations are increasingly trying to harness the expertise of highly specialized team members, regardless of their location. With increasing globalization and increasing use of the Internet, collaborators on projects or teams do not have to be collocated; rather, businesses increasingly form **virtual teams**, comprised of members from different geographic areas, assembled as needed to collaborate on a certain project (Sarker & Sahay, 2002) (see Figure 5.2). Membership on these virtual teams is fluid, with teams forming and disbanding as needed, with team size fluctuating as necessary, and with team members coming and going as they are needed; meetings typically take the form of **virtual meetings** using an online environment.

Virtual meetings can be done synchronously, like a teleconference, or asynchronously, using technologies such as online discussion boards. Employees may, at times, find themselves on multiple teams, and the life of a team may be very short. In addition, team members must have easy, flexible access to other team members, meeting contexts, and information. Think of these virtual teams as highly dynamic task forces. Virtual teams are commonly used for tasks such as developing systems and software; for example, the programmers are located in India, the project managers are in the United States, and the testers are in Europe. However, systems development is not the only place you will find virtual teams. For instance, the health care industry has embraced the idea of using technology to create superior care for patients. At the Rush University Medical Center in Chicago, team members may include dieticians, physicians, surgeons, pharmacists, and social workers from different cities, all of whom can coordinate care of the patient using various Web technologies to collaborate. This allows patients to get the best health care professionals regardless of where they reside. Rush University Hospital is finding that patients under "virtual team care" report fewer trips to the emergency room and gain a better understanding of the health care system.

THE EVOLVING WEB

Up until a few years ago, the Web was regarded as a one-way medium, with a relatively strict distinction between content creators and content consumers (sometimes referred to as "Web 1.0"). Some entities would create content (say, a Web site), and others would consume this content. However, changes in technology have enabled new uses of the Web; dynamic Web applications, often referred to as **Web 2.0** applications, allow people to collaborate and share information online. One of the basic concepts associated with Web 2.0 is a shift in the users' role from the passive consumer of content to its creator (see Figure 5.3). In contrast to the TV network ABC's site, where content is provided by ABC, the Web 2.0 application YouTube depends on content created and uploaded by other users; similarly, whereas the *Encyclopaedia Britannica* invests large sums

http://goo.gl/1Ja5b

FIGURE 5.3

Web 2.0 applications shift a Web user's role from a passive consumer of content to its creator.

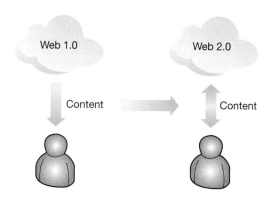

in professionally researched articles, the articles in the online encyclopedia Wikipedia are jointly written and edited by the online community (owing to societal changes and competition from Wikipedia, *Encyclopaedia Britannica* decided to stop producing printed encyclopedias in 2012, instead focusing on its online offerings). In addition to these applications, many organizations have successfully incorporated Web 2.0 concepts into their business models. For example, Amazon.com adds value to its site by incorporating book reviews from its customers. This way, they give customers a channel to voice their thoughts; at the same time, a larger number of reviews can help other customers make better decisions, thus attracting more visitors to Amazon .com's site. In the following sections, we will discuss technological and societal changes that both enable and necessitate changes in the way many organizations do business.

Evolving Web Capabilities

Many successful Web 2.0 applications rely on Web APIs (application programming interfaces) to function. A **Web API** provides a way for different components of software to interact and exchange data or functionality using common Web communication protocols. In other words, a Web site or service provider (such as Google) makes parts of its functionality or data (such as mapping data) available for others to use through one or more Web APIs; another Web site can utilize data or functionality offered by the provider without intimate knowledge about the provider's inner workings. Thus, Web APIs allow accessing remote or local data without having to know the complexities of this access, and thus enable creating unique and dynamic applications quickly and easily.

In the context of Web 2.0, Web APIs enable the creation of **mashups**. The idea of mashups came from popular music where many songs are produced by mixing two or more existing songs together; in Web 2.0 terminology, a mashup is a new application (or Web site) that uses data from one or more service providers. For example, a mashup could combine geospatial data, photos, reference information, hotel prices, and weather information to provide a comprehensive overview of travel destinations. Rather than having to collect or generate all of this information him- or herself, the creator of the mashup could simply draw on services provided by Flickr, Google Maps, Wikipedia, Expedia, and AccuWeather, all using the providers' Web APIs (see Figure 5.4). Using publicly accessible Web APIs, Craigslist developed a dynamic map of all available apartments in the United States (www.housingmaps.com). Likewise, users and

FIGURE 5.4

A mashup is a new application (or Web site) that uses data from one or more service providers.

companies can create mashups using Microsoft's Bing maps. The mashup "what's nearby" aggregates content from various sources on the Web so as to display information, reviews, or driving directions about businesses, restaurants, or medical facilities near a given location. Other mashups use information from airlines, radio stations, recommendation services, or any other sources of useful information. For a list of useful mashups, visit www.programmableweb.com.

Many organizations have recognized the power and benefits of offering Web APIs to the public. Why are companies doing this? By providing access to useful Web APIs, organizations extend their reach and build and strengthen customer relationships, providing a base for revenue-generating services (e.g., Google's Map API is free for low-volume usage, but is offered as a paid version for high-volume commercial usage, such as integration in a hotel booking site).

Evolving Social Interaction

Many successful Web 2.0 applications embody core Web 2.0 values such as collaboration and social sharing; these can be classified as **social media** (or **social software**), allowing people to communicate, interact, and collaborate in various ways. With Web 2.0 coming of age, people's behaviors as well as societies have undergone rapid changes. For example, many people have changed the ways they search for information. Whereas in the past people turned to paper encyclopedias as sources of unbiased information, people now increasingly turn to Web sites such as Wikipedia, or ask their friends and acquaintances on social networks such as Facebook or Google+ for personalized information. Similarly, there has been a marked shift in the way people view privacy and share information; although criticized by privacy advocates, people are sharing more personal information online than ever before. Repeatedly, you can read about people posting the most private information, without thinking about the consequences; as Facebook and other social Web sites have become pervasive in many people's lives, you have information about your friend's recent drinking escapades leading to a DUI, your coworker's breaking up with his girlfriend, and other things you may or may not want to know, all at your fingertips. Clearly, social software has strongly influenced the lives of many people. Table 5.1 highlights the shift in perspectives from the Web 1.0 to the Web 2.0 era.

Evolving Collaboration through Collective Intelligence

One major benefit of social software is the ability to harness the "wisdom of crowds," or collective intelligence (Surowiecki, 2004). The concept of **collective intelligence** is based on the notion that distributed groups of people with a divergent range of information and expertise will be able to outperform the capabilities of individual experts, as demonstrated by the online encyclopedia Wikipedia, which is entirely based on its users' contributions (see Figure 5.5). Likewise, open source software is another example of the power of collective intelligence. High-quality software such as the Firefox Web browser, the Linux operating system, or the Apache OpenOffice productivity suite are created, maintained, and updated by thousands of volunteers located all over the world. For organizations, making effective use of the collective intelligence of their employees, customers, and other stakeholders can prove extremely valuable. In addition to the benefits of harnessing the wisdom of crowds, societal changes (brought about by globalization, increasing wealth and consumerism, as well as the Web) are increasingly changing the way in which organizations interact with internal and external stakeholders.

TABLE 5.1 Shifting Perspectives from Web 1.0 to Web 2.0

Web 1.0	Web 2.0
Me	Me and you
Read	Read and write
Connect ideas	Connect ideas and people
Search	Receive and give recommendations to friends and others
Find	Share
Techies rule	Users rule
Organizations	Individuals

Source: Based on Sessums (2009).

FIGURE 5.5

The online encyclopedia Wikipedia is entirely based on user contributions.

Source: Courtesy of Wikimedia Foundation.

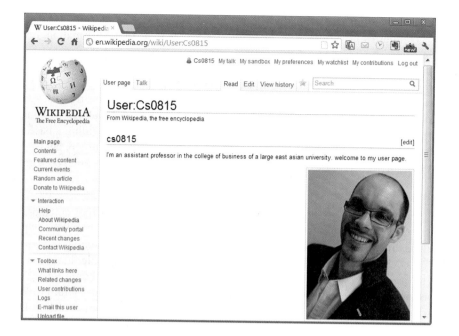

The Evolving Workspace

The "millennials," or "Generation Y," who grew up being tied to social software such as MySpace, YouTube, or Facebook, are joining the workforce and are having much different expectations from their workplace than prior generations. In his book *The CEO: The Chief Engagement Officer: Turning Hierarchy Upside Down to Drive Performance*, John Smythe (2007) argues that there are some fundamental shifts taking place in employer/employee relationships. For example, employees are now looking for a portfolio career rather than a cradle-to-grave job, tend to view themselves as citizens rather than employees, and "loan their talent" to the employer rather than being a "human resource." A recent global study by Accenture revealed that for 37 percent of 18- to 27-year-olds, state-of-the-art technology is a vital consideration in the choice

BRIEF CASE   Crowdsourcing a Constitution

When Iceland decided that the almost seven-decade-old Danish constitution being used to govern the country was outdated, the government turned to the Web for constructive ideas and opinions. Iceland is the world leader in Internet usage, with 94 percent of the population on the World Wide Web. Therefore, it came as no surprise in 2011 when the northern European country reached out to its citizens through various Web sites and social media—for example, government Web sites, Facebook, Twitter, YouTube, and Flickr—to solicit input to improve its constitution, fostering both outrage and engagement from Icelandic citizens.

Utilizing the Web as a platform for gathering recommendations, the Icelandic government successfully tried to leverage its citizens' collective intelligence for input to the new constitution. Members of the public offered ideas on a wide range of topics, ranging from how to improve the treatment of livestock to insights on how authorities can easier seize stolen property; net neutrality, transparency, and freedom of access were also discussed. After Icelanders verified their citizenship and submitted their suggestions, dedicated staff immediately worked to eliminate spam and other typical glitches. The drafts of various ideas and policies would then be published online to elicit further comments and discussion.

By the end of the process, hundreds of contributions from the Web were used to construct the country's new governing document, which would then be voted on by the citizens. This not only encouraged online participatory democracy, but ensured that Iceland would have a collectively accepted constitution that all Icelanders could be proud of.

Questions:

1. To what extent should ordinary citizens be included in governing a country?
2. What other applications can you envision for harnessing the wisdom of the crowds?

Based on:

Brown, M. (2011, August 1). Icelanders turn in first draft of crowdsourced constitution. *Wired.co.uk*. Retrieved July 5, 2012, from http://www.wired.co.uk/news/archive/2011-08/01/iceland-constitution.

IceNews (2011, October 5). Icelandic PM wants public vote on new constitution. *IceNews.is*. Retrieved July 5, 2012, from http://www.icenews.is/index.php/2011/10/05/icelandic-pm-wants-public-vote-on-new-constitution.

Siddique, H. (2011, June 9). Mob rule: Iceland crowdsources its next constitution. *The Guardian*. Retrieved July 5, 2012, from http://www.guardian.co.uk/world/2011/jun/09/iceland-crowdsourcing-constitution-facebook.

of workplace; of the working millennials, 55 percent use instant messaging, and 45 percent use social networking sites for work-related activities (Francis & Harrigan, 2010). The millennials bring with them many new and valuable skills, but also attitudes that may be difficult to integrate with more traditional business environments: over 19 percent of businesses worldwide ban social networking sites at work (Clearswift, 2011), but many millennials are skilled at finding creative work-arounds to circumvent such policies (which may result in increases in security breaches). A recent survey showed that 29 percent of college students would not join a company that bans social media applications, and a further 27 percent would find ways to circumvent the policies (Cisco, 2011). As a result, companies are increasingly starting to embrace social media to enhance communication, cooperation, collaboration, and connection (Cook, 2008).

Future Web Capabilities

Web technologies and collaboration are ever-evolving topics, and many developments have yet to be fully realized. This section briefly forecasts future capabilities of the Web, in particular, focusing on efforts to create the semantic Web and characteristics of Web 3.0.

THE SEMANTIC WEB. Since the Web opened up for public use, the number of Web pages and sites has grown exponentially. Although this increase in Web pages should mean that we have ever more information at our fingertips, it also means that the information is increasingly harder to find. What if the information on the Web was organized in a way that users could more easily find information or relevant content? At present, search engines cannot help to solve this formidable task, as Web pages can be understood by people but not by computers. For example, when you now go to Google.com and search for "what eats penguins," it returns Web sites that may have this information, but it is more likely that the sites just have the words or key terms "what" and "eats" and "penguins." For Larry Page, cofounder of Google, the perfect search engine would return only *one* result, namely, the one page that provides the best answer to the user's query. Currently, however, search engines are not sophisticated enough to be able to find, understand, and integrate information presented on Web pages. The **semantic Web**, originally envisioned by Tim Berners-Lee, one of the founders of the Internet, is a set of design principles that will allow computers to be able to better index Web sites, topics, and subjects. When Web pages are designed using semantic principles, computers will be able to read the pages, and search engines will be able to give richer and more accurate answers. In 2012, Google has started making strides toward implementing concepts related to the semantic Web in its "knowledge graph." When searching for terms in Google, the search engine now attempts to foresee what the user may mean; for example, when searching for "kings," the search engine not only provides a list of pages containing the keyword "kings," but also displays a box containing links to search results specific to the *Los Angeles Kings*, the *Sacramento Kings*, and the NBC TV series *Kings*. Similarly, when searching for "Los Angeles Kings," Google not only returns a list of Web pages, but also a summary of relevant information about the hockey team, culled from various Web sources. Although the semantic Web is largely unrealized, Google's efforts show that the semantic Web experience is getting closer.

WEB 3.0. In many ways, Web 2.0 has already replaced Web 1.0, and the question is "What will replace Web 2.0?" For some, Web 2.0 is just a short transitional period before the next wave of Internet technologies, which is predicted to last until 2020. There are several ideas on what this next wave, Web 3.0, will entail. Some, such as *Forbes* contributor Eric Jackson, envision the next wave of the Web to be centered around mobility, almost announcing the demise of the Web as we know it. Others see Web 3.0 as the "contextual Web," where the immense amounts of content available to users will be filtered by contextual factors such as time, location, social activities, and so on. You may have already seen some of these emerging technologies in practice, especially regarding the context of a user's location, and we may only know what Web 3.0 really is when we see it; it may even forever remain a buzzword. Nevertheless, we can see exciting new developments on the horizon, and the coming trends will likely involve true integration of devices and connectivity to create powerful socially aware Internet applications. Stay tuned to see what the future holds.

Enterprise 2.0

Having realized the opportunities brought about by these profound changes, many business organizations are continuously looking for ways to use social media to support their existing business processes; many organizations have built successful business models entirely based on core Web 2.0 values such as social sharing or collaboration. The use of social media within a company's boundaries or between a company and its customers or stakeholders (often referred to as **Enterprise 2.0**) can help in sharing organizational knowledge, making businesses more innovative and productive, and helping them to effectively connect with their customers and the wider public (McAfee, 2006a); such enterprises are sometimes also referred to as **social enterprises**. In the following sections, we will discuss traditional collaboration tools, before introducing various social media applications used by individual Web users as well as organizations.

http://goo.gl/aOQsm

TRADITIONAL COLLABORATION TOOLS

If you have ever worked on a team project for your class (and you probably have), you have noticed that there are many different communication needs, such as talking, sharing documents, and making decisions. Just as there are many things to discuss within your team project, there are also many ways that you can communicate and collaborate. One key distinction is between **synchronous** (i.e., at the same time) and **asynchronous** (i.e., not coordinated in time) communication media. For example, chatting online or making a telephone call are examples of synchronous communication, whereas e-mail is an example of asynchronous communication; a customer might send the customer service department an e-mail message at 7:00 A.M., and a customer service representative might reply at 5:00 P.M. Needless to say, such delays can create process inefficiencies or dissatisfied customers, and can thus be very costly for the organization. Thus, over the years, different tools have emerged to support various communication and collaboration needs (see Table 5.2).

Groupware

The term **groupware** refers to a class of software that enables people to work together more effectively. Groupware and other collaboration technologies are often distinguished along two key dimensions:

1. Whether the system supports groups working together at the same time (synchronous groupware) or at different times (asynchronous groupware)
2. Whether the system supports groups working together face-to-face or distributed

Using these two dimensions, groupware systems can be categorized as being able to support four types of group interaction methods, as shown in Figure 5.6. With the increased use of group-based problem solving and virtual teams, there are many potential benefits of utilizing groupware systems. These benefits are summarized in Table 5.3.

A large number of asynchronous groupware tools are becoming common in organizations, including e-mail, mailing lists, work flow automation systems, intranets (discussed below), group calendars, and collaborative writing tools. One widely used tool for group communication is discussion forums. Pre-dating the Web 2.0 era, **discussion forums** (also known as discussion boards or online forums) emulate traditional bulletin boards and allow for threaded discussions

TABLE 5.2 Categories of Collaborative Tools

Title	Description	Instances	Examples
Electronic communication tools	Tools allowing users to send files, documents, and pictures to each other and share information	Fax, e-mail, voice mail, blogs, wikis, static Web sites	MS Outlook, Blogger, Wikipedia
Electronic conferencing tools	Tools allowing information sharing and rich interactions between users	Internet forums, instant messaging, application sharing, video conferencing	Apple FaceTime, Skype, Google Talk, WebEx
Collaboration management tools	Tools used to facilitate virtual or collocated meetings and manage group activities	Electronic calendars, knowledge management systems, intranets, online document systems	Google Docs, MS Office 365, MS SharePoint

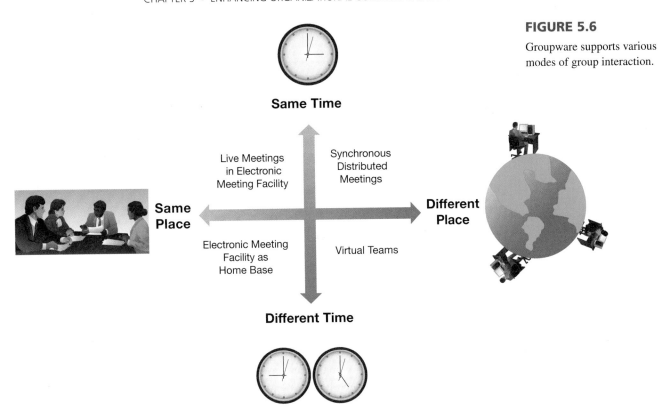

FIGURE 5.6

Groupware supports various modes of group interaction.

between participants. Typically, discussion forums are dedicated to specific topics, and users can start new threads (see Figure 5.7). Depending on the owner or host of the forum, the discussion forum may be moderated so that new postings appear only after they have been vetted by a moderator; further, some discussion forums may only allow posts from registered users, whereas others allow anyone to contribute. As the purpose of such forums is to enable discussion, there are usually multiple participants exchanging (typically rather short) thoughts. Many groupware systems combine functionalities such as e-mail, discussion boards, and so on. One of the most popular groupware systems—and arguably the system that put groupware into the mainstream— appeared in 1989 when Lotus Development released its Notes software product (today, Lotus is

TABLE 5.3 Benefits of Groupware

Benefit	Example
Process structuring	Keeps the group on track and helps it avoid costly diversions (i.e., doesn't allow people to get off topic or off the agenda)
Parallelism	Enables many people to speak and listen at the same time (i.e., everyone has an equal opportunity to participate)
Group size	Enables larger groups to participate (i.e., brings together broader perspectives, expertise, and participation)
Group memory	Automatically records member ideas, comments, and votes (i.e., allows members to focus on content of discussions rather than on recording comments)
Access to external information	Can easily incorporate external electronic data and files (i.e., plans and proposal documents can be collected and easily distributed to all members)
Spanning time and space	Enables members to collaborate from different places at different times (i.e., reduces travel costs or allows people from remote locations to participate)
Anonymity	Member ideas, comments, and votes are not identified to others, if desired (i.e., can make it easier to discuss controversial or sensitive topics without fear of identification or retribution)

FIGURE 5.7

Microsoft offers discussion forums for questions and feedback related to its various products and services.
Source: Courtesy of Microsoft, Inc.

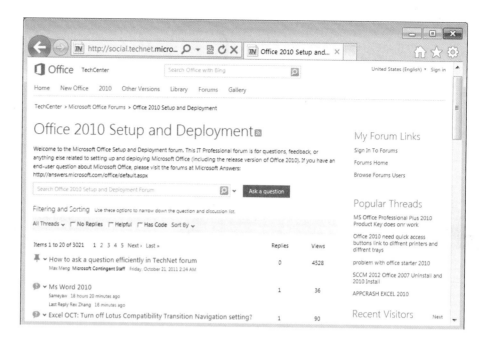

owned by IBM). In recent years, many new groupware products have emerged, most of which work through or with the Internet. Even with all these alternative groupware systems available, Notes continues to be an industry leader and is widely deployed throughout the world.

Like asynchronous groupware, there are also many forms of synchronous groupware available to support a wide variety of activities, including shared whiteboards, online chat, electronic meeting support systems, and, of course, video communication systems (discussed in the following section). Although many forms of groupware can be used to help groups work more effectively, one category of groupware focuses on helping groups have better meetings. These systems are commonly referred to as **electronic meeting systems (EMSs)**. An EMS is essentially a collection of personal computers networked together with sophisticated software tools to help group members solve problems and make decisions through interactive electronic idea generation, evaluation, and voting, as shown in Figure 5.8. EMSs have traditionally been housed within a dedicated meeting facility; increasingly, Web-based implementations support team members around the globe.

FIGURE 5.8

An electronic meeting system utilizes networked computers and sophisticated software to support various group tasks.
Source: Konstantinos Kokkinis/ Shutterstock

Videoconferencing

In the 1960's, at Disneyland and other theme parks and special events, the picturephone was first being demonstrated to large audiences. The phone companies estimated that we would be able to see a live picture with our phone calls in the near future. It took another 30 years, but that prediction has come true within many organizations. Many organizations are conducting videoconferencing to replace traditional meetings, using either desktop videoconferencing or dedicated videoconferencing systems that can cost from a few thousand dollars up to US$500,000.

Desktop videoconferencing has been enabled by the growing power of processors powering personal computers and faster Internet connections. A desktop videoconferencing system usually comprises a fast personal computer, a **webcam** (i.e., a small video camera that is connected directly to a PC), a speaker telephone or separate microphone, videoconferencing software (e.g., Skype, Google+, Yahoo! Messenger, or Windows Live Messenger), and a high-speed Internet connection. Similarly, people can now use apps such as FaceTime, FriendCaller, or Skype on their mobile devices, enabling them to make video calls on the go.

Dedicated videoconferencing systems are typically located within organizational conference rooms, facilitating meetings with customers or project team members across town or around the world. These systems can be highly realistic—as if you are almost collocated with your colleagues—but high-end systems can be extremely expensive. No matter what type of videoconferencing system utilized by an organization, this collaboration technology has come a long way from the demonstration at Disneyland in the 1960's, becoming mainstream in most modern organizations.

Intranets and Employee Portals

Internet technologies have given rise to another widely used tool for communicating and collaborating within organizational boundaries. Specifically, many large organizations have intranet-based employee portals. As discussed in Chapter 3, "Managing the Information Systems Infrastructure and Services," an intranet is a private network using Web technologies, used to facilitate the secured transmission of proprietary information within an organization. Intranets take advantage of standard Internet and Web protocols to communicate information to and from authorized employees. An intranet looks and acts just like a publicly accessible Web site, and uses the same software, hardware, and networking technologies to communicate information. Thus, users access their company's intranet using their Web browser. Many companies such as Boeing provide customized intranet pages for each employee depending on job functions or even geographical location. Whereas each employee's page has the same look and feel and draws on the same underlying data, each employee can access only the information he or she needs to perform his or her job function. For example, if an employee from human resources logs on to the employee portal, he or she would see only content that pertains to his or her job, such as payroll information or hiring statistics.

All intranet pages are behind the company's firewall, and in the simplest form of an intranet, communications take place only within the confines of organizational boundaries and do not travel across the Internet. However, increases in employees' mobility necessitate that an intranet be accessible from anywhere. Thus, most companies allow their employees to use VPNs to connect to the company's intranet while on the road or working from home (i.e., telecommuting). Figure 5.9 depicts a typical intranet system architecture (see Chapter 10, "Securing Information Systems" for more on firewalls and VPNs).

REAL-TIME ACCESS TO INFORMATION. A major benefit of corporate intranets is the ability to increase the efficiency and effectiveness of collaboration by providing real-time access to information. Unlike paper-based documents, which need to be continually updated and distributed to employees when changes occur, intranets make it less complicated to manage, update, distribute, and access corporate information. For instance, Boeing disseminates corporate news using multimedia files distributed over the company's intranet, allowing employees to view digital copies of company news releases as they occur, from the convenience of their desktops.

With intranet-based solutions such as those deployed at Boeing, up-to-date, accurate information can be easily accessed on a company-wide basis from a single source that is both efficient and user friendly. Companies can become more flexible with resources required to

FIGURE 5.9

Typical intranet system architecture.

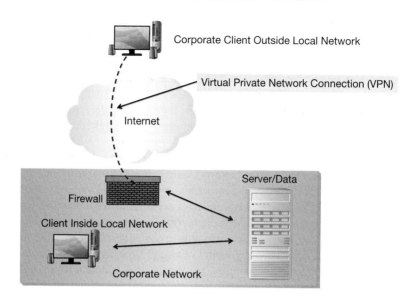

create, maintain, and distribute corporate documents, while in the process employees become more knowledgeable and current about the information that is important to them. Employees develop a sense of confidence and become self-reliant, reducing time spent dealing with employment-related issues and allowing them to focus on their work responsibilities.

ENTERPRISE SEARCH. Another component supporting employee productivity by providing real-time access to information is the integration of enterprise search functionality. As more and more content is accessible via a company's intranet, relevant information becomes increasingly more difficult to locate, especially if the information is in different languages and located on different servers or databases, as is the case in many large global organizations such as Nestlé. Hence, the requirements for enterprise search engines are very different from those of Internet search engines such as Google or Bing. Enterprise search engines such as Microsoft's Enterprise Search or the Google Search Appliance are designed to retrieve content from various internal data sources, including documents, databases, or applications linked to the company's intranet. For example, prior to Kimberly-Clark's implementation of the Google Search Appliance, their search engine could search only about 500,000 internal documents, and users' biggest complaint was that they were unable to find the information they were looking for; with Google Search Appliance, employees are now able to access more than 22 million documents located throughout the organization as well as external content. Thus, providing enterprise search functionality can enhance productivity and be an important factor contributing to users' satisfaction with the company's intranet.

COLLABORATION. One of the most common problems occurring in large corporations relates to the coordination of and collaboration on business activities in a timely fashion across divisions or functional areas. For instance, Boeing uses its intranet to facilitate collaborative efforts, such as in the process of designing new aircraft components. In this process, three-dimensional digital models of aircraft designs frequently need to be shared between aerospace engineers. Using Boeing's intranet, an engineer can share a drawing with another engineer at a remote location; the second engineer revises the drawing as necessary and uploads the updated drawing to a shared folder on the intranet. The Boeing intranet provides the company with the capability of reducing product development cycle times as well as the ability to stay abreast of current project, corporate, and market conditions.

Further, intranets are now being used to facilitate communication and collaboration within organizations outside of traditional workflows. For example, Atomic Energy of Canada Labs (AECL), the manufacturer of the CANDU, one of the world's most popular nuclear reactors, has been using an intranet to poll staff about current issues or to communicate new executive initiatives. The company's intranet collaboration tools empower employees to communicate with each other and executives in a secure non-public forum.

EMPLOYEE PORTALS. In addition to being used for communication and collaboration, organizational intranets are widely used for enabling employee self-service for administering benefits, managing retirement plans, or other human resources–based applications through **employee portals**. For example, for large companies, processing human resources–related forms can be a large cost factor. Depending on the complexity of the form, processing a paper-based form can cost US$20 to US$30, according to benefits administration solutions provider Workscape, Inc. Whereas interactive voice response–based telephone applications can cut these costs to US$2 to US$4, using intranet-based employee self-service applications can reduce this further, to a mere 5 to 10 cents per form (Wagner, 2002). Considering that employees, on average, conduct 15 human resources–related transactions per year, the savings can be significant. Using the intranet, report templates can be centrally managed, and modifications can be made instantaneously as conditions change; thus, employees can submit the appropriate template electronically with the assurance that they have used the correct version. Further, using online forms can help to significantly reduce error rates, as the entries can be checked for accuracy when the data are entered, thus preventing the user from inputting incorrect or illogical entries.

SOCIAL MEDIA AND THE ENTERPRISE

http://goo.gl/t5Lcn

You were likely familiar with many of the tools discussed previously, but there may have been some that you were not aware of. You are probably more comfortable or find more value using some tools over others. Similarly, organizations are increasingly trying to find the right tools for their different needs. In the following sections, we will discuss how different social media applications enable or support communication, cooperation, collaboration, or connection; needless to say, many of these applications cannot be neatly categorized, fitting into more than one category.

Enhancing Communication Using Social Media

A prime application of Enterprise 2.0 is facilitating and enhancing the communication within an organization as well as between an organization and its stakeholders. For organizations, social media have opened up a vast array of opportunities for presenting themselves to their (potential) customers; at the same time, these applications have opened up literally thousands of channels for customers to voice their opinions about an organization. In this section, we introduce various social media tools used for communication.

BLOGS. Blogging originally started out as a novice's way of expressing themselves using very simple Web pages. **Blogging** is the process of creating an online text diary (i.e., a **blog**, or Web log) made up of chronological entries that comment on everything from one's everyday life to wine and food, or even computer problems (see Figure 5.10). Rather than trying to produce

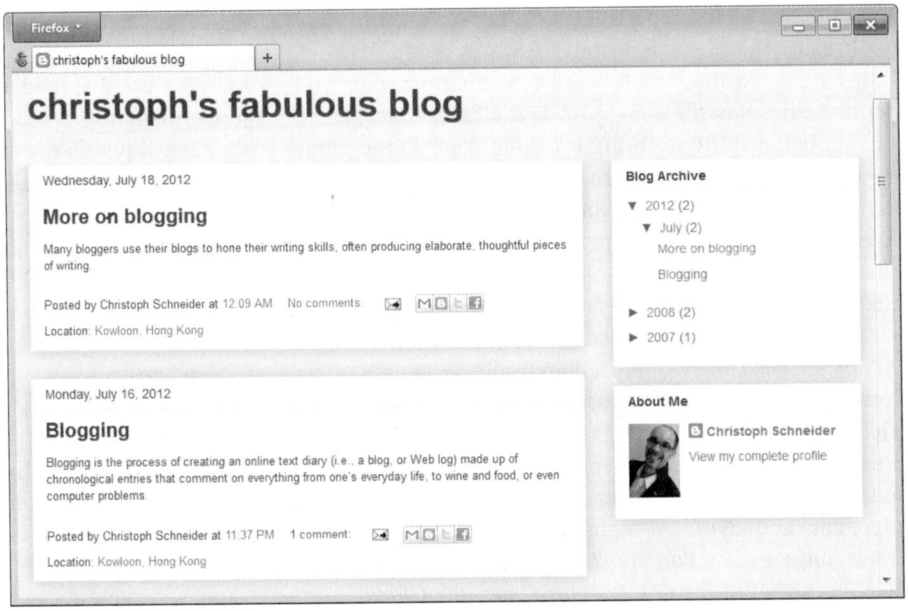

FIGURE 5.10

Blogging is the process of creating an online text diary (i.e., a blog, or Web log) made up of chronological entries.

TABLE 5.4 Examples of Prominent Blogs

Type of Blog	Example	Description
Technology	www.engadget.com	Consumer electronics blog
	news.cnet.com/tech-blogs	Various technology blogs
	www.roughtype.com	Blog of Nicholas Carr, author of the book *IT Doesn't Matter* and former executive editor of the *Harvard Business Review*
Financial	blogs.wsj.com/marketbeat	*Wall Street Journal's* blog on stock market happenings
	www.dvorak.org/blog	John Dvorak from *Market Watch* reports on various news events
Entertainment	www.perezhilton.com	A gossip and news blog run by TV personality Mario Armando Lavandeira, Jr.
	nymag.com/daily/fashion	*New York Magazine's* fashion blog
Political	corner.nationalreview.com	A blog run by *The National Review,* a magazine started in 1955 by William F. Buckley
	www.huffingtonpost.com	One of the most powerful political blogs; the *Huffington Post,* founded by Arianna Huffington, won the Pulitzer Prize in 2012 for a 10-part series covering wounded combat troops and their families

physical books to sell or use as gifts, bloggers (i.e., the people maintaining blogs) merely want to share stories about their lives or voice their opinions (although feedback is often encouraged through associated threaded discussions). Many bloggers use their blogs to hone their writing skills, often producing elaborate, thoughtful pieces of writing. Blogging has exploded into its own industry, and many companies, and even the mainstream media, embrace blogging (see Table 5.4). The influence of blogging has also hit the mainstream media. Many traditional media giants, such as CNN, now use blogs to paint a richer picture of the stories they produce. Anderson Cooper, one of CNN's anchors, currently edits and writes for CNN's flagship blog called Anderson Cooper 360.

Blogs are being used by small, medium-sized, and large organizations and have become important voices that can sway public opinion. One famous example of the power of blogging is the 2004 election scandal known as "Rathergate." Dan Rather, appearing on *60 Minutes,* reported on some suspect findings concerning President George W. Bush's record of military service. Bloggers soon after (correctly) reported that the documents used in this news story were falsified. Without the bloggers' visibility, this misrepresentation could have gone unnoticed. Because of the bloggers' reports, Dan Rather resigned from *60 Minutes,* and some say that this eventually caused his dismissal from CBS News.

Blogs are not without controversy. Nicholas Carr, noted technology journalist (and active blogger himself), classifies blogging as the **"amateurization" of journalism.** Often the value of blogging is the ability to bring breaking news to the public in the fastest possible way. By doing so, some bloggers cut journalistic corners, rendering some of the posts on the blogs less than accurate. For example, in May 2007, consumer electronics blog Engadget.com reported that Apple's iPhone and OSX operating system were going to be delayed. This news spurred a 4 percent downturn in Apple's stock price in less than 20 minutes. Soon after the story was released, users questioned the validity of the story, and Engadget.com retracted the story. Further, blogs have been criticized for frequently providing the biased opinions of the writers, particularly because many of the authors' sources cannot or have not been verified.

Nevertheless, blogs have massively influenced the way in which people gather and consume information. In fact, turning to free information from blogs and other online sources, many readers have cancelled newspaper subscriptions. In turn, diminishing readership in traditional newspapers has enticed advertisers to begin to withdraw from this traditional medium, leading to budget cuts and layoffs at reputable newspapers such as the *San Francisco Chronicle, The New York Times,* the *Washington Times,* and many others; in December 2008, newspaper giant Tribune Co., owner of the *Los Angeles Times,* the *Chicago Tribune,* and other newspapers, was forced to file for Chapter 11 bankruptcy protection, facing dwindling advertising revenues and a huge debt burden (as of mid-2012, it was regarded as likely that Tribune would finally exit from bankruptcy protection). Unfortunately—and ironically—this may erode the very sources that many bloggers base their information on. To show just how severe this problem is today, a mashup has been created to visually show where layoffs are occurring at newspapers across the United States (http://newspaperlayoffs.com/). These examples show both the power of the blogs and some of the problems associated with them. The influence of blogs has also been called the power of the **blogosphere** (i.e., the community of all blogs).

In addition to blogs created by and/or for individual readers, companies increasingly use blogs for connecting with their employees or customers. For example, IBM's business-oriented social software suite Lotus Connection includes blogs, helping people to voice ideas and obtain feedback from others. Similarly, companies such as Google maintain official company blogs at http://googleblog.blogspot.com to inform their stakeholders about news, rumors, or current thoughts.

MICROBLOGGING TOOLS. **Microblogging tools** (sometimes called **social presence tools**), similar to blogging, enable people to voice their thoughts; however, in contrast to blogs, which often contain lengthy posts, social presence tools are designed for broadcasting relatively short "status updates." In contrast to social networks, where a user can choose who can or cannot receive his or her status updates, typically, anyone can follow another person's microblog. A popular social presence tool is Twitter, which allows users to post short (up to 140 characters of text) "tweets" that are delivered to the author's followers or subscribers via mobile phone or Twitter applications (see Figure 5.11). The recipient can "retweet" (i.e., re-broadcast) interesting tweets to his or her followers. Whereas Twitter's initial focus was on personal status updates, the focus has now shifted to users tweeting "what's happening." Hence, Twitter has become a source for breaking news; for example, messages about US Airways Flight 1549 crashing in the Hudson River were spreading on Twitter 15 minutes before traditional media outlets started to broadcast news about the incident. Many social networking sites (discussed later in this chapter) also have social presence functionality built in; for example, users can update their status on Facebook, letting their friends know about their current thoughts and allowing them to post replies.

Many organizations have used this trend and created accounts on Twitter. For example, Coca-Cola has an official Twitter account used to post news or interact with its (as of mid-2012) over 570,000 followers; Coca-Cola follows more than 37,000 Twitter accounts and actively replies to and retweets Twitter messages. This way, Coca-Cola signals that it cares about its followers, and can increase its customers' brand loyalty. Tumblr, another popular microblogging tool, takes the concept a step further by allowing users to go beyond the 140-character limit and share any kind of digital content, including text, music, and videos.

INSTANT MESSAGING. In contrast to asynchronous discussion forums, blogs, and status updates, **instant messaging** (or online chat) enables real-time written conversations. Using instant messaging, multiple participants can have conversations and enjoy immediate feedback from their

FIGURE 5.11

Twitter allows posting short "tweets" that are delivered to the author's followers or subscribers via mobile phone or Twitter applications.
Source: Twitter.com

FIGURE 5.12

Virtual worlds consist of 3D environments where people can interact and build, buy, or sell virtual items, all using their personalized avatar.

Source: Photosani/Shutterstock

conversation partners. Some social networking sites such as Facebook have integrated instant messaging functionality; however, instant messaging is often regarded as somewhat artificial, although most instant messaging environments also support both video and voice communication. In addition, the increase in smartphone usage has merged instant messaging with cell phone–based text messaging by enabling cloud-based messaging services such as WhatsApp, allowing for group chat, free text messages (even internationally), and even the exchange of multimedia content between different devices, using the smartphone users' data plan. Many organizations have adopted Web-based instant messaging for internal communications, and also use live chat for sales and customer support functions. For example, the Chinese business-to-business marketplace Alibaba .com includes a chat interface so that interested buyers can immediately contact potential sellers.

VIRTUAL WORLDS. **Virtual worlds** take the concept of real-time communication a step further by allowing people to communicate using avatars. Popular virtual worlds such as Second Life, Meez, or IMVU consist of 3D environments where people can interact and build, buy, or sell virtual items, all using their personalized avatars (see Figure 5.12). While many companies have not been able to realize the full potential of those environments beyond just providing virtual showcases for their products, dedicated virtual worlds are increasingly used for rich communication; for example, virtual worlds are increasingly being used for education-related activities, employee training, or medical uses.

Enhancing Cooperation with Social Media

In addition to communication, companies and individuals can benefit from social media applications that enable cooperation. Cooperation between individuals or organizations creates win-win situations such that one participant's success improves the chances of success of other participants. Social media applications facilitating such cooperation rely on the **network effect** to provide the greatest benefits for users (various other applications, such as social networks or instant messaging applications also base their success on the network effect). The network effect refers to the notion that the value of a network (or tool or application based on a network) is dependent on the number of other users. In other words, if a network has few users, it has little or no value. For example, how useful would e-mail be if none of your friends or family members had access to it? Likewise, eBay would not be an effective auction Web site if only a few bidders were present: in order for eBay auctions to be valued, there must be a large number of users who are involved in the auctions. As more users hear about eBay and then become active buyers and sellers, the value of eBay continues to grow.

MEDIA SHARING. One example of cooperative social media applications making use of the network effect is media sharing. The sharing of pictures, videos, audio, and even presentations has become immensely popular on the Web, using applications such as Flickr or Instagram (images), Pinterest (pictures and interests), YouTube (videos), or SlideShare (presentations); using sites such as Pandora, users can even create their favorite music stream and share it with others who may

COMING ATTRACTIONS

Bio-Storing Files in Bacteria

You store your important files on a USB stick, which by now only has 30 MB left out of its total capacity; large parts of your music archive consume almost all of your smartphone's memory, and pictures from your recent trip to Europe are clogging up your laptop. In the United States, national archives occupy more than 500 miles of shelving, and in France they take up more than 100 miles. How can we find space to store all the information, which is growing by the minute? A group of students at the Chinese University of Hong Kong are suggesting a potential answer in a place you least expected—the E.coli bacterium. In the future, a box of bacteria housed right inside your refrigerator may serve as long-term storage for large datasets.

The idea of encoding and storing simple information in the DNA of bacteria was first concretely proposed in 2007 by a team at Keio University in Japan; using the notion that bacteria reproduce constantly, the researchers argued that information could potentially be stored for millennia. In 2011, the group of Hong Kong researchers developed ways to move beyond storing simple information, opening up the option of storing texts, images, music, and even video files in bacteria. Given the minuscule size of an E.coli cell, one gram of bacteria could hold the equivalent of 450 two-terabyte hard drives. In addition to the incredible storage capacity, biostorage promises high security: bacteria cannot be hacked, and are relatively immune from cyberattacks.

Where do we go after biostorage? It is hard to tell as the technology itself is still in a nascent stage, requiring much further analysis and research before it becomes practical. Yet, there are ideas for using biostorage for purposes other than storing text, music, or videos. For example, genetically modified crops could be equipped with a biological barcode, storing useful information such as product safety information, copyright information, and so on. Certainly, the possibilities of coming up with more innovations are unlimited—as environmental concerns are growing, scientists have come to suggest the use of micro-organisms in tackling various issues and crises humanity faces now and in the future. For now, at least we can say that cyber-attacks would no longer be a problem then. After all, WikiLeaks would find it rather challenging to poke into your refrigerator.

Based on:

Dillow, C. (2011, October 1). Biostorage scheme turns e. coli bacteria into hard drives. *Popsci*. Retrieved July 5, 2012, from http://www.popsci.com/science/article/2011-01/biostorage-scheme-turns-e-coli-bacteria-data-storing-hard-drives.

Evans, J. (2011, January 10). Bacteria work as hard drives. *Discovery-News.com*. Retrieved August 17, 2012, from http://news.discovery.com/tech/bacteria-work-as-hard-drives-110110.html.

have similar interests. Typically, the shared content is hosted on media sharing sites; however, the content can also be embedded into other sites, creating a win-win situation for the content creator and the site embedding the content. For example, embedding an interesting and relevant YouTube video into a blog post helps to increase the attractiveness of the blog while at the same time increasing the viewership of the video, thus creating positive returns for both parties.

Similarly, webcasting is increasingly used for media sharing. **Webcasting** (or **podcasting**) is the distribution of digital media, such as audio or video files for on-demand playback on digital media players. The increase in mobile devices such as smartphones and tablets has contributed to the tremendous growth of webcasts, as the consumption can be time shifted and place shifted; in other words, webcasts allow media content to be viewed at one's convenience, whenever or wherever. The term "podcasting," derived from combining the terms "broadcasting" and "iPod," is a misnomer, as **webcasts** (or **podcasts**) can be played on a variety of devices in addition to Apple's iPods. As with blogging, webcasting has grown substantially, with traditional media organizations now webcasting everything from shows on National Public Radio to Fox's *Family Guy* to the *Oprah Winfrey Show*. In addition to media organizations and independent webcasters, the educational sector uses webcasts for providing students access to lectures, lab demonstrations, or sports events; this allows students to review lectures or prepare for class during their morning and evening commutes. In 2007, Apple launched iTunes U, which offers free content provided by major U.S. universities, such as Stanford, Berkeley, and the Massachusetts Institute of Technology (see Figure 5.13). As webcasts can be enriched by allowing for interactive Q&A sessions or by embedding PowerPoint presentations, organizations increasingly use webcasts to provide access to shareholder meetings, online training, road shows, or other applications.

To receive the most current content, users can subscribe to blogs, webcasts, videos, and news stories through Apple's iTunes, or via **Real Simple Syndication (RSS)** feeds. RSS feeds are provided by content publishers so that the users get notified of updates to the content. Rather than users actively having to check multiple sources for updated content, RSS readers

FIGURE 5.13

A student listens to a podcast on iTunes U.

Source: Courtesy of Christoph Schneider

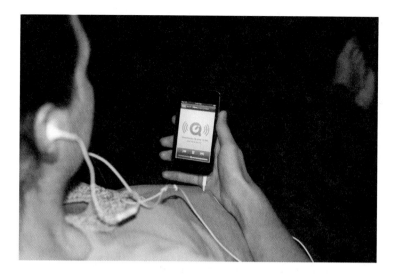

automatically check the feeds for updates. RSS feeds typically contain a synopsis of a document or the full text. For example, CNN.com publishes RSS feeds for each of its areas, such as world news, sports news, and entertainment news, and NBC uses RSS feeds to allow viewers to be notified about the most current version of shows such as *Meet the Press* and the *Nightly News*. RSS feeds can be read by most Web browsers and even e-mail clients such as Microsoft's Outlook, allowing users to browse different feeds as they would read e-mails; in addition, there are several stand-alone applications that can aggregate and present RSS feeds.

SOCIAL BOOKMARKING. Another category of social media applications relying on the network effect is social bookmarking. For many Web surfers, key challenges are finding information and finding it *again* at a later time; hence, people often keep long lists of bookmarks to sites they find interesting or visit frequently. Although this is useful for an individual, he or she may miss a plethora of other, related, and potentially interesting Web sites. **Social bookmarking** helps to address this by allowing users to share Internet bookmarks and to create categorization systems (referred to as **folksonomies**). As more people participate in social bookmarking, the value for each user grows as the bookmarks become more complete and more relevant to each user. Widely used public social bookmarking tools include reddit and delicious (see Figure 5.14). For organizations, social bookmarking can be extremely valuable for knowledge management and harnessing the collective intelligence of employees. Using enterprise-oriented social bookmarking tools, it is easy to map "islands" of knowledge within an organization, thus helping to easily find experts on a given topic.

FIGURE 5.14

delicious is a popular social bookmarking tool.

Source: Copyright © 2010 AVOS. All Rights Reserved.

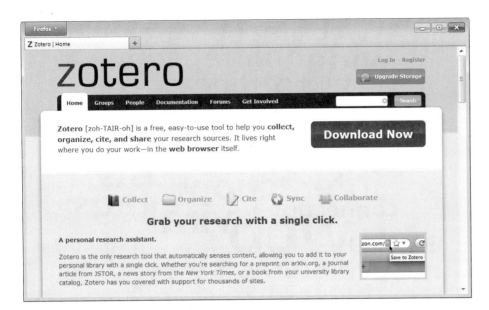

FIGURE 5.15

Zotero helps in organizing citations and research resources.

Source: Courtesy of Center for History and New Media, George Mason University.

SOCIAL CATALOGING. Similar to social bookmarking, **social cataloging** is the creation of a categorization system by users. Contributors build up catalogs regarding specific topics such as academic citations, wireless networks, books and music, and so on. For example, users can create virtual bookshelves with Google Books, organize their collections, write reviews, and then share this bookshelf with others on the Web. Similarly, students and researchers can use free tools such as Zotero (see Figure 5.15) to manage their citations, thus facilitating the creation of reference lists for research papers. Organizations are typically dealing with tremendous amounts of information, ranging from supplier information to frequent customer complaints, and can use social cataloging for structuring this information and making it more accessible and useful.

TAGGING. Social cataloging relies on the concept of **tagging**, or manually adding metadata to media or other content. **Metadata** can be simply thought of as data about data. In essence, metadata describe data in terms of who, where, when, why, and so on. For example, metadata about a Word document include the author, the time the document was created, and when it was last saved; metadata about a digital photo include date and time, focal length, shutter speed, aperture value, and so on (see Figure 5.16).

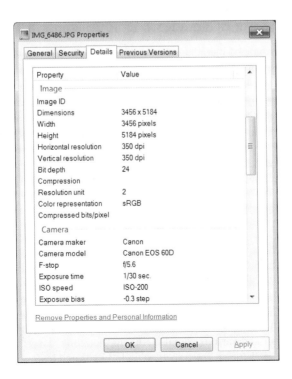

FIGURE 5.16

Metadata about a photo.

Source: Courtesy of Microsoft, Inc.

FIGURE 5.17

A tag cloud representing words and concepts that are key to social media.
Source: Shutterstock.

Whereas certain metadata about documents or media files are captured automatically (e.g., when saving a document in a word processor, or when taking a picture with a digital camera), there are various other important pieces of information that are not automatically captured, such as keywords about a document or the names of people in a picture. Tagging is the process of adding such metadata to pieces of information. Tags are commonly added to pictures and videos on Web sites such as Flickr, a picture and video hosting Web site that allows users to upload their content. Flickr, owned by Yahoo!, boasts millions of active users, and in August 2011 reached the milestone of 6 billion photos uploaded by its users, making it all but impossible to find images related to a certain topic. However, because many of the images have been tagged by users, they can be easily searched by various descriptive tags. For example, by adding the key word "Basketball" to a picture on Flickr, we are adding metadata about the context of the picture. The metadata will help return this picture as one of the results whenever a user searches Flickr for basketball pictures. A way to visualize user generated tags or content on a site is through **tag clouds** (see Figure 5.17). The size of a word in a tag cloud represents its importance or frequency, so that it is easy to spot the most important or frequent words or tags.

GEOTAGGING. Another type of metadata about media such as photos, videos, or even blogs or tweets is of geospatial nature; knowing where exactly a photo was taken and in what direction the camera was pointing, or knowing the location of a person sending out a breaking news update on Twitter, can be extremely valuable. Adding geospatial metadata (such as latitude, longitude, or altitude) to media is referred to as **geotagging**. Once the location of an item is known, it can easily be visualized on a map. For example, Google Maps can display various types of geotagged information, such as Wikipedia articles about places or landmarks, photos, webcams, or even Twitter posts. Thus, Google can offer a map experience containing pictures of attractions, reviews, and things to do without having to take a single picture or write a single review themselves.

Enhancing Collaboration with Social Media

Traditional office technologies, such as telephones or e-mail, are very useful to organizations; yet, such technologies are not well suited to support rich, rapid, multiple-person team collaboration. For example, the telephone is best suited for person-to-person communication; e-mail is a useful technology for teams, but it does not provide the structure needed for effective multiperson, interactive problem solving. Modern organizations need technologies that enable team members to interact through a set of media either at the same place and time or at different times and in different locations, with structure to aid in interactive problem solving and access to real-time information. The Internet and various social media applications, described next, provide many capabilities that have forever transformed the way individuals and teams can work together.

KEY PLAYERS

You, the Content Creator

In the ever-growing space of social media, many companies have found their place in their respective niche, from general-purpose social networks such as Facebook to microblogs such as Twitter to video sharing applications such as YouTube. In each niche, a few key players have emerged to become the most successful companies. These social media applications are centered around creating, sharing, or curating some form of digital content; yet, it is not the companies that do all this. Rather, in the world of social media, the user is the key player: the key to these companies' success is the network effect; as more users sign up for and use a service, the more valuable the service becomes for everyone. In the early days of social media, *Time Magazine* chose "you" as person of the year, recognizing the users' role in creating content. While the choice was not without criticism, the role of users has only gained in importance since.

As of mid-2012, Facebook was the undisputed leader in the social networking world, and its usage statistics demonstrate how valuable the users are in supporting Facebook's market hegemony. For example, in the first quarter of 2012, Facebook users uploaded 30 million photos per day, and shared more than 3.5 billion pieces of content. The power of the network effect is illustrated by the fact that Facebook's 900 million users are connected through 125 billion friend connections; given the flood of information each user receives in his or her newsfeed, it is no wonder that Facebook's users click the "Like" button 3.2 billion times per day. As more users generate, share, and like content, Facebook learns more about each individual user, and can thus better target its users with advertising. Ultimately, each Facebook user is not only Facebook's consumer, but also its product.

Likewise, LinkedIn, which has emerged as a key player in social networking for professionals, bases its success on its over 160 million users, who are connected in over one million groups. For its users, LinkedIn has become an indispensable tool for creating and maintaining their professional network, as well as an important source of information; it was estimated that in 2012, LinkedIn users would initiate 5.3 billion professionally oriented searches. For marketers looking for an audience that is relatively highly educated, influential, and affluent, LinkedIn is a treasure trove. LinkedIn's example clearly shows how the user is both consumer and product: on the one hand, using a freemium approach, LinkedIn generates revenue through professional subscriptions; on the other hand, LinkedIn is able to sell advertising space as well as hiring-related services based on the profile of its user community.

Other statistics further show the incredible contribution users have to the success of social media. Twitter has become the leader in microblogging; with over 750 tweets published per second, Twitter has become an important source of information about a variety of topics. Similarly, in mid-2012, the microblogging platform Tumblr boasted 63.6 million blogs containing 27 billion posts; it's not the 107 employees who generate this content, but the users, who, on a day in July 2012, created 69,224,951 posts.

Users of the video sharing site YouTube upload 829,000 videos per day; each minute, 72 hours of video are uploaded (including 3 hours of video per minute uploaded from mobile devices). YouTube is another prime example of not only the community creating and uploading content, but also actively participating: more than half of all videos posted on YouTube have received some response from the community in the form of ratings or comments, and every week, 100 million users engage in some form of social action. Users of the photo-sharing upstart Instagram have uploaded over 1 billion pictures, with 5 million photos being added per day. These photos generate on average 575 likes and 81 comments each second.

Together, these examples not only show the power of users creating content, but also of the network effect. The valuation of some of these companies is mindboggling, but they have found a clever way of both having the user *create their product* and *making the user* their product.

Based on:

Brown, D. (2012, June 8). 52 cool facts and stats about social media (2012 edition). *PR Daily*. Retrieved July 11, 2012, from http://www.prdaily.com/Main/Articles/52_cool_facts_and_stats_about_social_media_2012_ed_11846.aspx.

Facebook (2012). Key facts. *Facebook.com*. Retrieved July 11, 2012, from http://newsroom.fb.com/content/default.aspx?NewsAreaId=22.

Grossman, Lev (2006, December 25). You — yes, you — are TIME's person of the year. *Time Magazine*. Retrieved July 11, 2012, from http://www.time.com/time/magazine/article/0,9171,1570810,00.html.

Instagram (2012). Press center. *Instagram.com*. Retrieved July 11, 2012, from http://instagram.com/press.

LinkedIn (2012). About us. *LinkedIn.com*. Retrieved July 11, 2012, from http://press.linkedin.com/about.

Tumblr (2012) About. *Tumblr.com*. Retrieved July 11, 2012, from http://www.tumblr.com/about.

YouTube (2012). Statistics. *Youtube.com*. Retrieved July 11, 2012, from http://www.youtube.com/t/press_statistics.

TABLE 5.5 Benefits and Risks of Cloud-Based Collaboration Tools

Domain	Benefit	Risk
Information technology	Reduced costs and risks when using preexisting, easily deployed, and low-cost Web-based tools (versus in-house developed tools).	Loss of control regarding data and service quality (data and tools will likely reside on the provider's server).
Organization	Tools are easy to use, facilitating widespread adoption throughout an organization.	Little or no documentation, training, or support for system complexities or problems.
Competition	More efficient and effective than e-mail, FTP, or legacy collaboration tools, potentially speeding up product development cycles and enabling quick responses to competitors' actions.	Security and compliance policies are nearly impossible to enforce, which may increase the possibility of exposing sensitive corporate data; increased threat of industrial espionage.
Upgrade cycles	No need to purchase software upgrades.	Tools and features in the collaboration environment can change without notice, potentially causing problems with users and corporate IT strategy.

CLOUD-BASED COLLABORATION TOOLS. One key trend that has greatly facilitated collaboration is the rise of cloud computing. Traditionally, sharing and collaborating on documents was cumbersome; users typically had to e-mail documents back and forth, or had to worry about having the latest version of the software installed. **Cloud-based collaboration tools** have greatly facilitated collaboration; for example, cloud-based collaboration tools allow for easy access and easy transfer of documents or other files from one person to another; using services such as Dropbox, documents are not only stored on a user's computer, but also synced to other computers or devices via a copy of the document stored in the cloud. This way, a user can access a file from multiple devices, and always has the latest version at his or her fingertips, or collaborators can work on documents without needing to e-mail documents. Similarly, tools such as Evernote, Wunderlist, or Microsoft OneNote allow for synchronizing and sharing of notes, task lists, and the like. Cloud-based productivity suites take this concept a step further by not only storing the files in the cloud, but also enabling the access of office productivity tools from any computer (or even mobile device) with a Web browser and Internet connectivity. While this frees the user from having to locally install productivity software, using cloud-based collaboration tools requires a live Internet connection to work on shared documents, and thus users may not be able to work when traveling or when having Internet connectivity problems. Also, the applications are limited in what they can do. For example, many online spreadsheets can do only basic formulas. Table 5.5 outlines various benefits and risks of cloud-based collaboration tools.

Organizations and individuals can choose from different options for using cloud-based collaboration tools. One popular application is Google Apps, a family of cloud-based collaboration tools designed to function similarly to an offline office software suite while also allowing for easy collaboration. Google Apps include Gmail, a Web-based e-mail client allowing users to send large attachments and offering large storage space and superior filing and search capabilities; Google Calendar, a Web-based collaborative calendar that allows users to share events, send invitations to events, and subscribe to public calendars for new events (e.g., Netflix's calendar for new DVD releases); Google Talk, an instant messaging client; Google Docs, an online office suite comprised of a spreadsheet application, a word processor, and a presentation application; Google Sites, an enterprise-level collaboration tool that allows users to create group Web sites and share team information; and other tools. A variety of other providers offer similar cloud-based collaboration tools (see Table 5.6).

Given its comprehensive range of applications and its ease of use, Google Apps has been adopted by many users and organizations. Backed by Google, one of the world's most recognized companies, Google Apps are free for individual users and educational institutions and are provided on a per-user fee for commercial and governmental organizations. In fact, many

TABLE 5.6   Web-Based Collaboration Tools

Type	Names
Spreadsheets	Bad Blue, EditGrid, Google Drive, Zoho Sheet, Microsoft Office 365
Word processors	Adobe Buzzword, ThinkFree, Zoho Writer, Google Drive, ZCubes, Microsoft Office 365
Presentation	PresenterNet, Adobe Connect, Google Drive, Zoho Show, Microsoft Office 365
Office suites	eDesk Online, Zoho, Google Drive, Microsoft Office 365
Project	Trac, Redmine, eGroupWare, Collabtive
Notes/task management	Evernote, Wunderlist, Microsoft OneNote Web
Cloud storage/sharing	Dropbox, Google Drive, Microsoft SkyDrive, SugarSync

universities now use Google Apps for document sharing, communication, and collaboration. Similarly, Microsoft offers its Office 365 collaboration suite offering features such as online document sharing, instant messaging, e-mail, calendaring, or even video conferencing.

CONTENT MANAGEMENT SYSTEMS. A **content management system** allows users to publish, edit, version track, and retrieve digital content, such as documents, images, audio files, videos, or anything else that can be digitized. For example, organizations use open source content management systems such as Wordpress, Joomla, or Drupal to create blogs or Web sites; Carnival Cruise Lines uses WordPress for publishing company news, the French subsidiary of

WHO'S GOING MOBILE

Mobile Social Media

Social media seem to be made for the mobile context: mobile devices both constrain and enable ways in which people interact on the Web. On the one hand, mobile devices have limited screen sizes and often offer no physical keyboards; on the other hand, many people have their smartphone within their reach 24/7, and can post short status updates whenever, wherever. As smartphones are becoming ever more powerful, they enable more powerful apps, and users increasingly use their smartphones to create and consume multimedia content, be it sharing photographs using Facebook or Instagram or watching videos on YouTube. Having grown accustomed to consuming bite-sized content, the average length of a YouTube video of 2 minutes 46 seconds seems to be just right for being watched between two classes or two subway stations.

In the past, people spent much of their time on mobile devices playing games; in early 2012, however, this has shifted, with people now spending more time on mobile social networking than on playing games. For many people, the primary use of mobile phones is not making calls anymore; rather, people use their smartphones for everything from searching for information while on the go to social networking. One key capability of smartphones is to determine the exact location of users, enabling the convergence of social, local, and mobile (sometimes termed SoLoMo). For example, applications such as Yelp provide business listings based on a mobile user's location, along with reviews by other users. Similarly, Google Local lets mobile users search for attractions, restaurants, ATMs, and other places based on the user's location; the results are then augmented with Zagat reviews or recommendations from people the user is connected with on Google+, Google's social network. Especially for businesses that depend on local customer traffic, the combination of social networking, mobility, and location can help to better target potential customers with advertising campaigns and attract new business, as it allows targeting those who are in the vicinity, and are thus most likely to swing by to take advantage of a deal or a special offer.

Based on:

Loftus, T. (2012, April 20). New study shows boom in mobile social networking usage. *WSJ.com*. Retrieved July 11, 2012, from http://blogs.wsj.com/cio/2012/04/30/new-study-shows-boom-in-mobile-social-networking-usage.

SpeakyMagazine (2012, April 6). 24 Youtube facts and figures with infographic. *SpeakyMagazine*. Retrieved July 11, 2012, from http://www.speakymagazine.com/24-youtube-facts-and-figures-with-infographic.

Turner, J. (2012, May 17). 3 steps to determine if social local mobile is right for your business. *Social Media Examiner*. Retrieved July 11, 2012, from http://www.socialmediaexaminer.com/is-social-local-mobile-right-for-your-business/#more-18556.

FIGURE 5.18

Researchers at the University of Arizona use the Microsoft SharePoint content management system to assist in project collaboration.

Source: Courtesy University of Arizona.

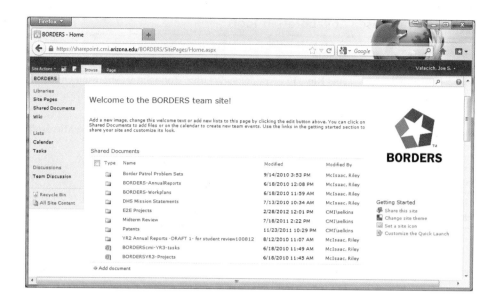

cereal manufacturer Kellogg's uses Joomla for its company Web site, and Turner Entertainment's Belgian site uses Drupal. Typically, such content management systems facilitate the creation and management of Web content by allowing the assignment of different roles for different users, such that some users can create and edit content, others can edit but not create, and yet others can only view content contained in the system. Many open source content management systems can even be used for building e-commerce sites, by incorporating functionality such as inventory management or shopping cart functionality. Yet, content management systems, also known by several other names, including digital asset management systems, document management systems, and enterprise content systems, can be used for collaboration beyond the creation and management of Web sites. For example, Microsoft SharePoint is a document management platform that can be used to host intranet sites, extranet sites, or public Web sites that enable shared workspaces and integrate other collaborative applications such as document sharing, *wikis* (discussed below) and blogs. SharePoint also includes workflow functionality such as to-do lists, discussion boards, and messaging alerts (see Figure 5.18). Because SharePoint has been designed to be easily customizable, it has been installed in a variety of businesses, which can personalize the collaborative SharePoint Web sites to meet their needs. For example, Mary Kay Cosmetics uses SharePoint to distribute product and company information to its over 30,000 Canadian beauty consultants. Microsoft also deploys its various Office products to support Web-based collaboration, where users can store, share, and collaborate on any type of Office document.

Learning Management Systems Similar to content management systems used for communication and collaboration, learning management systems such as BlackBoard, Sakai, or Moodle have facilitated business processes in educational settings. Typically, learning management systems enable uploading and viewing content, administering of exams, and self-service functions such as registering for courses or viewing grades. Increasingly, learning management systems offer additional tools for enabling team collaboration, class discussions, and the like.

PEER PRODUCTION. Another widely used Web 2.0 phenomenon is peer production. **Peer production** is the creation of goods or services by self-organizing communities. In peer production, the creation of the goods or services is dependent on the incremental contributions of the participants such that anyone can help in producing or improving the final outcome. Prime examples of peer production are open source projects (see Chapter 9, "Developing and Acquiring Information Systems") and wikis.

Wikis Ever since the inception of the online encyclopedia Wikipedia, wikis have become mainstream and are used for a variety of collaboration tasks. A **wiki** is a Web site allowing people to post, add, edit, comment, and access information. In contrast to a regular Web site, a wiki is

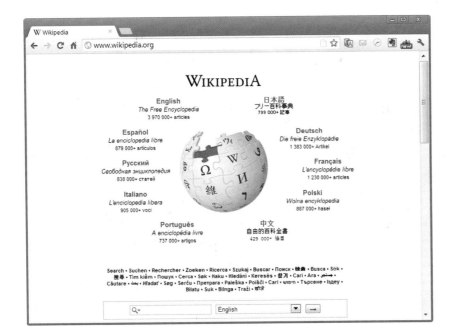

FIGURE 5.19

Wikipedia has over 22 million articles in more than 285 languages.
Source: Courtesy of Wikimedia Foundation.

linked to a database keeping a history of all prior versions and changes, and thus a wiki allows viewing prior versions of the site as well as reverting any changes made to the content. The idea behind wikis is that they allow anyone to contribute information or edit others' contributions. Whereas some wikis can be public and open to anyone who wishes to contribute, others are private so that only certain registered users can contribute. The most popular wiki is the online encyclopedia **Wikipedia**, which has over 22 million articles in 285 languages (see Figure 5.19).[1] These articles have been created by Wikipedia users, and almost any of these articles can be edited by either anonymous or registered users. By allowing easy access, Wikipedia has grown exponentially in a short amount of time. However, Wikipedia is not without its critics. Some argue that by allowing anyone to create and edit articles, a systematic bias in the content can occur. This includes the ability for users to add misinformation that is hard to verify. For example, recent news show that politicians, companies, and other entities of interest frequently edit their Wikipedia pages to portray a more positive image. Sometimes, so-called "wiki wars" arise, where contributors continuously edit or delete each others' posts. Also, Wikipedia has been found to have a significant cultural bias, as most contributors are males from either North America or Europe. Since the information is often not backed by verifiable sources, Wikipedia is not considered a credible source, and many universities discourage students from citing Wikipedia. In fact, in some instances professors have been failing students for using Wikipedia as their primary (or only) source. While a Wikipedia article may be a good starting point for researching about a topic, it is good practice to evaluate the sources used within the article, and to consult other sources as well. Wikipedia openly acknowledges this situation and encourages users to check the facts against multiple sources.

Wikis have been used for many more things than just an online encyclopedia. The ability for users to contribute and edit content has a wide variety of applications, such as designing software, helping people find media, and even helping people play video games. In fact, many organizations are using wiki technology to create internal knowledge repositories.

HUMAN-BASED COMPUTING (CROWDSOURCING). Another way individuals can collaborate with organizations is through crowdsourcing. When companies look for cheap labor, many immediately think about outsourcing work to *companies* in different countries, such as India, China, or Russia (see Chapter 1, "Managing in the Digital World"). However, companies have now found a way to use *everyday people* as a cheap labor force, a phenomenon called **crowdsourcing** (see Figure 5.20).

---

[1]Wikipedia:About. (2012, July 10). In *Wikipedia, the free encyclopedia.* Retrieved July 10, 2012, from http://en.wikipedia.org/w/index.php?title=Wikipedia:About&oldid=500845901.

FIGURE 5.20

Crowdsourcing uses everyday people from all over the world as a cheap labor force.

Source: Medioimages/Photodisc/ Thinkstock Royalty Free.

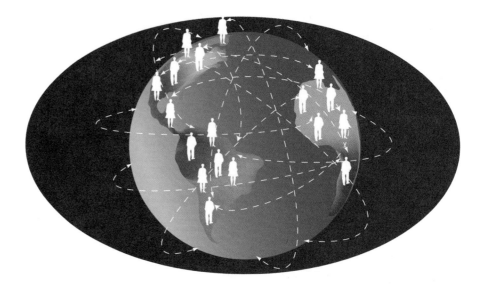

For example, up until a few years ago, book publishers such as Pearson Prentice Hall had to rely on so-called stock photography for many of a book's images; in other words, publishers had to pay large sums for pictures taken by professional photographers. Clearinghouses for stock photography had to charge high fees just to cover their expenses, as they had to purchase pictures from professional photographers. Today, high-quality digital cameras can be had for far less than US$1,000, and, with the right editing software, amateur photographers can create images that almost match those of professional photographers. Amateur photographers can upload their pictures to image sharing sites such as iStockphoto.com, where interested parties can license and download the images for US$1 to US$5 per image, which is a fraction of the price of a regular stock photo. Given that overhead costs are almost negligible, iStockphoto can make a profit while still sharing part of the revenue with the pictures' creators.

Similarly, companies are increasingly realizing that **open innovation**, or the process of integrating external stakeholders into the innovation process, can prove very beneficial. For example, pharmaceutical giant Eli Lilly created a site called InnoCentive, where companies can post scientific problems, and everybody can take a shot at solving the problem. Usually, a reward is paid to a successful solver. This way, an ad hoc research-and-development network is created, and companies have to rely less on a dedicated research-and-development department or on hiring specialists to solve a certain problem. At the same time, people can use their spare time and expertise to solve problems and earn rewards for their contributions.

Amazon.com took crowdsourcing mainstream with its mturk (mechanical turk) application. Using the mechanical turk, requesters can crowdsource so-called human intelligence tasks (HITs), which are small, self-contained tasks that humans can solve easily but would be difficult for a computer to solve. Examples of HITs include tagging images, generating potential search key words for a product, fixing product titles on e-commerce sites, and so on. Users can find HITs that are of interest to them, solve the tasks, and earn money that is credited to their Amazon.com account.

As you can see, for companies, crowdsourcing is an innovative way to reduce costs by using the expertise of the crowds. Similar to grid computing (see Chapter 3), a person's "idle time" is used for a certain business task, and many people are willing to provide their resources in exchange for a relatively small amount of money. Just imagine that you could pay for your textbooks using the money you earned from the collection of digital pictures you've taken, all for almost no extra effort. Another emerging trend is **e-lancing**. Traditionally, companies have used self-employed freelancers to work on individual projects or provide content. E-lancing takes this concept a step further by enabling people to work in more flexible ways on a variety of Internet-related projects.

Enhancing Connection with Social Media

Social media applications also aid in connecting people with each other, companies with their customers or stakeholders, or people with content. Without a doubt, social networking has become the most popular type of application in this category; we explore social networking and other, lesser-known applications in the following sections.

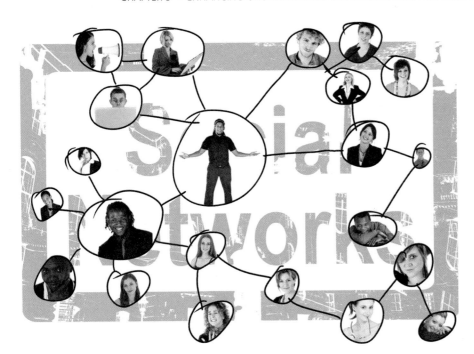

FIGURE 5.21

Individuals with a broad and diverse set of interests meet and communicate using social networks.
Source: Sean Nel/Shutterstock

SOCIAL NETWORKING. In addition to direct collaboration, **social networking** has become one of the most popular uses of the Internet over the past few years. Social networking sites create **social online communities** where individuals with a broad and diverse set of interests meet and collaborate (see Figure 5.21). Facebook.com exemplifies this trend, reaching 44 percent of global Internet users and accounting for over 5 percent of global page views (and being surpassed only by Google), according to Alexa.com. Facebook took the spot as the most frequented social network from MySpace.com, which originally was designed to be a social network based on musical interests, but then changed to a general interest social network used primarily by teens and young adults. Initially, MySpace had been so successful that in 2005 it was purchased by Rupert Murdoch's NewsCorp for US$580 million. Yet, the importance of MySpace has since declined tremendously, and in June 2011, NewsCorp sold MySpace for a mere US$35 million. Some have blamed MySpace's management for focusing too much on revenue, thus alienating users. Because of the network effect, as Facebook grew, it became ever more attractive for other people to join. In July 2012, Facebook announced that it had 900 million users, and it is still growing.

Social networks were initially largely popular among preteens, teens, and young adults, but social networking demographics have slowly shifted. Although in 2012 about 40 percent of Facebook's users were between 25 and 44 years old, 46 percent of the users were 45 years or older (onlinemba.com, 2012). In addition to general interest social networks, several social online communities are targeted at professional audiences, allowing users to meet business contacts, post career profiles, present themselves in a professional context, ask for expert advice, or be contacted regarding job opportunities. For example, LinkedIn has more than 150 million users, and Xing (which is widely popular in Europe) has more than 12 million users. Further, enterprise-oriented social software such as IBM Connections features social networking tools, allowing people within organizations to connect to one another; similarly, Yammer, part of Microsoft, is designed as a private social network for communication and collaboration within organizations. Designed to mirror consumer-oriented social media apps people are used to, applications such as Yammer are but one example of increasing consumerization of IT, where technologies and applications are first designed for the consumer marketplace and then make inroads into organizational settings.

Organizations also increasingly use social networks to connect to their customers. Numerous companies have their own Facebook pages to interact with their customers, get feedback on new products or services, or in general portray a positive brand image (similar to mobile phone applications developed by companies; see Chapter 4, "Enabling Business-to-Consumer Electronic Commerce").

ETHICAL DILEMMA

"Zucking" Up the Universe

As you're sitting in front of your most incredible lunch, you take a picture of your meal and instantaneously upload it to Facebook. As you scroll through the news feed, you see that your friend just got (or lost?) his driver's license and someone else invites you to join a house party on Saturday. Almost every aspect of our lives has become intertwined with Facebook. Although the social networking site works well for keeping in touch with people, concerns have been voiced over the possibility that Facebook is stealing the innocence from our generation.

As many people now spend more time interacting with virtual friends than interacting with people in the "real world," for many, there has been a shift in identity from the "real world" to a virtual world where the sense of self is closely linked to social media presence. In other words, as people define themselves by what others in the social media universe think of them (and how many friends they have on Facebook), they lose the sense of self. Traditionally, solitude was considered a driving force to nurturing good relationships; now, the social media world fills in that solitary absence with endless online updates, weakening our sense of self. In addition to losing that "human touch," social media can lead to narcissism and increase the need to be vain; instead of feeling good about oneself, confidence is built in status updates and picture posts. However, people should know better than to base self-assurance on such vulnerable grounds; professionals have warned that this leads to a vicious cycle: as pointed out by

entrepreneur and "professional skeptic" Andrew Keen, "The more we self-broadcast, the emptier we become and the emptier we become, the more we need to self-broadcast."

Making things worse is that with social networks becoming ubiquitous, it becomes increasingly challenging for children to grow up without being in danger of virtually exposing themselves to the entire world. In your childhood days, there was limited potential for losing your privacy (except for your "friends" revealing embarrassing secrets to others). Today, children risk losing their privacy to "Facebook parenting" (i.e., parents documenting their kids' every move during the infant and early childhood phases on Facebook) and later grow up assuming that it isn't a problem to reveal everything about themselves to the vast world of social networking. If one day Facebook becomes a normal means of attaining one's identity, and people lose their sense of what privacy entails, then our sense of self is no doubt facing the greatest crisis mankind has ever seen. Next time you feel an urge to post a picture of what you just had for breakfast, consider this: Is it more important to inform the virtual and transparent world of your every move than to enjoy quality time with the person who made the breakfast for you?

Based on:

Keen, A. (2012, May 30). Facebook threatens to 'Zuck up' the human race. *CNN*. Retrieved June 5, 2012, from http://edition.cnn.com/2012/05/30/tech/keen-technology-facebook-privacy/index.html.

SOCIAL SEARCH. As the Web has grown explosively since its early days (in the first six years, the growth rate was 850 percent, and after only 15 years, the number of Web sites was larger than 100 million; Nielsen, 2006), finding relevant information has become increasingly difficult. Early search engines such as Altavista were based on key words embedded within pages, and often tried to assemble "directories" of the Web (see http://dir.yahoo.com). In 1996, Sergey Brin and Larry Page came up with a new algorithm for Internet search. Called BackRub, the algorithm used the number of *other* pages linking to a Web page so as to return more relevant results to users; in 1998, Brin and Page founded Google (see Chapter 3). Although Google has become extremely successful, returning the most relevant results to each user is the holy grail for search engines. For Google, the optimum number of search results to be returned would be just one—the single result that perfectly answers the user's question. In order to increase the relevance of search results, search engines such as Google or Bing now offer social search functionality. **Social search** attempts to increase the relevance of search results by including content from social networks, blogs, or microblogging services. For example, a search on Bing may return relevant status updates from Facebook or Twitter; others go a step further and narrow the results to content from one's online social circle, arguing that content posted by friends is typically more relevant than content posted by complete strangers. Other social search approaches let users annotate or tag search results, making it easier for others to find relevant information; for example, Google users can recommend search results using a+1 button, helping their social circles obtain more relevant search results. This is especially valuable for enterprise search applications, where other users within an organization can tag internal documents, making it easier to find information as well as to find people who have certain information within the organization.

VIRAL MARKETING. In the offline world, marketing one's products or services is one of the most important aspects of successfully running a business. In an online context, marketing Web sites, products, and services is equally important, and business organizations use techniques such as search marketing, paid inclusion, and banner advertisements to promote their Web sites (see Chapter 4). Building on the foundations of social networking, advertisers are now using **viral marketing** to promote their Web sites, products, or services. Viral marketing is using the network effect to increase brand awareness. The term *viral marketing* was coined by Harvard business professor Jeffrey Rayport to describe how good marketing techniques can be driven by word-of-mouth or person-to-person communication, similar to how real viruses are transmitted through offline social networks. Rather than creating traditional banner ads or sending out massive amounts of spam, businesses create advertisements in a way that entices the viewers to share the message with their friends through e-mail or social networks so that the message will spread like a virus. Viral marketing can take many forms, such as video clips, e-books, flash games, and even text messages.

The power of viral marketing can be a great tool, and there are several techniques that are critical to making a successful viral marketing campaign. Writer and interaction designer Thomas Baekdal (2006) has outlined some critical factors in viral marketing, including the following:

1. Do something unexpected
2. Make people feel something
3. Make sequels
4. Allow sharing and easy distribution
5. Never restrict access to the viral content

Following these principles entices users to view content, share it with their friends, and revisit the site to look for new content. For example, BMW created a series of short films directed by popular directors. Rather than being traditional car ads, these films told stories, presenting the vehicles in a certain context. Viewers would watch the films because of the content, would share the films, and come back to the BMW films Web site to watch the next episode.

Another successful viral marketing campaign was used by Hotmail's founders during the launch of the free Hotmail e-mail service. One of the techniques involved adding a footer to every outbound message. This footer gave a short message about Hotmail.com's free e-mail service, and the message about the service was spread with every e-mail sent through the service. This campaign proved very effective (Hotmail spent only US$500,000 to get 12 million subscribers), and Microsoft later bought Hotmail.

MANAGING THE ENTERPRISE 2.0 STRATEGY

http://goo.gl/Z047Q

As you have seen, there are various tools that organizations can use for communicating with external stakeholders as well as for enhancing collaboration and connection of employees within the enterprise. In the following sections, we discuss factors to be examined when considering the use of Enterprise 2.0 tools within an organization. Then we highlight potential pitfalls brought about by these tools, when used by people within and outside an organization.

Organizational Issues

In the previous chapters, you have learned that in many cases, technology can be an important enabler of strategic advantage. Similarly, with internal Enterprise 2.0 tools, the technology is a critical success factor, but it is not the only component. Given that social media applications are based on close social interaction, information sharing, and network effects, corporate culture is key to successful Enterprise 2.0 implementations. Specifically, a corporate culture of knowledge sharing, trust, and honest feedback is conducive to Enterprise 2.0 implementations. In addition to culture, various other caveats have to be taken into consideration for any Enterprise 2.0 application (Khan, 2008) (see Figure 5.22).

ENTERPRISE≠WEB. While reading this chapter, you have learned about many Web-based technologies you are familiar with from your daily life. Although many of those technologies are hugely successful in a consumer environment, this success does not always translate to success in a corporate environment. On the Web, sites such as YouTube, Wikipedia, and Facebook have evolved

WHEN THINGS GO WRONG

Social Media Meltdown at Nestlé

In the past week, you've probably had something to eat that was made by Nestlé, the global producer of cereals, coffee, dairy, and other products. You probably know them best though for their wide range of confectionary treats like Kit Kat bars, Rolos, and anything from Willy Wonka. Life hasn't always been sweet for the company, however.

In early 2010, the environmental group Greenpeace began protesting Nestlé over their use of palm oil in some of their products. The group claimed that Nestlé was purchasing their oil from an Indonesian firm that was actively destroying vast swaths of rain forest in order to build palm oil plantations. The destruction of the rain forest, according to Greenpeace, was threatening Indonesia's orangutan population. Greenpeace's protest came in the form of a commercial (posted on YouTube) that showed an unsuspecting office worker opening a candy bar resembling a Kit Kat bar that had an orangutan finger inside. The shock parody got Nestlé's attention, and they quickly petitioned YouTube to remove the video.

The move by Nestlé to have the video taken down set off howls in the social media arena. Sites like Facebook were instantly abuzz about the orangutan story and the censorship Nestlé had imposed on the video. Although in the beginning the parody had fewer than 1,000 views on YouTube, it was picked up by other video sites and was linked to from multiple locations. Suddenly, the video was making the rounds on the Internet, and Nestlé's Facebook page was being overwhelmed with visitors decrying the company's censorship, their decision to buy palm oil from questionable suppliers, and the plight of the orangutan. Facebook posters were even changing their profile pictures to a modified Nestlé logo that read "Killer" in the Kit Kat font.

Surprisingly, instead of apologizing to their fans or explaining their position to attempt to control the growing controversy, Nestlé retaliated. On Facebook, the moderator of the page began deleting posts of protesters. A warning was posted that informed visitors to the site that although comments were welcome, any use of the company's logo would result in deleted posts. The moderator even began trading insults with users. The exchanges fueled the backlash even further, and the public relations nightmare began to snowball for Nestlé. By the time the company apologized for the online censorship and Facebook fighting, it was too late. The story had been picked up on Twitter, went viral, and quickly spread around the world.

The story is a lesson in the power of social media for all would-be public relations professionals and organizations. The global reach and lightning speed of these media allow messages, whether bitter or sweet, to spread like wildfire. Following this social media disaster, Nestlé made a commitment to eliminate deforestation from its supply chain; in 2011, 54 percent of Nestlé's palm oil came from sustainable sources, with a target of 80 percent for 2012.

Based on:

Eccleston, P. (2007, November 8). Need for cheap palm oil drives deforestation. *Telegraph.co.uk*. Retrieved July 10, 2012, from http://www.telegraph.co.uk/earth/earthnews/3313623/Need-for-cheap-palm-oil-drives-deforestation.html.

Hargrave-Silk, A. (2010, April 12). Social media blunder: Nestlé censorship fuels firestorm on Twitter and Facebook. *Campaign Asia*. Retrieved July 10, 2012, from http://www.campaignasia.com/Article/213070,social-media-blunder-nestle-censorship-fuels-firestorm-on-twitter-and-facebook.aspx.

Nestlé (2012). Combating deforestation. *Nestle.com*. Retrieved July 12, 2012, from http://www.nestle.com/csv/ruraldevelopment/sourcingoverview/Combatingdeforestation/Pages/Combatingdeforestation.aspx.

Titsworth, J. (2010, April 27). Nestlé, palm oil and social media, oh my! *Searchenginejournal.com*. Retrieved July 10, 2012, from http://www.searchenginejournal.com/nestle-palm-oil-and-social-media-oh-my/20400.

Toor, A. (2010, March 22). Nestlé's palm oil PR crisis pervades Facebook. *Switched.com*. Retrieved July 10, 2012, from http://www.switched.com/2010/03/22/nestles-palm-oil-pr-crisis-pervades-facebook.

over the years to become as successful as they are today, and examples such as MySpace show that success at one point in time is not guaranteed to continue. Further, what appears as seamless "magic" collaboration is sometimes based on intricate processes. For example, good articles in Wikipedia are based not only on the contributions of many editors, but also on many behind-the-scenes discussions over controversial issues or over how to improve an article. In contrast, many open source software projects closely guard changes to the software's programming code such that only a limited number of "committers" can actually implement suggested changes.

CULTURE. As highlighted earlier, organizational culture is a critical Enterprise 2.0 success factor, and many proposed projects face strong cultural resistance. Enterprise 2.0 applications, based on the premise of open communication, do not always do well within traditional top-down organizational structures based on rigid hierarchies and control. Further, social media applications base their success on user-driven self-expression (if no one were willing to update

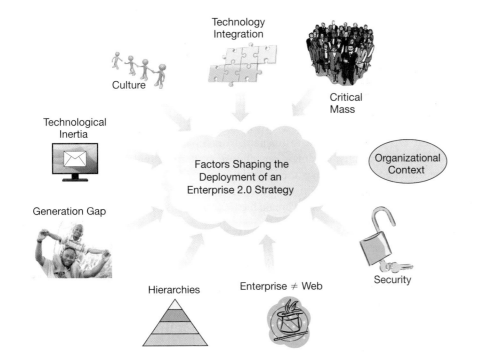

FIGURE 5.22

Various factors have to be taken into account for successful Enterprise 2.0 applications.

his or her status on Facebook, people would eventually stop visiting the site); on the Web, people participate by choice, but people in organizations cannot be forced to participate. Hence, organizations have to understand the multiple stakeholders, personalities, and perspectives of future users and ensure that any Enterprise 2.0 initiative will appeal to the organization's members.

ORGANIZATIONAL CONTEXT. Any implementation of Enterprise 2.0 applications should be driven by a specific usage context. Just as users choose popular social media applications such as YouTube or Wikipedia to fulfill a particular need, the work-related context should drive the choice of Enterprise 2.0 tools. In other words, organizations should always ask what objective is to be accomplished with the tool and only then decide which type of tool to implement. Merely setting up a wiki site and hoping that the employees will use it for the "right" purpose most likely will not lead to the intended results.

ORGANIZATIONAL HIERARCHIES. Often, Enterprise 2.0 initiatives are driven by user departments, and small-scale pilot implementations appear to work quite well. However, organization-wide Enterprise 2.0 implementations typically need changes in terms of organizational culture and processes, and often the flattening of organizational hierarchies. Therefore, to be successful, Enterprise 2.0 implementations need the support and active involvement of senior management so as to cope with the large magnitude of changes.

NETWORK EFFECTS AND CRITICAL MASS. Successful social media applications such as Wikipedia base their success on network effects and the Long Tail (see Chapter 4), and have needed some time to achieve a critical mass. For example, although Wikipedia enjoys millions of page views per day, there is only a small number of people who choose to actively participate in the creation of content. Within organizations, achieving the critical mass needed for an Enterprise 2.0 application is often difficult and takes considerable time and patience. Although for many smaller organizations collaborative Enterprise 2.0 tools can be beneficial, they will most likely not be able to harness the network effects that can be achieved with a larger user base.

GENERATION GAP. The success of an Enterprise 2.0 initiative is also heavily dependent on the composition of the organization's workforce. In organizations with high numbers of millennials, who have grown accustomed to highly interactive and communicative online social environments, Enterprise 2.0 initiatives have a higher likelihood of success; in contrast, many baby boomers are used to rigid hierarchies and organizational structures and are less likely to fully embrace the capabilities of Enterprise 2.0 tools. Further, senior organizational members may not fully grasp the potential and implications of social media applications in organizational settings.

TECHNOLOGICAL INERTIA. One factor hindering the adoption of many new technologies is technological inertia. In many cases, people are not willing to switch to new applications unless they see real, tangible benefits. This can be especially a hindrance with social media applications, many of which incorporate a variety of other tools (such as chat or message interfaces within social networking sites).

TECHNOLOGICAL INTEGRATION. Organizations will have to ensure that any Enterprise 2.0 applications are integrated well with the organization's existing information systems infrastructure so as to reap the greatest benefits from connecting people and connecting people with information. Typically, organizations choose systems provided by outside vendors such as Ning or Yammer, which allows the organization to create its own private social network. However, organizational users will use the tools they are used to as a benchmark, and public domain tools such as Facebook often create high expectations of usability for any internal tool.

SECURITY. A final issue is related to security and intellectual property. For organizations, securing their information systems infrastructure is of paramount concern (see Chapter 10). Any application that allows closer collaboration by increasing data sharing will necessarily incur greater risks of security breaches. Companies thus have to balance their desire for enhancing collaboration with the need to protect intellectual property and compliance with rules and regulations such as the Sarbanes-Oxley Act.

Pitfalls of Web 2.0 Marketing

Many organizations (and individuals) have learned painful lessons from public relations blunders and from not considering the fundamental rule: The Internet never forgets. Another fundamental rule brought about by social media applications is to constantly monitor social media and quickly and appropriately react to emerging issues. In this section, we highlight potential pitfalls of marketing using social media applications.

ONLINE PRODUCT REVIEWS. Online as well as offline consumers increasingly consult the Web before making a purchase decision. When making a purchase on Amazon.com, many potential buyers first consult the user reviews; relatedly, people read other travelers' reviews of hotels or restaurants on Tripadvisor.com, or consult Web sites dedicated to providing expert reviews. Unfortunately, such reviews are not always as unbiased as they seem; and sometimes, companies hire people to deliberately spread positive word-of-mouth across a variety of sites. Needless to say, the act of posting fake product reviews is unethical, to say the least. For companies operating globally, this is becoming even more problematic. For example, in China, where reviews are often posted by the millions, consulting the Web for advice is even more common, especially among online shoppers. As with the products being offered, fakes are a problem with product reviews as well. In fact, Chinese Internet marketing companies employ legions of people who do nothing but post positive comments about a client—and negative comments about competitors. To make matters even worse, a number of Internet marketing companies specialize in removing negative posts about their clients, usually by bribing forum managers or administrators. Fees for removing a negative post can be as high as US$1,500, depending on how urgent the request is or how popular the Web site or post is; for the companies paying for having negative posts removed, this is considered a regular advertising expense (Jiao, 2010). Companies operating globally should certainly be aware of such practices, and adjust their strategies accordingly.

MICROBLOGGING. Whereas **microblogging** can be very valuable for corporate communications, it has to be used carefully and is not without controversy. For example, in mid-2010, Utah's attorney general announced an impending execution on Twitter with the post, "I just gave the go ahead to Corrections Director to proceed with Gardner's execution. May God grant him the mercy he denied his victims," which was seen as distasteful by many observers and quickly made worldwide news. In the aftermath of BP's Gulf of Mexico oil spill disaster, a person frustrated with the oil giant's response to the spill set up a satirical Twitter account named "BP Public Relations (BPGlobalPR)," posting tweets such as "Cleaning up oil spills is expensive. Buying judges so we can keep drilling? Relatively cheap." BPGlobalPR became immensely popular, with over 178,000 followers, dwarfing BP's official account with 16,000 followers. Needless to say, BP soon found out about this account and asked the account holder to modify the account so as to make it clearer that the account was satirical. However, by that time, the satirical site had already gained much attention from the press, and the oil giant's attempt to deal with the mock account further tarnished its image.

For individuals, posting the wrong "tweets" can also have serious consequences, as they are more likely than not to reach the wrong readers—sooner or later. A Chicago woman was recently sued by her landlord for posting a tweet complaining about the management company's reaction to mold in her apartment. The management company sued her for defamation, arguing that the tweet was published on a global scale. Whereas the lady had a mere 22 followers on Twitter, the landlord's lawsuit was covered in major news outlets, online and offline, including the *Chicago Tribune,* the Associated Press, and the *New York Times.*

SOCIAL NETWORKS. While free to host, having a page on a social network is not free for organizations—the company should take great care to monitor what is happening on the page and take appropriate action. For example, Starbucks lets its customers upload their favorite Starbucks-related pictures to its Facebook page. However, people frequently post unrelated pictures, play pranks with the company logo, or post otherwise inappropriate content. A company then has to walk the fine line of removing inappropriate content to preserve the company's image while not alienating its fans. Starbucks chooses to liberally allow unrelated content.

As with most social software, posting the "wrong" content can quickly get you in trouble. Companies routinely check social networking sites before making hiring decisions, and many applicants have lost a job offer they almost had secured. Similarly, your posts may make it farther than you think; stories abound of people getting laid off after ranting about their jobs and their bosses in Facebook status updates—unfortunately, the boss was in the employee's contacts list and could immediately see the post. Further, many people never bother to adjust their accounts' privacy settings and inadvertently shout things out for the whole world to read. To see the extent of what people post on Facebook, try a search on sites such as http://www.openstatussearch.com; you'd be surprised by what you find out.

BAD VIBES GOING VIRAL. As with other social media, viral marketing can be a blessing or a nightmare (see also "When Things go Wrong: Nestlé's Social Media Meltdown"). In 2008, a musician on a tour witnessed from his airplane window how baggage handlers mishandled—and broke—his US$3,500 guitar. After not getting a satisfying response from the airline, the musician decided to write a song and post it on YouTube in 2009. The video quickly went viral, and the airline rushed to "make things right" for the musician. For the airline, however, the damage was done, and as of mid-2010, the video had already over 8 million views. Domino's Pizza faced a similar disaster in 2009, when two employees played not-so-harmless pranks and filmed each other preparing sandwiches with disgusting ingredients. After the videos were posted on YouTube, they quickly went viral and attracted more than a million viewers in just a few days. Domino's was initially slow in responding and decided not to respond to the crisis, fearing that a reaction may draw even more interest. After 48 hours, however, Domino's changed its strategy, opened a Twitter account to interact with concerned customers, and posted a video response by the president of Domino's on YouTube assuring that the culprits had been found, that the entire store had been closed and sanitized, and that everything would be done to avoid hiring the "wrong" people in the future. A nationwide survey by a media research company has found the response to be fairly successful, with over 90 percent of the respondents indicating that the response video was effective in restoring trust in the brand.

LESSONS LEARNED. As you probably know from your own experience and have seen from these stories, news travels fast in social media. For the companies in question, this is an enormous threat, as negative publicity can quickly reach millions of people. At the same time, the company's reaction is equally critical, as it can reach people just as fast and thus has to be carefully crafted. Richard Levick, president of Levick Strategic Communications, has provided some tips on how to prepare for and deal with such crises:

1. Identify a crisis team including members from within your organization (e.g., public relations or executive team) and from the outside (e.g., lawyers).
2. Identify your worst social media nightmare (and make sure to know the signs to look for, such as search engine key words your opposition could use).
3. Monitor your social media environment (such as YouTube, Facebook, and Twitter) and be connected and responsive.
4. Act fast. The first 24 hours count.

As in the offline world, companies should try to avoid such crises in the first place, but being prepared for a public relations disaster is crucial in today's fast-paced world. Many organizations have realized the need for social media monitoring; for example, Dell recently opened its "Social Media Listening Command Center" as a key part of their overall marketing efforts. Monitoring social media posts mentioning Dell in about a dozen languages enables Dell not only to respond to customers' problems before they go viral, but also serves as an effective means to gather business intelligence. We will discuss more about the role of social media monitoring and business intelligence in Chapter 8, "Strengthening Business-To-Business Relationships Via Supply Chain and Customer Relationship Management."

INDUSTRY ANALYSIS

Online Travel

Spring break is coming, and you've decided to go to Puerto Vallarta this year. Chances are that your first step will be to check the Web sites of Expedia, Priceline, Travelocity, and Orbitz for flights to and hotels in your chosen destination.

We all know the big four online travel agencies (OTAs). In today's digital world, they dominate the travel industry. They took the old brick-and-mortar travel industry and turned it into an online service where you can click to book flights and hotel reservations, change or cancel flights, reserve rental cars—even plan a vacation. In Internet terms, you can think of the big four as still being in Online Travel 1.0. But technology marches relentlessly on, and Online Travel 2.0 is in the works.

Travel service providers—airlines, hotels, and car rental companies—and travel customers pay fees to online travel agencies. And travel service providers selling through OTAs do not have the opportunity to build customer relationships. Therefore, some providers, including JetBlue and InterContinental Hotels, would rather have customers book directly from them. That way, they (and their customers) avoid OTA fees, and they are better able to satisfy customers since they can provide up-to-the-minute information.

Enter Online Travel 2.0—the travel search engines. They don't book travel services for you, but they locate and list URLs for hundreds of suppliers, and when you choose one, you can then click the link to the supplier's Web site. Travel search engines that are becoming increasingly popular with online consumers include Kayak, Vayama, Mobissimo, Yahoo! Travel, Google Flights, and Skyscanner. Some sites, such as the flight search engine Hipmunk, combine search functionality with innovative visualizations of the results, helping the users to navigate the tradeoffs between price, duration, number of layovers, and so on.

If you want to book a travel package, especially to an international destination, OTAs may be the best choice. But if you can navigate travel services yourself or want to deal directly with travel service providers, travel search engines can fill the bill.

More recently, a new trend is emerging. Following the retail industry, the travel sector is turning to mobile. Consumers increasingly choose mobile travel sites and applications so as to be able to book flights or hotel rooms, rent cars, or access information from anywhere at any time. For example, 12 million travelers booked travel using mobile devices in 2011 (the number is forecast to increase to 36 million by 2016), and in the first quarter of 2012, almost 10 percent of hotel bookings at Orbitz.com were made using mobile devices. Needless to say, travel and mobile devices are natural partners. Most major airlines offer smartphone apps, allowing users to book flights, check in, or receive mobile boarding passes in the form of QR codes; in addition, customers can get immediate notifications in case of flight delays. Other smartphone applications such as "Hotel Tonight" let users reserve hotel rooms at the last minute. In the future, we are likely to see many more useful applications combining contextual information such as location, time, and so on with increased mobility.

Questions:

1. Do you use online travel agencies for assisting you with travel plans? If so, which service provider do you use, and why did you make this choice? If not, why not?
2. Forecast the future of traditional travel agencies. How can travel agencies use social media to attract and retain customers?

Based on:

eMarketer (2012, April 17). Mobile use spurs digital travel sales. *eMarketer.com*. Retrieved July 12, 2012, from http://www.emarketer.com/Article.aspx?R=1008979.

King, D. (2012, June 26). Bookings via mobile soar. *Travel Weekly*. Retrieved July 12, 2012, from http://www.travelweekly.com/Travel-News/Online-Travel/Bookings-via-mobile-apps-soar.

Smith, B. (2006, April 27). Yahoo's FareChase: The stealth disruptor? *SearchEngineWatch*. Retrieved July 12, 2012, from http://searchenginewatch.com/searchday/article.php/3601971.

Stambor, Z. (2010, January 11). Mobile flying high in the online travel industry. *Internet Retailer*. Retrieved July 12, 2012, from http://www.internetretailer.com/2010/01/11/mobile-is-flying-high-in-the-online-travel-industry.

Key Points Review

1. *Explain organizations' needs for communication and collaboration.* In today's increasingly competitive world, organizations need to communicate and collaborate effectively and efficiently within and outside organizational boundaries. For example, different organizational locations or subunits need to share information, and companies have to communicate and collaborate with suppliers as well as customers. In addition, virtual teams, composed of team members located around the globe that are forming and disbanding as needed, have communication needs that often cannot be met by traditional communication media.

2. *Explain social media and Enterprise 2.0.* In contrast to traditional Web 1.0 sites, Web 2.0 applications allow people to collaborate and share information online. One of the basic concepts associated with Web 2.0 is a shift in the users' role from passive consumer of content to creator. Many Web 2.0 applications take the form of mashups, pulling data or functionality from various sources using Web APIs. Based on core values such as social sharing and collaboration, many successful Web 2.0 applications can be classified as social software that people widely use for communicating and socializing. One major benefit of social software is that it can help to harness the wisdom of the crowd by leveraging the collective intelligence of large groups of people. Owing to societal changes, using social media can be an important factor in being able to attract or retain employees as younger generations (who grew up using social software) are joining the workforce. Future Web capabilities extending Web 2.0 are the semantic Web, as well as the "contextual Web," which is characterized by devices providing the information and content needed depending on the user's specific context (such as time, location, and so on). To harness the opportunities brought about by these changes, organizations are increasingly using social software to connect with customers and internal or external stakeholders in order to become more innovative or productive.

3. *Describe traditional technologies to support communication and collaboration.* Organizations have long used tools for synchronous and asynchronous communication, such as e-mail, groupware systems, videoconferencing, and the like; in addition, intranets have become indispensable for enabling internal communication and collaboration, providing for real-time access to information, enterprise search, and collaboration functionalities.

4. *Describe various social media applications, and explain their role in enhancing communication, collaboration, cooperation, and connection.* Social software can enhance communication within organizations as well as between an organization and its stakeholders. Blogs, made up of chronological entries that comment on virtually any topic of interest to the author, are widely used by individuals and organizations to communicate with internal and external stakeholders. Microblogging tools allow sending relatively short status updates to one's followers. Instant messaging (or online chat) is used mainly for synchronous internal communication as well as for sales and customer support functions. Virtual worlds can be used to showcase products or hold rich interactive communication. Social media applications facilitating cooperation depend on the network effect to provide the greatest benefit to users. Media sharing applications allow people and organizations to share images, videos, slide shows, or podcasts with others. Social bookmarking allows users to share and categorize Internet bookmarks, which can be helpful in organizational knowledge management efforts. Similarly, social cataloging helps to categorize and share academic citations and information about books, music, and so on. Tagging refers to manually adding metadata to a piece of information such as a map, picture, or Web page, thus describing the content for others and making it searchable. Further, social media applications have enabled new forms of collaboration for organizations and individuals. These and other technologies have enabled cloud-based collaboration tools and content management systems. The users are central to the new Web environment and are no longer passive viewers of information. As the Web has evolved, individuals can now generate content using several methods, such as wikis, which are Web sites in which people can post, edit, comment, and access information. The idea behind wikis is that they allow anyone to contribute information or edit prior contributions. Another emerging topic is crowdsourcing, or the use of everyday people as a cheap labor force. Finally, social media applications aid in connecting people with each other. For individuals, social networking has become an important way to meet new friends, connect with family members, or meet new colleagues and business partners. Similarly, organizations use social networks for internal connections as well as to connect with their customers. Social search incorporates blog posts, status updates, and other information from people within and outside a person's social network so as to supplement generic search results and enhance the relevance of the search results. The reach of social networks is also used by business organizations to market their products

or services through viral marketing. Viral marketing resembles offline word-of-mouth communication, in which advertising messages are spread like viruses through social networks.

5. **Describe how companies can manage their Enterprise 2.0 strategy and deal with potential pitfalls associated with social media.** Social media applications can be an important enabler for organizations. However, organizations have to take into account that success in a consumer environment does not necessarily translate into corporate environments. Further, organizations have to take into account issues associated with culture, organizational context, and organizational hierarchies; further, lack of critical

mass, the generation gap, and technological inertia can hinder the success of Enterprise 2.0 initiatives. Finally, in organizational contexts, integration with existing technologies and security are of primary concern. As organizations can use social software for communicating with customers and viral marketing, an organization's opponents can use the same tools to spread damaging content or information to people all over the world within a very short time. Organizations should therefore plan for such incidents by identifying a crisis team, identifying crisis scenarios, monitoring the social media environment, and acting fast in case a crisis surfaces in the social media environment.

Key Terms

"amateurization" of journalism 224
asynchronous 218
blog 223
blogging 223
blogosphere 225
cloud-based collaboration tools 232
collaboration 212
collective intelligence 215
content management system 233
crowdsourcing 235
desktop videoconferencing 221
discussion forum 218
e-lancing 236
electronic meeting system (EMS) 220
employee portal 223
Enterprise 2.0 218
folksonomy 228
geotagging 230

groupware 218
instant messaging 225
mashup 214
metadata 229
microblogging 242
microblogging tools 225
network effect 226
open innovation 236
peer production 234
podcast 227
podcasting 227
Real Simple Syndication (RSS) 227
semantic Web 217
social bookmarking 228
social cataloging 229
social enterprise 218
social media 215
social networking 237

social online communities 237
social presence tools 225
social search 238
social software 215
synchronous 218
tag cloud 230
tagging 229
viral marketing 239
virtual meeting 213
virtual team 213
virtual world 226
Web API 214
Web 2.0 213
webcam 221
webcast 227
webcasting 227
wiki 234
Wikipedia 235

Review Questions

1. What are virtual teams, and how do they help to improve an organization's capabilities?
2. List some of the business-related benefits of social media.
3. What capabilities will define the Web of the future?
4. Compare Web 1.0 with Web 2.0. Explain why users are moving to the latter.
5. Why is using social media an important factor for attracting and retaining employees?
6. List some of the business benefits of blogging.
7. What is blogging, and why are blogs sometimes controversial?
8. List some of the benefits of groupware.
9. What is the network effect?
10. How can social bookmarking and social cataloging help in an organization's knowledge management efforts?
11. What is tagging, and how are organizations using it in their Web sites?

12. What is the difference between Twitter and instant messaging?
13. Explain what is meant by crowdsourcing and how the Web is enabling this form of collaboration.
14. What is social search, and how is it different from a regular Web search?
15. What is the role of a content management system? How does it help organizations in gaining a competitive advantage?
16. List some of the benefits and limitations of cloud-based collaboration tools.
17. Why do companies build Web services, widgets, and mashups?
18. How can organizations plan for social media disasters?

Self-Study Questions

1. Collective intelligence is based on the notion that distributed groups of people with a divergent range of information and expertise will be able to outperform the capabilities of _____.
   A. crowds
   B. customers
   C. individual experts
   D. virtual teams

2. Microblogging tools are used for _____.
   A. creating an online text diary
   B. providing location information
   C. short status updates
   D. customer support functions

3. Tagging is adding _____ to a piece of information such as a map, picture, or Web page.
   A. metadata
   B. comments
   C. blogs
   D. knowledge

4. The process of adding information such as latitude and longitude to pictures, videos, or other information is called _____.
   A. flagging
   B. posting
   C. geotagging
   D. tagging

5. Successful Enterprise 2.0 implementations consider _____.
   A. organizational culture
   B. organizational hierarchies
   C. technological inertia
   D. all of the above

6. _____ is the process of creating an online diary made up of chronological entries.
   A. Wikiing
   B. Tagging
   C. Blogging
   D. None of the above

7. Webcasts are also known as _____.
   A. podcasts
   B. blogcasts
   C. radiocasts
   D. blogging

8. RSS allows you to _____.
   A. publish a video blog
   B. publish current news stories
   C. subscribe to updates to content
   D. edit a Webcast

9. Wikis are a type of Web site where people can _____.
   A. post information
   B. comment on information
   C. access information
   D. all of the above

10. _____ communication is when people are all meeting at the same time or in real-time.
    A. Synchronous
    B. Asynchronous
    C. Collaboration
    D. None of the above

Answers are on page 249.

Problems and Exercises

1. Match the following terms with the appropriate definitions:
   i. Microblogging tools
   ii. Asynchronous
   iii. Metadata
   iv. Social networking
   v. Peer production
   vi. Social software
   vii. Webcasts
   viii. Folksonomy
   ix. Network effect
   x. Blogging

   a. Web 2.0 applications allowing people to communicate, interact, and collaborate in various ways
   b. Digital media streams that can be distributed to and played by digital media players
   c. The creation of goods or services by self-organizing communities
   d. The notion that the value of a network (or tool or application based on a network) is dependent on the number of other users
   e. User-created categorization system
   f. The process of creating an online text diary made up of chronological entries
   g. Data about data
   h. Tools enabling people to voice their thoughts using relatively short "status updates"
   i. Using Web-based services to link friends or colleagues
   j. Not coordinated in time

2. Visit popular social online communities (such as Facebook). What features entice you to visit such sites over and over again? Do you have an account in an online community? If yes, why? If no, what is keeping you from having such account? Is there any content you definitely would or would not post on such page?

3. Go to the Web site Programmable Web (www.programmableweb.com). List some interesting mashups you find. What factors do you think make a good mashup Web site?

4. Go to Amazon's Mechanical Turk Web site (www.mturk.com). Which of the HITs do you think could be completed using a computer, and which could not? Why?

5. Search the Web for a social networking site that you have not heard about before. Describe the users of this social online community. Are the features of this site different from those you are familiar with? If so, describe those features. If not, describe common features.

6. Visit Google Drive (drive.google.com) and Microsoft Office Web Apps (office.microsoft.com). Compare and contrast the features of each productivity suite. Which suite would you choose to use, and why?

7. Search the Web to identify the key success parameters for popular social networking Web sites. Identify who is taking the lead and in what areas.

8. Find an article you can contribute to on a wiki page. What do you like or dislike about this process? What would encourage you to contribute more to the wiki? Why?

9. Study social Web sites like Facebook and Twitter to determine how business organizations are using them to their advantage. Draw lessons for your own organization.

10. Describe an application or service you would like to be able to use on the Web today that is not yet available. Describe the potential market for this application or service. Forecast how long you believe it will take before this will occur.

11. Search the Web for public relations blunders involving social software. How did the companies in question react? In your opinion, were the reactions effective? Why or why not?

12. Have you listened to or watched a webcast (or podcast)? If so, describe your experience. If not, why?

13. Describe various social media applications and explain their role in enhancing communication, collaboration, cooperation, and connection.

14. Forecast the future of traditional travel agencies. How can travel agencies use social media to attract and retain customers?

Application Exercises

Note: The existing data files referenced in these exercises are available on the book's Web site: www.pearsonhighered.com/valacich.

**Spreadsheet Application:
Online Versus Traditional Spreadsheets**

Campus Travel is currently evaluating the possibility of using an online spreadsheet as opposed to the traditional locally installed spreadsheet. There are a variety of issues involved in this decision. The company wants you to investigate the possibilities that are currently available while also paying special attention to the company requirements. Campus Travel has the following requirements: (1) the ability to share spreadsheets easily, (2) the ability to secure this information, (3) the ability to save the spreadsheets into other forms (i.e., CSV files), and (4) the ability to do work from anywhere in the world. Prepare the following information:

1. On the Internet, find different options for online and traditional spreadsheets and list the available options.

2. Using the company requirements, list the pros and cons for each spreadsheet option.

3. Using an online spreadsheet, summarize the findings and provide a recommendation to the company. Present your findings with tables and/or graphs, if available.

**Database Application:
Tracking Web Site Visits**

As Campus Travel expands its Web presence, the importance of tracking what the competitors are doing has become very important. This includes making sure Campus Travel tracks the prices of packages and services that its closest competitor offers. To do so, a database must be created to track this information. Follow these steps to create the database:

1. Create a database called "tracking."

2. Create a table called "company_info." In this table, create fields for company_name and company_URL.

3. Create a table called "products." In this table, create fields for the company_name, product_name, product_description, product_price, and date_retrieved.

4. Create a table called "services." In this table, create fields for company_name, service_name, service description, service_price, and date_retrieved.

5. Once these tables are created, go to the relationship view (select "Relationships" under the "Database Tools" tab) and connect the company_info (one side) and products (many side) tables and the company_info (one side) and service (many side) tables.

6. Make sure that when you create the relationships, the referential integrity option is selected. (This will make sure that when you delete a company, the products associated with the company are also deleted.)

7. Test the referential integrity by adding data to the tables and make sure that when a company is deleted in the company table, the products table is updated too.

Team Work Exercise

 Net Stats:
Most Popular Facebook Fan Pages

More and more organizations have discovered Facebook as a way to connect with their customers and drive word-of-mouth advertising. Any company can create a Facebook page containing basic information about the business, a "wall" to share content, a space for uploading photos or pictures (many organizations use this to show "behind-the-scenes" content), and so on. Further, businesses can add apps (such as an app that allows customers to make a reservation at a restaurant) to further engage with their customers.

Facebook users who "like" a page automatically receive the business's status updates in their news feeds. As the liking of a page is announced to others in the user's news feed and his or her profile, the liking of the page can spread throughout the user's network of friends. Further, each business's page has a listing of all Facebook users who like the page. What businesses are liked by most Facebook users? As of July 12, 2012, the top 10 most-liked product pages were the following:

Rank	Page	Likes
1	Facebook for Every Phone	109,633,702
2	Facebook	69,407,098
3	Texas Holdem Poker	62,953,967
4	YouTube	60,435,402
5	Rihanna	58,701,595
6	The Simpsons	53,152,058
7	Shakira	52,685,540
8	Lady Gaga	52,666,640
9	Michael Jackson	50,697,698
10	Harry Potter	48,515,014

The first non-entertainment related page (besides Facebook) was Coca-Cola, with 44,950,392 likes.

Questions and Exercises

1. Search the Web for the most up-to-date statistics. Try to find the number of "likes" for pages that interest you most.
2. As a team, interpret these numbers. What is striking/important about these statistics?
3. How have the numbers changed since July 2012? Which categories seem to draw most attention in social networks? Why?
4. Using your spreadsheet software of choice, create a graph/figure most effectively visualizing the statistics/changes you consider most important.

Based on:
Facebook: Browse pages. Retrieved July 12, 2012, from https://www.facebook.com/directory/pages/.

Answers to the Self-Study Questions

1. C, p. 215	2. C, p. 225	3. A, p. 229	4. C, p. 230	5. D, p. 241
6. C, p. 223	7. A, p. 227	8. C, p. 227	9. D, p. 234	10. A, p. 218

CASE 1   Digg.com: The Rise and Fall of a Social Media Giant

Submit a news story or link to Digg.com, and if site users like it (i.e., "dig" it), the story moves to the front page. If the story proves unpopular, site users vote to "bury" it, and it disappears.

In October 2004, Kevin Rose, a former regular on the TechTV show *The Screen Savers,* and his friends Owen Byrne, Ron Gorodetzky, and Jay Adelson began playing around with the idea of a user-controlled, community-based news Web site. They launched the site on December 5, 2004, and it immediately began drawing visitors. The original design was advertisement free, but that has changed since Google AdSense was added to the site.

At one point, Digg had so many users that "digging" a news story or Web link posting could cause a phenomenon called the "Digg effect," whereby increased traffic to a linked Web site would cause it to either slow considerably or even crash. According to Compete.com, in May 2007 Digg attracted more unique visitors than Facebook, and attracted over 500 million unique visitors in its heyday in 2009.

In May 2007, when the Advanced Access Content System Consortium objected to Digg posts containing encryption-breaking code for HD-DVD and Blu-ray disks, management heeded advice from attorneys and took the offending articles and posts down. A user revolt followed that prompted Digg's Kevin Rose to post a comment that reversed direction: "We hear you, and effective immediately we won't delete stories or comments containing the code and will deal with whatever the consequences might be. If we lose, then what the hell, at least we died trying."

Yet, Digg's popularity has since dwindled, partly due to the following:

- The site gave users too much control over content, resulting in misinformation and sensationalism.
- Companies paying for submissions have skewed the site's original purpose.

- The site's operators, which were its founders, exerted too much control over front-page and forum content.
- The "bury" option was seen as undemocratic because those who vote to bury an item are allowed to remain anonymous (during its history, Digg removed the "bury" button, but reintroduced it in 2010).
- The site was too susceptible to "gaming"—to groups or Web site operators who deliberately tried to dictate content.

In 2009, Digg.com introduced the "Digg-Bar" to its Web site. The DiggBar was a toolbar that appeared at the top of the Digg home page that acted as a URL shortener. When a link was submitted to Digg, its URL was automatically shortened and prefixed with "www.digg.com." When a link was clicked by a user, instead of going to the corresponding Web site, the page appeared inside a framed Digg.com window. Using the DiggBar, users had immediate access to features such as sharing Digg links via e-mail or social media sites like Facebook or Twitter. In addition, users could instantly see what other Digg users had commented about on the story, check out related stories, and see the analytics surrounding the number of people that visited the link.

However, not long after the DiggBar's introduction, backlash from the Web community began to make news. Criticism of the toolbar centered around the way shortened URLs started with a Digg domain prefix. Links that normally opened a page at another domain (thereby giving that Web site a "hit" to statistics counters) opened in a frame and stayed within the Digg environment. Since the use of DiggBar was not optional, millions of potential lost "hits" were at stake. Web site owners and operators made an outpouring of negative feedback to Digg. Within a month of launch, Digg changed the way the toolbar operated and made it an opt-in for all

unregistered users, disabling the URL shortening and framing features.

The year 2009 also marked the year that cybercriminals used Digg to try to turn a profit. To set their trap, scammers loaded Digg with headlines promising readers a view of leaked personal celebrity videos. Once the reader followed the headline link, they were presented with a software download for viewing the videos. What actually installed on the unknowing user's computer was a program that supposedly scanned for malicious software. The bogus program, a type of malware, reported back serious problems found on the computer and offered to fix the issues for a small fee. To make the deception more realistic, the malware prevented the user's computer from operating correctly. Although it was unknown how many people fell into this trap, at least 50 user accounts were determined to be participating in the scam. Digg has since terminated over 300 user accounts suspected of spreading malicious software.

In April 2010, Digg's co-founder Jay Adelson left Digg. In August 2010, Digg tried to remain on top of the social networking world with a major redesign and update of the Digg.com home page. Yet, the redesign got off to a rocky start, and was fraught with problems. In March 2011, Kevin Rose, the other mastermind behind Digg, followed Adelson in leaving the company. Digg has never regained its prominent position, and, as of May 2012, had a meager 1.86 million unique visitors, 56 percent less than in May 2011. In July 2012, Digg was sold for a mere US$500,000, demonstrating that even social media giants are not immune from falling. Only six weeks after New-York-based company Betaworks purchased Digg, it released a completely reengineered site, complete with features such as improved integration with other social media sites such as Facebook and Twitter. Time will tell whether this revamp will be a success.

Questions:

1. What are the positives and negatives to a news site that organizes its stories using user input?
2. Can you imagine a similar fate happening to other social media sites such as Facebook? Why or why not?
3. What may be the next social media giant?

Based on:

Anonymous. (2009, March 5). Malware being distributed through comments and posts on Digg and YouTube. *PCHubs.com.* Retrieved July 12, 2012, from http://www.pchubs.com/blogs/malware-being-distributed-through-comments-and-posts-on-digg-and-youtube.

Anonymous. (2009, April 4). Digg launches the DiggBar. *Techtree.com.* Retrieved July 12, 2012, from http://www.techtree.com/India/News/Digg_launches_the_DiggBar/551-100776-643.html.

Arrington, M. (2006, March 18). The power of Digg. *Techcrunch.com.* Retrieved July 12, 2012, from http://www.techcrunch.com/2006/03/18/the-power-of-digg.

Compete (2007, June 20). Compete.com: Digg overtakes Facebook; both cross 20 million U.S. uniques. Retrieved July 12, 2012, from http://digg.com/news/story/

Compete_com_Digg_overtakes_Facebook_Both_cross_20_million_U_S_Uniques

Compete (2012, May). Digg.com. Retrieved July 12, 2012, from http://siteanalytics.compete.com/digg.com.

Dhaliwal, A. (2010, January 23). Digg founder Kevin Rose: Digg's "drastic" overhaul could "shock" users. *Topnews.us.* Retrieved July 12, 2012, from http://topnews.us/content/210231-digg-founder-kevin-rose-digg-s-drastic-overhaul-could-shock-users.

Gittleson, K. (2012, July 31). Digg reboots with added Twitter and Facebook integration. *BBC News.* Retrieved August 17, 2012, from http://www.bbc.com/news/technology-19072914.

Mello Jr., J.P. (2012, July 13). 7 ways Digg dug its own grave. *Computerworld.* Retrieved July 16, 2012, from http://www.computerworld.com/s/article/9229129/7_Ways_Digg_Dug_Its_Own_Grave.

Rose, K. (2007, May 1). Digg this: 09-f9-11-02-9d-74-e3-5b-d8-41-56-c5-63-56-88-c0. Retrieved July 12, 2012, from http://blog.digg.com/?p=74.

Wilson, J.L. (2010, August 25). Digg redesign: nice look, rocky start. *PCMag.com.* Retrieved July 12, 2012, from http://www.pcmag.com/article2/0,2817,2368297,00.asp.

CASE 2   Wikipedia: Who Is Editing?

Research almost any topic on the Web, and a URL for a Wikipedia entry will likely appear on the list of resources. Wikipedia is a free, online encyclopedia that gets its entries from users—be they amateurs, professionals, or pranksters with nothing better to do. ("Wiki wiki" is the Hawaiian term for "quick.") As of 2012, Wikipedia had over 22 million article pages in 285 languages and 17 million registered users in the English Wikipedia alone. It is the world's sixth most popular Web site, with over 470 million monthly visitors looking to read and edit its pages. Since Wikipedia's start in January 2001, there have been over 1.6 billion edits of content entries. Anybody is able to edit entries, but the Wikipedia site keeps detailed logs of the sources (IP addresses) of all changes (although editing of more controversial articles is limited to registered users). Users/editors are anonymous in that only their user names are known, but IP addresses can be traced back to the source.

Cal Tech computation and neural systems graduate student Virgil Griffith got curious about Wikipedia's anonymous editors in 2007 when he read that congressional aides had been editing entries about their employers—the senators and representatives of the U.S. Congress. Griffith wondered if other companies and organizations were doing the same thing, so he created a program to find out. Griffith created a database of all Wikipedia entries and changes, including the information logged each time an anonymous editor made a change. Griffith isolated the XML-based records of changes and IP addresses, then identified the owners of the IP addresses using public net-address lookup services, such as ARIN, as well as private domain name data obtained through http://IP2location.com.

Griffith's system revealed the following information about the editors:

■ Someone on a computer at voting-machine maker Diebold Election Systems deleted 15 paragraphs from a Wikipedia article about electronic voting that were critical of Diebold's machines.

■ Walmart made changes to improve its image.

■ Politicians are frequent editors. For instance, a former U.S. senator from Montana made changes to indicate that he was a voice for farmers in his state.

■ ExxonMobil deleted information about its nonpayment of damages to 32,000 Alaska fishermen after the *Exxon Valdez* oil spill.

■ A computer registered to Disney deleted information critical of the company's digital rights management software.

Griffith emphasizes that his system, WikiScanner, cannot identify Wikipedia editors as agents of certain companies or organizations. It can only identify IP addresses that come from networks registered by a company or organization.

Since Wikipedia entries can be written and edited by any user registered at the site, its accuracy should obviously not be completely trusted. If one uses other reputable sources in addition to Wikipedia, however, it can often be a starting point for further research on a topic. Just don't depend on it exclusively when researching a topic, and be sure to verify content read there before quoting it as fact.

Inaccuracies aside, the ability for anyone to contribute and edit entries has been seen as the main strength of Wikipedia, allowing knowledge to be built on, refined, and policed. The number of editors peaked in 2007. By the end of 2009, however, there had been a steep dropoff in the number of volunteers editing Wikipedia's pages. According to Spanish researcher Felipe Ortega, who analyzed the site's editing activities, Wikipedia's English-language pages lost over 49,000 editors compared to around 5,000 only a year earlier.

What is causing the plunge in editor activity? Some observers think that the perception that most of the relevant information is now on the site, leaving little to be done but maintain what is there, is driving down the number of those willing to contribute and edit. Others point to the inaccuracies that plague the site and the amount of time it takes to police the information. Although editors try to maintain factual articles, anyone is free to go in and change the information. At times, a back-and-forth battle begins between two legitimate editors over what the article contains (such battles are sometimes called "wiki wars"). At other times, mischievous pranksters revert legitimate edits to their original format, insert offensive content, or otherwise deface the article, forcing editors to go back in and make fixes. Still other explanations focus on the rules and protocols surrounding the actual editing of the content. Making changes to content requires navigating a complex interface and coding scheme.

Hoping to stop the exodus of volunteers from the site, Wikipedia got its first facelift in the spring of 2010. Besides some cosmetic and layout updates to the site, site navigation has been improved, making it easier for users to find essential functions. In addition, the editing system has gotten a major overhaul. Users can now make changes to data in tables and information boxes through simple forms. The edit page has been "decluttered" and rewritten in simpler language. An outline tool has also been added, making it easy to navigate longer articles.

Clearly, Wikipedia has plenty to offer when you need some quick information on a subject. Although editors have been in decline, Wikipedia clearly is aware of the problem and has made strides to correct the issue.

Questions:

1. Do you use Wikipedia for your research? Why or why not?
2. Have you ever made a change to a Wikipedia entry? If you were to see an obvious mistake (in your opinion), would you take the time to change it? Why or why not?
3. Anyone can edit entries on Wikipedia. Do you see this as a curse or as a blessing? Explain.

Based on:

Angwin, J., and Fowler, G. A. (2009, November 27). Volunteers log off as Wikipedia ages. *Wall Street Journal*. Retrieved July 12, 2012, from http://online.wsj.com/article/SB125893981183759969.html.

Anonymous. (2011, December 13). Seeing things. *The Economist*. Retrieved July 12, 2012, from http://www.economist.com/blogs/babbage/2011/12/changes-wikipedia.

Blakely, R. (2007, August 16). Wal-Mart, CIA, and ExxonMobil changed Wikipedia entries. *Foxnews.com*. Retrieved July 12, 2012, from http://www.foxnews.com/story/0,2933,293389,00.html.

Borland, J. (2007, August 14). See who's editing Wikipedia—Diebold, the CIA, a campaign. *Wired.com*. Retrieved July 12, 2012, from http://www.wired.com/politics/onlinerights/news/2007/08/wiki_tracker.

Crum, C. (2010, March 29). Will Wikipedia's new changes boost editing? *WebProNews*. Retrieved July 12, 2012, from http://www.webpronews.com/topnews/2010/03/29/will-wikipedias-new-changes-boost-editing.

Jones, M. W. (2010, March 27). Wikipedia user interface getting first overhaul. *Tech.Blorge*. Retrieved July 12, 2012, from http://tech.blorge.com/Structure:%20/2010/03/27/wikipedia-user-interface-getting-first-overhaul.

Wikipedia:About (2012, July 2). In *Wikipedia, The Free Encyclopedia*. Retrieved July 12, 2012, from http://en.wikipedia.org/w/index.php?title=Wikipedia:About&oldid=500845901.

Wikipedia:Statistics (2012, July 2). In *Wikipedia, The Free Encyclopedia*. Retrieved July 12, 2012, from http://en.wikipedia.org/w/index.php?title=Wikipedia:Statistics&oldid=500480091.

6

Enhancing Business Intelligence Using Information Systems

Preview

Today, organizations operate in a global, highly competitive, and rapidly changing environment. A key to effective management is high-quality and timely information to support decision making. This high-quality and timely information, or business intelligence, can be provided from a variety of information systems (IS). In this chapter, we first describe business intelligence, followed by a description of databases and data warehouses, two fundamental components for gaining business intelligence. Then we describe the primary IS components utilized by organizations to gain business intelligence. In Chapter 2, "Gaining Competitive Advantage Through Information Systems," you learned about general types of information systems supporting organizations' different decision-making levels and business functions that execute various business processes in order to realize the strategic goals of the organization. Here, we introduce different technologies utilized at various decision-making levels of modern organizations to gain business intelligence.

In recent years, social media has become pervasive throughout society. No one can deny that social media has completely changed the context of privacy, shaping and reshaping relationships, exaggerating ideals of sharing, and reconstructing daily routines in order to visit your online friends at least once a day. Thanks to social media, people can now share every wicked detail about the most minute things in life; personal pictures, snapshots from last night's party, or even collages of your pet's cutest poses. Sharing doesn't stop with pictures; personal feelings can be updated time and again, depending on how compulsive a personality you have (sometimes referred to as "over posting"). Updating where you are at any given moment alerts your friends what you are up to, but also allows enterprises to learn how to better market products and promote celebrities. Everything seems closer than ever when you can see what Rick, who sat beside you in third grade, looks like now, or when you can "get in touch" with Jessica Alba just by *liking* her personal posts and latest photos.

Responding to the growing influence of social media and in turn, demonstrating another crucial function of the phenomenon, all types of organizations are finding value in monitoring and digesting the non-stop flow of posts in the social media world (see Figure 6.1). For instance, Dell established the Social Media Listening Command Center; a team of employees using business intelligence applications to develop a better understanding of customer sentiments through the monitoring of social media. The center started with 10 employees who monitored, analyzed, and dealt with widespread social media content published in English. By June 2011, the center housed 70 employees monitoring and dealing with social media in 11 different languages (English, Japanese, Chinese, Portuguese, Spanish, French, German, Norwegian, Danish, Swedish, and Korean). Further, Dell's Radian 6–based monitoring and management tools record an enormous 25,000 social media events each day, responding within 24 hours to Tweets, Facebook posts, or other messages that deserve the attention of Dell.

Social media has not only become an important source of up-to-date information for businesses, but it is also emerging as a valuable resource for police and other first responders. Social media users have demonstrated that information about crises can travel at a rate that rivals 911 services. Indeed, analyzing public information is not unusual in the world of intelligence gathering either. During the Cold War, for instance, CIA operatives relied on Russian newspapers, television reports, and radio broadcasts to gather information about the Soviets. Today social media has people racing to express who they are and what they think, information that has never been this vast and openly accessible. Social media might be the FBI's next BFF (best friend forever), as the U.S. government is developing tools to forecast everything from revolutions to upheavals to economic changes. From business corporations to the FBI, insights about what is happening or about to happen can be gleaned from social media where people are compelled to share what they know or think with just about anyone.

Building business intelligence has gone beyond business. Twitter records on average 1 billion Tweets a day, and a large portion of those posts are related to consumer opinion and product criticism. Companies are starting to understand the plethora and usefulness of information provided by social media. The amount of posts in social media has reached an incomprehensible state

FIGURE 6.1

Organizations are analyzing social media content of various types.

for mere mortals, causing what is referred to as a "Big Data" problem. While cloud computing is helping organizations to better deal with the bombardment of information, a big challenge beyond the storage of tremendous amounts of data is the development of tools that teach computers how to understand and interpret social media messages and sentiments such as happiness and anger, as well as distinguish information generated by real users from information generated by software robots ("bots") which are lurking throughout the Web.

Have you checked your Facebook news feed today? Or, more accurately, how many times have you been on Facebook this morning? It is astonishing to see what a large part of our lives social media have become. By just keeping an eye on the number of posts your feed gets in an hour, you can easily imagine how analyzing these massive numbers of posts can quickly become a Big Data problem.

After reading this chapter, you will be able to answer the following:

1. How will organizations know what to look for when using social media for business intelligence?

2. How can government organizations analyze social media activities to predict social upheavals?

3. Given the speed and volume of activity on social media, what business analytics and visualization tools could be used to make sense of the information?

Based on:

George, B. (2010, December 16). Dell opens its Social Media Command Center. *Dell.com*. Retrieved July 17, 2012, from http://en.community.dell .com/dell-blogs/enterprise/b/inside-enterprise-it/archive/2010/12/16/ dell-opens-its-social-media-command-center.aspx.

Lohr, S. (2012, February 11). The age of Big Data. *The New York Times*. Retrieved July 17, 2012, from http://www.nytimes.com/2012/02/12/ sunday-review/big-datas-impact-in-the-world.html?pagewanted=all.

Menchaca, L. (2010, December 8). Dell's next step: The Social Media Listening Command Center. *Dell.com*. Retrieved July 17, 2012, from http://en.community.dell.com/dell-blogs/direct2dell/b/direct2dell/ archive/2010/12/08/dell-s-next-step-the-social-media-listening- command-center.aspx.

Tittel, E. (2011, July 21), How Dell really listens to its customers. *ReadWriteWeb*. Retrieved July 17, 2012, from http://www.readwriteweb .com/enterprise/2011/07/how-dell-really-listens-to-its.php.

Wohlsen, M. (2012, February 12). FBI seeks digital tool to mine entire universe of social media. *Chicago Sun-Times*. Retrieved July 17, 2012, from http://www.suntimes.com/news/nation/10605702-418/fbi-seeks- digital-tool-to-mine-entire-universe-of-social-media.html.

http://goo.gl/7H1nY

BUSINESS INTELLIGENCE

In Chapter 2, you learned about the importance of strategic planning for gaining and sustaining competitive advantage. To stay ahead of the competition, organizations have turned to **business intelligence**, or the use of information systems to gather and analyze data and information from internal and external sources in order to make better business decisions. To improve organizational performance, business executives are seeking answers to questions such as "How effective is this year's promotion as compared to last year's?" "Which customer segments should we focus on?" "Which customers are most likely to switch to a competitor if we raise prices by X percent?" or, even more important, "Do we care if those customers switch?" (Tapscott, 2008). Business intelligence also refers to the information gained from the use of such systems. Next, the need for business intelligence is examined.

Why Organizations Need Business Intelligence

Although a company's overall direction is decided on at the strategic level, business processes span all organizational levels and are highly interconnected. Recall from Chapter 2 that business processes refer to the activities that organizations perform in order to reach their business goals. Unfortunately, the business processes outlined within strategic plans are often not implemented as envisioned at the managerial and operational levels of the organization because the information needed to effectively monitor and control these processes is simply not available. This "missing" information, in fact, exists but often resides in disconnected spreadsheets, reports, or databases. A recent study surveying 154 senior executives from companies all around the world found that, for almost 80 percent of the respondents, data is the single most important input when making strategic and operational decisions, and 56 percent of the respondents fear making poor decisions due to inaccurate, incomplete, or faulty data; while data quality was clearly the most important criterion, only about 10 percent indicated that they would have the necessary data when needed (Economist Intelligence Unit, 2007). Similarly, Gartner research predicted that "through 2012, more than 35 percent of the top 5,000 global companies will regularly fail to make insightful decisions about significant changes in their business and markets" (Pettey and Stevens, 2009). The root causes of such failures are clearly linked to the ability to ask the right questions as well as the availability of data and systems to provide insights into its meaning. To realize the goals of their strategic plans, organizations must have up-to-date, accurate, and *integrated* information to monitor and fine-tune a broad range of business processes. Consequently, information systems that provide business intelligence—by collecting and analyzing data and delivering needed information to the right decision maker at the right time—facilitate the effective management of modern organizations. Additionally, business intelligence allows organizations to better respond to ongoing threats and opportunities as well as to better plan for the future.

RESPONDING TO THREATS AND OPPORTUNITIES. External factors such as globalization, competitive pressures, consumer demands, societal changes, and governmental regulations can create opportunities as well as threats for modern organizations. For example, increasing globalization provides opportunities to compete in new markets, but it also creates the challenge of gaining new types of information in order to effectively manage these opportunities. Globalization can also lead to the threat of increased competition from developing countries, forcing organizations to rethink strategies or to further improve business processes. Thus, as the world becomes increasingly flatter, market opportunities will expand, but, at the same time, markets will also become increasingly more competitive, forcing companies to develop new products at an ever-increasing rate. Similarly, today's consumers have increasing access to information via social media and mobile devices, and can much more easily switch to a competitor's products or services. Further, large corporate and banking failures have brought about more stringent rules and regulations (such as the Sarbanes–Oxley Act; see Chapter 10, "Securing Information Systems"), and organizations have to comply with ever-increasing government reporting requirements. In sum, today's business environment is characterized by factors such as unstable market conditions, fierce competition, shorter product life cycles, more stringent regulations, and wider choices for customers than ever before. Business intelligence can help organizations make better decisions in this increasingly complex, fast-changing, and competitive environment by more effectively collecting and analyzing both internal and external data (see Figure 6.2).

With increasing pressure to reduce costs, organizations have to focus on investing in systems that provide the greatest returns. Business intelligence solutions can provide quick returns, as they help to quickly react to problems by providing the right information at the right time. Further, business intelligence helps to leverage existing systems (such as enterprise-wide information systems; see Chapter 7, "Enhancing Business Processes Using Enterprise Information Systems") by enabling decision makers to extract and analyze data provided by those systems. Finally, quick returns can be provided by helping organizations to focus on customer satisfaction, helping to retain the most profitable customers.

BIG DATA MOVEMENT. One significant opportunity for organizations is the abundance of data available for decision making. While research has demonstrated a strong linkage between effective data management and organizational performance, many organizations are unable to harness the value of **Big Data**. Organizations have long tried to collect, analyze, and use internal and external data to gain and sustain competitive advantage. Yet, the increase in mobile

FIGURE 6.2

Business intelligence helps organizations swiftly respond to external threats and opportunities.

devices, social media, automated sensors, and other devices generate unprecedented amounts of *structured* and *unstructured data*. Big Data is typically characterized as being of high *volume*, *variety*, and *velocity*. One of the biggest opportunities is the sheer volume of data, which, for example, enables organizations to make business decisions based on more factors; at the same time, storing and managing increasing amounts of data poses tremendous challenges. The second characteristic is variety; useful data can come in the form of **structured data** (such as transaction data), which fit neatly into spreadsheets or databases, **semi-structured data**, such as clickstreams and sensor data, or **unstructured data**, such as audio and video data, comments on social networks and so on. Finally, Big Data is characterized based on its high velocity. On the one hand, data flow into organizations at increasingly higher rates; on the other hand, organizations have to process and use the data ever more quickly, such as when online retailer Amazon.com is providing recommendations for additional products. Thus, Big Data, ranging from geospatial data to customer sentiments, can prove invaluable for formulating and executing an organization's strategy. As data are becoming increasingly abundant, many organizations find themselves unable to use this data to make sound business decisions; being able to ask the right questions and successfully utilize Big Data remains elusive for many organizations. Realizing the opportunities and challenges brought about by Big Data and its management, high-level company executives are increasingly focusing on designing an organization-wide data management strategy.

EFFECTIVE PLANNING IS CONTINUOUS. In the past, organizations lacked the necessary information and tools to continuously plan for their future. Typically, organizations would first develop a strategic plan for some planning cycle (say, a year); then, once a strategic plan was agreed on, managers of various business units would prepare budgets for executing their portion of the plan. These budgets were often "backward looking" because they were typically based on historical data rather than being based on a clear understanding of current conditions and forecasts of future trends. Over time, managers would then execute their portion of the plan. For many organizations, this method of planning and managing was adequate given the relatively slow pace of change.

Today, however, given the need to swiftly respond to a highly competitive and rapidly changing environment, organizations must implement new ways of planning. In fact, successful organizations are utilizing a **continuous planning process** (see Figure 6.3). In a continuous planning process, organizations *continuously* monitor and analyze data and business processes; the results lead to ongoing adjustments to how the organization is managed, but these results are also reflected in ongoing updates to the organizational plans. It is only through timely and accurate business intelligence that continuous planning can be executed.

FIGURE 6.3

Effective business planning is continuous.

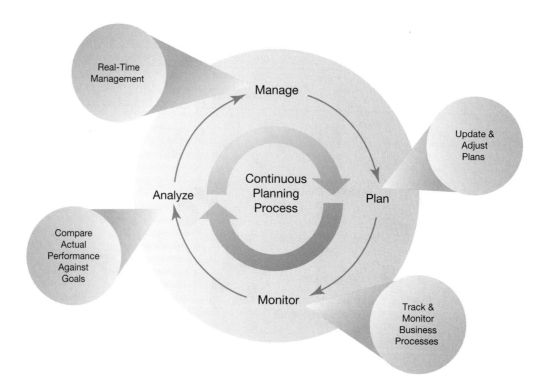

Responding to threats and opportunities and continuous planning are based on analyzing internal data (primarily from the operational level of the organization) as well as external data. In the next section, we describe how databases can be used to provide the necessary inputs to business intelligence applications.

Databases: Providing Inputs into Business Intelligence Applications

Data and knowledge are probably among the most important assets an organization has, as data and knowledge are essential for both executing business processes and gaining business intelligence. Databases, which are collections of related data organized in a way that facilitates data searches, are vital to an organization's success.

For instance, databases are essential for business processes such as supporting sales transactions and tracking inventory, but are also needed for marketing purposes, such as identifying potential customers in order to generate personalized marketing communications.

WHEN THINGS GO WRONG

Twitter Fever—Where Good Conscience Meets Bad Intelligence

Over the past few years, Twitter has successfully transformed both the ways of information transmission and the pulse of pop culture. Serving as a source of news for growing numbers of people, Twitter also works as a gathering place for expressing compassion, sharing grief, and spreading sympathetic messages, as witnessed during the devastating 2011 earthquake and tsunami in Japan. It was recorded that right after the earthquake, more than 1,200 Tweets were sent out from Tokyo in a single minute; relief organizations used Twitter to provide information on shelters where relief could be sought, and even the U.S. State Department resorted to tweeting emergency numbers to assist Japanese residents in America in contacting families back home.

Indeed, Twitter's ability to post thoughts in small snippets allows quick and easy dissemination of information to a broad audience. Thanks to microblogging and social networking, Twitter has become capable of gathering momentum so quickly that it is sometimes difficult to differentiate between truth and falsity. A Tweet cannot exceed 140 characters, and can thus easily be read out of context; the sheer number of Tweets, appearing at a rapid pace and often with little context, can easily result in endless confusion. In 2011, for instance, the phrase "RIP Jackie Chan" appeared for days on Twitter's Trending Topics list. The Tweet's life cycle started with initial expressions of sadness, continued with spammers hoping to profit by hopping on the bandwagon, and ended with annoyance and people becoming irritated as it became apparent that the rumor of Jackie Chan's death was a hoax but the topic would not stop trending.

In a more serious problem, Twitter raises questions over the legitimacy of a growing number of charity campaigns. Fueled by social media like Twitter and Facebook, Kony 2012, a short film about a Ugandan war criminal recruiting child soldiers, went viral. Initially, 77 percent of Twitter discussions concerning the campaign were positive, and many people supported the cause of Invisible Children, Inc., the creators of the video. Yet, when questions about exaggerated facts and criticisms of the organization arose, the tone immediately shifted. The sudden change of reaction opens up various other questions, but most importantly: How many people who sent out the Tweet actually really understood the message behind Kony 2012 (or even watched the video)?

When properly used for good, Twitter is undoubtedly a meaningful platform for reaching out to people. Going back to the case of the tragic earthquake in Japan, "Godzilla" simultaneously was a recurring topic on Twitter, circulated in an attempt to rebuke CNN anchor Rosemary Church for supposedly making a Godzilla joke against a backdrop of people running from the tsunami. In reality, Church only ever made reference to the waves of debris as resembling a monster movie. These stories show that many people seem to retweet first and ask questions later; yet, it may be better to do "due diligence" and try to Google first and retweet later, after establishing the veracity of some of the Tweets that are circulating.

Based On:

Dumenco, S. (2011, April 11). How Twitter can stop its descent into a cable-news style disinformation network. *AdAge Media News*. Retrieved June 26, 2012, from http://adage.com/article/the-media-guy/twitter-stop-descent-a-cable-news-style-disinformation-network/226894.

Fox, Z. (2012, March 16). Kony 2012: How social media fueled the most viral video of all time. *Mashable*. Retrieved June 26, 2012, from http://mashable.com/2012/03/16/kony-2012-pew-study.

Ingram, M. (2012, February 29). If you think Twitter doesn't break news, you're living in a dream world. *GigaOM*. Retrieved June 26, 2012, from http://gigaom.com/2012/02/29/if-you-think-twitter-doesnt-break-news-youre-living-in-a-dream-world.

Wallop, H. (2011, March 13). Japan earthquake: How Twitter and Facebook helped. *The Telegraph*. Retrieved June 26, 2012, from http://www.telegraph.co.uk/technology/twitter/8379101/Japan-earthquake-how-Twitter-and-Facebook-helped.html.

Additionally, database technology fuels electronic commerce on the Web, from tracking available products for sale to providing customer service.

ENABLING INTERACTIVE WEB SITES USING DATABASES. In today's highly dynamic digital world, any organization engaged in e-commerce makes extensive use of databases to provide dynamic and customized information on their Web pages. For example, many companies are enabling users of their Web site to view product catalogs, check inventory, and place orders—all actions that ultimately read and write to organizations' databases. Similarly, information about products (name, description, dimensions, shipping weight, and so on) is stored in databases and dynamically inserted into a Web page, freeing the company from having to develop a separate Web page for each individual product. For example, companies such as Amazon.com need only a few page templates for different product categories. Depending on what the user is looking for, these templates are then populated dynamically with the relevant product data that are pulled from a database; similarly, whenever a registered user places an order, the customer's billing and shipping information is retrieved from a database and displayed to the user for confirmation.

Some electronic commerce applications can receive and process millions of transactions per day. To ensure adequate system performance for customers, as well as to gain the greatest understanding of customer behavior, organizations must manage online data effectively. For example, Amazon.com is the world's largest bookstore, with more than 2.5 million titles. In contrast, the largest physical bookstores carry "only" about 170,000 titles, and it would not be economically feasible to build a physical bookstore the size of Amazon.com; a physical bookstore that carried Amazon.com's 2.5 million titles would need to be the size of nearly 25 football fields. As Amazon.com is open 24 hours a day, 365 days a year, its servers log millions of transactions per day, with dozens of database reads and writes for every single transaction. This is but one example that shows that the key to effectively designing an online electronic commerce business is the effective management of online data. Beyond Web sites and e-commerce, it is important to stress that database management systems are at the heart of your university's student registration system, the inventory system at the local grocery store, Apple's iTunes store, and virtually anything else you can think of that requires the recording and analysis of a large amount of data. Next we examine some basic concepts, advantages of the database approach, and database management.

DATABASES: FOUNDATION CONCEPTS. The database approach dominates nearly all computer-based information systems used today. To understand databases, we must familiarize ourselves with some terminology. In Figure 6.4, we compare database terminology (middle column) with

FIGURE 6.4

Computers make the process of storing and managing data much easier.

ID Number	Last Name	First Name	Street Address	City	State	Zip Code	Major
209345	Judson	Jackie	216 Main	Pullman	WA	99164	Information Systems
213009	Schirmer	Birgit	233 Webb	Pullman	WA	99163	History
345987	Valacich	Jordan	1212 Valley View	Pullman	WA	99163	Computer Science
457838	Wright	Elizabeth	426 Main	Pullman	WA	99163	Nursing
459987	Schmidt	Lisa-Marie	1824 Lamont	Pullman	WA	99164	Pre-Medicine
466711	Ferrell	Lauren	412 C Street	Pullman	WA	99164	Business Management
512678	Gatewood	Lael	200 Hill	Pullman	WA	99163	Psychology
691112	Fuller	Grace	312 Mountain Drive	Pullman	WA	99164	Veterinary Medicine
910234	Hardin	Ethan	200 Sunset	Pullman	WA	99164	Sociology
979776	Valacich	James	1212 Valley View	Pullman	WA	99163	Computer Science
983445	Kabbe	Joshua	825 Skylark	Pullman	WA	99164	Human Resources

FIGURE 6.5

This sample data table for the entity *Student* includes eight attributes and 11 records.

equivalents in a library (left column) and a business office (right column). We use database management systems (DBMSs) to interact with the data in databases. A DBMS is a software application with which you create, store, organize, and retrieve data from a single database or several databases. Microsoft Access is an example of a popular DBMS for personal computers. In the DBMS, the individual database is a collection of related attributes about entities. An **entity** is something you collect data about, such as people or classes (see Figure 6.5). We often think of entities as **tables**, where each row is a **record** and each column is an **attribute** (also referred to as field). A record is a collection of related attributes about a single instance of an entity. Each record typically consists of many attributes, which are individual pieces of information. For example, a name and a Social Security Number are attributes of a particular person.

DATABASES: ADVANTAGES. Before there were DBMSs, organizations used the file processing approach to store and manipulate data electronically. Data were usually kept in long, sequential computer files that were often stored on tape. Information about entities often appeared in several different places throughout the information system, and the data were often stored along with and sometimes embedded within the programming code that used the data. People had not yet envisioned the concept of separately storing information about entities in non-redundant databases, so different files often contained repetitive data about a customer, a supplier, or another entity. When someone's address changed, it had to be changed in every file where it occurred, an often tedious process. Similarly, if programmers changed the code, they typically had to change the corresponding data along with it. Further, the programmer would have had to know *how* the data were stored in order to make any changes. This was often no better than a pen-and-paper approach to storing data.

It is possible for a database to consist of only a single file or table. However, most databases managed under a DBMS consist of multiple tables or entities, often organized in several files. A DBMS can manage hundreds or even thousands of tables simultaneously by linking the tables as part of a single system. The DBMS helps us manage the tremendous volume and complexity of interrelated data so that we can be sure that the right data are accessed, changed, or deleted. For example, if a student or customer address is changed, that change is made through all the parts of the system where that data might occur. Using a database approach prevents unnecessary and problematic redundancies of the data, and the data are kept separate from the applications' programming code. This means that the database does not need to be changed if a change is made to an application. Consequently, there are numerous advantages to using a database approach to managing organizational data; these are summarized in Table 6.1. Of course, moving to the database approach comes with some costs and risks that must be recognized and managed (see Table 6.2). Nonetheless, most organizations have embraced the database approach because most feel that the advantages far exceed the risks or costs.

TABLE 6.1   Advantages of the Database Approach

Advantages	Description
Program–data independence	Much easier to evolve and alter software to changing business needs when data and programs are independent.
Minimal data redundancy	Single copy of data ensures that storage requirements are minimized.
Improved data consistency	Eliminating redundancy greatly reduces the possibilities of inconsistency.
Improved data sharing	Easier to deploy and control data access using a centralized system.
Increased productivity of application development	Data standards make it easier to build and modify applications.
Enforcement of standards	A centralized system makes it much easier to enforce standards and rules for data creation, modification, naming, and deletion.
Increased security	A centralized system makes it easier to enforce access restrictions.
Improved data quality	Centralized control, minimized redundancy, and improved data consistency help to enhance the quality of data.
Improved data accessibility	A centralized system makes it easier to provide access for personnel within or outside organizational boundaries.
Reduced program maintenance	Information changed in the central database is replicated seamlessly throughout all applications.

DATABASES: TYPES. Traditionally, organizations have used relational database management systems (RDBMS) to support their business processes. An **RDBMS** attempts to balance efficiency of storage needs, ease of retrieval, and other factors by storing data in tables linked via relationships. However, RDBMSs are not easily scalable in response to peaks in demand, as is often the case in data-intensive applications such as e-commerce and social media, and traditional RDBMSs may simply not be able to handle massive volumes of often unstructured "Big Data." Further, as RDBMSs tend to be highly complex, any changes need to be carefully planned and managed, potentially reducing the agility of a business. To overcome these limitations, a new breed of database management systems, called "NoSQL," are increasingly becoming popular. **NoSQL** databases such as Amazon.com's SimpleDB are highly scalable, as they can be distributed across multiple machines, which works especially well in a cloud computing infrastructure. Further, NoSQL databases often offer much flexibility in the types of data they handle (such as comments of various lengths made by Facebook users, or audio or video data). However, implementing NoSQL databases comes at a cost, as they are still in their early stages of development; thus, some needed features may be lacking, and it may be difficult to find experienced NoSQL developers. Further, it may not be possible to obtain support for NoSQL databases, as many of these are open source projects (see Chapter 9, "Developing and Acquiring Information Systems").

TABLE 6.2   Costs and Risks of the Database Approach

Cost or Risk	Description
New, specialized personnel	Conversion to the database approach may require hiring additional personnel.
Installation and management cost and complexity	Database approach has higher up-front costs and complexity in order to gain long-term benefits.
Conversion costs	Extensive costs are common when converting existing systems, often referred to as *legacy systems,* to the database approach.
Need for explicit backup and recovery	A shared corporate data resource must be accurate and available at all times.
Organizational conflict	Ownership—creation, naming, modification, and deletion—of data can cause organizational conflict.

DATABASES: EFFECTIVE MANAGEMENT. Now that we have outlined why databases are important to organizations, we can talk about how organizational databases can be managed effectively. The best database in the world is no better than the data it holds. Conversely, all the data in the world will do you no good if they are not organized in a manner in which there are few or no redundancies and in which you can retrieve, analyze, and understand them. The two key elements of an organizational database are the data and the structure of those data. The structure of the data is typically captured in a **data model**, that is, a map or diagram that represents entities and their relationships. Further, the structure of the data is documented to facilitate management of the database.

Each attribute in the database needs to be of a certain type. For example, an attribute may contain text, numbers, or dates. This **data type** helps the DBMS organize and sort the data, complete calculations, and allocate storage space. If tables are designed correctly, they will be easier to update and it will be faster to extract vital information to improve an organization's business intelligence capabilities.

Once the data model is created, the format of the data is documented in a **data dictionary**. The data dictionary (or metadata repository) is a document explaining several pieces of information for each attribute, such as its name, the type of data expected (dates, alphanumeric, numbers, and so on), and valid values. Data dictionaries can include information such as why the data item is needed, how often it should be updated, and on which forms and reports the data appears.

Data dictionaries can be used to document business rules. **Business rules**, such as who has authority to update a piece of data, are captured by the designers of the database and included in the data dictionary to prevent illegal or illogical entries from entering the database. For example, designers of a warehouse database could capture a rule in the data dictionary to prevent invalid ship dates from being entered into the database. Although NoSQL databases may not be as rigid as RDMBS, or may not enforce business rules at all (leaving the enforcing to applications), it is wise to create data models and to consider what data will be captured, how the data will be related, and what rules should be enforced.

ENTERING AND QUERYING DATA. At some point, data must be entered into the database. Traditionally, a clerk or other data entry professional would create records in the database by entering data. These data may come from telephone conversations, preprinted forms that must be filled out, historical records, or electronic files. Today, much organizational data are captured automatically, as is the case with transactional data from a point-of-sale terminal or a user's input in a Web form; whenever you place an order on the Web, sign up for a newsletter, or respond to an online survey, your input is directly stored in a database. A **form** (see Figure 6.6) typically has blanks where the user can enter information or make choices, each of which represents an

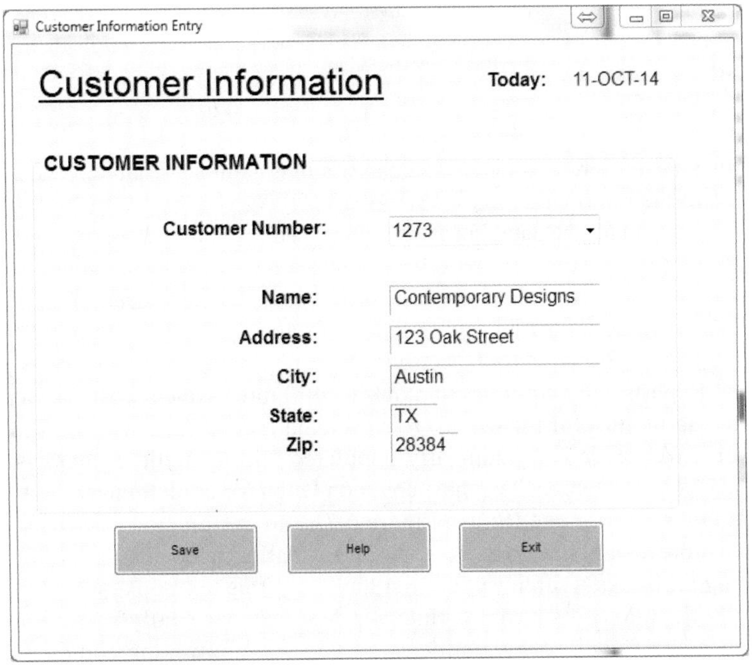

FIGURE 6.6

A computer-based form used for entering customer information

COMING ATTRACTIONS

The Internet of Things

How many different devices do you use to connect to the Internet? You certainly use your PC or laptop to surf the Web, and you may use your smartphone to access information on the go. You may have a tablet, and your television set may allow you to pull up Web pages. In 2008, more devices were connected to the Internet than there were people living on earth. Fueled by advances in chips and wireless radios, we will see more and more different devices connecting to the Internet in the not-too-distant future. Welcome to the Internet of things, where everything that can generate useful information will be equipped with sensors and wireless radios.

Your home may be equipped with sensors, allowing you to monitor temperatures when on vacation, and enabling you to remotely adjust the air-conditioning; your new fridge may allow you to check-in and check-out groceries, monitor expiration dates, and suggest recipes based on what you keep in there; similarly, your washing machine may send you an alert when the laundry is done. Yet, the Internet of Things doesn't end in people's homes. The potential for gathering useful sensor data is almost limitless. For example, sensors integrated in a road's surface could monitor temperatures, and trigger dynamic speed limits in case there is the risk of ice or snow. Similarly, sensors could monitor availability of parking spaces or traffic flow, alerting drivers of changes in conditions. Millions of sensors connected to the Internet could monitor weather conditions, helping to generate more accurate local weather predictions, or could monitor soil moisture in golf courses, reducing the need for watering. Cardiac monitors can alert physicians of health risks. Various types of sensors can be used in factories to monitor machinery, making production more efficient. In sum, the applications of sensor technology for home automation, smart cities, smart metering, smart farming, e-Health, and other areas are limitless. Or are they not?

Up until recently, the most prominent limit was the number of IP addresses, that is, the number of unique addresses that could be assigned to devices connecting to the Internet. When the Internet addressing system known as IPv4 was conceived, its creators envisioned that a 32-bit addressing system, allowing for 4.3 billion unique addresses, would be more than sufficient. Yet, given the tremendous increase in mobile devices, IPv4 was slowly running out of addresses, such that new devices would be unable to connect to the Internet unless a solution to this bottleneck was found. The solution came with IPv6, a 128-bit addressing system allowing for 340 trillion trillion trillion addresses. For now, this should be sufficient to pave the way for countless useful applications associated with the Internet of things. Until the next bottleneck looms: as more and more devices connect to the Internet and transmit and receive data, bandwidth will be the next problem to tackle.

Based on:

Anonymous. (n.d.) 50 Sensor applications for a smarter world. *Libelium.com*. Retrieved July 17, 2012, from http://www.libelium.com/top_50_iot_sensor_applications_ranking.

Anonymous. (2012). LG smart appliances for 2012 deliver connectivity, efficiency through Smart ThinQ™ technologies. *LG.com*. Retrieved July 17, 2012, from http://www.lgnewsroom.com/ces2012/view.php?product_code=95&product_type=95&post_index=1828.

Evans, D. (2011, July 15). The Internet of things [infographic]. *Cisco*. Retrieved July 17, 2012, from http://blogs.cisco.com/news/the-internet-of-things-infographic.

Proffitt, B. (2012, June 6). World IPv6 launch day is key for the Internet of Things. *ReadWriteWeb*. Retrieved July 17, 2012, from http://www.readwriteweb.com/enterprise/2012/06/world-ipv6-launch-day-is-key-for-the-internet-of-things.php.

attribute within a database record (such as the user's first name, last name, gender, and so on). This form presents the information to the user in an intuitive way so that the user can easily see the required items and enter the data. Forms are often used to capture data to be added, modified, or deleted from the database (e.g., for modifying your password or closing your e-mail account).

In addition to transaction support, data stored in a database are extensively used for analysis and reporting. A **report** is a compilation of data from the database that is organized and produced in printed format (either electronic or on paper). Sophisticated **report generators** such as Crystal Reports can help users to quickly build interactive reports and visualizations to present the data in a useful format. To retrieve data from a database, we use a **query**. In fact, whenever a Web page is dynamically populated with content, a query is executed to retrieve the data from a database. The most common language used to interface with RDBMSs is **Structured Query Language (SQL)**. Figure 6.7 is an example of an SQL statement that an online bookstore would use to retrieve the information needed to populate a summary page containing all books written by the first author of this textbook, sorted by publishing date. Writing SQL statements requires time and practice, especially when you are dealing with complex databases with many entities, or when you are writing complex queries with

```
SELECT AUTHOR, TITLE, PUBLICATION_DATE, PRICE
FROM BOOKS
WHERE AUTHOR="VALACICH"
ORDER BY PUBLICATION_DATE;
```

FIGURE 6.7

This sample SQL statement would be used to retrieve the information needed to populate a summary Web page containing all books written by the first author of this textbook, sorted by publication date.

multiple integrated criteria—such as adding numbers while sorting on two different attributes. Many desktop DBMS packages have a simpler way of interfacing with the databases—using a concept called **query by example (QBE)**. QBE capabilities in a database enable us to fill out a grid, or template, in order to construct a sample or description of the data we would like to see, typically using the drag-and-drop features of a graphical user interface to create a query quickly and easily. In Figure 6.8, we provide an example of the QBE grid from Microsoft Access's desktop DBMS package.

ONLINE TRANSACTION PROCESSING. The systems that are used to interact with customers and run a business in real-time are called **operational systems**. Examples of operational systems are sales order processing and reservation systems. As fast customer response is fundamental to having a successful Internet-based business, immediate automated responses to the requests of users are required. **Online transaction processing (OLTP)** systems provide this, and are designed to handle multiple concurrent transactions from customers. Typically, these transactions have a fixed number of inputs, such as order items, payment data, and customer name and address, and a specified output, such as total order price or order tracking number. In other words, the primary use of OLTP systems is gathering new information, transforming that information, and updating information in the system. Common transactions include receiving user information, processing orders, and generating sales receipts. Consequently, OLTP is a big part of interactive electronic commerce applications on the Internet. Since customers can be located virtually anywhere in the world, it is critical that transactions be processed efficiently. The speed with which DBMSs can process transactions is, therefore, an important design decision when building Internet systems. In addition to which technology is chosen to process the transactions, how the data are organized is also a major factor in determining system performance.

Although the database operations behind most transactions are relatively simple, designers often spend considerable time making adjustments to the database design in order to "tune" processing for optimal system performance. Once an organization has all this data, it must design

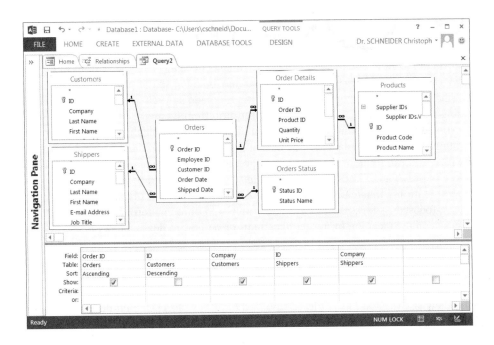

FIGURE 6.8

QBE provides a graphical interface to define what information you want to see.
Source: Courtesy of Microsoft, Inc.

TABLE 6.3 Comparison of Operational and Informational Systems

Characteristic	Operational System	Informational System
Primary purpose	Run the business on a current basis	Support managerial decision making
Type of data	Current representation of state of the business	Historical or point-in-time (snapshot)
Primary users	Online customers, clerks, salespersons, administrators	Managers, business analysts, and customers (checking status and history)
Scope of usage	Narrow and simple updates and queries	Broad and complex queries and analyses
Design goal	Performance	Ease of access and use

ways to gain the greatest value from its collection; each individual OLTP system could be queried individually, but the real power for an organization comes from analyzing the aggregation of data from different systems, or *data mining,* using methods such as *online analytical processing.*

OPERATIONAL SYSTEMS AND BUSINESS INTELLIGENCE. Operational systems can generate a wealth of data that can serve as useful inputs into business intelligence applications. For example, a grocery checkout system processes a specific transaction (the purchase) that can be linked to an inventory system (for reordering purposes), but it can also capture valuable data such as time of the purchase, items purchased together, form of payment, or loyalty program details. Coupled with external data (such as store location, weather data, or competitor information), these data can be analyzed for spending patterns, effectiveness of sales promotions, or customer profiling.

The systems designed to support decision making based on stable point-in-time or historical data are called **informational systems**. The requirements for designing and supporting operational and informational systems are quite different (see Table 6.3). In a distributed online environment, performing real-time analytical processing diminishes the performance of transaction processing. For example, complex analytical queries require the locking of data resources for extended periods of execution time, whereas transactional events—data insertions and simple queries from customers—are fast and can often occur simultaneously; further, the operational databases typically only contain current data. Thus, a well-tuned and responsive transaction processing system may have uneven performance for customers while analytical processing occurs. As a result, many organizations replicate all transactions on a second database server so that analytical processing does not slow customer transaction processing performance. This replication typically occurs in batches during off-peak hours, when site traffic volumes are at a minimum.

MASTER DATA MANAGEMENT. To make sound operational, tactical, and strategic business decisions, it is imperative that decisions made in different departments are based on the same underlying data, definitions, and assumptions; that is, there is a "single version of the truth." For example, do the marketing and accounting departments have the same definitions of a customer or a sale? Does a "customer" entail anyone who may be interested in the company's product or service (marketing view) or only those who actually made a purchase (accounting view)? Part of creating a single version of the truth is **master data management**. **Master data** are the data that is deemed most important in the operation of a business. Typically shared among multiple organizational units, master data include data about customers, suppliers, inventory, employees, and the like. You can think of master data as the "actors" in an organization's transactions; for example, a *customer* purchases something, an *employee* is paid, and so on. Given the importance of an organization's master data, master data management is a management rather than a technology-focused issue, as different business units and different corporate levels have to come to consensus on the meaning of master data items or on how to deal with duplicates. Especially for large organizations, arriving at a single version of the truth can be a challenge, as master data often have to be integrated from multiple systems. Likewise, after mergers or acquisitions, organizations have to try to consolidate the master data from two or more companies. Once the meaning and format of the master data have been agreed on, business intelligence applications can base their analyses on the single version of the truth by accessing multiple databases or by using a *data warehouse* that integrates data from various operational systems.

TABLE 6.4   Sample Industry Uses of Data Warehousing

Uses of Data Warehousing	Representative Companies
Analysis of scanner checkout data	Safeway
Tracking, analysis, and tuning of sales promotions and coupons	Costco, CVS Corporation
Inventory analysis and redeployment	Home Depot, Daimler AG
Price reduction modeling to "move" the product	Office Depot
Negotiating leverage with suppliers	Sears, General Motors
Frequent buyer program management	Target, T-Mobile
Profitability analysis and market segmentation	Walgreens, Toyota
Product promotions for focused market segments	Walmart, Williams-Sonoma
Resource and network utilization	Verizon
Problem tracking and customer service	Qwest Communications
Cross-segment marketing	Citigroup
Risk and credit analysis	HSBC
Merger and acquisition analysis	Goldman Sachs
Customer profiling	Morgan Stanley
Warranty tracking and analysis	Honda

DATA WAREHOUSES. Large organizations, such as Walmart, UPS, and Alaska Airlines, have built **data warehouses** that integrate multiple large databases and other information sources into a single repository. Such repository, containing both historic and almost current data for analysis and reporting, is suitable for direct querying, analysis, or processing. Much like a physical warehouse for products and components, a data warehouse stores and distributes data on computer-based information systems. A data warehouse is a company's virtual storehouse of valuable data from the organization's disparate information systems and external sources. It supports the online analysis of sales, inventory, and other vital business data that have been culled from operational systems. The purpose of a data warehouse is to put key business information into the hands of more decision makers, and an organization that successfully deploys a data warehouse has committed to pulling together, integrating, and sharing critical corporate data throughout the firm. Table 6.4 lists sample industry uses of data warehouses. Data warehouses can take up hundreds of gigabytes (even terabytes) of data. They usually run on fairly powerful mainframe computers and can cost millions of dollars.

While no changes to the existing, historical data contained in the data warehouse are made, the data in a data warehouse are periodically appended with "new" data from operational systems. Consequently, a crucial process for consolidating data from operational systems with other organizational data (to facilitate the use of data mining techniques to gain the greatest and broadest understanding from the data) is **extraction, transformation, and loading**. First, the data need to be extracted from various different systems. In the transformation stage, data are being cleansed and manipulated to fit the needs of the analysis (such as by creating new calculated fields or summary values). **Data cleansing** refers to the process of detecting, correcting (e.g., standardizing the format), or removing corrupt or inaccurate data retrieved from different systems (such as differences in the way dates or ZIP codes are stored). Finally, the transformed data are loaded into the data warehouse and are ready for being used for complex analyses (see Figure 6.9).

DATA MARTS. Rather than storing all enterprise data in one data warehouse, many organizations have created multiple data marts, each containing a subset of the data for a single aspect of a company's business, such as finance, inventory, or personnel. A **data mart** is a data warehouse that is limited in scope. It contains selected data from the data warehouse such that each separate data mart is customized for the decision support needs of a particular end-user group. Data marts have been popular among small and medium-sized businesses and among departments within larger organizations, all of which were previously prohibited from developing their own data warehouses because of the high costs involved.

FIGURE 6.9

Extraction, transformation, and loading are used to consolidate data from operational systems into a data warehouse.

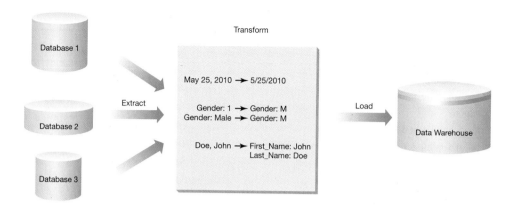

Williams-Sonoma, for example, known for its high-class home furnishing stores, is constantly looking to find new ways to increase sales and reach new target markets. Realizing the value of their data generated from catalog mailings, Williams-Sonoma built a data mart containing purchasing data from 33 million active U.S. households. Using SAS data mining tools and different statistical models, Williams-Sonoma was able to segment customers into groups of 30,000–50,000 households and to predict the profitability of those segments based on the prior year's purchases. These models resulted in the creation of a new catalog for a market segment that had up to then not been served by Williams-Sonoma. Now, for example, Williams-Sonoma markets a variety of new products, such as fringed lamps, chic furniture, and cool accessories, to an identified market segment using its Pottery Barn Teen catalog.

Data marts typically contain tens of gigabytes of data as opposed to the hundreds of gigabytes in data warehouses. Therefore, data marts can be deployed on less powerful hardware. The difference in costs between different types of data marts and data warehouses can be significant. The cost to develop a data mart is typically less than US$1 million, while the cost for a data warehouse can exceed US$10 million. However, with the advent of cloud computing, several vendors are offering data warehousing as a service, which can help to significantly lower the company's initial investment (see Chapter 3, "Managing the Information Systems Infrastructure and Services"); similarly, companies such as SAP are offering on-demand business intelligence as a service.

BUSINESS INTELLIGENCE COMPONENTS

http://goo.gl/44pH3

Various different vendors offer a wide variety of tools as business intelligence applications. In general, however, there are three categories of business intelligence tools: tools for aiding information and knowledge discovery, tools for analyzing data to improve decision making, and tools for visualizing complex data relationships. Although each type of application by itself can be very valuable to an organization, it is their convergence that enables organizations to gain and sustain competitive advantage through enhanced business intelligence. In the following sections, we discuss each of these categories as well as the various systems and technologies that each encompasses.

Information and Knowledge Discovery

Information and knowledge discovery tools are used primarily to extract information from existing data. Sometimes, information and knowledge discovery is completely atheoretical, and companies use business intelligence tools to search for hidden relationships between data, akin to searching for the "needle in the haystack." In other cases, business users formulate hypotheses (such as "customers with a household income of $150,000 are twice as likely to respond to our marketing campaigns as customers with an income of $60,000 or less"), and these hypotheses are tested against existing data. Business intelligence tools can support both forms of information and knowledge discovery; yet, being able to ask the right questions is the most crucial skill, and should come before jumping into technological solutions. In the following sections, we describe some of the applications used for discovering new and unexpected relationships and for testing hypotheses.

TABLE 6.5 Common Reports and Queries

Report/Query	Description
Scheduled reports	Reports produced at predefined intervals—daily, weekly, or monthly—to support routine decisions
Key-indicator reports	Reports that provide a summary of critical information on a recurring schedule
Exception reports	Reports that highlight situations that are out of the normal range
Drill-down reports	Reports that provide greater detail, so as to help analyze why a key indicator is not at an appropriate level or why an exception occurred
Ad hoc queries	Queries answering unplanned information requests to support a non-routine decision; typically not saved to be run again

AD HOC QUERIES AND REPORTS. Business users across an organization need the right information at the right time. Such information is typically presented as reports based on data stored in organizational databases and can take the form of **scheduled reports**, **drill-down reports**, **exception reports**, and **key-indicator reports** (see Table 6.5). These reports are either produced at prespecified intervals or created whenever a prespecified event happens. However, decision makers frequently have information needs that are unforeseen and may never arise again. In such instances, the users need to run **ad hoc queries** (i.e., queries created because of unplanned information needs that are typically not saved for later use). Ad hoc query tools provide an easy-to-use interface, allowing managers to run queries and reports themselves without having to know query languages or the structure of the underlying data. Installed on a person's desktop, notebook computer, or mobile device, these tools can be used to run queries and reports whenever an unplanned information need arises without having to resort to calling the IS department for help in creating a complex query or a special report.

ONLINE ANALYTICAL PROCESSING. **Online analytical processing (OLAP)** refers to the process of quickly conducting complex, multidimensional analyses of data stored in a database that is optimized for retrieval, typically using graphical software tools. OLAP tools enable users to analyze different dimensions of data beyond simple data summaries and data aggregations of normal database queries. A typical question asked would be "What were the profits for each week in 2013 by sales region and customer type?" In contrast to relatively simple ad hoc queries, running such multidimensional queries requires a deeper understanding of the underlying data. Given the high volume of transactions within Internet-based systems and the potential business value in the data, analysts must provide extensive OLAP capabilities to managers. The chief component of an OLAP system is the **OLAP server**, which understands how data are organized in the database and has special functions for analyzing the data. The use of dedicated databases allows for tremendous increases in retrieval speed. In the past, multidimensional queries against large transactional databases could take hours to run; in contrast, OLAP systems preaggregate data so that only the subset of the data necessary for the queries is extracted, greatly improving performance.

Measures and Dimensions Whenever a business transaction occurs, associated data can be stored and then analyzed from a variety of perspectives. To facilitate efficient processing of transactions, databases supporting online transaction processing systems treat all data in similar ways. In contrast, OLAP systems are designed for efficient retrieval of data and categorize data as measures and dimensions. **Measures** (or sometimes called **facts**) are the values or numbers the user wants to analyze, such as the sum of sales or the number of orders placed. **Dimensions** provide a way to summarize the data, such as region, time, or product line. Thus, sales (a measure) could be analyzed by product, time (year, quarter, or week), geographical region, or distributor (the dimensions). To enable the analysis of data at more or less detailed levels, the dimensions are organized as hierarchies (such as in year, quarter, month, or day). For example, when analyzing sales by geographical regions, a user can **drill down** from state, to county, to city, or to the individual store location, or **roll up** from state to sales region (northwest, south, southeast, and so on), to country, or to continent.

FIGURE 6.10

An OLAP cube allows for analyzing data by multiple dimensions.

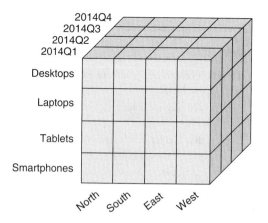

Cubes, Slicing, and Dicing To enable such multidimensional analyses, OLAP arranges the data in so-called cubes. An **OLAP cube** is a data structure allowing for multiple dimensions to be added to a traditional two-dimensional table (see Figure 6.10). Although the figure only shows three dimensions, data can be analyzed in more than three dimensions. Analyzing the data on subsets of the dimensions is referred to as **slicing and dicing**. For example, a slice may show sales by product type and region only for the second quarter of 2014. Another slice may only show sales for desktops in the western region (see Figure 6.11).

DATA MINING.   **Data mining** complements OLAP in that it provides capabilities for discovering "hidden" predictive relationships in the data. Using complicated algorithms on powerful multiprocessor computers or cloud computing architectures, data mining applications can analyze massive amounts of data to identify characteristics of profitable customers, purchasing patterns, or even fraudulent credit card transactions. Typically, data mining algorithms search for patterns, trends, or rules that are hidden in the data, so as to develop predictive models. Results from a data mining exercise (such as the characteristics of customers most likely to respond to a marketing campaign for a specific new product) can then be used in an ad hoc query (e.g., to identify customers sharing those characteristics so as to target them in the next campaign). It is important to note that any interesting predictive model derived from data mining should be tested against "fresh" data to determine if the model actually holds what it promises.

In order to increase predictive power, data mining algorithms are run against large data warehouses. Depending on the size of the data warehouse (large data warehouses often contain many terabytes of data), data mining algorithms can take a long time to run; thus, an important preparatory step to running data mining algorithms is **data reduction**, which reduces the complexity of the data to be analyzed. This can be achieved by rolling up a data cube to the smallest level of aggregation needed, reducing the dimensionality, or dividing continuous measures into discrete intervals.

Association Discovery One frequently used application of data mining is association discovery. **Association discovery** is a technique used to find associations or correlations among sets of items. For example, a supermarket chain wants to find out which items are typically purchased

FIGURE 6.11

Slicing and dicing allows for analyzing subsets of the dimensions.

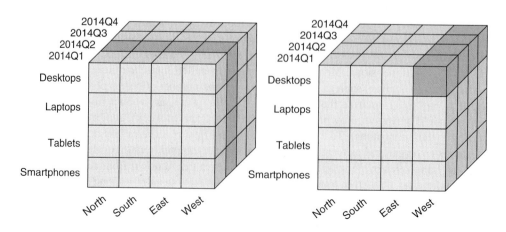

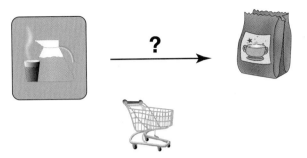

Coffee → Sugar [Support 20%, Confidence 80%]

together in order to redesign the store's layout and optimize the customers' "navigational path" through the store, or to launch a new promotion. Mining sales transactions over the past five years may reveal that 80 percent of the time, people who purchase coffee also purchase sugar (see Figure 6.12). Association rules typically contain two numbers: a percentage indicating support (e.g., the combination of coffee and sugar occurs in 20 percent of all transactions analyzed) and a confidence level indicating the reliability (e.g., 80 percent of all transactions that contain coffee also contain sugar). These numbers help managers decide if the association rule is meaningful and if any changes (e.g., to store layout or pricing) based on the findings are worthwhile. Similar to association discovery, **sequence discovery** is used to discover associations over time. For example, it may be discovered that 55 percent of all customers who purchase a new high-definition TV set also purchase a Blu-ray disc player within the next two months.

Clustering and Classification Another useful application of data mining is clustering and classification. **Clustering** is the process of grouping related records together on the basis of having similar values for attributes, thus finding structure in the data. For example, a manufacturer of consumer electronics may find clusters around model preferences, age groups, and income levels. These results can then be used for targeting certain groups of customers in marketing campaigns. In contrast, **classification** is used when the groups ("classes") are known beforehand, and records are segmented into these classes. For example, a bank may have found that there are different classes of customers who differ in their likelihood of defaulting on a loan. As such, all customers can be classified into different (known) risk categories in order to ensure that the bank does not exceed a desired level of risk within its loan portfolio. Typically, classification would use a decision tree to classify the records.

UNSTRUCTURED DATA ANALYSIS. Although the quantitative methods described above can help decision makers get a better view of their organization's performance or their customers' behavior, they only provide a partial picture. By focusing purely on structured data (such as transactions, credit lines, and so on), a wealth of unstructured data (such as customer sentiments voiced in online forums, letters, or service-related call center records) is left untapped; in fact, studies show that between 50 and 80 percent of all enterprise data consist of unstructured or semistructured data (Swoyer, 2007), and with the tremendous increase of user-generated content on the Web, this figure may be even higher in the future. Therefore, making important business decisions purely based on structured data can be dangerous, as the massive amounts of unstructured data could either strengthen or contradict findings derived from analyzing only structured data. Hence, organizations are trying not only to reach a single version of the truth, but also to get the whole truth by analyzing unstructured data using *text mining, Web content mining,* or *Web usage mining.*

Text Mining and Web Content Mining **Text mining** refers to the use of analytical techniques for extracting information from textual documents. For organizations, the analysis of textual documents can provide extremely valuable insights into business performance, competitors' activities, or regulatory compliance. Such textual documents can include internal data such as letters or e-mails from customers, customer calls, internal communications, or external data such as blog posts, wikis, Twitter messages, and Facebook posts, as well as competitor's Web pages, marketing materials, patent filings, and so on. Text mining systems analyze a document's linguistic structures to extract data such as places, companies, concepts, or dates. Most systems can easily extract a wide range of content and can be customized to meet an organization's needs by adding specific key words related to competitors, product names, persons of interest, and the like.

Web content mining refers to extracting textual information from Web documents. To extract information from the overall Internet (or from some subset of Web sites), a document collection spider, or *Web crawler* (discussed later in this chapter), would gather sites and documents that matched some prespecified criteria and place this information in a massive document warehouse. Once collected, the text mining system would apply a variety of analytical techniques to produce reports that can be used to gain additional insights beyond what is typically gained using data mining analytics alone (see Figure 6.13). The next challenge for organizations will be extracting useful information from audio or video streams on the Web.

Analyzing textual documents can help organizations in various ways:

- The marketing department can learn about customers' thoughts, feelings, and emotions, by analyzing not only customer e-mails or letters but also blogs, wikis, or discussion forums.
- The operations department can learn about product performance by analyzing service records or customer calls.
- Strategic decision makers can gather **competitive intelligence** by analyzing press releases, news article, or customer-generated Web content about competitors' products.
- The sales department can learn about major accounts by analyzing news coverage.
- The human resources department can monitor employee satisfaction or compliance to company policies by analyzing internal communications (this is especially important in order to comply with regulations such as the Sarbanes–Oxley Act; see Chapter 10).

Many major companies, including Capital One, Marriott International, United Airlines, and Walmart, use text mining solutions to assess customer sentiments and increase customer satisfaction. Similarly, raveable.com provides hotel ratings by aggregating information from sources such as tripadvisor.com, expedia.com, and travelocity.com as well as individual travel blogs; in addition to aggregating numerical ratings given for aspects such as cleanliness, value, or location, raveable.com uses text mining to analyze review comments based on key words such as "earplugs," "noise," or "clean" and the associated sentiments so as to categorize the reviews

FIGURE 6.13

Text mining the Internet.

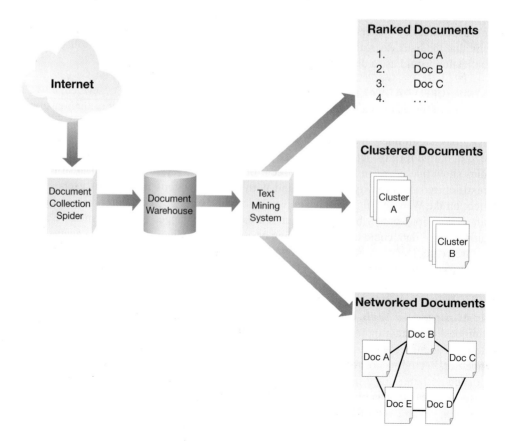

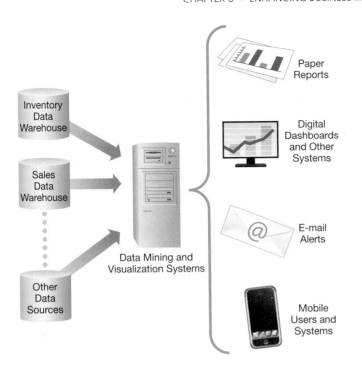

FIGURE 6.14

Data mining results can be delivered to users in a variety of ways.

and classify them as positive or negative. We will further discuss social media monitoring and their role in customer relationship management in Chapter 8, "Strengthening Business-to-Business Relationships Via Supply Chain and Customer Relationship Management."

Web Usage Mining **Web usage mining** is used by organizations such as Amazon.com to determine patterns in customers' usage data, such as how users navigate through the site or how much time they spend on different pages. By analyzing users' **clickstream data** (i.e., a recording of a user's path through a Web site), a business such as Amazon.com can assess its pages' **stickiness** (i.e., the ability to attract and keep visitors) and how customers navigate through different item categories, ultimately helping Amazon.com to optimize the structure of its Web site.

The tools used for information and knowledge discovery can be embedded into a broad range of managerial, executive, and functional area information systems, as well as into decision support and intelligent systems. Results from these analyses can be provided on digital dashboards, paper reports, Web portals, e-mail alerts (using monitoring or data mining agents), and mobile devices, as well as used by a variety of other information systems (see Figure 6.14).

Business Analytics to Support Decision Making

The second class of business intelligence applications comprises systems to support human and automated decision making. We first discuss applications designed to help predict future outcomes, followed by applications that support human decision makers in making unstructured decisions. Then we provide an overview of intelligent systems, which are designed to take some of these decisions out of the hands of the human decision makers, thus freeing up valuable resources. Finally, we examine various tools for managing organizational knowledge.

BUSINESS ANALYTICS. Traditional business intelligence applications for information and knowledge discovery are designed to focus on past and current performance, thus helping decision makers to get a detailed picture about the current state of a business. **Business analytics** augments business intelligence by using **predictive analysis** to help identify trends or predict business outcomes; whereas business intelligence is good for knowing what *is*, predictive analysis helps in foreseeing what *will be*. For example, predictive analysis can help in understanding how a certain customer segment would respond to targeted promotions or help in determining measures to retain the most valuable customers (Business Objects, n.d.). However, predictive analysis is heavily dependent on statistical models and their underlying assumptions.

BRIEF CASE

Princess D, Yoda, and Quality Assurance through Call Recording

Call recording may be one of the most random, unnoticed aspects in our busy lives. What exactly goes on after the automated message says "This call is being recorded for quality assurance"? Certainly, it's more than just pushing the little red button. Call recording company ELoyalty was built on a US$50 million foundation, and it took a total of six years to perfect its complex software algorithms that work not only to define specific complaints, but also to decode a caller's personality.

Founder and CEO Kelly Conway boasts that the technology categorizes people into one of six personality types—Spock, Princess Diana, Rush Limbaugh, Robin Williams, Donald Trump, and Yoda. For example, if you are rational and go directly for the facts, then you are Spock. For those who are opinion-based and tend to hold strong beliefs, Rush Limbaugh may be your personality type. People like Limbaugh tend to be more formal, and are most likely to lay out the reason for their call at the beginning of a conversation, looking in turn for concrete explanations rather than apologies. In contrast, emotions-based people look for a connection and will try to joke around or ask personal questions of the customer service representative. Expressions of sympathy work well in gaining control when interacting with such callers.

In addition, ELoyalty's algorithms use past experience and call analysis to come up with patterns that advise customer service representatives on how to handle particular customers and calls in the future. If a customer has called in the past, call center computers quickly flag his personality for the assessment of chances that he may call again to cancel his account; other hints of dealing with him are also provided by the computer. The software further syncs with company accounts to calculate how valuable a caller is—for example, the higher the caller's credit card limits, the greater priority he gets.

After using 1,000 servers, an algorithm utilized by Wall Street firms, and methodologies created by well-known psychologist Taibi Kahler to analyze 2 million speech patterns and 600 million conversations (totaling 600 terabytes of customer data), ELoyalty is able to work wonders in a business where time means money. If a minute usually costs around US$1–US$1.50, ELoyalty successfully lowers call center operating expenses by 20 percent because of more productive calls. In the near future, Conway is looking to bring his technology to the e-mail market—scanning e-mails to assess client relationships and simultaneously employee weaknesses, as well as spotting potential strains between large companies before it is too late.

Based on:

Singel, R. (2011, February 14). Meet the company that records your call for quality assurance. *Wired*. Retrieved July 17, 2012, from http://www.wired.com/epicenter/2011/02/eloyalty-call-recording/all/1.

Steiner, C. (2011, January 26). Make call centers really hum. *Forbes*. Retrieved July 17, 2012, from http://www.forbes.com/forbes/2011/0214/entrepreneurs-kelly-conway-software-eloyalty-your-pain.html.

Traditionally, such analyses were quite difficult for business users; in contrast, many of today's business analytics solutions offered by companies such as SAS or SAP guide the users through the process of conducting the desired analyses, selecting the right data, models, and so on, thus enabling "self-service business intelligence" and allowing business users to get self-service answers to the questions they have without relying on support staff.

DECISION SUPPORT SYSTEMS. A **decision support system (DSS)** is a special purpose information system designed to support organizational decision making related to a particular recurring problem. DSSs are typically used by managerial-level employees to help them solve semistructured problems such as sales and resource forecasting, yet DSSs can be used to support decisions at virtually all levels of the organization. A DSS augments human decision-making performance and problem solving by enabling managers to examine alternative solutions to a problem. One common approach is performing "what-if" analyses. A **what-if analysis** allows you to make hypothetical changes to the data associated with a problem (e.g., loan duration or interest rate) and observe how these changes influence the results. For example, a cash manager for a bank could examine what-if scenarios of the effect of various interest rates on cash availability. Some types of problems utilize a variety of input variables that each may have a different likelihood of occurring (e.g., there is 25 percent likelihood that inflation will stay the same and a 75 percent likelihood that inflation will increase). Sensitivity analysis allows you to understand how different input values and their probability of occurring (e.g., rate of inflation and its probability of occurring) will impact the results of a model. Similarly, goal-seeking analyses help in determining how input parameters need to be changed to achieve a desired end state. Finally, optimization models allow finding the best balance between certain parameters within given constraints. With a DSS, the manager uses decision analysis tools such as Microsoft

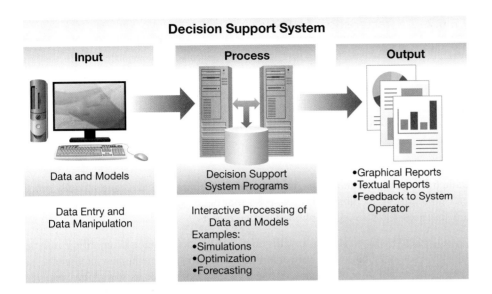

FIGURE 6.15

Architecture of a DSS using the basic systems model.

Excel—a widely used DSS environment—to either analyze or create meaningful information to support the decision making related to non-routine problems. In contrast to systems that primarily present the outputs in a passive way, a DSS is designed to be an "interactive" decision aid. The results from any analysis are displayed in both textual and graphical formats.

Architecture of a DSS Like the architecture of all systems, a DSS consists of input, process, and output components as illustrated in Figure 6.15 (Sprague, 1980). Specifically, a DSS uses **models** to manipulate data. For example, if you have some historic sales data, you can use many different types of models to create a forecast of future sales. One technique is to take an average of past sales, and adjust it for seasonal changes. The formula you would use to calculate and adjust the average is the model. A more complicated forecasting model might use time-series analysis or linear regression. See Table 6.6 for a summary of the ways organizations can use DSS to support decision making in organizations. Data for the DSS primarily come from transaction processing systems but can come from other sources as well.

TABLE 6.6   Common DSS Uses for Specific Organizational Areas

Area	Common DSS Uses
Corporate level	Corporate planning, venture analysis, mergers and acquisitions
Accounting	Cost analysis, discriminant analysis, breakeven analysis, auditing, tax computation and analysis, depreciation methods, budgeting
Finance	Discounted cash flow analysis, return on investment, buy or lease, capital budgeting, bond refinancing, stock portfolio management, compound interest, after-tax yield, foreign exchange values
Marketing	Product demand forecast, advertising strategy analysis, pricing strategies, market share analysis, sales growth evaluation, sales performance
Human resources	Labor negotiations, labor market analysis, personnel skills assessment, employee business expenses, fringe benefit computations, payroll and deductions
Production	Product design, production scheduling, transportation analysis, product mix, inventory levels, quality control, plant location, material allocation, maintenance analysis, machine replacement, job assignment, material requirements planning
Management science	Linear programming, decision trees, simulation, project planning and evaluation, queuing, dynamic programming, network analysis

TABLE 6.7   Characteristics of a DSS

Inputs	Data and models; data entry and data manipulation commands
Processing	Interactive processing of data and models; simulations, optimization, forecasts
Outputs	Graphs and textual reports; feedback to system user
Typical users	Midlevel managers (although a DSS could be used at any level of the organization)

Table 6.7 summarizes the characteristics of a DSS. Inputs are data and models. Processing supports the merging of data with models so that decision makers can examine alternative solution scenarios. Outputs are graphs and textual reports.

INTELLIGENT SYSTEMS. **Artificial intelligence (AI)** is the science of enabling information technologies—software, hardware, networks, and so on—to simulate human intelligence, such as reasoning and learning, as well as gaining sensing capabilities, such as seeing, hearing, walking, talking, and feeling. AI has had a strong connection to science fiction writers, who have written stories about AI-enabled technologies aiding humans (e.g., Mr. Data in *Star Trek: The Next Generation*), attempting world domination (e.g., *The Matrix*), or enabling humans to exist on an alien planet (e.g., *Avatar)*. The current reality of AI is that it is lagging far behind the imagination of most science fiction writers; nevertheless, great strides have been made. Most notably, the development of several types of intelligent systems is having great successes for a variety of applications. **Intelligent systems**—comprised of sensors, software, and computers embedded in machines and devices—emulate and enhance human capabilities. Intelligent systems are having a tremendous impact in a variety of areas, including banking and financial management, medicine, engineering, and the military. Three types of intelligent systems—expert systems, neural networks, and intelligent agents—are particularly relevant in business contexts and are discussed next.

Expert Systems An **expert system (ES)** is a type of intelligent system that uses reasoning methods based on knowledge about a specific problem domain in order to provide advice, much like a human expert. ESs are used to mimic human expertise by manipulating knowledge (understanding acquired through experience and extensive learning) rather than simply manipulating information (for more information, see Turban, Sharda, & Delen, 2011). Human knowledge can be represented in an ES by facts and rules about a problem coded in a form that can be manipulated by a computer. When you use an ES, the system asks you a series of questions, much as a human expert would. It continues to ask questions, and each new question is determined by your response to the preceding question. The ES matches the responses with the defined facts and rules until the responses point the system to a solution. A **rule** is a way of encoding knowledge, such as a recommendation, after collecting information from a user. Rules are typically expressed using an "if–then" format. For example, a rule in an ES for assisting with decisions related to the approval of automobile loans for individuals could be represented as follows: *If* personal income is US$50,000 or more, *then* approve the loan.

Given that most experts make decisions with limited information as well as use general categories of information when making judgments, researchers have developed **fuzzy logic** to broaden the capabilities of ESs and other intelligent systems. Specifically, fuzzy logic allows ES rules to be represented using approximations or subjective values in order to handle situations where information about a problem is incomplete. For example, a loan officer, when assessing a customer's loan application, may generally categorize some of the customer's financial information, such as income and debt level, as high, moderate, or low rather than using precise amounts. In addition to numerous business applications, fuzzy logic is used to better control antilock braking systems and household appliances as well as when making medical diagnoses or filtering offensive language in chat rooms.

The most difficult part of building an ES is acquiring the knowledge from the experts and gathering and compiling it into a consistent and complete form useful for making recommendations. ESs are used when expertise for a particular problem is rare or expensive, such as in the case of a complex machine repair or medical diagnosis. Using fuzzy logic, ESs are also utilized when knowledge about a problem is incomplete.

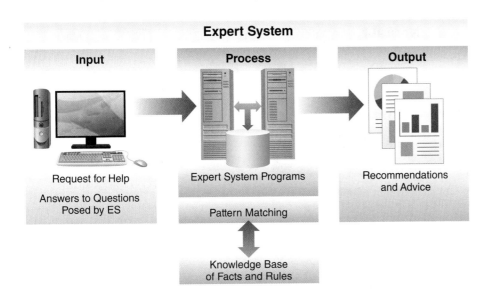

FIGURE 6.16

Architecture of an ES using the
basic systems model.

As with other information systems, the architecture of an ES (and other intelligent systems) can be described using the basic systems model (see Figure 6.16). Inputs to the system are questions and answers from the user. Processing is the matching of user questions and answers to information in the knowledge base. The processing in an ES is called **inferencing**, which consists of matching facts and rules, determining the sequence of questions presented to the user, and drawing a conclusion. The output from an ES is a recommendation. The general characteristics of an ES are summarized in Table 6.8.

Neural Networks Whereas "conventional" computers are very adept at processing large amounts of data by rapidly executing a program's instructions, they cannot easily adapt to different circumstances or deal with noisy data. If a conventional computer is presented with a novel problem that it is not programmed to solve, it cannot deal with this situation. Neural networks are a novel approach to problem solving; **neural networks**, composed of a network of processing elements (i.e., artificial "neurons") that work in parallel to complete a task, attempt to approximate the functioning of the human brain and can learn by example. Typically, a neural network is *trained* by having it categorize a large database of past information for common patterns. Once these patterns are established, new data can be compared to these learned patterns and conclusions drawn. For example, many financial institutions use neural network systems to analyze loan applications. These systems compare a person's loan application data with the neural network containing the *intelligence* of the success and failure of countless prior loans, ultimately making a loan acceptance (or rejection) recommendation (see Figure 6.17).

Intelligent Agent Systems An **intelligent agent**, or simply an *agent* (also called a **bot**—short for "software robot"), is a program that works in the background to provide some service when a specific event occurs. There are several types of agents for use in a broad range of contexts, including the following:

- **User Agents**. Agents that automatically perform a task for a user, such as automatically sending a report at the first of the month, assembling customized news, or filling out a Web form with routine information.

TABLE 6.8 Characteristics of an ES

Inputs	Request for help, users' answers to questions posed by the ES
Processing	Pattern matching and inferencing
Outputs	Recommendation or advice or further questions
Typical users	Midlevel managers (although an ES could be used at any level of the organization)

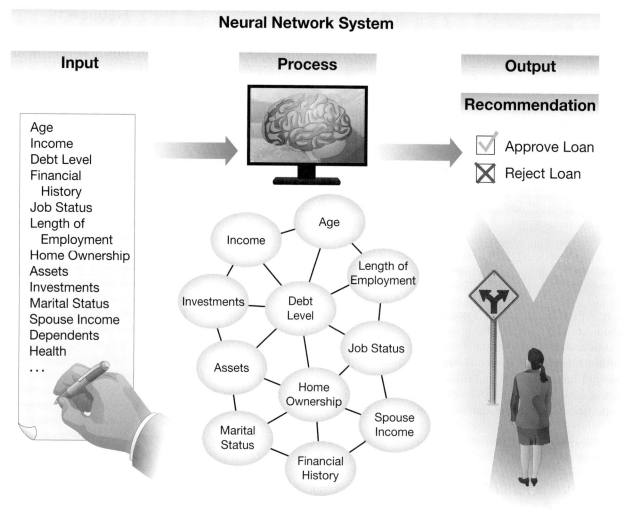

FIGURE 6.17

Neural networks approximate the functioning of the brain by creating common patterns in data and then comparing new data to learned patterns to make a recommendation.

- **Buyer Agents (Shopping Bots).** Agents that search to find the best price for a particular product you wish to purchase.
- **Monitoring and Sensing Agents.** Agents that keep track of key information, such as inventory levels or competitors' prices, notifying the user when conditions change.
- **Data Mining Agents.** Agents that continuously analyze large data warehouses to detect changes deemed important by a user, sending a notification when such changes occur.
- **Web Crawlers.** Agents that continuously browse the Web for specific information (e.g., used by search engines)—also known as **Web spiders**.
- **Destructive Agents.** Malicious agents designed by spammers and other Internet attackers to farm e-mail addresses off Web sites or deposit spyware on machines.

One example of an intelligent agent is Apple's Siri personal assistant, built into its iPhones. Similarly, Google Now! is an intelligent agent built into newer versions of the Android mobile phone operating system. Over time, Google Now! learns about a user's habits, and performs certain actions based on time of the day, location, and so on. For example, in the morning, the user automatically receives an alert about the weather in his or her current location; when passing by a subway station, public transport information is presented; when on a trip, the time to travel back home is automatically calculated (taking into consideration factors such as traffic situation); and so on (see Figure 6.18). Google also developed intelligent agents for its **augmented reality** applications built into Project Glass, eyeglasses with a tiny embedded screen, which augments reality by displaying information about the wearer's surroundings, including weather information, public transportation schedules, reviews about a restaurant the wearer is looking at, and other useful information (see Chapter 2).

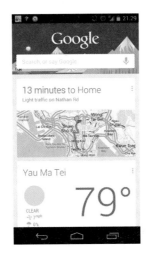

FIGURE 6.18

Google Now!, an intelligent agent built into the Android operating system, presents pertinent information based on factors such as the user's habits, location, and time of day.
Source: © 2012 Google

In sum, there are ongoing developments to make information systems *smarter* so that organizational decision makers gain business intelligence. Although systems such as ESs, neural networks, and intelligent agents have yet to realize the imagination of science fiction writers, they have taken great strides in helping information systems support business intelligence.

KNOWLEDGE MANAGEMENT SYSTEMS. There is no universal agreement on what exactly is meant by the term "knowledge management." In general, however, **knowledge management**

ETHICAL DILEMMA

Are You Being Tracked?

Consumer preference has always served as an important source for decisions about what to produce, or how to present, promote, or price products, and companies are always attempting to determine and/or influence buyer behavior. Most recently, a legal debate shed light on an innovative way of inferring individual shoppers' tastes simply by tracking them as they walk from store to store, tapping into shopping patterns and observing their behavior, all through the use of monitoring sensors that track mobile phone signals.

The technology, known as Footpath, was made possible by UK-based Path Intelligence. With the help of antennas that detect the TMSI (Temporary Mobile Subscriber Identifier) of mobile phones in the vicinity, Footpath senses the movement of customers by triangulation, thus following buyers as they stroll through the mall. To an extent, the system resembles Web usage mining, or the tracking of Web site visitors' paths when they are exploring the site or making a purchase, in that it allows brick-and-mortar retailers to track customers in an "offline" environment. Although Footpath was initially sold as an innovative method of collecting consumer information to boost revenue, two malls in the U.S. that carried the technology ended up receiving letters from a New York Senator warning of privacy violation and potential abuse of the tracking service.

How could online tracking have gone on for years without getting caught in legal complications when Footpath swiftly came face-to-face with ethical questioning? The fact is, in order to prevent Web sites and advertisers from tracking Web visitors without their consent, the U.S. and EU have so far recommended consumers be given the "do-not-track" and "Right-to-be-Forgotten" options for the sake of privacy protection. Sans the consent of either Web visitors or mall shoppers to track their preferences and compile data off the record, both online and offline tracking actually do raise a number of privacy red flags.

As businesses boom, competition has gotten stiffer and technology has become a viable solution to boosting revenue. However, privacy has simultaneously evolved as a crucial matter that requires further attention. If the only way to avoid being tracked by Footpath is to switch off one's mobile phone (which is rather vague considering it is not much of an option, especially when shoppers are not aware of the act), then it is up to corporate ethics and legal aid to ensure the protection of our privacy.

Based on:

Gallagher, S. (2011, November 26). We're watching: malls track shopper's cell phone signals to gather marketing data. *Ars Technica*. Retrieved July 18, 2012, from http://arstechnica.com/business/news/2011/11/were-watching-malls-track-shoppers-cell-phone-signals-to-gather-marketing-data.ars.

Goodin, D. (2011, November 29). Malls suspend plan to track shoppers' cellphones. *The Register*. Retrieved July 18, 2012, from http://www.theregister.co.uk/2011/11/29/cellphone_tracking_nixed.

refers to the processes an organization uses to gain the greatest value from its knowledge assets. In Chapter 1 "Managing in the Digital World," we contrasted data, information, and knowledge. Recall that data are raw material—recorded, unformatted symbols such as words or numbers. Information is data that have been formatted, organized, or processed in some way so that the result is useful to people. We need knowledge to understand relationships between different pieces of information. Consequently, what constitutes **knowledge assets** are all the underlying skills, routines, practices, principles, formulas, methods, heuristics, and intuitions, whether explicit or tacit. All databases, manuals, reference works, textbooks, diagrams, displays, computer files, proposals, plans, and any other artifacts in which both facts and procedures are recorded and stored are considered knowledge assets. From an organizational point of view, properly used knowledge assets enable an organization to improve its efficiency, effectiveness, and, of course, profitability. Additionally, as many companies are beginning to lose a large number of baby boomers to retirement, companies are using knowledge management systems to capture these crucial knowledge assets (Leonard, 2006). Clearly, effectively managing knowledge assets will enhance business intelligence.

Knowledge assets can be distinguished as being either explicit or tacit. **Explicit knowledge assets** reflect knowledge that can be documented, archived, and codified, often with the help of information systems. Explicit knowledge assets reflect much of what is typically stored in a DBMS. In contrast, **tacit knowledge assets** reflect the processes and procedures that are located in a person's mind on how to effectively perform a particular task (see Figure 6.19). Identifying key tacit knowledge assets and managing these assets so that they are accurate and available to people throughout the organization remains a significant challenge.

Tacit knowledge assets often reflect an organization's *best practices*—procedures and processes that are widely accepted as being among the most effective and/or efficient. Identifying how to recognize, generate, store, share, and manage this tacit knowledge is the primary objective for deploying a knowledge management system. Consequently, a **knowledge management system** is typically not a single technology but rather a collection of technology-based tools that include communication technologies—such as e-mail, groupware, instant messaging, and the like—as well as information storage and retrieval systems, such as wikis or DBMSs, to enable the generation, storage, sharing, and management of tacit and explicit knowledge assets (Malhotra, 2005).

Benefits of Knowledge Management Systems Many potential benefits can come from organizations' effectively capturing and utilizing their tacit knowledge assets (Levinson, 2010)

FIGURE 6.19

Explicit knowledge assets can easily be documented, archived, and codified, whereas tacit knowledge assets are located in a person's mind.

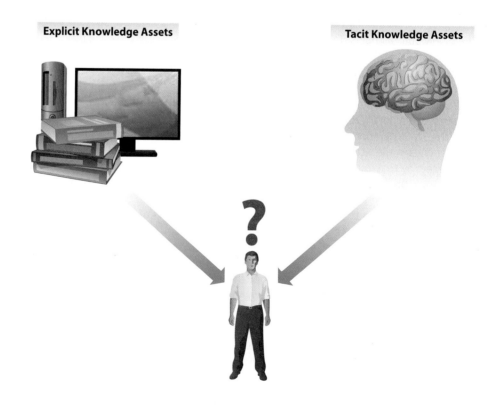

Table 6.9   Benefits and Challenges of Knowledge Management Systems

Benefits	Challenges
Enhanced innovation and creativity	Getting employee buy-in
Improved customer service, shorter product development, and streamlined operations	Focusing too much on technology
	Forgetting the goal
Enhanced employee retention	Dealing with knowledge overload and obsolescence
Improved organizational performance	

(see Table 6.9). For example, innovation and creativity may be enhanced by the free flow of ideas throughout the organization. Also, by widely sharing best practices, organizations should realize improved customer service, shorter product development times, and streamlined operations. Enhanced business operations will not only improve the overall organizational performance, but will also enhance employee retention rates by recognizing the value of employees' knowledge and rewarding them for sharing it. Thus, organizations can realize many benefits from the successful deployment of a knowledge management system.

Although there are many potential benefits for organizations that effectively deploy knowledge management systems, to do so requires that several substantial challenges be overcome (Table 6.9). First, effective deployment requires employees to agree to share their personal tacit knowledge assets and to take extra steps to utilize the system for identifying best practices. Therefore, to encourage employee buy-in and also to enable the sharing of knowledge, organizations must create a culture that values and rewards widespread participation. Second, experience has shown that a successful deployment must first identify what knowledge is needed, why it is needed, and who is likely to have this knowledge. Once an organization understands "why, what, and who," identifying the best technologies for facilitating knowledge exchange is a much easier task. In other words, the best practices for deploying knowledge management systems suggest that organizations save the "how"—that is, what collaboration and storage technologies to use—for last.

Third, the successful deployment of a knowledge management system must be linked to a specific business objective. By linking the system to a specific business objective and coupling that with the use of an assessment technique, such as return on investment, an organization can identify costs and benefits and can also be sure that the system is providing value in an area that is indeed important to the organization. Fourth, the knowledge management system must be easy to use, not only for entering, but also for retrieving knowledge. Similarly, the system cannot overload users with too much information or with information that is obsolete. Just as physical assets can erode over time, knowledge can also become stale and irrelevant. Therefore, an ongoing process of updating, amending, and removing obsolete or irrelevant knowledge must occur, or the system will fall into disarray and will not be used. In sum, an investment in a knowledge management system can offer a number of benefits, but organizations must take care to overcome various challenges.

How Organizations Utilize Knowledge Management Systems The people using a knowledge management system will be working in different departments within the organization, doing different functions, and will likely be located in different locations around the building, city, or even the world. Each person—or group of people—can be thought of as a separate island that is set apart from others by geography, job focus, expertise, age, and gender. Often, a person on one island is trying to solve a problem that has already been solved by another person located on some other island. Finding this "other" person is often a significant challenge. The goal of a successful knowledge management system is to facilitate the exchange of needed knowledge between these separate islands. To find and connect such separate islands, organizations use social network analysis. **Social network analysis** is a technique that attempts to find groups of people who work together, to find people who don't collaborate but should, or to find experts in particular subject areas. To do this, people's contacts are mapped so that connections or missing links within the organization can easily be discovered (see Figure 6.20). In addition to social network analysis, organizations use social bookmarking and social cataloging to capture and structure employees' knowledge and harness their collective intelligence (see Chapter 5, "Enhancing Organizational Communication and Collaboration Using Social Media").

FIGURE 6.20

Social network analysis can help to analyze collaboration patterns.

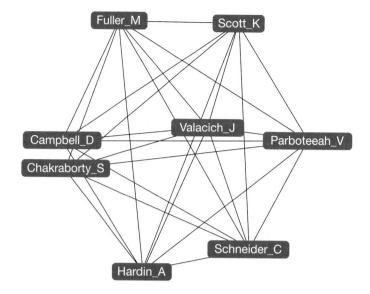

Once organizations have collected their knowledge into a repository, they must find an easy way to share it with employees (often using an intranet), customers, suppliers (often with an extranet), or the general public (often using the Internet). These **knowledge portals** can be customized to meet the unique needs of their intended users. For example, the U.S. Food and Drug Administration (FDA) uses a Web-based knowledge portal for keeping the public (e.g., citizens, researchers, and industry) informed on the most up-to-date information related to food (e.g., information on mad cow disease or product recalls) and drugs (e.g., the status of a drug trial) (see Figure 6.21).

In addition to the FDA, countless other organizations, such as Ford Motor Company, Eli Lilly, Walmart, and Dell Computers, are also rapidly deploying knowledge management systems. We are learning from these deployments that all organizations, whether for-profit or non-profit, struggle to get the right information to the right person at the right time. Through the use of a comprehensive strategy for managing knowledge assets, organizations are much more likely to gain a competitive advantage and a positive return on their IS investments.

Information Visualization

The third pillar of business intelligence applications is information visualization. **Visualization** refers to the display of complex data relationships using a variety of graphical methods, enabling managers to quickly grasp the results of the analysis. For example, Figure 6.22 shows the visualization of Hurricane Katrina in 2005 as the storm was gaining strength. The image

FIGURE 6.21

Countless organizations are using Web-based knowledge portals to provide information to employees, customers, and partners.

Source: Courtesy of the Food and Drug Administration.

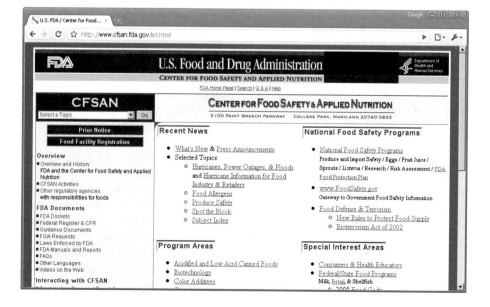

FIGURE 6.22

Visualization is the display of complex data relationships using a variety of graphical methods.
Source: NASA Headquarters

shows towering thunderclouds (in red), called hot towers, that were spotted just before Katrina intensified to a Category 5 hurricane. Once represented visually, analysts can view changes over time and perform what-if analyses to better understand the behavior of hurricanes. In similar ways, organizations around the world are utilizing visualization technologies to enhance business intelligence.

DASHBOARDS. **Digital dashboards** are commonly used to present key performance indicators and other summary information used by managers and executives to make decisions. To provide the greatest benefits for decision makers, digital dashboards typically support three usage models: push reporting, exception reporting and alerts, and pull reporting. Digital dashboards not only provide the decision makers with a quick, visual overview of key performance indicators and other key operational statistics and trends (i.e., push reporting), but also alert the user of any items that require immediate attention (i.e., exception reporting and alerts); if the user wants to analyze the root causes of an exception or perform other analyses, he or she can drill down or perform self-service ad hoc queries (i.e., pull reporting).

Digital dashboards (sometimes called executive dashboards) evolved from executive information systems designed to provide top-level managers with the needed information to support business processes, such as cash and investment management, resource allocation, and contract negotiation. Typically, executives require information presented in a highly aggregated form so that they can scan information quickly for trends and anomalies. Further, decisions made by executives typically require both "soft" and "hard" data. **Soft data** include textual news stories or other non-analytical information. **Hard data** include facts and numbers. While much of the hard data can be gathered from organizational databases and other systems, obtaining soft data typically involves the use of text mining technologies or input from dedicated personnel. For example, the executive dashboard offered by Dow Jones integrates information from an organization's internal systems with external information provided by Dow Jones; similarly, many dashboards integrate RSS readers to display news feeds to the users. In sum, digital dashboards deliver information from multiple sources to provide warnings, action notices, and summaries of business conditions.

Although data are typically provided in a very highly aggregated form, the executive also has the capability to drill down and see the details if necessary. For example, suppose a digital dashboard summarizes profits by region, as illustrated in Figure 6.23. If the executive wants to get a deeper understanding about a particular country, a selection on the screen can provide the details behind the aggregate numbers, as shown in Figure 6.24. By drilling down into the data, the executive can see that the majority of the profits were made in a particular region, or city, or even store. Also, the digital dashboard can connect the data in the system to the organization's

FIGURE 6.23

A digital dashboard showing profits by sales region.

Source: Courtesy of Microsoft, Inc.

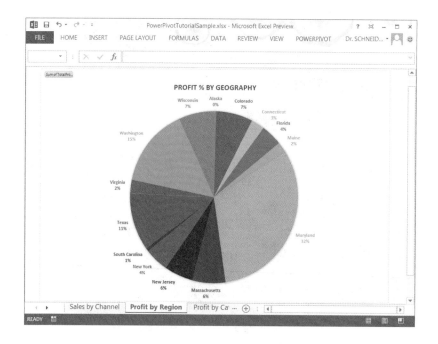

internal communication systems (e.g., electronic or voice mail) so that the executive can quickly send a message to the appropriate managers to discuss solutions to the problem discovered in the drill-down.

Dashboards make use of a variety of design elements to present the data in the most user-friendly way. To highlight deviations that need to be addressed or to symbolize changes over time, dashboards use maps, charts, spark lines, or graphics symbolizing traffic lights, thermometers, or speedometers (see Figure 6.25); conditional formatting is often used to highlight exceptions and draw the user's attention to deviations from the normal course of business. Many dashboards now combine business intelligence with technologies typically used to deliver rich Web applications (such as Adobe Flash) in order to provide the level of interactivity desired by users at different levels of an organization.

One recent trend influencing the design of dashboards is mobile business intelligence. With the advances in mobile communication technology, today's executives want to be in touch with their organizational performance anytime, anywhere. Further, most of today's knowledge workers are increasingly mobile in terms of the device they're using—during a

FIGURE 6.24

Drill-down numbers for profits by sales region.

Source: Courtesy of Microsoft, Inc.

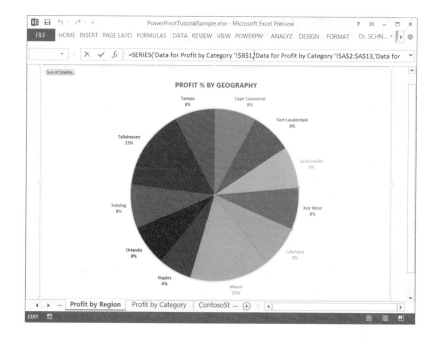

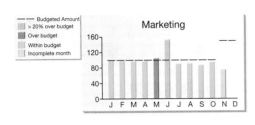

FIGURE 6.25

Dashboards use various graphical elements to highlight important information.

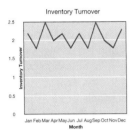

workday, one may use a desktop computer, a laptop, a smartphone, or an iPad. Hence, dashboard vendors are offering solutions for multiple devices and screen sizes so that the user can get the same information regardless of location and device used to access the information.

VISUAL ANALYTICS. As discussed in previous sections, business intelligence systems can provide business decision makers with a wide variety of analyses to support decision making. However, in the end, it is still the humans who have to interpret the output from these systems. With growing complexity of the underlying data (such as multiple dimensions, including spatial dimensions), interpreting the outputs becomes extremely challenging. **Visual analytics** is the combination of various analysis techniques and interactive visualization to solve complex problems. By combining human intelligence and reasoning capabilities with technology's retrieval and analysis capabilities, visual analytics can help in decision making, as the strengths of both the human and the machine are merged. With the humans' ability to make sense of "noisy" data, unexpected patterns or relationships in the data can be discovered, and results of complex queries can be quickly interpreted. Visual analytics is used in a variety of settings, ranging from homeland security to disaster relief.

GEOGRAPHIC INFORMATION SYSTEMS. One type of visualization system that is growing in popularity and is frequently incorporated into digital dashboards is called a **geographic information system (GIS)**. A GIS is a system for creating, storing, analyzing, and managing geographically referenced information. In other words, a GIS captures various characteristics about geographic locations, allowing these characteristics to be coupled with other data to support querying, analysis, and decision making. For example, a GIS could link the square footage of commercial real estate to its exact location in terms of latitude and longitude. These data could be paired with population density, average incomes of people living within an area, travel accessibility (e.g., interstate highways and major thoroughfares), proximity to services (e.g., fire, police, restaurants, public transportation stops), or virtually any other characteristic. A new business such as a restaurant could use this information to identify optimal locations for the placement of new locations. On a personal level, you probably frequently interact with GISs. For example, when you're accessing Google maps to search for a restaurant in your town, you can view geographic data (such as the map or the satellite image) as well as attribute data about restaurants, including name, address, opening hours, and customer reviews.

Businesses typically face many decisions with a spatial dimension: Where are my customers located? Where is the best location to open a new store? Which areas should be included in the next mailing? How far are my customers willing to drive? A GIS can help to create models used to answer questions such as where a company such as Levi Strauss should add authorized

KEY PLAYERS

SAS, MicroStrategy, and other Business Intelligence Leaders

With business intelligence, as with many other applications, the old mantra "garbage in, garbage out" applies, and any output from business intelligence applications is only as good as the inputs the applications are working with. Thus, it comes as no surprise that, in addition to "pure play" business intelligence (BI) vendors, those companies who support collection and storage of the data also venture into providing business intelligence applications. Whereas pure plays such as SAS and MicroStrategy are independent companies, companies such as SAP, IBM, Oracle, and Microsoft have gained prominence in the BI market through acquisitions.

Having started as a project to analyze agricultural research at North Carolina State University, SAS expanded into various other industries and geographic regions. SAS now has more than 13,000 employees and provides a variety of solutions related to business intelligence, including customer intelligence, financial intelligence, and supply chain intelligence, for industries ranging from casinos to utilities.

MicroStratey, the other major independent player in the BI arena, started out as a company offering data mining tools for businesses. Its innovativeness led to MicroStrategy becoming one of the first companies offering mobile BI solutions. Today, MicroStrategy is used by major companies ranging from eBay to Lowe's.

Given organizations' increasing interest in business intelligence solutions, other players in the enterprise software market started a shopping frenzy, so as to be able to offer end-to-end solutions to their customers. For example, as much input into business intelligence applications comes from enterprise systems (see Chapter 7, "Enhancing Business Processes Using Enterprise Information Systems"), the German enterprise software company SAP purchased BI vendor Business Objects

to provide self-service BI functionality to its users. Similarly, one of SAP's biggest contenders in the enterprise systems market, Oracle, is complementing its enterprise systems offerings with BI solutions after having acquired Hyperion in 2007.

IBM was traditionally known as a hardware company, but has since morphed into a provider of a variety of systems supporting diverse business processes and industries. Similar to SAP and Oracle, IBM jumped on the BI bandwagon by acquiring an independent BI vendor, Cognos. As IBM, software behemoth Microsoft has nearly uncountable product offerings focusing on diverse markets. Microsoft's BI solutions are designed with the end user in mind, and provide a familiar environment for many office workers.

Beyond these intelligent giants, various other companies focus on specific aspects related to business intelligence. While the companies presented here have emerged to become leaders in the overall business intelligence market, various specialized vendors should nevertheless remain on companies' watchlists.

Based on:

IBM. (n.d.) Business intelligence. Retrieved July 20, 2012, from http://www-142.ibm.com/software/products/us/en/category/SWQ20.

Microsoft. (n.d.) Microsoft Business Intelligence. Retrieved July 20, 2012, from http://www.microsoft.com/en-us/bi/default.aspx.

MicroStrategy. (n.d.) About MicroStrategy. Retrieved July 20, 2012, from http://www.microstrategy.com/about-us.

Oracle. (n.d.). Oracle and Hyperion. Retrieved July 20, 2012, from http://www.oracle.com/us/corporate/Acquisitions/hyperion/index.html.

SAP. (n.d.). Data-rich business intelligence. Retrieved July 20, 2012,from http://www.sap.com/solutions/analytics/business-intelligence/index.epx.

SAS. (n.d.). About SAS. Retrieved July 20, 2012, from http://www.sas.com/company/about/index.html.

resellers, or how, where, and what kinds of fertilizers farmers should apply, enabling precision farming (see Table 6.10 for various industry uses of GIS).

Using GIS, analysts can combine geographic, demographic, and other data for locating target customers, finding optimal site locations, or determining the right product mix at different locations; additionally, GIS can perform a variety of analyses, such as market share analysis and competitor analysis. Cities, counties, and states also use GIS for aiding in infrastructure design and zoning issues (e.g., where should the new elementary school be located?). For the various geospatial aspects you can map with GIS, refer to Table 6.11. How does a GIS help in analyzing geospatial and related data? Typically, a GIS provides a user with a blank map of an area. The user can then add information stored in different **layers**, each resembling a transparency containing different information about the area; for example, one layer may contain all roads, another layer may contain ZIP code boundaries, and yet another layer may contain floodplains, average household sizes, locations of coffee shops, or other information of interest (in Google Earth, you can view various layers, such as roads, traffic patterns, weather, earthquakes, golf courses, and so on; see Figure 6.26). Adding or removing those layers helps to view the relevant information needed to answer questions that have a spatial dimension.

TABLE 6.10   Various Industry Uses of GIS

Industry	Sample Uses
Agriculture	Analyze crop yield by location, soil erosion, or differences in fertilizer needs (precision farming)
Banking	Identify lucrative areas for marketing campaigns
Disaster response	Analyze historical events, set up evacuation plans, and identify areas most likely to be affected by disasters
Insurance	Risk analysis (e.g., earthquake insurance)
Government	Urban planning, zoning, and census planning
Law enforcement	Analyze high-crime areas
Marine biology	Track movement of fish swarms
Media	Create maps to visualize locations of events and analyze circulation
Mining and drilling	Locate potential areas for extraction of natural resources
Real estate	Create maps to visualize locations of properties
Retail	Analyze sales, inventory, customers, and so on by location; identify new retail locations; and visualize and present business data
Transportation and logistics	Route planning

Source: Based on ESRI, http://www.gis.com/content/who-uses-gis.

One question that organizations often face is where the customers come from. In order to answer this question, organizations typically use data from survey respondents (or the cashier asks for customers' ZIP codes); this data is then geocoded (i.e., transformed into coordinates) to create a layer containing customer information that can then be added to a map. Comparing customers' locations with the location of one's business can help in deciding whether the store has the optimal location or whether opening a new store would be warranted. Relatedly, trade area analysis helps to assess where customers are coming from by combining location information with, for example, drive time information to determine if certain areas are underserved or if two stores' trade areas overlap. Another way to visualize geospatial data is by using thematic maps. Thematic maps color code data that is aggregated for specific geographic regions. For example, a thematic map could display the median household income in different blocks, or it could display average household sizes, helping a business to identify areas with the most promising target population; similarly, an insurance company could use GIS to determine where certain crimes (such as car theft) most frequently occur (see Figure 6.27).

In addition to helping in analysis, GISs are also increasingly used by governments and organizations to effectively communicate with stakeholders. For example, many retail chains such as Best Buy or Walmart incorporate map-based store locators into their Web sites. When searching for a store by city, state, or ZIP code, the Web site returns a map showing the store's location (geographic data), along with attribute information such as distance, street address, phone

TABLE 6.11   Various Ways of Representing Geospatial Data

Mapping	Example
Features and patterns (i.e., distribution of features)	Earthquake epicenters (features) and areas where the hazard may be highest (patterns).
Quantities	The number of young families with a high income in a census district.
Densities	Number of high-income families per square mile in a census district.
What's inside	Does a luxury real estate development fall within a 15-minute driving radius of a store?
What's nearby	How many Starbucks stores are within 5 miles of my new coffee shop?
Change	How have store sales changed after a large ad campaign?

Source: Based on ESRI, http://www.gis.com/content/what-can-you-do-gis.

FIGURE 6.26

Google Earth uses layers to display information related to a specific geographical area.
Source: Courtesy of Google, Inc.

WHO'S GOING MOBILE

OpenStreetMap

Mobile devices and location are a perfect match for each other; many people carry their smartphones wherever they go, enabling them to receive useful information specific to their current location. Search engines such as Google or Bing provide users with information on nearby restaurants, ATMs, post offices, attractions, and so on. Review sites such as Yelp help users to find restaurants located in their vicinity. Online mapping services help users locate their position, and provide directions to wherever they want to go. These and other services make smartphones an ever more useful companion when being away from home or the office.

Where do these maps come from? One of the biggest contenders in the market for online mapping services is Google, which purchases or leases map data from various commercial entities. While Google provides its maps service for free for low-volume usage, it charges other providers for commercial usage of Google Maps data. Thus, many companies (including FourSquare or Apple) are increasingly turning to alternative mapping services. One popular alternative is OpenStreetMap. Similarly to the online encyclopedia Wikipedia, OpenStreetMap is maintained by a community of contributors, and anybody can help to fix bugs or add points of interest (also, companies such as Microsoft have recently started backing OpenStreetMap). This is where the combination of mobile devices and mapping services becomes extremely useful. On the one hand, OpenStreetMap can help people find their way around, but on the other hand, people can update or edit maps on the go. In other words, if you are standing on a street corner, and notice that some feature is mislabeled on OpenStreetMap, you can immediately help improving the service for others by providing a bug report; if you see a feature not included in OpenStreetMap, you can immediately provide the needed information.

Similar to Wikipedia, the more people contribute, the more accurate and useful the maps become. Various apps on different platforms now facilitate the editing of maps when on the go.

Recently, NGOs have discovered the use of online maps in the developing world, having realized the need for people to have access to location-based information about businesses, hospitals, schools, water points, or sanitation facilities. Given legal and technical restrictions of using commercial maps, projects such as Mapping Day Uganda contribute to OpenStreetMap by holding so-called "Mapping Days," where groups of students, armed with walking papers, GPS devices, and pens, help to "fill in the blanks" in Uganda's map. Similarly, supporters of Mapping Day Uganda have created a smartphone app that allows users to record information about businesses (such as name, address, opening times) directly from their mobile phone, making the editing even easier. This shows how the powerful combination of mobile devices, online maps, and crowdsourcing can help people even in the most remote places.

Based on:

About. (2012, April 15). OpenStreetMap Wiki. Retrieved July 20, 2012, from http://wiki.openstreetmap.org/w/index.php?title=About&oldid=760809.

Anonymous. (n.d.). About Mapping Uganda. Retrieved July 20, 2012, from http://www.mappingday.com/about-mapping-uganda.

Graham, F. (2012, July 17). Kenyan and Ugandan start-ups make location pay its way. *BBC News.* Retrieved July 20, 2012, from http://www.bbc.co.uk/news/business-18858897.

Gralla, P. (2012, March 26). Microsoft's secret weapon against Google Maps–open source. *Computerworld.* Retrieved June 7, 2012, from http://blogs.computerworld.com/19932/microsofts_secret_weapon_against_google_maps_open_source.

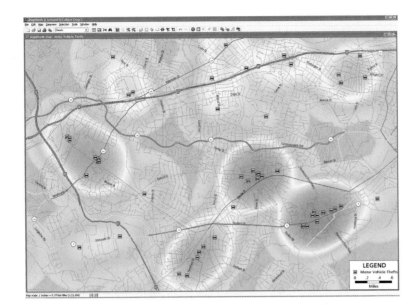

FIGURE 6.27

A thematic map showing car thefts in a town.
Source: Caliper Corporation/Maptitude Motor Vehicle Theft Map

number, and opening hours. Similarly, organizations use output from GISs to communicate to their stockholders about expansion plans, retail store density, and the like.

Clearly, GIS, like all the systems described in this chapter, are providing organizations with business intelligence to better compete in the digital world.

INDUSTRY ANALYSIS

Health Care

Do you remember the times when your doctor wrote a prescription and the handwriting was worse than your professor's, making you wonder how the pharmacist could ever decipher it and dispense the correct drugs? If you recently went to a doctor, you may have noticed that information systems have had a huge impact on the health care field; indeed, health informatics has become a key focus of health care providers, insurance companies, and governments. Now, many doctors carry laptops or tablets, allowing them to digitally store any diagnosis, facilitating the sharing of information between the physician, nurses, and even your medical insurance. In addition to providing access to electronic patient records, the laptop or tablet provides your physician access to medical and drug information, as offered by the *Physician's Desk Reference* Web site (www.pdr.net), where your physician can obtain the latest information about drugs and clinical guidelines or check interactions between different drugs. Electronic patient records are now even moving toward the Web. Pioneered by Microsoft's HealthVault and Google, Web-based electronic patient records free the patient from having to carry medical records from doctor to doctor (Google's initiative has since been discontinued due to limited public acceptance).

Information systems have also tremendously changed the diagnosis and monitoring of patients. For example, modern EEG and EKG devices heavily depend on computer technology, and, as the name implies, computer tomography (used

to produce images of internal organs) could not be performed without computer technology. Even diagnostic tests such as X-rays now use digital technology, allowing the doctor to digitally enhance the image for improved diagnosis or to electronically transmit the image to a remote specialist. Following the diagnosis of a serious condition, technology can even help in the operating room. For example, many modern clinics use surgical robots and endoscopes for delicate procedures such as neurosurgery or gastrointestinal surgery. Taken a step further, such systems can be used for what is referred to as telemedicine, including remote diagnosis and remote surgery. Whereas traditionally a patient had to travel thousands of miles to visit a specialized surgeon, many surgeries can now be performed remotely, reducing the strain on the patient and potentially saving precious time. Further, telemedicine applications can be used for remote locations, battlefields, or even prisons, reducing costs for transporting patients and improving care.

Although information technology can help to provide convenient health care to patients, privacy and data security may also be a concern for them. As vendors managing electronic health records have access to patient data, this can be an additional income stream; increasingly, such vendors are selling the "anonymized" patient data to pharmaceutical companies and other interested parties. These companies use data mining in order to detect disease patterns, cluster similar cases, or improve treatment. According to a *New York Times* report, however, such data can often be linked to other publicly available information, so that it loses its anonymity. Currently, the overall market for health record systems is between US$8 billion and US$10 billion annually, and vendors generate about 5 percent of this income from selling patient data. With the increasing use of electronic health care systems, this number is likely to grow considerably.

Just as physicians, insurance companies, and health care providers are turning to information systems to improve business processes and better serve patients' needs, consumers are increasingly using the Internet for health information. For example, WebMD is one of the most popular Web sites providing health-related information, priding itself on having high-quality, timely, and unbiased information. In addition to objective information, people use social media to obtain information beyond what's published by the experts. Specifically, people seeking physician and hospital rankings or recommendations frequent blogs, health-related discussion forums, or review sites such as ratemd.com or Angie's list (angieslist.com). Further, major search engines such as Microsoft's Bing are constantly refining their search algorithms to provide the most relevant information to health-related queries. Regardless of whether you're visiting your doctor regarding a condition or just for a routine checkup, or if you need more information about what your doctor is telling you, various information systems are likely to play a major role.

Questions

1. Discuss the benefits and drawbacks of online medical records.
2. Computer-aided diagnosis can replace years of experience, providing opportunities for young, inexperienced physicians. Contrast the benefits and drawbacks for the patients and the physicians.
3. Will there be a place for physicians without computer skills in the future? Why or why not?

Based on:

Anonymous. (n.d.). HealthVault. Retrieved July 19, 2012, from http://www.healthvault.com.

Anonymous. (n.d.). Welcome to PDR.net. Retrieved July 19, 2012, from http://www.pdr.net.

Anonymous. (2007, April 29). World's first image-guided surgical robot to enhance accuracy and safety of brain surgery. *Science Daily.* Retrieved July 19, 2012, from http://www.sciencedaily.com/releases/2007/04/070417114732.htm.

Anonymous. (2010, April 15). Consumers increasingly turning to Internet, social media for health care information. *iHealthBeat.* Retrieved July 19, 2012, from http://www.ihealthbeat.org/special-reports/2010/consumers-increasingly-turning-to-internet-social-media-for-health-care-information.aspx.

Zetter, K. (2009, October 19). Medical records: Stored in the cloud, sold on the open market. *Wired.* Retrieved July 19, 2012, from http://www.wired.com/threatlevel/2009/10/medicalrecords.

Key Points Review

1. *Describe the concept of business intelligence and how databases serve as a foundation for gaining business intelligence.* Businesses need business intelligence to quickly respond to external threats and opportunities arising from unstable market conditions, fierce competition, short product life cycles, government regulation, fickle customers, and Big Data. Business intelligence supports this by enabling a closed-loop approach to planning at all levels of the organization. Organizations use databases to capture and manage the data that can later be used as input to business intelligence applications. A database is a collection of related data organized in a way that facilitates data searches; databases are underlying all interactive Web sites. A database contains entities, attributes, records, and tables. Entities are things about which we collect data, such as people, courses, customers, or products. Attributes are the individual pieces of information about an entity, such as a person's last name or Social Security Number, that are stored in a database record. A record is the collection of related attributes about an entity; usually, a record is displayed as a database row. A table is a collection of related records about an entity type; each row in the table is a record, and each column is an attribute. A DBMS is a software application with which you create, store, organize, and retrieve data from a single database or several databases. The data within a database must be adequately organized so that it is possible to store and retrieve information effectively. To support more effective business processes, businesses use online transaction processing. Data from operational systems serve as an input to informational systems. Master data management helps organizations to arrive at a "single version of the truth" to gather business intelligence; data warehouses and data marts support the integration and analysis of large data sets.

2. *Explain the three components of business intelligence: information and knowledge discovery, business analytics, and information visualization.* Information and knowledge discovery tools are used to discover "hidden" relationships in data. Ad hoc query tools allow decision makers to run queries whenever needed. OLAP tools extend this capability by offering the ability to perform complex multidimensional queries. Data mining is used for association discovery

and clustering and classification. Unstructured data analysis is used to extract information from textual documents. Business analytics augments business intelligence by using predictive analysis to identify trends or predict business outcomes. Decision support and intelligent systems are used to support human and automated decision making. DSSs support organizational decision making and are typically designed to solve a particular recurring problem in the organization. DSSs are most commonly used to support semistructured problems that are addressed by managerial-level employees. A DSS is designed to be an interactive decision aid. Intelligent systems such as ESs, neural networks, and intelligent agents work to emulate and enhance human capabilities. ESs apply knowledge within some topic area to provide advice by mimicking human expertise (understanding acquired through experience and extensive learning). ESs are used when expertise for a particular problem is rare or expensive. Neural networks attempt to approximate the functioning and decision making of the human brain by comparing patterns in new data versus complex patterns learned from prior data. Intelligent agents are programs that can be applied to a broad variety of situations, typically operating in the background to provide some service when a special event occurs or when a request is made. Knowledge management systems are a collection of technology-based tools that enable the generation, storage, sharing, and management of knowledge assets. Visualization refers to the display of complex data relationships using a variety of graphical methods, enabling managers to quickly grasp the results of the analysis. Results of complex analyses as well as key performance indicators are displayed on digital dashboards, which are often used to provide decision makers with the right information in an easy-to-understand way. Visual analytics combines the human visual system and analysis techniques to aid in the analysis of complex relationships and make sense of "noisy" data. GISs aid in storing, analyzing, and managing geographically referenced information, such as for locating target customers or finding optimal store locations.

Key Terms

Review Questions

1. What is business intelligence and why do organizations need it?
2. What do you understand by normalization? Why it is important from a database perspective?
3. What is the importance of master data management?
4. What are the advantages of a DBMS?
5. Explain the differences between OLAP and OLTP.
6. List the differences between operational and informational systems.
7. What is the meaning of support and confidence in the context of data mining?
8. What is a data warehouse and how it is different from a data mart?
9. What is the relationship between measures and dimensions?
10. Describe and give examples of two types of Web mining.
11. What is a Web site's stickiness, and why is it important?
12. Explain the purpose of a model within a DSS.
13. Explain the difference between explicit and tacit knowledge.
14. What do you understand by ETL and why it is required for data warehousing?
15. What is a knowledge management system, and what types of technologies make up a comprehensive system?
16. How can visual analytics be used to gain business intelligence and improve decision making?
17. What are neural networks and what are their business applications?

Self-Study Questions

1. In a DBMS, an entity is represented as a(n) _____.
   A. attribute
   B. table
   C. row
   D. association
2. A(n) _____ report provides a summary of critical information on a recurring schedule.
   A. scheduled
   B. exception
   C. key indicator
   D. drill-down
3. In order to swiftly respond to a highly competitive and rapidly changing environment, organizations utilize a

   _____.
   A. continuous planning process
   B. structured decision-making process
   C. decision support process
   D. decision-making process
4. To determine the likelihood of new customers to default on a loan, a manager in a bank would typically use

   _____.
   A. association discovery
   B. sequence discovery
   C. classification
   D. clustering
5. Web usage mining entails analyzing _____.
   A. clickstream data
   B. page content
   C. associations among sets of items
   D. unstructured data
6. Market share analysis is typically used by the _____ function of an organization.
   A. marketing
   B. accounting
   C. production
   D. management science

7. Examples of the types of activities that can be supported by ESs include all of the following except _____.
   A. payroll calculations
   B. financial planning
   C. machine configuration
   D. medical diagnosis
8. _____ agents keep track of key information such as inventory levels, notifying the users when conditions change.
   A. User
   B. Buyer
   C. Monitoring and sensing
   D. Data mining
9. What is true about knowledge management?
   A. As baby boomers retire at an increasing rate, knowledge management is helping organizations capture their knowledge.
   B. A knowledge management system is not a single technology but a collection of technology-based tools.
   C. Finding the right technology to manage knowledge assets is much easier than identifying what knowledge is needed, why it is needed, and who has this knowledge.
   D. All of the above are true.
10. Which of the following is an example of attribute data commonly used in GIS applications?
    A. structured data
    B. longitude
    C. trade area
    D. annual sales

    Answers are on page 293.

Problems and Exercises

1. Match the following terms with the appropriate definitions:
   i. Social network analysis
   ii. Measures
   iii. Master data
   iv. Web content mining
   v. Continuous planning process
   vi. Data mining
   vii. Expert system
   viii. Digital dashboard
   ix. Geographic information system
   x. DSS

   a. An information system designed to analyze and store spatially referenced data
   b. A special-purpose information system designed to mimic human expertise by manipulating knowledge (understanding acquired through experience and extensive learning) rather than simply information
   c. A technique that attempts to find groups of people who work together, to find people who don't collaborate but should, or to find experts in particular subject areas
   d. A set of methods used to find hidden predictive relationships in a data set
   e. A strategic business planning process involving continuous monitoring and adjusting of business processes to enable rapid reaction to changing business conditions
   f. The values or numbers a user wants to analyze
   g. A special-purpose information system designed to support organizational decision making primarily at the managerial level of an organization
   h. Extracting textual information from Web documents
   i. A user interface visually representing summary information about a business's health, often from multiple sources
   j. The data that are deemed most important in the operation of a business

2. Interview a top-level executive within an organization with which you are familiar and find out their most important external threats. Can business intelligence help to respond to these threats? If so, how; if not, why not?

3. List some of the common data mining tools that are available. Explain with examples why a bank should use some of these tools.

4. Using a search engine, enter the key word "data warehousing." Who are the large vendors in this industry? What type of solutions do they offer to their clients? Do you see any common trend in data warehousing?

5. Visit CNN Money (http://cgi.money.cnn.com/tools/retirementplanner/retirementplanner.jsp) on the Web to plan your retirement using a DSS. What did you learn?

To what extent is the DSS useful in planning your retirement? If you browse through CNN Money, what other interesting stuff do you find?

6. Interview a top-level executive within an organization with which you are familiar and determine the extent to which the organization utilizes tools for information visualization or digital dashboards. Does this individual utilize these tools in any way? Why or why not? Which executives do utilize such tools?

7. Think about the junk mail you receive every day in your postal mail. Which mailings do you believe to be a result of data mining? How have the companies chosen you for their targeted mailings?

8. Using any program you choose or using the Web site www.moneycentral.com, find or create a template that you could use in the future to determine monthly payments on car or home loans. Compare your template with the one at www.bankrate.com/brm/auto-loan-calculator.asp. Would you have categorized the program you used to create this template as a DSS before doing this exercise?

9. Describe your experiences with ESs or go to www.exsys.com or www.easydiagnosis.com on the Web and spend some time interacting with their demonstration systems. Now choose a problem that you know a lot about and would like to build your own ES for. Describe the problem and list the questions you would need to ask someone in order to make a recommendation.

10. Go out onto the Web and compare three shopping bots for a product you are interested in (e.g., www.mysimon.com, www.bottomdollar.com, www.shopzilla.com, www.shopping.com, or www.pricegrabber.com). Did the different agents find the same information, or were there any differences? Did you prefer one over the others? Why?

11. Search the Web to identify the companies offering the most popular information visualization tools. What are their claims about the tools? Try to speak to some of their customers and find the applications for which they are using them.

12. Interview an IS manager within an organization. What types of information and knowledge discovery tools does the organization use? Was there an increase or decrease in the past few years? What predictions does this manager have regarding the future of these systems? Do you agree? Prepare a 10-minute presentation to the class on your findings.

13. Interview the top executives of two firms and find out their reasons for implementing the business intelligence system in their organization. Also find out the benefits they have gained after BI implementation.

14. A digital dashboard is powerful visual tool. At which level of the information systems hierarchy does it operate? What advantages does it offer to management?

15. Explain decision support systems and describe their characteristics. List some of the common DSS tools that are being used by the banking industry.

16. Visit Google maps (http://maps.google.com) and try out different layers provided under "More…" What other information would you like to see? Are there any publicly available mashups that offer this information as layers on top of Google maps?

Application Exercises

Note: The existing data files referenced in these exercises are available on the book's Web site: www.pearsonhighered.com/valacich.

Spreadsheet Application: Travel Loan Facility

A new aspect of the business has been added to Campus Travel. Students can apply for a loan to help pay for their travels. However, loans for travel are available only to students who are traveling outside the country for at least two weeks. Since the costs for this type of international travel differ depending on how you travel, where you stay, and what you do at the destination, different loan packages are available. For a month in Europe, you have decided to take out a loan. You have already taken a look at several offers but are unsure whether you can afford it. Set up a spreadsheet to calculate the payments per month for the following situations:

1. Two weeks in Eastern Europe; Price: $2,000; Percentage Rate: 5.5%; Time: one year
2. Two weeks in Western Europe; Price: $3,000; Percentage Rate: 6.0%; Time: one year
3. Three weeks in Eastern Europe; Price: $3,000; Percentage Rate: 6.5%; Time: two years
4. Three weeks in Western Europe; Price: $3,500; Percentage Rate: 5.5%; Time: two years
5. Four weeks in Eastern Europe; Price: $4,000; Percentage Rate: 6.0%; Time: two years
6. Four weeks in Western Europe; Price: $5,000; Percentage Rate: 6.5%; Time: three years

Once you have calculated the payments, calculate the total amount to be paid for each option as well as the total interest you would pay over the course of the loan. Make sure to use formulas for all calculations and print out a professionally formatted page displaying the results and a page displaying the formulas. (Hint: In Microsoft Excel, use the "PMT" function in the category "Financial" to calculate the payments. Use Ctrl+' [grave accent] to switch between formula and data views; calculate the number of payments before using the formula.)

Database Application: Tracking Regional Office Performance at Campus Travel

The general manager wants to know which offices were most profitable during the previous year and asks you to prepare several reports. In the file FY2012.mdb, you find information about the offices, sales agents, and destinations. Use the report wizard to generate the following reports:

1. List of all sales agents grouped by office (including total number of agents per office)
2. List of sales agents for each destination (grouped by destination, including total number of agents)
3. Destinations sold by each sales agent (including total number of destinations)

Hint: You will need to generate the necessary queries before creating the reports.

Team Work Exercise

 Net Stats:
The Demise of Broadcast TV

Recent studies of the TV industry indicate that it is in trouble. More and more people are choosing not to watch TV in the conventional "appointment" way. For example, in 2011, nearly 70 million people in the U.S. (or 29 percent of the population) watched television shows online; this number is forecast to increase to 99 million (or 40 percent of the population) by 2015. Similarly, according to Nielsen, in 2011, 288 million people in the U.S. watched TV/Video content via their TV set, compared with 143 million who watched content on the Internet, 111 million who watched timeshifted content, and 30 million who watched content on their mobile devices. A 2012 survey by Market Tool revealed that 57 percent of respondents are interested in viewing content on mobile devices, and 27 percent of respondent were currently users of mobile TV/video; of those, 43 percent consume mobile TV once per week, and 23 percent consume mobile TV on a daily basis. Further, the rise of tablets has increased mobile TV viewership. Juniper research forecasts that mobile TV consumption using tablets will grow by 58 percent between 2012 and 2016, and that by 2014, tablet users will on average watch 3 hours of video per month on their mobile devices.

Questions and Exercises

1. Search the Web for the most up-to-date statistics. Try to find the statistics for other countries as well.
2. As a team, interpret these numbers. What is striking/ important about these statistics? What may be the reason for differences between countries?
3. How have the numbers changed since 2012?
4. Using your spreadsheet software of choice, create a graph/ figure most effectively visualizing the statistics/changes you consider most important.

Based on:

Neill, G. (2012, March 6). Mobile TV consumption set to surge by 2016. *Mobile Today.* Retrieved July 21, 2012, from http://www.mobiletoday.co.uk/ News/14237/mobile_tv_consumption_surge.aspx.

Nielsen (2012). State of the media: Consumer usage report. Retrieved July 21, 2012, from http://blog.nielsen.com/nielsenwire/mediauniverse.

O'Neill, M. (2011, February 17). Nearly 100m adults to watch online TV by 2015. *SocialTimes.* Retrieved July 21, 2012, from http://socialtimes.com/ online-tv-2_b39066.

Petersen, A. (2012, April 11). U.S. survey finds TV everywhere hitting mainstream, with 57% of respondents interested in multiscreen viewing. *QuickPlay.* Retrieved July 21, 2012, from http://www.quickplay.com/2012/04/ u-s-survey-finds-tv-everywhere-hitting-mainstream-with-57-of-respondents-interested-in-multiscreen-viewing.

Answers to the Self-Study Questions

1. B, p. 259	2. C, p. 267	3. A, p. 256	4. C, p. 269	5. A, p. 271
6. A, p. 273	7. A, p. 274	8. C, p. 276	9. D, p. 278	10. D, p. 283

CASE 1   The Netflix Prize

Netflix is the world's largest online movie provider. For a flat monthly fee, subscribers have access to thousands of movies and television shows through mail delivery or by download. For DVDs coming in the mail, the subscriber maintains a title queue on Netflix's site that he or she wants to watch, listed in order of viewing preference. Netflix chooses which movies or shows to mail next from the queue, and when one disk is returned, another is mailed. Customers are never charged late fees, and after viewing the DVD simply drop it in a mailbox using the prepaid envelope Netflix provides.

Netflix has consistently ranked high in customer satisfaction surveys. In fact, the service has proved so successful that in April 2009, the company reported that it had shipped its two-billionth DVD. Its streaming "instant watch" service has proven extremely popular, with over 26 million subscribers in 2012.

A key feature of the Netflix service is customers' ability to rate the movies they have seen on a five-point scale from "hated it" to "loved it." Based on customers' ratings, Netflix's movie recommendation system, Cinematch, then displays other movie titles customers might enjoy. While the system works well for Netflix's purpose, it admits that improvements are possible. With that in mind, Netflix started a contest in 2006 to improve their movie rating/recommendation system. The grand prize was US$1 million, but to win the prize, contestants had to improve Cinematch's results by 10 percent—a difficult task. According to the contest rules published

at the Netflix Prize Web site, "It's 'easy' really. We provide you with a lot of anonymous rating data and a prediction accuracy bar that is 10 percent better than what Cinematch can do on the same training data set. (Accuracy is a measurement of how closely predicted ratings of movies match subsequent actual ratings.) If you develop a system that we judge most beats that bar on the qualifying test set we provide, you get serious money and the bragging rights. But (and you knew there would be a catch, right?) only if you share your method with us and describe to the world how you did it and why it works."

Contestants registered for the contest as teams, and entries were limited to one per day. Any team whose members came up with an algorithm that improved Cinematch performance by 1 percent would win US$50,000. The US$50,000 "progress prize" would be awarded once annually until someone reached the 10 percent increase or the contest ended. Entries would continue to be accepted in the Netflix Prize contest until the US$1 million prize was awarded or until 2011, whichever came first. On September 21, 2009, a team led by AT&T researchers known as "BellKor's Pragmatic Chaos" took the grand prize by improving over the Cinematch score 10.06 percent. Immediately following the close of the contest, Netflix announced plans for a second contest in which they would release anonymous information on 100 million Neflix users. The contest would center around predicting the movie preferences of users based on key information like age, gender, and geographic location.

However, two and a half months after the first contest ended, a lawsuit filed against Netflix put the second contest in jeopardy. The lawsuit, *Doe v. Netflix,* was filed in California by an anonymous lesbian mother claiming that Netflix invaded her privacy. The logic behind her claim was that by making the movie ratings available in the data set—along with the date of the rating, the movie information associated with the rating, and a unique identifier number for the subscriber that made the rating—anyone would be able to take that information and match it up against other publicly available data to determine someone's identity. In fact, that very scenario happened when two researchers working with the Netflix Prize data identified several users by comparing movie reviews on the Internet Movie Database (a popular movie information site) with the ratings in the "anonymous" data provided for the Netflix Prize contest. Information discovered about the identified users included political ideologies and sexual orientations.

In March 2010, the lawsuit was settled between the anonymous plaintiff and Netflix. Although Netflix did not admit to any wrongdoing, part of the settlement agreement was the cancellation of the second Netflix Prize contest. In 2012, Netflix announced that the algorithms created by the winners of the Netflix prize would not be implemented, as "the additional accuracy gains... did not seem to justify the engineering effort needed to bring them into a production environment" (Amatriain & Basilico, 2012).

Questions

1. In what ways could Netflix visualize movie ratings, preferences, or trends to provide its subscribers with additional "movie intelligence"?
2. What are the pros and cons of having the winner of the Netflix Prize share the improved Cinematch method?
3. Describe another problem in business or society that could utilize an approach similar to that for winning the Netflix Prize (i.e., a contest that anyone can try to solve).

Based on:

Amatriain, X, and Basilico, J. (2012, April 6). Netflix recommendations: Beyond the 5 stars (Part 1). *The Netflix Tech Blog.* Retrieved July 21, 2012, from http://techblog.netflix.com/2012/04/netflix-recommendations-beyond-5-stars.html.

Anonymous. (n.d.). The Netflix prize rules. Retrieved July 21, 2012, from http://www.netflixprize.com//rules.

Anonymous. (2009, September 18). Grand Prize awarded to team BellKor's Pragmatic Chaos. *Netflix Prize Forum.* Retrieved July 21, 2012, from http://www.netflixprize.com//community/viewtopic.php?id=1537.

Hunt, N. (2010, March 12). Netflix Prize update. *The Netflix Blog.* Retrieved July 21, 2012, from http://blog.netflix.com/2010/03/this-is-neil-hunt-chief-product-officer.html.

Lohr, S. (2009, September 22). A $1 million research bargain for Netflix, and maybe a model for others. *New York Times.* Retrieved July 21, 2012, from http://www.nytimes.com/2009/09/22/technology/internet/22netflix.html.

Singel, R. (2009, December 17). Netflix spilled your *Brokeback Mountain* secret, lawsuit claims. *Wired.* Retrieved July 21, 2012, from http://www.wired.com/threatlevel/2009/12/netflix-privacy-lawsuit.

CASE 2 Are We There Yet?—Online Map Services

Everyone who drives a car and/or uses a computer is familiar with online map services. Three of the best and most frequently used are Google maps (http://maps.google.com), Microsoft's Bing Maps (www.bing.com/maps), and Yahoo! Maps (http://maps.yahoo.com). The services are free for computer and mobile users who want to find the shortest route from point A to point B. Google has been especially popular for its satellite views and features such as real-time traffic information (in places like southern California) or the display of user-generated content (e.g., landmarks or restaurant reviews), although some of the overly inclusive satellite imagery of military bases has recently been taken down following a request by the U.S. military.

Although many online map services are free for consumers, the providers also offer fee-based enterprise versions. For example, all three of the above services provide a for-fee option for businesses wanting to add easy-to-use, interactive maps to their Web sites. With these applications, organizations can show customers how to reach stores or service centers in their areas, and employees on the road can more easily reach customers in various locations or find hotels and restaurants in their travel areas. Organizations can also track shipments or supply chains, manage employees and resources in the field, and insert relevant advertising into their customized maps when they are displayed on Web sites.

Online mapping has become a big component of the mobile phone experience as well. As more phones and tablets take advantage of location-based services and data networks, users can quickly find out what's around them through a simple Internet search. The search will return nearby businesses offering the products or services the user is looking for, and the user can choose a business to see a map and directions to the location.

Google took online mapping to the next level when they introduced "Street View" to their mapping services. Touted as the "last zoom level" by Google, Street View allows the user to actually view a complete 360 degree photographic view from the street. Originally, Street View photography was available for only five U.S. cities. As of 2010, all 50 U.S. states and over 14 countries had extensive street view coverage. Nearly all of the United Kingdom's and Australia's highways and roads have coverage. Google has recently begun collecting photography of college campuses and surrounding paths and trails while continuing to add more streets in smaller cities and in other countries.

Google's Street View has been criticized on fears of invasion of privacy and has come under increasing scrutiny in some countries, such as Germany. Many people have complained about having their home or license plate photographed. Although Google has gone through their photographic data and blurred faces, license plates, and other parts of photos, many are still troubled by Street View. Individuals who feel that their privacy is being violated can request imagery be blurred or removed from Google's data. Privacy fears aside, it appears that street-level imagery is here to stay and will continue to be updated. As of December 2009, Bing Maps started offering their own version of street-level photography with their "Streetside" feature.

Online mapping is now moving beyond the realm of the automobile alone and extending to bicycle riders. As of March 2010, a search on Google Maps can return biking directions and extensive bike trail data for many U.S. locations. Google map bike searches return efficient routing, allow users to customize their trips, locate biking lanes, and find "rider-friendly" routes that avoid big hills. Realizing the increasing smartphone penetration in many African countries, in 2012, Google released walking directions in 44 African countries.

Questions

1. Do you use Internet mapping sites? Why or why not?
2. As outlined in the case, there are many innovative mapping products and services; describe a new service that you want that doesn't yet exist.
3. Do you think that mapping software can be an invasion of privacy? Why or why not?

Based on:

Bass, S. (2005, June 29). Maps for fun and business. *PCWorld*. Retrieved July 21, 2012, from http://www.pcworld.com/article/121387/tips_and_tweaks_maps_for_fun_and_business.html.

Claburn, T. (2008, March 7). U.S. military restricts Google maps. *InformationWeek*. Retrieved July 21, 2012, from http://www.informationweek.com/news/206902500.

Fischman, J. (2009, June 22). Google's Street View eyeballs college campuses. *Chronicle of Higher Education*. Retrieved July 21, 2012, from http://chronicle.com/blogPost/Google-s-Street-View-/7231.

Guymon, S. (2010, March 10). Biking directions added to Google Maps. *The Official Google Blog*. Retrieved July 21, 2012, from http://googleblog.blogspot.com/2010/03/biking-directions-added-to-google-maps.html.

Rajuai, J., and Bengl, j. (2012, July 9). Google Maps for Africa gets better - walking directions launched! *Google Africa Blog*. Retrieved July 21, 2012, from http://google-africa.blogspot.hk/2012/07/google-maps-for-africa-gets-better_09.html.

7

Enhancing Business Processes Using Enterprise Information Systems

After reading this chapter, you will be able to do the following:

1. Explain core business processes that are common in organizations.

2. Describe what enterprise systems are and how they have evolved.

3. Describe enterprise resource planning systems and how they help to improve internal business processes.

4. Understand and utilize the keys to successfully implementing enterprise systems.

Preview

This chapter describes how companies are deploying enterprise-wide information systems to support and enable core business processes. Enterprise systems help to integrate various business activities, to increase coordination amongst various business departments and partners, to streamline and better manage interactions with customers, and to coordinate better with suppliers in order to more efficiently and effectively meet rapidly changing customer demands.

Companies continue to find that they need systems that span their entire organization to tie everything together. As a result, an understanding of enterprise systems is critical to succeed in today's competitive and ever-changing digital world. This chapter focuses on how organizations are utilizing enterprise-wide information systems to best support internal business processes. In Chapter 8, "Strengthening Business-to-Business Relationships Via Supply Chain and Customer Relationship Management," we focus on systems that support business processes spanning multiple organizations, critical in today's competitive global environment.

Managing in the Digital World:
Amazon.com

Remember the good old days when strolling through bookstores was an amusing, reposeful, enlightening experience that could easily consume an entire day? Today, there are many online alternatives, and book-shopping does not require making a trip to the nearest store any more. For instance, Amazon.com has millions of paper and electronic books to choose from (see Figure 7.1). Amazon.com has virtually transformed the notion of buying and enjoying a good book. With its innovative Amazon Kindle, the process of acquiring a book and reading it has never been so easy; simply, it enables users to electronically experience the satisfaction of reading a good book on a dedicated e-reader. A Kindle can store thousands of books, allowing its owner to easily and quickly shop for, download, and enjoy a broad range of content in a matter of minutes, all via wireless networking (using your Wi-Fi connection or a free connection over cellular phone providers). In addition to books, the Kindle allows you to enjoy newspapers, magazines, blogs, and other digital media.

Having evolved from just being an online bookseller, Amazon.com now provides basically anything and everything; kitchen appliances, garden furniture, clothing, sporting goods, and even groceries (in the Seattle area, there is "fresh.amazon.com"). Amazon.com's business model is

FIGURE 7.1

Companies can rent Amazon.com's warehouse infrastructure on an as-needed basis.

Source: Bombaert Patrick/Fotolia

to provide superior product selection well beyond the biggest mall and big box stores; all of these products can be purchased with "one click" from the convenience of your personal computer, tablet, or even mobile phone.

Beyond its retail offerings, Amazon.com provides the supporting infrastructure for many parts of your daily routine through its cloud computing services. Do you happen to read Newsweek online, read movie reviews on IMDb, or buy tickets through Ticketmaster.com? Those are just some of the services hosted by Amazon Web Services. If you are checking-in with Foursquare, streaming movies on Netflix, or watching Indy car races online, you are also benefitting from Amazon.com's superior infrastructure. Recently, the German software giant SAP even certified versions of its enterprise resource planning system for deployment on Amazon.com's cloud computing infrastructure.

Founded and headed by Jeff Bezos, Amazon.com started in 1994 with a commitment to be "customer-centric." The Amazon.com Web site greets you by name and remembers your recent purchases. Your home page is custom-tailored with recommendations for books, music, and DVDs that may entice you; these recommendations are provided by analyzing your prior purchases and comparing them to millions of other customers with similar tastes. Amazon.com offers free shipping when you place orders over US$25. "Amazon Prime" offers additional deals where customers can pay a small monthly fee to receive complimentary shipping upgrades.

In order to keep up with these features (and continually add more), Amazon.com needs more than just a sophisticated information systems (IS) infrastructure. The ability to excel at managing its supply chains provides another challenge; to be successful, Amazon.com needs to excel at acquiring and receiving the right goods at the right time from its suppliers, as well as at efficiently shipping physical goods to its customers. Such challenges can be generally categorized as belonging to the "upstream" or the "downstream" sides of the supply chain. By tackling the upstream side of the supply chain, Amazon.com faces challenges related to the seasonality of products, short product cycles, and changes in consumer tastes that make accurate demand forecasts almost impossible and control of inventory levels a pretty difficult job. All of these complexities are exacerbated by the myriad product lines that tend to be more fickle than seasonal climatic changes. On the downstream side, Amazon.com faces the issue of optimizing the operation of fulfillment centers to ensure efficient shipping of products to customers. Inventory levels have to be carefully managed to prevent unnecessary increases in shipping costs or stockouts. To aid in managing these downstream flows, Amazon.com relies on a few select shipping companies that have consistently provided superior and dependable service.

Amazon.com has worked rigorously to address the potential issues of its massive size and strong reputation for superior customer service, building a network of dozens of North American and international fulfillment centers with a sophisticated IS infrastructure. In 2007, the company started managing online stores and sales fulfillment for many large companies including Target.com. Amazon.com also discovered that their established infrastructure could be shared with numerous small Internet start-up companies looking to focus on attracting new customers and expanding their business without having to worry about building their own IS infrastructure. Amazon Web Services (AWS) provides a solid and reliable infrastructure that allows these companies to rent computing resources or storage space on an as-needed basis. In addition to shared IS infrastructure, Fulfillment by Amazon lets independent retailers, who list their goods on Amazon.com or elsewhere on the Web, use Amazon.com's network of distribution centers to store products and ship orders, all for a modest fee. This creates a win–win situation: for small, independent retailers, warehousing becomes a variable cost, and for Amazon.com, it creates additional revenue streams and helps to utilize excess capacity.

Clearly, Amazon.com is more than a vibrant online store. Its enterprise is growing by the minute and its management of the digital universe has provided a solid foundation for other companies to build on. Having designed an impressive IS infrastructure, Amazon.com is constantly developing new and innovative products and services that utilize this infrastructure. The AWS infrastructure has become so pervasive that researchers have estimated that one-third of North American Web users visit a site hosted by AWS at least once per day, and that 1 percent of consumer Internet traffic in North America is sent or received by Amazon's servers. What the future holds, either for Amazon.com, the supply chain, or both, is inconceivable, given Amazon.com's current rate of growth.

After reading this chapter, you will be able to answer the following:

1. How do the core business processes differ for Amazon.com's various product and service offerings?

2. How do enterprise-wide information systems enable Amazon.com's strategy?

3. What benefits would an organization realize by running their SAP enterprise resource planning system on Amazon.com's cloud computing infrastructure?

Based on:

Amazon Kindle. (2012, July 3). In *Wikipedia, The Free Encyclopedia*. Retrieved July 4, 2012, from http://en.wikipedia.org/w/index.php?title=Amazon_Kindle&oldid=500530492.

Anonymous. (n.d.). Amazon fulfillment Web service. Retrieved July 4, 2012, from http://aws.amazon.com/fws/.

Anonymous. (n.d.). History of e-commerce. Retrieved July 4, 2012, from http://www.ecommerce-land.com/history_ecommerce.html.

Anonymous. (2011). Amazon.com 2011 Annual Report. Retrieved July 4, 2012, from http://phx.corporate-ir.net/External.File?item=UGFyZW50SUQ9MTM0NDcwfENoaWxkSUQ9LTF8VHlwZT0z&t=1.

Anonymous. (2012). Trends and data. *Internet Retailer*. Retrieved July 4, 2012, from http://www.internetretailer.com/trends.

Labovitz, C. (2012, April 18). How big is Amazon's cloud? *DeepField.net*. Retrieved August 15, 2012, from http://www.deepfield.net/2012/04/how-big-is-amazons-cloud.

Ratcliffe, M. (2009, December 26). Updating Kindles sold estimate: 1.49 million. *ZDNet.com*. Retrieved July 4, 2012, from http://www.zdnet.com/blog/ratcliffe/updating-kindles-sold-estimate-1-49-million/486.

Stone, B. (2007, April 27). Sold on eBay, shipped by Amazon.com. *The New York Times*. Retrieved July 4, 2012, from http://www.nytimes.com/2007/04/27/technology/27amazon.html.

CORE BUSINESS PROCESSES AND ORGANIZATIONAL VALUE CHAINS

http://goo.gl/Wy8jm

Traditionally, companies are organized around five distinct functional areas; namely, marketing and sales, supply chain management, manufacturing and operations, accounting and finance, and human resources. Each of these functional areas is responsible for several well-defined business functions, such as: marketing a product; sales forecasting; procuring raw materials and components; manufacturing goods; planning and budgeting; or recruiting, hiring, and training. Although this model suggests that a company can be regarded as being comprised of distinct independent silos, the different functional areas are highly interrelated to perform value-added activities (see Figure 7.2). In fact, most business processes cross the boundaries of business functions, so it is helpful for managers to think in terms of business processes from a customer's (both internal and external) point of view.

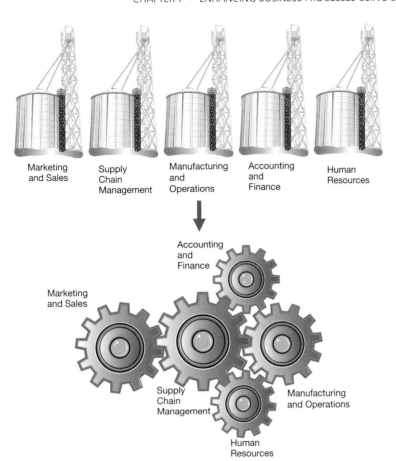

FIGURE 7.2

A company's functional areas should be interrelated.

Core Business Processes

In most cases, customers do not care about how things are being done; they care only that things are being done to their satisfaction. When you buy a book at Amazon.com, you typically do not care which functional areas are involved in the transaction; you care only about quickly getting the right book for the right price. Buying a book at Amazon.com can help to illustrate one of the core business processes, namely, *order-to-cash*. Similarly, *procure-to-pay* and *make-to-stock* are core business processes also common to most business organizations. Other important business processes are related to tracking a firm's revenues and expenses, managing employees, and so on. Next, we discuss the core business processes involved in generating revenue.

ORDER-TO-CASH. For business organizations, selling products or services are the main way of generating revenue. In the example of Amazon.com, you need to create an account and add items to your shopping cart. You then need to complete your order by entering shipping and billing information, and submitting the order. Amazon.com will then confirm that your address is valid and will check your credit card information. Many online retailers provide real-time information on available stock; however, in case an item is out of stock after placing an order, you will be notified or given the option to cancel your order. If the item is in stock, your order will be put together and shipped, and your credit card will be charged. Together, the processes associated with selling a product or service are referred to as the **order-to-cash process** (see Figure 7.3). As with all business processes, the order-to-cash process can be broken down into multiple subprocesses (most of which are common across organizations). For most businesses, the order-to-cash process entails subprocesses such as creating a customer record; checking the customer's creditworthiness; creating an order; checking and allocating stock; picking, packing, and shipping; invoicing; and collecting the payment. Depending on the nature of the transaction, the individual subprocesses and the time in which these are completed can differ considerably. For example, a sale in a convenience store may take only several seconds, and many of the subprocesses mentioned (such as creating a customer record) are not needed

FIGURE 7.3

The order-to-cash process.

(although many stores now try to gather information such as customers' ZIP codes for business intelligence). In contrast, sales of many big-ticket items (such as commercial aircraft or specialized manufacturing machinery) may take months or years to complete and may involve many more steps. The subprocesses can be further broken down to a more granular level.

Obviously, an ineffective order-to-cash process can have various negative effects for organizations; for example, the manual input of order information often causes errors, as do suboptimal picking and shipping processes. Together, such errors can lead to a high rate of disputes that have to be resolved, ineffective collection processes, and, ultimately, defecting customers. In contrast, an effective order-to-cash process can create customer satisfaction, speed up the collection process, and serve to provide valuable inputs into business intelligence and customer relationship management applications (see Chapter 8).

PROCURE-TO-PAY. In order to be able to sell books and other products, Amazon.com needs to acquire these from its suppliers. Amazon.com needs to manage literally thousands of suppliers, place purchase orders, receive the products, allocate warehouse space, receive and pay invoices, and handle potential disputes. These processes associated with procuring goods from external vendors are together referred to as the **procure-to-pay process** (see Figure 7.4). Subprocesses of the procure-to-pay process include price and terms negotiations, issuing of the purchase order, receiving the goods, and receiving and paying the invoice.

An ineffective procure-to-pay process can increase error rates in purchase order and invoice processing; further, it inhibits a company from developing close relationships with preferred vendors. Together, this can increase the cost per transaction, lead to an increase in disputes to be resolved, and prohibit the company from obtaining the most favorable conditions from its vendors. In contrast, an effective procure-to-pay process can help to obtain favorable conditions, reduce transaction costs, and, ultimately, create customer goodwill as it helps to efficiently fulfill customer orders.

MAKE-TO-STOCK/MAKE-TO-ORDER. A third set of core business processes is associated with producing goods (such as Amazon.com's Kindle e-book reader), and entails make-to-stock and make-to order. In the **make-to-stock process**, goods are produced based on forecasts and are stocked in a warehouse (i.e., a push-based approach); sales orders are then fulfilled from inventory. In contrast, in the **make-to-order process**, raw materials, subcomponents, and accessories are procured based on forecasts, but actual manufacturing does not start until sales orders are received (a pull-based approach); in extreme cases, even design and engineering start only when an order is received. For example, mass-produced goods, such as television sets or home appliances, are typically produced under a make-to-stock approach. Here, the organization stocks the produced goods, *pushing* the products out to customers after orders are received. In

FIGURE 7.4

The procure-to-pay process.

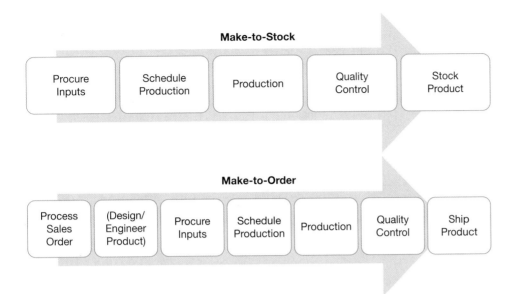

FIGURE 7.5

The make-to-stock versus the make-to-order process.

contrast, highly customizable or very expensive low-volume goods are often produced under a make-to-order approach, as is the case with Dell computers or with commercial aircraft, where the assembly starts only after a customer has placed an order. Here, the organization waits for an order, allowing it to initiate a *pulling* sequence to move the order through the production process. The processes associated with making products are comprised of processing sales orders, procuring the inputs to the manufacturing process, scheduling production, production, quality control, packaging, and stocking or shipping the product. Figure 7.5 illustrates the make-to-stock and make-to-order processes.

Together, these core business processes enable the creation of supply chains that are involved in transforming raw materials into products sold to the end consumer. A typical supply chain resembles a river, where the raw materials start out at the source and move downstream toward the end customer; at each step, the goods are transformed to make the end product. To meet the needs for various different inputs, each organization typically has multiple upstream suppliers; similarly, each organization typically sells to multiple downstream customers. Figure 7.6 shows the supply chain of a book. Within this supply chain, one company's sales-related processes overlap with the downstream company's procurement-related processes (supply chains are discussed in detail in Chapter 8).

Organizational Activities Along the Value Chain

To gain competitive advantage over their rivals, companies are trying to optimize the core business processes in different ways. One of the first challenges an organization must face is to understand how it can use information systems to support core and other business processes. For example, Amazon.com excels at using information systems to optimize both the procure-to-pay and the order-to-cash process. Generally, the set of business activities that add value to the end product is referred to as a *value chain* (Porter & Millar, 1985), in which information flows through functional areas that facilitate an organization's business processes. Figure 7.7 depicts the value chain framework. In Chapter 2, "Gaining Competitive Advantage Through Information Systems," we spoke of the strategic value of analyzing a value chain; now, we show you how the activities along the value chain support business processes.

Many business processes depend on activities performed by various functional areas within an organization; for example, Amazon.com's order-to-cash process involves activities performed by sales, shipping, accounting, and other functional areas. The functional areas directly involved in the process are responsible for the core activities, whereas other functional areas are performing support activities. In other words, *core activities* are performed by the functional areas that process inputs and produce outputs, and *support activities* are those activities that enable core activities to take place. In the following sections, we focus on core activities and then turn our attention to the support activities that make them possible.

FIGURE 7.6

Supply chain of a book.

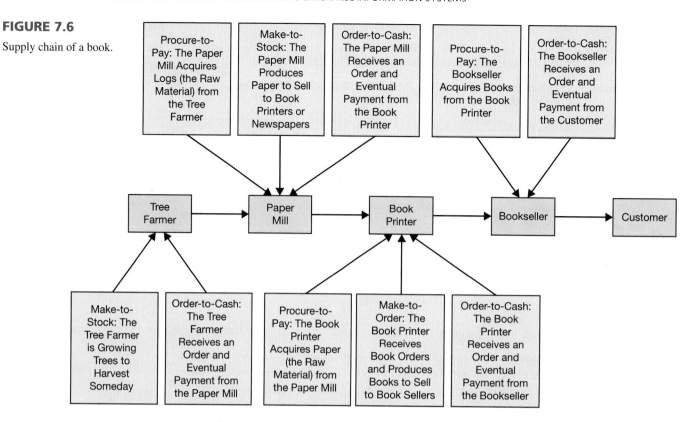

CORE ACTIVITIES. **Core activities** include inbound logistics (receiving), operations and manufacturing, outbound logistics (shipping), marketing and sales, and customer service. These activities may differ widely, depending on the unique requirements of the industry in which a company operates, although the basic concepts hold in most organizations.

Inbound Logistics Activities Inbound logistics involves the business activities associated with receiving and stocking raw materials, parts, and products. For example, inbound logistics at Amazon.com involves not only the receipt of books, e-book readers, and various other products for sale, but also the receipt of packaging materials and shipping labels. Shippers deliver these products to Amazon.com, where employees unwrap the packages and stock the products in the company's warehouse or directly route the products to operations in order to fill open orders. Amazon.com can automatically update inventory levels at the point of delivery, allowing purchasing managers access to up-to-date information related to inventory levels and reorder points. Inbound logistics, also referred to as supply chain management, activities are a crucial

FIGURE 7.7

Value chain framework.
Source: Based on Porter and Millar (1985).

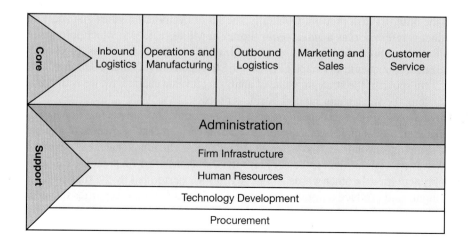

part of the procure-to-pay business process, as these activities enable the company to efficiently and effectively fill customer orders.

Operations and Manufacturing Activities Once the components have been stocked in inventory, operations and manufacturing activities transform the inputs into outputs. Operations and manufacturing can involve such activities as order processing (e.g., at Amazon.com) and/or manufacturing or assembly processes (e.g., at Dell) that transform raw materials and/or component parts into end products (i.e., the make-to-stock and make-to-order business processes). Companies such as Dell utilize Web-based information systems to allow customers to enter orders online. This information is used to coordinate the manufacturing of a customized personal computer in which the component parts are gathered and assembled to create the end product. During this process, inventory levels from inbound logistics are verified; if the appropriate inventory exists, workers pick the components from existing supplies and build the product to the customer's specifications. When components are picked, items are deducted from inventory; once the product is assembled, inventory levels for the final product are updated.

Outbound Logistics Activities The activities associated with outbound logistics mirror those of inbound logistics. Instead of involving the receipt of raw materials, parts, and products, outbound logistics focuses on the distribution of end products within the order-to-cash business process. For example, outbound logistics at Amazon.com involves the shipping of books that customers have ordered. Orders that have been processed by operations are forwarded to outbound logistics, which picks the products from inventory and coordinates shipment to the customer. At that point, items are packaged and deducted from the company's inventory, and an invoice is created that will be sent to the customer. Amazon.com can automatically update sales information at the point of distribution, allowing managers to view inventory and revenue information in real-time.

Marketing and Sales Activities Marketing and sales activities are associated primarily with the presales (i.e., before the sale) activities of the company. These activities include the creation of marketing literature, communication with potential and existing customers, and pricing of goods and services. As discussed in Chapter 4, "Enabling Business-to-Consumer Electronic Commerce," most companies support the business activity of marketing and sales by creating e-brochures, building pages on Facebook, or communicating on other social media such as Twitter. Many companies, especially those focused on selling products or services to the end consumer (e.g., passenger airlines such as United or online retailers such as Amazon.com), use information systems to update pricing information and/or schedules. This information is entered directly into the pricing and scheduling systems, allowing the information to become immediately accessible throughout the organization and to end consumers through the organization's Web site.

Customer Service Activities Whereas marketing and sales focus on presales activities, customer service focuses on postsales (i.e., after the sale) activities. Customers may have questions and need help from a customer service representative. For most companies, such as Amazon.com, utilizing information systems to provide customer service is essential, especially given the vast number of products offered. These applications allow customers to search for and download information related to the products that they have purchased or the purchase itself. For example, on Amazon.com customers can view their order status or can view and print invoices of current and past orders. Similarly, customers can find additional information and support about the Amazon Kindle or other digital products. Rather than calling a customer service representative, customers can easily find the needed information through a self-service customer support application. Information systems also enable customer service representatives to quickly locate information about products or services offered.

Companies can also use information systems to track service requests. When a customer calls in for repairs to a product, customer service representatives can access a bevy of information related to the customer. For instance, an agent can access technical information concerning the specific product as well as review any problems the customer has encountered in the past. This enables customer service representatives to react quickly to customer concerns, improving the customer service experience.

BRIEF CASE   Crowdsourcing Cinema at Amazon Studios

It is an online bookstore, a producer of consumer electronics, and the world's largest online retailer. Every year, it seems like Amazon.com continues to find new ways to innovate and add to its legendary success. Amazon Studios, one of its latest adventures, is an innovative film production venture that is radically different from your typical Hollywood studio. In contrast to traditional studios, Amazon Studios crowdsources ideas and scripts for movies, meaning that anyone interested is free to jump on the ride to Hollywood fame and fortune.

According to their official Web site, Amazon Studios aims to discover voices and talents as it accepts submissions from screenwriters and filmmakers who have yet to make it into the big league. Using prizes as incentives—that is, the best film of the year wins a captivating US$1 million and scores a chance to meet with Warner Bros. development executives—aspiring filmmakers are encouraged to upload a screenplay, make improvements to someone else's screenplay, or turn submitted screenplays into a test movie. Amazon Studios initially provided the creative democracy of allowing anyone unbridled editing of the screenplay submissions of others. Unfortunately this experiment proved too radical and was stopped after only two months. Amazon Studios revised its policy, allowing writers to control the extent of input from others, setting permission levels at "open," "closed," or "revisable by permission."

A number of other criticisms surrounded Amazon Studios, including doubts over the crowdsourcing of creativity where screenwriters, in particular, have expressed dissenting voices. The possibilities of winning the prize, or having one's movie made to fit the silver screen, is also pretty low, considering Amazon Studios received 6,000 screenplays and more than 600 movies the first year it was launched. For instance, consider Marty Weiss, who won the first ever best movie of the year award in 2010; he is still waiting and hoping for his movie to be produced.

Looking on the brighter side, the notion of crowdsourcing cinema has been gaining more recognition and getting more exposure in different venues. For example, Ridley Scott's Life in a Day and the UN-backed One Day on Earth are two highly acclaimed examples that demonstrate that crowdsourcing can be used to create meaningful films that touch millions of viewers. Indeed, it appears that true creativity can indeed be crowdsourced, with or without million-dollar budgets or a shot at Hollywood fame.

Based on:

Amazon Studios. (n.d.). *Amazon Studios*. Retrieved July 5, 2012, from http://studios.amazon.com.

Bishop, T. (2011, December 18). Amazon signs big-name Hollywood producers for its first crowdsourced films. *GeekWire*. Retrieved July 5, 2012, from http://www.geekwire.com/2011/amazon-studios-signs-big-producers-crowdsourced-films.

Jones, E.E. (2011, December 1). The Amazon movie revolution . . . one year on. *The Guardian*. Retrieved July 5, 2012, from http://www.guardian.co.uk/film/2011/dec/01/amazon-studios-revolution.

SUPPORT ACTIVITIES. **Support activities** are business activities that enable the primary activities to take place. Support activities include administrative activities, infrastructure, human resources, technology development, and procurement.

Administrative Activities Administrative activities focus on the processes and decision making that orchestrate the day-to-day operations of an organization, particularly those processes that span organizational functions and levels. Administration includes systems and processes from virtually all functional areas—accounting, finance, marketing, operations, and so on—as well as both the executive and the managerial levels of an organization.

Infrastructure Activities Infrastructure refers to the hardware and software that must be implemented to support the applications that the primary activities use. An order entry application requires that employees who enter orders have a computer and the necessary software to accomplish their business objectives. In turn, the computer must be connected via the network to a database containing the order information so that the order can be saved and recalled later for processing. Infrastructure provides the necessary components to facilitate the order entry process (see Chapter 3, "Managing the Information Systems Infrastructure and Services").

Human Resource Activities Human resource activities encompass all business activities associated with employee management, such as hiring, interview scheduling, payroll, and benefits management. Human resource activities are classified as support activities since the primary activities cannot be accomplished without the employees to perform them. In other words, all the primary activities rely on human resource–related business activities. For example, if a company needs a new customer service representative to serve the growing volume of customers, the request is processed through the human resource function, which creates the job description and locates the appropriate person to fill the job.

Technology Development Activities Technology development includes the design and development of applications that support the primary business activities, so as to improve products and/or services. If you are planning on pursuing a career in the management information systems (MIS) field, you will frequently participate in activities related to the development or acquisition of new applications and systems. Technology development can involve a wide array of responsibilities, such as the selection of packaged software or the design and development of custom software to meet a particular business need. Many companies are leveraging the technology development business activity to build Internet, intranet, extranet, or mobile applications to support a wide variety of primary business activities.

Procurement Activities Procurement refers to the purchasing of goods and services that are required as inputs to the primary activities. Allowing each functional area to send out purchase orders can create problems for companies, such as maintaining relationships with more suppliers than necessary and not taking advantage of volume discounts. The procurement business activity can leverage information systems by accumulating purchase orders from the different functional areas within the organization. Procurement personnel can then combine multiple purchase orders containing the same item into a single purchase order. Ordering larger volumes from its suppliers means that the company can achieve dramatic cost savings through volume discounts. Procurement receives, approves, and processes requests for goods and services from the primary activities and coordinates the purchase of those items. This allows the primary activities to concentrate on running the business rather than adding to their workload.

Value Systems: Connecting Multiple Organizational Value Chains

The flow of information can be streamlined not only within a company but outside organizational boundaries as well. A company can create additional value by integrating internal applications with suppliers, business partners, and customers. Companies accomplish this by connecting their internal value chains to form a **value system** (Porter & Millar, 1985), in which information flows from one company's value chain to another company's value chain. Figure 7.8 depicts the value system framework. In this diagram, three companies are aligning their value chains to form a value system. First, Company A processes information through its value chain and forwards the information along to its customer, Company B, which processes the information through its value chain and sends the information along to its customer, Company C, which processes the information through its value chain. Adding additional suppliers, business partners, and customers can create complex value systems. However, for our purposes, we simply view an organization's information systems as a value chain that interacts with the value chains of other organizations.

As information systems can be used to streamline an organization's internal value chain, information systems can also be used to coordinate a company's value chain with another company's value chain or with consumers (such as in business-to-consumer electronic commerce).

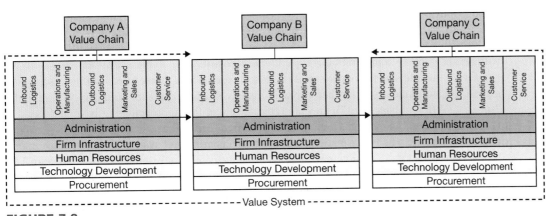

FIGURE 7.8

Three companies combine their value chains, forming a value system.
Source: Based on Porter and Millar (1985); Christensen (1997).

Any information that feeds into a company's value chain, whether its source is another company's value chain or an end consumer, is considered part of the value system.

As discussed previously, a supply chain can be viewed as a river, where physical goods "flow" from a source to an ultimate destination. Like a river, at any particular point there is a flow coming from upstream and progressing downstream. In a similar way, a value system can be viewed as a river of information, comprising upstream and downstream information flows. An **upstream information flow** consists of information that is received from another organization, whereas a **downstream information flow** relates to the information that is produced by a company and sent along to another organization. For instance, in the value system depicted in Figure 7.8, the upstream and downstream information flows for Company B become quite evident. In this case, Company B receives information from its upstream supplier, processes the information through its internal value chain, and subsequently passes information downstream to its distributors and/or customers (see Chapter 8 for a discussion of product and information flows in the opposite direction). These flows of external information into and from a company can be leveraged to create additional value and competitive advantage.

http://goo.gl/YfdO1

ENTERPRISE SYSTEMS

Businesses have leveraged information systems to support business processes for decades, beginning with the installation of individual, separate applications to assist companies with specific business tasks, such as issuing paychecks. However, in order to efficiently and effectively conduct the core business processes (as well as other business processes), the different functional areas within a company need to share data. For example, data about your book order need to be shared between accounting (for billing purposes), marketing and sales (e.g., to feed into product recommendations for other customers), and supply chain management and operations (e.g., to fulfill the order and replenish the inventory).

The Rise of Enterprise Systems

As companies begin to leverage IS applications, they typically start out by fulfilling the needs of particular business activities in a particular department within the organization. Systems that focus on the specific needs of individual departments are typically not designed to communicate with other systems in the organization and are therefore referred to as **stand-alone applications**. Stand-alone applications usually run on a variety of computing hardware platforms, such as mainframes, servers, or employees' PCs. However, although such departmental systems enable departments to conduct their daily business activities efficiently and effectively, these systems often are not very helpful when people from one part of the firm need information from another part of the firm (e.g., people in manufacturing need forecasts from sales).

Organizations used to purchase a variety of proprietary software systems from different software vendors to support different business processes; these systems, however, were not designed to share data with other vendors' systems. Similarly, different employees or departments of a company often develop or purchase a department-specific type of software (e.g., accounting) to meet their needs, and IS managers are then faced with the problem of "knitting together" a hodgepodge portfolio of discordant proprietary applications into a system that shares information. This can be challenging, as applications running on different computing platforms are difficult to integrate; often, custom interfaces are required in order for one system to communicate with another, and such integration is typically very costly.

Given that old stand-alone systems (both software and hardware) were not necessarily designed to communicate with other applications beyond departmental boundaries (essentially "speaking different languages"), they are typically either fast approaching or beyond the end of their useful life within the organization and are referred to as **legacy systems**. Legacy systems can prove problematic when information from multiple departmental systems is required to support business processes and decision making (as is often the case). For example, if the applications for inbound logistics and operations are not integrated, companies will lose valuable time in accessing information related to inventory levels. When an order is placed through operations, personnel need to verify that the components are available in inventory before the order can be processed.

If the inventory and order-entry systems are not integrated, personnel may have to access two separate applications or use a custom interface that pulls information from both systems.

ETHICAL DILEMMA

Too Much Intelligence? RFID and Privacy

Radio frequency identification (RFID) tags are the latest in technological tracking devices. Each tag contains unique identification information that can be accessed by an RFID reader. The identification is then sent to the information system that can identify the product that was tagged. For example, the pharmaceutical industry tags certain drugs in large quantities, such as 100-pill bottles of Viagra and Oxycontin, in order to track them as they move through the supply chain and thus prevent counterfeits from reaching the public.

As is true with all electronic tracking devices, privacy advocates are concerned about misuse. Since, theoretically, RFID tags can be read by anyone who has an RFID reader, the tags have the potential of revealing private consumer information. For example, if you buy a product that has an RFID tag, someone with an RFID reader can possibly identify where you bought the product and how much you paid for it. The amount of information imprinted on an RFID tag is limited, however, and since few retail businesses have purchased RFID writers, readers, or the erasers that can clear information from the tags before they leave the store, the likelihood of privacy abuse is currently slim. Although pharmaceutical companies use RFID tags to track certain products, drug company spokespersons say it is highly unlikely that consumers will take home tracking devices with their heart medications or birth control pills.

In June 2012, a Texas school district disclosed plans to track students using an RFID chip implanted in all student ID cards. The district argued that RFID tags would improve student safety by allowing the district to instantly locate students and count them more accurately throughout the school day. Although some parents looking to keep their children glued to the school seats are supportive of the move, questions of invasion of privacy are certainly hard to ignore. What would happen if someone were to hack into the system? Is it appropriate to monitor the students' every move as if the school were prison grounds? The ACLU is vigorously opposing the RFID tracking initiative because they don't want to see this kind of "intrusive surveillance infrastructure gain inroads into our culture, and because we should not be teaching our children to accept such an intrusive surveillance technology." While RFID has become well accepted for tracking valuable products, society is still debating whether RFID should be used to track people.

Based on:

Anonymous. (2010, February 16). New Hampshire seeks to outlaw biometric IDs. *Infosecurity.* Retrieved July 3, 2012, from http://www.infosecurity-us.com/view/7360/new-hampshire-seeks-to-outlaw-biometric-ids.

Jones, K. (2007, September 4). California passes bill to ban forced RFID tagging. *InformationWeek.* Retrieved July 3, 2012, from http://www.informationweek.com/news/security/showArticle.jhtml?articleID=201803861.

Long, M. (2005, December 29). Mind being tracked by a tiny chip? *Newsfactor.* Retrieved July 3, 2012, from http://www.newsfactor.com/story.xhtml?story_id=40435.

Stanley, J. (2012, June 29). Newest school RFID scheme is reminder of technology's surveillance potential. *ACLU.* Retrieved July 3, 2012, from http://www.aclu.org/blog/technology-and-liberty-lgbt-rights-religion-belief-reproductive-freedom/newest-school-rfid.

Vara-Orta, R. (2012, May 26). Students will be tracked via chips in IDs. *mysanantonio.com.* Retrieved July 3, 2012, from http://www.mysanantonio.com/news/education/article/Students-will-be-tracked-via-chips-in-IDs-3584339.php.

Figure 7.9 provides an example of how information flows through stand-alone systems within an organization. As the diagram depicts, information is generated by the inbound logistics business activity, but it does not flow through to the next business activity, in this case operations; in other words, there are too many "rocks" in the river, impeding the flow of information. Since the inbound logistics and operations departments use different stand-alone systems, information cannot readily flow from one business activity to another. Understandably, this creates a highly inefficient process for operations personnel, who must have access to two systems or a common interface that pulls information together in order to get both the order entry and the inventory information. In some cases, inventory information may be stored on both systems, creating redundancy. Should data be updated in one system but not the other, the data become inconsistent. In addition, there are further unnecessary costs associated with entering, storing, and updating data redundantly.

To utilize data stored in separate stand-alone systems to facilitate business processes and decision making, information must be reentered from one system to the next (by either manual typing, copying and pasting, or even downloads to Excel) or be consolidated by a third system. Further, the same data may also be stored in several (sometimes conflicting) versions throughout the organization, making the information harder to consolidate, often causing the business to lose money because of inefficiencies or missed business opportunities. In addition, organizations need integrated data to demonstrate compliance with standards, rules, or government

FIGURE 7.9

Information flows using stand-alone systems.

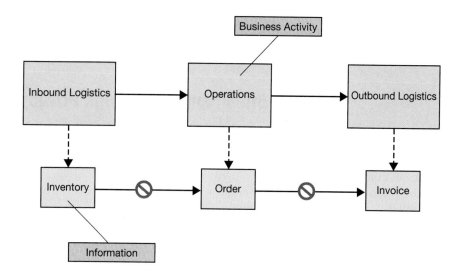

regulations. To address these challenges, organizations have turned to enterprise-wide information systems. An **enterprise-wide information system** (or **enterprise system**) is an integrated suite of business applications for virtually every department, process, and industry, allowing companies to integrate information across operations on a company-wide basis using one large database. Rather than storing information in separate places throughout the organization, enterprise systems provide a central repository common to all corporate users. This, along with a common user interface, allows personnel to share information seamlessly, no matter where the user is located or who is using the application (see Figure 7.10).

The emergence of the Internet and the Web has resulted in the globalization of customer and supplier networks, opening up new opportunities and methods to conduct business. For example,

FIGURE 7.10

Enterprise systems allow companies to integrate information across operations on a company-wide basis.

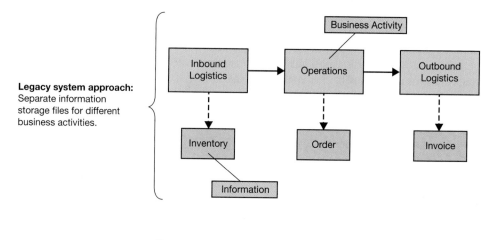

Legacy system approach: Separate information storage files for different business activities.

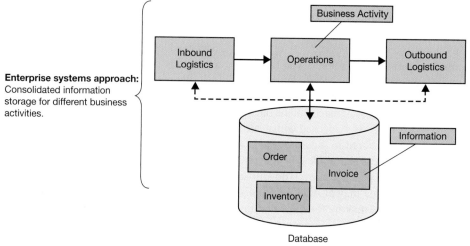

Enterprise systems approach: Consolidated information storage for different business activities.

raw materials and component parts for a computer may come from China and be shipped to Europe for fabrication, and the final products are assembled and shipped to customers across the globe (see Chapter 1, "Managing in the Digital World"). Customers have an increasing number of options available to them, so they are demanding more sophisticated products that are customized to their unique needs. They also expect higher levels of customer service. If companies cannot keep their customers satisfied, the customers will not hesitate to do business with a competitor. Therefore, companies need to provide quality customer service and develop products faster and more efficiently to compete in global markets. Enterprise systems can support this by streamlining communications with global customers and suppliers. For example, the enterprise systems of SAP, the German enterprise systems pioneer, support over 30 different languages and currencies and perform translation and currency exchange seamlessly. Rather than focusing only on internal operations, these systems can also focus on business activities that occur outside organizational boundaries. Enterprise systems can help companies find innovative ways to increase accurate on-time shipments, avoid (or at least anticipate) surprises (such as shortages in raw materials or weather problems), minimize costs, and ultimately increase customer satisfaction and the overall profitability of the company.

Enterprise systems come in a variety of shapes and sizes, each providing a unique set of features and functionality. When deciding to implement enterprise solutions, managers need to be aware of a number of issues. One of the most important involves selecting and implementing applications that meet the requirements of the business as well as of its customers and suppliers. In the following sections, we examine the ways in which information systems can be leveraged to support business processes. This is followed by an in-depth analysis of how enterprise systems have evolved and how companies are using these systems to support their internal and external operations.

Supporting Business Processes

As discussed previously, information systems can be used to gain and sustain competitive advantage by supporting and/or streamlining activities along the value chain. For example, an information system could be used to support a billing process in such a way that it reduces the use of paper and, more important, the handling of paper, thus reducing material and labor costs. This system can help managers keep track of that same billing process more effectively because they will have more accurate, up-to-date information about the billing process, enabling them to make smart, timely business decisions.

Information systems can be used to support either internally or externally focused business processes. **Internally focused systems** support functional areas, business processes, and decision making *within* an organization. These activities can be viewed as a series of links in a chain along which information flows within the organization. At each stage (or link) in the process, value is added in the form of the work performed by people associated with that process, and new, useful information is generated. Information begins to accumulate at the point of entry and flows through the various links, or business processes, within the organization, progressing through the organization with new, useful information being added every step of the way (see Figure 7.11).

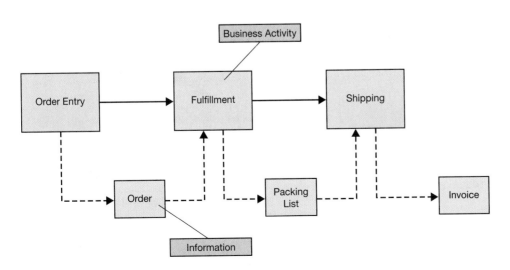

FIGURE 7.11

Information flow for a typical order.

Companies can gain several advantages by integrating and converting legacy systems so that information stored on separate computing platforms can be consolidated to provide a centralized point of access, which typically comes in the form of *enterprise resource planning* applications (discussed later in this chapter). Although such applications do an excellent job of serving the needs of internal business operations on an organization-wide basis, they are not necessarily designed to completely accommodate the communication of information outside the organization's boundaries.

Externally focused systems coordinate business processes with customers, suppliers, business partners, and others who operate *outside* an organization's boundaries. A system that communicates across organizational boundaries is sometimes referred to as an **interorganizational system (IOS)** (Kumar & Crook, 1999). The key purpose of an IOS is to streamline the flow of information from one company's operations to another's (e.g., from a company to its potential or existing customers).

Competitive advantage can be accomplished here by integrating multiple business processes in ways that enable a firm to meet a wide range of unique customer needs. Sharing information between organizations helps companies to adapt more quickly to changing market conditions. For instance, should consumers demand that an additional component be added to a product, a company can gain this information from its information systems that support sales and instantaneously pass it along to its component suppliers. Information systems allow the company and its suppliers to satisfy the needs of customers efficiently since changes can be identified and managed immediately, creating a competitive advantage for companies that can respond quickly. We can view processes and information flows across organizations just as we previously viewed the processes and information flows within an organization. At each stage (or link) in the process, value is added by the work performed, and new, useful information is generated and exchanged between organizations (see Figure 7.12). Using an IOS, one company can create information and transmit it electronically to another company.

Systems that facilitate interorganizational communications focus on the upstream and downstream information flows. *Customer relationship management* applications concentrate on the activities involved in promoting and selling products to the customers as well as providing customer service and nourishing long-term relationships. In contrast, *supply chain management* applications integrate the value chains of business partners within a supply chain, improving the coordination of suppliers, product or service production, and distribution (both types of applications are discussed in Chapter 8). Integrating internally focused and externally focused applications can be extremely valuable for companies operating in global markets. For example, the enterprise systems offered by SAP have multilingual interfaces and automatically convert measurement units (e.g., kilograms versus pounds or centimeters versus inches) and currencies. This way, engineers in Germany, Spain, or Italy can input the bill of materials,

FIGURE 7.12

Information flow for a typical shipment across organizational boundaries.

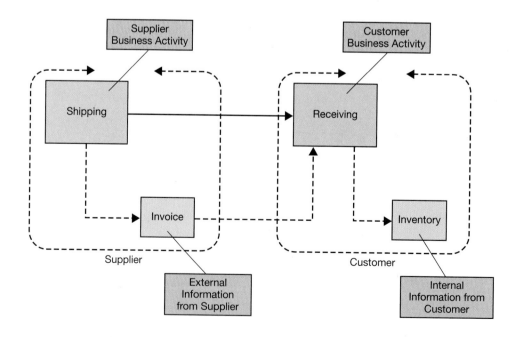

COMING ATTRACTIONS

Power of the Swarm

Social insects, such as ants, bees, termites, and wasps, have very powerful problem-solving skills with sophisticated collective intelligence. For instance, ants use pheromone trails to mark the routes they use to find food. The more traveled trails accumulate more pheromones, which attract new ants. Conversely, pheromones deposited on less traveled paths will evaporate eventually. The problems social insects solve—finding food, dividing labor among nestmates, building nests, responding to external challenges—have important counterparts in engineering and computer science. Swarm intelligence, inspired by the observation of these social insects, attempts to mimic the highly efficient behavior of social insects by combining hundreds or even thousands of relatively simple robots to generate behavior more complex than any individual device could achieve alone.

As a branch of artificial intelligence, swarm intelligence has many potential application areas, including the military, surveillance and monitoring, health, micromanufacturing, and space exploration. For instance, maybe the only way we will truly explore the solar system and beyond is to build vast numbers of small robots that will be able to land on planetary bodies. Then they might build copies of themselves as well as new vehicles, eventually generating millions of robots spread throughout the galaxy.

Based on:

Boothroyd, D. (2010, August 3). By imitating insects, microrobots could open new avenues of research and application. *NewElectronics.* Retrieved July 3, 2012, from http://www.newelectronics.co.uk/article/22890/Hive-mentality-Microrobots.aspx.

Bradley, R. (2012, June 26). Bee-school: Why is everyone suddenly so interested in the hive mind. *CNN Money.* Retrieved July 3, 2012, from http://management.fortune.cnn.com/2012/06/26/bees/.

Greenemeier, L. (2010, January 13). Group thinker: Researcher gets $2.9 million to further develop swarm intelligence. *Scientific American.* Retrieved July 3, 2012, from http://www.scientificamerican.com/article.cfm?id=swarm-intelligence-research.

Swarm intelligence. (2012, June 30). In *Wikipedia, The Free Encyclopedia.* Retrieved July 3, 2012, from http://en.wikipedia.org/w/index.php?title=Swarm_intelligence&oldid=500011530.

---

manufacturing engineers and factory specialists can buy the parts and set up the production run, and marketing and sales staff in the United States can easily communicate with their clients. Most large enterprise systems vendors offer a suite of integrated core business applications that combine internally focused and externally focused applications (see Table 7.1 for the core applications available in SAP's Business Suite).

IMPROVING BUSINESS PROCESSES THROUGH ENTERPRISE SYSTEMS. Software programs come in two forms—packaged and custom. **Packaged software**, sometimes referred to as **off-the-shelf software**, are applications written by third-party vendors for the needs of many different users and organizations, whereas **custom software** are applications that are designed and developed exclusively for a specific organization (see Chapter 9, "Developing and Acquiring Information Systems"). Packaged software that you are likely familiar with is Microsoft Office, which you can purchase off the shelf (or download) to help you with your personal documents and communications. Packaged software is highly useful for standardized, repetitive tasks, such as writing a report or preparing a presentation or a tax return. These programs can be quite cost effective since the vendor that builds the application can spread out development costs through selling to a large number of users.

Yet, packaged software may not be well suited for tasks that are unique to a particular business. In these cases, companies may prefer to develop (or have developed for them) custom software that can accommodate their particular business needs. The development costs of custom software are much higher than for packaged software because of the time, money, and resources that are required to design and develop them. Furthermore, applications need to be maintained internally when changes are required. With packaged software, the vendor makes the changes

---

TABLE 7.1 Core Applications of SAP's Business Suite

SAP Customer Relationship Management	SAP Supplier Relationship Management
SAP Enterprise Resource Planning	SAP Supply Chain Management
SAP Product Life Cycle Management	

and distributes new versions to its customers. In all, there are trade-offs when choosing between the packaged and custom software routes. Managers must consider whether packaged software can meet the business requirements and, if not, conduct a cost–benefit analysis to ensure that taking the custom software approach will prove worthwhile to the company.

Because all companies are different, no packaged software application will exactly fit the unique requirements of a particular business. Thus, enterprise systems come in a variety of shapes and sizes, each designed to accommodate certain transaction volumes, industries, and business processes. Enterprise systems vendors such as SAP, Oracle, or Microsoft offer different **modules**, which are components that can be selected and implemented as needed. In essence, each module is designed to replace a legacy system, be it a finance, human resources, or manufacturing system; thus, after the conversion to an enterprise system, each business function has access to various modules that serve its needs, but the modules (and the underlying data) are tightly integrated and share the same look and feel (see Figure 7.13). For example, Oracle's JD Edwards EnterpriseOne offers more than 70 different modules to support a variety of business functions. Similarly, SAP offers a variety of modules related to four major groups of functions (see Table 7.2). The modules provided by different vendors may vary in the specific business processes they support as well as in what they are called.

Vanilla versus Customized Software As the naming and capabilities differ between the software vendors, it is critical for managers to understand the vendors' naming conventions and software modules to gain an understanding of how these features can be implemented to support the company's business processes. The features and modules that an enterprise system comes with out of the box are referred to as the **vanilla version**. If the vanilla version does not support a certain business process, the company may require a customized version. **Customization** provides either additional software that is integrated with the enterprise system or consists of direct changes to the vanilla application itself. SAP, for example, includes literally thousands of elements in its various enterprise systems that can be customized, and it also offers many industry-specific versions that have already been customized for a particular industry based on SAP's perceptions of the best way to do things (i.e., industry best practices). Companies must take special care when dealing with customization issues. Customizations can be extremely costly, and maintaining and upgrading customizations can be troublesome. For example, a customization made to the vanilla version will need to be reprogrammed when a new release of the system is implemented because subsequent releases of the software will not include the previous customizations. In other words, new vanilla versions must be continually upgraded

FIGURE 7.13

Each module in an enterprise system is designed to replace a stand-alone legacy system.
Source: Courtesy of Microsoft, Inc.

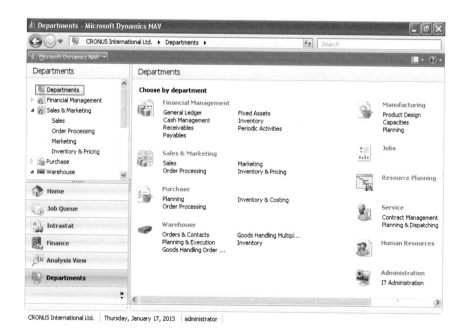

TABLE 7.2 Key Capabilities of SAP's Enterprise Systems

Capability	Explanation
Financials	Allows organizations to manage corporate finance functions by automating financial supply chain management, financial accounting, and management accounting
Human capital management	Gives organizations the tools needed to maximize the profitability potential of the workforce, with functionality for employee transaction management and employee life cycle management
Operations	Empowers organizations to streamline operations with integrated functionality for managing end-to-end logistics processes while expanding collaborative capabilities in supply chain management, product life cycle management, and supplier relationship management
Corporate services	Allows organizations to optimize centralized and decentralized services for managing real estate, corporate travel, and incentives and commissions

to accommodate the company-specific customizations. This process can involve a substantial investment of time and resources, diverting attention away from other key business activities and reducing company profits.

Best Practices–Based Software One of the major hurdles facing companies that implement enterprise systems involves changing business processes to accommodate the manner in which the software works. Enterprise system implementations are often used as a catalyst for overall improvement of underlying business processes. As with SAP, most enterprise systems are designed to operate according to industry-standard business processes, or **best practices**. Best practices reflect the techniques and processes, identified through experience and research, that have consistently shown results superior to those achieved with other means. In fact, because they have proven to consistently lead to superior performance, most enterprise system vendors build best practices into their applications to provide guidelines for management to identify business activities within their organizations that need to be streamlined. Implementations and future upgrades to the system will go more smoothly when companies change their business processes to fit the way the enterprise system operates.

However, many organizations have spent years developing business processes that provide them with a competitive advantage in the marketplace. Adopting their industry's best practices may force these companies to abandon their unique ways of doing business, putting them on par with their industry competitors. In other words, companies can potentially lose their competitive advantages by adopting the best practices within their industry. Best practices is an area that managers must carefully consider before selecting any type of enterprise system, because some enterprise system vendors build their entire systems around best practices, and companies that reject these best practices are in for a long and time-consuming implementation (although the vendors and external consultants typically offer help in the process). Other vendors provide a series of options that companies select before implementing the software, allowing them some (but not complete) flexibility in changing their business processes to accommodate the enterprise system modules. Given the importance and difficulty of changing business processes with enterprise and other systems implementations, we now briefly describe business process management.

Business Process Management Since the first publishing of *The Principles of Scientific Management* by Fredrick Taylor in 1911 (and probably even before that), organizations have focused on improving business processes. Over the years, various approaches for improving business processes have been developed (see Table 7.3). Given the magnitude of change that an enterprise system can impose on an organization's business processes, understanding the role of business process management in the implementation of an enterprise system is necessary. **Business process management (BPM)** is a systematic, structured improvement approach by all or part of an organization whereby people critically examine, rethink, and redesign business processes in order to achieve dramatic improvements in one or more performance measures,

TABLE 7.3 Some Other Terms Closely Related to Business Process Management

Business activity modeling	Business process redesign
Business activity monitoring	Business process reengineering
Business architecture modernization	Functional process improvement
Business process improvement	Work flow management

such as quality, cycle time, or cost. BPM became very popular in the 1990s (and was then called **business process reengineering [BPR]**) when Michael Hammer and James Champy published their best-selling book *Reengineering the Corporation.*

Hammer and Champy and their proponents argued that radical redesign of an organization was sometimes necessary in order to lower costs and increase quality, and that information systems were the key enabler for that radical change. The basic steps in BPM can be summarized as follows:

1. Develop a vision for the organization that specifies business objectives, such as reducing costs, shortening the time it takes to get products to market, improving quality of products and/or services, and so on
2. Identify the critical processes that are to be redesigned
3. Understand and measure the existing processes as a baseline for future improvements
4. Identify ways that information systems can be used to improve processes
5. Design and implement a prototype of the new processes

At the heart of BPM initiatives are information systems that enable the streamlining of business processes. Given the importance of information systems in such endeavors, organizations are increasingly hiring information systems (IS) consultants and business analysts who have a sound understanding of the business but who are also well versed in technology. In fact, business analysts and business systems analysts are often listed among the hottest jobs because of good job prospects, high salaries, and the diversity of work. In enterprise systems projects, business analysts are deeply involved in analyzing and improving business processes and mapping the processes to the different enterprise systems modules.

BPM is similar to quality improvement approaches such as *total quality management* and *continuous process improvement* in that they are intended to be cross-functional approaches to improve an organization. BPM differs from these quality improvement approaches, however, in one fundamental way. These quality improvement approaches tend to focus on incremental change and gradual improvement of processes, while the intention behind BPM is radical redesign and drastic improvement of processes.

When BPR was introduced in the 1990s, many efforts were reported to have failed. These failures occurred for a variety of reasons, including the lack of sustained management commitment and leadership, unrealistic scope and expectations, and resistance to change. In fact, BPR gained the reputation of being a nice way of saying "downsizing."

Nevertheless, BPR (and its successors such as BPM) lives on today and is still a popular approach to improving organizations. No matter what it is called, the conditions that appear to lead to a successful business process improvement effort include the following:

- Support by senior management
- Shared vision by all organizational members
- Realistic expectations
- Participants empowered to make changes
- The right people participating
- Sound management practices
- Appropriate funding

In any event, it is clear that successful business process change, especially involving enterprise systems, requires a broad range of organizational factors to converge that are far beyond the technical implementation issues.

Benefits and Costs of Enterprise Systems Beyond the improvements in critical business processes, there are various types of benefits and costs associated with the acquisition and development of enterprise systems. According to industry research, implementation costs run over budget 56 percent of the time (Panorama, 2012). On average, projects costs were around US$10 million, but running nearly US$2 million over budget. Top reasons cited for budget overruns are that the initial project scope was expanded, and that unanticipated technical or organizational change management issues resulted in additional costs.

Gaining a better understanding of both project benefits and costs can help to develop an improved understanding of the project's total cost of ownership, and help make the business case for a particular investment decision (see Chapter 9). Benefits of enterprise systems that can be used to make the business case include:

- Improved availability of information
- Increased interaction throughout the organization
- Improved (reduced) lead times for manufacturing
- Improved customer interaction
- Reduced operating expenses
- Reduced IS costs
- Improved supplier integration
- Improved compliance with standards, rules, and regulations

The two mostly likely benefits realized from utilizing enterprise systems are improvements in information availability and increased interaction across the organization as a result of streamlining business processes.

Just as there are many possible benefits that can be realized when implementing an enterprise system, there are also many potential costs that can impact the total cost of ownership of these large and complex systems. Many companies underestimate these costs and, as a result, ultimately go over budget. Understanding all of the items that make up the total cost of ownership will help guide organizations into making better financial projections and project approval decisions. Beyond the system acquisition costs—for example, software licenses and maintenance costs, technical implementation, and hardware costs—other costs that are often overlooked when estimating project costs include:

- Travel and training costs for personnel
- Ongoing customization and integration costs
- Business process studies
- Project governance costs

If all costs are not considered, it can result in unexpected budget increases, delayed project timelines, and angry management. Next, we examine enterprise resource planning systems.

ENTERPRISE RESOURCE PLANNING

When companies realize that legacy systems can create dramatic inefficiencies within their organizations, the next step is to integrate legacy information on a company-wide basis. As previously described, applications that integrate business activities across departmental boundaries are often referred to as **enterprise resource planning (ERP)** systems. In the 1990s, we witnessed companies' initial push to implement integrated applications, as exhibited by skyrocketing ERP sales at that time. Be aware that the terms "resource" and "planning" are somewhat misnomers, meaning that they only partially describe the purpose of ERP, since these applications do much more than just planning or managing resources. The reason for the term "enterprise resource planning" is that these systems evolved in part during the 1990s from material requirements planning and manufacturing resource planning packages. Do not get hung up on the words "resource" and "planning." The key word to remember from the acronym ERP is "enterprise."

http://goo.gl/DDSrj

Integrating Data to Integrate Applications

ERP replaces stand-alone applications by providing various modules based on a common database and similar application interfaces that service the entire enterprise rather than portions of it. Information stored on legacy systems is converted into a large, centralized database that stores

KEY PLAYERS

The Titans of ERP

Titan: Noun. A person or thing of great size or power.
In the ERP world, the three largest and most powerful ERP providers are SAP, Oracle, and Microsoft. Founded in 1972, SAP is a German multinational software corporation that makes enterprise software to manage business operations and customer relations. SAP has developed close relationships with numerous partners who help to provide an abundance of add-on products and consulting that work in conjunction with SAP products. Many of the world's largest and most complex ERP implementations utilize SAP software. Headquartered in Walldorf, Germany, with regional offices around the world, SAP is the market leader in enterprise application software. In 2011, SAP had nearly 60,000 employees and revenues over US$17.6 billion. In 2010, SAP captured about 24 percent of the ERP market.

Oracle Corporation is an American multinational computer technology corporation that specializes in developing and marketing computer hardware systems and enterprise software products. Oracle is best known for its database systems rather than its ERP systems. However, the company has rapidly expanded its ERP market share through natural sales growth and several high-profile acquisitions of ERP applications, including JD Edwards, PeopleSoft, and Siebel CRM. Oracle targets mid-to-large organizations with ERP solutions that are highly customizable to a particular organization and industry. Headquartered in Redwood City, California, Oracle employs approximately 115,000 people worldwide, with revenues exceeding US$37.1 billion in 2011. In 2010, Oracle captured about 18 percent of the ERP market.

Microsoft Corporation, also an American multinational corporation, is headquartered in Redmond, Washington. Microsoft is a very diverse company that develops, manufactures, licenses, and supports a wide range of products and services related to computing. Microsoft is the largest software corporation in the world, with over 92,000 employees and revenues exceeding US$69.9 billion in 2011. Microsoft entered the ERP marketplace in 2000 with the acquisition of Great Plains accounting software. Over the past decade, Microsoft acquired several other companies to expand its Dynamics ERP product line, which is targeted at small- to mid-sized businesses desiring a simple, out-of-the-box ERP solution. In 2010, Microsoft captured about 11 percent of the ERP market.

SAP, Oracle, and Microsoft have different strengths, weaknesses, and tradeoffs. As different organizations have different needs, organizations typically work with consultants to find the right vendor and the right product to meet their needs. An analysis of investment payback by Panorama Consulting found that it takes most organizations about 2.5 years to achieve payback on an ERP implementation; Oracle was ranked as having the slowest payback, while Microsoft was ranked as having the fastest. SAP-based projects were reported to cost in excess of US$19 million, Oracle projects exceeded US$1.5 million, and Microsoft projects exceeded US$0.4 million. Clearly, SAP is being used for extremely large ERP implementations, while Oracle and Microsoft are being utilized by relatively smaller organizations, respectively. Each of these titans, however, have acquired their size and strength using a different approach, with SAP exclusively focusing on ERP-related solutions, Oracle focusing on a variety of organizational solutions that include ERP, and Microsoft focusing on a broad range of computing products to serve organization and consumer marketplaces. For organizations looking to purchase an ERP solution, they will need to carefully consider their business circumstances and contrast these with the distinct strengths, weaknesses, and tradeoffs of the various product offerings.

Based on:

Microsoft. (2012, June 30). In *Wikipedia, The Free Encyclopedia*. Retrieved July 5, 2012, from http://en.wikipedia.org/w/index.php ?title=Microsoft&oldid=500062036.

Oracle Corporation. (2012, June 29). In *Wikipedia, The Free Encyclopedia*. Retrieved July 5, 2012, from http://en.wikipedia.org/w/ index.php?title=Oracle_Corporation&oldid=499867811.

Panorama Consulting Solutions (2011). Clash of the titans: An independent comparison of SAP, Oracle, and Microsoft Dynamics. Retrieved July 4, 2012, from http://panorama-consulting.com/ resource-center.

SAP AG. (2012, July 2). In *Wikipedia, The Free Encyclopedia*. Retrieved July 5, 2012, from http://en.wikipedia.org/w/index.php?title= SAP_AG&oldid=500350524.

information related to the various business activities of an organization. The central database alleviates the problems associated with multiple computing platforms by providing a single place where all information relevant to the company and particular departments can be stored and accessed, as depicted in Figure 7.14.

In contrast to legacy systems, where it is difficult to share information between business activities, ERP applications make accessing information easier by providing a central information repository. For example, where an ERP solution is used, both inbound logistics and operations have access to current inventory data because both business activities have access to the same information. Rather than information flowing from one department to the next, it can be accessed and updated at will, meaning that the next business activity can access information in the

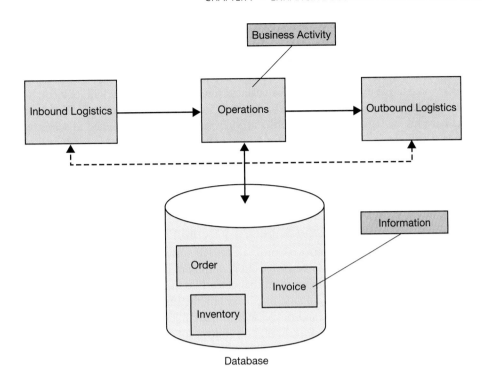

FIGURE 7.14

Information storage using an ERP solution.

database whenever it needs to. This gives personnel access to accurate, up-to-date information. The beauty of ERP lies in the fact that information can be shared throughout the organization. For example, inventory information is accessible not only to inbound logistics and operations, but also to accounting, sales, and customer service personnel. If a customer calls to inquire about the status of an order, customer service representatives can find out by accessing the database through the ERP application (see Figure 7.15). Prior to the emergence of ERP, customer service representatives may have had to retrieve information from two or more separate computing systems or, worse yet, call someone who would be able to access the information, making their job extremely difficult while potentially resulting in dissatisfied customers. Storing data in a single place and making it available to everyone within the organization empowers everyone in the organization to be aware of the current state of business and to perform their jobs better.

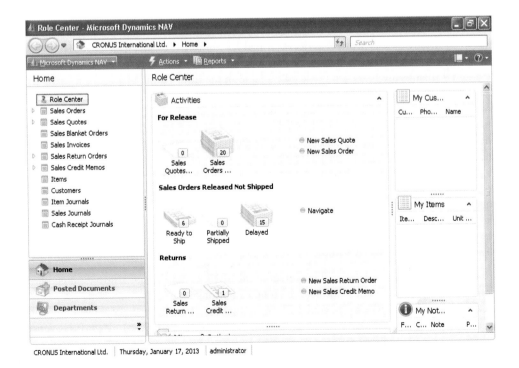

FIGURE 7.15

An ERP system can provide employees with relevant up-to-date information.
Source: Courtesy of Microsoft, Inc.

ERP applications that access the database are designed to have the same look and feel regardless of the unique needs of a particular department. Inbound logistics and operations personnel will use a common user interface to access the same pieces of information from the shared database. Although the inbound logistics module and the operations module will have different features tailored to the unique needs of the business functions, the screens will look comparable, with similar designs, screen layouts, menu options, and so on. The Microsoft Office products provide a useful analogy. Microsoft Word and Microsoft Excel are designed to serve separate functions (word processing and spreadsheets, respectively), but overall the products look and feel very similar to one another. Word and Excel have similar user interfaces but differ vastly in the purpose, features, and functionality that each application offers. Likewise, the look and feel of Microsoft Dynamics (Microsoft's suite of enterprise-wide information systems) resembles that of Microsoft Office so as to reduce the learning curve for new users.

Responding to Compliance and Regulatory Demands

In addition to helping improve business processes, ERP systems improve and ease an organization's ability to implement audit controls and government imposed compliance regulations. Compliance with far-reaching government mandates like the Sarbanes–Oxley Act and other evolving and emerging regulatory standards is based on the implementation and documentation of internal controls, procedures, and processes. All ERP systems are being designed to have an abundance of control features built in that can mirror an organization's business processes (e.g., controlling who has access to information and process steps, segregating duties across job functions, etc.). Such enterprise-wide capabilities provide organizations with tested solutions for developing and deploying a comprehensive compliance strategy. While the ERP system may not provide answers to all regulation requirements, deploying an ERP has been a central strategy for many organizations struggling to adhere to the myriad legal, regulatory, and supply chain mandates that are common in today's highly regulated business environment.

Choosing an ERP System

When selecting an appropriate ERP application for an organization, management needs to take many factors into careful consideration. ERP applications come as packaged software, which means that they are designed to appeal to many different companies. However, businesses have unique needs even within their own industries. In other words, like snowflakes, no two companies are exactly alike. Management must carefully select an ERP application that will meet the unique requirements of its particular company, and must consider a number of factors in the ERP selection. Among the most prevalent issues facing management are ERP control and ERP business requirements.

ERP CONTROL. ERP control refers to the locus of control over the computing systems and data contained in those systems, as well as decision-making authority. Companies typically either opt for centralized control or allow particular business units to govern themselves. In the context of ERP, these decisions are based on the level of detail in the information that must be provided to management. Some corporations want to have as much detail as possible made available at the executive level, whereas other companies do not require such access. For instance, an accountant in one company may want the ability to view costs down to the level of individual transactions, while an accountant in another company may want only summary information. Another area related to control involves the consistency of policies and procedures. Some companies prefer that policies and procedures remain consistent throughout an organization. Other companies want to allow each business unit to develop its own policies and procedures to accommodate the unique ways that they do business. ERP applications vary widely in their allowance for control, typically assuming either a corporate or a business-unit locus of control. Some ERP applications allow users to select or customize the locus of control. In either case, management must consider the ERP's stance on control to ensure that it will meet the business requirements of the company.

ERP BUSINESS REQUIREMENTS. When selecting an ERP system, organizations must choose which modules to implement from a large menu of options—most organizations adopt only a subset of the available ERP components. There are two major categories of ERP components— ERP *core* components and ERP *extended* components (see Figure 7.16). Most ERP vendors provide components that are tailored to specific industry best practices and, of course, allow customization if desired by the customer.

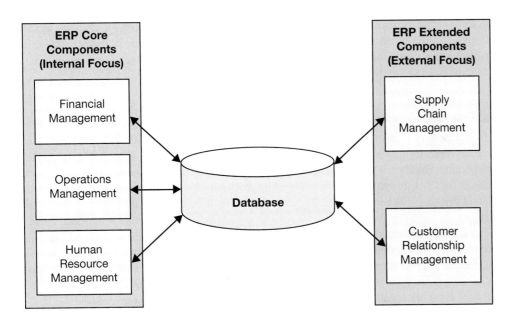

FIGURE 7.16

An ERP system consists of core and extended components.

ERP Core Components **ERP core components** support the important *internal* activities of the organization for producing their products and services. These components support internal operations such as the following:

1. *Financial Management.* Components to support accounting, financial reporting, performance management, and corporate governance
2. *Operations Management.* Components to simplify, standardize, and automate business processes related to inbound and outbound logistics, product development, manufacturing, and sales and service
3. *Human Resource Management.* Components to support employee recruitment, assignment tracking, performance reviews, payroll, and regulatory requirements

Whereas the operations management components enable the core activities of the value chain, financial management and human resources management are associated with activities supporting the core activities (see Figure 7.17).

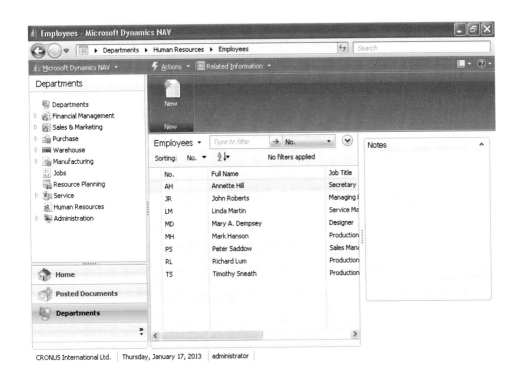

FIGURE 7.17

The human resources management component of an ERP enables core value chain activities to take place.

Source: Courtesy of Microsoft, Inc.

ERP Extended Components ERP **extended components** support the primary *external* activities of the organization for dealing with suppliers and customers. Specifically, ERP extended components focus primarily on supply chain management and customer relationship management. Both are discussed in detail in Chapter 8.

Enabling Business Processes Using ERP Core Components

To fit the needs of various businesses in different industries, an ERP system's core components are typically implemented using a building-block approach through a series of modules. For example, SAP's ERP application is built around modules that are modeled after the best practices for 25 different industries. Depending on the industries, the modules are localized for different countries: Whereas the modules for the automotive industry are localized for Japan or Germany, the modules for apparel and footwear industries are localized for China and India, the modules for the pharmaceutical industry are localized for Germany and the United States, and so on. Similarly, Microsoft offers its Dynamics ERP system for various industries, including construction, health care, manufacturing, retail, and others (see Table 7.4). Depending on the way processes are typically performed in an industry, the modules within each industry-specific ERP package work together to enable the business processes needed to run a business efficiently and effectively. ERP vendors typically package the various modules that enable industry-specific processes and offer such systems as "industry solutions." This way, organizations have to spend less effort in selecting the needed modules and can more easily implement the ERP system.

ORDER-TO-CASH. As discussed above, the order-to-cash process entails the processes related to selling goods or services. Depending on the industry, the order-to-cash process can be very simple or extremely complex. In a retail environment, this process can be as simple as capturing product data, modifying the sale price (if needed), processing payment cards, and processing loyalty cards for customer profiling purposes. For a wholesale distributor, the order-to-cash process is more elaborate and consists of price quotation, stock allocation, credit limit check, picking, packing, shipping, billing, and receiving payment. For these processes to take place, different modules of the financial and operations management components work together. For example, the financial management component provides modules for checking credit limits, billing, and processing incoming payments. The operations management component provides modules related to sales and warehouse management operations, such as price quotation, stock allocation, picking, packing, and shipping (see Figure 7.18).

PROCURE-TO-PAY. To recall, a generic procure-to-pay process entails negotiating price and terms, issuing purchase orders, receiving the goods, receiving the invoice, and settling the payment. As the order-to-cash process differs between industries, so does the procure-to-pay process. A grocery store, for example, typically orders a standard assortment of products, but also faces additional constraints such as having to optimize order quantities, taking into account not only demand and storage costs but also seasonality and perishability of products. In contrast, a construction company procures diverse materials, depending on the project at hand, and the procurement process could entail a lengthy sourcing process, including requests for quotations, a bidding process, reviewing of bids, awarding the contract, and thoroughly inspecting the delivered products or materials (see also Chapter 9 for the process of purchasing a new information system). Similar to the order-to-cash process, different modules of the financial management and operations management ERP components work together to enable the different activities related to the procure-to-pay process (see Figure 7.19).

TABLE 7.4 Industry-Specific Versions of the Microsoft Dynamics ERP System

Construction	Distribution
Education	Financial services
Government	Health care
Manufacturing	Not-for-profit
Professional services	Retail

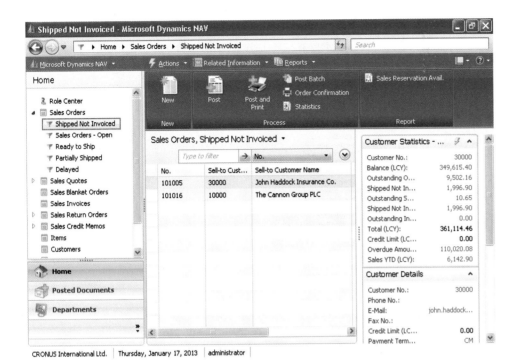

FIGURE 7.18

An ERP system can support all aspects of the order-to-cash process.
Source: Courtesy of Microsoft, Inc.

MAKE-TO-STOCK/MAKE-TO-ORDER. The processes related to producing goods differ widely between different industries. The biggest distinction is between the make-to-stock and make-to-order processes. As indicated above, the make-to-stock process is typically used for commodities, whereas the make-to-order process is used for highly customizable goods or big-ticket items (such as aircraft or highway bridges). Many beverage companies, for instance, use a make-to-stock approach, involving production planning, manufacturing, and quality control. In contrast, an aerospace company has to start with planning the project and ordering subassemblies or raw materials with long lead times before planning and executing the production for each specific project, and finally checking quality and shipping the product. Many of the activities associated

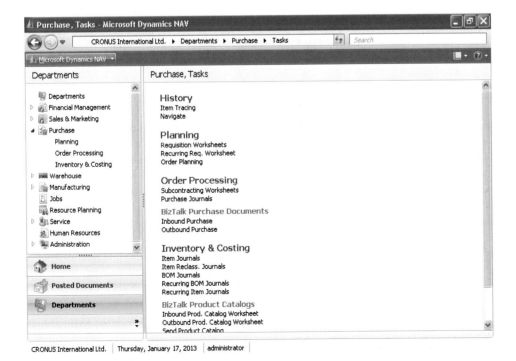

FIGURE 7.19

An ERP system can support all aspects of the procure-to-pay process.
Source: Courtesy of Microsoft, Inc.

FIGURE 7.20

An ERP system can support all aspects of the production process.
Source: Courtesy of Microsoft, Inc.

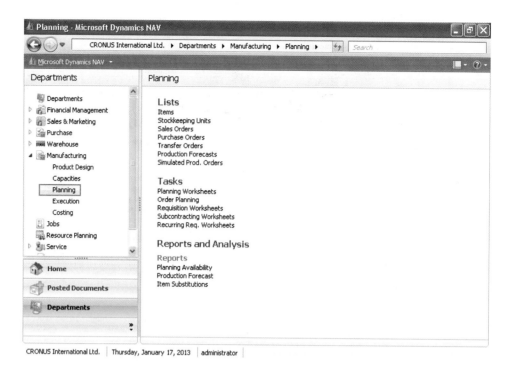

with the production process are supported by the operations management component of an ERP (see Figure 7.20).

OTHER BUSINESS PROCESSES. In addition to these business processes, ERP systems typically enable a variety of other generic as well as industry-specific business processes. Any business needs to manage its workforce, including managing the hiring processes, scheduling the workforce, recording time and attendance, processing payroll, managing benefits, and so on. All these processes are supported by the human resources management component of an ERP. Similarly, the financial management component supports generic processes, such as financial and managerial accounting, corporate governance, and the like. Industry-specific processes and the modules supporting these can vary widely. For example, the business of an aircraft manufacturer consists to a large extent of aftermarket support; a retail chain, in contrast, needs modules supporting retail space planning and price and markdown management; a commercial real estate company needs modules for managing assets, leases, and common spaces; and a large part of an airline's operations is related to maintenance, repair, overhaul, flight operations, catering, and customer care.

ERP Installation

Previously, we discussed how organizations can benefit from the integration of stand-alone systems; further, you learned how business processes can differ between industries. Thus, any organization considering the implementation of an ERP system has to carefully evaluate the different options available not only in terms of the overall systems offered by different vendors but also in terms of the industry-specific solutions offered by the software vendors. An evaluation should entail the assessment of how far the different modules can support existing business processes, which modules may have to be added, and the extent to which existing business processes have to be modified in order to fit the modules offered by the ERP system.

An activity that is widely underestimated, however, is the *configuration* of ERP systems. Whereas customization involves the programming of company-specific modules or changing how business processes are implemented within the system and is often discouraged, configuration is an activity to be performed during any ERP implementation. Specifically, the system must be configured to reflect the way an organization does business and the associated business rules. As one of the most important parts of an ERP system is the underlying company-wide database, setting up the database is key to a successful ERP implementation, and organizations have to make countless decisions on how to configure hundreds or thousands of database tables

WHO'S GOING MOBILE

Big ERP Systems Embracing Small Mobile Devices

ERP technologies are transforming organizations of all sizes in all industries. ERP vendors are rapidly evolving their systems to better support road warriors with a variety of mobile ERP applications. With mobile ERP, workers will be able to take advantage of the functionality, data, and benefits of their ERP application not only in the office, but also on the road. Mobile ERP applications can provide many benefits to an organization, including:

1. **Improving Service Quality**–Mobile ERP will allow remote workers access to relevant customer information, improving service quality and responsiveness.
2. **Improving Productivity**–Mobile ERP will allow remote workers to access key resources when commuting or waiting in airports, improving productivity and reducing downtime.
3. **Strengthening Customer Relationships**–Mobile ERP will allow remote workers to have key customer information when needed to strengthen customer relationships.
4. **Improving Competitive Advantage**–Mobile ERP can speed responsiveness to customer needs, improving competitive advantage.
5. **Improving Data Timeliness and Accuracy**–Mobile ERP allows for easier, less redundant, and more timely data

capture, allowing workers in the field to capture critical data as it emerges without having to re-key it into multiple systems where errors and inconsistencies can occur.

In 2011, SAP announced 19 new mobile applications, including apps for iPhone, iPad, BlackBerry, and Android devices. Microsoft is also developing a suite of mobile applications for reporting and dashboarding for its Dynamics ERP system. As mobility is a megatrend that will only become more and more prevalent in the workplace, organizations should choose ERP systems that have the capability and flexibility to integrate with an expanding array of mobile devices and platforms.

Based on:

Borek, R. (2011, July 22). 5 Benefits to mobile ERP. *ERP Software-Blog*. Retrieved July 3, 2012, from http://www.erpsoftwareblog.com/2011/07/5-benefits-to-mobile-erp.

Kearns, J. (2012, March 17). The Advent of the mobile ERP. *Accounting Micro Systems*. Retrieved July 3, 2012, from http://www.accountingmicro.com/blog/item/35-the-advent-of-the-mobile-erp.html.

Maycockk, D. (2011, August 17). SAP going mobile: How big ERP is embracing small technology. *ZDNet*. Retrieved July 3, 2012, from http://www.zdnet.com/news/sap-going-mobile-how-big-erp-is-embracing-small-technology/6280204.

to fit the business's needs. Similarly, organizations have to make thousands of decisions related to the different business processes. For example, what should be the format of the unique identifier for a customer, when will a bill be considered overdue, what is considered the "standard" method of shipping, and so on? To make all these decisions, a good understanding of the way the company does its business is needed. Hence, many organizations hire experienced business analysts or outside consultants to assist with these configuration tasks.

ERP Limitations

Since ERP core components are designed primarily to support internal business activities, they tend not to be well suited for managing value system activities. Companies wanting to integrate their value chains with the business activities of their suppliers, business partners, and customers typically choose to implement systems other than (or in addition to) ERP to manage the upstream and/or downstream flows of information. These types of applications, designed to coordinate activities outside organizational boundaries, are discussed in Chapter 8.

THE FORMULA FOR ENTERPRISE SYSTEM SUCCESS

To summarize, the main objective of enterprise systems is to create competitive advantage by streamlining business activities within and outside a company. However, many implementations turn out to be more costly and time consuming than originally envisioned. It is not uncommon to have projects that run over budget, meaning that identifying common problems and devising methods for dealing with these issues can prove invaluable to management. Industry surveys have shown that over 90 percent of companies that undertake enterprise system implementations realize some benefits; around 50 percent realize about half of the expected benefits and 6 percent report that they did not realize any benefits (Panorama, 2012).

http://goo.gl/BKZXh

Given these numbers, should businesses even attempt to tackle large IS projects? The answer is, in most cases, yes. Typically, organizations do not (or should not) start such projects for the sake of starting the projects; rather, organizations are trying to fix certain problems, such as inefficient or ineffective distribution, pricing, or logistics, or lack of compliance with government regulations. Further, businesses have realized that it is all but impossible to improve business processes without the support of information systems. Thus, it should come as no surprise that more than 85 percent of IS executives of companies who have installed ERP systems regard the system as core to their business and indicate that they could not live without it, as shown by a survey of almost 400 IS executives (Wailgum, 2008a). Companies that have successfully installed enterprise systems are found to follow a basic set of recommendations related to enterprise system implementations. As with all large projects, governance and risk mitigation are critical to success, and companies should attempt to share both risks and rewards with the vendors. Although the following list is not meant to be comprehensive, these recommendations will provide an understanding of some of the challenges involved in implementing enterprise systems:

Recommendation 1. Secure executive sponsorship

Recommendation 2. Get help from outside experts

Recommendation 3. Thoroughly train users

Recommendation 4. Take a multidisciplinary approach to implementations

Recommendation 5. Look beyond ERP

Secure Executive Sponsorship

The primary reason that enterprise system implementations fail is believed to be a lack of top-level management support. Although executives do not necessarily need to make decisions concerning the enterprise system, it is critical that they buy into the decisions made by project managers. Many problems can arise if projects fail to grab the attention of top-level management. In most companies, executives have the ultimate authority regarding the availability and distribution of resources within the organization. If executives do not understand the importance of the enterprise system, this will likely result in delays or stoppages because the necessary resources may not be available when they are needed.

A second problem that may arise deals with top-level management's ability to authorize changes in the way the company does business. When business processes need to be changed to incorporate best practices, these modifications need to be completed. Otherwise, the company will have a piece of software on its hands that does not fit the way people accomplish their business tasks. Lack of executive sponsorship can also have a trickle-down effect within the organization. As people, in general, are reluctant to change the way they are working, there is bound to be resistance to the implementation of an ERP system. If users and midlevel management perceive the enterprise system to be unimportant, they are not likely to view it as a priority. Enterprise systems require a concentrated effort, and executive sponsorship can propel or stifle the implementation. Executive sponsorship can obliterate many obstacles that arise.

Get Help from Outside Experts

Enterprise systems are complex. Even the most talented IS departments can struggle in coming to grips with ERP, customer relationship management, and supply chain management applications. Most vendors have trained project managers and experienced consultants to assist companies with installing enterprise systems. Outside consultants can prove invaluable when helping the organization to stick to the implementation schedule and resist changes in project scope. Using consultants tends to move companies through the implementation more quickly and tends to help companies train their personnel on the applications more effectively. However, companies should not rely too heavily on support from the vendors. The salespeople's job is, after all, selling a system, and they are unlikely to thoroughly understand the company's exact business needs. Thus, organizations should also draw on external consultants to help define the functionality *before* selecting a vendor, and to ensure that all requirements are incorporated in the contract with the vendor. In addition, companies should plan for the consultants leaving once the implementation is complete. When consultants are physically present, company personnel tend to rely on them for assistance. Once the application goes live and the consultants are no longer there, users have to do the job themselves. A key focus should therefore be facilitating user learning.

Thoroughly Train Users

Training is often the most overlooked, underestimated, and poorly budgeted expense involved in planning enterprise system implementations. Enterprise systems are much more complicated to learn than stand-alone systems. Learning a single application requires users to become accustomed to a new software interface, but enterprise system users typically need to learn a new set of business processes as well. Once enterprise systems go live, many companies initially experience a dramatic drop-off in productivity. This issue can potentially lead to heightened levels of dissatisfaction among users, as they prefer to accomplish their business activities in a familiar manner rather than doing things the new way. By training users before the system goes live and giving them sufficient opportunities to learn the new system, a company can allay fears and mitigate potential productivity issues.

Take a Multidisciplinary Approach to Implementations

Enterprise systems affect the entire organization; thus, companies should include personnel from different levels and departments in the implementation project (Kumar & Crook, 1999). In customer relationship management and supply chain management environments in which other organizations are participating in the implementation, it is critical to enlist the support of personnel in their organizations as well. During implementation, project managers need to include personnel from midlevel management, the IS department, external consultants, and, most important, end users.

WHEN THINGS GO WRONG

Time Is a Lot of Money in the Big Apple

If you Google the phrase "ERP failure" you will find millions of search results. In 2012, if you add the word "biggest" to your search and click on any of the links, you will surely find New York City's "CityTime" project. While most ERP industry experts know that far too many ERP projects run over budget and fail to live up to expected benefits, the CityTime project demonstrates just how bad a failure can be.

The CityTime project had great expectations. It was meant to modernize a flawed payroll system for its municipal employees. Many employees were billing the city for overtime and work that couldn't be tracked or accounted for; millions of dollars each year were wasted on fraudulent time cards and expenses. CityTime was going to fix this corruption.

Beginning in 1998, the project was originally budgeted at US$63 million; in 2012, the still incomplete project had run up a bill of more than US$700 million. The project had been plagued by cost overruns and delays since it began in 1998. More seriously, in 2010, federal prosecutors charged several CityTime consultants with a multimillion-dollar fraud scheme that began in 2005, accusing them of manipulating the city into paying out expensive contracts to businesses that they controlled, and then redirecting some of the money to enrich themselves. According to the federal indictment, "... virtually all of the US$600 million that the City paid ... was tainted, directly or indirectly, by fraud." Additionally, the "[a]lleged criminal scheme extended across virtually every level of [the]

CityTime [project]; contractors and subcontractors systematically inflated costs, overbilled for consultants' time, and artificially extended [the] completion date."

There are many ways to enhance project success that weren't followed by the CityTime project. It will take years for auditors to untangle the depth of the corruption and the flaws in the system development and acquisition processes. Arguably, failing to adopt strong project management, planning, governance, and controls was a cornerstone to this failure. Each year, massive ERP failures are in the headlines. Organizations need to learn from these failures or become another "first page" story on a future "ERP failure" Google search.

Based on:

Anonymous. (2012, March 14). CityTime. *The New York Times.* Retrieved July 4, 2012, from http://topics.nytimes.com/top/reference/timestopics/organizations/o/office_of_payroll_administration_nyc/citytime/index.html.

Charette, R. (2011, June 21). New York City's $720 million City Time project a vehicle for unprecedented fraud says US prosecutor. *IEEE Spectrum.* Retrieved July 4, 2012, from http://spectrum.ieee.org/riskfactor/computing/it/new-york-citys-720-million-citytime-project-a-vehicle-for-unprecedented-fraud-says-us-prosecutor.

Kanaracus, C. (2011, December 20). 10 biggest ERP software failures of 2011. *PC World.* Retrieved July 4, 2012, from http://www.pcworld.com/businesscenter/article/246647/10_biggest_erp_software_failures_of_2011.html.

Failing to include the appropriate people in the day-to-day activities of the project can prove problematic in many areas. From a needs-analysis standpoint, it is critical that all the business requirements be sufficiently captured before selection of an enterprise solution. Since end users are involved in every aspect of daily business activities, their insights can be invaluable. For instance, an end user might make salient a feature that no one on the project team had thought of. Having an application that does not meet all of the business's requirements can result in poorly fitting software or customizations. Another peril in leaving out key personnel is the threat of alienation. Departments and/or personnel that do not feel included may develop a sense of animosity toward the new system and view it in a negative light. In extreme cases, users will refuse to use the new application, resulting in conflicts and inefficiencies within the organization.

Evolving the ERP Architecture

As you can see, implementing ERP systems is a highly complex undertaking; although a successful implementation can have huge payoffs for an organization, some organizations fear losing the ability to quickly respond to changing business requirements, particularly since large ERP systems are difficult to install, maintain, and upgrade. In addition, the lifecycle of a large ERP installation is typically 10–15 years. A recent trend is to move away from such large, comprehensive systems to a **service-oriented architecture (SOA)**. Using SOA, business processes are broken down into individual components (or **services**) that are designed to achieve the desired results for the service consumer (which can either be an application, another service, or a person). To illustrate this concept, think about the next oil change for your car. As you can't be expert in everything, it is probably more effective to have someone change the oil for you. You may take your car to the dealership, you may go to an independent garage or oil change service, or you may ask your friend to do it for you. For you, all that matters is that the service will be provided at the expected level of quality and cost, but you typically do not care if different service providers do things differently or use different tools.

By breaking down business processes into individual services, organizations can more swiftly react to changing business needs. For example, using an ERP approach, one module would handle all aspects of the customer order process; in contrast, using an SOA approach, multiple services (such as "check inventory" or "order supplies") would be orchestrated to handle the individual tasks associated with the order process and could be changed relatively easily if the business process changes.

To facilitate online collaboration with suppliers, business partners, and customers, organizations need to allow outsiders to connect to their data, typically using the Internet. However, the Internet was originally designed to enable human-to-computer interaction, with Web pages being a collection of text that hyperlinked to other Web pages. A computer could not use data from other computers without explicit knowledge of the physical location and the security configuration of the remote computer network. Today, **Web services** are one of the critical components of sharing data. Web services allow data to be accessed without intimate knowledge of other organizations' systems, enabling machine-to-machine interaction over the Internet. By using and reusing individual services as "building blocks," systems can be easily built and reconfigured as requirements change. To achieve these benefits, services have to follow three main principles:

1. *Reusability.* A service should be usable in many different applications.
2. *Interoperability.* A service should work with any other service.
3. *Componentization.* A service should be simple and modular.

Following these principles, multiple applications can invoke the same services. For example, both an organization's point-of-sale system and e-commerce Web site could invoke the service "process credit card," and the executive dashboard could invoke the services "display products," "display inventory," and "display sales" (see Figure 7.21). Using SOA can be very beneficial for an organization. For example, the Virgin Entertainment Group, which, at one time, had 23 mega–record stores in North America, implemented a real-time loss prevention system to prevent employee theft and shrinkage in its stores. SOA was used to develop a system that could monitor point-of-sale activity, along with receiving systems. By breaking this complex business process into several small services, the theft prevention system could easily be integrated into the company's current enterprise system. The SOA approach was successful for Virgin, as losses and employee theft decreased 50 percent. Whereas an SOA approach appears to be appealing for

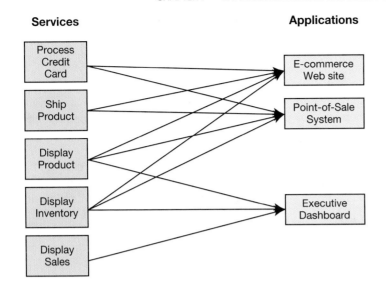

FIGURE 7.21

Using SOA, multiple applications can invoke multiple services.

many companies, it requires tremendous effort and expertise to plan the architecture, select the right services from hundreds or thousands of available services, and orchestrate and deploy the services. Hence, while an SOA approach helps to increase flexibility, the integration of various services can be extremely complex and can be well beyond the means of small enterprises.

Recently, large ERP vendors such as Oracle and SAP introduced platforms enabling companies to harness the benefits of both ERP and SOA. Whereas mission-critical back-end systems are based on ERP, additional functionality can be added as needed using an SOA approach. Further, these solutions allow the use of services from other systems or vendors, increasing an organization's flexibility.

Although expansive enterprise system implementations, as well as SOA approaches, are often cumbersome and difficult, the potential payoff is huge. As a result, organizations are compelled to implement these systems. Further, given the popularity and necessity of integrating systems and processes on an organization-wide basis, you are likely to find yourself involved in the implementation and/or use of such a system. We are confident that after reading this chapter, you will be better able to understand and help with the development and use of such systems.

INDUSTRY ANALYSIS

The Automobile Industry

There are more than 800 million cars and light trucks on the road throughout the world. The Boston Consulting Group predicts that by 2014, one-third of world demand will be in the four BRIC markets (Brazil, Russia, India, and China). These emerging auto markets already buy more cars than established markets in North America, Europe, and Japan. According to a J.D. Power study, emerging markets accounted for 51 percent of the global light-vehicle sales in 2010; the pace of globalization suggests that this trend will not only continue, it will accelerate.

In the U.S. and around the world, the 2008 recession devastated the automobile industry. America's car and light truck market, for instance, dropped dramatically, from more than 16 million units in 2007 to around 13 million in 2008; 2009 was even worse with sales totaling around 10 million units. As a result, two giant U.S. manufacturers (GM and Chrysler) filed for bankruptcy, while a large number of dealerships, suppliers, parts manufacturers, and other auto-related businesses also failed. By 2011, Chrysler was 50 percent owned by Italian car maker Fiat, thanks to agreements and financing that had enabled Chrysler to exit bankruptcy. GM was 61 percent owned by the U.S. federal government. Only U.S.-based Ford Motor Company escaped bankruptcy during those turbulent years. By 2012, the global auto industry had stabilized and growth reemerged. Low interest rates, as well as pent-up demand (in the U.S., the average car is more than 10 years old), fueled the U.S. rebound despite anxiety about the broader economy.

Auto industry experts have claimed for years that globalization—the flattening of the world—would result in a widespread consolidation of automakers. What is happening within the auto industry is indicative of globalization in general. A "flattened" world implies that the world is becoming more homogeneous. As the process continues, distinctions between national markets are fading and, for some products, may disappear entirely.

For instance, for decades manufacturers within the automobile industry have worked toward developing a "world car"—a basic car that with a few modifications can be sold all over the world. In the 1990s, three attempts were made to produce and market a world car: Honda's Accord, Ford's Mondeo/Contour, and GM's Cadillac Catera/Opel Omega. None of the models sold as well as hoped in North America, Europe, and Asia for several reasons:

- Consumers in different areas of the world have different tastes in automobiles. For example, small cab size has long been accepted in Europe, but American consumers prefer larger cabs.
- Europeans prefer steel construction over plastic, as in door panels, which are largely used in car manufacturing in the United States.
- Differences in infrastructure among countries lead to varying preferences in cars. Asians, for example, prefer smaller-sized cars that can maneuver well through narrow and crowded streets, while many Americans prefer sport-utility vehicles and pickups.
- The price of gasoline varies throughout the world. Europeans typically carefully consider fuel economy when buying a car, while, until recently because of sharp spikes in gas prices, most Americans have not heavily weighed this criterion.
- Variations in regulations governing cars, such as emission standards, also vary with countries and affect car buyers' choices.

While globalization is driving the search for the perfect world car, the diversity of the various markets makes this objective elusive. There is, however, growing global demand for small, energy efficient autos. Since 2006, the "World Car of the Year" has been selected by a jury of 48 international automotive journalists from 22 countries. Cars nominated for this award need to have been sold in at least five countries and on at least two continents. In 2011, the innovative Nissan Leaf was selected; in 2012, Volkswagen's up! was chosen as winner. Both vehicles are small and highly efficient.

In the meantime, the automobile industry continues to move beyond traditional geographic boundaries. U.S.-based auto companies are moving plants overseas, and foreign manufacturers are moving production facilities to the United States. The Japanese auto manufacturer Toyota operates production plants in many U.S. states, including Alabama, Texas, and West Virginia. The Ford Motor Company is based in the United States but operates satellite companies in Asia and Europe. A Chinese car manufacturer recently bought Volvo and moved production to China. In fact, in 2011, more than 18 million vehicles were produced in China (by a variety of manufactures), more than doubling the combined production of vehicles within Japan and the U.S.

Another significant change in the auto industry involves sales channels. Traditionally, U.S. automakers maintain localized franchises that handle auto sales in a specific region. Now there are Internet franchises that have also created worldwide sales centers that did not previously exist.

Clearly, the global marketplace has changed the automobile industry profoundly by allowing the automakers to build global networks of suppliers (such as Bosch and Continental from Germany, Magna and Lear from the United States, or Yazaki from Japan) and selling to customers from all over the world. Although this has created new opportunities, the recent auto crisis has shown that in the age of globalization, the success or failure of any major global firm has ripple effects far beyond its home country.

Questions:

1. How is globalization changing in the auto industry?

2. Examine how cultural differences make it difficult to create a world car.

Based on:

Anonymous. (n.d.). Automobile industry introduction. *Plunkett Research, Ltd.* Retrieved July 8, 2012, from http://www.plunkettresearch.com/automobiles-trucks-market-research/industry-and-business-data.

Anonymous. (2010, April 20). Geely automobile picking sites for China-made Volvo. *TradingMarket*. Retrieved July 8, 2012, from http://www.tradingmarkets.com/news/stock-alert/volvo_geely-automobile-picking-sites-for-china-made-volvo-922498.html.

Automotive industry. (2012, June 28). In *Wikipedia, The Free Encyclopedia*. Retrieved July 8, 2012, from http://en.wikipedia.org/w/index.php?title=Automotive_industry&oldid=499757272.

Chandler, C. (2000, May 22). Globalization: The automobile industry's quest for a "world car" strategy. Retrieved July 8, 2012, from http://globaledge.msu.edu/newsandviews/views/papers/globalization_automotive_industry_strategy.pdf.

Chrysler Chapter 11 reorganization. (2012, March 21). In *Wikipedia, The Free Encyclopedia*. Retrieved July 8, 2012, from http://en.wikipedia.org/w/index.php?title=Chrysler_Chapter_11_reorganization&oldid=483155991.

General Motors Chapter 11 reorganization. (2012, May 29). In *Wikipedia, The Free Encyclopedia*. Retrieved July 8, 2012, from http://en.wikipedia.org/w/index.php?title=General_Motors_Chapter_11_reorganization&oldid=494897034.

Modica, M. (2012, June 12). Akerson admits GM bankruptcy not well thought out. *NLPC.org*. Retrieved July 8, 2012, from http://nlpc.org/stories/2012/06/12/akerson-admits-gm-bankruptcy-not-well-thought-out.

World Car of the Year. (2012, April 18). In *Wikipedia, The Free Encyclopedia*. Retrieved July 8, 2012 from http://en.wikipedia.org/w/index.php?title=World_Car_of_the_Year&oldid=487986618.

Key Points Review

1. ***Explain core business processes that are common in organizations.*** Most organizations are organized around five distinct functional areas that are responsible for well-defined business functions: marketing and sales, supply chain management, operations and manufacturing, accounting and finance, and human resources. These separate functional areas work together to execute core business processes. These core processes are order-to-cash, procure-to-pay, and make-to-stock/order. Order-to-cash refers to the various processes associated with selling a product or service to a customer. Procure-to-pay refers to the various processes associated with procuring goods from external vendors. The make-to-stock and make-to-order processes refer to those activities associated with producing goods to hold in inventory or after a customer order. Together, these core business processes enable the creation of supply chains that are involved in transforming raw materials into products sold to the end consumer. Supply chains are composed of both core and support activities. Core activities include inbound logistics (receiving), operations and manufacturing, outbound logistics (shipping), marketing and sales, and customer service. These activities may differ widely, depending on the unique requirements of the industry in which a company operates, although the basic concepts hold in most organizations. Support activities include administrative activities, infrastructure, human resources, technology development, and procurement. Companies connect their value chains with suppliers and customers, creating value systems such that information flows from one company's value chain to another company's value chain.

2. ***Describe what enterprise systems are and how they have evolved.*** Enterprise systems are information systems that span the entire organization and can be used to integrate business processes, activities, and information across all the functional areas of a firm. Enterprise systems can be either prepackaged software or custom-made applications. The implementation of enterprise systems often involves business process management, a systematic, structured improvement approach by all or part of an organization that critically examines, rethinks, and redesigns processes in order to achieve dramatic improvements in one or more performance measures, such as quality, cycle time, or cost. Enterprise systems evolved from legacy systems that supported distinct organizational activities by combining data and applications into a single comprehensive system.

3. ***Describe ERP systems and how they help to improve internal business processes.*** ERP systems evolved from "material requirements planning" systems during the 1990s and are, for the most part, used to support internal business processes. ERP systems allow information to be shared throughout the organization through the use of a large database, helping to streamline business processes and improve customer service. When selecting an ERP system, organizations must choose which modules to implement from a large menu of options—most organizations adopt only a subset of the available ERP components. ERP core components support the major internal activities of the organization for producing their products and services, while ERP extended components support the primary external activities of the organization for dealing with suppliers and customers.

4. ***Understand and utilize the keys to successfully implementing enterprise systems.*** Experience with enterprise system implementations suggests that there are some common problems that can be avoided and/or should be managed carefully. Organizations can avoid common implementation problems by (1) securing executive sponsorship, (2) getting necessary help from outside experts, (3) thoroughly training users, (4) taking a multidisciplinary approach to implementations, and (5) looking beyond ERP.

Key Terms

best practices   313

business process management (BPM)   313

business process reengineering (BPR)   314

core activities   302

custom software   311

customization   312

downstream information flow   306

enterprise resource planning (ERP)   315

enterprise system   308

enterprise-wide information system   308

ERP core components   319

ERP extended components   320

externally focused system   310

internally focused system   309

interorganizational system (IOS)   310

legacy system   306

make-to-order process   300

make-to-stock process   300

module   312

off-the-shelf software   311

order-to-cash process   299

packaged software   311

procure-to-pay process   300

service   326

service-oriented architecture (SOA)   326

stand-alone application   306

support activities   304

upstream information flow   306

value system   305

vanilla version   312

Web service   326

Review Questions

1. What are core business processes?
2. Describe and contrast order-to-cash, procure-to-pay, make-to-stock, and make-to-order business processes.
3. What are the core and support activities of a value chain?
4. What do you understand by business process management? List some of the terms related to it.
5. Describe what enterprise systems are and how they have evolved.
6. List the core applications of SAP's Business Suite.
7. What are the five trends shaping the way in which social media is viewed and used by organizations?
8. List the basic steps in business process management.
9. List the benefits of enterprise systems that can improve business case development.

Self-Study Questions

1. _____ are information systems that allow companies to integrate information and support operations on a company-wide basis.
   A. Customer relationship management systems
   B. Enterprise systems
   C. Wide area networks
   D. Interorganizational systems

2. Which of the following is a core activity according to the value chain model?
   A. firm infrastructure
   B. customer service
   C. human resources
   D. procurement

3. According to the value chain model, which of the following is a support activity?
   A. technology development
   B. marketing and sales
   C. inbound logistics
   D. operations and manufacturing

4. All of the following are true about legacy systems except _____.
   A. they are stand-alone systems
   B. they are older software systems
   C. they are ERP systems
   D. they may be difficult to integrate into other systems

5. The processes associated with obtaining goods from external vendors are referred to as _____.
   A. make-to-order processes
   B. make-to-stock processes
   C. procure-to-pay processes
   D. order-to-cash processes

6. The processes associated with selling a product or service are referred to as _____.
   A. make-to-order processes
   B. make-to-stock processes
   C. procure-to-pay processes
   D. order-to-cash processes

7. Which processes are most often associated with pull-based manufacturing of products?
   A. make-to-order processes
   B. make-to-stock processes
   C. procure-to-pay processes
   D. order-to-cash processes

8. Information systems that focus on supporting functional areas, business processes, and decision making within an organization are referred to as _____.
   A. legacy systems
   B. enterprise-wide information systems
   C. interorganizational systems
   D. internally focused systems

9. An enterprise system that has not been customized is commonly referred to as _____.
   A. a vanilla version
   B. a root version
   C. a core version
   D. none of the above

10. _____ is a systematic, structured improvement approach by all or part of an organization that critically examines, rethinks, and redesigns processes in order to achieve dramatic improvements in one or more performance measures, such as quality, cycle time, or cost.
   A. Systems analysis
   B. Business process management
   C. Customer relationship management
   D. Total quality management
   Answers are on page 332.

Problems and Exercises

1. Match the following terms with the appropriate definitions:
   i. Enterprise systems
   ii. Legacy systems
   iii. Value system
   iv. ERP extended components
   v. Stand-alone applications
   vi. Vanilla version
   vii. Make-to-stock process
   viii. Business process management
   ix. Procure-to-pay process
   x. Internally focused systems

   a. Components that support the primary *external* activities of the organization for dealing with suppliers and customers
   b. Systems that focus on the specific needs of individual departments
   c. The processes associated with producing goods based on forecasted demand
   d. Older systems that are not designed to communicate with other applications beyond departmental boundaries
   e. Information systems that allow companies to integrate information on a company-wide basis
   f. The features and modules that a packaged software system comes with out of the box
   g. The processes associated with acquiring goods from suppliers
   h. A systematic, structured improvement approach by all or part of an organization whereby people critically examine, rethink, and redesign business processes in order to achieve dramatic improvements in one or more performance measures, such as quality, cycle time, or cost
   i. Information systems that support functional areas, business processes, and decision making within an organization
   j. A collection of interlocking company value chains

2. Find an organization that you are familiar with and determine how many software applications it is utilizing concurrently. Are the company's information systems cohesive, or do they need updating and streamlining?

3. Select an organization in the manufacturing sector and draw a complete value chain structure for it by identifying the core and support activities.

4. SAP AG, the leading ERP solutions provider, claims that it offers business solutions based on the best practices. What do they mean by "best practices"? List some of these "best practices" offered by SAP. You may use their official Web site and other resources available on the Internet.

5. Using Figure 7.6 as a guide, develop a supply chain diagram for some other product.

6. Based on your own experiences with applications, have you used customized or off-the-shelf applications? What is the difference, and how good was the system documentation?

7. Search the Web for the phrase "best practices," and you will find numerous sites that summarize the best practices for a variety of industries and professions. Choose one and summarize these best practices into a one-page report.

8. Examine and contrast the differences between packaged and custom software. When is one approach better or worse than the other?

9. You are hired as an enterprise consultant by one of the leading financial institutions. During the requirement study, you found that the company uses a number of legacy systems. Identify the challenges that you would face in converting them to enterprise applications.

10. RFID is an emerging data capturing and management technology. Search the Web to find major applications of RFID in the health-care industry.

Application Exercises

Note: The existing data files referenced in these exercises are available on the book's Web site: www.pearsonhighered.com/valacich.

 Spreadsheet Application: Choosing an ERP System at Campus Travel

Campus Travel is interested in integrating its business processes to streamline processes such as purchasing, sales, human resource management, and customer relationship management. Because of your success in implementing the e-commerce infrastructure, the general manager asks you for advice on what to do to streamline operations at Campus Travel. Use the data provided in the file ERPSystems.csv to make a recommendation about which ERP system to purchase. The file includes ratings of the different modules of the systems and the weights assigned to these ratings. You are asked to do the following:

1. Determine the product with the highest overall rating (Hint: Use the SUMPRODUCT formula to multiply each vendor's scores with the respective weights and add the weighted scores).
2. Prepare the necessary graphs to compare the products on the different dimensions and the overall score.
3. Be sure to professionally format the graphs before printing them out.

Database Application: Creating Forms at Campus Travel

After helping Campus Travel off to a good start with its databases, you have decided that it should enter data using forms rather than doing it from tables. From your experience, you know that employees have an easier time being able to browse, modify, and add records from a form view. As this can be implemented using your existing database, you decide to set up a form. You can accomplish this by doing the following:

1. Open the employees' database (employeeData.mdb).
2. Select the employee table in the database window.
3. Create a form using the table (Hint: This can be done by selecting "More Forms >> Form Wizard" under "Forms" in the "Create" tab).
4. Save the form as "employees."

Team Work Exercise

Net Stats: The Changing Value of Social Media in the Workplace

Not long ago, the idea of using Facebook at work was viewed by most as a non–work-related activity. However, today, as more organizations are working to have personal relationships with customers and suppliers, social media are no longer taboo in the office. Social media sites like Facebook, LinkedIn, and Twitter are increasingly being viewed as providing improved methods for connecting, sharing, and collaborating with customers and suppliers. A recent white paper by toolbox.com reports five trends that are shaping the way in which social media are viewed and being used by organizations:

- *Trend 1: Social media are increasingly being used to improve decision making.* Organizations are finding that important information can be obtained by actively participating in online communities.
- *Trend 2: The value of social media has expanded beyond networking.* Organizations are realizing that social media provide numerous benefits beyond networking of individuals, such as market intelligence, improved customer service, and loyalty.
- *Trend 3: Best practices communities are emerging, easing the search for key human resources.* Organizations are more easily finding individuals with unique and hard-to-find talents.

- *Trend 4: Talented personnel are attracted to organizations embracing social media as a part of their organizational strategy and tactics.* Organizations are finding that some of the best users of social media in their personal lives also want to work for companies who share these same values.
- *Trend 5: Talented personnel place strong value on organizations demonstrating transparency and responsiveness to the use of social media.* Individuals have greater trust and loyalty to organizations they believe to be honest and accessible.

Questions and Exercises

1. Social media are increasingly being used by organizations in the hiring process; search the Web to identify a recent story about how organizations are using social media in the hiring process.
2. As a team, interpret this article. What is striking/important about the article?
3. As a team, discuss how this may look like in 5 years and 10 years. How will things differ between the U.S. market and across the world? Where will things move faster/slower? Why?
4. Using your presentation software, create two or three slides that summarize the findings you consider most important.

Based on:
Toolbox.com (2010). Top 5 trends in B2B social media usage. Retrieved July 8, 2012 from http://www.toolbox.com.

Answers to the Self-Study Questions

1. B, p. 308	2. B, p. 302	3. A, p. 304	4. C, p. 306	5. C, p. 300
6. D, p. 299	7. A, p. 300	8. D, p. 309	9. A, p. 312	10. B, p. 313

CASE 1   Software as a Service: ERP by the Hour

As you know by now, an organization's IS infrastructure is not simple to construct or maintain, but is a complex infrastructure of servers and databases useful for managing large amounts of information. Although corporations can ask IS personnel to build an infrastructure to support an organization's goals, building such infrastructure generally proves to be time consuming and expensive. Alternatively, the IS department can design from scratch or purchase off-the-shelf software to meet the organization's data processing needs.

However, a new model of IS infrastructure and software has appeared and is rapidly changing the way many organizations do business. Software as a service, or SaaS, is a way for organizations to use cloud-based Internet services to accomplish the goals that traditional IS infrastructure and software models have in the past. Utilizing SaaS, organizations now have the opportunity to downsize their infrastructure, save money on software implementation, and move to a computing-by-the-hour frame of mind.

SaaS allows software application vendors to deploy their products over the Internet through Web-based services. SaaS customers pay to use applications on demand, giving them the freedom to access a software service only when needed. Applications and software are developed, hosted, and operated by SaaS vendors. Once customers finish using the software, their "license" expires, and they no longer have to carry the cost of the software. If a future need for the software arises, the customer simply orders it again to have access. SaaS products can be licensed for single or multiple users within the organization, making them flexible and scalable.

Using the SaaS model has several advantages. Through SaaS applications, organizations can move their data storage into the cloud, reducing the cost of buying storage and diminishing the risk of catastrophic data loss. Software on demand allows for less resource expenditure on long-term software licensing because an organization can get what they need when they need it. Infrastructure operation costs are shifted to the SaaS vendor, freeing up resources for use in other areas. Implementation of SaaS products is also quick, increasing an organization's agility in responding to new challenges as they occur. In addition, it is in the vendor's financial interest to keep the services they provide running at peak performance, or they risk losing customers to other vendors. This incentive ensures that the SaaS vendor's infrastructure is regularly updated and modernized to minimize customer downtime. SaaS utilization also allows organizations to become more productive outside the physical confines of their buildings. Since SaaS services are in the cloud, employees can access services in remote offices, on the road, from their smart phone, or from their home PC.

One of the main disadvantages to SaaS is that customers must give up some autonomy over their applications and data. Not having the software in-house means organizations must use it "as is." This point leads to another issue in that some organizations require specialized software solutions and are used to customizing software in-house to meet their needs. Although some SaaS vendors are beginning to offer customizable solutions, the problem is still a roadblock for some. Computing off-site also means that security may be at issue. Organizational operations and data are effectively running on someone else's computer. Security concerns are another roadblock that organizations must overcome in order to use SaaS products. It is impossible for some types of organizations to keep their data—and their secrets—in the cloud.

These disadvantages aside, organizations are reaping the benefits of SaaS, utilizing them for human resources activities, e-mail services, collaboration efforts, storage solutions, and financial tasks, such as billing, invoicing, and timekeeping. In addition to more general purpose applications, many organizations are deploying ERP capabilities via SaaS vendors. And the growth of the SaaS industry doesn't appear to be slowing. In fact, a recent study by Gartner found that by 2015, SaaS revenues should reach US$22 billion.

Companies like Google, Amazon.com, and Microsoft have become well-known SaaS vendors offering a range of services to organizations. For instance, Google has a variety of cloud-based services available across their different platforms, including shared-document management, communication services, cloud-based e-mail, calendaring, photo and video sharing, Web and intranet page management, and data storage services, just to name a few.

Likewise, while Amazon.com is known as a top e-commerce destination to most consumers, they also have SaaS solutions that many organizations employ. One of their offerings is SimpleDB—a service for organizations that can't afford in-house databases or simply want the convenience of letting a hosted service do most of the work. Database developers sign up for the service, which operates in conjunction with Amazon.com's Simple Storage Service (S3), and pay only for time and storage space used. Amazon.com S3 customers are provided with a Web interface that allows them to store and retrieve any amount of data, any time they want, from anywhere there is an Internet connection available. S3 has redundant storage across several Amazon.com sites, ensuring data security, availability, and integrity.

Another household name in the computing industry, Microsoft, has also followed suit, offering their own cloud-based SaaS solution called Microsoft Azure. Although Microsoft came into the SaaS market later than others, they have the experience and resources to quickly become a formidable competitor to other already established vendors. Azure offers its customers a similar range of services as other SaaS vendors, from application data storage and hosted services to a framework for interconnecting resources and services. This linking framework, known as the AppFabric, allows developers to create "cloud-aware" services and applications for use within their organizations. Azure, like many other services, has a pay-as-you-go pricing structure. Alternatively, customers can take the "commitment" option and pay for a six-month obligation of use of service. The commitment option makes the customer eligible for discount pricing for purchasing six months of service.

Because of the issues associated with enterprise systems, ERP vendors are increasingly offering their software as a service as well. For example, SAP offers SAP Business ByDesign, an integrated on-demand ERP solution for small and medium-sized enterprises. Similarly, Microsoft offers its Dynamics customer relationship management system as a service, and Oracle offers the subscription-based Oracle On Demand customer relationship management solution.

Computing-by-the-hour has now become a viable and legitimate business model for many organizations. As more continue to adopt SaaS services as a way of carrying on their day-to-day activities, vendors will continue to upgrade and expand the available technologies for use. The question of whether organizations will adopt SaaS services has, for the most part, been answered. The question has now become how much of their business they will put in the cloud.

Questions:

1. Would you trust an external provider with your organization's data? Why or why not? What would be needed to raise your trust in the reliability, security, and privacy of the data?

2. What are the potential drawbacks of using a relatively simple in-house database with limited capabilities versus a more robust, SaaS database solution? Do the benefits outweigh these limitations? Why or why not?

3. Are there any types of applications that should only be purchased rather than obtained through a SaaS relationship? If so, why or why not?

Based on:

Anonymous. (n.d.). Amazon SimpleDB. Retrieved July 5, 2012, from http://aws.amazon.com/simpledb.

Anonymous. (n.d.). What is SAAS? Retrieved July 5, 2012, from http://www.whatissaas.net.

Anonymous. (2009, July 1). Amazon's cloud: A SaaS solution. Retrieved July 5, 2012, from http://www.istockanalyst.com/article/viewarticle/articleid/3325300.

Biddick, M. (2010, January 16). Why you need a SaaS strategy. *InformationWeek*. Retrieved July 5, 2012, from http://www.informationweek.com/news/services/saas/showArticle.jhtml?articleID=222301002.

Foley, J. (2010, January 28). Microsoft to launch pennies-per-hour Azure cloud service Monday. *InformationWeek*. Retrieved July 5, 2012, from http://www.informationweek.com/news/services/saas/showArticle.jhtml?articleID=222600247.

Kanaracus, C. (2012, March 27). Gartner: SaaS market to grow 17.9% to $14.5B. *ComputerWorld*. Retrieved July 5, 2012, from http://www.computerworld.com/s/article/9225590/Gartner_SaaS_market_to_grow_17.9_to_14.5B.

Levine, B. (2007, December 17). Amazon launching database-as-a-service. *Newsfactor.com*. Retrieved July 5, 2012, from http://www.newsfactor.com/story.xhtml?story_id=110003L9MFM8.

Olsen, G. (2010, March 18). Microsoft Azure's place in the cloud. Retrieved July 5, 2012, from http://searchwinit.techtarget.com/tip/0,289483,sid1_gci1488526,00.html.

Software as a service. (2012, July 5). In *Wikipedia, The Free Encyclopedia*. Retrieved July 7, 2012, from http://en.wikipedia.org/w/index.php?title=Software_as_a_service&oldid=500768579.

CASE 2   ERP Systems: Do They Satisfy?

ERP systems are the backbone of many business ventures and are found in organizations of all shapes and sizes around the globe. They are powerful systems designed to unify and economize operations across an organization's scope of operations. But these powerful systems also have drawbacks, and the mere utterance of the acronym ERP is enough to send some IS professionals reaching for the aspirin bottle.

ERPs systems sprang from manufacturers' requirements-planning software that was used to control inventory, manage manufacturing and delivery schedules, and handle purchasing activities. As these software platforms matured, they began appearing in organizations other than manufacturing. Modern ERP systems are designed to be an integrated computer system that stretches across every aspect of an organization, allowing users to access and build on information to meet task requirements and goals.

ERP systems are made up of modules that work together from a centralized database to form the enterprise system. With an ERP in place, each department within the organization will have a specialized module that allows them to accomplish their departmental tasks. Accounting, for instance, will have a specialized module that handles all accounting related tasks. Since the modules are interconnected across the system through the central database, employees can call up information they need from outside their immediate department. If a shipping manager needs to know how many workers to schedule, he or she can call up information from the manufacturing module to see how many widgets are projected to come off the line and will need to be shipped that week. The scalability (the ability to handle organizational growth) of this modular system is a key strength of ERP systems. If an organization adds new departments, new modules can be added to the ERP system to meet the needs of the expanded operation without interrupting the existing modules.

Although these powerful systems have the ability to aggregate huge amounts of data and manage organizational resources and activities, many users are dissatisfied with their ERP's performance and return on investment (ROI). This is partially due to the fact that organizations don't always consider the total cost of an ERP implementation. Buying new computer hardware and infrastructure upgrades to run the ERP system is not the only expense associated with project execution. Since the technology of ERP systems is either foreign or too complex for most "in-house" experts to handle, a consulting firm is usually hired to manage the implementation. Consultants help the organization map out how the new system will interact with business processes, customize the ERP software to meet task requirements, and train users on how to work with the new systems—all with a hefty price tag. Unfortunately for many organizations, the implementation stage can last much longer than expected, driving consultant fees and dissatisfaction with the project ever higher. Add to these costs software licensing fees and the possibility of vendor "lock-in" on a range of services within the ERP system, and it becomes clear that organizations should consider a wide range of costs before undertaking an ERP project. According to a study by the Panorama Consulting Group, 54 percent of ERP implementations take longer than expected, and 56 percent exceed their budget.

Another cost that must be considered may not always have a price tag associated with it: that of organizational change. New ERP processes will likely involve members of the organization learning how to do their daily tasks differently than they're used to doing them. ERP systems may also consolidate or eliminate the need for certain activities to be accomplished, leaving some to feel that their job or position is threatened. Additionally, since one of the ERP's main functions is to allow users across the organization to share data, it is more difficult to control the flow of information. For example, before an ERP implementation, departments can disseminate data as they see fit or even not at all. But after the ERP is in place, the power of the gatekeeper is diminished as data becomes more freely available to other users. Having open access to information can lead employees to having a sense of being watched or feeling that their positions are threatened. Issues like these can make organizational change difficult and sometimes painful. Resistance to change is an expected human response, and ERP implementations typically do not escape this reality.

The Panorama study also found that about 42 percent of the organizations that implement ERP systems get less than 50 percent of the business benefit they expected after project completion. This statistic is not completely surprising, however. With ERP implementations historically running over on budget and time, organizations are often just happy to have the flow of organization money to consultants stopped and the project completed. Little thought is given as to whether the new system is an improvement over the old or if it is giving them as much return on investment as it can.

Traditional ERP implementations are challenging for organizations, so much so that many projects have outright failed, resulting in millions of dollars lost, organizational cohesiveness destroyed, and employees quitting. Today, tales of troublesome implementation projects are filling the pages of tech-industry magazines, and many others are having less than stellar track records.

Questions:

1. What are the advantages to using an ERP system? What are the disadvantages?
2. If you were the chief information officer of a large company, would you recommend implementing an ERP system? Why or why not?
3. How can a small business avoid experiencing "just another ERP failure"?

Based on:

Enterprise resource planning. (2012, July 6). In *Wikipedia, The Free Encyclopedia*. Retrieved July 7, 2012, from http://en.wikipedia.org/w/index .php?title=Enterprise_resource_planning&oldid=500941803.

Eresource. (2010). Why some people think ROI on ERP is low? *Eresource.com*. Retrieved July 5, 2012, from http://www.eresourceerp.com/Why-some-people-think-ROI-on-ERP-is-low.html.

Kanaracus, C. (2010, March 17). Widespread discontent persists with ERP projects. *PC World*. Retrieved July 5, 2012, from http://www.pcworld.com/businesscenter/ article/191750/widespread_discontent_persists_with_erp_projects.html.

Kanaracus, C. (2010, March 31). Lawson puts its ERP on Amazon's cloud. *BusinessWeek*. Retrieved July 5, 2012, from http://www.businessweek.com/ idg/2010-03-31/lawson-puts-its-erp-on-amazon-s-cloud.html.

Krigsman, M. (2010, February 3). ERP failure: New research and statistics. *Enterprise Irregulars*. Retrieved July 5, 2012, from http://www .enterpriseirregulars.com/11871/erp-failure-new-research-and-statistics.

Panorama Consulting Solutions. (2012). 2012 ERP report. Retrieved July 5, 2012, from http://Panorama-Consulting.com/resource-center/2012-erp-report.

Sootkoos, R. (2010, January 28). ERP and cloud computing trends. *ERP .com*. Retrieved July 5, 2012, from http://www.erp.com/section-layout/51-erp-success-stories/5674-erp-and-cloud-computing-trends.html.

8

Strengthening Business-to-Business Relationships via Supply Chain and Customer Relationship Management

After reading this chapter, you will be able to do the following:

1. Describe supply chain management systems and how they help to improve business-to-business processes.

2. Describe customer relationship management systems and how they help to improve the activities involved in promoting and selling products to customers as well as providing customer service and nourishing long-term relationships.

Preview

This chapter extends the prior discussion regarding how companies are deploying enterprise-wide information systems to build and strengthen organizational partnerships. Enterprise systems help integrate various business activities, streamline and better manage interactions with customers, and coordinate better with suppliers in order to meet changing customer demands more efficiently and effectively. In this chapter, two additional powerful systems are introduced: supply chain management (SCM) systems supporting business-to-business (B2B) transactions and customer relationship management (CRM) systems for promoting and selling products and building and nourishing long-term customer relationships. When added to enterprise resource planning (ERP) systems, both of these systems tie the customer to the supply chain that includes the manufacturer and suppliers all the way back to the raw materials that ultimately become the product no matter where in the world they originate.

More and more companies find that they need systems that span their entire organization to tie everything together. As a result, an understanding of supply chain management and customer relationship management is critical to succeed in today's competitive and ever-changing digital world.

Managing in the Digital World:
Supply Chain Havoc

Information systems have assisted in the creation of global supply networks that allow for the worldwide procurement of raw materials and components needed as inputs into production processes. For the purpose of achieving an optimal balance between quality and costs, manufacturers often have had to rely on a complicated and fragile supply chain. Imagine that you are the manufacturer of a trendy new gadget that is gaining popularity worldwide. Also imagine that a tsunami just rolled over the key manufacturer of a certain critical component in your device. At best, you may encounter long shipment delays and lost sales; at worst, your opportunity in the marketplace fades and you go out of business. Thus, shielding the delicate supply chain from negative impacts arising from external events is a tremendous challenge for many organizations, especially in a reality where disruptions can rarely be forecast and the results can be devastating.

One example of such external events is the serious flooding in Thailand during the 2011 monsoon season. The World Bank estimated a mighty US$47.5 billion in economic loss and a massive disruption in production within the country. Yet, this disruption was not limited to the country itself, but sent shockwaves through global supply chains. Thailand is the second biggest producer of computer hard drives in the world, as well as a critical supplier of key components; for instance, 70 percent of all hard drive motors are produced in the Southeast Asian country. Because the floods caused tremendous damage to concerned factories, hard drive production all around the world dropped about 30 percent compared to the previous quarter. The cost of this disruption was a surge in the price of hard drives; in some temporary yet exceptional cases, prices were up to 150 percent higher. In the quarter following the floods, hard drive prices were still about 5–15 percent higher than before the natural disaster. Consumers, producers, and organizations alike suffered from the natural disaster. In fact, over a year after the floods, huge shortages still lingered for some types of hard drives.

The flooding in Thailand shows a domino effect that can eventually disrupt entire global supply networks; the collapse of one piece of the network leads to the fall of another, until eventually the entire chain crumbles. The flooding started the dominoes toppling, leading to the shortage of hard drives, which triggered computer manufacturers to focus on building higher-margin, more expensive computers. Thus, manufacturers reduced production of lower-margin low-end PCs, netbooks, and the like, ultimately resulting in an increase in prices for these devices as well. Likewise, two other well-known consumer electronics companies experienced severe disruptions of their supply chains during and after the devastating floods. Nikon suffered greatly as the entire first floor of one of its primary factories assembling digital single-lens reflex (DSLR) cameras was submerged in water. The company subsequently announced that the production of 90 percent of their DSLR cameras—from low to mid-range—was affected by the flood and had reached a state of non-recovery. Similarly, Sony, 100 percent of whose DSLRs were made in a factory damaged by the flood, found itself scrambling to resume production. Both Nikon and Sony were unable to quickly bring production back to prior levels, and were even forced to postpone the release of various newly introduced camera models, resulting in net losses for both companies.

It is not just damage to production facilities that can wreak havoc on global supply networks. The 2010 volcanic eruption of Eyjafjallajokull in Iceland proved that unexpected events could severely disrupt global supply networks by crippling transportation and communication networks (see Figure 8.1). As the volcano was spewing ash into the atmosphere, flights had to be canceled, severely disrupting the supply chains of numerous companies and industries and stranding countless tourists and business travelers throughout the world. For instance, flowers and vegetables worth millions of dollars withered in African warehouses, waiting to be shipped to Europe. At the same time, disruption in the distribution of perishable goods like Italian mozzarella cheese and fresh fruits cost producers about US$14 million per day. BMW had to halt production in several German plants, and parts that had already been produced could not be flown to its assembly plant in South Carolina. Likewise, diamond cutters in India could not ship gems to trading dealers in Belgium and logistic companies such as UPS and DHL had to divert planes, cancel flights, and organize ground transport for shipments throughout Europe. Clearly, the disruptions of freight movements to and from Europe had global impacts on the supply chain of countless organizations.

FIGURE 8.1

A major blast from the Icelandic volcano Eyjafjallajokull sent tons of volcanic ash into the jet stream.
Source: sumos/Fotolia

In their quest to achieve sustainable competitive advantage, many companies face a dilemma when trying to maximize efficiency and effectiveness of their global supply chains. Without doubt, supply chain management systems have contributed tremendously to improving interorganizational business processes, such as by allowing to build highly efficient supply chains that minimize inventory levels. However, minimum inventory levels, short product cycles, and inadequate risk management all contribute to the fragile nature of many global supply networks, and the danger of unforeseen external events disrupting these supply networks always lingers.

After reading this chapter, you will be able to answer the following:

1. What are the benefits of a global supply network?

2. What are the trade-offs when developing a supply chain strategy?

3. How can information systems help organizations minimize the impacts of disruptions to their global supply network?

Based on:

Anonymous. (2010, April 20). Flugverbote treffen Autoindustrie mit voller Wucht. *Die Welt.* Retrieved July 9, 2012, from http://www.welt.de/wirtschaft/article7258797/Flugverbote-treffen-Autoindustrie-mit-voller-Wucht.html.

Anonymous. (2010, June 10). Supply chain: What can supply chain executives learn from the Iceland volcano? Retrieved July 9, 2012, from http://www.scmr.com/article/supply_chain_what_can_supply_chain_executives_learn_from_the_iceland_volcan.

Bell, R. (2010, April 20). Volcano disrupts BMW supply chain to S.C. Retrieved July 9, 2012, from http://www.thestate.com/2010/04/20/1251405/volcano-disrupts-bmw-supply-chain.html.

Cooke, J. A. (2010, April 22). Commentary: Volcano's effects prove importance of managing supply chain risk. Retrieved July 9, 2012, from http://www.dcvelocity.com/print/article/20100422managing_supply_chain_risk.

Fuller, T. (2011, November 6). Thailand flooding cripples hard-drive supply. *The New York Times.* Retrieved July 9, 2012, from http://www.nytimes.com/2011/11/07/business/global/07iht-floods07.html.

Mearian, L. (2011, December 20). Hard drive prices slide as Thai flood aftermath subsides. *ComputerWorld.* Retrieved July 9, 2012, from http://www.computerworld.com/s/article/9222871/Hard_drive_prices_slide_as_Thai_flood_aftermath_subsides.

Nicolai, B., & Siegmud, H. (2010, April 18). Vulkan macht iPhones und Papaya zur Mangelware. *Die Welt.* Retrieved July 9, 2012, from http://www.welt.de/wirtschaft/article7237211/Vulkan-macht-iPhones-und-Papaya-zur-Mangelware.html.

Riberiro, J. (2011, October 31). Thai floods hit Q4 hard drive production, says research firm. *PC World.* Retrieved July 9, 2012, from http://www.pcworld.com/businesscenter/article/242913/thai_floods_hit_q4_hard_drive_production_says_research_firm.html.

Sowinski, L. L. (2010, April 24). Iceland's volcano does a number on global supply chains. Retrieved July 9, 2012, from http://www.worldtradewt100.com/blogs/14-wt100-blog/post/iceland-s-volcano-does-a-number-on-global-supply-chains.

Thompson, H. (2011, November 11). Floods in Thailand leading to higher hard drive and computer prices. *Digital Home.* Retrieved July 9, 2012, from http://www.digitalhome.ca/2011/11/floods-in-thailand-leading-to-higher-hard-drive-and-computer-prices.

http://goo.gl/FHxuC

SUPPLY CHAIN MANAGEMENT

In the previous chapter, we discussed the need to share internal data in order to streamline business processes, improving coordination within the organization to improve efficiency and effectiveness. Now we turn our attention to collaborating with partners along the supply chain. Getting the raw materials and components that a company uses in its daily operations is an important key to business success. When deliveries from suppliers are accurate and timely, companies can convert them to finished products more efficiently. Coordinating this effort with suppliers has become a central part of many companies' overall business strategy, as it can help them reduce costs associated with inventory levels and get new products to market more quickly. Ultimately, this helps companies drive profitability and improve their customer service since they can react to changing market conditions swiftly. Collaborating or sharing information with suppliers has become a strategic necessity for business success. In other words, by developing and maintaining stronger, more integrated relationships with suppliers, companies can more effectively compete in their markets through cost reductions and responsiveness to market demands.

FIGURE 8.2
A typical supply network.

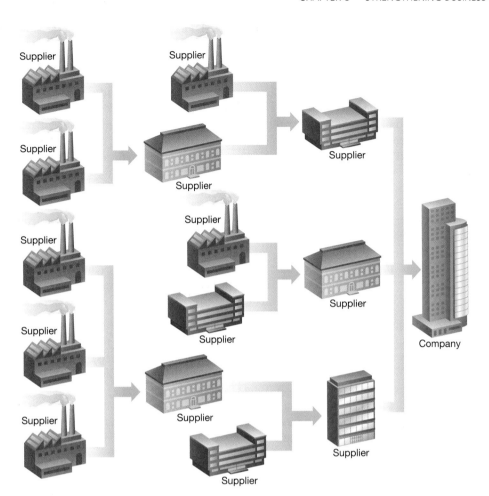

What Is a Supply Chain?

The term **supply chain** is commonly used to refer to a collection of companies and processes involved in moving a product from the suppliers of raw materials to the suppliers of intermediate components, then to final production, and, ultimately, to the customer. Companies often procure specific raw materials and components from many different "upstream" suppliers. These suppliers, in turn, work with their own suppliers to obtain raw materials and components; their suppliers work with additional suppliers, and so forth. The further out in the supply chain one looks, the more suppliers are involved. As a result, the term "chain" becomes somewhat of a misnomer since it implies one-to-one relationships facilitating a chain of events flowing from the first supplier to the second to the third and so on. Similarly, on the "downstream" side, the products move to many different customers. The flow of materials from suppliers to customers can thus be more accurately described as a **supply network** because of the various interrelated parties involved in moving raw materials, intermediate components, and finally, the end product within the production process (see Figure 8.2).

Business-to-Business Electronic Commerce: Exchanging Data in Supply Networks

As defined earlier, transactions conducted between different businesses in a supply network, not involving the end consumer, are referred to as business-to-business electronic commerce, which accounts for 90 percent of all EC in the United States (U.S. Census Bureau, 2012). B2B transactions require proprietary information (such as orders for parts) to be communicated to an organization's business partners. For many organizations, keeping such information private can be of strategic value; for example, Apple tries to keep news about potential new product launches to a minimum, as any information about orders for key components (such as touch screens) could give away hints of what a new product may be. Prior to the introduction of the Internet and Web, the secure communication of proprietary information in B2B EC was facilitated using **Electronic Data Interchange (EDI)**. EDI refers to computer–computer communication (without human intervention) following certain standards as set by the UN Economic Commission (for Europe) or the American National Standards Institute. Traditionally, using EDI, the exchange of business documents and other information took place via dedicated telecommunication networks between suppliers and customers, and thus the use of EDI was generally limited to large corporations that could afford the associated expenses. Today, the Internet has become an economical medium over which this business-related information can be transmitted, enabling even small to midsized enterprises to use EDI; many large companies (such as the retail giant Walmart) require their suppliers to transmit information such as advance shipping notices using Web-based EDI protocols. Further, companies have devised a number of innovative ways to facilitate B2B transactions using Web-based technologies. We introduce these technologies in the following sections.

The use of extranets (see Chapter 3, "Managing the Information Systems Infrastructure and Services") has increased due to the development of a common set of applications that have been found to be particularly beneficial to organizations. The primary use of extranets in organizations is for managing their supply chains; in other words, organizations exchange data and handle transactions with their suppliers or organizational customers, and extranets have evolved as a popular alternative to proprietary supply linkages.

PORTALS. **Portals**, in the context of B2B supply chain management, can be defined as access points (or front doors) through which a business partner accesses secured, proprietary information that may be dispersed throughout an organization (typically using extranets). By allowing direct access to critical information needed to conduct business, portals can thus provide substantial productivity gains and cost savings for B2B transactions.

Most companies are depending on a steady source of key supplies needed to produce their goods or services. For example, luxury restaurants require their produce to be consistently of high quality; similarly, car manufacturers need steel, paint, or electronic components in the right quantities, at the right quality and price, and at the right time. Thus, most companies are seeking long-term B2B relationships with a limited number of carefully selected suppliers—rather than one-time deals—and invest considerable efforts in selecting their suppliers or business partners; often, suppliers are assessed not only on product features such as price or quality but also on supplier's characteristics, such as trustworthiness, commitment, or viability. As a result, in contrast to B2C EC, where anyone can set up a customer account with a retailer, the suppliers or customers in B2B transactions are typically pre-screened by the business, and access to the company's extranet will be given depending on the business relationship (typically, after a review of the supplier's or buyer's application). To support different types of business relationships, portals come in two basic forms: supplier portals and customer portals. Supplier portals automate the business processes involved in purchasing or procuring products between a single buyer and multiple suppliers. On the other end of the spectrum, customer portals automate the business processes involved in selling or distributing products from a single supplier to multiple buyers. B2B marketplaces are typically run by separate entities and connect multiple buyers and multiple suppliers (see Figure 8.3).

Supplier Portals Many companies that are dealing with large numbers of suppliers (e.g., The Boeing Company, Lilly, P&G, and Hewlett-Packard [HP]) set up **supplier portals** (sometimes

FIGURE 8.3

Supplier portals, B2B marketplaces, and customer portals.

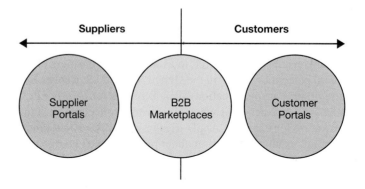

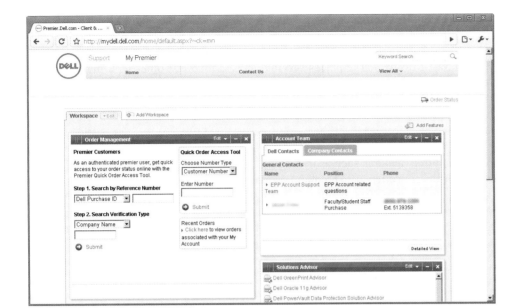

referred to as sourcing portals or procurement portals). A supplier portal is a subset of an organization's extranet designed to automate the business processes that occur before, during, and after sales have been transacted between the organization (i.e., a single buyer) and its multiple suppliers. For example, on the HP Supplier Portal, companies can register their interest in becoming a supplier for HP; access terms and conditions or guidelines (such as guidelines related to labeling, shipment, or packaging); and, once a business relationship is established with HP, manage interorganizational business processes associated with ordering and payment.

Customer Portals **Customer portals** are designed to automate the business processes that occur before, during, and after sales have been transacted between a supplier and multiple customers. In other words, customer portals provide efficient tools for business customers to manage all phases of the purchasing cycle, including reviewing product information, order entry, and customer service. For example, MyBoeingFleet, the customer portal of The Boeing Company, is part of Boeing's extranet and allows airplane owners, operators, and other parties to access information about their airplanes' configurations, maintenance documents, or spare parts. In other cases, customer portals are set up as B2B Web sites that provide custom-tailored offers or specific deals based on sales volume, as is the case with large office retailers such as OfficeMax (www.officemaxsolutions.com) or computer manufacturer Dell, which services business customers through its customer portal Dell Premier (see Figure 8.4).

B2B Marketplaces

The purpose of supplier portals and customer portals is to enable interaction between a single company and its many suppliers or customers. Being owned/operated by a single organization, these portals can be considered a subset of the organization's extranet. However, setting up such portals tends to be beyond the reach of small to midsized businesses because of the costs involved in designing, developing, and maintaining this type of system. Many of these firms do not have the necessary monetary resources or skilled personnel to develop large-scale supply chain management applications on their own, and the transaction volume does not justify the expenses. To service this market niche, a number of **business-to-business marketplaces** have sprung up. B2B marketplaces are operated by third-party vendors, meaning they are built and maintained by a separate entity rather than being associated with a particular buyer or supplier. These marketplaces generate revenue by taking a small commission for each transaction that occurs, by charging usage fees, by charging association fees, and/or by generating advertising revenues. Unlike customer and supplier portals, B2B marketplaces allow many buyers and many sellers to come together, offering firms access to real-time trading with other companies in their **vertical markets** (i.e., markets comprised of firms operating within a certain industry sector). Such B2B marketplaces can create tremendous efficiencies for companies since they bring together numerous participants along the supply network. Some popular B2B marketplaces include www.steellink.com (steel), www.paperindex.com (paper), and www.fibre2fashion.com (textile and fashion supplies).

In contrast to B2B marketplaces serving vertical markets, other B2B marketplaces are not focused on any particular industry. One of the most successful examples is the Chinese marketplace Alibaba.com. Alibaba.com brings together buyers and suppliers from around the globe, from almost every industry, selling almost any product, ranging from fresh ginger to manufacturing machinery. Alibaba.com offers various free services, such as posting item leads, displaying products, and contacting buyers or sellers. In addition to providing item listings, Alibaba.com offers features such as trading tips or price watch for raw materials. To generate revenue, Alibaba.com offers paid premium membership for sellers; the "Gold Supplier" premium membership entails a verified identity (signaling prospective buyers that the supplier is indeed a legitimate business entity) as well as unlimited product listings. Offering various trading tools including online storefronts, virtual factory tours, and real-time chat, such B2B marketplaces have enabled many small or little-known suppliers to engage in trade on a global basis.

Managing Complex Supply Networks

A prime example of a company having to manage extremely complex supply networks is Apple and its latest extremely successful mobile devices, such as the iPhone 5 or the iPad. Apple sold 3 million iPads within the first 80 days of its release (or roughly 26 iPads per minute on average), and sold over 5 million iPhone 5 during the first weekend after launching the product. In fact, the iPhone 5 has been so successful that Apple was facing supply shortages, forcing the company to delay shipping pre-ordered phones for several weeks. How does Apple manage to produce such an incredible amount of these products? If you take a close look at the devices, you will find a statement saying "Designed by Apple in California Assembled in China." Every time a new Apple device is launched, industry observers disassemble these devices to get a sneak peek into Apple's supply chain. The iPhone, like other Apple devices, is by no means *manufactured* by Apple. The components of the iPhone are sourced from dozens of companies located in various different countries. For example, according to market research firm iSuppli, the iPhone's flash memory and central processing unit are produced by Korean Samsung; the display is sourced from Korean LG; the phone chips are made by German Infineon (manufactured in Germany or Southeast Asia); the Wi-Fi and Global Positioning System chips are produced by U.S.-based Broadcom (but possibly assembled in China, Korea, Singapore, or Taiwan); the touch-screen controller is made by Texas Instruments; many other parts, such as the camera, are possibly made in Taiwan; and so on. The final product is assembled in a factory owned by Taiwanese electronics giant Foxconn, located in Shenzhen, China (a city of almost 9 million people, located just north of Hong Kong), from where the finished iPhones are shipped by air to the different countries where the iPhone is on sale (see Figure 8.5). Although many have never heard of Foxconn, it is the largest electronics manufacturer in the world, producing components, cell phones, gaming consoles, and so on for various other companies, including Dell, HP, and Sony.

Coordinating such extensive supply network requires considerable expertise, especially when facing unexpected events such as shortages in touch-screen panels, other issues at suppliers' factories, or natural disasters. In 2010, for example, the eruption of a volcano in Iceland led to the closing of the northern European airspace for several days, causing delays in iPhone shipments to Europe; similarly, the earthquake and associated tsunami that devastated Japan in March 2011 devastated the supply chains of electronics and automobile manufacturers who had to shut down plants around the world, as key components could not be produced in Japan and delivered to assembly lines. A shrinking pool of suppliers for critical components exacerbates such problems, as companies have fewer options to switch suppliers if necessary. It is thus important not only to monitor one's own direct suppliers but also to constantly monitor the company's extended supply chain so as to anticipate any issues that may have an impact on one's direct suppliers.

Benefits of Effectively Managing Supply Chains

Whereas effectively managing the supply chain can create various opportunities, many problems can arise when firms within the network do not collaborate effectively. For example,

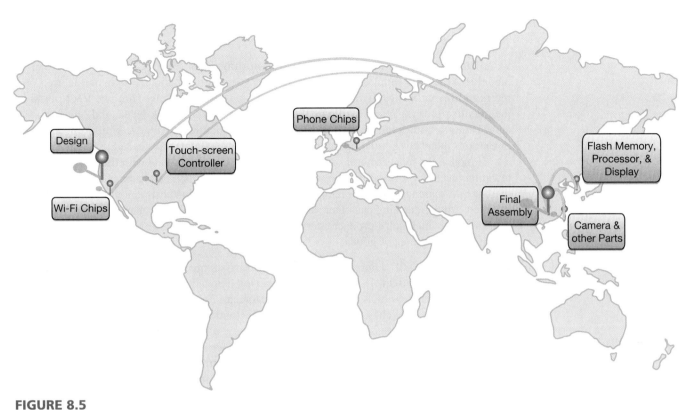

FIGURE 8.5

The iPhone is assembled in China from globally sourced components.

collaboration within supply networks has enabled process innovations such as just-in-time manufacturing and vendor-managed inventory (discussed in the following sections). On the other hand, if firms do not collaborate effectively, information can easily become distorted as it moves from one company down through the supply network. Problems such as excessive inventories, inaccurate manufacturing capacity plans, and missed production schedules can run rampant, causing huge ripple effects that lead to degradations in profitability and poor customer service by everyone within the supply network. Further, effectively managing the supply chain is becoming increasingly important in terms of corporate social responsibility.

JUST-IN-TIME PRODUCTION. One of the most significant advances to production has been the use of **just-in-time (JIT)** strategies. Based on the notion that keeping inventory is costly (in terms of both storage costs and the capital that is tied up) and does not add value, companies using a JIT method are trying to optimize their ordering quantities such that parts or raw material arrive just when they are needed for production. As the orders arrive in smaller quantities (but at higher frequency), the investment in storage space and inventory is minimized. Pioneered by Japanese automaker Toyota, many other businesses have now adopted a JIT approach. For example, computer maker Dell realized the problems with keeping large inventories, especially because of the fast rate of obsolescence of electronics components. To illustrate, recall our discussion of Moore's Law (see Chapter 3), which suggests that processor technology is doubling in performance approximately every 24 months. Because of this, successful computer manufacturers have learned that holding inventory that can quickly become obsolete or devalued is a poor strategy for success. In fact, Dell now only keeps about two hours of inventory in its factories. Obviously, using a JIT method is heavily dependent on tight cooperation between all partners in the supply network, not only including suppliers, but also other needed partners, such as shipping and logistics companies. In 2002, a labor lockout effectively shut down 29 U.S. West Coast ports for 10 days; events such as this can wreak havoc for companies requiring goods shipped from overseas for their business. For a computer maker such as Dell, which sources most of its components from Southeast Asia and depends on a steady stream of supplies for its JIT manufacturing processes, this could have potentially been devastating. However, foreseeing those potential problems in the supply network, Dell chartered 18 Boeing 747 freighter aircraft to shuttle parts from its Asian suppliers to the U.S. assembly facilities so as to keep business running. In the end, Dell successfully managed to weather this storm without having to delay any customer orders.

VENDOR-MANAGED INVENTORY. **Vendor-managed inventory (VMI)** is a business model in which the suppliers to a manufacturer (or retailer) manage the manufacturer's (or retailer's) inventory levels based on preestablished service levels. To make VMI possible, the manufacturer (or retailer) allows the supplier to monitor stock levels and ongoing sales data. Under a traditional inventory model, the manufacturer or retailer would manage their inventories themselves, sending out requests for additional items as needed. In contrast, under a VMI model, the manufacturer or retailer shares real-time sales data with their suppliers, who maintain inventory levels based on preestablished agreements. Such arrangements can help to optimize the manufacturer's (or retailer's) inventory, both saving costs and minimizing stockout situations (thus enhancing customer satisfaction); the supplier, in turn, benefits from the intense data sharing, which helps produce more accurate forecasts, reduces ordering errors, and helps prioritize the shipment of goods.

THE BULLWHIP EFFECT. One major problem affecting supply chains are ripple effects referred to as the **bullwhip effect**. Each business forecasting demand typically includes a safety buffer in order to prevent possible stockouts. However, forecast errors and safety stocks multiply when moving up the supply chain, such that a small fluctuation in demand for an end product can lead to tremendous fluctuation in demand for parts or raw materials farther up the supply chain. Like someone cracking a bullwhip, a tiny "flick of the wrist" will create a big movement at the other end of the whip. Likewise, a small forecasting error at the end of the supply chain can cause massive forecasting errors farther up the supply chain. Implementing integrated business processes allows a company to better coordinate the entire supply network and reduce the impact of the bullwhip.

CORPORATE SOCIAL RESPONSIBILITY. Effectively managing the supply chain has also become tremendously important for aspects related to corporate social responsibility. Specifically, transparency and accountability within the supply chain can help organizations save costs and/ or create a good image. Two related issues are product recalls and sustainable business practices; both are discussed next.

Product Recalls Given that a typical supply network comprises tens, hundreds, or sometimes thousands of players, many of which are dispersed across the globe, there are myriad possibilities where shortcuts are being taken or quality standards are not being met. Often, such issues are caught somewhere along the supply chain, but sometimes such incidents go unnoticed until the product reaches the end consumer. For example, the Discovery Kids Animated Marine and Safari Lamp was imported from China and sold through various online and offline retailers throughout the U.S. In mid-2012, more than 300,000 lamps had to be recalled after it was detected that they could pose a fire and burn hazard due to a design flaw. This shows that problems can be exacerbated if companies are sourcing their products or raw materials globally, as more potential points of failure are added due to differences in quality or product safety regulations in the originating countries.

Hence, it is extremely important to have the necessary information to trace back the movement of the product through the supply chain so as to be able to quickly identify the problematic link. Being able to single out the source of the problem helps the company to perform an appropriate response, helping to save goodwill and limiting the costs of a recall. Further, in many cases, only some batches of a product may be problematic (such as when certain raw materials or components are sourced from different suppliers). If a company is not able to clearly identify the affected batches, the recall will have to be much broader, costing the company much more (in both goodwill and money) than just having to recall the affected batches. Hence, companies need to have a clear picture of their supply chain, and also need to store these data in case of problems at a later point in time.

Sustainable Business Practices Another aspect related to corporate social responsibility is a growing emphasis on sustainable business practices. Particularly, organizations have come under increasing scrutiny for issues such as ethical treatment of workers (especially overseas) or environmental practices. For example, since 2010, more than 20 employees at Foxconn's

Shenzhen plant have committed suicide. As the suicides happened at the plant manufacturing iPhones for Apple, many blamed Apple for the working conditions at the plant. Although Apple is certainly aware of the negative effects that a supplier's action can have on a company's reputation, it also faces a conundrum, as few (if any) companies besides Foxconn have sufficient production capacity to meet the demand for hugely popular products such as the iPhone.

Other companies are trying to portray a "green" image and attempt to minimize their carbon footprint. For example, HP takes a proactive approach, being the first major information technology company to publish its aggregate supply chain greenhouse gas emissions, restrict the use of hazardous materials, implement environmentally friendly packaging policies, and so on. In order to do that and to provide sound, convincing numbers to back their "green" image, a company such as HP needs to have a clear view of its entire supply chain. Similarly, U.S. regulations require 95 percent of computers purchased by the U.S. federal government to carry the EPEAT eco-label. To achieve this certification, a manufacturer has to possess and produce extensive evidence that the products meet EPEAT's strict requirements.

Optimizing the Supply Chain through Supply Chain Management

Information systems focusing on improving supply chains have two main objectives: to accelerate product development and innovation and to reduce costs. These systems, called **supply chain management (SCM)**, improve the coordination of suppliers, product or service production, and distribution. When executed successfully, SCM helps in not only reducing inventory costs, but also enhancing revenue through improved customer service. SCM is often integrated with ERP to leverage internal and external information in order to better collaborate with suppliers. Like ERP and customer relationship management applications, SCM packages are delivered in the form of modules (see Table 8.1) that companies select and implement according to their differing business requirements.

As discussed previously, ERP systems are primarily used to optimize business processes *within* the organization, whereas SCM is used to improve business processes that *span* organizational boundaries. Whereas some stand-alone SCM systems only automate the logistics aspects of the supply chain, organizations can reap the greatest benefits when the SCM system is tightly integrated with ERP and customer relationship management systems modules; this way, SCM systems can use data about customer orders or sales forecasts (from the customer relationship management system), data about payments (from the ERP system), and so on. Given

TABLE 8.1 Functions That Optimize the Supply Network

Module	Key Uses
Demand planning and forecasting	Forecast and plan anticipated demand for products
Safety stock planning	Assign optimal safety stock and target stock levels in all inventories in the supply network
Distribution planning	Optimize the allocation of available supply to meet demand
Supply network collaboration	Work with partners across the supply network to improve accuracy of demand forecasts, reduce inventory buffers, increase the velocity of materials, and improve customer service
Materials management	Ensure that the materials required for production are available where needed when needed
Manufacturing execution	Support production processes taking into account capacity and material constraints
Order promising	Provide answers to customer relationship management queries regarding product availability, costs, and delivery times
Transportation execution	Manage logistics between company locations or from company to customers, taking into account transportation modes and constraints
Warehouse management	Support receiving, storing, and picking of goods in a warehouse
Supply chain analytics	Monitor key performance indicators to assess performance across the supply chain

Source: Based on http://www.sap.com.

WHEN THINGS GO WRONG

Apple's "Very Angry Birds" Disrupt App Store Supply Chain

Snorting pigs, chirping birds, and the sound of a slingshot. Those are some of the all too familiar sound effects of the hugely successful game Angry Birds. Initially released for Apple's iOS in December 2009, it is now available for Android mobile devices and even as a version for Google's Chrome browser, so players can enjoy the quest on their monitors in HD. Since its release, more than 700 million copies of the game have been downloaded. In early July 2012, technical teams within Apple spent hours fixing a problem related to Digital Rights Management (DRM). The problem kept millions of users from successfully downloading and updating apps like Angry Birds, and even prevented developers from accessing their own apps. According to Apple, a server wrongly inserted DRM code into various apps, making them inoperable. To make matters worse, Apple's servers prompted customers to update various infected apps, impacting more than 100 different apps. Of course, customers were unaware of the corrupted code, so many customers complied with the update requests. Once "updated" the apps would crash upon launch. Consequently, a large number of very angry customers sent a flood of negative reviews to Apple's App Stores for the various products that wouldn't work. Because the errors that occurred had nothing to do with the apps themselves, Apple subsequently removed the negative app reviews that occurred over this period. However, with hundreds of millions of consumers relying on Apple's App Store every day, when things go wrong, many people are impacted.

Based on:

Allsopp, A. (2012, July 9). Apple removes negative app reviews caused by update crashing bug. Retrieved July 9, 2012, from http://www.macworld.co.uk/ipad-iphone/news/?newsid=3368620.

Angry Birds. (2012, July 9). In *Wikipedia, The Free Encyclopedia*. Retrieved July 9, 2012, from http://en.wikipedia.org/w/index.php?title=Angry_Birds&oldid=501441789.

Ashford, W. (2012, July 9). Rogue Apple server corrupts Angry Birds Space and other apps. Retrieved July 9, 2012, from http://www.computerweekly.com/news/2240159273/Rogue-Apple-server-corrupts-Angry-Birds-Space-and-other-apps.

Ferrence, P. (2012, July 9). Apple Inc (AAPL) app store technical glitch leaves millions affected. Retrieved July 9, 2012, from http://www.pt-news.org/apple-inc-aapl-app-store-technical-glitch-leaves-millions-affected/125718.

Hardawar, D. (2012, July 6). Instapaper founder: Apple's app corruption issues affected more than a "small number" of users. Retrieved July 9, 2012, from http://venturebeat.com/2012/07/06/instapaper-founder-apples-app-corruption-issues-affected-more-than-a-small-number-of-users.

Seitz, D. (2012, July 6). How Apple accidentally trashed Angry Birds, Max Payne Mobile and more. Retrieved July 9, 2012, from http://www.gametrailers.com/side-mission/20584/how-apple-accidentally-trashed-angry-birds-max-payne-mobile-and-more.

its scope, SCM is adopted primarily by large organizations with a large and/or complex supplier network. At the same time, many smaller suppliers are interacting with the systems of large companies. To obtain the greatest benefits from the SCM processes and systems, organizations need to extend the system to include all trading partners regardless of size, providing a central location for information integration and common processes so that all partners benefit.

For an effective SCM strategy, several challenges have to be overcome. First and foremost, as with any information system, an SCM system is only as good as the data entered into it. This means that to benefit most from an SCM system, the organization's employees have to actually use the system and move away from traditional ways of managing the supply chain, as an order placed by fax or telephone will most likely not find its way into the system. Another challenge to overcome is distrust among partners in the supply chain; for many companies, sales and supply chain data are strategic assets, and no one wants to show his or her cards to other members in the supply chain. Further, many organizations (such as Apple) tend to be very clandestine about their suppliers, as such information could reveal their pricing strategies or give clues about new product development. In addition, more and more organizations are reluctant to share data along the supply chain because of an increase in intellectual property theft, especially in China, a major source of supplies for many companies. A final challenge is to get all partners within the supply chain to adopt an SCM system. Several years ago, the retail giant Walmart began mandating its suppliers use its RetailLink supply chain system, and refused to engage in a business relationship with any supplier who was not willing to use the system. Whereas large companies can force their suppliers or partners to use a system, smaller companies typically do not have this power.

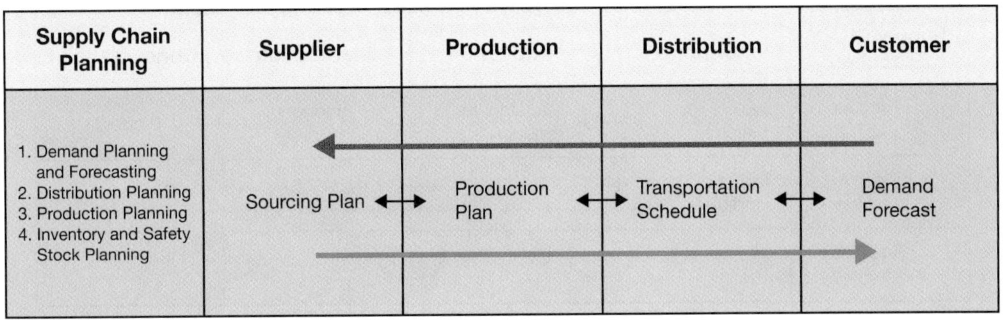

Supply Chain Planning	Supplier	Production	Distribution	Customer
1. Demand Planning and Forecasting 2. Distribution Planning 3. Production Planning 4. Inventory and Safety Stock Planning	Sourcing Plan ↔	Production Plan ↔	Transportation Schedule ↔	Demand Forecast

FIGURE 8.6

SCP includes (customer) demand planning and forecasting, distribution planning, production planning, and (supplier) inventory and safety stock planning.

SCM Architecture

An SCM system includes more than simply hardware and software; it also integrates business processes and supply chain partners. As shown in Table 8.1, an SCM system consists of many modules or applications. Each of these modules supports either supply chain planning, supply chain execution, or supply chain visibility and analytics. All are described next.

SUPPLY CHAIN PLANNING. **Supply chain planning (SCP)** involves the development of various resource plans to support the efficient and effective production of goods and services (see Figure 8.6). Four key processes are generally supported by SCP modules:

1. *Demand Planning and Forecasting.* SCP begins with product demand planning and forecasting. To develop demand forecasts, SCM modules examine historical data to develop the most accurate forecasts possible. The accuracy of these forecasts will be influenced greatly by the stability of the data. When historic data are stable, plans can be longer in duration, whereas if historic data show unpredictable fluctuations in demand, the forecasting time frame must be narrowed. SCM systems also support collaborative demand and supply planning such that a sales representative can work together with the demand planner, taking into account information provided by the organization's point-of-sale system, promotions entered in the customer relationship management system, and other factors influencing demand. Demand planning and forecasting leads to the development of the overall *demand forecast.*
2. *Distribution Planning.* Once demand forecasts are finalized, plans for moving products to distributors can be developed. Specifically, distribution planning focuses on delivering products or services to consumers as well as warehousing, delivering, invoicing, and payment collection. Distribution planning leads to the development of the overall *transportation schedule.*
3. *Production Scheduling.* Production scheduling focuses on the coordination of all activities needed to create the product or service. When developing this plan, analytical tools are used to optimally utilize materials, equipment, and labor. Production also involves product testing, packaging, and delivery preparation. Production scheduling leads to the development of the *production plan.*
4. *Inventory and Safety Stock Planning.* Inventory and safety stock planning focuses on the development of inventory estimates. Using inventory simulations and other analytical techniques, organizations can balance inventory costs and desired customer service levels to determine optimal inventory levels. Once inventory levels are estimated, suppliers are chosen who contractually agree to preestablished delivery and pricing terms. Inventory and safety stock planning leads to the development of a *sourcing plan.*

As suggested, various types of analytical tools—such as statistical analysis, simulation, and optimization—are used to forecast and visualize demand levels, distribution and warehouse locations, resource sequencing, and so on. Once these plans are developed, they are used to guide supply chain execution. Additionally, it is important to note that SCM planning is an ongoing process—as new data are obtained, plans are updated. For example, as shortages in the capacity for manufacturing touch-screen displays became evident in late 2012, Apple had to dynamically adjust its plans so as to obtain the needed quantities to meet customer demand.

SUPPLY CHAIN EXECUTION. **Supply chain execution (SCE)** is the execution of SCP. Essentially, SCE puts the SCM planning into motion and reflects the processes involved in improving the collaboration of all members of the supply chain—suppliers, producers, distributors, and

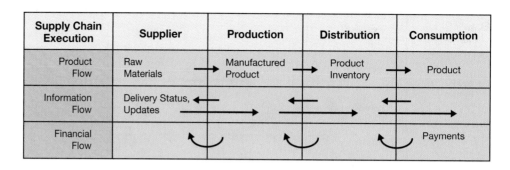

customers. SCE involves the management of three key elements of the supply chain: product flow, information flow, and financial flow (see Figure 8.7). Each of these flows is discussed next.

Product Flow **Product flow** refers to the movement of goods from the supplier to production, from production to distribution, and from distribution to the consumer. Although products primarily "flow" in one direction, an effective SCM system will also support the activities associated with product returns. Effectively processing returns and customer refunds is a critical part of SCE. Thus, an SCM system should support not only the physical product production process but also the necessary processes in place to efficiently receive excessive or defective products from customers (and ship replacements or credit accounts).

Information Flow **Information flow** refers to the movement of information along the supply chain, such as order processing and delivery status updates. Like the product flow, information can also flow up or down the supply chain as needed. The key element to the information flow is the complete removal of paper documents. Specifically, all information about orders, fulfillment, billing, and consolidation is shared electronically. These paperless information flows save not only paperwork but also time and money. Additionally, because SCM systems use a central database to store information, all supply chain partners have at all times access to the most current information necessary for scheduling production, shipping orders, and so on.

Financial Flow **Financial flow** refers primarily to the movement of financial assets throughout the supply chain. Financial flows also include information related to payment schedules, consignment and ownership of products and materials, and other relevant information. Linkages to electronic banking and financial institutions allow payments to automatically flow into the accounts of all members within the supply chain.

SUPPLY CHAIN VISIBILITY AND ANALYTICS. **Supply chain visibility** refers to the ability not only to track products as they move through the supply chain but also to foresee external events. Being able to see where a shipment is at any given time can be of tremendous help, especially when using JIT methods or when maintaining low inventory levels. For example, knowing where a shipment is and being able to expedite it can help in not losing a sale or help in taking away a sale from a competitor. Further, knowing where a supplier's facilities are located can help to anticipate and react to issues arising from adverse weather conditions, natural disasters, or political issues; if I don't know where in Taiwan my suppliers' factories are located, how will I know whether they might be affected by a fast-approaching typhoon? Similarly, some companies even want to know when labor contracts of key suppliers' workers expire in order to plan for potential labor disputes (Penfield, 2008). Needless to say, such levels of information sharing throughout the supply chain require tremendous trust among the partners.

Supply chain analytics refers to the use of key performance indicators to monitor performance of the entire supply chain, including sourcing, planning, production, and distribution. For example, a purchasing manager can identify the suppliers that are frequently unable to meet promised delivery dates (see Figure 8.8). Being able to access key performance metrics can help to identify and remove bottlenecks, such as by switching suppliers, spreading orders over multiple suppliers, expediting shipping for critical goods, and so on.

BRIEF CASE   The Formula for Success: Demand Media

Imagine Google, YouTube, and Wikipedia all merged into a single comprehensive system ready to help you answer any question you might have. You type in a typical question and receive an informative response, in the form of an instructional video, or a simple article focused on your exact question. Demand Media and its various sites on the Web provide such answers, offering intellectual nourishment to random inquiries that range from instructions for making banana pancakes to running a vintage clothing shop (and thereby generating considerable advertising revenue).

Demand Media, Inc., an American content and social media company, developed an algorithm that uses search engine query data and bids on advertising auctions to identify topics with high advertising potential. These topics are typically in the advice and how-to field. For example, they have learned that the key words "best" and "how" tend to bring in high search traffic and click-through rates. Once the algorithm identifies a search query that is likely to draw traffic, Demand Media then crowdsources the production of corresponding text or video content to answer the algorithm-generated search query (e.g., "Where can I donate a car in Dallas?"). The content is then posted on the company's own sites such as eHow, Livestrong.com, Trails.com, GolfLink.com, Mania.com, and Cracked.com (as well as various other sites, such as YouTube), and Demand Media generates revenue through advertisements placed on these sites.

Demand Media is on the rise, and many freelancers are scrambling to grab the best titles, add them to their assignment queue, and start rolling with the least amount of effort. The average writer earns US$15 per piece for articles containing a few hundred words, whereas a filmmaker receives US$20 per clip, both of which are paid on a weekly basis through PayPal. Demand Media also offers opportunities to copyedit, fact-check, approve the quality of a film, or transcribe, with pay ranging from 25 cents to $2.50 depending on the type of work. Although the pay is not too inviting, the high demand for professional contributions, which exceeds several hundred thousand articles per year and thousands of videos per month, has had filmmakers and writers around the world racing against time to produce the 4,000 videos and articles that Demand Media publishes every single day. For many, shooting a couple of videos each day for a week can be a good opportunity to earn more than US$500.

The volume and exposure that Demand Media creates and receives has been impressive; its 170,000 uploads to YouTube is twice the content of CBS, the Associated Press, Universal Music Group, CollegeHumor, Al Jazeera English, and Soulja Boy combined. Its network of 45 B-list sites manages to bring in more traffic than Web sites like ESPN and NBC Universal combined. It is no wonder that Internet giant Google has reached out to the company and is now working as Demand Media's top distribution partner, closely collaborating with Demand Media to generate more revenue from the algorithm of profiting from advertisers.

Questions:

1. Would you be interested in working for Demand Media to produce content? Why or why not?
2. Does Demand Media have a competitive advantage? If so, what is it and how will they sustain it? If not, why not?

Based on:

Anonymous. (n.d.). *Demand Media.* Retrieved July 12, 2012, from http://www.demandmedia.com/about.

Demand Media. (2012, June 22). In *Wikipedia, The Free Encyclopedia.* Retrieved July 12, 2012, from http://en.wikipedia.org/w/index.php?title=Demand_Media&oldid=498846959.

Roth, D. (2009, October 19). The answer factory: Demand Media and the fast, disposable, and profitable as hell media model. *Wired.* Retrieved July 12, 2012, from http://www.wired.com/magazine/2009/10/ff_demandmedia/all/1.

Developing an SCM Strategy

When developing an SCM strategy, an organization must consider a variety of factors that will affect the efficiency and effectiveness of the supply chain. **Supply chain efficiency** is the extent to which a company's supply chain is focusing on minimizing procurement, production, and transportation costs, sometimes by sacrificing excellent customer service. In contrast, **supply chain effectiveness** is the extent to which a company's supply chain is focusing on maximizing customer service, with lesser focus on procurement, production, and transportation costs (see Figure 8.9). In other words, the design of the supply chain must consider natural trade-offs between a variety of factors and should reflect the organization's competitive strategy to reap the greatest benefits. For example, an organization utilizing a low-cost provider competitive strategy would likely focus on supply chain efficiency. In contrast, an organization pursuing a superior customer service differentiation strategy would focus on supply chain effectiveness.

SCM systems typically allow for making trade-offs between efficiency and effectiveness for individual components or raw materials. For example, if a hurricane is likely to delay the arrival of a key component by sea, the company can perform simulations to evaluate the effect of the delay on production and can assess the feasibility of temporarily switching suppliers, switching modes of transportation (e.g., expediting the shipment via air freight), or substituting the component altogether. In such cases, making changes to the original plans may be more costly but can help the organization

FIGURE 8.8

Supply chain analytics helps to monitor the performance of the supply chain.

Source: Courtesy of Microsoft, Inc.

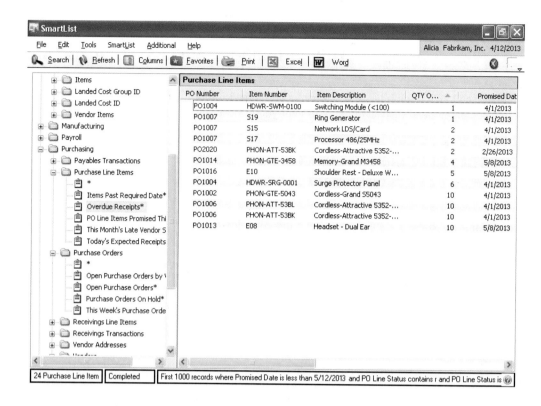

meet promised delivery deadlines, thus maintaining goodwill and avoiding possible contract penalties. On the other hand, companies can dynamically adjust schedules for noncritical components or raw materials so as to minimize costs while still meeting the targets set in the production schedule.

Managing B2B Financial Transactions

In B2C electronic commerce, most transactions are settled using credit cards or electronic payment services such as PayPal; in contrast, B2B payments are lagging far behind. In fact, according to some estimates, about 75 percent of all noncash B2B payments in the United States are made by check. While this may sound archaic, the time needed to process a check serves as a form of trade credit, which can amount to a significant part of an organization's working capital. For smaller purchases, organizations also often use purchasing cards. However, although productivity gains can be realized from using purchasing cards instead of checks, such cards are typically not used for large B2B transactions because of preset spending limits. In global B2B transactions, organizations often use letters of credit issued by a bank to make payments. While letters of credit help to reduce credit risk, these are often used only for relatively large amounts. Alternatively, businesses can make payments using providers such as Western Union. In any case, making a B2B payment is far from being as simple as making a purchase at Amazon.com

FIGURE 8.9

A supply chain strategy requires balancing supply chain efficiency and effectiveness.

Supply Chain Strategy	Procurement	Production	Transportation
Effectiveness	More Inventory Multiple Inventory Sources ...	General Purpose Facilities More Facilities Higher Excess Capacity ...	Fast Delivery Times More Warehouses ...
Efficiency	... Single Inventory Source Less Inventory	... Less Excess Capacity Fewer Facilities Special Purpose Facilities	... Fewer Warehouses Longer Delivery Times

using your credit card, and making B2B payments easier can greatly enhance efficiency as well as reduce costs for organizations. Thus, it is no wonder that businesses have started asking for payment methods as simple as PayPal for B2B transactions.

When dealing with new, unknown suppliers, there is considerable fraud risk involved; this is especially of concern in global EC. This can become a limiting factor for B2B marketplaces such as Alibaba.com, which allow many smaller and lesser-known manufacturers to participate in global B2B EC. In 2004, the Alibaba Group (the parent company of Alibaba.com) founded Alipay, a third-party payment and escrow service. When businesses pay for orders using Alipay, payment is released only when the buyer has confirmed satisfactory delivery of the goods, reducing the risks for the buyer.

Key Technologies for Enhancing SCM

As is the case with all technologies, SCM is evolving. As discussed previously, one key trend is the development of supplier portals, customer portals, and business-to-business marketplaces, all of which provide an alternative to proprietary supply linkages, such as linkages using electronic data interchange. In addition, new technologies are helping to add greater value to SCM. In this section, we briefly review two technologies that are providing significant benefits to managing supply chains.

EXTENSIBLE MARKUP LANGUAGE. **Extensible Markup Language (XML)** is a data presentation standard first specified by the World Wide Web Consortium, an international consortium of organizations whose purpose is to develop open standards for the Web. XML allows designers of Web documents to create their own customized tags, enabling the definition, transmission, validation, and interpretation of data between applications and between organizations.

As described in the Technology Briefing, Hypertext Markup Language (HTML) uses HTML tags to instruct a Web browser how data on a Web page should be laid out cosmetically on a user's screen. Much like HTML, XML also uses tags, but they go well beyond HTML. XML does not specify any particular formatting; rather, it specifies the rules for tagging elements. An **XML tag** is a label that is inserted into an XML document in order to specify how the document or a portion of the document should be interpreted and/or used. For example, the tags <item_no>...</item_no> would instruct the application reading the XML file that the numbers enclosed in the tags should be interpreted as a product's item number (see Figure 8.10). The application could use this information when displaying a product on a Web page or when updating inventory records. As a result, XML is a powerful tagging system that can be tailored to share

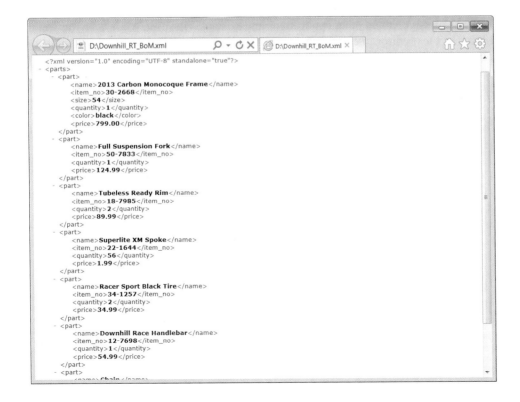

FIGURE 8.10

An XML file for transmitting a bill of materials for a bicycle.
Source: Courtesy of Mozilla

FIGURE 8.11

An XBRL file for sharing Securities and Exchange Commission filings.

Source: Courtesy of Microsoft, Inc.

similar data across applications over the Web. With these advanced data definition capabilities built into Web applications, organizations can then use the Web as the worldwide network for electronic commerce and SCM.

Many people think that XML is on its way to becoming the standard for automating data exchange between business information systems and may well replace all other formats for electronic data interchange. Companies can, for example, use XML to create applications for doing Web-based ordering, for checking on and managing inventory, for signaling to a supplier that more parts are needed, for alerting a third-party logistics company that a delivery is needed, and so on. All these various applications can work together using the common language of XML.

XML is customizable, and a number of variations of XML have been developed. For example, **Extensible Business Reporting Language (XBRL)** is an XML-based specification for publishing financial information. XBRL makes it easier for public and private companies to share information with each other, with industry analysts, and with shareholders. XBRL includes tags for data such as annual and quarterly reports, Securities and Exchange Commission filings, general ledger information, and net revenue and accounting schedules (see Figure 8.11).

XML is not, however, a panacea for SCM. Support for and use of XML is growing rapidly, and most necessary standards and agreements are in place to enable XML-based applications to work seamlessly with all other applications and systems. However, while nearly anyone can learn to use a text editor to create a basic HTML document, XML is far more complex and requires not only knowledge of XML but also expertise in distributed database design and management. Nevertheless, XML holds great promise for managing supply chains by its ability to inject more information into the process.

RADIO FREQUENCY IDENTIFICATION.   Another exciting technology now being used within SCM systems is radio frequency identification (RFID), which is starting to replace the standard bar codes you find on almost every product. RFID is the use of electromagnetic energy to transmit information between a reader (transceiver) and a processing device, or RFID tag.

RFID tags can be used just about anywhere a unique identification system might be needed, such as on clothing, pets, cars, keys, missiles, or manufactured parts. RFID tags can range in size from being a fraction of an inch, which can be inserted beneath an animal's skin, up to several inches across and affixed to a product or shipping container (see Figure 8.12). The tag can carry information as simple as the name of the owner of a pet or as complex as how a product is to be manufactured on the shop floor.

RFID systems offer advantages over standard bar code technologies in that RFID eliminates the need for line-of-sight reading. RFID also does not require time-consuming hand scanning, and RFID information is readable regardless of the entity's position or whether the tag is plainly visible. RFID tags can also contain more information than bar codes. Further, a company can program any information that it wants or needs onto an RFID tag, enabling a vast array of potential uses. Thus, it is possible to retrieve information about an entity's version,

FIGURE 8.12

RFID tags can range in size from being a fraction of an inch up to several inches across.
Source: Albert Lozano-Nieto/Fotolia

origin, location, maintenance history, and other important information, and to manipulate that information on the tag. RFID scanning can also be done at greater distances than can bar code scanning. *Passive tags* are small and relatively inexpensive (starting from 10 cents) and typically have a range up to a few feet. *Active tags,* on the other hand, cost upward of US$5, include a battery, and can transmit hundreds of feet.

COMING ATTRACTIONS

Saving Lives through 3D Bioprinting

When building prototypes or manufacturing parts, companies have traditionally used machine tools to drill, cut, or mill the part out of a solid piece of material. As you can imagine, such traditional forms of machining are not very efficient, often leaving up to 90 percent of a slab of metal (or other material) ready to go in the garbage dump (or, hopefully, to being recycled) on any given day. Recently, 3D printing has become a viable alternative for producing various parts using different materials. 3D printing works by adding successive layers of material onto a surface, thus building a 3D model out of myriad individual slices. In addition to being extremely precise, 3D printing creates significantly less waste. Successful applications of 3D printing range from Airbus using 3D printers to make lighter airplane parts to custom-made prosthetics, benefitting people who have missing limbs by creating prosthetics that exactly fit their personal shape and size. Three-dimensional printing is about to bring about another revolution; this time in the world of medicine, where this new technology could save lives where existing drugs cannot.

At Wake Forest University, 3D printing is being used to print new skin directly onto burn wounds for U.S. troops wounded in Afghanistan; the entire process only takes an hour. It is believed that 3D "bioprinting" will potentially lead to the direct printing of organs that would be ready for implantation. In other words, this innovation has the potential to do away with organ transplants. People would no longer be troubled by long waiting lists for transplants and the limits of age restrictions: every body part that wears out due to age or medical complications, from faces to eyeballs to lungs, could be replaced with relative ease.

Furthermore, the 3D bioprinter promises to save time and money, particularly with drug companies spending billions of dollars each year for clinical trials, many of which fail because cell cultures and animals can react very differently from human tissue. This is where the 3D printing system comes in as a feasible answer to the problem. Since the bioprinter creates skin and organs similar to human tissue, the technology could help drug researchers determine drugs that would fail long before they reach clinical trials.

If the development of 3D bioprinting continues making great strides, uncountable lives around the world will surely benefit from the technology. Statistics provided by Donate Life America show that every day, 18 people die from a lack of available organs for transplants and another name is added to the waiting list every 10 minutes, with more than 100,000 people already needing life-saving organ transplants in the U.S. alone. Then there is the other problem of the rejection of transplanted organs due to incompatibility. The bioprinter is expected to get rid of both problems as its ultimate goal is set to print complete organs for transplants—literally printing and growing a heart for someone through the use of their own cells, just as you saw in movies like *Star Trek*.

Based on:

Fitzwater, R. (2012, March 12). Organovo's 3D bioprinting: A win for pharmaceuticals? *Seeking Alpha.* Retrieved July 9, 2012, from http://seekingalpha.com/article/428421-organovo-s-3d-bioprinting-a-win-for-pharmaceuticals.

Draeger, D. (2012, May 9). Future tech: How 3D printing will change the world. *AlterNet.* Retrieved July 9, 2012, from http://www.alternet.org/visions/155254/future_tech%3A_how_3d_printing_will_change_the_world.

RFID systems offer great opportunities for managing supply chains. For example, airlines are strapped for cash and think a lot about those metal, rolling serving carts that are used on airplanes and that can cost as much as US$1,000 each. "We've heard horrific stories of airlines losing up to 1,500 of these things in three months," says Tony Naylor, vice president of in-flight solutions for eLSG.SkyChefs, a technology provider for the airline catering industry based in Irving, Texas (Edwards, 2003). To keep tabs on their vanishing carts, eLSG.SkyChefs now uses an RFID system with an RFID tag on each cart (LSG, 2010).

Additionally, virtually all major retailers are adopting RFID to better manage their supply chains, as are governments for tracking military supplies and weapons, drug shipments and ingredients (i.e., for eliminating counterfeit drugs), and citizens with RFID chips on passports. While RFID's deployment is growing rapidly, the systems are still relatively expensive, there isn't yet a clear set of data standards, and radio frequencies allocated to RFID differ between countries. Fortunately, these hurdles are being overcome by cooperation between vendors and regulating authorities. In any event, RFID is clearly a valuable new technology for managing supply chains.

http://goo.gl/YRCwJ

CUSTOMER RELATIONSHIP MANAGEMENT

With the changes introduced by the Web, in most industries a company's competition is simply a mouse click away. It is increasingly important for companies not only to generate new business but also to attract repeat business from existing customers. This means that to remain competitive, companies must keep their customers satisfied. In today's highly competitive markets, customers hold the balance of power because, if they become dissatisfied with the levels of customer service they are receiving, they have many alternatives readily available. The global nature of the Web has affected companies worldwide in virtually all industries. An economic transformation is taking place, shifting the emphasis from conducting business transactions to managing relationships. If a company successfully manages the relationship with a customer—satisfying them and solving their problems—the customer is less price sensitive. Hence, leveraging and managing customer relationships is equally as important as product development. Indeed, customer relationship management systems often collect data that can be mined to discover the next product line extension that consumers covet.

The Internet, Web 2.0, and social media have tremendously changed the way organizations need to interact with their customers. Some researchers argue that we have moved from the Internet age to the "age of the customer" (Bernoff et al., 2011). The age of the customer is characterized by customers being part of social circles, and being increasingly empowered by social media (see Figure 8.13). For example, customers have much more access to information from various sources; at the same time, customers' word of mouth has a much wider reach through social media such as blogs, Twitter, or Facebook; this can pose tremendous challenges for organizations trying to present and maintain a positive public image, as unmonitored information can have huge negative impacts, and monitoring and participating in ongoing conversations can be an important part of shaping public opinion. In addition, companies face significant changes to the traditional competitive forces (see Chapter 2, "Gaining Competitive

FIGURE 8.13

Today's empowered customers have many ways to obtain and spread information and opinions about companies.

Advantage Through Information Systems"). For example, the Internet has freed customers from having to purchase goods locally, and has thus lowered the barriers to entry for potential rivals. Similarly, many products have been replaced or marginalized by digital substitutes. The power of buyers has increased, as people can quickly and easily find information, reviews, or prices at a competitor's store. At the same time, employees, an important source of supply, have more mobility, and thus have higher power. Last but not least, not only other customers, but also competitors have tremendous amounts of information about a company's products (and its strengths and weaknesses) available at their fingertips, and can more easily predict the company's next strategic move. Thus, businesses have to rethink their interactions with customers; rather than seeing customers as an audience, organizations need to engage in conversations with their customers.

Many of the world's most successful corporations have realized the importance of developing and nurturing relationships with their customers. For example, Starbucks Coffee uses a variety of means to engage with their customers: Like many other businesses, Starbucks uses a loyalty card to entice people to return to its stores; further, Starbucks actively solicits feedback and new product ideas from its customers, not only within the stores but also via its open innovation platform mystarbucksidea.com, and it has one of the most successful fan pages on Facebook. Computer manufacturer Dell, in contrast, has various other needs when interacting with its customers. For instance, when Dell sales representatives are dealing with large corporate clients who routinely make large computer purchases, issues of quantity pricing and delivery are likely to be paramount; whereas when dealing with less computer-savvy individuals ordering a new notebook for personal use, questions about compatibility with an older printer or the ability to run a specific program may be asked. No matter the customer, Dell attempts to provide all customers with a positive experience during both the presale and the ongoing support phases. Large banks and insurance companies, in contrast, are trying to widen and deepen relationships with customers so as to be able to sell more financial services and products, maximizing the lifetime value of each individual customer. Chase Card Services, for example, has more than 4,000 agents, handling 200 million customer calls a year. Being able to increase **first-call resolution**, that is, addressing the customers' issues during the first call, can help to save costs tremendously while increasing customer satisfaction.

Marketing researchers have found that the cost of trying to get back customers who have gone elsewhere can be up to 50 to 100 times as much as keeping a current one satisfied. Thus, companies are finding it imperative to develop and maintain customer satisfaction and widen (by attracting new customers), lengthen (by keeping existing profitable customers satisfied), and deepen (by transforming minor customers into profitable customers) the relationships with their customers in order to compete effectively in their markets (see Figure 8.14). To achieve this, companies need to not only understand who their customers are but also determine the lifetime value of each customer. With the increasing popularity of social media such as social networks, blogs, and microblogs, companies have more ways than ever to learn about their customers.

FIGURE 8.14

Companies search for ways to widen, lengthen, and deepen customer relationships.

Widen
Attract New Customers

Lengthen
Keep Current
Customers Satisfied

Deepen
Transform Minor
Customers into
Profitable Customers

To assist in deploying an organization-wide strategy for managing these increasingly complex customer relationships, organizations are deploying **customer relationship management (CRM)** systems. CRM is not simply a technology, but also a corporate-level strategy to create and maintain, through the introduction of reliable systems, processes, and procedures, lasting relationships with customers by concentrating on downstream information flows. Applications focusing on downstream information flows have three main objectives: to attract potential customers, to create customer loyalty, and to portray a positive corporate image. The appropriate CRM technology combined with the management of sales-related business

KEY PLAYERS

Salesforce.com

Customer Relationship Management (CRM) is a critical component for the success of most medium to large organizations. More and more, CRM is becoming a necessity for many small organizations as well. There are many benefits to CRM, including enhanced productivity, increased revenue, better customer service, and increased customer satisfaction and retention. Not to mention, the benefits of having all customer data in one place that is accessible to all staff members, whether in the office or on the road.

In the not too distant past, to deploy a CRM system, organizations would need to run one or more in-house servers and databases and have the necessary IT admin skills to install and maintain their CRM system. Because of this big investment, CRM remained a tool primarily used by larger organizations. However, given the ease with which systems can be adopted and deployed using a cloud-based software as a service (SaaS) model, this is no longer true. Organizations of any size can easily deploy CRM solutions. The benefits of a cloud-based SaaS deployment are notable, including quicker implementations, lower initial costs, and accelerated return on investment (ROI). The leader in cloud-based SaaS CRM is Salesforce.com, which provides a suite of tools to support all CRM-related needs. Some key capabilities of Salesforce.com's solutions include:

1. **The Sales Cloud:** This application provides sales representatives with a complete customer profile and account history, allows the user to manage marketing campaign spending and performance across a variety of channels from a single application, tracks all opportunity-related data including milestones, decision makers, customer communications, and any other information unique to the company's sales process. Automatic e-mail reminders can be scheduled to keep teams up-to-date on the latest information.

2. **The Service Cloud:** This application allows organizations to create and track service cases coming in from every sales or communication channel, automatically routing and escalating cases as needed. A customer portal also provides customers with the ability to track their own cases 24 hours a day. A social networking plug-in enables the user to join the conversation about their company on social networking Web sites, and provides analytical tools and other services including e-mail services, chatting tools, Google search, and access to customers' entitlement and contracts.

3. **Force.com:** This product provides an infrastructure platform for external developers to create add-on applications that can be integrated into the main Salesforce.com application and are hosted on Salesforce.com's infrastructure.

4. **Chatter:** This application is a real-time collaboration platform for a sales team. The service sends information proactively via a real-time news stream. A sales team can follow coworkers and data to receive broadcast updates about project and customer statuses. The team can also form groups and post messages on each other's profiles to collaborate on projects. Chatter helps organizations to communicate better and provide improved customer service.

5. **AppExchange:** This online marketplace allows customers to buy and sell cloud computing applications, developed by third-party developers and customers, for their Salesforce.com environment. In early 2012, more than 1,400 applications, developed by 450 independent software vendors, were available for purchase.

All Salesforce.com applications are accessible on traditional computers and a variety of mobile devices. These capabilities are transforming organizations of all sizes. Clearly, the advanced capabilities of CRM systems are not just for the big boys anymore.

Based on:

Anonymous. (n.d.). 2012 Compare Best CRM Software. Retrieved July 12, 2012, from http://crm-software-review.toptenreviews.com.

Salesforce.com. (n.d.). Retrieved July 12, 2012, from http://www.salesforce.com/.

Salesforce.com. (2012, July 10). In *Wikipedia, The Free Encyclopedia*. Retrieved July 12, 2012, from http://en.wikipedia.org/w/index.php?title=Salesforce.com&oldid=501590205.

Schnackenburg, P. (2011, November 29). The best CRM suite. Retrieved July 12, 2012, from http://www.zdnet.com/the-best-crm-suite_p2-1339324237.

TABLE 8.2   Benefits of a CRM System

Benefit	Examples
Enables 24/7/365 operation	Web-based interfaces provide product information, sales status, support information, issue tracking, and so on.
Individualized service	Learn how each customer defines product and service quality so that customized product, pricing, and services can be designed or developed collaboratively.
Improved information	Integrate all information for all points of contact with the customers—marketing, sales, and service—so that all who interact with customers have the same view and understand current issues.
Speeds problem identification/resolution	Improved record keeping and efficient methods of capturing customer complaints help to identify and solve problems faster.
Speeds processes	Integrated information removes information handoffs, speeding both sales and support processes.
Improved integration	Information from the CRM can be integrated with other systems to streamline business processes and gain business intelligence as well as make other cross-functional systems more efficient and effective.
Improved product development	Tracking customer behavior over time helps to identify future opportunities for product and service offerings.
Improved planning	Provides mechanisms for managing and scheduling sales follow-ups to assess satisfaction, repurchase probabilities, time frames, and frequencies.

processes can have tremendous benefits for an organization (see Table 8.2). To pursue customer satisfaction as a basis for achieving competitive advantage, organizations must be able to access information and track customer interactions throughout the organization regardless of where, when, or how the interaction occurs. This means that companies need to have an integrated system that captures information from retail stores, Web sites, social networks, microblogs, call centers, and various other ways that organizations communicate downstream within their value chain. More important, managers need the capability to monitor and analyze factors that drive customer satisfaction (as well as dissatisfaction) as changes occur according to prevailing market conditions.

CRM applications come in the form of packaged software that is purchased from software vendors. CRM applications are commonly integrated with a comprehensive ERP implementation to leverage internal and external information to better serve customers. Thus, most large vendors of ERP packages, such as Oracle, SAP, and Microsoft, also offer CRM systems; further, specialized vendors, such as Salesforce.com or Sugar CRM, offer CRM solutions on a software-as-a-service basis. Like ERP, CRM applications come with various features and modules. Management must carefully select a CRM application that will meet the unique requirements of their business processes.

Companies that have successfully implemented CRM can experience greater customer satisfaction and increased productivity of their sales and service personnel, which can translate into dramatic enhancements to the company's profitability. CRM allows organizations to focus on driving revenue as well as on reducing costs, as opposed to emphasizing only cost cutting. Cost cutting tends to have a lower limit because there are only so many costs that companies can reduce, whereas revenue generation strategies are bound only by the size of the market itself. The importance of focusing on customer satisfaction is emphasized by findings from the National Quality Research Center, which estimates that a 1 percent increase in customer satisfaction can lead to a threefold increase in a company's market capitalization.

Developing a CRM Strategy

To develop a successful CRM strategy, organizations must do more than simply purchase and install CRM software. The first consideration is whether a comprehensive CRM system is even needed for a company; for example, the closer an organization is to the end customer, the more

FIGURE 8.15

A successful CRM strategy requires enterprise-wide changes.

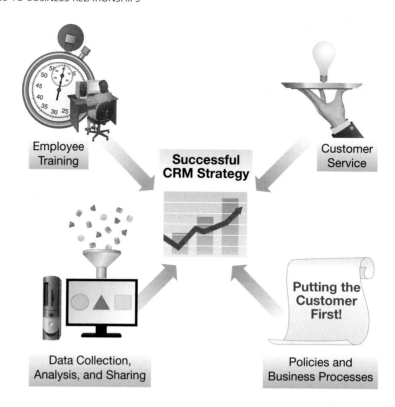

important CRM becomes. Further, companies have to realize that a successful CRM strategy must include enterprise-wide changes, including changes to:

- *Policies and Business Processes.* Organizational policies and procedures need to reflect a customer-focused culture.
- *Customer Service.* Key metrics for managing the business need to reflect customer-focused measures for quality and satisfaction as well as process changes to enhance the customer experience.
- *Employee Training.* Employees from all areas—marketing, sales, and support—must have a consistent focus that values customer service and satisfaction.
- *Data Collection, Analysis, and Sharing.* All aspects of the customer experience—prospecting, sales, support, and so on—must be tracked, analyzed, and shared to optimize the benefits of the CRM.

In sum, the organization must focus and organize its activities to provide the best customer service possible (see Figure 8.15). Additionally, a successful CRM strategy must carefully consider the ethical and privacy concerns of customers' data (discussed later in this chapter).

Architecture of a CRM System

A comprehensive CRM system comprises three primary components:

1. *Operational CRM.* Systems for automating the fundamental business processes—marketing, sales, and support—for interacting with the customer
2. *Analytical CRM.* Systems for analyzing customer behavior and perceptions (e.g., quality, price, and overall satisfaction) in order to provide business intelligence
3. *Collaborative CRM.* Systems for providing effective and efficient communication with the customer from the entire organization

Operational CRM enables direct interaction with customers; in contrast, analytical CRM provides the analysis necessary to more effectively manage the sales, service, and marketing activities. Whereas analytical CRM aids in the development of a company's CRM strategy, operational CRM aids in the execution of CRM strategy; thus, either component alone provides no real benefit for a business. Finally, collaborative CRM provides the communication capabilities of the CRM environment (see Figure 8.16). Next, we examine each of these components.

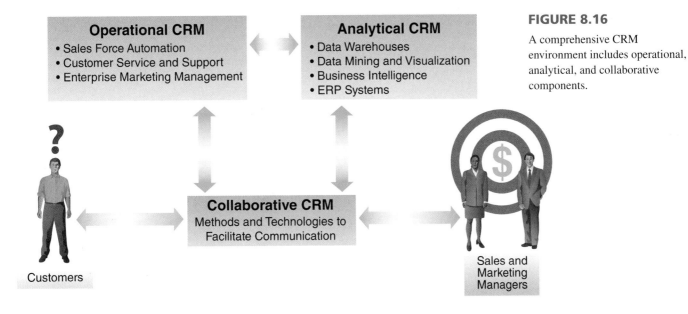

FIGURE 8.16

A comprehensive CRM environment includes operational, analytical, and collaborative components.

OPERATIONAL CRM. **Operational CRM** includes the systems used to enable customer interaction and service. For example, operational CRM systems help create the mass e-mail marketing campaigns wherein each consumer receives an individualized e-mail based on their prior purchase history (although many consumers just consider the unsolicited e-mails nothing but spam). With an effective operational CRM environment, organizations are able to provide personalized and highly efficient customer service. Customer-focused personnel are provided complete customer information—history, pending sales, and service requests—in order to optimize interaction and service. It is important to stress that the operational CRM environment provides *all* customer information regardless of the touch point (i.e., technical support, customer service, and in-store sales, as well as Web site interactions such as downloading content and e-commerce clickstream data). This means that marketing, sales, and support personnel see *all* prior and current interactions with the customer regardless of where it occurred within the organization. To facilitate the sharing of information and customer interaction, three separate modules are utilized (see Figure 8.17).

Sales Force Automation The first component of an operational CRM is **sales force automation (SFA)**. SFA refers to systems to support the day-to-day sales activities of an organization. For example, companies such as Dell have thousands of sales staff in various different countries, working with many different clients. Unless sales personnel and sales managers have an integrated view of Dell's entire sales pipeline, Dell sales staff may be competing with each other for the same contracts, unbeknownst to each other. SFA supports a broad range of sales-related business processes, such as order processing and tracking, managing accounts, contacts, opportunities, and sales, and tracking and managing customer history and preferences (both in terms of product and communication). Together, this can help in creating more accurate sales forecasts and analyzing sales performance.

SFA systems provide advantages for sales personnel, sales managers, and marketing managers. For sales personnel, SFA reduces the potentially error-prone paperwork associated with the selling process. Because all the information is within the system, personnel can more easily handoff work and collaborate; it is also easier to train new personnel. Sales personnel can then use their time more efficiently, and ultimately focus more on selling than on paperwork and other non-selling tasks. Likewise, for sales managers, the SFA system provides tremendous benefits. Most notably, the manager is provided with accurate, up-to-the-minute information on all customers, markets, and sales personnel. This improved information allows better planning, scheduling, and coordination. Ultimately, SFA provides better day-to-day management of the sales function. For example, SFA allows sales managers to track a plethora of sales performance measures, such as the sales pipeline for each salesperson, including rating and probability (see Figure 8.18), revenue per salesperson, per territory, or as a percentage of sales quota, or number of calls per day, time spent per contact, revenue per call, cost per call, or ratio of orders to calls.

FIGURE 8.17

An operational CRM is used to enable customer interaction and service.

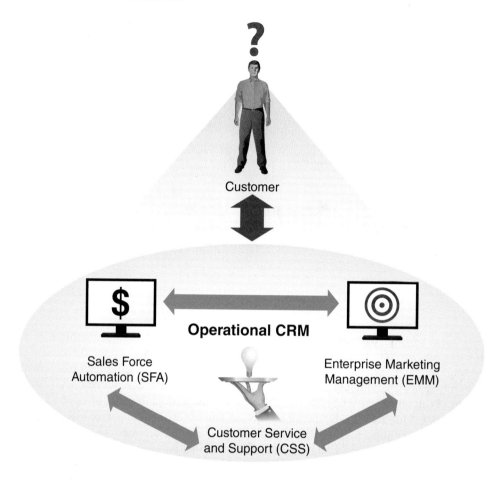

The Power of Mobile CRM

While not all companies deploy sales mobility, those that do outperform those that do not across a myriad of measures...
—Aberdeen Group Benchmark Report (2010)

Mobile CRM allows employees on the go to use mobile devices—smartphones and tablets—to access, update, and interact with customer data wherever they are. The best mobile CRM solutions let mobile workers do everything they could do with CRM at their desktop. CRM mobility, in organizations where the sales staff is frequently in the field, is a critical component to the CRM solution and has a significant impact on sales performance for staff and the company. A recent report by the Aberdeen Group found that companies utilizing mobile CRM solutions had many benefits, including:

- Better year-over-year revenue growth
- Increased customer renewals
- Increased deal size
- Increased CRM user adoption
- Higher sales team quota attainment
- Lower personnel turnover

CRM is one of the hottest software investments for organizations of all sizes. In 2011, Gartner predicted that CRM spending will increase faster than any other area of application software investment. Much of this investment is focused on providing mobile CRM capabilities so that sales forces can be highly responsive to customer needs.

Based on:

Aberdeen Group. (2010, December 9). Improving sales effectiveness through a mobile sales team. Retrieved July 8, 2012, from http://www.aberdeen.com/Press/Details/Sales-Mobility/100.aspx.

Anonymous. (n.d.). About mobile CRM. *Tendigits*. Retrieved July 8, 2012, from http://www.tendigits.com/about-mobile-crm.html.

Anonymous. (n.d.). Mobile CRM report. *Tendigits*. Retrieved July 8, 2012, from http://www.tendigits.com/aberdeen-report.html.

Robb, D. (2011, March 17). Top ten mobile CRM apps. *Enterprise-Today*. Retrieved July 8, 2012, from http://www.enterpriseappstoday.com/crm/top-ten-mobile-crm-apps.html.

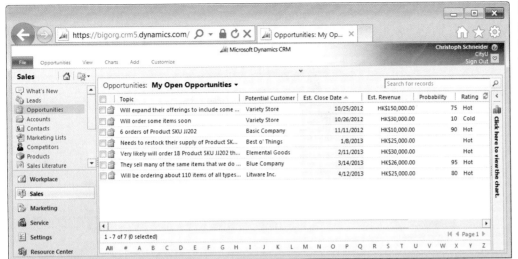

FIGURE 8.18

SFA allows sales managers to track sales performance.
Source: Courtesy of Microsoft, Inc.

Similarly, sales managers can obtain other useful information such as number of lost customers per period or cost of customer acquisition; product-related information such as margins by product category, customer segment, or customer; or percentage of goods returned, number of customer complaints, or number of overdue accounts. All of these measures aid in assessing sales performance and detecting potential problems in certain regions, or issues with product or service quality.

Finally, SFA improves the effectiveness of the marketing function by providing an improved understanding of market conditions, competitors, and products. This enhanced information will provide numerous advantages for the management and execution of the marketing function. Specifically, SFA aids in gaining a better understanding of markets, segments, and customers, as well as competitors and the overall economic structure of the industry. Such broad and deep understanding of the competitive landscape can help organizations assess their unique strengths and weaknesses, thereby facilitating new product development and improving strategic planning.

In sum, the primary goals of SFA are to better identify potential customers, streamline selling processes, and improve managerial information. Next, we examine systems for improving customer service and support.

Customer Service and Support The second component of an operational CRM system is **customer service and support (CSS)**. CSS refers to systems that automate service requests, complaints, product returns, and information requests. In the past, organizations had *help desks* and *call centers* to provide customer service and support. Today, organizations are deploying a **customer interaction center (CIC)**, using multiple communication channels to support the communication preferences of customers, such as the Web, the company's Facebook page, industry blogs, face-to-face contact, telephone, and so on (see the section "Collaborative CRM" later in this chapter). The CIC utilizes a variety of communication technologies for optimizing customers' communications with the organization. For example, automatic call distribution systems forward calls to the next available person; while waiting to connect, customers can be given the option to use key or voice response technologies to check account status information. Southwest Airlines improves customer service by using "virtual hold technology," where customers can choose to stay on the line or be called back when the next agent is available; this helped to save almost 25 million toll minutes in 2009, and reduced the number of abandoned calls, which provides additional opportunities for ticket sales and signals increased customer satisfaction. In essence, the goal of the CSS is to provide great customer service—anytime, anywhere, and through any channel—while keeping service and support costs low. For example, many CICs use powerful self-service diagnostic tools that guide consumers to their needed information. Customers can log service requests or gain updates to pending support requests using a variety of self-service or assisted technologies (see Figure 8.19). Successful CSS systems enable faster response times, increased first-contact resolution rates, and improved productivity of service and support personnel. Managers can utilize digital dashboards to monitor key metrics such as first-contact resolution and service personnel utilization, which allows for improved

FIGURE 8.19

A CIC allows customers to use a variety of self-service and assisted technologies to interact with the organization.

management of the service and support functions (see Chapter 6, "Enhancing Business Intelligence Using Information Systems").

Enterprise Marketing Management The third component of an operational CRM system is **enterprise marketing management (EMM)**. EMM tools help a company in the execution of the CRM strategy by improving the management of promotional campaigns (see Figure 8.20). Today, many companies use a variety of channels (such as e-mail, telephone, direct mail, Facebook pages and YouTube channels, Twitter status updates, and so on; see Chapter 4, "Enabling Business-to-Consumer Electronic Commerce" and Chapter 5, "Enhancing Organizational Communication and Collaboration Using Social Media") to reach potential customers and drive them to Web sites customized for their target market (based on demographics and lifestyle). Using EMM tools can help integrate those campaigns such that the right messages are sent to the right people through the right channels. This necessitates that customer lists are managed carefully to avoid targeting people who have opted out of receiving marketing communication and to be able to personalize messages that can deliver individualized attention to each potential customer. At the same time, EMM tools provide extensive analytical capabilities that can help to analyze the effectiveness of marketing campaigns and can help to efficiently route sales leads to the right salespeople, leading to higher conversion rates.

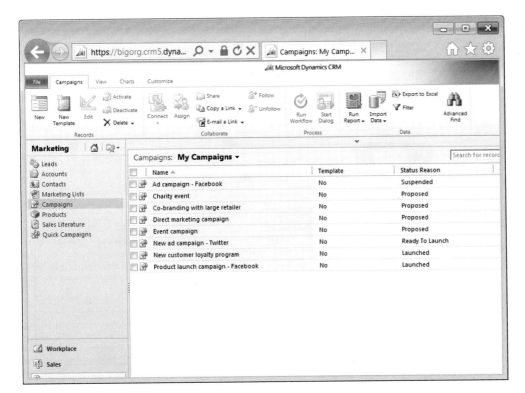

FIGURE 8.20

CRM systems allow for managing various types of promotional campaigns.
Source: Courtesy of Microsoft, Inc.

ANALYTICAL CRM. **Analytical CRM** focuses on analyzing customer behavior and perceptions in order to provide the business intelligence necessary to identify new opportunities and to provide superior customer service. Organizations that effectively utilize analytical CRM can more easily customize marketing campaigns from the segment level to even the individual customer. Such customized campaigns help to increase cross- or up-selling (i.e., selling more profitable products or identifying popular bundles of products and services tailored to different market segments) as well as retain customers by having accurate, timely, and personalized information. Analytical CRM systems are also used to spot sales trends by ZIP code, state, and region as well as specific target markets within those areas.

Key technologies within analytical CRM systems include data mining, decision support, and other business intelligence technologies that attempt to create predictive models of various customer attributes (see Chapter 6). These analyses can focus on enhancing a broad range of customer-focused business processes; for example, marketing campaign analysis can help organizations to optimize campaigns by improving customer segmentation and sales coverage, as well as by optimizing the use of each customer's preferred communication channels. Similarly, analytical CRM tools can help in analyzing customer acquisition and retention. In addition, analytical CRM tools help in pricing optimization by building models of customer demand, taking into consideration not only factors such as product usage and customer satisfaction, but also price, quality, and satisfaction of competitors' products or services.

Once these predictive models are created, they can be delivered to marketing and sales managers using a variety of visualization methods, including digital dashboards and other reporting methods (see Figure 8.21). To gain the greatest value from analytical CRM applications, data collection and analysis must be continuous so that all decision making reflects the most accurate, comprehensive, and up-to-date information.

One goal that customer-focused organizations are constantly striving for is to get a 360-degree view of the customer so as to be able to maximize the outcomes of sales and marketing campaigns and to identify the most profitable customers. In order to get the most complete picture of a sales prospect or a customer, marketers have to tie together information from various sources, such as demographic information provided when signing up for a loyalty card program, the customer's address, purchase and contact history, clickstream data on the company's Web site, and so on. In addition to the data captured when interacting with a person, marketers can complete the picture with publicly available information posted on the person's Facebook or LinkedIn profile or the person's Twitter updates. Unfortunately, many

FIGURE 8.21

Digital dashboards help to visualize key CRM performance metrics.
Source: Courtesy of Microsoft, Inc.

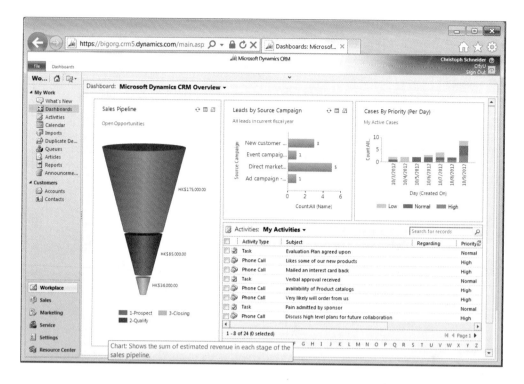

people have various different online identities (e.g., for different social networks), use multiple e-mail addresses, and access Web sites from different computers (see Figure 8.22). Analytical CRM systems can help merge different identities by using fuzzy logic–based algorithms (see Chapter 6) to identify multiple records belonging to the same person.

Finally, social media applications enable customers to interact with each other in various ways, greatly facilitating the spreading of information as well as misinformation. Monitoring such conversations can help organizations to measure public perceptions, and participating can help organizations to keep customers satisfied and maintain a positive brand image. For example, monitoring online conversations can help to assess customer sentiments, find out what people really think about a product, and discover ways for improving a product: Whereas most customers do not bother to fill out a survey about a product, they are very likely to voice their thoughts on Facebook or Twitter if they are very satisfied or very dissatisfied with a product. Similarly, many people participate in online discussion forums related to a product or company, and the company should monitor the conversation and step in when needed (e.g., when customers have questions about a product, but no other customer answers within a certain time frame).

FIGURE 8.22

Many people interact with a company in many different ways using various online identities.

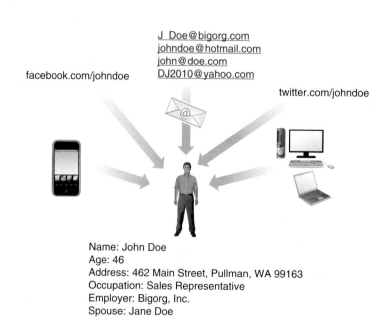

Name: John Doe
Age: 46
Address: 462 Main Street, Pullman, WA 99163
Occupation: Sales Representative
Employer: Bigorg, Inc.
Spouse: Jane Doe

ETHICAL DILEMMA

CRM: Targeting or Discriminating?

CRM systems could be called a marketer's dream because they promise companies the capability of getting to know their customers and at the same time maximize the benefit gained from every customer. Through the use of sophisticated features, CRM software can let companies take a close look at customer behavior, drilling down to smaller and smaller market segments. Once so segmented, customers can be targeted with specific "special offers" or promotions. For the company, this process reaps the greatest returns from marketing efforts since only those customers are targeted who are likely to respond to the marketing campaign.

From a customer's perspective, CRM systems seem like a great idea. Finally, you stop receiving advertisements for reams of stuff that don't interest you. But what if a company uses its CRM software in a more discriminating way? Where do companies draw the line between using CRM data to offer certain clients customized deals and unethically discriminating against other customers? For example, banks, which often segment their customers according to their creditworthiness, might use this credit risk data to target customers having a low credit rating. Although these customers are more risky for the banks, the higher fees and interest charged for credit make these customers especially lucrative.

A fine line exists between using CRM data for targeted marketing purposes and using such data to take advantage of certain groups. Some companies sell the customer data they have collected through CRM programs—without customer knowledge or consent. For example, a card found in the wallet of almost every person in Hong Kong is the "Octopus Card,"

an RFID-based stored value card that is accepted throughout Hong Kong's vast public transport network but can also be used to make payments at convenience and grocery stores, vending machines, or parking meters, and can even be used as a keyless access card for residential buildings. Along with these features, Octopus Cards (the company managing this card) offers a reward program where users have to provide various personal details when signing up and can, in return, earn rewards at participating merchants; the merchants benefit from a widely accepted rewards program and can provide tailored offers to their clients. In 2010 it became known that the operator of the card system had, despite claims to the contrary, sold customer data to the insurance company CIGNA, resulting in a public relations nightmare for Octopus Cards. Such data sharing alliances benefit from the use of CRM programs, and they are legal—but are they ethical?

Based on:

Chan, S. (2010, July 27). Tentacle of lies. *The Standard*. Retrieved July 8, 2012, from http://www.thestandard.com.hk/news_detail.asp?pp_cat=30&art_id=101004&sid=29033262&con_type=3&d_str=20100727&sear_year=2010.

Jourdier, A. (2002, May 1). Privacy & ethics: Is CRM too close for comfort? *CIO.com*. Retrieved July 8, 2012, from http://www.cio.com/article/31062/Privacy_Ethics_Is_CRM_Too_Close_for_Comfort_.

Octopus Cards Limited. (2011, April 4). In *Wikipedia, The Free Encyclopedia*. Retrieved July 9, 2012, from http://en.wikipedia.org/w/index.php?title=Octopus_Cards_Limited&oldid=422386365.

Shermach, K. (2006, August 25). Data mining: Where legality and ethics rarely meet. *CRMBuyer.com*. Retrieved July 8, 2012, from http://www.crmbuyer.com/story/52616.html.

Analytical CRM applications such as the Social Networking Accelerator add-on for Microsoft Dynamics CRM help in monitoring and analyzing ongoing conversations on social media sites, helping to spot potential perception issues or to discover trends in customer sentiment (the use of social media for customer relationship management is often referred to as **social CRM**). Needless to say, an organization should have an appropriate social CRM strategy in place and should have clear policies, such as when to step into an online discussion, which (or how many) tweets to reply to, or how to strike a balance between grassroots marketing and deceiving people by posing as casual conversation partners.

Given the rise and importance of social media for reaching out and communicating with customers, many organizations are creating a formal organizational group to engage in social media monitoring. **Social media monitoring** is the process of identifying and assessing the volume and sentiment of what is being said about a company, individual, product, or brand. To collect this information, organizations utilize a variety of tools to track and aggregate social media content from blogs, wikis, news sites, micro-blogs such as Twitter, social networking sites like Facebook, video/photo sharing Web sites like YouTube and Flickr, forums, message boards, blogs, and user-generated content in general. Depending on the goal of the social media monitoring program, a simple tool like Google Alerts might be adequate; to gain deep and timely understanding of evolving customer sentiment, specialized applications that provide sophisticated analyses and full integration with existing CRM applications are available. As organizations increasingly rely on social media, social media monitoring will become a central part of analyzing and understanding evolving market trends and customer sentiments. In addition, social media monitoring helps in identifying the "influencers" who are most likely to share their views through social media. Even though social media allow anybody to voice their opinions, not everyone does so. For example, while many people regularly read blogs, only a few people write their own blogs; yet, these blogs can be influential in swaying others' opinions. The importance of social media monitoring is exemplified by large companies such as Dell, which established a Social Media Listening Command Center, where a number of full-time staff monitor over 22,000 daily posts made about the company on various social media. Having a dedicated team helps to quickly react to customer complaints or changes in public sentiment about the company, enabling near-real-time communication with the customers through social media.

COLLABORATIVE CRM. **Collaborative CRM** refers to systems for providing effective and efficient communication with the customer from the entire organization. Collaborative CRM systems facilitate the sharing of information across the various departments of an organization in order to increase customer satisfaction and loyalty. Sharing useful customer information on a company-wide basis helps improve information quality and can be used to identify products or services a customer may be interested in. A collaborative CRM system supports customer communication and collaboration with the entire organization, thus providing more streamlined customer service with fewer handoffs. The CIC (as described previously) enables customers to utilize the communication method they prefer when interacting with the organization. In other words, collaborative CRM integrates the communication related to all aspects of the marketing, sales, and support processes in order to better serve and retain customers. Collaborative CRM enhances communication in the following ways:

- *Greater Customer Focus.* Understanding customer history and current needs helps to focus the communication on issues important to the customer.
- *Lower Communication Barriers.* Customers are more likely to communicate with the organization when personnel have complete information and when they utilize the communication methods and preferences of the customer.
- *Increased Information Integration.* All information about the customer as well as all prior and ongoing communication is given to all organizational personnel interacting with the customer; customers can get status updates from any organizational touch point.

In addition to these benefits, collaborative CRM environments are flexible such that they can support both routine and non-routine events.

Ethical Concerns with CRM

Although CRM has become a strategic enabler for developing and maintaining customer relationships, it is not viewed positively by those who feel that it invades customer privacy and facilitates coercive sales practices. Proponents of CRM warn that relying too much on the "systems" profile of a customer, based on statistical analysis of past behavior, may categorize customers in a way that they will take exception to. Additionally, given that a goal of CRM is to better meet the needs of customers by providing highly *personalized* communication and service (such as Amazon.com's recommendations), at what point does the communication get *too* personal? It is intuitive to conclude that when customers feel that the system knows too much about them, personalization could backfire on a company. Clearly, CRM raises several ethical concerns in the digital world (see Chapter 1, "Managing in the Digital World," for a comprehensive discussion of information privacy). Nevertheless, as competition continues to increase in the digital world, CRM will remain a key technology for attracting and retaining customers.

INDUSTRY ANALYSIS

Manufacturing

Regardless of whether you're thinking about a new computer, a TV, an automobile, or a toy for your baby brother, most of today's consumer products have undergone an elaborate design and manufacturing process, and few companies fail to make heavy use of information systems in the process. Traditionally, designers and engineers used large drawing boards to sketch detailed drawings of each component of a product. Today, designers use **computer-aided design (CAD)** software for this task, allowing them to create drawings faster and more accurately, thus cutting down cycle time (i.e., the time from inception to the shipment of the first product) tremendously. At the same time, CAD allows easier sharing of designs and can be used to produce three-dimensional (3D) drawings of a new product. However, although you can create realistic 3D drawings of a new product, people often still prefer holding a physical model in their hands to evaluate it. 3D printing, sometimes known as "fabbing," can greatly speed up the creation of models and an increasing range of finished products. In essence, 3D printers add successive layers of material onto a surface, thus building a 3D model out of myriad individual slices. In fact, some 3D printers even use materials such as titanium, allowing battleships to produce spare parts on an as-needed basis rather than carrying warehouses full of parts. 3D printing is rapidly evolving. For instance, in 2012, Airbus announced that it is exploring the building of future airplanes using giant 3D printers. Such printers would need to be as large as an aircraft hangar; Airbus expects to transition from building small components to the entire plane over the next 40 years.

Engineers use **computer-aided engineering (CAE)** tools to test the designs produced using CAD systems. Whereas traditionally many features of a new product could be tested only after building prototypes, CAE allows for the testing and modification of features before the first prototypes are ever built, resulting in substantial savings of both time and money. For example, almost all automobile manufacturers now use CAE tools to perform tests for wind resistance, noise, vibrations, or simulating crashes or wear and tear. Rather than

having to build prototype after prototype to test different design changes, these are tested on the computer, and the first working prototype is closer than ever to the final model.

Finally, **computer-aided manufacturing (CAM)** is the use of information systems to control the production of the final product. CAM systems take design input from a CAD system and then automatically control the manufacturing of a product's components, ranging from sheet metal presses to the spray painting of a car's exterior by "painting robots." This integration of design, engineering, and manufacturing has reduced manufacturing costs and at the same time improved product quality.

The use of technology doesn't stop there. Inventory planning, job scheduling, or warehouse management are all supported by information systems, often in the form of ERP and SCM systems. Once a product leaves the manufacturer, information systems are being used throughout the distribution of the product, from transportation scheduling to route optimization to improvement of a trucking company fleet's fuel efficiency. Clearly, information systems have changed and will continue to change the process of designing, manufacturing, and shipping products to you.

Based on:

3D printing. (2012, July 12). In *Wikipedia, The Free Encyclopedia.* Retrieved July 12, 2012, from http://en.wikipedia.org/w/index .php?title=3D_printing&oldid=501858773.

Gardiner, B. (2007, November 21). 3-D printers redefine industrial design. *Wired.* Retrieved July 12, 2012, from http://www.wired.com/ gadgets/miscellaneous/news/2007/11/3d_printers.

Groover, M. (2008). *Automation, production systems, and computer-integrated manufacturing* (3rd ed.). Upper Saddle River, NJ: Prentice Hall.

Leberecht, T. (2007, December 17). Trends 2008: Will 3D printing finally go mainstream? *CNET News.com.* Retrieved July 12, 2012, from http://news.cnet.com/8301-13641_3-9835160-44.html.

Olson, P. (2012, July 11). Airbus explores building planes with giant 3D printers. *Forbes.* Retrieved July 12, 2012, from http://www .forbes.com/sites/parmyolson/2012/07/11/airbus-explores-a-future-where-planes-are-built-with-giant-3d-printers.

Key Points Review

1. ***Describe SCM systems and how they help to improve business-to-business processes.*** SCM focuses on improving interorganizational business processes in B2B relationships and has two main objectives: to accelerate product development and to reduce costs associated with procuring raw materials, components, and services from suppliers. Supplier and customers portals provide secure access points for established business partners, allowing organizations to implement JIT and VMI strategies. For smaller organizations, B2B marketplaces, which are operated by third-party vendors, have proven to be extremely valuable for automating supply chains. At the same time, effectively managing the supply chain has become important to avoid the bullwhip effect, effectively manage quality problems, and pursue sustainable business practices. SCM systems consist of SCP, SCE, and supply chain visibility and analytics components. SCP

involves the development of various resource plans to support the efficient and effective production of goods and services. SCE puts the SCP into motion and reflects the processes involved in improving the collaboration of all members of the supply chain—suppliers, producers, distributors, and customers. SCE involves the management of three key elements of the supply chain: product flow, information flow, and financial flow. Supply chain visibility and analytics help in foreseeing the impacts of external events and monitoring the performance of the supply chain to address performance issues. When developing an SCM strategy, an organization must consider a variety of factors that will affect the efficiency and effectiveness of the supply chain. Specifically, organizations must match their overall supply chain strategy to their overall competitive strategy to reap the greatest benefits. SCM is continuously advancing, using technologies such as XML and RFID.

2. *Describe CRM systems and how they help to improve the activities involved in promoting and selling products to customers as well as providing customer service and nourishing long-term relationships.* CRM is a corporate-level strategy to create and maintain lasting relationships with customers by concentrating on downstream information flows through the introduction of reliable systems, processes, and procedures. Applications focusing on downstream information flows have three main objectives: to attract potential customers, to create customer loyalty, and to portray a positive corporate image. Social media applications have not only introduced various ways to communicate with customers, but have also brought about challenges for companies trying to portray a positive brand image. To develop a successful CRM strategy, organizations must do more than simply purchase and install CRM software; they must also make changes to policies and business processes, customer service, employee training, and data utilization. A CRM consists of three primary components: operational CRM, analytical CRM, and collaborative CRM. Operational CRM focuses on activities that deal directly with customers and includes modules such as SFA, customer service and support, and EMM. Analytical CRM focuses on activities that aid managers in analyzing the sales and marketing functions as well as monitoring ongoing conversations in social media. Finally, collaborative CRM provides effective communication capabilities within the organization and externally with customers. When implementing a CRM strategy, organizations have to be sure to carefully consider ethical concerns associated with profiling customers or treating them in ways they may object to.

Key Terms

analytical CRM   363
bullwhip effect   344
business-to-business marketplace   341
collaborative CRM   366
computer-aided design (CAD)   367
computer-aided engineering (CAE)   367
computer-aided manufacturing (CAM)   367
customer interaction center (CIC)   361
customer portal   341
customer relationship management (CRM)   356
customer service and support (CSS)   361
Electronic Data Interchange (EDI)   340

enterprise marketing management (EMM)   362
Extensible Business Reporting Language (XBRL)   352
Extensible Markup Language (XML)   351
financial flow   348
first-call resolution   355
information flow   348
just-in-time (JIT)   343
operational CRM   359
portal   340
product flow   348
radio frequency identification (RFID)   352
RFID tag   352

sales force automation (SFA)   359
social CRM   365
social media monitoring   365
supplier portal   340
supply chain   339
supply chain analytics   348
supply chain effectiveness   349
supply chain efficiency   349
supply chain execution (SCE)   347
supply chain management (SCM)   345
supply chain planning (SCP)   347
supply chain visibility   348
supply network   339
vendor-managed inventory (VMI)   344
vertical market   341
XML tag   351

Review Questions

1. What are upstream suppliers and downstream suppliers? Describe their roles in supply chain systems.
2. Contrast B2B portals with B2B marketplaces.
3. What do you understand by just-in-time production and how it is different from vendor-managed inventory?
4. Explain how effectively managing the supply chain can help an organization be a responsible social citizen.
5. How does SCP differ from SCE?
6. How does supply chain visibility help an organization react to external events?
7. Contrast supply chain effectiveness and supply chain efficiency.
8. What is XML, and how does it impact SCM?
9. List four key processes of SCP.

10. How does CRM differ from SCM?
11. List some of the key functions of the supply chain management system that help an organization to optimize their supply networks.
12. What do you understand by sales force automation? How does it help in developing CRM?
13. Contrast operational and analytical CRM.
14. What is mobile CRM and what are its benefits?

Self-Study Questions

1. Which of the following is commonly used to refer to the producers of supplies that a company uses?
   A. procurement
   B. sales force
   C. supply network
   D. customers

2. Under a VMI model, _____ .
   A. a manufacturer has to signal restocking quantities to the supplier
   B. the suppliers to a manufacturer manage the manufacturer's inventory levels based on preestablished service levels
   C. the vendor has access only to stock levels
   D. stockout situations are more likely to occur

3. The bullwhip effect refers to _____ .
   A. contract penalties resulting from a supplier's inability to deliver raw materials on time
   B. small forecasting errors at the end of the supply chain causing massive forecasting errors farther up the supply chain
   C. pressure to use a specific SCM system by a company in a supply chain
   D. rising stock values due to effective SCM practices

4. Which type of flow does SCE not focus on?
   A. procurement flow
   B. product flow
   C. information flow
   D. financial flow

5. RFID tags can be used for _____ .
   A. tracking military weapons
   B. eliminating counterfeit drugs
   C. tracking passports
   D. all of the above

6. A comprehensive CRM system includes all but which of the following components?
   A. operational CRM
   B. analytical CRM
   C. diagnostic CRM
   D. collaborative CRM

7. SFA is most closely associated with what?
   A. operational CRM
   B. analytical CRM
   C. cooperative CRM
   D. collaborative CRM

8. All the following are channels used for promotional campaigns except _____ .
   A. Twitter
   B. telephone
   C. direct mail
   D. all of the above are used

9. A metric for being able to quickly resolve customers' issues is called _____ .
   A. customer satisfaction and complaint management
   B. customer communication optimization
   C. virtual-hold technology
   D. first-call resolution

10. Categorizing customers based on statistical analysis of past behavior is _____ .
    A. illegal
    B. a common but sometimes ethically questionable business practice
    C. ethical and a common business practice
    D. technically impossible

Answers are on page 371.

Problems and Exercises

1. Match the following terms with the appropriate definitions:
   i. JIT
   ii. Supply chain efficiency
   iii. Supply chain
   iv. Supply chain visibility
   v. CRM
   vi. CIC
   vii. SCM
   viii. VMI
   ix. CAM
   x. RFID

   a. The ability not only to track products as they move through the supply chain but also to foresee external events
   b. The use of information systems to control production processes
   c. The use of electromagnetic energy to transmit information between a reader (transceiver) and a processing device, used to replace bar codes and bar code readers
   d. The extent to which a company's supply chain is focusing on minimizing procurement, production, and transportation costs
   e. An SCM innovation that optimizes ordering quantities such that parts or raw materials arrive just when they are needed for production
   f. Applications that help to create and maintain lasting relationships with customers by concentrating on the downstream information flows
   g. Commonly used to refer to the network of producers of supplies that a company uses
   h. A business model in which the suppliers to a manufacturer (or retailer) manage the manufacturer's (or retailer's) inventory levels based on preestablished service levels
   i. A part of operational CRM that provides a central point of contact for an organization's customers
   j. Applications that help to improve interorganizational business processes to accelerate product development and innovation and to reduce costs

2. Find an organization that you are familiar with and determine how it manages its supply chain. Is the company effective in managing the supply chain, or does it need closer integration and collaboration with its suppliers?

3. Identify a service sector organization in your area and study its supply chain model. Identify its upstream and downstream suppliers. Have they implemented any SCM solution?

4. Search the Web for companies using sustainable SCM practices. Are those attempts convincing? Why or why not? Under what circumstances would such practices influence your purchasing decisions?

5. Analyze the supply chain of your favorite electronic gadget and compare this with the supply chain of your favorite pair of jeans. How do the supply chains differ? What are potential reasons for this?

6. Discuss how companies are using the power of social media sites like Facebook, LinkedIn, and Twitter to build relationships with their customers.

7. Choose a company you are familiar with and examine how efficiently or effectively it has designed the procurement, production, and transportation aspects of its business.

8. What applications other than those mentioned in the chapter are there for RFID tags? What must happen in order for the use of RFID to become more widespread?

9. Assume you are a sales manager. What sales performance measures would you want the CRM system to provide you in order to better manage your sales force? For each measure, describe how you would use it and at what interval you would need to update this information.

10. Find an organization that is utilizing CRM (visit vendor Web sites for case studies or industry journals such as *CIO Magazine* or *Computerworld*). Who within the organization is most involved in this process, and who benefits?

11. When you last contacted a company with a product or service request, which contact options did you have? Which option did you choose, and why?

12. Search the Web for recent articles on social CRM. What is the current state-of-the-art application for managing customer relationships in social media?

13. Use the Web to visit sites of three companies offering CRM systems. Do these companies sell only CRM systems? What do they have in common? What do they have that is unique?

14. Search on Facebook for your favorite company's page. How does this company present itself in the social media? How does it handle customer conversations? Is the organization's strategy effective?

15. Discuss the ethical trade-offs involved when using large databases that profile and categorize customers so that companies can more effectively market their products. Think about products that are "good" for the consumer versus those that are not.

Application Exercises

Note: The existing data files referenced in these exercises are available on the book's Web site: www.pearsonhighered.com/valacich.

Spreadsheet Application:
Tracking Web Site Visits at Campus Travel

Campus Travel has recently started selling products on the Internet; the managers are eager to know how the company's Web site is accepted by the customers. The file CampusTravel.csv contains transaction information for the past three days, generated from the company's Web server, including IP addresses of the visitors, whether a transaction was completed, and the transaction amount. You are asked to present the current status of the e-commerce initiative. Use your spreadsheet program to prepare the following graphs:

1. A graph highlighting the total number of site visits and the total number of transactions per day
2. A graph highlighting the total sales per day

Make sure to format the graphs in a professional manner, including headers, footers, and the appropriate labels, and print each graph on a separate page (Hint: To calculate the total number of site visits and the total number of transactions, use the "countif" function to count the number.)

Database Application:
Managing Customer Relations at Campus Travel

Not all frequent fliers accumulate large amounts of miles. There are many who never travel for years but have frequent-flier accounts. As manager of sales and marketing, you want to find out how to target these individuals with promotions and special offers. To accomplish this task, you will need to create the following reports:

1. A report displaying all frequent fliers, sorted by distance traveled
2. A report displaying all frequent fliers, sorted by the total amount spent on air travel.

In the file InfrequentFliers.mdb, you find travel data of the members of a frequent-flier program for the year 2012. Prepare professionally formatted printouts of all reports, including headers, footers, dates, and so on. (Hint: Use the report wizard to create the reports; use queries to sum up the fares and distances for each traveler before creating the respective reports.)

Team Work Exercise

Net Stats:
RFID on the Rise

The market for RFID tags, those high-tech devices that let businesses keep track of certain products via radio frequency transmitters and receivers, has been steadily increasing for the past few years. According to a recent research report, the global RFID market is expected to grow at a compound annual rate of 18 percent between 2011 and 2014, generating approximately US$19.3 billion in revenue by the end of 2014. As RFID becomes more mainstream in more industries, the software and services segment of this industry will play an increasingly larger role to help companies better utilize the data collected by these devices. The report also found that the adoption of RFID technology in health care, retail, automotive, consumer packaged goods, government, and transportation sectors has been quite impressive in light of the challenging global economic conditions. While the adoption of RFID technology may require a large start-up investment for organizations, it provides a strong long-term return on investment.

Questions and Exercises

1. Search the Web for the most up-to-date statistics on the forecast and use of RFID technology.
2. As a team, interpret these numbers (or stories). What is striking/important about these findings?
3. As a team, discuss how these findings will look like in 5 years and 10 years. How are things in the U.S. market the same or different across the world? Where are things moving faster/slower? Why?
4. Using your spreadsheet software of choice, create a graph/figure most effectively visualizing the finding you consider most important.

Based on:
Anonymous. (2012, March 13). Global RFID market forecast to 2014. Retrieved August 17, 2012, from http://www.prnewswire.com/news-releases/global-rfid-market-forecast-to-2014-142456625.html.

Answers to the Self-Study Questions

1. C, p. 339	2. B, p. 344	3. B, p. 344	4. A, p. 348	5. D, p. 352
6. C, p. 358	7. A, p. 359	8. D, p. 362	9. D, p. 355	10. B, p. 366

CASE 1   The Battle for the Dashboard

Competition is stiff among electronics manufacturers as they battle for dominance of consumers' living rooms, desktops, and mobile devices. Now the battle extends to the automobile industry. It is clear that the tech industry sees the automobile industry as a key target for bringing new technologies to consumers.

Most recently, Ford Motor Corporation's president and chief executive officer Alan Mulally reported in his address that more than 1 million Ford customers were driving automobiles equipped with its "Sync" technology. The Sync system, co-developed with Microsoft, allows drivers to operate mobile phones and media players with voice controls. In addition, Sync can deliver traffic and direction services, provide auto-911 dialing in the event of an emergency, and give a vehicle health report; it will even read text messages aloud to drivers if they arrive on their mobile phone while driving. Sync also allows drivers to use their smartphones to connect to the Internet, allowing Twitter messages to be read aloud, as well as compose and send replies—all through the voice-enabled, hands-free interface. In addition, users can stream Internet radio from Pandora through the car's sound system; the system is also Wi-Fi capable in addition to having an optional USB port and keyboard plugin jack.

Ford has also released a system called myFord Touch that incorporates all of Sync's features, as well as navigation, information, and data collected by the car, serving as a platform for adding other technologies as they are developed. One such planned development program is called American Journey 2.0, which will allow university students to take data collected by cars' onboard computers and combine it with other Web information in a sort of "mashup" to create new applications. For example, if the system determined that other cars on a particular stretch of road turned on their windshield wipers and fog lights, this information could be delivered to the car's computer through a social networking site to alert people of adverse weather conditions. The goal is to leverage emerging Web 2.0 applications with the data being produced by cars within the Sync network.

Ford is not the only automaker that has brought information and entertainment to the dashboard. In fact, there has been an explosion of high-tech gadgetry appearing in car dashboards of all makes and models. These advances have brought plenty of new conveniences to drivers, but many question how safe they are. Studies have revealed that text-messaging drivers increase their time with eyes off the road by 400 percent, leading to a higher chance that they will not see something on the road that could lead to an accident. Drivers dialing on a cell phone are nearly three times as likely to be involved in an accident as those not dialing on a phone. So what will all these new gadgets, giving drivers a whole new set of possible distractions, mean for safety on the road? Safety advocates worry that increasing the amount of distraction for drivers will result in more crashes and injuries. In 2010, more than 3,000 people died in crashes that were reported to involve a distracted driver and about 416,000 people were injured in the U.S. alone.

With these fears in mind, some new dashboard technology has been designed to enhance driver safety. For example, Mercedes has a feature called "Attention-Assist," which monitors more than 70 streams of sensor data about the driver, looking for actions that might indicate that they are beginning to doze at the wheel. The system will warn these sleepy drivers that it's time to take a break with a flashing coffee cup and an audible warning.

Safety concerns aside, many cars already incorporate many of the electronics consumers (and drivers) have grown to love, such as the Global Positioning System, TV screens, touch-screen monitors, smartphone-enabled ports, hands-free mobile dialing, and automated park assist systems. Coming soon are cars that talk to each other and cars that drive themselves. Cars of the near future will contain electronic sensors to alert drivers to objects in the road ahead (or behind if the vehicle is in reverse), and vehicle-to-vehicle transponder systems will let other cars know when conditions are changing, as when one car in a row of cars is braking. Electronics will also eventually keep cars spaced appropriately during highway driving, make cars obey all traffic signals, and allow cars to communicate with highway information centers along main routes. One good example of such technology in operation is Google's Driverless Car project. As of 2012, Google has tested several vehicles equipped with the system, driving more than 250,000 miles without any human intervention in a variety of terrain and driving conditions, and the use of Google's self-driving cars has been approved in the state of Nevada.

As the electronics and auto industries merge, the technology-dominated home and workplace environments will no longer be separate from the automobile environment. According to Larry Burns, head of research and development at General Motors, "Consumers don't want to have a different experience when they're in their car versus when they're outside their car, so I think that tying in with consumer electronics is going to be really important for the future of our industry. Connectivity will be mainstream with the auto industry."

Questions:

1. How can interorganizational systems help companies like General Motors better manage supplier and customer relationships, especially as the automobile industry is transformed?
2. Which capabilities of interorganizational systems will be most critical for manufacturing or selling the cars of the future?
3. What capabilities would you like to see in the car of the future?

Based on:

Barrett, L. (2010, January 7). CES 2010: Ford promises a smarter digital dashboard. *InternetNews.com*. Retrieved July 12, 2012, from http://itmanagement.earthweb.com/entdev/article.php/3857151/CES-2010-Ford-Promises-a-Smarter-Digital-Dashboard.htm.

Ford Sync. (2012, July 7). In *Wikipedia, The Free Encyclopedia*. Retrieved July 12, 2012, from http://en.wikipedia.org/w/index.php?title=Ford_Sync&oldid=501073311.

Google driverless car. (2012, June 19). In *Wikipedia, The Free Encyclopedia*. Retrieved July 12, 2012, from http://en.wikipedia.org/w/index.php?title=Google_driverless_car&oldid=498312405.

Hartley, M. (2008, January 9). The battle for the dashboard. *The Globe and Mail*. Retrieved July 12, 2012, from http://www.theglobeandmail.com/news/technology/article658735.ece.

MyFord Touch. (2012, July 5). In *Wikipedia, The Free Encyclopedia*. Retrieved July 12, 2012, from http://en.wikipedia.org/w/index.php?title=MyFord_Touch&oldid=500802913.

National Highway Traffic Safety Administration. (2012). Key facts and statistics. Retrieved August 17, 2012, from http://www.distraction.gov.

Vance, A., & Richtel, M. (2010, January 6). Despite risks, Internet creeps onto car dashboards. *The New York Times*. Retrieved on July 12, 2012, from http://www.nytimes.com/2010/01/07/technology/07distracted.html.

CASE 2   CRM 2.0

Organizations are attempting to learn more about customers' needs and behaviors in order to widen, lengthen, and deepen their relationships with them. CRM is a broadly recognized and implemented methodology for managing an organization's interactions with its customers and potential clients. It involves the use of technology for organizing and automating a number of organizational activities, such as marketing, customer service, tech support, and, most often, sales.

Visualizing CRM as just technology, however, is the wrong way to think about it; technology is merely one of the tools that enable CRM. CRM is a customer-centric business philosophy that helps organizations bring together information about their products, services, customers, and the market forces that are driving them. Data are gathered and aggregated from as many internal and external sources as possible to give an actual, real-time picture of the customer base. CRM allows an organization to provide better customer service, discover new customers, sell products more effectively, and simplify marketing and sales processes. Although there are many facets, the following are some core CRM components:

- CRM helps an organization enable its marketing departments to identify and target their best customers, manage marketing campaigns, and generate quality leads for the sales team.
- CRM assists an organization in improving its customer accounts and sales management by optimizing information shared across the employee base and streamlining existing processes.
- CRM enables the formation of individualized relationships with an organization's customers, with the aim

of improving customer satisfaction and maximizing profits.
- CRM provides employees with the information and processes necessary to build relationships between the company, its customer base, and distribution partners.
- Once the best and most profitable customers are identified through CRM, organizations can ensure that they are providing them the highest level of service.

In addition to these features, CRM environments support collaboration and communication within the organization. Just as Facebook, LinkedIn, Twitter, and other social media are becoming a preferred way to stay connected to friends and family members, CRM applications are also evolving to reflect the movement toward social media. In fact, CRM pioneer Salesforce.com provides a product called Salesforce Chatter, which provides a similar set of capabilities found on many of the popular social media sites, allowing individuals throughout an organization to collaborate more effectively using methods that have become extremely popular. For instance, with a Web-based interface that looks very similar to Facebook, Chatter allows individuals within organizations to post profiles, provide real-time status updates about themselves or activities, organize groups, monitor feeds, share documents, and so on. Clarence So, senior vice president for Salesforce.com, when talking about how individuals within organizations are working together, states, "Increasingly, instead of using the Web for search, they're using platforms such as Facebook and YouTube. Instead of communicating by e-mail, they're using instant messaging and texts. And instead of accessing the Web from

a desktop, they're turning to smartphones and other mobile devices." Chatter is designed to bring the best collaboration features found on the most popular Web sites into a single collaboration environment, allowing people within an organization to more effectively work together and collaborate. As So adds, "It's a Facebook-like feed interface that lets a user follow objects, which could be fellow employees, a customer record, a project, a document, anything that's an object within Salesforce.com. They can interact with and receive updates on the objects they follow in their Chatter feed." Chatter is also offered for mobile devices such as the iPad, helping to support a mobile CRM strategy.

Interacting with customers via social media, however, still presents many challenges for most organizations that are increasingly finding themselves being left out of conversations that customers are having about them. Traditional CRM communication channels have been built on the telephone and e-mail, but many customers are moving to social media. Strategies for understanding which customers to connect with through social media are still developing, but organizations are moving to embrace the technology via products like Chatter in order to keep pace with ever-changing communication styles. Social media are actually very synergistic with CRM tools, since social media are about interacting with someone on the other end. Organizations will do well to understand that social media are not just about pushing advertising or making announcements, but also about connecting with their customers and building relationships. Expect CRM tools and the sophistication of their use to continue to evolve, transforming CRM into an Enterprise 2.0 technology.

Questions:

1. What role does technology play in CRM? Is CRM mostly about technology or mostly about relationships?
2. What types of communication (e.g., e-mail, texting, Facebook, and so on) methods would you want to have with a company you do business with? Explain.
3. If you were the chief executive officer of a Fortune 500 company, would you be comfortable using social media sites like Facebook or Twitter as part of your CRM strategy? Why or why not?

Based on:

Anonymous. (2010, February 19). What is CRM? *DestinationCRM.com*. Retrieved July 12, 2012, from http://www.destinationcrm.com/Articles/CRM-News/Daily-News/What-Is-CRM-46033.aspx.

Jedras, J. (2010, July 19). Salesforce.com says stage set for cloud 2.0. *itbusiness.ca*. Retrieved July 12, 2012, from http://www.itbusiness.ca/it/client/en/home/News.asp?id=58434.

Lau, K. (2010, March 19). Social CRM's 18 use cases: Altimeter. *NetworkWorld*. Retrieved July 12, 2012, from http://www.networkworld.com/news/2010/031910-social-crms-18-use-cases.html.

Salesforce.com. (2012). Salesforce Chatter. Retrieved July 12, 2012, from http://www.salesforce.com/chatter/overview.

Columbus, L. (2012, April 23). What's hot in CRM applications, 2012. *Forbes*. Retrieved July 12, 2012, from http://www.forbes.com/sites/louiscolumbus/2012/04/23/whats-hot-in-crm-applications-2012.

Vile, D. (2010, July 22). The significance of Salesforce.com's "Chatter." *Computing.co.uk*. Retrieved July 12, 2012, from http://freeform.computing.co.uk/2010/07/the-significance-of-salesforcecoms-chatter.html.

Williams, E. (2006, October 25). CRM. Retrieved July 12, 2012, from http://searchcrm.techtarget.com/definition/CRM.

9

Developing and Acquiring Information Systems

After reading this chapter, you will be able to do the following:

1. Describe how to formulate and present the business case for technology investments.
2. Describe the systems development life cycle and its various phases.
3. Explain how organizations acquire systems via external acquisition and outsourcing.

Preview

As you have read throughout this book and have experienced in your own life, information systems and technologies are of many different types, including high-speed Web servers to rapidly process customer requests, decision support systems to aid managerial decision making, and customer relationship management systems to provide improved customer service. Given this variety, when we refer to "systems" in this chapter, we are talking about a broad range of technologies, including hardware, software, and services. Just as there are different types of systems, there are different approaches for developing and acquiring them. If you are a business student majoring in areas such as marketing, finance, accounting, or management, you might be wondering why we have a chapter on developing and acquiring information systems. The answer is simple: No matter what area of an organization you are in, you will be involved in the systems development or technology acquisition process. In fact, research indicates that spending on systems in many organizations is controlled by the specific business functions rather than by the information systems (IS) department. What this means is that even if your career interests are in something other than information systems, it is very likely that you will be involved in the development and acquisition of systems, technologies, or services. Understanding this process is important to your future success.

Managing in the Digital World:
Microsoft Is "Kinecting" Its Ecosystem

How useful would an iPhone or a Samsung smartphone be without the apps available on different marketplaces? How useful would a blu-ray player be without a large selection of movies available in that format? The value of any device or system does not stand on its own. Instead, it grows with the size of its ecosystem, which refers to the users, application or content developers, sellers, and marketplace that help to increase its popularity. Like a tree standing still in a world without rain, birds, flowers, and other species—a tree that would likely not be able to survive—the iPhone *sans* the "apps" would be much less useful, would trigger much less excitement, and would likely be much less successful in the marketplace. Similarly, Google, Microsoft, and, not surprisingly, Amazon.com are trying to build large ecosystems around their products and services.

In the mobile device industry, these ecosystems are not just based on product or services developed by the original creators, but are instead fueled by a pool of independent developers that work the behind-the-scenes magic to expand the ecosystem's capabilities. This collective expansion in capabilities in turn generates additional marketing buzz and market demand. To create such an expanded ecosystem, a cooperative development approach is the norm, as has been common in many successful software, hardware, and, more recently, consumer electronics marketplaces. This mutually dependent approach is characterized by systems development activities constantly shifting back-and-forth between the big well-known product developers like Apple and Microsoft to small, virtually unknown independent app developers who build creative extensions that broaden market appeal. Indeed, both parties benefit from the initial device development and the mad rush by the independent developers to use their creativity and brainpower to expand the ecosystem. As independent developers provide new applications beyond the imagination of the original developers, market demand for the product grows. For each iteration in a product's lifecycle, the original product developer provides new capabilities, such as enhanced performance or security or entirely new product features. The broader ecosystem responds to these enhancements by identifying new apps to leverage these new capabilities with a hope of further expanding the ecosystem. When product's developers fail to effectively evolve their products, users are often quick to adopt alternative products, creating another ecosystem around another device. One example of an ecosystem evolving around a device is Microsoft's Kinect. We are still in the early stages of the evolution of Kinect's ecosystem, but here is a quick overview of its development.

On November 4, 2010, Microsoft launched the Kinect, a US$150 body motion capture device for the Xbox (see Figure 9.1). A controller-free add-on, the Kinect provided a completely new way of interacting with the device, creating sheer unlimited possibilities for the innovative mind. For instance, some tinkerers saw an affordable, lightweight camera in the Kinect which can capture 3D images in real-time while others saw bright prospects in the Kinect that could be used to control robotics. However, one key element to make these visions reality remained missing: supplementary drivers to capture the data stream generated by the Kinect, so as to to make it work with PCs, Macs, and other devices. Soon after the Kinect's release, hackers started trying to find ways to access and use the device's data stream. Despite the fact that Microsoft threatened to sue those

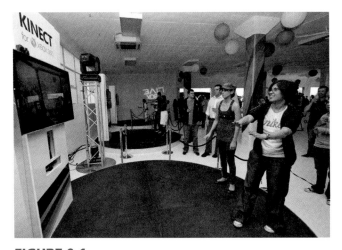

FIGURE 9.1

Microsoft Kinect.
Source: pcruciatti/Shutterstock

who attempted to hack the system, the stakes still ran high. DIY electronics e-tailer Adafruit Industries initially offered a US$1,000 bounty to the first person to pioneer such drivers. Needless to say, Microsoft immediately reacted with additional threats, but Adafruit responded with raising the bounty with every retaliating statement from Microsoft. Within several days, the first hacker won the race to develop drivers and claimed the bounty, which, by that time, had reached US$3,000. The source code of the hack was published under an open source license, and it did not take long before various innovative applications were fast on the way. A Kinect strapped to a Roomba was used to maneuver the robot vacuum cleaner with the wave of a hand. Others used the device to control characters in the game "World of Warcraft" with their bodies, while virtual puppets projected onto a wall were manipulated with hand gestures through the help of the Kinect.

All the excitement pushed Microsoft to get in on the commotion; in June 2011, the company made a U-turn and released an official software development toolkit (SDK), consisting of a set of tools needed to develop applications for the Kinect. As a result, Microsoft's reputation in the open source community improved rapidly. In late 2011, Microsoft even announced the "Kinect Accelerator," a three-month incubation program to support startups in developing innovative Kinect applications. Since that time, a lot of interesting apps have emerged.

Imagine what happens when an electric skateboard is reengineered with a Kinect and a Samsung Windows 8 tablet. Apart from video recognition, speech recognition, location data, and accelerometer data, the user's gestures and movements are transmitted to control the speed of the electric skateboard, which goes up to 32 miles per hour. Just as the iPhone and Android smartphones have gone beyond just being phones, the Kinect has become far more than a just gaming controller, thanks to the innovative ideas from techies around the globe.

After reading this chapter, you will be able to answer the following:

1. How can a company make a business case for/against allowing access to an SDK?

2. What are potential pitfalls if established practices (such as the SDLC) are not followed when developing third-party applications?

3. How is the "open sourcing" of systems development different from traditional outsourcing?

Based on:

Anonymous. (n.d.). Chaotic Moon Labs' Board of Awesomeness. *Chaoticmoon.com.* Retrieved May 28, 2012, from http://www.chaoticmoon.com/labs/board-of-awesomeness.

Anonymous. (n.d.). The Microsoft Accelerator for Kinect. *Microsoft.com.* Retrieved May 28, 2012, from http://www.microsoft.com/bizspark/kinectaccelerator.

Gohring, J. (2011, June 16). Microsoft releases Kinect SDK for PCs. *Networkworld.com.* Retrieved May 28, 2012, from http://www.networkworld.com/news/2011/061611-microsoft-releases-kinect-sdk-for.html.

Tanz, J. (2011, June 28). Kinect hackers are changing the future of robotics. *Wired.* Retrieved May 28, 2012, from http://www.wired.com/magazine/2011/06/mf_kinect/all/1.

Vance, A. (2011, January 13). Microsoft's ambivalence about Kinect hackers. *BusinessWeek.* Retrieved May 28, 2012, from http://www.businessweek.com/magazine/content/11_04/b4212028870272.htm.

MAKING THE BUSINESS CASE

http://goo.gl/0b0A8

Before people are willing to spend money to acquire or develop a new system, or spend more money on an existing one, they want to be convinced that this will be a good investment. **Making the business case** refers to the process of identifying, quantifying, and presenting the value provided by a system.

Business Case Objectives

What does making the business case mean? Think for a moment about what defense lawyers do in court trials. They carefully build a strong, integrated set of arguments and evidence to prove that their clients are innocent to those who will pass judgment on their clients. In much the same way, a manager has to build a strong, integrated set of arguments and evidence to prove that an information system (or any type of investment) is adding value to the organization or its constituents. This is, in business lingo, "making the business case" for a system.

As a business professional, you will be called on to make the business case for systems and other capital investments, or you will have to make the case for a new system or application you may need for your work to improve certain business processes. Thus, as a finance, accounting, marketing, or management professional, you are likely to be involved in this process and will therefore need to know how to effectively make the business case for a system (or other capital expenditures) and need to understand the relevant organizational issues involved. It will be in the organization's best interest—and in your own—to ferret out systems that are not adding value. In these cases, you will need to either improve the systems or replace them. Traditionally, business units turned to IS departments for new systems or applications. Today, business units often directly purchase applications from outside vendors, and expect these applications to function on the infrastructure provided by the IS departments. As more and more applications are purchased from external vendors, organizations have to make sure to go through a proper process in selecting the right applications.

Making the business case is as important for proposed systems as it is for the continued investment in an existing system. For a proposed system, the case will be used to determine whether the new system is a "go" or a "no-go." For an existing system, the case will be used to determine whether the company will continue to fund the system. Whether a new system or an existing one is being considered, your goal is to make sure that the investment adds value, that it helps the firm achieve its strategy and competitive advantage over its rivals, and that money is being spent wisely.

The Productivity Paradox

Unfortunately, while it is easy to quantify the costs associated with developing an information system, it is often difficult to quantify tangible productivity gains from its use. Over the past several years, the press has given a lot of attention to the impact of IS investments on worker productivity. In many cases, IS expenditures, salaries, and the number of people on the IS staff have all been rising, but results from these investments have often been disappointing. For instance, the information and technology research firm Gartner reports that worldwide spending on systems and technologies surpassed US$3.6 trillion in 2012, and is forecasted to exceed US$4.4 trillion by 2016. American and Canadian companies are spending, on average, around 4 percent of company revenues on system-related investments. As a result, justifying the costs for IS investments has been a hot topic among senior managers at many firms. In particular, "white-collar" productivity, especially in the service sector, has not increased at the rate one might expect, given the trillions of dollars spent.

Why has it been difficult to show that these vast expenditures on technologies have led to productivity gains? Have information systems somehow failed us, promising increases in performance and productivity and then failing to deliver on that promise? Determining the answer is not easy. Information systems may have increased productivity, but other forces may have simultaneously worked to reduce it, the end results being difficult to identify. Factors such as government regulations, more complex tax codes, stricter financial reporting requirements (such as the Sarbanes–Oxley Act; see Chapter 10, "Securing Information Systems"), and more complex products can all have major impacts on a firm's productivity.

It is also true that information systems introduced with the best intentions may have had unintended consequences. A paramount example is giving employees access to e-mail and the Internet—now employees are spending excessive amounts of time surfing the Web to check sports scores on the ESPN Web site, to read volumes of electronic junk mail received from Internet marketing companies or from personal friends, post status updates on social networking sites, or use company PCs to download and play software games (see Figure 9.2); recently, it was reported that visits to social networking sites such as Facebook and Twitter cost U.K. firms alone

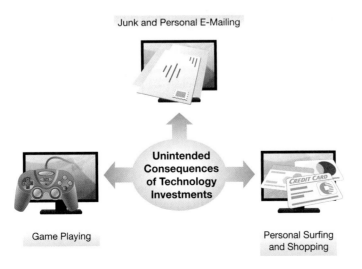

Junk and Personal E-Mailing

Unintended Consequences of Technology Investments

Game Playing

Personal Surfing and Shopping

FIGURE 9.2

Unintended consequences can limit the productivity gains from IS investments.

FIGURE 9.3

Factors leading to the IS
productivity paradox.

approximately US$2.25 billion in lost productivity every year. In these situations, information systems can result in less efficient and less effective communication among employees and less productive uses of employee time than before the systems were implemented. Nevertheless, sound technology investments should increase organizational productivity. If this is so, why have organizations not been able to show larger productivity gains? A number of reasons have been given for the apparent **productivity paradox** of technology investments (Figure 9.3). This issue is examined next.

MEASUREMENT PROBLEMS. In many cases, the benefits of information systems are difficult to pinpoint because firms may be measuring the wrong things. Often, the biggest increases in productivity result from increased **system effectiveness** (i.e., the extent to which a system enables people and/or the firm to accomplish goals or tasks well). Unfortunately, many business metrics focus on **system efficiency** (i.e., the extent to which a system enables people and/or the firm to do things faster, at lower cost, or with relatively little time and effort).

A good example of measurement problems associated with a technology investment is the use of online banking. How much has online banking contributed to banking productivity? Traditional statistics might look at the adoption rate of the service and associated reductions in branch-based services and locations. While informative, such statistics may not work well for evaluating online banking, at least at this point in time. For instance, some older customers may not want to bank online, so a reduction in the number of traditional branches could threaten a potentially large number of very good customers while at the same time inflating the percentage of online banking users (i.e., if the number of traditional banking customers leave the bank because of a reduction of branches, the adoption rate of online customers as a percentage will be increased). So, investing in online banking may be unimportant for an important segment of customers while essential for others. Nevertheless, can you imagine a bank staying competitive without offering online services? Deploying technologies such as online banking has become a *strategic necessity*—something an organization must do in order to survive (see Chapter 2, "Gaining Competitive Advantage Through Information Systems"). The value of necessary investments is often difficult to quantify.

TIME LAGS. A second explanation for why productivity is sometimes difficult to demonstrate for some technology investments is that a significant time lag may occur from when a company makes the investment until that investment is translated into improvement in the bottom line. Let us return to our online banking example. In some markets, it may take years from the first implementation of this new system before the magnitude of benefits may be felt by the organization.

REDISTRIBUTION. A third possible explanation for why IS productivity figures are not always easy to define is that a new type of system may be beneficial for individual firms but not for a particular industry or the economy as a whole. Particularly in competitive situations, new innovations may be used to redistribute the pieces of the pie rather than making the whole pie bigger. The result for the industry or economy as a whole is a wash—that is, the same number of products are being sold, and the same number of dollars are being spread across all the firms.

MISMANAGEMENT. A fourth explanation is that the new system has not been implemented and managed well. Some believe that people often simply build bad systems, implement them poorly, and rely on technology fixes when the organization has problems that require a joint technology/process solution. Rather than increasing outputs or profits, IS investments might merely be a temporary bandage and may serve to mask or even increase organizational slack and inefficiency. Also, as we mentioned in Chapter 1, "Managing in the Digital World," an information system can be only as effective as the business model that it serves. Bad business models can't be overcome by good information systems.

If it is so difficult to quantify the benefits of information systems for individual firms and for entire industries, why do managers continue to invest in information systems? The answer is that competitive pressures force managers to invest in information systems whether they like it or not. Also, for many organizations, information systems are an important source of competitive advantage. You might ask, then, so why waste time making the business case for a system? Why not just acquire or develop them? The answer: Given the vast number of potential systems and technologies that could be selected, a strong business case aids the decision-making process and helps direct resources in more strategic ways.

Making a Successful Business Case

People make a variety of arguments in their business cases for information systems. When managers make the business case for an information system, they typically base their arguments on faith, fear, and/or facts (Wheeler, 2002; Wheeler also adds a fourth "F" for "fiction," and notes that, unfortunately, managers sometimes base their arguments on pure fiction, which is not only bad for their careers but also not at all healthy for their firms.) Table 9.1 shows examples of these three types of arguments.

Do not assume that you must base your business case on facts only. It is entirely appropriate to base the business case on faith, fear, or facts (see Figure 9.4). Indeed, the strongest and most

TABLE 9.1 Three Types of Arguments Commonly Made in the Business Case for an Information System

Type of Argument	Description	Example
Faith	Arguments based on beliefs about organizational strategy, competitive advantage, industry forces, customer perceptions, market share, and so on	"I know I don't have good data to back this up, but I'm convinced that having this customer relationship management system will enable us to serve our customers significantly better than our competitors do and, as a result, we'll beat the competition.... You just have to take it on faith."
Fear	Arguments based on the notion that if the system is not implemented, the firm will lose out to the competition or, worse, go out of business	"If we don't implement this enterprise resource planning system, we'll get killed by our competitors because they're all implementing these kinds of systems.... We either do this or we die."
Fact	Arguments based on data, quantitative analysis, and/or indisputable factors	"This analysis shows that implementing the inventory control system will help us reduce errors by 50 percent, reduce operating costs by 15 percent a year, increase production by 5 percent a year, and pay for itself within 18 months."

BRIEF CASE   The Cold War in Software Patents

In the seventies, when key technologies that made the Internet possible were being developed, intellectual property and patent claims were not as much a big deal. The idea then was to make the technology an international standard, and opening it up for public use. For some time after that, the threat of a "mutually assured destruction" among key technology players like IBM and Microsoft made sure that the danger of a patent war was limited to a controllable state. Come the twenty-first century and a Cold War in technological innovation is formally taking place, especially in the mobile market where the stakes are high. Companies are increasingly fighting patent wars to protect market share and clever technologies and applications.

An overview of the mobile patent wars looks something like this: Microsoft is suing Motorola for video coding, Motorola is counter-suing Microsoft's use of e-mail, instant messaging, and Wi-Fi; on the other side of the game, Google, which faces lawsuits from Oracle for its implementation of the Java programming language in its Android system, has just acquired Motorola to gain access to its patent portfolio. In another story, HTC is fighting against Apple, and Apple has made use of patent rights to prevent Samsung Electronics from selling its Galaxy Tab 10.1 tablet in Australia and Germany. Without hesitation, Samsung has retaliated by attempting to ban iPhone sales in Japan and Australia. In recent times, Apple has won several battles in court; yet, it may be too late to win the war using patents. Whereas companies are still waiting for court decisions about hardware introduced the year before, new generations of phones are already hitting the shelves. In mid-2012, partly due to the growing market penetration of Google's Android operating system, Apple's earnings were below analysts' forecasts. Given the number of patent disputes being fought in courts, many argue that the mobile world is at war, and if the war drags on, the consequences may not look rosy for everyone involved. Further exacerbating the situation are so-called "patent trolls," who buy up patents with the sole intent to sue large companies over the use of their patents.

For companies (and ultimately for consumers as well), these battles come at a huge costs. Over the past few years, the number of mobile handset patent infringement filings to the U.S. courts has grown from 24 cases in 2006 to 84 cases in 2010; the number is expected to continue to rise. Similarly, the direct costs incurred by companies dealing with patent trolls were estimated to be US$29 billion in 2011, a number

that amounts to over 10 percent of the US$247 billion U.S. businesses spent on research and development in 2009. To mobile technology innovators, this is an ugly battle that discourages creativity, and the costs of filing a lawsuit and fighting in court may well result in higher prices that will later be passed on to the consumers, resulting in higher prices, limited functionality, or both. Considering that the U.S. patent system offers inventors a limited monopoly on their ideas for 20 years, consumers may actually find fewer choices in the market the next time they look for a new handset.

Questions:

1. Some companies, referred to as "patent trolls," buy patents from other companies with no intention of using them other than to sue another company for infringing on their recently acquired patented technology. How does this practice help and hurt consumers?

2. Many feel that the patent wars act to destroy small players in the marketplace who cannot afford expensive and lengthy legal battles. What other impacts do the patent wars have on this industry?

Based on:

Anonymous. (2011, October 26). Apple patents touchscreen unlock gestures. *BBC News.* Retrieved May 28, 2012, from http://www.bbc.com/news/technology-15461732.

Anonymous. (2011, November 9). Do the patent wars threaten innovation? *BBC News.* Retrieved May 28, 2012, from http://www.bbc.com/news/technology-15652385.

Bessen, J. E. and Meurer, M. J. (2012, June 28). The direct costs from NPE disputes. *Boston Univ. School of Law, Law and Economics Research Paper No. 12-34.* Retrieved August 3, 2012, from http://ssrn.com/abstract=2091210.

Fuest, B. (2012, July 29). Apples 80er-Fluch und Googles Umsonst-Strategie. *Die Welt.* Retrieved August 3, 2012, from http://www.welt.de/wirtschaft/webwelt/article108407064/Apples-80er-Fluch-und-Googles-Umsonst-Strategie.html.

Kelion, L. (2011, October 23). Mobile phone makers wage war to protect their patents. *BBC News.* Retrieved May 28, 2012, from http://www.bbc.co.uk/news/business-15343549.

Neiger, C. (2012, May 22). What you need to know about mobile patent wars. *SFGate.com.* Retrieved May 28, 2012, from http://www.sfgate.com/cgi-bin/article.cgi?f=/g/a/2012/05/22/investopedia82513.DTL.

Neild, B. (2011, August 16). Google's Motorola deal seen as Cold War arms race. *CNN.com.* Retrieved May 28, 2012, from http://edition.cnn.com/2011/TECH/mobile/08/16/google.motorola.patents/index.html?iref=allsearch.

comprehensive business case will include a little of each type of argument. In the following sections, we talk about each of these types of arguments for the business case.

BUSINESS CASE ARGUMENTS BASED ON FAITH. In some situations, arguments based on faith (or fear) can be the most compelling and can drive the decision to invest in an information system despite the lack of any hard data on system costs, or even in the face of some data that say that the dollar cost for the system will be high. Arguments based on faith often hold that an information system must be implemented in order to achieve the organization's strategy effectively and to gain or sustain a competitive advantage over rivals.

FIGURE 9.4

A successful business case will be based on faith, fear, and fact.

For example, a firm has set as its strategy that it will be the dominant, global force in its industry. As a result, this firm must adopt a variety of collaboration technologies, such as desktop videoconferencing and groupware tools, in order to enable employees from different parts of the globe to work together effectively and efficiently. Similarly, a firm that has set as its strategy that it will have a broad scope—producing products and services across a wide range of consumer needs—may need to adopt some form of an enterprise resource planning system to better coordinate business activities across its diverse product lines.

In short, successful business case arguments based on faith should clearly describe the firm's mission and objectives, the strategy for achieving them, and the types of information systems that are needed in order to enact the strategy. A word of caution is warranted here. In today's business environment, cases based solely on strategic arguments, with no hard numbers demonstrating the value of the information system under consideration, are not likely to be funded.

BUSINESS CASE ARGUMENTS BASED ON FEAR. There are several different factors to take into account when making a business case in which you will provide arguments based on fear. These include a number of factors involving competition and other elements of the industry in which the firm operates. For example, a mature industry, such as the automotive industry, may need systems simply to maintain the current pace of operations. While having the newest systems and technologies available may be nice, they may not be needed to stay in business. However, a company in a newer, expanding industry, such as the mobile phone industry, may find it more important to be on the leading edge of technology in order to compete effectively in the marketplace. Likewise, some industries are more highly regulated than others. In these cases, companies can use technology investments to better control processes and ensure compliance with appropriate regulations. The argument for the business case here would be something like "If we do not implement this system, we run the risk of being sued or, worse, being thrown in jail" (see Chapter 10).

Probably the most important industry factor that can affect technology investments is the nature of competition or rivalry in the industry. For example, when competition in an industry is high and use of the newest technologies is rampant, as it is in the mobile phone industry, strategic necessity, more than anything else, forces firms to adopt new systems. Given how tight profit margins are in this industry, Apple, Samsung, and other manufacturers must use inventory control systems, Web-based purchasing and customer service, and a host of other systems that help them to be more effective and efficient. If they do not adopt these systems, they will likely go out of business. Introduced in Chapter 2, a common way for assessing the level of competition within an industry is the five forces model (Porter, 1979). By assessing the various competitive forces, you can determine which specific technologies may be more or less useful. For instance, in a highly price-competitive market, where buyers have strong bargaining power, investments to reduce production costs might be advantageous. Business case arguments formulated this way sound something like "If we do not implement this system, our competitors are going to beat us on price, we will lose market share, and we will go out of business."

BUSINESS CASE ARGUMENTS BASED ON FACT. Many people, including most chief financial officers, want to see the business case for an information system based on a convincing, quantitative analysis that proves beyond the shadow of a doubt that the benefits of the system will outweigh the costs. The most common way to prove this is to provide a detailed cost–benefit analysis of the information system. Although this step is critical, the manager must remember that there are inherent difficulties in, and limits to, cost–benefit analyses for information systems. To illustrate how a cost–benefit analysis could be used to build a fact-based business case, let us consider the development of a Web-based order entry system for a relatively small firm.

Identifying Costs One goal of a cost–benefit analysis is to accurately determine the **total cost of ownership (TCO)** for an investment. TCO is focused on understanding not only the total cost of *acquisition* but also all costs associated with ongoing *use and maintenance* of a system. Consequently, costs can usually be divided into two categories: **non-recurring costs** and **recurring costs**. Non-recurring costs are one-time costs that are not expected to continue after the system is implemented. These include costs for things such as site preparation and technology purchases. These one-time costs may also include the costs of attracting and training a Webmaster or renovating some office space for new personnel or for hosting the Web servers.

Recurring costs are ongoing costs that occur throughout the life of the system. Recurring costs include the salary and benefits of the Webmaster and any other personnel assigned to maintain the system, upgrades and maintenance of the system components, monthly fees paid to a local Internet service provider, and the continuing costs for the space in which the Webmaster works or the data center where the servers reside. Personnel costs are usually the largest recurring costs, and the Web-based system is no exception in this regard. These recurring expenses can go well beyond the Webmaster to include expenses for customer support, content management, ongoing maintenance, and so on.

The sample costs described thus far are **tangible costs** that are relatively easy to quantify. Some **intangible costs** ought to be accounted for as well, even though they will not fit neatly into the quantitative analysis. These might include the costs of reduced traditional sales, losing some customers that are not "Web ready," or losing customers if the Web application is poorly designed or not on par with competitors' sites. You can choose to either quantify these in some way (i.e., determine the cost of losing a customer) or simply reserve these as important costs to consider outside of—but along with—the quantitative cost–benefit analysis.

Identifying Benefits Next, you determine both **tangible benefits** and **intangible benefits**. Some tangible benefits are relatively easy to determine. For example, you can estimate that the increased customer reach of the new Web-based system will result in at least a modest increase in sales. Based on evidence from similar projects, you might estimate, say, a 5 percent increase in sales the first year, a 10 percent increase the second year, and a 15 percent increase the third year. In addition, you might also include as tangible benefits the reduction of order entry errors because orders will now be tracked electronically and shipped automatically. You could calculate the money previously lost on faulty and lost orders, along with the salaries and wages of personnel assigned to find and fix these orders, and then consider the reduction of these costs as a quantifiable benefit of the new system. Cost avoidance is a legitimate, quantifiable benefit of many systems. Similarly, the new system may enable the company to use fewer order entry clerks or redeploy these personnel to other, more important functions within the company. You could consider these cost reductions as benefits of the new system.

A Web-based system may have intangible benefits as well. Some intangible benefits of this new system might include improvements in customer service resulting from faster turnaround on fulfilling orders. These are real benefits, but they might be hard to quantify with confidence. Perhaps an even more intangible benefit would be the overall improved perception of the firm. Customers might consider it more progressive and customer service–oriented than its rivals; in addition to attracting new customers, this might increase the value of the firm's stock if it is a publicly traded firm. Another intangible benefit might be simply that it was a strategic necessity to offer customers Web-based ordering to keep pace with rivals. While these intangibles are difficult to quantify, they must be considered along with the more quantitative analysis of benefits. In fact, the intangible benefits of this Web-based system might be so important that they could carry the day despite an inconclusive or even negative cost–benefit analysis.

COMING ATTRACTIONS

Microsoft's PixelSense—Any Place, Any Time

If you have ever watched the television show *CSI Miami*, you have seen PixelSense in action (not the actual machine but a demonstration of the technology). A technician uses her fingers to manipulate images—photos, microscope slides, and documents—on a flat horizontal surface in front of her, and she can "throw" the images to a larger screen that displays them vertically. If you thought the concept was still science fiction, you were wrong. The technology exists, and Microsoft introduced it to the public commercially in April 2008 (see Figure 9.5).

With PixelSense, Microsoft reveals, "We can actually grab data with our hands and move information between objects with natural gestures and touch." No keyboards, no mice, just a 30-inch tabletop display where fingers do the walking—and drawing and writing and tapping; moreover, multiple users can simultaneously manipulate data. Users can also place physical objects, like cell phones and even drinks, on the PixelSense to see additional information revealed, such as the features present in the cell phone or the ingredients in a drink. PixelSense uses cameras to sense objects, hand gestures, and touch. User input is processed, and the results are projected on the tabletop surface.

According to Microsoft Chairman Bill Gates, PixelSense computing will eventually become so pervasive that it won't be limited to tabletops and walls. He said, "Our view is that all surfaces—horizontal, vertical—will eventually have an inexpensive screen display capability, and software that sees what you're doing there, so it's completely interactive." Today, in addition to CSI Miami, PixelSense can be found in high-end restaurants and hotel lobbies; this technology has simply been too expensive for most households to afford. In addition to its high cost, current versions of PixelSense are also quite large and bulky, making it difficult to have in a cramped dorm room or apartment.

To overcome these constraints, Microsoft is spending a great deal on research and development to evolve the PixelSense to lower its cost and size. They have also partnered with consumer electronics giant Samsung, releasing the PixelSense 2.0 in early 2012. The new and improved device is thinner, faster, and less expensive. Current research at Microsoft is moving the touch interface beyond a dedicated tabletop, called the Mobile PixelSense project. Prototypes for the Mobile PixelSense can be powered by a laptop computer or even a smartphone, and be projected onto a wall or even your hand. Although the Mobile PixelSense is still just a prototype, it shows that many of the limitations of table-based interfaces can someday be overcome. This technology has numerous potential applications that can transform how we interact with technology.

Based on:

Chang, J. (2011, October 17). Two extremes of touch interaction. *Microsoft Research*. Retrieved on June 3, 2012, from http://research.microsoft.com/en-us/news/features/touch-101711.aspx.

Chen, J. (2008, May 8). Microsoft Surface + Xbox 360 = What? *Gizmodo*. Retrieved June 3, 2012, from http://gizmodo.com/388749/microsoft-surface-%252B-xbox-360-what.

Costa, D. (2007, May 30). Hands on with "Microsoft Surface": The coffee-table PC. *PC Magazine*. Retrieved June 3, 2012, from http://www.pcmag.com/article2/0,1759,2138251,00.asp.

Derene, G. (2007, July). Microsoft Surface: Behind-the-scenes first look. *Popular Mechanics*. Retrieved June 3, 2012, from http://www.popularmechanics.com/technology/industry/4217348.html.

McLaughlin, K. (2010, March 3). Microsoft working on mobile version of surface. *Channelweb*. Retrieved March 18, 2010, from http://www.crn.com/software/223101445.

Microsoft PixelSense. (2012, June 22). In *Wikipedia, The Free Encyclopedia*. Retrieved June 22, 2012, from http://en.wikipedia.org/w/index.php?title=Microsoft_PixelSense&oldid=498887855.

Ulanoff, L. (2012, February 2). Hands on with Microsoft Surface 2. *Mashable.com*. Retrieved June 3, 2012, from http://mashable.com/2012/02/02/microsoft-surface-2-demo.

FIGURE 9.5

The Microsoft PixelSense.
Source: JP5\ZOB/WENN/Newscom

Performing Cost–Benefit Analyses An example of a simplified **cost–benefit analysis** that contrasts the total expected tangible costs versus the tangible benefits is presented in Figure 9.6. Notice the fairly large investment up front, with another significant outlay in the fifth year for a system upgrade. You could now use the net costs/benefits for each year as the basis of your conclusion about this system. Alternatively, you could perform a **break-even analysis**—a type

FIGURE 9.6

Worksheet showing a simplified cost–benefit analysis for the Web-based order fulfillment system.

		2012	2013	2014	2015	2016
Costs						
Non-recurring						
Hardware		$ 20,000				
Software		$ 7,500				
Networking		$ 4,500				
Infrastructure		$ 7,500				
Personnel		$100,000				
Recurring						
Hardware			$ 500	$ 1,000	$ 2,500	$ 15,000
Software			$ 500	$ 500	$ 1,000	$ 2,500
Networking			$ 250	$ 250	$ 500	$ 1,000
Service fees			$ 250	$ 250	$ 250	$ 500
Infrastructure				$ 250	$ 500	$ 1,500
Personnel			$ 60,000	$ 62,500	$ 70,000	$ 90,000
Total costs		$139,500	$ 61,500	$ 64,750	$ 74,750	$110,500
Benefits						
Increased sales		$ 20,000	$ 50,000	$ 80,000	$115,000	$175,000
Error reduction		$ 15,000	$ 15,000	$ 15,000	$ 15,000	$ 15,000
Cost reduction		$100,000	$100,000	$100,000	$100,000	$100,000
Total benefits		$135,000	$165,000	$195,000	$230,000	$290,000
Net costs/benefits		$ (4,500)	$103,500	$130,250	$155,250	$179,500

of cost–benefit analysis to identify at what point (if ever) tangible benefits equal tangible costs (note that break-even occurs early in the second year of the system's life in this example)—or a more formal **net-present-value analysis** of the relevant cash flow streams associated with the system at the organization's **discount rate** (i.e., the rate of return used by an organization to compute the present value of future cash flows). In any event, this cost–benefit analysis helps you make the business case for this proposed Web-based order fulfillment system. It clearly shows that the investment for this system is relatively small, and the company can fairly quickly recapture the investment. In addition, there appear to be intangible strategic benefits to deploying this system. This analysis—and the accompanying arguments and evidence—goes a long way toward convincing senior managers in the firm that this new system makes sense.

Comparing Competing Investments One method for deciding among different IS investments or when considering alternative designs for a given system is **weighted multicriteria analysis**, as illustrated in Figure 9.7. For example, suppose that for a given application being considered for purchase, there are three alternatives that could be pursued—A, B, or C. Let's also suppose that early planning meetings identified three key system requirements and four key constraints that could be used to help make a decision on which alternative to pursue. In the left column of Figure 9.7, three system requirements and four constraints are listed. Because not all requirements and constraints are of equal importance, they are weighted on the basis of their relative importance. In other words, you do not have to weight requirements and constraints equally; it is certainly possible to make requirements more or less important than constraints. Weights are arrived at in discussions among the analysis team, users, and managers. Weights tend to be fairly subjective and, for that reason, should be determined through a process of open discussion to reveal underlying assumptions, followed by an attempt to reach consensus among

Criteria	Weight	Alternative A		Alternative B		Alternative C	
		Rating	Score	Rating	Score	Rating	Score
Requirements							
Web-based HCI	18	5	90	5	90	5	90
Security Capabilities	18	1	18	5	90	5	90
BI Capabilities	14	1	14	5	70	5	70
	50		122		250		250
Constraints							
Software costs	15	4	60	5	75	3	45
Hardware costs	15	4	60	4	60	3	45
Operating costs	15	5	75	1	15	5	75
Ease of training	5	5	25	3	15	3	15
	50		220		165		180
Total	100		342		415		430

FIGURE 9.7

Decisions about alternative projects or system design approaches can be assisted using a weighted multicriteria analysis.

stakeholders. Notice that the total of the weights for both the requirements and constraints is 100 percent.

Next, each requirement and constraint is rated on a scale of 1–5. A rating of 1 indicates that the alternative does not meet the requirement very well or that the alternative violates the constraint. A rating of 5 indicates that the alternative meets or exceeds the requirement or clearly abides by the constraint. Ratings are even more subjective than weights and should also be determined through open discussion among users, analysts, and managers. For each requirement and constraint, a score is calculated by multiplying the rating for each requirement and each constraint by its weight. The final step is to add up the weighted scores for each alternative. Notice that we have included three sets of totals: for requirements, for constraints, and for overall totals. If you look at the totals for requirements, alternative B or C is the best choice because each meets or exceeds all requirements. However, if you look only at constraints, alternative A is the best choice because it does not violate any constraints. When we combine the totals for requirements and constraints, we see that the best choice is alternative C. Whether alternative C is actually chosen for development, however, is another issue. The decision makers may choose alternative A because it has the lowest cost, knowing that it does not meet two key requirements. In short, what may appear to be the best choice for a systems development project may not always be the one that ends up being developed or acquired. By conducting a thorough analysis, organizations can greatly improve their decision-making outcomes.

Presenting the Business Case

Up to this point, we have discussed the key issues to consider as you prepare to make the business case for a system. We have also shown you some tools for determining the value that a system adds to an organization. Now you are actually ready to make the case—to present your arguments and evidence to the decision makers in the firm.

KNOW THE AUDIENCE. Depending on the firm, a number of people from various areas of the firm might be involved in the decision-making process. People from different areas of the firm typically hold very different perspectives about what investments should be made and how those investments should be managed (see Table 9.2). Consequently, presenting the business case for a new system investment can be quite challenging. Ultimately, a number of factors come into play in making investment decisions, and numerous outcomes can occur (see Figure 9.8). Understanding the audience and the issues important to them is a first step in making an effective presentation. Various ways to improve the development of a business case are examined next.

CONVERT BENEFITS TO MONETARY TERMS. When making the case for an IS investment, it is desirable to translate all potential benefits into monetary terms. For example, if a new system saves department managers an hour per day, try to quantify that savings in terms of dollars.

ETHICAL DILEMMA

Genetic Testing

The Human Genome Project has been big news since its beginning in 1990. Funded by the U.S. government, the project encourages scientists around the world to map the 20,000 to 25,000 genes within the 23 pairs of human chromosomes—groundbreaking science, for sure, but also a source of ethical dilemmas in a number of industries because of the personal information genetic testing can reveal. Do you carry genes for chronic diseases that may make you a bad risk for health insurance companies or for potential employers who provide health insurance for their employees? Would you want to know if you carry the gene or genes for a fatal disease for which there is currently no treatment or cure, such as Alzheimer's disease? How ethical are mail-order genetic testing laboratories that offer genetic analyses without counseling to help clients interpret results? Is genetic testing another example of technology outpacing legal and ethical issues?

In May 2008, Congress passed the Genetic Information Nondiscrimination Act to bar discrimination based on genes. "People know we all have bad genes, and we are all potential victims of genetic discrimination," said Representative Louise M. Slaughter of New York, who proposed the legislation. The bill prohibited health insurance companies from using genetic information to deny benefits or raise premiums for individual policies. Furthermore, employers who use genetic information to make decisions about hiring, firing, or salaries could face hefty fines.

Technology has opened the door to the possibility of not only genetic discrimination but also new ways for unscrupulous doctors to take advantage of patients. Today, a plethora of genetic testing laboratories can be found online. "Paternity tests for $79," one lab advertised. A more extensive genetic profile could be obtained for around US$300 from a number of testing facilities. Companies will take a sample of your DNA from cheek cells (you spit into a vial), scan it, and send you information about your genetic future as well as your family tree. You and members of your family can track inherited traits, such as athletic endurance, heart disease, breast cancer, colorectal cancer, and lactose intolerance. Other companies focus on matching the genes you have discovered you have to current medical research, calculating your genetic risk for developing a wide range of diseases. Some doctors in several Third World countries are going a step further, promising miracle cures using untested stem cell therapies for people with devastating conditions and injuries.

The new genomics age comes with great promise and opportunity, but it also raises ethical questions that will be difficult to answer. How will knowing your genetic profile affect your life and your future? And how can we protect such information from those who would abuse it? Linda Avey and Anne Wojcicki (the wife of Google's cofounder Sergei Brin), cofounders of a genetic testing company called "23andMe," emphasize that one's genome is simply information. Information about our health or potential health to add to the information we're already collecting, such as blood pressure, cholesterol level, and height/weight comparisons. Using such information wisely and without prejudice is the challenge for the twenty-first century. As an "Alpha tester" for 23andMe, Sergei Brin discovered that he has a 50 percent chance of developing Parkinson's disease; Brin has donated nearly US$150 million to studying Parkinson's, primarily through the Michael J. Fox Foundation, which is the world's largest private funder of Parkinson's research, hoping to contribute to finding a cure for the disease.

Based on:

Anonymous. (2012, May 12). Google's Sergey Brin makes strides to find Parkinson's cure. *The Times of India*. Retrieved May 28, 2012, from http://articles.timesofindia.indiatimes.com/2012-05-12/strategy/31679109_1_wojcicki-james-parkinson-disease.

Goetz, T. (2007, November 17). 23AndMe will decode your DNA for $1,000. Welcome to the age of genomics. *Wired*. Retrieved May 28, 2012, from http://www.wired.com:80/medtech/genetics/magazine/15-12/ff_genomics.

Goetz, T. (2010, June). Sergey Brin's search for a Parkinson's cure. *Wired*. Retrieved May 28, 2012, from http://www.wired.com/magazine/2010/06/ff_sergeys_search.

Harmon, A. (2008, May 2). Congress passes bill to bar bias based on genes. *The New York Times*. Retrieved May 28, 2012, from http://www.nytimes.com:80/2008/05/02/health/policy/02gene.html.

Human genome project information. (n.d.). Retrieved May 28, 2012, from http://www.ornl.gov/sci/techresources/Human_Genome/home.shtml.

Judson K., & Harrison, C. (2012). *Law and ethics for medical careers*, 6th Ed. Boston: McGraw-Hill.

Nolen, S. (2010, March 19). The stem-cell black market: Delhi doctor claims wonder cures. *The Globe and Mail*. Retrieved May 28, 2012, from http://www.theglobeandmail.com/news/technology/science/the-stem-cell-black-market-delhi-doctor-claims-wonder-cures/article1506296.

Pollack, A. (2009, March 11). Google co-founder backs vast Parkinson's study. *The New York Times*. Retrieved May 28, 2012, from http://www.nytimes.com/2009/03/12/business/12gene.html.

The Michael J. Fox Foundation. (2012, May 21). The Michael J. Fox Foundation announces second quarter participants in partnering program between awardees and industry. Retrieved May 28, 2012, from http://www.sacbee.com/2012/05/21/4505387/the-michael-j-fox-foundation-announces.html.

TABLE 9.2   Characteristics of Different Stakeholders Involved in Making IS Investment Decisions

Stakeholder	Perspective	Focus/Project Characteristics
Management	Representatives or managers from each of the functional areas within the firm	Greater strategic focus; largest project sizes; longest project durations
Steering committee	Representatives from various interest groups within the organization (they may have their own agendas at stake when making investment decisions)	Cross-functional focus; greater organizational change; formal cost–benefit analysis; larger and riskier projects
User department	Representatives of the intended users of the system	Narrow, non-strategic focus; faster development
IS executive	Has overall responsibility for managing IS development, implementation, and maintenance of selected systems	Focus on integration with existing systems; fewer development delays; less concern with cost–benefit analysis

Source: Based on Hoffer, George, & Valacich (2014) and McKeen, Guimaraes, & Wetherbe (1994).

Figure 9.9 shows how you might convert time savings into dollar figures. While merely explaining this benefit as "saving managers' time" makes it sound useful, managers may not consider it a significant enough inducement to warrant spending a significant amount of money. Justifying a US$50,000 system because it will "save time" may not be persuasive enough. However, an annual savings of US$90,000 is more likely to capture the attention of decision makers and is more likely to result in project approval. Senior managers can easily rationalize a US$50,000 expense for a US$90,000 savings and can easily see why they should approve such a request. They can also more easily rationalize their decision later on if something goes wrong with the system.

DEVISE PROXY VARIABLES. The situation presented in Figure 9.9 is fairly straightforward. Anyone can see that a US$50,000 investment is a good idea because the return on that investment is US$90,000 the first year. Unfortunately, not all cases are this clear-cut. In cases in which it is not as easy to quantify the impact of an investment, you can come up with **proxy variables** (i.e., alternative measures of outcomes) to help clarify what the impact on the firm will be. Proxy variables can be used to measure changes in terms of their perceived value to the organization. For example, if mundane administrative tasks are seen as a low value (perhaps a 1 on a 5-point scale), but direct contact with customers is seen as a high value (a rating of 5), you can use these perceptions to indicate how new systems will add value to the organization. In this example, you can show that a new system will allow personnel to have more contact with customers while at the same time reducing the administrative workload. Senior managers can quickly see that individual workload is being shifted from low-value to high-value activities.

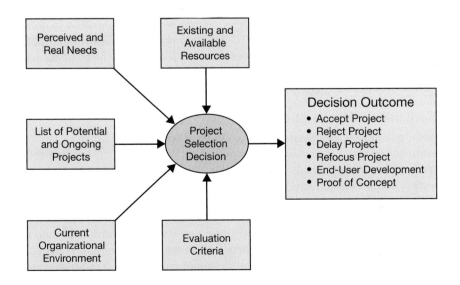

FIGURE 9.8

Investment selection decisions must consider numerous factors and can have numerous outcomes.

FIGURE 9.9

Converting time savings into dollar figures.

Benefit:	
New system saves at least one hour per day for 12 mid-level managers.	
Quantified as:	
Manager's salary (per hour)	$30.00
Number of managers affected	12
Daily savings (one hour saved × 12 managers)	$360.00
Weekly savings (daily savings × 5)	$1,800.00
Annual savings (weekly savings × 50)	$90,000.00

You can communicate these differences using percentages, increases or decreases, and so on—whatever best conveys the idea that the new system is creating changes in work, in performance, and in the way people think about their work. This gives decision makers some relatively solid data on which to base their decision.

MEASURE WHAT IS IMPORTANT TO MANAGEMENT. One of the most important things you can do to show the benefits of a system is one of the simplest: measure what senior managers think is important. You may think this is trivial advice, but you would be surprised how often people calculate impressive-looking statistics in terms of downtime, reliability, and so on, only to find that senior managers disregard or only briefly skim over those figures. You should concentrate on the issues senior business managers care about. The "hot-button" issues with senior managers should be easy to discover, and they are not always financial reports. Hot issues with senior managers could include cycle time (how long it takes to process an order), regulatory or compliance issues, customer feedback, and employee morale. By focusing on what senior business managers believe to be important, you can make the business case for systems in a way that is more meaningful for those managers, which makes selling systems to decision makers much easier. Managers are more likely to buy in to the importance of systems if they can see the impact on areas that are important to them. Now that you understand how to make the business case for new information systems, we now examine the development process.

THE SYSTEMS DEVELOPMENT PROCESS

http://goo.gl/e4mnV

No matter if a software company such as Microsoft is planning to build a new version of its popular Office software suite, or if a company such as Netflix is trying to build a system to improve its movie recommendations, companies follow a standardized approach. This process of designing, building, and maintaining information systems is often referred to as **systems analysis and design**. Likewise, the individual who performs this task is referred to as a **systems analyst**. Because few organizations can survive without effectively utilizing information and computing technology, the demand for skilled systems analysts is very strong. In fact, the *Wall Street Journal* named being a systems analyst one of the 10 best jobs for 2012. Likewise, the U.S. Bureau of Labor Statistics ranks systems analysts near the top of all professions for job stability, income, and employment growth through 2016, with average growth exceeding 29 percent. Organizations want to hire systems analysts because they possess a unique blend of managerial and technical expertise—systems analysts are not just "techies." Systems analysts remain in demand precisely because of this unique blend of abilities.

Customized versus Off-the-Shelf Software

When deciding to deploy new systems to support their operations in order to gain or sustain a competitive advantage, organizations can typically choose between customized and off-the-shelf software. For example, many types of application software (such as word processors, spreadsheet, or accounting software) can be used by a variety of businesses within and across industries. These types of general purpose systems are typically purchased off the shelf. Often, however, organizations have very specific needs that cannot be met by generic technologies. This is especially true for companies trying to capitalize on a first-mover advantage, and therefore may not be able to purchase a preexisting system to meet their specific needs. For example, pioneers in online retailing (such as Amazon.com) or budget air travel (such as Southwest Airlines) needed entirely new systems and technologies to support their revolutionary business models and had to develop (or have someone else develop) customized solutions. The approaches to developing or acquiring customized and off-the-shelf software are quite different, but they also have many similarities. Before going into the details of developing or acquiring such systems, we'll first contrast these two types of systems.

CUSTOMIZED SOFTWARE. Customized software is developed to meet the specifications of an organization. These technologies may be developed (or configured) in-house by the company's own IS staff, or the development may be contracted, or outsourced, to a specialized vendor charged with developing the system to the company's contractual specifications. Customized systems have two primary advantages over general purpose commercial technologies:

1. *Customizability.* The software can be tailored to meet unique organizational requirements. Such requirements, for example, can reflect a desire to achieve a competitive advantage through a specific type of system (e.g., Amazon.com's one-click ordering) or to better fit business operations, characteristics of the organizational culture, or proprietary security requirements, or to better interface with existing systems.
2. *Problem Specificity.* The company pays only for the features specifically required for its users. For example, company- or industry-specific terms or acronyms can be included in a new software application, as can unique types of required reports. Such specificity is not typically possible in off-the-shelf systems that are targeted to a more general audience.

Today, building a complete system from scratch is quite rare; most information systems that are developed within an organization for its internal use typically include a large number of preprogrammed, reusable modules as well as off-the-shelf hardware technologies that are purchased from development organizations or consultants.

OFF-THE-SHELF SOFTWARE. Although customized software has advantages, it is not automatically the best choice for an organization. Off-the-shelf software (or packaged software) is typically used to support common business processes that do not require any specific tailoring. In general, off-the-shelf systems, whether hardware or software, are less costly, faster to procure, of higher quality, and less risky than customized systems. Table 9.3 summarizes examples of off-the-shelf application software.

Traditionally, the most common option for packaged software was so-called commercial off-the-shelf (COTS) software; this type of software is typically developed by software companies that spread the development costs over a large number of customers. An alternative to commercial off-the-shelf software is open source software.

Open Source Software

Open source is a philosophy that promotes developers' and users' access to the source of a product or idea. Particularly in the area of software development, the open source movement has taken off with the advent of the Internet; and people around the world are contributing their time and expertise to develop or improve software, ranging from operating systems to applications software. As the programs' source code is freely available for use and/or modification,

TABLE 9.3   Examples of Off-the-Shelf Application Software

Category	Application	Description	Examples
Business information systems	Payroll	Automation of payroll services, from the optical reading of time sheets to generating paychecks	ZPAY Intuit Payroll
	Inventory	Automation of inventory tracking, order processing, billing, and shipping	Intuit QuickBooks InventoryPower 5
Office automation	Personal productivity	Support for a wide range of tasks from word processing to graphics to e-mail	OpenOffice Corel WordPerfect Microsoft Office

this software is referred to as **open source software**. Open source software owes its success to the inputs from a large user base, helping to fix problems or improve the software. Linux, one of the most prevalent examples of open source software, was developed as a hobby by the Finnish university student Linus Torvalds in 1991. Having developed the first version himself, he made the source code of his operating system available to everyone who wanted to use it and improve on it. Since then, various Linux distributions (such as Ubuntu, Red Hat, and Debian) have been released; each distribution integrates the core part of the Linux operating system with different utilities and software applications, depending on the intended use (e.g., desktop computer, tablet, Web server, embedded system, and so on). With most distributions, users can only *suggest* modifications for official releases; for example, users can contribute to program code or provide new designs for the system's user interface, but only a small group of carefully selected "committers" can implement these modifications into the official releases of the software, which helps to ensure the quality and stability of the software. Because of its un-rivaled stability, Linux has become the operating system of choice for Web servers, **embedded systems** (such as TiVo boxes and network routers), and supercomputers alike (as of June 2012, 92 percent of the world's 500 fastest supercomputers ran Linux operating systems; [Top 500, 2012]). In addition to the Linux operating system, other open source software has been gaining increasing popularity because of its stability and low cost. For example, in 2012, 65 percent of all Web sites were powered by the Apache Web server, another open source project (Netcraft, 2012). Other popular examples of open source application software include the Firefox Web browser and the office productivity suite Apache OpenOffice. While there are many benefits to open source software, vendors of proprietary software are still highlighting "hidden" costs of running open source software, such as obtaining reliable customer support. On the other hand, however, commercial open source vendors are providing customer support, installation, train-ing, and so on to their paying customers. H&R Block, AVIS Sweden, and many other large companies are using a CRM system offered by SugarCRM, Inc., a commercial open source vendor that offers free "community editions" as well as other, more feature-rich paid editions of its software. Similarly, the popular MySQL database, which is used by Yahoo!, Facebook, the Associated Press, and many other companies is provided under an open source license for personal use, but the company employs its own developers and offers commercial licenses (in-cluding dedicated 24/7 technical support, consulting, and indemnification clauses) to business users. Further, many open source projects are now backed by major information technology (IT) companies such as IBM, which give money and human resources to Linux projects, or Oracle, which donated the source code of the OpenOffice productivity suite to the Apache Soft-ware Foundation.

Combining Customized, Open Source, and Off-the-Shelf Systems

It is possible to combine the advantages of customized, open source, and off-the-shelf sys-tems. Companies can purchase off-the-shelf technologies and then have these modified for their specific needs. For example, an online retailer may want to purchase an off-the-shelf inven-tory management system and then modify it to account for the specific products, outlets, and reports it needs to conduct its day-to-day business. This system could be based on the open source database MySQL; further, the online retailer could use the open source Apache Web server to power its online shopping site. In some cases, companies selling off-the-shelf soft-ware make customized changes for a fee. Other vendors, however, may not allow their software to be modified.

Commercial, off-the-shelf systems are always acquired from an external vendor (unless you *are* the vendor, such as personnel within Microsoft using Word for their word processing tasks), whereas customized systems can be either developed in-house or developed by an outside ven-dor (see Figure 9.10). Regardless of the source of the new system—customized, open source, or off-the-shelf—the primary role of managers and users in the organization is to make sure that it will meet the organization's business needs.

IS Development in Action

The tools and techniques used to develop information systems are continually evolving with the rapid changes in IS hardware and software. As you will see, the IS development approach is a fairly disciplined and structured process that moves from step to step. Systems analysts become

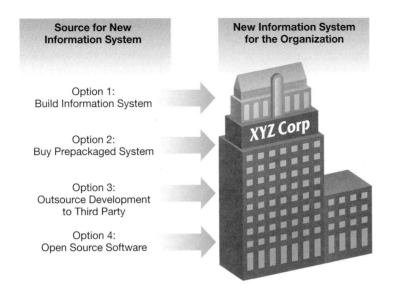

FIGURE 9.10

There are a variety of sources for information systems.

adept at decomposing large, complex problems into many small, simple problems. The goal of the systems analyst is to design the final system by piecing together many small programs and technologies into one comprehensive system (see Figure 9.11). For example, think about using LEGO™ blocks for building a model of a space station. Each individual block is a small, simple piece that is nothing without the others. When put together, the blocks can create a large and very complex design (Google co-founder Larry Page had gained some notoriety for building a working printer out of LEGO bricks). When systems are built in this manner, they are much easier to design, build, and, most important, maintain.

Although many people in organizations, such as managers and users, are responsible and participate in a systems development project, the systems analyst has primary responsibility. Some projects may have one or several systems analysts working together, depending on the size and complexity of the project. The primary role of the systems analyst is to study the problems and needs of an organization in order to determine how people, methods, and information technology can best be combined to bring about improvements in the organization. A systems analyst helps systems users and other business managers define their requirements for new or enhanced information systems.

A systems analyst typically also *manages* the development project. As the **project manager**, the systems analyst needs a diverse set of management, leadership, technical, conflict management, and customer relationships skills. The project manager is the person most responsible for ensuring that a project is a success. The project manager must deal with continual change and

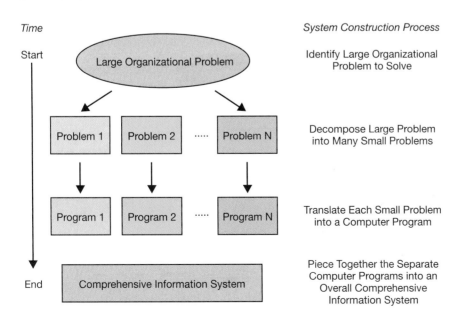

FIGURE 9.11

Problem decomposition makes solving large, complex problems easier.

problem solving. Successful projects require effective resource and task management as well as effective communication as the project moves through its various steps. Project management is an important aspect of the system development or acquisition process and a critical skill for successful systems analysts. The focus of project management is to ensure that projects meet customer expectations and are delivered within budget and time constraints. Clearly, a systems analyst is an agent of change and innovation in modern organizations.

The Role of Users in the Systems Development Process

Many organizations have a huge investment in transaction processing and management information systems. These systems are most often designed, constructed, and maintained by systems analysts within the organization, using a variety of methods. When building and maintaining information systems, systems analysts rely on information provided by system users, who are involved in all phases of the system's development process. To effectively participate in the process, it is important for all members of the organization to understand what is meant by systems development and what activities occur. A close, mutually respectful working relationship between analysts and users is key to project success.

Steps in the Systems Development Process

Just as the products that a firm produces and sells follow a life cycle, so do organizational information systems. For example, a new type of tennis shoe follows a life cycle of being designed, introduced to the market, being accepted into the market, maturing, declining in popularity, and ultimately being retired. The term **systems development life cycle (SDLC)** describes the life of an information system from conception to retirement (Hoffer et al., 2014). The SDLC has four primary phases:

1. Systems planning and selection
2. Systems analysis
3. Systems design
4. Systems implementation and operation

Figure 9.12 is a graphical representation of the SDLC containing four boxes connected by arrows. Within the SDLC, arrows flow from systems planning and selection, to systems analysis, to systems design, and, finally, to systems implementation and operation. Once a system is in operation, it moves into an ongoing maintenance phase that parallels the initial development process. For example, when new features are added to an existing system, analysts must first plan and select which new features to add, then analyze the possible impact of adding these features to the existing system, then design how the new features will work, and, finally, implement these new features into the existing system. While some consider maintenance another SDLC phase, it is really a repeated application of the core SDLC phases. In this way, the SDLC becomes an ongoing *cycle*. During ongoing system maintenance, the entire SDLC is followed to implement system repairs and enhancements.

FIGURE 9.12

The SDLC defines the typical process for building systems.

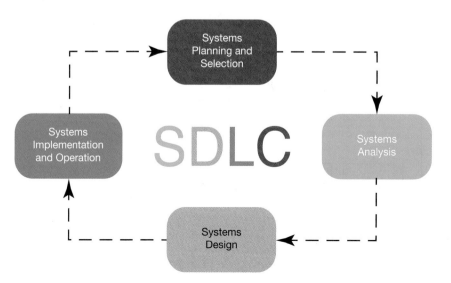

WHO'S GOING MOBILE

Creating Mobile Apps

With the rapid rise of smartphone usage, various useful and entertaining applications (apps) are rapidly being developed, greatly enhancing the phones' capabilities. In June 2012, Apple reported that it had more than 500,000 apps in the iTunes store; Google Play (a marketplace for Android apps) reported over 456,000 apps, with many more apps appearing on the various marketplaces every day. The primary reason for this tremendous increase is that anyone can build and try to sell apps, from software companies with teams of highly skilled programmers focused on translating their existing products (such as Adobe Reader) onto mobile platforms, to individuals who have a clever idea for a game, or even parents working on educational apps for their children.

Owing to the intense competition between hundreds of thousands of apps, it is not surprising that only relatively few are highly successful. Among the most successful apps is *Angry Birds,* which, as of May 2012, had more than 1 billon downloads, including free and paid versions. Other apps have not seen such success. In fact, market data from 2010 show that about 26 percent of downloaded mobile apps get used only once by the customer. So, while a lot of apps are being developed, only a small number are widely successful. Given the diversity of people building apps, you might ask yourself, "How do you design a winning app?"

Like the SDLC, the first step in this process is to come up with your initial idea for a product. Is your new app a game, a productivity tool for students, or a better way to keep track of your passwords? To make sure you select a good product idea, you will want to do some market research. Are there competitors to your idea? If so, what is their revenue model? Why is your solution better than existing ones? These are critical questions. If you cannot clearly see that your product is unique and has a large potential market, then you need to come up with a new idea. Your goal is to find a unique idea, or a new spin on an old idea, that will be well received in the marketplace.

Once you have your initial idea, your development process should mirror the SDLC as outlined in this chapter. These next steps include: analysis, design, and implementation. During analysis, you need to analyze the capabilities of the mobile platform to support your product idea. For instance, will the limited screen size be adequate for the type of app you are building? As you get a better idea of the requirements for your app, you will also want to continue your market analysis. For example, you will want to know how your intended customers react to your idea. What features do they think would be most important?

Once you have carefully analyzed the requirements for your new app, and you feel you still have a winning idea, you will then need to translate this analysis and market understanding into a design. Your design should include a clear description of how the app will look and operate. For instance, you will want to design the look and feel of the screens (in the beginning,

designing the app on paper works best), identify what information might need to be stored on the device, and so on. When your design is complete, you should again test your ideas with your target market and friends; in fact, you will want to go through several rounds of design and refinement. Don't build any software until you know exactly what you intend to build! However, once you settle all the design questions, you are then ready to implement your app. Your implementation approach will also leverage your target market and friends, who will need to test and provide suggestions for further improvements.

Finally, once you are happy with your new app, you will then have to get it listed in your intended marketplace. One question you will have to deal with is pricing. If you are new to the app development game, you may want to start your career as an app developer with a free product, or price your new app at the lower end of the pricing scale. In June 2012, for example, more than 72 percent of the apps on Google Play (an Android market) were free; about 20 percent changed between $0.01 and $2.50. The goal in the app world is to develop a following of people who love your app and recommend it to others. In other words, you want your app to go "viral" on the social web (e.g., Facebook, YouTube)! In fact, if your app becomes popular, you can then release an enhanced version of your app, and this time charge a fair price that people will be willing to pay. This successful revenue model is executed to perfection by Finnish computer game developer Rovio Mobile, who owns the Angry Birds franchise, with a combination of free and paid versions and levels. Creating a winning app is not as easy as it looks, after all, a good combination of creativity, determination, and fortunate timing is needed to be successful. On the other hand, many software development newbies have launched a successful apps business. Good luck!

Based on:

Angry Birds. (2012, June 5). In *Wikipedia, The Free Encyclopedia*. Retrieved June 8, 2012, from http://en.wikipedia.org/w/index.php?title=Angry_Birds&oldid=496186105.

Anonymous. (n.d.). Android market stats. *Appbrain.com*. Retrieved June 8, 2012, from http://www.appbrain.com/stats.

Cashmore, P. (2011, March 19). How to build an iPhone app: a guide. *Mashable Tech*. Retrieved June 7, 2012, from http://mashable.com/2009/02/21/how-to-build-an-iphone-app.

Francis, R. (2012, February 15). An insider's guide to developing mobile applications. *The Guardian*. Retrieved June 7, 2012, from http://www.guardian.co.uk/media-network/media-network-blog/2012/feb/15/developing-mobile-applications-business.

Gross, D. (2011, February 1). Report: one-quarter of download apps only get used once. *CNN Tech*. Retrieved June 7, 2012, from http://articles.cnn.com/2011-02-01/tech/apps.used.once_1_apps-windows-phone-mobile-users.

Tahnk, J.L. (2011, March 19). HOW TO: Create a blockbuster mobile app. *Mashable Tech*. Retrieved June 7, 2012, from http://mashable.com/2011/03/18/create-blockbuster-mobile-app.

TABLE 9.4 Possible Evaluation Criteria for Classifying and Ranking Projects

Evaluation Criteria	Description
Strategic alignment	The extent to which the project is viewed as helping the organization achieve its strategic objectives and long-term goals
Potential benefits	The extent to which the project is viewed as improving profits, customer service, and so forth, and the duration of these benefits
Potential costs and resource availability	The number and types of resources the project requires and their availability
Project size and duration	The number of individuals and the length of time needed to complete the project
Technical difficulty and risks	The level of technical difficulty involved in successfully completing the project within a given time and resource constraint

Source: Based on Hoffer, George, & Valacich (2014).

Phase 1: Systems Planning and Selection

The first phase of the SDLC is **systems planning and selection** (see Figure 9.12). Understanding that it can work on only a limited number of projects at a given time because of limited resources, an organization must take care that only those projects that are critical to enabling the organization's mission, goals, and objectives are undertaken. Consequently, the goal of systems planning and selection is simply to identify, plan, and select a development project from all possible projects that could be performed. Organizations differ in how they identify, plan, and select projects. Some organizations have a formal **information systems planning** process whereby a senior manager, a business group, an IS manager, or a steering committee identifies and assesses all possible systems development projects that the organization could undertake. Project managers present the business case for the new system and it is accepted or rejected. Others follow a more ad hoc process for identifying potential projects. Nonetheless, after all possible projects are identified, those deemed most likely to yield significant organizational benefits, given available resources, are selected for subsequent development activities.

Just as there are often differences in the source of systems projects within organizations, there are often different evaluation criteria used within organizations when classifying and ranking potential projects (Table 9.4). During project planning, the analyst works with the customers—the potential users of the system and their managers—to collect a broad range of information to gain an understanding of the project size, potential benefits and costs, and other relevant factors. After collecting and analyzing this information, the analyst builds the business case that can be reviewed and compared with other possible projects. Table 9.4 provides a sample of the criteria often used by organizations. If the organization accepts the project, systems analysis begins.

Phase 2: Systems Analysis

The second phase of the SDLC is called **systems analysis** (see Figure 9.12). One purpose of the systems analysis phase is for designers to gain a thorough understanding of an organization's current way of doing things in the area for which the new information system will be constructed. The process of conducting an analysis requires that many tasks, or subphases, be performed. The first subphase focuses on determining system requirements. To determine the requirements, an analyst works closely with users to determine what is needed from the proposed system. After collecting the requirements, analysts organize this information using data, process, and logic modeling tools.

COLLECTING REQUIREMENTS. The collection and structuring of requirements is arguably the most important activity in the systems development process because how well the IS requirements are defined influences all subsequent activities. The old saying "garbage in, garbage out" very much applies to the systems development process. **Requirements collection** is the process of gathering and organizing information from users, managers, customers, business processes, and documents to understand how a proposed information system should function. Systems analysts

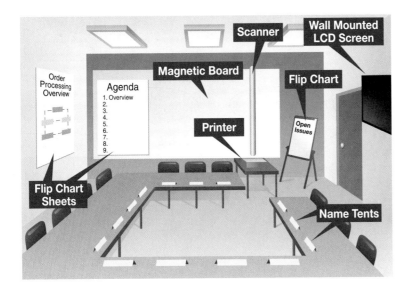

FIGURE 9.13

A JAD room.

Source: Based on Wood & Silver (1989); Hoffer et al. (2014).

use a variety of techniques for collecting system requirements, including the following (Hoffer et al., 2014):

- *Interviews.* Analysts interview people informed about the operation and issues of the current or proposed system.
- *Questionnaires.* Analysts design and administer surveys to gather opinions from people informed about the operation and issues of the current or proposed system.
- *Observations.* Analysts observe system users at selected times to see how data are handled and what information people need to do their jobs.
- *Document Analysis.* Analysts study business documents to discover issues, policies, and rules, as well as concrete examples of the use of data and information in the organization.
- *Joint Application Design.* **Joint application design (JAD)** is a group meeting–based process for requirements collection (see Figure 9.13). During this meeting, the users *jointly* define and agree on system requirements or designs. This process can result in dramatic reductions in the length of time needed to collect requirements or specify designs.

MODELING DATA. Data are facts that describe people, objects, or events. A lot of different facts can be used to describe a person: name, age, gender, race, and occupation, among others. To construct an information system, systems analysts must understand what data the information system needs in order to accomplish the intended tasks. To do this, they use data modeling tools to collect and describe the data to users to confirm that all needed data are known and presented to users as useful information. Figure 9.14 shows an *entity-relationship diagram,* a type of data model describing students, classes, majors, and classrooms at a university. Each box in the diagram is referred to as a data entity, and each entity is related to other entities. Data modeling tools enable the systems analyst to represent data in a form that is easy for users to understand and critique. For more information on databases and data modeling, see the Technology Briefing.

MODELING PROCESSES AND LOGIC. The next step in this phase is to model how data are being input, processed, and presented to the users. As the name implies, **data flows** represent the movement of data through an organization or within an information system. For example, your registration for a class may be captured in a registration form on paper or in an interactive form on the Web. After it is filled out, this form probably flows through several processes to validate and record the class registration, as shown as "Data Flows" in Figure 9.15. After all students have been registered, a repository of all registration information can be processed for developing class rosters or for generating student billing information, which is shown as "Data" in Figure 9.15. **Processing logic** represents the way in which data are transformed. Processing logic is often expressed in **pseudocode**, which is a representation of the program's internal functioning, independent of the actual programming language being used. As there are no standards for pseudocode, the level of detail can vary. For example, pseudocode to calculate students'

FIGURE 9.14

A sample entity-relationship diagram for students.

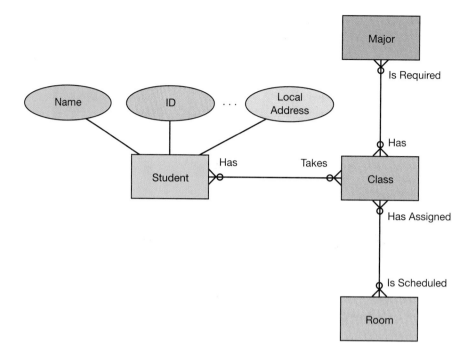

grade-point averages at the conclusion of a term is shown in the "Processing Logic" section in Figure 9.15.

After the data, data flow, and processing logic requirements for the proposed system have been identified, analysts develop one or many possible overall approaches—sometimes called designs—for the information system. For example, one approach for the system may possess only basic functionality but has the advantage of being relatively easy and inexpensive to build. An analyst might also propose a more elaborate approach for the system, but it may be more difficult and more costly to build. Analysts evaluate alternative system design approaches with the knowledge that different solutions yield different benefits and different costs. After a system approach is selected, details of that particular system approach can be defined.

Phase 3: Systems Design

The third phase of the SDLC is **systems design** (see Figure 9.12). As its name implies, it is during this phase that the proposed system is designed; that is, the details of the chosen approach are elaborated. As with analysis, many different activities must occur during systems design. The elements that must be designed when building an information system include the following:

- Human–computer interface
- Databases and files
- Processing and logic

DESIGNING THE HUMAN–COMPUTER INTERFACE. Just as people have different ways of interacting with other people, information systems can have different ways of interacting with people. A **human–computer interface (HCI)** is the point of contact between a system and users. Companies like Facebook, Twitter, and Amazon.com spend considerable time and effort designing easy-to-use systems. In addition to the HCI, analysts take great care in designing data entry forms and management reports. A form is a business document containing some predefined data, often including some areas where additional data can be filled in (see Figure 9.16). Similarly, a report is a business document containing only predefined data for online viewing or printing (see Figure 9.17). For more on forms and reports, see Chapter 6, "Enhancing Business Intelligence Using Information Systems."

DESIGNING DATABASES AND FILES. To design databases and files, a systems analyst must have a thorough understanding of an organization's data and informational needs. For example,

FIGURE 9.15

Four key elements to the development of a system: requirements, data, data flows, and processing logic.

Requirements

Data

Name	Class	GPA
Patty Nicholls	Senior	3.7
Brett Williams	Grad	2.9
Mary Shide	Fresh	3.2

Data Flows

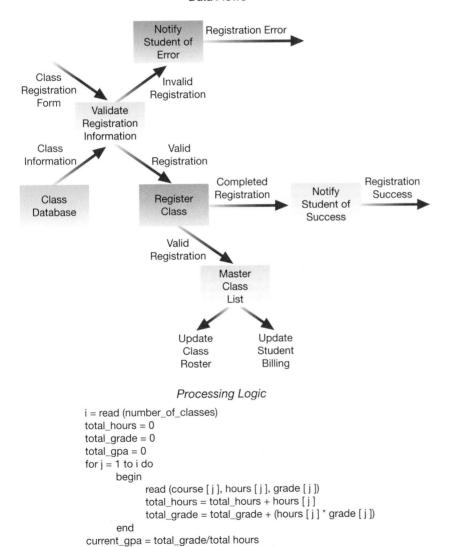

Processing Logic

```
i = read (number_of_classes)
total_hours = 0
total_grade = 0
total_gpa = 0
for j = 1 to i do
        begin
                read (course [ j ], hours [ j ], grade [ j ])
                total_hours = total_hours + hours [ j ]
                total_grade = total_grade + (hours [ j ] * grade [ j ])
        end
current_gpa = total_grade/total hours
```

Figure 9.18 shows the database design to keep track of student information in a Microsoft Access database. The database design is more complete (shows each attribute of the student) and more detailed (shows how the information is formatted) than a conceptual data model built during systems analysis (as was shown in Figure 9.14).

FIGURE 9.16

A data entry form.

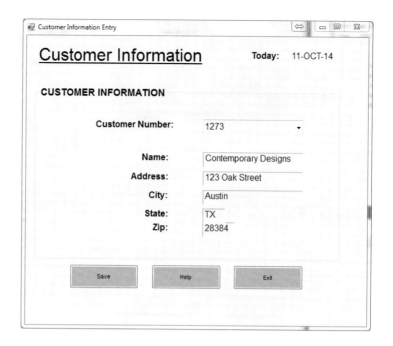

DESIGNING PROCESSING AND LOGIC. The processing and logic operations of an information system are the steps and procedures that transform raw data inputs into new or modified information. For example, when calculating your grade-point average, your school needs to perform the following steps:

1. Obtain the prior grade-point average, credit hours earned, and list of prior courses
2. Obtain the list of each current course, final grade, and course credit hours
3. Combine the prior and current credit hours into aggregate sums
4. Calculate the new grade-point average

The logic and steps needed to make this calculation can be represented in many ways, including structure charts, decision trees, pseudocode, programming code, and so on (see Figure 9.15). Regardless of how the logic is represented, the process of converting pseudocode, structure charts, or decision trees into actual program code during system implementation is a relatively straightforward process.

Phase 4: Systems Implementation and Operation

Many separate activities occur during **systems implementation**, the fourth phase of the SDLC (see Figure 9.12). One group of activities focuses on transforming the system design into a working information system. These activities include software programming and testing. A second group of activities focuses on preparing the organization for using the new information

FIGURE 9.17

Sales summary report.

Ascend Systems Incorporated
SALESPERSON ANNUAL SUMMARY REPORT 2014

REGION	SALESPERSON	SSN	QUARTERLY ACTUAL SALES			
			FIRST	SECOND	THIRD	FOURTH
Northwest and Mountain						
	Wachter	999-99-0001	16,500	18,600	24,300	18,000
	Mennecke	999-99-0002	22,000	15,500	17,300	19,800
	Wheeler	999-99-0003	19,000	12,500	22,000	28,000
Midwest and Mid-Atlantic						
	Spurrier	999-99-0004	14,000	16,000	19,000	21,000
	Powell	999-99-0005	7,500	16,600	10,000	8,000
	Topi	999-99-0006	12,000	19,800	17,000	19,000
New England						
	Speier	999-99-0007	18,000	18,000	20,000	27,000
	Morris	999-99-0008	28,000	29,000	19,000	31,000

```
C:\MSOFFICE\ACCESS\STUDENT.MDB                    Monday, June 23, 2014
Table: Students                                              Page: 1


Properties
Date Created:   6/23/14 10:35:41 PM        Def. Updatable:   Yes
Last Updated:   6/23/14 10:35:43 PM        Record Count:     0


Columns
        Name                        Type                   Size
        StudentID                   Number (Long)             4
        FirstName                   Text                     50
        MiddleName                  Text                     30
        LastName                    Text                     50
        Address                     Text                    255
        City                        Text                     50
        State                       Text                     50
        Region                      Text                     50
        PostalCode                  Text                     20
        PhoneNumber                 Text                     30
        EmailName                   Text                     50
        Major                       Text                     50
        Note                        Memo                      -
```

FIGURE 9.18

The database design for student information from an Access database.

Source: Courtesy of Microsoft, Inc.

system. These activities include system conversion, documentation, user training, and support. This section briefly describes what occurs during systems implementation.

SOFTWARE PROGRAMMING AND TESTING. Programming is the process of transforming the system design into a working computer system. During this transformation, both processing and testing should occur in parallel. As you might expect, a broad range of tests are conducted before a system is complete, including **developmental testing**, **alpha testing**, and **beta testing** (see Table 9.5).

SYSTEM CONVERSION, DOCUMENTATION, TRAINING, AND SUPPORT. **System conversion** is the process of decommissioning the current way of doing things (automated or manual) and installing the new system in the organization. Effective conversion of a system requires not only that the new software be installed but also that users be effectively trained and supported. System conversion can be performed in at least four ways, as shown in Figure 9.19.

Many types of documentation must be produced for an information system. Programmers develop system documentation that details the inner workings of the system to ease future maintenance and to ensure reliability of the system. A second type of documentation is user-related documentation, which is typically written not by programmers or analysts but by users or professional technical writers. The range of documents can include the following:

- User and reference guides
- User training manuals and tutorials
- Installation procedures and troubleshooting suggestions

TABLE 9.5   General Testing Types, Their Focus, and Who Performs Them

Testing Type	Focus	Performed by
Developmental	Testing the correctness of individual modules and the integration of multiple modules	Programmer
Alpha	Testing of overall system to see whether it meets design requirements	Software tester
Beta	Testing of the capabilities of the system in the user environment with actual data	Actual system users

FIGURE 9.19

Software conversion strategies.

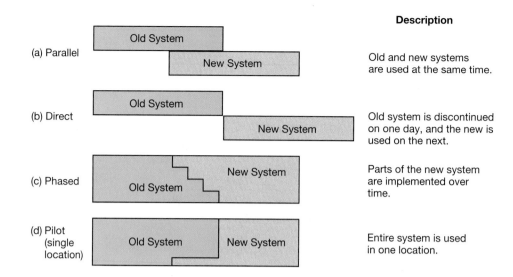

Description

(a) Parallel — Old and new systems are used at the same time.

(b) Direct — Old system is discontinued on one day, and the new is used on the next.

(c) Phased — Parts of the new system are implemented over time.

(d) Pilot (single location) — Entire system is used in one location.

In addition to documentation, users may also need training and ongoing support to use a new system effectively. Different types of training and support require different levels of investment by the organization. Self-paced training and tutorials are the least expensive options, and one-on-one training is the most expensive. Table 9.6 summarizes various user training options.

Besides training, providing ongoing education and problem-solving assistance for users may also be necessary. This is commonly referred to as system support, which is often provided by a special group of people in the organization who make up an information center or help desk. Support personnel must have strong communication skills and be good problem solvers in addition to being expert users of the system. An alternative option for a system not developed internally is to outsource support activities to a vendor specializing in technical system support and training. Regardless of how support is provided, it is an ongoing issue that must be managed effectively for the company to realize the maximum benefits of a system.

Repeating the SDLC: Systems Maintenance

After an information system is installed, it is essentially in the maintenance phase, in which an information system is systematically repaired and/or improved. During maintenance, it is typical that one person within the systems development group is responsible for collecting maintenance requests from system users. Periodically, these requests are analyzed to evaluate how a proposed change might alter the system and what business benefits might result from such a change. As with developing or acquiring new systems, any changes to an existing system need to be carefully managed. Unmanaged change can have a variety of negative consequences, including system malfunction, system failure, increasing unreliability (as errors tend to build up over time, making the system more fragile), or opening the door for fraud or deliberate misuse (e.g., if a "backdoor" is introduced during changes to a system). If the change request is approved, a system

TABLE 9.6 User Training Options

Training Option	Description
Offline Tutorial	One person taught at a time by a human or by paper-based exercises
Course	Several people taught at a time
Computer-aided instruction	One person taught at a time by the computer system
Interactive training manuals	Combination of tutorials and computer-aided instruction
Resident expert	Expert on call to assist users as needed
Software help components	Built-in system components designed to train users and trouble-shoot problems
External sources	Vendors and training providers to provide tutorials, courses, and other training activities

KEY PLAYERS

Game Development Studios

Have you ever wondered how and where tech companies generate so much money each year? For example, in 2011, some of the largest tech companies, including mainstays like HP (US$126 billion in total revenue), IBM (US$100 billion in total revenue), and Apple (US$76 billion in total revenue), generated their massive revenues with a mix of hardware, services, and software sales. For these three giants, however, software revenue was a relatively modest portion, amounting to 5.3 percent (US$6.7 billion) for HP, 22.5 percent (US$22.5 billion) for IBM, and only 1.8 percent (US$1.4 billion) for Apple. In contrast, Microsoft, one of world's largest firms, with total revenue topping US$67 billion, generated about 81 percent (US$54 billion) of their revenue through software sales, making Microsoft the highest grossing software company in the world. Software sales revenue includes revenue from sales of licenses, maintenance, subscription, and support, but does not include revenue generated from custom software development.

A closer analysis of the sources of revenue of the top-100 "software companies" in the world shows that most derive income from a variety of sources beyond software sales. Few software companies are capable of standing out solely by relying on software revenue; that is, with the exception of gaming. Game development is certainly no less competitive than the market of general software development. In the 2011 Global Software Top 100 list, game developers Activision Blizzard (e.g., Guitar Hero, World of Warcraft), Electronics Arts (e.g., Madden NFL, SimCity, Need for Speed), and Take-two Interactive (e.g., Grand Theft Auto, Duke Nukem) landed on the 9th, 13th, and 36th spots respectively. Notably, however, these gaming giants generated 100 percent of their revenue from software sales.

While all software development follows a methodology like the SDLC, game development has some unique characteristics given the high entertainment or educational goals of this type of software. In a normal SDLC, analysis and design activities are carried out by a relatively narrow group of system and business analysts, while programming and testing is carried out by programmers and software testers. Like any software project, game development begins with the establishment of a general project goal, that is, to solve a particular problem or take advantage of an opportunity (such as to have a bestselling game or to produce a game associated with a certain sports event). From there, things change quite a bit.

Designing a bestselling game more or less resembles the process of a heavily invested movie production. Like high-budget, blockbuster movies, games targeted for massive markets can be extremely expensive to create. In fact, leading games have been reported to cost more than US$100 million to develop. So, building a poor selling game can literally bankrupt a game studio. The most remarkable stage of game development—and most difficult—is the process of developing the central idea or general concept of the game (e.g., What is the game about? What market is it for? What will be unique about the game? Why will people want to play it?). Once this basic idea is established, storyboards and rough sketches of possible game sequences are made up to depict flow and different levels within the game; a diverse combination of game designers, artists, and trusted gamers work together to develop these central "mechanics" of the game (how the game will be played and how this mechanic will "hook" the players). These designs are repeatedly refined and tested using various means before any software is developed.

For instance, the game is first developed on "paper" and is tested with people to see how people react to the flow and action in the design. This is called "paper play testing." It is much easier to change the paper-based design before building the software. Once the details of the game are worked out, the game's "design document" is produced, incorporating all of the above into something that looks a lot like a movie script. Once this document is completed, skilled game developers go to work with artists as well as music and sound technicians to translate the design into a working prototype. This prototype is refined and fine-tuned through repeated play testing by a broad range of testers and naïve players. During this testing and refinement, the fun factor, as well as the educational value, of the tested game is placed under focus. Ultimately the game is transitioned into the marketplace, usually with an expensive marketing campaign. Given the complexity, expense, and deep specialization required to develop top-selling games, it is easy to see why those companies focus their efforts solely on software sales to create the next best seller.

Based on:

Game development life cycle. (n.d.). Retrieved June 6, 2012, from http://games.ubuntuvancouver.com/wiki/doku.php?id=tutorials:panda3d:life.

LaMothe, A. (n.d.). Designing video games. *Dummies.com*. Retrieved June 6, 2012, from http://www.dummies.com/how-to/content/designing-video-games.html.

Van Kooten, M. (2011, August 23). Global Software Top 100- Edition 2011. *Software Top 100*. Retrieved June 6, 2012, from http://www.softwaretop100.org/global-software-top-100-edition-2011.

change is designed and then implemented (see Figure 9.20). As with the initial development of the system, implemented changes are formally reviewed and tested before being installed into operational systems. Thus, **change request management** is a formal process that ensures that any proposed system changes are documented, reviewed for potential risks, appropriately

FIGURE 9.20

Change request management is
used during systems maintenance.

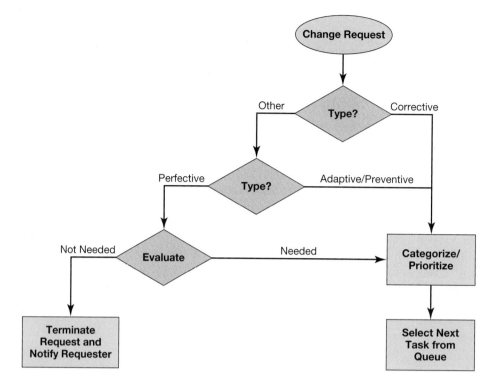

authorized, prioritized, and carefully managed (to establish an audit trail; to be able to trace back who reviewed, authorized, implemented, or tested the changes). In other words, the **systems maintenance** process parallels the process used for the initial development of the information system, as shown in Figure 9.21. Interestingly, it is during system maintenance that the largest part of the system development effort occurs.

The question must be, then, why does all this maintenance occur? It is not as if software wears out in the physical manner that cars, buildings, or other physical objects do. Correct? Yes, but software must still be maintained. The types of maintenance are summarized in Table 9.7.

As with **adaptive maintenance**, both **perfective maintenance** and **preventive maintenance** are typically a much lower priority than **corrective maintenance**, which deals with repairing flaws in the system. Corrective maintenance is most likely to occur after initial system installation as well as over the life of a system after major system changes. This means that

FIGURE 9.21

Mapping of system maintenance
activities to the SDLC.

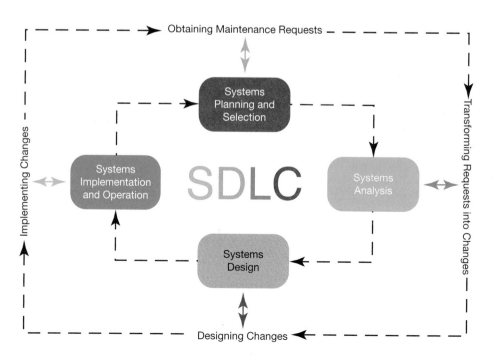

TABLE 9.7   Types of Software Maintenance

Maintenance Type	Description
Corrective maintenance	Making changes to an information system to repair flaws in the design, coding, or implementation
Adaptive maintenance	Making changes to an information system to evolve its functionality, to accommodate changing business needs, or to migrate it to a different operating environment
Preventive maintenance	Making changes to a system to reduce the chance of future system failure
Perfective maintenance	Making enhancements to improve processing performance or interface usability, or adding desired but not necessarily required system features (in other words, "bells and whistles")

adaptive, perfective, and preventive maintenance activities can lead to corrective maintenance activities if they are not carefully designed and implemented.

Today, vendors of commercial off-the-shelf software packages incorporate **patch management systems** to facilitate the different forms of software maintenance for the user; patch management systems use the Internet to check the software vendor's Web site for available patches and/or updates. If the software vendor offers a new patch, the application will download and install the patch in order to fix the software flaw. An example of a patch management system in wide use is the Windows Update Service, which automatically connects to a Microsoft Web service to download critical operating system patches for corrective maintenance (e.g., to fix bugs in the Windows operating system) or preventive maintenance (e.g., to fix security holes that could be exploited by malicious hackers).

As you can see, there is more to system maintenance than you might think. Lots of time, effort, and money are spent in this final phase of a system's development, and it is important to follow prescribed, structured steps. In fact, the approach to systems development described in this chapter—from the initial phase of identifying, selecting, and planning for systems to the final phase of system maintenance—is a very structured and systematic process. Each phase is fairly well prescribed and requires active involvement by systems people, users, and managers. It is likely that you will have numerous opportunities to participate in the acquisition or development of a new system for an organization for which you currently work or will work in the future. Now that you have an understanding of the process, you should be better equipped to make a positive contribution to the success of any systems development project.

Other Approaches to Designing and Building Systems

The SDLC is one approach to managing the development process, and it is a very good approach to follow when the requirements for the information system are highly structured and straightforward—for example, for a payroll or inventory system. Today, in addition to "standard" systems such as payroll and inventory systems, organizations need a broad variety of company-specific information systems, for which requirements either are very hard to specify in advance or are constantly changing. For example, an organization's Web site is likely to evolve over time to keep pace with changing business requirements. How many Web sites have you visited in which the content or layout seemed to change almost every week? For this type of system, the SDLC might work as a development approach, but it would not be optimal.

A commonly used alternative to the SDLC is **prototyping**, which uses a trial-and-error approach for discovering how a system should operate. You may think that this does not sound like a process at all; however, you probably use prototyping all the time in many of your day-to-day activities, but you just do not know it. For example, when you buy new clothes, you likely use prototyping—that is, trial and error—by trying on several shirts before making a selection.

Figure 9.22 diagrams the prototyping process when applied to identifying/determining system requirements. To begin the process, the system designer interviews one or several users of the system, either individually or as a group, using a JAD session. After the designer gains a general understanding of what the users want, he or she develops a prototype of the new system as quickly as possible to share with the users. The users may like what they see

FIGURE 9.22

The prototyping process uses a trial-and-error approach to discovering how a system should operate.

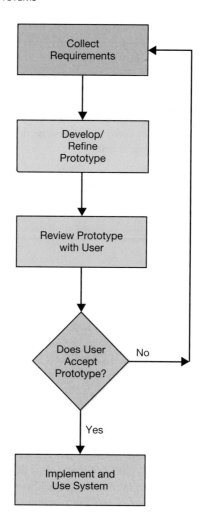

or ask for changes. If the users request changes, the designer modifies the prototype and again shares it with them. This process of sharing and refinement continues until the users approve the functionality of the system.

Beyond the SDLC and prototyping, there are many more approaches for designing and constructing information systems (e.g., Agile Methodologies, Extreme Programming, RAD [Rapid Application Development], object-oriented analysis and design, and so on). Each alternative approach has its strengths and weaknesses, providing a skilled systems analyst with a variety of tools to best meet the needs of a situation (for more, see Hoffer et al., 2014).

http://goo.gl/2nfcU

ACQUIRING INFORMATION SYSTEMS

We have now explained some of the general approaches that organizations follow when building systems in-house with their own IS staff. Many times, however, this is not a feasible solution. The following are four situations in which you might need to consider alternative development strategies.

- *Situation 1: Limited IS Staff.* Often, an organization does not have the capability to build a system itself. Perhaps its development staff is small or deployed on other activities and does not have the capability to take on an in-house development project.
- *Situation 2: IS Staff Has Limited Skill Set.* In other situations, the IS staff may not have the skills needed to develop a particular kind of system. This has been especially true with the explosive growth of the Web; many organizations are having outside groups develop and manage their sites.
- *Situation 3: IS Staff Is Overworked.* In some organizations, the IS staff may simply not have the time to work on all the systems that the organization requires or wants.

WHEN THINGS GO WRONG

Conquering Computer Contagion

Blue Security, an Israel-based Internet security company start-up, thought it had the answer to spammers. For every unwanted spam message that the half million clients of the company's e-mail service, Blue Frog, received, a message was returned to the advertiser. As a result, six of the top 10 spammers were inundated by the opt-out messages and were forced to eliminate Blue Frog's clients from their mailing list. One spamming company, however, decided to fight back. According to Blue Security, PharmaMaster responded by sending so many spam messages to Blue Frog's clients that several Internet service providers' servers crashed. Under PharmaMaster's threat of continuing and expanded attacks, Blue Security folded after a mere two weeks. "We cannot take the responsibility for an ever-escalating cyberwar through our continued operations," said Eran Reshef, chief executive officer (CEO) and founder of Blue Security.

Like PharmaMaster, all authors of malware (destructive computer code such as viruses, Trojan horses and worms, and intrusive pop-up and spam ads) have continued to flout efforts to cleanse the Internet of their disruptive and exasperating wares. As the Internet evolves so have the approaches taken by attackers; Table 9.8 lists the top malware issues of 2012.

Unfortunately, the battle against malware will probably rage as long as the Internet exists. On the plus side, however, the battle has given rise to new enterprises dedicated solely to protecting Internet users—the "white knights" who will continue to come to the rescue as long as the malware threat exists.

Based on:

Kitten, T. (2012, May 30). Top 4 Malware-Related Issues for 2012. *BankinfoSecurity.com.* Retrieved June 3, 2012, from http://www.bankinfosecurity.com/top-4-malware-related-issues-for-2012-a-4808/op-1.

Lemos, R. (2006, May 17). Blue Security folds under spammer's wrath. *SecurityFocus.* Retrieved June 12, 2012, from http://www.securityfocus.com/news/11392.

TABLE 9.8   Top 4 Malware Issues for 2012

Rank	Issue	Description
1	Mobile Malware	As iPhone and Android devices gain popularity and are used for more than communication, a new platform for attacks is emerging.
2	Social Network Spreads Trojans	Twitter, Facebook and other social networking sites are increasingly being used to spread Trojans and other malicious software.
3	More Man-in-the-Browser Attacks	Use of Web site pop-up ads to launch attack to infiltrate a person's bank account.
4	Dealing with BYOD Growth	Allowing employees to use their own devices in organizations causes new security concerns.

■ *Situation 4: Problems with Performance of IS Staff.* Earlier in this book, we discussed how and why systems development projects could sometimes be risky. Often, the efforts of IS departments are derailed because of staff turnover, changing requirements, shifts in technology, or budget constraints. Regardless of the reason, the result is the same: another failed (or flawed) system.

When it isn't possible or advantageous to develop a system in-house, organizations are pursuing two popular options:

1. External acquisition of a prepackaged system
2. Outsourcing systems development

These options are examined next.

External Acquisition

Purchasing an existing system from an outside vendor such as IBM, HP Enterprise Services, or Accenture is referred to as **external acquisition**. How does external acquisition of an information

FIGURE 9.23

Taking software for a "test-drive" prior to purchase.
Source: Yuri Arcurs/Fotolia

system work? Think about the process that you might use when buying a car. Do you simply walk into the first dealership you see, tell them you need a car, and see what they try to sell you? You had better not. Probably you have done some up-front analysis and know how much money you can afford to spend and what your needs are. If you have done your homework, you probably have an idea of what you want and which dealership can provide the type of car you desire.

This up-front analysis of your needs can be extremely helpful in narrowing your options and can save you a lot of time. Understanding your needs can also help you sift through the salespeople's hype that you are likely to encounter from one dealer to the next as each tries to sell you on why his or her model is perfect for you. After getting some information, you may want to take a couple of promising models for a test-drive, actually getting behind the wheel to see how well the car fits you and your driving habits. You might even talk to other people who have owned this type of car to see how they feel about it. Ultimately, you are the one who has to evaluate all the different cars to see which one is best for you. They may all be good cars; however, one may fit your needs just a little better than the others.

The external acquisition of an information system is very similar to the purchase of a car. When you acquire a new system, you should do some analysis of your specific needs. For example, how much can you afford to spend, what basic functionality is required, and approximately how many people will use the system? Next, you can begin to "shop" for the new system by asking potential vendors to provide information about the systems that they have to offer. After you evaluate this information, it may become clear that several vendors have systems that are worth considering. You may ask those vendors to come to your organization and set up their systems so that you and your colleagues are able to "test-drive" them (see Figure 9.23). Seeing how people react to the systems and seeing how each system performs in the organizational environment can help you "see" exactly what you are buying. By seeing the actual system and how it performs with real users, with real or simulated data, you can get a much clearer idea of whether that system fits your needs. When you take a car for a test-drive, you learn how the car meets your needs. By seeing how the system meets your needs before you buy, you can greatly reduce the risk associated with acquiring that system.

STEPS IN EXTERNAL ACQUISITION. In many cases, your organization will use a competitive bid process for making an external acquisition. In the competitive bid process, vendors are given an opportunity to propose systems that meet the organization's needs. The goal of the competitive process is to help the organization ensure that it gets the best system at the lowest possible price. Most competitive external acquisition processes have at least five general steps:

1. Systems planning and selection
2. Systems analysis

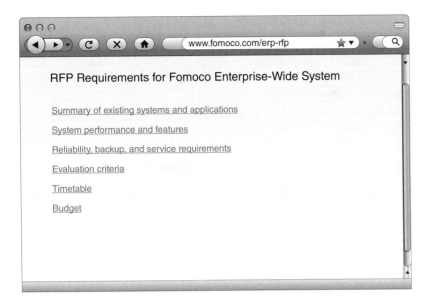

FIGURE 9.24
Sample RFP Web site for an information systems project.

3. Development of a request for proposal
4. Proposal evaluation
5. Vendor selection

You have already learned about the first two steps because they apply when you build a system yourself as well as when you purchase a system through an external vendor. Step 3, development of a request for proposal, is where the external acquisition process differs significantly from in-house development.

DEVELOPMENT OF A REQUEST FOR PROPOSAL. A **request for proposal (RFP)** is simply a document that is used to tell vendors what your requirements are and to invite them to provide information about how they might be able to meet those requirements. An RFP is sent to vendors who might potentially be interested in providing hardware and/or software for the system.

Among the areas that may be covered in an RFP are the following:

- A summary of existing systems and applications
- Requirements for system performance and features
- Reliability, backup, and service requirements
- The criteria that will be used to evaluate proposals
- Timetable and budget constraints (how much you can spend)

The RFP is then sent to prospective vendors along with an invitation to present their bids for the project. Eventually, you will likely receive a number of proposals to evaluate. If, on the other hand, you do not receive many proposals, it may be necessary to rethink the requirements—perhaps the requirements are greater than the budget limitations or the timetable is too short. In some situations, you may first need to send out a preliminary request for information simply to gather information from prospective vendors. This will help you determine whether, indeed, the desired system is feasible or even possible. If you determine that it is, you can then send out an RFP. Often, rather than trying to identify all potential vendors and sending out RFPs, companies set up a project Web site, allowing potential bidders to find out more about the organization and its current and planned information systems (see Figure 9.24).

PROPOSAL EVALUATION. The fourth step in external acquisition is to evaluate proposals received from vendors. This evaluation may include viewing system demonstrations, evaluating the performance of those systems, examining criteria important to the organization, and judging how the proposed systems "stack up" to those criteria. Demonstrations are a good way to get a feel for the different systems' capabilities. Just as you can go to the showroom to look at a new car and get a feel for whether it meets your needs, it is also possible to screen various systems through a demonstration from the vendor. During a demonstration, a sales team from the vendor gives an oral presentation about their system, its features and cost, followed by a demonstration

TABLE 9.9   Commonly Used Evaluation Criteria

Hardware Criteria	Software Criteria	Other Criteria
Clock speed of CPU	Memory requirements	Installation
Memory availability	Help features	Testing
Secondary storage (including capacity, access time, and so on)	Usability	Price
Video display size	Learnability	
Printer speed	Number of features supported	
	Training and documentation	
	Maintenance and repair	

of the actual system. Although such demonstrations are often useful in helping you understand the features of different systems being proposed, they are rarely enough in and of themselves to warrant purchasing the system without further evaluation.

One of the methods you can use to evaluate a proposed system is **systems benchmarking**, which is the use of standardized performance tests to facilitate comparison between systems. Benchmark programs are sample programs or jobs that simulate your computer workload. You can have benchmarks designed to test portions of the system that are most critical to your needs, based on your systems analysis. A benchmark might test how long it takes to calculate a set of numbers, how long it takes to access a set of records in a database, or how long it would take to access certain information given a certain number of concurrent users. Some common system benchmarks include the following:

- Response time given a specified number of users
- Time to sort records
- Time to retrieve a set of records
- Time to produce a given report
- Time to read in a set of data

In addition, vendors may also supply benchmarks that you can use, although you should not rely solely on vendor information. For popular systems, you may be able to rely on system benchmarks published in computer trade journals such as *PC Magazine* or on industry Web sites, such as www.cnet.com. However, in most cases, demos and benchmarks alone do not provide all the information you need to make a purchase. The systems analysis phase should have revealed some specific requirements for the new system. These requirements may be listed as criteria that the organization can use to further evaluate vendor proposals. Depending on what you are purchasing—hardware, software, or both—the criteria you use will change. Table 9.9 provides examples of commonly used evaluation criteria.

VENDOR SELECTION.   In most cases, more than one system will meet your needs, just as more than one car will usually meet your needs. However, some probably "fit" better than others. In these cases, you should have a way of prioritizing or ranking competing proposals. One way of doing this is by devising a scoring system for each of the criteria and benchmarking results as described when making the business case.

Companies may use other, less formalized approaches to evaluate vendors. Sometimes they use simple checklists; other times they use a more subjective process. Regardless of the mechanism, eventually a company completes the evaluation stage and selects a vendor, ending the external acquisition process.

MANAGING SOFTWARE LICENSING.   When purchasing commercial, off-the-shelf software, companies usually have to agree to a license agreement. In general, software licenses can be classified based on their restrictiveness or the freedom they offer to use or modify the software. Software licensing has been a hot-button topic for software companies as they lose billions in piracy and mislicensed customers (see Chapter 10). Traditionally, software licensing is defined as the permission and rights that are imposed on applications; the use of software without a proper license is illegal in most countries.

Most software licenses differ in terms of restrictiveness, ranging from no restrictions at all to completely restricted. Note that although freeware or shareware is freely available, the copyright

TABLE 9.10   Different Types of Software Licenses

Restrictiveness	Software Types	Rights	Restrictions	Examples
Full rights	Public domain software	Full rights	No restrictions; owner forsakes copyright	Different programs for outdated IBM mainframes
	Non-protective open source (e.g., Berkeley software development [BSD] license)	Freedom to copy, modify, and redistribute the software; can be incorporated into a commercial product	Creator retains copyright	Free BSD operating system; BSD components in (proprietary) Mac OS X operating system
	Protective open source (e.g., general public license [GPL])	Freedom to copy, modify, and redistribute the software	Modified or redistributed software must be made available under the same license; cannot be incorporated into commercial product	Linux operating system
	Proprietary software	Right to run the software (for licensed users)	Access to source code severely restricted; no rights to copy or modify software	Windows operating system
No rights	Trade secret	Software typically only used internally	Access to source code severely restricted; software is not distributed outside the organization	Google PageRank™ algorithm

owners often retain their rights and do not provide access to the program's source code. For organizations using proprietary software, two types of licenses are of special importance. The first type includes the **shrink-wrap licenses** and **click-wrap licenses** that accompany the software, which are used primarily for generic, off-the-shelf application and systems software. The shrink-wrapped contract has been named as such because the contract is activated when the shrink wrap on the packaging has been removed; similarly, a click-wrap license refers to a license primarily used for downloaded software that requires computer users to click on "I accept" before installing the software. The second type of license is an **enterprise license** (also known as a **volume license**). Enterprise licenses can vary greatly and are usually negotiated. In addition to rights and permissions, enterprise licenses usually contain limitations of liability and warranty disclaimers that protect the software vendor from being sued if their software does not operate as expected.

As shown in Table 9.10, there are a variety of software licenses. For different business needs, organizations often depend on a variety of software, each having different licenses, which can cause headaches for many organizations. Not knowing about the software an organization has can have a variety of consequences. For example, companies are not able to negotiate volume licensing options, unused licenses strain the organization's budget, or license violations can lead to fines or public embarrassment. **Software asset management** helps organizations to avoid such negative consequences. Usually, software asset management consists of a set of activities, such as performing a software inventory (either manually or using automated tools), matching the installed software with the licenses, reviewing software-related policies and procedures, and creating a software asset management plan. The results of these processes help organizations to better manage their software infrastructure by being able to consolidate and standardize their software titles, decide to retire unused software, or decide when to upgrade or replace software.

EXTERNAL ACQUISITION THROUGH THE CLOUD. Undoubtedly, managing the software infrastructure is a complex task, often resulting in high operating costs for organizations; further, many systems are not scalable in response to large increases in demand. To deal with these issues, business organizations increasingly use Software as a Service—that is, clients access applications in the cloud on an as-needed basis using standard Web-enabled interfaces (see Chapter 3, "Managing the Information Systems Infrastructure and Services"). For organizations, using SaaS provides a variety of benefits, such as a reduced need to maintain or upgrade software, variable costs based on the actual use of the services (rather than fixed IS costs), and the ability to rely on a provider that has gained considerable expertise because of a large number of clients.

Outsourcing Systems Development

Outsourcing systems development is a way to acquire new systems that closely resembles the process of in-house development. However, in the case of outsourcing, the responsibility for some or all of an organization's information systems development (and potentially the day-to-day management of its operation) is turned over to an outside firm. Information systems outsourcing includes a variety of working relationships. The outside firm, or service provider, may develop your information systems applications and house them within their organization; they may run your applications on their computers; or they may develop systems to run on existing computers within your organization. Anything is fair game in an outsourcing arrangement. Today, outsourcing has become a big business and is a very popular option for many organizations (see Chapter 1 for more information on outsourcing).

WHY OUTSOURCING? A firm might outsource some (or all) of its information systems services for many reasons. Some of these are old reasons, but some are new to today's environment (Applegate, Austin, & Soule, 2009):

- *Cost and Quality Concerns.* In many cases it is possible to achieve higher-quality systems at a lower price through economies of scale, better management of hardware, lower labor costs, and better software licenses on the part of a service provider.
- *Problems in IS Performance.* IS departments may have problems meeting acceptable service standards because of cost overruns, delayed systems, underutilized systems, or poorly performing systems. In such cases, organizational management may attempt to increase reliability through outsourcing.
- *Supplier Pressures.* Perhaps not surprisingly, some of the largest service providers are also the largest suppliers of computer equipment (e.g., IBM or Hewlett-Packard). In some cases, the aggressive sales forces of these suppliers are able to convince senior managers at other organizations to outsource their IS functions.
- *Simplifying, Downsizing, and Reengineering.* Organizations under competitive pressure often attempt to focus on only their "core competencies." In many cases, organizations simply decide that running information systems is not one of their core competencies and decide to outsource this function to companies such as IBM and HP Enterprise Services, whose primary competency is developing and maintaining information systems.
- *Financial Factors.* When firms turn over their information systems to a service provider, they can sometimes strengthen their balance sheets by liquidating their IT assets. Also, if users perceive that they are actually paying for their IT services rather than simply having them provided by an in-house staff, they may use those services more wisely and perceive them to be of greater value.
- *Organizational Culture.* Political or organizational problems are often difficult for an IS group to overcome. However, an external service provider often brings enough clout, devoid of any organizational or functional ties, to streamline IS operations as needed.
- *Internal Irritants.* Tension between end users and the IS staff is sometimes difficult to eliminate. At times this tension can intrude on the daily operations of the organization, and the idea of a remote, external, relatively neutral IS group can be appealing. Whether the tension between users and the IS staff (or service provider) is really eliminated is open to question; however, simply having the IS group external to the organization can remove a lingering thorn in management's side.

MANAGING THE IS OUTSOURCING RELATIONSHIP. The ongoing management of an outsourcing alliance is the single most important aspect of the outsourcing project's success. Some advice includes the following:

1. A strong, active chief information officer (CIO) and staff should continually manage the legal and professional relationship with the outsourcing firm.
2. Clear, realistic performance measurements of the systems and of the outsourcing arrangement, such as tangible and intangible costs and benefits, should be developed.
3. The interface between the customer and the outsourcer should have multiple levels (e.g., links to deal with policy and relationship issues and links to deal with operational and tactical issues).

Managing outsourcing alliances in this way has important implications for the success of the relationship. For example, in addition to making sure a firm has a strong CIO and staff, McFarlan and Nolan (1995) recommend that firms assign full-time relationship managers and coordinating groups lower in the organization to "manage" the project. The structure and nature of the internal system activities change from exclusively building and managing systems to also including managing relationships with outside firms that build and manage systems under legal contract.

NOT ALL OUTSOURCING RELATIONSHIPS ARE THE SAME. Most organizations no longer enter into a strictly legal contract with an outsourcing vendor but rather into a mutually beneficial relationship with a strategic partner. In such a relationship, both the firm and the vendor are concerned with—and perhaps have a direct stake in—the success of the other. Yet other types of relationships exist, meaning that not all outsourcing agreements need to be structured the same way. In fact, at least three different types of outsourcing relationships can be identified:

- Basic relationship
- Preferred relationship
- Strategic relationship

A basic relationship can best be thought of as a "cash-and-carry" relationship in which you buy products and services on the basis of price and convenience. Organizations should try to have a few preferred relationships in which the buyer and the supplier set preferences and prices to the benefit of each other. For example, a supplier can provide preferred pricing to customers that do a specified volume of business. Most organizations have just a few strategic relationships in which both sides share risks and rewards.

INDUSTRY ANALYSIS

Broadcasting

Only a few years ago, radio and television were among the primary sources for satisfying the desire for both entertainment and up-to-date news and information. Over the past few years, this situation has changed dramatically, with many people turning to the Internet for both information and entertainment. In fact, in 2010, for the first time, more Americans would give up their TVs than the Internet. For traditional broadcasting media, this evolution in their consumers' habits has caused both tremendous opportunities and tremendous headaches.

For many television news companies, the Internet has opened opportunities, as news features can be easily transmitted over the Internet, allowing easier connection between the newsrooms and the "action" on the field. At the same time, viewing habits have changed, and many viewers prefer to obtain their latest news via the Internet or while on the move. As a reaction, television stations (both focusing on news and entertainment) are increasingly using the Internet as a distribution medium for their content. Internet TV uses the Internet's TCP/IP protocol to transmit content, and viewers can watch parts of a provider's content at their home computers or while on the go using their iPad or smartphone. Integration of content across devices is a strategy being pursued by many broadcasters. The shift in people's viewing habits has

also prompted television stations to change the format of their broadcasts—typically to include shorter segments to cater to ever-shortening attention spans. Some stations even started to produce limited-budget episodes of popular TV shows specifically for the Internet. In late 2011, YouTube launched "Original Channels," featuring content produced by professional content providers, in an attempt to rival traditional TV channels.

These changes force TV stations to adjust their revenue models. Whereas traditionally large revenues were derived from TV advertising, advertisers are now less willing to pay high advertising fees in light of dwindling viewership. On the other hand, TV stations can potentially charge more for advertising tied to online shows, as the Internet offers benefits such as advertising targeted at the individual viewer and provides detailed tracking metrics such as click-through rates, allowing the advertiser to directly assess the success of a campaign.

For radio stations, the situation is similar. With more and more people listening to various Internet radio stations, music services like Pandora, or downloading music (legally or illegally), the number of listeners to traditional radio has dwindled and along with it advertising revenues. Online advertising now surpasses radio advertising spending. Facing competition from Internet radio, satellite radio, podcasting, and a plethora of other online diversions, many radio stations (as well as all forms of broadcasting) will have to find innovative ways to prosper in these times of profound change.

Questions:

1. What is the effect of the Internet on television and radio content? With revenues from advertising in traditional channels diminishing, how can television and radio stations continue to produce high-quality content?

2. Today there are thousands of AM/FM stations competing with Internet radio stations and music downloading. Forecast their future and provide a strategy for retaining and gaining market share.

Based on:

Anonymous. (2008, April 20). TV networks looking for new eyeballs online. *Todayshow.com*. Retrieved June 3, 2012, from http://www.msnbc.msn.com/id/24096815.

Edison Research. (2010, April 8). The infinite dial 2010: Digital platforms and the future of radio. Retrieved June 3, 2012, from http://www.edisonresearch.com/The_Infinite_Dial_2010.pdf.

Macklin, B. (2007, August). Radio trends: On air and online. *eMarketer*. Retrieved June 3, 2012, from http://www.emarketer.com/Report.aspx?code=emarketer_2000409.

Marshall, C. & Venturini, F. (2011). The future of broadcasting: a new storm is brewing. *Accenture*. Retrieved June 3, 2012, from http://www.accenture.com/SiteCollectionDocuments/PDF/Accenture_The_Future_of_Broadcasting_A_New_Storm_is_Brewing.pdf.

Key Points Review

1. *Describe how to formulate and present the business case for technology investments.* Making the business case is the process of building and presenting the set of arguments that show that an information system investment is adding value to an organization. It is often difficult to quantify the value that a system provides because of measurement problems, time lags before benefits are realized, industry redistribution, and mismanagement. You must also understand your organization's particular business strategy in order to make an effective business case for systems. In short, technology investments should be closely linked to the organization's business strategy, because these investments are becoming one of the major vehicles by which organizations can achieve their strategy. After you gain an understanding of your organization's position in the marketplace, its strategy for investing in systems that add value, and firm-level implementation factors, you can quantify the relative costs and benefits of the system. Considering all of these factors simultaneously will help you formulate an effective business case. In order to make a convincing presentation, you should be specific about the benefits this investment will provide for the organization. To do this, you must convert the benefits into monetary terms, such as the amount of money saved or revenue generated. If you have difficulty identifying specific monetary measures, you should devise some proxy measures to demonstrate the benefits of the system. Finally, make sure that you measure things that are important to the decision makers of the organizations. Choosing the wrong measures can yield a negative decision about a beneficial system.

2. *Describe the SDLC, its various phases, and alternatives to the SDLC.* The development of information systems follows a process called the SDLC. The SDLC is a process that first identifies the need for a system and then defines the processes for designing, developing, and maintaining an information system. The process is very structured and formal and requires the active involvement of managers and users. The SDLC has four phases: systems planning and selection, systems analysis, systems design, and systems implementation and operation. Systems identification, selection, and planning are the first phase of the SDLC, in which potential projects are identified, selected, and planned. Systems analysis is the second phase of the SDLC, in which the current ways of doing business are studied and alternative replacement systems are proposed. Systems design is the third phase of the SDLC, in which all features of the proposed system are described. Systems implementation and operation is the fourth phase of the SDLC, in which the information system is programmed, tested, installed, and supported. Systems maintenance is an ongoing process after initial system implementation that focuses on repairing and improving the system. Beyond the SDLC, there are many alternative systems development methods. One approach, prototyping, is an iterative systems development process in which requirements are converted into a working system that is continually revised through a close working relationship between analysts and users. A variety of other approaches are available to enhance the development process for different types of systems and contexts.

3. *Explain how organizations acquire systems via external acquisition and outsourcing.* It is not feasible for an organization to build a system in-house in at least four situations. First, some organizations have limited IS staffing and therefore do not have the capability to build a system themselves. Second, an organization may have IS staff with a limited skill set. Existing IS staff may be highly skilled at

producing traditional applications, but they may not have the skills to build new types of systems or systems that require emerging development tools. Third, in many organizations, the IS staff does not have the time to work on all the systems that the organization desires. Fourth, some organizations have performance problems with their IS staff whereby staff turnover, changing requirements, shifts in technology, or budget constraints have resulted in poor results. In any of these situations, it may be advantageous to an organization to consider an alternative to in-house systems development. External acquisition is the process of purchasing an existing information system from an external organization or vendor. External acquisition is a five-step process. Steps 1 and 2 mirror the first two steps of the SDLC.

Step 3 is the development of a request for proposal (RFP). An RFP is a communication tool indicating an organization's requirements for a given system and requesting information from potential vendors on their ability to deliver such a system. Step 4 is proposal evaluation, which focuses on evaluating proposals received from vendors. This evaluation may include viewing system demonstrations, evaluating the performance of those systems, and examining criteria important to the organization and the ways the proposed systems meet those criteria. Step 5 is vendor selection, which focuses on choosing the vendor to provide the system. Outsourcing refers to the turning over of partial or entire responsibility for information systems development and management to an outside organization.

Key Terms

adaptive maintenance   402
alpha testing   399
beta testing   399
break-even analysis   383
change request management   401
click-wrap license   409
corrective maintenance   402
cost–benefit analysis   383
data flows   395
developmental testing   399
discount rate   384
embedded system   390
enterprise license   409
external acquisition   405
human–computer interface
   (HCI)   396
information systems planning   394
intangible benefit   382
intangible cost   382

joint application design
   (JAD)   395
making the business case   376
net-present-value analysis   384
non-recurring cost   382
open source software   390
patch management system   403
perfective maintenance   402
preventive maintenance   402
processing logic   395
productivity paradox   378
project manager   391
prototyping   403
proxy variable   387
pseudocode   395
recurring cost   382
request for proposal (RFP)   407
requirements collection   394
shrink-wrap license   409

software asset management   409
system conversion   399
system effectiveness   378
system efficiency   378
systems analysis   394
systems analysis and design   388
systems analyst   388
systems benchmarking   408
systems design   396
systems development life cycle
   (SDLC)   392
systems implementation   398
systems maintenance   402
systems planning and selection   394
tangible benefit   382
tangible cost   382
total cost of ownership (TCO)   382
volume license   409
weighted multicriteria analysis   384

Review Questions

1. Define system analysis and design.
2. Describe how to make a successful business case, contrasting faith-, fear-, and fact-based arguments.
3. Compare and contrast tangible and intangible benefits and costs.
4. Contrast the perspectives of different stakeholders involved in making information systems investment decisions.
5. Define a proxy variable and give an example.
6. What are the four phases of the systems development life cycle (SDLC)?
7. What is joint application development? Where is this technique used?
8. What are the three major components/tasks of the systems design phase of the SDLC?

9. What are the four options for system conversion? How do they differ from each other?
10. List the types of testing done on software during the transformation stage.
11. What are the advantages and disadvantages of prototyping?
12. How do hackers find security holes and how can they be fixed?
13. What is an application service provider? What are the different types of application service providers?
14. What is a request for proposal? To whom is it sent?
15. List and describe two main types of software licenses.
16. What is software asset management, and why is it important for organizations?
17. What is system benchmarking, and what are some common benchmarks?

Self-Study Questions

1. Which of the following is not one of the four phases of the systems development life cycle?
   A. systems analysis
   B. systems implementation
   C. systems design
   D. systems resource acquisition

2. _____ is the process of gathering and organizing information from users, managers, business processes, and documents to understand how a proposed information system should function.
   A. Requirements collection
   B. Systems collection
   C. Systems analysis
   D. Records archiving

3. Which of the following is the correct order of phases in the systems development life cycle?
   A. analysis, planning, design, implementation
   B. analysis, design, planning, implementation
   C. planning, analysis, design, implementation
   D. design, analysis, planning, implementation

4. In the systems design phase, the elements that must be designed when building an information system include all of the following except _____.
   A. the human–computer interface
   B. questionnaires
   C. databases and files
   D. processing and logic

5. _____ maintenance involves making enhancements to improve processing performance or interface usability or adding desired (but not necessarily required) system features (in other words, "bells and whistles").
   A. Preventive   B. Perfective
   C. Corrective   D. Adaptive

6. Which of the following is not one of the three types of arguments commonly made in the business case for an information system?
   A. fear   B. fact
   C. faith   D. fun

7. A _____ is a document that an organization uses to tell vendors what its requirements are and to invite them to provide information about how they might be able to meet those requirements.
   A. request letter
   B. vendor request
   C. request for proposal
   D. requirements specification

8. Which of the following is not a type of outsourcing?
   A. basic
   B. elite
   C. strategic
   D. preferred

9. Which of the following factors is a good reason to outsource?
   A. problems in IS performance
   B. supplier pressures
   C. financial factors
   D. all of the above

10. Most competitive external acquisition processes have at least five general steps. Which of the following is not one of those steps?
    A. vendor selection
    B. proposal evaluation
    C. development of a request for proposal
    D. implementation
    Answers are on page 417.

Problems and Exercises

1. Match the following terms with the appropriate definitions:
   i. Request for proposal
   ii. Systems benchmarking
   iii. Alpha testing
   iv. Systems development life cycle
   v. Productivity paradox
   vi. Prototyping
   vii. Pilot conversion
   viii. Systems analysis
   ix. Outsourcing
   x. External acquisition
   xi. Data flows
   xii. Requirements collection

   a. The movement of data through an organization or within an information system
   b. Term that describes the life of an information system from conception to retirement
   c. The second phase of the systems development life cycle
   d. The process of gathering and organizing information from users, managers, business processes, and documents to understand how a proposed information system should function
   e. Testing performed by the development organization to assess whether the entire system meets the design requirements of the users
   f. Using a new system in one location before rolling it out to the entire organization
   g. A systems development methodology that uses a trial-and-error approach for discovering how a system should operate
   h. The practice of turning over responsibility for some or all of an organization's information systems development and operations to an outside firm

i. The observation that productivity increases at a rate that is lower than expected when new technologies are introduced

j. The process of purchasing an existing system from an outside vendor

k. A way to evaluate a proposed system by testing a portion of it with the system workload

l. A report that is used to tell vendors what the requirements are and to invite them to provide information about how they might be able to meet those requirements

2. After reading this chapter, it should be fairly obvious why an IS professional should be able to make a business case for a given system. Why, however, is it just as important for non-IS professionals? How are they involved in this process? What is their role in making IS investment decisions?

3. Read the references given in this book and search the Web to identify current international standards with respect to software development. List some of the companies that follow these in your country.

4. List the various options that an organization can choose from while deciding on new systems that support their operations to gain or sustain a competitive advantage.

5. Why can it be difficult to develop an accurate cost–benefit analysis? What factors may be difficult to quantify? How can this be handled? Is this something that should just be avoided altogether? What are the consequences of that approach?

6. Within a small group of classmates, describe any involvement you have had with making the business case for buying something for yourself or within an organization. To whom were you making the case? Was it a difficult sell? Why? To what extent did you follow the guidelines set forth in this chapter? Were your arguments based on faith, fear, fact, or fiction? How did your business case differ from those of others in your group? Were you successful? Why or why not? Were they successful? Why or why not?

7. Discuss the following in a small group of classmates or with a friend. Describe a situation from your own experience in which something was purchased where a cost–benefit analysis showed it to have a negative return when based on tangible factors. Was the purchase decision based on intangible factors? Have these intangible factors proven themselves to be worth the investment? Was it harder to convince others of the purchase because of these intangible factors?

8. Contrast the total cost of acquisition versus the total cost of ownership for the purchase of a new car. Demonstrate how the type of car, year, make, model, and so on change the values of various types of costs and benefits.

9. Identify and describe three different situations where fear, faith, or fact arguments would be most compelling when making an information systems investment decision.

10. Talk to an information systems manager and have him or her describe a system that took some length of time to improve organizational productivity in some significant way. Specifically, find out how long and why it took this much time. Was the time frame longer than expected? Why or why not? Was this a typical situation or a unique one?

11. Contrast the differing perspectives of different stakeholders involved in making information systems investment decisions.

12. Explain the differences between data and data flows. How might systems analysts obtain the information they need to generate the data flows of a system? How are these data flows and the accompanying processing logic used in the system design phase of the life cycle? What happens when the data and data flows are modeled incorrectly?

13. When Microsoft posts a new version of Internet Explorer on its Web site and states that this is a beta version, what does it mean? Is this a final working version of the software, or is it still being tested? Who is doing the testing? Search the Web to find other companies that have beta versions of their products available to the public. You might try Corel (www.corel.com) or Adobe (www.adobe.com). What other companies did you find?

14. Search the Web to identify different types of model-driven analysis methods commonly used in the industry. Prepare a comparative note stating which approach needs to be used and when.

15. Conduct a search on the Web for "systems development life cycle." Check out some of the hits. Compare them with the SDLC outlined in this chapter. Do all these life cycles follow the same general path? How many phases do the ones you found on the Web contain? Is the terminology the same or different? Prepare a 10-minute presentation to the class on your findings.

16. Choose an organization with which you are familiar that develops its own information systems. Does this organization follow an SDLC? If not, why not? If so, how many phases does it have? Who developed this life cycle? Was it someone within the company, or was the life cycle adopted from somewhere else?

17. Describe your experiences with information systems that were undergoing changes or updates. What kind of conversion procedure was being used? How did this affect your interaction with the system as a user? Who else was affected? If the system was down altogether, for how long was it down? Do you or any of your classmates have horror stories, or were the situations not that bad?

18. Choose an organization with which you are familiar and determine whether it builds its applications in-house. How many IS staff members does the organization have, and how large is the organization they support?

19. Think about the requirements of a career in IS. Do IS positions generally require people to work 40 hours a week or more if a project has a deadline? Do positions in the IS department require people skills? To find these answers, visit the IS department at your university,

a local business, or an online clearinghouse of jobs, such as hotjobs.yahoo.com or www.job-hunt.org.

20. Find an organization on the Internet (e.g., at www .computerworld.com or www.infoworld.com) or a company you may want to work for in the future that outsources work. What are the managerial challenges of outsourcing, and why is this a popular alternative to hiring additional staff?

21. Interview an IS professional about his or her company's use of software asset management processes. How does the company keep track of the different software installed? If anyone asked you about the software installed on your computer, would you know what you have installed? Would you be able to produce the licenses for all software installed?

22. A number of organizations have outsourced their routine applications like the payroll and customer service support. Identify some of these organizations to ascertain their experience about outsourcing.

Application Exercises

Note: The existing data files referenced in these exercises are available on the book's Web site: www.pearsonhighered.com/valacich.

Spreadsheet Application: Outsourcing Information Systems at Campus Travel

Campus Travel wants to increase its customer focus and wants to be able to better serve its most valued customers. Many members of the frequent flier program have requested the ability to check on the status of their membership online; furthermore, the frequent fliers would welcome the opportunity to book reward flights online. As you know that there are a number of companies specializing in building such transactional systems, you have decided to outsource the development of such a system. The following weights are assigned to evaluate the different vendors' systems:

- Online booking capability: 20 percent
- User friendliness: 25 percent
- Maximum number of concurrent users: 20 percent
- Integration with current systems: 10 percent
- Vendor support: 10 percent
- Price: 15 percent

To evaluate the different offers, you need to calculate a weighted score for each vendor using the data provided in the Outsourcing.csv spreadsheet. To calculate the total points for each vendor, do the following:

1. Open the file Outsourcing.csv.
2. Use the SUMPRODUCT formula to multiply each vendor's scores with the respective weights and add the weighted scores.
3. Use conditional formatting to highlight all vendors falling below a total of 60 percent and above a total of 85 percent to facilitate the vendor selection.

Database Application: Building a Special Needs Database for Campus Travel

In addition to international travel, travel reservations for people with special needs is an area of specialty of Campus Travel. However, to be able to recommend travel destinations and travel activities, you should know what facilities are available at each destination. Therefore, you have been asked to create a database of the destinations and the type of facilities that are available for people with special needs. In order to make the system as useful as possible for all, you need to design reports for the users to retrieve information about each destination. Your manager would like to have a system that contains the following information about the destinations:

- Location
- Availability of facilities for the physically handicapped
- Distance to medical facilities
- Pet friendliness

Each location may have one or more handicap facility (e.g., hearing, walking, sight, and so on). A type of handicap facility can be present at multiple locations. Also, each location has to have one pet-friendly accommodation/activity and may also have accommodation for different types of pets (dogs, cats, and so on). After designing the database, please design three professionally formatted reports that (1) list the locations in alphabetical order, (2) list all locations that have the handicap facilities for those that find it difficult to walk, and (3) list all locations that have a cat-friendly policy.

Hint: In Microsoft Access, you can create queries before preparing the reports. Enter a few sample data sets and print out the reports.

Team Work Exercise

 Net Stats:
Moore's Law and the Laggards

The technology industry, laboring under Moore's Law, depends on technology users to regularly adopt new hardware and software. Millions of users, however, accustomed to the tried and true, would rather stick with those products they know—at least as long as possible. Sometimes the reason for not rushing to replace the old with the new is familiarity with and an acquired expertise in using the older version of a product or service:

- In February 2012, 12 percent of U.S. adults had not yet purchased a mobile phone.
- In May 2012, Windows XP, long retired by Microsoft, was still on 45 percent of desktop PCs.
- In June 2012, more than 3.1 million people still used AOL's dial-up Internet access service, even when broadband was available at comparable prices.

Other reasons why people may be slow to adopt new technologies are prohibitive costs or user views that the new product or service has yet to prove itself as superior to the old. Microsoft's Vista versus Windows 7 operating systems is a case in point. While Vista was viewed as an improvement over the prior Windows version, XP, most consumers did not adopt Vista, viewing its cost and high system requirements to be excessive. In mid-2010, just a few months after its release, the adoption rate for Windows 7 outpaced that of Vista over a similar period by more than two to one. Also, by May 2012, Windows 7 had 41 percent and Vista had about 7 percent of the desktop market share; note that Windows XP, initially released in 2001, still retained the largest market share!

Individual computer users are free to opt to be tortoises or hares regarding the adoption of new technology. Information technology (IT) directors, however, must usually follow company culture and management preferences when opting whether to adopt new technology. If management is comfortable with risk and likes to be on the cutting edge, for example,

IT directors can probably feel safe in adopting new technology early on. A staid, risk-averse management attitude, however, would probably not appreciate an IT director who rushes to adopt new technology. In any event, whether to adopt new technology immediately as it becomes available is a decision that will always be with us.

Questions and Exercises

1. In 2012, 46 percent of Americans owned a smartphone; search the Web for the most up-to-date statistics on this technology.
2. As a team, interpret the changes in numbers (or stories). What is striking/important about these findings?
3. As a team, discuss how these findings will look like in 5 years and 10 years. How are things in the U.S. market the same or different across the world? Where are things moving faster/slower? Why?
4. Using your spreadsheet software of choice, create a graph/figure most effectively visualizing the finding you consider most important.

Based on:

Anonymous. (2012, June 4). Subscriber data from Internet service providers. *Boston.com.* Retrieved June 8, 2012, from http://articles.boston.com/2012-06-04/business/31368613_1_dial-up-access-customers-fios-internet-dsl-internet.

Anonymous. (2012). *Netmarketshare.com.* Retrieved June 8, 2012, from http://www.netmarketshare.com/.

Helft, M. (2008, March 12). Tech's late adopters prefer the tried and true. *The New York Times.* Retrieved June 12, 2012, from http://www.nytimes.com/2008/03/12/technology/12inertia.html.

History of Microsoft Windows. (2012, June 7). In *Wikipedia, The Free Encyclopedia.* Retrieved June 8, 2012, from http://en.wikipedia.org/w/index.php?title=History_of_Microsoft_Windows&oldid=496382691.

Oiaga, M. (2010, February 22). Windows 7 crushes Vista. *Softpedia.* Retrieved June 12, 2012, from http://news.softpedia.com/news/Windows-7-Crushes-Vista-135712.shtml.

Pew Internet. (2012, March 1). 46% of American adults are smartphone owners. *Pew Internet.* Retrieved on June 12, 2012, from http://pewinternet.org/~/media//Files/Reports/2012/Smartphone%20ownership%202012.pdf.

Warren, S. (2005, November 17). Adopting new tech: Conservative or Aggressive? *Earthweb.* Retrieved June 8, 2012, from http://itmanagement.earthweb.com/erp/article.php/3565056.

Answers to the Self-Study Questions

1. D, p. 392
2. A, p. 394
3. C, p. 392
4. B, p. 396
5. B, p. 403
6. D, p. 379
7. C, p. 407
8. B, p. 411
9. D, p. 410
10. D, p. 406

CASE 1	Next Generation Identification: FBI, ICE Databases Expand and Join Forces

As crime-solving aides, first there was finger-printing; decades later came DNA analysis. Next is the FBI's US$1 billion "Next Generation Identification" (NGI) database, used to store biometric identification ranging from palm prints to iris eye patterns, photos of scars and tattoos, and distinctive facial characteristics for criminal identification. In the past, fingerprints have been the most widely used means of uniquely identifying people, with the FBI keeping 55 million sets of fingerprints in its current database dubbed "Integrated Automated Fingerprint Identification System" (IAFIS). The next step includes storing additional biometric characteristics. Unfortunately, taken alone, many of those have been proven to be rather unreliable (facial recognition accuracy in public places can be as low as 10 to 20 percent, depending on lighting conditions), such that a real increase in identification accuracy can come only from combining the results of multiple biometrics.

In defense of the FBI's extensive program, Kimberly Del Greco, the FBI's Biometric Services section chief, said that adding to the database is "important to protect the borders to keep the terrorists out, protect our citizens, our neighbors, our children so they can have good jobs and have a safe country to live in."

Similar to the FBI's IAFIS database, the Department of Homeland Security (DHS) maintains the massive "Automated Biometric Identification System" (IDENT) database. The Immigration and Customs Enforcement Agency (ICE), part of the DHS, uses this database in its "Secure Communities" initiative to aid in capturing criminal aliens. The Secure Communities program is a federal, state, and local government partnership that allows state and local law enforcement officials to quickly share information with ICE on captured suspects. The data forwarded to ICE are used to make immigration processing and removing more efficient if the suspect turns out to be a criminal alien. At the heart of the Secure Communities program is the automatic integration of the IAFIS and IDENT databases. When someone is arrested, local law enforcement puts the suspect's fingerprints into the FBI's database. However, the fingerprints are not only checked against the FBI's IAFIS system, but also against the DHS' IDENT database to see if the suspect is in the country legally. If the suspect isn't legal, ICE can immediately begin the deportation process. The system also prioritizes removal of criminal aliens based on their risk to national security and the local community. The prioritization helps ensure that serious criminals (aliens or otherwise) are not inadvertently released and cuts down on the time criminal aliens must be held in custody before being returned to their home country. In 2011, the IDENT/IAFIS interoperability, which allows for automatic information sharing between these databases, was deployed in 937 jurisdictions, and close to 7 million submissions resulted in almost 350,000 matches, leading to nearly 80,000 deportations. As of June 2012, the IDENT and IAFIS databases were integrated in 97 percent of U.S. jurisdictions, and ICE's goal is to have Secure Communities operating in each of the 3,181 jurisdictions across the United States by 2013. The FBI's Next Generation Identification database will take this a step further, as it will not only be based on data from both existing databases, but will also include a host of other biometric identifiers.

Both the FBI and Secure Communities programs have been criticized by privacy advocates. Critics say that Secure Communities, for example, can lead to unnecessary or prolonged detention, make accessing a lawyer difficult, and prevent release on bail. There is also a fear that there is no complaint mechanism associated with the systems. Opponents believe that victims of system errors will have little redress if they are erroneously identified as a criminal or illegal alien. In addition, opponents to the Secure Communities program argue that the integration of databases undermines the trust between immigrant communities and local law enforcement agencies. Fearing that illegal immigrants may be dissuaded from reporting crimes or may not be willing to serve as witnesses, Washington, D.C. mayor Vincent Gray announced in June 2012 that law enforcement officers would be prohibited from asking about people's immigration status.

While the FBI and ICE maintain that their programs are strictly limited to criminals and those in the country illegally, privacy and civil rights activists are watching the developments to ensure that the government respects the rights of its citizens.

Questions:

1. List a set of tangible and intangible benefits as well as tangible and intangible costs for the FBI database system.
2. Develop a set of faith-, fear-, and fact-based arguments to support the continued and ongoing expansion of the FBI database. Which arguments do you think are the strongest? Why?
3. Some privacy advocates argue that biometric systems can become unreliable and single out innocent people, especially over time as these databases become less accurate because of a person's natural aging process, weight loss, weight gain, injury, or permanent disability. Discuss the problems associated with having these systems single out innocent people.

Based on:

American Immigration Council. (2009, November 23). Secure Communities: A fact sheet. *Immigrationpolicy.org*. Retrieved April 4, 2012, from http://www .immigrationpolicy.org/just-facts/secure-communities-fact-sheet.

Howell, J. (2012, June 4). D.C. prepares to walk fine line on deportations. *The Washington Times*. Retrieved June 6, 2012, from http://www.washingtontimes .com/news/2012/jun/4/dc-prepares-to-walk-fine-line-on-deportations.

Lynch, J. (2011, July 8). The FBI's Next Generation Identification: Bigger and faster but much worse for privacy. *Electronic Frontier Foundation*. Retrieved June 6, 2012, from https://www.eff.org/deeplinks/2011/07/ fbis-next-generation-identification-database.

McNeill, J. (2010, January 6). Secure Communities: A model for Obama's 2010 Immigration Enforcement Strategy. *Heritage.org*. Retrieved April 4, 2012, from http://www.heritage.org/Research/Reports/2010/01/Secure-Communities-A-Model-for-Obamas-2010-Immigration-Enforcement-Strategy.

U.S. Immigrations and Customs Enforcement. (2011, October 14). Secure Communities IDENT/IAFIS Interoperability monthly statistics through September 30, 2011. Retrieved June 6, 2012, from http://www.ice.gov/doclib/ foia/sc-stats/nationwide_interoperability_stats-fy2011-to-date.pdf.

U.S. Immigrations and Customs Enforcement. (2012, June 5). Activated Jurisdictions. Retrieved June 6, 2012, from http://www.ice.gov/doclib/secure-communities/pdf/sc-activated.pdf.

CASE 2   The Emergence of Open Source Software

You're probably well aware by now that some software, such as the Linux operating system and the Firefox browser, is *open source*. That is, creators of the programs made the source code available so that anyone could program changes to improve the software's performance.

Bruce Perens and Eric S. Raymond, two prominent proponents of open source software, formed the Open Source Initiative (OSI) in 1998, a non-profit organization dedicated to promoting open source software. The OSI formulated an *open source definition* to determine whether software can be considered for an open source license. An open source license is a copyright license for software that specifies that the source code is available for redistribution and modification without programmers having to pay the original author.

Open source software continues to make inroads into a broad range of personal and business applications. In particular, open source software is having an ever-expanding role in data warehousing and business intelligence solutions.

Open source software can also be found in many government applications, but advocates are pushing for more. For instance, several open source industry leaders sent a letter to President Obama asking him to consider the role that open source software could play in the government. In the letter, the authors point out that open source's transparency could help lead to more efficient government through its open platform.

Microsoft, the proprietary software giant, is even lending a more supportive role to the open source community. In September 2009, Microsoft started the CodePlex Foundation in an effort to "complement existing open source foundations and organizations, providing a forum in which best practices and shared understanding can be established by a broad group of participants, both software companies and open source communities." Time will tell if Microsoft's CodePlex Foundation can advance the cause of open source software and help smooth over some of the rough relations the company has had with the open source community.

Open source, making use of the wisdom of the crowds, fuels some of the big IT megatrends, including cloud computing, mobile applications, and Big Data. For example, in March 2010, the Free Cloud Alliance was formed, bringing together open source software publishers to build cloud-based, open source solutions for "high-performance, mission-critical applications." Its goal is to provide the same type of service that's currently delivered by SaaS providers like Amazon.com but in an open source format, giving users access to the source code and their data.

Another megatrend fueled by open source is mobility; in particular, the Android operating system has made inroads into the mobile operating system market, now having the largest market share of all mobile phone operating systems. Likewise, another battlefield in the mobile (and stationary) world is map services. For years, Google Maps has been the gold standard, even being integrated into Apple's iPhones and iPads. As Google started charging high fees for commercial use of its maps, many companies moved away from Google maps; in 2012, Apple even released its own mapping service, and Foursquare has moved to Open Street Map (OSM), an open source mapping service that is similar to the online encyclopedia Wikipedia, in that everyone can contribute by providing updates on new buildings or roads, or correct errors.

Finally, open source projects have become indispensable for Big Data initiatives ranging from storing and managing vast amounts of unstructured data to analyzing these data. Not only do open source applications provide the tools to deal with Big Data, the openness of the source code also helps instill confidence as to why and where the results come from. For example, recently, the oil company Chevron turned to the open source project Hadoop for storing and managing huge amounts of seismic data needed to locate oil or gas deposits on the ocean floor.

As with the Internet, servers, cloud computing, mobility, and Big Data, open source seems to have been at the forefront of many megatrends. What will be the next megatrend fuelled by open source?

Questions:

1. What are the pros and cons of having so much open source software enabling the Internet?
2. For what types of applications do you think open source is better than proprietary software? When is it worse?
3. Find a for-profit company that is distributing open source software. What is the software? How does the company make money? Is its revenue model sustainable?

Based on:

Bloom, B. (2012, May 29). The open-source answer to big data. *ITWorld.com*. Retrieved June 6, 2012, from http://www.itworld.com/open-source/279090/open-source-answer-big-data.

Free Cloud Alliance Press Release. (2010, March 29). Free Cloud Alliance formed: Open source IaaS, PaaS and SaaS for the Enterprise. *Freecloudalliance.org*. Retrieved June 4, 2012, from http://www.freecloudalliance.org/fca-Home/news-free-cloud-alliance.

Gralla, P. (2012, March 26). Microsoft's secret weapon against Google Maps–open source. *Computerworld*. Retrieved June 7, 2012, from http://blogs.computerworld.com/19932/microsofts_secret_weapon_against_google_maps_open_source.

King, R. (2012, June 5). Chevron explores open source using Hadoop. *Wall Street Journal*. Retrieved June 6, 2012, from http://blogs.wsj.com/cio/2012/06/05/chevron-explores-open-source-using-hadoop.

Kunkel, R. G. (2002, September). Recent developments in Shrinkwrap, Clickwrap and Browsewrap licenses in the United States. *E Law*. Retrieved June 4, 2012, from http://www.murdoch.edu.au/elaw/issues/v9n3/kunkel93.html.

Montalbano, E. (2009, September 10). Microsoft forms, funds new open-source foundation. *PC World*. Retrieved June 4, 2012, from http://www.pcworld.com/businesscenter/article/171756/microsoft_forms_funds_new_opensource_foundation.html.

Open Source Initiative. (2012, June 4). In *Wikipedia, The Free Encyclopedia*. Retrieved June 5, 2012, from http://en.wikipedia.org/w/index.php?title=Open_Source_Initiative&oldid=495987156.

Ricknäs, M. (2010, March 31). Companies create alliance to push open source clouds. *PC World*. Retrieved June 4, 2012, from http://www.pcworld.com/businesscenter/article/193008/companies_create_alliance_to_push_open_source_clouds.html.

Rooney, P. (2012, May 22). Open source driving cloud, big data, mobile, survey finds. *ZDNet.com*. Retrieved June 6, 2012, from http://www.zdnet.com/blog/open-source/open-source-driving-cloud-big-data-mobile-survey-finds/11015.

Scannell, E. (2009, March 13). 1 in 3 IT shops uses combo proprietary, open source software. *InformationWeek*. Retrieved June 4, 2012, from http://www.informationweek.com/news/software/open_source/showArticle.jhtml?articleID=215900159.

Tiemann, M. (2006, September 19). History of the OSI. *Open Source Initiative*. Retrieved June 4, 2012, from http://opensource.org/history.

Securing Information Systems

Preview

As organizations become more dependent on information systems for enabling organizational strategy, they also become more vulnerable to catastrophic security disasters. Because of this, organizations are focusing more of their attention on information systems security. In this chapter, we first examine various threats to information systems security, followed by a discussion of various approaches for securing information systems and the critical information they hold.

Managing in the digital world requires careful attention to IS security. Having thorough plans for dealing with IS security attacks and natural disasters is critical for effectively managing IS resources within organizations.

Managing in the Digital World:
Not So "Anonymous"—Activists, Hacktivists, or Just Plain Criminals?

Online piracy is a serious problem eating away at the profits from most of today's media corporations, from software to videos to music. With online piracy constantly breathing down their necks, publishers, studios, and labels lobbied the U.S. legislature to introduce legislation to fight, or at least limit, the activities of online piracy through controversial bills; namely SOPA (Stop Online Piracy Act) and PIPA (Protect Intellectual Property Act). One provision of the bills related to the DNS (Domain Name System)—databases residing on the Internet that are used to store and translate relatively easy to remember domain names (www.arizona.edu) into IP addresses (128.196.134.37); if passed, both bills would allow the Justice Department to seize the domain name of any blog or Web site found engaging in piracy, so that users would not be able to access the site using the domain name (this provision has since been removed from the proposed legislation). However, many questioned the effectiveness of the bills, perceiving them as culprits that will cost millions of jobs, infringe on free speech, or even hamper innovation instead of stopping piracy.

File-sharing sites like Megaupload.com, best known for its massive size and volume of downloaded content, are the hotbeds of online piracy. After being shut down by U.S. authorities, Megaupload.com formally bade goodbye in 2012 as New Zealand police raided several homes and businesses linked to its founder Kim Dotcom (a name he took on after making a fortune during the dotcom bubble). With only a slight warning from a tweet reading, "One thing is certain: EXPECT US!," hacktivist group Anonymous launched "Operation Payback" (see Figure 10.1); utilizing 5,635 *zombie computers* distributed throughout the Internet, Anonymous delivered a retaliatory attack resulting in a string of highly coordinated takedowns of Web sites managed by the Department of Justice and a number of other organizations that have publicly supported anti-piracy legislation, including the Recording Industry of America, the Motion Picture Association, and Universal Music.

Who is Anonymous? Having no formal organization and no formal leadership, Anonymous is often considered a loose collective of hacktivists; Internet users practicing civil disobedience by taking part in cyber-attacks on Web sites. Anonymous' deadliest tool for targeting Web sites is known as a *denial-of-service attack*, that is, overwhelming sites with junk traffic to crash the targeted Web servers. The group has participated in several cyber-attacks; the best known concerned a vigilante movement against VISA, MasterCard, and PayPal as a protest for their freezing the accounts of the whistleblower site WikiLeaks. Another example which helped Anonymous garner much public sympathy is the 2011 "Operation Darknet"; in an attempt to battle child pornography, Anonymous took down a number of domains hosting child pornography and related content.

Having been referred to as "The Punisher" of the World Wide Web, Anonymous is well-known for their Internet vigilantism. Although Anonymous claims to have good

FIGURE 10.1

The symbol of the Anonymous group is a mask depicting the historical figure Guy Fawkes.
Source: dny3d/Shutterstock

intentions, what they do is nevertheless illegal, and Anonymous and its supporters face a dilemma between pursuing (sometimes worthwhile) ideological goals and crossing the boundaries of legality.

After reading this chapter, you will be able to answer the following:

1. Who is more responsible for software, music, or movie piracy, the hosting Web site, or the individual downloading the content?

2. When is a hacktivist a criminal, and when are they an activist?

3. What are the ethical tradeoffs for allowing people to have access to any type of information (e.g., child pornography, hate speech, bomb making recipes)?

Based on:

Anonymous. (group). (2012, May 21). In *Wikipedia, The Free Encyclopedia*. Retrieved May 21, 2012, from http://en.wikipedia.org/w/index.php?title=Anonymous_(group)&oldid=493701394.

Gallagher, S. (2011, October 24). Anonymous takes down darknet child porn site on Tor network. *Arstechnica.* Retrieved August 15, 2012, from http://arstechnica.com/business/2011/10/anonymous-takes-down-darknet-child-porn-site-on-tor-network.

Gillmor, D. (2011, October 27). WikiLeaks payments blockade sets dangerous precedent. *The Guardian.* Retrieved August 15, 2012, from http://www.guardian.co.uk/commentisfree/cifamerica/2011/oct/27/wikileaks-payments-blockade-dangerous-precedent.

Taylor, L., and Connelly, C. (2012, January 20). FBI shuts down Megaupload.com, Anonymous shut down FBI. *News.com.au.* Retrieved August 15, 2012, from http://www.news.com.au/technology/fbi-shuts-down-megauploadcom-charges-seven-with-online-piracy/story-e6frfro0-1226249114650.

COMPUTER CRIME

http://goo.gl/6ncJh

Everyone who uses an information system (IS) knows that disasters can happen to stored information or to entire systems. Some disasters are accidents caused by power outages, inexperienced computer users, or mistakes, while others are caused on purpose by malicious hackers. The primary threats to the security of information systems include the following (see Figure 10.2):

- *Natural Disasters.* Power outages, hurricanes, floods, and so on.
- *Accidents.* Inexperienced or careless computer operators (or cats walking across keyboards!).

FIGURE 10.2

Threats to IS security.

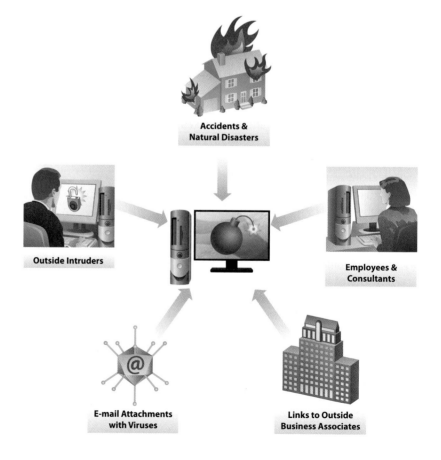

Accidents & Natural Disasters

Outside Intruders

Employees & Consultants

E-mail Attachments with Viruses

Links to Outside Business Associates

- *Employees and Consultants.* People within an organization who have access to electronic files.
- *Links to Outside Business Contacts.* Electronic information can be at risk when it travels between or among business affiliates as part of doing business.
- *Outsiders.* Hackers and crackers who penetrate networks and computer systems to snoop or to cause damage (viruses, perpetually rampant on the Internet, are included in this category).

For individuals as well as organizations, trying to recover from disasters can cost a lot in terms of time and money; in addition, organizations can lose much goodwill if their systems are unavailable (no matter what the reason is) or are compromised by malicious hackers. Hence, for organizations, it is essential to carefully manage IS risk and to ensure business continuity by securing their IS infrastructure. Because *any* information system can be compromised, organizations must engage in **IS risk management**, which refers to gaining an understanding of the interplay between

- threats (i.e., undesirable events that can cause harm),
- vulnerabilities (i.e., weaknesses in an organization's systems or security policies that can be exploited to cause damage), and
- impacts (i.e., the severity of the consequences if a threat indeed causes damage by exploiting a vulnerability).

By understanding and evaluating these factors, organizations can make informed decisions about whether and how to implement controls to eliminate vulnerabilities or reduce impacts (see Figure 10.3). While you may not need the level of security or protection large organizations such as Amazon.com need, you will certainly realize the need to protect your own information systems and data from disaster and computer criminals.

What Is Computer Crime?

Computer crime is defined as the act of using a computer to commit an illegal act. This broad definition of computer crime can include the following:

- Targeting a computer while committing an offense. For example, someone gains unauthorized entry to a computer system in order to cause damage to the computer system or to the data it contains.
- Using a computer to commit an offense. In such cases, computer criminals may steal credit card numbers from Web sites or a company's database, skim money from bank accounts, or make unauthorized electronic fund transfers from financial institutions.
- Using computers to support a criminal activity despite the fact that computers are not actually targeted. For example, drug dealers and other professional criminals may use computers to store records of their illegal transactions.

According to the 2010/11 Computer Security Institute (CSI) Computer Crime and Security Survey, the overall trend for computer crime has been declining over the past several years (CSI, 2011). Nevertheless, the reported losses for organizations due to computer crime have been

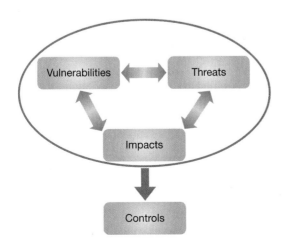

FIGURE 10.3

Organizations have to understand the interplay between threats, vulnerabilities, and impacts to plan and implement effective IS controls.

FIGURE 10.4

Financial impact of virus attacks, 1995–2006, and beyond.

Source: Based on http://www .computereconomics.com.

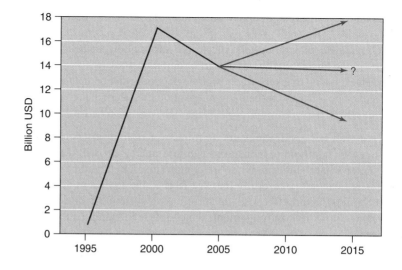

tremendous. For example, in an extreme case, one of the 351 organizations surveyed reported losses exceeding US$25 million for 2010. Additionally, worldwide losses for computer viruses alone were estimated to exceed US$13.3 billion in 2006, and a 2009 estimate by the White House suggested that cybercrime and industrial espionage approached US$1 trillion a year— nearly 2 percent of global GDP (Glenny, 2011). Nevertheless, the trends for losses in the future are unknown, as some experts believe that better security measures may be counteracted by increased sophistication of the criminals (see Figure 10.4). Many organizations do not report incidents of computer crime because of fear that negative publicity could hurt stock value or provide advantages to competitors. Thus, experts believe that many incidents are never reported and that real losses exceed these estimates. It is clear, however, that computer crime is a fact of life. In this section, we briefly introduce this topic of growing importance.

Hacking and Cracking

Those individuals who are knowledgeable enough to gain access to computer systems without authorization have long been referred to as **hackers**. The name was first used in the 1960s to describe expert computer users and programmers who were students at the Massachusetts Institute of Technology. Based on curiosity and the desire to learn as much as possible about computers, they wrote programs for the mainframes they used that allowed them to roam freely through computer systems, and freely exchanged information about their "hacks;" however, they followed unwritten rules against damaging or stealing information belonging to others.

As computer crime became more prevalent and damaging, true hackers—those motivated by curiosity and not by a desire to do harm (sometimes referred to as "white hats")—objected to use of the term to describe computer criminals. Today, those who break into computer systems with the intention of doing damage or committing a crime are usually called **crackers** or "black hats." Some computer criminals attempt to break into systems or deface Web sites to promote political or ideological goals (such as free speech, human rights, and antiwar campaigns); these Web vandals are referred to as **hacktivists**.

Types of Computer Criminals and Crimes

Computer crimes are almost as varied as the users who commit them. Some involve the use of a computer to steal money or other assets or to perpetrate a deception for money, such as advertising merchandise for sale on a Web auction site, collecting orders and payment, and then sending either inferior merchandise or no merchandise at all. Other computer crimes involve stealing or altering information. Some of those thieves who steal information or disrupt a computer system have demanded a ransom from victims in exchange for returning the information or repairing the damage. Cyberterrorists have planted destructive programs in computer systems, and then threatened to activate them if a ransom is not paid (see more on cyberterrorism later in this chapter). Crimes in the form of electronic vandalism cause damage when offenders plant viruses, cause computer systems to crash, or deny service on a Web site.

Use of the Internet has fostered other types of criminal activity, such as the stalking of minors by sexual predators through newsgroups and chat rooms. Those who buy, sell, and distribute pornography have also found in the Internet a new medium for carrying out their activities.

WHO COMMITS COMPUTER CRIMES? When you hear the term "cracker" or "computer criminal," you might imagine a techno-geek, someone who sits in front of his or her computer all day and night, attempting to break the ultra-super-secret security code of one of the most sophisticated computer systems in the world, perhaps a computer for the U.S. military, a Swiss bank, or the Central Intelligence Agency. While this fits the traditional profile for a computer criminal, there is no clear profile today. More and more people have the skills, the tools, and the motives to hack into a computer system. A modern-day computer criminal could be a disgruntled, middle-aged, white-collar worker sitting at a nice desk on the fourteenth floor of

ETHICAL DILEMMA

Industrial Espionage

Industrial espionage describes covert activities, such as the theft of trade secrets, bribery, blackmail, and technological surveillance. Many notable companies have been victims of industrial espionage, including Procter & Gamble, IBM, DuPont, Gillette, Kodak, Starwood, and Microsoft. As most companies expect to fall victim to some form of industrial espionage, many large companies try to take active countermeasures, such as employing security personnel that work specifically to guard against such spying.

Industrial espionage is most commonly associated with technology-heavy industries, such as the computer hardware and software industries, but also with any other industry in which a significant amount of money is spent on research and development (R&D), such as the defense and pharmaceutical industries. Often, competitors attempt to steal prototypes, so as to gain access to new technological developments. In some cases, governmental agencies are suspected of industrial espionage when searching laptops at airports, where trade secrets can be stolen or spyware can be deposited on laptops; thus, many organizations provide their employees with "forensically clean" laptops to be used for travel. Industrial espionage is also often carried out by compromising someone who works for a targeted company through bribery, coercion, or blackmail.

Another target for industrial espionage is recently laid-off or fired employees. These ex-employees may be disgruntled and willing to trade their valuable secrets for a price. Similarly, a person currently working within a targeted company, often referred to as an insider threat, may trade their secrets for a price. While earning money this way may seem lucrative for the people involved, penalties for a person giving private information away can include not only being fired, but also criminal charges if the employee signed a confidentiality agreement, or worked on projects which required a governmental security clearance.

The proliferation of the Internet and mobile devices is providing additional avenues for industrial espionage. Cracking into a company's computer system has become a fairly common practice, where criminals steal information and trade secrets that might be sold to others. Critical information can also be downloaded off unattended computers in offices by interns, visiting cleaners, or repairmen. Laptops, mobile devices, and USB drives can be stolen or accessed while left unattended in hotel rooms or can be stolen while in transit (e.g., stolen out of checked baggage when traveling). In the Information Age, critical information is always vulnerable to attacks, and the loss of strategic information may give an organization's rivals a competitive advantage and can have devastating impacts on the company's bottom line.

Today, with many organizations and countries engaging in industrial espionage, it seems like almost everyone is engaged in stealing ideas from their competitors. Imagine you were the owner of a company that fell victim to industrial espionage, and is on the verge of bankruptcy. At a trade show, the USB drive (on which you suspect some trade secrets) of a competitor's salesperson is within your direct reach, and no one would notice it's missing until after the show. You suspect the competitor to have copied your products and ideas before, and the contents of the USB drive could save your company, as well as your employees' jobs. What would you do?

Based on:

Anonymous. (2011, April 25). 10 Most notorious acts of corporate espionage. Retrieved October 17, 2012, from http://www .businesspundit.com/10-most-notorious-acts-of-corporate-espionage.

Benetton, L. (n.d.). How to secure your laptop before crossing the border. CBA.org. http://www.cba.org/cba/practicelink/tayp /laptopborder.aspx.

Ellis-Christensen, T. (2012). What is industrial espionage? *wiseGEEK.com*. Retrieved October 17, 2012, from http://www.wisegeek.com/ what-is-industrial-espionage.htm.

Industrial espionage. (2012, October 5). In *Wikipedia, The Free Encyclopedia*. Retrieved October 17, 2012, from http://en.wikipedia.org/w/ index.php?title=Industrial_espionage&oldid=516223741.

the headquarters building of a billion-dollar software manufacturer. Computer criminals have been around for decades. For the most part, we associate hackers and crackers with their pranks and crimes involving security systems and viruses. Nevertheless, hackers and crackers have caused the loss of billions of dollars' worth of stolen goods, repair bills, and lost goodwill with customers.

Studies attempting to categorize computer criminals show that they generally fall into one of four groups. These groups are listed next, from those who commit the most infractions to those who commit the fewest infractions:

1. Current or former employees who are in a position to steal or otherwise do damage to employers; most organizations report insider abuses as their most common crime (CSI, 2011).
2. People with technical knowledge who commit business or information sabotage for personal gain.
3. Career criminals who use computers to assist in crimes.
4. Outside crackers simply snooping or hoping to find information of value—crackers commit millions of intrusions per year, but most cause no harm. Estimates are that only around 10 percent of cracker attacks cause damage.

Some crackers probe others' computer systems, electronically stored data, or Web sites for fun, for curiosity, or just to prove they can. Others have malicious or financial motives and intend to steal for gain or do other harm. Whatever the motives, discovery, prosecution, fines, and jail terms can result.

UNAUTHORIZED ACCESS. **Unauthorized access** occurs whenever people who are not authorized to see, manipulate, or otherwise handle information look through electronically stored information files for interesting or useful data, peek at monitors displaying proprietary or confidential information, or intercept electronic information on the way to its destination. Here are a few additional examples from recent media reports:

- Employees steal time on company computers to do personal business.
- Intruders break into government Web sites and change the information displayed.
- Thieves steal credit card numbers and Social Security numbers from electronic databases, and then use the stolen information to charge thousands of dollars in merchandise to victims.
- Competitor's employees posing as interns steal proprietary information about products or corporate strategies (i.e., engage in industrial espionage).

When computer information is shared by several users, as in an organization, in-house system administrators can prevent casual snooping or theft of information by requiring correct permissions. Further, administrators can log attempts of unauthorized individuals trying to obtain access. Determined attackers, however, will try to gain access by giving themselves system administrator status or otherwise elevating their permission level—sometimes by stealing passwords and logging on to a system as authorized users (see Figure 10.5).

INFORMATION MODIFICATION. Often related to unauthorized access, **information modification** occurs when someone accesses electronic information and then changes the information in some way, such as when crackers hack into government Web sites and change information or when employees give themselves electronic raises and bonuses (see Figure 10.6).

OTHER THREATS TO IS SECURITY. Many times, IS security is breached simply because organizations and individuals do not exercise proper care in safeguarding information. Some examples follow:

- Employees keep passwords or access codes on slips of paper in plain sight.
- Individuals have never bothered to install antivirus software, or they install the software but fail to keep it up to date.
- Computer users within an organization continue to use default network passwords after a network is set up instead of passwords that are more difficult to break.
- Employees are careless about letting outsiders view computer monitors, or they carelessly give out information over the telephone.
- Organizations fail to limit access to company files and system resources.

FIGURE 10.5

Unauthorized access can occur in many ways.

FIGURE 10.6

Information modification attack.

- Organizations fail to install effective firewalls or intrusion detection systems, or they install an intrusion detection system but fail to monitor it regularly.
- Proper background checks are not done on new hires.
- Employees are not properly monitored, and they steal company data or computer resources.
- Fired employees are resentful and install harmful code, such as computer viruses, when they leave the company.

While there are many threats to IS security, there are also ways to combat those threats. Later in this chapter, we discuss safeguards organizations can use to improve IS security.

Computer Viruses and Other Destructive Code

Malware—short for "malicious software" such as viruses, worms, and Trojan horses—continues to have a tremendous economic impact on the world, costing organizations more than US$13 billion in 2006 (computereconomics.com, 2008). Accurate estimates of real costs to organizations and society are difficult to obtain, as many organizations choose not to report major incidents (CSI, 2011); most organizations do not want to alarm customers and shareholders of malware and other security events. Whatever the true costs are, antivirus Web vendors report thousands of new forms of malware each month.

COMPUTER VIRUSES. A **virus** is a destructive program that disrupts the normal functioning of computer systems. Viruses differ from other types of malicious code in that they can reproduce themselves. Some viruses are intended to be harmless pranks, but more often they do damage to a computer system by erasing files on the hard drive or by slowing computer processing or otherwise compromising the system. Viruses infect a single computer only, potentially spreading to other computers if infected files are shared. Viruses are planted in host computers in a number of ways (Figure 10.7), but are most often spread through malicious e-mail attachments, the sharing of removable media (such as USB sticks), or file downloads from malicious Web sites.

WORMS, TROJAN HORSES, AND OTHER SINISTER PROGRAMS. Viruses are among the most virulent forms of computer infections, but other destructive code can also be damaging. A **worm**, a variation of a virus that is targeted at networks, is designed to spread by itself, without the need for an infected host file to be shared. Worms take advantage of security holes in operating systems and other software to replicate endlessly across the Internet, thus causing servers to crash, which denies service to Internet users.

Another category of destructive programs is called **Trojan horses**. Like the Trojan horse in Greek mythology, Trojan horses appear to be legitimate, benign programs, but carry a destructive payload. Unlike viruses, Trojan horses typically do not replicate themselves, but, like viruses, can do much damage, such as by giving the creator unauthorized access to a system. When a Trojan horse is planted in a computer, its instructions remain hidden. The computer appears to function normally, but in fact it is performing underlying functions dictated by the intrusive code. For example, under the pretext of playing chess with an unsuspecting systems operator, a cracker group installed a Trojan horse in a Canadian mainframe. While the game appeared to be proceeding normally, the Trojan horse program was sneakily establishing a powerful unauthorized account for the future use of the intruders.

FIGURE 10.7

How a computer virus is spread.

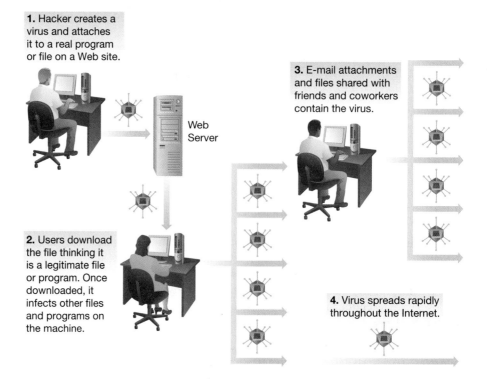

1. Hacker creates a virus and attaches it to a real program or file on a Web site.

2. Users download the file thinking it is a legitimate file or program. Once downloaded, it infects other files and programs on the machine.

Web Server

3. E-mail attachments and files shared with friends and coworkers contain the virus.

4. Virus spreads rapidly throughout the Internet.

Logic bombs or **time bombs** are variations of Trojan horses. They also do not reproduce themselves, and are designed to operate without disrupting normal computer function. Instead, they lie in wait for unsuspecting computer users to perform a triggering operation. Time bombs are set off by specific dates, such as the birthday of a famous person. Logic bombs are set off by certain types of operations, such as entering a specific password or adding or deleting names and other information to and from certain computer files. Disgruntled employees have planted logic and time bombs on being fired, intending for the program to activate after they have left the company. In at least one instance in recent history, a former employee in Minnesota demanded money to deactivate the time bomb he had planted in company computers before it destroyed employee payroll records.

DENIAL OF SERVICE. **Denial-of-service attacks** occur when electronic intruders deliberately attempt to prevent legitimate users of a service (e.g., customers accessing a Web site) from using that service, often by using up all of a system's resources. To execute such attacks, intruders often create armies of **zombie computers** by infecting computers that are located in homes, schools, and businesses with viruses or worms. Any computer connected to the Internet can be infected if it is not protected by firewalls and antivirus software and is, therefore, open to attacks and to being used as a zombie computer (in fact, some security experts believe that more than 10 percent of all computers connected to the Internet are used as zombies, unbeknownst to the owners). The zombie computers, without users' knowledge or consent, are used to spread the virus to other computers and to launch attacks on popular Web sites. The Web site servers under attack crash under the barrage of bogus computer-generated visitors, causing a denial of service to those Internet users who are legitimately trying to visit the sites (see Figure 10.8). For example, MyDoom was able to recruit an army of zombies that bombarded Microsoft's Web site with traffic and literally locked out legitimate customers. (Microsoft is a popular target for virus writers, and the company must constantly provide downloadable patches to those using its software in order to prevent unauthorized intrusion.)

SPYWARE, SPAM, AND COOKIES. Three additional ways in which information systems can be threatened is by spyware, spam, and cookies.

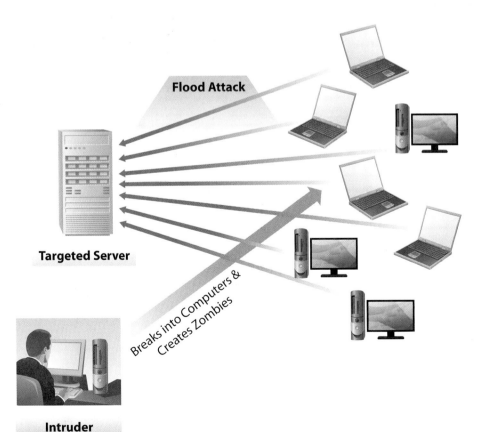

FIGURE 10.8

Denial-of-service attack.

Spyware **Spyware** is any software that covertly gathers information about a user through an Internet connection without the user's knowledge. Spyware is sometimes hidden within freeware or shareware programs. In other instances, it is embedded within a Web site and is downloaded to the user's computer, without the user's knowledge, in order to track data about the user for marketing and advertisement purposes. Spyware can monitor your activity (such as Web site visits) and secretly transmit that information to someone else. **Keyloggers** can capture every keystroke and thus gather information such as e-mail addresses, passwords, and credit card numbers (note that keyloggers may be installed on companies' computers to monitor employees). Spyware presents problems because it uses your computer's memory resources; eats network bandwidth as it sends information back to the spyware's home base via your Internet connection; causes system instability or, worse, system crashes; and exposes users to identity theft, credit card fraud, and other types of crime. **Adware** (free software paid for by advertisements appearing during the use of the software) sometimes contains spyware that collects information about a person's Web surfing behavior in order to customize Web site banner advertisements. It is important to note that spyware is not currently illegal, although there is ongoing legislative hype about regulating it in some way. Fortunately, firewalls and spyware protection software can be used to scan for and block spyware.

Spam Another prevalent form of network traffic that invades our e-mail is spam. **Spam** is electronic junk mail or junk newsgroup postings, usually for the purpose of advertising for some product and/or service (see Figure 10.9). In addition to being a nuisance and wasting our time, spam also eats up huge amounts of storage space and network bandwidth. Today, according to websense.com, nearly 90 percent of all e-mail is spam! Although there are federal, state, and international laws related to spam, most notably the CAN-SPAM Act of 2003, very little can be done to stop a motivated spammer (see www.spamlaws.com for more information). Spammers commonly use zombie computers to send out millions of e-mail messages, unbeknownst to the computer users. Some spam consists of hoaxes, asking you to donate money to nonexistent causes or warning you of viruses and other Internet dangers that do not exist. Other times, spam includes attachments that carry destructive computer viruses. As a result, Internet service providers and those who manage e-mail within organizations often use **spam filters** to fight spam. Typical spam filters use multiple defense layers—and can utilize both hardware and software—to help reduce the amount of spam processed by the central e-mail servers and delivered to users' in-boxes. Spam filters fight not only spam but also other e-mail threats, such as directory harvest

FIGURE 10.9

Spam is rampant and consumes an enormous amount of human and technology resources.

Source: Courtesy of Microsoft, Inc.

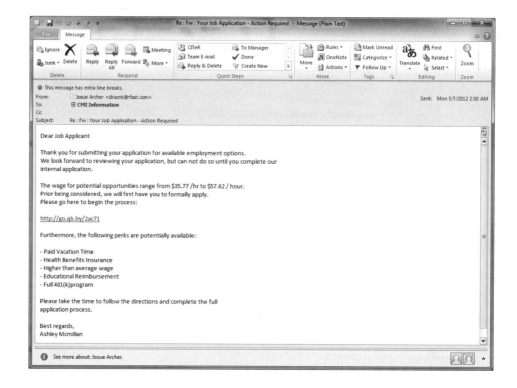

attacks (i.e., attempts to determine valid e-mail addresses for spam databases), phishing attacks, viruses, and more.

Some spam e-mail is used for **phishing** (or spoofing), which are attempts to trick financial account and credit card holders into giving away their authentication information, usually by sending spam messages to literally millions of e-mail accounts (i.e., attackers are "phishing" [fishing] for victims). These phony messages contain links to Web sites that duplicate legitimate sites to capture account information. For example, most e-mail users regularly receive phishing attempts from various spoofed banks, eBay, or PayPal (see Figure 10.10). As people learn that generically addressed e-mail from a bank is not likely legitimate, criminals have turned to spear phishing. **Spear phishing** is a more sophisticated fraudulent e-mail attack that targets a specific person or organization by personalizing the message (phishing with a spear rather than a broad net) in order to make the message appear as if it is from a trusted source such as an individual within the recipient's company, a government entity, or a well-known company. While spear phishing can be very effective, the attacker needs some basic information in order to optimally target the phishing message. Many fear that social media sites like Facebook will increasingly provide valuable information about potential victims to criminals designing spear phishing attacks.

In addition to e-mail–based spam, spam over text messaging and spam over instant messaging—called **spim**—are becoming increasingly used. Spim is particularly tricky because messages—typically a Web site link and some text saying how great the site is when using instant messaging—are formatted to mimic communication chat sessions. Commonly, spammers try to impersonate a known contact by hijacking his or her account, or try to find victims by sending contact requests to millions of subscribers to instant messaging services. Once contact is made, the spammers try to lure their victims to a Web site containing malware. Cell phones are also not immune to spam; the number of spam text messages in the U.S. rose 45 percent in 2011, to more than 4.5 billion messages (Kharif, 2012).

Often, spammers post their spam messages in online forums, blogs, or wikis, or create thousands of e-mail accounts at free providers such as Yahoo! or Hotmail to send out their messages. Rather than manually going through such tedious tasks to set up these accounts or post thousands of messages, spammers use bots (i.e., software robots that work in the background to provide services to their owners; see Chapter 6, "Enhancing Business Intelligence Using Information Systems") to do this. Faced with this problem, e-mail providers and managers of online forums are attempting to prevent spammers from using bots to automatically submit online forms. One commonly used approach for preventing bots from submitting forms is the use of CAPTCHAs. A **CAPTCHA** (Completely Automated Public Turing Test to Tell Computers and Humans Apart) typically consists of a distorted image displaying a combination of letters and/

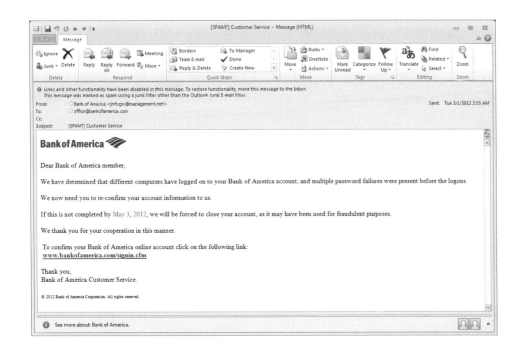

FIGURE 10.10

A phishing e-mail message.
Source: Courtesy of Microsoft, Inc.

or numbers that a user has to input into a form (in addition to other required information) before submitting it. As the image is distorted, (currently) only humans can interpret the letters/ numbers, preventing the use of automated bots for creating accounts or posting spam to forums, blogs, or wikis. CAPTCHAs are also used to prevent bots from trying to break passwords using a brute force approach (see Figure 10.11).

Unfortunately, in addition to posing challenges for the disabled, CAPTCHAs are becoming increasingly ineffective. Whereas some spammers try to break CAPTCHAs using sophisticated character recognition technology, others use cheap human labor; recently, inventive spammers created a striptease game, where the "players" had to solve CAPTCHAs for "Melissa" to expose herself. Unbeknownst to the users, the program would send the results to a remote server that would use the information for malicious purposes. Increasingly, Web masters are using a combination of multiple techniques to stop spammers, such as detecting mouse movements (as automated agents do not use a mouse), or detecting the rate at which text is entered into forms, or incorporating invisible fields (which would be "seen" and filled out by an automated agent but not a human user), together with CAPTCHAs in order to distinguish between malicious bots and legitimate users.

Cookies Another nuisance in Internet usage is cookies. A **cookie** is a small text file passed to a Web browser on a user's computer by a Web server. The browser then stores the message in a text file, and the message is sent back to the server each time the user's browser requests a page from that server.

Cookies are normally used for legitimate purposes, such as identifying a user in order to present a customized Web page or for authentication purposes. Although you can choose to not accept the storage of cookies, you may not be able to visit the site, or it may not function properly. For example, to read the *New York Times* online, you must register by entering your name and other information. When you go through the registration process, cookies are stored on your machine. If you don't accept cookies or you delete the stored cookies, you are not allowed to access the online newspaper without reregistering. Similarly, you will have to accept cookies when purchasing from many e-tailers, as most online shopping carts require cookies to function properly. In some cases, cookies may contain sensitive information (such as credit card numbers) and thus pose a security risk in case unauthorized persons gain access to the computer.

Specific cookie management or cookie killer software can be used to manage cookies, but an even simpler way to manage cookies is through the settings in your Web browser. In the settings for the Firefox Web browser, for example, you can set levels of restrictions on the use of cookies, you can stop the use of them altogether, and, if you do allow them, you can go in periodically and delete them from your computer.

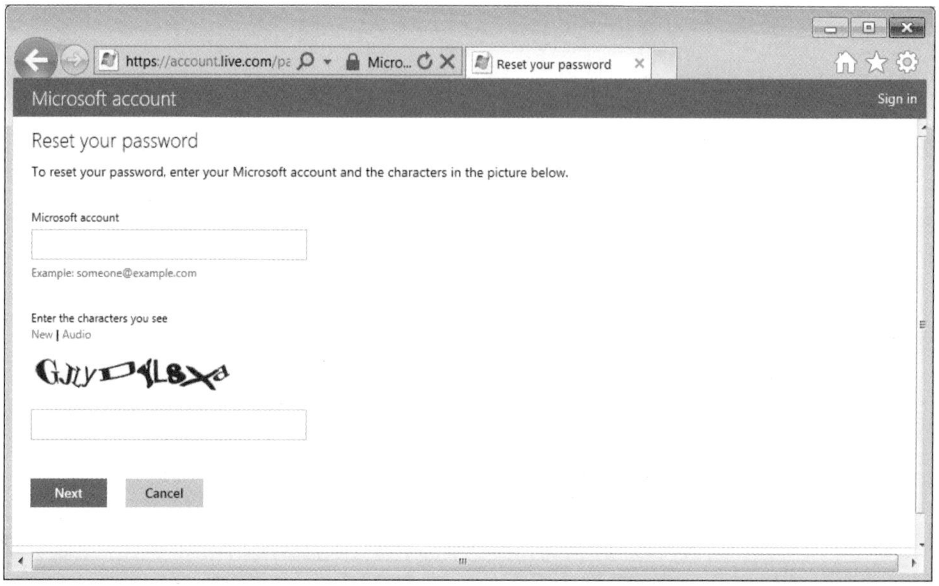

FIGURE 10.11

A CAPTCHA is used to prevent bots from submitting an online form.
Source: Courtesy of Microsoft, Inc.

THE RISE OF BOTNETS AND THE CYBERATTACK SUPPLY CHAIN. Destructive software robots called bots (see Chapter 6), working together on a collection of zombie computers via the Internet, called **botnets**, have become the standard method of operation for professional cybercriminals. For example, about 85 percent of all e-mail spam is sent out by only six major botnets. Attacks using botnets are emerging into a global supply chain of highly specialized criminals. For instance, a phishing attack can involve the following:

1. A *programmer* writes a phishing attack template and makes this available for purchase.
2. A *phisher* who wants to run an attack purchases the template and designs an attack (e.g., ask recipients of a spam e-mail to update their banking information at the Wells Fargo Bank).
3. The *phisher* contracts with a *cracker* to provide hosting space for the phishing Web sites.
4. The *phisher* contacts a **bot herder**—a criminal who has a botnet residing on a collection of zombie computers—to send out the spam e-mail that carries the attack to unsuspecting people.
5. After launching the attack and collecting information from those who responded to the phishing attack, the *phisher* provides the stolen personal information to a *collector* who specializes in removing funds from the affected financial institutions.
6. The *collector* works with a criminal called a *mule herder* who has a network of people who carry out the withdrawals from affected banks.

Each member of the supply chain has very specialized skills and can be located anywhere in the world. In fact, one of the difficulties in stopping this global crime syndicate is the difficulty of not only tracking the locations of these villains but also prosecuting criminals across international borders. Today, a would-be cybercriminal does not need highly specialized computer skills to build a botnet; rather, the criminal can easily "rent" space on a botnet (including technical support from the bot herder, tremendous resources, and bandwidth) starting at US$150, depending on the size of the botnet.

IDENTITY THEFT. One of the fastest-growing "information" crimes in recent years has been **identity theft** (see Figure 10.12). Identity theft is the stealing of another person's Social Security Number, credit card number, and other personal information for the purpose of using the victim's credit rating to borrow money, buy merchandise, and otherwise run up debts that are never repaid. In some cases, thieves even withdraw money directly from victims' bank accounts. Since many government and private organizations keep information about individuals in accessible databases, opportunities abound for thieves to retrieve it. Reclaiming one's identity and restoring a good credit rating can be frustrating and time consuming for victims.

FIGURE 10.12

Identity theft is one of the fastest-growing information crimes.
Source: Getty Images - IStock Exclusive RF

The solution to identity theft lies in the government and private sector working together to change practices used to verify a person's identity. For example, a mother's maiden name and an individual's Social Security Number are too easily obtained. Other methods of personal identification, such as biometrics and encryption, may need to be used if the problem is to be solved. Methods of information security, including biometrics and encryption, are discussed later in this chapter.

Internet Hoaxes

An **Internet hoax** is a false message circulated online about new viruses; funds for alleged victims of the March 11, 2011 Japan earthquake and tsunami; kids in trouble; cancer causes; or any other topic of public interest. In most cases, the consequences of passing on a hoax will be small, and your friends will just ridicule you; in other cases, spammers might "harvest" e-mail addresses from hoaxes, potentially causing your in-box to be flooded with junk mail. Several Web sites, such as Hoaxbusters (www.hoaxbusters.org), Symantec, or McAfee, publish lists of known hoaxes, and you should always check to see if a message is a hoax before you forward it to others.

Cybersquatting

An issue related to information property is **cybersquatting**, the dubious practice of registering a domain name and then trying to sell the name for big bucks to the person, company, or organization most likely to want it. Domain names are one of the few scarce resources on the Internet, and victims of cybersquatting include Panasonic, Hertz, Avon, and numerous other companies and individuals. Fortunately, the U.S. government passed the Anti-Cybersquatting Consumer Protection Act in 1999, which made it a crime to register, traffic in, or use a domain name to profit from the goodwill of a trademark belonging to someone else. Fines for cybersquatting can reach as high as US$100,000, in addition to the forfeiture of the disputed domain name. As a result, recent court cases have not been kind to cybersquatters. Many feel, however, that it is often much easier simply to pay the cybersquatter because that will likely be much faster and cheaper than to hire a lawyer and go through the lengthy legal process. Others, such as rapper Eminem, who won a case against a company that had registered the domain name eminemmobile.com, use a fast-track procedure of the World Intellectual Property Organization of the United Nations to stop others from using their names without permission. No matter how companies or individuals deal with this problem, valuable resources of time and money are wasted resolving these disputes.

Cyberharassment, Cyberstalking, and Cyberbullying

The Internet has become a place where people utilize its anonymity to harass, stalk, and bully others. **Cyberharassment**, a crime in many states and countries, broadly refers to the use of a computer to communicate obscene, vulgar, or threatening content that causes a reasonable person to endure distress. A single offensive message can be considered cyberharassment.

Repeated contacts with a victim are referred to as **cyberstalking**. Cyberstalking can take many forms, including the following:

- Making false accusations that damage the reputation of the victim on blogs, Web sites, chat rooms, or e-commerce sites (e.g., eBay)
- Gaining information on a victim by monitoring online activities, accessing databases, and so on
- Encouraging others to harass a victim by posting personal information about the victim on Web sites or in chat rooms
- Attacking data and equipment of the victim by sending e-mail viruses and other destructive code
- Using the Internet to place false orders for goods and services, such as magazines, pornography, and other embarrassing items, as well as having such items delivered to work addresses

Many states, the U.S. government, and many countries have anti-cyberstalking laws. Unfortunately, law enforcement has a difficult time catching most cyberstalkers. While cyberstalking can take many forms and can go undetected by the victim, the intent of **cyberbullying** is to *deliberately* cause emotional distress in the victim. Cyberharassment, cyberstalking, and cyberbullying are typically targeted at a particular person or group as a means of revenge or expressing hatred.

In contrast, **online predators** typically target vulnerable people, usually the young or old, for sexual or financial purposes. While typically online chat rooms and instant messaging systems have been the playground for online predators, these villains are also targeting many social networking sites like Facebook. To combat these online predators, parents must educate their children not to share personal information and possibly must use monitoring software to track online activity. Fortunately, most social networking and online chat sites also provide ways to report abuse by these predators.

Software Piracy

Software developers and marketers want you to buy as many copies of their products as you want, of course. But commercial software vendors do not want you or anyone else to buy one copy and then bootleg additional copies to sell or to give to others. Vendors also take a dim view of companies that buy one copy of a software application and then make many copies to distribute to employees. In fact, the practice is called **software piracy**, and it is illegal.

When you buy commercial software, it is typically legal for you to make one (1) backup copy for your own use (although the software vendor can make it very difficult to copy the software). It is also legal to offer shareware or public domain software for free on a Web site. But **warez** peddling—offering stolen proprietary software for free over the Internet—is a crime. ("Warez" is the slang term for such stolen software.) To discover and understand any protection mechanisms (such as registration or license keys) built into the software by its original developer, computer criminals typically disassemble the software, a practice referred to as **reverse engineering**. Once the crackers understand the inner workings of the protection mechanism, they can build a **key generator** that can be used to generate fake keys to circumvent the protection mechanism. (Reverse engineering is not always destructive and may be legally used to improve a program, but use of the term here implies using the process for gaining unauthorized access to a program's internal structure.)

Both patent and copyright laws can apply to software, which is a form of intellectual property—creations of the mind (e.g., music, software, and so on), inventions, names, images, designs, and other works used in commerce. Patents and copyrights are recognized and enforced by most countries, giving the creator exclusive rights to benefit from the creation for a limited period of time. **Patents** typically refer to process, machine, or material inventions. For example, Amazon.com's "one-click buying" process is protected by patent law, and Apple has patented its multitouch technology (including the "pinch" for shrinking and expanding items) used in the iPhone and iPad. **Copyrights** generally refer to creations of the mind such as music, literature, or software. Copyright laws covering software include the 1980 Computer Software Copyright Act, a 1992 act that made software piracy a felony, and the 1997 No Electronic Theft Act, which made copyright infringement a criminal act even when no profit was involved.

Software piracy has become a problem because it is so widespread, costing the commercial software industry and the entire economy billions of dollars a year. A 2010 study conducted by the Business Software Alliance (BSA) suggested that reducing software piracy by only 10 percent over the next four years could generate 500,000 new jobs, infuse US$142 billion into the global economy, and generate US$32 billion in tax revenues for governments (BSA, 2011). The crime is difficult to trace, but many individuals and even companies have been successfully prosecuted for pirating software. Many software vendors are trying to limit software piracy by requiring the users to enter license keys or verifying the key before allowing the customer to register or update the software.

SOFTWARE PIRACY IS A GLOBAL BUSINESS. A major international issue that businesses deal with is the willingness (or unwillingness) of governments and individuals to recognize and enforce the ownership of intellectual property—in particular, software copyrights. Piracy of software and other technologies is widespread internationally (see Figure 10.13). The BSA (2012) points to countries such as Georgia (91 percent), Zimbabwe (92 percent), and Bangladesh (90 percent) as those with the highest percentages of illegal software. Worldwide losses due to piracy exceeded US$63 billion in 2011. Countries with the lowest piracy rates include the United States (19 percent), Japan (21 percent), Luxembourg (20 percent), and New Zealand (22 percent). Because technology usage varies significantly by region, average piracy levels and dollar losses greatly differ across regions (see Table 10.1). For instance, even though the United States has

FIGURE 10.13

In many parts of the world, using pirated software is a common practice.

Source: Courtesy of Christoph Schneider

the lowest piracy rate, it also is the country where the greatest losses occur (more than US$9.7 billion) because of its high level of computer usage.

In addition to being a crime, is software piracy also an ethical problem? Perhaps in part, but businesspeople must acknowledge and deal with other perspectives as well. In part, the problem stems from other countries' differing concepts of ownership. Many of the ideas about intellectual property ownership stem from long-standing cultural traditions. For example, the concept of individual ownership of knowledge is traditionally a strange one in many Middle Eastern countries, where knowledge is meant to be shared. Plagiarism does not exist in a country where words belong to everyone. By the same token, piracy does not exist either. This view is gradually changing; the Saudi Arabia Patent Office granted its first patents several years ago, and its piracy rates have plummeted from 79 percent in 1996 to 51 percent in 2011.

In other cases, there are political, social, and economic reasons for piracy. In many countries, software publishers are not catering to the needs of consumers, who often simply do not have the funds to purchase software legitimately. This is true in many areas of South America, Africa, and other regions with low per capita income. It is particularly true of students and other members of university communities whose needs are critical in some areas.

Other factors leading to piracy or infringement of intellectual property agreements throughout the world include lack of public awareness about the issue and the increasingly high demand for computers and other technology products. The United States has repeatedly pressured and threatened other countries accused of pirating. It is interesting to note, however, that despite the fact that few of these cultural and economic explanations are valid in the United States, the United States leads the world in the sheer volume of illegal software in use. Businesses that operate in glass offices should surely not throw stones.

TABLE 10.1 Software Piracy Levels and Dollar Losses by Region

Region	Piracy Level	Dollar Loss (in US$ millions)
North America	19%	10,958
Western Europe	32%	13,749
Asia/Pacific	60%	20,998
Latin America	61%	7,459
Middle East/Africa	58%	4,159
Eastern Europe	62%	6,133
Worldwide	42%	63,456

Source: Based on Business Software Alliance (2012). Extracted from unnumbered Tables on pages 8–9 from http://portal.bsa.org/globalpiracy2011/downloads/study_pdf/2011_BSA_Piracy_Study-Standard.pdf.

Federal and State Laws

In the United States, there are two main federal laws against computer crime: the Computer Fraud and Abuse Act of 1986 and the Electronic Communications Privacy Act of 1986. The Computer Fraud and Abuse Act of 1986 prohibits the following:

- Stealing or compromising data about national defense, foreign relations, atomic energy, or other restricted information
- Gaining unauthorized access to computers owned by any agency or department of the U.S. government
- Violating data belonging to banks or other financial institutions
- Intercepting or otherwise intruding on communications between states or foreign countries
- Threatening to damage computer systems in order to extort money or other valuables from persons, businesses, or institutions
- Threatening the US President, vice president, members of congress, and other administrative members (even if it's just in a critical e-mail)

In 1996, the Computer Abuse Amendments Act expanded the Computer Fraud and Abuse Act of 1986 to prohibit the dissemination of computer viruses and other harmful code.

The Electronic Communications Privacy Act of 1986 makes it a crime to break into any electronic communications service, including telephone services. It prohibits the interception of any type of electronic communications. Interception, as defined by the law, includes listening in on communications without authorization and recording or otherwise taking the contents of communications. In 2002, however, the U.S. Congress passed the USA PATRIOT Act (Patriot Act) to extend the Computer Fraud and Abuse Act. Prior to the Patriot Act, investigators could not monitor voice communication—or stored voice communication—when investigating someone suspected of violating the Computer Fraud and Abuse Act. Under the Patriot Act, investigators can gain access to voice-related communications much more easily, and this makes it a very controversial law. Many civil libertarians feel that the Patriot Act greatly erodes many existing constitutional protections, and it is likely to be hotly debated long into the future.

In addition to the primary laws discussed here, other federal laws may apply to computer crime. Patent laws protect some software and computer hardware, and contract laws may protect trade secrets that are stored on computers. In 1980, the U.S. Copyright Act was amended to include computer software, making it a violation of this act to post online written compositions, photos, sound files, and software without the permission of the copyright holder.

The Federal Bureau of Investigation (FBI) and the U.S. Secret Service jointly enforce federal computer crime laws. The FBI is in charge when crimes involve espionage, terrorism, banking, organized crime, and threats to national security. The Secret Service investigates crimes against U.S. Treasury Department computers and against computers that contain information protected by the Right to Financial Privacy Act. Information protected by the Financial Privacy Act includes credit card usage, credit reporting, and bank loan application data. In some federal computer crime cases, the U.S. Customs Department, the Commerce Department, or the military may have jurisdiction. In addition to federal laws against computer crime, all 50 states have passed laws prohibiting computer crime. Many foreign countries also have similar laws.

Some violations of state and federal computer crime laws are charged as misdemeanors. These violations are punishable by fines and by not more than one year in prison. Other violations are classified as felonies and are punishable by fines and by more than one year in prison. The Patriot Act converted many misdemeanors into felony-level offenses. Nevertheless, intent can often determine whether crimes are prosecuted as misdemeanors or felonies. If intruders breach computer systems with intent to do harm, they may be charged with a felony. If a break-in is classified as reckless disregard but causes no damage, the offense may be classified as a misdemeanor.

Some critics argue that laws do not go far enough to prosecute computer crimes, while others believe that they should not be invoked when systems are breached but no damage is done. Even the definition of "damage" is debatable. For instance, has damage occurred if someone gains unauthorized access to a computer system but does not steal or change information?

There are additional difficulties in legislating and enforcing laws that affect global networks. Since many countries can be involved when break-ins and other crimes occur, who has jurisdiction? Should e-mail messages be monitored for libelous or other illegal content, and, if so, who should have monitoring responsibility? Should e-mail be subject to the same laws as mail delivered by the U.S. Postal Service, or should it be more akin to telephone conversations and the laws that apply to them?

WHO'S GOING MOBILE

Mobile Security

Computer hacking has long been a serious problem that both security experts and computer users have been battling. While the problem of viruses and spyware in computers and laptops may always remain a cat-and-mouse game, the rise of smartphones and tablets adds another level to security threats—mobile malware. With smartphones becoming both increasingly powerful and popular, new categories of threats have emerged. Today's smartphone owners can download hundreds of thousands of apps from various sources; for example, there are over 400,000 apps available on Google Play (Google's market for Android apps), and over 500,000 apps on Apple's App Store. Yet, when installing various apps on their devices, many users run the risk of installing mobile malware on their devices.

Such malware could be capable of issuing commands to an attacked device, could steal the user's contacts and photos, or worse, it could turn on the device's camera or send text messages. For instance, SMS Trojans contained in unsuspicious-looking apps can send bogus text messages to malware authors, charging victims US$2-3 per text.

Another mobile security-related threat is apps for snooping on a targeted smartphone. Such malware, once installed and activated, is capable of tracking the target's location in real-time, recording phone calls, and saving and displaying chats and text messages, even if the user has deleted them. Spyware apps typically work by disguising themselves so that they never show up in one's list of installed apps. Although such apps can be used for legitimate purposes (such as law enforcement, following a court order), in the wrong hands, these apps can cause tremendous damage.

As concerns grow for potential threats to mobile security, computer security companies have already eyed the problem and are consequently coming out with feasible solutions. McAfee, for one, introduced a mobile security system for businesses; AT&T also partnered with Juniper Networks to build mobile security apps for consumers and corporations; Lookout is another app that can be downloaded free for Android, BlackBerry, and Windows phones.

It is agreed that mobile hackers are not much of a threat at the moment, but with the rapid increase of smartphones and their functionality, the threat of mobile malware is growing. For example, research firm Juniper Networks analyzed the availability of malware apps across all mobile phone platforms, and reported a 155 percent increase in mobile malware apps from 2010 to 2011; between June and December 2011, the number of Android-focused malware samples found increased from 400 to over 13,000. Analysts to a large extent attribute this to the openness of the Android platform: As opposed to Apple's App Store, applications submitted to the marketplace are often not vetted for potentially harmful code (in early 2012, Google introduced a malware-scanning feature called "bouncer" to Google Play; however, several other Android markets do not have such a feature). Yet, not even owners of Apple's iPhone and iPad are completely protected, as evidenced by a recent demonstration by a security researcher who managed to circumvent the App Store's vetting system to show that it is indeed possible to introduce malware into the App Store. Further, many users who are frustrated with the closeness of Apple's platform choose to "jailbreak" their phone, so as to be able to download apps from sources other than the official App Store; this, however, exposes them to various potential threats. Considering the rapid increase in malware, it is no surprise that even the Defense Department has called for a search of innovative ways to protect mobile devices from malware.

Based on:

Budmar, P. (2011, November 21). Cyber criminals to target mobile devices and London Olympics in 2012: M86. *ARN.com*. Retrieved on May 21, 2012, from http://www.arnnet.com.au/article/408045/cyber_criminals_target_mobile_devices_london_olympics_2012_m86/?fp=4&fpid=1382389953#closeme.

Gahran, A. (2011, June 17). Mobile phone security: What are the risks? *CNN.com*. Retrieved May 21, 2012, from http://articles.cnn.com/2011-06-17/tech/mobile.security.gahran_1_android-app-android-phone-apple-s-app-store/3?_s=PM:TECH.

Keizer, G. (2011, November 8). Researcher plants rogue app in Apple's App Store. *Computerworld*. Retrieved May 21, 2012, from http://www.computerworld.com/s/article/9221615/Researcher_plants_rogue_app_in_Apple_s_App_Store.

Miller, C.C. (2011, September 27). For hackers, the next lock to pick. *The New York Times*. Retrieved May 21, 2012, from http://www.nytimes.com/2011/09/28/technology/companies-see-opportunity-in-stopping-cellphone-hackers.html.

Tynan, D. (2011, November 20). Mobile malware epidemic looms. *PC World*. Retrieved May 21, 2012, from http://www.pcworld.com/article/244346/mobile_malware_epidemic_looms.html.

http://goo.gl/iv68Y

CYBERWAR AND CYBERTERRORISM

Over the past several years, individual computer criminals have caused billions of dollars in losses through the use of viruses, worms, and unauthorized access to computers. In the future, many believe that coordinated efforts by national governments or terrorist groups have the potential to do hundreds of billions of dollars in damage as well as put the lives of countless people at stake (Boyle & Panko, 2013). Most experts believe that cyberwar and cyberterrorism are imminent threats to the United States and other technologically advanced countries. A major attack that cripples a country's information infrastructure or power grid or even the global Internet could have devastating implications for a country's (or the world's) economic system and make transportation systems, medical capabilities, and other key infrastructure extremely vulnerable to disaster, especially given the proliferation of cloud computing for many personal, commercial, and governmental applications.

Cyberwar

Cyberwar refers to an organized attempt by a country's military to disrupt or destroy the information and communication systems of another country. Cyberwar is often executed simultaneously with traditional methods to quickly dissipate the capabilities of an enemy. For example, the United States reportedly conducted its first cyberwar campaign during the 78-day Serbia/Kosovo war by establishing a team of information warriors to support its bombing campaign against Serbia. The U.S. information operation cell electronically attacked Serbia's critical networks and command-and-control systems. However, given that the United States and NATO alliance is the most technologically sophisticated war machine in the world—and also the most dependent on its networking and computing infrastructure—it is also the most vulnerable to cyberwar (or cyberterrorism) attacks.

CYBERWAR VULNERABILITIES. The goal of cyberwar is to turn the balance of information and knowledge in one's favor in order to enhance one's capabilities while diminishing those of an opponent. Cyberwar utilizes a diverse range of technologies, including software, hardware, and networking technologies, to gain an information advantage over an opponent. These technologies can be used to electronically blind, jam, deceive, overload, and intrude into an enemy's computing and networking capabilities in order to diminish various capabilities, including the following:

- Command-and-control systems
- Intelligence collection, processing, and distribution systems
- Tactical communication systems and methods
- Troop and weapon positioning systems
- Friend-or-foe identification systems
- Smart weapons systems

Additionally, controlling the content and distribution of propaganda and information to an opponent's civilians, troops, and government is a key part of a cyberwar strategy. At the simplest level, **Web vandalism** can occur by simply defacing Web sites. Likewise, cyberpropaganda can be quickly and easily distributed through chat rooms, Web sites, and e-mail. Espionage—stealing of secrets or modifying information—can occur if data and systems are not adequately protected and secure.

A recent example of a cyberwar event was discovered in June 2010 when a Belarus-based computer security company discovered a computer worm called **Stuxnet** on a computer system belonging to an Iranian client. Stuxnet is a computer worm designed to find and infect a particular piece of industrial hardware inside Iranian nuclear plants. Once Stuxnet found its intended target, centrifuges within Iran's nuclear enrichment program, it was programmed to manipulate their motor speeds. The manipulation of the motor speeds beyond normal operating tolerances would ultimately destroy the equipment; slowing and degrading the nuclear program. Since its discovery computer security experts around the globe have studied its design. Stuxnet is a very sophisticated and unprecedented method for attacking an adversary. While most experts agreed that Stuxnet was most likely designed by a nation state, from the time of its discovery, no country had come forward to admit their involvement in its creation. This suspicion ended in June 2012, when it was revealed that both Israel and the USA worked together to design Stuxnet. It is one of the first examples where cyber warfare was used to inflict physical damage to critical infrastructure of a nation state. Another (admittedly less damaging attack) on the Iranian nuclear program happened in 2012, when malware introduced into Iranian nuclear facilities caused computers to play AC/DC's "Thunderstruck" at full volume in the middle of the night. In traditional war, destroying equipment by dropping a bomb is an act of war. Time will tell how nation states will respond to cyber-based attacks that ultimately cause similar damage.

FIGURE 10.14

The Cuban missile crisis was the height of the Cold War.

Source: John Wollwerth/Shutterstock

THE NEW COLD WAR. According to the 2007 annual report of the Internet security company McAfee, a *cyber cold war* is an imminent threat for the world's computers. It reports that more than 120 nations are developing ways to use the Internet as a weapon to target financial markets, governmental computer systems, and key infrastructure. Reminiscent of the Cold War—a period of conflict, tension, and competition between the United States and the Soviet Union and their respective allies from the mid-1940s until the early 1990s (see Figure 10.14)—intelligence agencies from countries around the world are secretly testing networks and looking for weaknesses in their potential enemies' computer systems. There are several known attacks, although most governments deny involvement. Typically, governments accused of cyberwar activities blame uncontrolled **patriot hackers**—independent citizens or supporters of a country that perpetrate attacks on perceived or real enemies. Regardless of the source of these attacks, it is clear that one of the big challenges for governments moving forward will be to fully integrate a cyberwar strategy into their overall plans and capabilities.

Cyberterrorism

Unlike cyberwar, **cyberterrorism** is launched not by governments but by individuals and organized groups. Cyberterrorism is the use of computer and networking technologies against persons or property to intimidate or coerce governments, civilians, or any segment of society in order to attain political, religious, or ideological goals. One of the great fears about cyberterrorism is that an attack can be launched from a computer anywhere in the world—no borders have to be crossed, no bombs smuggled and placed, and no lives lost in carrying out the attack. Because computers and networking systems control power plants, telephone systems, and transportation systems, as well as water and oil pipelines, any disruption in these systems could cause loss of life or widespread chaos (Volonino & Robinson, 2004). Just as physical terrorist attacks have physical and psychological effects, so also do cyberattacks. Dealing with the unknown—where, when, and how—of an indiscriminant terrorist attack is what leads to "terror."

WHAT KINDS OF ATTACKS ARE CONSIDERED CYBERTERRORISM? Cyberterrorism could involve physical destruction of computer systems or acts that destroy economic stability or infrastructure. Cyberterrorist acts could likely damage the machines that control traffic lights, power plants, dams, or airline traffic in order to create fear and panic. Attacks launched in cyberspace could take many forms, such as viruses, denial of service, destruction of government computers, stealing classified files, altering Web page content, deleting or corrupting vital information, disrupting media

TABLE 10.2 Categories of Potential Cyberterrorist Attacks

Category	Description
Coordinated bomb attacks	To distribute a number of devices—from small explosive devices to large weapons of mass destruction—that communicate with each other through the Internet or cellular phone networks and are made to simultaneously detonate if one device stops communicating with the others
Manipulation of financial and banking information	To disrupt the flow of financial information with the objective of causing fear and lack of confidence in the world's or a country's financial system
Manipulation of the pharmaceutical industry	To make hard-to-detect changes in the formulas of medications in order to cause fear and lack of confidence in this important industry
Manipulation of transportation control systems	To disrupt airline and railroad transportation systems, possibly leading to disastrous collisions
Manipulation of the broader civilian infrastructures	To compromise the communication, broadcast media, gas lines, water systems, and electrical grids in order to cause panic and fear within the population
Manipulation of nuclear power plants	To disrupt cooling systems in order to cause a meltdown that would disperse radiation

broadcasts, and otherwise interrupting the flow of information. Table 10.2 summarizes several categories of attacks that experts believe cyberterrorists will try to deliver.

The goal of cyberterrorists is to cause fear, panic, and destruction. Through the power of computer technology and global networks, terrorists can gain access to critical parts of the world's infrastructure to produce both physical and virtual terror. Given the great potential for cyberterrorism, many experts believe that it will, unfortunately, become the weapon of choice for the world's most sophisticated terrorists.

HOW THE INTERNET IS CHANGING THE BUSINESS PROCESSES OF TERRORISTS. Virtually all modern terrorist groups utilize the Internet (Weimann, 2006). Beyond using the Internet to wage cyberattacks, the Internet is a powerful tool for improving and streamlining the business processes of the modern terrorist (see Table 10.3). Just as the Internet has fueled globalization

TABLE 10.3 How Terrorists Are Using the Internet

Use	Description
Information dissemination	The use of Web sites to disseminate propaganda to current and potential supporters, to influence international public opinion, and to notify potential enemies of pending plans.
Data mining	The use of the vast amount of information available on the Internet regarding virtually any topic for planning, recruitment, and numerous other endeavors.
Fund-raising	The use of Web sites for bogus charities and nongovernmental organizations to raise funds and transfer currencies around the world.
Recruiting and mobilization	The use of Web sites to provide information for recruiting new members as well as utilizing more interactive Internet technologies, such as roaming online chat rooms and cybercafés for receptive individuals.
Networking	The use of the Internet to enable a less hierarchical, cell-based organizational structure that is much more difficult to combat; networking capabilities also allow different groups with common enemies to better share and coordinate information.
Information sharing	The use of the Internet as a powerful tool for announcing events as well as sharing best practices.
Training	The use of the Internet to disseminate training materials. For example, the official Hamas Web site details how to make homemade poisons and gases, and Syrian rebels use YouTube to disseminate weapons training videos.
Planning and coordinating	The use of communication and information dissemination capabilities to facilitate designing and executing plans.
Information gathering	The use of mapping software such as Google Earth to locate potential targets for terrorist attacks.
Location monitoring	The use of public Web cams to monitor and study potential attack sites (e.g., Times Square or public resources such as tunnels or power generation facilities).

for organizations and societies, it too has fueled global terrorism. Clearly, the Internet is transforming the "business processes" of the modern terrorist.

ASSESSING THE CYBERTERRORISM THREAT. Some experts claim that because of the general openness of access, the Internet infrastructure is extremely vulnerable to cyberterrorism. Each year, cyberattacks on critical infrastructure such as nuclear power plants, dams, and power grids are increasing. While the majority of such attacks have not done damage at this point, a few have been alarmingly successful and concerning:

- During the Gulf War in 1991, a group of Dutch crackers stole electronic information about U.S. troop movements and offered it for sale to Iraq. The Iraqis turned down the offer, thinking it was a hoax.
- In 1998, a 20-year-old Israeli cracker, Ehud Tennebaum, also known as "The Analyzer," joined two crackers in California to disrupt U.S. troop movements by disabling computers at the Pentagon, the National Security Agency, and national labs.
- In 1999, crackers allegedly gained control of a British military communication satellite and held it for ransom. The British military denied that the satellite had ever been under the control of intruders.
- Also in 1999, during the Serbia/Kosovo war, Serb crackers allegedly gained access to NATO Web pages and flooded e-mail accounts with pro-Serb messages.
- During the 2000 presidential election in the United States, Web attacks were reported that involved intruders with various political motives. Information was changed on targeted Web sites, snooping on political sites was rampant, and many denial-of-service attacks were launched.
- In May 2003, Romanian crackers compromised systems that housed life support control for 58 scientists and contractors in Antarctica. FBI agents assisted in the arrest of the crackers, who attempted to extort money from the research station.
- In May 2007, government networks and commercial banks within Estonia came under a very sophisticated cyberattack by cyberterrorists in retaliation for the removal of a Soviet-era memorial to fallen soldiers (see Figure 10.15).
- In early 2010, Chinese-based hackers attacked Google, prompting the search engine giant to threaten to no longer filter searches within China deemed objectionable by the Chinese government (e.g., democracy, pornography, Tibet, the Tiananmen Square protests, and so on).
- In 2010–2012, "The Jester," believed to be a former U.S. solider, claimed responsibility for attacks on WikiLeaks (see When Things Go Wrong for more on WikiLeaks), Islamists' Web sites, and even the Web site of Iranian President Mahmoud Ahmadinejad. After a successful attack, The Jester broadcasts "TANGO DOWN"—a military term that means a target has been injured or killed—on Twitter.

While cyberterrorism obviously remains a threat to computer and network security, some experts point out that there are disadvantages to using acts of cyberterrorism as a weapon, including the following:

1. Computer systems and networks are complex, so cyberattacks are difficult to control and may not achieve the desired destruction as effectively as physical weapons.
2. Computer systems and networks change and security measures improve, so it requires an ever-increasing level of knowledge and expertise on the part of intruders for cyberattacks to be effective. This means that perpetrators will be required to continuously study and hone their skills as older methods of attack no longer work.
3. Cyberattacks rarely cause physical harm to victims; therefore, there is less drama and emotional appeal than for perpetrators using conventional weapons.

FIGURE 10.15

The removal of a Soviet-era memorial motivated patriot hackers to attack networks in Estonia.

Source: Andrei Nekrassov/Shutterstock

While cyberterrorism and cyberwar may be methods of choice for future generations with advanced computer knowledge, experts are hopeful that the increasing sophistication of computer security measures will help reduce the number of such incidents.

THE GLOBALIZATION OF TERRORISM. With the proliferation of and dependence on technology increasing at an astronomical rate, the threat of cyberterrorism will continue to increase. As has been true with virtually all governments and business organizations, fueled by the digitization of information and the Internet, terrorism has become a global business. To be adequately prepared, national governments along with industry partners must design coordinated responses to various attack scenarios. In addition to greater cooperation and preparedness, governments must improve their intelligence-gathering capabilities so that potential attacks are thwarted before they begin. Industry must also be given incentives to secure their information resources so that losses and disruptions in operations are minimized. International laws and treaties must rapidly evolve to reflect the realities of cyberterrorism, where attacks can be launched from anywhere in the world to anywhere in the world. Fortunately, experts believe that the likelihood of a devastating attack that causes significant disruption in the major U.S. infrastructure systems is quite low because the attackers would need "$200 million, intelligence information, and years of preparation" to succeed (Volonino & Robinson, 2004). Nevertheless, small attacks have been occurring for years and are likely to increase in frequency and severity—even a "small" attack, like an individual suicide bomber, can cause tremendous chaos to a society. Clearly, there are great challenges ahead.

BRIEF CASE   3D Crime Scenes

3D technology is now widely used for the re-creation of crime scenes, from comparing footprints to testing crime theories. Modern 3D forensic ballistics is capable of handling an enormous amount of data and provides powerful graphics capabilities. The process of 3D modeling uses laser scanning equipment to capture every minute detail of a crime scene and document the positions and location of bloodstains. It is also capable of creating a 3D image of a bullet that has been fired and then finding a match from previous criminal cases. Once the crime scene is re-created, technology further allows detectives and/or police to revisit the scene in three dimensions, from any vantage point desired, in real-time. Three-dimensional images of cities and buildings are also being stored to help police foil future terrorist attacks. 3D home security systems also play a role in protecting your home and belongings from fire or burglary. Users of this technology can check for potential loss and search for probable causes, the same way the police do at crime scenes.

Questions:

1. How does the rapid evolution of technology change the way crimes are investigated and cases are presented in court proceedings?
2. Advanced technology used in solving crimes has created the so called CSI effect, named after the popular TV program

CSI: Crime Scene Investigation. The CSI effect refers to the belief that jurors demand more forensic evidence in criminal trials due to advances in forensic and investigative technology that is learned by watching modern police shows, thereby raising the effective standard of proof for prosecutors. Will 3D crime scene capabilities increase or decrease the CSI effect? Why?

Based on:

Adcock, S. (2012, January 23). NC State forensic sciences: Virtual crime scene. Retrieved May 21, 2012, from http://www.ncsu.edu/features/2012/01/virtual-crime-scene.

Cheshire, T. (2011, November 24). Return to the scene of the crime—in 3D. *Wired.com.* Retrieved May 21, 2012, from http://www.wired.co.uk/magazine/archive/2011/12/start/return-to-the-scene-of-the-crime.

CSI effect. (2012, April 22). In *Wikipedia, The Free Encyclopedia.* Retrieved June 6, 2012, from http://en.wikipedia.org/w/index.php?title=CSI_effect&oldid=488619644.

Robison, D. (2011, January 20). 3-D camera keeps crime scenes intact. *InnovationTrail.com.* Retrieved May 21, 2012, from http://innovationtrail.org/post/3-d-camera-keeps-crime-scenes-intact.

WKBW News. (2011, January 20). Erie County has new high tach crime scene tool. *Wkbw.com.* Retrieved May 21, 2012, from http://www.wkbw.com/news/crime/Erie-County-Has-New-High-Tach-Crime-Scene-Tool-114291674.html.

http://goo.gl/hau6U

INFORMATION SYSTEMS SECURITY

How do you secure information systems from dangers such as natural disasters, criminal activity, cyberterrorism, and other threats? The rule of thumb for deciding whether an information system is at risk is simple: All systems connected to networks are vulnerable to security violations from outsiders as well as insiders as well as to virus infections and other forms of computer crime. Further, no information system is immune to intentional or unintentional physical harm. In short, threats to information systems can come from a variety of places inside and external to an organization. **Information systems security** refers to precautions taken to keep all aspects of information systems (e.g., all hardware, software, network equipment, and data) safe from destruction, manipulation, or unauthorized use or access. That means that you have to secure not only the personal computers on people's desks but also the notebook computers, the mobile devices, and the servers: all levels of the network and any gateway between the network and the outside world.

As use of the Internet and related telecommunications technologies and systems has become pervasive, use of these networks now creates a new vulnerability for organizations. These networks can be infiltrated and/or subverted in a number of ways. As a result, the need for tight computer and network security has increased dramatically. Fortunately, there are a variety of managerial methods and security technologies that can be used to manage IS security effectively. In the remaining sections of this chapter, we address this new reality.

Safeguarding IS Resources

Any good approach to securing information systems begins first with a thorough audit of all aspects of those systems, including hardware, software, data, networks, and any business processes that involve them. By doing this, you can then decide which aspects of the various systems within the organization are most vulnerable to harm/destruction, break-ins by unauthorized users, and/or misuse by authorized users. After such an audit, you can then design and implement a security plan that makes the best use of the available resources in order to protect the systems and guard against (or at least minimize) any risks. People within the IS department are usually responsible for implementing the security measures chosen, though people from throughout the organization should participate in the systems security audit. Some organizations even go so far as to pay an external consulting firm to attempt to break in and breach their systems so that vulnerabilities will be uncovered and fixed.

It would not make sense to spend literally millions of dollars a year to protect an asset, the loss of which would cost the organization only a few thousand dollars. As a result, organizations frequently conduct IS audits (discussed later in this chapter). One critical component of a good IS audit is a thorough risk analysis. **Risk analysis** is a process in which you assess the value of the assets being protected, determine their probability of being compromised, and compare the probable costs of their being compromised with the estimated costs of whatever protections you might have to take. Protecting an asset only makes economic sense if the cost of protecting the asset is less than (or equal to) the value of the asset (and the associated data that can be lost) multiplied by the probability of a disaster. Thus, people in organizations often perform risk analyses for their systems to ensure that IS security programs make sense economically (Stallings & Brown, 2012).

Risk analysis then enables us to determine what steps, if any, to take to secure systems. There are three general ways to react:

1. *Risk Reduction.* Taking active countermeasures to protect your systems, such as installing firewalls like those described later in this chapter.
2. *Risk Acceptance.* Implementing no countermeasures and simply absorbing any damages that occur.
3. *Risk Transference.* Having someone else absorb the risk, such as by investing in insurance, by outsourcing certain functions to another organization with specific expertise, or using cloud computing service providers for critical infrastructure needs.

Large organizations typically use a balance of all three approaches, taking steps in **risk reduction** for some systems, accepting risk and living with it in other cases (i.e., **risk acceptance**), and also insuring all or most of their systems activities as well (i.e., **risk transference**). A fourth category—risk avoidance (e.g., by not engaging in e-commerce, not having a Web site, or not using e-mail)—is normally impractical or even infeasible in today's networked environment. There are two broad categories of safeguards for reducing risk—technological- and human-based approaches—and any comprehensive security plan will include both.

Technological Safeguards

There are six commonly used methods in which technology is employed to safeguard information systems:

- Physical access restrictions
- Firewalls
- Encryption
- Virus monitoring and prevention
- Audit-control software
- Secure data centers

Within any type of safeguard, there are a variety of ways in which it can be deployed. Next, we briefly review each of these methods.

PHYSICAL ACCESS RESTRICTIONS. Organizations can prevent unauthorized access to information systems by keeping stored information safe and allowing access only to those employees who need it to do their jobs. Of course, organizations can protect computers and data resources by physically securing computers to desks or requiring users to lock hard drives with keys when leaving a computer unattended. However, most organizations don't go to such lengths and control access only by requiring some form of **authentication**. The most common form of authentication is the use of passwords, which are effective only if chosen carefully and changed frequently (see Figure 10.16). Besides passwords, employees may be asked to provide an ID combination, a security code sequence, or personal data, such as their mother's maiden name. Employees authorized to use computer systems may also be issued keys to physically

COMING ATTRACTIONS

Speeding Security Screening

Just about everyone who uses airline travel today dreads the invasive and time consuming airport security screening process. Researchers at the University of Arizona are developing an interactive screening kiosk called AVATAR to naturally interact with people, conduct interviews, and detect changes in arousal, behavior, and cognitive effort by using psychophysiological information systems. The kiosk uses embodied intelligent agents (avatars) to ask people questions and then has a variety of sensors to non-invasively monitor their responses. The AVATAR kiosk assesses cues through sensors in body movement, vocalics (e.g., voice pitch changes), pupillometry (e.g., eye dilation and blinking), and eye tracking. The kiosk is an interactive screening technology designed to be on the front lines of border crossings and airports. It is envisioned that individuals will approach the AVATAR kiosk, scan their identification, answer a few simple questions, and then move on. Meanwhile, the AVATAR kiosk uses non-invasive sensor technology and artificial intelligence algorithms to gauge suspicious behavior. The AVATAR kiosk is not intended to be a replacement of officers, but is envisioned to help them to better utilize their valuable time. For instance, several AVATAR kiosks could be operated by a single officer who would step in to work directly with individuals whose behavior has been flagged as abnormal. In 2010, the kiosk was tested in Warsaw, Poland, with a participating group of European Union border guards. In a controlled test of the AVATAR, half of the guards assumed the identity of a terrorist, constructing mock bombs, packing them into a suitcase, and then trying to get through the AVATAR kiosk interview. The AVATAR detected all of the mock bombers, but also flagged a few other non-bombers for additional screening. In 2012, the AVATAR was tested for several months at the Nogales, Arizona border crossing with Mexico, supporting agents in the U.S. Customs and Border Protection Trusted Travel program. With each test of the AVATAR kiosk, the researchers learn more and improve its design. Someday, you too may be interviewed by AVATAR before entering the restricted area of an airport or when crossing international borders.

Based on:

Anonymous. (2011, February). AVATAR kiosk aims to automate, augment border enforcement. *Eller Buzz.* Retrieved on May 21, 2012, from http://www.eller.arizona.edu/buzz/2011/feb/avatar.asp.

FIGURE 10.16

The most common form of authentication is through passwords.
Source: Courtesy of Google, Inc.

FIGURE 10.17

A smart card.
Source: al62/Fotolia

unlock a computer, photo ID cards, smart cards with digital ID, and other physical devices allowing computer access. In sum, access is usually limited by making it dependent on one of the following:

- *Something You Have.* Keys, picture identification cards, smart cards, or smart badges that contain memory chips with authentication data on them (see Figure 10.17)
- *Something You Know.* Passwords, code numbers, PIN numbers, lock combinations, or answers to secret questions (your pet's name, your mother's maiden name, and so on)
- *Something You Are.* Unique attributes, such as fingerprints, voice patterns, facial characteristics, or retinal patterns (collectively called *biometrics*)

Some measures that limit access to information are more secure than others. For example, smart cards and smart badges, passwords, lock combinations, and code numbers can be stolen. Biometric devices are difficult to fool, but determined intruders may sometimes devise ways to bypass them. Any of the previously mentioned single items can be used, but it is safer to use combinations of safeguards, such as a password *and* a smart card. Next, we examine various methods for implementing physical access control.

Biometrics **Biometrics** is one of the most sophisticated forms of restricting computer user access. Biometrics is a form of authentication used to govern access to systems, data, and/or facilities. With biometrics, employees may be identified by fingerprints, retinal patterns in the eye, facial features, or other bodily characteristics before being granted access to use a computer or to enter a facility (see Figure 10.18). Biometrics has the promise of providing very high security while at the same time authenticating people extremely efficiently, so many governments and companies are investigating how best to use this technology. For example, many laptops and computer keyboards now incorporate fingerprint readers; similarly, residents of Hong Kong can quickly pass through immigration checkpoints by using a smart card and their thumbprints.

Access-Control Software Special software can also be used to help keep stored information secure. **Access-control software**, for example, may allow computer users access only to those files related to their work. The user might even be restricted to these resources only at certain times or for specified periods of time, and, depending on the access level, the user can be restricted to being able to only read a file, to read and edit the file, to add to the file, and/or to delete the file. Many common business systems applications now build in these kinds of security features so that you do not have to have additional, separate access-control software running on top of your applications software.

FIGURE 10.18

Biometric devices are used to verify a person's identity.
Source: Kilukilu/Dreamstime

Wireless LAN Control Given how easy and inexpensive wireless local area networks (LANs) are to install and use, their use has skyrocketed, leaving many systems open to attack. On an unsecured network, for instance, unauthorized people can thus easily "steal" company resources (e.g., by surfing the Web for free, which is illegal in many countries) or do considerable damage to the network. A new form of attack known as **drive-by hacking** has arisen, where an attacker accesses the network, intercepts data from it, and even uses network services and/or sends attack instructions to it without having to enter the home, office, or organization that owns the network (see Figure 10.19). Wireless LAN control refers to methods of configuring the LAN so that only authorized users can gain access.

Virtual Private Networks A **virtual private network (VPN)** is a network connection that is constructed dynamically within an existing network—often called a secure tunnel—in order to connect users or nodes (see Figure 10.20). For example, a number of companies and software solutions enable you to create VPNs within the Internet as the medium for transporting data. These systems use authentication and encryption (discussed later) and other security

FIGURE 10.19

Drive-by hacking is on the rise given the proliferation of unsecured wireless LANs.

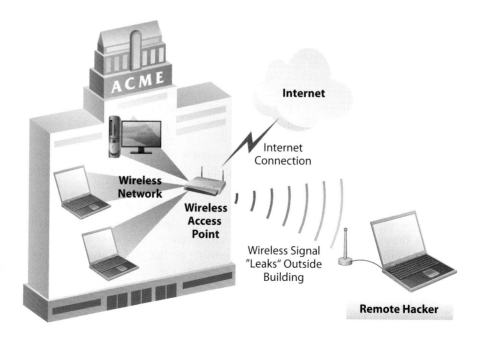

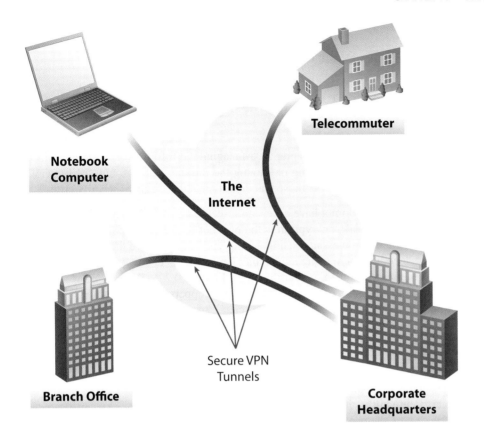

FIGURE 10.20

A virtual private network (VPN) allows remote sites and users to connect to organizational network resources using a secure tunnel.

mechanisms to ensure that only authorized users can access the VPN and that the data cannot be intercepted and compromised; this practice of creating an encrypted "tunnel" to send secure (private) data over the (public) Internet is known as **tunneling**. For example, The University of Arizona requires VPN software to be used when accessing some critical information resources from remote (off-campus) locations.

FIREWALLS. A **firewall** is a part of a computer system designed to detect intrusion and prevent unauthorized access to or from a private network (see Figure 10.21). Think of a firewall essentially as a security fence around the perimeter of an organization that spots any intruders that try to penetrate the organization's outer defenses. Firewalls can be implemented in hardware, in software, or in a combination of both. Firewalls are frequently used to prevent unauthorized Internet users from accessing private networks connected to the Internet, especially private

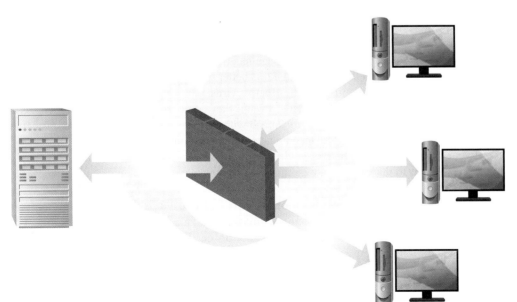

FIGURE 10.21

A firewall blocks unauthorized access to organizational systems and data, while permitting authorized communication to flow in and out of the organization to the broader Internet.

FIGURE 10.22

Encryption is used to encode information so that unauthorized people cannot understand it.

```
Ciphertext letters:
JOGPSNBUJPO TZTUFNT UPEBZ
Equivalent plaintext letters:
INFORMATION SYSTEMS TODAY
```

corporate intranets, described in Chapter 3, "Managing the Information Systems Infrastructure and Services." All messages entering or leaving the intranet pass through the firewall, which examines each message and blocks those that do not meet the specified security criteria.

ENCRYPTION. When you do not have access to a secure channel for sending information over a wired or wireless network, encryption is the best bet for keeping snoopers out. **Encryption** is the process of encoding messages using an encryption key before they enter the network or airwaves, then decoding them using a matching key at the receiving end of the transfer so that the intended recipients can read or hear them (see Figure 10.22). The process works because if you scramble messages before you send them, eavesdroppers who might intercept them cannot decipher them without the decoding key. (The science of encryption is called *cryptography*.) All encryption methods use a key—the code that scrambles and then decodes messages. Encryption is used to protect data that are transmitted over the Internet (e.g., your new purchase at Amazon.com), your call on your mobile phone, or the information between your notebook and Bluetooth-connected printer.

Implementing encryption on a large scale, such as on a busy Web site, requires a third party, called a **certificate authority**, to help manage the distribution of keys. The certificate authority acts as a trusted middleman between computers and verifies that a Web site is a trusted site. The certificate authority knows that each computer is who it says it is and provides the encryption/decryption keys to each computer. **Secure Sockets Layer**, developed by Netscape, is a popular public key encryption method used on the Internet. There are many different encryption approaches for different types of data transmission.

VIRUS MONITORING AND PREVENTION. **Virus prevention**, which is a set of activities for detecting and preventing computer viruses, has become a full-time, important task for IS departments within organizations and for all of us with our personal computers. While viruses often have colorful names—Melissa, I Love You, Naked Wife—they can be catastrophic from a computing perspective. Here we describe some precautions you can take to ensure that your computer is protected:

- Purchase and install antivirus software, then update frequently to be sure you are protected against new viruses.
- Do not use flash drives or shareware from unknown or suspect sources and be equally careful when downloading material from the Internet, making sure that the source is reputable.
- Delete without opening any e-mail message received from an unknown source. Be especially wary of opening attachments. It is better to delete a legitimate message than to infect your computer system with a destructive virus.
- Do not blindly open e-mail attachments, even if they come from a known source (such as a friend or coworker). Many viruses are spread without the sender's knowledge, so it is better to check with the sender before opening a potentially unsafe attachment.
- If your computer system contracts a virus, report the infection to your school or company's IS department so that appropriate measures can be taken.

AUDIT-CONTROL SOFTWARE. **Audit-control software** is used to keep track of computer activity so that auditors can spot suspicious activity and take action. Any user—authorized or unauthorized—leaves electronic footprints that auditors can trace. Audit-control software helps creating an audit trail, a record showing who has used a computer system and how it was used. For the software to effectively protect security, of course, auditors within an organization—most often someone in the IS department or information security department—must monitor and interpret results.

SECURE DATA CENTERS. Specialized facilities are an important component of creating a reliable and secure IS infrastructure. Data and the ability to process the data are the lifeblood for many of today's large organizations, such as Amazon.com, Travelocity.com, or Facebook. Storing and processing massive amounts of data needs a lot of power as well as air-conditioning to keep the equipment running within the optimal temperature range (which helps to increase the life span of the equipment). In addition to these requirements, organizations need to protect important equipment from both outside intruders and the elements, such as water or fire. The most prominent threats to an organization's IS facilities come from floods, seismic activity, rolling blackouts, hurricanes, and the potential of criminal activities (see Figure 10.23). How can an organization reliably protect its facilities from such threats?

Ensuring Availability As many potential causes of disasters cannot be avoided (there's no way to stop a hurricane), organizations should attempt to plan for the worst and protect their infrastructure accordingly. For companies operating in the digital world, the IS infrastructure is often critical for most business processes, so special care has to be taken to secure it. Whereas some applications can tolerate some downtime in case something malfunctions or disaster strikes, other applications (such as UPS's package tracking databases) can't tolerate any downtime—these companies need 24/7/365 reliability (see Figure 10.24).

Securing the Facilities Infrastructure An organization's IS infrastructure always needs to be secured to protect it from outside intruders. Absolute protection against security breaches remains out of reach, but here are a few additional safeguards organizations can employ:

■ *Backups.* Organizations and individual computer users should perform **backups** of important files to external hard drives, CDs, tapes, or online backup service providers at regular intervals. Some systems can be set to perform automatic backups at specified intervals, such as at the end of a working day. Information maintained in current databases and transferred to backup tapes should be encrypted so that if crackers enter databases or thieves steal tapes, the information is useless to them.

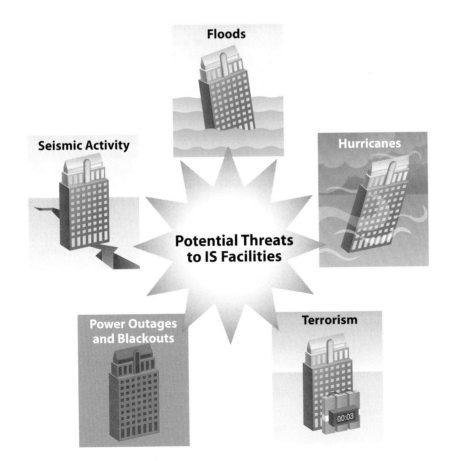

FIGURE 10.23

Potential threats to IS facilities include floods, hurricanes, terrorism, power outages, and seismic activity.

FIGURE 10.24

UPS's servers handle up to 20 million requests per day.
Source: Alejandro Mendoza R/ Shutterstock

- *Backup Sites.* **Backup sites** are critical for business continuity in the event a disaster strikes; in other words, backup sites can be thought of as a company's office in a temporary location. Commonly, a distinction is made between cold and hot backup sites. A **cold backup site** is nothing more than an empty warehouse with all necessary connections for power and communication but nothing else. In the case of a disaster, a company has to first set up all necessary equipment, ranging from office furniture to Web servers. While this is the least expensive option, it also takes a relatively longer time before a company can resume working after a disaster. A **hot backup site**, in contrast, is a fully equipped backup facility, having everything from office chairs to a one-to-one replication of the most current data. In the event of a disaster, all that has to be done is to relocate the employees to the backup site to continue working. Obviously, this is a very expensive option, as the backup site has to be kept fully equipped and all the IS infrastructure duplicated. Further, hot backup sites also have a redundant backup of the data so that the business processes are interrupted as little as possible. To achieve this redundancy, all data are **mirrored** on separate servers (i.e., everything is stored synchronously on two independent systems). This might seem expensive, but for a critical business application involving customers, it may be less expensive to run a redundant backup system in parallel than it would be to disrupt business or lose customers in the event of catastrophic system failure.
- *Redundant Data Centers.* Often, companies choose to replicate their data centers in multiple locations. Thinking about the location of redundant systems is an important aspect of disaster planning. If a company relies on redundant systems, all of which are located within the same building, a single event can incapacitate all the systems. Similarly, events such as a hurricane can damage systems that are located across town from each other. Thus, even if the primary infrastructure is located in-house, it pays to have a backup located in a different geographic area to minimize the risk of a disaster happening to both systems.
- *Closed-Circuit Television.* While installing and monitoring a closed-circuit television system is costly, the systems can monitor for physical intruders in data centers, server rooms, or collocation facilities. Video cameras display the physical interior and/or exterior

of a facility and record all activity on tape. In-house security personnel or an outside security service can watch computer monitors and immediately report suspicious activity to the police. Digital video recording can be used to store this information digitally, even from remote cameras connected to the system via a company's intranet, wireless LANs, or the Internet.

■ *Uninterruptible Power Supply.* An uninterruptible power supply does not protect against intruders, but it does protect against power surges and temporary power failures that can cause information loss.

For reasons of business continuity, companies such as UPS maintain large data centers in different geographic areas. Many (especially smaller) organizations do not need facilities the size of one of the UPS data centers; instead, they may just need space for a few servers. For such needs, companies can turn to **collocation facilities**. Organizations can rent space (usually in the form of cabinets or shares of a cabinet; see Figure 10.25) for their servers in such collocation facilities, and the organizations managing collocation facilities provide the necessary infrastructure in terms of power, backups, connectivity, and security. Alternatively, organizations increasingly attempt to transfer risk by using cloud computing services.

Clearly, there are a broad range of technology-based approaches for securing information systems, and no matter whether your server is located in a cabinet within your organization or you have rented space in a collocation facility, you should have physical safeguards in place to secure the equipment. A comprehensive security plan will include numerous technological methods. Next, we examine human-based methods.

Human Safeguards

In addition to the technological safeguards, there are various human safeguards that can help to protect information systems, specifically ethics, laws, and effective management (see Figure 10.26). *IS ethics*, discussed in Chapter 1, "Managing in the Digital World," relates to a broad range of standards of appropriate conduct by users. Educating potential users at an early age as to what constitutes appropriate behavior can help, but unethical users will undoubtedly always remain a problem for those wanting to maintain IS security. Additionally, there are numerous federal and state laws against unauthorized use of networks and computer systems. Unfortunately, individuals who want unauthorized access to networks and computer systems usually find a way to exploit them; often, after the fact, laws are enacted to prohibit that activity in the future.

FIGURE 10.25

Collocation facilities allow organizations to rent secure space for their infrastructure.
Source: Shutterstock

FIGURE 10.26

Human safeguards for
IS security.

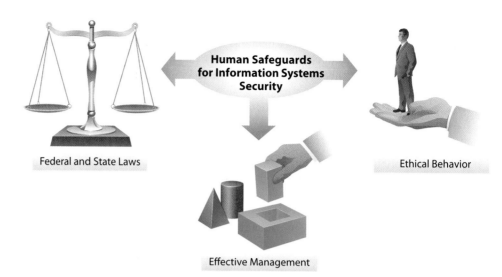

Federal and State Laws

**Human Safeguards
for Information Systems
Security**

Ethical Behavior

Effective Management

Computer Forensics

As computer crime has gone mainstream, law enforcement has had to become much more sophisticated in their computer crime investigations. **Computer forensics** is the use of formal investigative techniques to evaluate digital information for judicial review. Most often, computer forensics experts evaluate various types of storage devices to find traces of illegal activity or to gain evidence in related non-computer crimes. In fact, in most missing-person or murder cases today, investigators immediately want to examine the victim's computer for clues or evidence.

Organizations and governments are increasingly utilizing *honeypots* to proactively gather intelligence to improve their defenses or to catch cybercriminals. A **honeypot** is a computer, data, or network site that is designed to be enticing to crackers so as to detect, deflect, or counteract illegal activity. For instance, the FBI operated a cybercrime clearinghouse called "DarkMarket" where unsuspecting hackers, credit card swindlers, and identity thieves bought and sold products and information (Poulsen, 2008). Products for sale included electronic banking logins, stolen personal data, and even specialized hardware for producing counterfeit credit cards. The FBI operated DarkMarket for more than two years to collect information on the global marketplace for cybercriminals. In late 2008, DarkMarket was shut down because it had become known to the criminals. It is without question that countless other honeypots are being operated by governments and computer forensics experts to track criminals and gather information.

Although computer forensics experts are extremely skilled in investigating prior and ongoing computer crime, many computer criminals are also experts, making the forensics process extremely difficult in some cases. Some criminals, for example, have special "booby-trap" programs running on computers to destroy evidence if someone other than the criminal uses the machine. Using special software tools, computer forensics experts can often restore data that have been deleted from a computer's hard drive. Clearly, computer forensics will continue to evolve as criminals utilize more sophisticated computer-based methods for committing and aiding criminal activities.

Additionally, beyond human and technological safeguards, the quality of information security in any organization depends on *effective management*. Managers must continuously check for security problems, recognize that holes in security exist, and take appropriate action. We discuss methods for effectively managing IS security next.

KEY PLAYERS

White Knights of the Internet Age

Ever since organizational and personal computing became ubiquitous, computer criminals have attempted to infect computers with malicious software. Crimes such as robbing a bank can be complex undertakings involving relatively high risks; even criminals mugging someone on the street face relatively high risks. In contrast, using malicious software to gain access to an unsuspecting computer user's password, or stealing the user's credit card data is a relatively "clean" and easy endeavor, and is comparatively less risky.

Because every computer is vulnerable to an attack, computer criminals have many different ways to attack unsuspecting users. Given the way in which antivirus software works, criminals typically have a certain amount of time before their malicious software is detected. First, a machine has to be infected before the virus is detected. Additionally, users typically do not expect to become victims, and are thus not constantly on alert. Finally, as computer criminals continually come up with new ways to exploit vulnerabilities, neither users nor virus protection software know what to look for, making protection from malware a cat-and-mouse game.

A common recommendation is to install antivirus software, so as to minimize the potential threat of "known" viruses exploiting certain vulnerabilities of a computer. Antivirus software attempts to detect viruses and protect users by deleting, quarantining, or repairing any files deemed malicious. If no one knows what to look for, which is the case with new viruses, how are viruses detected?

There are three basic ways in which security software detects malware. The first approach, often referred to as *signature detection* (or dictionary-based approach) compares the content of files with known pieces of code of malicious software. However, as the malware has to be known to the software, this is a reactive strategy that does not work for new malware; in addition, frequent updates to the security program's malware database are needed for this approach to be reasonably effective. The second approach is behavior based: security software attempts to detect anomalous behavior, and alerts the user of such activity. However, the increasing complexity of modern software makes it ever harder to detect anomalies, and "false positives" are the norm, desensitizing or annoying users. Further, if the malware behaves like a normal program, it will not be detected by security software. A final approach is specification-based, which curtails insecure activities based on predefined policies (such as preventing files downloaded from the Web from executing); malware that reflects these defined activities is stopped before it can do any harm. Typically, security software uses a combination of these approaches to maximize effectiveness.

Given the continuous threat by computer criminals, it is no surprise that security software is big business. Even with the global economy slowing, spending on security software hasn't slowed; according to research firm Gartner, the market for security software increased by 7.5 percent from 2010 to 2011, totaling more than US$17.7 billion in 2011. The biggest players in the market for security software include specialized computer security companies such as Symantec, TrendMicro, McAfee, Check Point, Kaspersky, Verint, and AVG. Other players in the market are companies focusing on a broad range of software and services, such as EMC, CA, or IBM. Interestingly, two companies well-known for highly effective security software, AVG and Kaspersky, originated in countries of the former Eastern bloc (the Czech Republic and Russia, respectively), which is infamous for being the origin of many threats to information systems security. Many of these companies offer full suites of security software, including virus and malware detection, e-mail protection, and other safeguards. In addition, many of the key players have discovered mobile phone security as the next big area.

As you see, there are plenty of options to choose from, depending on the nature of the systems to protect and the potential impact of a threat exploiting a potential vulnerability. Yet, a global survey conducted by security firm McAfee revealed that in 2011, 17 percent of users had their security software disabled, or had no protection to begin with (in the United States, almost 20 percent of users were unprotected). These figures show that even in light of high profile computer attacks (such as the Stuxnet or Flame malware targeted at rogue countries' infrastructures) and frequent coverage of malware in the news, people seem to be unaware of the threats. As in many other situations, not only technological safeguards are needed, but user education seems to be key.

Based on:

Kassner, M. (2010, January 19). How antivirus software works: Is it worth it? *Techrepublic*. Retrieved June 12, 2012, from http://www.techrepublic.com/blog/security/how-antivirus-software-works-is-it-worth-it/3015.

McAfee. (2012, May 30). Consumer alert: McAfee releases results of global unprotected rates study. *McAfee.com*. Retrieved June 12, 2012, from https://blogs.mcafee.com/consumer/family-safety/mcafee-releases-results-of-global-unprotected-rates.

Pettey, C., and van der Meulen, R. (2012, April 26). Gartner says security software market grew 7.5 percent in 2011. *Gartner*. Retrieved June 12, 2012, from http://www.gartner.com/it/page.jsp?id=1996415.

Van Kooten, M. (2009, November 10). Strong growth for security software top 12. *Software Top 100*. Retrieved June 12, 2012, from http://www.softwaretop100.org/strong-growth-for-security-software-top-12.

Van Kooten, M. (2011, August 23). Global software top 100 – Edition 2011. *Software Top 100*. Retrieved June 12, 2012, from http://www.softwaretop100.org/global-software-top-100-edition-2011.

http://goo.gl/kvTpZ

MANAGING IS SECURITY

Very often some of the best things that people can do to secure their information systems are not necessarily technical in nature. Instead, they may involve changes within the organization and/or better management of people's use of information systems. For example, one of the outcomes of the systems security risk analysis described here may well be a set of computer and/or Internet use policies (sometimes referred to as **acceptable use policies**) for people within the organization, with clearly spelled out penalties for noncompliance (see Figure 10.27). Organizations often require employees to acknowledge the acceptance of acceptable use policies in order to mitigate downstream risks for employee noncompliance. More fundamental to security than management techniques such as these is that you make every effort to hire trustworthy employees and treat them well. Trustworthy employees who are treated well are less likely to commit offenses affecting the organization's information systems.

Developing an IS Security Plan

All organizations should develop an IS security plan. An **information systems security plan** involves assessing risks, planning ways to reduce risk, implementing the plan, and ongoing monitoring. This planning process should be ongoing and include these five steps:

1. *Risk Analysis.* Organizations should do the following:
   a. Determine the value of electronic information
   b. Assess threats to confidentiality, integrity, and availability of information
   c. Determine which computer operations are most vulnerable to security breaches
   d. Assess current security policies
   e. Recommend changes to existing practices and/or policies that will improve computer security
2. *Policies and Procedures.* Once risks are assessed, a plan should be formulated that details what action will be taken if security is breached. Policies and procedures related to computer security generally include the following:
   a. *Information Policy.* Outlines how sensitive information will be handled, stored, transmitted, and destroyed.
   b. *Security Policy.* Explains technical controls on all organizational computer systems, such as access limitations, audit-control software, firewalls, and so on.

FIGURE 10.27

Most organizations provide employees or customers with an acceptable use policy.

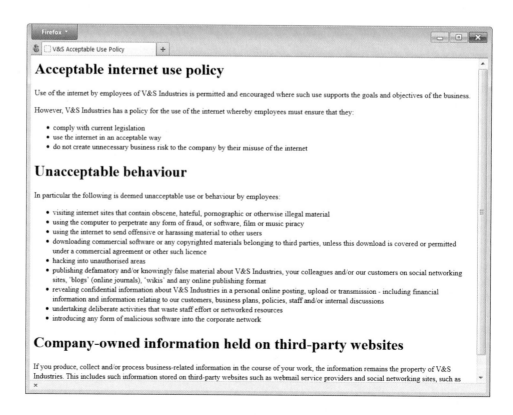

c. *Use Policy.* Outlines the organization's policy regarding appropriate use of in-house computer systems. May mandate no Internet surfing, use of company computer systems only for employment-related purposes, restricted use of social networking and e-mail, and so on.

d. *Backup Policy.* Explains requirements for backing up information.

e. *Account Management Policy.* Lists procedures for adding new users to systems and removing users who have left the organization.

f. *Incident Handling Procedures.* Lists procedures to follow when handling a security breach.

g. *Disaster Recovery Plan.* Lists all the steps an organization will take to restore computer operations in case of a natural or deliberate disaster. Each department within the organization generally has its own disaster recovery plan (see the following discussion).

3. *Implementation.* Once policies and plans are established, organizations can decide which security mechanisms to use and train personnel regarding security policies and measures. During this phase, network security mechanisms such as firewalls are put in place, as are intrusion detection systems, such as antivirus software, manual and automated log examination software, and host- and network-based intrusion detection software. Encryption information, passwords, and smart cards and smart badges are also disseminated and explained during this phase. The IS department is usually responsible for instituting security measures.

4. *Training.* Personnel within an organization should know the security policy and the plan for disaster recovery and be prepared to perform assigned tasks in that regard—both routinely on a daily basis and disaster related.

5. *Auditing.* Auditing is an ongoing process that assesses policy adherence, the security of new projects, and whether the organization's computer security can be penetrated. Penetration tests are conducted in-house and/or by an outside contractor to see how well the organization's computer security measures are working. Can the intrusion detection system detect attacks? Are incident response procedures effective? Can the network be penetrated? Is physical security adequate? Do employees know security policies and procedures?

DISASTER PLANNING. In some cases, all attempts to provide a reliable and secure IS infrastructure are in vain, and disasters cannot be avoided. Thus, organizations need to be prepared for when something catastrophic occurs. The most important aspect of preparing for disaster is creating a **business continuity plan**, which describes how a business resumes operation after a disaster. A subset of the business continuity plan is the **disaster recovery plan**, which spells out detailed procedures for recovering from systems-related disasters, such as virus infections and other disasters that might cripple the IS infrastructure. This way, even under the worst-case scenario, people will be able to replace or reconstruct critical files or data, or they will at least have a plan readily available to begin the recovery process. A typical disaster recovery plan includes information that answers the following questions:

- What events are considered a disaster?
- What should be done to prepare the backup site?
- What is the chain of command, and who can declare a disaster?
- What hardware and software are needed to recover from a disaster?
- Which personnel are needed for staffing the backup sites?
- What is the sequence for moving back to the original location after recovery?
- Which providers can be drawn on to aid in the disaster recovery process?

DESIGNING THE RECOVERY PLAN. When planning for disaster, two objectives should be considered by an organization: recovery time and recovery point objectives. **Recovery time objectives** specify the maximum time allowed to recover from a catastrophic event. For example, should the organization be able to resume operations in minutes, hours, or days after the disaster? Companies using cloud-based backup services often forget that restoring large quantities of data from the cloud can take a long time, and having completely redundant systems helps to minimize the recovery time and might be best suited for mission-critical applications, such as e-commerce transaction servers. For other applications, such as data mining, while important, the recovery time can be longer without disrupting primary business processes.

Additionally, **recovery point objectives** specify how current the backup data should be. Imagine that your computer's hard drive crashes while you are working on a term paper. Luckily, you recently backed up your data. Would you prefer the last backup to be a few days old, or would you rather have the last backup include your most recent changes to the term paper? Having completely redundant systems that mirror the data helps to minimize (or even avoid) data loss in the event of a catastrophic failure.

RESPONDING TO A SECURITY BREACH. Organizations that have developed a comprehensive IS security plan, as outlined previously, will have the ability to rapidly respond to any type of security breach to their IS resources or to a natural disaster. In addition to restoring lost data using backups, common responses to a security breach include performing a new risk audit and implementing a combination of additional (more secure) safeguards (as described previously). Additionally, when intruders are discovered, organizations can contact local law enforcement agencies and the FBI for assistance in locating and prosecuting them. Several online organizations issue bulletins to alert businesses and individuals to possible software vulnerabilities or attacks based on reports from organizations that have experienced security breaches. The Computer Emergency Response Team Coordination Center, established by the U.S. federal government in 1988 as a major center of Internet security expertise, provides additional resources for organizations by publishing security alerts, conducting and publishing research, and providing training to incident response professionals (see www.cert.org).

The State of Systems Security Management

We continue to hear and read about cases where a breach of computer security was catastrophic and/or had potentially dire consequences. For example, a stolen laptop computer in May 2006 reportedly put 26.5 million U.S. military personnel at risk for identity theft because it contained a large database that included Social Security Numbers, birth dates, and other personal information. Nevertheless, despite these highly publicized incidents, systems security measures are paying off for most organizations. According to the annual CSI Computer Crime and Security Survey (2011), the total financial losses resulting from cybercrime are decreasing. Key findings from their survey include the following (Courtesy of Computer Security Institute):

- Financial fraud attacks result in the greatest financial losses for organizations; other significant costs were due to viruses, data theft, unauthorized access, and denial-of-service attacks.
- Relatively few organizations (about 28 percent) report computer intrusions to law enforcement because of various fears, such as how negative publicity would hurt stock values or how competitors might gain an advantage over news of a security incident.
- Most organizations do not outsource security activities.
- Nearly all organizations conduct routine and ongoing security audits.
- The majority of organizations believed security training of employees is important, but most respondents said their organization did not spend enough on security training.

In addition to these findings, organizations use a broad variety of security technologies, including the following:

- Activity logging and intrusion detection
- Antivirus and antispyware software
- Firewalls and VPNs
- Encryption for data in transit and at rest

Clearly, because malicious crackers won't become complacent anytime soon, it is encouraging that organizations appear to be gaining ground to guard against attacks. The lesson learned here is that we need to continue to implement vigilant approaches to better manage systems security in the digital world.

WHEN THINGS GO WRONG

Stopping Insider Threats: WikiLeaks and Bradley Manning

Insider threats—a trusted adversary who operates within an organization's boundaries—are a significant danger to both private and public sectors, and are often cited as the greatest threat to an organization. Insider threats include disgruntled employees or ex-employees, contractors, business partners, or auditors. The damage caused by an insider threat can take many forms, including workplace violence; the introduction of malware into corporate networks; the theft of information, corporate secrets, or money; the corruption or deletion of data; and so on. The identification of insider threats, however, is an extremely difficult, expensive, error prone, and time-consuming task. This identification process is heightened in very large organizations. For instance, identifying a small number of potential insider threats within an organization with thousands of employees is a literal "needle in the haystack" problem.

Bradley Manning, a U.S. Army soldier, was arrested in May 2010 on suspicion of having passed classified material to whistleblower Web site **WikiLeaks**. Today, Manning is considered to be one of the world's most infamous examples of an insider threat. WikiLeaks is a very controversial information disclosure portal that works a lot like Wikipedia, where volunteers submit and analyze classified and restricted material provided by whistleblowers. WikiLeaks, edited by Julian Assange, an Australian Internet activist, is principled on the belief that all citizens have the right to access the documents and proceedings of governments to allow for effective public oversight. Opponents of this view believe that sites like WikiLeaks are dangerous and put governments and personnel at tremendous risk.

Manning was an intelligence analyst in Iraq and had unfettered access to several databases that were used by the U.S. government to transmit and store classified information. Using a blank CD with "Lady Gaga" written on it, Manning managed to easily download and store massive amounts of information, and smuggle it outside the base. Manning was arrested after confiding to a former computer hacker that he had provided classified information to WikiLeaks; the former hacker, Adrian Lamo, who is now rumored to have been a consultant to various governmental security agencies after his hacking days, contacted the FBI about Manning's admissions. Lamo is now considered a "snitch" by many in the hacker community, but others view him as a patriot who is likely to have saved many lives by his actions. It is estimated that Manning provided WikiLeaks with the largest set of restricted documents ever leaked to the public. This information included videos of a 2007 helicopter gun attack in Baghdad and the 2009 Granai airstrike in Afghanistan; 250,000 United States diplomatic cables (including communication between U.S. government officials and those from various countries); and 500,000 army reports that came to be known as the Iraq and Afghan War logs. The leaks were both embarrassing and created an unprecedented security concern for diplomats and governments around the world.

Manning is scheduled to go on trial in September 2012. If convicted of espionage, Manning will face life imprisonment. Reactions to Manning's actions are mixed. Many feel that Manning's actions were a catalyst for political reforms, while others question how an Army private had unrestricted access to such massive amounts of critical information with little or no oversight. From the U.S. government's perspective, WikiLeaks will forever be a wakeup call; improved policies, monitoring, and a host of other human and technical safeguards are being deployed throughout the military and governmental agencies. Protecting against another WikiLeaks type event and the identification of possible insider threats has become a paramount concern.

Based on:

Adrian Lamo. (2012, May 3). In *Wikipedia, The Free Encyclopedia*. Retrieved May 20, 2012, from http://en.wikipedia.org/w/index.php?title=Adrian_Lamo&oldid=490489696.

Bradley Manning. (2012, May 16). In *Wikipedia, The Free Encyclopedia*. Retrieved May 20, 2012, from http://en.wikipedia.org/w/index.php?title=Bradley_Manning&oldid=492931636.

Poulsen, K. and Zetter, K. (2010, June 6). U.S. intelligence analyst arrested in Wikileaks video probe. *Wired.com*. Retrieved August 15, 2012, from http://www.wired.com/threatlevel/2010/06/leak.

WikiLeaks. (2012, May 19). In *Wikipedia, The Free Encyclopedia*. Retrieved May 20, 2012, from http://en.wikipedia.org/w/index.php?title=WikiLeaks&oldid=493319019.

http://goo.gl/OjbKo

INFORMATION SYSTEMS CONTROLS, AUDITING, AND THE SARBANES–OXLEY ACT

As you have seen, there are a variety of issues to consider when managing IS security. To ensure security, control costs, gain and protect trust, remain competitive, and comply with internal or external governance (e.g., the Sarbanes–Oxley Act, discussed later in this section), **information systems controls** have to be put into place. Such controls, which help ensure the reliability of information, can consist of a variety of different measures, such as systems security policies and their physical implementation, access restrictions, or record keeping, to be able to trace actions and transactions and who is responsible for these. IS controls thus need to be applied throughout the entire IS infrastructure. To be most effective, controls should be a combination of three types of controls:

- Preventive controls (to prevent any potentially negative event from occurring, such as by preventing outside intruders from accessing a facility)
- Detective controls (to assess whether anything went wrong, such as unauthorized access attempts)
- Corrective controls (to mitigate the impact of any problem after it has arisen, such as restoring compromised data)

One way to conceptualize the different forms of controls is by a hierarchy ranging from high-level policies to the implementation at the application level (see Figure 10.28 for the hierarchy of controls); Table 10.4 gives a brief explanation of the different types of controls and presents examples for each. While reading this book, you have learned about a variety of IS controls, and you will continue to come across the different elements of control in the following sections when we will describe how companies use IS auditing to assess the IS controls in place and whether further IS controls need to be implemented or changed.

IS Auditing

Analyzing the IS controls should be an ongoing process for organizations. However, often it can be beneficial for organizations to periodically have an external entity review the controls so as to uncover any potential problems. An **information systems audit**, often performed by external auditors, can help organizations assess the state of their IS controls to determine necessary changes and to help ensure the information systems' availability, confidentiality, and integrity. The response to the strengths and weaknesses identified in the IS audit is often determined by the potential risks an organization faces. In other words, the IS audit has to assess whether the IS controls in place are sufficient to address the potential risks. Thus, a major

FIGURE 10.28

Hierarchy of IS controls.
Source: Based on http://infotech.aicpa.org.

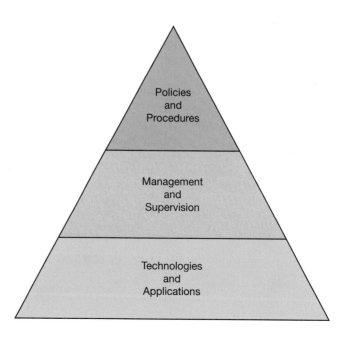

TABLE 10.4 Different Types of IS Controls

Type of Control	What Is It For?	Examples
Policies	Define aims and objectives of the organization	General policies about: Security and privacy Rights of access Data and systems ownership Access to sensitive areas (e.g., high-availability facilities) Disaster planning
Standards	Support the requirements of policies	Standards about: Systems development process Systems software configuration Application controls Data structures Documentation
Organization and management	Define lines of reporting to implement effective control and policy development	Policies about: Security and use Account authorization Backup and recovery Incident reporting
Physical and environmental controls	Protect the organization's IS assets	High-availability facilities Collocation facilities
Systems software controls	Enable applications and users to utilize the systems	Control access to applications Generate activity logs Prevent outside intrusion (e.g., by hackers)
Systems development and acquisition controls	Ensure that systems meet the organization's needs	Document user requirements Use formal processes for systems design, development, testing, and maintenance
Application-based controls	Ensure correct input, processing, storage, and output of data; maintain record of data as the data move through the system	Input controls (such as automated checking of the inputs into a Web form) Processing controls Output controls (comparing the outputs against intended results) Integrity controls (ensure that data remain correct) Audit trail (keep record of transactions to be able to locate sources of potential errors)

component of the IS audit is a risk assessment (discussed in prior sections), which aims at determining what type of risks the organization's IS infrastructure faces, the criticality of those risks to the infrastructure, and the level of risks the organization is willing to tolerate.

Once the risk has been assessed, auditors have to evaluate the organization's internal controls. During such audits, the auditor tries to gather evidence regarding the effectiveness of the controls. However, testing all controls under all possible conditions is very inefficient and often infeasible. Thus, auditors frequently rely on **computer-assisted auditing tools**, or specific software that tests applications and data using test data or simulations. In addition to using specific auditing tools, auditors use audit sampling procedures to assess the controls, enabling the audit to be conducted in the most cost-effective manner. Once the audit has been performed and sufficient evidence has been gathered, reports are issued to the organization. Usually, such reports are followed up with a discussion of the results and potential courses of action.

The Sarbanes–Oxley Act

Performing an IS audit can help an organization reduce costs or remain competitive by identifying areas where IS controls are lacking and need improvement. Another major factor that has contributed to a high demand for IS auditors is the need to comply with government regulations, most notably the **Sarbanes–Oxley Act** of 2002 (hereafter S-OX). Formed as a reaction to large-scale accounting scandals that led to the downfall of corporations such as WorldCom and Enron, and to protect investors from fraudulent practices by organizations, S-OX mandates companies to demonstrate compliance with accounting standards and to establish controls and corporate governance. Commonly used controls include limiting a single employee's influence over transactions, such as by segregation of duties and establishing proper checks and balances. For example, if the employee who creates a purchase order also has the authority to approve the purchase order, this opens up a possibility for creating fraudulent orders; similarly, if the same employee is responsible for disbursing cash, recording the disbursements, and reconciling the related accounts, the employee can devise schemes to embezzle money. Implementing proper controls not only helps to reduce the potential for fraud, but also helps to prevent unintentional errors. To demonstrate S-OX compliance, public companies are required, among other things, to have external auditors assess the effectiveness of their internal controls, as well as audit their financial statements. While S-OX addresses primarily the accounting side of organizations, it is of major importance to include IS controls in compliance reviews, given the importance of an IS infrastructure and IS controls for an organization's financial applications.

According to S-OX, companies have to demonstrate that there are controls in place to prevent misuse or fraud, controls to detect any potential problems, and effective measures to correct any problems; S-OX goes so far that corporate executives face jail time and heavy fines if the appropriate controls are not in place or are ineffective. The IS architecture plays a key role in S-OX compliance, given that many controls are IS based, providing capabilities to detect information exceptions and to provide a management trail for tracing exceptions. However, S-OX itself barely addresses IS controls specifically; rather, it addresses general processes and practices, leaving companies wondering how to comply with the guidelines put forth in the act. Further, it is often cumbersome and time consuming for organizations to identify the relevant systems to be audited for S-OX compliance. Thus, many organizations find it easier to review their entire IS infrastructure, following objectives set forth in guidelines such as the **control objectives for information and related technology (COBIT)**—a set of best practices that helps organizations both maximize the benefits from their IS infrastructure and establish appropriate controls.

Another issue faced by organizations because of S-OX is the requirement to preserve evidence to document compliance and for potential lawsuits. Since the inception of S-OX, e-mails and even instant messages have achieved the same status as regular business documents and thus need to be preserved for a period of time, typically up to seven years. Failure to present such documents in the case of litigious activity can lead to severe fines being imposed on companies and their executives, and courts usually will not accept the argument that a message could not be located. For example, the investment bank Morgan Stanley faced fines up to US$15 million for failing to retain e-mail messages. On the surface, it seems easiest for an organization to simply archive all the e-mail messages sent and received. However, such a "digital landfill," where everything is stored, can quickly grow to an unmanageable size, and companies cannot comply with the mandate to present evidence in a timely manner. Thus, many organizations turn to e-mail management software that archives and categorizes all incoming and outgoing e-mails based on key words. Even using such specialized software, finding e-mails related to a certain topic within the archive can pose a tremendous task: Some analysts estimate that a business with 25,000 employees generates over 4 billion e-mail messages over the course of seven years (not counting any increase in e-mail activity), which would be hard to handle for even the most sophisticated programs.

INDUSTRY ANALYSIS

Cybercops Track Cybercriminals

The *CSI* (crime scene investigation) television shows have made "DNA testing" a household phrase. Virtually everyone knows that a criminal who leaves body cells or fluids—hair and skin cells, saliva, blood, semen, and so on—at the scene of a crime can be linked to the crime through DNA analysis. (DNA, or deoxyribonucleic acid, is present in all living tissue—plant or animal.) The CSI shows have helped to illustrate that just as crime laboratories have had to keep technologically current, so, too, have law enforcement officers at national, state, and local levels.

Because technological advancement has been rapid, law enforcement has lagged behind, but it is catching up. At the U.S. federal level, the Computer Crime and Intellectual Property Section within the Justice Department is devoted to combating cybercrime. In addition, the FBI has created computer crime squads in 16 metropolitan areas around the country specifically to investigate cybercrime. In Washington, D.C., the FBI's National Infrastructure Protection Center acts as a clearinghouse for information and expertise relating to cybercrime. And each federal judicial district has at least one assistant U.S. attorney, called a computer and telecommunications crime coordinator, who has received special training in how to investigate and prosecute cybercrime.

Furthermore, every state now has a computer crime investigation unit available as a resource to local law enforcement agencies, and many municipal police departments have their own computer crime investigative units.

Software tools available to law enforcement agencies have also improved. Programs such as the Software Forensic Tool Kit provide police with the ability to search and recreate deleted files on computers. Also digitized for law enforcement use are criminal identification systems, such as the Statewide Network of Agency Photos (SNAP). Law enforcement officers can search SNAP's digital database for mug shots that show a criminal's distinguishing marks, such as scars and tattoos, making criminal identification simpler. SNAP is connected to the FBI's Integrated Automatic Fingerprint Identification System, which electronically transmits fingerprints at the time a person is arrested.

Similarly, the Classification System for Serial Criminal Patterns, developed by the Chicago Police Department, allows detectives to look for possible patterns connecting crimes.

Like many of us who use social networking sites to stay connected to our family and friends, cybercops are also utilizing these valuable tools to reach out to their communities. In fact, Facebook, Twitter, and other social networking sites are being increasingly used to gather tips and solve crimes.

Radio communication has also been updated to provide a secure means of voice communication for law enforcement officers. No longer can any interested civilian buy a receiver and monitor police calls since digital voice communication can now be encrypted, allowing for a higher level of security.

It's an unfortunate fact that criminals have discovered how to use the Internet to their advantage. Clearly, however, law enforcement is gaining on them, as officers also use technological advancement to track, arrest, and prosecute online and offline criminals.

Questions:

1. Today, is it harder or easier to be a criminal? Why?
2. Argue whether law enforcement can or cannot ever get ahead of criminals.

Based on:

Anonymous. (2010, April 27). Fighting crime on Facebook. *BBC News.* Retrieved May 20, 2012, from http://news.bbc.co.uk/2/hi/uk_news/northern_ireland/8646428.stm.

Ashcroft, J. (2001, May 22). Remarks of Attorney General John Ashcroft. Retrieved April 24, 2010, from http://www.usdoj.gov/criminal/cybercrime/AGCPPSI.htm.

Justice Technology Information Network. (n.d.). Retrieved May 24, 2012, from http://www.justnet.org/Pages/home.aspx.

Key Points Review

1. ***Define computer crime and describe several types of computer crime.*** Computer crime is defined as the act of using a computer to commit an illegal act, such as targeting a computer while committing an offense, using a computer to commit an offense, or using computers in the course of a criminal activity. A person who gains unauthorized access to a computer system has also committed a computer crime. Those individuals who are knowledgeable enough to gain access to computer systems without authorization have long been referred to as hackers. Today, those who break into computer systems with the intention of doing damage or committing a crime are usually called crackers. Hackers and crackers can commit a wide variety of computer crimes, including unauthorized access and information modification. Crackers are

also associated with the making and distributing of computer viruses and other destructive codes. People are increasingly using information systems to aid in crimes against individuals, including identity theft, cyberharassment, cyberstalking, and cyberbullying. Finally, making illegal copies of software, a worldwide computer crime, is called software piracy.

2. *Describe and explain the differences between cyberwar and cyberterrorism.* Cyberwar refers to an organized attempt by a country's military to disrupt or destroy the information and communication systems of another country. The goal of cyberwar is to turn the balance of information and knowledge in one's favor in order to diminish an opponent's capabilities and also to enhance those of the attacker. Cyberterrorism is the use of computer and networking technologies by individuals and organized groups against persons or property to intimidate or coerce governments, civilians, or any segment of society to attain political, religious, or ideological goals. Now that terrorist groups are increasingly using the Internet for their purposes, one of the great fears about cyberterrorism is that an attack can be launched from a computer anywhere in the world.

3. *Explain what is meant by the term "information systems security" and describe both technology- and human-based safeguards for information systems.* "Information systems security" refers to precautions taken to keep all aspects of information systems (e.g., all hardware, software, network equipment, and data) safe from unauthorized use or access. There are five general categories of technological safeguards: physical access restrictions, firewalls, encryption, virus monitoring and protection, and audit-control software. Physical access restrictions prevent unauthorized access using authentication through something a person has (e.g., identification card), something a person knows (e.g., password), or something a person is (e.g., unique human attribute). Many organizations use some combination of methods to best control IS assets. A variety of technologies can be deployed to enhance system security, including firewalls, biometrics, virtual private networks, encryption, and virus protection tools. Firewalls are hardware or software used to detect intrusion and prevent unauthorized access to or from a private network. Biometrics is the use of technology to better authenticate users by matching fingerprints, retinal patterns in the eye, body weight, or other bodily characteristics before granting access to a computer or a facility. Virtual private networks use authentication and encryption to provide a secure tunnel within a public network such as the Internet so that information can pass securely between two computers. Encryption—the process of encoding messages before they enter the network or airwaves— is very useful for securing information when you do not have access to a secure telecommunications channel. Virus monitoring and protection utilizes a set of hardware and software to detect and prevent computer viruses. Audit-control software is used to keep track of computer activity so that auditors can spot suspicious activity and take action if necessary. Other technological safeguards include backups, closed-circuit television, and uninterruptible power supplies. Human safeguards include ethical standards, federal and state laws, and effective management. Organizations typically utilize a combination of both technological and human safeguards when protecting their IS resources.

4. *Discuss how to better manage IS security and explain the process of developing an IS security plan.* Because no system is 100 percent secure, organizations must utilize all available resources for implementing an effective IS security plan. The planning process includes a risk analysis, the development of policies and procedures, implementation, training, and ongoing auditing. Relatedly, organizations should develop a business continuity plan and a disaster recovery plan that specifies how to react to a disaster. After a security breach, organizations should perform new audits, implement new countermeasures, and possibly inform law enforcement agencies of the breach.

5. *Describe how organizations can establish IS controls to better ensure security.* IS controls can help ensure a secure and reliable infrastructure; such controls should be a mix of preventive, detective, and corrective controls. To assess the efficacy of these controls, organizations frequently conduct IS audits to determine the risks an organization faces and how far the IS controls can limit any potentially negative effects. Further, organizations perform IS audits to comply with government regulations, most notably the Sarbanes–Oxley Act of 2002. According to this act, companies have to demonstrate that there are controls in place to prevent misuse or fraud, controls to detect any potential problems, and effective measures to correct any problems; the act goes so far that a business executive could face heavy fines or substantial jail time if appropriate controls are not in place or are ineffective. Performing thorough IS audits on a regular basis can help assess compliance to these regulations.

Key Terms

acceptable use policy   456
access-control software   447
adware   430
audit-control software   450
authentication   445
backup   451
backup site   452
biometrics   447
bot herder   433
botnet   433
business continuity plan   457
CAPTCHA   431
certificate authority   452
cold backup site   452
collocation facility   453
computer-assisted auditing tool   461
computer crime   423
computer forensics   454
control objectives for information and
    related technology (COBIT)   462
cookie   432
copyright   435
cracker   424
cyberbullying   434
cyberharassment   434
cybersquatting   434
cyberstalking   434
cyberterrorism   440

cyberwar   439
denial-of-service attack   429
disaster recovery plan   457
drive-by hacking   448
encryption   450
firewall   449
hacker   424
hacktivist   424
honeypot   454
hot backup site   452
identity theft   433
information modification   426
information systems audit   460
information systems controls   460
information systems security   444
information systems security plan   456
industrial espionage   425
insider threat   459
Internet hoax   434
IS risk management   423
key generator   435
logic bomb   429
malware   428
mirror   452
online predator   435
patent   435
patriot hacker   440
phishing   431

recovery point objective   458
recovery time objective   457
reverse engineering   435
risk acceptance   445
risk analysis   445
risk reduction   445
risk transference   445
Sarbanes–Oxley Act   462
Secure Sockets Layer   450
software piracy   435
spam   430
spam filter   430
spear phishing   431
spim   431
spyware   430
Stuxnet   439
time bomb   429
Trojan horse   428
tunneling   449
unauthorized access   426
virtual private network (VPN)   448
virus   428
virus prevention   450
warez   435
Web vandalism   439
WikiLeaks   459
worm   428
zombie computer   429

Review Questions

1. List and describe the primary threats to IS security.
2. Define denial of service. What is the role of zombie computers?
3. Explain the purpose of the Computer Fraud and Abuse Act of 1986 and the Electronic Communications Privacy Act of 1986.
4. Contrast hackers versus crackers.
5. Define unauthorized access and give several examples from recent media reports.
6. Define cybersquatting and give some examples.
7. Define virus and give some examples.
8. Define and contrast cyberharassment, cyberstalking, and cyberbullying.
9. Define and contrast cyberwar and cyberterrorism.
10. List some of the threats to information systems security that are not considered as standard security threats.
11. What are physical access restrictions, and how do they make an information system more secure?
12. Describe several methods for preventing and/or managing the spread of computer viruses.
13. What are bots and how do they affect the supply chain?
14. What is an IS security plan, and what are the five steps for developing such a plan?
15. List the six different technological safeguard methods that are employed by organizations.

Self-Study Questions

1. What is the common rule for deciding if an information system faces a security risk?
   A. Only desktop computers are at risk.
   B. Only network servers are at risk.
   C. All systems connected to networks are vulnerable to security violations.
   D. Networks have nothing to do with computer security.

2. Those individuals who break into computer systems with the intention of doing damage or committing a crime are usually called _____.
   A. hackers
   B. crackers
   C. computer geniuses
   D. computer operatives

3. Which of the following does *not* pose a threat to electronic information?
   A. unauthorized access
   B. lack of proper care and procedures
   C. unauthorized information modification
   D. all of the above can compromise information

4. Information modification attacks occur when _____.
   A. an authorized user changes a Web site address
   B. a Web site crashes
   C. the power is cut off
   D. someone who is not authorized to do so changes electronic information

5. Technological safeguards used to protect information include _____.
   A. laws
   B. effective management
   C. firewalls and physical access restrictions
   D. ethics

6. Limiting access to electronic information usually involves _____.
   A. something you have
   B. something you know
   C. something you are
   D. all of the above

7. Which of the following is the process of determining the true, accurate identity of a user of an information system?
   A. audit
   B. authentication
   C. firewall
   D. virtual private network

8. The use of computer and networking technologies by individuals and organized groups against persons or property to intimidate or coerce governments, civilians, or any segment of society in order to attain political, religious, or ideological goals is known as _____.
   A. cyberwar
   B. cybercrime
   C. cyberterrorism
   D. none of the above

9. A(n) _____ is a system composed of hardware, software, or both that is designed to detect intrusion and prevent unauthorized access to or from a private network.
   A. encryption
   B. firewall
   C. alarm
   D. logic bomb

10. _____ is the process of encoding messages before they enter the network or airwaves, then decoding them at the receiving end of the transfer so that recipients can read or hear them.
    A. Encryption
    B. Biometrics
    C. Authentication
    D. Disaster recovery

Answers are on page 469.

Problems and Exercises

1. Match the following terms to the appropriate definitions:
   i. Acceptable use policy
   ii. Authentication
   iii. Cyberwar
   iv. Biometrics
   v. Firewall
   vi. Phishing
   vii. Risk analysis
   viii. Spyware
   ix. Unauthorized access
   x. Zombie computer

   a. A type of security that grants or denies access to a computer system through the analysis of fingerprints, retinal patterns in the eye, or other bodily characteristics

   b. Specialized hardware and software that are used to keep unwanted users out of a system or to let users in with restricted access and privileges

   c. An organized attempt by a country's military to disrupt or destroy the information and communication systems of another country

   d. The process of identifying that the user is indeed who he or she claims to be, typically by requiring something that the user knows (e.g., a password) together with something that the user carries with him or her or has access to (e.g., an identification card or file)

   e. Computer and/or Internet use policy for people within an organization, with clearly spelled-out penalties for noncompliance

f. A process in which the value of the assets being protected is assessed, the likelihood of their being compromised is determined, and the costs of their being compromised are compared with the costs of the protections to be taken

g. An e-mail that attempts to trick financial account and credit card holders into giving away their private information

h. A computer that has been infected with a virus allowing an attacker to control it without the knowledge of the owner

i. Software that covertly gathers information about a user through an Internet connection without the knowledge of the owner

j. An IS security breach where an unauthorized individual sees, manipulates, or otherwise handles electronically stored information

2. Take a poll of classmates to determine who has had personal experience with computer virus infections, identity theft, or other computer/information system intrusions. How did victims handle the situation? What are classmates who have not been victimized doing to secure computers and personal information?

3. Banks and financial institutions have moved their applications to the Internet. Study some of these organizations to find out how they protect their information systems from hackers and other threats.

4. Visit the Web site for the Computer Emergency Response Team at www.cert.org/tech_tips/denial_of_service.html and answer the following:

a. What are the three basic types of denial-of-service attacks?

b. What impact can denial-of-service attacks have on an organization?

c. What other devices or activities within an organization might be impacted by denial-of-service attacks?

d. Name three steps organizations might take to prevent denial-of-service attacks.

If the previously given URL is no longer active, conduct a Web search for "denial-of-service attacks." Other active links can provide answers to the questions.

5. A number of countries across the globe have IT policies and laws. Study the IT policy of your country and prepare a small report highlighting its salient features.

6. Identity theft is a new type of theft. Visit www.fraud.org to find ways to protect yourself. Search the Internet for additional sources that provide information on identity theft and make a list of other ways to safeguard against it. What are some of the losses in addition to stolen documents and additional bills to pay that may result from identity theft?

7. Search the Internet for information about the damaging effects of software piracy and/or look at the following Web sites: www.bsa.org and www.microsoft.com/piracy. Is software piracy a global problem? What can you do to mitigate the problem? Prepare a short presentation to present to the class.

8. Search the Web to find out how many types of hackers there are. Identify the role of good hackers and offer arguments that support the contention that every organization must hire good hackers.

9. What laws should be enacted to combat cyberterrorism? How could such laws be enforced?

10. Contrast cyberharassment, cyberstalking, and cyberbullying using real-world examples found from recent news stories.

11. There are many brands of software firewalls, with ZoneAlarm, Norton 360, and Comodo Firewall being three popular choices. Search for these products on the Web and learn more about how a firewall works and what it costs to give you this needed protection; prepare a one-page report that outlines what you have learned.

12. Search for further information on encryption. What is the difference between 128-bit and 40-bit encryption? What level of encryption is used in your Web browser? Why has the U.S. government been reluctant to release software with higher levels of encryption to other countries?

13. What levels of user authentication are used at your school and/or place of work? Do they seem to be effective? What if a higher level of authentication were necessary? Would it be worth it, or would the added steps cause you to be less productive?

14. Should the encryption issue be subject to ethical judgments? For instance, if an absolutely unbreakable code becomes feasible, should we use it with the knowledge that it may help terrorists and other criminals evade the law? Should governments regulate which encryption technology can be used so that government law enforcement agents can always read material generated by terrorists and other criminals? Explain your answer. Should the government continue to regulate the exportation of encryption technology to foreign countries, excluding those that support terrorism as it does now? Why or why not?

15. Assess and compare the security of the computers you use regularly at home, work, and/or school. What measures do you use at home to protect your computer? What measures are taken at work or school to protect computers? (If possible, interview IT/IS personnel at work and/or at school to determine how systems are protected in the workplace and in classrooms.) Describe any security vulnerabilities you find and explain how they might be corrected.

16. In some cases, individuals engage in cybersquatting in the hope of being able to sell the domain names to companies at a high price; in other cases, companies engage in cybersquatting by registering domain names that are very similar to their competitors' product names in order to generate traffic from people misspelling Web addresses. Would you differentiate between these practices? Why or why not? If so, where would you draw the boundaries?

17. Find your school's guidelines for ethical computer use on the Internet and answer the following questions: Are there limitations as to the type of Web sites and material that can be viewed (e.g., pornography)? Are students allowed to change the programs on the hard drives of the

lab computers or download software for their own use? Are there rules governing personal use of computers and e-mail?

18. To learn more about protecting your privacy, visit www.cookiecentral.com and www.epubliceye.com. Did you learn something that will help protect your privacy? Why is privacy more important now than ever?

19. List some of the technological solutions that are deployed by your institution for ensuring authentication, integrity, confidentiality, and privacy of data moving across the network.

20. Insider threats are not new. Use the web and find two examples of insider threats throughout history that have had a big negative impact on their organization or government.

21. Microsoft and other software producers make free upgrades available to legitimate buyers of applications when security risks are exposed, but those using pirated copies are not eligible to receive security downloads. Should security patches for popular software be given for free to everyone, no questions asked? Why or why not?

Application Exercises

Note: The existing data files referenced in these exercises are available on the book's Web site: www.pearsonhighered.com/valacich.

Spreadsheet Application:
Analyzing Ethical Concerns at Campus Travel

Because of the employees' increased use of IS resources for private purposes at Campus Travel, you have announced that a new IS use policy will be implemented. You have set up a Web site for the employees to provide feedback to the proposed changes; the results of this survey are stored in the file EthicsSurvey.csv. Your boss wants to use the survey results to find out what the greatest concerns in terms of ethical implications are for the employees, so you are asked to do the following:

1. Complete the spreadsheet to include descriptive statistics (mean, standard deviation, mode, minimum, maximum, and range) for each survey item. Use formulas to calculate all statistics for the responses to the individual questions. (Hint: In Microsoft Excel, you can look up the necessary formulas in the category "Statistical"; you will have to calculate the ranges yourself.)

2. Format the means using color scales to highlight the items needing attention.
   Make sure to professionally format the pages before printing them out.

Database Application:
Tracking Software Licenses at Campus Travel

Recently, you have taken on the position of IS manager at Campus Travel. In your second week at work, you realize that many of the software licenses are about to expire or have already expired. As you know about the legal and ethical implications of unlicensed software, you have decided to set up a software asset management system that lets you keep track of the software licenses. You have already set up a database and stored some of the information, but you want to make the system more user friendly. Using the SWLicenses.mdb database, design a form to input the following information for new software products:

- Software title
- Installation location (office)
- License number
- Expiration date

Furthermore, design a report displaying all software licenses and expiration dates (sorted by expiration dates). (Hint: In Microsoft Access, use the form and report wizards to create the forms and reports; you will find the wizards under the "Create" tab.)

Team Work Exercise

Net Stats:
Top Cyberthreats

Robert Morris's worm, a bug that crashed a record 6,000 computers (a statistic compiled from an estimate that there were 60,000 computers connected to the Internet at the time and the worm affected 10 percent of them), now seems as antiquated as the 1911 Stutz Bearcat automobile. Morris was a student at Cornell University in 1988 when he devised a program that he later insisted was intended simply to gauge how many computers were connected to the Internet. Errors in Morris's program turned it into a self-replicating monster that overloaded computers and threatened frightened Internet users. Dubbed simply the Internet Worm, Morris's program was the precursor for today's multitude of malevolent codes.

According to Kaspersky Lab, a leading developer of content management security solutions, attackers are having to continuously change their methods in response to the growing competition among the IT security companies that investigate and protect against targeted attacks. Increased public attention to security lapses will also force the attackers to search for new instruments. For example, conventional methods of attacks involving e-mail attachments will gradually become less effective, while browser attacks will gain in popularity. For 2012 and beyond, they expected to see an increase in the following:

1. "Hacktivism" will continue to increase in frequency and destruction.

2. Cloud computing will create a security nightmare for many organizations.

3. Cyber-espionage by state actors will become a common practice.
4. Increased attacks on certificate authorities (CA), increasing the concerns with the security of electronic commerce.
5. Cyberwar will continue to mature, using targeted attacks like Stuxnet.
6. Online games sites like the Sony PlayStation Network will be attacked to gain access to player profiles and credit card information.
7. Law enforcement will continue to increase their capabilities to take down botnets and cyber criminals.
8. As Android devices gain popularity, so will the malware on those devices due to Android's freely available documentation about its platform and the weak screening of applications on Google Play.
9. More privacy concerns related to the tracking and logging of mobile devices.
10. Mac OS malware will be on the rise.

In addition to these various trends, an old favorite, the Windows operating system, will continue to be a popular target. Nevertheless, given some major security improvements within Windows 7 and Windows 8, many experts believe that this is driving criminals to other, easier targets.

Questions and Exercises

1. Search the Web for the most up-to-date statistics and events related to IS security.
2. As a team, interpret these numbers (or stories). What is striking/important about these findings?
3. As a team, discuss how these findings will look like in 5 years and 10 years. What will the changes mean for globalization? What issues/opportunities do you see arising?
4. Using your spreadsheet software of choice, create a graph/figure most effectively visualizing the findings you consider most important.

Based on:

Anonymous. (2012, January 9). Kaspersky Lab Cyberthreat 2012 forecast. Retrieved May 21, 2012, from http://www.kaspersky.com/images/Kaspersky%20 report-10-134377.pdf.

Markoff, J. (1990, May 5). Computer intruder is put on probation and fined $10,000. *The New York Times*. Retrieved May 21, 2012, from http://query.nytimes .com/gst/fullpage.html?res=9C0CE1D71038F936A35756C0A966958260.

Answers to the Self-Study Questions

1. C, p. 444	2. B, p. 424	3. D, p. 422	4. D, p. 426	5. C, p. 445
6. D, p. 447	7. B, p. 445	8. C, p. 440	9. B, p. 449	10. A, p. 450

CASE 1 Under Attack

By now you know the scam. You receive an e-mail from eBay, PayPal, or your bank or credit card company that says they are "updating" your account information. The e-mail letterhead looks legitimate, so you read on. If you will just use the Web site address provided, the e-mail promises, the problem can be remedied, and your account won't be canceled. If you visit the URL provided, the site looks legitimate—that is, it's been "spoofed" to fool you—but the scam artists have posted it to steal your account information. By now you probably also know better than to respond to such a request. The scam is called "phishing"—meaning to "fish" for user information—and it's akin to identity theft. If you are conned into revealing account numbers, the scam artists will use that information to steal from you.

Phony e-mail is just one version of the phishing scam. Others include the following:

- Phishing via instant message, whereby users are sent a link to click on. Similar to the e-mail phishing, the user is directed to a fraudulent Web site that asks for sensitive information.
- Phishing via malware. Malware (short for "malicious software") is a malicious program that is installed on an unsuspecting user's computer via a virus or Trojan horse. This malware then runs in the background waiting for the user to go to, for example, a financial site. As soon as the malware detects the user going to a prime site, a pop-up window appears asking for sensitive information. This pop-up cannot be blocked since it is generated from the infected PC, not the Web server.

Phishing con artists also like to take advantage of special times of the year, such as April 15, when tax returns are due. Taxpayers must now beware of bogus e-mails from the Internal Revenue Service that say something like this: "You are eligible to receive a tax refund of $285.67. To access the form for your tax refund, please click here." Clicking on the URL provided, of course, takes you to a counterfeit form, asking for personal information that the phishing thieves can use to steal from you. Fake IRS sites have also bilked taxpayers of personal information.

All types of phishing are a significant problem for Internet businesses and consumers. The Anti-Phishing Working Group estimated that over 115,000 e-mail phishing attacks were launched in 2010, down from over 180,000 separate attacks in 2009. These attacks target millions of consumers, often multiple times per day. While the overall trend is down for these massive attacks, the impacts are enormous. For instance, according to the security company Trusteer, while only a small number of online banking customers visit phishing sites each year (around 1 percent), nearly half of these victims divulge their login credentials to these fraudulent Web sites impersonating the bank. With millions of consumers attacked daily, losses cost consumers and banks millions of dollars a year. Although determining exact figures for how much financial damage is done due to phishing is difficult, the Gartner group reported that over 5 million people were affected by phishing scams in 2008 and lost an average of US$351. A report in 2011 found that cyber romance scams alone cost U.S. victims over US$50 million.

What is even more troublesome is the fact that in 2010, over 3,800 brands were hijacked or spoofed. As of February 2010, the top targets for phishing attacks were PayPal, eBay, and Facebook. As social media sites become more popular, so are they becoming hotbeds of phishing activity. In fact, a 2011 security report by Microsoft found that from the beginning of 2010 to the end of the year, phishing attacks based on social networks increased by 1200 percent. At the beginning of the year, those kinds of phishing attacks accounted for about 8.3 percent of phishing attempts and in December that number had jumped to 84.5 percent. Another trend is spear phishing, a personalized attack on a particular individual or group. While phishing messages usually appear to come from a large well-known company like eBay or PayPal, spear phishing messages often appear to come from an individual within the recipient's own company and generally someone in a position of authority. Such customized attacks have been found to be highly effective.

In an effort to defeat phishers, banks and other online entities are taking steps to protect their customers. PayPal, for instance, has stopped using e-mail to contact account holders. Instead, PayPal has its own proprietary messaging system that handles all transactions. If PayPal needs to contact you regarding your account, they will send a single e-mail message saying that there is a message waiting on the Web site messaging system. This procedure may further complicate access for an account holder, but it also adds a necessary layer of security.

Questions:

1. What types of companies are most susceptible to phishing attacks?
2. Assume you have replied to a phishing e-mail; research on the Web what steps you should follow to limit any possible consequences.
3. Research on the Web for the telltale signs of a phishing message.

Based on:

Anonymous. (2011, May 12). Microsoft releases security intelligence report: Cybercriminals increasingly targeting consumers. *Microsoft.* Retrieved May 21, 2012, from http://blogs.technet.com/b/microsoft_on_the_issues/archive/2011/05/12/microsoft-releases-security-intelligence-report-cybercriminals-increasingly-targeting-consumers.aspx.

Anonymous. (2012). 2011 Internet crime report. *Internet Crime Complaint Center.* Retrieved July 29, 2012, from http://www.ic3.gov/media/annualreport/2011_IC3Report.pdf.

Anonymous. (2007, December 17). Gartner survey shows phishing attacks escalated in 2007; more than $3 billion lost to these attacks. *Gartner.* Retrieved May 21, 2012, from http://www.gartner.com/it/page.jsp?id=565125.

Anonymous. (2009, December 2). Measuring the effectiveness of in-the-wild phishing attacks. *Trusteer.com.* Retrieved May 21, 2012, from http://www.trusteer.com/sites/default/files/Phishing-Statistics-Dec-2009-FIN.pdf.

Anonymous. (2010, March 24). Social network brands highly abused in phishing. *Spamfighter.com.* Retrieved May 21, 2012, from http://www.spamfighter.com/News-14084-Social-Network-Brands-Highly-Abused-in-Phishing.htm.

Anti-Phishing Working Group. (2011). Phishing activity trends report. www.antiphishing.org. Retrieved May 21, 2012, from http://www.antiphishing.org/reports/APWG_GlobalPhishingSurvey_2H2010.pdf.

Carr, D.F. (2012, March 26). Social phishing spikes as spam declines, IBM Finds. *InformationWeek.* Retrieved May 21, 2012, from http://www.informationweek.com/thebrainyard/news/social_networking_consumer/232700191.

Dignan, L. (2008, January 14). Phishing for your tax return. *ZDNet.* Retrieved May 21, 2012, from http://blogs.zdnet.com/security/?p=805.

Fraud Protection. (n.d.). Retrieved May 21, 2012, from http://www.americanexpress.com/gns/fraud_protection.html.

Tetzlaff, R. (2010, April 2). A history of phishing. *BrightHub.com.* Retrieved May 21, 2012, from http://www.brighthub.com/internet/security-privacy/articles/67965.aspx.

CASE 2   China's Great (Fire) Wall

Welcome to modern-day China, where the government blocks Web site access to the country's 513 million Internet users on such subjects as democracy, Tibet, Taiwan, health, education, news, entertainment, religion, and revolution. Chat rooms, blogs, photo and video sharing sites, gaming and podcasting sites, and bulletin boards are also forbidden stops on the Web, and don't even think about googling "Tiananmen Square massacre" or anything remotely considered pornographic.

Building censorship into China's Internet infrastructure is the first step for the country's government in controlling access to politically sensitive material. To accomplish this, the Chinese government prevents Internet service providers (ISPs)—many of them privately held businesses, some with foreign investments—from hosting any material the government calls politically objectionable by holding the ISPs liable for content and imposing severe penalties for violations, including imprisonment.

In addition, the Chinese government targets Internet content providers (ICPs—organizations and individuals who post Web sites, both nonprofit and for profit), who are required to register for and post a license to operate legally, and like ISPs are held liable for politically incorrect content. To keep a license, ICPs must police sites for objectionable content and must take down those sites that violate regulations governing content. Yahoo!, Microsoft's MSN, and Google all act as ICPs in China and have been criticized for complying with China's strict Internet censorship policy.

Managing ISPs and ICPs is not the only tool China has for controlling what content its citizens can access. Beginning operations in 2003, China instituted the Golden Shield Project. More popularly known as "The Great Firewall of China," the system can automatically filter and block content that the government deems inappropriate. Through IP tracking, blocking, DNS/URL filtering, and redirection, the Golden Shield not only blocks and filters content but acts as a surveillance system as well. However, the Great Firewall creates a sluggish and congested network infrastructure, although some believe this is intentional to discourage Internet use.

In 2012, a reported 2,600 popular Web sites were blocked in China, including Facebook, Twitter, IMDB, and YouTube.

Historically, many foreign ICPs have cooperated with the Chinese government by censoring information in order to operate in the country. Yahoo!, the only non-Chinese company providing e-mail service in China, has even turned over e-mail content to the authorities, resulting in the prosecution and conviction of at least four persons for criticizing the government. In 2010, however, Google took a different course with China.

In late 2009, Google was hit with a sophisticated attack on their Gmail servers and some of their other corporate networks. Google believed that the attack was an attempt to access the Gmail accounts of human rights activists. Up until then, Google had been censoring content like other ICPs, tailoring results to remove topics deemed subversive or pornographic. However, after the network attack, tensions began to rise between Google and China, as it was widely believed that the attacks came from the Chinese government or were at least sponsored by them in an effort to root out political dissidents. As a result, Google threatened to end its practice of censoring search results or even completely pull their business out of China.

Early in 2010, Google made the decision to redirect all its search traffic in China to servers in Hong Kong, where greater civil liberties remain, effectively ending its practice of censoring results and opening unrestricted searches to the Chinese public. Within days of the move, China began filtering and blocking searches directed to the Hong Kong servers using the Golden Shield system, and even pulled out of lucrative agreements to use Google's Android operating system on a number of mobile platforms. In March 2010, Google's annual license to be an ICP in China expired. In summer 2010, China renewed Google's license, but it remains to be seen how this standoff between the search giant and China will end. Today, Google is "back to normal," operating in China with government imposed limitations on its search results; several Google applications including Docs, Drive, and Picasa are also blocked.

As is true of most attempts to censor the Internet, tech-savvy users in China find ways to circumvent the government's firewall. Proxy servers have helped poke holes in the wall, and users with the right knowledge can configure browsers to access the Internet through proxy servers located in other countries, allowing them to visit "forbidden" Web sites. However, many Chinese Internet users have been unwilling or unable to use proxy servers. That has begun to change as sites like Facebook, Twitter, and YouTube were blocked after a Tibetan uprising in the summer of 2008. The loss of access to these popular sites has led to a greater number of Chinese Internet users finding ways to *fanqiang*, or "scale the wall." One Chinese Internet activist believes that the rise of social networking sites is causing the government censors to lose ground. He says that "China's censorship was built for Web 1.0, but everything now is Web 2.0."

Questions:

1. Should foreign companies provide their technologies to China, knowing that the technologies are used to limit the individual freedom of Chinese citizens? Why or why not?

2. Given that China has the largest number of Internet users, do you think they can ultimately succeed in controlling information? Why or why not?

3. Should the rest of the world care if China limits information access within China? Why or why not? Now that Google has moved against censorship, do you think other companies will follow suit? Why or why not?

Based on:

Anonymous. (2006, August). Race to the bottom: Corporate complicity in Chinese Internet censorship. *Human Rights Watch*. Retrieved May 21, 2012, from http://www.hrw.org/reports/2006/china0806.

August, O. (2007, October 23). The great firewall: China's misguided—and futile—attempt to control what happens online. *Wired*. Retrieved May 21, 2012, from http://www.wired.com/politics/security/magazine/15-11/ff_chinafirewall.

Fallows, J. (2008, March). The connection has been reset. *The Atlantic*. Retrieved May 21, 2012, from http://www.theatlantic.com/magazine/archive/2008/03/-ldquo-the-connection-has-been-reset-rdquo/6650.

Fang, Y. (2010, July 22). China confirms Google's operation license renewed. *Xinhua*. Retrieved May 21, 2012, from http://news.xinhuanet.com/english2010/china/2010-07/11/c_13394498.htm.

Helft, M., & Wines, M. (2010, March 23). Google faces fallout as China reacts to site shift. *The New York Times*. Retrieved May 21, 2012, from http://www.nytimes.com/2010/03/24/technology/24google.html.

List of websites blocked in the People's Republic of China. (2012, May 16). In *Wikipedia, The Free Encyclopedia*. Retrieved May 21, 2012, from http://en.wikipedia.org/w/index.php?title=List_of_websites_blocked_in_the_People%27s_Republic_of_China&oldid=492849752.

Pierson, D. (2010, January 16). Despite censorship, cracks widen in China's Great Firewall. *Los Angeles Times*. Retrieved May 21, 2012, from http://articles.latimes.com/2010/jan/16/business/la-fi-china-firewall16-2010jan16/3.

Technology Briefing

Foundations of Information Systems Infrastructure

After reading this briefing, you will be able to do the following:

1. Discuss foundational information systems (IS) hardware concepts.

2. Describe foundational topics related to system software as well as those of various types of programming languages and application development environments.

3. Describe foundational networking and Internet concepts.

4. Explain foundational database management concepts.

Preview

In Chapter 3, "Managing the Information Systems Infrastructure and Services," you learned about the key components of a comprehensive IS infrastructure and why its careful management is necessary. This Technology Briefing will expand that discussion, providing you with a deeper understanding of those topics. Each of the major sections within this briefing provides optional material that is stand-alone from the other sections as well as the entire book. Likewise, the end-of-chapter material is presented in separate sections to facilitate this independence.

FOUNDATIONAL TOPICS IN IS HARDWARE

IS hardware is an integral part of the IS infrastructure and is broadly classified into three types: input, processing, and output technologies. In this section, we examine foundational topics related to IS hardware.

http://goo.gl/2QjfK

Input Technologies

Input technologies are used to enter information into a computer, laptop, tablet, or smartphone (see Figure TB1). Well known input devices include various types of keyboards or pointing devices like track pads and mice. Other, more specialized, pointing devices include biometric fingerprint readers to authenticate people (for access control, such as for secure laboratories, or for border controls), RFID scanners to track valuable inventory in a warehouse (see Chapter 8, "Strengthening Business-to-Business Relationships Via Supply Chain and Customer Relationship Management"), and eye-tracking devices, an innovative pointing device developed primarily for the disabled for help with operating computers.

ENTERING BATCH DATA. Large amounts of routine data, referred to as **batch data**, are often entered into the computer using scanners that convert printed text and images into digital data. Scanners range from small handheld devices that look like a mouse to large desktop boxes that resemble personal photocopiers. Rather than duplicating the image on another piece of paper, the computer translates the image into digital data that can be stored or manipulated by the computer. Insurance companies, universities, and other organizations that routinely process a large number of forms and documents are typically using scanner technology to increase employee productivity; entering a large number of separate forms or documents into a computer system and manipulating these data at a single time is referred to as **batch processing**.

Once a document is converted into digital format, **text recognition software** uses **optical character recognition** to convert typed, printed, or handwritten text into the computer-based characters that form the original letters and words. Other special-purpose scanning technologies include **optical mark recognition** devices, **bar code readers**, and **magnetic ink character recognition**, as summarized in Table TB1.

Other Input Technologies Used in many European and Asian countries, as well as at many colleges and universities, **smart cards** are special credit card–sized cards containing a microprocessor chip, memory circuits, and often a magnetic stripe. Smart cards can be used for

(a)

(b)

(c)

FIGURE TB1

All computing devices utilize input technologies.

Sources: (a) Nikolai Sorokin/Fotolia; (b) Aaron Amat/Fotolia; (c) Jan Engel/Fotolia

TABLE TB1 Specialized Scanners for Inputting Information

Scanner	Description
Optical mark recognition	Used to scan questionnaires and test answer forms ("bubble sheets") where answer choices are marked by filling in circles using pencil or pen
Optical character recognition	Used to read and digitize typewritten, computer-printed, and even handwritten characters such as on sales tags on department store merchandise, patient information in hospitals, or the address information on a piece of postal mail
Bar code reader	Used mostly in grocery stores and other retail businesses to read bar code data at the checkout counter; also used by libraries, banks, hospitals, utility companies, and so on
Magnetic ink character recognition	Used by the banking industry to read data, account numbers, bank codes, and check numbers on preprinted checks
Biometric scanner	Used to scan human body characteristics of users to enable everything from access control to payment procurement

various applications, including identification, providing building access, or making payments (e.g., at vending machines or checkout counters). Some smart cards allow for contactless transmission of data using RFID technology (e.g., the Exxon Speedpass for purchasing gasoline). Biometric devices, discussed in more detail in Chapter 10, "Securing Information Systems," are being used primarily for identification and security purposes. These devices read certain body features, including iris, fingerprints, and hand or face geometry, and compare them with stored profiles. Biometric devices are now also being included in consumer products such as laptops or keyboards, allowing users to log on to the computer by scanning their fingerprint rather than typing their user name and password. Finally, most modern smartphones use various sensors to obtain data about the device's location (GPS sensor), orientation (compass and gyroscope), acceleration (accelerometer), altitude (barometer), proximity to the user's body, or ambient light.

ENTERING AUDIO AND VIDEO. When entering **audio** (i.e., sound) or **video** (i.e., still and moving images) data into a computer, the data have to be digitized before they can be manipulated, stored, and played or displayed. In addition to the manipulation of music, audio input is helpful for operating a computer when a user's hands need to be free to do other tasks. Video has become popular for assisting in security-related applications, such as room monitoring and employee verification. It has also gained popularity for videoconferencing and chatting on the Internet, using your PC and a webcam.

Voice Input With the increased interest in such applications as Internet-based telephone calls and videoconferencing, microphones have become an important component of computer systems. A process called **speech recognition** also makes it possible for your computer or smartphone to understand speech. **Voice-to-text software** is an application that uses a microphone to monitor a person's speech and then converts the speech into text. There are consumer versions of voice-to-text software that are relatively cheap, but the professional software used by the disabled can be very expensive. Speech recognition technology can also be especially helpful for physicians and other medical professionals, airplane cockpit personnel, factory workers whose hands get too dirty to use keyboards, mobile users who don't want to type while walking or driving, and computer users who cannot type and do not want to learn. Increasingly, **interactive voice response**, based on speech recognition technology, is used for telephone surveys or to guide you through the various menu options when calling a company's customer service line.

Other Forms of Audio Input In addition to using a microphone, users can enter audio using electronic keyboards, or they can transfer audio from another device (such as an audio recorder). The users can then analyze and manipulate the sounds via sound editing software for output to MP3 files, CDs, or other media.

Video Input A final way in which data can be entered into a computer is through video input. Digital cameras record still images or short video clips in digital form on small, removable memory cards rather than on film. File size is primarily influenced by the resolution and file format you select for pictures or the length of the recording for video. Digital camera technology has become so portable that it is used in a variety of products, including cell phones and laptops. As webcams have become very popular with people wanting to use the Internet for chatting with friends and family, using programs like Skype, Google Talk, Windows Live Messenger, or Yahoo! Messenger, protocols to transmit data in a continuous fashion are needed. In contrast to discrete files (such as audio or image files), which have to be completely downloaded before they can be opened, **streaming audio** and **streaming video** (together referred to as **streaming media**) are data streams transmitted using specific protocols that are available for immediate playback on the recipient's computer. Similarly, the video sharing site YouTube, online radio stations, or Netflix use specific protocols to stream media content.

Processing: Transforming Inputs into Outputs

In this section we provide a brief overview of computer processing. **Processing technologies**, contained inside any computing devices (including smartphones, tablets, or wireless routers), transform inputs into outputs.

HOW A COMPUTER WORKS. Inside any computing device, you will find the **motherboard**, a plastic or fiberglass circuit board that holds or connects to all of the computer's electronic components (see Figure TB2). The motherboard holds the **central processing unit (CPU)** or **microprocessor**, which is the main component of a computing device, and connects it to the power supply, primary and secondary storage, as well as to various peripherals (such as input and output devices, or expansion cards, such as dedicated sound or video cards). The CPU is often called the computer's brain, as it is responsible for performing all the operations of the computer (see Figure TB3). Its job includes loading the *operating system* (e.g., Windows 8, Mac OS X, or Ubuntu Linux) when the machine is first turned on and performing, coordinating, and managing all the calculations and instructions relayed to it while the computer is running. The CPU, a small device made of silicon, is composed of millions of tiny transistors arranged in complex patterns that allow it to interpret and manipulate data. In addition to the number of transistors on the CPU, three other factors greatly influence its speed—its system *clock speed* (the number of instructions a CPU can execute in a fixed amount of time), registers, and *cache memory* (described below). The CPU consists of two main sections: the **arithmetic logic unit**

FIGURE TB2

A computer's motherboard holds or connects to all of the computer's electronic components.

Source: Bretislav Horak/Shutterstock

FIGURE TB3

A CPU performs all operations of a computer.

Source: Tatiana Popova/Shutterstock

(ALU) and the **control unit**. The ALU performs calculations and logical operations, which involves comparing packets of data and then executing appropriate instructions. Combined in various ways, these functions allow the computer to perform complicated operations rapidly. The control unit works closely with the ALU, fetching and decoding instructions as well as retrieving and storing data.

Inside all computers, data are represented in the form of binary digits, or **bits** (i.e., the 0s and 1s a computer understands); a sequence of 8 bits is referred to as a **byte**. Different **binary codes** have been developed to represent characters or numbers as strings of bits. A widely used standard is the **American Standard Code for Information Interchange (ASCII)**, where, for example, the binary digits "01100001" represent the letter "a." Due to limitations in the number of characters that can be represented, as well as for specialized applications, various other codes have been developed. For example, **Unicode** has gained widespread acceptance, as it allows for representing characters and scripts beyond the Latin alphabet, including Chinese, Cyrillic, Hebrew, and Arabic. Any input your computer receives (say, a keystroke or mouse movement) is **digitized**, or translated into binary code, and then is processed by the CPU.

Within the computer, an electronic circuit generates pulses at a rapid rate, setting the pace for processing events to take place, rather like a metronome marks time for a musician. This circuit is called the **system clock**. A single pulse is a **clock tick**, and a fixed number of clock ticks is required to execute a single instruction. In microcomputers, the processor's **clock speed** is measured in hertz (Hz) or multiples thereof. One megahertz (MHz) is 1 million clock ticks, or instruction cycles, per second. Personal computer speeds are most often indicated in gigahertz (GHz, or 1 billion hertz). Microprocessor speeds improve so quickly that faster chips are on the market about every six months. Today, most new PCs operate at more than 3 GHz. To give you an idea of how things have changed, the original IBM PC had a clock speed of 4.77 MHz.

As its inner workings are very complex, for most of us it is easiest to think of a CPU as being a "black box" where all the processing occurs. The CPU uses registers and cache memory (both located inside the CPU) and RAM as *primary*, or temporary, storage space for data that are currently being processed. The CPU interacts with *secondary storage* (such as a *hard drive*, *optical disk*, or *flash drive*) for permanently storing data; as primary storage is considerably faster than secondary storage, the amount of primary storage greatly influences a computer's performance. The different types of storage are discussed next.

STORAGE. A computer has various different types of storage, each serving a specific purpose. The primary differences between different types of storage are capacity, volatility, and read/write speed (see Table TB2 for a comparison of different storage technologies).

Primary Storage Primary storage (such as **random-access memory [RAM]**), also called main memory, is located on the motherboard and is used to store the data and programs currently in use; primary storage uses memory chips (consisting of transistors and capacitors) to store data. Because instructions and work stored in RAM are lost when the power to the computer

TABLE TB2 Different Storage Technologies

Name	Volatility	Speed	Access	Capacity	Usage
Register	Volatile	Extremely fast	Random	Less than 200 bytes	Data directly used by CPU
Cache	Volatile	Extremely fast	Random	Typically up to 8 MB	Data and instructions used by CPU
RAM	Volatile	Very fast	Random	Depends on configuration; typically up to 32 GB	Programs and data currently used
ROM	Nonvolatile	Fast	Random	Very low	Instructions used before the operating system is loaded
Hard drive	Nonvolatile	Relatively slow	Random	High	Storage of programs and data
SSD	Nonvolatile	Fast	Random	High	Storage of programs and data
Optical disks	Nonvolatile	Slow	Random	Medium	Backup and long-term storage; software distribution; music and movies
Tape	Nonvolatile	Very slow	Sequential	Medium	Archiving of data

is turned off, it is referred to as **volatile memory**. Within the CPU itself, registers provide temporary storage locations where data must reside while being processed or manipulated. For example, if two numbers are to be added together, both must reside in registers, with the result placed in a register. Consequently, the number and size of the registers can also greatly influence the speed and power of a CPU.

A **cache** (pronounced "cash") is a small block of memory used by processors to store those instructions most recently or most often used. Just as you might keep file folders that you use most in a handy location on your desktop, cache memory is located within the CPU. Thanks to cache memory, before performing an operation, the processor does not have to go directly to main memory, which is slower, farther away from the microprocessor, and takes longer to reach. Instead, it can check first to see if needed data are contained in the cache. Cache memory is another way computer engineers have increased processing speed.

Modern CPUs have a hierarchy of cache memory (level 1, level 2, or even level 3); the lower levels of cache memory are faster but also smaller and more expensive. The more cache available to a CPU, the better the overall system performs because more data are readily available (although at a certain size, factors such as heat emission and power consumption become prohibitive to increasing the CPU cache).

Read-only memory (ROM) is used to store programs and instructions that are automatically loaded when the computer is turned on (before the operating system is loaded), such as the **basic input/output system (BIOS)**. In contrast to other forms of primary storage, ROM is **nonvolatile memory**, which means that it retains the data when the power to the computer is shut off.

Secondary Storage **Secondary storage** refers to methods for permanently storing data to a large-capacity, nonvolatile storage component, such as a **hard drive**. Most of the software run on a computer, including the operating system, is stored on the hard drive (or hard disk). Hard drives are usually installed internally but additional hard drives may be externally located and attached via cables to ports on the computer case.

The storage capacity of the hard drives for today's microcomputers is typically measured in gigabytes (GB, billions of bytes) or terabytes (TB, trillions of bytes). It is not unusual for PCs currently on the market to come equipped with hard drives with 500 GB to 1000 GB (i.e., 1 TB) storage capacities. Modern supercomputers can have millions of terabytes of storage. To make sure critical data are not lost, some computers employ **redundant array of independent disks (RAID)** technology to store redundant copies of data on two or more hard drives. RAID is not typically used on an individual's computer, but it is very common for Web servers and many business applications. RAID is sometimes called a "redundant array of *inexpensive*

FIGURE TB4

A hard drive consists of several disks that are stacked on top of one another and read/write heads to read and write data.

Source: Studio Foxy/Shutterstock

disks" because it is typically less expensive to have multiple redundant disks than fewer highly reliable and expensive ones.

Hard drives consist of several disks, or platters, stacked on top of one another so that they do not touch (see Figure TB4). Each disk within a disk pack has an access arm with two **read/write heads**—one positioned close to the top surface of the disk and another positioned close to the bottom surface of the disk—to inscribe or retrieve data. (Both surfaces of each disk are used for data storage.) When reading from or writing to the disks, the read/write heads are constantly repositioned to the desired storage location for the data while the disks are spinning at speeds of 5,400 to 15,000 revolutions per minute. The read/write heads do not actually touch either surface of the disks. In fact, a **head crash** occurs if the read/write head for some reason touches the disk, leading to a loss of data. Because of the mechanical action needed to position the read/write heads, hard drives are comparably slow; it takes a permanent storage device such as a hard disk about 3–10 milliseconds to access data. Within a CPU, however, a single transistor can be changed from a 0 to a 1 in about 10 picoseconds (10-trillionths of a second). Changes inside the CPU occur about 1 billion times faster than they do in a fixed disk because the CPU operates only on electronic impulses, whereas the fixed disks perform both electronic and mechanical activities, such as spinning the disk and moving the read/write head. Mechanical activities are extremely slow relative to electronic activities; however, modern hard drives use cache memory to decrease the time needed to access frequently used data. A new secondary storage technology called **solid-state drive (SSD)** uses nonvolatile memory chips (i.e., *flash memory*) to store data; as SSDs have no moving parts, they are typically faster (with access times of 0.1–0.5 milliseconds), quieter, and more reliable, but also more expensive than traditional hard disk-based drives. Solid-state drives have become increasingly popular due to the rise of smartphones and tablets. Given their performance, weight, and reliability, they are also increasingly used for laptops and even high performance servers and supercomputers.

Removable Storage Media Today, there are different types of removable storage: flash memory, optical disks, and tapes. **Flash memory** is a memory-chip-based nonvolatile computer storage method that is used in USB flash drives, solid-state hard drives, and memory cards (such as SD cards) for storing music and pictures in digital cameras and music players. A **flash drive** is a data storage device that includes flash memory with an integrated USB interface. Flash drives are a relatively inexpensive storage device typically having capacities of 16 to 128 GB; as of 2012, the highest-capacity flash drive could store 256 GB of data.

Optical disks (i.e., disks that are written/read using laser beam technology) are very inexpensive removable nonvolatile storage media used to store data (e.g., photos and videos) and distribute software, video games, and movies. Optical disks store binary data in the form of pits and flat areas on the disk's surface (where the pits and flats represent the 0s and 1s, respectively); an optical disk drive's laser beam can then read the data based on the reflection of the disk's surface. For many years, CD-ROMs (compact disc—read-only memory) were the standard for distributing data and software because of their low cost and their storage capacity of 700 MB. As CD-ROMs cannot be written to, most computers support another type of optical disk that data can be written to, the **CD-R (compact disc–recordable)**. Whereas a CD-R can be written onto only once, a **CD-RW (compact disc–rewritable)** can be written onto multiple times. The **DVD-ROM (digital versatile disc–read-only memory)** has more storage space than a CD-ROM, because DVD-ROM (or typically referred to as simply DVD) drives use a shorter-wavelength laser beam that allows more optical pits to be deposited on the disk. Like compact discs, there are recordable (DVD-R) and rewritable (DVD-RW) versions of this storage technology. DVDs used for the distribution of movies are also called **digital video disks**. The increasing demand for high-definition video content led to the creation of Blu-ray, a DVD format that provides up to 50 GB of storage.

Tapes are removable, high capacity, secondary storage media; allowing only for sequential access, tapes are typically only used for archiving data and long-term storage. Magnetic tapes used for data storage consist of narrow plastic tape coated with a magnetic substance. Storage tapes are typically enclosed in a cartridge, similar to a music cassette, and must be inserted into a tape reader. As with other forms of magnetic storage, data are stored in tiny magnetic spots. The storage capacity of tapes is expressed as **density**, which equals the number of **characters per inch** or **bytes per inch** that can be stored on the tape.

Having a life span of several decades, magnetic tape is still used for backing up or archiving large amounts of computer data, but it is gradually being replaced by high-capacity disk storage, since disk storage is equally reliable. In fact, data stored on disks are easier and faster to locate, because computers do not have to scan an entire tape to find a specific data file when using disks.

PORTS AND POWER SUPPLY. To use the full functionality of a computer, you need to be able to connect various types of peripheral devices, such as mice, printers, and cameras, to the system unit. A **port** provides a hardware interface—plugs and sockets—for connecting devices to computers. The characteristics of various types of ports are summarized in Table TB3. A final key component of any computing device is the **power supply**, which converts electricity from

TABLE TB3 Common Computer Ports, Their Applications, and Description

Port Name	Used to Connect	Description
Serial	Modem, mouse, keyboard, terminal display, MIDI	• Used to transfer one bit at a time • Slowest data transfer rates
Parallel	Printer	• Used to transfer several bits concurrently • Many times faster than serial
USB	Printer, scanner, mouse, keyboard, digital camera and camcorders, external disk drives	• A very high-speed data transfer method • Up to 4.8 billion bits per second using USB3.0 • Up to 127 devices simultaneously connected
IEEE 1394 ("Fire Wire")	Digital cameras and camcorders, external disk drives	• Extremely high-speed data transfer method • Up to 800 million bits per second • Up to 63 devices simultaneously connected
Thunderbolt	Up to six peripheral devices to a single port	• Allows for simultaneous transmission of Display Port (video and audio), PCI Express (data), and power • Up to 10 billion bits per second
Ethernet	Network	• Most common standard for local area networks
VGA (Video Graphics Array), DVI (Digital Visual Interface)	Monitors	• VGA is designed for transmission of analog video signals • DVI allows for digital transmission of video signals
HDMI (High Definition Multimedia Interface)	Monitors, home theater	• HDMI allows for simultaneous transmission of digital audio and video signals

the wall socket to a lower voltage. Whereas typically power supplied by the utility companies can vary from 100 to 240 volts AC, depending on where you are in the world, a PC's components use lower voltages—3.3 to 12 volts DC. The power supply converts the power accordingly and also regulates the voltage to eliminate spikes and surges common in most electrical systems. For added protection against external power surges, many PC owners opt to connect their systems to a separately purchased voltage surge suppressor. The power supply includes one or several fans for air cooling the electronic components inside the system unit—that low humming noise you hear while the computer is running is the fan.

Now that you understand how data are input into a computer and how data can be processed and stored, we can turn our attention to the third category of hardware—output technologies.

Output Technologies

Output technologies, such as a computer monitor or printer, deliver information to you in a usable format. A **printer** is an output device that produces a paper copy of alphanumeric or graphic data from a computer. Printers vary in price, performance and capabilites (e.g., document size, color or black and white, technology, speed, resolution quality). Ink-jet, LED, or laser technology are used in most personal printers.

Monitors are used to display information from a computer and, like printers, can vary in price, performance, and capabilities (e.g., screen size, color, technology, resolution, and so on). Monitors can be color, black and white, or monochrome (meaning all one color, usually green or amber). Today, monochrome monitors are used primarily in cash registers and other point-of-sale applications. Most monitors use **liquid crystal display (LCD)** technology, because they are lighter and thinner than the bulky **cathode ray tubes** used in old computer displays and televisions. Because display monitors are embedded into a broad range of products and devices, such as cell phones, digital cameras, and automobiles (e.g., to display route maps and other relevant information), they must be sturdy, reliable, lightweight, energy efficient, and low in cost. Recent developments in monitor technologies have thus focused on other display technologies, such as **organic light-emitting diodes**, which require far less power and are much thinner than traditional LCD panels. Finally, projectors are often used for presentation to an audience (and by many as a way to project a large video image in a home theater). Projectors have gone from large, very expensive equipment (US$5,000 or more) to very small, relatively inexpensive equipment (US$200). This is due primarily to the development of LCD technology, as previously discussed.

In addition to traditional monitors, touch screen displays have become extremely popular with the development of high resolution smartphones, tablet computers like the iPad, and a variety of technology gadgets. A **touch screen** is a display screen that is also an input device; a user interacts with the device by touching pictures or words on the screen with a finger or a stylus. In addition to your smartphone or tablet PC, touch screens are used in ATM machines, retail point-of-sale terminals, car navigation, and industrial control computers. Touch screens provide great flexibily in how an input device can look and operate.

Especially for mobile computing, monitor technology is still a challenge. In addition to screen size and power requirements of commonly used display technologies, glare is often an issue, and many laptop screens are hard to read in bright sunlight. For years, many futurists have envisioned a day when computer displays would be lightweight, thin, and flexible like paper, as well as be inexpensive and not require external power to retain an image. Recently, devices using **electronic paper** (or **e-paper**) have been introduced into the market. E-paper uses microscopic beads that change color (and retain this image indefinitely) in response to small electrical charges. These beads are encased between very thin sheets of flexible material. The primary benefits of e-paper are that it needs no backlight (as LCD displays do) and reflects like ordinary paper. Current applications of e-paper include electronic signs (that can be automatically updated by a wireless network), infinitely reusable newspapers and magazines, improved displays for mobile phones, and e-book readers such as the Amazon Kindle. Recently, manufacturers have introduced flexible glass for touchscreens, which allows for new form factors of mobile devices.

Now that you have learned more about IS hardware, we will focus on software, another key component of the IS infrastructure.

FOUNDATIONAL TOPICS IN IS SOFTWARE

http://goo.gl/Dchgx

Software refers to programs, or sets of instructions, that allow all the hardware components in your computer system to speak to each other and to perform the desired tasks. Throughout the book, we have discussed a variety of application software, from large business systems (e.g., an enterprise resource planning system) to office automation and personal productivity tools. Without software, the biggest, fastest, most powerful computer in the world is nothing more than a fancy paperweight. Software is intertwined with all types of products and services—toys, music, appliances, health care, and countless other products. Here, we provide some background on this critical component to all computer-based products.

System Software

In Chapter 3, you learned about one type of system software, the operating system, and its many different tasks. More specifically, common tasks of an operating system include the following:

- Booting (or starting) your computer
- Reading programs into memory and managing memory allocation
- Managing where programs and files are located in secondary storage
- Maintaining the structure of directories and subdirectories
- Formatting disks
- Controlling the computer monitor
- Sending documents to the printer

Just as there are many kinds of computers, there are many different kinds of operating systems (see Table TB4). In general, operating systems—whether for large mainframe computers or for small notebook computers—perform similar operations. Obviously, large multiuser supercomputers are more complex than small desktop systems; therefore, the operating system must account for and manage that complexity. However, the basic purpose of all operating systems is the same.

A second type of system software, **utilities** (or **utility programs**), are designed to manage computer resources and files. Some utilities are included in operating systems, while others must be purchased separately and installed on your computer. Table TB5 provides a sample of a few utility programs that are considered essential.

TABLE TB4 Common Operating Systems

Operating System	Description
z/OS	A proprietary operating system developed specifically for large IBM mainframe systems.
Unix	A multiuser, multitasking operating system that is available for a wide variety of computer platforms. Commonly used because of its superior security.
Windows	Currently, the Windows desktop operating system is by far the most popular in the world. Variations are also used to operate large servers, small handhelds, and cell phones.
Mac OS	The first commercial graphical-based operating system, making its debut in 1984. The operating system of Apple computers.
Linux	An open source operating system designed in 1991 by a Finnish student. Known as a secure, low-cost, multiplatform operating system. Linux powers about one-third of all Web servers. Linux users can choose between different "flavors" (or distributions) depending on their needs (such as the novice-friendly Ubuntu).
Android	Google's Linux-based operating system for mobile devices.
iOS	Apple's mobile operating system, previously named iPhone OS; also used on the iPod Touch and iPad.

TABLE TB5 Common Types of Computer Software Utilities

Utility	Description
Backup	Archives files from the hard disk to tapes, flash drives, or other storage devices
File defragmentation	Converts fragmented files (i.e., files not stored contiguously) on your hard disk into contiguous files that will load and be manipulated more rapidly
Disk and data recovery	Allows the recovery of damaged or erased data from hard disks and flash drives
Data compression	Compresses data by substituting a short code for frequently repeated patterns of data, much like the machine shorthand used by court reporters, allowing more data to be stored on a storage medium
File conversion	Translates a file from one format to another so that it can be used by an application other than the one used to create it
Antivirus	Scans files for viruses and removes or quarantines any virus found
Device driver	Allows adding new hardware to your computer system, such as a game controller, printer, scanner, and so on, to function with your operating system
Spam blocker	Monitors incoming e-mail messages and filters or blocks unwanted messages from arriving
Spyware detection and removal	Scans a computer for spyware and disables or removes any spyware found
Media player	Allows listening to music or watching video on a computer

Programming Languages and Development Environments

Each piece of software is developed using some programming language. A programming language is the computer language the software vendor uses to write programs. For application software, such as spreadsheets or database management systems (DBMSs), the underlying programming language is invisible to the user. However, programmers in an organization's IS group, and in some instances end users, can use programming languages to develop their own specialized applications. The **source code** (i.e., the program written in a programming language) must be translated into object code—called assembly or machine language—that the hardware can understand. Normally, the source code is translated into machine language using programs called *compilers* and *interpreters*.

COMPILERS AND INTERPRETERS. A **compiler** takes an entire program's source code written in a programming language and converts it into an **executable**, that is, a program in machine language that can be read and executed directly by the computer (see Figure TB5). Although the compilation process can take quite some time (especially for large programs), the resulting executables run very fast; thus, programs are usually compiled before they are sold as executables to the customers. As in such cases, the customers purchase only the executable and do not have access to the program's source code; they can run the program but not make any modifications to it.

Some programming environments do not compile the entire program into machine language. Instead, each statement of the program is converted into machine language and executed "on the fly" (i.e., one statement at a time), as depicted in Figure TB6. The type of program that does the conversion and execution is called an **interpreter**. As the source code is translated each

FIGURE TB5

A compiler translates the entire computer program into machine language, then the CPU executes the machine language program.

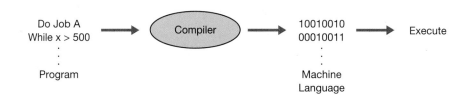

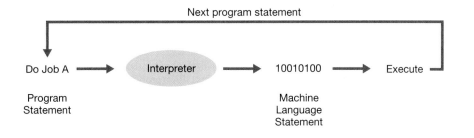

FIGURE TB6

Interpreters read, translate, and execute one line of source code at a time.

time the program is run, it is easy to quickly evaluate the effects of any changes made to the program's source code. However, this also causes interpreted programs to run much slower than compiled executables. Programming languages can be either compiled or interpreted.

PROGRAMMING LANGUAGES. Over the past few decades, software has evolved. As software has evolved, so have the programming languages. Each programming language has been designed at a particular time, for a particular use, and the first generations of programming languages were quite crude by today's standards. Some popular programming languages are listed in Table TB6.

Of course, programming languages continue to evolve, with object-oriented languages, visual programming languages, and Web development languages rapidly gaining popularity. We discuss these next.

Object-Oriented Languages **Object-oriented languages** are the most recent in the progression of high-level programming languages and are extremely popular with application developers. Object-oriented languages use common modules (called objects), which combine properties and behaviors to define the relevant system components. An example of an object would be a specific student who has a name, an address, and a date of birth (i.e., the properties), but can also perform certain operations, such as register for a course (the behaviors). If an object-oriented programming language is being used, it enables the design and implementation of the objects to happen quickly and simultaneously, as oftentimes preexisting objects can be reused or adapted. For important concepts related to object-oriented languages, see Table TB7.

TABLE TB6 Examples of Popular Programming Languages

Language	Application	Description
BASIC	General purpose	Beginner's All-Purpose Symbolic Interaction Code. An easy-to-learn language, BASIC works on almost all PCs.
C/C++	General purpose	C++ is a newer version of C. Developed at AT&T Bell Labs. Complex languages used for a wide range of applications.
COBOL	Business	COmmon Business-Oriented Language. Developed in the 1960s, it was the first language for developing business software. COBOL is still frequently used for many business transaction processing applications on mainframes.
FORTRAN	Scientific	FORmula TRANslator. The first commercial high-level language developed by IBM in the 1950s. Designed for scientific, mathematical, and engineering applications.
Java	World Wide Web	An object-oriented programming language developed by Sun Microsystems in the early 1990s. It is a popular programming language for the Internet because it is highly transportable from one computer to another.
.NET Framework	World Wide Web	A variety of programming languages (e.g., ASP.NET and C#) offered by Microsoft that can easily be integrated into Web applications.
LISP	Artificial Intelligence	LISt Processor. Dates from the late 1950s. One of the main languages used to develop applications in artificial intelligence and high-speed arcade graphics.
PERL	World Wide Web	A dynamic programming language commonly used for writing scripts for Web sites, as well as for batch processing of large amounts of data.
Objective-C	App development	Evolved from C, Objective-C is used for developing Apps for iPhones, iPads, and Apple computers.

TABLE TB7 Concepts Related to Object-Oriented Languages

Concept	Description	Examples
Class	A set of objects having the same properties and behaviors (but the values of the properties can differ for each individual object). Classes can be reused for different programs.	A "student" has an address and a grade-point average (GPA) (properties) and can enroll in courses (behavior).
Object	Instantiation of a class.	Student Jeff Smith has a GPA of 3.94, and enrolls in MIS250.
Encapsulation	Data and behavior of a class are hidden from other classes and are thus protected from unexpected changes.	The registrar doesn't need to know how the GPA is calculated within the "student" class; the registrar cares only that it is updated.
Inheritance	More specific classes include the properties and behaviors of the more general class.	Both "distance degree student" and "on-campus student" inherit properties (such as address and GPA) and behaviors (such as enroll in a course) from the general class "student."
Event-driven program execution	The programmer does not determine the sequence of execution for the program; the flow is determined by user input (e.g., mouse clicks) or messages from other applications.	A word processor reacts to your typing and clicking.

Visual Programming Languages Just as you may have found it easier to use a computer operating system with a **graphical user interface (GUI)**, such as Windows 8 or Mac OS X, programmers using **visual programming languages** may also take advantage of the GUI. For instance, programmers can easily add a command button to a screen with a few clicks of a mouse (see Figure TB7) instead of programming the button pixel by pixel and using many lines of code. Visual Basic.NET and Visual C# (pronounced as "C-sharp") are two popular examples of visual programming languages.

Web Development Languages If you have been surfing the Web for a while, you may have thought of creating a personal Web page or already have one. In that event, you have some experience with using a markup language. The markup language you used to create your Web page is called Hypertext Markup Language (HTML). HTML is a text-based file format

FIGURE TB7

Visual Basic.Net, a visual programming language, is used to create standard business forms.

TABLE TB8 Common HTML Tags

Tag	Description
\<html\>…\</html\>	Delineates an HTML document
\<head\>…\</head\>	Sets off the title and other information that is not displayed on the Web page itself
\<body\>…\</body\>	Sets off the visible portion of the document
\<b\>…\</b\>	Creates bold text
\<a href="URL"\>…\</a\>	Creates a hyperlink
\<a href=mailto:EMAIL\>…\</a\>	Creates a link creating a new e-mail message
\<p\>…\</p\>	Creates a new paragraph
\<table\>…\</table\>	Creates a table

that uses a series of codes (i.e., tags) to set up a document; **HTML tags** are used to instruct the Web browser on how a document should be formatted and presented to the user. Because HTML editing programs are visually oriented and easy to use, you do not need to memorize the language to set up a Web page. Programs for creating Web pages (such as Microsoft Expression Web and Adobe Dreamweaver) are called **Web page builders** or **HTML editors**.

In HTML, the tags used to identify different elements on a page and to format the page are set apart from the text with angle brackets (\<\>). Specific tags are used to mark the beginning and the ending of an element or a formatting command. For example, if you want text to appear in bold type, the HTML tag to begin bolding is \<b\>. The tag to turn off bolding, at the end of the selected text, is \</b\>. The "a href" command sets up a hyperlink from a word or image on the page to another HTML document. Tags also denote document formatting commands, such as text to be used as a title, sizes of text in headings, the ends of paragraphs, underlining, italics, bolding, and places to insert pictures and sound (see Table TB8).

A good way to understand how HTML works is to find a Web page you like, then use the "View Source" command on your browser to see the hypertext that created the page (see Figure TB8). Once you have created your own Web page and saved it to a disk, you can upload it to an account you have created through your Web site's host.

FIGURE TB8

A Web page and the html source code used to create it.

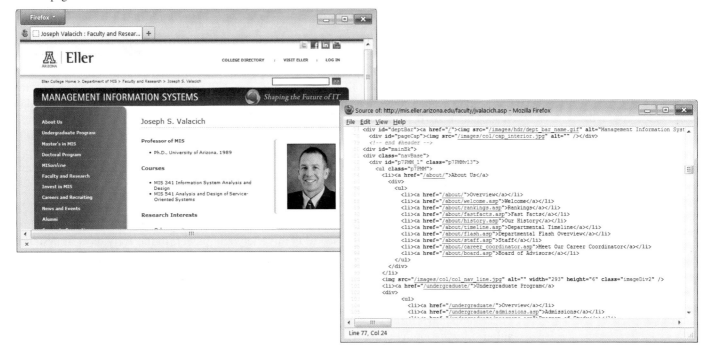

Markup languages such as HTML are for laying out or formatting Web pages. If you want to add dynamic content or have users interact with your Web page other than by clicking on hypertext links, then you will need to use special purpose programming languages such as Java or use Web services, a scripting language, and so on.

Java is a programming language that was developed by Sun Microsystems in the early 1990s to allow adding dynamic, interactive content to Web pages. For example, the chat feature in the Blackboard learning environment uses Java. You can add Java applications to a Web page in one of two ways: by learning Java or a similar language and programming the content you want, or by downloading free general purpose **applets** from the Web to provide the content you want on your Web page. Applets are small programs that are executed within another application, such as a Web page. When a user accesses your Web page, the applets you inserted are downloaded from the server along with your Web page to the user's browser, where they perform the desired action. Later, when the user leaves your Web page, the Web page and the applets disappear from his or her computer.

Microsoft .NET is a programming platform that is used to develop applications that are highly interoperable across a variety of platforms and devices. For example, using the .NET framework, developers can create an application that runs on desktop computers, mobile computers, or smartphones. A suite of visual programming languages including Visual C#, ASP .NET, and Visual Basic.NET can be used to construct .NET applications. To gain its interoperability, the .NET framework utilizes Web APIs (see also Chapter 5, "Enhancing Organizational Communication and Collaboration Using Social Media").

Scripting languages can also be used to supply interactive components and dynamic content to a Web page. These languages let you build programs or scripts directly into HTML page code. Web page designers frequently use them to check the accuracy of user-entered information, such as names, addresses, and credit card numbers. Two common scripting languages are Microsoft's VBScript and JavaScript.

JavaScript bears little resemblance to Java. The two are similar, however, in that both Java and JavaScript are useful component software tools for creating dynamic, interactive Web pages. That is, both allow users to add or create applets that lend dynamic content to Web pages. Both are also cross-platform programs, meaning that they can typically be executed by computers running Windows, Linux, Mac OS, and other operating systems.

The development of programming languages is an ongoing process of change and innovation, and these changes often result in more capable and complex systems for the user. The popularity of the Internet has further spurred the creation of innovative and evolving software. From the pace of change that is occurring, it is clear that many more innovations are on the horizon.

Another common way to add dynamic content to Web sites is Flash. Using the application development suite Adobe Flash, developers can create animation and video that can be compressed small enough for fast download speeds. When you browse the Web and see animation or complex data streams, this is often done in Flash. Flash animation is displayed on your screen using the Adobe Flash player. Flash can also include Web services to allow data-driven animation. Some examples of data-driven flash animation on Web sites are the bag builder at Timbuk2 (www.timbuk2.com) and the live Major League Baseball game update at Yahoo!'s sports site (http://sports.yahoo.com/mlb/gamechannel). Yet, Flash content is not well suited for mobile devices, and in 2010, Apple announced that it would not support Flash on its iPhones and iPads, rather advocating the use of HTML5 (the newest standard of the HTML markup language), which allows for rich, interactive Web applications.

Along with commercial products, there are several open source tools in wide use today. The most common is PHP, originally designed as a high-level tool for producing dynamic Web content.

AUTOMATED DEVELOPMENT ENVIRONMENTS. Over the years, the tools for developing information systems have increased in both variety and power. In the early days of systems development, a developer was left to use a pencil and paper to sketch out design ideas and program code. Computers were cumbersome to use and slow to program, and most designers worked out on paper as much of the system design as they could before moving to the computer. Today, system developers have a vast array of powerful computer-based tools at their disposal. These tools have forever changed the ways in which systems are developed. **Computer-aided software engineering (CASE)** refers to the use of automated software tools by systems developers to design and implement information systems. Developers can use CASE tools to automate or support activities throughout the systems development process with the objective of increasing productivity and improving the overall quality of systems. The capabilities of CASE tools are continually evolving and being integrated into a variety of development environments. Next we briefly review some of the interesting characteristics of CASE.

Types of CASE Tools Two of the primary activities in the development of large-scale information systems are the creation of design documents and the management of information. Over the life of a project, thousands of documents need to be created—from screen prototypes to database content and structure to layouts of sample forms and reports. At the heart of all CASE environments is a repository for managing information.

CASE also helps developers represent business processes and information flows by using graphical diagramming tools. By providing standard symbols to represent business processes, information flows between processes, data storage, and the organizational entities that interact with the business processes, CASE eases a very tedious and error-prone activity (see Figure TB9). The tools not only ease the drawing process, but also ensure that the drawing conforms to development standards and is consistent with other design documents created by other developers.

Another powerful capability of CASE is its ability to generate program source code automatically. CASE tools keep pace with contemporary programming languages and can automatically produce programming code directly from high-level designs in languages such as Java, Visual Basic.NET, and C#. In addition to diagramming tools and code generators, a broad range of other tools assists in the systems development process. The general types of CASE tools used throughout the development process are summarized in Table TB9.

Open Source Software

Open source software refers to systems software, applications, and programming languages in which the source code (i.e., the program code written in a programming language) is freely available to the general public for use and/or modification. Many large mainstream software companies are actively involved in the open source community. For example, IBM is playing a leading role in evolving the Linux operating system. Likewise, Oracle was active in developing and extending the OpenOffice Productivity Suite before donating it to the Apache Foundation.

Open source is a philosophy that promotes developers' and users' access to the source of a product or idea. Particularly in the area of software development, the open source movement has taken off with the advent of the Internet; people around the world are contributing their time and expertise to develop or improve software, ranging from operating systems to applications software. Open source software owes its success to the inputs from a large user base, helping to

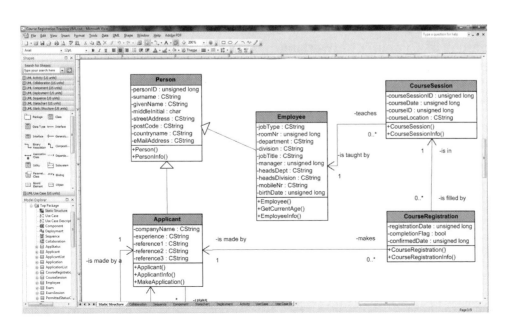

FIGURE TB9

System design diagram from Microsoft Visio.

Source: Courtesy of Microsoft, Inc.

TABLE TB9 General Types of CASE Tools

CASE Tool	Description
Diagramming tools	Tools that enable a system's process, data, and control structures to be represented graphically.
Screen and report generators	Tools that help model how systems look and feel to users. Screen and report generators also make it easier for the systems analyst to identify data requirements and relationships.
Analysis tools	Tools that automatically check for incomplete, inconsistent, or incorrect specifications in diagrams, screens, and reports.
Repositories	Tools that enable the integrated storage of specifications, diagrams, reports, and project management information.
Documentation generators	Tools that help produce both technical and user documentation in standard formats.
Code generators	Tools that enable the automatic generation of program and database definition code directly from the design documents, diagrams, screens, and reports.

Source: Hoffer, George, & Valacich (2014).

fix problems or improve the software; however, with large open source projects, such as different variants of the operating system Linux, only a small group of contributors is ultimately responsible for ensuring the quality and stability of the software. Linux, one of the most prevalent examples of open source software, was developed as a hobby by the Finnish university student Linus Torvalds in 1991. Having developed the first version himself, he made the source code of his operating system available to everyone who wanted to use it and improve on it. Since then, various Linux distributions (such as Ubuntu, Red Hat, and Debian) have been released; each distribution integrates the core part of the Linux operating system with different utilities and software applications, depending on the intended use (e.g., desktop computer, netbook, Web server, embedded system, and so on). With most distributions, users can only *suggest* modifications for official releases; for example, users can contribute to program code or provide new designs for the system's user interface, but only a small group of carefully selected "committers" can implement these modifications into the official releases of the software.

http://goo.gl/xbEZS

FOUNDATIONAL TOPICS IN NETWORKING

Telecommunications and networking technologies have become very important as almost all organizations rely on computer-based information systems to support various business processes. Understanding how the underlying networking technologies work and where these technologies are heading will help you better understand the potential of information systems. The discussion begins with a description of the evolution of computer networking.

Evolution of Computer Networking

Over the past decades, computer networking underwent an evolution from centralized computing to distributed computing to collaborative computing. These eras of computer networking are discussed next.

CENTRALIZED COMPUTING. **Centralized computing**, depicted in Figure TB10, remained largely unchanged through the 1970s. In this model, large centralized computers, called mainframes, were used to process and store data. During the mainframe era (beginning in the 1940s), people entered data on mainframes through the use of local input devices called **terminals**. These devices were called "dumb" terminals because they did not conduct any processing, or "smart," activities. The centralized computing model is not a true network because there is no sharing of data and capabilities. The mainframe provides all the capabilities, and the terminals are only input/output devices. Computer networks evolved in the 1980s when organizations needed separate, independent computers to communicate with each other.

DISTRIBUTED COMPUTING. The introduction of personal computers in the late 1970s and early 1980s gave individuals control over their own computing. Organizations also realized that they could use multiple small computers to achieve many of the same processing goals of a single

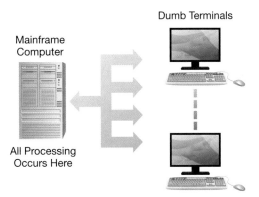

FIGURE TB10

In the centralized computing model, all processing occurs in one central mainframe.

large computer. People could work on subsets of tasks on separate computers rather than using one mainframe to perform all the processing. To achieve this goal, computer networks were needed so that data and services could be easily shared between these distributed computers. The 1980s were characterized by an evolution to a computing model called **distributed computing**, shown in Figure TB11, in which multiple types of computers are networked together to share data and services.

COLLABORATIVE COMPUTING. In the 1990s, a new computing model, called **collaborative computing**, emerged. Collaborative computing is a synergistic form of distributed computing in which two or more networked computers are used to accomplish a common processing task. That is, in this model of computing, computers are not simply communicating data but are also sharing processing capabilities. For example, one computer may be used to store a large employee database. A second computer may be used to process and update individual employee

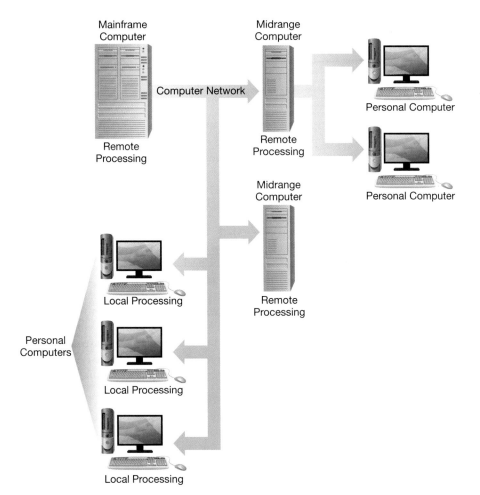

FIGURE TB11

In the distributed computing model, separate computers work on subsets of tasks and then pool their results by communicating over a network.

FIGURE TB12

In the collaborative computing model, two or more networked computers are used to accomplish a common processing task.

records selected from this database. The two computers collaborate to keep the company's employee records current, as depicted in Figure TB12. Many organizations' information systems encompass a large number of different servers, connected via high-speed networks.

NETWORK SERVICES. Computer networks allow for sharing various capabilities between devices. For example, computer networks allow for efficiently storing, retrieving, and moving data between computers, or allow for accessing network printers and fax equipment; similarly, e-mail, instant messaging, and the sending and receiving of pictures or video and audio data require the sender and recipient to be connected to a network. Finally, networks enable computers to share processing power, in that processing can be distributed between the client and server. Clients request data or services from the servers. The servers store data and application programs. For example, the physical search of database records may take place on the server, while the user interacts with a much smaller database application that runs on the client.

When an organization decides to network its computers and devices, it must decide what services will be provided; typically, different services on the network are offered by different servers, such as print servers, e-mail servers, and so on. In addition to those servers, networks typically have specialized systems for managing the network, its users, and its resources. These include computers providing **authentication services** for granting users and devices access rights to resources on a network, or **directory services**, which are repositories (or "address books") containing information about users, user groups, resources on a network, access rights, and so on.

Types of Networks

Computing networks today include all three computing models: centralized, distributed, and collaborative. The emergence of new computing models did not mean that organizations completely discarded older technologies. Rather, a typical organizational computer network includes mainframes, servers, personal computers, and a variety of other devices. Computer networks are commonly classified by size, distance covered, and structure. The most common are described next.

PRIVATE BRANCH EXCHANGE. A private branch exchange (PBX) is a telephone system that serves a particular location, such as a business (see Figure TB13). It connects telephone extensions within the system and connects internal extensions to the outside telephone network. It can also connect computers within the system to other PBX systems, to an outside network, or to various office devices, such as fax machines or photocopiers. Since they use ordinary telephone lines, PBX systems have limited bandwidth, preventing them from transmitting such forms of data as interactive video, digital music, or high-resolution photos. Using PBX technology, a business requires few outside phone lines, but has to purchase or lease the PBX equipment. Many organizations now use *Internet protocol*–based PBX systems, which make use of the organizations' data networks and allow for low cost voice over IP calling.

LOCAL AREA NETWORK. A local area network (LAN), shown in Figure TB14, is a computer network that spans a relatively small area, allowing all computer users to connect with each other to share data and peripheral devices, such as printers. LAN-based communications may involve the sharing of data, software applications, or other resources between several users. LANs typically do not exceed tens of kilometers in size and are typically contained within a single building or a limited geographical area.

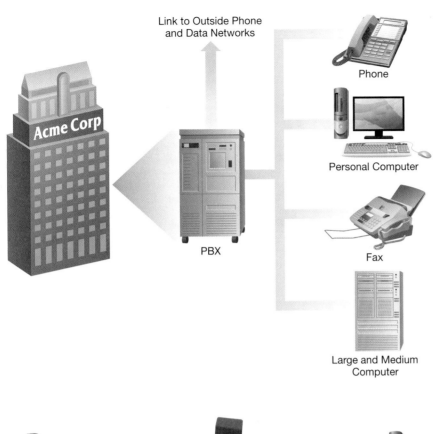

FIGURE TB13

A PBX supports local phone and data communications as well as links to outside phone and data networks.

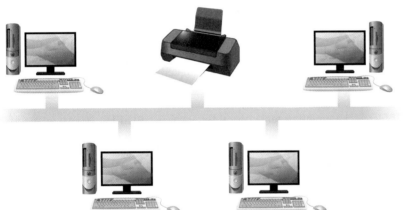

FIGURE TB14

A LAN allows multiple computers located near each other to communicate directly with each other and to share peripheral devices, such as a printer.

CAMPUS AREA NETWORK. A campus area network (CAN) is a computer network that is used (and owned or leased) by a single organization to connect multiple LANs. A CAN typically spans multiple buildings, such as at a corporate or university campus.

WIDE AREA NETWORK. A wide area network (WAN) is a computer network that spans a relatively large geographical area. WANs are typically used to connect two or more LANs. Different hardware and transmission media are often used in WANs because they must cover large distances efficiently. Used by multinational companies, WANs transmit and receive data across cities and countries. A discussion follows of four specific types of WANs: metropolitan area networks, enterprise WANs, value-added networks, and global networks.

Metropolitan Area Networks A metropolitan area network is a computer network of limited geographic scope, typically a citywide area, which combines both LAN and high-speed fiber-optic technologies. Such networks are attractive to organizations that need high-speed data transmission within a limited geographic area.

Enterprise WANs An **enterprise WAN** is a WAN connecting disparate local area networks of a single organization into a single network (see Figure TB15).

FIGURE TB15

An enterprise network allows an organization to connect distributed locations into a single network.

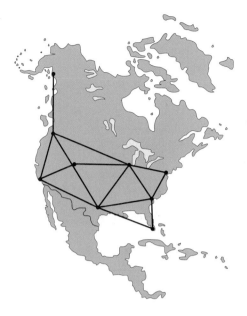

Value-Added Networks **Value-added networks** (VANs) are private, third-party-managed WANs typically used for B2B communications. With much B2B data communication now happening over the Internet, VAN providers focus on offering services such as secure e-mail and translation of EDI standards to facilitate communication between a business and its suppliers and/or customers.

Global Networks A **global network** spans multiple countries and may include the networks of several organizations. The Internet is an example of a global network. The Internet is the world's largest computer network, consisting of thousands of individual networks connecting billions of computers, smartphones, and other devices in almost every country of the world.

PERSONAL AREA NETWORKS. A final type of computer network, called a personal area network (PAN), is an emerging technology that uses wireless communication to exchange data between computing devices using short-range radio communication, typically within an area of 10 meters (30 feet). The enabling technology for PAN is called **Bluetooth**, a specification for personal networking of desktop computers, peripheral devices, mobile phones, portable stereos, and various other devices. Bluetooth is integrated into a variety of personal devices to ease interoperability and information sharing (see Figure TB16).

FIGURE TB16

Bluetooth is used by many to provide hands-free communication. Getty images–thinkstock.

Source: Getty Images–Thinkstock

Now that you have an understanding of the general types of networks, the next sections examine some further fundamental concepts. After discussing packet switching as a concept for sharing communication channels, we will delve deeper into network standards and technologies. Together, these sections provide a foundation for understanding various types of networks.

Packet Switching

Telecommunications advances have enabled individual computer networks—constructed with a variety of hardware and software—to connect together in what appears to be a single network. Networks are increasingly being used to dynamically exchange relevant, value-added knowledge and information throughout global organizations and institutions. To enable rapid transmission of massive amounts of data, most data networks rely on packet switching. **Packet switching** is based on the concept of turn taking and enables millions of users to send large and small chunks of data across the network concurrently. To minimize delays, network technologies limit the amount of data that any computer can transfer on each turn. Consider a conveyor belt as a comparison. Suppose that the conveyor belt connects a warehouse and a retail store. When a customer places an order, it is sent from the store to the warehouse, where a clerk assembles the items in the order. The items are placed on the conveyor belt and delivered to the customer in the store. In most situations, clerks finish sending items from one order before proceeding to send items from another order. This process works well when orders are small, but when a large order with many items comes in, sharing a conveyor belt can introduce delays for others. Consider waiting in the store for your one item while another order with 50 items is being filled.

Local area networks (LANs), WANs, PANs, and the Internet all use packet-switching technologies so that users can share the communication channel and minimize delivery delays. Figure TB17 illustrates how computers use packet switching. Computer A wants to send a message to computer C; similarly, computer B wants to send a message to computer D. For example, computer A is trying to send an e-mail message to computer C, while computer B is trying to send a word processing file to computer D. The outgoing messages are divided into smaller packets of data, and then each sending computer (A and B) takes turns sending the packets over the transmission medium. The incoming packets are reassembled at their respective destinations, using previously assigned packet sequence numbers.

For packet switching to work, each computer attached to a network must have a unique network address, and each packet being sent across a network must be labeled with a header containing the network address of the source (sending computer) and the network address of the destination (receiving computer). As packets are transmitted, network hardware detects whether a particular packet is destined for a local machine. Packet-switching systems adapt instantly to changes in network traffic. If only one computer needs to use the network, it can send data continuously. As soon as another computer needs to send data, packet switching, or turn taking, begins. Next, we explain the importance of network standards and protocols to enable data communication.

Network Standards and Protocols

Standards play a key role in creating networks. The physical elements of networks—adapters, cables, and connectors—are defined by a set of standards that have evolved since the early 1970s. Standards ensure the interoperability and compatibility of network devices, and each standard combines a media access control technique, network topology, and transmission media in different ways. The dominant standard for wired local area networks is 802.3, typically

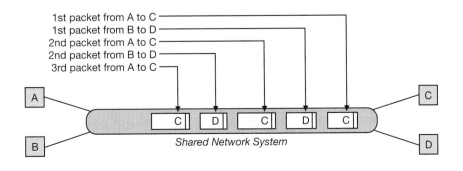

FIGURE TB17

Computers A and B use packet switching to send messages or files to computers C and D.

referred to as Ethernet; wireless local area networks are based on the 802.11 family of standards. Any other competing standards for local area networks have all but vanished. Software interacts with hardware to implement protocols that allow different types of computers and networks to communicate successfully.

PROTOCOLS. All networks employ protocols to make sure communication between computers is successful. Protocols are agreed-on formats for transmitting data between connected computers. They specify how computers should be connected to the network, how errors will be checked, what data compression method will be used, how a sending computer will signal that it has finished sending a message, and how a receiving computer will signal that it has received a message. Protocols allow packets to be correctly routed to and from their destinations. There are literally thousands of protocols to choose from, but a few are a lot more important than the others. In this section, we will first review the worldwide standard, called the OSI model, for implementing protocols. Next, we briefly review TCP/IP, the protocol used by the Internet, and Ethernet, a commonly used protocol for local area networks.

The OSI Model The need of organizations to interconnect computers and networks that use different protocols has driven the industry to an open system architecture in which different protocols can communicate with each other. The International Organization for Standardization defined a networking model called Open Systems Interconnection (OSI), which divides computer-to-computer communications into seven connected layers. The **Open Systems Interconnection (OSI) model** represents a group of specific tasks (represented in Figure TB18) as successive layers that enable computers to communicate data. Each successively higher layer builds on the functions of the layers below. For example, suppose you are using a PC running Windows and are connected to the Internet, and you want to send a message to a friend who is connected to the Internet through a large workstation computer running Unix—two different computers and two different operating systems. When you transmit your message, it is passed down from layer to layer in the Windows protocol environment of your system. At each layer, special bookkeeping information specific to the layer, called a header, is added to the data. Eventually, the data and headers are transferred from the Windows layer 1 to Unix's layer 1 over some physical pathway. On receipt, the message is passed up through the layers in the Unix application. At each layer, the corresponding header information is stripped away, the requested task is performed, and the remaining data package is passed on until your message arrives as you sent it, as shown in Figure TB19. In other words, protocols represent an agreement between different parts of the network about how data are to be transferred.

Transmission Control Protocol/Internet Protocol (TCP/IP) Because so many different networks are interconnected throughout the world, they must have a common language, or protocol, to communicate. The protocol used by the Internet is called Transmission Control Protocol/Internet Protocol (TCP/IP). The first part, TCP, breaks data into small chunks and manages the transfer of those packets from computer to computer via packet switching. For example, a single document may be broken into several packets, each containing several hundred characters, as well as a destination address (the IP part of the protocol). The IP part defines

FIGURE TB18

The OSI model has seven layers and provides a framework for connecting different computers with different operating systems to a network.

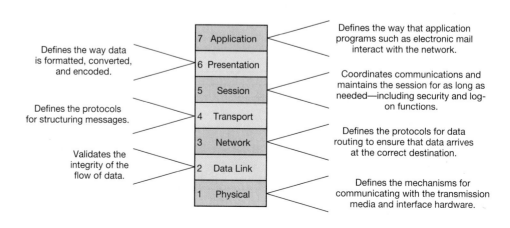

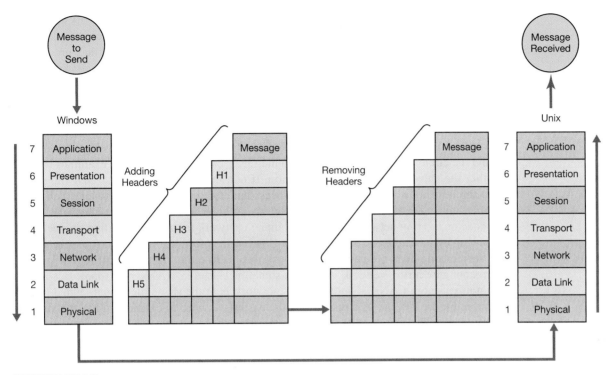

FIGURE TB19

Message passing between two different computers.

how a data packet must be formed and to where a **router** (an intelligent device used to connect two or more individual networks) must forward each packet. Packets travel independently to their destination, sometimes following different paths and arriving out of order. The destination computer reassembles all the packets on the basis of their identification and sequencing information. Together, TCP and IP provide a reliable and efficient way to send data across the Internet.

A data packet that conforms to the IP specification is called an **IP datagram**. Datagram routing and delivery are possible because, as previously mentioned, every computer and router connected to the Internet is assigned a unique address, called its IP address. When an organization connects to the Internet, it obtains a set of IP addresses that it can assign to its computers. TCP helps IP guarantee delivery of datagrams by performing three main tasks. First, it automatically checks for datagrams that may have been lost en route from their source to their destination. Second, TCP collects the incoming datagrams and puts them in the correct order to re-create the original message. Finally, TCP discards any duplicate copies of datagrams that may have been created by network hardware.

Ethernet **Ethernet** is a LAN protocol using packet switching developed by the Xerox Corporation in 1976. Different types of data (including IP datagrams) can travel on Ethernets by being enclosed in another set of headers to form packets called Ethernet frames. The original Ethernet protocol supports data transfer rates of 10 Mbps. A later version, called 100Base-T or Fast Ethernet, supports transfer rates of 100 Mbps; the latest version, called 100GB Ethernet, supports transfer rates of 100 gigabits, or 100,000 megabits, per second over relatively large distances. Most new computers have a **network interface card (NIC)** (also known as network adapter or Ethernet card) installed, allowing you to use this type of network connection to connect to broadband modems, home networks, or work networks. Each NIC has a unique identifier (called MAC address, assigned by the manufacturer) that is used to identify the computer on the network. The PC is then connected to other network components via transmission media, such as Ethernet cables.

NETWORK TOPOLOGIES. **Network topology** refers to the shape of a network. The four basic network topologies are star, ring, bus, and mesh. A **star network** is configured, as you might expect, in the shape of a star, as shown in Figure TB20a. That is, all nodes or workstations are connected to a central hub through which all messages pass. The workstations represent the points of the star. Star topologies are easy to lay out and modify. However, they are also the most costly because they require the largest amount of cabling. Although it is easy to diagnose problems at individual workstations, star networks are susceptible to a single point of failure at the hub that would result in all workstations losing network access. This topology is used in switched Ethernet local area networks, where all devices are connected to a central switch. A **ring network** is configured in the shape of a closed loop or circle with each node connecting to the next node, as shown in Figure TB20b. In ring networks, messages move in one direction around the circle. As a message moves around the circle, each workstation examines it to see whether the message is for that workstation. If not, the message is regenerated and passed on to the next node. This regeneration process enables ring networks to cover much larger distances than star or bus networks can. Relatively little cabling is required, but a failure of any node on the ring network can cause complete network failure. Self-healing ring networks avoid this by having two rings with data flowing in different directions; thus, the failure of a single node does not cause the network to fail. In either case, it is difficult to modify and reconfigure a ring network. Although sometimes used in WANs, ring topologies are not commonly used in LANs anymore. A **bus network** is in the shape of an open-ended line, as shown in Figure TB20c; as a result, it is the easiest network to extend and has the simplest wiring layout. This topology enables all network nodes to receive the same message through the network cable at the same time. However, it is difficult to diagnose and isolate network faults. Whereas early variants of Ethernet used bus networks, they are not commonly used any more. Finally, a **mesh network** consists of computers and other devices that are either fully or partially connected to each other. In a *full* mesh design, every computer and device is connected to every other computer and device. In a *partial* mesh design, many but not all computers and devices are connected (see Figure TB20d). Like a ring network, mesh networks provide relatively short routes from one node to another. Mesh networks also provide many possible routes through the network—a design that prevents one circuit or computer from becoming overloaded when traffic is heavy. Given these benefits, most WANs, including the Internet, use a partial mesh design.

MEDIA ACCESS CONTROL. **Media access control** is the set of rules that governs how a given node or workstation gains access to the network to send or receive data. Without access control, collisions are likely to happen if two or more workstations simultaneously transmit messages onto the network. There are two general types of access control: distributed and random access. With distributed access control, only a single workstation at a time has authorization to transmit its data. One method of authorization is token passing, where authorization is transferred sequentially from workstation to workstation. Ring networks normally use a token-passing media access control method to regulate network traffic. Another method, polling, uses a master device which centrally controls access to the network by sequentially polling each connected device whether it needs to transmit data. Under random access control (sometimes referred to as contention-based), any workstation can transmit its data by checking whether the medium is available. No specific permission is required. A commonly used method of random access control in wireless LANs is called **carrier sense multiple access/collision avoidance (CSMA/CA)**. In CSMA/CA, each connected device "listens" to traffic on the transmission medium to determine whether a message is being transmitted. If no traffic is detected, the device sends its message; otherwise, it waits. Modern Ethernet local area networks use *switches* to do away with the problem of collisions altogether: each device is connected to a switch, which connects the different devices as needed for transmitting data; in other words, the switch creates separate point-to-point circuits between devices, such that a message is not broadcast to all devices, but only travels between the sender and the receiver.

Network Technologies

Typically, devices in a network are not connected directly to each other; rather, computer networks rely on different networking hardware components to connect computers and route messages. In addition, individual devices and hardware components are connected using different wired or wireless media. These are discussed next.

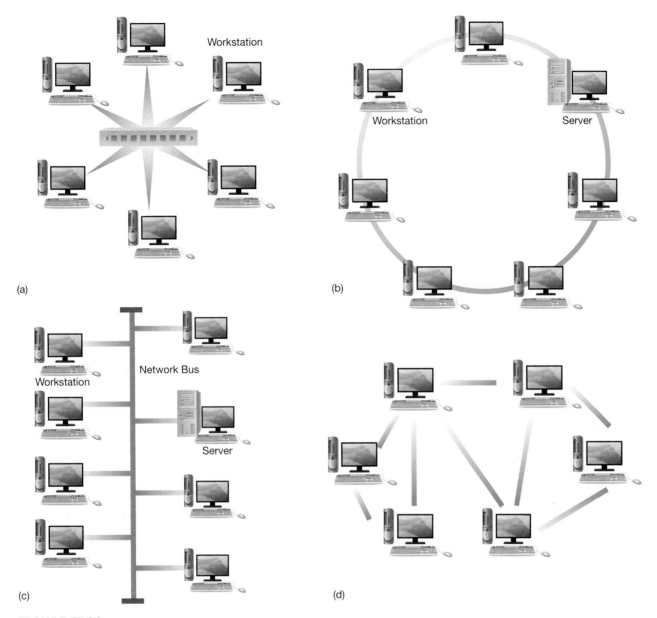

FIGURE TB20

(a) The star network has several workstations connected to a central hub. (b) The ring network is configured in a closed loop, with each workstation connected to another workstation. (c) The bus network is configured in the shape of an open-ended line where each workstation receives the same message simultaneously. (d) The mesh network consists of computers and other devices that are either fully or partially connected to each other.

NETWORKING HARDWARE. Because of the complexity of current networks, a variety of specialized pieces of equipment have been developed for computers to connect and transfer data. However, not all pieces of equipment are necessary in order to connect computers together, and the use of this equipment is dependent on the intended use and configuration of the network. Table TB10 presents some commonly used types of networking equipment to meet businesses' networking needs. Some of these devices are also commonly used in home networks; for example, your DSL modem may also act as a router and wireless access point. Other networking devices used by telecommunications companies are beyond the scope of this discussion.

CABLE MEDIA. Cable media physically link computers and other devices in a network. The most common forms of cable media are twisted pair, coaxial, and fiber-optic.

TABLE TB10   Networking Hardware

Networking Hardware	Description
Switch	A **switch** is used to connect multiple computers, servers, or printers to create a network. Switches typically inspect data packets received and forward them to the correct addressee.
Router	A router is an intelligent device used to connect two or more individual networks. When a router receives a data packet, it looks at the network address and passes the packet on to the appropriate network. Routers are commonly used to connect a LAN to a WAN, such as the Internet.
Wireless access point	A **wireless access point** transmits and receives wireless (Wi-Fi) signals to allow wireless devices to connect to the network.
Wireless controller	A **wireless controller** manages multiple access points and can be used to manage transmission power and channel allocation to establish desired coverage throughout a building and minimize interference between individual access points. Further, wireless controllers can be used to manage authentication and other security features.

Twisted-Pair Cable Twisted-pair (TP) cable is made of two or more pairs of insulated copper wires twisted together (see Figure TB21). TP cables are rated according to quality (in terms of the ability to transmit high frequency signals and the "crosstalk" between individual wires); category 3 (Cat 3), Cat 5, and Cat 6 cables are often used in network installations. Depending on the rating, TP cables have a capacity up to 10 gigabits per second (Gbps) at distances up to 100 meters (330 feet). The cable may be unshielded (UTP) or shielded (STP). Telephone wire installations as well as many local area networks use UTP cabling, as it is cheap and easy to install. However, like all copper wiring, it has rapid attenuation and is very sensitive to electromagnetic interference (EMI) and eavesdropping—the undetected capturing of data transmitted over a network. STP uses wires wrapped in insulation, making it less prone to EMI and eavesdropping. STP cable is more expensive than unshielded TP cable, and it is more difficult to install because it requires special grounding connectors to drain EMI. Ethernet cables typically use RJ-45 connectors so that they can be plugged into an NIC or into other network components.

Coaxial Cable Coaxial (or coax) cable contains a solid inner copper conductor surrounded by plastic insulation and an outer braided copper or foil shield (see Figure TB22). Coax cable comes in a variety of thicknesses—thinnet coax and thicknet coax—based on resistance to EMI. Although less costly than TP, thinnet coax is not commonly used in networks anymore;

(a)
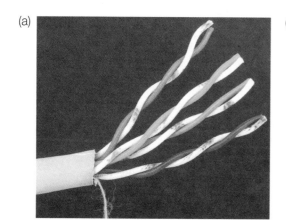

(b)

FIGURE TB21

(a) A cable spliced open showing several twisted pairs. (b) A sample network installation that utilizes many TP cables at once.

Sources: (a) Georgios Alexandris/Shutterstock; (b) Inara Prusakova/Shutterstock

FIGURE TB22

These coaxial cables are ready
to be connected to a computer or
other device.

Source: Kasia/Shutterstock

thicknet coax is more expensive than TP. Coax cable is most commonly used for cable television installations and for networks operating at 10 to 100 megabits per second (Mbps). Its attenuation is lower than TP cable's, and it is moderately susceptible to EMI and eavesdropping.

Fiber-Optic Cable Fiber-optic cable is made of a light-conducting glass or plastic core surrounded by more glass, called cladding, and a tough outer sheath (see Figure TB23). The sheath protects the fiber from changes in temperature as well as from bending or breaking. This technology uses pulses of light sent along the optical cable to transmit data. Fiber-optic cable transmits clear and secure data because it is immune to EMI and eavesdropping. Transmission signals do not break up because fiber-optic cable has low attenuation. It can support bandwidths from 100 Mbps to greater than 2 Gbps and distances up to 25 kilometers (15 miles). Fiber-optic cable is more expensive than copper wire because the cost and difficulties of installation

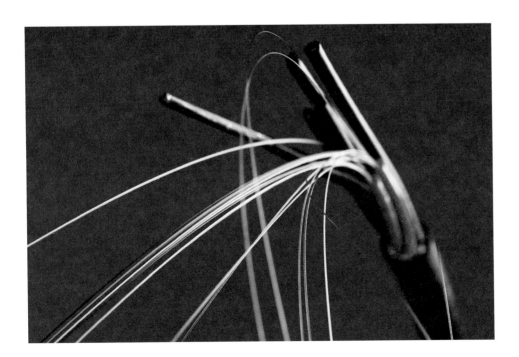

FIGURE TB23

Fiber-optic cable consists of a
light-conducting glass or plastic
core, surrounded by more glass,
called cladding, and a tough outer
sheath.

Source: Thinkstock Images Royalty Free/
Jupiter Images/Goodshoot

and repair are higher for fiber-optic. Fiber-optic cables are used for high-speed **backbones**—the high-speed central networks to which many smaller networks can be connected. A backbone may connect, for example, several different buildings in which other, smaller LANs reside. Submarine telecommunications cables (used for telephone and Internet traffic between continents) also use fiber-optic cable. In home environments, fiber-optic cable can be used to connect digital audio devices.

WIRELESS MEDIA. With the popularity of mobile devices such as laptops, tablets, and smartphones, wireless media are rapidly gaining popularity. Wireless media transmit and receive electromagnetic signals using methods such as infrared line of sight, high-frequency radio, and microwave systems.

Infrared Line of Sight Infrared line of sight uses high-frequency light waves to transmit signals on an unobstructed path between nodes. While commonly being used in remote controls for most audiovisual equipment, such as TVs, stereos, and other consumer electronics equipment, infrared systems are not well suited for rapidly transmitting large amounts of data; thus, this technology has since been surpassed by Wi-Fi and Bluetooth for data communication.

High-Frequency Radio High-frequency radio signals can transmit data at rates of up to several hundred Mbps to network nodes from 12.2 up to approximately 40 kilometers (7.5 to 25 miles) apart, depending on the nature of any obstructions between them. The flexibility of the signal path makes high-frequency radio ideal for mobile transmissions. For example, most police departments use high-frequency radio signals that enable police vehicles to communicate with each other as well as with the dispatch office. This medium is expensive because of the cost of antenna towers and high-output transceivers. Installation is complex and often dangerous because of the high voltages. Although attenuation is fairly low, this medium is very susceptible to EMI and eavesdropping.

Two common applications of high-frequency radio communication are cellular phones and wireless networks. A **cellular phone** gets its name from how the signal is distributed. In a cellular system, a coverage area is divided into **cells** with a low-powered radio antenna/receiver in each cell; these cells are monitored and controlled by a central computer (see Figure TB24). Any given cellular network has a fixed number of radio frequencies. When a user initiates or receives a call, the mobile telephone switching office assigns the caller a unique frequency for the duration of the call. As a person travels within the network, the central computer at the switching office monitors the quality of the signal and automatically assigns the call to the closest cellular antenna. Cellular phones have gone through rapid changes since their first commercial use in the mid-1980s (see Table TB11). Because of the costs involved in setting up fixed telephone lines, cellular phones have become very popular in many African countries and are a key factor in bridging the digital divide.

FIGURE TB24

A cellular network divides a geographic region into cells.

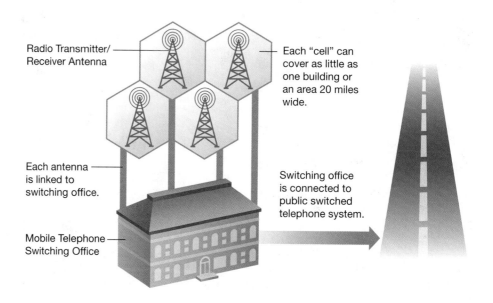

Radio Transmitter/
Receiver Antenna

Each "cell" can cover as little as one building or an area 20 miles wide.

Each antenna is linked to switching office.

Switching office is connected to public switched telephone system.

Mobile Telephone Switching Office

TABLE TB11 Evolution of Cell Phone Technology

Generation	Description	Data Transfer	Advantages
0G	Preceded modern cellular mobile telephony and was usually mounted in cars or trucks; it was a closed circuit, so you could call only other radio telephone users.	Analog	Enabled communicating on the go.
1G	This technology, introduced in the 1980s, used circuit switching; it had poor voice quality, unreliable handoffs between towers, and nonexistent security.	Analog	Enabled users to communicate with other cell phones and land lines.
2G	The first all-digital signal that was divided into TDMA and CDMA standards. Allowed for SMS (text) messaging and e-mails to be sent/received.	Digital (up to 9.6-Kbps transfer)	Lower-powered radio signals allowed for longer battery life. Digital format allowed for clearer signal and reduced signal noise.
2.5G	Allows for faster data transmission via a packet-switched domain in addition to the circuit-switched domain.	Digital (up to 115-Kbps transfer)	Higher data speeds allow for more complex data to be transmitted (e.g., sports scores and news stories).
3G	Even faster. Requires a new cellular network, different from that already available in 2G systems.	Digital (minimum of 384 Kbps when moving and 2 Mbps when stationary)	Transfer full video and audio.
4G	Emerging standards for high-speed mobile connectivity. Different standards on different networks and locations.	Digital (up to 100 Mbps when moving and 1 Gbps when stationary)	Data speeds similar to wired networks.

One of the most significant advances in cellular technology was the introduction of packet switching for data transmission as operators moved from 2G to 2.5G. Although connection speeds have increased significantly since, many cellular customers around the world who rely on their mobile devices are anticipating the widespread deployment of 4G cellular networks. A 4G network provides mobile broadband Internet access, supporting mobile Web access, IP telephony (e.g., Skype), game services, high definition mobile TV, and video conferencing. There are competing standards for deploying 4G services; three notable standards are: HSPA+, WiMAX, and LTE (long-term evolution). Each standard supports different data rates and distances. Nevertheless, they all are significantly faster than what would be considered existing 3G networks. HSPA+ (High Speed Packet Access) is a family of high-speed 3G and 4G digital data services available to mobile carriers worldwide that helps to extend the capabilities of existing infrastructures; as an upgrade of 3G technologies, some do not consider it "true" 4G. WiMax, or Worldwide Interoperability for Microwave Access, is notable for supporting extremely long distances (up to 30 miles). LTE uses an all IP-based architecture where everything (including voice) is handled as data, similar to the Internet. Each standard continues to evolve and gain (or lose) market share and acceptance with different global carriers; given advantages in terms of speed, LTE is currently the predominant 4G standard in the U.S. Over the next decade, industry insiders believe that standards will further advance and converge, making high-speed mobile connectivity a reality for much of the world.

High-frequency radio-wave technology is increasingly being used to support wireless local area networks (WLANs). WLANs based on a family of standards called 802.11 are also referred to as Wi-Fi (wireless fidelity). The 802.11 family of standards has been universally adopted and has transmission speeds up to 450 Mbps (using the 802.11n standard), with even faster standards being under development. The ease of installation has made WLANs popular for business and home use. For example, some homes and many buildings have (or want) multiple computers and need to share Internet access, files, and peripheral devices. Unfortunately, many older buildings and homes do not have a wired infrastructure to easily connect computers and devices, making wireless networking particularly attractive. Through the use of wireless technologies, many organizations are transforming their work environments into better team collaboration environments.

Microwave Transmission Microwave transmission uses high-frequency radio signals that are sent through the air using either terrestrial (earth-based) systems or satellite systems (microwaves are typically of shorter wavelength, and thus higher frequency than radio waves used by cellular or Wi-Fi networks). Terrestrial microwave, shown in Figure TB25, uses antennae that require an unobstructed path or line of sight between nodes. The cost of a terrestrial microwave system depends on the distance to be covered. Typically, businesses lease access to these microwave systems from service providers rather than invest in antenna equipment. Data may be transmitted at up to 274 Mbps. Over short distances, attenuation is not a problem, but signals can be disrupted over longer distances by environmental conditions such as high winds and heavy rain. EMI and eavesdropping are significant problems with microwave communications.

Satellite microwave, shown in Figure TB26, uses satellites orbiting the earth as relay stations to transfer signals between ground stations located on earth. Satellites orbit from 400 to 22,300 miles above the earth and have different uses and characteristics (see Table TB12). Because of the distance signals must travel, satellite transmissions are delayed (also known as **propagation delay**). Satellite transmission has become very viable for media such as TV and radio, including the digital radio stations XM and Sirius, both of which have their own satellites that send out scrambled signals to proprietary receivers.

Another strength of satellite communication is that it can be used to access very remote and undeveloped locations on the earth. Such systems are extremely costly because their use and installation depends on space technology. Companies such as AT&T sell satellite services with typical transmission rates ranging from less than 1 to 10 Mbps, but the rates can be as high as

FIGURE TB25

Terrestrial microwave requires a line-of-sight path between a sender and a receiver.

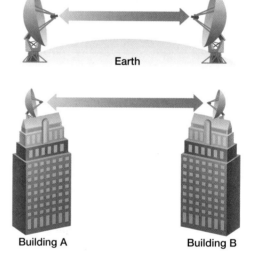

FIGURE TB26

Communications satellites are relay stations that receive signals from one earth station and rebroadcast them to another.

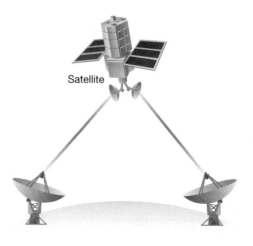

TABLE TB12 Characteristics of Satellites with Different Orbits

Name	Distance from Earth	Characteristics/Common Application
Low Earth Orbit (LEO) Satellite	400–1,000 miles	• Not fixed in space in relation to the rotation of the earth; circles the earth several times per day. • Photography for mapping and locating mineral deposits; monitoring ice caps, coastlines, volcanoes, and rain forests; researching plant and crop changes; monitoring wildlife habitats and changes; search and rescue for downed aircraft or ships that are in trouble; research projects in astronomy and physics.
Medium Earth Orbit (MEO)	1,000–22,300 miles	• Not fixed in space in relation to the rotation of the earth; circles the earth more than one time per day. • Primarily used in geographical positioning systems (such as the Global Positioning System) for navigation of ships at sea, spacecraft, airplanes, automobiles, and military weapons.
Geosynchronous Earth Orbit (GEO)	22,300 miles	• Fixed in space in relation to the rotation of the earth; circles the earth one time per day. • Because it is fixed in space, transmission is simplified. • Transmission of high-speed data for television, weather information, remote Internet connections, digital satellite radio, and telecommunications (satellite phones).

TABLE TB13 Relative Comparison of Wireless Media

Medium	Expense	Speed	Attenuation	EMI	Eavesdropping
Infrared line of sight	Low	Up to 16 Mbps	High	High	High
High-frequency radio	Moderate	Up to 300 Mbps	Low	High	High
Terrestrial microwave	Moderate	Up to 274 Mbps	Low	High	High
Satellite microwave	High	Up to 90 Mbps	Moderate	High	High

90 Mbps. Like terrestrial microwave, satellite systems are prone to attenuation and are susceptible to EMI and eavesdropping. Table TB13 compares wireless media across several criteria.

The Internet

The name "Internet" is derived from the concept of *internetworking*, which means connecting host computers and their networks to form even larger networks. The Internet is a large worldwide collection of networks that uses a common protocol to communicate. In the following sections, we discuss in more detail how independent networks are connected to form the Internet, who manages the Internet, and how home and business users can connect to the Internet.

HOW DID THE INTERNET GET STARTED? You can trace the roots of the Internet back to the late 1960s, when the U.S. **Defense Advanced Research Projects Agency** began to study ways to interconnect networks of various kinds. This research effort produced the **Advanced Research Projects Agency Network (ARPANET)**, a large wide area network (WAN) that linked many universities and research centers. The first two nodes on the ARPANET were the University of California, Los Angeles, and the Stanford Research Institute, followed by the University of California, Santa Barbara, and the University of Utah.

ARPANET quickly evolved and was combined with other networks. For example, in 1986, the U.S. **National Science Foundation (NSF)** initiated the development of the **National Science Foundation Network (NSFNET)**, which became a major component of the Internet. Other networks throughout the United States and the rest of the world were interconnected and/ or morphed into the growing "Internet." Throughout the world, support for the Internet has come from a combination of federal and state governments, universities, national and international research organizations, and industry.

FIGURE TB27

Routers connect independent networks.

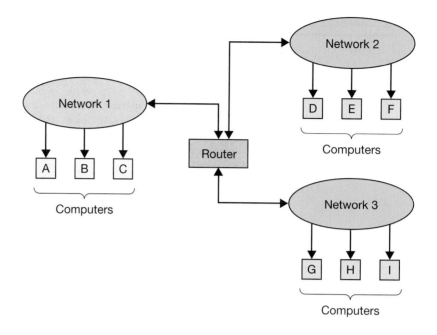

CONNECTING INDEPENDENT NETWORKS. The Internet uses routers to interconnect independent networks. For example, Figure TB27 illustrates a router that connects networks 1, 2, and 3. A router, like a conventional computer, has a central processor, memory, and network interfaces. However, routers do not use conventional software, nor are they used to run applications. Their only job is to interconnect networks and forward data packets from one network to another. As illustrated in Figure TB28, computers A and F are connected to independent networks. If computer A generates a data packet destined for computer F, the packet is sent to the router that interconnects the two networks. The router forwards the packet onto network 2, where it is delivered to its destination at computer F.

Routers are the fundamental building blocks of the Internet because they connect thousands of LANs and WANs. LANs are connected to backbone WANs, as depicted in Figure TB28. A backbone network manages the bulk of network traffic and typically uses a higher-speed connection than the individual LAN segments. For example, a backbone network might use fiber-optic cabling, which can transfer data at a rate of 100 Gbps, whereas a LAN connected to the backbone may use Ethernet with TP cabling, transferring data at a rate of 10 Mbps to 10 Gbps. To gain access to the Internet, an organization installs a router between one of its own networks and the closest Internet site. Business organizations typically connect to the Internet not only with personal computers but with Web servers as well.

FIGURE TB28

LANs connect to wide area backbones.

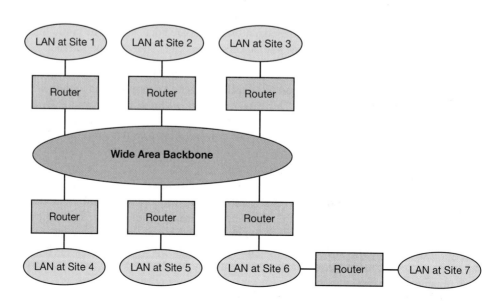

WHO MANAGES THE INTERNET? Individual computers on the Internet are identified by their IP addresses. So who keeps track of these IP addresses on the Internet? A number of national and international standing committees and task forces have been used to manage the development and use of the Internet. Most notably, the Internet Assigned Numbers Authority is responsible for managing global and country code top-level domains, as well as global IP number space assignments. Similarly, the Internet Assigned Numbers Authority also provides central maintenance of the **Domain Name System (DNS)** root database, which points to distributed DNS servers replicated throughout the Internet. This database is used to associate Internet host names with their Internet IP addresses. Users can access Web sites using domain name or IP addresses. The functionality of the DNS is to provide users easy-to-remember domain names to access Web sites. In other words, it is far easier to remember www.apple.com than it is to remember 17.149.160.10 (the IP address of a server mirroring Apple's content as of mid-2012), but both will work as a Uniform Resource Locator in any Web browser, as the DNS servers will translate the domain names into the accompanying IP address.

In 1993, the NSF created **InterNIC**, a government–industry collaboration, to manage directory and database services, domain registration services, and other information services on the Internet. In the late 1990s, this Internet oversight was transitioned more fully out into industry when InterNIC morphed into the **Internet Corporation for Assigned Names and Numbers**, a nonprofit corporation that assumed responsibility for managing IP addresses, domain names, and root server system management. The number of unassigned Internet addresses is running out, so new classes of addresses are being added as **IPv6**, the latest version of the IP, was adopted in June 2012.

HOW TO CONNECT TO THE INTERNET. Now you can see how the Internet works and how it is managed. How do you connect to the Internet? For personal use (i.e., from home), we typically connect to the Internet through an **Internet service provider (ISP)**, also called an Internet access provider. ISPs provide several different ways to access the Internet from home (see Table TB14).

ISPs connect to one another through **Internet exchange points (IXPs)**. Much like railway stations, these IXPs serve as access points for ISPs and are an exchange point for Internet traffic. They determine how traffic is routed and are often the points of most Internet congestion. IXPs are a key component of the **Internet backbone**, which is the collection of main network connections and telecommunications lines that make up the Internet (see Figure TB29).

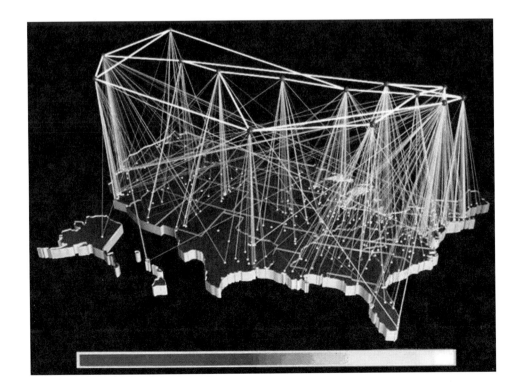

FIGURE TB29

The Internet backbone.

TABLE TB14 Methods for Connecting to the Internet

Service	Current Status and Future Outlook	Typical Bandwidth
Dial-up	Although still used in the United States, there are very few new dial-up customers. This market should dry up as broadband is moved to rural areas and developing nations.	52 Kbps
Integrated Services Digital Network	This technology has limited market share because of its expense. Typically, these connections are more expensive than broadband connections, although they offer less bandwidth.	128 Kbps
Cable	Coaxial cable used for cable TV provides much greater bandwidth than telephone lines and therefore is the market leader in broadband use for home users. Overselling of bandwidth that causes slower-than-average speeds tends to be a major problem for home users.	Upload: 2–10 Mbps Download: 12–50 Mbps
DSL	DSL technology has gained market share from cable. With many companies offering higher speeds at lower cost, DSL should continue to cut into cable's market share.	Upload: up to 10 Mbps Download: 1.5–50 Mbps
Satellite	Although satellite connectivity had a promising future, many users are moving away from this expensive technology in order to access faster and cheaper cable or DSL connections.	Upload: 50 Kbps Download: 5 Mbps
Wireless broadband	Wireless broadband offers the most promise of any of the current technologies, as the speeds are increasing while the coverage areas continue to grow.	Up to 54 Mbps
Fiber to the home	Fiber to the home has been adopted by several major players in the ISP industry. Although the technology typically can be placed only in new developments, the demand for fast connections is helping make this a significant technology for ISPs.	Up to 100 Mbps

The Internet follows a hierarchical structure, similar to the interstate highway system. High-speed central network lines are like interstate highways, enabling traffic from midlevel networks to get on and off. Think of midlevel networks as city streets that, in turn, accept traffic from their neighborhood streets or member networks. However, you cannot get on an interstate or city street whenever you want to. You have to share the highway and follow traffic control signs to arrive safely at your destination. The same holds true for traffic on the Internet, and people can connect to the Internet in a number of ways. In the next section, we outline how typical home users connect to the Internet.

Dial-Up Traditionally, most people connected to the Internet through a telephone line at home or work. The term we use for standard telephone lines is **plain old telephone service (POTS)** (the POTS system is also called the **public switched telephone network (PSTN)**). Because the dial-up telephone system was designed to pass the sound of voices in the form of analog signals, it cannot pass the electrical pulses—**digital signals**—that computers use. The only way to pass digital data over conventional voice telephone lines is to convert it to audio tones—**analog signals**—that the telephone lines can carry. A **modem** (MOdulator/DEModulator) converts digital signals from a computer into analog signals so that telephone lines may be used as a transmission medium to send and receive electronic data, as shown in Figure TB30. As the speed, or bandwidth, of POTS is generally only about 52 Kbps (52,000 bits per second), today, most people connect to the Internet using some form of digital, high-speed connection.

Integrated Services Digital Network Integrated services digital network (ISDN) is a standard for worldwide digital communications. ISDN was designed in the 1980s to replace all analog systems, such as most telephone connections in the United States, with a completely digital transmission system. ISDN uses existing TP telephone wires to provide high-speed data service. ISDN systems can transmit voice, video, and data. Because ISDN is a purely digital network, you can connect your PC to the Internet without the use of a traditional modem. Removing the analog-to-digital conversion for sending data and the digital-to-analog conversion for receiving data and higher bandwidth greatly increase the data transfer rate. However, a small

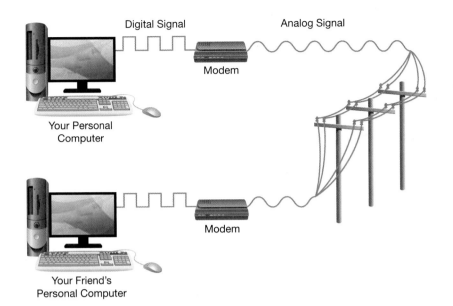

FIGURE TB30

Modems convert digital signals into analog and analog signals into digital.

electronic box called an "ISDN modem" is typically required so that computers and older, analog-based devices such as telephones and fax machines can utilize and share the ISDN-based service. While ISDN has had moderate success in various parts of the world, it has largely been surpassed by DSL and cable modems.

Digital Subscriber Line Digital subscriber line (DSL) is a popular way of connecting to the Internet. DSL is referred to as a "last-mile" solution because it is used only for connections from a telephone switching station to a home or office and generally is not used between telephone switching stations.

The abbreviation DSL is used to refer collectively to **asymmetric digital subscriber line (ADSL)**, **symmetric digital subscriber line (SDSL)**, and other forms of DSL. DSL enables more data to be sent over existing copper telephone lines by sending digital pulses in the high-frequency area of telephone wires. Because these high frequencies are not used by normal voice communications, DSL enables your computer to operate simultaneously with voice connections over the same wires. ADSL speeds range from 1.5 to 50 Mbps downstream and from 16 Kbps to 10 Mbps upstream. SDSL is said to be symmetric because it supports the same data rates for upstream and downstream traffic (up to 3 Mbps). Like ISDN, ADSL and SDSL require a special modem-like device. As most Internet users primarily download content, ADSL is most popular in consumer environments. SDSL is offered primarily to business customers.

Cable Modems In most areas, the company that provides cable television service also provides Internet service. With this type of service, a special **cable modem** is designed to transmit data over cable TV lines. Coaxial cable used for cable TV provides much greater bandwidth than telephone lines, and millions of homes in the United States are already wired for cable TV, so cable modems are a fast, popular method for accessing the Internet. Cable modems offer download speeds up to 50 Mbps.

Satellite Connections In many regions of the world, people can only access the Internet via satellite, referred to as **Internet over satellite (IoS)**. IoS technologies allow users to access the Internet via satellites that are placed in a geostationary orbit above the earth's surface. With these services, your PC is connected to a satellite dish hanging out on the side of your home or placed out on a pole (much like satellite services for your television); you are able to maintain a reliable connection to the satellite in the sky because the satellite orbits the earth at the exact speed of the earth's rotation. Given the vast distance that signals must travel from the earth up to the satellite and back again, IoS is slower than high-speed terrestrial (i.e., land-based) connections to the Internet over copper or fiber-optic cables. In remote regions of the world, however, IoS is the only option available because installing the cables necessary for an Internet connection is not economically feasible or, in many cases, is just not physically possible.

Wireless Broadband **Wireless broadband** is a technology that is becoming more prevalent with home users today. With speeds similar to DSL and cable, wireless broadband is usually found in rural areas where other connectivity options, such as DSL and cable, are not available. A common scenario is that the ISP will install an antenna at a high point, such as a large building or radio tower, and the consumer will mount a small dish to the roof and point it at the antenna. Wireless broadband can bridge a distance of up to 50 kilometers (30 miles).

Mobile Wireless Access In addition to the fixed wireless approach, there are also many new **mobile wireless** approaches for connecting to the Internet. For example, with a subscription to a data plan, smartphones give you Internet access nearly anywhere. Also, special network adapter cards or USB "dongles" from a cellular service provider allow a notebook computer, tablet, or desktop computer to connect to cellular networks. The advantage of these systems is that as long as you are in the coverage area of that cell phone provider you have access to the Internet. Most mobile wireless service providers limit the amount of data that can be downloaded per month without incurring expensive fees, making this a relatively expensive option for a person's exclusive method for accessing the Internet.

Fiber to the Home Fiber to the home (FTTH), also known as **fiber to the premises**, refers to connectivity technology that provides a superspeed connection to people's homes. This is usually done by fiber-optic cabling running directly into new homes. FTTH is currently available only in major metropolitan areas. The growth in FTTH is dependent on new home building, as it is currently cost prohibitive to distribute the technology to existing structures.

Until now, we have talked about ways that individuals typically access the Internet. In the following section, we talk more about ways that organizations typically access the Internet.

BUSINESS INTERNET CONNECTIVITY. Although home users have enjoyed a consistent increase in bandwidth availability, the demand for corporate use has increased at a greater pace; therefore, the need for faster speeds has become of great importance. In addition to the home connectivity options, business customers also have several high-speed options, described next.

T1 Lines To gain adequate access to the Internet, organizations are turning to long-distance carriers to lease dedicated **T1 lines** for digital transmissions. The T1 line was developed by AT&T as a dedicated digital transmission line that can carry 1.544 Mbps of data. In the United States, companies such as MCI that sell long-distance services are called **interexchange carriers** because their circuits carry service between the major telephone exchanges. A T1 line usually traverses hundreds or thousands of miles over leased long-distance facilities.

AT&T and other carriers charge as little as US$200 per month for a dedicated T1 circuit, and some providers will waive the installation fee if you sign up for some specified length of service. If you need an even faster link, you might choose a **T3 line**. T3 provides about 45 Mbps of service at about 10 times the cost of leasing a T1 line. Alternatively, organizations often choose to use two or more T1 lines simultaneously rather than jump to the more expensive T3 line. Higher speeds than the T3 are also available, but are not typically used for normal business activity. For example, fiber-optic networks offer speeds considerably faster than T3 lines. See Table TB15 for a summary of telecommunication line capacities, including optical carrier (OC) lines that use the Synchronous Optical Network standard.

TABLE TB15   Capacity of Telecommunication Lines

Type of Line	Data Rate
T1	1.544 Mbps
T3	44.736 Mbps
OC-1	51.85 Mbps
OC-3	155.52 Mbps
OC-12	622.08 Mbps
OC-24	1.244 Gbps
OC-48	2.488 Gbps

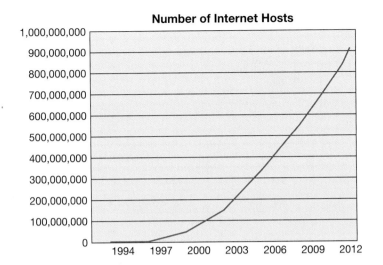

FIGURE TB31

Growth in Internet servers (hosts).
Source: Based on Internet Systems Consortium. http://www.isc.org/solutions/survey.

THE CURRENT STATE OF INTERNET USAGE. The Internet is now the most prominent global network. Internet World Stats (www.internetworldstats.com) reports that, as of 2012, over 2.2 billion people worldwide use the Internet. This means that over 32 percent of the world's population has Internet access at home, an increase of almost 528 percent since 2000. Most Internet users are found in Asia, but North America has the largest percentage of users (78.6 percent of the North American population have access to the Internet). Africa, on the other hand, has the smallest percentage of its population using the Internet since 2000 (just 13.5 percent), but is experiencing rapid growth (2,988 percent).

One other way to measure the rapid growth of the Internet, in addition to the number of users, is to examine the growth in the number of **Internet hosts**—that is, computers working as servers on the Internet—as shown in Figure TB31.

FOUNDATIONAL TOPICS IN DATABASE MANAGEMENT

In Chapter 6, you were introduced to database concepts such as attributes, entities, and relationships, as well as managerial aspects related to databases. In the following sections, we delve deeper into the topic of relational database management to give you a better idea of the intricacies involved in designing a sound database. Note that the design of non-relational databases, such as NoSQL databases, are beyond the scope of this discussion.

http://goo.gl/3Zhya

Relational Database Design

Much of the work of creating an effective relational database is in the creation of the data model. If the model is not accurate, the database will not be effective. A poor data model will result in data that are inaccurate, redundant, or difficult to search. If the database is relatively small, the effects of a poor design might not be too severe. A corporate database, however, contains many entities, perhaps hundreds or thousands. In this case, the implications of a poor data model can be catastrophic. A poorly organized database is difficult to maintain and process—thus defeating the purpose of having a DBMS in the first place. Undoubtedly, your university maintains databases with a variety of entity types—for example, students and grades—with both of these entities having several attributes. Attributes of a Student entity might be Student ID, Name, Campus Address, Major, and Phone. Attributes of a Grades entity might include Student ID, Course ID, Section Number, Term, and Grade (see Figure TB32).

For the DBMS to distinguish between records correctly, each instance of an entity must have one unique identifier. For example, each student has a unique Student ID. Note that using the student name (or most other attributes) would not be adequate because students may have the exact same name, live at the same address, or have the same phone number. Consequently, when designing a database, we must always create and use a unique identifier, called a **primary key**, for each type of entity in order to store and retrieve data accurately. In some instances, the primary key can also be a combination of two or more attributes, in which case it is called a **combination primary key**. An example of this is the Grades entity, shown in Figure TB32, where the

FIGURE TB32

The attributes for and links between two entities—students and grades.

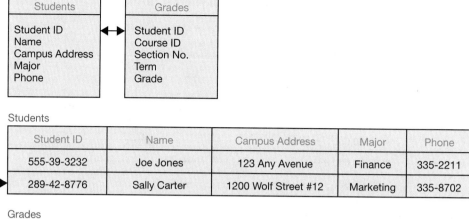

Students

Student ID	Name	Campus Address	Major	Phone
555-39-3232	Joe Jones	123 Any Avenue	Finance	335-2211
289-42-8776	Sally Carter	1200 Wolf Street #12	Marketing	335-8702

Grades

Student ID	Course ID	Section No.	Term	Grade
555-39-3232	MIS 250	2	F'05	D+
555-39-3232	MIS 250	1	F'06	A–
289-42-8776	MIS 250	3	S'07	B+

combination of Student ID, Course ID, Section Number, and Term uniquely refers to the grade of an individual student in a particular class (section number) in a particular term. Attributes not used as the primary key can be referred to as **secondary keys** when they are used to identify one or more records within a table that share a common value. For example, a secondary key in the Student entity shown in Figure TB32 would be Major when used to find all students who share a particular major.

ASSOCIATIONS. To retrieve information from a relational database, it is necessary to associate or relate information from separate tables. The three types of **relationships** (or **associations**) among entities are one-to-one, one-to-many, and many-to-many. Table TB16 summarizes each of these three associations and shows how they should be handled in database design for a basketball league.

To understand how relationships work, consider Figure TB33, which shows four tables—Home Stadium, Team, Player, and Games—for keeping track of the information for a basketball league. The Home Stadium table lists the Stadium ID, Stadium Name, Capacity, and Location, with the primary key underlined. The Team table contains two attributes, Team ID and Team Name, but nothing about the stadium where the team plays. If we wanted to have such information, we could gain it only by creating a relationship between the Home Stadium and Team tables. For example, if each team has only one home stadium and each home stadium has only one team, we have a one-to-one relationship between the Team and the Home Stadium entities. In situations in which we have one-to-one relationships between entities, we place the primary

TABLE TB16 Rules for Expressing Relationships Among Entities and Their Corresponding Data Structures

Relationship	Examples	Instructions
One-to-one	Each team has only one home stadium, and each home stadium has only one team.	Place the primary key from one table (e.g., Stadium) into the other (e.g., Team) as a foreign key.
One-to-many	Each player is on only one team, but each team has many players.	Place the primary key from the table on the "one" side of the relationship (e.g., Team) as a foreign key in the table on the "many" side of the relationship (e.g., Player).
Many-to-many	Each player participates in many games, and each game has many players.	Create a third table (e.g., Player Statistics) and place the primary keys from each of the original tables (e.g., Player and Team) together in the third as a combination primary key.

Home Stadium

Stadium ID	Stadium Name	Capacity	Location

Team

Team ID	Team Name

Player

Player ID	Player Name	Position

Games

Team ID (1)	Team ID (2)	Date	Final Score

FIGURE TB33

Tables used for storing information about several basketball teams, with no foreign key attributes added; thus, associations cannot be made.

key from one table in the table for the other entity and refer to this attribute as a **foreign key**. In other words, a foreign key refers to an attribute that appears as a non-primary key attribute in one entity and as a primary key attribute (or part of a primary key) in another entity. By sharing this common—but unique—value, entities can be linked, or associated, together. We can choose in which of these tables to place the foreign key of the other. After adding the primary key of the Home Stadium entity to the Team entity, we can identify which stadium is the home for a particular team and then be able to find all the details about that stadium (see section A in Figure TB34).

When we find a one-to-many relationship—for example, each player plays for only one team, but each team has many players—we place the primary key from the entity on the "one" side of the relationship, the Team entity, as a foreign key in the table for the entity on the "many" side of the relationship, the Player entity (see section B in Figure TB34). In essence, we take from the one and give to the many, a Robin Hood strategy.

When we find a many-to-many relationship (e.g., each player plays in many games, and each game has many players), we create a third (new) entity—in this case, the Player Statistics entity and corresponding table. We then place the primary keys from each of the original entities together into the third (new) table as a combination primary key (see section C in Figure TB34).

You may have noticed that by placing the primary key from one entity in the table of another entity, we are creating a bit of redundancy. We are repeating the data in different places. We are willing to live with this bit of redundancy, however, because it enables us to keep track of the interrelationships among the many pieces of important organizational data that are stored in different tables. By keeping track of these relationships, we can quickly answer questions such as "Which players on the SuperSonics played in the game on February 16 and scored more than 10 points?" In a business setting, the question might be "Which customers purchased a 2012 Toyota Prius from a salesperson named Jeff at the James Toyota dealership in Pullman, Washington, during the first quarter of 2012, and how much did each customer pay?" This kind of question would be useful in calculating the bonus money Jeff should receive for that quarter or in recalling those specific vehicles in the event of a recall by the manufacturer.

A. One-to-one relationship: Each team has only one home stadium, and each home stadium has only one team.

Team

Team ID	Team Name	*Stadium ID*

B. One-to-many relationship: Each player is on only one team, but each team has many players.

Player

Player ID	Player Name	Position	*Team ID*

C. Many-to-many relationship: Each player participates in many games, and each game has many players.

Player Statistics

Team 1	*Team 2*	*Date*	*Player ID*	Points	Minutes	Fouls

FIGURE TB34

Tables used for storing information about several basketball teams, with foreign key attributes added in order to make associations.

ENTITY-RELATIONSHIP DIAGRAMMING. A diagramming technique that creates an **entity-relationship diagram (ERD)** is commonly used when designing relational databases, especially when showing associations between entities. To create an ERD, you draw entities as boxes and draw lines between entities to show relationships. Each relationship can be labeled on the diagram to give it additional meaning. For example, Figure TB35 shows an ERD for the basketball league data previously discussed. From this diagram, you can see the following associations:

- Each Home Stadium has a Team.
- Each Team has Players.
- Each Team participates in Games.
- For each Player and Game, there are Game Statistics.

When you are designing a complex database, with numerous entities and relationships, ERDs are very useful. They allow the designer to talk with people throughout the organization to make sure that all entities and relationships have been found.

THE RELATIONAL MODEL. Now that we have discussed associations and data models, we need a mechanism for joining entities that have natural relationships with one another. For example, in the University database we described previously, there are several relationships among the four entities: students, instructors, classes, and grades. Students are enrolled in multiple classes. Likewise, instructors teach multiple classes and have many students in their classes in a semester. At the end of the semester, instructors assign a grade to each student, and each student earns grades in multiple classes. It is important to keep track of these relationships. We might, for example, want to know which courses a student is enrolled in so that we can notify her instructors that she will miss courses because of an illness. The primary DBMS approach, or model, for keeping track of these relationships among data entities is the relational model. Other models—the hierarchical, network, and object-oriented models—are also used to join entities with commercial DBMSs, but this is beyond the scope of our discussion (see Hoffer, Ramesh, & Topi, 2011).

The most common DBMS approach in use today is the **relational database model**. A DBMS package using this approach is referred to as a relational DBMS. With this approach, the DBMS views and presents entities as two-dimensional tables, with records as rows and attributes as columns. Tables can be joined when there are common columns in the tables. The uniqueness of the primary key, as mentioned earlier, tells the DBMS which records should be joined with others in the corresponding tables. This structure supports very powerful data manipulation capabilities and linking of interrelated data. Database files in the relational model are three-dimensional: a table has rows (one dimension) and columns (a second dimension) and can contain rows of attributes in common with another table (a third dimension). This three-dimensional database is potentially much more powerful and useful than traditional, two-dimensional, "flat-file" databases (see Figure TB36).

A good relational database design eliminates unnecessary data duplications and is easy to maintain. To design a database with clear, non-redundant relationships, you perform a process called normalization.

FIGURE TB35

An entity-relationship diagram showing the relationships between entities in a basketball league database.

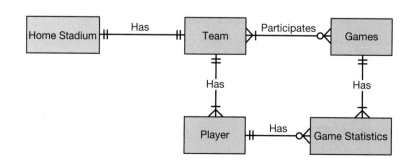

Department Records

Dept No	Dept Name	Location	Dean
Dept A			
Dept B			
Dept C			

Instructor Records

Instructor No	Inst Name	Title	Salary	Dept No
Inst 1				
Inst 2				
Inst 3				
Inst 4				

FIGURE TB36

With the relational model, we represent these two entities, department and instructor, as two separate tables and capture the relationship between them with a common column in each table.

NORMALIZATION. To be effective, databases must be efficient. Developed in the 1970s, **normalization** is a technique to make complex relational databases more efficient and more easily handled by the DBMS (Hoffer et al., 2011). Normalization makes sure that each table contains only attributes that are related to the entity; hence, normalization helps to eliminate data duplication. To understand the normalization process, let us return to the scenario in the beginning of this section. Think about your report card. It looks like nearly any other form or invoice. Your personal information is usually at the top, and each of your classes is listed, along with an instructor, a class day and time, the number of credit hours, and a location. Now think about how these data are stored in a relational database. Imagine that this database is organized so that in each row of the database, the student's identification number is listed on the far left. To the right of the student ID are the student's name, local address, major, phone number, course and instructor information, and a final course grade (see Figure TB37). Notice that there are redundant data for students, courses, and instructors in each row of this database. This redundancy means that this database is not well organized. If, for example, we want to change the phone number of an instructor who has hundreds of students, we have to change this number hundreds of times. In addition, this redundancy wastes valuable storage space.

Elimination of data redundancy is a major goal and benefit of using data normalization techniques. After the normalization process, the student data is organized into five separate tables (see Figure TB38). This reorganization helps simplify the ongoing use and maintenance of the database and any associated analysis programs.

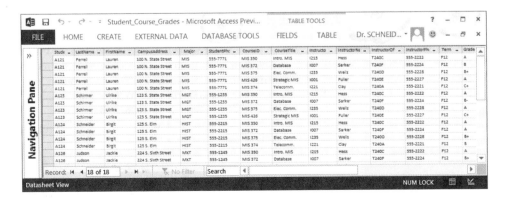

FIGURE TB37

Database of students, courses, instructors, and grades with redundant data.

Source: Courtesy of Microsoft, Inc.

FIGURE TB38

Organization of information on students, courses, instructors, and grades after normalization.

Source: Courtesy of Microsoft, Inc.

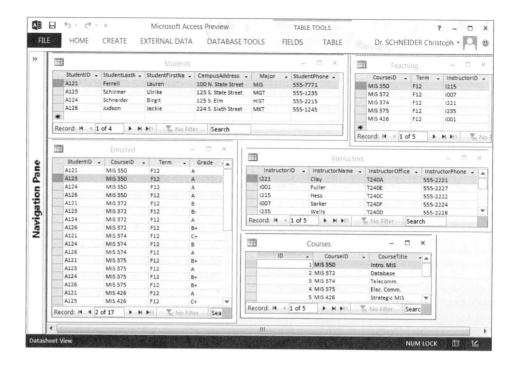

Key Points Review

1. ***Discuss foundational IS hardware concepts.***
   IS hardware is classified into three types: input, processing, and output technologies. Input hardware consists of devices used to enter data into a computer. Processing hardware transforms inputs into outputs. The CPU is the device that performs this transformation, with the help of several other closely related devices that store and recall data. Data are stored on primary and secondary storage devices. Finally, output-related hardware focuses on delivering information in a usable format to users.

2. ***Describe foundational topics related to system software as well as the characteristics of various types of programming languages and application development environments.*** System software, or the operating system, performs many different tasks. Some of these tasks include booting your computer, reading programs into memory, managing memory allocation to those programs, managing where programs and files are located in secondary storage, maintaining the structure of directories and subdirectories, and so on. A programming language is the computer language that programmers use to write application programs. In order to run on a computer, programs must be translated into binary machine language. Programming languages are translated into machine language through special types of programs, called compilers and interpreters. As computing devices continue to evolve, so too do the programming languages in order to provide innovative services and to best take advantage

of the evolving hardware capabilities. In addition to this evolution, object-oriented programming, visual programming, and Web development languages are relatively new enhancements to programming languages. Finally, CASE environments help systems developers construct large-scale systems more rapidly and with higher quality. Open source software refers to systems software, applications, and programming languages in which the source code is freely available to the general public for use and/or modification.

3. ***Describe foundational networking and Internet concepts.*** Networks provide for services such as transmitting files, sharing printers, or sending and receiving messages. There are several types of computer networks, classified according to their use and distance covered. To enable rapid transmission of massive amounts of data, most data networks rely on packet switching. Protocols are agreed-on formats for transmitting data between connected computers; the most prominent standards are TCP/IP and Ethernet. Networks exchange data by using cable or wireless transmission media, and media access control refers to the rules that govern how a given workstation gains access to the transmission media. The shape of a network can vary; the four most common topologies are star, ring, bus, and mesh configurations. The Internet is composed of networks that are developed and maintained by many different entities; it follows a hierarchical structure, similar to the interstate highway system. High-speed central networks called backbones

are like interstate highways, enabling traffic from midlevel networks to get on and off. Routers are used to interconnect independent networks.

4. ***Explain foundational database management concepts.*** In order to get the most of their data, organizations have to take care to create an accurate data model. Often, entity-relationship diagrams are used when designing relational databases. A primary key is used to uniquely identify records in a database. A foreign key is used to link entities together. A useful diagramming technique is entity-relationship diagramming, displaying entities and the associations between them. Normalization is used to reduce redundancy in a database.

Key Terms

Foundational Hardware Key Terms

American Standard Code for Information Interchange (ASCII)   476
arithmetic logic unit (ALU)   475
audio   474
bar code reader   473
basic input/output system (BIOS)   477
batch data   473
batch processing   473
binary code   476
bit   476
byte   476
bytes per inch   479
cache   477
cathode ray tube   480
CD-R (compact disc–recordable)   479
CD-RW (compact disc–rewritable)   479
central processing unit (CPU)   475
characters per inch   479
clock speed   476
clock tick   476
control unit   476
density   479
digital video disc   479
digitize   476
DVD-ROM (digital versatile disc–read-only memory)   479
electronic paper   480
e-paper   480
flash drive   478
flash memory   478
hard drive   477
head crash   478
input technologies   473
interactive voice response   474
liquid crystal display (LCD)   480
magnetic ink character recognition   473
microprocessor   475
motherboard   475
nonvolatile memory   477
optical character recognition   473

optical disk   478
optical mark recognition   473
organic light-emitting diode   480
output technologies   480
port   479
power supply   479
primary storage   476
printer   480
processing technologies   475
random-access memory (RAM)   476
read-only memory (ROM)   477
read/write head   478
redundant array of independent disks (RAID)   477
secondary storage   487
smart card   473
solid-state drive (SSD)   478
speech recognition   474
streaming audio   475
streaming media   475
streaming video   475
system clock   476
tape   479
text recognition software   473
touch screen   480
Unicode   476
video   474
voice-to-text software   474
volatile memory   477

Foundational Software Key Terms

applet   486
compiler   482
computer-aided software engineering (CASE)   486
executable   482
graphical user interface (GUI)   484
HTML editor   485
HTML tag   485
interpreter   482
Java   486
JavaScript   486
Microsoft.NET   486
object-oriented language   483
scripting language   486

source code   482
utilities   481
utility program   481
visual programming language   484
Web page builder   485

Foundational Networking Key Terms

Advanced Research Projects Agency Network (ARPANET)   503
analog signals   506
asymmetric digital subscriber line (ADSL)   507
authentication service   490
backbone   500
Bluetooth   492
bus network   496
cable modem   507
carrier sense multiple access/collision avoidance (CSMA/CA)   496
cell   500
cellular phone   500
centralized computing   488
collaborative computing   489
Defense Advanced Research Projects Agency   503
digital signals   506
digital subscriber line (DSL)   506
directory service   490
distributed computing   489
Domain Name System (DNS)   505
enterprise WAN   491
Ethernet   495
fiber to the home (FTTH)   508
fiber to the premises   508
global network   492
integrated services digital network (ISDN)   506
interexchange carrier   508
Internet backbone   505
Internet Corporation for Assigned Names and Numbers   505
Internet exchange point (IXP)   505
Internet host   509
Internet over satellite (IoS)   507
Internet service provider (ISP)   505

Review Questions

Foundational Hardware Review Questions

1. IS hardware is classified into what three major types?
2. Describe various methods for entering data into and interacting with a computer.
3. How do computers represent data internally?
4. Describe the role of a motherboard.
5. What determines the speed of a CPU?
6. Compare and contrast the different types of secondary data storage.
7. What are output devices? Describe various methods for providing computer output.

Foundational Software Review Questions

1. Define the term *software* and list several software packages and their uses.
2. Describe at least four different tasks performed by an operating system.
3. Describe the similarities and differences between at least two major operating systems in use today.
4. Name and describe four functions of utility programs.
5. What is HTML, and why is it important?
6. Describe various options for adding dynamic content to a Web page.
7. What is CASE, and how can it help in the development of information systems?
8. What is open source software? Why would business choose to implement open source software?

Foundational Networking Review Questions

1. Compare and contrast centralized, distributed, and collaborative computing.

2. How are LANs, WANs, PANs, and global networks related to each other?
3. What are the roles of authentication services and directory services?
4. What is packet switching, and why is it useful?
5. What is the purpose of the OSI model?
6. What is a network topology? Describe the four basic topologies.
7. What are three common types of transmission media that use cabling?
8. What are four common methods of wireless transmission media for networking, and how do they differ from each other?
9. What is the Internet, and why was it created?
10. Other than dial-up, what are three alternatives for connecting to the Internet at home?

Foundational Database Review Questions

1. Describe why database design is important for modern organizations.
2. Compare and contrast the primary key, combination key, and foreign key within an entity.
3. Describe the three types of relationships in a relational database.
4. What is the purpose of a secondary key?
5. What is an entity-relationship diagram and why is it useful?
6. What is the relational model?
7. What is the purpose of normalization?
8. Why is redundancy undesired?

Self-Study Questions

Foundational Hardware Self-Study Questions

1. All of the following are considered primary storage except _____.
   A. SSDs
   B. RAM
   C. Registers
   D. Cache

2. Which of the following is not an input device?
   A. biometric scanner
   B. touch screen
   C. LCD screen
   D. stylus

3. Which of the following is an output device?
   A. cathode ray tube
   B. scanner
   C. video camera
   D. keyboard

4. _____ can convert handwritten text into computer-based characters.
   A. Scanners
   B. Bar code/optical character readers
   C. Text recognition software
   D. Audio/video

5. A _____ card is a special credit card with a microprocessor chip and memory circuits.
   A. smart
   B. master
   C. universal
   D. proprietary
   Answers are on page 520.

Foundational Software Self-Study Questions

1. An operating system performs which of the following tasks?
   A. booting the computer
   B. managing where programs and files are stored
   C. sending documents to the printer
   D. all of the above

2. What is the name of the programming language developed by Sun Microsystems in the 1990s?
   A. Latte
   B. Java
   C. Mocha
   D. none of the above

3. Which of the following programming languages would most likely *not* be used for building Web applications?
   A. HTML
   B. JavaScript
   C. XML
   D. Fortran

4. A utility program may provide _____.
   A. antivirus protection
   B. file conversion capability
   C. file compression and defragmentation
   D. all of the above

5. CASE tools support all of the following except: _____.
   A. diagramming
   B. consistency checking
   C. generating code
   D. compiling code
   Answers are on page 520.

Foundational Networking Self-Study Questions

1. Which of the following is *not* a type of cable medium?
   A. twisted pair
   B. coaxial
   C. fiber-optic
   D. shielded pair

2. All of the following are common applications of high-frequency radio communication except _____.
   A. pagers
   B. cellular phones
   C. wireless networks
   D. facsimiles

3. Which of the following is the protocol of the Internet, allowing different interconnected networks to communicate using the same language?
   A. Ethernet
   B. C++
   C. TCP/IP
   D. router

4. Which is the fastest connection available for home users?
   A. dial-up
   B. DSL
   C. wireless broadband
   D. FTTH

5. Which of the following is a typical way large corporations connect to the Internet?
   A. satellite
   B. cable
   C. T1 lines
   D. all of the above
   Answers are on page 520.

Foundational Database Self-Study Questions

1. A(n) _____ is a unique identifier that can be a combination of one or more attributes.
   A. secondary key
   B. primary key
   C. tertiary key
   D. elementary key

2. Which of the following is *not* true in regard to the relational database model?
   A. Entities are viewed as tables, with records as rows and attributes as columns.
   B. Databases use keys and redundant data in different tables in order to link interrelated data.
   C. Entities are viewed as children of higher-level attributes.
   D. A properly designed table has a unique identifier that may consist of one or more attributes.

3. Each team has only one home stadium, and each home stadium has only one team. This is an example of which of the following relationships?
   A. one-to-one
   B. one-to-many
   C. many-to-many
   D. many-to-one

4. A popular diagramming technique for designing databases is called _____.
   A. flowcharting
   B. database diagramming
   C. entity-relationship diagramming
   D. none of the above

5. _____ is a technique to make a complex database more efficient by eliminating redundancy.
   A. Extraction, transformation, and loading
   B. Associating
   C. Normalization
   D. Standardization

Answers are on page 520.

Problems and Exercises

Foundational Hardware Problems and Exercises

1. Match the following terms with the appropriate definitions:
   i. Motherboard
   ii. Audio
   iii. DVD-ROM
   iv. Smart card
   v. Streaming video

   a. Sound that has been digitized for storage and replay on the computer
   b. A special type of credit card with a magnetic stripe that includes a microprocessor chip and memory circuits
   c. An optical storage device that has more storage space than a CD-ROM disk and uses a shorter-wavelength laser beam, which allows more optical pits to be deposited on the disk
   d. A sequence of moving images, sent in a compressed form over the Internet and displayed on the receiver's screen as the images arrive
   e. A large printed plastic or fiberglass circuit board that contains all the components that do the actual processing work of the computer and holds or connects to all the computer's electronic components

2. Visit a computer shop or look on the Web for mice or touch pads. What is new about how these input devices look or how they are used? What are some of the advantages and disadvantages of each device?

3. What types of printers are most common today? What is the cost of a color printer versus a black-and-white one? Compare and contrast laser and ink-jet printers in terms of speed, cost, and quality of output. What kind of printer would you buy or have you bought?

4. Based on your experiences with different input devices, which do you like the best and least? Why? Are your preferences due to the devices' design or usability, or are they based on the integration of the device with the entire information system?

5. Choose a few of the computer hardware vendors that sell computers to the general public. These include Dell, HP, Lenovo, Gateway, Apple, and many lesser-known brands. Using each company's home page on the Web, determine what options these vendors provide for input devices, processing devices, and output devices. Does it seem that this company has a broad range of choices for its customers? Is there something that you did not find available from this company? Present your findings in a 10-minute presentation to the rest of the class.

Foundational Software Problems and Exercises

1. Match the following terms with the appropriate definitions:
   i. Applet
   ii. Visual programming language
   iii. Scripting language
   iv. Interpreter
   v. Compiler

   a. A software program that translates an entire program's source code into machine language that can be read and executed directly by the computer
   b. Programming language that provides a graphical user interface and is generally easier to use than non-GUI languages
   c. A program designed to be executed within another application (such as a Web page)
   d. A software program that translates a programming language into machine language one statement at a time
   e. Used to supply interactive components to a Web page by building programs or scripts directly into HTML page code

2. What are the implications for an organization of having more than one operating system? What might be the advantages? What are some of the disadvantages? Would you recommend such a situation? Prepare a 10-minute presentation to the rest of the class on your findings.

3. Imagine that you are in charge of procuring software applications for your division of a company. You are in need of a powerful business IS software application that will control most of the accounting and bookkeeping functions. Based on your current knowledge of the intricacies of the accounting profession and its practices, would you be more likely to purchase this application as a customized software application or an off-the-shelf software application? Why did you select this choice? What would make you choose the other option?

4. Based on your own experiences with computers and computer systems, what do you like and dislike about different operating systems that you have used? Were these uses on a professional or a personal level or both? Who made the decision to purchase that particular operating system? Did you have any say in the purchase decision?

5. Imagine that you and a friend are at a local ATM getting some cash from your account to pay for a movie. The ATM does not seem to be working. It is giving you an error message every time you press any button. Is this most likely a software-related problem, a hardware-related problem, or a network-related problem? Why? Use the information in this and other briefings to help you make your decision.

Foundational Networking Problems and Exercises

1. Match the following terms with the appropriate definitions:
   i. Protocols
   ii. Ethernet
   iii. FTTH
   iv. T1 line
   v. Domain name

   a. A dedicated digital transmission line that can carry 1.544 Mbps of information
   b. Used in Uniform Resource Locators to identify a source or host entity on the Internet
   c. High-speed network connectivity to homes and offices that is implemented using fiber-optic cable
   d. The most widely used local area network protocol, supporting data rates of up to 100 gigabits per second.
   e. The procedures that different computers follow when they transmit and receive data

2. Discuss the difference between PBX networks and LANs. What are the advantages of each? What are possible disadvantages of each? When would you recommend one over the other?

3. Personal area networks using Bluetooth are becoming increasingly popular. Visit www.bluetooth.com and investigate the types of products that this wireless technology is being used to enhance. Find three products that you find interesting and prepare a 10-minute presentation on what these products are and how Bluetooth is enhancing their operation and usage.

4. Describe one of your experiences with a computer network. What type of topology was being used? Was the network connected to any other networks? How?

5. Working in a group, have everyone describe what type of network would be most appropriate for a small office with about 10 computers, one printer, and one scanner, all within one floor in one building and relatively close to one another. Be sure to talk about transmission media, network topology, and hardware. Did all group members come up with the same option? Why or why not? What else would you need to know to make a good recommendation?

6. Investigate the options for high-speed, broadband Internet access into your home. What options are available to you, and how much do they cost?

7. You have probably experienced several different types of connection—from the university T1 connections to a home DSL or even dial-up connection. If you had to balance between cost and speed, which connection would you choose?

8. Explain in simple language how the Internet works. Be sure to talk about backbones, packet switching, networks, routers, TCP/IP, and Internet services. What technologies, hardware, and software do you utilize when using the Internet? What would you like to use that isn't available to you?

Foundational Database Problems and Exercises

1. Match the following terms with the appropriate definitions:
   i. Primary key
   ii. Foreign key
   iii. Relational database model
   iv. Relationship
   v. Secondary key

   a. Attributes not used as the primary key that can be used to identify one or more records within a table that share a common value
   b. An attribute that appears as a nonprimary key attribute in one entity and as a primary key in another
   c. A field included in a database table that ensures that each instance of an entity is stored or retrieved accurately
   d. An association between entities in a database to enable data retrieval
   e. A data management approach in which entities are presented as two-dimensional tables that can be joined together with common columns

2. You see an announcement for a job as a database administrator for a large corporation but are unclear about what this title means. Research this on the Web and obtain a specific job announcement.

3. Why would it matter what data type is used for the attributes within a database? How does this relate to programming? How does this relate to queries and calculations? Does the size of the database matter?

4. Have several classmates interview database administrators within organizations with which they are familiar. To whom do these people report? How many employees report to these people? Is there a big variance in the responsibilities across organizations? Why or why not?

5. Based on your understanding of a primary key and the information in the following sample grades table, determine the best choice of attribute(s) for a primary key.

Student ID	Course	Grade
100013	Visual Programming	A
000117	Telesystems	A
000117	Introduction to MIS	A

6. Search the Web for an organization with a Web page that utilizes a link between the Web page and the organization's own database. Describe the data that the browser enters and the organization's possible uses for these data. Can you retrieve company information, or can you only send information to the company? How are the data displayed on the Web page?

Answers to the Foundational Hardware Self-Study Questions

1. A, p. 476 **2.** C, p. 473 **3.** A, p. 480 **4.** C, p. 473 **5.** A, p. 473

Answers to the Foundational Software Self-Study Questions

1. D, p. 481 **2.** B, p. 486 **3.** D, p. 483 **4.** D, p. 481 **5.** D, p. 488

Answers to the Foundational Networking Self-Study Questions

1. D, p. 497 **2.** D, p. 500 **3.** C, p. 494 **4.** D, p. 508 **5.** C, p. 508

Answers to the Foundational Database Self-Study Questions

1. B, p. 509 **2.** C, p. 509 **3.** A, p. 510 **4.** C, p. 512 **5.** C, p. 513

Acronyms

ADSL: Asymmetric Digital Subscriber Line

AI: Artificial Intelligence

ALU: Arithmetic Logic Unit

API: Application Programming Interface

ARPANET: Advanced Research Projects Agency Network

ASCII: American Standard Code for Information Interchange

ATM: Automated Teller Machine

B2B: Business-to-Business

B2C: Business-to-Consumer

BI: Business Intelligence

BIOS: Basic Input-Output System

BPI: Bytes per Inch

BPM: Business Process Management

BPR: Business Process Reengineering

BYOD: Bring Your Own Device

C2B: Consumer-to-Business

C2C: Consumer-to-Consumer

CAAT: Computer-Assisted Auditing Tool

CAD: Computer-Aided Design

CAE: Computer-Aided Engineering

CAM: Computer-Aided Manufacturing

CAN: Campus Area Network

CAPTCHA: Completely Automated Public Turing Test to Tell Computers and Humans Apart

CASE: Computer-Aided Software Engineering

CD-R: Compact Disc–Recordable

CD-RW: Compact Disc–Rewritable

CIC: Customer Interaction Center

CIO: Chief Information Officer

COBIT: Control Objectives for Information and Related Technology

COPA: Child Online Protection Act

CPI: Characters per Inch

CPM: Cost per Mille

CPU: Central Processing Unit

CRM: Customer Relationship Management

CRT: Cathode Ray Tube

CSF: Critical Success Factor

CSMA/CA: Carrier Sense Multiple Access/ Collision Avoidance

CSS: Customer Service and Support

CVV2: Card Verification Value

DARPA: Defense Advanced Research Projects Agency

DBA: Database Administrator

DBMS: Database Management System

DNS: Domain Name System

DoS: Denial of Service

DRM: Digital Rights Management

DSL: Digital Subscriber Line

DSS: Decision Support System

DVD-ROM: Digital Versatile Disc–Read-Only Memory

DVD: Digital Video Disc

DVI: Digital Visual Interface

EC: Electronic Commerce

ECPA: Electronic Communications Privacy Act

EDI: Electronic Data Interchange

EEPROM: Electrically Erasable Programmable Read-Only Memory

EMI: Electromagnetic Interference

EMM: Enterprise Marketing Management

EMS: Electronic Meeting System

ERD: Entity-Relationship Diagram

ERP: Enterprise Resource Planning

ES: Expert System

ETL: Extraction, Transformation, and Loading

FTTH: Fiber to the Home

FTTP: Fiber to the Premises

G2B: Government-to-Business

G2C: Government-to-Citizens

G2G: Government-to-Government

GB: Gigabyte

Gbps: Gigabits per second

GEO: Geosynchronous Earth Orbit

GHz: Gigahertz

GIS: Geographic Information System

GPS: Global Positioning System

GUI: Graphical User Interface

HCI: Human–Computer Interface

HDMI: High Definition Multimedia Interface

HIPAA: Health Insurance Portability and Accountability Act

HTML: Hypertext Markup Language

HTTP: Hypertext Transfer Protocol

Hz: Hertz

IaaS: Infrastructure as a Service

ICANN: Internet Corporation for Assigned Names and Numbers

IoS: Internet over Satellite

IOS: Interorganizational System

IP: Intellectual Property

IP: Internet Protocol

IS: Information System

ISDN: Integrated Services Digital Network

ISP: Internet Service Provider

IT: Information Technology

IVR: Interactive Voice Response

IXP: Internet Exchange Point

JAD: Joint Application Design

JIT: Just-In-Time

KB: Kilobyte

Kbps: Kilobits per second

KPI: Key Performance Indicator

LAN: Local Area Network

LCD: Liquid Crystal Display

LEO: Low Earth Orbit

LTE: Long-Term Evolution

MAN: Metropolitan Area Network

MB: Megabyte

Mbps: Megabits per second

MEO: Middle Earth Orbit

MHz: Megahertz

MICR: Magnetic Ink Character Recognition

MIS: Management Information System

NAT: Network Address Translation

NIC: Network Interface Card

NOS: Network Operating System

NPV: Net Present Value

NSF: National Science Foundation

NSFNET: National Science Foundation Network

OAS: Office Automation System

OCR: Optical Character Recognition

OLAP: Online Analytical Processing

OLPC: One Laptop per Child

OLED: Organic Light-Emitting Diode

OLTP: Online Transaction Processing

OMR: Optical Mark Recognition

OSI: Open Systems Interconnection

P2P: Peer-to-Peer

PaaS: Platform as a Service

PAN: Personal Area Network

PBX: Private Branch Exchange

PC: Personal Computer

PDA: Personal Digital Assistant

PIN: Personal Identification Number

POTS: Plain Old Telephone Service

PSTN: Public Switched Telephone Network

QBE: Query by Example

RAD: Rapid Application Development

RAID: Redundant Array of Independent Disks

RAM: Random Access Memory

RDBMS: Relational Database Management System

RFID: Radio-Frequency Identification

RFP: Request for Proposal

ROM: Read-Only Memory

RSS: Real Simple Syndication

SaaS: Software as a Service

SAD: Systems Analysis and Design

SAM: Software Asset Management

SCE: Supply Chain Execution

SCM: Supply Chain Management

SCP: Supply Chain Planning

SDLC: Systems Development Life Cycle

SDSL: Symmetric Digital Subscriber Line

SEO: Search Engine Optimization

SFA: Sales Force Automation

SLA: Service-Level Agreement

SOA: Service-Oriented Architecture

SOX: Sarbanes-Oxley Act

SQL: Structured Query Language

SSD: Solid-State Drive

SSL: Secure Sockets Layer

STP: Shielded Twisted Pair

TB: Terabyte

TCO: Total Cost of Ownership

TCP/IP: Transmission Control Protocol/Internet Protocol

TP: Twisted Pair

TPS: Transaction Processing System

URL: Uniform Resource Locator

USB: Universal Serial Bus

UTP: Unshielded Twisted Pair

VAN: Value-Added Network

VGA: Video Graphics Array

VMI: Vendor Managed Inventory

VoIP: Voice over IP

VPN: Virtual Private Network

Wi-Fi: Wireless Fidelity

WAN: Wide Area Network

WiMax: Worldwide Interoperability for Microwave Access

WLAN: Wireless Local Area Network

WWW: World Wide Web

XBRL: Extensible Business Reporting Language

XML: Extensible Markup Language

Glossary

"Amateurization" of journalism: The replacement of professional journalism by amateur bloggers.

Acceptable use policies: Computer and/or Internet usage policies for people within an organization, with clearly spelled-out penalties for noncompliance.

Access-control software: Software for securing information systems that allows only specific users access to specific computers, applications, or data.

Ad hoc query: A request for information created due to unplanned information needs that is typically not saved for later use.

Adaptive maintenance: Making changes to an information system to make its functionality meet changing business needs or to migrate it to a different operating environment.

Administrative heritage: The corporate culture that has evolved in the environment of a firm's home country.

Advanced Research Projects Agency Network (ARPANET): A wide area network linking various universities and research centers; forerunner of the Internet.

Adware: Free software paid for by advertisements appearing during the use of the software.

Affiliate marketing: A type of marketing that allows individual Web site owners to earn commission by posting other companies' ads on their Web pages.

Alpha testing: Testing performed by the development organization to assess whether the entire system meets the design requirements of the users.

American Standard Code for Information Interchange (ASCII): Character encoding method for representing characters of the English alphabet that provides binary codes to represent symbols.

Analog signals: Audio tones used to transmit data over conventional voice telephone lines.

Analytical CRM: Systems for analyzing customer behavior and perceptions in order to provide business intelligence.

Applet: A program designed to be executed within another application, such as a Web page.

Application software: Software used to perform a specific task that the user needs to accomplish.

Arithmetic logic unit (ALU): A part of the central processing unit (CPU) that performs mathematics and logical operations.

Artificial intelligence (AI): The science of enabling information technologies to simulate human intelligence as well as gain sensing capabilities.

Association: *See* Relationship.

Association discovery: A data mining technique used to find associations or correlations among sets of items.

Asymmetric digital subscriber line (ADSL): A variant of DSL offering faster download speeds than upload speeds.

Asynchronous: Not coordinated in time.

Attribute: An individual piece of information about an entity in a database.

Audio: Analog or digital sound data.

Audit-control software: Software used to keep track of computer activity, enabling auditors to spot suspicious activity.

Augmented reality: The use of information systems to enhance a person's perception of reality by providing relevant information about the user's surroundings

Authentication: The process of confirming the identity of a user who is attempting to access a restricted system or Web site.

Authentication service: A service on a network granting users and devices access rights to resources on the network.

Automating: Using information systems to do an activity faster, cheaper, and perhaps with more accuracy and/or consistency.

Backbone: A high-speed central network to which many smaller networks can be connected.

Backup: A copy of critical data on a separate storage medium.

Backup site: A facility allowing businesses to continue functioning in the event a disaster strikes.

Bandwidth: The transmission capacity of a computer or communications channel.

Bar code reader: A specialized scanner used to read bar code data.

Basic input-output system (BIOS): Programs and instructions that are automatically loaded when the computer is turned on.

Batch data: Large amounts of routine data.

Batch processing: The processing of transactions after some quantity of transactions is collected; the transactions are processed together as a "batch" at some later time.

Best practices: Procedures and processes used by business organizations that are widely accepted as being among the most effective and/or efficient.

Best-cost provider strategy: A strategy to offer products or services of reasonably good quality at competitive prices.

Beta testing: Testing performed by actual system users with actual data in their work environment.

Big Data: Extremely large and complex datasets, typically characterized as being of high volume, variety, and velocity.

Binary code: The digital representation of data and information using sequences of zeros and ones.

Biometrics: Body characteristics such as fingerprints, retinal patterns in the eye, or facial characteristics that allow the unique identification of a person.

Bit: A basic unit of data in computing. Short for "binary digit"; the individual ones and zeros that make up a byte.

Blog: Short for "Web log." Chronological online text diary that can focus on anything the user desires.

Blogging: The creation and maintenance of a blog. Also called "Weblogging."

Blogosphere: The community of all blogs.

Bluetooth: A wireless specification for personal area networking (PAN) of desktop computers, peripheral devices (such as headsets, keyboards, mice, and printers), mobile phones, tablets, and various other devices.

Bot: Short for "software robot"; a program that works in the background to provide some service when a specific event occurs.

Bot herder: A computer criminal who "owns" a botnet.

Botnet: A collection of zombie computers used for destructive activities or spamming.

Breakeven analysis: A type of cost–benefit analysis to identify at what point (if ever) tangible benefits equal tangible costs.

Brick-and-mortar business strategy: A business approach exclusively utilizing physical locations, such as department stores, business offices, and manufacturing plants, without an online presence.

Bricks-and-clicks business strategy: *See* Click-and-mortar business strategy.

Bullwhip effect: Large fluctuations in suppliers' forecasts caused by small fluctuations in demand for the end product and the need to create safety buffers.

Bus network: A network in the shape of an open-ended line.

Business analytics: Applications that augment business intelligence by using predictive analysis to help identify trends or predict business outcomes.

Business continuity plan: A plan describing how a business resumes operation after a disaster.

Business intelligence: The use of information systems to gather and analyze information from both external and internal sources to make better decisions, and the data derived from these processes.

Business model: The summary of a business's strategic direction, outlining how the objectives will be achieved; a business model specifies how a company will create, deliver, and capture value.

Business process: A set of related activities an organization performs in order to reach its business goals.

Business process management (BPM): A systematic, structured improvement approach by all or part of an organization, including a critical examination and redesign of business processes in order to achieve dramatic improvements in one or more performance measures such as quality, cycle time, or cost.

Business process reengineering (BPR): Legacy term for business process management (BPM).

Business rules: Policies by which a business runs.

Business/IT alignment: The alignment of information systems with a business's strategy.

Business-to-business (B2B): Electronic commerce transactions between business partners, such as suppliers and intermediaries.

Business-to-business marketplace: A trading exchange operated by a third-party vendor, not associated with a particular buyer or supplier.

Business-to-consumer (B2C): Electronic commerce transactions between businesses and consumers.

Buyer agent: An intelligent agent used to find the best price for a particular product a consumer wishes to purchase. Also known as a "shopping bot."

BYOD: Bring your own device; the trend of employees increasingly using their own devices for work-related purposes.

Byte: A unit of data typically containing 8 bits, or about one typed character.

Bytes per inch (BPI): The numbers of bytes that can be stored on one inch of magnetic tape.

Cable modem: A specialized piece of equipment that enables a computer to access Internet service via cable TV lines.

Cache: A small block of special high-speed memory used by processors to store those instructions most recently or most often used (pronounced "cash").

Campus area network (CAN): A type of network spanning multiple buildings, such as a university or business campus.

Capabilities: An organization's ability to leverage its resources.

CAPTCHA: Short for "Completely Automated Public Turing Test to Tell Computers and Humans Apart." A system designed to prevent automated mechanisms from repeatedly attempting to submit forms or gain access to a system. A CAPTCHA requires the user to enter letters or numbers that are presented in the form of a distorted image before submitting an online form.

Card verification value 2 (CVV2): A three-digit code located on the back of a credit card; used in transactions when the physical card is not present.

Carrier sense multiple access/collision avoidance (CSMA/CA): A random access control method in which each workstation "listens" to the traffic on the transmission medium to determine whether a message is being transmitted. If no traffic is detected, the workstation sends its message; otherwise, it waits. When a workstation gains access to the medium and sends data onto the network, messages are broadcast to all workstations on the network; however, only the destination with the proper address is able to "open" the message.

Cathode ray tube (CRT): Display technology similar to a television monitor.

CD-R (compact disc–recordable): A type of optical disk that data can be written to.

CD-RW (compact disc–rewritable): A type of optical disk that can be written onto multiple times.

Cell: A geographic area containing a low-powered radio antenna/receiver for transmitting telecommunications signals within that area; monitored and controlled by a central computer.

Cellular phone: Mobile phone technology using a communications system that divides a geographic region into sections called cells.

Central processing unit (CPU): Responsible for performing all the operations of the computer. Also called a microprocessor, processor, or chip.

Centralized computing: A computing model utilizing large centralized computers, called mainframes, to process and store data and local input devices called "terminals"; no sharing of data and capabilities between mainframes and terminals.

Certificate authority: A trusted middleman between computers that verifies that a Web site is a trusted site and that provides large-scale public-key encryption.

Change request management: A formal process that ensures that any proposed system changes are documented, reviewed for potential risks, appropriately authorized, prioritized, and carefully managed.

Characters per inch (CPI): The number of characters that can be stored on one inch of magnetic tape.

Classification: A data mining technique used for grouping instances into predefined categories.

Click fraud: The abuse of pay-per-click advertising models by repeatedly clicking on a link to inflate revenue to the host or increase the costs for the advertiser.

Click-and-mortar business strategy: A business approach utilizing both physical locations and virtual locations. Also referred to as "bricks-and-clicks."

Click-only business strategy: A business approach that exclusively utilizes an online presence. Companies using this strategy are also referred to as virtual companies.

Clickstream data: A recording of the users' path through a Web site.

Click-through rate: The ratio of surfers who click on an ad (i.e., clicks), divided by the number of times it was displayed (i.e., impressions).

Click-wrap license: A type of software license primarily used for downloaded software that requires computer users to accept the license terms by clicking a button before installing the software.

Client: Any computer or software application that requests and uses the services provided by a server.

Client-server network: A network in which servers and clients have defined roles.

Clock speed: The speed of the system clock, typically measured in hertz (Hz) or multiples thereof.

Clock tick: A single pulse of the system clock.

Cloud computing: A computing model enabling ubiquitous, convenient, on-demand network access to a shared pool of configurable computing resources (e.g., networks, servers, storage, applications, and services) that can be rapidly provisioned and released with minimal management effort or service provider interaction (NIST, 2011).

Cloud-based collaboration tools: Tools enabling teams to collaborate on projects using the Internet.

Clustering: Data mining technique grouping related records on the basis of having similar attributes.

Cold backup site: A backup facility consisting of an empty warehouse with all the necessary connections for power and communication but nothing else.

Collaboration: Two or more people working together to achieve a common goal.

Collaborative computing: A synergistic form of distributed computing in which two or more networked computers are used to accomplish common processing tasks.

Collaborative CRM: Systems for providing effective and efficient communication with the customer from the entire organization.

Collective intelligence: A concept based on the notion that distributed groups of people with a divergent range of information and expertise will be able to outperform the capabilities of individual experts.

Collocation facility: A facility in which businesses can rent space for servers or other information systems equipment.

Combination primary key: A unique identifier consisting of two or more attributes.

Competitive advantage: A firm's ability to do something better, faster, cheaper, or uniquely when compared with rival firms in the market.

Competitive click fraud: A competitor's attempt to inflate an organization's online advertising costs by repeatedly clicking on an advertiser's link.

Competitive intelligence: Information about competitors, used to enhance a business's strategic position.

Compiler: A software program that translates an entire program's source code into machine language that can be read and executed directly by the computer.

Computer crime: The use of a computer to commit an illegal act.

Computer ethics: A broad range of issues and standards of conduct that have emerged through the use and proliferation of information systems.

Computer fluency: The ability to independently learn new technologies as they emerge and assess their impact on one's work and life.

Computer forensics: The use of formal investigative techniques to evaluate digital information for judicial review.

Computer literacy: The knowledge of how to operate a computer.

Computer networking: The sharing of data or services between computers using wireless or cable transmission media.

Computer-aided design (CAD): Software used to create design drawings and three-dimensional models during the product design process.

Computer-aided engineering (CAE): Software used to complement or replace the process of building prototypes during product development.

Computer-aided manufacturing (CAM): The use of information systems to control the production process of a product.

Computer-aided software engineering (CASE): The use of software tools that provide automated support for some portion of the systems development process.

Computer-assisted auditing tool: Software used to test information systems controls.

Computer-based information system: A combination of hardware, software, and telecommunication networks that people build and use to collect, create, and distribute data.

Consumerization of IT: The trend of technological innovations first being introduced in the consumer marketplace before being used by organizations.

Consumer-to-business (C2B): Electronic commerce transactions in which consumers sell goods or services to businesses.

Consumer-to-consumer (C2C): Electronic commerce transactions taking place solely between consumers.

Content management system: An information system enabling users to publish, edit, version track, and retrieve digital information (or content).

Continuous planning process: A strategic business planning process involving continuous monitoring and adjusting of business processes to enable rapid reaction to changing business conditions.

Control objectives for information and related technology (COBIT): A set of best practices that help organizations to both maximize the benefits from their information systems infrastructure and establish appropriate controls.

Control unit: Part of the central processing unit (CPU) that works closely with the ALU (arithmetic logic unit) by fetching and decoding instructions as well as retrieving and storing data.

Conversion rate: The percentage of visitors to a Web site who perform the desired action.

Cookie: A small text file (typically containing certain information collected from/about a user or data related to the user's browsing session) passed by a Web server to a Web browser to be stored on a user's computer; this message is then sent back to the server each time the user's browser requests a page from that server.

Copyright: A form of intellectual property, referring to creations of the mind such as music, literature, or software.

Core activities: The activities within a value chain that process inputs and produce outputs, including inbound logistics, operations and manufacturing, outbound logistics, marketing and sales, and customer service.

Corrective maintenance: Making changes to an information system to repair flaws in its design, coding, or implementation.

Cost–benefit analysis: Techniques that contrast the total expected tangible costs versus the tangible benefits for an investment.

Cracker: An individual who breaks into computer systems with the intention of doing damage or committing a crime.

Crowdsourcing: The use of everyday people as cheap labor force, enabled by information technology.

Custom software: Software programs that are designed and developed for a company's specific needs as opposed to being bought off the shelf.

Customer interaction center (CIC): A part of operational CRM that provides a central point of contact for an organization's customers, employing multiple communication channels to support the communication preferences of customers.

Customer portal: An enterprise portal designed to automate the business processes that occur before, during, and after sales between a supplier and multiple customers.

Customer relationship management (CRM): A corporate-level strategy designed to create and maintain lasting relationships with customers by concentrating on the downstream information flows through the introduction of reliable systems, processes, and procedures.

Customer service and support (CSS): A part of operational CRM that automates service and information requests, complaints, and product returns.

Customization: Modifying software so that it better suits user needs.

Cyberbullying: The use of a computer to intentionally cause emotional distress to a person.

Cyberharassment: The use of a computer to communicate obscene, vulgar, or threatening content that causes a reasonable person to endure distress.

Cybersquatting: The dubious practice of registering a domain name, then trying to sell the name to the person, company, or organization most likely to want it.

Cyberstalking: The use of a computer to repeatedly engage in threatening or harassing behavior.

Cyberterrorism: The use of computer and networking technologies against persons or property to intimidate or coerce governments, individuals, or any segment of society to attain political, religious, or ideological goals.

Cyberwar: An organized attempt by a country's military to disrupt or destroy the information and communications systems of another country.

Data: Raw symbols, such as words and numbers that have no meaning in and of themselves, and are of little value until processed.

Data cleansing: The process of detecting, correcting (e.g., standardizing the format), or removing corrupt or inaccurate data retrieved from different systems.

Data dictionary: A document prepared by database designers to describe the characteristics of all items in a database.

Data flows: Data moving through an organization or within an information system.

Data mart: A data warehouse that is limited in scope and customized for the decision support applications of a particular end-user group.

Data mining: Methods used by companies to discover "hidden" predictive relationships in data to better understand their customers, products, markets, or any other phase of their business for which data have been captured.

Data mining agent: An intelligent agent that continuously analyzes large data warehouses to detect changes deemed important by a user, sending a notification when such changes occur.

Data model: A map or diagram that represents the entities of a database and their relationships.

Data privacy statement: A statement on a Web site containing information about what data are gathered, what they are used for, who will have access to the data, whether provision of the data is required or voluntary, and how confidentiality will be ensured.

Data reduction: A preparatory step to running data mining algorithms, performed by rolling up a data cube to the smallest level of aggregation needed, reducing the dimensionality, or dividing continuous measures into discrete intervals.

Data type: The type (e.g., text, number, or date) of an attribute in a database.

Data warehouse: A repository containing data from multiple large databases and other sources that is suitable for direct querying, analysis, or processing.

Database: A collection of related data organized in a way to facilitate data searches.

Database management system (DBMS): A software application used to create, store, organize, and retrieve data from a single database or several databases.

Decision support system (DSS): A special-purpose information system designed to support organizational decision making.

Dedicated grid: A grid computing architecture consisting of homogeneous computers that are dedicated to performing the grid's computing tasks.

Defense Advanced Research Projects Agency (DARPA): The U.S. governmental agency that began to study ways to interconnect networks of various kinds, leading to the development of the ARPANET (Advanced Research Projects Agency Network).

Denial of service attack: An attack by crackers—often using zombie computers—that makes a network resource (e.g., Web site) unavailable to users or available with only a poor degree of service.

Density: The storage capacity of magnetic tape; typically expressed in characters per inch (CPI) or bytes per inch (BPI).

Desktop videoconferencing: The use of integrated computer, telephone, video recording, and playback technologies—typically by two people—to remotely interact with each other using their desktop computers.

Destructive agent: A malicious agent designed by spammers and other Internet attackers to farm e-mail addresses off Web sites or deposit spyware on machines.

Developmental testing: Testing performed by programmers to ensure that each module of a new program is error free.

Differentiation strategy: A strategy in which an organization differentiates itself by providing better products or services than its competitors.

Digital dashboard: A display delivering summary information to managers and executives to provide warnings, action notices, and summaries of business conditions.

Digital divide: The gap between those individuals in our society who are computer literate and have access to information resources such as the Internet and those who do not.

Digital rights management (DRM): A technological solution that allows publishers to control their digital media (music, movies, and so on) to discourage, limit, or prevent illegal copying and distribution.

Digital signals: The electrical pulses that computers use to send bits of information.

Digital subscriber line (DSL): A high-speed data transmission method that uses special modulation schemes to fit more data onto traditional copper telephone wires.

Digital video disc: A DVD used for storing movies.

Digitize: Convert analog input into digital data.

Dimension: A way to summarize data, such as region, time, or product line.

Directory service: A repository (or "address book") containing information about users, user groups, resources, access rights, etc. on a network.

Disaster recovery plan: An organizational plan that spells out detailed procedures for recovering from systems-related disasters, such as virus infections and other disasters that might strike critical information systems.

Discount rate: The rate of return used by an organization to compute the present value of future cash flows.

Discussion forum: An electronic bulletin board that allows for threaded discussions between participants.

Disintermediation: The phenomenon of cutting out the "middleman" in transactions and reaching customers more directly and efficiently.

Disruptive innovation: A new technology, product, or service that eventually surpasses the existing dominant technology, product, or service in a market.

Distinctive competency: Any unique strength possessed by an organization (e.g., innovation, agility, quality, or low cost) that helps to pursue an organizational strategy.

Distributed computing: Using separate computers to work on subsets of tasks and then pooling the results by communicating over a network.

Domain name: Used in Uniform Resource Locators (URLs) to identify a source or host entity on the Internet.

Domain Name System (DNS): A collection of databases used to associate Internet host names with their IP addresses.

Domestic company: A company operating solely in its domestic market.

Downsizing: The practice of slashing costs and streamlining operations by laying off employees.

Downstream information flow: An information flow that relates to the information that is produced by a company and sent along to another organization, such as a distributor.

Drill down: To analyze data at more detailed levels of a specific dimension.

Drill-down report: A report that provides details behind the summary values on a key-indicator or exception report.

Drive-by hacking: A computer attack in which an attacker accesses a wireless computer network, intercepts data, uses network services, and/or sends attack instructions without entering the office or organization that owns the network.

DVD-ROM (digital versatile disc–read-only memory): A DVD that can be read but not written to.

E-auction: An electronic auction.

E-business: A term used to refer to the use of a variety of types of information technologies and systems to support every part of the business.

E-business innovation cycle: A model suggesting that the extent to which modern organizations use information technologies and systems in timely, innovative ways is the key to success.

Economic opportunities: Opportunities that a firm finds for making more money and/or making money in new ways.

Edge computing: The location of relatively small servers close to the end users to save resources in terms of network bandwidth and provide improved responsiveness.

E-government: The use of information systems to provide citizens, organizations, and other governmental agencies with information about and access to public services.

E-information: The use of the Internet to provide electronic brochures and other types of information for customers.

E-integration: The use of the Internet to provide customers with the ability to gain personalized information by querying corporate databases and other information sources.

E-lancing: Self-employed work, similar to freelancing, typically on Internet-related projects.

Electronic bill pay: The use of online banking for bill paying.

Electronic commerce (EC): The exchange of goods and services via the Internet among and between customers, firms, employees, business partners, suppliers, and so on.

Electronic data interchange (EDI): The digital, or electronic, transmission of business documents and related data between organizations via dedicated telecommunications networks.

Electronic meeting system (EMS): A collection of personal computers networked together with sophisticated software tools to help group members solve problems and make decisions through interactive electronic idea generation, evaluation, and voting.

Electronic paper: A flexible output medium using microscopic beads that change color in response to small electrical charges.

Embedded system: A microprocessor-based system designed to perform only a specific, predefined task (such as a digital video recorder [TiVo] or a network router).

Employee portal: An intranet portal used for enabling employee self-service for administering benefits, managing retirement plans, or other human resources–based applications.

Enabling technology: An information technology that enables a firm to accomplish a task or goal or to gain or sustain a competitive advantage in some way.

Encryption: The process of encoding messages or files so that only intended recipients can decipher and understand them.

Enterprise 2.0: The use of social media within a company's boundaries or between a company and its customers or stakeholders.

Enterprise license: A type of software license that is usually negotiated and covers all users within an organization. Also known as a "volume license."

Enterprise marketing management (EMM): CRM tools used to integrate and analyze marketing campaigns.

Enterprise resource planning (ERP): An information system that integrates business activities across departmental boundaries, including planning, manufacturing, sales, marketing, and so on.

Enterprise system: An information system that spans the entire organization and can be used to integrate business processes, activities, and information across all functional areas of a firm.

Enterprise WAN: A WAN connecting disparate networks of a single organization into a single network.

Enterprise-wide information systems: *See* Enterprise system.

Entity: Something data are collected about, such as people or classes.

Entity-relationship diagram (ERD): A diagram used to display the structure of data and show associations between entities.

E-paper: Electronic paper.

ERP core components: The components of an ERP that support the internal activities of an organization for producing products and services.

ERP extended components: The components of an ERP that support the primary external activities of an organization for dealing with suppliers and customers.

E-tailing: Electronic retailing; the online sales of goods and services.

Ethernet: The most widely used local area network protocol, supporting data rates of up to 100 gigabits per second.

E-transaction: The use of the Internet to allow customers to place orders and make payments.

Exception report: A report providing users with information about situations that are out of the normal operating range.

Executable: A program in machine language that can be read and executed directly by a computer.

Executive level: The top level of the organization, where executives focus on long-term strategic issues facing the organization.

Expert system (ES): A special-purpose information system designed to mimic human expertise by manipulating knowledge—understanding acquired through experience and extensive learning—rather than simply information.

Explicit knowledge asset: A knowledge asset that can be documented, archived, and codified.

Extensible Business Reporting Language (XBRL): An XML-based specification for publishing financial information.

Extensible Markup Language (XML): A data presentation standard that allows designers to create customized features that enable data to be more easily shared between applications and organizations.

External acquisition: The process of purchasing an existing information system from an external organization or vendor.

Externally focused system: An information system that coordinates business activities with customers, suppliers, business partners, and others who operate outside an organization's boundaries.

Extraction, transformation, and loading (ETL): The process of consolidating, cleansing, and manipulating data before loading it into a data warehouse.

Extranet: A private part of the Internet that is cordoned off from ordinary users, that enables two or more firms to use the Internet to do business together.

Fact: *See* Measure.

Fiber to the home (FTTH): *See* Fiber to the premises.

Fiber to the premises (FTTP): High-speed network connectivity to homes and offices that is implemented using fiber-optic cable. Also known as "fiber to the home."

Financial flow: The movement of financial assets throughout the supply chain.

Firewall: Hardware or software designed to keep unauthorized users out of network systems.

First-call resolution: Addressing the customers' issues during the first call.

First-mover advantage: Being the first to enter a market.

Flash drive: A portable, removable data storage device using flash memory.

Flash memory: A memory-chip-based non-volatile computer storage method.

Folksonomy: A categorization system created by Internet users (as opposed to experts).

Foreign key: An attribute that appears as a non-primary key attribute in one entity and as a primary key attribute (or part of a primary key) in another entity.

Form: A business document that contains some predefined data and may include some areas where additional data is to be filled in, typically for modifying data related to a single record.

Forward auction: A form of e-auctions that allows sellers to post goods and services for sale and buyers to bid on those items.

Freeconomics: The leveraging of digital technologies to provide *free* goods and services to customers as a business strategy for gaining a competitive advantage.

Functional area information system: A cross-organizational-level information system designed to support a specific functional area.

Functional convenience: A Web site's characteristics that make the interaction with the site easier or more convenient.

Fuzzy logic: A type of logic used in intelligent systems that allows rules to be represented using approximations or subjective values in order to handle situations where information about a problem is incomplete.

Geographic information system (GIS): A system for creating, storing, analyzing, and managing geographically referenced information.

Geotagging: Adding geospatial metadata (such as latitude, longitude, or altitude) to digital media.

Global business strategy: An international business strategy employed to achieve economies of scale by producing identical products in large quantities for a variety of different markets.

Global information dissemination: The use of the Internet as an inexpensive means for distributing an organization's information.

Global network: A network spanning multiple countries that may include the networks of several organizations. The Internet is an example of a global network.

Globalization: The integration of economies throughout the world, enabled by innovation and technological progress.

Government-to-business (G2B): Electronic commerce that involves a country's government and businesses.

Government-to-citizen (G2C): Online interactions between federal, state, and local governments and their constituents.

Government-to-government (G2G): Electronic interactions that take place between countries or between different levels of government within a country.

Graphical user interface (GUI): A computer interface that enables the user to select or manipulate pictures, icons, and menus to send instructions to the computer.

Green computing: Attempts to use computing resources more efficiently to reduce environmental impacts.

Grid computing: A computing architecture that combines the computing power of a large number of smaller, independent, networked computers (often regular desktop PCs) into a cohesive system in order to solve large-scale computing problems.

Group buying: Special volume discounts negotiated with local businesses and offered to people in the form of "daily deals"; if enough people agree to purchase the product or service, everyone can purchase the product at the discounted price.

Groupware: Software that enables people to work together more effectively.

Hacker: An individual who gains unauthorized access to computer systems.

Hacktivist: A cybercriminal pursuing political, religious, or ideological goals.

Hard data: Facts and numbers that are typically generated by transaction processing systems and management information systems.

Hard drive: A magnetic storage device used for secondary storage. Also called "hard disk."

Hardware: Physical computer equipment, such as the computer monitor, central processing unit, or keyboard.

Head crash: A hard disk failure occurring when the read/write head touches the disk, resulting in the loss of the data and/or irreparable damage to the hard disk.

Home-replication strategy: An international business strategy that views the international business as an extension of the home business.

Honeypot: A computer, data, or network site that is designed to be enticing to crackers so as to detect, deflect, or counteract illegal activity.

Hot backup site: A fully equipped backup facility, having everything from hardware, software, and current data to office equipment.

HTML editor: *See* Web page builder.

HTML tag: A command that is inserted into the source document of a Web page to specify how an element on the page is to be formatted or used.

Human–computer interface (HCI): The point of contact between an information system and its users.

Hyperlink: A reference or link on a Web page to another document that contains related information.

Hypertext: Text in a Web document that is linked to other text or files.

Hypertext Markup Language (HTML): The standard method of specifying the format of Web pages. Specific content within each Web page is enclosed within codes (called HTML tags) that stipulate how the content should appear to the user.

Hypertext Transfer Protocol (HTTP): The standard regulating how servers process user requests for Web pages.

Identity theft: Stealing another person's Social Security number, credit card number, and other personal information for the purpose of using the victim's credit rating to borrow money, buy merchandise, or run up debts that are never repaid.

Industrial espionage: Covert activities, such as the theft of trade secrets, bribery, blackmail and technological surveillance to gain an advantage over rivals.

Inferencing: The matching of user questions and answers to information in a knowledge base within an expert system in order to make a recommendation.

Information: Data that have been formatted and/or organized in some way as to be useful to people.

Information age: A period of time in society when information became a valuable or dominant currency.

Information flow: The movement of information along the supply chain.

Information modification: The intentional change of electronic information by unauthorized users.

Information privacy: An ethical issue that is concerned with what information an individual should have to reveal to others through the course of employment or through other transactions such as online shopping.

Information system (IS): Assumed to mean a computer-based information system; a combination of hardware, software, and telecommunications networks that people build and use to collect, create, and distribute useful data; this term is also used to represent the field in which people develop, use, manage, and study computer-based information systems in organizations.

Information systems audit: An assessment of the state of an organization's information systems controls to determine necessary changes and to help ensure the information systems' availability, confidentiality, and integrity.

Information systems controls: Controls helping to ensure the reliability of information, consisting of policies and their physical implementation, access restrictions, and record keeping of actions and transactions.

Information systems infrastructure: The hardware, software, networks, data, facilities, human resources, and services used by organizations to support their decision making, business processes, and competitive strategy.

Information systems planning: A formal process for identifying and assessing all possible information systems development projects of an organization.

Information systems security: Precautions taken to keep all aspects of information systems safe from unauthorized use or access.

Information systems security plan: An ongoing planning process to secure information systems that involves risk assessment, risk-reduction planning, and plan implementation as well as ongoing monitoring.

Information technology (IT): The hardware, software, and networking components of an information system.

Informational system: A system designed to support decision making based on stable point-in-time or historical data.

Infrastructure: The interconnection of various structural elements to support an overall entity, such as an organization, city, or country.

Infrastructure as a service (IaaS): A cloud computing model in which only the basic capabilities of processing, storage, and networking are provided.

Innovator's dilemma: The notion that disruptive innovations can cause established firms or industries to lose market dominance, often leading to failure.

Input technologies: Hardware that is used to enter information into a computer.

Insider threat: A trusted adversary who operates within an organization's boundaries.

Instant messaging: An online chat emulating real-time written conversations.

Intangible benefit: A benefit of using a particular system or technology that is difficult to quantify.

Intangible cost: A cost of using a particular system or technology that is difficult to quantify.

Integrated Services Digital Network (ISDN): A standard for worldwide digital telecommunications that uses existing twisted-pair telephone wires to provide high-speed data service.

Integration: The use of Web technologies to link Web sites to corporate databases to provide real-time access to personalized information.

Intellectual property (IP): Creations of the mind that have commercial value.

Intelligent agent: A program that works in the background to provide some service when a specific event occurs.

Intelligent system: A system comprised of sensors, software, and computers embedded in machines and devices that emulates and enhances human capabilities.

Interactive communication: Immediate communication and feedback between a company and its customers using Web technologies.

Interactive voice response (IVR): A system using speech recognition technology to guide callers through online surveys or menu options.

Interexchange carrier (IXC): A company selling long-distance services with circuits that carry signals between the major telephone exchanges.

Internally focused system: An information system that supports functional areas, business processes, and decision making within an organization.

International business strategy: A set of strategies employed by organizations operating in different global markets.

Internet: A large worldwide collection of networks that use a common protocol to communicate with each other.

Internet backbone: The collection of primary network connections and telecommunications lines making up the Internet.

Internet Corporation for Assigned Names and Numbers (ICANN): A nonprofit corporation that is responsible for managing IP addresses, domain names, and the root server system.

Internet exchange point (IXP): An access point for ISPs and an exchange point for Internet traffic.

Internet hoax: A false message circulated online about any topic of public interest, typically asking the recipient to perform a certain action.

Internet host: A computer working as a server on the Internet.

Internet over Satellite (IoS): A technology that allows users to access the Internet via satellites that are placed in a geostationary orbit.

Internet service provider (ISP): An organization that enables individuals and organizations to connect to the Internet.

Internet Tax Freedom Act: An act mandating a moratorium on electronic commerce taxation in order to stimulate electronic commerce.

Internetworking: Connecting host computers and their networks to form even larger networks.

InterNIC: A government–industry collaboration created by the NSF in 1993 to manage directory and database services, domain registration services, and other information services on the Internet.

Interorganizational system (IOS): An information system that communicates across organizational boundaries.

Interpreter: A software program that translates a program's source code into machine language one statement at a time.

Intranet: An internal, private network using Web technologies to facilitate the secured transmission of proprietary information within an organization, thereby limiting access to authorized users within the organization.

IP address: A numerical address assigned to every computer and router connected to the Internet that serves as the destination address of that computer or device and enables the network to route messages to the proper destination.

IP convergence: The use of the Internet protocol for transporting voice, video, fax, and data traffic.

IP datagram: A data packet that conforms to the Internet protocol specification.

IPv6: The latest version of the Internet protocol.

IS risk management: Understanding and evaluating the interplay between threats, vulnerabilities, and impacts to information systems resources in order to implement effective IS controls.

Java: An object-oriented programming language developed by Sun Microsystems in the early 1990s that is used primarily for developing Web-based applications.

JavaScript: A scripting language created by Netscape that allows developers to add dynamic content to Web sites.

Joint application design (JAD): A special type of a group meeting in which all (or most) users meet with a systems analyst to jointly define and agree on system requirements or designs.

Just-in-time (JIT): A method to optimize ordering quantities so that parts or raw materials arrive just when they are needed for production.

Key generator: Software used to generate fake license or registration keys to circumvent a program's protection mechanism.

Key performance indicator (KPI): A metric deemed critical to assessing progress toward a certain organizational goal.

Key-indicator report: A report that provides a summary of critical information on a recurring schedule.

Knowledge: A body of governing procedures such as guidelines or rules that are used to organize or manipulate data to make it suitable for a given task.

Knowledge assets: The set of skills, routines, practices, principles, formulas, methods, heuristics, and intuitions (both explicit and tacit) used by organizations to improve efficiency, effectiveness, and profitability.

Knowledge management: The processes an organization uses to gain the greatest value from its knowledge assets.

Knowledge management system: A collection of technology-based tools that includes communications technologies and information storage and retrieval systems to enable the generation, storage, sharing, and management of tacit and explicit knowledge assets.

Knowledge portal: A specific portal used to share knowledge collected into a repository with employees (often using an intranet), with customers and suppliers (often using an extranet), or the general public (often using the Internet).

Knowledge society: A term coined by Peter Drucker to refer to a society in which education is the cornerstone of society and there is an increase in the importance of knowledge workers.

Knowledge worker: A term coined by Peter Drucker to refer to professionals who are relatively well-educated and who create, modify, and/or synthesize knowledge as a fundamental part of their jobs.

Layer: In a GIS, related data can be made visible or invisible when viewing a map; each *layer* acts like a transparency that can be turned on or off and provides additional information, such as roads, utilities, ZIP code boundaries, floodplains, and so on.

Legacy system: Older stand-alone computer systems within an organization with older versions of applications that are either fast approaching or beyond the end of their useful life within the organization.

Liquid crystal display (LCD): A type of monitor used for most current notebook and desktop computers.

Local area network (LAN): A computer network that spans a relatively small area, allowing all computer users to connect with each other to share information and peripheral devices, such as printers.

Location-based services: Highly personalized mobile services based on a user's location.

Logic bomb: A type of computer virus that lies in wait for unsuspecting computer users to perform a triggering operation before executing its instructions.

Long tail: The large parts of consumer demand that are outside the relatively small number of mainstream tastes.

Low-cost leadership strategy: A strategy to offer the best prices in the industry on goods or services.

Magnetic ink character recognition (MICR): Scanning technology used by the banking industry to read data, account numbers, bank codes, and check numbers on preprinted checks.

Mainframe: A very large computer typically used as the main, central computing system by major corporations and governmental agencies.

Make-to-order process: The set of processes associated with producing goods based on sales orders.

Make-to-stock process: The set of processes associated with producing goods based on demand forecasts.

Making the business case: The process of identifying, quantifying, and presenting the value provided by an information system.

Malware: Malicious software, such as viruses, worms, or Trojan horses.

Management information system (MIS): An information system designed to support the management of organizational functions at the managerial level of the organization.

Managerial level: The middle level of the organization, where functional managers focus on monitoring and controlling operational-level activities and providing information to higher levels of the organization.

Mashup: A new application or Web site created by integrating one or more Web services.

Mass customization: Tailoring products and services to meet particular needs of individual customers on a large scale.

Master data: The data that are deemed most important in the operation of a business; typically the "actors" in an organization's transactions.

Master data management: Consolidating master data so as to facilitate arriving at a single version of the truth.

M-commerce (mobile commerce): Any electronic transaction or information interaction conducted using a wireless, mobile device and mobile networks that leads to a transfer of real or perceived value in exchange for information, services, or goods.

Measure: The values and numbers a user wants to analyze. Also referred to as "facts."

Media access control: The rules that govern how a given node or workstation gains access to a network to send or receive information.

Menu-driven pricing: A pricing system in which companies set and present non-negotiable prices for products to consumers.

Mesh network: A network that consists of computers and other devices that are either fully or partially connected to each other.

Metadata: Data about data, describing data in terms of who, where, when, why, and so on.

Metropolitan area network (MAN): A computer network of limited geographic scope, typically a citywide area that combines both LAN and high-speed fiber-optic technologies.

Microblogging: Voicing thoughts through relatively short "status updates" using social presence tools.

Microblogging tools: Tools enabling people to voice thoughts through relatively short "status updates."

Microprocessor: *See* Central processing unit.

Microsoft.NET: A programming platform that is used to develop applications that are highly interoperable across a variety of platforms and devices.

Middleware: A software layer on top of individual machines' operating systems that is designed to shield programmers from having to build applications for different underlying operating systems, particularly in heterogeneous, distributed environments.

Mirror: To store data synchronously on independent systems to achieve redundancy for purposes of reliability and/or performance.

Mobile wireless: The transfer of data to a moving computer or handheld device.

Model: A conceptual, mathematical, logical, or analytical formula used to represent or project business events or trends.

Modem: Short for "modulator-demodulator"; a device or program that enables a computer to transmit data over telephone or cable television lines.

Module: A component of a software application that can be selected and implemented as needed.

Monitoring and sensing agent: An intelligent agent that keeps track of key information and notifies the user when conditions change.

Moore's Law: The prediction that computer processing performance would double every 24 months.

Motherboard: A large printed plastic or fiberglass circuit board that holds or connects to all the computer's electronic components.

Multidomestic business strategy: A decentralized international business strategy using a federation of associated business units, employed to be flexible and responsive to the needs and demands of heterogeneous local markets.

National Science Foundation (NSF): A United States government agency responsible for promoting science and engineering; the NSF initiated the development of the NSFNET (National Science Foundation Network), which became a major component of the Internet.

National Science Foundation Network (NSFNET): A network developed by the United States in 1986 that became a major component of the Internet.

Net-present-value analysis: A type of cost–benefit analysis of the cash flow streams associated with an investment.

Network: A group of computers and associated peripheral devices connected by a communication channel capable of sharing data and other resources among users.

Network click fraud: A form of click fraud where a site hosting an advertisement creates fake clicks in order to receive higher payments from the advertiser.

Network effect: The notion that the value of a network (or tool or application based on a network) is dependent on the number of other users.

Network interface card (NIC): An expansion board that plugs into a computer so that it can be connected to a network.

Network topology: The shape of a network; the four common network topologies are star, ring, bus, and mesh.

Neural network: An information system that attempts to approximate the functioning of the human brain.

Non-recurring cost: A one-time cost that is not expected to continue after a system is implemented.

Nonvolatile memory: Memory that does not lose its data after power is shut off.

Normalization: A technique for making complex relational databases more efficient and more easily handled by a database management system.

NoSQL: Highly scalable databases that do not confirm to RDBMS schemas.

Object-oriented language: A programming language that groups together data and its corresponding instructions into manipulable objects.

Office automation system (OAS): A collection of software and hardware for developing documents, scheduling resources, and communicating.

Off-the-shelf software: Software designed and used to support general business processes that does not require any specific tailoring to meet an organization's needs.

OLAP cube: A data structure allowing for multiple dimensions to be added to a traditional two-dimensional table for detailed analysis.

OLAP server: The chief component of an OLAP system that understands how data is organized in the database and has special functions for analyzing the data.

Online analytical processing (OLAP): The process of quickly conducting complex analyses of data stored in a database, typically using graphical software tools.

Online banking: The use of the Internet to conduct financial transactions.

Online investing: The use of the Internet to obtain information about stock quotes and manage financial portfolios.

Online predator: A cybercriminal using the Internet to target vulnerable people, usually the young or old, for sexual or financial purposes.

Online transaction processing (OLTP): Immediate automated responses to the requests from multiple concurrent transactions of customers.

Open innovation: The process of integrating external stakeholders into an organization's innovation process.

Open source software: Software for which the source code is freely available for use and/or modification.

Open systems interconnection (OSI) model: A networking model that represents a group of specific communication tasks as successive layers.

Operating system: Software that coordinates the interaction between hardware devices, peripherals, application software, and users.

Operational CRM: Systems for automating the fundamental business processes—marketing, sales, and support—for interacting with the customer.

Operational level: The bottom level of an organization, where the routine, day-to-day business processes and interactions with customers occur.

Operational systems: The systems that are used to interact with customers and run a business in real time.

Optical character recognition (OCR): Scanning technology used to read and digitize typewritten, computer-printed, or handwritten characters.

Optical disk: A storage disk coated with a metallic substance that is written to (or read from) when a laser beam passes over the surface of the disk.

Optical mark recognition (OMR): Scanning technology used to scan questionnaires and test answer forms ("bubble sheets") where answer choices are marked by filling in circles using a pencil or pen.

Opt-in: To signal agreement to the collection/further use of one's data, e.g., by checking a box.

Opt-out: To signal that data cannot be collected/used in other ways, e.g., by checking a box.

Order-to-cash process: The set of processes associated with selling a product or service.

Organic light-emitting diode (OLED): A display technology using less power than LCD technology.

Organizational learning: The ability of an organization to learn from past behavior and information, improving as a result.

Organizational strategy: A firm's plan to accomplish its mission and goals as well as to gain or sustain competitive advantage over rivals.

Output technologies: Hardware devices that deliver information in a usable form.

Outsourcing: The moving of routine jobs and/or tasks to people in another firm.

Packaged software: A software program written by a third-party vendor for the needs of many different users and organizations.

Packet switching: The process of breaking information into small chunks called data packets and then transferring those packets from computer to computer via the Internet, based on the concept of turn taking.

Paid inclusion: The inclusion of a Web site in a search engine's listing after payment of a fee.

Patch management system: An online system that utilizes Web services to automatically check for software updates, downloading and installing these "patches" as they are made available.

Patent: A type of intellectual property typically referring to process, machine, or material inventions.

Patriot hacker: Independent citizens or supporters of a country that perpetrate computer attacks on perceived or real enemies.

Pay-per-click: A payment model used in online advertising where the advertiser pays the Web site owner a fee for visitors visiting a certain link.

Peer: Any computer that may both request and provide services.

Peer production: The creation of goods or services by self-organizing communities.

Peer-to-peer networks: Networks that enable any computer or device on the network to provide and request services.

Perfective maintenance: Making enhancements to improve processing performance, to improve interface usability, or to add desired but not necessarily required system features.

Personal area network (PAN): A wireless network used to exchange data between computing devices using short-range radio communication, typically within an area of 10 meters.

Personal computer (PC): A stationary computer used for personal computing and small business computing.

Phishing: Attempts to trick financial account and credit card holders into giving away their authorization information, usually by sending spam messages to literally millions of e-mail accounts. Also known as "spoofing."

Plain old telephone service (POTS): Standard analog telephone lines with a bandwidth of generally about 52 Kbps (52,000 bits per second); also called "public switched telephone network (PSTN)."

Planned obsolescence: The design of a product so that it lasts for only a certain life span.

Platform as a service (PaaS): A cloud computing model in which the customer can run his or her own applications that are typically designed using tools provided by the service provider; the customer has limited or no control over the underlying infrastructure.

Podcast: *See* Webcast.

Podcasting: *See* Webcasting.

Port: A hardware interface by which a computer communicates with another device or system.

Portal: An access point (or front door) through which a business partner accesses secured, proprietary information from an organization (typically using extranets).

Post-PC era: An era characterized by the proliferation of new device form factors, such as tablets or smartphones, which complement or even replace traditional PCs and laptops.

Power supply: A device that converts electricity from the wall socket to a lower voltage appropriate for computer components and regulates the voltage to eliminate surges common in most electrical systems.

Predictive analysis: Business intelligence techniques focusing on identifying trends or predicting business outcomes.

Preventive maintenance: Making changes to a system to reduce the chance of future system failure.

Primary key: A field included in a database table that contains a unique value for each instance of an entity to ensure that it is stored or retrieved accurately.

Primary storage: Temporary storage for current calculations.

Printer: An output device that produces a paper copy of alphanumeric or graphic data from a computer.

Private branch exchange (PBX): A telephone system that serves a particular location, such as a business, connecting one telephone extension to another within the system and connecting the internal extensions to the outside telephone network.

Private cloud: Cloud infrastructure that is internal to an organization.

Processing logic: The steps by which data is transformed or moved, as well as a description of the events that trigger these steps.

Processing technologies: Computer hardware that transforms inputs into outputs.

Procure-to-pay process: The set of processes associated with procuring goods from external vendors.

Product flow: The movement of goods from the supplier to production, from production to distribution, and from distribution to the consumer.

Productivity paradox: The observation that productivity increases at a rate that is lower than expected when new technologies are introduced.

Project manager: The person most responsible for ensuring that a project is a success.

Propagation delay: The delay in the transmission of a satellite signal because of the distance the signal must travel.

Protocols: Procedures that different computers follow when they transmit and receive data.

Prototyping: An iterative systems development process in which requirements are converted into a working system that is continually revised through close work between analysts and users.

Proxy variable: An alternative measurement of outcomes; used when it is difficult to determine and measure direct effects.

Pseudocode: A way to express processing logic independent of the actual programming language being used.

Public cloud: Cloud infrastructure offered on a commercial basis by a cloud service provider.

Public switched telephone network: *See* Plain old telephone service (POTS).

QR code: A two-dimensional barcode with a high storage capacity.

Query: A method used to retrieve information from a database.

Query by example (QBE): A capability of a DBMS that enables data to be requested by providing a sample or a description of the types of data the user would like to see.

Radio-frequency identification (RFID): The use of electromagnetic energy to transmit information between a reader (transceiver) and a processing device; used to replace bar codes and bar code readers.

Random-access memory (RAM): A type of primary storage that is volatile and can be accessed randomly by the CPU.

RDBMS: A database management system based on the relational model.

Read-only memory (ROM): A type of nonvolatile primary storage that is used to store programs and instructions that are automatically loaded when the computer is turned on.

Read/write head: A device that inscribes data to or retrieves data from a hard disk or tape.

Real Simple Syndication (RSS): A set of standards for sharing updated Web content, such as news and sports scores, across sites.

Record: A collection of related attributes about a single entity.

Recovery point objective: An objective specifying how timely backup data should be preserved.

Recovery time objective: An objective specifying the maximum time allowed to recover from a catastrophic event.

Recurring cost: An ongoing cost that occurs throughout the life cycle of systems development, implementation, and maintenance.

Redundant array of independent disks (RAID): A secondary storage technology that makes redundant copies of data on two or more hard drives.

Reintermediation: The design of a business model that reintroduces middlemen in order to reduce the chaos brought on by disintermediation.

Relational database model: The most common DBMS approach; entities are presented as two-dimensional tables, with records as rows and attributes as columns.

Relationship: An association between entities in a database to enable data retrieval.

Report: A compilation of data from a database that is organized and produced in printed format.

Report generator: A software tool that helps users build reports quickly and describe the data in a useful format.

Representational delight: A Web site's characteristics that stimulate a consumer's senses.

Request for proposal (RFP): A communication tool indicating buyer requirements for a given system and requesting information or soliciting bids from potential vendors.

Requirements collection: The process of gathering and organizing information from users, managers, customers, business processes, and documents to understand how a proposed information system should function.

Resources: An organization's specific assets that are utilized to create cost or product differentiation from their competitors.

Revenue model: Part of a business model that describes how the organization will earn revenue, generate profits, and produce a superior return on invested capital.

Reverse auction: A type of auction in which buyers post a request for proposal (RFP) and sellers respond with bids.

Reverse engineering: Disassembling a piece of software in order to understand its functioning.

Reverse pricing: A pricing system in which customers specify the product they are looking for and how much they are willing to pay; this information is routed to appropriate companies who either accept or reject the customer's offer.

RFID tag: The processing device used in an RFID system that uniquely identifies an object.

Ring network: A network that is configured in the shape of a closed loop or circle, with each node connecting to the next node.

Risk acceptance: A computer system security policy in which no countermeasures are adopted and any damages that occur are simply absorbed.

Risk analysis: The process in which the value of the assets being protected are assessed, the likelihood of their being compromised is determined, and the costs of their being compromised are compared with the costs of the protections to be taken.

Risk reduction: The process of taking active countermeasures to protect information systems.

Risk transference: A computer system security policy in which someone else absorbs the risk, as with insurance.

Roll up: To analyze data at less detailed levels of a certain dimension.

Router: An intelligent device used to connect and route data traffic across two or more individual networks.

Rule: A way of encoding knowledge, typically expressed using an "if–then" format, within an expert system.

Sales force automation (SFA): CRM systems to support the day-to-day sales activities of an organization.

Sarbanes–Oxley Act: A U.S. government regulation mandating companies to demonstrate compliance with accounting standards and establishing controls and corporate governance.

Scalability: The ability to adapt to increases or decreases in demand for processing or data storage.

Scheduled report: A report produced at predefined intervals—daily, weekly, or monthly—to support the routine informational needs of managerial-level decision making.

Scripting language: A programming language for integrating interactive components into a Web page.

Search advertising: Advertising that is listed in the sponsored search results for a specific search term.

Search engine optimization (SEO): Methods for improving a site's ranking in search engine results.

Secondary key: An attribute that can be used to identify two or more records within a table that share a common value.

Secondary storage: Methods for permanently storing data to a large-capacity storage component, such as a hard disk, CD-ROM disk, or tape.

Secure Sockets Layer (SSL): A popular public-key encryption method used on the Internet.

Semantic web: A set of design principles that will allow computers to be able to index Web sites, topics, and subjects, enabling computers to read Web pages and search engines to give richer and more accurate answers.

Semistructured data: Data (such as clickstreams and sensor data) which does not fit neatly into relational database structures.

Semistructured decision: A decision where problems and solutions are not clear-cut and often require judgment and expertise.

Sequence discovery: A data mining technique used to discover associations over time.

Server: Any computer on the network that enables access to files, databases, communications, and other services available to users of the network; it typically has a more advanced microprocessor, more memory, a larger cache, and more disk storage than a single-user computer.

Service: An individual software component designed to perform a specific task.

Service-level agreement: A contract specifying the level of service provided in terms of performance (e.g., as measured by uptime), warranties, disaster recovery, and so on.

Service-oriented architecture (SOA): A software architecture in which business processes are broken down into individual components (or services) that are designed to achieve the desired results for the service consumer (which can be either an application, another service, or a person).

Shopping bot: *See* Buyer agent.

Shrink-wrap license: A type of software license that is used primarily for consumer products; the contract is activated when the shrink wrap on the packaging has been removed.

Slicing and dicing: Analyzing data on subsets of certain dimensions.

Smart card: A special credit card–sized card containing a microprocessor chip, memory circuits, and often a magnetic stripe.

Social bookmarking: The sharing and categorization of Internet bookmarks by Internet users.

Social cataloging: The creation of categorizations by Internet users.

Social CRM: The use of social media for customer relationship management.

Social enterprise: A company using social media within its boundaries or between the company and its customers or stakeholders.

Social media: Web-based applications embodying core Web 2.0 values such as collaboration and social sharing, allowing people to communicate, interact, and collaborate in various ways.

Social media monitoring: The process of identifying and assessing the volume and sentiment of what is being said in social media about a company, individual, product, or brand.

Social network analysis: A technique that attempts to find groups of people who work together, to find people who don't collaborate but should, or to find experts in particular subject areas.

Social networking: Connecting to colleagues, family members, or friends for business or entertainment purposes.

Social online community: A community within a social network.

Social presence tools: *See Microblogging tools.*

Social search: A search functionality that attempts to increase the relevance of search results by including content from social networks, blogs, or microblogging services.

Social software: *See* Social media.

Soft data: Textual news stories or other nonanalytical information.

Software: A program (or set of programs) that tells the computer to perform certain processing functions.

Software as a service (SaaS): A cloud computing model in which a service provider offers applications via a cloud infrastructure.

Software asset management (SAM): A set of activities performed to better manage an organization's software infrastructure by helping to: consolidate and standardize software titles, decide when to retire unused software, or decide when to upgrade or replace software.

Software piracy: A type of computer crime where individuals make illegal copies of software protected by copyright laws.

Solid-state drive (SSD): A secondary storage technology using flash memory to store data.

Source code: A computer program's code written in a programming language.

Spam: Electronic junk mail.

Spam filter: A hardware or software device used to fight spam and other e-mail threats, such as directory harvest attacks, phishing attacks, viruses, and more.

Spear phishing: A sophisticated fraudulent e-mail attack that targets a specific person or organization by personalizing the message in order to make the message appear as if it is from a trusted source, such as an individual within the recipient's company, a government entity, or a well-known company.

Speech recognition: The process of converting spoken words into commands and data.

Spim: Spam sent via instant messaging.

Sponsored search: *See* Search advertising.

Spyware: Software that covertly gathers information about a user through an Internet connection without the user's knowledge.

Stand-alone application: A system that focuses on the specific needs of an individual department and is not designed to communicate with other systems in the organization.

Star network: A network with several workstations connected to a central hub.

Stickiness: A Web site's ability to attract and keep visitors.

Strategic: A way of thinking in which plans are made to accomplish specific long-term goals.

Strategic necessity: Something an organization must do in order to survive.

Strategic planning: The process of forming a vision of where the organization needs to head, converting that vision into measurable objectives and performance targets, and crafting a plan to achieve the desired results.

Streaming audio: Audio data streams, transmitted via specific protocols, that are available for immediate playback on the recipient's computer.

Streaming media: An umbrella term for streaming audio and streaming video; audio and video data streams, transmitted via specific protocols, that are available for immediate playback on the recipient's computer.

Streaming video: Video data streams, transmitted via specific protocols, that are available for immediate playback on the recipient's computer.

Structural firmness: A Web site's characteristics related to security and performance.

Structured data: Data (such as transaction data), which fit neatly into spreadsheets or databases.

Structured decision: A decision where the procedures to follow for a given situation can be specified in advance.

Structured Query Language (SQL): The most common language used to interface with databases.

Stuxnet: A computer worm designed to find and infect a particular piece of industrial hardware; used in an attack against Iranian nuclear plants.

Supercomputer: The most expensive and most powerful category of computers. It is primarily used to assist in solving massive research and scientific problems.

Supplier portal: A subset of an organization's extranet designed to automate the business processes that occur before, during, and after sales have been transacted between a single buyer and multiple suppliers. Also referred to as a "sourcing portal" or "procurement portal."

Supply chain: The collection of companies and processes involved in moving a product from the suppliers of raw materials, to the suppliers of intermediate components, to final production, and ultimately to the customer.

Supply chain analytics: The use of key performance indicators to monitor performance of the entire supply chain, including sourcing, planning, production, and distribution.

Supply chain effectiveness: The extent to which a company's supply chain is focusing on maximizing customer service, with lesser focus on procurement, production, and transportation costs.

Supply chain efficiency: The extent to which a company's supply chain is focusing on minimizing procurement, production, and transportation costs, sometimes by reducing customer service.

Supply chain execution (SCE): The execution of supply chain planning, involving the management of product flows, information flows, and financial flows.

Supply chain management (SCM): Information systems focusing on improving upstream information flows with two main objectives—to accelerate product development and to reduce costs associated with procuring raw materials, components, and services from suppliers.

Supply chain planning (SCP): The process of developing various resource plans to support the efficient and effective production of goods and services.

Supply chain visibility: The ability to track products as they move through the supply chain and to foresee external events.

Supply network: The network of multiple (sometimes interrelated) producers of supplies that a company uses.

Support activities: Business activities that enable the primary activities to take place. Support activities include administrative activities, infrastructure, human resources, technology development, and procurement.

Switch: A device used to connect multiple computers, servers, or printers to create a network.

Symmetric digital subscriber line (SDSL): A variant of DSL that supports the same data rates for upstream and downstream traffic.

Synchronous: Coordinated in time.

System clock: An electronic circuit inside a computer that generates pulses at a rapid rate for setting the pace of processing events.

System conversion: The process of decommissioning the current system and installing a new system into the organization.

System effectiveness: The extent to which a system enables people and/or the firm to accomplish goals or tasks well.

System efficiency: The extent to which a system enables people and/or a firm to do things faster, at lower cost, or with relatively little time and effort.

System software: The collection of programs that controls the basic operations of computer hardware.

Systems analysis: The second phase of the systems development life cycle in which the current ways of doing business are studied and alternative replacement systems are proposed.

Systems analysis and design: The process of designing, building, and maintaining information systems.

Systems analyst: The primary person responsible for performing systems analysis and design activities.

Systems benchmarking: A standardized set of performance tests designed to facilitate comparison between systems.

Systems design: The third phase of the systems development life cycle in which details of the chosen approach are developed.

Systems development life cycle (SDLC): A model describing the life of an information system from conception to retirement.

Systems implementation: The fourth phase of the systems development life cycle in which the information system is programmed, tested, installed, and supported.

Systems integration: Connecting separate information systems and data to improve business processes and decision making.

Systems maintenance: The process of systematically repairing and/or improving an information system.

Systems planning and selection: The first phase of the systems development life cycle in which potential projects are identified, selected, and planned.

T1 line: A dedicated digital transmission line that can carry 1.544 Mbps of data.

T3 line: A dedicated digital transmission line that can carry about 45 Mbps of data.

Table: A collection of related records in a database where each row is a record and each column is an attribute.

Tacit knowledge assets: Knowledge assets that reflect the processes and procedures located in employees' minds.

Tag cloud: A way to visualize user generated tags or content on a site, where the size of a word represents its importance or frequency.

Tagging: Adding metadata to media or other content.

Tangible benefit: A benefit of using a particular system or technology that is quantifiable.

Tangible cost: A cost of using a particular system of technology that is quantifiable.

Tape: A removable, high capacity, secondary storage medium allowing only for sequential access; typically used for archiving data.

Telecommunications network: A group of two or more computer systems linked together with communications equipment.

Terminal: A local input device used to enter data into mainframes in centralized computing systems.

Text mining: Analytical techniques for extracting information from textual documents.

Text recognition software: Software designed to convert handwritten text into computer-based characters.

Time bomb: A type of computer virus that lies in wait for a specific date before executing its instructions.

Top-level domain: A URL's suffix (i.e., .com, .edu, or .org) representing the highest level of Internet domain names in the domain name system.

Total cost of ownership (TCO): The cost of owning and operating a system, including the total cost of acquisition, as well as all costs associated with its ongoing use and maintenance.

Touch screen: A pointing device using a touch-sensitive computer display.

Transaction: Anything that occurs as part of daily business of which an organization must keep a record.

Transaction processing system (TPS): An information system designed to process day-to-day business-event data at the operational level of the organization.

Transaction support: Utilizing the Web to provide automatic support to clients and firms for conducting business online without human assistance.

Transmission Control Protocol/Internet Protocol (TCP/IP): The protocol of the Internet, which allows different interconnected networks to communicate using the same language.

Transmission media: The physical pathways to send data and information between two or more entities on a network.

Transnational business strategy: An international business strategy that allows companies to leverage the flexibility offered by a decentralized organization (to be more responsive to local conditions) while at the same time reaping economies of scale enjoyed by centralization; characterized by a balance between centralization and decentralization and interdependent resources.

Trojan horse: A program that appears to be a legitimate, benign program, but carries a destructive payload. Trojan horses typically do not replicate themselves.

Tunneling: A technology used by VPNs to encapsulate, encrypt, and securely transmit data over the public Internet infrastructure, enabling business partners to exchange information in a secured, private manner between organizational networks.

Unauthorized access: An information systems security breach where an unauthorized individual sees, manipulates, or otherwise handles electronically stored information.

Unicode: Character encoding method for representing characters and scripts beyond the Latin alphabet, including Chinese, Cyrillic, Hebrew, and Arabic.

Uniform Resource Locator (URL): The unique Internet address for a Web site and specific Web pages within sites.

Unstructured data: Data (such as audio and video data, comments on social networks, and so on) which does not have any identifiable structure.

Unstructured decision: A decision where few or no procedures to follow for a given situation can be specified in advance.

Upstream information flow: An information flow consisting of information received from another organization, such as from a supplier.

User agent: An intelligent agent that automatically performs specific tasks for a user, such as automatically sending a report at the first of the month, assembling customized news, or filling out a Web form with routine information.

Utilities: *See* Utility programs.

Utility computing: A form of on-demand computing where resources in terms of processing, data storage, or networking are rented on an as-needed basis. The organization only pays for the services used.

Utility program: Software designed to manage computer resources and files.

Value chain: The set of primary and support activities in an organization where value is added to a product or service.

Value chain analysis: The process of analyzing an organization's activities to determine where value is added to products and/or services and the costs that are incurred for doing so.

Value creation: An organization providing products at a lower cost or with superior (differentiated) benefits to the customer.

Value proposition: The utility that the product/service has to offer to customers.

Value system: A collection of interlocking company value chains.

Value-added network (VAN): Private, third-party–managed WANs typically used for B2B communications, offering services such as secure e-mail and translation of EDI standards to facilitate communication between a business and its suppliers and/or customers.

Vanilla version: The features and modules that a packaged software system comes with out of the box.

Vendor-managed inventory (VMI): A business model in which the suppliers to a manufacturer (or retailer) manage the manufacturer's (or retailer's) inventory levels based on preestablished service levels.

Vertical market: A market comprised of firms within a specific industry sector.

Video: Still and moving images that can be recorded, manipulated, and displayed on a computer.

Videoconferencing over IP: The use of Internet technologies for videoconferences.

Viral marketing: A type of marketing that resembles offline word-of-mouth communication in which advertising messages are spread similar to how real viruses are transmitted through offline social networks.

Virtual company: *See* Click-only business strategy.

Virtual meeting: A meeting taking place using an online environment.

Virtual private network (VPN): A network connection that is constructed dynamically within an existing network—often called a "secure tunnel"—in order to securely connect remote users or nodes to an organization's network.

Virtual team: A work team that is composed of members that may be from different organizations and different locations that forms and disbands as needed.

Virtual world: An online environment allowing people to communicate synchronously using 3D avatars.

Virus: A destructive program that disrupts the normal functioning of computer systems.

Virus prevention: A set of activities designed to detect and prevent computer viruses.

Visual analytics: The combination of various analysis techniques and interactive visualizations to solve complex problems.

Visual programming language: A programming language that has a graphical user interface (GUI) for the programmer and is designed for programming applications that will have a GUI.

Visualization: The display of complex data relationships using a variety of graphical methods.

Voice over IP (VoIP): The use of Internet technologies for placing telephone calls.

Voice-to-text software: An application that uses a microphone to monitor a person's speech and then converts the speech into text.

Volatile memory: Memory that loses its contents when the power is turned off.

Volume license: *See* enterprise license.

Warez: A slang term for stolen proprietary software that is sold or shared for free over the Internet.

Watermark: A digital or physical mark that is difficult to reproduce; used to prevent counterfeiting or to trace illegal copies to the original purchaser.

Web 2.0: A term used to describe dynamic Web applications that allow people to collaborate and share information online.

Web analytics: The analysis of Web surfers' behavior in order to improve a site's performance.

Web API: A Web application programming interface that provides a way for different components of software to interact and exchange data or functionality using common Web communication protocols.

Web browser: A software application that can be used to locate and display Web pages including text, graphics, and multimedia content.

Web content mining: Extracting textual information from Web documents.

Web crawler: An intelligent agent that continuously browses the Web for specific information (e.g., used by search engines). Also known as a "Web spider."

Web page: A hypertext document stored on a Web server that contains not only information, but also references or links to other documents that contain related information.

Web page builder: A program for assisting in the creation and maintenance of Web pages.

Web server: A computer used to host Web sites.

Web service: A component that allows data to be accessed without intimate knowledge of other organizations' systems, enabling machine-to-machine interaction over the Internet.

Web site: A collection of interlinked Web pages typically belonging to the same person or business organization.

Web spider: *See* Web crawler.

Web usage mining: An analysis of a Web site's usage patterns, such as navigational paths or time spent.

Web vandalism: The act of defacing Web sites.

Webcam: A small camera that is used to transmit real-time video images within desktop videoconferencing systems.

Webcast: A digital media stream that can be distributed to and played by digital media players.

Webcasting: The process of publishing Webcasts.

Weighted multicriteria analysis: A method for deciding among different information systems investments or alternative designs for a given system in which requirements and constraints are weighted on the basis of their importance.

What-if analysis: An analysis of the effects hypothetical changes to data have on the results.

Wide area network (WAN): A computer network that spans a relatively large geographic area; typically used to connect two or more LANs.

Wi-Fi network (wireless fidelity): Wireless LAN, based on the 802.11 family of standards.

Wiki: A Web site allowing people to post, edit, comment, and access information. In contrast to a regular Web site, a wiki is linked to a database that keeps a history of all prior versions and changes; therefore, a wiki allows viewing prior versions of the site as well as reversing any changes made to the content.

WikiLeaks: An information disclosure portal where volunteers submit and analyze classified and restricted material provided by whistleblowers.

Wikipedia: An online encyclopedia using wiki technology.

Wireless access point: A networking device that transmits and receives wireless (Wi-Fi) signals to allow wireless devices to connect to the network.

Wireless broadband: Wireless transmission technology with speeds similar to DSL and cable that requires line of sight between the sender and receiver.

Wireless controller: A networking device that manages multiple access points and can be used to manage transmission power and channel allocation to establish desired coverage throughout a building and minimize interference between individual access points.

Wireless local area network (WLAN): A local area network that uses a wireless transmission protocol.

Workstation: A computer offering lower performance than mainframes but higher performance than personal computers that is designed for medical, engineering, or animation and graphics design uses, and is optimized for visualization and rendering of three-dimensional models.

World Wide Web (WWW): A system of Internet servers that support documents formatted in HTML, which supports links to other documents as well as graphics, audio, and video files.

Worm: A destructive computer code that is designed to copy and send itself throughout networked computers.

XML tag: A command that is inserted into a document in order to specify how information should be interpreted and used.

Zombie computer: A virus-infected computer that can be used to launch attacks on Web sites.

References

CHAPTER 1

Ackoff, R. L. (1989). From data to wisdom. *Journal of Applied Systems Analysis*, 16, 3–9.

Anand, G. (2011, April 5). India graduates millions, but few are fit to hire. *The Wall Street Journal*. Retrieved July 26, 2012, from http://online.wsj.com/article/SB10001424052748703515504576142092863219826.html.

Anonymous. (2012, July). Information technology manager salary. *Salary.com*. Retrieved July 20, 2012, from http://www1.salary.com/Information-Technology-Manager-salary.html.

Battelle, J. (2010, March 5). The database of intentions is far larger than I thought. *Searchblog*. Retrieved July 26, 2012, from http://battellemedia.com/archives/2010/03/the_database_of_intentions_is_far_larger_than_i_thought.php.

Brandel, M. (2009, December 29). 6 hottest IT skills for 2010. *Computerworld*. Retrieved July 20, 2012, from http://www.computerworld.com/s/article/345529/6_hottest_IT_skills_for_2010.

Bureau of Labor Statistics. (2012, March 27). Occupational employment and wages, May 2011. *BLS.gov*. Retrieved July 20, 2012, from http://www.bls.gov/oes/current/oes113021.htm.

Bureau of Labor Statistics. (2012, July 11). Occupational outlook handbook: Computer and information systems managers. *BLS.gov*. Retrieved July 20, 2012, from http://www.bls.gov/oco/ocos258.htm.

Carr, N. (2003). IT doesn't matter. *Harvard Business Review, 81*(5), 41–49.

Carr, N. (2004). *Does IT matter? Information technology and the corrosion of competitive advantage*. Boston: Harvard Business School Press.

Collett, S. (2006). Hot skills, cold skills: The IT worker of 2010 won't be a technology guru but rather a "versatilist." *Computerworld*. Retrieved July 20, 2012, from http://www.computerworld.com/s/article/112360/Hot_Skills_Cold_Skills.

Drucker, P. (1959). *Landmarks of tomorrow*. New York: Harper.

Elgan, M. (2010, February 20). Mike Elgan: How Buzz, Facebook and Twitter create "social insecurity." *Computerworld*. Retrieved July 20, 2012, from http://www.computerworld.com/s/article/9159679/Mike_Elgan_How_Buzz_Facebook_and_Twitter_create_social_insecurity_.

Epps, S.R., Gownder, J.P., Golvin, C.S., Bodine, K., & Corbett, A.E. (2011, May 17). *What the post-PC era really means*. Cambridge, MA: Forrest Research.

Farrell, D., Kaka, N., & Stürze, S. (2005, September). Ensuring India's offshoring future. *McKinsey Quarterly*. Retrieved July 20, 2012, from https://www.mckinseyquarterly.com/Ensuring_Indias_offshoring_future_1660.

Friedman, T. L. (2007). *The world is flat 3.0: A brief history of the twenty-first century*. New York: Farrar, Straus and Giroux.

Galbraith, J. K. (1987). *The affluent society*. New York: Houghton Mifflin.

Gartner (2011, December 21). Forecast analysis: IT outsourcing, worldwide, 2010-2015, 4Q11 update. Retrieved July 26, 2012, from http://www.gartner.com/id=1881228.

Healey, M. (2012, May). 2012 consumerization of IT survey. *InformationWeek*. Retrieved July 31, 2012, from http://reports.informationweek.com.

Heath, N. (2009, November 19). Outsourcers to fall victim to cloud computing rush? *ZDNet*. Retrieved July 20, 2012, from http://www.zdnet.com/outsourcers-to-fall-victim-to-cloud-computing-rush-3040153103.

Hinchcliffe, D. (2011, October 2). The "Big Five" IT trends of the next half decade: Mobile, social, cloud, consumerization, and big data. *ZDNet*. Retrieved July 26, 2012, from http://www.zdnet.com/blog/hinchcliffe/the-big-five-it-trends-of-the-next-half-decade-mobile-social-cloud-consumerization-and-big-data/1811.

Hofmann, P. (2011, October 15). The big five IT megatrends. *Slideshare*. Retrieved July 26, 2012, from http://www.slideshare.net/paulhofmann/the-big-five-it-mega-trends.

International Monetary Fund. (2002). Globalization: Threat or opportunity? Retrieved July 20, 2012, from http://www.imf.org/external/np/exr/ib/2000/041200to.htm.

King, J. (2003, September 15). IT's global itinerary: Offshore outsourcing is inevitable. *Computerworld*. Retrieved July 20, 2012, from http://www.computerworld.com/managementtopics/outsourcing/story/0,10801,84861,00.html.

King, J. (2011, June 6). Extreme automation: FedEx Ground hubs speed deliveries. *Computerworld*. Retrieved July 26, 2012, from http://www.computerworld.com/s/

article/356328/Extreme_automation_FedEx_Ground_hubs_speed_deliveries.

Leung, L. (2009). 10 hot skills for 2009. *Global Knowledge*. Retrieved July 20, 2012, from http://www.globalknowledge.com/training/generic.asp?pageid=2321.

Lundberg, A. (2004, May 1). Interview with N. Carr. *CIO.com*. Retrieved July 20, 2012, from http://www.cio.com/article/32264/Interview_Nicholas_Carr_The_Argument_Over_IT.

Mallaby, S. (2006, January 2). In India, engineering success. *Washington Post*. Retrieved July 20, 2012, from http://www.washingtonpost.com/wp-dyn/content/article/2006/01/02/AR2006010200566.html.

Mason, R. O. (1986). Four ethical issues of the information age. *MIS Quarterly, 10*(1), 5–12.

Michaeli, R. (2009). *Competitive intelligence: Competitive advantage through analysis of competition, markets and technologies*. New York: Springer.

NACE (2011, April 14). Top-paid majors for 2010-2011. *Naceweb.org*. Retrieved July 31, 2012, from http://www.naceweb.org/s04142011/top_paid_graduates.

Osterman, M. (2011, August). Embracing and empowering the consumerization of IT. *Yousendit.com*. Retrieved July 31, 2012, from http://resources.yousendit.com/rs/yousendit/images/Embracing%20and%20Empowering%20the%20Consumerization%20of%20IT.pdf.

Overby, S. (2006, September 5). Global outsourcing guide 2006. *CIO.com*. Retrieved July 20, 2012, from http://www.cio.com.au/article/170687/global_outsourcing_guide_2006.

Pettey, C. (2011, November 8). Gartner says consumerization will drive at least four mobile management styles. *Gartner*. Retrieved July 26, 2012, from http://www.gartner.com/it/page.jsp?id=1842615.

Porter, M. E. (1985). *Competitive advantage: Creating and sustaining superior performance*. New York: Free Press.

Porter, M. E., & Millar, V. (1985). How information gives you competitive advantage. *Harvard Business Review, 63*(4), 149–161.

Rosen, E. (2011, January 11). Every worker is a knowledge worker. *BusinessWeek*. Retrieved July 26, 2012, from http://www.businessweek.com/managing/content/jan2011/ca20110110_985915.htm.

Savitz, E. (2012, February 20). Consumerization of IT: Getting beyond the myths. *Forbes*. Retrieved July 26, 2012, from http://www.forbes.com/sites/ciocentral/2012/02/20/consumerization-of-it-getting-beyond-the-myths.

Sipior, J. C., & Ward, B. T. (1995). The ethical and legal quandary of e-mail privacy. *Communications of the ACM, 38*(12), 48–54.

Tapscott, D. (2004, May 1). The engine that drives success: The best companies have the best business models because they have the best IT strategies. *CIO.com*. Retrieved July 20, 2012, from http://www.cio.com/article/32265/IT_The_Engine_That_Drives_Success.

Todd, P., McKeen, J., & Gallupe, R. (1995). The evolution of IS job skills: A content analysis of IS jobs. *MIS Quarterly, 19*(1), 1–27.

TrendMicro. (2011). Consumerization of IT. Retrieved July 26, 2012, from http://www.trendmicro.com/cloud-content/us/pdfs/business/reports/rpt_consumerization-of-it.pdf.

United States Census. (2011, September). Education and synthetic work-life earnings estimates. Retrieved June 15, 2012, from http://www.census.gov/prod/2011pubs/acs-14.pdf.

Vellante, D. (2011, November 14). When IT consumers become technology providers. *Cliff Davies*. Retrieved July 26, 2012, from http://cliffdavies.com/blog/cloudcomputing/when-it-consumers-become-technology-providers.

Veritude (2009). 2009 IT hiring outlook. Retrieved July 20, 2012, from https://www.vtrenz.net/imaeds/ownerassets/1010/Ver_WP_2009%20IT%20Outlook%20Report_FINAL.pdf.

Voorhout, M. (2012, January 23). Big data: It ain't over till it's over. *Capgemini*. Retrieved July 26, 2012, from http://www.capgemini.com/technology-blog/2012/01/big-data/.

Weisband, S. P., & Reinig, B. A. (1995, December). Managing user perceptions of e-mail privacy. *Communications of the ACM, 38*(12), 40–47.

CHAPTER 2

Alavi, M., & Young, G. (1992). Information technologies in international enterprise: An organizing framework. In S. Palvia, P. Palvia, & R. Zigli (Eds.), *Global issues in information technology management* (pp. 495–516). Harrisburg, PA: Idea Group.

Anderson, C. (2009). *Free: The future of a radical price*. New York: Hyperion.

Applegate, L. M., Austin, R. D., & Soule, D.L. (2009). *Corporate information strategy and management* (8th ed.). New York: McGraw-Hill.

Bakos, J. Y., & Treacy, M. E. (1986). Information technology and corporate strategy: A research perspective. *MIS Quarterly, 10*(2), 107–120.

Bartlett, C., & Ghoshal, S. (1998). *Managing across borders: The transnational solution*. Boston: Harvard Business School Press.

Christensen, C. M. (1997). *The innovator's dilemma*. Boston: Harvard Business School Press.

Christensen, C. M., & Raynor, M. E. (2003). *The innovator's solution: Creating and sustaining successful growth*. Boston: Harvard Business School Press.

Christensen, C. M., Roth, E. A., & Anthony, S. D. (2004). *Seeing what's next: Using theories of innovation to predict industry change*. Boston: Harvard Business School Press.

Garvin, D. A. (1993). Building a learning organization. *Harvard Business Review, 71*(4), 78–91.

Ghoshal, S. (1987). Global strategy: An organizing framework. *Strategic Management Journal, 8*(5), 425–440.

Hitt, M. A., Ireland, R. D., & Hoskisson, R. E. (2013). *Strategic management: Competitiveness and globalization* (10th ed.). Boston: South-Western.

Karimi, J., & Konsynski, B. R. (1991). Globalization and information management strategies. *Journal of Management Information Systems, 7*(4), 7–26.

Maddox, J. (1999, December). The unexpected science to come. *Scientific American, 281*, 62–67.

McKeen, J. D., Guimaraes, T., & Wetherbe, J. C. (1994). A comparative analysis of MIS project selection mechanisms. *Database, 25*(2), 43–59.

Osterwalder, A., & Pigneur, Y. (2010). *Business model generation*. Hoboken, NJ: Wiley.

Porter, M. E. (1979, March–April). How competitive forces shape strategy. *Harvard Business Review, 57*, 137–145.

Porter, M. E. (1985). *Competitive advantage: Creating and sustaining superior performance*. New York: Free Press.

Porter, M. E. (2001). Strategy and the internet. *Harvard Business Review, 79*(3), 62–78.

Prahalad, C. K., & Doz, Y. L. (1987). *The multinational mission: Balancing local demands and global vision*. New York: Free Press.

Ramarapu, N. K., & Lado, A. A. (1995). Linking information technology to global business strategy to gain competitive advantage: An integrative model. *Journal of Information Technology, 10*, 115–124.

Rogers, E. (2003). *Diffusion of innovations* (5th ed.). New York: Free Press.

Rubin, H. (2004, June 1). Practical counsel for capturing IT value: The elusive value of infrastructure. *CIO.com*. Retrieved July 20, 2012, from http://www.cio.com/article/32321/Real_Value_The_Elusive_Value_of_Infrastructure.

Shank, J., & Govindarajan, V. (1993). *Strategic cost management: Three key themes for managing costs effectively*. New York: Free Press.

Wheeler, B. C. (2002). NeBIC: A dynamic capabilities theory for assessing net-enablement. *Information Systems Research, 13*(2), 125–146.

Zuboff, S. (1988). *In the age of the smart machine: The future of work and power*. New York: Basic Books.

CHAPTER 3

Amazon. (2012). Amazon Web services. *Amazon.com*. Retrieved July 20, 2012, from http://aws.amazon.com.

Berghel, H. (1996). U.S. technology policy in the information age. *Communications of the ACM, 39*(6), 15–18.

Belson, D. (2012). The state of the Internet. 4th quarter, 2011 report. *Akamai*. Retrieved July 31, 2012, from http://akamai.com/stateoftheinternet.

Golden, B. (2009, January 22). The case against cloud computing, part one. *CIO.com*. Retrieved June 4, 2012, from http://www.cio.com/article/477473/The_Case_Against_Cloud_Computing_Part_One.

Google. (2012). Google's green initiatives. *Google.com*. Retrieved July 20, 2012, from http://www.google.com/green.

Hoffer, J. A., George, J. F., & Valacich, J. S. (2014). *Modern systems analysis and design* (7th ed.). Upper Saddle River, NJ: Pearson Prentice Hall.

Hoffer, J., Ramesh, V., & Topi, H. (2013). *Modern database management* (11th ed.). Upper Saddle River, NJ: Pearson Prentice Hall.

Hofmann, P., & Woods, D. (2010). Cloud computing: The limits of public clouds for business applications. *IEEE Internet Computing, November/December*, 90–93.

Laberta, C. (2011). *Computers are your future* (11th ed.). Upper Saddle River, NJ: Pearson Prentice Hall.

National Institute of Standards and Technology. (2011, September). The NIST definition of cloud computing. Retrieved July 20, 2012, from http://csrc.nist.gov/publications/nistpubs/800-145/SP800-145.pdf.

Netcraft. (2012, May 12). May 2012 Web server survey. *Netcraft.com*. Retrieved July 20, 2012, from http://news.netcraft.com/archives/2012/05/02/may-2012-web-server-survey.html.

Panko, R., & Panko, J. (2013). *Business data networks and security* (9th ed.). Upper Saddle River, NJ: Pearson Prentice Hall.

Stallings, W. (2011). *Network security essentials: Applications and standards* (4th ed.). Upper Saddle River, NJ: Pearson Prentice Hall.

Tebutt, D. (2010, February 9). Ten green issues for CIOs. *Techworld*. Retrieved July 20, 2012, from http://features.techworld.com/green-it/3212282/ten-green-issues-for-cios.

Te'eni, D., Carey, J. M., & Zhang, P. (2007). *Human-computer interaction: Developing effective organizational information systems*. New York: Wiley.

Top 500. (2012, June). Retrieved July 20, 2012, from http://www.top500.org/lists/2012/06.

Violino, B. (2011, December 5). Preparing for the real cost of cloud computing. *Computerworld*. Retrieved June 4, 2012, from http://www.computerworld.com/s/article/359383/The_Real_Costs_of_Cloud_Computing.

Wheeland, M. (2007, May 2). Green computing at Google. Retrieved July 20, 2012, from http://www.greenbiz.com/news/2007/05/02/green-computing-google.

CHAPTER 4

ABI Research. (2010, February 19). Shopping by mobile will grow to $119 billion in 2015. Retrieved July 20, 2012, from http://www.abiresearch.com/press/1605-Shopping+by+Mobile+Will+Grow+to+$119+Billion+in+2015.

Adobe.com (2012). The impact of tablet visitors on retail websites. *Adobe.com*. Retrieved June 15, 2012, from http://success.adobe.com/assets/en/downloads/whitepaper/13926_digital_index_tablet_report.pdf.

Alipay. (2012). About Alipay. Retrieved July 20, 2012, from https://www.alipay.com/static/aboutalipay/englishabout.htm.

Anderson, C. (2004). The long tail. *Wired*. Retrieved July 20, 2012, from http://www.wired.com/wired/archive/12.10/tail.html.

Anderson, C. (2006). *The long tail: Why the future of business is selling less of more*. New York: Hyperion.

Anonymous. (2012, July 31). Industry adoption updates. *CheckImage Central*. Retrieved July 31, 2012, from http://www.checkimagecentral.org/industryAdoptionUpdates.

Benson, C. (2009, April 2). The problem with B2B payments. *Paymentsviews*. Retrieved July 20, 2012, from http://paymentsviews.com/2009/04/02/the-problem-with-b2b-payments.

California Office of Privacy Protection (2012, June 7). Identity theft. Retrieved June 15, 2012, from http://www.privacy.ca.gov/consumers/identity_theft.shtml.

Chatterjee, D., & Sambamurthy, V. (1999). Business implications of Web technology: An insight into usage of the World Wide Web by U.S. companies. *Electronic Markets, 9*(2), 126–131.

CNet Australia (2012, June 13). Do we really need DRM? *CNet.com.au*. Retrieved June 15, 2012, from http://www.cnet.com.au/do-we-really-need-drm-339339633.htm.

EFF (2010). Is your printer spying on you? *Electronic Frontier Foundation*. Retrieved July 31, 2012, from http://www.eff.org/issues/printers.

Evan, P., & Wurster, T. (1999). *Blown to bits: How the new economics of information transforms strategy*. Boston: Harvard Business School Press.

eMarketer. (2012, April 5). Apparel drives US retail ecommerce sales growth. *eMarketer.com*. Retrieved June 15, 2012, from http://www.emarketer.com/PressRelease.aspx?R=1008956.

Federal Trade Commission. (2010, May 21). A consumer's guide to e-payments. *ftc.gov*. Retrieved July 20, 2012, from http://www.ftc.gov/bcp/edu/pubs/consumer/tech/tec01.shtm.

Firstdata. (2009, October 26). Why b2b payments need a "BizPal": An international perspective. Retrieved July 20, 2012, from http://www.firstdata.com/en_au/insights/b2b_payments_intl_marketinsights.

Google. (2007). Marketing and advertising using Google. Retrieved July 20, 2012, from books.google.com/intl/en/googlebooks/pdf/MarketingAndAdvertisingUsingGoogle.pdf.

Internet Crime Complaint Center. (2010, March 12). 2011 IC3 annual report. Retrieved July 20, 2012, from http://www.ic3.gov/media/annualreport/2011_IC3Report.pdf.

Jayaraman, K., & Blank, P. (2012, February). 2012 Identity fraud report: Consumers taking control to reduce their risk of fraud. *Javelinstrategy.com*. Retrieved June 15, 2012, from https://www.javelinstrategy.com/uploads/web_brochure/1201.R_2012%20Identity%20Fraud%20Consumer%20Report.pdf.

Kalakota, R., Oliva, R. A., & Donath, E. (1999). Move over, e-commerce. *Marketing Management, 8*(3), 23–32.

Laudon, K., & Guercio Traver, C. (2010). *E-commerce 2010* (6th ed.). New York: Pearson Addison Wesley.

Lee, M., & Lin, D. (2009, November 24). Alipay to become world's No 1 e-payment firm. *Reuters.* Retrieved July 20, 2012, from http://www.reuters.com/article/idUSSHA32192420091124.

Li, S. (2012, April 12). Many people see risks in online banking and shopping, survey says. *Los Angeles Times.* Retrieved June 15, 2012, from http://articles.latimes.com/2012/apr/12/business/la-fi-mo-banking-shopping-online-20120411.

Looney, C., & Chatterjee, D. (2002). Web enabled transformation of the brokerage industry: An analysis of emerging business models. *Communications of the ACM, 45*(8), 75–81.

Looney, C., Jessup, L., & Valacich, J. (2004). Emerging business models for mobile brokerage services. *Communications of the ACM, 47*(6), 71–77.

MacMillan, D. (2009, August 31). Can Hulu's high prices hold? *BusinessWeek.* Retrieved July 20, 2012, from http://www.businessweek.com/the_thread/techbeat/archives/2009/08/can_hulus_high.html.

MobileInfo. (2008). M-commerce. *MobileInfo.com.* Retrieved July 20, 2012, from http://www.mobileinfo.com/Mcommerce/index.htm.

Nystedt, D. (2009, October 12). Researchers advise cyber self defense in the cloud. *PCWorld.* Retrieved July 20, 2012, from http://www.pcworld.com/businesscenter/article/173467/researchers_advise_cyber_self_defense_in_the_cloud.html.

Priceline. (2012). 2011 annual report. Retrieved July 20, 2012, from http://ir.priceline.com/common/download/download.cfm?companyid=PCLN&fileid=561766&filekey=CB103EAD-2799-49FD-991C-F192C5F8223A&filename=PCLN_2011_Annual_Report.pdf.

Quelch, J. A., & Klein, L. R. (1996, Spring). The Internet and internal marketing. *Sloan Management Review, 63,* 60–75.

Rao, L. (2011, June 17). Forrester: U.S. Mobile commerce to reach $31 billion by 2016. *Techcrunch.* Retrieved June 13, 2012, from http://techcrunch.com/2011/06/17/forrester-u-s-mobile-commerce-to-reach-31-billion-by-2016.

Seideman, T. (1996) What Sam Walton learned from the Berlin airlift. *Audacity: The Magazine of Business Experience*, Spring, 52–61.

Szuprowicz, B.O. (1998). *Extranets and Intranets: E-Commerce business strategies for the future.* Charleston, SC: Computer Technology Research.

Turban, E., King, D., Lee, J., Liang, T. P., & Turban, D. (2012). *Electronic commerce 2012: A managerial perspective* (7th ed.). Upper Saddle River, NJ: Pearson.

U.S. Census Bureau. (2012, May 10). E-stats 2010. Retrieved July 20, 2012, from http://www.census.gov/econ/estats/2010/2010reportfinal.pdf.

U.S. Census Bureau News. (2012, May 17). Quarterly retail e-commerce sales 1st quarter 2012. Retrieved June 15, 2012, from http://www.census.gov/retail/mrts/www/data/pdf/ec_current.pdf.

Valacich, J. S., Parboteeah, D. V., & Wells, J. D. (2007). The online consumer's hierarchy of needs. *Communications of the ACM, 50*(9), 84–90.

VanBoskirk, S. (2011, August 24). *US interactive marketing forecast, 2011 to 2016.* Cambridge, MA: Forrester Research.

Visa (2008). Visa e-commerce merchants' guide to risk management. Retrieved June 15, 2012, from http://usa.visa.com/download/merchants/visa_risk_management_guide_ecommerce.pdf.

Wells, J., & Gobeli, D. (2003). The three R framework: Improving e-strategy across reach, richness and range. *Business Horizons, 46*(2), 5–14.

Wells, J. D., Valacich, J. S., & Hess, T. J. (2011). What signals are you sending? How website quality influences perceptions of product quality and purchase intentions. *MIS Quarterly, 35*(2), 373–396.

Yang, A., & Birge, J. (2011). How inventory is (should be) financed? Trade credit in supply chains with demand uncertainty and costs of financial distress. Retrieved July 20, 2012, from http://papers.ssrn.com/sol3/papers.cfm?abstract_id=1734682.

Zwass, V. (1996). Electronic commerce: Structures and issues. *International Journal of Electronic Commerce, 1*(1), 3–23.

CHAPTER 5

Anonymous. (2012, July 31). Facebook.com site info. *Alexa.com.* Retrieved July 31, 2012, from http://www.alexa.com/siteinfo/facebook.com.

Arrington, M. (2007). Engadget knocks $4 billion off Apple market cap on bogus iPhone email. *Techcrunch.* Retrieved July 20, 2012, from http://www.techcrunch.com/2007/05/16/engadget-knocks-4-billion-of-apple-market-cap-on-bogus-iphone-email.

Baekdal, T. (2006, November 23). 7 tricks to viral Web marketing. *Baekdal.com.* Retrieved July 20, 2012, from http://www.baekdal.com/media/viral-marketing-tricks.

Brown, D. (2010, June 21). PR disaster aside, BP should leave satire alone. *CNN.com.* Retrieved July 20, 2012, from http://www.cnn.com/2010/TECH/web/06/21/bp.fake.twitter.norm/index.html.

Carr, N. (2005). The amorality of Web 2.0. Retrieved July 20, 2012, from http://www.roughtype.com/archives/2005/10/the_amorality_o.php.

CBS. (2005). CBA ousts 4 for Bush guard story. *CBS News.* Retrieved July 20, 2012, from http://www.cbsnews.com/stories/2005/01/10/national/main665727.shtml.

Cisco. (2011). 2011 Cisco connected world technology report. Retrieved July 12, 2012, from http://www.cisco.com/en/US/solutions/ns341/ns525/ns537/ns705/ns1120/2011-CCWTR-Chapter-3-All-Finding.pdf.

Clearswift. (2011, September 6). Worldwide clampdown on technology as businesses overreact to high profile data breaches. Retrieved July 12, 2012, from http://www.clearswift.com/news/press-releases/worldwide-clampdown-on-technology-as-businesses-overreact-to-high-profile-data-breaches.

Cook, N. (2008). *Enterprise 2.0: How social software will change the future of work.* Burlington, VT: Gower.

Flandez, R. (2009, April 20). Domino's response offers lesson in crisis management. *Wall Street Journal.* Retrieved July 20, 2012, from http://blogs.wsj.com/independentstreet/2009/04/20/dominos-response-offers-lessons-in-crisis-management.

Francis, J. A., & Harrigan, G. M. (2010). Jumping the boundaries of corporate IT: Accenture global research on Millennials' use of technology. Retrieved July 20, 2012, from http://nstore.accenture.com/technology/millennials/global_millennial_generation_research.pdf.

Gaudin, S. (2009, October 6). Study: 54% of companies ban Facebook, Twitter at work. *Computerworld.* Retrieved July 20, 2012, from http://www.computerworld.com/s/article/9139020/Study_54_of_companies_ban_Facebook_Twitter_at_work.

Gonzalez, N. (2012, July 31). Facebook marketing statistics, demographics, reports, and news. Retrieved July 31, 2012, from http://www.checkfacebook.com.

Hinchcliffe, D. (2010, April 14). Enterprise 2.0 and improved business performance. *ZDNet*. Retrieved July 20, 2012, from http://www.zdnet.com/blog/hinchcliffe/enterprise-20-and-improved-business-performance/1355.

Jackson, E. (2012, April 30). Here's why Google and Facebook might completely disappear in the next 5 years. *Forbes.com*. Retrieved July 11, 2012, from http://www.forbes.com/sites/ericjackson/2012/04/30/heres-why-google-and-facebook-might-completely-disappear-in-the-next-5-years.

Jiao, P. (2010, August 17). The traits that separate China's Net from rest. *South China Morning Post*. Retrieved August 17, 2012, from http://www.scmp.com.

Keen, W. (2007). *The cult of the amateur: How today's Internet is killing our culture*. New York: Doubleday.

Khan, S. (2008, June 24). Enterprise 2.0—Giving the hype a second thought. *CIOUpdate.com*. Retrieved July 20, 2012, from http://www.cioupdate.com/reports/article.php/11050_3755056_1/Enterprise-20—Giving-the-Hype-a-Second-Thought.htm.

Kravets, D. (2010, June 18). Utah attorney general announces execution on Twitter. *Wired.com*. Retrieved July 20, 2012, from http://www.wired.com/threatlevel/2010/06/execution-announced-on-twitter.

MacManus, R. (2007, August 7). Eric Schmidt defines Web 3.0. Retrieved July 20, 2012, from http://www.readwriteweb.com/archives/eric_schmidt_defines_web_30.php.

Madden, M., & Zickuhr, K. (2011, August 26). 65% of online adults use social networking sites. *Pew Research*. Retrieved July 31, 2012, from http://pewinternet.org/Reports/2011/Social-Networking-Sites.aspx.

Mascarenhas, A. (2010, June 4). BP's global PR vs. BPGlobalPR. *Newsweek*. Retrieved July 20, 2012, from http://www.newsweek.com/2010/06/04/bp-s-global-pr-vs-bpglobalpr.html.

McAfee, A. (2006a, April 1). Enterprise 2.0: The dawn of emergent collaboration. *MIT Sloan Management Review, 47*(3), 21–28.

McAfee, A. (2006b, May 27). Enterprise 2.0, version 2.0. Retrieved July 20, 2012, from http://andrewmcafee.org/2006/05/enterprise_20_version_20.

Meyerson, B., & Wang, A. (2009, July 29). Tweet lawsuit: Chicago landlord sues ex-tenant over tweet complaining about apartment. *Chicago Tribune*. Retrieved July 20, 2012, from http://www.chicagotribune.com/news/local/chi-twitter-suit-29-jul29,0,2500898.story.

Microsoft Corporation. (2007a, February 15). Major cosmetics producer deploys Microsoft search technology to increase efficiency. Retrieved October July 20, 2012, from http://www.microsoft.com/en-us/download/details.aspx?id=836.

Microsoft Corporation. (2007b, February 20). Leading global coffee retailer improves business processes and enhances store Web portal with Microsoft Office SharePoint Server. Retrieved July 20, 2012, from http://www.microsoft.com/en-us/download/details.aspx?id=8178.

Newman, C. (2012, May 1). A new internet for a new decade—are we in Web 3.0? *OttoPilot Media*. Retrieved July 11, 2012, from http://info.ottopilotmedia.com/blog/bid/124993/A-New-Internet-For-A-New-Decade-Are-We-In-Web-3-0.

Nielsen, J. (2006, November 6). 100 million Websites. *Jacob Nielsen's Alertbox*. Retrieved July 20, 2012, from http://www.useit.com/alertbox/web-growth.html.

Nielsen (2011). State of the media: Social media report Q3. *Nielsen.com*. Retrieved July 31, 2012, from http://www.nielsen.com/content/corporate/us/en/insights/reports-downloads/2011/social-media-report-q3.html.

Preidt, R. (2008, May 2). "Virtual" health teams boost patient care. Retrieved July 20, 2012, from http://abcnews.go.com/Health/Healthday/story?id=4777948.

Prescott, L. (2010, February 10). 54% of US Internet users on Facebook, 27% on MySpace. *SocialBeat*. Retrieved July 20, 2012, from http://venturebeat.com/2010/02/10/54-of-us-internet-users-on-facebook-27-on-myspace.

Rayport, J. (1996, December 31). The virus of marketing. *Fast Company.com*. Retrieved July 20, 2012, from http://www.fastcompany.com/magazine/06/virus.html.

Reynolds, C. (2009, July 7). Smashed guitar, YouTube song—United is listening now. *Los Angeles Times*. Retrieved July 20, 2012, from http://articles.latimes.com/2009/jul/07/travel/la-tr-smash-guitar-united-07072009.

Salesforce.com. (2012). The little blue book of social enterprise transformation. *Salesforce.com*. Retrieved July 31, 2012, from https://www.salesforce.com/form/pdf/social-enterprise-bluebook.jsp.

Sarker, S., & Sahay, S. (2002). Understanding virtual team development: An interpretive study. *Journal of the AIS, 3*, 247–285.

Sessums, C. D. (2009, December 17). A simple definition: Web 2.0. Retrieved July 20, 2012, from http://www.csessums.com/2009/12/a-simple-definition-web-2-0.

Smythe, J. (2007). *The CEO: The chief engagement officer: Turning hierarchy upside down to drive performance*. Burlington, VT: Gower.

Surowiecki, J. (2004). *The wisdom of crowds*. New York: Doubleday.

Wagner, M. (2002, May 23). Saving trees and serving up benefits. *Internet Retailer*. Retrieved July 20, 2012, from http://www.internetretailer.com/2002/05/23/saving-trees-and-serving-up-benefits.

Wikipedia. (2012, July 20). In *Wikipedia, The Free Encyclopedia*. Retrieved July 20, 2012, from http://en.wikipedia.org/w/index.php?title=Wikipedia&oldid=503214889.

World Wide Web Consortium. (2008). Widgets 1.0: Requirements. Retrieved July 20, 2012, from http://www.w3.org/TR/2008/WD-widgets-reqs-20080625.

CHAPTER 6

Alavi, M., & Leidner, D. (1999). Knowledge management systems: Issues, challenges, and benefits. *Communications of the AIS, 1*(Article 7).

Awad, E. M., & Ghaziri, H. M. (2004). *Knowledge management*. Upper Saddle River, NJ: Pearson Prentice Hall.

Blumberg, R., & Atre, S. (2003, February 1). The problem with unstructured data. *Information Management Magazine*. Retrieved July 20, 2012, from http://www.information-management.com/issues/20030201/6287-1.html.

Business Objects. (2008). Business intelligence—Now more than ever. Retrieved July 20, 2012, from http://www.clariba.com/pdf/bi_nowmorethanever.pdf.

Business Objects. (n.d.). Expanding BI's role by including predictive analytics. Retrieved July 20, 2012, from http://www.infoworld.com/t/business-intelligenceanalytics/wp/expanding-bi%E2%80%99s-role-including-predictive-analytics-638.

Checkland, P. B. (1981). *Systems thinking, systems practice*. Chichester, UK: Wiley.

Clarke, K. C. (2011). *Getting started with geographic information systems* (5th ed.). Upper Saddle River, NJ: Pearson Prentice Hall.

Dumbill, E. (2012, January 19). Volume, velocity, variety: What you need to know about Big Data. *Forbes.* Retrieved July 19, 2012, from http://www.forbes.com/sites/oreillymedia/2012/01/19/volume-velocity-variety-what-you-need-to-know-about-big-data.

Economist Intelligence Unit. (2007). In search of clarity: Unravelling the complexities of executive decision-making. Retrieved July 20, 2012, from http://graphics.eiu.com/upload/EIU_In_search_of_clarity.pdf.

Economist Intelligence Unit. (2011). Big data: Harnessing a game-changing asset. Retrieved July 20, 2012, from http://www.sas.com/resources/asset/SAS_BigData_final.pdf.

Gantz, J., Reinsel, D., Chute, C., Schlichting, W., McArthur, J., Minton, S., et al. (2007, March). The expanding digital universe. *IDC.* Retrieved July 20, 2012, from http://www.emc.com/about/destination/digital_universe/pdf/Expanding_Digital_Universe_IDC_WhitePaper_022507.pdf.

Harrison, G. (2010, August 26). 10 things you should know about NoSQL databases. *Techrepublic.* Retrieved July 19, 2012, from http://www.techrepublic.com/blog/10things/10-things-you-should-know-about-nosql-databases/1772.

Larose, D. T. (2006). *Data mining methods and models.* New York: Wiley.

Leonard, D. (2006, January 30). How to salvage your company's deep smarts. *CIO.com.* Retrieved July 20, 2012, from http://www.cio.com.au/article/182425/how_salvage_your_company_deep_smarts.

Levinson, M. (2010). Knowledge management definition and solutions. *CIO.com.* Retrieved July 20, 2012, from http://www.cio.com/article/40343/Knowledge_Management_Definition_and_Solutions.

Lo, C. P., & Yeung, A. K. W. (2007). *Concepts and techniques of geographic information systems* (2nd ed.). Upper Saddle River, NJ: Pearson Prentice Hall.

Malhotra, Y. (2005). Integrating knowledge management technologies in organizational business processes: Getting real time enterprises to deliver real business performance. *Journal of Knowledge Management, 9*(1), 7–28.

Markoff, J. (2012, June 25). How many computers to identify a cat? 16,000. *The New York Times.* Retrieved July 20, 2012, from http://www.nytimes.com/2012/06/26/technology/in-a-big-network-of-computers-evidence-of-machine-learning.html.

Myatt, G. J., & Johnson, W. P. (2009). *Making sense of data: A practical guide to data visualization, advanced data mining methods, and applications.* New York: Wiley.

Pettey, C., & Stevens, H. (2009, January 15). Gartner reveals five business intelligence predictions for 2009 and beyond. *Gartner.* Retrieved July 20, 2012, from http://www.gartner.com/it/page.jsp?id=856714.

Saarenvirta, G. (2004). The untapped value of geographic information. *Business Intelligence Journal, 9*(1), 58–63.

Sprague, R. H., Jr. (1980). A framework for the development of decision support systems. *MIS Quarterly, 4*(4), 1–26.

Stubbs, E. (2011). *The value of business analytics.* New York: Wiley.

Swoyer, S. (2007, September 5). Unstructured data: Attacking a myth. *TDWI.* Retrieved July 20, 2012, from http://tdwi.org/articles/2007/09/05/unstructured-data-attacking-a-myth.aspx.

Tapscott, D. (2008). Actionable insights for business decision makers. Retrieved July 20, 2012, from http://www.businessobjects.com/campaigns/forms/q109/apj/everyone/tapscott/BI_for_Decision_Makers.pdf.

Turban, E., Sharda, R., & Delen, D. (2011). *Decision support systems and business intelligence systems* (9th ed.). Upper Saddle River, NJ: Pearson Prentice Hall.

Turban, E., Sharda, R., Delen, D., & King, D. (2011). *Business intelligence* (2nd ed.). Upper Saddle River, NJ: Pearson Prentice Hall.

White, C. (2005). Bridging the planning and business performance gap. *SAP BI Research.* Retrieved July 20, 2012, from http://www.sap.com/belux/platform/netweaver/pdf/BWP_AR_BI_Research.pdf.

CHAPTER 7

Brown, P. C. (2007). *Succeeding with SOA: Realizing business value through total architecture.* New York: Addison-Wesley.

Christensen, C. M. (1997). *The innovator's dilemma.* Boston: Harvard Business School Press.

Erl, T. (2008). *SOA principles of service design.* Upper Saddle River, NJ: Pearson Prentice Hall.

Hammer, M., & Champy, J. (1993). *Reengineering the corporation: A manifesto for business revolution.* New York: Harper Business Essentials.

Jacobs, F. R., & Whybark, D. C. (2000). *Why ERP? A primer on SAP implementation.* Boston: Irwin/McGraw-Hill.

Kumar, R. L., & Crook, C. W. (1999). A multi-disciplinary framework for the management of interorganizational systems. *Database for Advances in Information Systems, 30*(1), 22–36.

Langenwalter, G. A. (2000). *Enterprise resource planning and beyond.* Boca Raton, FL: St. Lucie Press.

Larson, P. D., & Rogers, D.S. (1998), Supply chain management: Definition, growth and approaches. *Journal of Marketing Theory and Practice, 6*(4), 1–5.

Olson, D. (2004). *Managerial issues of enterprise resource planning systems.* Boston: McGraw-Hill/Irwin.

Panorama Consulting Solutions. (2012). 2012 ERP report. Retrieved July 5, 2012, from http://Panorama-Consulting.com/resource-center/2012-erp-report.

Porter, M. E., & Millar, V. E. (1985). How information gives you competitive advantage. *Harvard Business Review*, July–August, 149–160.

Taylor, F. W. (1911). *The Principles of Scientific Management.* New York: Harper Bros.

Wagner, B., & Monk, E. (2013). *Concepts in enterprise resource planning* (4th ed.). Boston: Cengage.

Wailgum, T. (2008, January 29). Why ERP systems are more important than ever. *CIO.com.* Retrieved July 20, 2012, from http://www.cio.com/article/177300/Why_ERP_Systems_Are_More_Important_Than_Ever.

Wailgum, T. (2008, April 17). ERP definition and solutions. *CIO.com.* Retrieved July 20, 2012, from http://www.cio.com/article/40323/ERP_Definition_and_Solutions.

CHAPTER 8

Anonymous. (2009). CRM and social networking: Engaging the social customer. Retrieved July 20, 2012, from http://www.techrepublic.com/whitepapers/crm-and-social-networking-engaging-the-social-customer/1145249.

Anonymous. (2010). About vendor managed inventory. *Vendor Managed Inventory.com.* Retrieved July 20, 2012, from http://www.vendormanagedinventory.com/about.php.

Arano, N. (2010, July 21). Canadian university offers social CRM course. *CIO.com.* Retrieved July 20, 2012, from http://www.cio.com/article/600257/Canadian_University_Offers_Social_CRM_Course.

Barboza, D. (2010, July 5). Supply chain for iPhone highlights costs in China. *New York Times.* Retrieved July 20, 2012, from http://www.nytimes.com/2010/07/06/technology/06iphone.html.

Bernoff, J., Cooperstein, D., de Lussanet, M., & Madigan, C.J. (2011, June 6). *Competitive strategy in the age of the customer.* Cambridge, MA: Forrester Research.

Breen, B. (2004, November 1). Living in Dell time. *Fastcompany.* Retrieved July 20, 2012, from http://www.fastcompany.com/magazine/88/dell.html.

Dean, J. (2007, August 11). The forbidden city of Terry Gou. *Wall Street Journal.* Retrieved July 20, 2012, from http://online.wsj.com/article/NA_WSJ_PUB:SB118677584137994489.html.

Edwards, J. (2003, February 15). RFID creates fast asset identification and management. *CIO.com.* Retrieved July 20, 2012, from http://www.cio.com/article/31724/RFID_Creates_Fast_Asset_Identification_and_Management.

Harrison, A., & Van Hoek, R. (2011). *Logistics management and strategy: Competing through the supply chain* (4th ed.). Upper Saddle River, NJ: Pearson Prentice Hall.

Kanaracus, C. (2009, July 9). Microsoft ties Dynamics CRM to Twitter. *CIO.com.* Retrieved July 20, 2012, from http://www.cio.com/article/496978/Microsoft_Ties_Dynamics_CRM_to_Twitter.

Keller, K. (2010, June 28). iPhone 4 carries bill of materials of $187.51, according to iSuppli. *iSuppli.com.* Retrieved July 20, 2012, from http://www.isuppli.com/Teardowns-Manufacturing-and-Pricing/News/Pages/iPhone-4-Carries-Bill-of-Materials-of-187-51-According-to-iSuppli.aspx.

Keuky, R., & Clarke, S. (2011). Socializing CRM: Merits and approaches to deploying social CRM solutions. *Capgemini.* Retrieved July 31, 2012, from http://www.capgemini.com/discover/pdf/dilemma_4/Socializing%20CRM.pdf.

Lager, M. (2008, April). The 2008 CRM Service Awards: Elite—JPMorgan Chase Card Services. *destinationCRM.com.* Retrieved July 20, 2012, from http://www.destinationcrm.com/Articles/ReadArticle.aspx?ArticleID=46576.

Larson, P. D., & Rogers, D. S. (1998). Supply chain management: Definition, growth, and approaches. *Journal of Marketing Theory and Practice, 6*(4), 1–5.

LSG. (2010, May 11). Quantum Lightweight Trolley receives airworthiness certificate. Retrieved July 20, 2012, from http://www.lsgskychefs.com/en/press-room/information/quantum-lightweight-trolley-receives-airworthiness-certificate.html.

Menchaca, L. (2010, December 8). Dell's next step: The Social Media Listening Command Center. *Dell.com.* Retrieved July 17, 2012, from http://en.community.dell.com/dell-blogs/direct2dell/b/direct2dell/archive/2010/12/08/dell-s-next-step-the-social-media-listening-command-center.aspx.

Nash, K. (2007, October 22). Beyond Peter Pan: How ConAgra's pot pie recall bakes in hard lessons for supply chain management. *CIO.com.* Retrieved July 20, 2012, from http://www.cio.com/article/148054/Beyond_Peter_Pan_How_ConAgra_s_Pot_Pie_Recall_Bakes_In_Hard_Lessons_for_Supply_Chain_Management.

Penfield, P. (2008, August 26). Visibility within the supply chain. *MHIA.org.* Retrieved July 20, 2012, from http://www.mhia.org/news/industry/7960/visibility-within-the-supply-chain.

Sebor, J. (2010, March). The 2010 CRM Service Awards: The service elite—Southwest Airlines. *destinationCRM.com.* Retrieved July 20, 2012, from http://www.destinationcrm.com/Articles/Editorial/Magazine-Features/The-2010-CRM-Service-Awards-The-Service-Elite—Southwest-Airlines-61390.aspx.

Taber, D. (2009, September 28). Marketing automation: Unique kid on the CRM block. *CIO.com.* Retrieved July 20, 2012, from http://www.cio.com/article/503436/Marketing_Automation_Unique_Kid_on_the_CRM_Block.

Taber, D. (2010, February 22). CRM's identity crisis: Duplicate contacts, part 2. *CIO.com.* Retrieved July 20, 2012, from http://www.cio.com/article/551313/CRM_s_Identity_Crisis_Duplicate_Contacts_Part_2.

Taber, D. (2010, May 19). CRM problems come in threes. *CIO.com.* Retrieved July 20, 2012, from http://www.cio.com/article/594235/CRM_Problems_Come_in_Threes.

U.S. Census Bureau. (2012, May 10). E-stats 2010. Retrieved July 20, 2012, from http://www.census.gov/econ/estats/2010/2010reportfinal.pdf.

Wagner, W., & Zubey, M. (2006). *Customer relationship management.* Boston: Course Technology.

Wailgum, T. (2008, November 20). Supply chain management definition and solutions. *CIO.com.* Retrieved July 20, 2012, from http://www.cio.com/article/40940/Supply_Chain_Management_Definition_and_Solutions.

CHAPTER 9

Anonymous. (2009, October 26). Twitter "costs businesses £1.4bn." *BBC News.* Retrieved July 20, 2012, from http://news.bbc.co.uk/2/hi/business/8325865.stm.

Anonymous. (2012, April 10). Best and worst jobs 2012. *Wall Street Journal.* Retrieved June 3, 2012, from http://online.wsj.com/article/SB10001424052702304587704577335703058909284.html.

Anonymous. (2012, July 9). Gartner says worldwide IT spending on pace to surpass $3.6 trillion in 2012. *Gartner.* Retrieved July 20, 2012, from http://www.gartner.com/it/page.jsp?id=2074815.

Applegate, L. M., Austin, R. D., & Soule, D.L. (2009). *Corporate information strategy and management* (8th ed.). New York: McGraw-Hill.

Fuller, M. A., Valacich, J. S., & George, J. F. (2008). *Information systems project management: A process and team approach.* Upper Saddle River, NJ: Pearson Prentice Hall.

Great American Group. (2011). *Technology Monitor,* December 2011-Vol. 4. Retrieved on June 3, 2012, from http://www.greatamerican.com/news_media/downloads/Dec_Tech_Monitor.pdf.

Hoffer, J. A., George, J. F., & Valacich, J. S. (2014). *Modern systems analysis and design* (7th ed.). Upper Saddle River, NJ: Pearson Prentice Hall.

McFarlan, F. W., & Nolan, R. L. (1995). How to manage an IT outsourcing alliance. *Sloan Management Review, 36*(2), 9–24.

McKeen, J. D., Guimaraes, T., & Wetherbe, J. C. (1994). A comparative analysis of MIS project selection mechanisms. *Database, 25*(2), 43–59.

Netcraft. (2012, May 12). May 2012 Web server survey. *Netcraft.com.* Retrieved July 20, 2012, from http://news.netcraft.com/archives/2012/05/02/may-2012-web-server-survey.html.

Porter, M. E. (1979, March–April). How competitive forces shape strategy. *Harvard Business Review, 57,* 137–145.

Top 500. (2012, June). Retrieved July 20, 2012, from http://www.top500.org/lists/2012/06.

Valacich, J. S., George, J. F., & Hoffer, J. A. (2012). *Essentials of systems analysis and design* (5th ed.). Upper Saddle River, NJ: Pearson Prentice Hall.

Wheeler, B. C. (2002). Making the business case for IT investments through facts, faith, and fear: Online teaching case and teaching note. Retrieved July 15, 2012, from http://collopy.case.edu/articles/ConsumerProductsIntl.

Wood, J., & Silver, D. (1989). *Joint Application Design.* New York: Wiley.

CHAPTER 10

Ackerman, S. (2012, July 17). Syrian rebels use YouTube, Facebook for weapons training. *Wired.com.* Retrieved September 6, 2012, from http://www.wired.com/dangerroom/2012/07/syria-youtube-facebook.

Addison-Hewitt Associates. (2005). The Sarbanes-Oxley Act. Retrieved May 20, 2012, from http://www.soxlaw.com/index.htm.

Bielski, Z. (2008, June 21). World unprepared for coming catastrophes, warn experts. *National Post.* Retrieved May 20, 2012, from http://www2.canada.com/cars/story.html?id=602830.

Bocij, P. (2004). *Cyberstalking: Harassment in the Internet age and how to protect your family.* Westport, CT: Greenwood.

Boyle, R.E. & Panko, R. (2013). *Corporate computer security* (3rd ed.). Upper Saddle River, NJ: Pearson Prentice Hall.

Burgess-Proctor, A., Patchin, J. W., & Hinduja, S. (2008). Cyberbullying and online harassment: Reconceptualizing the victimization of adolescent girls. In V. Garcia & J. Clifford (Eds.), *Female crime victims: Reality reconsidered* (pp. 162–176). Upper Saddle River, NJ: Pearson Prentice Hall.

Business Software Alliance. (2007). The fight for cyber space. Retrieved May 20, 2012, from http://www.bsa.org/country/Research%20and%20Statistics/~/media/9CA4C9DFEDE24250AA16F16F0ED297A6.ashx.

Business Software Alliance. (2011). Eighth annual BSA global 2010 software piracy study. Retrieved July 31, 2012, from http://portal.bsa.org/globalpiracy2010/downloads/study_pdf/2010_BSA_Piracy_Study-Standard.pdf.

Business Software Alliance. (2012). Ninth annual BSA global 2011 software piracy study. Retrieved July 31, 2012, from http://portal.bsa.org/globalpiracy2011/downloads/study_pdf/2011_BSA_Piracy_Study-Standard.pdf.

CAPTCHA. (2010). Telling humans and computers apart automatically. Retrieved May 20, 2012, from http://www.captcha.net.

CERT. (2012). CERT Coordination Center (CERT/CC). Retrieved May 20, 2012, from http://www.cert.org/certcc.html.

Champlain, J. (2003). *Auditing information systems.* Hoboken, NJ: Wiley.

Chen, H., Reid, E., Sinai, J., Sike, A., & Ganor, B. (2008). *Terrorism informatics: Knowledge management and data mining for homeland security.* Berlin: Springer.

Cobb, M. (2012) Measuring risk: A security pro's guide. *InformationWeek.* Retrieved July 31, 2012, from http://reports.informationweek.com.

Computer Security Institute. (2011). *2010/2011: The 15th annual computer crime and security survey.* Retrieved May 21, 2012, from http://gocsi.com/members/reports.

Federal Bureau of Investigation. (2008, October 16). FBI coordinates global effort to nab "Dark Market" cyber criminals. Retrieved May 21, 2012, from http://www.fbi.gov/news/pressrel/press-releases/fbi-coordinates-global-effort-to-nab-2018dark-market2019-cyber-criminals.

Finneran, M. (2012). 2012 state of mobile security. *InformationWeek.* Retrieved July 31, 2012, from http://reports.informationweek.com.

Fitzgerald, T. (2008). The ocean is full of phish. *Information Systems Security.* Retrieved May 21, 2012, from http://www.infosectoday.com/Articles/Phishing.htm.

Geers, K. (2008). A new approach to cyber defense. *Internet Evolution.* Retrieved May 21, 2012, from http://www.internetevolution.com/author.asp?id=628&doc_id=151762.

Glenny, M. (2011, September 21). Cybercrime: is it out of control? *The Guardian.* Retrieved May 21, 2012, from http://www.guardian.co.uk/technology/2011/sep/21/cybercrime-spam-phishing-viruses-malware.

Kabay, M. E. (2007). How far could cyberware go? *NetworkWorld.* Retrieved May 21, 2012, from http://www.networkworld.com/newsletters/sec/2007/0723sec2.html.

Keizer, G. (2010). Botnets "the Swiss Army knife of attack tools" (hacker militias can turn to botnets for instant cyberattacks). *Computerworld.* Retrieved May 21, 2012, from http://www.computerworld.com/s/article/9174560/Botnets_the_Swiss_Army_knife_of_attack_tools.

Kharif, O. (2012, April 30). Mobile spam texts hit 4.5 billion raising consumer ire. *BusinessWeek.* Retrieved May 25, 2012, from http://www.businessweek.com/news/2012-04-30/mobile-spam-texts-hit-4-dot-5-billion-raising-consumer-ire.

Leyden, J. (2002, March 27). Drive-by hacking linked to cyberterror. *The Register.* Retrieved May 21, 2012, from http://www.theregister.co.uk/2002/03/27/driveby_hacking_linked_to_cyberterror.

National Audit Office. (2004, February). Review of information systems controls. Retrieved July 17, 2012, from http://www.auditnet.org/Guides/NAOReviewofISWorkbook2004.pdf.

Poulsen, K. (2008, October 13). Cybercrime supersite "DarkMarket" was FBI sting, documents confirm. *Wired.com.* Retrieved May 21, 2012, from http://www.wired.com/threatlevel/2008/10/darkmarket-post.

Reuters. (2006). Morgan Stanley offers $15M fine for e-mail violations. *Computerworld.* Retrieved May 21, 2012, from http://www.computerworld.com/hardwaretopics/storage/story/0,10801,108687,00.html.

Salek, N. (2008, June 24). Does cyberterrorism exist? *CRN.com.au.* Retrieved May 21, 2012, from http://www.crn.com.au/Feature/4652,does-cyberterrorism-exist.aspx.

SearchCIO. (2007). Business continuity and disaster recovery planning guide for CIOs. *SearchCIO.com.* Retrieved May 21, 2012, from http://searchcio.techtarget.com/generic/0,295582,sid182_gci1206807,00.html.

Stallings, W. (2011). *Network security essentials: Applications and standards* (4th ed.). Upper Saddle River, NJ: Pearson Prentice Hall.

Stallings, W., & Brown, L. (2012). *Computer security: Principles and practices* (2nd ed.). Upper Saddle River, NJ: Pearson Prentice Hall.

Stuxnet. (2012, June 6). In *Wikipedia, The Free Encyclopedia.* Retrieved June 6, 2012, from http://en.wikipedia.org/w/index.php?title=Stuxnet&oldid=496267822.

The Jester. (2012, May 19). In *Wikipedia, The Free Encyclopedia.* Retrieved May 21, 2012, from http://en.wikipedia.org/w/index.php?title=The_Jester&oldid=493315662.

US News. (2007). Top computer crimes of 2007. *USNEWS.com.* Retrieved May 21, 2012, from http://www.usnews.com/usnews/news/badguys/070515/top_computer_crimes_of_2007_fi.htm.

Volonino, L., & Robinson, S. R. (2004). *Principles and practice of information security.* Upper Saddle River, NJ: Pearson Prentice Hall.

Weber, T. (2007, January 25). Criminals "may overwhelm the web." *BBC News.* Retrieved May 20, 2012, from http://news.bbc.co.uk/1/hi/business/6298641.stm.

Websense. (2012). Websense 2012 threat report. Retrieved July 31, 2012, from http://www.websense.com/content/websense-2012-threat-report-download.aspx.

Wehner, M. (2012, July 24). Iran nuclear energy facility hit with malware that plays AC/DC at full volume. *Yahoo! News.* Retrieved September 6, 2012, from http://news.yahoo.com/blogs/technology-blog/iran-nuclear-energy-facility-hit-malware-plays-ac-203806981.html.

Weimann, G. (2006). *Terror on the Internet: The new arena, the new challenges.* Washington, DC: United States Institute of Peace Press.

TECHNOLOGY BRIEFING

Comer, D. E. (1997). *The Internet book* (2nd ed.). Upper Saddle River, NJ: Pearson Prentice Hall.

Hoffer, J. A., George, J. F., & Valacich, J. S. (2014). *Modern systems analysis and design* (7th ed.). Upper Saddle River, NJ: Pearson Prentice Hall.

Hoffer, J., Ramesh, V., & Topi, H. (2013). *Modern database management* (11th ed.). Upper Saddle River, NJ: Pearson Prentice Hall.

Laberta, C. (2012). *Computers are your future complete* (12th ed.). Upper Saddle River, NJ: Pearson Prentice Hall.

Panko, R., & Panko, J. (2013). *Business data networks and security* (9th ed.). Upper Saddle River, NJ: Pearson Prentice Hall.

Stallings, W. (2011). *Network security essentials: Applications and standards* (4th ed.). Upper Saddle River, NJ: Pearson Prentice Hall.

Te'eni, D., Carey, J. M., & Zhang, P. (2007). *Human-computer interaction: Developing effective organizational information systems.* New York: Wiley.

Name Index

Organization Index

Subject Index

Key terms and the page numbers where they are defined appear in boldface.

P

Packaged software, 311–312
Packet switching, 493
Paid inclusion, 186
Passive tags, 353
Patch management system, 403
Patent, 352, 435
PATRIOT Act, 437
Patriot hacker, 440
Pay by Fingerprint, 202
Payment Card Industry Data Security
　　Standard, 154
Payment failure, 194
Payments
　global, 77
　mobile, 77, 195
　securing, 196–198
　services for, 198
Pay-per-click, 189
Peer production, 234–235
Peer, 138
Peer-to-peer (P2P) networks, 139
Perfective maintenance, 402–403
Personal area network (PAN), 139,
　492–493
Personal Computer (PC), 133
Personal digital assistants (PDAs), 41
Personnel, IS, 54
Phishing, 431, 470
Physical access restrictions, 445–449
Pippin, 60
Piracy, software, 435–436
PixelSense (Microsoft), 383
Plain old telephone service
　(POTS), 506
Planned obsolescence, 146
Platform as a service (PaaS), 151–**152**
Podcast, 227
Podcasting, 227
Port, 479
Portal, 340–341
Post-PC devices, 41
Post-PC era, 33
PowerMac G4 Cube, 60
Power supply, 479–480
Predictive analysis, 271
Preferred relationships, 411
Preventive maintenance, 402–403
Pricing models, 189
Primary key, 509–510
Primary storage, 476–477
Principles of Scientific Management
　(Taylor), 313
Printer, 480
Privacy
　of the cloud, 154
　email, 64
　information, 62–66

maintaining, 65–66
online, 64–66, 131, 215
RFID technology and, 307
Private branch exchanges (PBXs),
　139, 490, 491
Private cloud, 152, 153
Processing logic, 395–396, 397, 398
Processing technologies, 475–480
Procurement activities, 305
Procure-to-pay process, 300, 320,
　321
Product flow, 348
Production/operations, 84, 273
Productivity measurement, 378
Productivity paradox, 377–379
Product recalls, 344
Programming languages, 482–486
Project classification/ranking, 394
Project Glass, 103
Project manager, 391–392
Propagation delay, 502
Proposal evaluation, 407–408
Proprietary software, 409
Protected Intellectual Privacy Act
　(PIPA), 421
Protective open source software, 409
Protocols, 137, 494–496
Prototyping, 403–404
Proxy variables, 387–388
Pseudocode, 395–396, 397
Public cloud, 152, 153
Public domain software, 409
Public switched telephone network
　(PSTN), 506
Puck mouse, 60

Q

QR code, 182
Query, 262
Query by example (QBE), 263
Questionnaires, 395

R

Radio frequency identification (RFID)
　technology, 202, 307, 352–354,
　474
Random access control, 496
Random-access memory (RAM),
　476–477
RDBMS (Relational database
　management system), 260
Read-only memory (ROM), 477
Read/write head, 478
Real Simple Syndication (RSS),
　227–228
Record, 259
Recovery point objective, 458

Recovery plans, 457–458
Recovery time objective, 457
Recurring cost, 382
Redistribution and productivity, 379
Redundant array of independent
　disks (RAID), 477–478
Redundant data centers, 452
Reengineering the Corporation
　(Hammer and Champy), 314
Regulations, ERP, 318
Regulatory/compliance value, 92
Reintermediation, 174
Relational database design, 509–510
Relational database management
　system (RDBMS), 260
Relational database model, 512–513
Relationship, 510–511
Removable storage media, 478–479
Report generator, 262
Report, 262, 267
Representational delight, 183
Reputation management, 178
Request for proposal (RFP), 407
Requirements collection, 394–395
Resources, 88–89, 151
Retail industry, 202
Revenue model, 93
Reverse auction, 193
Reverse engineering, 435
Reverse pricing, 179
RFID (radio frequency identification)
　technology, 202, 307, 352–354,
　474
RFID tags, 352–353
Right to Financial Privacy Act, 437
Ring network, 496, 497
Risk acceptance, 445
Risk analysis, 445
Risk avoidance, 445
Risk management, 196–198
Risk reduction, 445
Risk transference, 445
Rivalry, industry, 381
Roll up, 267
Router, 495, 498, 504
RSS (Real Simple Syndication),
　227–228
Rule, 274

S

Salaries, IS professionals, 50, 51
Sales Cloud (Salesforce), 356
Sales force automation (SFA),
　359–361
Sarbanes–Oxley Act (S-OX), 135,
　154, **462**
Satellite connections, 506, 507–508